CHILD PSYCHOLOGY

A CONTEMPORARY VIEWPOINT

FIFTH EDITION

E. Mavis Hetherington
University of Virginia

Ross D. Parke
University of California
Riverside

Revised by Ross D. Parke
and Virginia Otis Locke

**McGraw-Hill
College**

Boston   Burr Ridge, IL   Dubuque, IA   Madison, WI
New York   San Francisco   St. Louis
Bangkok   Bogotá   Caracas   Lisbon   London   Madrid   Mexico City
Milan   New Delhi   Seoul   Singapore   Sydney   Taipei   Toronto

McGraw-Hill College

A Division of The **McGraw·Hill** *Companies*

CHILD PSYCHOLOGY: A CONTEMPORARY VIEWPOINT, FIFTH EDITION

This book is printed on acid-free paper.

1 2 3 4 5 6 7 8 9 0 VNH/VNH 9 3 2 1 0 9 8

ISBN 0-07-028469-5

Editorial director: *Jane E. Vaicunas*
Executive editor: *Mickey Cox*
Senior developmental editor: *Meera Dash*
Editorial assistants: *Sarah Thomas, Kristen Mellitt*
Senior marketing manager: *James Rozsa*
Project manager: *Donna Nemmers*
Production supervisor: *Laura Fuller*
Freelance coordinator: *Mary L. Christianson*
Photo research coordinator: *Lori Hancock*
Art editor: *Jodi K. Banowetz*
Senior supplement coordinator: *David A. Welsh*
Compositor/illustrator: *Shepard Poorman Communications Corp.*
Typeface: *10/12 Stempel Garamond*
Printer: *Von Hoffmann Press, Inc.*

Freelance interior designer: *Wanda Siedlecka*
Freelance cover designer: *Kristyn A. Kalnes*
Cover photograph: © *Chip Henderson/Tony Stone Images*

The credits section for this book begins on page C-1 and is considered an extension of the copyright page.

Library of Congress Cataloging-in-Publication Data

Hetherington, E. Mavis (Eileen Mavis), 1926–
    Child psychology: a contemporary viewpoint/E. Mavis
Hetherington, Ross D. Parke, Virginia Otis Locke. — 5th ed.
       p. cm.
    Includes bibliographical references and indexes.
    ISBN 0-07-028469-5. — ISBN 0-07-115728-X (ISE)
    1. Child psychology.   I. Parke, Ross D.   II. Locke, Virginia Otis
III. Title.
BF721.H418   1999
155.4—dc21
                                    98-15013
                                    CIP

www.mhhe.com

To my wife, Barbara, my children, Gillian, Timothy, Megan, Sarah, Jennifer, and Zachary, and my grandson, Ben

To the memory of my sister, Mary Eleta Locke Schmidt, educator, who helped many children to grow and flourish

Contents in Brief

Contents

About the Authors

Ross D. Parke is Distinguished Professor of Psychology and director of the Center for Family Studies at the University of California, Riverside. He is a past President of Division 7, the Developmental Psychology Division, of the American Psychological Association, and in 1995 received the G. Stanley Hall Award from this APA division. Parke was elected a Fellow of the American Association for the Advancement of Science in 1997. He is currently editor of the *Journal of Family Psychology* and has served as editor of *Developmental Psychology* and as associate editor of *Child Development*. Parke is author of *Fatherhood*; co-author of *The Throwaway Father*, with Armin Brott; and co-editor of *Family-Peer Relationships: In Search of the Linkages*, with Gary Ladd, *Children in Time and Place*, with Glen Elder and John Modell, and *Exploring Family Relationships with Other Social Contexts*, with Sheppard Kellam. Parke's research has focused on early social relationships in infancy and childhood. He obtained his Ph.D. from the University of Waterloo, Ontario, Canada and is well known for his early work on the effects of punishment, aggression, and child abuse and for his work on the father's role in infancy and early childhood. His current work focuses on the links between family and peer social systems and on the impact of economic stress on families of diverse ethnic backgrounds.

Virginia Otis Locke has been a professional writer and editor for more than twenty years. She is an author of *Introduction to Theories of Personality*, with Calvin Hall, Gardner Lindzey, John Loehlin, and Martin Manosevitz, and of several other books. Both while a senior development editor at Prentice Hall and as a freelance writer-editor, Locke has developed many books in the behavioral sciences. As writer-editor at Cornell Medical College/New York Hospital Medical Center, she also wrote and edited professional and lay articles in the field of cardiovascular medicine. Locke received her B.A. from Barnard College and earned her M.A. in the doctoral clinical psychology program at Duke University. For several years she was a staff psychologist at St. Luke's-Roosevelt Medical Center, New York City. Her biography is included in *Who's Who in America* and *Who's Who of American Women*. Locke is studying elementary education and plans to teach in the early grades.

This is an exciting time in the field of child psychology, for the study of children's development is undergoing rapid change. Theorists and researchers have made remarkable breakthroughs in the last few years. For example, they have offered the field new insights into the biological underpinnings of behavior, they have revealed some remarkable cognitive skills in infants, and they have explored the effects of our many new family arrangements on children's development.

In the fifth edition of our book we continue to reflect the dynamic nature of the field of child psychology. We discuss a wealth of new research that highlights the central processes that account for developmental change within the different domains of child development. Designed primarily for use in courses in child psychology or child development in either two- or four-year colleges, our book approaches the course material in a topical fashion. This allows us to introduce the student to such subjects as the impact on children's development of the continuing interaction between genetic and environmental factors, the growing body of knowledge about how children learn language and continually sharpen their cognitive skills, and the way children develop social skills through interaction with peers.

We hope *Child Psychology: A Contemporary Viewpoint*, fifth edition, lives up to its title—an up-to-date and exciting overview of the best that our field has to offer to both instructors and students. Although we have made many revisions in each new edition of our book, our primary goal has never wavered: to present the most important contemporary ideas and issues in child psychology in a way that all students will understand, enjoy, and find useful in their lives and, in some cases, their professional careers. We hope that the academic community will find this new edition a comprehensive and current resource as well as an invaluable teaching tool

DISTINGUISHING CHARACTERISTICS OF THIS BOOK

Several characteristics continue to distinguish *Child Psychology: A Contemporary Viewpoint*. We offer balanced theoretical discussions, explore both basic research and its practical applications, and integrate multicultural and cross-cultural research throughout the book.

Balanced Theoretical Perspectives

The topical approach lends itself to a sophisticated presentation of theories, such as those of Piaget and Freud, that guide research in the many areas of child development. The few universal theories of child behavior that have been advanced have raised questions and produced far-reaching insights that have stimulated decades of research activity. But as the research evidence accumulates, the limitations and flaws in these wide-ranging theories have become more evident. In place of a few grand universal theories that provide accounts of many aspects of development, increasingly we are realizing the value of smaller theories that guide research in specific topic areas, such as language, motor development, or emotional understanding. In our first chapter we survey a range of theoretical viewpoints including Piagetian thought, the information processing approach, behavioral views, and psychoanalytic theory. New to this edition is an expanded discussion of Vygotskian sociocultural theory and a section on dynamic systems theory, a recent and exciting approach to understanding development. This theory has been applied extensively to the study of motor development (Chapter 6) as well as to research on the family as a system (Chapter 12). Variants of dynamics systems theory are being used in many areas of developmental psychology.

Child Psychology: A Contemporary Viewpoint strives to be theoretically eclectic and to emphasize the multiply determined nature of development. Biological factors predominate in our coverage of genetics and early development. These same factors, however, also receive attention in our discussion of other topics, such as language and gender typing. For example, although cognitive learning theories such as those of Vygotsky, Piaget, and information processing specialists necessarily dominate our discussions of language, cognition, and intellectual development, sociocultural concepts are also viewed as major modifiers of cognitive growth and development. Similarly, whereas social and affective factors predominate in our coverage of the family and peers, in these discussions we are equally concerned with cognitive, behavioral, and biological issues. This approach to theoretical material reflects the discipline's increasing recognition of the interplay among biological, cognitive, and social factors in children's development and reflects the fact that development in all domains is multiply determined. The newer theoretical approaches—sociocultural theory and dynamics systems theory—reflect this increasing connectedness across the domains of development.

Process Orientation.   If we have any bias, it is one that emphasizes the *processes* of development, which is one of the hallmarks of contemporary child psychology. By focusing on the processes that are responsible for changes in the child's development, the student not only learns the content of development and what changes take place across time but also comes to understand the dynamics of why these changes happen across development.

Themes of Development.   *Child Psychology: A Contemporary Viewpoint* continues to characterize theoretical perspectives, in part, by a number of specific themes of development. In this edition we have trimmed the number of these themes to six, and we have added a new theme, that of risk versus resilience, which has captured the interest of psychologists in recent years. The themes of development are more salient in some chapters than others. For example, the question of genetic versus environmental influences on the child is perhaps of most concern in Chapters 3 and 11, but it informs discussions in almost every other chapter as well. The theme of continuity of development versus discontinuity is particularly at issue in Chapters 9 and 10, but it too is reprised in many other chapters. In our Epilogue we link the developmental themes with broad principles that summarize our views about child development and the theory-building and research needs of the field.

Basic and Applied Research: A Reciprocal Relationship

We present child psychology as a scientific discipline, illustrating and discussing the techniques used by psychologists in the field. Students must become familiar with the methodological approaches unique to child psychology if they are to understand, interpret, and use the results of research intelligently. We present many research findings in sufficient detail to enable the student to appreciate the steps that are involved in the research process as well as the complexity of how psychologists arrive at their conclusions about how children develop.

Although some instructors express a preference for a basic research focus and others for an applied approach, we think this an unnecessary and artificial distinction. Instead, we try to show how research and its application inform each other. Basic information about the processes of development can help us understand a wide range of real-life problems and, conversely, insights we gain from applications of research—for example, from early intervention programs like Head Start (Chapter 11)—can help improve research and sharpen our theoretical understanding. New research on homesickness shows the relevance of attachment theory for real-life problems, and research on early mother-infant attachment has clear implications for understanding the effects of day care (Chapter 7). Social learning theory and basic research on imitation have helped us understand the effects of television on children's cognitive and social development (Chapters 1 and 14). Bilingual education (Chapter 8), the use of computers in the classroom (Chapter 14), and child abuse and its consequences (Chapter 12) are other applied topics highlighted in this edition. Throughout the book, teachers and students will find fascinating examples that demonstrate the dynamic interplay between basic and applied research.

Sociocultural Diversity in Child Development

In the fifth edition, we have intensified our focus on the ethnic, racial, and cultural diversity of heterogeneous societies like the United States as well as on differences between cultures around the world. Our expanded discussions of Vygotskian theory, with its strong emphasis on the role of culture in development, provides one framework for understanding how culture and development interact. This theme of cultural pluralism, introduced in Chapter 1, is reprised in every chapter of the book; we integrate research from the American culture as well as from other nations around the world into each topical discussion. In addition, one of our box series highlights cross-cultural and intra-cultural studies of particular interest.

ORGANIZATION

Several organizational decisions and changes in the fifth edition also spotlight our book among the array of developmental texts. First, recognizing the field's increased focus on the interplay among emotion regulation, emotional understanding, and attachment, we continue to treat attachment as part of our discussion of early emotional development (Chapter 7). Moreover, we view this major development as a foundation for later cognitive (Chapters 8–11) and social development (Chapters 12–16).

Second, we have resequenced material in Chapters 9 and 10, in order to present theories and supporting data together. In Chapter 9, we present Piaget, Vygotsky, and related research, and we devote Chapter 10 to information-processing theory and the associated research evidence. We hope that this arrangement will make it easier for students to understand the theories and to interpret the research evidence.

Third, we have included new material on the self throughout the book. Because we view the self as relevant to multiple aspects of development and as best understood in the context of other topics, we have chosen not to isolate the discussion of the self in a separate chapter. For example, we emphasize the role of the self in the emergence of early emotions and attachment (Chapter 7) and in the beginnings of cognitive awareness of selfhood and the child's theory of mind (Chapters 9 and 10). We explore the role of peers in the refinement of self image and self-esteem (Chapter 13) and the links between self-esteem and achievement (Chapter 14). Finally, the self plays a significant role in our discussions of moral development and aggression (Chapter 16).

Although we have organized our book with the one-semester course in mind, instructors can easily adapt the content for use in shorter courses and for those with specific emphases. For example, instructors who teach a brief course focusing on early development could concentrate on Chapters 1 through 7. Alternatively, instructors who are particularly interested in cognitive development could use Chapters 1, 2, 8, 9, 10, and 11. And instructors who emphasize the development of social skills might focus on Chapters 1, 2, 12, 13, 14, 15, and 16.

To allow greater flexibility in teaching the course, we have reduced the book from 18 to 16 chapters. Our former Chapter 18 is now an epilogue that summarizes the principles of theory and research in development. Our former Chapter 17 is now a separate, fully updated *Developmental Psychopathology Module* in which we discuss the DSM-IV classification of psychological disorders, offer new data on treatment of attention-deficit hyperactivity disorder and depression in childhood, present new statistics on child victims of violent crime, and explore the role of prevention in alleviating many childhood problems. This module is available to all instructors who wish to use it. See your McGraw-Hill sales representative for details.

SOME HIGHLIGHTS OF THE FIFTH EDITION

We have rewritten *Child Psychology: A Contemporary Viewpoint* to feature the most recent developments in theory and research. Every chapter includes new information and new discussions. The following are some highlights in this new coverage:

Chapter 1: Themes and Theories of Child Development
- New material on dynamic systems theory
- Introduction to Vygotsky's sociocultural theory and the idea of cultural pluralism
- Six themes of development, including the new theme of "risk and resilience"
- New work on microgenetic approach

Chapter 2: Research Methods in Child Psychology
- New material on the importance of including minority members as participants in developmental research
- Expanded discussion and illustration of the sequential research design
- New illustrations aid student understanding of the correlational method

Chapter 3: Heredity and the Environment
- Expanded section on the role of temperament in development
- New discussion of the Human Genome Project
- New discoveries of genetic markers for diseases, such as cystic fibrosis
- Expanded discussion of shared and nonshared environment

Chapter 4: Prenatal Development and Birth
- New discussion of studies of the impact of drugs and environmental toxins on the fetus and young infant
- New material on children's resilience in the face of early difficulties
- New data on AIDS
- New data on fathers' participation in the birth of their children

Chapter 5: Infancy: Sensation, Perception, and Learning
- Expanded information on infant assessment
- New data on babies' musical preferences
- New data on intermodal perception

Chapter 6: The Child's Growth: Brain, Body, Motor Skills, and Sexual Maturation
- Expanded coverage of brain anatomy and function
- New data on the use of PET scans to detect changes in the brain
- New research on motor development stimulated by dynamic systems theory
- Expanded discussion of multicultural perspectives on physical growth

Chapter 7: Emotional Development
- New and expanded discussion of the role of the self in early socioemotional development, including self awareness, self recognition, and self permanence
- New research on the intergenerational continuity of attachment patterns, and new data on fathers in this connection
- New section on the consequences in later life of early attachment quality

- New discussion of the use of the Strange Situation in different cultures
- New studies on the effects of day care including the results of the new National Collaborative Study of Day Care
- New work on the determinants of homesickness

Chapter 8: Language and Communication

- New work on the early emergence of infants' preference for the sounds of their native language and their "tuning out" of the sounds of other languages
- New evidence of infants' ability to segment speech
- New section on bilingualism and language development, including new studies of how the brain processes two languages

Chapter 9: Cognitive Development: Piaget and Vygotsky

- Complete reorganization of chapter, focusing on Piaget and Vygotsky
- New work on Piagetian notions of when children achieve certain concepts, such as the understanding of physical laws; updates on René Baillargeon's and others' research with infants
- New discussion of how children learn to distinguish self from other and to take others' perspectives
- New work on application of Vygotskian theory to classroom learning
- Expanded evaluation of Piagetian theory

Chapter 10: Cognitive Development: Information Processing

- Thorough reorganization of chapter, now devoted to information-processing theory and associated research
- New discussion of Robert Siegler's microgenetic analysis of developmental change
- New research on the development of children's attention
- New research on the role of processing speed
- New research on children's eyewitness testimony

Chapter 11: Intelligence

- Updated discussion of the controversy on genetic versus environmental contributions to intelligence
- New research on the prediction of intelligence from infant attentional tests
- New section on the development of creativity in children
- New work on multicultural and cross-cultural differences in intellectual achievement

Chapter 12: The Family

- New material on cross-cultural/multicultural differences in parenting styles
- New section on teen pregnancy and parenting
- New section on the effects of parenting after age 30
- New section on gay and lesbian parents
- New material on the effects of marital conflict on children

Chapter 13: Peers and Friends

- Expanded section on infants' interactions with peers
- New section on peers and the development of self
- New research on cultural differences in pretend play
- Updated model of social information-processing approach to peer relationships
- New work on victimization by peers
- Expanded and updated work on cross-cultural variations in peer relationships

Chapter 14: Schools, Technology, and Television

- Updated discussion of textbooks and of computers in the classroom
- Updated discussion of integration, affirmative action, and the schools
- New perspectives on effective strategies for improving the achievement of minority children
- New information on the beneficial and harmful effects of TV viewing

Chapter 15: Gender Roles and Gender Differences

- Updates on cognitive schema models of gender roles
- New work on gender differences in mathematics achievement

- New research on the gender roles of children raised in gay and lesbian families
- New work on biological bases of gender differences

Chapter 16: Morality, Altruism, and Aggression

- Expanded discussion of moral judgments, including the personal domain
- Expanded perspectives on cross-cultural variations in moral judgments and the perception of moral obligation
- The role of temperament in the development of self-control
- New work on gender differences in empathy and prosocial behavior
- New research on the development of intervention programs for reducing aggression
- New work on cross-cultural differences in aggressive behavior

SPECIAL FEATURES

In the fifth edition of *Child Psychology: A Contemporary Viewpoint* we have expanded and refined our special features, and for the first time we present the text in full color. We are confident that our enhanced and visually appealing complement of pedagogical aids will both promote student learning and assist instructors in presenting important material.

- **Chapter Outlines and Summaries.** Our chapter outlines facilitate students' survey of a chapter's contents, and our comprehensive, bulleted summaries reiterate the chapter's key concepts and main ideas. By also repeating key terms, the summaries enable students quickly to return to significant sections and discussions.
- **Box Program.** Our boxed discussions highlight three important themes: the application of basic research to real problems of children's lives; the importance of understanding and supporting the resilience displayed by many children in the face of risk; and the similarities and differences that characterize children of many different cultures. Instructors who have used earlier editions will recognize these themes as having permeated the book's pages for years. Our decision to highlight them reflects our continuing conviction that these topics are among the most important issues in child development. Our 50 boxes either are wholly new or have been updated and completely rewritten for this edition.

  Child Psychology in Action boxes pick up the thread of our research-application theme, focusing on how the results of basic research can be and are being applied daily to the solution of significant problems in children's development. For example, in Chapter 4, the box "Of Babies and Bears and Postnatal Care" describes Evelyn Thoman's research on the ability of infants born prematurely to actively regulate their own breathing. As a result of Thoman's findings, the "breathing bear" that simulates the sound of gentle quiet-sleep respiration is now available across the country to parents who are concerned about their babies' well being. In Chapter 10, the new box "Should Young Children Testify in Court?" shows that although children's memory may be accurate, children are susceptible to such influences as the circumstances under which they acquired their original information and the characteristics and attitude of the person who later interviews them.

  Risk and Resilience boxes follow the new theme introduced in Chapter 1. These boxes explore the sometimes astounding resilience that children can display in the face of a wide variety of risks, including physical and mental disabilities, disease, poverty, deteriorated neighborhoods, and broken or dysfunctional families. These discussions focus not only on how we can support and encourage such resilience but how we can work to alleviate or eliminate the risk factors. For example, in Chapter 4, the new box "What Factors Help Children Overcome Early Adversity?" focuses on Emmy Werner's classic and continuing work on risk and resilience on Hawaii's island of Kauai. In Chapter 8, the new box "Children at Risk for Failure to Develop Language" discusses the System for Augmenting Language developed by Mary Ann Romski and Rose Sevcik, by which nonspeaking children with mild to severe mental retardation have been able, for the first time, to communicate with others by using a system of lexigrams and a computerized keyboard.

Perspectives on Diversity boxes tie in with another of our major themes, examining research on the development of children's abilities, behaviors, and skills that not only spans nations and continents but explores differences among children of the many different cultural groups who make up the U. S. population. These boxes recognize the increasing importance of understanding and respect for all peoples, attitudes that need to be rooted in the world of the child. For example, in Chapter 12, the new box "Parental Childrearing Styles Carry Different Meanings in Different Cultures," discusses the work of Ruth Chao in illuminating the different ways in which the *authoritarian* style of parenting is expressed in American and Chinese cultures. In Chapter 16, the new box "Justice versus Interpersonal Obligations: India and the United States" demonstrates that Hindu Indians are much more likely to accord interpersonal considerations importance in making moral judgments than are Americans.

- **Key Terms and Margin Glossary.** In this edition we have carefully reviewed key terms for their usefulness and significance for the student and have added new terms that we consider crucial to the student's learning of new material. These terms, set in boldface type, and their definitions are repeated on the same page in a margin glossary, new to this edition, which helps students to recognize and learn the terminology. Terms that may be unfamiliar but are not crucial to learning the text material are shown in italics. All key terms and their definitions also appear in the alphabetized Glossary at the back of the book.

- **Turning Points Charts.** New to the fifth edition are a series of charts, titled *Turning Points,* which help students view children's evolving skills and abilities in terms of their chronology over the child's development. It is important to note that these charts record what is *typical* and do not take account of individual differences. These charts appear in Chapters 4–10, 13, 15, and 16. We also highlight the chronologies of various specific evolving characteristics and skills in briefer tables throughout the book. Examples include Table 7-2, Children's Understanding of Multiple and Conflicting Emotions; Table 9-2, Acquiring the Concept of Object Permanence; and Table 16-2, Evolution of Prosocial Reasoning.

- **Updated Research.** As the title of our book, *A Contemporary Viewpoint,* promises, we continue to provide the most up-to-date and current perspectives on the field. Of the 2800 references in *Child Psychology,* fifth edition, more than 900 are entirely new to the book. Nearly half of our references are from the 1990s, and of these more than a third date from 1995 onward. We continue to include research classics, however, because they often provide the frameworks for more recent studies and thus are critical for understanding contemporary research.

- **Illustration Program.** In the new edition we have expanded our program of illustrations considerably. The addition of color has enhanced our ability to convey graphic information in a way that is both instructive and appealing. We have revised many graphics and tables to achieve better clarity and have added many new illustrations. A majority of our photographs are in full color, which heightens not only their appeal to the reader but the impact of the information they convey. Clear captions help the student understand figures and photos and relate data clearly to text discussions.

SUPPLEMENTS

A complete package of multimedia ancillaries has been prepared for this book. The supplements listed here may accompany the fifth edition of Hetherington/ Parke, *Child Psychology: A Contemporary Viewpoint*. Please contact your local McGraw-Hill representative for details concerning policies, prices, and availability, as some restrictions may apply.

The **Student Study Guide** (0-07-289692-2) was prepared by Katherine Kipp of the University of Georgia. Each chapter of the Study Guide opens with a chapter summary and list of learning objectives. Key terms, with references to the pages on which they appear in the textbook, are also included. A matching exercise, activities with ready-to-use handouts, and self-tests containing both multiple-choice and essay items allow students to gauge their comprehension of the chapter material. An answer key, complete with feedback explaining each answer and distractor (wrong answer) for all multiple-choice items, is also included.

The **Instructor's Manual** (0-07-289693-0), also prepared by Katherine Kipp, is a comprehensive resource that provides numerous ideas for lectures, class discussions, demonstrations, and student activities. Learning objectives presented here correspond with those in the study guide and the test bank. Lists of relevant films and videos and ready-to-use handouts are also included.

The **Test Bank** (0-07-289694-9), prepared by Gail Walton of Southern Methodist University, contains more than 1,500 multiple-choice, short-answer, and essay questions. Each multiple-choice item is classified by cognitive type—factual, conceptual, or applied—and by level of difficulty, and is keyed to the appropriate learning objective and page number in the textbook. Items that test knowledge of material in the textbook's boxes are indicated for easy reference as well.

Computerized Test Banks, available in Windows (0-07-289696-5) and Macintosh (0-07-289695-1) formats, make the items from the Test Bank easily available to instructors. MicroTest III, a powerful but easy-to-use test-generating program by Chariot Software Group, facilitates both selection of questions from the Test Bank and printing tests and answer keys. Instructors can customize questions, headings, and instructions and add or import their own questions.

The **Critical Thinker** (0-697-26685-0), written by Richard Mayer and Fiona Goodchild of the University of California at Santa Barbara, uses excerpts from introductory psychology textbooks to help students think critically about psychology.

Taking Sides: Clashing Views on Controversial Issues in Childhood and Society, 2/e, (0-697-39104-3) is available to instructors interested in encouraging classroom discussion and helping students to develop their critical thinking skills. This reader is designed to introduce students to controversies in childhood and development by taking a pro/con approach to issues. Featured readings represent the arguments of leading child behaviorists and social commentators, and reflect a variety of lively, current viewpoints.

McGraw-Hill's **Videocases in Human Development** is a four-tape set of videos featuring spontaneous interviews on topics of human development. The Prenatal Issues video (0-07-292971-5) is the first of the four part series, providing excerpts from the lives of real people as they talk about issues such as alternative ways to parenthood, teratogens, preterm babies, and the birth process. The Childhood Issues video (0-07-292972-3) is the second of the series, addressing topics such as biracial adoption, attention deficit-hyperactivity disorder, chronic life-threatening illness, and child prostitution. Videos on Adolescent Issues (0-07-292973-1) and Adulthood Issues (0-07-292974-X) complete the set.

The **McGraw-Hill Developmental Psychology Image Database CD-ROM** (0-07-289691-4) is a dynamic presentation manager that contains 200 color images. Developmental psychology instructors can use the database to create a customized slide show for their courses.

Instructors can also supplement their lectures with a set of 175 full-color **Overhead Transparencies** (0-07-366079-5). This set of transparencies comes with a resource guide that shows how to coordinate each piece with the *Child Psychology: A Contemporary Viewpoint*, fifth edition, textbook.

The *Child Psychology: A Contemporary Viewpoint*, **fifth edition, Web Page** can be accessed from the McGraw-Hill Developmental Psychology site (http://www.mhhe.com/developmental) by choosing Child Development Topical. The pages for *Child Psychology*, fifth edition, display the book's table of contents and offer other information including the book's features and its supplements packages. From these pages instructors and students can also access the Child Development Image Gallery, where they can view and download a number of figures and tables from the Image Database as well as a group of 127 images specifically selected for their relevance to *Child Psychology*, fifth edition. In addition, the *Child Psychology*, fifth edition, pages allow viewers to access information on available audio-visual materials and on many other websites relevant to the study of child development.

The **AIDS Booklet** (0-697-26261-8) is a brief but comprehensive introduction to the acquired immune deficiency syndrome (AIDS).

ACKNOWLEDGMENTS

First and foremost, we want to express our admiration, respect, and gratitude to **E. Mavis Hetherington**, who inspired this project at its inception and who, through four editions, has consistently enriched the field of child psychology through her impeccable sense of scholarship, her rich insights, and her keen eye for new and exciting work in the field. Her earlier research continues to inform *Child Psychology*, 5/e, and many pages of this edition highlight her seminal and continuing work on gender roles, divorce, stepparenting, and behavior genetics. We are indebted to Mavis Hetherington for all she has given to this ongoing book project, and we are grateful for her continuing and significant contributions to the field of child psychology.

We are grateful to the many contributors to the fifth edition of the *Handbook of Child Psychology* who kindly made prepublication copies of their chapters available to us. As this multivolume work's general editor, William Damon, notes, "This fifth edition of the *Handbook of Child Psychology* belongs to an invaluable scholarly tradition: the presentation, at approximately 15-year intervals, of a well-planned, comprehensive, authoritative account of the current state of the field" (1998, p. ix). The current edition includes four volumes: *Theoretical models of human development*, volume editor Richard M. Lerner; *Cognition, perception, and language*, volume editors Deanna Kuhn and Robert S. Siegler; *Social, emotional, and personality development*, volume editor Nancy Eisenberg; and *Child psychology as a practice*, volume editors Irving E. Sigel and K. Anne Renninger. The 131 authors of the 71 chapters in these four volumes are leading experts in their subfields of child psychology. We know that readers of *Child Psychology: A Contemporary Viewpoint* will benefit greatly from discussions throughout our book that draw on portions of this significant work.

We wish to thank Nancy Lees, of the University of California, at both Riverside and Los Angeles, for her contribution to the revision of Chapters 9 and 10, and for her bibliographic assistance on other chapters. Thanks also to Ross Parke's step-daughter, Sarah Tinsley, and to Bob Schemerhorn, who spent many busy nights at the computer tracking down references and helping update the material that formed the basis for this new edition. Their help was invaluable, and their skill and care were greatly appreciated. We also want to thank Tracy Bunker and Heather Guzman for their patient and professional assistance in preparing the manuscript.

We are fortunate to have had a number of people who teach the child development course offer us their insights and suggestions for the manuscript of this book. For this invaluable assistance we thank **Mark Alcorn**, University of Northern Colorado; **Barbara Biales**, College of St. Catherine; **K. Robert Bridges**, Pennsylvania State University—New Kensington; **David Cross**, Texas Christian University; **Trisha Folds-Bennett**, College of Charleston; **Marie Hayes**, University of Maine; **Katherine Kipp**, University of Georgia; **Pat Lefler**, Lexington Community College; **Robert Lickliter**, Virginia Polytechnic Institute and State University; **Dennis R. Papini**, Western Illinois University; **Dana Plude**, University of Maryland; **Laura Thompson**, New Mexico State University; **Gail Walton**, Southern Methodist University; and **Beth Wildman**, Kent State University.

We are particularly grateful to several people who lent their specialized expertise to reviews and recommendations for key areas. Many thanks to **Michael Bailey**, Northwestern University (chapter on intelligence); **Douglas Behrend**, University of Arkansas (chapter on language and communication); **Patricia Kerig**, Simon Fraser University (module on developmental psychopathology); and **David Uttal**, Northwestern University (chapters on cognitive development).

For the fifth time this book has benefited from the expertise and dedication of the McGraw-Hill College Division staff. We express our appreciation to Jane Vaicunas, editorial director, who has continued to support this project through many editions. Mickey Cox, executive editor for psychology, has overseen the entire project with great competence. Leslye Jackson and Beth Kaufman were supportive in the early stages of the project. Throughout the entire process of creating this new edition, Meera Dash, senior developmental editor, has offered us her keen insight and innumerable helpful recommendations, as well as her unfailing and sensitive support. Her assistant, Kristen Mellitt, helped keep the supplements on track and has responded to all our requests with great efficiency. Donna Nemmers, project manager, has supervised the production process smoothly, and Laurie McGee, copyeditor, Inge King, photo researcher, and Connie Dowcett, permissions editor, have made important contributions to the readability, artistry, and accuracy of this book. The designer, Mary Christianson, has provided an elegant framework for the new edition. Jim Rozsa, senior marketing manager, has brought great creativity to the development of a plan for putting our book into the hands of the talented McGraw-Hill sales force.

Finally, Ross Parke thanks his wife, colleague, and friend, Barbara Tinsley, for her insights, suggestions, and feedback that improved the book, as well as her understanding and support through the several years required to prepare this edition. Ginny Locke thanks family and friends for understanding why for so long she couldn't come out and play.

Ross D. Parke
Virginia Otis Locke

CHILD PSYCHOLOGY
A CONTEMPORARY VIEWPOINT

Themes and Theories of Child Development

C H A P T E R 1

A HISTORICAL INTERLUDE

THEMES OF DEVELOPMENT

THEORETICAL PERSPECTIVES ON DEVELOPMENT

DEVELOPMENTAL THEMES AND THEORETICAL PERSPECTIVES: AN OVERVIEW

SUMMARY

At 2 Mariela can put all her red blocks in one group and all the blue ones in another. By the time she's 5 she can sort and re-sort a collection of objects that have several different sizes, different shapes, different colors. And when Mariela is 7 or so she can use this strategy of categorization in learning new information; for example, if her teacher gives her a list of words including *shirt, eyes, carrot, apple, nose, shoes, pants, cereal,* and *mouth* she can learn the words more efficiently by classifying them into groups: clothing, parts of the body, and foods.

Justin, who is a year and a half, plays with his toys next to another child but doesn't talk to the other child or interact with him except, perhaps, to grab one of his companion's toys or scream if the other child has taken one of his. When Justin is 6 or 7 he can and does engage in group play. He also understands that people have different points of view, although he believes that people act from their own self-interest. By the time he is in his midteens, Justin understands the need for positive human relationships, the desirability of being "good" rather than "bad," and the concept of societal law and order.

What accounts for this gradual but steady evolution in the child's ability to perceive and describe complex relationships among things, to learn new things efficiently, and to relate to, interact with, and feel responsibility toward other people? The field of **child development,** or child psychology, seeks to answer this complex question in two major ways: first, by identifying and describing *changes* in the child's cognitive, emotional, motor, and social capacities and behaviors from the moment of conception through the period of adolescence; second, by uncovering the *processes* that underlie these changes and help to explain how and why they occur. Moreover, child developmentalists are interested in the specific *strategies* that children use to help them achieve new skills and behaviors; for example, the cognitive strategy of categorization and the social strategy of cooperating with others offer children powerful aids in learning new information and in becoming successful participants in their social worlds.

Like the broader field of *developmental psychology,* which concerns itself with changes in human abilities and behavior across the entire life span, child development takes both an empirical and an applied approach to the study of growth and change. For some scientists, unraveling the mysteries of childhood is a goal in itself. We study children to increase our knowledge about how development evolves and about what processes further or impede this evolution. We can also derive information about adults from studies of children's development: understanding earlier forms of behavior may help us understand later forms. Moreover, we can observe some processes in simpler forms in children than in adults.

Researchers who study children also undertake their work with many practical and policy implications in mind (Table 1-1 lists some of the issues that this book explores). Better information about child development can assist all members of society who care about the well-being of children, including parents, teachers, health professionals, and legislators. Research findings can lead to helpful advice on a wide range of current issues, from creating and selecting effective day-care programs and handling children's temper tantrums to dealing with the impact of busing and the effects on children of television violence. Finally, information on normal child development helps all those who work with and care for children to detect problems of both physical and mental development, thus facilitating both the prevention and the treatment of developmental difficulties.

Throughout our exploration of contemporary child psychology we will continue to keep these two levels of scientific inquiry in mind. Thus we will repeatedly ask how specific processes and strategies account for different aspects of the child's development. In addition, we will seek to discover how we can use what we learn about these dynamics to improve children's functioning and self-confidence in all the important areas of their lives—their relations with family, friends, and peers; their academic pursuits; and their initial forays into the adult world of work, love, friendship, and societal responsibility.

child development   A field of study that seeks to account for the gradual evolution of the child's cognitive, social, and other capacities first by describing changes in the child's observed behaviors and then by uncovering the processes and strategies that underlie these changes.

TABLE 1-1   Some Interesting Facts about Children's Development

	Where Discussed in the Text
■ A mother's single use of cocaine can adversely affect her developing fetus.	Chapter 3
■ Waterbeds can help premature babies develop.	Chapter 4
■ Newborns can recognize their own mothers by smell.	Chapter 5
■ Babies can learn in the womb.	Chapter 5
■ Even 2-year-olds can be jealous.	Chapter 7
■ Children learn a new language more easily than their parents.	Chapter 8
■ Divorce affects boys' development more adversely than that of girls.	Chapter 12
■ Aggressive behavior in an 8-year-old can sometimes predict criminal behavior at the age of 30.	Chapter 16

A HISTORICAL INTERLUDE

The scientific study of child psychology is a relatively young enterprise that got its start just a century ago with the pioneering work of Charles Darwin. In his research on infants' early sensory and perceptual capacities and children's emotions, Darwin (1872) clearly demonstrated that scientists could study infants and children. Later, John Watson continued the formal analysis of children's learning capacities. Freud and Piaget, about whom you will read shortly in this chapter, were two other important early contributors to our understanding of children.

Why is this field so young? Part of the reason is that our appreciation of childhood as a unique period is a relatively modern phenomenon. As the French historian Philipe Aries, in his classic work *Centuries of Childhood,* documents, for many years people viewed children as miniature adults. Another reason is that people did not value children as we do today. This was, in part, because children often died very young. Many infants died at birth or in the first few months of life, owing largely to people's lack of understanding of germs and infection and to the limited medical knowledge of the times. Another indication of the undervaluation of children was the way adults treated them. Children were often laborers in factories and mines, and it was only in the nineteenth century that child labor laws were introduced to protect children from this kind of exploitation. Even today, child labor laws are not universal, and young children continue to be drafted into the workforce in many countries.

Since the early 1900s the field of child psychology has been concerned not only about improving scientific knowledge about children but about using this knowledge to shape social policy on behalf of children (Sears, 1975, Sigel, 1998). Throughout this book we will see many examples of this historically based commitment to both science and public policy.

THEMES OF DEVELOPMENT

As scientists have studied children's development they have continued to confront and debate a number of significant themes. These themes generally pose basically conflicting views: For example, are children's behavior and development the result of biological, or hereditary, influences, or are they formed by environmental forces? Today scientists agree that both our biology and the social and physical

TABLE 1-2 Overview of Developmental Themes and Theoretical Perspectives

Theoretical Perspectives	Chapters in Which Discussed	Developmental Themes					
		Biology vs. Environment	Active vs. Passive Child	Continuity vs. Discontinuity	Situation vs. Individual	Cultural Universals vs. Cultural Relativism	Risk and Resilience
Learning Perspectives							
Behaviorism (classical and operant conditioning)	5, 7, 16	Environment	Passive child	Continuity (no stages)	High on situational influences	Cultural universals	Low on resilience
Cognitive social learning theory	5, 7, 14, 16	Environment	Moderately active child	Continuity (no stages)	High on situational influences	Cultural universals	Emphasizes both risk and resilience
Cognitive Developmental Perspectives							
Piagetian theory	9, 16	Interaction between biology and environment	Highly active child	Discontinuity (stages of development)	Emphasis on individual characteristics (cognitive frameworks)	Cultural universals	Low in focus on risk and resilience
Vygotsky's sociocultural theory	9, 10	Interaction between biology and environment	Active child	Discontinuity (stages of development)	Situation and context are important	Culture-bound principles	Emphasizes child's resilience
Information processing theory	10, 15, 16	Focus on environment but recognition of biology	Active, reflective child	Continuity (no stages)	Both characteristics of the person and the situation are important	Cultural universals but culture-bound products	No focus on this issue

		Nature and nurture	Activity–passivity	Continuity–discontinuity	Individual/situational	Cultural	Risk/resilience
Psychodynamic Perspectives							
Freudian theory	7, 12, 15	Interaction between biology and environment	Initially passive but increasingly active child	Discontinuity (stages of development)	High on individual traits	Cultural universals	Emphasis on risks and adaptive mechanisms
Erikson's theory	12	Interaction between biology and environment	Initially passive but increasingly active child	Discontinuity (stages of development across entire life span)	High on individual traits	Culture-bound principles	Emphasis on both risk and resilience
Systems Theory Perspectives							
Dynamic systems theory	6, 10, 12	Interactions among all systems—biological, psychosocial, environmental	Active child	Continuity (no stages)	Interaction between situation and individual	Both cultural universals and culture-bound principles	Emphasis on both risk and resilience
Bronfenbrenner's ecological theory	12, 13, 16	Focus on environment but recognition of biology	Highly active child	Continuity (no stages)	High on situational influences	Culture-bound principles	High on resilience
Ethological Theory	7, 12, 13	Emphasis on biology but environment plays role in eliciting and modifying behavior patterns	Moderately active child	Discontinuity (stages of development)	High on situational influences	Cultural universals	Focus on adaptation
Life Span Perspective	12, 13, 16	Focus on environment but recognition of biological constraints	Highly active child	Continuity (no stages)	High on situational influences	Culture-bound principles	Emphasizes both risks (transitions) and resilience

environment that surrounds us affect our development, although they may influence different aspects of development in different degrees. Do children play an active role in their own development or only a passive role? Although among modern psychologists the view of the active child is dominant, some investigators still support the passive view. Does development take place in similar ways in children of all cultures and races, or is the experience of each culture distinct and separate? Here again, each view probably owns a little of the truth.

We will encounter these and other themes repeatedly as we discuss the many sides of development—biological, cognitive, linguistic, emotional, and social. We will also see that different theories of child development—discussed in the next major section—emphasize one or more themes in differing degrees (see Table 1–2). Thus it's important to understand the issues reflected in these themes. The more we try to solve the puzzle of children's development the more we learn about the nature and evolution of all human behavior.

Biological versus Environmental Influences

Most modern viewpoints recognize that both biological and environmental factors influence human development, but they disagree about the relative importance of each of these factors for different aspects of development. Biological extremists of the past argued that biology is destiny, and that development is merely a matter of maturation. They believed that the course of development was largely predetermined by genetic factors; these genetic or biological processes led to the naturally unfolding course of growth called **maturation.** One early advocate of this view was Arnold Gesell, who suggested, "All things considered, the inevitableness and surety of maturation are the most impressive characteristics of early development. It is the hereditary ballast which conserves and stabilizes the growth of each individual infant" (Gesell, 1928, p. 378). Opposing this view, other early theorists, such as the behaviorist John B. Watson, placed their emphasis strictly on the environment. Watson (1928) assumed that genetic factors place no restrictions on the ways that environmental events can shape the course of a child's development and claimed that by properly organizing the environment he could produce a Mozart, a Babe Ruth, or an Al Capone.

maturation   A genetically determined process of growth that unfolds naturally over a period of time.

Today no one supports either of these extreme positions. The challenge to modern developmentalists is to explore how biological and environmental factors interact to produce developmental variations in different children. The interplay between biology and environment is evident in many ways. For example, both certain hormones and exposure to experiences of aggression influence an individual's development of aggressive behavior, both genetic inheritance and nutrition affect physical and social development, and both an infant's temperament and its early environment influence the child's social and personality development.

Thus the question is not which factor is more important, but how the expression of the biological program that we inherit is shaped, modified, and directed by our particular set of environmental circumstances. Anticipating our discussion of language development (Chapter 8), consider the fact that although infants around the world are biologically equipped to learn to recognize and produce language, before the end of their first year they begin to "tune out" linguistic sounds to which they have not been exposed. For example, Dutch babies can discriminate sounds in both Dutch and English but gradually become unresponsive to English words (Kuhl et al., 1997). The environment clearly shapes the form that the infant's biologically based language capacity can assume.

The Active versus the Passive Child

Although early developmentalists viewed the child as a passive organism who is shaped mainly by external forces in the environment, the prevailing view today is that the child is an active seeker of information and of ways to use it. Those modern theorists who do still hold to the passive view assert, for example, that children are either assertive or shy largely as a result of parental childrearing practices. According to this view, a talented teacher encourages a child to become interested in history or geometry, or association with an antisocial peer group causes a child to become delinquent. In general, however, modern developmentalists disagree sharply with this view, holding instead that children are usually active agents who shape, control, and direct the course of their own development (Bell, 1968; Bugental & Goodnow, 1998). Children, they assert, are curious information seekers who intentionally try to understand and explore the world about them. Moreover, socializing agents like parents, peers, or teachers do not simply mold the child; instead, influence is a two-way process. Children actively modify the actions of their parents and other people whom they encounter in their daily lives.

Continuity versus Discontinuity

One of the major questions that confronts developmental psychologists is how to characterize the nature of developmental change. Some view development as a continuous process whereby, in an orderly way, each new event or change builds on earlier experiences. They see development as smooth and gradual, without any abrupt shifts along the path (Figure 1-1*a*). Others, however, view development as occurring in a series of discrete steps or stages and see the organization of behavior as qualitatively different at each new stage or plateau. The concerns of each phase of development and the skills learned in that phase are different from those of every other phase. Consider, for example, the period of adolescence: In the discontinuous view, we should treat adolescence as a distinctive phase of development that marks an abrupt change in biological, social, and cognitive functioning. A little later in this chapter we consider the theories of Jean Piaget and Sigmund Freud, both of whom proposed stage theories of development (Figure 1-1*b* displays the Piagetian model). Each theorist proposed that at every stage, new strategies for understanding and acquiring knowledge and for managing interpersonal relationships come into play and displace the prior ways of dealing with the world. In contrast, scientists like Albert Bandura who endorse the continuous view think of the changes in adolescence as part of an ongoing series of smaller shifts that have been going on throughout childhood.

Recently, some theorists (e.g., Siegler, 1998) have suggested that our judgment of continuity or discontinuity depends on the power of the lens we use in examining changes across development. If we look from a distance or over a fairly long period of time, it is clear that there are marked differences between, say, the young infant's tentative motor abilities and the toddler's motor gymnastics or between the fourth grader's and the adolescent's competence at solving problems of logic. Clearly, both level and quality of skill vary greatly in such comparisons. And as we'll see in Chapter 10, younger and older children approach a memory task differently. Young children try to memorize a list of words by rehearsing the list as it's given to them; older children, on the other hand, tend to group the list into categories, just as the 7-year-old in our opening paragraph does. Categorizing words in order to remember them more efficiently is an illustration of a *qualitative* change in memory. Thus, there are indeed qualitative changes across development.

If we look more closely, however, we find that a change such as a shift to a more efficient memory strategy is not abrupt. In fact, when we examine the ways children solve problems, we find a great deal of variability in the strategies they use at the same point in time: For example, a child may sometimes use a developmentally advanced strategy and at other times a relatively primitive one. Through microscopic examination of this sort, we see a very different picture of development—one of gradual change in which the child only slowly learns to adopt the best and developmentally most advanced approach (Figure 1-1*c*). So over time, qualitative changes proceed in a less coherent and linear way than stage notions of development suggest.

Most contemporary child psychologists hold a more or less middle-of-the-road view of the continuity-discontinuity issue, seeing development as basically

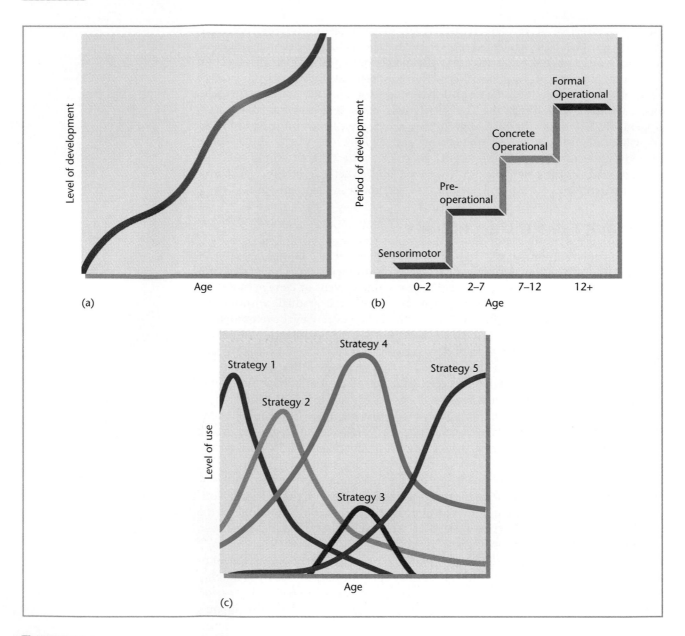

■ FIGURE 1-1

Continuity and discontinuity in the child's development.

The continuous view (a) sees development as a gradual series of shifts in capacities, skills, and behavior without any abrupt changes. Those who hold the opposite perspective (b), in which development is discontinuous, propose just such abrupt, steplike changes, each qualitatively different from the one that precedes it. Most contemporary developmentalists believe a third view, which holds that development is fundamentally continuous but interspersed with transitions that may appear sudden, most accurately represents the progress of development over time. Siegler's "overlapping waves" model (c) suggests that children use a variety of strategies in thinking and learning and that cognition involves constant competition among different strategies rather than the use of a single strategy at a given age. Although each strategy may take a qualitative step forward in effectiveness, at any given point in time the child uses several strategies of varying levels of sophistication. The use of each strategy ebbs and flows with increasing age and expertise, and it is only gradually that the most successful strategies predominate. As a result, from a macroscopic perspective, development appears generally continuous, but at a microscopic level we can observe specific qualitative changes. (Source: part (c) from *Children's Thinking, 3rd ed.* by Siegler, R., p. 92. Copyright © 1998 Prentice-Hall, Inc., Upper Saddle River, NJ. Reprinted with permission.)

continuous but interspersed with periods of transition in which change may be quite sudden or pronounced. These transitional periods are important because developmental processes are often revealed most clearly during such times of change. And transitions come in a variety of forms: Some are biological, such as walking, which may result in a reorganization of the household so that the child cannot reach breakable or dangerous items. Others may be both biological and psychological; the onset of puberty, for example, is often accompanied by changes in how adolescents think about their world and their relationships with family and peers (Caspi, 1998). Still other changes are culturally determined, like the timing of entry into junior high school when the child first confronts new academic subjects and the necessity to move among multiple classrooms and teachers. Moving to a new neighborhood may constitute a major transition if it involves leaving old friends and making new ones. And the transitions posed by divorce or remarriage often present both children and adults with the need for major adjustments. Each transition the individual experiences offers both challenges and opportunities, and the success with which the person handles these challenges gives us insight into the nature of his or her development. We will explore many of these transitions in later chapters.

Situational Influences versus Individual Characteristics

Children grow up in a variety of diverse settings such as homes, schools, playgrounds, and streets. How much do the contexts in which we study children affect what we learn about them? Do children behave differently in certain settings than in others, or do their individual predispositions and personality characteristics cause them to behave similarly across a broad range of situations? Can we describe certain children as honest, dependent, aggressive, or helpful and expect them to exhibit these qualities at all times? How will these traits be manifested in different situations—a difficult test, a confrontation with an angry parent or teacher, a competitive game, or a friend in need? Developmental psychologists differ in terms of the importance they assign to personality or person factors in contrast to situational or setting variables. Many resolve the controversy by adopting an interactionist viewpoint, which stresses the dual role of personality and situational factors (Magnusson, 1996; Magnusson & Stattin, 1998). For example, children who have aggressive personality traits may often seek out contexts in which they can display these characteristics; thus they're more likely to join a gang or enroll in a karate class than opt for the church choir or a stamp collector's club (Bullock & Merrill, 1980). But these same children, in settings that don't allow or promote aggressive behavior, may be friendly, reasonable, and cooperative.

Cultural Universals versus Cultural Relativism

Children who grow up on a farm in China or a kibbutz in Israel, in a village in Peru, or in a suburb in the United States have very different kinds of experiences. Developmental psychologists differ in how they view the importance of culture. Some argue that culture-free laws of development will be discovered to apply to all children in all cultures. Others argue that the cultural setting in which children grow up plays a major role in formulating the laws that govern development. Between these extreme views is one suggesting that development proceeds everywhere in the same orderly fashion but that the rates at which children in different societies progress may vary. For example, in some cultures, children are encouraged to walk very early and are given opportunities to exercise their new skills. In other cultures, infants are carried or swaddled for long periods of time, which reduces their chances to walk until they are older.

Cultures differ not only across national boundaries but within single countries. The United States, Australia, and Russia, for example, all contain a wide range of subcultural groups representing very diverse racial and ethnic traditions (Fisher, Jackson, & Villaruel, 1998). In the United States it is not uncommon to find Native

In the world's many varied cultures children begin, often at an early age, to develop specialized skills. In Somalia a son learns the care and management of camels from his father. In Kotzebue, Alaska, an Inupiat mother guides her daughter in mending fishnets.

American, African American, Japanese American, Hispanic American, European American, and other racial-ethnic children together in a single school or classroom. In spite of the controversy about how culture influences development, today most child developmentalists recognize the importance of considering cultural contexts in their accounts of development (Rogoff, 1998). Later in this chapter we will encounter a theorist, Lev Vygotsky, who put special emphasis on the important role that culture plays in development.

Cultures are, of course, constantly undergoing change. U.S. society, for example, has seen dramatic changes since the 1950s: To mention just a few of these changes, divorce and remarriage are more common, delayed childbearing is on the rise, the majority of women work outside the home, and personal computers are becoming almost as common in households as the television set. Are the laws that govern children's behavior affected by these changes, or do children develop in much the same way regardless of shifts in the culture that surrounds them? Theories differ considerably in the seriousness with which they regard these kinds of shifts, but all recognize that such changes may play a part in influencing a child's development.

Risk and Resilience

Our final theme of child development is the role played by the combination of risk and resilience in childrens development. As we grow and mature, we encounter a variety of risks that may alter our developmental trajectories for better or for worse. Such risks or challenges may alter a child's course of development from normal to nonnormal or from a nonnormal course to a normal one. And risk comes in many forms. Some risks are genetic or biological: for example, a serious illness, or having to live with a psychotic parent. Other risks are demographic: family income, education, or membership in a minority group. Other risks include divorce, the death or remarriage of a parent, physical accidents, multiple shifts in home or caregivers, and institutionalization or repeated hospitalization.

Individual children respond to such risks in very different ways. Many seem to suffer permanent developmental disruptions or delays. Others show "sleeper" effects; they seem to cope well initially, but exhibit problems later in development. Still others, however, exhibit resilience under the most difficult of circumstances, and some not only are able to cope with risk but seem actually to be enhanced by it. Moreover, when they confront new risks later in life these children seem better able to adapt to challenges than children who have experienced little or no risk; in a kind of inoculation effect, they appear to have learned from their experiences (Hetherington, 1991b; Rutter, 1987; Rutter & Rutter, 1993).

Researchers who have studied resilient individuals have identified three primary types of protective factors, or personal attributes and environmental conditions, that appear to buffer the child—and later, the adult—from the effects of risk and stress and to promote coping and good adjustment in the face of adversity. The first set of factors consists of positive individual attributes. Children who have easy temperaments and high self-esteem and who are intelligent and independent are more adaptable in the face of stressful life experiences (Hetherington, 1991b; Rutter, 1987; Werner, 1988). Girls and women seem to have a slight edge on resiliency in comparison with boys and men. The second set of protective factors are combined in a supportive family environment. For example, the presence of one warm supportive parent can help to buffer the adverse effects of poverty, divorce, family discord, and child abuse (Luthar & Zigler, 1991). The final set of factors comprises people outside the family as well as societal agencies and institutions: for example, the school system, peer groups, and churches that support both children's and parents' coping efforts. The effects of these protective factors are not automatic; that is, it is only the individuals who actually make use of such potentially supportive resources who benefit from them.

Studies of risk and resilience show clearly that, contrary to what traditional theories often proposed, development does not proceed along a single, common pathway. Contemporary viewpoints stress that, as they develop, individual children often follow very diverse pathways. Differences in the types and the timing of experiences have profound influences on a child's course of development. A child who experiences serious health problems, fails a grade, reaches puberty early, and drops out of high school will have a radically different developmental pathway from the one traversed by the child who encounters, say, parental divorce and frequent changes in residence but no academic failure. At the same time, we know that children whose pathways are difficult may still mature into well-adjusted adults. Throughout our exploration of children's development we will continually encounter both risk and protective factors, and by tracing how, at different points in development, individual children respond to these challenges we can increase our understanding of the process of development.

THEORETICAL PERSPECTIVES ON DEVELOPMENT

Theories about the way children grow and mature play a central part in the scientific process of understanding children's development. Theories serve two main functions. First, they help organize and integrate existing information into coherent and interesting accounts of how children develop. Second, they lead to testable hypotheses or predictions about children's behavior. No theory is able to account for all aspects of human development, and, as you will see, many of the theories we discuss try to explain and predict a limited area of behavior. For example, the behavioral and cognitive social learning theories we discuss first have focused particularly on learning and on social and emotional behavior; the perspectives of Piaget, Vygotsky, and those who study information processing tend to emphasize cognition, language, and social interaction; the theories advanced by Freud and Erikson place much more emphasis on emotional development and psychopathology. Systems theory perspectives tend to be rather eclectic, as is the life span perspective, which carries the concept of development beyond adolescence into adulthood. Ethological theory, too, endeavors to encompass all areas of behavior, especially biological and social aspects of development.

As we will see, different theories vary both in the emphasis they give to the developmental themes we have just discussed and in the positions they take on the questions these themes pose. It may be helpful to you, as you read this section on theoretical views of development, to refer occasionally to Table 1-2 (see pages 6–7), which locates major discussions of the theories throughout the book and provides an overview of the way the themes and the theories are related. Although we have given some theories more space than others, you should not take this as a sign of their relative importance but a reflection of our decision to give certain theories more in-depth treatment in later chapters. Our goal here is simply to give you the flavor and diversity of different theoretical approaches to development. In the last section of this chapter we will revisit the table as we summarize our discussions of how the various theoretical perspectives view and interpret the themes of development.

Learning Perspectives

The study of learning is one of the oldest subdisciplines of human psychology. In this section we explore some of the principal learning theories that have been applied to developmental issues. We begin with the work of the behaviorists and then consider the approach of the cognitive social learning theorists.

Behavioral Theories

The behaviorist approach to development is exemplified in the work of John B. Watson, Ivan Pavlov, and B. F. Skinner, who developed central ideas of learning and applied these ideas to children's development. **Behaviorism,** which holds that theories of behavior must be based on observations of actual behavior rather than on speculation about motives or other unobservable factors, views development as a continuous process, not a discontinuous or stagelike process. On this view, the same principles of learning shape development throughout childhood and, indeed, across the entire life span. Children play a relatively passive role in their own development; like computers, which can do only what programmers tell them to do, children do only what the environment directs that they do. Modern developmentalists do not generally accept these radical assumptions, but in the history of child psychology the behaviorist view did play a prominent role. A good example of the behaviorist approach is Pavlov's famous experiment in which he showed that a dog would learn to salivate at the sound of a bell if that sound were always associated with the presentation of food. The dog typically salivated at the appearance of food; if the food was repeatedly paired with the sound of a bell, eventually the dog learned to salivate at the sound of the bell whether or not it was accompanied by food. This type of learning is called **classical conditioning.** Watson, following Pavlov's demonstration, used classical conditioning to explain many aspects of children's behavior, especially emotions such as fear. For example, he conditioned an 11-month-old infant to fear furry animals by showing the baby, who was easily frightened by noises, a white rat and simultaneously making a loud noise.

Another form of conditioning, studied by B. F. Skinner, focuses on the impact of the consequences of a person's behavior, rather than on the results of simply pairing particular stimuli. According to Skinner's theory of **operant conditioning,** behavior is modified by the types of rewarding or punishing events that follow it. If we apply this theory to children's behavior, positive reinforcement of a particular behavior in the form of a friendly smile, specific praise, or a special treat can increase the likelihood that a child will exhibit that behavior again. On the other hand, punishment in the form of a frown, criticism, or the withdrawal of such privileges as watching television can decrease the chance that a child will engage in that same behavior again.

Using operant reinforcement principles, Skinner explained a wide range of behaviors, and many later researchers have shown the value of his approach for understanding both how children's behaviors develop and how we can change such behaviors. Gerald Patterson (Patterson, 1982, 1993; Patterson & Capaldi, 1991), for example, has shown how children's aggressive behavior is often increased rather than decreased by the very attention that parents pay to such acts as hitting and

behaviorism A school of psychology that holds that theories of behavior must be based on direct observations of actual behavior and not on speculations about such unobservable things as human motives.

classical conditioning A type of learning in which individuals learn to respond to unfamiliar stimuli in the same way they are accustomed to respond to familiar stimuli if the two stimuli are repeatedly presented together.

operant conditioning A type of learning in which learning depends on the consequences of behavior; rewards increase the likelihood that behavior will recur, whereas punishment decreases that likelihood.

teasing. Patterson has also shown that punishment of these kinds of acts by "time-out"—a brief period of isolation away from other family members—can help diminish aggressive behavior. Operant conditioning has been incorporated into many applied programs to help teachers and parents change children's behavior, including hyperactivity (restlessness, inattention, impulsivity) and aggression.

Cognitive Social Learning Theory

According to **cognitive social learning theory,** children learn not only through classical and operant conditioning but also by observing and imitating others (Bandura, 1989). In a series of classic studies, Bandura showed that if children were exposed to the aggressive behavior of another person they were likely to imitate that behavior. A group of nursery school children watched an adult punch, kick, and pummel a large Bobo doll (a clownlike, inflated rubber doll that pops back up after each attack) either live or on videotape. When the children were later given the chance to play with this doll, they were more likely to attack and play aggressively with it than were a group of children who had not seen the model. Moreover, the child observers reproduced many of the adult model's behaviors quite accurately and precisely. Neither the adult model nor the children had received any apparent reinforcement, yet quite clearly the children had learned some specific behaviors.

Since Bandura's original studies, many researchers who have explored children's learning by observation and imitation have concluded that such learning has both positive and negative aspects. Box 1-1, which describes the impact on children's intellectual development of watching the television program "Sesame Street," gives us one example of the beneficial effects such learning can have. On the negative side, as we discuss in Chapters 2 and 14, there is evidence that children who watch a great deal of television violence are more likely to develop aggressive attitudes and behaviors (Comstock, 1991; Huston & Wright, 1998).

The clues that social learning theory provided as to how the process of imitation works led to experimentation that revealed the important contribution of cognition to the process of observational learning. Discovering that children do not imitate blindly, or automatically, but rather select specific behaviors to imitate, contemporary social learning theorists became increasingly interested in the role of cognitive factors in observation and imitation. As Figure 1-2 illustrates, Bandura has suggested four sets of processes that govern how well a child will learn by observing another person. First, many factors determine whether a child will *attend* to a model's behavior. Children interpret and process the social behaviors they observe on the basis of their own personality variables, their past experience, their relationship with the model or models they observe, and the situations in which observation takes place. Second, specific cognitive skills involved in *retention* play an important role in observational learning. In order to imitate, children must be capable of remembering the many nuances of the behavior a model is displaying, and children who use active strategies (see the chapter's opening paragraph) in rehearsing, organizing, and recalling the observed behaviors are the most effective learners. Third, the observer must have the capacity to *reproduce* the observed behaviors. Fourth and last, the child must be *motivated* or have an incentive to reproduce a model's actions. Together these four sets of processes determine how effectively a child will learn by observing the behavior of others.

■ FIGURE 1-2
Bandura's model of observational learning.
To produce a behavior that matches that of a model, a child goes through four sets of processes. Her ability to attend to the modeled behavior is influenced by factors in her own experience as well as in the situation; her skill in retaining what she has observed reflects a collection of cognitive skills; her reproduction of the behavior depends on other cognitive skills including the use of feedback from others; and she will be motivated to produce the behavior by various incentives, her own standards, and her tendency to compare herself with others. (*Source:* Based on Bandura, 1989)

cognitive social learning theory A learning theory that stresses learning by observation and imitation mediated by cognitive processes and skills.

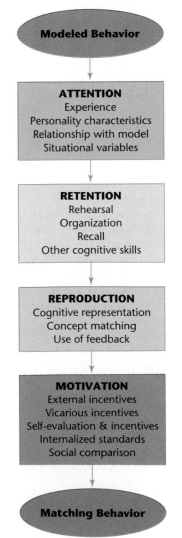

BOX 1-1

Child Psychology in Action

"Sesame Street" as an Educational Tool

Can children learn new intellectual skills by watching television? In the late 1960s, the producers of "Sesame Street" attempted to answer this question by introducing their new show to millions of American children. The specific aim of the show was to improve preschoolers' cognitive skills in order to prepare them better for elementary school education. Through the medium of television, the Children's Television Workshop hoped to bring the educational message to a large number of preschool children. In fact, among its target group of 3- to 5-year-olds, "Sesame Street" is very popular; according to one authority (Chen, 1996), 16 million children watch this program regularly, and on average, children among the target group watch it for three to four hours each week. "Sesame Street" is the only educational children's television show that comes close to being ranked among the top-viewed shows across all television programming (Wartella, 1995).

"Sesame Street" introduced Cookie Monster, Big Bird, Bert, Ernie, and a host of other zany characters to its viewing audience. However, it was not merely the clever puppets and attention-holding tactics but a well-defined set of educational goals that made "Sesame Street" so successful. And according to research findings, the show achieved its goals. Both before and after a six-month viewing period, Ball and Bogatz (1972) tested children on a variety of skills such as identifying letters, numbers, geometric forms, and parts of the body as well as sorting and classifying objects and found marked improvement in a variety of the children's cognitive skills.

These researchers compared the amount of time that children from both low- and middle-income families spent viewing "Sesame Street" with the scores the children received on the various skills measures and found that all the children made measurable gains in test scores. In addition, because they divided the children into groups according to the numbers of hours they typically spent watching the program, they were able to show that the more time children spent viewing, the more gains they made in test scores (see Fig. 1-3). Critics of these studies argued that Ball and Bogatz hadn't sampled "normal" home viewing, that is, viewing without any outside intervention, but when another group of researchers designed a study that did sample natural home viewing, the same positive effects of viewing this popular program emerged. Even controlling for such factors as parents' education levels, parental attitudes, and family size, these investigators (Rice, Huston, Truglio, & Wright, 1990) found that 3- to 5-year-olds showed more improvement in vocabulary over a two-year viewing period than did infrequent viewers.

In an even more ambitious study, researchers measured school readiness, letter and number skills, and vocabulary in 5-year-olds who had viewed "Sesame Street" between the ages of 2 and 4. Children who had watched this program had higher scores than children who had watched it rarely or never viewed it, and these findings held when a number of significant factors were held constant: the children's initial language competency, their parents' educational levels, the family income, the primary language spoken at home, and a score based on the quality of the home environment (Huston & Wright, 1996; 1998). Although reading skills were improved among this group, by the time these children had entered school and reached the age of 7, their earlier TV viewing did not predict their reading skills. This may suggest that the impact of "Sesame Street" is greatest for preschoolers. Older children's reading skills may reflect other, more recent experiences with books and other print media, such as being read to and reading on their own.

In discussing these findings, Huston and Wright (1996) point out that young TV viewers generally do not as often succumb to couch potatohood as their adult counterparts do. Indeed, these researchers assert, the data show that even very young children watch television actively and selectively. When the material is comprehensible and interesting, they attend closely. And according to Chen (1996), young viewers are often physically engaged, singing, clapping, and otherwise following with their favorite characters on screen, particularly when the shows encourage them to do so. These positive effects are not limited to the United States (Cole & Richman, 1997). A study of "Rua Sésamo" in Portugal found that the program helped children and their parents gain a better, more positive perspective about school (Brederode-Santos, 1993). Similarly, learning games from watching "Susam Sokagi" in Turkey and "Plaza Sésamo" in Mexico have been found as well (Sahin, 1990; UNICEF, 1996).

It seems clear both that children learn by observation and that television can be an important educational tool. The passage of the Children's Television Act of 1990 and the National Ready to Learn Act of 1993 were hopeful signs that both the federal government and the broadcast industry have recognized the need to serve the educational and informational needs of children. Parental involvement in pushing for better and better programming will be of great importance, particularly inasmuch as children's television viewing patterns are closely related to parents' and other family members' viewing preferences and influences (Huston & Wright, 1998).

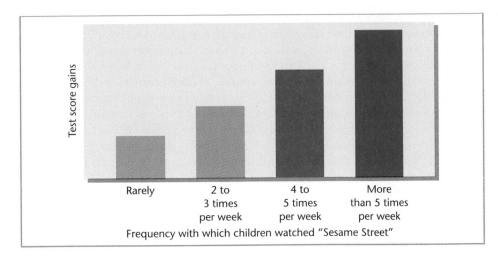

■ FIGURE 1-3
Watching "Sesame Street" makes test scores rise.
In one of the first studies of the effects on children of watching "Sesame Street," researchers found that on such tests as identification of body parts; recognition of letters, numbers, and geometric forms; and classifying and sorting, preschoolers who watched the show frequently performed significantly better than those who watched little.

Together, classical, operant, and cognitive social learning approaches have been highly influential in helping researchers understand children's development. Throughout this book, as we examine children's social, emotional, and intellectual development, we will repeatedly encounter evidence of these different types of learning.

Cognitive Developmental Perspectives

Contributing to the realization that cognitive factors play a major role in children's learning and development were the so-called *organismic* theories of development, theories that hold that psychological structures and processes within the child help to determine his or her development. As you may guess, this perspective sees children as the active organizers of their experience. The best-known organismic theory of development is Swiss psychologist Jean Piaget's cognitive structural theory. Piaget's view has had a profound influence on our thinking about human development. In this section we also introduce the work of Lev Vygotsky who, like Piaget, saw the child as playing an active role but put more emphasis on the notion of development as a joint enterprise between the child and his social environment.

Piagetian Theory

According to **Piagetian theory**, two complementary cognitive processes play a major role in promoting change and increasing children's cognitive understanding of their world. On one hand, children use their current knowledge of how the world works as a framework for the absorption or *assimilation* of new experiences. On the other hand, children modify their existing knowledge base by incorporating new information into its frameworks, or mental structures. Through the process of *accommodation* they modify these frameworks in response to the new input from their environment. As they develop, children reach a better and more meaningful understanding of their world through the interplay between these complementary processes; in Chapter 9 we discuss both processes in greater detail.

Piagetian theory A theory of cognitive development that sees the child as actively seeking new information and incorporating it into his knowledge base through the processes of assimilation and accommodation.

A child psychologist at the universities of Geneva and Lausanne, Switzerland, Jean Piaget (1896–1980) framed a theory of the child's cognitive development that has had great impact on developmentalists, educators, and others concerned with the course and determinants of children's development. The literature on child development today continues to examine Piagetian concepts and techniques as it also refines and expands his work.

According to this viewpoint, children actively interpret and make sense of the information and events they encounter. They are not passive receivers of experience, shaped by the reinforcements and models to which they are exposed; they actively seek experience in order to build their cognitive worlds. Because of this continual interpretation and reorganization of experience, children construct their own reality, a reality that may differ from the objective reality that adults perceive. In addition, the way a child organizes new information depends on her level of cognitive development. Piaget proposed that all children go through several stages of cognitive development, each characterized by qualitatively different ways of thinking, organizing knowledge, and solving problems. Thus, as you can see in Figure 1-1*b*, the Piagetian stage concept sees development as discontinuous.

Young children are more bound than adolescents and adults to sensory and motor information, and they are also less flexible and less able to think symbolically and abstractly. It is not until adolescence that the ability to use logic and to engage in deductive reasoning appears. Young children are also more *egocentric*—that is, they are more centered on their own perspectives than older children and less able to take the viewpoints or understand the feelings and perceptions of others. According to Piaget, we may think of cognitive development as a decentering process, in which the child shifts from a focus on self, immediate sensory experience, and single-component problems to a more complex, multifaceted, and abstract view of the world.

Vygotsky's Sociocultural Theory

The developmental theory proposed by Lev Vygotsky is unique in placing particular emphasis on the impact of children's social and cultural worlds on their development. Despite his early death as the age of 38, Vygotsky, who was a contemporary of Piaget, has had a major impact on our thinking about cognitive development. At the time Vygotsky wrote, the communist revolution had just come into full bloom in the Soviet Union, and much of his theory reflects the philosophy of the times. Vygotsky's work was banned in the early 1940s when Stalin came to power, and as a result it is only rather recently that Western psychologists have begun to give his theory the attention it deserves (Belmont, 1989; Wertsch & Tulviste, 1994).

sociocultural theory A theory of development, proposed by Lev Vygotsky, that sees development as evolving out of children's interactions with more-skilled others in their social environment.

Vygotsky's **sociocultural theory** of development contrasts markedly with those of Piaget and other Western developmentalists. Whereas the latter generally focus on development as it is achieved by the individual child, Vygotsky's theory proposes that the child's development is best understood as a product of social interaction, that it evolves as the child and her more-sophisticated partners—parents, teachers, and others—solve such problems as learning to count or to read. Thus Vygotskian theory focuses on dyadic interaction rather than on individual behavior. It is through the assistance provided by others in her social environment that the child gradually learns to function intellectually on her own, as an individual. According to Vygotsky, every child has a set of innate abilities, such as perceptual and memory skills. It is input from the child's society, in the form of interactions with adults and peers who are more skilled than the child, that molds these basic abilities into more complex, higher-order cognitive functions.

By emphasizing the socially mediated nature of cognitive processes Vygotsky's approach offers a fresh perspective from which to view cognitive development. In addition, his theory has given direction to new ways of assessing children's cognitive potential and new ways of teaching reading, mathematics, and writing (Belmont, 1989; Brown & Campione, 1990; Rogoff, 1998). A vivid example of Vygotskian theory in action in the modern classroom is peer tutoring, in which an older child helps a younger pupil learn to read, write, add, subtract, and so on. Vygotsky has also increased our appreciation of the profound importance of cultural variation in development, as Box 1-2 illustrates.

BOX 1-2

How Culture Can Affect Children's Cognitive Development

Lev Vygotsky's theory placed particular emphasis on the significance of culture in children's development. Vygotsky enunciated two important principles of cultural influence in his theory. First, cultures vary in the institutions and settings they provide to facilitate children's cognitive development. Consider an example from Uzbekistan, a former member of the old Soviet Union: Traditional Uzbekis, for the most part illiterate, responded to reasoning problems using concrete examples based on their own experience. On the theory that education can transform the ways in which we think, Alexander Luria (1971), an early collaborator of Vygotsky, showed that Uzbekis who learned to read and write began to approach problems in different ways. For example, they treated reasoning problems such as syllogisms as logical (and abstract) puzzles (Scribner, 1985).

Other researchers have come up with similar findings in other cultures of the world. For example, Saxe (1982) found that the Oksapmim people of Papua, New Guinea, relied on a rudimentary number system based on their own body parts to help them deal with the demands of daily life (rather like the Western child's counting on his fingers). However, as a result not only of education but of new occupational and trading activities, the system is changing: Not only paper and pencil notations but calculators are transforming the Oksapmim's traditional counting methods.

Consider another example in which a visitor to a culture was frustrated, in attempting to learn a skill, by culturally determined teaching methods: A U.S. college student undertook to study loom weaving with an experienced weaver of the Zinacantan culture, in Mexico. For two months the student observed while the weaver created her fabric; the weaver would often call the student's attention to a fine point of her technique, but she never allowed the student to lay a hand on the loom. Instead, she would say from time to time that inasmuch as the student had seen her do the weaving, she had learned it herself. Although the student kept silent, she did not agree; indeed, she wanted to shout, "Let me try it myself!" Understandably, perhaps, she was more than chagrined when, at last given the loom, her inevitable mistakes elicited the weaver's criticism that she hadn't watched and therefore hadn't learned (Greenfield & Childs, 1991).

In the Zinacanteco culture, motoric quietude and a habit of responding rather than initiating have been valued qualities. Perhaps a Zinacanteco student of weaving would have sat more quietly and attended more closely to the actions of the weaving master than did the U.S. student. On the other hand, the authors point out, at the time they began their study of development and cultural context weavers produced a limited number of patterns, but within a few years new patterns were becoming common; one wonders if the teaching method has changed as well.

Vygotsky's second principle was that we must consider cultural contexts in assessing children's cognitive development. Cognitive tasks should be embedded in their appropriate cultural context; we may seriously underestimate children's development if we ignore the culturally specific nature of children's learning (Greenfield & Cocking, 1995; Greenfield & Suzuki, 1998; Rogoff, 1990).

Like Piaget, Vygotsky was a stage theorist, defining development in terms of abrupt shifts rather than steady, incremental change, and he believed in studying the processes by which development occurs, not just its end products. He was also interested in what he considered the psychological tools children use to understand their world. These tools, or *mediators*—which can take a variety of forms—include language, counting, mnemonic devices, algebraic symbols, art, and writing. As children develop, different tools emerge to permit them to function more effectively in solving problems and understanding their cognitive world.

Information-Processing Approaches

Unlike Piaget's and Vygotsky's stage theories of development, **information-processing theories** emphasize the continuous flow of development: "The quality of children's thinking at any stage depends on what information they represent in a particular situation, how they operate on the information to achieve their goal, and how much information they can keep in mind at one time" (Siegler, 1991, p. 59).

Theorists in this tradition often use computer analogies and flowcharts to describe the precise steps that a child must take to solve a problem and generate an answer (see Figure 10-1 in Chapter 10). These models are not meant to imply that human beings think in the same way that computers process information; the strategies are designed simply to help researchers plot expected steps in a precise

information-processing theories Theories of development that focus on the flow of information through the child's cognitive system and that are particularly interested in the specific operations the child performs between input and output phases.

19

manner. Information-processing theorists focus on the flow of information through the cognitive system, beginning with an input or stimulus and ending with an output or response (Klahr, 1989; Klahr & MacWhinney, 1998). Output may take a variety of forms including an action, a decision, an insight, a verbalization, or simply a memory that is stored for later use.

So far, this sounds similar to the behavioral approach, but information-processing theorists are most interested in the steps or operations that a child performs between input and output. What operations does the child perform to achieve the output? He attends to information, changes it into a mental or cognitive representation, stores it in memory, compares it to other memories, generates various responses, makes a decision about the most appropriate response, and, finally, takes some specific action. These operations are analogous to the way computers deal with information; information in the form of symbols is entered into the system and this input undergoes a series of transformations—it is registered, organized, and stored, and finally it provides an answer or output. We can also draw analogies between the human brain and computer hardware, and between the human being's cognitive operations like attention, evaluation, decision making, and memory storage and retrieval and the software that enables the computer to function.

Consider this illustration of the information-processing approach in which we trace the steps that a child goes through in trying to understand a new story, Dr. Dolittle's tale of the pushmi-pullyu, a horselike creature that has a head at each end.

> The delighted child attends to the picture of the creature while ignoring other objects on the page and encodes it visually, as an image, or verbally, as a "pushmi-pullyu" or a "two-headed horse." He processes this visual or verbal representation further as he compares it with previously stored information about horses or fantastic creatures such as unicorns. Furthermore, the child may [pose questions based on the] implications [of] having two heads ("How does it know if it's coming or going?"), store the new information in a way that allows him to recognize pushmi-pullyus on future occasions, and finally laugh, ask his father to reread the page, or look ahead in the book for more pictures of the pushmi-pullyu (Miller, 1993, p. 235).

As this example illustrates, according to the information-processing perspective, the child, in order to understand or achieve meaning about some external event, engages in a series of cognitive operations by which information is changed, transformed, and manipulated over time. The hallmark of this perspective is the precise way in which it specifies the steps that the child takes to achieve this understanding.

The information-processing approach has been applied particularly to a wide range of problems of cognitive development, including attention, memory, problem solving, and planning. In Chapter 10 we give particular attention to this developmental approach. Information-processing theory is also proving to be a highly valuable approach to the study of how children develop an understanding of reading, mathematics, and science (Siegler, 1991; 1998). And, interestingly, this approach has also provided a powerful analytic tool for understanding social behavior, such as social problem solving and aggression (Crick & Dodge, 1994).

Psychodynamic Perspectives

With his introduction of *psychoanalytic theory*, Sigmund Freud initiated a revolution in thinking about human motivation and personality. Freud's general views on the critical role played in the development of personality by events occurring in the early years of development—especially those having to do with basic drives such as hunger and sexual urges—and by instinctual and unconscious motivation were seen as radical in the early 1900s. Today, however, Freudian views are accepted at least in part by many Western psychologists. An innovative theorist who constantly revised his theory, Freud has had an enormous influence on psychological and psychiatric thinking. Many of his specific concepts, however, continue to invite debate and controversy. Today those who follow in his footsteps generally hold to what is called *psychodynamic theory,* which, in its simplest form, proposes that dynamic forces within the individual determine motivation and behavior. Psychodynamic theories have been more influential in clinical, or applied, settings than in scientific research, and for this reason they have been less often incorporated into the study of child development than other theories discussed here.

In this section we examine not only traditional Freudian theory but the developmental theory of Erik Erikson, who accepted many of Freud's basic ideas but expanded them to include the full life span from childhood to adulthood and old age. Erikson also gave more recognition to the importance, in both child and adult development, of social interaction, social influence, and culture.

Freudian Theory

According to Freud's **psychoanalytic theory of development,** psychological growth and change are governed by unconscious drives and instincts. Freud stressed the role of biologically based drives such as sex, aggression, and hunger in determining behavior. At the same time, he held that these drives were shaped by encounters with the environment, especially other family members. For Freud, the developing personality consists of three interrelated parts: the id, the ego, and the superego. The roles that each of these three components of personality play change across development as the infant, who is largely under the control of the **id,** or its instinctual drives, gradually becomes more rational and reality bound. The id operates on the *pleasure principle,* which is oriented toward maximizing pleasure and satisfying needs immediately. As the infant develops, the **ego,** or the rational, controlling part of personality, emerges and attempts to gratify needs through appropriate, socially constructive behavior. The third component of personality, the **superego,** emerges when the child *internalizes*—that is, accepts and absorbs—parental or societal morals, values, and roles and develops a *conscience,* or the ability to apply moral values in judging her own acts.

To Freud, development was a discontinuous process. In each of five discrete stages, biological forces orchestrate the relations between the developing child and his world (see also Table 1-3). In the first, *oral* stage, which extends through the first year of life, the infant is preoccupied with activities such as eating, sucking, and biting and with objects, such as food, that can be put in the mouth. Freud assumed that the infant derived great enjoyment and satisfaction from these oral behaviors. In the second or sometimes third year, priorities change: In this *anal* stage, the child is forced to learn to postpone the pleasure of expelling feces, as his parents struggle with the task of toilet training. From here until the fifth or sixth year, the *phallic* stage holds sway: Children's sexual curiosity is aroused. Their preoccupation with their own sexual anatomy and the pleasures of genital stimulation alerts them as well to the differences in sexual anatomy between the genders.

During the phallic period, boys become enmeshed in the **Oedipus complex,** in which they are attracted to their mothers and feel themselves jealous rivals of their fathers but also fear the latter will punish them by cutting off their genitals. The Oedipus complex is resolved when boys give up their sexual feelings for their mothers and identify with their fathers. In the **Electra complex,** girls blame their mothers for their own lack of a penis and focus their sexual feelings on their fathers, who possess the penis Freud believed they wanted. When they finally realize that they cannot possess their fathers as mates, girls transfer their feelings to other males. They relinquish their resentment of their mothers and instead begin to identify with her. These dramatic events are followed by the *latency* period, when Freud believed that sexual drives are temporarily submerged. During this period, which lasts from about 6 years of age to puberty, children avoid relationships with opposite-gender peers and become intensely involved with peers of the same gender. As we will discuss further in Chapter 13, this turning from the family to the

---

psychoanalytic theory of development Freud's theory that development, which proceeds in discrete stages, is determined largely by biologically based drives shaped by encounters with the environment and through the interaction of three components of personality—the *id, ego,* and *superego.*

id The person's instinctual drives; the first component of the personality to evolve, the id operates on the basis of the *pleasure principle.*

ego The rational, controlling component of the personality, which tries to satisfy needs through appropriate, socially acceptable behaviors.

superego The personality component that is the repository of the child's internalization of parental or societal values, morals, and roles.

Oedipus complex A primary dynamic of the *phallic* stage of Freudian development theory in which the boy is sexually attracted to his mother, is a rival with his father, and fears his father's retribution.

Electra complex A primary dynamic of Freud's *phallic* stage in which a girl resents her mother for having deprived her of a penis and transfers her affections to her father.

TABLE 1-3   Freud's and Erikson's Developmental Stages

	Stage of Development	
Age Period	Freudian	Eriksonian
0–1	**Oral.** Focus on eating and taking things into the mouth	**Infancy.** Task: To develop *basic trust* in oneself and others. Risk: *mistrust* of others and lack of self confidence
1–3	**Anal.** Emphasis on toilet training; first experience with discipline and authority	**Early Childhood.** Task: To learn self-control and establish *autonomy*. Risk: *shame* and *doubt* about one's own capabilities
3–6	**Phallic.** Increase in sexual urges leads to Oedipus complex in males and Electra complex in females	**Play Age.** Task: To develop *initiative* in mastering environment. Risk: Feelings of *guilt* over aggressiveness and daring
6–12	**Latency.** Sexual urges repressed; emphasis on education and the beginnings of concern for others	**School Age.** Task: To develop *industry*. Risk: Feelings of *inferiority* over real or imagined failure to master tasks
12–20	**Genital.** Altruistic love joins selfish love; need for reproduction of species underlies adoption of adult responsibilities*	**Adolescence.** Task: To achieve a sense of *identity*. Risk: *Role confusion* over who and what individual wants to be
20–30		**Young Adulthood.** Task: To achieve *intimacy* with others. Risk: Shaky identity may lead to avoidance of others and *isolation*
30–65		**Adulthood.** Task: To express oneself through *generativity*. Risk: Inability to create children, ideas, or products may lead to *stagnation*
65+		**Mature Age.** Task: To achieve a sense of *integrity*. Risk: Doubts and unfulfilled desires may lead to *despair*

*Freud's *genital* stage encompassed both adolescence and adulthood.

peer group is associated with the acquisition of the social skills necessary to function effectively in the world. In Freud's last stage, the *genital* period, sexual desires reemerge, but this time they are more appropriately directed toward peers. Once again, biological change—in this case, puberty—plays a significant role in defining developmental focus.

According to Freud, the ways in which the child negotiates each of these stages has a profound impact on his later, adult personality. For example, infants who have unsatisfied needs for oral stimulation may be more likely to smoke as adults. Or toddlers whose parents toilet trained them extremely early and in a very rigid manner may later be obsessively concerned with neatness and cleanliness. Research has in fact supported very few of these predictions, but the general view that events in infancy and childhood have a formative impact on later development remains a central issue in the study of child development.

Erikson's Theory

Erik Erikson, one of Freud's most influential disciples, is a good example of the many followers who accepted a considerable number of Freud's general concepts but turned gradually to a view that gave greater emphasis to the effects of the social environment on the individual's development. Erikson's **psychosocial theory** held, as did Freudian theory, that development was discontinuous, proceeding through a

psychosocial theory Erikson's theory of development that sees children developing through a series of stages largely through accomplishing tasks that involve them in interaction with their social environment.

series of stages. However, as you can see from Table 1-3, Erikson proposed eight specific developmental stages across the life span, whereas Freud left his last stage open-ended, suggesting that is encompassed both adolescence and adulthood. For every one of his stages, Erikson specified the personal and social tasks that the individual must accomplish as well as the risks the individual confronts if she fails at the tasks of that particular stage.

Erik Erikson (1902–1990) left his native Germany after finishing school and wandered through Europe, sketching and writing about what he saw, in search of his own identity. This journey led him eventually to the practice of psychoanalysis and to one of his best-known concepts, that of the child-adolescent's *identity crisis*. Erikson's psychosocial theory of development, spanning the entire life course, continues to inform the thinking of many psychologists and other social scientists.

In the first stage, of infancy, the challenge of acquiring a sense of basic trust is the main task. By learning to trust his parents or caretakers the infant learns to trust not only his environment but himself. If he finds others not trustworthy, he may develop mistrust of both himself and the world. In early childhood, children must learn self-control and develop autonomy but may develop shame and self-doubt if they remain worried and concerned about their continuing dependency and their inability to live up to adult expectations. During the play age, between about 3 and 6, children struggle to develop initiative and to master their environment but at the same time often feel guilty if they are too aggressive, too daring. Between 6 and 12, during the school age, children try to develop industry, largely by succeeding in school. This is also a period of constant social comparison whereby children evaluate their skills in relation to their peers. Real or imagined failure at either academic or social tasks may bring feelings of inferiority.

In Erikson's stage of adolescence, the child's main focus is the search for a stable definition of the self—that is, for a self-identity—and the danger is role confusion, in which the individual cannot get a grip on who or what she wants to be. In young adulthood, the task is to achieve intimacy with others and, in particular, a stable intimate and sexual relationship with one other. Problems in earlier stages, such as a shaky sense of identity, may lead to the avoidance of relations with others and thus to isolation. The task that confronts the individual in adulthood is to create something—children, ideas, or products. If not given expression, this quality of generativity can deteriorate into stagnation. In Erikson's last stage, that of mature age, ego integrity is the goal. When reflection on one's past accomplishments and failures leads to doubt and regret, despair may be the result.

Psychodynamic theories have helped shape many of the concerns of modern child psychology, including the impact of early experience on later behavior, the role of the family in socialization, and—particularly through Erikson's work—the impact of social interaction on children's development. For some years few researchers actively tested psychodynamic theories, and their concepts and principles were of most interest to professional psychologists and others working with people who were psychologically distressed. Beginning about the 1980s there was a revival of interest in certain issues, such as Erikson's concept of the formation of self-identity in adolescence (Grotevant, 1986; Waterman, 1985). More recently, investigators have examined the concept of generativity, especially the effects of being a parent on this quality in adulthood (Hawkins & Dollahite, 1997; Snarey, 1993).

Systems Theory Perspectives

For a long time developmentalists and other psychologists have realized that children as well as adults function not only in many different settings—such as home, school, workplace—but in broader contexts, such as communities and societies. As we have seen, some theorists, notably Vygotsky and Erikson, have taken particular account of the effects of social and cultural surroundings on the developing individual. Nevertheless, until recently the notion of the responsible individual—the independent self, rational, and self-constructed—that evolved out of Cartesian and other Enlightenment thinking held sway in psychology as in philosophy and other fields (Fogel, 1993). Beginning in the late nineteenth century, thinkers in such diverse fields as evolutionary science (Charles Darwin), physics (Albert Einstein), and economics (Karl Marx) began to emphasize the importance of the physical and social surround, and out of their thought came the notion that "the idea of human interdependence, of social relativity, of people and their products as individuals who construct the social order, of freedom from hereditary predestination and from the constraints of centralized leadership, cannot be traced to a single individual but to a socio-historical process that shaped the character of Western science and thought" (Fogel, 1993, p. 45). We consider two theoretical perspectives that illustrate a systems theory approach to development: dynamic systems theory and ecological systems theory.

Dynamic Systems Theory

Around the turn of the last century, scientists began to think in terms of *process*—a concept we have alluded to before—and in terms of the *system,* which can be defined most simply as a regularly interacting or interdependent group of parts. What makes the system more than just a collection of parts is its dynamism; because its parts are in constant motion, the processes in which they engage and the relationships they form and maintain become the primary focus of the system. Thus in **dynamic systems theory,** individuals and their achievements remain significant but must be understood and interpreted within the framework of interacting, dynamic systems in which contributing relations among the members of the system have equal importance and in which change is the only constant. Table 1-4 summarizes some important principles of this theory.

Because systems are dynamic and their members are active organisms, the latter are constantly changing the environment, and this brings about some interesting contradictions. According to Piaget, development occurs as a result of the contradictions between what the individual knows and the existing environment. However, as Sameroff (1989) points out, the contradiction may become compounded, for "the act of knowing is already changing what one is trying to know" (p. 226). On this view, the challenge the young child faces in trying to understand and interact with his environment is formidable. On the other hand, the support his environment gives him in the form of continuing interrelations with members of the systems and subsystems within which he functions can help him meet the challenge. Systems theory has been applied to a variety of developmental issues, including motor development, perception, language, cognition, and social behavior (Smith & Thelen, 1993); we discuss some of these efforts in later chapters (see Table 1-4).

According to Fogel (1993), one of the problems that psychologists have with systems thinking is that it "democratizes the process of developmental change" (p. 49). From a systems perspective, the brain and central nervous system are not the absolute rulers of the human being, nor are the genes the sole determinants of human development. For example, Fogel says, the organism inherits not only its parents' genes but the genes' environment, that is, the original cell (the *zygote,* which we will meet in Chapter 3) created by the act of sexual reproduction, in which the genes reside. Thus because the genes are already interacting with an environment as the organism that has been created begins to grow, the organism has inherited developmental processes, not simply genes. Again we see that the emphasis of dynamic systems theory is on process: "life is process, not substance" (Weiss, quoted in Fogel, 1993, p. 47). The actions of a system and its members are constantly changing in response to ongoing interactions within the system as well as among the system and other systems and their members. We will encounter

dynamic systems theory
A theory that proposes that individuals develop and function within systems and that studies the relationships among individuals and systems and the processes by which these relationships operate.

TABLE 1-4   Some Principles of Systems Theory Perspectives

Complexity   Each part of a system is unique but also related to one or more of the system's other parts. For example, an extended family comprises individual members—mother, brother, niece—and subsystems—a married couple; their daughter and her husband and children; their son and his wife and children. Each family member and family subsystem influences and is influenced not only by each other member and subsystem but by the relationships among different members and subsystems.

Wholeness and Organization   The whole system is organized and more than just the sum of its parts. Its collective behavior can be described in terms that do not necessarily apply to the system's parts and their interrelationships. To understand a family system's functioning we must study not only the characteristics of individual family members and the relationships between them but the organization of all family relationships and the whole family as an interacting unit.

Identity and Stabilization   No matter how the components of a system may change or how external forces may influence it, the identity of the system remains intact. The family unit continues even when new members join it and older members die. The system's tendency toward stability is maintained over time by the ongoing interactions among individual members and their relationships with one another. The continuing care given children by their parents, the children's dependence on their parents, and the relations among this nuclear group and the extended family help to maintain the family as a system.

Morphogenesis   A system must be able to grow and adapt to internal and external changes. Children go to school, leave home, marry, and establish new family subsystems. Parents raise children, change jobs, retire, and may become dependent on their children. Catastrophic change, like divorce, may force a family system to reorganize itself by, say, adapting to a stepparent or accommodating to a new mode of functioning in which a single parent assumes responsibility for the entire family. The family must also adapt to historical change and to changes in social values and institutions, such as economic cycles, social ills like crime, substance abuse, discrimination.

Equifinality   Although the dynamics of certain kinds of systems may be quite different, over time they tend to develop similarities. Family systems across different societies and cultures share many common characteristics, yet the particular customs of a culture may dictate quite different expressions of these characteristics.

Source: Based on Fogel, 1993; Novak, 1996; Sameroff, 1989, 1994; Thelen, 1992.

many different applications of systems theory later in the book; in the next section we look at one particularly influential application, that of Urie Bronfenbrenner's ecological systems theory.

Bronfenbrenner's Ecological Theory

Ecological theory stresses the importance of understanding not only the relationships between the organism—such as the child—and various environmental systems—such as the family and the community—but the relationships among environmental systems themselves. The theory views children as active participants in creating their own environments and considers children's subjective experiences of their relationships and their surroundings just as important as the objective aspects of these phenomena.

Urie Bronfenbrenner (1979, 1986, 1989; Bronfenbrenner & Morris, 1998), a major advocate of ecological theory, has offered a framework for organizing sets of environmental systems. In his view, the child's world is organized "as a set of nested structures, each inside the next, like a set of Russian dolls" (1979, p. 22). As Figure 1-4 illustrates, these structures, or systems, range from the most immediate

ecological theory   A theory of development that stresses the importance of understanding not only the relationships between the organism and various environmental systems but the relations between such systems themselves.

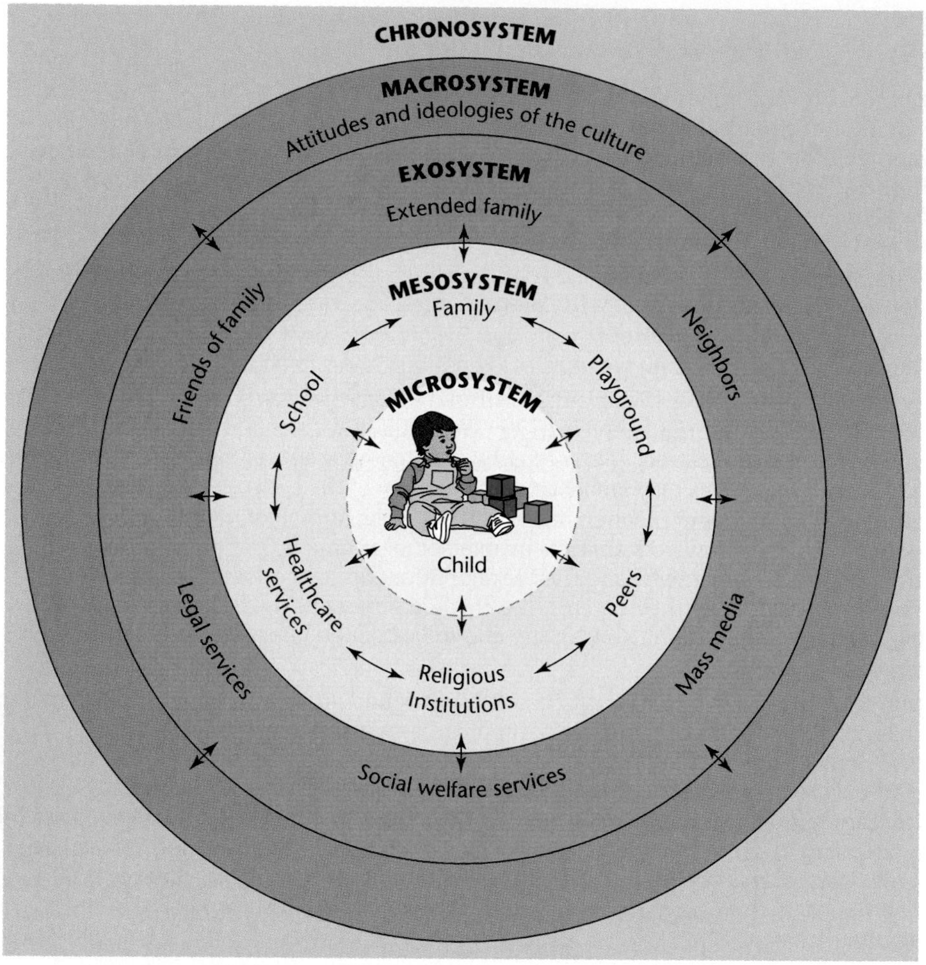

■ FIGURE 1-4
Bronfenbrenner's ecological model of development. Bronfenbrenner emphasizes the importance of the developing child's interactions with the people and institutions closest to her within the *microsystem* and *mesosystem,* as well as the effects on her life of a widening array of social and cultural institutions, attitudes, and beliefs within the *exosystem* and the *macrosystem.* The fact that all of these systems change over time is represented by the *chronosystem. (Source:* Adapted from Garbarino, 1982)

microsystem In Bronfenbrenner's ecological theory, the context in which children live and interact with the people and institutions closest to them, such as parents, peers, and school.

mesosystem The inter-relations that obtain among the components of the *microsystem* with which the child interacts.

exosystem The collection of settings that impinge on a child's development but in which the child does not play a direct role.

macrosystem The system that surrounds the *microsystem, mesosystem,* and *exosystem,* and that represents the values, ideologies, and laws of the society or culture.

settings, such as the family or peer group, to more remote contexts in which the child is not directly involved, such as the society's value and legal systems. Both these systems and the relationships among them can change over the course of development. The **microsystem** is the setting in which the child lives and interacts with the people and institutions closest to her. Over time, the relative importance of these different interactions may change. For example, family may be most important in infancy, whereas peers and school may become important foci in middle childhood and adolescence. The **mesosystem** comprises the interrelations among the components of the microsystem. Thus, parents interact with teachers and the school system; both family members and peers may maintain relations with a religious institution; health-care services interact both with a child's family and her school.

The **exosystem** is composed of settings that impinge on a child's development but with which the child has largely indirect contact. For example, a parent's work may affect the child's life if it requires that he travel a great deal or suddenly go on shift work. Or, if a local planning commission decides to run a highway through the neighborhood playground, the child's recreational life may suffer. The **macrosystem,** which surround Bronfenbrenner's first three systems, represents the ideological and institutional patterns of a particular culture or subculture. Broad patterns of beliefs and ideology distinguish different cultures and countries, as well as different subcultures within a single country. Children who grow up in China experience a different social ideology than children who grow up in the United

States. Children who live in an inner-city ghetto are exposed to a different set of values and beliefs than children in an affluent suburb.

Finally, these four systems—the micro-, meso-, exo-, and macrosystems—change over time. Bronfenbrenner's term for the time-based dimension of his model is the **chronosystem.** The chronosystem can alter the operation of all ecological levels, from microsystem to macrosystem. Over time both the child and his environment undergo change, and change can originate within the individual (e.g., puberty, severe illness, an accident) or in the external world (e.g., the birth of a sibling, entering school for the first time, divorce, winning the lottery). Bronfenbrenner suggests that understanding both kinds of changes is crucial to an appreciation of how the other components of his model shift and, in turn, how all these changes affect development. "Whatever the origin, the critical feature of such events is that they alter the existing relation between person and environment, thus creating a dynamic that may instigate developmental change" (Bronfenbrenner, 1989, p. 201). Development involves the interaction of a changing child with a changing matrix of ecological systems.

chronosystem The time-based dimension that can alter the operation of all other levels, from *microsystem* through *macrosystem.*

Ethological Theory

Another perspective that stresses the importance of context in development is ethological theory. Since Charles Darwin proposed that only the "fittest" survive in the world of infrahumans, other scientists, like the European zoologists Konrad Lorenz and Niko Tinbergen, have sought to understand both the evolution of behavior and its adaptive, or survival, value to the species exhibiting it (Hinde, 1987, 1989, 1994). Central to this line of thought is the necessity to view and understand behavior as occurring in a particular context. For example, in studying social interactions among monkeys, one must consider habitat; that is, the kind of vegetation that is available to a band of monkeys for food and protection is a powerful determinant of such things as social organization and social dominance. Similarly, in attempting to understand human children's behavior, ethologists stress the critical importance of the nature of the setting in which behavior takes place, such as a classroom, playground, or library.

Increasingly, **ethological theory** and the research it has generated have captured the attention of child developmentalists, who observe many behaviors in human infants and children that are "species-specific" (unique to their species) and that they believe may play an important role in ensuring that others meet children's basic needs. This hypothesis is supported by the finding that some behaviors are common to all human children regardless of the culture into which they are born and in which they grow to maturity. Studies have found, for example, that emotional expressions like those of joy, sadness, disgust, and anger are similar across a wide range of modern cultures, including those of Brazil, Japan, and the United States, as well as of older cultures such as the Fore and Dori tribes of New Guinea (Ekman, 1972, 1994; Ekman et al., 1987).

Many behaviors such as smiling and crying that are seen across a range of cultures have a biological basis and play an important role in ensuring that caregivers meet children's needs. Crying can be viewed as an "elicitor" of parental behavior; it serves to communicate the fact that a child is distressed or hungry. It thus has clear survival value, for it ensures that parents give the young infant the kind of attention she needs for adequate development. Although human ethologists view many elicitors such as crying as biologically based, they also assume that these types of behaviors are modified by environmentally based experiences. For example, children may learn to mask their emotions by smiling even when they are unhappy (Saarni, Mumme, & Campos, 1998). Thus modern ethologists view children as open to learning and input from the environment; children are not solely captives of their biological roots.

ethological theory A theory that holds that behavior must be viewed and understood as occurring in a particular context and as having adaptive or survival value.

Proposing one of the first theories of children's emotional development, Charles Darwin (1809–1882) based much of his theorizing on his infant son's earliest emotional expressions. Although Darwin is more widely known for his theory of organic evolution, his work on children's emotional behavior continues to have considerable influence on the field of child development.

A powerful concept that we will encounter in Chapter 4 comes from ethology—this is the notion of the *critical period*, or the specific time in an organism's development during which certain external factors have a particular impact on the organism. Related to this notion is John Bowlby's theory of attachment, discussed in Chapter 7, which proposes that a child's early development of a warm and intimate relationship with a caretaker is crucial to her social relationships in later life.

One of ethologists' major interests is the organization of social behavior between individuals— for example, between brother and sister or between two peers. Ethologists frequently study the role of nonverbal behavior in regulating social exchanges among children. We know that monkeys often use threat gestures, such as a stare and bared teeth, to ward off attackers or appeasement signs, such as baring the neck, to call a halt to a struggle. As Darwin observed over a century ago, "making oneself smaller" is an appeasement gesture that can inhibit aggression. Do children use similar tactics? When researchers observed elementary school boys at play during school recess, they found that such behaviors as kneeling, bowing, and lying down—all behaviors that involved "making themselves smaller"—were successful appeasement tactics (Ginsburg, Pollman, & Wauson, 1977). When the playground bully was on a rampage, boys who displayed these behaviors were more likely to be successful in stopping an attack. Darwin was right—and modern ethologists continue to explore ways in which social behavior is regulated by gestures, postures, facial expressions, and other nonverbal cues. As we will see in Chapter 13, ethologists have also made important contributions to our understanding of how children's groups are organized. It turns out that monkeys and chickens are not the only ones to develop dominance hierarchies. According to Hinde (1994), children develop specific organizational structures and "pecking orders" as well!

Ethologists' basic methodology is the observation of children in their natural surroundings, and their goals are to develop detailed descriptions and classifications of behavior. They seek to understand how behavior is organized into meaningful patterns. For example, high rates of hitting, poking, kicking, and yelling are often used to define the construct of aggression, whereas a slight lift of the eyebrows, a suggestive smile, and a tilt of the head suggest a pattern of flirtatious behavior. Ethology has been very influential in increasing the popularity of observational approaches in modern developmental psychology.

Life Span Perspective

life span theory   A theory that sees development as a process that continues throughout the life cycle, from infancy through adulthood and old age.

The **life span theory** of development has gained increasing recognition in recent years. In contrast to traditional development perspectives, which span the period of infancy through adolescence, the life span view recognizes that development is a process that continues throughout the life cycle into adulthood and old age (Baltes, 1987; Baltes, Lindenberger, & Staudinger, 1998; Elder, 1998). Erik Erikson, whose work we discussed earlier, was one of the first to extend the notion of development

BOX 1-3

Risk and Resilience

Children of the Great Depression

What happens to children when economic disaster strikes? To find out, Elder (1974) studied children who, at the time of the Great Depression, were part of an ongoing longitudinal study in California of social and intellectual development. Some of the children were just entering school when the U.S. economy collapsed; others were teenagers. The fact that not all families suffered or lost their jobs enabled Elder to compare families who were severely deprived with those who remained relatively well off.

In the economically deprived families, dramatic changes in family roles and relationships affected children's development. The division of labor and power within the family shifted. As fathers' jobs disappeared and income dropped, mothers entered the labor market or took in boarders. As a result, the mother's power increased and the power, prestige, and emotional significance of the father decreased. The rates of divorce, separation, and desertion rose, especially among couples whose relationship was shaky even before the onset of bad economic times (Liker & Elder, 1983).

Roles changed for children, too. Girls were drafted into more household work, and the older boys took more outside jobs. Parent-child relationships changed in response to economic hardship; fathers especially became more punitive, less concerned, and less supportive of their children. Boys tended to move away from the family, becoming more peer-oriented. They also frequently became ill-tempered and angry. Both boys and girls were moodier, more easily slighted, and less calm (Elder, 1984). Because younger children were more dependent on their parents and thus exposed to the altered situation at home for a longer period of time, the effects of the Depression were greater for children who were young when catastrophe struck.

Many of the effects on children were long lasting. When these children became adults, their values, work patterns, and marriages bore the marks of these earlier experiences. Men who were forced to enter the job market as teenagers because of economic hardship preferred secure but modest jobs over riskier but higher-status positions. However, they were also less satisfied with their work and income. In addition to vocational problems, men and women who had experienced adjustment problems in response to the Depression in the 1930s had marriages that were less successful. The marriages of men and women who had been ill-tempered children were less stable, and women with childhood difficulties often married men who were lacking in ambition and achievement (Caspi, Elder, & Bem, 1987). Finally, girls who were prone to temper outbursts as children became ill-tempered parents. Thus we see a three-generational impact of the Depression. Clearly, economic hardship left its imprint on the lives of many of these families. On the other hand, some families managed well in spite of economic hardship, particularly if the family ties were strong before the onset of the Depression.

---

to the years of maturity and aging. Modern life span theory, however, does not endorse psychoanalytic principles and instead seeks to understand developmental shifts by examining the commonality of events among people over the life course.

Life span theory views childhood as of equal importance with other stages but does not accord it special significance in the shaping or forming of later stages of development. At all points in development, the individual is open or susceptible to change. According to the life span perspective, change over time can be traced to three sets of causes. First, there are *normative events,* or age-graded experiences that most children and adults undergo at roughly the same age or time in their lives. Some of these experiences, such as the beginning of walking in early childhood or the onset of menstruation in adolescent girls, are biological or maturational. The timing of these and other similar events does vary among individuals, but there is an average or normative schedule for such biological events. Other normative events are programmed by our society to follow schedules that most people adhere to: For example, children enter school at approximately the age of 5 and begin college at about 17 or 18 years of age; young people generally marry in the midtwenties or, nowadays, even later.

Development does not always conform to a previously prescribed schedule; a second set of causative factors are the unexpected events that often push development in new directions. Life span theorists term these *nonnormative events,* for they neither happen to everyone in the normal course of development nor follow

These children, shown on their Missouri farm in 1940, were among the many whose families, whether on farms or in urban tenements and ghettos, were victims of the Great Depression. Although the stock market crash of 1929 triggered an economic collapse that hit its peak by 1933, the U.S. economy did not fully recover until the country began heightened defense spending, in 1941, just before entering the second World War.

any preset schedule. Instead, these are events that can happen to any child or family at any time and often without much warning or anticipation. Divorce, job loss, or residence change are events that may have a profound impact on the child but are not normal, expected occurrences. We will explore the effects of some of these nonnormative events in Chapter 12.

Finally, according to the life span perspective, a third set of factors influences development, namely, cohort effects. *Cohort* is a term used to describe a group of children who were born in the same year (e.g., 1980) or the same general period (1980–1985). As cohorts develop, they share the same historical experiences. Children who were born in 1980, for example, were in late childhood when the Communist monopoly in Europe collapsed and the Cold War ended. In contrast, children born in 1950 were adolescents during the 1960s—the turbulent Vietnam era in North American society—and their adolescence was marked by considerable upheaval and social unrest. For another example of the effects of societal events on life span development, see Box 1-3, which describes the experience of children and adults who lived through the Great Depression of the 1930s. As you can see, historical context is an important source of influence on the developing child, making development different for different cohorts of children.

DEVELOPMENTAL THEMES AND THEORETICAL PERSPECTIVES: AN OVERVIEW

As we will stress throughout the chapters of this book, the understanding of children's development can be approached from many perspectives and with a number of important themes in mind. If you will look back at Table 1-2, which summarizes the relationships between these themes and theoretical perspectives, you will see that some perspectives offer better and more complete accounts of certain aspects of development than do others. For example, Piaget's organismic theory is especially helpful in explaining children's cognitive development, whereas Bandura's cognitive social learning theory offers a useful perspective for explaining social development. Freudian theory is especially useful for understanding problems of emotional dysfunction, whereas ethological approaches have been particularly helpful in describing the development of emotional expression and communication.

Many problems and issues benefit from the application of several different theoretical perspectives. Increasingly we recognize that different aspects of development such as language and emotional and social behavior are interlinked. For example, children's learning takes place in social contexts with other people—parents and peers. The ways that children perceive the environment may be influenced by the development of their motor skills. Similarly, language and cognitive development are better understood by recognizing their mutual interdependence. In short, every aspect of development is related to several others. This increasing acceptance of the interdependence of domains of development is leading to a greater acceptance of systems approaches to development. In fact, many theories share at least some of the assumptions of a systems approach. Recall our discussions of Erikson, Vygotsky, the ethological perspective, and even life span theories; with their focus on multiple levels of analysis and an appreciation of context, these views are quite clearly related to a systems theory approach to development. Thus, all perspectives have a place in the researcher's repertoire. It is often helpful to draw on several theories to help understand children's development; in combination, they can tell us a great deal more about the causes and course of children's development than any single theory alone can tell us.

SUMMARY

- **Child development** attempts to account for the gradual evolution of children's abilities and behaviors by describing the changes in children's behaviors as they develop and by uncovering the processes that underlie these changes. It also seeks to understand the strategies that children use, at different points of development, to accomplish tasks in many areas of behavior, including motoric abilities and emotional, social, and cognitive behaviors.
- Scientists also study children to develop practical information that can help those who care for children, such as parents, teachers, health professionals, and legislators.

A Historical Interlude

- The field of child psychology began to form with Charles Darwin's study of children's emotions and perceptual capacities. Until the end of the nineteenth century children were regarded as small adults, were often exploited as cheap labor, and were not valued in their own right. Today, child psychologists are concerned both to increase scientific knowledge about children and to shape social policy on behalf of children.

Themes of Development

- Although in the past development was held by many to be the result of **maturation,** most modern developmentalists recognize the importance of both biological and environmental influences. Many psychologists and others continue to disagree over the relative contributions of each set of factors to human development but are concerned primarily with discovering the ways in which biological and environmental factors interact to produce developmental differences.
- Most contemporary developmentalists believe that children actively shape, control, and direct the course of their own development. Some, however, still hold that children are the passive recipients of environmental influence.
- A number of theorists view development as a continuous process, whereby change over time takes place smoothly and gradually, but others see development as a series of qualitatively different steps or stages. The more closely and more frequently we examine the child's development, the more gradual the process appears.
- Some developmentalists continue to debate the question of whether situational influences or individual personality characteristics are more important in determining how stable a child's behavior will be across varying contexts. Many contemporary psychologists avoid this debate by taking an interactionist viewpoint that stresses the complementary roles of personality and situational factors.

- Developmental psychologists who emphasize cultural universals seek culture-free laws of development that can be applied across all societies and cultures. Those who stress cultural relativism study the effects of distinctive cultural settings on children's development. Most developmentalists agree, however, that cultural contexts must be considered in any account of development.
- A number of child psychologists have become interested in the contradictions posed to a child's development by the presence, early in life, of high-risk factors and the evolution in the child of the quality of resilience. These researchers study how children are able to cope with such negative influences as family disintegration, poverty, and illness and create a satisfying and useful life for themselves.

Theoretical Perspectives on Development

- Theories serve two functions. First, they help organize and integrate existing knowledge into a coherent account of how children develop. Second, they foster research by providing testable predictions about behavior. Different theories take different positions on the issues or themes of development, and in general they also account for different aspects of development. In this sense they can be seen as complementary rather than as competing with each other.
- According to traditional **behavioral** perspectives, development is a continuous process, which uses the same principles of learning across the life span. On this view, the child is relatively passive, molded by environmental factors that modify behavior by either **classical** or **operant conditioning.**
- **Cognitive social learning theory** has extended the behavioral perspective to include imitation as another form of learning. Studies based on this perspective have focused our attention particularly on the positive and negative aspects of television, a common source of models for children's imitation. According to this theory, children are selective about who and what behaviors they imitate.
- **Piagetian theory** describes the child as actively seeking information and new experiences. Children adapt to their environment by assimilating new information when possible or by accommodating their existing frameworks to new information. Development results from increasingly complex reorganizations of mental frameworks as the child moves through an invariant sequence of stages to more advanced levels of cognitive functioning.
- In his **sociocultural** theory of development, Vygotsky emphasized the interaction between the active child and her social environment. According to Vygotsky, the child grows and changes as a function of her own efforts and supported by the guidance and help of more-skilled others.
- **Information-processing theories** focus on children's representations of information and how they operate on information to achieve their goals in particular situations. Theorists in this tradition often use computer analogies and flowcharts to help describe the steps involved in solving a problem. This approach has been applied to a wide range of problems in studies of cognitive development and social behavior.
- Freud's **psychoanalytic theory** presents a discontinuous view of development in which the child is motivated by a set of basic biological drives that are focused on different sensory zones and different activities during the early years of development. The concepts of **id, ego,** and **superego** are integral to Freud's notion of the development of personality, as are his formulations of the **Oedipus** and **Electra complexes.** According to Freudian theory, later adult personality is a direct result of whether or not the child's drives were deprived or satisfied at each earlier stage.
- Erikson expanded Freud's theory to include social and cultural factors as influences on the child's development as well as to extend the theory to cover the entire life span. Erikson's **psychosocial theory** is organized around a series of

fundamental personal and social tasks that the individual must accomplish at each stage.

- **Dynamic systems theories** view the developing individual as a member of a system or series of systems that are complex, self-stabilizing, and self-reorganizing. The continuing interactions among system members and among systems make development a highly dynamic enterprise in which relationships and processes are the primary focus.

- **Ecological theory** stresses the importance of understanding the relationship between the organism and various environmental systems, such as the family, school, community, and culture. Development involves the interplay between children and their changing relationships with these different ecological systems—the **microsystem, mesosystem, exosystem, macrosystem,** and **chronosystem.** The child's subjective experience or understanding of the environment and the child's active role in modifying the environment are important aspects of this perspective.

- **Ethological theory** takes a biological-evolutionary approach to describing development. Ethologists, whose primary mode of study is direct observation of behavior in natural settings, seek similar patterns of behaviors across human and infrahuman species and across human societies and cultures.

- **Life span theory** emphasizes development over the entire life course. According to this view, developmental change can be traced to normative age-graded events, nonnormative events, and historical or cohort events.

Developmental Themes and Theoretical Perspectives: An Overview

- Some theoretical perspectives on child development are particularly useful in explaining certain aspects of children's growth and change, whereas other perspectives illuminate other aspects more successfully.

- Because every aspect of development is related to several others, however, it is often useful to apply several different theoretical perspectives to the analysis and study of a particular problem or issue. The interrelatedness of different domains of development makes a systems approach increasingly attractive.

Research Methods
in Child
Psychology

C H A P T E R 2

A theory can provide us with insights, hunches, and ideas about human development, but if it is to be useful, a theory must enable us to predict with some degree of accuracy such things as how children change as they grow older and why development unfolds as it does. In this chapter we investigate some of the many strategies and methods that psychologists who study child development use to help answer these and other questions.

Like other scientists, child psychologists use the **scientific method** in their research; that is, they formulate hypotheses on the basis of a theory and use measurable and replicable techniques to collect, study, and analyze data in an effort to test the theory's usefulness. This chapter follows the steps of the scientific method, considering first how developmental researchers select a group of children to study. The chapter then explores ways in which researchers gather the data they need to test their hypotheses and examines the principal research strategies, or designs, used to investigate issues of child development. Among the designs we discuss, the correlational and experimental methods are the most commonly used, and most designs have the option of using one of several techniques that are particularly useful in revealing how children change over time: the cross-sectional, the longitudinal, and the sequential methodologies. The scientific method culminates in the analysis of data gathered in a search for a meaningful pattern and support for the original hypothesis and, often, in a replication of the study to ensure that its results are trustworthy. Throughout this entire process, researchers are guided by the ethical principles that we discuss at the conclusion of the chapter.

SELECTING A SAMPLE

If you wanted to study the typical weekend activities of college freshmen, how would you go about collecting your data? How many college freshmen do you suppose there are at a given time in the United States? Rather a lot. Thus, you couldn't possibly study all of them, but you could select a **sample,** or a group of manageable size and made up of individuals who, you hope, are representative of the entire population of first-year college students. Because it is rarely possible to look at all the members of a given population, researchers must limit their focus in some way, and sampling is the most common solution.

Some Solutions to the Problem of Representativeness

If we want our research conclusions to be applicable to the population our sample is designed to reflect, we must ensure the **representativeness** of that sample. That is, the persons we choose to study must possess nearly the same characteristics evidenced by the larger population in which we are interested; depending on that population we may need a very broad sample in which, say, all social classes or many ethnic backgrounds are represented. Consider the following example:

> A researcher wants to study the way children's vocabularies change over time. Living near a private nursery school in a rather affluent suburban community, she selects thirty 3-year-olds and thirty 5-year-olds from the school population and carefully tests their vocabulary levels. Based on the performance of these children of professional parents the investigator reports that she now has a set of norms or guidelines for what may be expected of preschoolers' vocabulary knowledge. What's wrong with the researcher's conclusion?

The investigator has chosen her sample poorly, for, other things being equal, the children of professionals are likely to have verbal skills that surpass those of children of less well educated parents. It's also possible that direct teaching at the school, where the ratio of teachers to students may be more favorable than in public schools, facilitates children's learning. Clearly, we can't generalize about the average vocabulary accomplishment of all children of 3 and 5 unless we sample a wide range of children from different backgrounds and in different instructional settings.

scientific method The use of measurable and replicable techniques in framing hypotheses and collecting and analyzing data to test a theory's usefulness.

sample A group of individuals who are representative of a larger population.

representativeness The degree to which a sample actually possesses the characteristics of the larger population it represents.

Selecting a sample is a crucial step in the research process. For example, if scientists include children of different cultural backgrounds in their research they may be able to draw useful conclusions about the universal or culture-specific nature of the phenomena they study.

Here's another example:

Suppose you are interested in the development of aggressive behavior in children. You select a sample of children who have been brought to a psychological clinic because of family problems. There are 30 boys and 5 girls in the sample, and all come from a poor part of a large urban area. You evaluate various aspects of the children's behavior by watching them play with other children and by asking them how they would resolve a dispute with a peer. To begin the search for causes, you assess how well each child's parents get along and how much TV the children watch. Ultimately you conclude that boys are more aggressive than girls, and that aggression in children is related both to watching a lot of TV viewing and to parental fighting.

Problems plague this study. Perhaps children who are brought to a clinic because of behavior problems are different from children whose families do not or cannot seek this kind of help. It is possible that boys are in fact more aggressive than girls, but the sample of girls in this study is disproportionate to the sample of boys, and it is also too small to support such a conclusion. Given the nonrepresentativeness of this sample, there is no basis for connecting excessive TV viewing and parental conflict with aggressiveness in children. To draw such a conclusion legitimately you would have to test equal numbers of girls and boys (perhaps as many as 50 of each) and divide them equally among varying socioeconomic backgrounds and between those who were and were not attending a clinic for behavioral problems.

These examples illustrate one of the major problems that a researcher faces in selecting a sample—namely, to try to recruit a group of people that is representative of the larger population about which the researcher wishes to make general statements. Great care must be taken in generalizing to a larger population from a sample that is restricted in some way (e.g., by race, gender, social class, or region of the country). Increasingly, investigators are finding it helpful to select several samples, each made up of people who vary in race, gender, and social class. By selecting multiple samples, they can be more certain that their conclusions about development do, in fact, apply to a broad range of people. This strategy is often used in developmental research when investigators in different parts of the country tackle the same issues. When researchers use multiple samples to collect their data, and if several researchers draw similar conclusions, we can have greater confidence in the generalizability of the findings.

Another Approach: The National Survey

national survey   A method of sampling in which a very large, nationally representative group of people are selected for a particular study.

In an innovative approach to sampling called the **national survey,** researchers interested in a particular issue or issues select a very large, nationally representative group of people. For example, the National Longitudinal Survey of Youth (NLSY), begun in 1979 with a sample of young men and women who ranged then in age from 14 to 24, has interviewed its participants annually on such topics as the role of family factors, school performance, and early work experience in the employment patterns of young adults. The survey participants were drawn from 235 geographic areas that included 485 counties and cities across the United States. This broad sampling strategy has the advantage of allowing researchers to make general statements that may be applied to all Americans in the same age groups. It has a major disadvantage, however, in that national surveys are costly. Consider the time and labor required in 1979 to interview the nearly 12,000 original participants in the NLSY and, in 1986, to interview the 5,000 children of women who had participated in the original survey!

In recent years, the NLSY has begun to investigate such issues as the impact of day care, maternal employment, and divorce on children and families (Chase-Lansdale, Mott, Brooks-Gunn, & Phillips, 1991). The survey's researchers have found, for example, that maternal employment during the first year of a child's life has significant long-term effects on children's cognitive, social, and emotional development. Because both middle-class and lower-class families were included in the survey, the researchers were able to show that these relationships varied across social class. Among poor families, early maternal employment was linked to some positive developmental factors, but among middle-class families it was linked to some negative ones (Desai, Chase-Lansdale, & Michael, 1989; Desai, Michael, & Chase-Lansdale, 1990). We discuss these findings in greater detail in Chapters 7 and 12. The important point here is that, because of the way this sample was selected, relationships found in the NLSY are generalizable across the entire U.S. population of young adults and their children. Without such a large representative sample from which to draw findings researchers would not know whether any pattern they discovered was confined only to people who shared the characteristics of those they studied.

In addition to being expensive, national surveys are also limited by their inability to examine the factors that influence development in detail. Although these surveys' large samples allow them to reveal overarching patterns in people's behavior and relationships among particular factors, these broad-based studies are less suited to answering specific questions about the processes that may account for different aspects of development. To study 5,000 children in detail, for example, would take much more time than most investigators have at their disposal (and, incidentally, would also be far too costly). For this reason, a national survey is sometimes used in combination with a more intensive look at a smaller sample of people. Of our 5,000 children, for example, we might select a subsample of 100 or 200 and then observe, study, and test these children in some depth in order to achieve a better understanding of the processes that underlie changes over time in their thinking and behavior.

Finally, sampling needs not only to ensure broad representativeness on such fairly obvious parameters as age, gender, and socioeconomic status; researchers must recognize that many aspects of development vary across different cultural, ethnic, and racial backgrounds. As a result, samples within the United States need to represent the growing diversity of the U.S. population. Unless there is a special effort to target particular ethnic groups such as Hispanic Americans or African Americans, we may be losing significant opportunities to discover important ethnic differences (Box 2-1). These differences may be lost when we average the responses of people in these ethnic groups into the larger population of children. Thus we need *both* representative samples as well as samples of important ethnic groups if we are to appreciate fully the similarities and differences among different groups within our society. As we discuss later, psychologists are increasingly recognizing the importance of research that informs us about children around the world.

METHODS OF GATHERING DATA ABOUT CHILDREN

Once researchers have decided what group or groups they want to study, they must decide how they will study these youngsters. This next step involves deciding on a method of gathering information relevant to the development issues in which the investigators are interested. Essentially, there are three approaches: We can ask children about themselves; we can ask people who are close to these children about them; or we can ourselves observe the children in various situations. Each approach has its advantages and limitations, and researchers' choices depend on the kinds of questions they want to answer.

Children's Self-Reports

A **self-report** is information that a person provides about himself or herself, typically by answering a set of questions devised by a researcher. Soliciting such information from a child, as you may imagine, presents special problems. Compared with adults, children—especially younger ones—are apt to be less attentive, slower to respond, and to have more trouble understanding the questions that researchers ask. Children are no less truthful than adults; in an interview study of a national sample of 2,279 children between 7 and 11 years of age and their parents, the interviewers rated the apparent truthfulness of parents and children equally (Zill, 1986), although they rated younger children as less reliable reporters than older children. Interestingly, researchers also rated children as less truthful if a parent was present and listening closely during the interview. Barring the possibility that younger children are sometimes simply less knowledgeable about certain matters, we may increase the truthfulness of children's answers by interviewing them alone.

Despite these limitations on children's self-reports, some kinds of information are difficult to obtain in any other way. Zill (1986), for example, points out that interviewing children directly "permits a glimpse at a child's life from his or her unique perspective. The child is the best authority on his own feelings, even if he has some trouble verbalizing those feelings. And even in matters of fact—where adults have the advantage of a more fully developed sense of where, or when and of

> **self-report** Information that people provide about themselves, either in a direct interview or in some written form, such as a questionnaire.

BOX 2–1

Perspectives on Diversity

Minority Groups in Child Development Research

In 1990 the non-European, nonwhite proportion of the U.S. population was 25 percent, and by 2020 it's expected to reach 30 percent (U.S. Department of Commerce, 1996). Today about 50 percent of the U.S. population is either working-class or poor (Children's Defense Fund, 1997). Despite these statistics, most developmental research has virtually ignored non-European, non-middle-class children and families (Fisher et al., 1998). For example, as late as 1989 only 1.5 percent of articles in *Developmental Psychology* and other journals in the field pertained to African Americans, and, despite the fact that the non-white U.S. population has been *increasing* steadily, this was a *decrease* from the proportion of articles (5.5%) found in the early 1970s (Graham, 1992)!

Many minority people have moved from lower social classes into the middle class. Nevertheless, when researchers do include nonwhite, non-European individuals in their studies, they tend to sample only those of low socioeconomic status (Fisher et al., 1998). This practice may reinforce a stereotypic view of racial-ethnic people as monolithic—that is, as a group of people who are uniformly poor and "different" from middle-class people—when in fact there are minority people in all social classes. In addition, research studies typically use materials and procedures that have been developed from a "monocultural" perspective and that therefore often elicit responses from minority participants that are seen as deficient in some way (Fisher et al., 1998). As we will see in Chapter 11, this is particularly likely when measures of cognitive functioning or intelligence are used.

This "deficit" orientation essentially rules out the possibility of exploring the assets, strengths, skills, and resiliencies of people whose heritage and cultural patterns are different from the dominant North American patterns (Fisher et al., 1998). It also prevents researchers from understanding the sociocultural bases for minorities' beliefs, attitudes, behaviors, and lifestyles from the points of view of minorities themselves and leads to the evaluation of research participants on the basis of the dominant group's perception of social reality. According to Fisher et al. (1998), such a failure to give ethnic minority members a voice in a scientific enterprise that's designed to characterize their individual and collective natures seriously challenges the ability of the social sciences "to respond to the full diversity of human nature" (p. 1181).

Stimulated in part by such increasingly popular theoretical perspectives as Vygotsky's sociocultural theory, dynamic systems theory, and Bronfenbrenner's ecological theory (Chapter 1), a new research paradigm that emphasize cross-cultural and multicultural comparisons is emerging (Fisher et al., 1998). This model proposes that to understand human growth and development, researchers must add cultural context as a parameter of equal importance with the biological, psychological, and social aspects of human life. Thus, to carry out useful research with ethnic minority participants, researchers need to understand the fundamental cultural values and practices of the groups they seek to study. New methods, such as ethnographic approaches that involve rich descriptions of the cultural practices of minority groups in their everyday environments are becoming commonly used to improve our understanding of the unique characteristics and mores of different ethnic groups. In addition, using the language of participants can facilitate communication between investigators and research participants.

Cultural understanding needs to inform research instruments and methodology as well; questionnaires, interview protocols, and tests need to be adapted to the cultural characteristics of the group being studied. Some psychologists have pointed out that the most widely used tests of intelligence draw on white middle-class language, experience, and values. For example, the vocabulary used on such tests often differs from the language or dialect some children use every day. On this view, some researchers have argued that minority children's lower verbal scores may reflect cultural bias, not lack of intelligence.

---

how many—there are aspects of a child's daily life that his parents or teacher know little or nothing about" (pp. 23–24).

Reports by Family Members, Teachers, and Peers

Our second strategy for collecting data on child development issues is to solicit information from people who know a child or children well. These people may include parents, siblings, teachers, peers, other relatives, and sometimes other people in the community; most commonly, child development researchers seek this information from family members, teachers, and peers.

Family Members

A strength of interviews with parents and other family members—and this includes children's own self-reports—is that these reports are generally based on many

As Miller-Jones (1989) argues, the way a person interprets a task influences the way she or he performs it and, significantly, this interpretation is related not only to the specific features of the task but to the person's earlier cultural experiences. Consider the effect of experience on a minority child's success or failure on a question from the Stanford-Binet, a widely used intelligence test (we discuss this test in Chapter 11). For the question "What's the thing for you to do if another child hits you without meaning to do it?" the correct responses suggested include "I'd say, 'That's all right. I know it was an accident' and walk away." In some minority communities, children must fight to survive. A child who took a chance like that might end up with a knife or bullet in the back (Williams, 1970).

Children who have not been exposed to information about tests and what they are for may not understand the context of the testing situation. Once again, the child's interpretation of the context will influence her behavior in that context.

Tester: "What is a ball?"
Child: "You kick balls."
Tester: "What is a hat?"
Child: "You put it on your head."
Tester: "What is a stove?"
Child: "You cook. That's what you writing down?"
Tester: "Yeah. I'm writing down what you say so I can remember it later."
Child: [Incredulously] "'Cause you don't know what it's for?"

If all children taking a particular test do not understand and interpret both the goal of the testing situation and the meaning of each specific test item in the same way, can the tester legitimately compare the responses of different children? Equating tasks or test items in terms of familiarity or cultural appropriateness is very difficult, but it is reasonable to suppose that the more psychologists try to use culturally relevant materials and procedures and to ensure that the individual being asked to perform understands both the nature of the task and the examiner's sincere interest in his or her responses, the more likely it is that the person will perform competently.

Theorizing that children from minority and low-income groups may feel uncomfortable with European American examiners and may become anxious in unfamiliar testing situations, especially when pressed to respond within rigid time limits, some researchers have tried a number of ways of facilitating children's performance (Golden & Birns, 1971; Zigler & Seitz, 1982). For example, they have tried to familiarize children with the test environment and test materials, to give them specific encouragement and feedback on various tasks, and to use material rewards like candy or toys to motivate performance. The fact that such efforts have had much more effect on economically deprived children than on middle-class children supports the notion that minority children may be just as competent as nonminority children but unable to perform under the conditions ordinarily set for them.

The new research paradigm points out that culture is not static and, in accord with contemporary psychologists' emphasis on the processes rather than the products of development, encourages investigators to design studies that seek to understand and describe the processes that reflect the dynamic nature of culture (Fisher et al., 1998). For example, regardless of their relative positions in a social-class hierarchy, cultural subgroups constantly influence each other: The music of American jazz, now a universal art form, is largely the creation of African Americans; conversely, among talented interpreters of classical (European) ballet today is the Dance Theatre of Harlem. Cultural borrowing as well as cultural shock affects the development of children and youth from every group within a society. If research is to be useful in developing policies, services, and institutions to promote the healthy development of all children, it must be sensitive to and explore the basic values and characteristics of society's many groups.

observations made over time in a variety of situations. As we will see, in most direct observational studies the observer sees the participant for only a short time and in a single situation.

Another advantage of reports by family members is that even if parents and siblings are not totally accurate in their reporting, their perceptions, expectations, beliefs, and interpretations of events and behavior may be just as important as what we can only assume is objective reality (Bugental & Goodnow, 1998; Goodnow & Collins, 1991). For example, a son may feel rejected by a father who really loves him but who believes that men don't show emotion and that high standards and strict discipline are necessary to develop strong moral character in the young. The child's belief that his father does not find him worthy of love, rather than the father's real attitude, may well result in the development of feelings of inadequacy and low self-esteem in the son.

Researchers can use measures of such things as the images family members have of one another and the ways family members interact to differentiate problem families from families that are functioning well. If family members perceive the family and each other in very different ways, these discrepancies tend to be associated with conflict and distress (Grych & Fincham, 1990). Many family therapists focus on helping family members discover such discrepancies in their perceptions of each other and communicate more openly as a way of reducing family conflict.

There are some clear disadvantages in soliciting parental and other family reports about a child's growth and development. For example, we cannot always take at face value what parents tell us about their childrearing practices (Holden, 1997; Holden & Edwards, 1989), in part because human memory is not completely reliable. When asked to recall details of past interactions with their children, people may simply not be able to remember exactly how they handled certain situations. Also, because people are motivated to remember themselves in the best light possible, they often tend to recall what they wish they had done rather than what they did and to remember themselves as having been more consistent, patient, and even-tempered with their children than more objective assessments might have revealed them to be.

A classic study by Robbins (1963) compared parents' retrospective reports of their childrearing practices with the same parents' reports made regularly over the course of the first three years of a longitudinal study. Robbins found that distortions in parents' recall of events tended to cast the parents in the light of greater agreement with the opinions of then-contemporary experts such as the pediatrician Benjamin Spock. For example, Dr. Spock, in the 1957 edition of his book, *Baby and Child Care,* disapproved of allowing a child to suck its thumb and instead approved giving the child a pacifier. In Robbins's study, all mothers who gave inaccurate reports of their children's thumb-sucking and even those who had earlier indicated concern to their physicians about their children's thumb-sucking, denied that the children had ever sucked their thumbs. Similarly, most of the mothers who reported inaccurately on their use of pacifiers said that they had used a pacifier when the actual records showed that they had not.

When parents see their children as extensions of themselves, they are unlikely to report problems as honestly as we would hope. Few parents report their children's development as slow, and instead recall the children as having walked and talked a little earlier than they really did and as having achieved better grades in school than they actually earned. Such parents may be telling us more about themselves than about their children. And many parents will gloss over certain aspects of their children's behavior that others view more negatively. Thus, a father may describe his son as a rough-and-tumble "real boy" who is full of good-natured mischief rather than the scourge of the neighborhood that others have described.

Recently, in an effort to increase the accuracy of parents' reports about their children, investigators have devised a number of new interview strategies. For example, they may have parents report only very recent events so as to ensure more reliable memories, or they may specifically train parents to be more accurate, impartial observers. They may phone parents every evening and ask which of a list of specific behaviors (such as hitting, crying, yelling, or refusing to comply) their children have exhibited in the past 24 hours (Patterson, 1996; Patterson & Bank, 1989). Or they may ask parents to carry a structured diary and to record, every half hour, where they are, with whom they are, what they are doing, and what they are feeling (Hetherington, 1991a). Child development researchers have even used the pagers carried by physicians for emergency calls: Parents carry a monitor and are "beeped" at random times and asked to record their activities or feelings or those of their children (Larson & Lampman-Petraitis, 1989; Larson & Richards, 1994). This approach allows for a random sampling not only of behaviors but of the situations in which these behaviors occur.

Teachers and Peers

For some questions, such as how well a child attends to classroom activities and work or how cooperative she is on the playground, parents may not always be good sources of information. Indeed, some parents are unaware of whether their child is the class clown or the worst nerd in the school. To learn about a child's behavior in these and other settings when parents aren't present, researchers can ask other people, such as teachers and peers.

One technique researchers often use is to ask peers to rate how well a particular child's peers accept him. For example, investigators might ask all the youngsters in a classroom to rate each of their peers in terms of "how much I like to play with" him or her. The researchers then combine all the ratings to yield a picture of each child's social status in the classroom (Coie & Dodge, 1988; Rubin, Bukowski, & Parker, 1998; Terry & Coie, 1991). Or sometimes investigators may ask teachers to rate children on a specific series of dimensions such as attentiveness, disruptiveness, dependability, and sociability. Both peers and teachers can provide important information about children's behaviors that are useful supplements to children's self-reports and the information provided by family members (Parke et al., 1997).

Although children's self-reports, parental reports, and reports by others have their limitations, researchers have found that these reports offer them the best understanding of many issues. In addition, as we will see next, these kinds of reports are often used in conjunction with other data-gathering strategies.

Direct Observation

There is often no substitute for the researchers' own **direct observation** of people, and students of child development may make such observations in naturalistic settings, such as participants' own homes, or in laboratories where they give children and sometimes parents some highly structured task to perform. Observational data, however, are valid only to the extent that the presence of an observer or other demands of the situation do not distort participants' behavior and responses.

direct observation A method of observation in which researchers go into settings in the natural world to observe behaviors of interest.

These distorting factors are sometimes hard to avoid because children and parents often do behave differently in different kinds of settings, or when they know they are being watched. Mothers, for instance, often respond to a toddler's temper tantrum quite differently at home than they do in a crowded supermarket. Studies also suggest that when families are shifted from familiar to unfamiliar settings (from the home to a laboratory, for instance), or from unstructured settings to situations in which they must perform specific tasks in a very structured fashion, they tend to express less negative emotion and to exhibit more socially desirable behavior (Johnson & Bolsted, 1973; Lamb, Suomi, & Stephenson, 1979). Conversely, parents are less likely to exhibit stereotyped gender-role behavior at home, where, in addition, mothers participate more actively in decision making and fathers display more emotion (O'Rourke, 1963).

Even at home, customary behavior can be distorted by the presence of an outside observer. Parents, for instance, tend to behave in ways that enhance their images as parents and to inhibit negative behavior when they are being watched (Russell, Russell, & Midwinter, 1991). Although this is especially true of fathers, even mothers behave in a warmer, more involved style with their children when an observer is in the home (Zegoib, Arnold, & Forehand, 1975).

Attempts to minimize such distortions in studies in people's homes include the use of less obtrusive observational methods, such as video or tape recordings. Sustained observation of this kind can apparently encourage people to "be themselves" (Jacob et al., 1994; Patterson & Bank, 1989). Some researchers have monitored families by video or tape recorder during all their waking hours for periods as long as a month. Others have arrived at a family's home each dinner hour over a period of several weeks (Feiring & Lewis, 1987). Although you might think

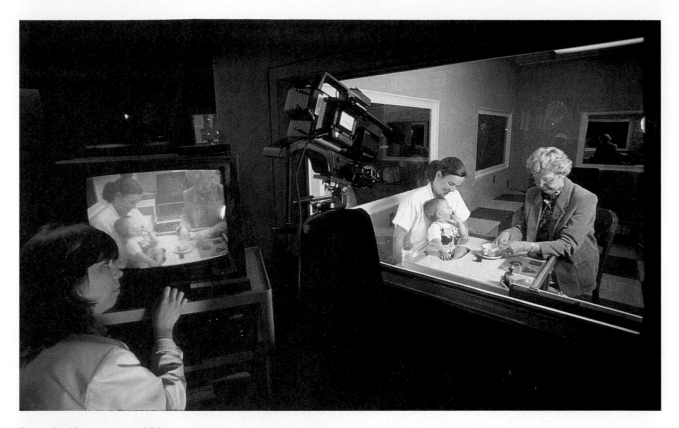

Research with very young children, like this six-month-old infant, is becoming increasingly common as psychologists seek to expand our knowledge about the beginnings of development. As we mention later in the chapter, researchers today are more commonly using designs that do not include such things as observation through one-way windows. This is in line with ethical guidelines that prohibit measures or manipulations that in any way deceive research participants.

specimen record A technique by which researchers record everything a person does within a given period of time.

event sampling A technique by which investigators record subjects' behavior only when an event of particular interest occurs, not at other times.

time sampling A technique by which researchers record any of a set of predetermined behaviors that occur within a specified time period.

it would be hard to get used to an observer appearing every evening with the entree, wearing dark glasses (to conceal the direction of his gaze), and taking notes on a clipboard, families do report that they gradually become almost unaware of being observed. The veracity of their statements is reflected in gradual increases in less socially accepted behaviors, such as quarreling, criticizing, punishing, and using obscene language (Boyum & Parke, 1995).

When researchers decide to observe children and their families directly they must decide what kinds of behaviors to record (Bakeman & Gottman, 1997). If they're interested in a broad range of behaviors, they may use a **specimen record,** in which they record everything a subject does for a specified period of time. If they're interested in studying only a particular type of behavior, such as the way a child responds to her parents' directives, they may use a technique called **event sampling,** in which they record individuals' behavior whenever the event of interest occurs but not at other times. For example, an investigator interested in a child's response to parental directives would start recording information when a parent issued a command and stop recording when the child had clearly either obeyed or disobeyed the command.

In the **time sampling** approach, the researcher checks off any of the behaviors listed on a sheet of paper that occur during a predetermined time period. Thus, if an investigator were going to observe a family for an hour, she might divide the hour into 120 thirty-second units, prepare a grid showing behaviors and time blocks, and then put a check beside each behavior that occurs in each block of time. This approach would yield the frequency of different kinds of behaviors during the hour. If the researcher wanted to examine the stream of behavior, however, a better strategy would be to record events continuously and sequentially for a stated period of time (Mann et al., 1991). For example, suppose that a baby throws his cereal bowl to the floor, his mother scolds him, the baby cries, and the mother then picks the baby up and comforts him. This clear stream of behavior gives us a model of mother–child interaction and enables us to ask such questions as, When the baby misbehaves (in this and other ways), what is the mother's most common response? How does the baby respond to her behavior? How does she react to the baby's response?

When a child development specialist is interested in some relatively rare behavior that is unlikely to occur in a naturalistic observation setting he may structure a situation so that the behavior is more likely to happen; this method is called **structured observation.** Suppose that a researcher is interested in the way parents respond to their child's request for help. By giving the child tasks that are very difficult to do, the investigator may increase the likelihood that the child will ask his parents for help, thus giving the researcher an opportunity to observe the parents' responses to their child's request (Zahn-Waxler, Robinson, and Emde, 1992).

Because of the limitations inherent in all these methods of gathering data, many investigators have begun using multiple measures of the same behavior. For example, a researcher might ask a child whether he is afraid of snakes, ask his friends if they think he is afraid of snakes, observe him closely on a field trip to the local woods, and watch his reaction when he is shown pictures of snakes or when his class adopts a snake as a classroom pet. The idea behind this approach is that if the findings of a variety of assessment techniques converge, researchers can reasonably conclude that the findings are valid. Moreover, researchers assume that different methods will shed light on different facets of children's development.

> **structured observation**
> A form of observation in which researchers structure a situation so that behaviors they wish to study are more likely to occur.

RESEARCH DESIGN: ESTABLISHING RELATIONSHIPS AND CAUSES

Selecting a sample and a method of gathering information enables us to describe some aspect of human development in which we are interested, but what will this information do for us? To make use of it, we need to know how the various factors of development that we have described are related and interact and to determine the reasons why development occurs as it does. We begin this section by discussing the correlational research design, which enables us to establish not only the existence but the strength of relationships among various factors, and then move on to the laboratory experimental design, in which researchers attempt to demonstrate causality among factors in child development. After we explore both field and natural experimental designs we examine an approach that combines laboratory and field designs. In the last part of this section we discuss the case study, a design that allows for the intensive study of a single individual.

The Correlational Method

Many people have wondered whether "Sesame Street" and other educational children's programs on TV can help young viewers perform better when they enter school. As we discussed in Chapter 1 (Box 1-1), some evidence indicates that "Sesame Street" offers young children this kind of help. To illustrate the correlational research design, let's examine one of the studies that has contributed to this evidence. Using the **correlational method,** a design that enables researchers to establish not only that one or more factors are related to each other but the strength of these relationships, John Wright and Aletha Huston (1995) studied the TV-viewing behavior of preschool children in more than 250 families, all from low-income areas. The children were either 2 or 4 years old at the start of the study, and either 5 or 7 at its conclusion. Their parents were asked to make detailed reports on how their preschoolers spent their time, including which TV shows they watched and for how long each day.

> **correlational method** A research design that permits investigators to establish relationships among variables as well as the strength of those relationships.

Every year the children were given a variety of cognitive achievement tests, such as measures of mathematical skills, letter and word knowledge, and vocabulary size. The researchers found that children who watched children's educational programs, particularly "Sesame Street," tended to have a higher level of cognitive achievement. That is, the more such programming children watched, the higher they scored on the tests. Regular viewing of children's cartoons or adult TV programs, on the other hand, was negatively related to children's performance on tests of cognitive abilities: The more time they spent watching cartoons or adult programs, the lower they scored on these tests.

Do these findings mean that watching "Sesame Street" caused these children's high test scores? No, they do not. Why? Because any number of factors other than watching this children's show could have caused the improved scores. For example, suppose that "Sesame Street" appeals particularly to children who have superior cognitive skills. Or, suppose that children who watch "Sesame Street" have parents who give them a great deal of encouragement and guidance in reading, writing, math, and other school subjects. Either of these factors could be the real cause of their achievement, and watching "Sesame Street" might have relatively little to do with it. Well, then, couldn't the researchers have somehow taken these factors into account? In fact, they did. They made certain that all the children had the same or nearly the same level of cognitive skills, and they ensured that all the parents were equated on level of education, socioeconomic status, and the degree to which they actively stimulated and encouraged their children to learn. The result was, as we reported, that more watching of educational TV was related to higher test scores.

Surely now we can say that "Sesame Street" was the cause of the children's achievement. Unfortunately, we cannot. A cardinal rule in correlational research is that correlation is not the same thing as causation. A relation between two factors may be established, but the method does not tell us which factor is "causing" the other. No matter how strong the relationship between two factors, at best we can say that one is a likely cause of the other. If correlational research doesn't allow us to determine causation, why then do we use it? For one thing, as we will see in the next section, the controlled laboratory experiment, which can in fact demonstrate causality, is often more difficult to implement. For another, as we will also see, ethical concerns associated with lab experiments may interfere with their design or make their execution questionable. In most cases, however, researchers are careful to design experiments that are scientifically meaningful and ethically acceptable.

Before we turn to the more formal, laboratory experiment, let's look at the statistical tool used by researchers in the correlational design. Commonly known as the **correlation coefficient,** this statistic is a numerical measure, or index, of how closely two factors are related to each other. Correlation coefficients range along a continuum from +1, which is the highest possible positive correlation, to –1, the lowest possible negative correlation (see Fig. 2-1). (At the midpoint of the continuum, the coefficient of .00, or zero, means that factors are totally unrelated; for example, if we compared physical height and intelligence measures for different people, it would be clear that they would have nothing to do with each other.) This index expresses both the direction and the strength of the relationship. For example, the direction of the relationship between watching "Sesame Street" and getting high test scores is positive, because when one of the variables is high, so is the other. In Wright and Huston's study, this relationship was expressed by correlation coefficients ranging from +.05 to +.25. On the other hand, the relationship in this study between watching cartoons or adult programs and test scores was negative. When the first of these factors was high—when children watched a lot—the second was low—they got low scores on cognitive skills tests. In the "Sesame Street" study this relationship was expressed by coefficients ranging from –.05 to –.20.

The second dimension illuminated by the correlation coefficient is the strength of a relationship, and this is indicated by the size of the coefficient number. In the study of child psychology, researchers generally find relationships on the order of .30 to .50, indicating a moderately strong correlation. By comparison, Wright and Huston's correlation coefficients were quite modest. What does this suggest to you? Might it be that still other factors are at work in the children's high achievement test scores that will have to be discovered and controlled for in subsequent studies?

correlation coefficient A numerical measure of how closely two factors are related to each other.

The Laboratory Experiment

A more convincing way of investigating causal connections among factors is to conduct a formal experiment. In a **laboratory experiment,** researchers are able to

laboratory experiment A research design that allows investigators, through controlling variables and treatments and assigning participants randomly to treatments, to determine cause and effect.

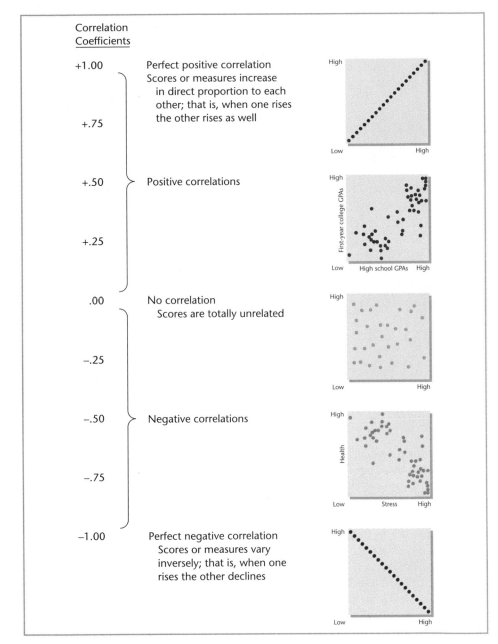

Correlation
Coefficients

+1.00   Perfect positive correlation
         Scores or measures increase
            in direct proportion to each
            other; that is, when one rises
            the other rises as well

+.75

+.50 ⟩ Positive correlations

+.25

.00   No correlation
         Scores are totally unrelated

−.25

−.50 ⟩ Negative correlations

−.75

−1.00   Perfect negative correlation
         Scores or measures vary
            inversely; that is, when one
            rises the other declines

■ FIGURE 2-1
The correlation coefficient: establishing relationships between factors.
The closer the correlation coefficient gets to 1.00, whether positive or negative, the stronger the relationship depicted. All the scatter plots on the right are hypothetical, but the second and fourth illustrate two commonly found relationships: Grade point averages in high school and in the first year of college are generally positively related; that is, if one is high the other is high, and if one is low the other is also. Health and stress level, on the other hand, are generally negatively related; thus if your health is good (high), your stress level is likely to be low, whereas if you are under a lot of stress, your health may suffer.

control so many factors that may possibly influence the variable in which they are interested that their results allow them to draw conclusions about cause and effect. First, they hold constant, or equate in some way, every possible influence except the one factor that they have hypothesized as the cause of the variable they want to study. Second, investigators create two groups of subjects. They then subject one, called the **experimental group,** to the proposed causative factor; the second, **control group,** does not receive or experience this factor. In a third manipulation designed to rule out the possibility that the people in each of the groups differ from one another in some way that could distort the results of the experiment (more highly skilled people in the experimental group, for instance, and fewer highly skilled people in the control group), researchers use the technique of **random assignment** to decide which individuals will join the experimental or the control group. Because their assignment is purely a matter of chance, it is unlikely that the people in each group will differ from each other in any systematic fashion.

To understand how these various controls enable the laboratory experimenter to determine causality, let's look at a classic study of the relationship between

experimental group   In a formal experiment, the group that is exposed to the treatment, that is, the independent variable.

control group   In a formal experiment, the group that is not exposed to the treatment, that is, the independent variable.

random assignment   The technique by which researchers assign individuals randomly to either an experimental or a control group.

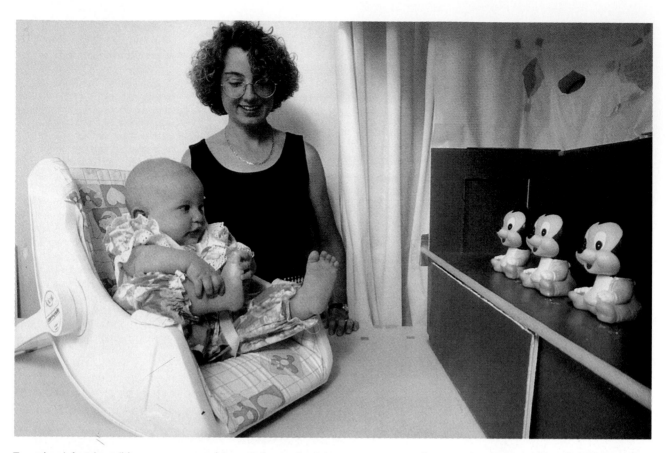

To explore infants' possible mathematical skills, Karen Wynn, development psychologist at the University of Arizona, showed a 5-month-old infant varying combinations of three Mickey Mouse figurines. Wynn concluded that the baby demonstrated rudimentary awareness of enumeration by staring more protractedly when, say, 3 figurines appeared after she had seen Wynn place only two behind a screen. Some psychologists found the research sound. Others held that the infant may simply have understood that the display violated her expectation, not that she understood the specific change in quantity.

watching violent television programs and aggressive behavior. Liebert and Baron (1972) randomly assigned 136 boys and girls ranging in age from 5 to 9 in either an experimental group or a control group. When each child arrived at the laboratory, an experimenter took him or her to an individual waiting room that contained a television set and suggested that the child watch TV for a few minutes until the study was ready to begin. In actual fact, what each child watched on TV was the substance of either the experimental or the control condition. The researchers believed it was necessary to deceive them into thinking that watching TV was incidental in order to keep them from guessing the true purpose of the study and thus perhaps altering their reactions. However, this deception raises ethical questions about the researchers' procedures, as does the manipulation we will discuss shortly.

During this portion of the study, the children in both groups first saw two brief commercials selected for their humor and attention-getting value. Then half the children—those in the experimental group—saw three and a half minutes of a program from the TV series "The Untouchables," in which federal agents battled organized crime in Chicago of the 1920s. The film sequence contained a chase, two fistfights, two shootings, and a knifing. In contrast, the children in the control group watched a highly active, but nonviolent sports sequence of the same time length in which athletes competed in hurdle races and high jumps. Finally, the children in both groups watched another 60 seconds of a tire commercial. Notice that the only difference in the material in which the two groups were exposed was in the three-and-a-half-minute video they watched; one group saw violent episodes, the other no violence at all. The researchers thus hypothesized that if later the children in the experimental group behaved differently than those in the control group, it would be reasonable to conclude that exposure to TV violence was the cause.

In the second phase of the study, the experimenters told each of the children that they were to play a game with another child in an adjoining room (whom they could not see and who, in fact, was purely imaginary). The researchers seated each child before a panel that had two buttons labeled "Hurt" and "Help" and told the child that the buttons were connected to a panel that the child in the other room sat before. This child was playing a game that required turning a handle, the experimenter explained, and if the child wanted to make it easier for her "partner" to turn the handle she could press the "Help" button; on the other hand, if the participant wanted to hinder the other child, pressing the "Hurt" button would turn the handle burning hot. Of course, this entire scenario was a deception, and nothing a child did hurt anyone else. But the researchers believed that with this story line and by measuring how long and how often children depressed the "Hurt" button they could gauge how aggressively children in both the experimental and the control groups would behave toward another child. Do you think the deceptive manipulation in this part of Liebert and Baron's study was justified? We'll return to this question when we discuss the issue of ethics in research at the end of the chapter.

You can now see how an experiment assesses the relationship between two factors, or variables: the **independent variable,** which is the factor the researchers deliberately manipulate, and the **dependent variable,** the factor researchers expect to change as a function of change in the independent variable. Thus, changes in the dependent variable *depend* on changes in the independent variable. In this case, the independent variable was the kind of TV program the children watched, and the dependent variable was the amount of aggressiveness children might display toward other children. Liebert and Baron discovered that children who had seen the violent "Untouchables" segment showed significantly more willingness to engage in interpersonal aggression than children who had watched the fast-paced but nonviolent sports program. This finding supported the researchers' hypothesis that exposure to TV violence can cause interpersonal aggression.

Note, however, that even the best-controlled laboratory experiment has limitations that prevent easy generalization from the experimental situation to the natural world. Ensuring a study's **ecological validity,** or its accurate representation of events and processes that occur in the natural environment, is often difficult, and laboratory findings don't necessarily reflect how people act in the everyday world. For example, Liebert and Baron edited their violent TV program to include more acts of violence in three and a half minutes than would normally occur in a randomly chosen TV segment of this length, even from a show that has a lot of violence. In addition, the researchers used an artificially contrived test setting and measure of aggression, something children would not normally encounter in real life. Based on such an unusual situation, is it fair to make a blanket statement that watching TV violence causes people to behave more hostilely toward others than they normally would?

One way to overcome some of the problem of artificiality in a laboratory study is to conduct a **laboratory analogue experiment,** in which researchers try to duplicate in the lab many of the features or events that occur naturally in everyday life. For instance, laboratory investigators have staged angry interactions between mothers and other adults and then videotaped the reactions of the mothers' children (Cummings & Davies, 1994; Cummings et al., 1989). These interactions, which the researchers tried to make as realistic as possible, were like ones that might take place in natural settings such as stores, malls, streets, or the home, but because the experimenters controlled their timing and venue, they were able to measure the children's responses as they could rarely hope to do in the natural environment.

Of course, "naturalism" isn't demanded in all developmental studies. For example, as you will see in later chapters, experimenters usually gain important insights about people's perceptual capacities, such as how well they see and hear, through laboratory assessments. This is because, in the laboratory, researchers can precisely control the critical features of perceptual stimuli. For instance, they can increase the loudness of a sound by a single decibel to determine if people can detect the change in loudness. Because many basic perceptual skills don't vary across contexts, a laboratory is just as valid a place to assess them as anywhere else (Seitz, 1988).

independent variable The variable, or factor, that researchers deliberately manipulate in a formal experiment.

dependent variable The variable, or factor, that researchers expect to change as a function of change in the independent variable.

ecological validity The degree to which a research study accurately represents events and processes that occur in the natural world.

laboratory analogue experiment An experiment in which investigators try to duplicate in the laboratory features or events of everyday life.

Clearly, research strategies must be matched to the questions being asked. And even though correlational designs do not allow us to determine causality, researchers are often constrained to use them because some issues—for example, residential mobility, divorce, or child abuse—simply do not lend themselves to the experimental approach.

Field and Natural Approaches

When we want to avoid artificiality and some of the other problems associated with the lab or even laboratory analogue experiment, we can sometimes conduct experiments in people's natural environments. In field experiments, clever investigators may deliberately introduce changes in the normal environment; in natural experiments, they may take advantage of naturally occurring changes in the everyday world.

The Field Experiment

field experiment An experiment in which researchers deliberately create a change in a real-world setting and then measure the outcome of their manipulation.

In another study of the impact of viewing TV violence on aggressive behavior in children, Friedrich and Stein (1973) offer us an example of the **field experiment,** in which investigators deliberately bring about a change in a real-world setting and then measure the outcome in that setting. Thus, instead of bringing participants into a laboratory, these experimenters entered the participants' world, that of a summer nursery school. During the first three weeks of the study, the researchers simply observed the children during their usual play sessions to achieve a baseline measure of the degree of aggressive behavior each child manifested under normal circumstances. Then, for the next four weeks, they showed the children a half-hour TV program each day. Randomly assigned to three groups, some children always saw programs depicting interpersonal aggression, such as Batman and Superman cartoons; others saw programs with a message of caring and kindness toward others, such as "Mister Rogers' Neighborhood"; and still others watched neutral shows, such as nature programs or circus movies.

observer bias The tendency of researchers-observers to be influenced in their judgments by their knowledge of the hypotheses guiding the research.

To minimize **observer bias,** that is, the tendency of observers who are knowledgeable about a research design to be influenced in their evaluations by that knowledge, the researchers assessing the children's subsequent behavior did not know the types of programs that different children had been viewing. Friedrich and Stein found that children who had been rated high in aggressive behavior before the TV watching started behaved even more aggressively after repeated exposure to aggressive cartoons, but not after exposure to the other two kinds of shows. For children who were rated low in aggression during the initial assessment period, watching interpersonal aggression seemed to have no effect; they were still less likely to behave aggressively. And, as you might guess, the behavior of the third group, who watched neutral shows, did not change either. The researchers concluded that exposure to TV violence can increase aggression in children, but only among children already likely to behave aggressively.

One advantage of the field experiment over the laboratory experiment is that the results can be generalized more readily to natural environments. Friedrich and Stein did not edit the TV programs the children saw in any way, and these programs were among those that many of the children watched in their homes. Moreover, the children's aggressive behavior was measured in an everyday setting, not in a situation contrived to allow or encourage them to behave aggressively. Both these factors enhance the study's generalizability to the world beyond the researchers' domain.

At the same time, the field experiment retains some important features of a laboratory experiment. Because the independent variable—the type of TV program—was still under the control of the researchers and the participants were still randomly assigned to the various groups, Friedrich and Stein could be reasonably confident that they had demonstrated a causal connection, namely that exposure to TV violence may encourage aggressive children to behave even more aggressively.

The Natural Experiment

When for ethical or practical reasons researchers can't introduce changes into the natural world, they may elect to do a **natural experiment,** in which they can measure the effects of events or changes that occur naturally in the real world. This approach is often called a *quasi-experiment,* because investigators don't assign the research participants randomly to experimental conditions; instead, they select the children they study because the children are exposed to a set of conditions that are of interest to the researcher, such as enrollment in day care or a nutritional supplement program. One example of a natural experiment is a study that investigated the way the introduction of television into a community affected aggressive behavior among children (Williams, 1986). By monitoring the level of aggressiveness in children's play both before and after the debut of television in a small town in Canada, the investigator was able to show that aggressive behavior did in fact increase after TV arrived in town.

Because this research did not contrive the introduction of television to the provincial town it studied, its findings may have more ecological validity than those of laboratory studies on TV's impact. On the other hand, the independent variable—TV viewing—is very broadly defined; children watch all kinds of programs, and the study did not attempt to examine or control what shows they chose. As a result, we cannot say precisely what aspect of television might have caused the behaviors the researcher observed. Moreover, the researchers neither divided participants into experimental and control groups nor assigned them randomly to such groups, so we can neither distinguish between the presence or absence of the independent variable nor rule out the influence of personal characteristics.

In the United States, a great deal of research has been devoted to children's television viewing. Both academic investigators and researchers employed by television companies have attempted to study the nature of children's viewing and, most important, the effects that watching specific kinds of programs have on children's development. As Box 2-2 discusses, although this research has been instrumental in the adoption of legislation aimed at regulating the material available to children through television, most laws passed so far have had few teeth, and the responsibility for such regulation continues to lodge with parents, teachers, and caregivers.

natural experiment An experiment in which researchers measure the results of events that occur naturally in the real world.

Combination Designs in Developmental Research

No research strategy is without its limitations. We've seen that the correlational approach, which is a relatively simple design and which avoids some of the pitfalls of experimental methods, such as the ethics of manipulating people and events, exerts minimal control over variables, says nothing about cause and effect, and is very limited in generalizability. Among laboratory, field, and natural experiments, on the other hand, there is often a trade-off between control of variables and the generalizability of findings. Table 2-1 summarizes the differences among the research designs we've examined so far.

It is important to remember that each method can play a particular role in helping the investigator understand human behavior. Often a researcher may start off in an unexplored area by using a correlational approach simply to establish some possible relationships. Then she may use formal experimental approaches to achieve a clearer view of the causal links among the variables established by the earlier method. In the field of child development, the use of multiple methodological strategies is becoming increasingly common.

One way to deal with the control-generalizability trade-off is to combine field and laboratory approaches in a single research design. As Figure 2-2 suggests, there are two ways to do this: In a combined laboratory-field design, we can introduce the independent variable in the lab and measure the dependent variable in the field (upper right-hand cell) or we can introduce the independent variable in the field and

BOX 2-2

Child Psychology in Action

How Can We Make Better Use of Research on Children and Television?

The impact on children of the amazing growth of communications media within the twentieth century cannot be denied. From early radio, movies, and comic books to television and its electronic cousins—videotapes, video games, CD-ROM, and the Internet—children have been bombarded with material of often questionable value and sometimes dangerous potential. As we have seen in this chapter and in Chapter 1, some educational programs, like "Sesame Street," have had a useful impact on their young audiences. Many have expressed the fear, however, that television may displace other, more valuable activities and turn children into TV addicts rather than intelligent, inquiring, social adults (Huston & Wright, 1998). Yet, despite a considerable body of research and the passage of a half dozen laws in response to these fears, TV programming remains essentially uncontrolled.

What has the wealth of research on children and television—much of it instigated by federal commissions and agencies—revealed? It has shown that some programs do help young children learn, but it has also made a strong case for the negative effects on children of watching programs that focus on violence and sex as well as advertising that preys on the young child's credulousness, which evolves largely from lack of information. Why then have we no laws that protect children from negative programming and advertising and require the media to provide educational and informational programming?

Although the U.S. Congress and the Federal Communications Commission have passed laws intended to influence commercial media, these laws have often failed to impose specific directives, such as banning certain content, mandating certain types of programs, or setting limits as to the period of time (e.g., early evening) or amount of time they allot to child-oriented programming. And the laws that have imposed such directives have often not been enforced. For example, although the Children's Television Act of 1990, drafted on the basis of research, required broadcasters to provide programs that would serve children's educational and informational needs, it had little initial impact not only because enforcement was minimal but also because some stations claimed an educational thrust for programs that few would call informative (e.g., "Teenage Mutant Ninja Turtles," and "Bugs and Tweety Show") (Kunkel & Canepa, 1994).

Attempts to legislate television programming run the risk of violating First Amendment rights to freedom of expression. When broadcasters, journalists, and those who seek to protect civil liberties raise this issue we may ask why anyone should be free to teach young children to be violent. Nevertheless, we must confront the difficult problem of protecting a principle from challenges that could set dangerous precedents. Yet another barrier to the regulation of media content is economic. The television industry itself makes use of research to support its positions, and it maintains a powerful lobby in the nation's capital (Wartella, 1995).

Another barrier to regulation is the difficulty of reaching consensus as to just what kinds of things regulations

---

measure the dependent variable in the lab (lower left-hand cell). An example of the lab-field experiment would be bringing shy youngsters into the lab and showing them films designed to foster positive social interaction and then measuring any changes in their behavior with peers in the classroom. An example of the field-lab experiment would be controlling children's TV viewing in their homes by allowing one group to watch only aggressive programs and a second group to watch only nonviolent and prosocial programs, and then conducting a laboratory assessment of any changes in the two groups' level of aggressiveness. The first design offers more precise control over the independent variable, while allowing the dependent variable to be measured in a way that isn't too contrived; the second manipulates the independent variable in a natural way, while still allowing tight control over measurement of the dependent variable. Both approaches enhance the generalizability of the findings without loosening control enough to call reliability into question.

The Case Study Approach

case study method A form of research in which investigators study individual persons.

Can we learn anything about development by studying a single child, or must we always study groups of people? The study of individual persons, called the **case study method,** does have a useful role in developmental research. The case study allows investigators to explore phenomena that they do not often encounter, such as an unusual talent or a rare developmental disorder. It also facilitates more intensive investigation because the researcher's efforts are not spread across a large number of participants. In the 1800s, in one of the first recorded case studies, Charles

should target. For example, the 1996 Telecommunications Act required television manufacturers to install in every set a special chip that would allow the consumer to block programs assigned particular ratings similar to the ratings used by the film industry. However, agreement on such a system initially ran into obstacles, not only the problem of deciding on a rating for a particular program but also arguments raised as to whether labeling programs would be counterproductive, attracting rather than turning away viewers.

If television programming is unsuitable for children and essentially uncontrolled, what can parents and others do to protect their young charges beyond seeking stricter laws and government policies? According to Huston and Wright such efforts may pale in the face of our need to recognize and act on our own enormous influence on children's use of television. "What, how, and how much television parents view has a direct impact on children not only because it provides a model, but because children are directly exposed to programs that parents are viewing" (Huston & Wright, 1998, p. 41). Setting an example is a time-honored prescription, although admittedly it is not always effective and it is unappealing to some adults. And perhaps today in the swelling rapids of the media flow it is not enough.

On the basis of research that has highlighted positive effects of coviewing by parents and children of suitable television programs, a number of psychologists have recommended this practice. If parents or others reinforce a program's content, helping young children identify and discuss characters and events, and generally providing what Lev Vygotsky has called scaffolding (Chapter 9) for their understanding and interpretations, the children may benefit (St. Peters, 1993; Watkins et al., 1980). Research has also shown that parents can help children cope with fears aroused by specific television content (Wilson & Weiss, 1993). However, the evidence is that families don't engage often in such coviewing, at least not of programs that are child-oriented. Other techniques for mitigating the effects of disturbing content, such as telling children to turn off the TV or close their eyes, are not very useful.

Other more positive approaches may have better results. Huston and Wright (1998) point out that parents and others who reject television as a source of beneficial learning may waste an important opportunity, not only that of using television to teach children but of teaching children how to use television. There is some research evidence that supplementary (printed) materials distributed by programs like "Sesame Street" and "Mr. Rogers' Neighborhood" have been useful in helping children understand educational and prosocial messages and generalize them to their own environments. There is also some evidence that giving children specific lessons about television violence can decrease the amount of aggressive behavior they display (Chapter 16).

Clearly, television viewing is a family affair, and families as well as networks and the government need to take responsibility for what children watch. In Chapter 16 we revisit this issue and explore further ways of gaining control over children's television viewing.

Darwin kept a highly detailed diary of his infant son's emotional expressions, a record that became the basis for his theory of emotional development in infants and children. This early work provided useful hunches, insights, and hypotheses that later investigators pursued in a more systematic fashion.

Sometimes a case study leads into a kind of experiment in which a psychologist or other researcher tries to bring about a change in a particular behavior, most often a behavior that is self-destructive or that involves aggressive behavior toward other people. Consider the case of a 4-year-old whom we'll call Joey. During every play period on the nursery school playground Joey hit other children two or three times. At first, every time Joey hit another child, his teachers rushed over to stop him, often lingering with him to explain why he shouldn't hit other people. But Joey kept right on hitting just the same. The school psychologist, who thought that Joey hit other children in part to gain the teachers' attention, told the teachers to ignore Joey whenever he was aggressive and to instruct the other children just to walk away from these incidents. At first, Joey reacted to this new response with an increase in aggressive attacks. However, after a few days of the "silent treatment" his rate of hitting began to drop. Then, to determine whether or not Joey's behavior was changing in response to the new strategy, the psychologist asked the teachers to resume paying attention to him when he hit. Sure enough, his rate of hitting increased, suggesting that his need for attention was indeed controlling the behavior. The teachers were then instructed once again to ignore Joey's hitting, and once more his rate of hitting dropped.

TABLE 2-1   Research Designs: Advantages and Limitations

Design	Control over Independent Variable	Control over Dependent Variable	Generalizability of Findings
Correlational method	Low	Low	Medium
Laboratory experiment	High	High	Low
Field experiment	Medium	Low	High
Natural experiment	Low	Low	High

ABAB design   A technique in which an experimental treatment is administered, withdrawn, and readministered in order to measure its effects. Also called a *reversal* design.

This is an example of what is called a *reversal*, or ABAB, experimental design intended to diminish an undesirable behavior. In the **ABAB design,** A is the control, or normal condition of the subject and B is the experimental condition. Thus Joey's initial hitting behavior is represented by the first A, and the experimental treatment—ignoring Joey's behavior and walking away from him—by the first B. The second A reflects the psychologist's instruction that everyone return to the original condition, and the second B reflects the reinstatement of the experimental treatment as a result of Joey's having reverted to his aggressive behavior. If the reinstatement of the experimental treatment again diminishes the undesirable behavior—and it did—we can be pretty certain that the treatment works.

The chief limitation of the single-case approach is the impossibility of generalizing from one individual to other people in other settings. Joey's treatment might or might not work with another child; nothing in the study of a single individual gives us a clue as to the generalizability of the research.

STUDYING CHANGE OVER TIME

The study of child development makes use of certain research techniques that are intended to measure differences among individuals that are related to age and the progression of time: the cross-sectional, longitudinal, and sequential methods. Other fields use these methods as well, but because of their special usefulness in studying change over time, they are of particular relevance to developmental topics.

As we explore these different research methods, keep in mind that they are independent of both the data-collection methods and the research designs chosen by an investigator. Thus, for example, a longitudinal study could use self-reports or observational data, and it could be fitted to a correlational or an experimental research design. However, longitudinal studies are usually correlational, whereas cross-sectional investigations more often use experimental research designs.

The Cross-Sectional Method

cross-sectional method   A research method in which researchers compare groups of individuals of different age levels at approximately the same point in time.

The most common strategy for investigating age-related differences in development is the **cross-sectional method,** in which researchers compare different individuals representing different age levels at approximately the same point in time. This method lends itself well to the important cross-cultural research that helps us discover whether we can generalize findings about children's development in one country, say the United States, to children in other countries, such as Cameroon, Mexico, or Zambia. Box 2-3 discusses some interesting examples of cross-cultural research. The cross-sectional method has both advantages and limitations, however, as we will see in our discussion of Rheingold and Eckerman's (1970) classic study of the growth of independence in young children.

Selecting different groups of children at different age levels, these researchers used a cross-sectional design to investigate the way children's independence differs across a range of ages. They recruited children at nine different ages—three girls

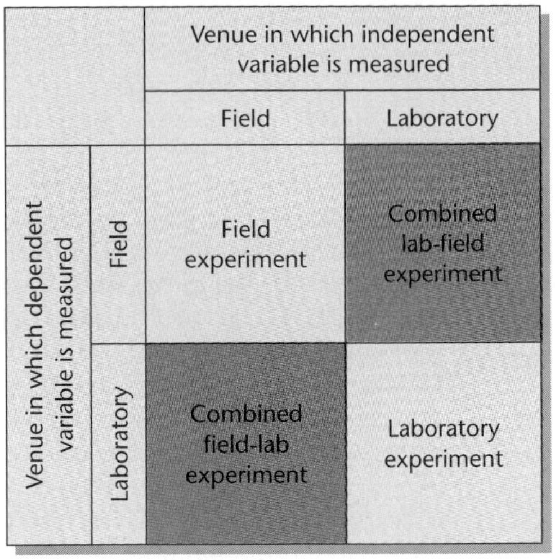

		Venue in which independent variable is measured	
		Field	Laboratory
Venue in which dependent variable is measured	Field	Field experiment	Combined lab-field experiment
	Laboratory	Combined field-lab experiment	Laboratory experiment

■ FIGURE 2-2
Combining field and laboratory experimental approaches.
In the ordinary field and laboratory experiments, both independent and dependent variables are manipulated or measured in the same place. In the combined approaches shown in the upper-right and lower-left cells, by varying the location of these operations on the variables, experimenters have two options for balancing control with generalizability.

and three boys at each half year of age between 12 and 60 months—and the children's mothers. Choosing a seminaturalistic setting, they placed the mothers and children at one end of a large lawn; the mothers sat in chairs, and the children were free to roam. Observers were stationed in nearby windows to track the paths of the children's excursions.

A clear, linear relationship between age and distance traveled emerged. The average farthest distance for 1-year-olds was about 23 feet (6.9 meters); by 2 years of age children ventured about 50 feet (15.1 meters); 3-year-olds went 57 feet (17.3 meters); and 4-year-olds ventured 68 feet (20.6 meters). For each month of age the children went almost a foot, or a third of a meter, farther.

The significance of this study is that Rheingold and Eckerman were able to determine how independence differs across age levels by comparing the behaviors of groups of different children at different ages during the same period of time. In fact, their study was unusual in that they collected their data across a wide age range in a very short time—just a couple of months. Thus these investigators did not have to wait until the 12-month-old infant became a 4-year-old toddler to evaluate developmental advances. This advantage, of course, becomes very clear when the comparisons involve even wider age ranges. And had they spent only a little more time, they could easily have included 8-, 12-, and 16-year-olds, tracking the way independence changes in adolescence.

However, the distinctive characteristic of the cross-sectional approach, that is, its examination of different children at several ages levels, has disadvantages. It yields no information about the possible past determinants of the apparently age-related changes observed because we can't know what these children were like at younger ages. In addition, the method gives us no information about the ways in which individual children develop. How stable is independence? Is the child who is independent at 1 year likely to be more independent at 5 than a peer who exhibited little independence until he was 2? Because the cross-sectional approach cannot answer these kinds of questions, we must turn to the longitudinal method to tackle these issues.

The Longitudinal Method

One of the most ambitious projects in the study of child development is the Fels Longitudinal Study, which began in 1929 and continued until the 1970s to follow groups of children from birth to the age of 18, hoping to unravel some of the mysteries of development. Parents enrolling their newborns in this study agreed to have the child weighed, measured, observed, and tested until he or she was old enough to graduate from high school.

This type of **longitudinal method,** in which researchers study the same individuals repeatedly at various points in their lives in order to assess patterns of

longitudinal method A method in which investigators study the same people repeatedly at various times in the participants' lives.

BOX 2–3

Perspectives on Diversity

Studying Development Cross-Culturally

Child developmentalists are becoming increasingly aware of the importance of establishing the limitations of their findings and determining whether the developmental insights gained by studies in one culture apply to children in other cultures as well. Is the timing of the onset of crawling and walking universal? Do children show the same emotions in all cultures?

We can often address fundamental development issues such as the relative roles of nature and nurture by comparing child development in different cultures. A finding that some aspect of development evolves similarly in a wide variety of cultures may suggest not only that some behavior patterns are universal in nature but also that genetic factors may play a central role in the emergence of these patterns. On the other hand, the discovery that a behavior differs markedly across cultures may suggest that environmental variables play a significant role in its evolution.

Consider the timing of motor development. Although we might expect it to be universal, it is not. For example, in some African cultures, such as the Kipsigis people of Kenya or the people of Zambia, babies learn to crawl and walk at earlier ages than do infants in the United States (Harkness & Super, 1995). In these cultures parents teach their children to sit up, stand, and walk very soon after birth. In contrast, cultures like the Ache who live in the rainforest of Paraguay discourage early motor development and keep children in close physical contact with

their mothers. As a result, motor development is slowed down.

In another interesting example of cross-cultural difference, the Nso children of Cameroon assume much more responsibility for the rearing of their siblings than do U.S. children (Nsamenang & Lamb, 1994). What implications may this behavior of Cameroon children have for the assumption of responsibility later in life? And consider patterns of play in Mexico. Whereas U.S. and Canadian adults serve as play partners for their children, in Mexican families sisters and brothers are more often play partners than are adults (Farver & Howes, 1993). These and other differences in socialization patterns may have profound effects on children's development, and these naturally occurring variations in cultural practices may provide important information about the impact of different childrearing conditions on later development.

Cross-cultural research is often difficult and expensive. Language barriers and lack of familiarity with the underlying meanings of different customs and practices can often lead researchers to form erroneous conclusions. Successful cross-cultural studies often benefit from the participation of cultural informants, usually local people who serve as translators and interpreters, who help researchers gain the trust of officials and other people with whom they need to collaborate and who often assist in interpreting research findings (Rogoff, 1998; Greenfield & Suzuki, 1998). As awareness of cross-cultural differences and of their significance for development research increases, cross-cultural research is becoming a more frequently used method in child psychology.

stability and change over time, has clear advantages over cross-sectional studies. A longitudinal design allows researchers to follow the development of individuals rather than of groups of people over time and to explore possible causes of any observed patterns. Longitudinal research requires great patience, but it is a powerful method of evaluating the impact of earlier events on later behavior, a topic of enormous interest to child psychologists.

But the longitudinal method also has disadvantages, many of which are related to time. It takes years to collect longitudinal data, and researchers often want to obtain information more quickly. Moreover, they may find it hard to keep up the funding for a project that spans decades. In addition, there is the problem of losing subjects—and sometimes staff—from a lengthy longitudinal study. Over time, people move, become ill, or simply lose interest, and the result is a shrinking sample that can bias the results and reduce their reliability. Even the sample of individuals who initially agree to participate in a longitudinal project may not be very representative of the general population. Would you want to be observed, measured, and questioned annually for 18 years?

Another problem is one of inflexibility: The theories and research that generate hypotheses in child development are constantly changing, but it is hard for researchers to take advantage of new insights or methods in a study that is already under way. For example, in a longitudinal study of IQ, if a new test is discovered 10 years after a study has begun, what can the longitudinal investigators do? Several options are available: Researchers can start over with a new sample and the

new test, or, alternatively, they can begin to give the new test to their 10-year-olds (the "old" sample). But then they lose the possibility of comparing the earlier results with the later findings, because the test instruments are not comparable. Here is a solution. The researchers can give both the old and the new test at the same time to the same subjects and thus judge the comparability of the two tests. Another problem is presented by what we call *practice effects,* or the effects of repeated testing. Since the same measures may be used in several successive years, participants' altered answers may be as a result of their familiarity with the items or questions. In contrast, individuals who responded to these issues for the first time may give different answers.

For the same reasons that have encouraged psychologists to study young infants, developmentalists also study preschoolers, exploring the depth and breadth of their cognitive, emotional, and social development.

A way to avoid some of these problems is to conduct a short-term longitudinal study. Here researchers track a group of people for a limited time period of a few months to a few years. Their focus is less broad and usually limited to a few key questions. For instance, Roger Brown and his colleagues (Brown, 1973) at Harvard University tracked the language development of three children, Adam, Eve, and Sarah, for a period of five years. In a later chapter we will discuss some of the wealth of detailed information about the development of language and grammar that this project yielded. What is important to us here is that the research had the advantage of shortening the period of data collection compared with longer-term studies, avoiding dropouts in the sample, and allowing the researchers to maintain the same staff and measurement procedures. In addition, findings from the first project could be used to help design another, thus keeping the research effort up-to-date in theory and methods, building on its own insights and those of other researchers.

A different kind of drawback to lengthy longitudinal studies is the problem of generalizing to generations other than the one being studied. As times change, people become exposed to different influences. Children today, for instance, grow up with many experiences virtually unknown to children growing up in their parents' or grandparents' generations: for example, television, computers, two parents working outside the home, day care, single mothers who have never married. Who is to say that findings from a much earlier longitudinal study are still applicable today? Thus, perhaps some of the patterns observed in the people who were studied are

age cohort   People born within the same generation.

specific only to an **age cohort,** that is, members of the same generation. The Fels study circumvented this problem by continuing to study a small sample of new children year after year, to provide a basis of comparison with the earlier subjects. This method, however, further increases the length of a study and adds additional expense.

The Sequential Method

sequential method   A research method that combines features of both the cross-sectional and the longitudinal methods.

Another way around the problem of separating age-related changes from changes that are caused by the unique experiences of a particular age cohort is to use the **sequential method,** which combines features of both cross-sectional and longitudinal studies. Researchers may begin by selecting samples of children of different ages, as they would in cross-sectional research. Suppose, for example, that we wanted to study the change in the development of children's reading skills throughout childhood. We might begin by recruiting and testing three samples of children: 2-year-olds, 4-year-olds, and 6-year-olds. This would constitute a cross-sectional study. We would then test these children again at periodic intervals, let's say every two years, thus transforming the study into a longitudinal one. At each of the two-year measuring points, we could also add a new sample of 2-year-olds to the pool of subjects, thus expanding the scope of the study and enabling us to compare a larger number of age cohorts. Figure 2-3 displays the design of this study.

Notice the advantages of this sequential approach. First, it allows us to examine age-related changes in children, because the longitudinal feature allows us to test the same children every four years. Second, the cross-sectional aspect of this approach allows us to examine the impact of the year of evaluation, because in each such year at least three different groups of children are assessed. Third, in following each age cohort, it allows us to explore generational effects, or effects of the particular time period in which each group of children was born and raised. For example, some of the 6-year-olds recruited in 1994 for this study were entering kindergartens at a time when educators were engaged in vigorous debate about whether phonics, stressed during the 1960s and 1970s, or the study of good literature, which many began to advocate in the 1980s, should predominate. By comparing these and other age cohorts we might be able to assess changes in children's reading abilities as instructional techniques either continued to change or settled into an accepted methodology. And finally, the design has a time-saving advantage. Six years after the start of the study, in 2006, we would have data on changes in reading ability that, in terms of factors that influence these changes, actually span a period of 10 years (look again at Fig. 2-3). This is a four-year saving over a traditional longitudinal study.

When studying change over time, developmental researchers clearly have a number of design and methodological options. What they choose depends on the particular kinds of data they want to gather, on the availability of participants, and on the time and money they have to carry out the project (see Table 2-2 for a comparison of the pluses and minuses of all three strategies). No one strategy is best in all situations. This is why different researchers use different methods, and the same researchers use different methods at different times.

THE ETHICS OF RESEARCH WITH CHILDREN

A major consideration for the student of child development in deciding on a research strategy is the potential effects of the strategy's procedures on the children to be studied. In recent decades there has been a growing awareness of the ethical issues involved in doing research with children. Various government review boards and professional organizations, such as the American Psychological Association and the Society for Research in Child Development, have suggested guidelines for the participation of children in research projects in an effort to protect children from dangerous and harmful procedures (see Table 2-3). In addition, all legitimate research

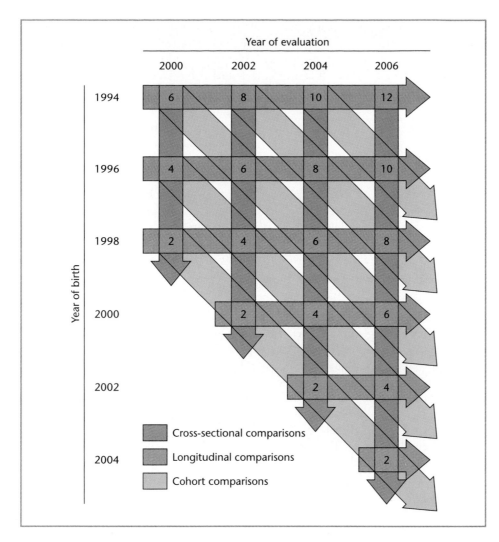

Year of evaluation

Year of birth	2000	2002	2004	2006
1994	6	8	10	12
1996	4	6	8	10
1998	2	4	6	8
2000		2	4	6
2002			2	4
2004				2

Cross-sectional comparisons
Longitudinal comparisons
Cohort comparisons

■ FIGURE 2-3
Design for a sequential study. This combination of the cross-sectional and longitudinal designs yields a third, historical dimension of measurement, that of comparing cohorts, or people of the same age, at different points in time. The numbers within the network of arrows representing type of comparison are the ages of the groups of children to be studied. For example, in the year 2000 we would do a cross-sectional study of three groups of children, ages 2, 4, and 6. In 2002 we would do another cross-sectional study, this time of children aged 2, 4, 6, and 8 (the latter were 6 in our first study). In a longitudinal study we would then compare the scores of the 8-year-olds with their own scores of two years earlier. And in a cohort study, we would compare the scores of 6-year-old children at different points in time—for example, those who were 6 years old in 2000 and 6-year-olds in 2002.

projects involving children (and adults) are scrutinized and approved by review boards at the institutions where the research is carried out, including, of course, colleges and universities. This scrutiny ensures that researchers follow ethical guidelines.

The right to be fully informed about the nature of a study and fully aware of its procedures is high on any list of ethical guidelines. As a result of growing sensitivity to this right, fewer psychologists can be found peering into waiting rooms, watching people behind one-way windows, and observing through the lens of a hidden camera. Laboratory research involving deception (in which participants are deliberately misled about the true purpose of the study) are also becoming less common. Investigators are increasingly accepting the view that lack of full disclosure is no longer acceptable, and that participants have a right to know beforehand all that a study entails.

Another central right of subjects is the right to give consent before being included in a study. Although it is important to gain agreement from the children themselves to participate in the research process, very often children are too young to fully appreciate the complex issues that are involved in making informed decisions. Some investigators suggest that children under the age of 8 are too young to offer fully **informed consent,** or agreement to participate in research based on a clear understanding of the purposes and procedures to be employed in the study. In cases involving such children, parents must question researchers and others and make choices for their children, protecting them at all times. In addition, if children are recruited through a school or other institution, teachers and administrators provide another layer of query and consent that is particularly important when

informed consent
Agreement to participate in a research study that is based on a clear and full understanding of the purposes and procedures of that study.

TABLE 2-2   Comparative Characteristics of Methods of Studying Developmental Change over Time

	Cross-sectional	Longitudinal	Sequential
Time required	Short	Long	Moderate
Ability to control costs	High	Low	Moderate
Ability to maintain potential pool of participants	Excellent	Very problematic	Moderate to good
Continuity of staff	High	Medium to low	Moderate to high
Flexibility in adapting to new tests and measures	High	Low	Moderate
Likelihood of practice effects	High	Low	Medium
Ability to assess research issues:			
Normative development data at different ages	Excellent	Excellent	Excellent
Impact of early events on later behavior	Poor	Excellent	Good
Stability vs. instability of behavior	Poor	Excellent	Good
Developmental paths of individuals	Poor	Excellent	Good
Historical or cohort issues	Excellent	Poor	Good

parents don't pay close attention to school activities, or when, for one reason or another, they are neglectful of their children's interests (Thompson, 1990).

A third major right of research participants is the right not to be harmed. This includes protection not only from physical harm, but from psychological and emotional harm as well. Children have the right not to be made to feel uncomfortable by participation in a study and a right not to be encouraged to act in ways that lessen their own view of themselves or the way other people view them. Investigators have an obligation to conduct their research in ways that respect the feelings and needs of the children they study. For example, in an experimental procedure called the Strange Situation, which is used to assess children's social relationships with their caregivers, infants are left alone briefly, and sometimes they fuss and cry. As we will see in Chapter 7, this procedure has yielded a great deal of information about early social-emotional development, but is the infant's distress justified?

As easy as it is to list such rights of child participants in research, it is not always easy to determine the ethical course of action in a particular situation. For instance, suppose you are a psychologist who wants to study the long-term effects of being born very prematurely. Should you inform parents whose children you wish to include in the study of all the hypotheses you want to test? What if revealing this information could encourage the parents to act toward the baby in ways that turned the hypotheses into self-fulfilling prophecies, causing the infant to develop less favorably than he or she otherwise might? In other words, does the end justify the means? If you suspect that full disclosure might somehow cause a child harm, is restricting information justified? Or should you not do the study in the first place?

Let us look at another ethical issue in research: To study children's persistence in the face of failure, researchers gave children a task so difficult that they could not possibly master it. In order, they hoped, to eliminate negative effects of the failure experience, the researchers followed the first task with one in which all the children could—and did—succeed. Because failure is a common experience in school for many children, were the researchers justified in forcing their child participants to experience failure? Did the long-term goal of the study—to find out how to teach children to continue to work even after a failure experience—justify this experiment?

And what about the experiment by Liebert and Baron (1972) that we discussed in the section "The Laboratory Experiment"? Was it ethical to encourage the child participants in this study to choose to push the "Hurt" button and to let them believe that they were not only keeping another child from winning the game she was presumably playing but causing her actual physical harm? Even though the entire scenario was a deception and therefore no child was being frustrated in play or physically harmed, how might the child participants have viewed themselves,

TABLE 2-3　A Bill of Child Participants' Rights in Child Development Research

1. *The right to be fully informed.* Every child has the right to full and truthful information about the purposes of a study in which he or she is to participate and about the procedures to be used.
2. *The right to give informed and voluntary consent.* Every child has the right to agree, either orally or in writing, to participate in a research project. If a child is too young to understand the aims and procedures of the study and to make an informed decision, researchers must request the informed consent of the child's parents.
3. *The right not to be harmed in any way.* Every child has the right to know that he or she will not experience any physical or psychological harm or damage as a result of the research procedures.
4. *The right to withdraw voluntarily from research.* Every child has the right to withdraw at any time from continued participation in any research project.
5. *The right to be informed of the results of research.* Every child has the right to information about the results of the research project. If the child is too young to fully understand this information, it must be provided to the child's parents. It is understood that sometimes information is in the form of group measures or scores on a task rather than individual scores.
6. *The right to confidentiality.* Every child has the right to know that personal information gathered as part of the research project will remain private and confidential, and that it will not be shared with any other individuals or agencies.
7. *The right to full compensation.* Every child has the right to be fully compensated for her or his time and effort as a research participant, even if the child withdraws and does not complete her or his participation.
8. *The right to beneficial treatments.* Every child has the right to profit from any beneficial treatments provided to other participants in the research project. When experimental treatments are deemed beneficial—for example, participation in a program designed to enhance reading or math skills—participants in control groups, who do not receive this treatment during the research study proper, have the right to the same participation in the beneficial treatment after the project is completed.

Sources: American Psychological Association, 1992; Society for Research on Child Development Committee on Ethical Conduct in Child Development Research, 1993.

the researchers, their parents (if they agreed to the children's participation in the research), and anyone else involved in the study? Might they have felt ashamed of themselves? Angry that adults would deceive them? Shocked that adults would condone such an experiment? Encouraged to go out and frustrate and harm other people because all these adults said it was okay?

In the final analysis, a careful cost-benefit analysis is usually the guiding principle. What effects, if any, might participation in the research project have on the children to be studied, and how do those effects weigh against the possible gains from whatever information may be obtained from the research? Developmental research is a tool for increasing our knowledge about children, and through this knowledge, children will, it is hoped, benefit. The ethics of research in child psychology is a continuing debate, and the last word is yet to be heard. As you read descriptions of studies throughout the rest of this book, think carefully about the ethical issues that surround them.

SUMMARY

- Child psychologists use the **scientific method** in their research. They formulate hypotheses on the basis of theories, and they use measurable and replicable techniques to collect, study, and analyze data to test the usefulness of these theories.

Selecting a Sample

- Selecting a **sample** is an important first step in doing research because it determines the extent to which the researcher's conclusions can be applied, or generalized, to people other than those who were studied. To ensure the **representativeness** of a sample, or the degree to which it accurately reflects the larger national population, it must include individuals who vary by such factors as race, sex, and social class. Conducting a **national survey** is one way to ensure that a sample is representative of a broad range of people.

Methods of Gathering Data About Children

- Soliciting **self-reports** from children, usually by means of interviews, is one way to gather information about child development issues. Getting self-reports from children can be more difficult than getting them from adults, for children tend to be less attentive, slower to respond, and less likely to understand the questions put to them. Self-reports, however, are the only way to obtain information about such things as children's feelings and their unique perspectives on their lives.
- Another data-gathering method is to solicit information about a child from other people who know that child well, such as parents, siblings, teachers, and peers. Attempts to increase the accuracy of parents' reports about their children include focusing on specific current issues in the child's life, training the parents to be more accurate observers, using structured diaries to guide their observations, and "beeping" them at various times to tell them when to record information.
- Often, of course, there is no substitute for researchers' own **direct observation** of children. Such observations can occur in natural settings, such as a child's home, or in a laboratory; in the latter case, a **structured observation** allows researchers to observe the child as he performs some highly structured task. One limitation of direct observation is that, when children and parents know they are being watched, they act in more socially acceptable ways than they ordinarily would. To minimize such distortions, researchers try to observe unobtrusively for relatively long periods to enable subjects to adapt to the situation.
- When researchers use direct observations, they must decide what kinds of behaviors to record. They can write down everything the participant does (a **specimen record**), record only particular events (**event sampling**), or check off from a list of behaviors those that occur during a predetermined period (**time sampling**). If the researcher wishes to examine the stream of behavior, a better strategy is to record events in sequence. To observe a behavior that occurs infrequently, the researcher can structure the situation to increase the likelihood that the behavior will take place. Because of the limitations of all data-gathering methods, researchers often use multiple measures of the same behaviors.

Research Design: Establishing Relationships and Causes

- The **correlational method** involves examining the relationship between two variables, such as children's aggressive behavior and the amount of aggression they watch on TV. The **correlation coefficient** is expressed in terms of the direction (positive or negative) and the strength (0 to –1 or 0 to +1) of the relationship. If two factors are correlated, they are systematically related to each other, but a correlation alone does not tell us whether one factor causes the other.
- A **laboratory experiment** permits researchers to establish cause-and-effect relationships by assessing a specific behavior (such as trying to hurt another person) in a controlled setting where a certain factor of interest (such as viewing TV violence) is introduced to an **experimental group** of participants while a **control group** is exposed to some neutral factor. Researchers use **random assignment** to assign participants to either of these groups. The **dependent variable** is the behavior that is affected by manipulation of the **independent variable.**
- The problem with laboratory experiments is that they rarely have **ecological validity** and cannot easily be generalized to real-world settings. In a **laboratory analogue experiment** a researcher duplicates in a laboratory many of the features of a natural setting. This approach allows control over the situation while

preserving some of the "naturalism" of real situations. Even less artificial is a **field experiment,** in which a researcher deliberately produces a change in a real-life setting and measures the outcome there. Nevertheless, researchers have to guard against **observer bias** when working in the field. Another alternative to increase the generalizability of findings is to conduct a **natural experiment.** In this case, the investigator measures the impact on children's behavior of some naturally occurring change. But because of lack of control over the independent variable and other factors that could affect behavior, it is often difficult to interpret the results of a natural experiment.

- The various types of experiments available to researchers illustrate an important trade-off between experimental control and the generalizability of findings. No single strategy is always best. Rather, investigators are increasingly using multiple research strategies to study relationships and causes.

- The **case study method** takes an in-depth look at a single child, often (but not always) one with some rare disorder, an unusual ability, or some other uncommon feature that makes him or her of special interest to developmentalists. One form of the case study is the **ABAB design,** in which researchers first measure a child's baseline behavior and then introduce, withdraw, and reintroduce the independent variable to discover its effects on behavior.

Studying Change Over Time

- The most common strategy for investigating developmental change over time is the **cross-sectional method,** in which researchers compare groups of children of different ages at a given point in time. This approach is economical in terms of both time and money, but it yields no information about change nor about the causes of any observed age-related differences in the child participants. The **longitudinal method** overcomes these two drawbacks of cross-sectional research because the researcher examines the same children at different points in their lives. But longitudinal research has its own disadvantages, including high cost, gradual loss of subjects, limited flexibility in using new insights or methods once the study has begun, and the question of the applicability of findings to other **age cohorts.**

- To overcome some of these limitations, researchers can use the **sequential method,** which combines features of both cross-sectional and longitudinal studies. This design enables researchers to compare not only groups of different ages at one point in time, and to track individual children over a period of years, but also to track age cohorts over a number of years.

The Ethics of Research with Children

- A major consideration when deciding on a research strategy is the effects of the procedures on participants. Various government and institutional review boards, in addition to professional organizations, are involved in setting and maintaining guidelines for the proper treatment of human subjects in research. These guidelines include the right to be fully informed about the nature of a study and its procedures, the right to give **informed consent** before participating, and the right not to be harmed.

- But as easy as it is to list such rights of human subjects, it is not always easy to determine the ethical course of action in a particular situation. To determine if certain research procedures are ethical or not, the costs to participants must be carefully weighed against the potential benefits of increased knowledge about development.

Heredity and the Environment

C H A P T E R 3

One of the most striking things about newborns in a hospital nursery is their diversity. From the moment they're born, babies differ from one another not only in physical appearance but in behavior. One baby may sleep most of the time; another may be quite alert, visually scanning the surroundings as if exploring them; a third baby may often be irritable and cry a lot. What contributes to these individual differences at such a young age? Before birth—according to some researchers, even before conception—transactions among a vast array of hereditary and environmental factors begin. Such transactions between genes and the environment make each newborn unique, and they continue to shape the individual's characteristics throughout his or her life span.

The concepts of genotype and phenotype provide a framework for exploring the interactions of genes and environment. A **genotype** is a person's particular set of genes inherited from his or her parents. With the exception of identical twins, no two people have exactly the same genotype. During the course of development the genotype interacts with the environment in complex ways to produce the **phenotype,** which is the observable and measurable expression of an individual's physical and behavioral characteristics. It is these kinds of characteristics—for example, motor abilities, intellectual skills, social behavior, emotionality, and personality traits— that psychologists study in an effort to increase our understanding of how genetic and environmental factors interact to produce each unique human being.

We begin this chapter by exploring what genes are and how they are transmitted from generation to generation. Next we look at the ways in which genes guide development, from determining a child's sex and many other of his or her characteristics to causing or predisposing children and adults to particular disorders. We go on to examine genetic testing and counseling for would-be parents who face the prospect of having a child with a troubling disorder, and we explore the growing field of genetic engineering. Then we consider heredity-environment interactions: We discuss both the ways environmental factors influence the actual expression of an individual child's genetic makeup and, conversely, the way that genetic makeup can shape the environment. Finally, to further our understanding of how genes and the environment interact, we explore the relative contributions of these two forces to intellectual characteristics and functioning, to temperament and personality, and to the presence or absence in a child of mental and emotional distress.

THE PROCESS OF GENETIC TRANSMISSION

In the dark, warm, moist environment of a woman's *oviduct,* sperm and egg unite to create a new living organism that has the potential to develop into a human being. This new organism, called a *zygote,* owes its existence to this union of the male and female germ, or reproductive, cells, both of which carry genetic information. The egg, or **ovum,** the largest human cell, is about 90,000 times as heavy as the sperm that penetrates it; nevertheless, it is still quite small, smaller even than the period at the end of this sentence. The **sperm,** the smallest of all human cells, packs its hereditary information in its head and uses the rest of its tiny body, composed of a long, whiplike tail, to propel itself through the woman's reproductive system in search of the ovum. One of the marvels of human development is that from these microscopic beginnings and within a period of just nine months, a 7- or 8-pound baby, 20 or so inches long, grows and is ready to enter the world.

Chromosomes and Genes

At the moment of human conception, when sperm and egg unite, 23 chromosomes from each of these cells join together to create 23 chromosome *pairs,* or 46 chromosomes in all. **Chromosomes** are threadlike structures—located in the nucleus, or central portion, of a cell—that carry genetic information that helps direct devel-

genotype The particular set of genes that a person inherits from his or her parents.

phenotype Created by the interaction of a person's genotype, or genetic makeup, with the environment; the visible expression of the person's particular physical and behavioral characteristics.

ovum The female germ cell, or egg.

sperm The male germ cell.

chromosomes Threadlike structures, located in the central portion, or nucleus, of a cell, that carry genetic information to help direct development.

opment. An individual's 46 chromosomes are said to come in 23 pairs because each chromosome contributed by the father's sperm is *homologous* (similar in shape and function) to one of the chromosomes contributed by the mother's egg. Copies of these original 23 homologous pairs of chromosomes are passed on to every cell in a person's body with one exception: the reproductive cells. Each reproductive cell contains only 23 single chromosomes instead of the usual 46 because during its development it undergoes a special form of cell division, called **meiosis**, in which its 23 chromosome pairs are halved (see Figure 3-1). The reason for this halving becomes clear when sperm and egg unite. Now 23 chromosomes from the sperm combine with 23 chromosomes from the egg to produce the correct number of 46 chromosomes for a new human being.

Both meiosis and sexual reproduction are crucial to the process of genetic transmission because each facilitates the production of a tremendous diversity of genetic combinations. During meiosis, when a male's or a female's set of chromosomes is halved to produce a germ cell—sperm or egg—that halving process mixes chromo-

meiosis The process by which a germ cell divides to produce new germ cells with only half the normal complement of chromosomes; thus male and female germ cells (sperm and ovum) each contain only 23 chromosomes so that when they unite, the new organism they form will have 46 chromosomes, half from each parent.

■ FIGURE 3-1
Meiosis.
As meiosis, a type of cell division that produces male and female reproductive cells, begins in both sexes, all the chromosomes in the cell replicate themselves, as if they were about to undergo *mitosis,* or normal cell division (see Figure 3-2). In (a) we see the results of this replication (we show cells with only 4 chromosomes, or 2 pairs, rather than the full complement of 46 chromosomes, or 23 pairs). In (b) *crossing over* between chromosomes ensures the zygote's unique genetic inheritance. In (c), the male chromosome pairs separate to form 2 cells, each with 23 chromosomes. In the female, 2 cells are also formed but one is nonfunctional and may or may not produce 2 more nonfunctional cells. In (d) the chromosomes separate once again, in the male forming 4 sperm cells and in the female a single ovum and a fourth nonfunctional cell. (The genetic material in the female's 4 nonfunctional cells degenerates.) When a sperm cell fertilizes an ovum (e), a zygote is formed (f), with 23 chromosome pairs, or 46 in all.

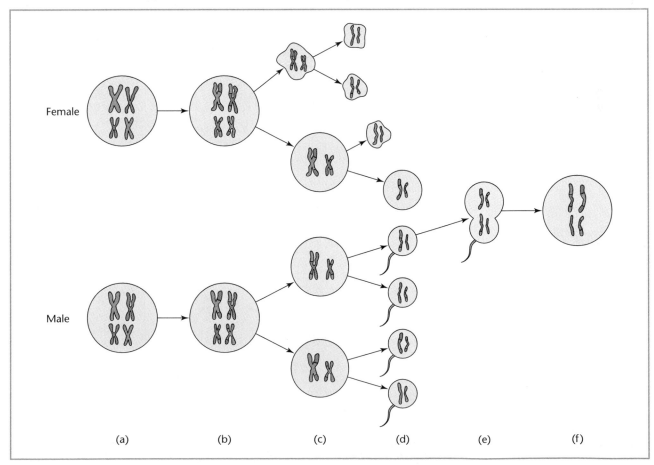

Female

Male

(a)   (b)   (c)   (d)   (e)   (f)

somes that originated from the individual's father with chromosomes that originated from the individual's mother. (Note that all female germ cells, or ova, are created before the time of a female child's birth, whereas male germ cells, or sperm, are created continuously throughout most of a male's life.) Moreover, this mixing process is totally random. The only requirement is that one of each pair of homologous chromosomes end up in the new reproductive cell. This random assortment of homologous chromosomes makes possible the production of about 8 million different chromosome combinations in both a female's eggs and a male's sperm. Further genetic variability is added during meiosis by a process called **crossing over**, in which equivalent sections of homologous chromosomes randomly switch places (Figure 3-1), so that genetic information is shuffled even more. No wonder that the chances of any given man and woman producing two genetically identical children is one in many trillion (except, of course, when a single fertilized egg splits into identical twins).

In Chapter 4 we will follow the progress of the fertilized egg, or zygote, as it develops within the mother's body, becoming an embryo, then a fetus, and finally, at birth, a living human infant. Here we may ask, however, how the single cell created by the union of egg and sperm, becomes that complex, living being. By a process called **mitosis,** which occurs in all **autosomes**, or non-sex chromosomes, as well as in the sex chromosomes, a cell duplicates its chromosomes and then divides into daughter cells that have the exact same number of chromosomes as their parent cell (see Figure 3-2). Thus the zygote divides and continues to divide, each time producing new cells that have the full complement of 46 chromosomes and gradually becoming a multicellular organism.

Genes, DNA, and Proteins

Scientists know that the binding element of a chromosome is a long, thin molecule of **deoxyribonucleic acid,** or **DNA** for short. This molecule, which stores genetic information and transmits it during reproduction, is made up of building blocks called nucleotides that are held together by two long, twisted parallel strands that resemble the two side rails of a spiral staircase (see Figure 3-3). From each **nucleotide,** which is a compound consisting of a nitrogen base, a simple sugar, and a phosphate group, one of four different nitrogen-containing bases projects out toward the base opposite it to form one of the staircase's "risers." Only bases that are compatible with each other will bond together. As Figure 3-3 shows, adenine and thymine form a bond, as do cytosine and guanine, but no other combination of these four is possible.

crossing over   The process by which equivalent sections of homologous chromosomes switch places randomly, shuffling the genetic information each carries.

mitosis   The process in which a body cell divides in two, first duplicating its chromosomes so that the new, daughter cells each contain the usual 46 chromosomes.

autosomes   The 22 paired non-sex chromosomes.

deoxyribonucleic acid (DNA)   A ladderlike molecule that stores genetic information in cells and transmits it during reproduction.

nucleotide   A compound containing a nitrogen base, a simple sugar, and a phosphate group.

■ FIGURE 3-2
Mitosis. The zygote divides and keeps dividing to produce a multicellular organism.
In (a) we show a zygote with only 4 chromosomes rather than the 46 each cell normally contains. In (b), each chromosome splits in half (lengthwise) to produce a duplicate of itself. Next, in (c), the duplicates move away from each other as the cell begins to divide. Finally, in (d), the cell has divided in two, and each new cell has the same set of chromosomes as the other and as the original, parent cell (a).

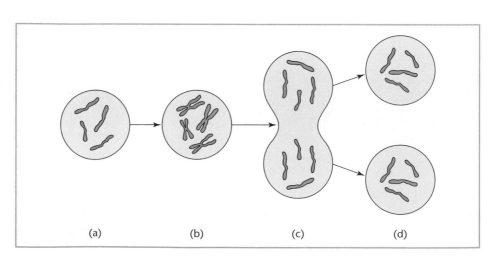

(a)   (b)   (c)   (d)

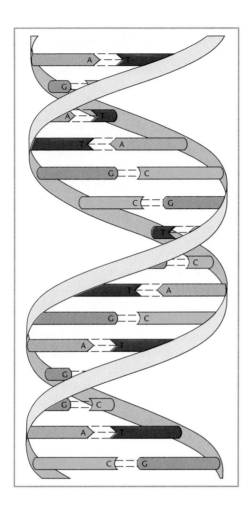

■ FIGURE 3-3
The structure of DNA.
The two twisted strands of DNA
form a kind of spiral staircase
whose risers are composed of the
complementary base pairs of
nucleotides, adenosine-thymine
or guanine-cytosine.

How do chromosomes carry the units of hereditary information? Portions of the chromosome's DNA molecule, called **genes,** are located at particular sites on the chromosome, where they code for the production of certain kinds of proteins. The genetic code is "written" in the order in which the four bases are included in the gene, much as the code for the meaning of a word is written in the order of its letters. Genes trigger the production of proteins only when a particular change in the environment signals them to become activated. Now the gene, or DNA segment, splits down the middle so that its pairs of bases are no longer joined. According to the rules by which the four bases bond with each other, "free" nucleotides surrounding the gene connect to the exposed bases to form new pairs. The resulting copy of the gene then travels from the cell nucleus to the body of the cell, where protein synthesis takes place. The copy acts as a template for building protein molecules: Each sequence of three bases codes for one of the many amino acids (organic compounds) from which different kinds of proteins are built.

When the protein molecule is assembled, it is ready to begin its work in the body. Each of the many different types of proteins serves a different function. Some proteins give cells their characteristic physical properties. For example, bone cells get their hardness, skin cells their elasticity, and nerve cells their capacity to conduct electrical impulses from the different kinds of proteins they possess. Other proteins do many other jobs within the body, such as triggering chemical reactions, carrying chemical messages, fighting foreign invaders, and regulating genes. It's the combined action of all the proteins in a human body that compose a living organism, each of whose specialized cells and organ systems has distinctive characteristics.

gene A portion of DNA that is located at a particular site on a chromosome and that codes for the production of certain kinds of proteins.

GENETIC INFLUENCES ON DEVELOPMENT

Scientists are learning more and more about how genes exert their influences on development. The central message they have gleaned is that, at least with respect to behavior, *genes never work in isolation, but always in combination with environmental influences* (Plomin & McClearn, 1993). A gene alone is useless. Its coded message cannot be "read" unless it is embedded in an environment that signals when and how it should respond. But because the topic of genetic-environmental interactions is so complex, in this and the next major section we'll focus on genetic influences apart from environmental ones and return to the critical determining process of gene-environment interaction in the last two sections of the chapter.

The Transmission of Traits: A Basic Model

Two basic concepts are crucial to understanding genetic influences on development. First, at any given gene's position on two homologous chromosomes, there can be more than one form of that gene; these alternate forms are called the gene's **alleles.** One of these alleles comes from the person's mother, the other from the person's father. Second, if the alleles from both parents are the same, the person is said to be **homozygous** for that particular gene or for the trait associated with it. If the two alleles are different, the person is said to be **heterozygous** for that particular characteristic. If *A* represents one allele and *a* another, the individual clearly can have one of three possible combinations: *AA, aa,* or *Aa (aA).*

When a person has one of the first two of these combinations (*AA* or *aa*), she or he is homozygous for the trait coded by the two identical alleles. Thus, for example, a person with two alleles for dark skin will have dark skin, and a person with two alleles for light skin will be light. When a person has a variant of the third combination, however, he or she is heterozygous for the trait for which each allele codes, and the result of this combination is more variable. Sometimes the combination of two dissimilar alleles will produce an outcome intermediate between the traits for which each allele alone codes. For instance, a light-skinned parent and a dark-skinned parent may produce a child of intermediate skin color. A second possibility is that both alleles will express their traits simultaneously; that is, the two traits will combine but will not blend. For example, the allele for blood type A in combination with the allele for blood type B produces the blood type AB, which has both kinds of antigens, A and B, on the surface of red blood cells. This pattern is called **codominance** of the two alleles. A third possibility is that in a heterozygous combination, the characteristic associated with only one of the alleles may be expressed. The more powerful allele is said to be **dominant** over the weaker, **recessive** allele. An example is the dominant allele for curly hair combined with the recessive allele for straight hair; this combination produces a person whose hair is curly (Table 3-1). Fortunately, many deleterious alleles are recessive, which greatly reduces the incidence of genetic abnormalities in people. One of the reasons why many societies prohibit marriage between close blood relatives is that a harmful recessive allele possessed by one relative is more apt to be possessed by other relatives as well, thus increasing the chances that children of their intermarriage will be homozygous for the harmful trait.

Genes on the Sex Chromosomes: Exceptions to the Rule

The genes on the sex chromosomes provide an exception to the rule we've just discussed, for not all of these genes have two alleles. But before we examine this special situation, we must back up a bit in our story. In every human being, 1 of the 23 pairs, or 2 of the 46 of human chromosomes we have discussed are called **sex chromosomes;** these chromosomes have the important function of determining the individual's sex, and they differ in males and females (see Figure 3-4). A female has

---

allele An alternate form of a gene; typically, a gene has two alleles, one inherited from the individual's mother, and one from the father.

homozygous Describing the state of an individual whose alleles for a particular trait from each parent are the same.

heterozygous Describing the state of an individual whose alleles for a particular trait from each parent are different.

codominance A genetic pattern in which heterozygous alleles express the variants of the trait for which they code simultaneously and with equal force.

dominant Describing the more powerful of two alleles in a heterozygous combination.

recessive Describing the weaker of two alleles in a heterozygous combination.

sex chromosomes In both males and females, the 23rd pair of chromosomes, which determine the individual's sex and are responsible for sex-related characteristics; in females, this pair normally comprises two X chromosomes, in males an X and a Y chromosome.

TABLE 3-1 Some Common Dominant and Recessive Traits	
Dominant	*Recessive*
Curly hair	Straight hair
Normal amount of hair	Baldness
Dark hair	Light or blond hair
Blond or brunette hair	Red hair
Normal skin coloring	Albinism (lack of skin pigmentation)
Roman nose	Straight nose
Thick lips	Thin lips
Cheek dimples	No dimples
Double-jointedness	Normal joints
Normal color vision	Color "blindness" (red and green not distinguished)
Farsightedness	Nearsightedness (myopia)
Immunity to poison ivy	Susceptibility to poison ivy
Normal hearing	Congenital deafness
Normal blood clotting	Failure of blood to clot (hemophilia)
Normal protein metabolism	Phenylketonuria
Normal red blood cells	Sickle-cell anemia

two large, homologous sex chromosomes, the so-called XX chromosomes, one from her mother, the other from her father. A male, on the other hand, has one X chromosome from his mother and a smaller, Y chromosome from his father; this pattern is referred to as XY. Because an X chromosome is about five times longer than a Y chromosome, it carries more genes. This means that some genes on a male's X chromosome will have no equivalent genes on his Y chromosome and as a result, any recessive **X-linked genes** will automatically be expressed; the male's Y chromosome has no counteracting dominant genes. In females, X-linked recessive genes are expressed much less frequently because females, who have two X chromosomes, have a chance of inheriting a dominant and counteracting allele on the other X chromosome.

Hemophilia, a disorder in which the blood fails to clot, is an example of an X-linked recessive characteristic. Because the allele for hemophilia is recessive, a female who inherits it will have normally clotting blood as long as her second allele, inherited from her other parent, does not code for hemophilia. Only if she is homozygous for the recessive allele will her blood clotting be impaired. If a male is unfortunate enough to receive the hemophilia allele on his X chromosome, he is in greater danger of developing hemophilia. Like the female, he will develop the disorder if he receives another hemophilia allele on his Y chromosome; however, he will also develop hemophilia if he receives no counteracting gene on his Y chromosome. Only if the small collection of alleles on his Y chromosome happens to include one for normal blood clotting will he escape the disorder.

Many other X-linked recessive disorders are more common in men than in women. Some of these are diabetes, color blindness, certain forms of night blindness, atrophy of the optic nerve, one form of muscular dystrophy, and a disorder resulting in an inability to produce antibodies to fight certain bacterial infections. Males' higher rates of mortality as compared with those of females—whether through miscarriage before they're born, death in infancy, or early death in adulthood—are partly attributable to males' greater vulnerability to X-linked disorders. Even resistance to certain childhood diseases appears to be X-linked. Thus, although 120 males are conceived for every 100 females and 106 males are born for every 100 females, this numerical imbalance between the sexes is rapidly eliminated over the course of development.

X-linked genes Genes that are carried on the X chromosome and that, in males, may have no analogous genes on the Y chromosome.

hemophilia A disorder caused by an X-linked recessive gene in which the blood fails to clot; found more often in males than in females.

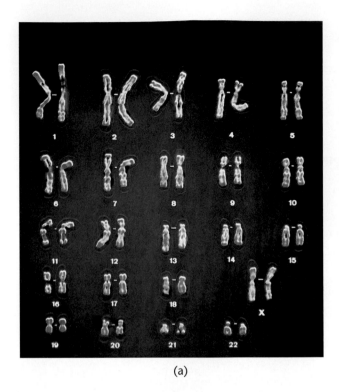

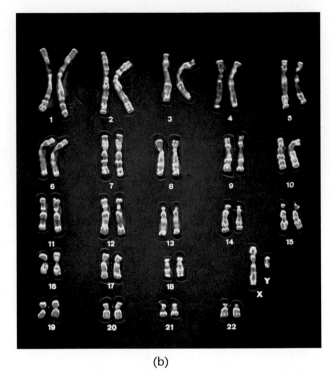

(a)   (b)

■ FIGURE 3-4
Normal chromosome arrangements.
These *karyotypes*, or photographs, show the normal lineup of chromosomes in a female (a) and a male (b). As you can see, the 22 pairs are similar in both sexes, but the 23rd pair is different: In the female this pair shows an XX pattern, and in the male an XY pattern.

modifier genes   Genes that exert their influence indirectly, by affecting the expression of still other genes.

Interactions among Genes

So far we have presented a relatively simple genetic model in which a single allele or a single pair of alleles determines a particular characteristic. Although this model applies to certain human traits, many other characteristics are determined not by one pair of alleles, but by many pairs acting together. In fact, most of the characteristics that are of the greatest interest to psychologists, such as intelligence, creativity, sociability, and style of emotional expression, are probably influenced by the interaction of multiple genes.

This interaction may help explain why some traits that are influenced by genes do not tend to run in families. The development of such traits usually depends on a certain configuration of many genes, and that particular configuration is not likely to be passed on from parent to child. A likely example is genius. Why are geniuses sometimes born to parents of quite ordinary intelligence, and why do geniuses go on to produce children of their own who are not unusually talented? Such cases make sense if you consider genius a trait that emerges from a particular configuration of many genes, all interacting with each other (Lykken, McGue, Tellegen, & Bouchard, 1992).

To further complicate the nature of genetic inheritance, we now know that a single pair of alleles may influence more than one trait. Moreover, they may do this not directly, but indirectly through their effects on the expression of still other genes. Genes that act in this manner are called **modifier genes.** One example is the modifier gene that affects the early development of *cataract,* a condition in which the lens of the eye becomes clouded, obscuring vision. Although the occurrence of early cataract is determined by a dominant gene, the nature of cataract formation is influenced by modifier genes. It is these kinds of genes that determine, for example, whether the cloudiness forms along the periphery of the lens or in its center.

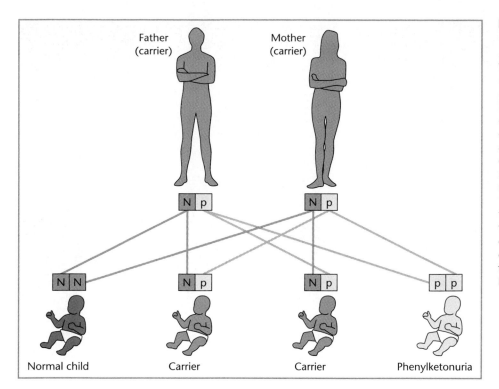

FIGURE 3-5
Genetic transmission of phenylketonuria.
When both parents carry the recessive allele for phenylketonuria, they have a one in four chance of producing a child with the disorder. If their dominant genes for normality (N) are passed to their offspring, the child will be normal. If the child receives one dominant and one recessive gene (p) it will be a "carrier"; that is, it will not have the disorder itself, but it may pass the recessive allele to its own children. And of course if the child receives recessive genes from both of its parents, it will have phenylketonuria.

Genetic Disorders

Genes can have both positive and negative effects on development. As we've seen, people can inherit harmful allele of certain genes such as the ones that cause hemophilia or early cataract. It's also possible for a person to receive whole sets of genes that are not only harmful but fatal. In this section we will look at some of the genetic abnormalities that can interfere with normal development. Table 3-2 summarizes the chief characteristics of some of the disorders that these abnormalities cause.

Why Harmful Alleles Survive

A major reason why potentially harmful alleles survive is that they are not harmful in the heterozygous state, that is, when a person inherits both a normal allele and a recessive one. A good example is the allele that causes **phenylketonuria**, or **PKU.** PKU is caused by a recessive allele that fails to produce an enzyme necessary to metabolize the protein phenylalanine that is present in milk, the basic diet of infants. As long as a person also possesses a normal allele, the PKU allele has no ill effects. In fact, about 1 out of every 20 European Americans carries the recessive PKU allele and doesn't even know it. It is only in infants unfortunate enough to be homozygous for the recessive gene that problems arise. After birth, when they start ingesting milk, their bodies cannot break down phenylalanine. If infants are not treated, toxic substances accumulate in their bodies, damaging the nervous system and causing mental retardation. Figure 3-5 shows that two heterozygous parents have a one in four chance of producing an infant who is homozygous for PKU. Most people who carry the PKU allele also have a normal allele, so they do not succumb to the disorder. Because these individuals survive and reproduce, however, the defective allele also survives from generation to generation, even though it is activated only 25 percent of the time.

Some potentially harmful alleles may survive because they are actually beneficial in combination with a normal allele. An example of this kind of survival is provided by a disease to which some African Americans as well as people in some

phenylketonuria (PKU)
A disease caused by a recessive allele that fails to produce an enzyme necessary to metabolize the protein phenylalanine; if untreated immediately at birth, damages the nervous system and causes mental retardation.

TABLE 3-2 Some Disorders That Are Caused by Genetic Defects

Disorder and Its Nature	U.S. Incidence	Cause	Method of Diagnosis	Current Methods of Treatment and Prevention
Hemophilia Blood disease characterized by poor clotting ability	1/10,000 (80–90% males)	Heredity: X-linked recessive trait	Blood tests	Hemophilia is treated at present by transfusions of clotting factors. New gene-splicing techniques may make it possible to provide these factors without running the risk of the transmission of blood-borne infections by donated blood products. Genetic counseling can help determine whether a couple risk bearing a child with this disorder.
Diabetes mellitus Body's inability to metabolize carbohydrates and maintain proper glucose levels	1/2,500 children (usually adult onset)	Heredity: X-linked recessive trait; exaggerated by environmental factors	Blood and urine tests	Sufferers can often control this disorder by special diet alone. In other cases oral medication, and/or insulin injections are required to maintain the body's equilibrium. Genetic counseling can determine a couple's risk factors.
Muscular dystrophy Impairment of voluntary muscular function	1/3,000–5,000 (data for males)	Heredity: X-linked recessive trait	Symptoms and disability are apparent at onset	Physical therapy is treatment of choice. New genetic techniques may permit localization of the gene for this disorder on the X chromosome, thus screening for presence of the disorder before symptoms appear or even before birth.
Cataract (early) Clouding of the lens of the eye	1.2–6/10,000 infants	Heredity in most cases	Eye exams and subjective experience of decreasing visual acuity	Surgical removal of lens and its replacement with artificial implant; subsequent fine-tuning of vision with eyeglasses or contact lenses.
Phenylketonuria (PKU) Inability to convert phenylalanine to tyrosine; untreated, leads to mental retardation	1/10,000	Heredity: recessive allele	Blood tests prenatally or at birth	Genetic counseling can indicate risk that a couple will have a PKU child. Modern genetic techniques can detect recessive alleles before such a child's birth, and immediately after birth a special diet can be instituted that will prevent the disorder's toxic effects.
Sickle-cell anemia Blood disease characterized by malformation of red blood cells that are low in oxygen	5% of African Americans; 0.1% of European Americans	Heredity: two recessive alleles in combination	Blood tests	Blood transfusions have until recently been the only treatment. However, the recent in utero treatment of a fetus for an autoimmune disorder has brought hope that sickle-cell anemia and other similar diseases may be treated successfully before birth.
Down syndrome (trisomy 21) Physically and mentally retarded development; sometimes cardiovascular and respiratory abnormalities	1/1,000	Heredity: extra full or partial chromosome attached to chromosome pair 21	Amniocentesis, alphafetoprotein assay, chorionic villi sampling, chromosome analysis	Special physical training; special education, including speech therapy. Surgical corrections of problems with the heart and with hearing are sometimes necessary. In future, because the defective allele for Down syndrome has now been located, gene therapy may be successful in preventing this disorder.

Syndrome	Incidence	Cause	Prenatal Diagnosis	Treatment
Turner (XO) syndrome Underdeveloped secondary sex characteristics; infertility; short stature; social immaturity	1/1,200–3,000 (females)	Chromosomal abnormality: only one X chromosome instead of two	Blood tests	Hormone therapy can promote development of secondary sex characteristics. Counseling; special education to lessen deficits in spatial understanding.
Triple X (XXX) syndrome Some physical abnormalities, including menstrual irregularities and premature menopause; some limitations on cognitive abilities	1/1,000 females	Chromosomal abnormality: extra X chromosome	Blood tests	Special education to improve cognitive skills.
Klinefelter's (XXY) syndrome Some female physical characteristics; sterility; mild to severe cognitive difficulties	1/1,000 males	Chromosomal abnormality: extra X chromosome	Blood tests	Testosterone treatments can enhance development of male secondary sex characteristics as well as sexual interest and assertiveness. Special education to improve cognitive skills.
XYY syndrome Unusual height; lowered fertility; some cognitive impairment	1/1,000 males	Chromosomal abnormality: extra Y chromosome	Blood tests	Special education
Fragile X syndrome Physical abnormalities; mental retardation that deepens with time; psychological and social problems	1/1,200 males 1/2,000 females	Heredity: breaking of an X chromosome near its tip	Blood test	No known treatment
Huntington disease Increasing difficulty in performing voluntary and involuntary movements; gradual decline in cognitive functioning	1/18,000–20,000	Heredity: destruction of certain neurons in the brain	Blood test for Huntington gene, now known to be located at one end of chromosome 4	No known treatment, but gene therapy may hold future promise of prevention before birth.

Sources: Lambert & Drack, 1996; Lin, Verp, & Sabbagha, 1993; Martini, 1995; Money, 1993; Nightingale & Meister, 1987; Postlethwait & Hopson, 1995. Data on early Infantile Cataracts by Lambert S., & Drack, A. Infantile Cataracts (1996). Survey of Ophthalmology, 40, 427–438.

BOX 3-1

Perspectives on Diversity

Sickle-Cell Anemia: A Double-Edged Sword

Sickle-cell anemia, a severe and often fatal disorder, affects about 60,000 people in the United States (Postlethwait & Hopson, 1995). It is far more common, however, among African Americans than among other Americans; about 9 percent of African Americans carry a recessive sickle-cell allele. The term **sickle-cell anemia** gets its name from the peculiar shape that the red blood cells of an afflicted person assume when they are low in oxygen (for instance, when they have just released oxygen to hard-working muscle cells). Rather than remaining disk shaped, as normal red blood cells do, these cells become elongated and bent into the shape of a sickle (see Figure 3-6). This shape causes them to get stuck in small blood vessels, especially in the joints and the abdomen, resulting in severe pain, tissue damage, and possible death if critical vessels in the brain and lungs are blocked. Moreover, because these cells are abnormal, the spleen continually removes them from the blood, giving rise to chronic *anemia* (too few red blood cells). An allele on chromosome number 11 is the cause of sickle-cell anemia. When its companion allele is also recessive for this trait, the person develops the disorder. Among people who have one sickle-cell allele and one normal one, however, red blood cells rarely sickle except under conditions of low oxygen, such as in mountain climbing or under anesthesia, and, as a result, such people usually suffer no harmful effects of the defective allele.

Scientists were once puzzled as to why the sickle-cell allele is so prevalent among African Americans, in many African communities, and in some societies in the Middle East (Postlethwait & Hopson, 1995). Among the Baamba, for instance, 39 percent of the population has the sickle-cell gene. The mystery was solved with the discovery that the sickle-cell allele also has a positive effect: It confers protection against malaria, another deadly disease of almost exactly the same areas in which the sickle-cell allele is found. When malaria parasites take up residence in the red blood cells of someone who is heterozygous for this disorder or who has one sickle-cell allele and one normal one, the former cells become sickle-shaped when low in oxygen, just as such cells typically behave in people who are homozygous for the allele. But in this case, when the spleen removes the parasite-containing cells from the blood, it removes the malaria parasites as well. As a result, for these people with only one sickle-cell allele, having built-in resistance to malaria is an enormous aid to survival.

Because the defective allele enables these people to fight off malaria, they tend to live longer than people who haven't a sickle-cell gene to protect them, and they reproduce more often; thus they pass the gene on to subsequent generations in increasing numbers. In this way, a potentially harmful gene not only survives but flourishes. Of course, for the person who is homozygous for sickle-cell anemia, or has two recessive genes for this disorder, the illness itself is so life-threatening that the person's enhanced resistance to malaria is of little benefit to him or her.

---

sickle-cell anemia A disorder, caused by a recessive gene, in which the red blood cells become distorted when low in oxygen, causing fatigue, shortness of breath, and severe pain and posing a threat to life from blockage of crucial blood vessels.

Down syndrome A form of chromosome abnormality in which the person suffers disabling physical and mental development and is highly susceptible to such illnesses as leukemia, heart disorders, and respiratory infections.

African countries are subject: sickle-cell anemia. Box 3-1 describes this disorder and how its allele actually helps some people survive another life-threatening disease: malaria.

Chromosome Abnormalities

Developmental disorders can be caused not only by single genes or gene groups but also by defects in entire chromosomes. Almost 1 percent of all newborns have diagnosable chromosome abnormalities, and it has been estimated that 60 percent of early spontaneous abortions and 5 percent of later miscarriages are attributable to aberrations in chromosomes. Normally, such chromosome defects are not present in a child's parents, as are the defective alleles we've been discussing. Instead, they generally arise during the process of meiosis, when eggs or sperm are formed. In a great many instances the aberration proves lethal, and the zygote produced by the union of sperm and egg spontaneously aborts. But sometimes, particularly when certain chromosomes are involved, a zygote is able to survive the abnormal condition, and a baby with a chromosome defect is born.

Down Syndrome. **Down syndrome** is characterized by physical and mental retardation and a distinctive physical appearance. People with this syndrome are typically of short stature and usually have almond-shaped eyes with a fold in the eyelid, as well as one or more other unusual physical characteristics. More troublesome is their heightened susceptibility to such illnesses as leukemia, heart disorders, and respiratory infections and their moderate to severe mental

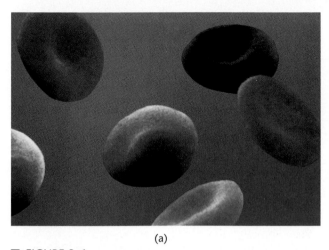
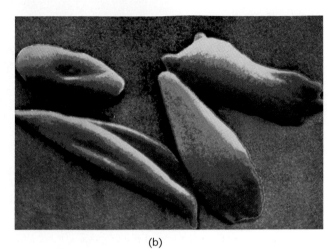

(a)   (b)

■ FIGURE 3-6
Red blood cell changes in sickle-cell anemia.
Normal red blood cells are disk shaped (a), but in sickle-cell anemia these cells become sickled, or distorted, when they are low in oxygen (b). Among the symptoms of this disorder are pain in the joints and abdomen, chronic fatigue, and shortness of breath.

Until recently, there had been little hope for victims of sickle-cell anemia. The successful in utero treatment of a 4-month-old fetus for a condition called *severe combined immunodeficiency*, however, has made it possible now to think of treating sickle-cell anemia and many other immune-deficiency and blood diseases before birth. In this groundbreaking surgery, physicians injected bone marrow cells from the fetus's father into its abdomen by means of a long needle inserted through the mother's abdomen, using ultrasound as a guide (Flake et al., 1996). (The father's bone marrow was used in this case to minimize stress on the pregnant mother.) Nearly a year and a half after his birth, the child was healthy and showed no sign of the rare genetic disease that had threatened his not-yet-begun life.

retardation. However, with advances in the treatment of these physical disorders (such as the use of antibiotics for pneumonia), the life spans of people with Down syndrome have greatly increased; currently about 70 percent of individuals with Down syndrome live into their sixties. Unfortunately, they are at greater risk for developing Alzheimer's disease in later life than the average person (Hayes & Batshaw, 1993).

Probably the most well known chromosome disorder, Down syndrome is caused by a deviation in the set of chromosomes labeled number 21. Instead of a pair of these chromosomes, the person with Down syndrome has three chromosomes, which is why the disorder is also called *trisomy 21*. The extra 21st chromosome most often comes from the mother's egg, when her homologous pair of 21st chromosomes fails to separate during meiosis. Male sperm carries the extra chromosome in only about 5 percent of cases (Antonarakis & Down Syndrome Collaboration Group, 1991). And, for reasons that are not yet fully understood, this error occurs more often as women age (see Table 3-3). The father's age matters too; the rates of Down syndrome births are higher for men over 50 (Hayes & Batshaw, 1993). Scientists have recently identified a gene that may play a role in the mental retardation associated with Down syndrome, but it is likely that other genes play a role as well (Smith et al., 1997).

Infants with Down syndrome may develop fairly normally for their first 6 months, but unless they receive special therapy their rate of intellectual growth begins to decline after about a year. These children are generally slow to learn to

TABLE 3-3   Risk of Giving Birth to a Down Syndrome Infant, by Maternal Age

Maternal Age	Frequency of Down Syndrome Infants among All Births
25	1/2,000
30	1/885
35	1/365
40	1/109
45	1/40
50	1/10

Sources: Gaulden, 1992; Hook, 1982.

Note: Age of father is the causative factor in some cases.

speak and often have difficulty articulating words. They also have trouble attending to, discriminating, and interpreting complex or subtle information in their environments. These difficulties are reflected in problems in communication between children with Down syndrome and their caregivers; often parents are induced to talk more and be more directive than the parents of normal children (Hodapp, 1995; Kopp, 1983; Loveland, 1987). Children with Down syndrome develop more competence when their caregivers provide them with stimulation and encourage them to be attentive to and involved in their environments. Although these efforts are more apt to enhance emotional, social, and motor development than cognitive development, training can help children with Down syndrome learn to read and write (Crawley & Spiker, 1983; Gibson & Harris, 1988; Hodapp, 1995). A number of children with Down syndrome become competent adults who hold jobs and live independently in group homes. A few people with Down syndrome have become actors and authors (Papalia & Olds, 1996).

Sex Chromosome Anomalies. Abnormalities may also arise in the sex chromosomes, where they are rarely fatal to a developing organism but lead to various physical and physiological defects. For example, some females are born with only one X chromosome rather than the normal XX pattern. Usually this occurs because the father's sperm contained neither an X nor a Y chromosome. Girls with this XO pattern, called

With some special help, the Down child in this affectionate family may complete school, get a job, and have loving friends and a satisfying life, much like anyone else.

Turner syndrome, remain short, with stubby fingers, webbed necks, and unusually shaped mouths and ears. They usually have normal intelligence, and they tend to be docile, pleasant, and not easily upset. As teenagers, they do not develop secondary sex characteristics, such as breasts and pubic hair, unless given female hormones. Because their internal reproductive organs do not develop normally, they remain sterile throughout their lives. Women with Turner syndrome tend to have problems in social relationships because they are immature and lacking in assertiveness (McCauley, Ito, & Kay, 1986). These problems are related in part to others' responses to these women's physical appearance. More important, women with Turner syndrome have difficulty discriminating and interpreting emotional cues and facial expressions in others, skills essential for appropriate social interactions (McCauley, Kay, Ito, & Treeler, 1987).

Another sex chromosome abnormality found in females is the XXX pattern, in which a girl inherits three X sex chromosomes instead of the normal two. These *triple-X* girls appear normal physically and have normal secondary sexual development, but their cognitive abilities are affected, especially their short-term memory and verbal skills (Robinson, Bender, & Linden, 1992; Rovet & Netley, 1983). When a male inherits an extra X chromosome, producing an XXY pattern known as **Klinefelter's syndrome,** he is sterile and has many female characteristics, such as breast development and a rounded, broad-hipped figure. Like the triple-X female, he tends to have verbal language deficits and reading problems and is sometimes retarded (Netley, 1986; Robinson et al., 1992). Also likely to suffer some cognitive impairment is the male who inherits an extra Y chromosome, the XYY pattern once thought to be accompanied by excessive aggressiveness. Although XYY men are generally taller than normal men, they have not been shown to be any more aggressive or violent than others (Burns & Bottino, 1989; Schaivi, Thelgaard, Owen, & White, 1984).

Finally, some people carry an X chromosome that appears to be pinched or narrowed in some areas, causing it to be quite fragile. This **fragile X syndrome** is more frequent in males than females. It accounts for about 5 percent of retarded males whose IQ scores range between 30 and 55, although not all males with the syndrome are retarded (Barnes, 1989; Jacobs, 1991). In addition, people with fragile X syndrome often have physical abnormalities and psychological and social problems. Cleft palate, seizures, abnormal EEGs, and disorders of the eyes are some of the more common physical symptoms. Psychological and social problems include anxiety, hyperactivity, attention deficits, and abnormal communication patterns. Males may have deficits in social interaction, and females may be more likely to suffer from depression (Hagerman & Sobesky, 1989; Reiss & Freund, 1990).

In considering these chromosomal anomalies it is important to remember the influence of the environment on the way genes are expressed. The severity of the symptoms that arise with hereditary disorders is often related to the degree to which the person has a supportive environment (Bender, Linden, & Robinson, 1987; Hodapp, 1995). We will return to the topic of how environmental conditions can lessen the effects of genetic abnormalities a little later in this chapter. It is also important to remember that with special therapeutic and educational methods, some manifestations of these abnormalities may be modified (see Table 3-2).

GENETIC COUNSELING AND GENETIC ENGINEERING

Advances in biology and genetics have opened new opportunities for shaping and controlling some aspects of development. For some time now it has been possible to sample cells from a developing fetus to determine whether the fetus carries genes

Turner syndrome A form of abnormality of the sex chromosomes found in females, in which secondary sex characteristics develop only if female hormones are administered and in which abnormal formation of internal reproductive organs leads to permanent sterility.

Klinefelter's syndrome A form of chromosome abnormality in which a male inherits an extra X sex chromosome, resulting in the XXY pattern, and has many feminine physical characteristics as well as language deficits and, sometimes, mental retardation.

fragile X syndrome A form of chromosome abnormality, more common in males than in females, in which an X chromosome is narrowed in some areas, causing it to be fragile and leading to a variety of physical, psychological, and social problems.

for any of the disorders we have discussed, as well as for many others. With this knowledge, gained through *genetic counseling,* parents may choose either to abort the birth of a child with abnormalities or to prepare for the arrival of such a child, who will need special care. For many people this is a very difficult choice. For example, ethical and religious beliefs prevent some couples from deciding for abortion. In addition, because environmental factors can affect genetic predispositions, we cannot know for sure whether the anomalies we detect will inevitably result in serious problems. For example, although some XYY males engage in criminal activity, such men are relatively few; what would be the ethics, then, of a parental decision to abort a male fetus with this chromosomal pattern?

More recent advances in the study of genes and their influence have made it possible to offer what we might call preventive genetic counseling. In this work, couples wanting to have a child can themselves be tested for various defective genes. If they find that they carry defective alleles, they may elect to adopt a child or to conceive a child through one of various *assisted reproductive techniques* in which a donor's egg or sperm may be substituted for one of their own germ cells. These techniques were originally developed to make parenting possible for couples who could not conceive and bear a child of their own. Box 3-2 describes some of the most common of these techniques.

Prenatal Diagnostic Techniques

It is possible that some day we may be able to replace defective genes in a fetus through gene therapy, thus preventing a genetically determined disorder before it even happens. Already, physicians have been successful in injecting healthy bone marrow into a fetus to counteract an autoimmune disorder (Anderson, 1995). Before we discuss the exciting new work in this area, however, let us look at the major existing methods for testing the viability and health of a fetus.

Commonly Used Tests

The risk of disorder, as in an older expectant mother, may prompt testing of a fetus. In **amniocentesis,** the most widely used technique for sampling fetal cells, a physician inserts a needle into the amniotic sac, or the fluid-filled membranous cover that surrounds and protects the fetus, and withdraws a little of the amniotic fluid. This fluid contains cells sloughed off from the fetus (such as skin cells), which pathologists can then analyze for their chromosomal and genetic makeup. The 16th week of pregnancy seems optimal for performing amniocentesis. By this time there are enough cells in the amniotic fluid to draw an adequate sample, yet the fetus is still small enough not to be injured by the insertion of the needle. Nevertheless, this technique does carry a small risk of miscarriage.

Slightly more risky is **chorionic villi sampling,** which can be done as early as the 9th or 10th week of pregnancy. Physicians draw cells from the *chorionic villi,* finger-like projections from the *chorion,* the outermost membrane that surrounds the amniotic sac. The villi help the zygote to embed itself in the uterine lining and then multiply to form the placenta. Although the villi are not part of the embryo itself, the chromosomes and genes in them are identical to the embryo's because they all arise from the same fertilized egg.

With a prenatal sample of cells in hand, it is possible to examine the fetus's chromosomes and genes for any signs of chromosome disorder. The critical abnormalities (such as missing or extra chromosomes) are clearly visible under a high-powered microscope. In addition, scientists have identified particular pieces of DNA, called *genetic markers,* that can serve as indicators of many disorders caused by one or more defective genes. For example, the gene for cystic fibrosis has been located on the midsection of chromosome 7, and a gene for familial Alzheimer's disease is found on the long arm of chromosome 21 (Lander, 1996; Martin, 1987). The latter discovery may in part account for the fact that children

amniocentesis A technique for sampling and assessing fetal cells for indications of abnormalities in the developing fetus; performed by inserting a needle through the abdominal wall and into the amniotic sac and withdrawing a small amount of the amniotic fluid.

chorionic villi sampling A technique for sampling and assessing cells withdrawn from the chorionic villi, projections from the chorion that surrounds the amniotic sac; cells are withdrawn either through a tube inserted into the uterus through the vagina or through a needle inserted through the abdominal wall.

BOX 3-2

Child Psychology in Action

The New Reproductive Technologies

The technique of *in vitro fertilization*—literally, fertilization "in glass" or in a glass dish—is most often used to make childbearing possible for a woman whose fallopian tubes are blocked. Physicians administer hormones to the woman to stimulate ovulation and then remove mature eggs from her ovary. They then place the eggs in a nourishing solution in a glass *petri* dish where they are mixed with the husband's sperm. If fertilization is successful, the zygote begins to divide, and when it is at the eight-cell stage, approximately two to four days later, it is inserted into the woman's uterus. For the pregnancy to be successful, the embryo must implant itself in the lining of the uterus. If the woman's uterus is not at the optimum stage to facilitate implantation, the embryo may be frozen and stored until the uterus reaches the proper stage.

In vitro fertilization was a remarkable breakthrough when Louise Joy Brown, the first baby conceived outside of her mother's body, was born in England in 1978. Since then, however, more than 5,000 such babies have been born in different countries around the world by this and other, more advanced assisted reproduction techniques. For example, when a husband has an insufficient supply of sperm or when the sperm are weak or otherwise inadequate, physicians may use a male donor's sperm to fertilize the wife's egg. Or if the woman cannot produce an egg, the husband's sperm may be used to fertilize a female donor's egg, which may then be implanted in the wife's uterus. Or the zygote produced by a husband's sperm and a wife's egg may be implanted in the uterus of another woman—a surrogate mother—who carries the child to term. Using this technique, in 1991 a woman carried her own grandchild for her daughter, who had been born without a uterus. This feat of becoming a mother and a grandmother at the same time has since been repeated by other women.

Like many other medical breakthroughs, these new reproductive technologies have presented some ethical dilemmas (McGinty & Zafran, 1988; Ryan, 1989). How should prospective parents be screened? What criteria should be used in selecting sperm donors and in matching sperm to eggs? For example, should parents be offered sperm from a Nobel Prize winner (a bank of such sperm was actually started some years ago)? What possibly unrealistic expectations might such parents have? What legal rights does a male donor have? What should be done if one or both parents die while their zygote is frozen in storage, as happened in a recent Australian case? What legal rights to the child she bears has a woman who has agreed to be a surrogate mother for another couple? In spite of these difficult questions, the hope, joy, and prospect of parenthood that these procedures have given to many couples unable to conceive or bear children on their own seem to outweigh other considerations.

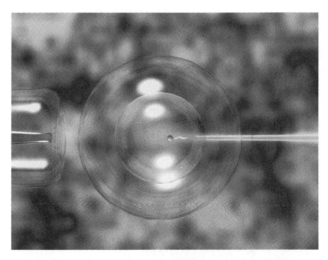

In this computerized rendering of the microscopic in vitro fertilization procedure, we can see that the egg (rounded, greenish) lying in a petri dish has just been penetrated by a micro-needle (green, at right), allowing one tiny sperm cell (pinkish head, with yellow tail) to enter and fertilize the egg. The device at the left, called a pipette (green and white), holds the egg steady as the needle is inserted.

---

with Down syndrome, who have an extra chromosome 21, face a greater chance of developing Alzheimer's disease, although without further research we cannot be certain that this is so.

One of the more personal hunts for a genetic marker was led by neuropsychologist Nancy Wexler, whose mother had died of **Huntington disease,** a fatal deterioration of the nervous system that begins in midadulthood, one that Wexler had a 50 percent chance of inheriting. Wexler charted patterns of Huntington disease in 5,000 Venezuelans who were all descendants of a woman who died of the disease more than 100 years ago. By using DNA samples from living relatives who had the disorder, Wexler and geneticist James Gusella (Gusella et al., 1983) were able to identify a Huntington marker that was located near one end of chromosome 4. This discovery made it possible to develop a test for the Huntington gene.

> **Huntington disease** A genetically caused, fatal disorder of the nervous system that begins in midadulthood and is manifested chiefly in uncontrollable, spasmodic, movements of the body and limbs and eventual mental deterioration.

alphafetoprotein assay (AFP) A blood test performed prenatally to detect such problems as Down syndrome, the presence of multiple embryos, and defects of the central nervous system.

ultrasound A technique that uses sound waves to visualize deep body structures; commonly used to reveal the size and structure of a developing fetus. Also called *ultrasonography*.

Two other prenatal tests are now routinely done for most pregnancies, not just in cases of suspected risk based on family history. The **alphafetoprotein assay (AFP)** is a blood test that can reveal fetal problems such as Down syndrome or defects of the central nervous system, as well as the presence of multiple embryos. If the test does uncover difficulties, physicians undertake further tests. **Ultrasound** (ultrasonography), a method of visualizing deep body structures, is now commonly used to detect gross physical abnormalities in a fetus. The technique, which scans the uterus by means of sound waves, produces a sonogram, or film, that shows the size and structure of the developing fetus and that has the added feature of determining the baby's sex. If parents want to know this—many prefer to be surprised—they can stock up on blue or pink blankets with confidence. Ultrasound has other benefits as well. The opportunity to observe that the developing fetus is healthy and normal probably reduces parent's anxieties. Field and her coworkers (1985) found that women who had periodic ultrasound tests were less anxious as pregnancy progressed, had fewer birth complications, and delivered heavier, more alert, more responsive, and less irritable infants.

Ethical and Policy Issues

When prenatal genetic testing reveals some major chromosomal or genetic abnormality in an unborn child, parents have the option of aborting the pregnancy. But this raises the ethical dilemma of deciding when an abnormality is severe enough to warrant an abortion. If a fetus has a lethal genetic disorder that will lead to a painful death in a few months or years, the choice is often easier than if the disorder is one that is not so devastating. What about a female fetus with Turner's syndrome, the XO chromosome pattern, or a male with the XXY pattern that gives rise to Klinefelter's syndrome? Although these children have both physical abnormalities and some cognitive impairments, they are capable of leading very productive lives. Confronting prospective parents with such difficult ethical choices is one result of developing the new technology to analyze chromosomes and genes (Murray, 1996). Even nongenetic testing, like ultrasound, is associated with some ethical problems. For example, in some cultures where male children are preferred over females, this kind of prenatal assessment could lead to an increase in the rate of abortions of female fetuses (Murray, 1996).

The new availability of genetic information also raises troubling issues of ethics and policy in such areas as employment and personal insurance and among people who oppose abortion. For example, it's conceivable that employers might decide to require in-depth genetic screening for potential employees and to reject individuals who have a gene that may someday put them at risk for cancer, heart trouble, or other diseases. Some writers have even suggested that industrial concerns might try to select employees for their lower likelihood of being affected by exposure to chemical toxins—and then fail to institute necessary procedures to protect employees. Equally disturbing is the possibility that insurance companies might decide to use information about the genetic risks people may have for certain diseases to exclude such individuals from insurance protection or to adjust rates for insurance coverage (Murray, 1996; Wadman, 1996). Finally, religious and social groups are concerned about the rising rate of abortion owing to increased use of genetic screening. The best route to developing guidelines for addressing such dilemmas may be to heighten public awareness of these issues (Bentley, 1996).

Gene Therapy

Scientists hope not only to locate the genes responsible for inherited disorders, but also to use gene therapy to ameliorate or even cure these problems. Gene therapy involves inserting normal alleles into patients' cells to compensate for defective alleles. The most effective current technique uses modified viruses (viruses from which harmful properties have been removed) to carry the new genes into the patient's cells. Scientists have adopted this strategy because viruses are by nature adapted to penetrate another organism's cells. Most often, target cells in the patient are first removed from the person's body, infused with the new gene by way of the virus, and then returned to the body. With federal approval, this procedure was first used in 1990 in treating a 4-year-old girl who had a deadly genetic disorder that shut down her immune system, leaving her defenseless against infections. Doctors inserted into some of the child's blood the gene needed to produce a critical enzyme that her immune system lacked. Five years later, after just a few additional booster treatments, the child was a healthy, active 9-year-old with an immune system that functioned well (Anderson, 1995).

Scientists suspect that in another 20 years, gene therapy will be used routinely to treat the many disorders caused by a single defective gene (currently, more than 4,000 are known). At the same time, gene therapy may be employed to treat conditions that are caused in part by impairment of genes that are involved in the body's mechanisms for maintaining and defending itself. This kind of therapy would include new treatments for such disorders as cancer, heart disease, and AIDS. Even more exciting, we are nearing the ability to alter reproductive cells genetically to prevent hereditary disorders from arising in the first place. Theoretically at least, normal genes could replace defective ones in sperm or ova, or they could be inserted into a newly created zygote (Anderson, 1995). Box 3-3 describes the work of the Human Genome Project, whose aim is to map the exact identities and locations of the entire panoply of human genes—perhaps more than 100,000 genes—in the hope of ultimately being able to prevent and/or treat the more than 4,000 diseases to which our genes make one or another of us susceptible.

But again, as science enters this new age of genetic engineering, we confront significant ethical issues (Murray, 1996). As greater genetic manipulation becomes possible, how should we use it? And how, for the good of humankind, should we limit its use? It is one thing to replace a defective allele in a person who is seriously ill, and quite another to attempt to create a race of superhumans. Even more troublesome to many is our newfound ability to clone living creatures. Whether or not the U.S. Congress outlaws the cloning of human beings, scientists who are determined to accomplish this feat will undoubtedly find ways to achieve their goal. The potential benefits of many of our new technologies are great, but the dangers of using them unwisely may be even greater.

HEREDITY-ENVIRONMENT INTERACTIONS

In the past, many scientists took up opposing positions on what was familiarly referred to as the nature-nurture issue. Scholars who were more biologically oriented emphasized the role of heredity and maturational factors in human development, whereas those who were more environmentally oriented emphasized the role of learning and experience. In the United States, where political and social philosophy stressed the importance of opportunity, education, and initiative, theories of biological determinism fell on rocky ground. In contrast, the environmentalist position of John B. Watson and the behaviorists flourished. In 1926, in the heat of the nature-nurture debate, Watson boasted:

> Give me a dozen healthy infants, well-formed, and my own specific world to bring them up in and I'll guarantee to take any one at random and train him to become any type of specialist I might select—a doctor, lawyer, artist, merchant-chief and, yes, even into beggar-man and thief, regardless of his talents, penchants, tendencies, abilities, vocations and race of his ancestors. (Watson, 1926, p. 10)

Contemporary psychologists, both in the United States and in other countries, see neither nature nor nurture as wholly responsible for the development of a

BOX 3-3

Child Psychology in Action

The Human Genome Project

An international effort, the Human Genome Project (HGP) aims to identify and locate all human genes and to make genes accessible for further biological study. Begun in October 1990, within its first two years this enormous undertaking had determined the location of more than 2,000 genes and was well on its way to discovering the 50,000 to 100,000 additional genes that comprise the human genome. A second goal is to determine the nucleotide sequence of all 3 billion bases in human DNA. And a final aim is to develop the technology to interpret human gene function (Collins & Galas, 1993; Lander, 1996).

The Human Genome Project will cost more and take longer than it took to build the atom bomb or to land people on the moon (Postlethwait & Hopson, 1995). The goal is to complete the job by 2005, and the tab will be nearly $3 billion! The implications of this project are sweeping. Not only will it give us insight into the basic workings of the human body, but it will provide us with important insights into genetic diseases such as sickle-cell anemia, Huntington disease, and Turner syndrome. These and several hundred other diseases are carried on single genes, but most illnesses, such as cancer or heart disease, are determined by interactions among multiple genes; figuring out the origins of the bulk of genetically caused illnesses will be a truly daunting task.

Despite the incredible scope of their assignment, researchers have made progress in identifying genes that may in part account for diseases such as Lou Gehrig's disease, some forms of Alzheimer's disease, epilepsy, and even cardiovascular disease and resistance to HIV (Lander, 1996). As of mid-1996, approximately half of all human genes had been sampled. Consider this description of the cataloging of the human genome:

> Some geneticists compare these segments (of genes) to books on a library shelf and for chromosomes 21 and Y, all the books now shelved are in correct order. Researchers still can't decipher the locations or meanings of most phrases (genes) and letters (nucleotide sequences) within these volumes. At least, though, once an experimenter does discover which large segment contains a gene or base sequence of interest, he or she gets it straight off the "library shelf." (Postlethwait & Hopson, 1995, p. 281)

As with genetic testing, there are ethical concerns about how doctors, employers, and insurance companies will use the data and about possible abuses of the new genetic information. For example, even if scientists determine that a person is genetically prone to develop a disease, he may never do so; as a result, caution in the use of this information is critical.

Not all are as wary as others. As James Watson, the Nobel Prize winner argued, "When finally interpreted, the genetic message encoded within our DNA molecules will provide the ultimate answers to the chemical underpinnings of human existence" (Postlethwait & Hopson, 1995, p. 281).

A geneticist examines a computer display of a DNA sequencing pattern. The different colors represent the four nitrogen-containing bases—adenine, thymine, cytosine, and guanine—that by their sequencing "write" the genetic codes for protein production and for various structural and functional characteristics that are transmitted from generation to generation.

human being. Instead, scholars focus today on how heredity and environment constantly interact to shape the developing person. Although they see genetic endowment as to some extent constraining what a person can become and do, most psychologists believe that social and environmental experience exerts a tremendous influence on the developing child. Moreover, they see gene-environment interactions as highly complex. Not only do environments influence how genes are expressed, but genes can help to shape the environments to which people are exposed. We will explore both sides of this complex story.

How the Environment Influences the Expression of Genes

The concept of **range of reaction** helps explain how environments influence genes (Gottesman, 1963; Plomin, 1995). According to this concept, heredity does not rigidly fix behavior but instead establishes a range of possible developmental outcomes that may occur in response to different environments. As you might expect, individuals with different genetic makeups also have different ranges of reaction; their particular sets of genes set boundaries on their range of developmental possibilities. But within those boundaries, it is largely the environment that determines how the person will develop.

A good example of the interaction between range of reaction and the environment is provided by the hypothetical example illustrated in Figure 3-7. Each of the three children represented by curves A, B, and C has a different range of possible scores on an achievement test. If all three children experience exactly the same level of environmental stimulation, child C will always outperform the other two. However, child B could achieve a substantially higher score than C, if B experiences a more enriched environment than C does. (An enriched environment may have a high level of physical stimulation, such as a wide array of toys and books; social-emotional stimulation, such as the presence of highly responsive and attentive caregivers; or cognitive-linguistic stimulation, such as caregivers who talk and read a lot to a child.) Notice too that child C has the widest range of reaction: That is, the difference between child C's potential performance in either restricted or enriched environments is much greater than the analogous difference for child B and child A. Child A has both the lowest and the most limited range of reaction. This child not only scores below average (50) whether raised in a stimulating or unstimulating setting, but also shows less ability to respond to environmental enrichment.

When a reaction range is extremely narrow, even narrower than child A's, it is said to show strong **canalization** (Waddington, 1962, 1966). When a trait is highly canalized, development is restricted to just a few pathways, and intense or more specific environmental pushes are required to deflect the course of development. For example, a baby's tendency to repetitively utter consonant-vowel combinations (called babbling) is strongly canalized, because babbling occurs even in babies who are born deaf and have never heard a human voice (Lenneberg, 1967). In contrast, intelligence is less highly canalized, for it can be modified by a variety of physical, social, and educational experiences.

range of reaction The notion that the human being's genetic makeup establishes a range of possible developmental outcomes, within which environmental forces largely determine how the person actually develops.

canalization The genetic restriction of a phenotype to a small number of developmental outcomes, permitting environmental influences to play only a small role in these outcomes.

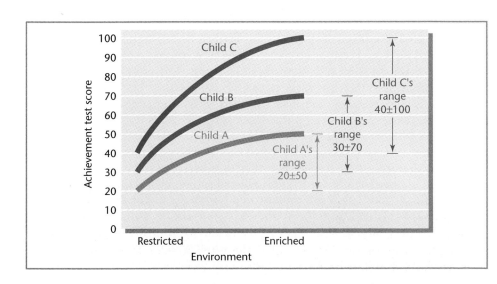

■ FIGURE 3-7
Interaction between environment and genotype. Providing any child with an enriched, stimulating environment can substantially improve the child's performance on various measures of achievement. However, each child's genotype—in this hypothetical illustration these are represented by the labels "Child A," "Child B," and "Child C"—will determine the limits within which his or her performance may vary. (*Source:* Adapted from Gottesman, 1963.)

■ FIGURE 3-8
Bidirectional influence in gene-environment interactions.
In the developmental systems view, the influence wielded by each of the four levels of individual development is bidirectional; that is, each level influences both the one above and the one below it. Any level may also influence nonadjacent levels. (*Source*: Gottlieb, 1992)

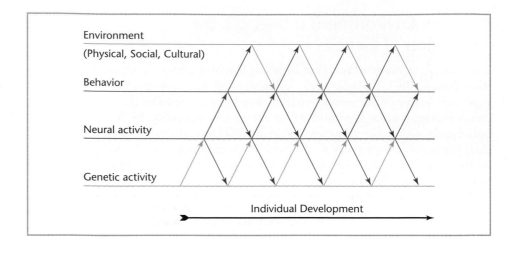

Gilbert Gottlieb (1991, 1992; Gottlieb, Wahlsten, & Lickliter, 1998) has offered a modified view of gene-environment interaction, in which genes play a less determining role in shaping development. According to Gottlieb's developmental systems view, "the concept of the genetic determination of traits is truly outmoded" (Gottlieb, 1991, p. 5). Instead, Gottlieb argues, individual development is organized into multiple levels—for example, genetic activity, neural activity (activity of the nervous system), behavior, and environment—all of which influence each other. As Figure 3-8 shows, this influence is bidirectional; that is, both from bottom to top and from top to bottom. The figure offers a simplified explanation of how genes and environment mutually influence each other; for example, the prenatal environment could alter the expression of the genes, and the postnatal environment, in part, will determine whether a genetic predisposition finds full expression in behavior. Thus, although each of the figure's levels generally influences the level directly above or below it, other interactions across nonadjacent levels are possible as well. In his work on mallard ducklings, Gottlieb found that ducklings' usual preference for the sounds of other ducks—a genetically governed preference—could be modified if the duckling were exposed before birth to sounds made by chickens. The duckling exposed to "chicken sounds" preferred these sounds over duck sounds.

The most important point of this systems view is the recognition that genes are part of an overall system and that their activity—that is, the expression of the characteristics they carry—is affected by events at other levels of the system, including the organism's environment.

Another factor in gene-environment interaction is the stage of the child's development. Both developmental stage and the environment determine the likelihood that a genetically based trait or characteristic will be influenced by environmental forces. For example, as we discuss further in Chapter 4, if a fetus is exposed early in its development to the virus that causes German measles, the child after birth is very likely to evidence some damage to its hearing. After the third month of pregnancy, however, fetal exposure to this virus generally does not affect the child's hearing. The window of opportunity for this particular environmental influence has largely closed because the fetus has reached a more mature stage of development.

Another example of the importance of critical periods can be seen in the treatment for PKU, the genetic disorder we discussed earlier. Babies today are routinely tested for PKU, and if they are found to be homozygous for the trait, they are placed on a special diet low in phenylalanine to prevent the buildup of toxins that results in mental retardation. In Figure 3-9 we see once again that in the interaction between genotype and environment there is a window of opportunity. The special PKU diet must begin immediately after birth, for delays of even a few months can

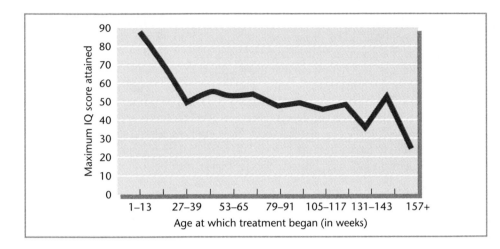

■ FIGURE 3-9
Diet and intelligence in PKU children.
Clearly, delaying the age at which a special diet for the child born with phenylketonuria is begun can have seriously negative effects on the child's intellectual functioning. If the diet is begun at birth, however, the child can eventually achieve an IQ score close to average (which would be 100; see Chapter 11). (*Source:* Adapted from Baumeister [1967] by permission of the publisher and the author)

have devastating effects on a child's intellectual development. On the other hand, if this diet is begun at once and continued until the nervous system is mature, a PKU child can develop intellectual abilities that are close to normal. Whether a child must stay on this diet indefinitely is subject to controversy; at present, most experts recommend that women, at least, remain on it for life if they plan to bear children. If they don't do this, they may have to go back on the diet in pregnancy; if they fail to do this early enough in a pregnancy, they may miscarry or the fetus may develop mental retardation (Verp, 1993). This example illustrates not only the importance of the timing of environmental influences but the complex way in which developmental outcomes—even those involving a genetically based predisposition—arise from the interaction between genes and environment.

How Genetic Makeup Helps to Shape the Environment

Although it is now widely accepted that the expression of genes is influenced by the environment, that genes can shape the environment is an even newer idea and one that is less commonly acknowledged. Scientists have proposed several ways in which people's genetic makeup can influence their environments (Plomin, 1995; Scarr, 1992, 1996; Scarr & McCartney, 1983). In one of these pathways, parents with certain genetic predispositions may create a home environment that suits those predispositions and that may also suit and encourage the inherited predispositions of their children. Thus intelligent, well-educated parents may provide a home with books and stimulating conversation that enhances their children's inherited tendencies to be bright and encourages them to learn. Another way in which genes can influence environment is for people's inherited tendencies to evoke certain responses from others, that is, from their social environment. For instance, babies with an inborn tendency to smile often will probably elicit more positive stimulation from others than do very sober, unresponsive infants (Lytton, 1980; Plomin, 1995). In this paradigm, the environment that has been altered by genetic expression has reciprocal effects on genetic makeup: The evoked stimulation reinforces the babies' smiling and ultimately, by a circular process, tends to magnify the babies' genetic predisposition.

Finally, genes can influence environment in a third way: People's genetic makeups may encourage them to actually seek out experiences that are compatible with their inherited tendencies (Scarr, 1996; Scarr & McCartney, 1983). In a process called **niche picking,** people search for, select, or build environments that are compatible with their predispositions. Thus, people who are genetically predisposed to be extraverted or gregarious actively seek the company of other people and become involved in a wide range of social activities. These experiences, in turn, enhance the

niche picking   Seeking out or creating environments that are compatible with one's own (genetically based) predispositions.

expression of their genes for sociability. The importance of niche picking probably increases from childhood to adolescence and adulthood, as people gain more freedom to choose their own activities and companions.

These influences of genes on environment underscore the difficulty of determining the relative contributions of heredity and environment to individual differences in development (Baumrind, 1993; Hoffman, 1991). If genes influence environmental experiences, which in turn influence genes, it is difficult to separate the factors involved in these complex feedback loops. Nevertheless, as we will see in the next section, researchers have attempted to calculate the relative influences of heredity and environment on individual differences in a large number of characteristics.

HEREDITY, ENVIRONMENT, AND INDIVIDUAL DIFFERENCES

An important issue with which researchers contend is the question of why people develop in such widely different ways. Why, for example, does one child achieve an IQ score of 105, whereas his sister has a score of 150? Why is one child so outgoing and sociable, another more introverted and shy? How can we explain why some children—and adults—are chronically aggressive, whereas others seek to cooperate with others and to avoid confrontation? For years, psychologists interested in human personality struggled with questions like these. The field of **human behavior genetics** arose in the 1960s when some scientists began to focus their attention particularly on the relative contributions that heredity and environment make to the array of individual differences observed in human behavior (Plomin, 1990a).

Unlike biologists who study heredity, behavior geneticists can conduct their research without ever directly measuring chromosomes, DNA, or genes. Instead, using sophisticated statistical techniques, they calculate what are called **heritability factors,** or percentage estimates of the contribution that heredity makes to a particular ability or type of behavior. When discussing heritability factors, a caution is in order: These percentage contributions of heredity to individual differences should not be viewed as applicable to all groups of children or adults at all points in their development. The relative contribution of heredity to an observed difference in human behavior depends on how wide a range of environmental influences the people studied have been exposed to. For example, when children experience virtually the same environment, we may assume that heredity plays the greater role in any individual differences in their behaviors. When environments are extremely different, however, things get more complex: Whereas environmental factors may exert greater influence on people's behavior, their very abundance may sometimes obscure the genetic influences that are at work.

British psychiatrist Sir Michael Rutter (1992) believes that people have many misconceptions about what the study of genetics contributes to our knowledge of human development (see Table 3-4). According to Rutter, the field of behavior genetics has as much to say about environmental influences as about genetic effects on the human being. With the right research strategies, Rutter claims, it is possible not only to reveal the interaction between these two forces but also to distinguish them and to estimate the extent to which each contributes to any given trait or ability.

Methods of Studying Individual Differences

The method used most often to investigate the contributions of heredity and environment to individual differences is the study of family members whose degrees of biological relatedness are known. Studies of this type generally compare adopted children with their biological and adoptive parents, examine similarities

human behavior genetics   The study of the relative influences of heredity and environmental forces on the evolution of individual differences in traits and abilities.

heritability factor   A statistical estimate of the contribution made by heredity to a particular trait or ability.

TABLE 3-4 Some Misconceptions about the Study of Behavior Genetics

■ *Genes limit potential.* Wrong. Genetic factors do affect potential, but that potential in turn is affected by a child's environment. Change the environment, and the potential changes, too.

■ *Strong genetic effects mean that environmental influences are not important.* Wrong. Although genetic effects account for individual variability, the environment may effect changes in the average expression of a characteristic. For example, the range of individual differences in IQ of children from disadvantaged families who are adopted into more advantaged families is more closely related to the IQ range of the children's biological parents. Nevertheless, these children show a general rise in IQ levels, demonstrating the effect of a stimulating environment.

■ *Nature and nurture are separate.* Wrong. Both genes and environment are necessary for an individual to develop: "No genes, no organism; no environment, no organism" (Scarr & Weinberg, 1983).

■ *Genetic influences diminish with age.* Wrong. The relation between genes and aging is highly complex. Some hereditary characteristics are most evident in early stages of development; some are more evident in later stages. For example, the age at which puberty occurs is largely under genetic control, whereas the contribution of genetic factors to individual differences in intelligence is more evident in older than in younger children.

■ *Genes regulate only static characteristics.* Wrong. Genes are concerned with developmental change as well. Deviations in the normally expected environment can upset the timetable for the child's physical and psychological development, producing gross delay. However, the time at which particular characteristics emerge and the sequence in which they appear are determined primarily by the child's genetic makeup.

Sources: Rutter, 1992; Shaffer, 1996.

and differences between fraternal and identical twins, or explore the effects of similar and different environments on twins and ordinary siblings.

Adoption Studies

In adoption studies, researchers usually compare characteristics of adopted children with those of both their adoptive and biological parents. Although the adoptive parents exert environmental influences on their adopted children, investigators can assume that there is no genetically determined similarity between these adoptive parents and children. Adopted children of course have genes in common with their biological parents, but the latter exert no postnatal environmental influences on the children. (These kinds of studies include only adopted children who have no contact with their biological parents.) Based on these assumptions and conditions, researchers reason that any similarity of adopted children to their adoptive parents must be due to their social environment, whereas any similarity of the children to their biological parents must be the result of similar genetic makeup. Adoption studies also sometimes study the similarities and differences between biological siblings and adopted children who live in the same home.

Twin Studies

Twin studies take a different approach to uncovering the contributions of heredity and environment to human differences. Often these studies involve comparing the similarities of identical and fraternal twins raised together in the same home. Identical, or **monozygotic,** twins are created when a single zygote splits in half and each half becomes a distinct embryo with exactly the same genes; both embryos come from one zygote (*mono* means "one"). In contrast, fraternal, or **dizygotic,** twins develop from two different eggs that have been fertilized by two different sperm, producing two different zygotes (*di* means "two").

monozygotic Characterizing *identical* twins, who have developed from a single fertilized egg.

dizygotic Characterizing *fraternal* twins, who have developed from two separate fertilized eggs.

Because they are conceived independently of each other, fraternal twins are no more similar genetically than any other pair of siblings; on average, they have half their genes in common. When comparing sets of identical and fraternal twins, researchers assume that each set has been raised in essentially the same type of environment. Thus, if identical twins show more resemblance on a particular trait than fraternal twins do, we can assume that the resemblance is strongly influenced by genes. On the other hand, if on a given trait the two kinds of twins resemble each other almost equally, we can assume that the resemblance is strongly influenced by the environment.

Shared and Nonshared Environments

Is it legitimate to make these assumptions? Some investigators have questioned the proposition that each member of a twin pair experiences the same environmental conditions. These investigators argue that identical twins, because of their identical genes and inherited predispositions, are treated more similarly by their parents, evoke more similar responses from people outside the family, and select more similar settings, companions, and activities for themselves than do fraternal twins (Baumrind, 1993; Scarr, 1996; Scarr & McCartney, 1983). Thus, these critics claim, identical twins have more **shared environments** than fraternal twins, and so any similarities in their traits must be attributed to both the environment and their genetic makeup (Plomin, 1986, 1995). Fraternal twins and siblings, they suggest, have more **nonshared environments,** or experiences and activities of varied sorts.

This viewpoint stresses that people are active creators of their own environments, not just passive recipients of environmental influences. In both deliberate and unintentional ways, people help to shape the many experiences to which they're exposed. With this in mind, consider whether two siblings who live together in the same home encounter exactly the same family environment (Dunn & Plomin, 1991; Dunn, Stocker, & Plomin, 1990). In fact there are differences in people's experiences even within the same setting, differences based in part on who the people are as individuals. This perspective helps explain why adoptive siblings, and even biologically related ones, often show only a modest similarity on behavioral traits. Moreover, the initially modest similarity caused by a shared childhood home tends to decline with age, as personal niche picking exerts more and more influence on people's behavior (Reiss, Hetherington, & Plomin, 1994; Reiss, Plomin, & Hetherington, 1991).

Children raised in the same family, then, have both shared and nonshared experiences. Conditions shared would include such factors as being poor or well off, living in a good or a bad neighborhood, and having parents who are employed or unemployed, in good heath or physically or mentally ill (Reiss et al., 1991). Experiences not shared, in contrast, would include factors or events related to the individual characteristics of a particular child; for example, what specific activities that child engages in, or how he or she is treated because of age, gender, temperament, illness, or physical and cognitive abilities. Studies show that siblings, even twins, have many nonshared experiences that affect their development (Plomin, 1995; Plomin & Bergeman, 1991; Plomin & Daniels, 1987). Even small differences in nonshared experiences may cause differences in how siblings develop. Furthermore, siblings' perceptions that their experiences—for example, the way their parents treat them—are different can affect their behavior whether or not these perceptions are accurate. Clearly, researchers in individual differences can no longer assume a homogeneous home environment for all siblings, and you must be alert to this fact when you read the reports and conclusions of such studies.

Some Individual Differences and Their Contributors

In this section we have chosen to look at some of the findings of research in behavior genetics in three important areas. We begin by examining the effects of heredity and environment on differences in intellectual abilities; we then explore differences

---

shared environment A set of conditions or experiences that is shared by children raised in the same family with each other; a parameter commonly examined in studies of individual differences.

nonshared environment A set of conditions or activities that is experienced by one child in a family and not shared with another child in the same family.

in temperament and personality; and we conclude with a look at differences in the tendency to develop behavioral disorders.

Intellectual Characteristics

Interestingly, studies comparing the intelligence quotient, or IQ, scores of twins have been remarkably consistent in their findings (we discuss intelligence at length in Chapter 11). This research indicates that similarities and differences in individual performance on intelligence tests are heavily influenced by genes. Generally, the closer the genetic links between two people, the more similar their IQ scores. As you can see from Table 3-5, which summarizes more than 100 family resemblance studies of twins, siblings, and other relatives, identical twins reared in the same household are most similar in IQ scores (+.86 is a very high positive correlation, as you'll recall from Chapter 2). The least similar in IQ scores are cousins, who have relatively few genes in common and are not raised in the same home (only +.15). As genetic similarity decreases, so does similarity in intelligence scores. Even identical twins raised apart have IQ scores that are more similar than are those of fraternal twins raised in the same home. Furthermore, although twin correlations of IQ decrease with age as the influence of a shared family environment diminishes, that decrease is greater for fraternal twins than for identical ones (McCartney, Harris, & Berniere, 1990).

Genes contribute not only to differences in general intellectual performance but to differences in specific mental abilities as well, some more so than others. Differences in spatial and verbal abilities, for instance, are more influenced by genetic factors than are differences in memory and perceptual speed (Plomin, 1989). In a surprising finding, however, differences in creativity, that aspect of cognitive behavior that includes scientific and artistic innovation, show less genetic influence than differences in any other specific cognitive ability. It looks as if geniuses are largely made, not born!

Heredity affects not just differences in the level of mental development but also differences in the timing and rate of development. Just as children show spurts and plateaus in their physical growth, they also show variations in the rate and timing of their mental growth. Heredity apparently contributes substantially to these individual differences, as suggested by the fact that identical twins are more similar in this regard than fraternal twins (Wilson, 1983). For example, Figure 3-10 shows how the scores achieved by four sets of identical twins on infant intelligence tests rose and fell in very much the same patterns over their first two years. Tests of infants typically show wide fluctuations like these over time; what is remarkable here is how similar the patterns of the fluctuations were for each pair of twins.

TABLE 3-5 Resemblance in Intelligence Scores among Family Members[a]

Relationship of Family Members	Correlation between IQ Scores
Identical twins reared together	.86
Identical twins reared apart	.79
Fraternal twins reared together	.60
Siblings reared together	.47
Parent and child	.40
Foster parent and child	.31
Siblings reared apart	.24
Cousins	.15

Source: Adapted from Bouchard & McGue (1981).

[a]Correlations are compiled from 111 different studies from all parts of the world. In general, the closer the genetic relationship of two people, the higher the correlation between their IQ scores.

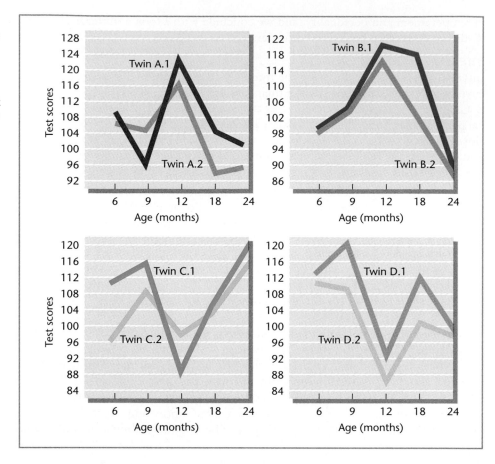

Adoption studies also reveal significant genetic contributions to individual differences in intellectual development (Burks, 1928; Leahy, 1935; Plomin & McClearn, 1993; Scarr & Weinberg, 1977). Even if children have been adopted in their first year of life, their intellectual performance at school age correlates more closely with their biological parents' intelligence ratings or scores than it does with those of their adoptive parents; moreover, the correlation with foster or adoptive parents declines with age (Scarr & Weinberg, 1983).

Bear in mind that the results of adoption studies do not mean that adoptive parents fail to influence their adopted children's intellectual performance (Schiff & Lewontin, 1986; Turkheimer, 1991). In one classic adoption study, adopted children often averaged 20 or more IQ points higher than their biological mothers (Skodak & Skeels, 1949). Because in this study the adoptive parents tended to be more highly educated and more socially and economically advantaged than the biological parents, this result was probably due to the more stimulating home environments that the adoptive parents provided. But note also that, despite this environmental influence on development, individual differences seemed still to be substantially influenced by genetic inheritance. The rank ordering of the children's IQ scores more closely resembled that of their biological mothers than that of their adoptive parents. The children whose biological mothers had the lowest IQ scores were likely to have lower IQ scores than the children whose biological mothers scored higher. Thus, although the absolute level of intellectual development was apparently boosted by the environmental influences provided by the adoptive parents, individual differences among the adopted children in intellectual performance—that is, their relative standings in this regard—appeared to stem more from their biological inheritance than from the increased intellectual stimulation provided in their adoptive homes.

Another qualification of the findings of this research is that because it studied primarily children who were adopted into middle-class families, it may have limited the expression of environmental influences. Among children adopted into families from a wider range of socioeconomic backgrounds, environment probably makes a greater contribution to individual differences in intellectual performance. For example, studies have shown that adopted children in economically disadvantaged homes have lower IQ scores and are more likely to drop out of school than those placed with more well-to-do families (Capron & Duyme, 1989; Duyme, 1988).

Thus, although twin studies and adoptive studies are in agreement in showing that genetic factors make an important contribution to individual differences in IQ, environmental factors can also be important contributors to these differences, especially when there are wide disparities in the contexts in which individuals live. As you will see in Chapter 11, very poor or stressful environments can dramatically lower IQ scores, and cognitively stimulating environments or intervention programs can raise them.

Temperament and Personality

Even in infants' earliest days of life, we can see marked differences in what we call **temperament,** or the individual's typical mode of response to the environment, including such things as activity level, adaptability to new situations, and intensity of emotional expression. We use the term *temperament* to describe these kinds of individual differences in infants and children. In adolescence and adulthood these styles of responding to the world are often discussed as different aspects of *personality,* such as emotionality, activity, and sociability.

> **temperament** The individual's typical mode of response to the environment, including such things as activity level, emotional intensity, and attention span; used particularly to describe infants' and children's behavior.

Thomas and Chess (1986) have proposed a typology of temperament that has been widely accepted. This framework classifies infants as *difficult, easy,* or *slow-to-warm-up,* and each of these types is associated with a distinctive pattern of behavioral responses (Rothbart & Bates, 1998; Thomas & Chess, 1986). Difficult infants (about 10% of all babies) sleep and eat irregularly, become easily upset by new situations, and experience extremes of fussiness and crying. In contrast, easy babies (about 40%) are friendly, happy, and adaptable. Even in the same family, babies may exhibit both of these dramatically different temperaments:

> Nothing was easy with Chris. Mealtimes, bedtimes, toilet training were all hell. It would take me an hour and a half to get part of a bottle into him and he'd be hungry two hours later. I can't remember once in the first two years when he didn't go to bed crying. I'd try to rock him to sleep but as soon as I'd tiptoe over to put him in his crib his head would lurch up and he'd start bellowing again. He didn't like any kind of changes in his routine. New people and places upset him so it was hard to take him anywhere.
>
> John was my touchy feely baby. From the first day in the hospital he cuddled and seemed so contented to be held I could hardly bear to put him down. He didn't cry unless something was wrong—he was wet, or hungry, or tired. We took him everywhere because he seemed to enjoy new things. You could always sit him in a corner and he'd entertain himself. Sometimes I'd forget he was there until he'd start laughing or prattling.

The *slow-to-warm-up* child is low in activity level and tends to respond negatively to new stimuli at first but to adapt slowly to new objects or novel experiences after repeated contact with them. Essentially, these children fall somewhere between difficult and easy children; on first exposure to something strange they may look like difficult children, but they gradually show quiet interest, much like an easy child.

Rothbart (1981) and colleagues have developed an alternative and increasingly popular measure of temperament known as the Infant Behavior Questionnaire. The six scales of this instrument are (1) positive affect, (2) irritable distress, (3) fearful distress, (4) activity level, (5) attention span/persistence, and (6) rhythmicity (Table 3-6). They have also developed a similar temperament measure for toddlers,

TABLE 3-6	Components of Infant Temperament
Component	Description
Positive affect	Measured by a child's smiling, laughter, cooperativeness, and manageability
Irritable distress	Indexed by a child's irritability, fussiness, anger, frustration, and distress at limitations on her behavior
Fearful distress	Assessed by the length of time a child requires to adjust to a new situation, or his adaptability, and by the child's tendency to withdraw and show distress in new situations
Activity level	Indexed by the child's tendency to be more or less active
Attention span/persistence	Measured by a child's ability to concentrate, focus on a task, and continue to work at a problem
Rhythmicity	Assessed by the predictability or regularity of a child's behavior patterns

Sources: Rothbart & Bates, 1998; Rothbart & Mauro, 1990.

children, early adolescents, and adults (Capaldi & Rothbart, 1992; Goldsmith, in press; Rothbart, Ahadi, & Hershey, 1994; Rothbart & Bates, 1998). The fact that there are comparable scales across the span of development makes this approach to temperament an influential one. Temperament, of course, is expressed in different ways as the individual grows older. For example, in infancy we may index persistence by the length of time a baby looks at an object, whereas in childhood we may measure this component by the length of time a child continues to work on a puzzle or problem.

Researchers have also compiled evidence for differences in newborn temperament among children of different ethnicities and race. For instance, Chinese American babies, in contrast to European American and Irish infants, have been described as generally calmer, easier to console, more able to quiet themselves after crying, and faster to adapt to external stimulation or changes (Freedman, 1974, 1976; Kagan, Kearsley, & Zelazo, 1978; Kagan et al., 1994). Similarly, Lewis, Ramsey, and Kawakami (1993) reported that Japanese infants between the ages of 2 and 6 months were less reactive than European American infants during well-baby examinations and that they were less likely to display intense distress at being inoculated.

A variety of cultural differences in infant temperament have been found for different East African societies. The Digo, for example, view the infant as active and able to learn within a few months after birth, whereas the Kikuyu view their infants as passive, keep them swaddled for the first year, and believe that serious education is not possible until the second year (DeVries & Sameroff, 1984). These findings underscore the ways in which cultural beliefs about the nature of infant temperament may, in part, shape the nature of the infant's early emotional regulatory capacities. Culture shapes temperament, just as temperament shapes the ways in which caregivers behave (Sameroff, 1994; Rothbart & Bates, 1998).

A higher rate of developmental problems is found in later life among children described by their mothers as difficult babies (Rothbart & Bates, 1998; Pettit & Bates, 1989; Rutter, Quinton, & Yule, 1977; Thomas, Chess, & Korn, 1982). Two factors may contribute to this relationship: A first is that a less malleable child is likely to find it harder to adapt to environmental demands and so is more prone to stress and the toll it takes on emotional well-being. A second factor, which has been demonstrated in research studies, is that a child with a difficult temperament is more apt to elicit adverse reactions from other people and thus to suffer the

As children develop and have more freedom to choose companions and contexts they may, in what is called niche-picking, select activities that are compatible with their genetic predispositions. Thus they give expression to these predispositions by choosing endeavors that support them.

psychological damage caused by social rejection. Children with difficult temperaments have been found to serve as targets for parental irritability, especially when the parents are under stress. Stressed mothers are especially likely to withdraw affection from temperamentally difficult boys and to show irritation with them (Hetherington, 1991b). If a mother is under multiple stresses and lacks a supportive family or friendship network, dealing with a difficult baby may disrupt the development of a secure attachment relationship and increase the likelihood that the child will exhibit later developmental problems (Crockenberg, 1981). On the other hand, a difficult baby is not likely to suffer any long-term negative effects if its parents are calm and supportive (Hetherington, 1991b).

How do heredity and environment affect temperament and personality? Scientists assumed for some time that both are at least in part genetically determined, although there have been arguments on both sides of the issue. Recent studies have suggested that prenatal environment and environmental factors at birth may make larger contributions than heredity to infant temperament (Riese, 1990). At the same time, genetic influences on temperament seem to become increasingly prominent throughout early childhood (Dunn & Plomin, 1991; Stevenson & Fielding, 1985; Wilson & Matheny, 1986). It may be that although some individual differences are partly genetic in origin, they are nevertheless susceptible to environmental influences, particularly interactions among family members (Loehlin, Willerman, & Horn, 1988). Personality traits show some stability over time, which might suggest a genetic influence, but most psychologists today consider that both heredity and environmental factors contribute to personality.

Studies have shown that heredity contributes to individual differences in a number of temperament characteristics and personality traits, including some of the components identified by Rothbart and his colleagues: affect, or emotionality; fears and anxieties; activity level; attention span and persistence; and the tendencies to maintain high moral standards and to obey authority (Goldsmith, 1983; Kochanska, 1993b; Plomin, 1989; Tellegan et al., 1988). According to Plomin (1995), inheritance apparently contributes most to emotionality, activity level, and sociability. Temperament and personality show a declining link with genetic factors as people age, however, and among older people differing life experiences seem more significant (Plomin, McClearn, Pedersen, Nesselroade, & Bergeman, 1988).

Psychopathology

Behavior geneticists have also studied the relative contributions of heredity and environment to the differential development of psychological disorders. Again using twin and adoption studies, researchers have found that genetic factors may play a role in the development of a wide range of disorders that fall under the heading of **psychopathology**, such as childhood behavior disorders, depression, suicidal tendencies, manic-depressive disorder, and schizophrenia. Among these, researchers have focused most often on schizophrenia.

Schizophrenia is a severe mental and emotional disorder that is often characterized by bizarre beliefs and behavior. Like many other qualities and characteristics that we've discussed, schizophrenia appears to be caused by a combination of genetic vulnerability and environmental stresses, although the contribution of genetic makeup to the evolution of this disorder seems quite strong. For example, the **concordance rate**—the percentage of cases in which a characteristic or trait exhibited by one member of a twin pair is also exhibited by the other twin—is more than three times as high for identical twins (46%) as for fraternal twins (14%) and close to five times as high as for first-degree relatives (10%) (Gottesman, 1993; Gottesman & Shields, 1982). The fact that the concordance rate is not higher reminds us that genes alone do not determine outcomes; even identical twins raised in their family of origin may experience different interactions with their parents or encounter other different environmental events. Having an adoptive parent who is schizophrenic doesn't usually place a child at significantly greater risk for developing the disorder as long as the child's biological parents are normal. In one study, the incidence of schizophrenia was 11 percent among children of normal biological parents who were adopted by a schizophrenic adult, and 10 percent among those for whom both biological and adoptive parents were normal (Wender et al., 1974). In contrast, almost twice as many children (19%) with a schizophrenic biological parent but normal adoptive parents later developed this mental disorder, even when the children were separated from a schizophrenic biological parent at an early age (Mednick, Schulsinger, & Schulsinger, 1975).

Having a biological parent who is schizophrenic puts a child at greater risk for other disorders as well. A classic study compared children of schizophrenic mothers who were separated from those mothers at birth with children whose mothers were not schizophrenic (Heston, 1966). About half of each group were in adoptive homes, and half were in institutions. Both groups were compared on a variety of disorders at about age 35. The higher rates of behavioral problems in the children of schizophrenics suggests that the genetic influences involved may manifest themselves in a range of psychopathologies, depending on the effects of life experiences. The results of this study have been confirmed in recent years (Plomin, 1990b; Plomin & McClearn, 1993).

Researchers have also focused their attention on the developmental risks of having a mother who is depressed. Somewhat surprisingly, having a depressed mother may be even more detrimental to a child than having a mother who is schizophrenic. Schizophrenic mothers are at least responsive to their children, albeit in an erratic and sometimes strange fashion. But depressed parents are more likely to be unresponsive, irritable, tense, withdrawn, and disorganized (Campbell, Cohn, & Meyers, 1995; Cohn & Campbell, 1992; Field, 1992). The link between depression in mothers and depression in their children has been attributed to this inept parenting. Depression in mothers has also been related to a pattern of behavior in young children in which the child avoids contact with the mother even in times of stress (Radke-Yarrow, Cummings, Kuczynski, & Chapman, 1985). Other developmental problems seen in the children of depressed women are attention deficits,

psychopathology
Psychological and behavioral dysfunction as it occurs in various types of mental disorder.

concordance rate The percentage of cases in which a characteristic or trait exhibited by one member of a twin pair is also exhibited by the other twin.

separation anxiety, conduct disorders, and lack of competence in school and in peer relations (Hammen, 1997; Zahn-Waxler, Denham, Ianotti, & Cummings, 1992; Zahn-Waxler, Kochanska, Krupnick, & McKnew, 1990). Which of these various outcomes tends to arise is probably determined by complex interactions among genetic and environmental influences.

SUMMARY

- During the course of development, the **genotype** interacts with the environment in complex ways to produce the **phenotype.** It is the phenotypic expression of individual physical and behavioral characteristics that scientists study in an effort to understand how genes and the environment interact to produce each unique human being.

The Process of Genetic Transmission

- Within each cell nucleus are threadlike structures called **chromosomes,** on which **genes** containing the genetic code are located. Genetic variability is the result of the huge number of chromosome combinations that are possible during the formation of sperm and egg cells, and to **crossing over,** which occurs during the kind of cell division called **meiosis** and involves the exchange of genes on homologous chromosomes. Sexual reproduction, or the union of **ovum** with **sperm,** also contributes to genetic variability, as 23 chromosomes from a woman unite with 23 chromosomes from a man to form the **zygote.** Through the process of **mitosis,** this new **autosome** divides and continues to divide, eventually producing a new, multicellular organism.
- Chromosomes are bound by molecules of **deoxyribonucleic acid (DNA),** which in turn are made up of **nucleotides.** Genes, portions of the DNA molecule, are located at particular sites on the chromosome where they code for the production of certain kinds of protein. When a gene is activated, a copy of it travels from the cell nucleus to the body of the cell where it serves as a template for building a protein molecule. Each of the many different kinds of proteins in the human body serves a different function. All of them, working together, are what make a living organism.

Genetic Influences on Development

- At any given gene's position on two homologous chromosomes, there can be more than one form of that gene, called the gene's **alleles.** If the alleles are the same, the person is **homozygous** for that particular characteristic; if the alleles are different, the person is **heterozygous.** Heterozygous combinations may be expressed in three ways: (1) the person may have a trait intermediate between the traits that each of the two alleles codes for; (2) both alleles may express their traits simultaneously, an outcome called **codominance;** and (3) a **dominant** allele may overcome the other, **recessive** allele, resulting in the expression of the dominant allele's trait.
- The 23rd pair of human chromosomes are the **sex chromosomes,** differing in males and females. Females have two large homologous sex chromosomes, forming an XX pattern; males have one X and a smaller Y chromosome, an XY pattern. Because an X chromosome is about five times longer than a Y chromosome, it carries more genes. This means that, in males, some genes on the X chromosome have no equivalent genes on the Y chromosome; the person inherits only one each of these **X-linked genes.** If the inherited gene happens to be a

harmful recessive allele, the associated genetic disorder will automatically be expressed. **Hemophilia,** a disease in which the blood fails to clot, is an example of an X-linked recessive trait.

- Many human characteristics are influenced by complex interactions among multiple genes acting together. This interaction of multiple genes may help explain why some traits that are influenced by genes do not tend to run in families. Their development depends on a configuration of many genes, and that whole configuration is not likely to be passed on from parent to child. Further adding to the complexity of genetic influences on development, a single pair of alleles may influence more than one trait, and, if they are **modifier genes** they may do so not directly but indirectly through the effects they have on how other genes are expressed.

- Harmful alleles survive generally because, as in **phenylketonuria (PKU),** they are not harmful in the heterozygous state. They may also survive, as they do in people who carry the allele for **sickle-cell anemia,** when, in addition to threatening people with that disease, they also protect people who carry them from malaria.

- **Down syndrome** is one example of the many identifiable human chromosome disorders. It is caused by inheriting three 21st chromosomes instead of the normal two and is characterized by both physical and mental retardation and a distinctive physical appearance. Abnormalities can also arise in the sex chromosomes. Examples are **Turner syndrome** (an XO pattern), the triple-X syndrome, **Klinefelter's syndrome** (an XXY pattern), the double-Y syndrome (an XYY pattern), and **fragile X syndrome.** The physical, psychological, and emotional characteristics of people with these chromosome aberrations vary widely depending upon the specific chromosome pattern and environmental factors.

Genetic Counseling and Genetic Engineering

- Advances in biology and genetics have opened new opportunities for diagnosing genetic disorders before birth. The two methods most commonly used to collect samples of fetal cells for genetic analysis are **amniocentesis** and **chorionic villi sampling.** Other diagnostic methods include the **alphafetoprotein assay** and **ultrasound.**

- Scientists hope eventually to locate the genes responsible for all inherited disorders. A breakthrough occurred when researchers identified the genetic marker for **Huntington disease,** making it possible to develop a test for the Huntington gene. With the aim of treating or curing genetic disorders, scientists are exploring gene therapy, which involves inserting normal alleles into patient's cells to compensate for defective alleles. Theoretically, normal genes could even replace defective ones in sperm or egg cells, or they could be inserted into a newly created zygote.

Heredity-Environment Interactions

- The concept of the **range of reaction** helps shed light on how environments influence genes. According to this concept, heredity does not rigidly fix behavior, but instead establishes a range of possible developmental outcomes that may occur in response to different environments. When a reaction range is extremely narrow, it is said to exhibit **canalization.** With a highly canalized trait, there are few pathways that development can take, and intense or more specific environmental pushes are required to deflect the course of development.

- Not only does environment influence genes, but genes also influence the environments to which people are exposed. One way this can happen is for parents with certain genetic predispositions to create a home environment that suits those predispositions, and which may also suit and encourage the inherited predispositions of their children. Another way is for people's inherited tendencies to evoke certain environmental influences from others. A third way is for genes to encourage people to engage in **niche picking,** seeking out experiences that are compatible with their inherited tendencies.

Heredity, Environment, and Individual Differences

■ An important question researchers ask is why significant differences exist in the ways that people develop. **Human behavior genetics** seeks to answer this question by calculating **heritability factors**—percentage estimates of the contribution that genes make to some observed individual difference. Commonly, researchers study family members with known degrees of biological relatedness, such as **monozygotic** and **dizygotic** twins and adopted children, as well as the degree to which they inhabit **shared** or **nonshared environments.**

■ Family resemblance studies consistently show that individual differences in IQ scores are substantially influenced by genetic factors. In addition, individual differences in certain more specific cognitive abilities, including spatial skills and verbal proficiency, are also influenced by genes, as are differences in the timing and rate of mental development. Nevertheless, an enriched environment can boost a child's level of intellectual development considerably.

■ Heredity contributes to many individual differences in **temperament** and personality, especially differences in emotionality, activity level, and sociability. However, the contribution of heredity to differences in these traits appears to decline with age, as people's personalities become increasingly influenced by their life experiences. In the area of **psychopathology** we find an influence of genes as well. Whether a person develops a certain psychological disorder or not often depends on a combination of genetic vulnerability and environmental stresses.

Prenatal Development and Birth

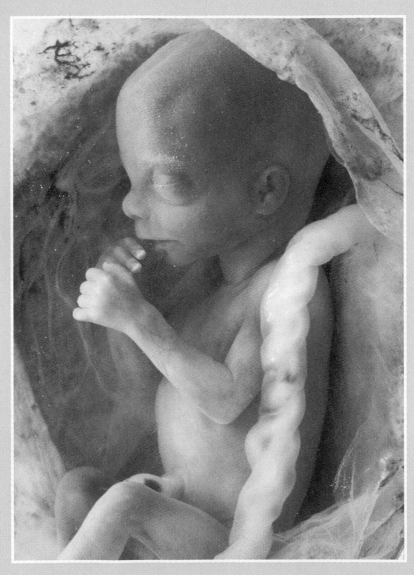

C H A P T E R 4

Anticipating the birth of a child can be one of the most joyous times in peoples' lives. Couples look forward to becoming parents and enjoy preparing for their baby's arrival. And they may even try to influence the new family member by playing favorite music or reading to their unborn child!

Whether it's possible to influence a baby in such positive ways during pregnancy is not entirely certain, although as we will see, there is some evidence of babies' learning in utero. Unfortunately, however, clear evidence indicates that the developing organism is vulnerable to a variety of negative influences. Some of these influences are genetic, as we saw in the last chapter, and others are variations in the prenatal environment caused by factors and events that impinge on the mother as her pregnancy develops. A quite amazing number of adverse agents including medications and diagnostic procedures; prescription, nonprescription, and other legal and illegal drugs; maternal age and *parity* (whether a woman has had a child before); illness, dietary deficiencies, and emotional distress; and environmental toxins—can contribute to deviations in the normal development of a child from its first weeks of gestation. In addition, events occurring during childbirth may threaten the viability or the good health of an infant, and, as we might guess, the economic and social conditions under which a child is raised can affect its development from the very earliest days of its life outside the womb.

We begin this chapter by exploring the normal development of the human being from conception to delivery and then discuss the many factors that can threaten this normal development throughout a pregnancy. We look at normal childbirth and at some of the complications of labor and delivery, including the problems of prematurity and low birthweight. We conclude the chapter with a review of research that has explored the long-term effects of pregnancy and birth complications and some children's resilience in the face of such difficulties. Throughout these discussions we will ask several questions: What are the most significant of these complicating factors? How does the timing of their appearance in the *prenatal* environment modify their impact on the developing infant? And, perhaps most important, how do *perinatal* factors (those occurring shortly before and/or after birth) affect the child's later development, and what *postnatal* events and conditions serve to sustain or modify the effects of prenatal and perinatal factors?

STAGES OF PRENATAL DEVELOPMENT

Over the approximately nine months of prenatal development, the new organism shows many varieties of change. The kinds, numbers, positions, sizes, and shapes of cells, tissues, and bodily systems change, and such systems—for example, the central nervous system, which includes the brain and spinal cord—usually increase in size and complexity. On the other hand, some prenatal structures actually decrease in size or disappear. For example, at the end of the third week of pregnancy gill arches appear in the developing organism, but by the middle of the second month these remnants of an ancestral past have been transformed into parts of the inner ear, the larynx, and the neck. The external tail that emerges between the second and fourth months also disappears.

The nine months of prenatal development are characterized in two ways. Traditionally, pregnancy has been described as occurring in three *trimesters*, or three periods of three months each, and we often speak of a particular event as occurring in one or another trimester. Increasingly, however, we talk about the three periods of (1) the zygote, (2) the embryo, and (3) the fetus. Although they are distinct in many ways, these periods should be thought of as comprising continuous phases of development, for from the moment the sperm penetrates the ovum, development involves a systematic series of sequential changes by which the organism becomes increasingly complex and differentiated. Figure 4-1 illustrates this series, from ovulation, when the ovum embarks on its journey to the uterus, to the end of the second trimester, when the fetus appears fully human.

The Zygote

The period of the zygote includes approximately the first 2 weeks of life, extending from the time a sperm fertilizes the ovum until that ovum, now a **zygote,** proceeds down the mother's fallopian tube into her uterus, where it becomes implanted in the wall of the uterus. When this occurs, about eight days after conception, the zygote is so tiny that probably 100 to 200 zygotes placed side by side would measure only an inch and some 5 million would weigh only an ounce (Meredith, 1975). Gradually, tendrils from the zygote penetrate the blood vessels in the wall of the uterus, and the zygote forms the physiologically dependent relationship with the mother that will continue throughout the course of prenatal development.

zygote The developing organism from the time of the union of sperm and egg to about the second week of gestation; the period of the zygote comprises the implantation of the fertilized egg in the wall of the uterus.

The Embryo

The establishment of the zygote's secure relationship with the mother marks the beginning of the second prenatal period, the period of the embryo, a state of rapid growth that lasts from the beginning of the third week of gestation until the end of the eighth week. During this brief phase, in which the organism's most important physiological structures and systems become differentiated, the **embryo** also becomes recognizable as a partially functioning tiny human being. From the time of fertilization until the end of this period the infant increases 2 million percent in size! During this period, three crucial structures develop to protect and sustain the growing life within the mother's uterus: the amniotic sac, the placenta, and the umbilical cord. The **amniotic sac** contains the *amniotic fluid*, a watery liquid in which the developing embryo floats and which serves as a protective buffer against physical shocks and temperature changes. The tendrils that attach the embryo to the uterine wall increase in size and complexity to form a fleshy disclike structure called the **placenta**. The embryo is joined to the placenta at the abdomen by a third apparatus, the **umbilical cord,** a tube that contains the blood vessels that carry blood back and forth between the infant and placenta. (The umbilical cord attains a final length slightly greater than that of the growing organism, permitting it considerable mobility within the uterine environment.) However, semipermeable membranes within the placenta separate the bloodstreams of the mother and child, allowing some substances to pass through but not others. The placenta and umbilical cord thus serve to transmit oxygen and nutrients to the infant and to remove carbon dioxide and waste products from it, but they do not permit direct exchange of blood. Early in gestation the nutrients in the mother's bloodstream exceed the needs of the embryo and are stored by the placenta for later use. Unfortunately, certain potentially destructive substances, such as drugs, hormones, viruses, and antibodies from the mother, do pass through the placenta to the embryo.

During this period, the inner mass of the new organism differentiates into three layers: the ectoderm, the mesoderm, and the endoderm. It is from the *ectoderm* that the hair, nails, parts of the teeth, the outer layer of the skin and skin glands, and the sensory cells and the nervous system develop. The muscles, skeleton, the circulatory and excretory systems, and the inner skin layer evolve from the *mesoderm,* and from the *endoderm* come the gastrointestinal tract, the trachea, bronchia, eustachian tubes, glands, and vital organs such as the lungs, pancreas, and liver. The especially rapid development and differentiation that occurs at this time makes the embryo more susceptible during this period than any other to environmental assault, and as a result it is the period when most gross congenital anomalies occur. For example, about the fourth or fifth week of gestation the *neural folds* (formations that evolve ultimately into the central nervous system) begin to close; if something occurs to prevent them from closing completely, the child will have *spina bifida,* a disorder in which the spinal cord and the membranes that protect it may protrude from the spinal column (Corner, 1961, p. 14).

By the end of the period of the embryo, the growing organism's face and features are delineated, and fingers, toes, and external genitalia are present. Even at 6 weeks the embryo is recognizable as a human being, although a rather strangely

embryo The developing organism between the second and eighth week of gestation; the period of the embryo comprises the differentiation of the major physiological structures and systems.

amniotic sac A membrane containing a watery fluid that encloses the developing organism, protecting it from physical shocks and temperature changes.

placenta A fleshy, disclike structure formed by cells from the lining of the uterus and from the zygote, and that, together with the *umbilical cord,* serves to protect and sustain the life of the growing organism.

umbilical cord A tube that contains blood vessels going between the growing organism and its mother by way of the *placenta*; carries oxygen and nutrients to the growing infant and removes carbon dioxide and waste products.

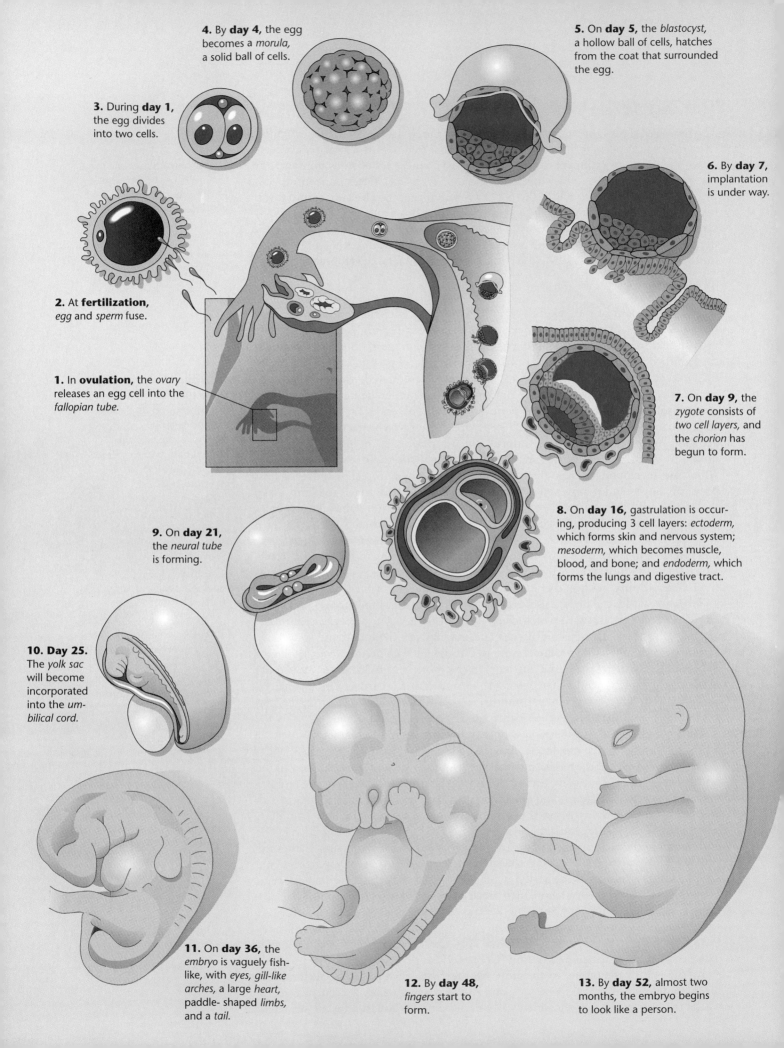

4. By **day 4,** the egg becomes a *morula*, a solid ball of cells.

5. On **day 5,** the *blastocyst*, a hollow ball of cells, hatches from the coat that surrounded the egg.

3. During **day 1,** the egg divides into two cells.

6. By **day 7,** implantation is under way.

2. At **fertilization**, *egg* and *sperm* fuse.

1. In **ovulation**, the *ovary* releases an egg cell into the *fallopian tube.*

7. On **day 9,** the *zygote* consists of *two cell layers,* and the *chorion* has begun to form.

8. On **day 16,** gastrulation is occurring, producing 3 cell layers: *ectoderm,* which forms skin and nervous system; *mesoderm,* which becomes muscle, blood, and bone; and *endoderm,* which forms the lungs and digestive tract.

9. On **day 21,** the *neural tube* is forming.

10. Day 25. The *yolk sac* will become incorporated into the *umbilical cord.*

11. On **day 36,** the *embryo* is vaguely fish-like, with *eyes, gill-like arches,* a large *heart,* paddle- shaped *limbs,* and a *tail.*

12. By **day 48,** *fingers* start to form.

13. By **day 52,** almost two months, the embryo begins to look like a person.

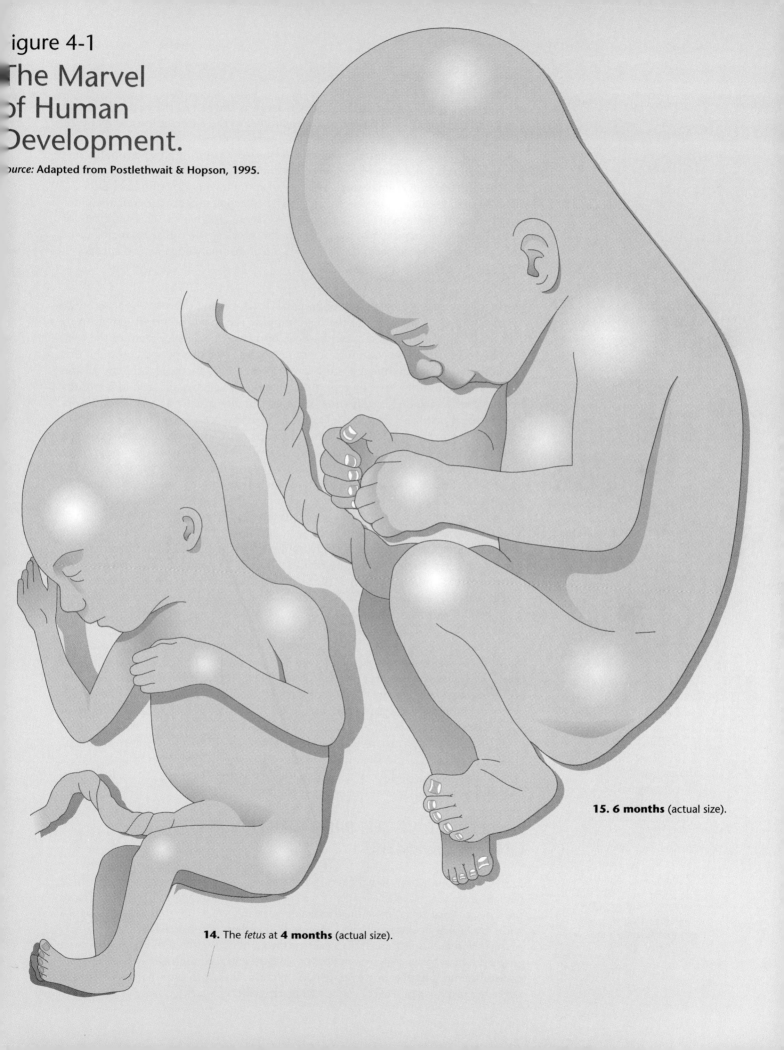

Figure 4-1

The Marvel of Human Development.

Source: Adapted from Postlethwait & Hopson, 1995.

15. 6 months (actual size).

14. The *fetus* at **4 months** (actual size).

proportioned one for the head is almost as large as the rest of the body. Primitive functioning of the heart and liver, as well as waves of the contractile movements of ingestion, have been reported late in this period.

Most *miscarriages*, or spontaneous abortions, occur during this period; for one reason or another the embryo becomes detached from the wall of the uterus and is expelled through the vaginal canal. The rate of spontaneous abortion has been estimated as high as one in four pregnancies, but many such miscarriages remain undetected because they occur in the first few weeks of pregnancy. This high rate of natural abortion may be advantageous to the species, for the great majority of embryos aborted in this manner have gross chromosomal and genetic disorders.

The Fetus

During the third and final period of prenatal development, the **fetus**—the term for the developing organism from the beginning of the third month of gestation to delivery—experiences rapid muscular development. The development of the central nervous system also continues at a rapid pace during this period, although this development is not completed until several years after birth. By the end of the fourth month, mothers usually report movement of the fetus. At around 5 months reflexes such as sucking, swallowing, and hiccoughing usually appear. In addition, a *Babinski reflex,* or a fanning of the toes in response to stroking of the foot, occurs. After the fifth month, the fetus develops nails and sweat glands, a coarser, more adultlike skin, and a soft hair, called **lanugo,** which covers the body. Most fetuses shed this hair in utero, but some continue to shed it after birth. By 6 months the eyes have developed and can open and close. If an infant is born prematurely at 6 months, the regulatory processes and nervous and respiratory systems are usually not mature enough for survival without intensive intervention. At this time the fetus cannot produce and maintain an adequate amount of *surfactant,* a liquid that allows the lungs to transmit oxygen from the air to the blood. Without surfactant, infants are often unable to breathe adequately, and they may develop **respiratory distress syndrome,** a condition of the newborn marked by labored breathing and a bluish discoloration of the skin or mucous membranes. This syndrome, which is often heralded by such symptoms as flaring nostrils and a gruntlike sound on expiration, can result in death.

The age of 28 weeks (about 6-1/2 months), sometimes referred to as the **age of viability,** is an important point in fetal development, because by this time the fetus's physical systems are sufficiently advanced so that if born prematurely, the child has a reasonable probability of surviving. With the exceptional resources available in modern intensive-care nurseries, infants as immature as 25 weeks can sometimes live. Notice in this chapter's Turning Points chart (pp. 108–109), however, that many systems are still developing; the respiratory system in particular continues to evolve into the ninth month of gestation. Not uncommonly, babies born before 28 weeks display developmental deviations later on, especially if they encounter other, adverse environmental conditions.

THE EFFECT OF THE PRENATAL ENVIRONMENT ON DEVELOPMENT

During the course of prenatal development, many agents may cause developmental deviations in the fetus. These agents are called **teratogens,** a term that derives from the Greek word *teras,* meaning "monster" or "marvel." Teratogens encompass a wide variety of agents, including maternal age, diet, emotional state, and illness; prescription and nonprescription medications and drugs given to the mother; and environmental toxins, such as pollution. As you can see, teratogens are essentially environmental factors; however, genetic factors within the mother or child will affect the response of each to any given teratogenic agent.

fetus The developing organism from the third month of gestation through delivery; during the fetal period development of bodily structures and systems becomes complete.

lanugo A fine, soft hair that covers the fetus's body from about the fifth month of gestation on; may be shed before birth or after.

respiratory distress syndrome A condition of the newborn marked by labored breathing and a bluish discoloration of the skin or mucous membranes and which often leads to death.

age of viability The age of 28 weeks from conception, by which point the fetus's physical systems are well enough advanced that it has a chance at survival if born prematurely.

teratogen An environmental agent, such as a drug, medication, dietary imbalance, or polluting substance, that may cause developmental deviations in a growing human organism; most threatening in the embryonic stage but capable of causing abnormalities in the fetal stage as well.

In considering the effects of adverse prenatal and childbirth factors on development we often tend to concentrate on the resulting gross physical defects or mental impairments that sometimes result. However, an equally important issue is how these factors change the life experiences of the child and the responses of those around the child. How does a parent with a child at risk because of prematurity treat the baby? How is the emotional bond that usually forms between parent and child affected by an infant's being kept longer in the hospital because of prematurity, low birthweight, or other physical problems? Is the parent more anxious, or more protective? Or may the parent sometimes even reject the child? What happens to parent-child interaction if the infant is lethargic and unresponsive because of drugs administered during its delivery? Experiential factors like these may ultimately be the most important in sustaining or minimizing the long-term effects of early adversity.

Before we begin to explore some of the many possible threats to the health of the fetus or newborn, let us consider some general principles that guide the effects of teratogens on prenatal development (Moore, 1989; Vorhees & Mollnow, 1987).

1. *A teratogen exerts its effects largely during critical periods.* The effects of a teratogen vary with the developmental stage of the embryo. As we've said and as Figure 4-2 shows, it is during the embryonic stage that the organism is most vulnerable to assault; teratogens acting on newly differentiated cells may damage developing but yet unformed organ systems. Moreover, each organ system, developing at its own pace, has a different critical period (Little, 1992). For example, the most vulnerable period for the heart is between 20 and 40 days of life (Moore, 1989; Tuchmann-Deuplessis, 1965). During the fetal stage, teratogen-induced abnormalities tend to occur only in locations or systems that are still maturing, such as the central nervous system and the genitalia (Clegg, 1971).

2. *Each teratogen exerts certain specific effects.* Because individual teratogens influence specific developmental processes, they produce specific patterns of developmental deviations. For example, *rubella,* or German measles, in the mother affects mainly the fetus's heart, eyes, and brain. The drug thalidomide (which we discuss later) causes primarily malformations of the limbs.

3. *Either maternal or fetal genotypes may counteract a teratogen's effects.* Both maternal and fetal genotypes can affect the developing organism's response to teratogenic agents and may play an important role in whether offspring will display abnormalities. For example, not all pregnant women who have German measles or poor diets produce defective infants. Infants who develop disabilities or defects may do so because of their own genetic vulnerability or that of their mothers to a particular teratogen.

4. *The effects of one teratogen may intensify the effects of another.* The physiological status of the mother will influence the action of a teratogen. Factors such as nutrition and hormonal balance may modify the impact of a teratogen. For example, nutritional deficiencies, which may interfere with healthy prenatal development, may also intensify adverse effects to the fetus of drugs that the mother has ingested, such as cortisone.

5. *A particular teratogen may affect the fetus but have no discernible effect on the mother.* Levels of teratogenic agents that will produce malformations in the offspring may have no appreciable detrimental effects on the mother. Thus although the mother may take drugs, experience disease or irradiation, and maintain a deficient diet without visible ill effect, her child may exhibit gross abnormalities.

6. *A particular teratogen may produce a variety of deviations, whereas several different teratogens may produce the same deviation.* For example, if the mother contracts rubella early in her pregnancy, her child risks deafness. However, not only maternal rubella but also the mother's ingestion of drugs such as quinine or streptomycin may cause deafness in her infant.

TURNING POINTS: An Overview of Prenatal Development

Month	Size & Weight	Nervous & Sensory Systems	Cardiovascular & Respiratory Systems	Musculo-Skeletal & Dermal Systems	Digestive & Urinary Systems	Endocrine & Reproductive Systems	Other Events
1 (Zygote / Embryo)	0.2 in. .007 oz	Neural tube (B) Eyes, ears (B)	Heartbeat (B) Trachea and lungs (B)		Intestinal tract, liver, pancreas (B)		
2 (Embryo)	1.1 in. .09 oz	Nervous system organization, growth of cerebrum (B) Taste buds, olfactory system (B)	Heart structure, major blood vessels, lymph nodes (B) Blood formation in liver (B) Bronchial branching (B) Diaphragm (C)	Cartilage formation (B) Muscles that support central portion of body framed (C)	Intestinal subdivisions including salivary glands (B) Kidney formation (B)	Thyroid, pituitary, adrenal glands (B) Mammary glands (B)	
3	3.2 in. 1.6 oz	Basic spinal cord & brain structure (C)	Tonsils; blood formation in bone marrow (B)	Cartilage replaced with bone (B) Muscles that support appendages (e.g., legs, arms) formed (C) Skeleton visible in X rays by 14 weeks	Gallbladder, pancreas (C)	Genitalia (B) Differentiation of gonads into ovaries and testes	Fetus responds to stimulation Form is recognizably human Mother's abdomen visibly distended Mother can feel baby's movements
4	5.3 in. 5 oz	Rapid expansion of cerebrum (B) Eye & ear structure complete (C)	Blood formation in spleen (B) Lymphocytes migrate to lymphatic organs (B)	Lanugo & head hair form (B) Skin thin, wrinkled, translucent Sweat glands (C)		Genitalia distinct by 16 weeks	
5	8 in. 17 oz	Myelination of spinal cord (B)	Nostrils open (C)	Adultlike skin Eyelashes & eyebrows Nail production (B)	Intestinal subdivisions (C)		Fetus sucks, swallows, & hiccoughs Evidence of Babinski & grasping reflexes

First trimester: Months 1–3

Second trimester: Months 4–5

TURNING POINTS: An Overview of Prenatal Development (*continued*)

Month	Size & Weight	Nervous & Sensory Systems	Cardiovascular & Respiratory Systems	Musculo-Skeletal & Dermal Systems	Digestive & Urinary Systems	Endocrine & Reproductive Systems	Other Events
6 *(Fetus)*	11.2 in. 1 lb, 10 oz	CNS tract formation; layering of cerebral cortex (B)	Spleen, liver, & bone marrow (C) Formation of lung alveoli (B)	Perineal (sphincter) muscles (C)		Adrenal glands (C)	Survival outside womb relatively rare
7 *(Third trimester)*	14–15 in. 2 lb, 11 oz	Eyelids open; retina sensitive to light		Nail & hair formation (B)		Pituitary gland (C) Descent of testes into scrotum (B)	Survival outside womb not uncommon Rapid weight gain begins Sensitivity to sounds
8 *(Third trimester)*	15–17 in. 4 lb, 6 oz	Taste receptors become functional	Pulmonary branching and alveolar formation (C)		Kidney structure (C)		
9 *(Third trimester)*	19–21 in. 6 lb, 10 oz to 7 lb, 10 oz					Descent of testes complete at or near time of delivery	Normal birth
Postnatal development		CNS tract formation continues	Immune system becomes operative	Hair changes in consistency and distribution Skeletal growth continues Muscle mass and control increase			

Sources: Based on Fisher & Lazarson, 1984; Martini, 1995.

Key: B = Begins to form
C = Completes formation

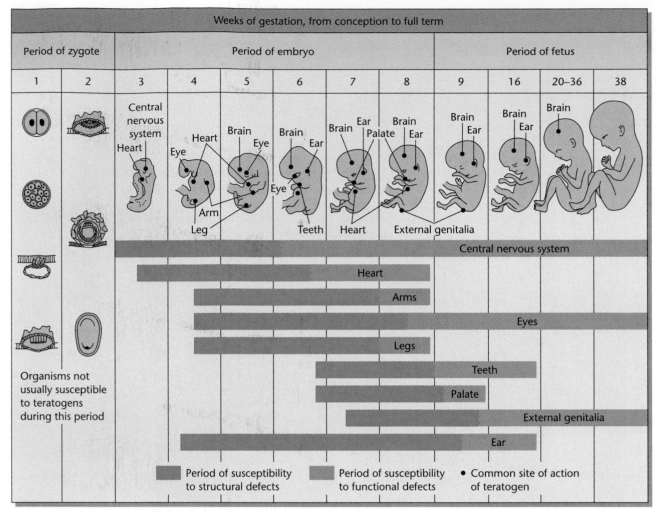

■ FIGURE 4-2
The child's prenatal susceptibility to teratogenic agents.
Sensitivity of the growing embryo to teratogens is greatest in the first 4 to 8 weeks of gestation, peaking about the fifth week. Normally, the zygote is not susceptible to specific teratogens, but if it does succumb to a teratogenic agent, its tiny mass is usually so defenseless that it dies. The defects that occur early in development, when critical organs are being formed, are generally structural; teratogenic agents that impinge on the fetus in later weeks are more likely to stunt its growth or cause functional problems. (*Source:* Adapted from Moore, 1989)

7. *The longer a fetus is exposed to a particular teratogen and the greater the intensity of the teratogen's effects, the more likely it is that the fetus will be seriously harmed.*

Maternal Characteristics

For the fetus, all teratogenic agents or their influences are mediated by the mother's body; however, some factors are directly related to characteristics of the mother herself. In this section we discuss how a mother's age, choice of diet, and emotional state may affect her unborn child. In the next section we will explore the diseases and disorders that may also have a negative impact on a developing fetus. As you read on you may find it useful to look at Table 4-1, which gives an overview of this material.

Age and Parity

A woman's age and *parity*, or the number of children she has already borne, may interact in influencing the development of her fetus. Women who have their first child when they are under 15 or over 35 are likely to experience more problems during pregnancy and complications during delivery than other women. In the past this was attributed either to the immaturity of the reproductive system in teenagers or the deterioration in the reproductive system in older mothers. It is now recognized, however, that these risks in both groups are more closely associated with maternal health than with age.

Teenage mothers tend to encounter greater risks to their health and the health of their infants because they are often of low socioeconomic status and thus suffer

TABLE 4-1 Maternal Characteristics, Diseases, and Disorders That Can Have a Negative Impact on Prenatal Development

Potential Negative Effects

Characteristics of the Mother

Age	Teenage mothers tend to live in risky environments, to neglect their health and diets, and to use drugs, thus risking premature and low-birthweight babies; older mothers risk bearing a Down syndrome child as well as problems posed by illnesses that are more common as people age.
Diet	Malnourishment can lead to miscarriage, stillbirths, prematurity, low birthweight, physical and neural defects, smaller size in newborns, and sometimes cognitive difficulties.
Emotional state	Mothers who are stressed may have more-troubled pregnancies, miscarriages, long labor and delivery complications, and more need for childbirth anesthesia; their infants may be hyperactive and irritable and have feedings and sleep problems.

Diseases and Disorders

Mumps	Infant may suffer malformation of some kind.
Rubella (German measles)	Infant may be born deaf or mentally retarded or have cardiac disorders or cataract formation.
Rh factor incompatibility	If mother's and infant's blood types are incompatible (mother's negative, infant's positive), on second and subsequent pregnancies antibodies produced by mother's blood can kill the fetus.
Hypertension (high blood pressure)	Fetal abnormalities, miscarriage, fetal death.
Diabetes	Preeclampsia or eclampsia, associated with hypertension; possible stillbirth or death of newborn.
Gonorrhea	Infant may be infected in the birth canal.
Syphilis	Miscarriage; if infant survives it may be born blind, mentally retarded, or have other physical abnormalities.
Chlamydia	Miscarriage or stillbirth; surviving infant may acquire disease in birth process, or develop pneumonia or a form of conjunctivitis.
Genital herpes	Infected infant may be blind, mentally retarded, or have motor abnormalities or a wide range of neurological disorders. Half of surviving infants are seriously disabled.
Acquired immune deficiency syndrome (AIDS)	Infants infected often suffer neurological impairments, defects in mental and physical development, microcephaly (small head), and other physical abnormalities. Infants survive an average of nine months; three-fourths are dead within two years.

from poor nutrition and a lack of prenatal care. Moreover, they tend to live in environments characterized by high rates of disease and environmental pollutants. One study of such young mothers, more than two-thirds from minority groups, showed that postnatally their children were at risk for delays in developing intellectual, language, and social skills (Sommer, Keogh, & Whitman, 1995). Another study of young mothers of similar backgrounds found that a mother's "cognitive readiness" for parenting—defined as knowledge of child development, parenting style preferences, and parenting attitudes—significantly affected her child's tendencies to develop anxiety and depression and to exhibit aggressive behavior (Miller, Heysek, & Whitman, 1995). Other studies have shown that because teenagers are more likely to have unhealthy personal habits, such as the use or abuse of drugs, they are more likely to have pregnancy complications like *toxemia* (a condition that results from the spread of bacterial products in the bloodstream) and to bear infants with lower birthweights (Smith, 1994). In addition, the failure of many teenagers to seek formal prenatal care contributes to the relatively high rate of infant mortality in the United States (see Box 4-1).

BOX 4-1

Perspectives on Diversity

Prenatal Health Care and Infant Mortality

It seems astonishing that more babies die at or soon after birth in the United States than in 15 countries of western Europe, 6 countries of Asia and the Pacific Rim, and Canada (Grant, 1993). After all, U.S. medicine and technology lead the world. Why, then, are our infant mortality rates so high? The answer is tied in large part to our less than adequate provision of prenatal health care to pregnant women (Wegman, 1993).

In any 1 of 10 western European countries—Belgium, Denmark, England, France, Germany, Ireland, Netherlands, Norway, Spain, and Switzerland—pregnant women automatically receive prenatal and postnatal care that costs very little, because it is supported by their governments, as well as paid maternity leave from work that ranges from 9 to 40 weeks. (These services vary within the countries cited.) Even in developing countries, between 1985 and 1991 many advances were made in the provision of prenatal care: Research revealed about 35 percent improvement for these countries overall and about 17 percent for the least developed of this group of nations (World Health Organization, 1993).

Many pregnant women in the United States face a difficult situation. There are no uniform national standards to guarantee them consistent high-quality maternity care or, equally important, financial coverage. Nationwide, at least 1.3 million U.S. women receive insufficient prenatal care each year, and many of these women are those who need this care most (Healy, 1995; Wymelenberg, 1990). The groups least likely to receive care are teens, the unmarried, the poor, the less educated, recent immigrants, and minorities (African Americans, Latinos, and American Indians). It is these women who are at greatest risk of bearing babies with complications such as prematurity and low birthweight.

The data also reveal clear distinctions among racial-ethnic groups, with those at the lowest rung of the socioeconomic ladder receiving the least adequate care. As you can see from Figure 4-3, Cuban, Japanese, and Chinese American mothers are more likely to get first-trimester prenatal care and less likely to go without such care or to seek it only in the third trimester than women in all other groups. European Americans and Filipino Americans follow closely behind these three groups. There is a sharp break between these women and those of Hawaiian, Latino, African, and Native American origin; these groups of women are the least likely to get early prenatal care and the most likely to seek it late or not at all. African Americans, Mexican Americans, Native Americans, and Central and South Americans receive the least prenatal care. Latinos, who may come from any Spanish or Portuguese-speaking country in the Western Hemisphere, are the fastest growing minority in the United States, and they are also among the most seriously affected by poverty, unemployment or underemployment, lack of health insurance, and inadequate education (Council on Scientific Affairs, 1991).

According to Young and her colleagues (Young, McMahon, Bowman, & Thompson, 1989), other reasons why women do not seek prenatal care include motivational problems and multiple social problems. For example, in one study African American women in particular reported problems with scheduling and keeping appointments for prenatal care as a reason for delaying such care, whereas European Americans often noted that they didn't feel they needed prenatal care. Scheduling difficulties were more often cited by women under 20 than older women. Among social problems, those most often cited were unemployment (presumably implying lack of money), being a single parent (perhaps time and money), psychological stress, interpersonal conflicts with the father of the baby, and family crises. Another reason may be women's fear and/or dislike of doctors (Kotelchuck, 1995).

Young and her associates also found that their participants often tended to deny the symptoms of pregnancy and to be reluctant to assume the role of expectant mother. A majority of participants were single mothers with infants and toddlers, and many lacked social support. Research findings on the effect of social support on women's seeking prenatal care, however, seem to indicate that such support may not guarantee that a woman will seek medical help and guidance. In one study, researchers found living with a husband or partner was more likely to impel a woman to seek prenatal care than having access to a supportive network (Casper & Hogan, 1990). Another group of researchers found that women who were enclosed within strong, mostly familial networks were less likely to seek prenatal care (St. Clair, Smeriglio, Alexander, & Celentano, 1989).

Within the United States the rates of infant (both fetal and neonatal) deaths have generally declined since 1960, but over the years the rates for African American infants have remained about twice those for European Americans. For example, in 1993, all infant deaths among European Americans totaled 6.8 per 1,000 live births (0.7%), but among African Americans there were 14.1 per 1,000 live births (1.4%).

What can we do about this situation? The resistance in the United States to national health standards and/or a national health-care system has been monumental. As a result of this resistance and of the marked discrepancy between the wealthy and poor sectors of the population, a large group of poor mothers either have no access to prenatal care or do not take advantage of opportunities they do have. In view of the costs, both emotional and financial, of high infant mortality and high rates of premature and handicapped infants, it is important to make prenatal services widely available to women of all racial, ethnic, and socioeconomic groups.

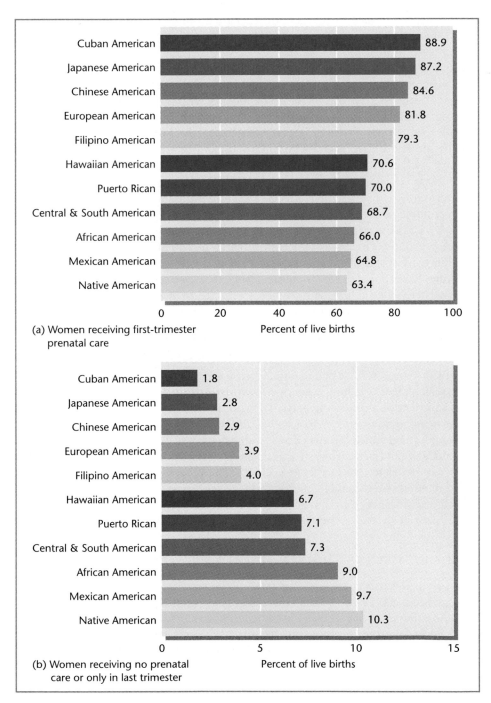

(a) Women receiving first-trimester prenatal care

(b) Women receiving no prenatal care or only in last trimester

■ FIGURE 4-3
Inequities in care for pregnant women in the United States, 1993.
The discrepancies between the best and least prenatal care given to expectant mothers in different U.S. racial-ethnic groups have been very great. For example, in 1993, Cuban American mothers were likely to receive 33 percent more care in the first trimester than were Native American women (a), and conversely, pregnant Native American women were five times more likely than Cuban American women to receive no care at all or only in the third trimester (b). (*Source:* U.S. Department of Health and Human Services, May 1996)

When teenage mothers have adequate diets and prenatal care they do not show higher rates of complications in birth or pregnancy than mothers in their twenties (Brooks-Gunn & Chase-Lansdale, 1995; Smith, 1994). Among older mothers, rather than age per se, it is emerging health risks, such as an increase in hypertension, diabetes, alcoholism, and other health problems, that contribute to difficulties in pregnancy and birth. Thus, except for the threat of bearing a Down syndrome child (Chapter 3), healthy mothers over 35 are unlikely to have serious complications (Spellacy, Miller, & Winegar, 1986).

Choice of Diet

It is difficult to separate the effects of maternal malnourishment from those of a variety of other deleterious factors. The mother who is malnourished often exists in an environment of poverty and disadvantage characterized by poor education, inferior sanitation and shelter, and inadequate medical care. In the United States, malnutrition and high maternal and infant mortality are associated not only with negative socioeconomic factors but with ethnicity. People who are both nonwhite and poor are exposed to more of these harmful environmental factors and experience more of their destructive effects. U.S. nonwhites tend to be less affluent, to begin childbearing early and to end it later, and to have poorer diets and poorer prenatal and delivery care. In addition, unwed mothers are more likely to be from minority groups. The environment of poverty to which the new mother returns with her baby sustains and compounds all of these effects.

Studies have shown that gross dietary deficiencies, especially of some vitamins and proteins, in the diets of pregnant women are related to increased rates of miscarriage, stillbirths, and infant mortality, and that such deficiencies are more likely to lead to prematurity, physical and neural defects, and smaller size in neonates (Kirksey & Wasynczuk, 1993; Sigman, 1995). Studies of severely malnourished animals and infants suggest that early malnutrition may interfere with the development of the nervous system. Again we find that the specific form the damage takes depends on the age at which the threatening event or condition—in this case, malnutrition—occurs.

Impairment of a child's intellectual development that is associated with prenatal malnutrition appears most marked when the mother's malnutrition has been severe and long lasting, and when the effects of this dietary deprivation are sustained after childbirth by adverse nutritional, social, and economic factors (Sigman, 1995). Thus a network of deleterious factors associated with prenatal malnutrition leads to continued ill effects on the child. Studies of short-term periods of famine attributable to such things as war suggest that no long-lasting intellectual deficits are found in children if previously well-nourished mothers go through a temporary period of malnourishment during pregnancy and if the child has a reasonably good diet and responsive caretakers following birth (Stein & Susser, 1976). On the other hand, studies of the impact of a drought in Kenya found that school-age children who suffered the worst malnutrition showed decreased playground activity, social involvement, and classroom attentiveness (McDonald, Sigman, Espinosa, & Neumann, 1994).

Although it has been generally assumed that malnutrition had its greatest impact on social and motor development (Riciutti, 1993), a number of researchers have found that cognitive abilities are affected by poor nutrition as well (Grantham-McGregor, Powell, Walker, & Hines, 1991; Pollitt, Gorman, & Metallinos-Katsaras, 1992; Rose, 1994; Sigman, 1995). Thus cognitive or academic difficulties may not necessarily be the result of biological changes in the brain but may be linked instead with the sequelae of malnutrition—lowered energy, inattention, and lack of motivation and responsiveness. Nutrition supplement studies in Jamaica, Indonesia, and Colombia found that both motor and cognitive abilities improved when infants were given enriched diets (Grantham-McGregor et al., 1991).

Finally, the effects of prenatal malnutrition on an infant may be compounded if tired, malnourished parents respond to their irritable or nonresponsive malnourished infants with lack of support or rejection (Lozoff, 1989). For this reason, besides providing dietary supplements for malnourished families of low socioeconomic status, many successful intervention programs have focused on training economically deprived parents to interact with their children in a more sensitive, involved, and stimulating manner (Grantham-McGregor et al., 1994; Ramey & Campbell, 1992).

Emotional State

The emotional state of the mother during pregnancy may have adverse effects on the fetus and newborn (Parker & Barrett, 1992). Emotional characteristics may be transmitted genetically. A pregnant woman's emotionality may induce metabolic or biochemical changes that affect the fetus, and a woman who is emotionally disturbed during pregnancy may be emotionally unstable after childbirth and bring inadequate caretaking skills to her important role as the main socializing influence on her baby. Thus, in the findings of the studies we discuss next, genetic or prenatal factors or early infant learning and experiences could all have played a role.

Studies have found that women who suffer sustained emotional distress tend to experience complications during both pregnancy and delivery. Some of these difficulties include nausea during pregnancy, premature delivery, spontaneous abortion, prolonged labor, delivery complications, and greater need for anesthesia during childbirth (Katz, Jenkins, Haley, & Bowes, 1991; Parker & Barrett, 1992). Predictably, such difficulties are more common among women who have been diagnosed as having formal, psychiatric disorders, but the severity of the disorder rather than a specific classification is the major determinant of perinatal and obstetrical outcomes (Sameroff & Zax, 1973).

Women who are anxious and under emotional stress during pregnancy tend to have infants who are physically more active in utero. After their birth, these infants tend to be hyperactive and irritable, to cry more, and to have feeding and sleep problems (Van Den Bergh, 1992). Stresses during pregnancy can encompass a wide array of problems, such as marital discord, disagreement about whether to continue the pregnancy, moving to a new locality, and illness and death in relatives. A woman's emotional distress during pregnancy may be of a temporary nature, or it may signal ongoing difficulties. Women who have positive attitudes toward their pregnancies typically have enjoyed happy childhoods and close family relationships and regard themselves as having satisfying marital, sexual, and social relationships. The reverse is true of women whose attitudes toward pregnancy are negative. In the latter case, fear and distress during pregnancy may be part of a broader pattern of maladjustment, and this pattern of disturbance may be continued later in these women's handling of their infants.

Interestingly, the effects of stress may be moderated by the support available to a pregnant woman. One study found that when pregnant women were going through severe life stresses, those with supportive relatives and friends had only a 33 percent rate of complications in pregnancy and childbirth in comparison to a 91 percent rate for women lacking in social support (Nickolls, Cassel, & Kaplan, 1972). Another study demonstrated the effects on labor and delivery of the actual presence of a supportive companion (Sosa, Kennell, Klaus, Robertson, & Urrutia, 1980). These researchers studied the childbirth experiences of healthy Guatemalan women. The women in the experimental group were assigned a *doula,* a supportive female companion who talked to them, reassured them, rubbed their backs, and held their hands until delivery. The control group went through the normal hospital routine with no supportive person present. The mean length of labor was 19.3 hours for the control group and 8.7 hours for the women who had supportive companions. The latter women also had fewer complications such as the need for cesarean sections, and their infants were less likely to experience fetal distress. Similar beneficial effects of having a trained, supportive companion have been found for women having babies in U.S. hospitals (Kennell, Klaus, McGrath, Robertson, & Hinckley, 1991).

In the United States in the mid-1970s, hospitals began allowing the husbands of pregnant women to be present, first, during their wives' labor and then during delivery itself. Researchers have found that, in general, fathers' presence during labor and delivery has a beneficial effect on mothers, particularly in reducing their felt pain and their needs for medication and in making their view of the birth experience more positive (Entwisle & Doering, 1981; Lindell, 1988; Parke, 1996). Moreover, fathers can play a special role in the delivery room: Because they have just one job they can be a continuous source of support to their wives (Parke, 1996).

On the other hand, it has also been found that the presence of the father alone may be less effective in reducing the need for cesarean deliveries than the presence of both the father and a support figure (Kennell & McGrath, 1993). Father's presence may thus be helpful, but dads may need more training and support if they are to realize their full potential as labor partners. At the same time, being present may benefit fathers themselves. For example, more fathers than mothers get to hold the baby while still in the delivery room, and many fathers have expressed high levels of emotional pleasure during this experience (Entwisle & Doering, 1981; Mosedale, 1991). One elated father remembered being "as joyful as I've ever been in my life. . . . [It was] the greatest experience of anything I've ever done."

Diseases and Disorders

A wide range of maternal diseases and disorders can affect an infant's development either prenatally or during the birth process. Like the effects of other teratogenic agents, the effects of these disorders are often mediated by their appearance at a critical time. For example, if the pregnant woman contracts the viral disease of *mumps* during her first trimester, her infant is much more likely to suffer some kind of malformation than if she were to contract the disease later in her pregnancy. Similarly, if a woman contracts *rubella* during the first month of her pregnancy, even if the attack is a mild one her fetus risks cardiac disorders, cataract formation, deafness, and mental retardation (Cochi et al., 1989). If she contracts this illness in her third month, however, the likelihood that her infant will suffer disability declines from 50 percent to 17 percent, and after the third month, there is virtually no chance of fetal abnormality.

Timing is also an issue in the potentially life-threatening condition of **Rh factor incompatibility,** in which an infant's blood is Rh positive (Rh+) whereas its mother's blood is Rh negative (Rh−). (Rh factors are antigens, or substances in the blood that can induce specific immune responses.) Because positive and negative blood types are incompatible, if by some chance fetal and maternal blood should commingle (as we've said, normally they do not), the mother's blood could produce antibodies that would attack the fetal blood cells, bringing about the death of the fetus. Because such antibodies are scarce in a woman who is pregnant for the first

Rh factor incompatibility A condition in which an infant's Rh negative blood opposes its mother's Rh positive blood and threatens fetuses in second, third, and later births when the mother's body has had time to produce antibodies that will attack fetal blood cells.

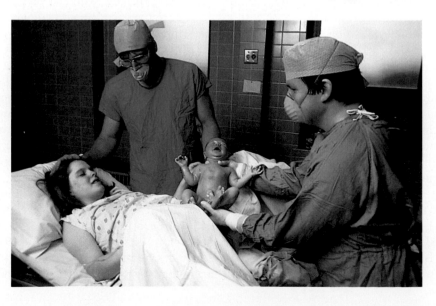

More and more fathers are electing to be in the delivery room these days, and many couples report their shared experience of the birth of a child as one of great joy and happiness.

time, Rh incompatibility is not an issue during a first birth. To prevent it from ever becoming an issue, Rh immune globulin can be administered to the mother after the birth of each child to prevent antibody formation and ensure the birth of other healthy children (Turner & Rubinson, 1993).

A number of other maternal conditions may increase rates of fetal abnormalities, miscarriage, and death. In the case of *hypertension,* also known as high blood pressure, the higher the mother's blood pressure, the greater the likelihood of prenatal complications. Women who suffer from *diabetes* face the possibility of delivering a stillborn child or a baby who will die shortly after birth. Diabetic women also have a greater chance of developing *preeclampsia* or, in its more serious form, *eclampsia* (also known as *toxemia of pregnancy*), which has such symptoms as very high blood pressure and excessive weight gain. Untreated, the condition can lead to death of the mother (10%–15% of cases), the child (50%), or both. Despite these rather alarming statistics, when diabetic mothers receive special care during their pregnancies, their babies have an 85 percent chance of survival.

The other maternal disorders that can affect the infant adversely are generally considered sexually transmitted diseases. In most cases contracted through sexual intercourse, these include gonorrhea, syphilis, chlamydia-pelvic inflammatory disease, herpes, and HIV/AIDS. Note that AIDS can be transmitted also by infected blood or by infected needles used in blood transfusions, in treating *hemophilia* (a disease in which the absence of a clotting factor leads to excessive bleeding), or in illegal drug ingestion. We may subdivide these illnesses according to whether they're caused by bacterial or viral infections.

Bacterial Infections

Gonorrhea, which is spread for the most part by direct sexual contact with an infected person, can usually be treated with antibiotics. Left untreated, however, it can cause cardiovascular difficulties, arthritis, sterility, and, in women, *pelvic inflammatory disease,* which itself can cause an *ectopic,* or tubal, pregnancy. In an ectopic pregnancy, the zygote implants in the woman's fallopian tube rather than in her uterus, and to save the mother's life the pregnancy must be terminated (Turner & Rubinson, 1993). Although gonorrhea in the mother can be transmitted prenatally, most commonly an infant is infected as it passes through the birth canal. If not treated, the disease can cause blindness; for this reason, in most hospitals in the United States, a few drops of silver nitrate or penicillin are placed in the eyes of newborns to prevent infection.

Some chronic infections invade the developing embryo and remain active but do not exert their worst effects until later stages of development. For example, the deleterious effects on the fetus of maternal **syphilis** do not occur before 18 weeks of gestation, and therefore early treatment of a syphilitic mother may avert abnormalities in the child. If the mother is untreated, however, invasion of the fetus by bacteria from the mother may result in spontaneous abortion, blindness, mental retardation, or other physical abnormalities. Moreover, in some cases the negative effects of syphilis are not apparent even at birth but emerge gradually during the early years of development. In this case they are expressed in the form of deterioration in thought processes, judgment, and speech; in a decline in motor and mental abilities; and, eventually, in death. Although years ago syphilis was virtually a death sentence, today if it is detected and treated early with antibiotics, it can be cured.

Although less well known, **chlamydia** is probably the most widespread bacterial infection among sexually transmitted diseases. Babies born to women with this infection often acquire it in the birth process and may develop pneumonia or a form of conjunctivitis. Mothers with chlamydia also risk spontaneous abortion and stillbirth. In addition, like gonorrhea, chlamydia can lead to pelvic inflammatory disease.

Viral Infections

One of the most common sexually transmitted diseases is **genital herpes,** which is spread primarily through intimate sexual contact. Of the approximately 4 million

gonorrhea   A sexually transmitted bacterial infection that, in a pregnant woman, can cause blindness in her infant; normally treatable with antibiotics.

syphilis   A sexually transmitted bacterial disease that today can usually be treated with antibiotics but that untreated in the pregnant woman can lead to miscarriage or blindness, mental retardation, or other physical abnormalities in her baby.

chlamydia   Probably the most widespread bacterial sexually transmitted disease; can cause pneumonia or a form of conjunctivitis in a pregnant woman's baby.

genital herpes   A common viral infection spread through sexual contact; if contracted by an infant during birth can cause blindness, motor abnormalities, mental retardation, and a wide range of neurological disorders.

babies born in the United States each year, between 1,500 and 2,200 come into the world infected with herpes (National March of Dimes Foundation, 1996). If a herpes infection is detected in a pregnant woman before labor, a cesarean delivery will usually succeed in preventing the infant from coming in contact with the disease and thus protect it from contagion. Herpes can be transmitted by exposure to the virus after birth, although this occurs less frequently. Because an infant does not have a fully developed immune system before it is 5 weeks old, if it is infected with herpes, the disease can cause blindness, motor abnormalities, mental retardation, and a wide range of neurological disorders. Sixty percent of these babies will die; roughly 90 percent of the babies who survive are left with serious problems, including skin and mouth ulcers, and eye and brain infections. Nearly half have major developmental disorders (Healy, 1995).

Of course, the viral infection that has caused the greatest alarm in recent years is the *human immunodeficiency virus (HIV)* infection and its expression in **acquired immune deficiency syndrome (AIDS).** Although at its first appearance in the United States, in the early 1980s, AIDS was labeled a disease primarily of gay men, gradually it became apparent that the disease affected not only gay and bisexual men but their heterosexual partners, the offspring of these people, drug abusers who shared needles, and the recipients of blood transfusions, where the blood came from infected persons.

In the decade that followed the U.S. debut of AIDS, more than 2,000 cases of childhood AIDS were identified. By mid-1996 more than 7,000 children under 12 years of age had been diagnosed with AIDS, and nearly 6,000 of these were children younger than 5. Another 2,600 cases of adolescent AIDS were reported by 1996 (Centers for Disease Control, 1996; Kalichman, 1996). Most children are infected prenatally—through passage of the virus through the placenta during the birth process—or through the mother's milk. A few contract the disease through blood transfusions, usually for the treatment of hemophilia. About three-quarters of infected pregnant women are intravenous (IV) drug users or the sexual partners of IV drug users (Brooks-Gunn, Boyer, & Hein, 1988; Henggeler, Melton, & Rodrigue, 1992), and an infected pregnant woman has a 15 to 30 percent chance of transmitting the AIDS virus to her child. Recent advances in drug therapy, however, have reduced the likelihood of HIV transmission to newborns by two-thirds; one study found a reduction from 26 to 8 percent (Connor et al., 1994). As most children who develop AIDS are infected from birth, and because the disease progresses more rapidly in children than in adults, some 80 percent of children with AIDS are less than 5 years of age (Centers for Disease Control, 1996). As Figure 4-4 shows, more than half of these children are African American and almost a quarter are Latino. European Americans make up 18 percent; the rest are Asian, Pacific Islander, or Native American (Centers for Disease Control, 1996).

Among children who contract HIV from their mothers, almost 14 percent will be diagnosed with AIDS in their first year, and 11 to 12 percent will be diagnosed each year after that through age 7. On average, AIDS is diagnosed at 4 years of age, and 54 percent of cases are diagnosed by the age of 7 (Whinney, 1993). These children often suffer neurological impairments, delays in mental and physical development, and such structural deformities as *microcephaly,* or an unusually small head, a square forehead, and widely spaced, slanted eyes. Of greater significance, of course, is the fact that AIDS is an autoimmune disease, or one in which the body's immunological forces are disabled and/or attack the body's healthy cells. Thus, it is these children's vulnerability to disease and infections of all sorts that is the cause of their early deaths. Once diagnosed with HIV/AIDS, children survive an average of nine months; three-quarters die within two years. If children are diagnosed before the age of 1 they have an even shorter survival time.

The parents of children with AIDS often have few resources; they are often drug users and both ill and poor. As a result they are frequently unable or unwilling to care for their HIV-infected children. It is very difficult to obtain foster care for such children, but infected children and their families are desperately in need of

---

acquired immune deficiency syndrome (AIDS)   A viral disease that attacks the body's immune systems; transmitted to a fetus or newborn in the form of the *human immunodeficiency virus (HIV)*, this disorder weakens the child's immune system and may ultimately cause its death.

specialized care and support systems. Because at this time we have no cure for AIDS, many experts think that concentrating on preventive efforts, through education and programs aimed at modifying high-risk sexual behavior and drug abuse, is the only effective means of dealing with the problem (Dryfoos, 1994). Unfortunately, most such programs have not been evaluated so we have no idea how successful they may be. Moreover, because they are often school based, they do not serve the groups most vulnerable to AIDS: school dropouts, runaways, prostitutes, juvenile prisoners, and drug users in general (Brooks-

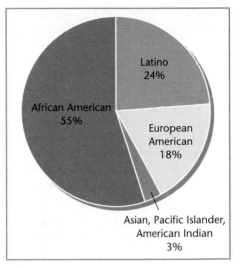

■ FIGURE 4-4
U.S. children under five with AIDS, 1996.
Children in different ethnic and racial groups are at different levels of risks for AIDS. African American children are at highest risk for this disease, whereas Asian and American Indian children are the least likely to be affected with AIDS. *Source:* Based on data from Centers for Disease Control, 1996.

Gunn et al., 1988; Dryfoos, 1994). Clearly, we need more research on the prevention of high-risk behaviors in adolescents and young adults.

Legal and Illegal Drugs

Although most physicians and parents would probably agree that it is not good for pregnant women to take too many drugs, 60 to 80 percent of women take some sort of drug during pregnancy (Schnoll, 1986). According to one source, the average pregnant American woman consumes about 10 different drugs during her pregnancy (Truss, 1981). In this section we discuss the potential effects on the pregnant woman of the drugs people most commonly take for stimulation, tension release, or pleasure: Nicotine, in the form of cigarette smoking, and alcohol are legal drugs; heroin, cocaine, and some others are illegal. In the next section we will consider the potential effects of drugs that are often prescribed by treating physicians as well as the effects of some over-the-counter drugs. Again, in Table 4-2 we provide you with an overview of this section as well as of the next two sections, on medical interventions and environmental toxins.

Nicotine and Alcohol

Despite the efforts of many groups in recent years to convince the public that nicotine and alcohol are just as dangerous and addictive as the so-called hard drugs like heroin and cocaine, people persist in using these substances. Researchers have found that both smoking and drinking are associated with disturbances in placental functioning and with changes in maternal physiology that lead to oxygen deprivation and may produce structural and functional changes in the brain of the fetus (Day & Richardson, 1988; Edmondson, 1994). Nevertheless, it has been estimated that over 80 percent of pregnant women in the United States drink alcohol and over 30 percent smoke.

The rate of abortions, prematurity, and low-birthweight babies is higher for mothers who smoke or drink than for those who do neither (Aaronson & MacNee, 1989). In addition, *sudden infant death syndrome (SIDS),* in which infants under the age of 6 months stop breathing and die, without apparent cause, is more common in the offspring of mothers who smoke, drink, or take narcotic drugs (Stechler & Halton, 1982). Women who are chronic smokers have premature infants almost twice as often as do nonsmokers, and the more a particular woman smokes, the more likely she is to deliver prematurely. Babies born to nonsmokers, whether prematurely or not, are heavier (Meredith, 1975) and less wakeful (Landesman-Dwyer & Sackett, 1983) than smokers' infants.

Recent studies have indicated that passive smoke, that is, the smoking of people in the vicinity of nonsmokers, can also contribute to low birthweight even in babies of mothers who don't smoke (Schwartz-Bickenbach, Sculte-Hobein, Abt,

TABLE 4-2   The Effect of Drugs, Medications, and Environmental Toxins on Prenatal Development

	Potential Negative Effects
Legal Drugs	
Nicotine	Prematurity, low birthweight, delayed intellectual and behavioral development, risk of pneumonia, bronchitis, laryngitis, inner ear infections; fathers' smoking may transmit risk of cancer to offspring
Alcohol	Fetal alcohol syndrome (physical defects, short stature, mental retardation, hyperactivity, stereotyped behaviors, congenital addiction leading to withdrawal syndrome); father's abuse of alcohol may cause genetic damage that leads to birth defects. The combination of parental smoking and drinking may cause miscarriages, prematurity, low birthweight, and sudden infant death syndrome
Illegal Drugs	
Heroin, morphine, methadone	In mother, difficulty conceiving; in infant, prematurity, low birthweight, addiction, withdrawal, death
Marijuana	In mother, difficulty conceiving; in infant, prematurity, low birthweight, high-pitched crying; no long-term effects
Cocaine	In mother, difficulty conceiving; in infant, prematurity, low birthweight; see text for further discussion
Lysergic acid diethylamide (LSD)	Chromosomal breakage
Medications/Treatments	
Diethylstilbestrol (DES)	In mother, miscarriage; in infant, prematurity, low birthweight; female child may develop cancer of the cervix; male child may have reproductive abnormalities and increased risk of testicular cancer
Thalidomide	Deformations of infant's face, limbs, fingers and toes; malformations of heart and digestive and genitourinary tracts; malformations or absence of limbs
Quinine	Deafness in infant
Reserpine (tranquilizer)	Respiratory problems in infant
Tetracyclines	Defective skeletal growth in infant
Aspirin	Blood disorders in infant
Some anticonvulsant medications	Cleft lip and palate in infant; failure of blood coagulation
Anesthetics, local or general; epidural blocks	Short-term depression of infant's responsiveness, disruptions in feeding, behavioral disorganization, impaired attention and motor abilities
Environmental Toxins	
Lead	Miscarriage, anemia, hemorrhage in mother
Methyl mercury	Cerebral palsy in infant
Radiation	In mother, miscarriage, stillbirth; in infant, microcephaly, stunted growth, leukemia, cancer, cataract

fetal alcohol syndrome A disorder exhibited by infants of alcoholic mothers and characterized by stunted growth, a number of physical and physiological abnormalities and, often, mental retardation.

Plum, & Nau, 1987). One study found that if fathers smoked during pregnancy, babies were 3 pounds (88 grams) lighter at birth than babies of nonsmoking fathers (Martinez, Wright, & Taussig, 1994). Other studies have shown that passive smoke can cause delays in intellectual and behavioral development (Rush & Callahan, 1989) and that babies exposed in utero to passive smoke are at increased risk for a variety of illnesses such as pneumonia, bronchitis, laryngitis, and otitis media, an inner ear infection (Charlton, 1994). Clearly it is difficult for nonsmoking pregnant women to protect their unborn children from the dangers of nicotine, when friends, coworkers, and even husbands smoke.

As early as 1800, abnormalities in children of alcoholic mothers were reported in England. Concerns were expressed that the high consumption of gin, euphemistically known as "mother's ruin," was leading to increased rates of dwarfism in women's offspring. Today, we know that **fetal alcohol syndrome** characterizes 6 percent of infants of alcoholic mothers (Day & Richardson, 1994).

Even before birth the fetus's spontaneous movements may be suppressed, and young infants often display motor deficits (Streissgath et al., 1994). Infants with this disorder have a high incidence of facial, heart, and limb defects; they are 20 percent shorter than the average child of their age and are often mentally retarded (Aaronson & MacNee, 1989; Streissgath, 1994; Streissgath, Sampson, & Barr, 1989). The mental retardation may be related to the loss of oxygen by the fetal brain when the fetus's breathing movements cease temporarily: It has been demonstrated that if in their last trimester women who are not heavy drinkers drink just 1 ounce of 80-proof vodka, their fetuses may stop breathing for more than half an hour (Fox et al., 1978). Indeed, the fetal damage from alcohol appears to be greatest in the last trimester. If women can cease drinking in this period, their babies tend to be longer, weigh more, and have a larger head circumference than those of women who continue heavy drinking (Aaronson & MacNee, 1989).

Children with fetal alcohol syndrome may exhibit a wide range of abnormal behaviors: They may be excessively irritable, distractible, and hyperactive and may engage in behaviors such as repeatedly banging their heads or rhythmically rocking their bodies. They may also exhibit failure to become accustomed to repeated stimuli, and they may be slow or unable to learn to perform such actions as turning their heads or even sucking (Jacobson, Jacobson, Sokol, Martier, & Ager, 1993; Streissgath, Bookstein, Sampson, & Barr, 1993). Many babies born to alcoholic mothers go through withdrawal from the drug: They shake, vomit, are irascible, and generally exhibit symptoms akin to *delirium tremens,* the extreme withdrawal syndrome seen in adult alcoholics.

Although the worst cases of fetal alcohol syndrome are seen in babies born to clearly alcoholic mothers, even a pregnant woman's moderate social drinking—say, an ounce and a half of hard liquor or a glass of beer or wine per day—can cause abnormal behavior patterns in her baby. (Jacobson & Jacobson, 1996; Streissgath et al., 1989). Furthermore, studies of older children indicate that many children whose mothers smoke or drink exhibit cognitive deficits, get lower IQ test scores, and have more problems with attention and academic achievement than other children (Barr, Streissgath, Darby, & Sampson, 1990; Streissgath et al., 1989; Streissguth et al., 1995). For example, studying more than 500 children, Streissgath and colleagues (Streissgath et al., 1995) found that prenatal alcohol consumption affected attention even in 14-year-olds. Finally, smoking and drinking seem to interact negatively with each other: Infants whose mothers use both alcohol and tobacco show more prenatal growth deficiencies than do infants whose mothers use only one of these substances (Little, 1975).

If it seems as if all the blame for prenatal damage to infants is placed on the mother, note that research has suggested that men who drink heavily may sustain genetic damage that leads to birth defects in their offspring (Cicero, 1994). In addition, British scientists have reported that men who smoke may transmit the risk of cancer to their offspring. Studying 1,500 parents whose children died of cancer in the early 1950s, these researchers found that fathers who smoked a pack or more of cigarettes a day had a 42 percent increased risk of having a child with cancer (Sorahan, Lancashire, Hulten, Peck, & Stewart, 1997). Note, however, that these data are only correlational; as we noted in Chapter 2, we cannot infer causation from such evidence. It is possible that some other factor, such as socioeconomic status, is responsible for these findings.

Heroin, Cocaine, and Other Drugs

Although drug use and abuse in the United States have waxed and waned in recent years, neither has gone away nor is either likely to in the foreseeable future. As a result, the prenatal effects of drugs such as heroin, morphine, methadone, cocaine, and lysergic acid diethylamide (LSD) are of increasing concern. Mothers who are addicted to heroin, which is a form of morphine, or to morphine itself or who use cocaine have offspring who are also addicted or who sustain toxic effects from these drugs. Babies addicted to one of these drugs go through withdrawal symptoms, some of which are similar to those we described in infants born to alcoholics: irritability, minimal ability to regulate their state of arousal, trembling, shrill crying, rapid respiration, and hyperactivity. Moreover, because these infants are often premature and of low birthweight, it is even more difficult for them to cope with the trauma of withdrawal symptoms (Zuckerman et al., 1989). In general, the severity of the newborn's symptoms is related to the length, continuity, and intensity of the mother's addiction. If the mother stops taking drugs in the last trimester preceding birth, the infant is usually not affected appreciably (Chasnoff, Griffith, MacGregor, Dirkes, & Burns, 1989; Edmondson, 1994). However, in some cases, symptoms can be severe enough to result in an infant's death in the first few days of its life (Chasnoff & Griffith, 1991; Edmondson, 1994; Lester, 1991; Phillips, Sharma, Premachandra, Vaugn, & Reyes-Lee, 1996; Zuckerman et al., 1989).

At a time when an infant needs special attention and loving care, these infants' behavior may elicit the opposite kind of behavior from drug-using parents who have problems of their own. Although addicted babies' symptoms are likely to get the attention of a caregiver, these infants when held do not readily cuddle or cling to an adult. Moreover, when adults physically stimulate these infants or place them on their shoulders, they don't elicit the alertness that normal babies evidence. Clinging, alerting, and eye contact are the main behaviors by which infants initiate and sustain social interactions with their caregivers (Field, 1990), and the lack of these behaviors in addicted newborns may disrupt parenting and have long-term adverse outcomes for parent-child relationships (Phillips et al., 1996).

As many as 200,000 American babies a year have mothers who used cocaine during pregnancy and in some inner-city areas, one in four births are to cocaine-addicted mothers (Atkins, 1988; Hawley & Disney, 1992). Some estimate that by the year 2000, more than 50,000 infants and children will have been exposed prenatally to cocaine (Hawley & Disney, 1992). Not all mothers who take cocaine have babies with developmental anomalies, and symptoms in early infancy are sometimes temporary (Mayes, 1995). Among the few long-term studies of the effects of maternal cocaine use, some have reported that children born to cocaine-using women appear to be impulsive, highly distractible, and difficult to control and to have problems in language development as they grow older. Lester (1991) reports that two common patterns are found in the children of such mothers: One pattern is characterized by excitable, irritable behavior, and high-pitched prolonged crying; the other is one of depressed, unresponsive behavior with less crying of lower amplitude. The first pattern, which Lester suggests is associated with direct toxic effects of cocaine on the neurological system, is also accompanied by irregular, accelerated heartbeat, elevated blood pressure, and constriction in the upper airways. The second pattern, he suggests, is an indirect result of the effects of cocaine use and related to low birthweight and stunted growth. Some children show a combination of both patterns, appearing lethargic and sleeping a great deal but then waking up screaming and resisting all efforts to soothe them.

The question of whether and how severely maternal cocaine use affects the developing fetus remains controversial (Mayes & Bornstein, 1996). Although some researchers have concluded that prenatal exposure to cocaine may indeed have negative effects, such as interfering with maternal-infant bonding (Phillips et al., 1996), others have found no appreciable effects on the children of cocaine-using mothers (e.g., Neuspiel, Hamel, Hochberg, Greene, & Campbell, 1991). Researchers who reviewed studies that targeted mothers' cocaine use as a cause of infants' difficulties concluded that methodological errors, such as failure either to include a control group or to follow up on the infants in the study, may have accounted for these studies' findings (Lutiger, Graham, Einarson, & Koren, 1991; Mayes, 1995).

The evidence for the adverse effects of LSD during pregnancy is less conclusive than that for heroin and cocaine. Chromosomal breakages have been found in both humans and animals exposed to high and sustained doses of LSD. In animal studies some developmental anomalies have been associated with this drug, but in human studies no firm conclusions can be drawn about the relation between defects in children and maternal drug use (Eriksson, Catz, & Yaffe, 1973; Schardein, 1985). In studies of maternal use of LSD, as in those of other illegally used drugs, it is difficult to isolate the specific effects of the drugs. Frequently, these mothers have been multiple-drug users, are malnourished, and have poor prenatal and delivery care; all of these factors may contribute to producing anomalies in their infants (Gonzalez & Campbell, 1994; Hawley & Disney, 1992). Finally, the effects of marijuana use on either fetal or infant development are less clear. Although investigators have observed reduced weight and size, as well as some short-term changes in behavior such as increased startle and a high-pitched cry, we have no evidence of long-term adverse effects on infant development (Dreher, Nugent, & Hudgins, 1994; Lester & Dreher, 1989; Zuckerman & Breshahan, 1991).

Environmental Toxins

A wide range of dangerous substances in the everyday environment are harmful to children. Some of the most commonly encountered are radiation, lead, mercury, pesticides, household cleaners, and even food additives and cosmetics. We have known for many years that radiation can harm the developing fetus, and it is for this reason that health personnel routinely advise pregnant women to avoid X rays (Smith, 1992).

Lead is another well-documented problem for both pregnant women and children. Women may be exposed to lead, for example, by inadvertently inhaling automobile exhaust or by drinking water contaminated by industrial waste. Exposure to lead during pregnancy has been associated with a variety of problems in newborns, including prematurity and low birthweight, brain damage, and physical defects, as well as with long-term problems in cognitive and intellectual functioning (Bellinger et al., 1991; Dietrich, Berger, Succop, Hammond, & Bornschein, 1993). Lead also threatens babies and young children who eat peeling lead-based paint, which is often found in older homes. Ingestion of lead has been linked to poorer cognitive and academic abilities (Needleman, Leviton, & Bellinger, 1982; Voorhees & Mollnow, 1987).

Joseph and Sandra Jacobson (1996) have alerted us to the dangerous effects on pregnant women of another environmental hazard: polychlorinated biphenyls (PCBs), which were used routinely in electrical transformers and capacitators. This use of these substances has been banned since the mid-1970s, when it was discovered that pregnant women who ate PCB-contaminated fish gave birth to infants with various deficits (Jacobson, Jacobson, Fein, Schwartz, & Dowler, 1984). These babies were smaller, less responsive, and less neurologically advanced than infants who had not been exposed to PCBs. More recently, the Jacobsons and their colleagues have reported long-term effects of prenatal exposure to PCBs: Among these effects were lower IQ and poorer memory in 4-year-old children (Jacobson & Jacobson, 1992; Jacobson, Padgett, Brumitt, & Billings, 1992).

Even fathers' exposure to environmental toxins can have harmful effects on a developing fetus. Men who work in occupations that expose them to toxic substances such as radiation, mercury, or lead may develop chromosomal abnormalities that may affect their fertility or may increase the risk that their pregnant wives will miscarry or will bear infants with birth defects (Bentur & Koren, 1991; Stone, 1992). It would seem that both wife and husband who are planning to have a child should monitor their exposure to environmental toxins. Some individual manufacturing companies have developed policies that protect pregnant women from job-related exposure to such toxins, and it looks as though these policies ought to include men as well.

Medical Interventions in Pregnancy and Childbirth

Because even many normal pregnancies are not without discomfort and symptoms that are distressing to the mother, physicians may prescribe drugs or diagnostic procedures to alleviate such problems. Medical X rays are now known to be harmful to the developing fetus and are avoided during pregnancy; other procedures, such as ultrasound, which we discussed in Chapter 3, are now used to examine the fetus and to check for irregularities.

Some Therapeutic Disasters

diethylstilbestrol (DES)
A synthetic hormone once prescribed for pregnant women to prevent miscarriage but discontinued when cancer and precancerous conditions were detected in the children of such women.

Between 1947 and 1964, the synthetic hormone **diethylstilbestrol (DES)** was often prescribed to help prevent pregnant women from miscarrying. Tragically, this drug turned out to be anything but therapeutic, for in the late 1960s scientists discovered its delayed effects. Many female offspring of the perhaps 2 million U.S. women who had taken DES during pregnancy developed vaginal abnormalities and cancer of the cervix in adolescence (Nevin, 1988). In addition, these young women also experienced a high rate of problems in pregnancy: spontaneous abortion (the very thing the drug had been intended to prevent in their mothers), premature deliveries, and babies with low birthweight (Linn et al., 1988). Moreover, although researchers thought at first that DES had affected only female offspring adversely, it is now recognized that sons of women who ingested DES during pregnancy may have not only abnormalities of the reproductive tract such as seminal fluid abnormalities but also fertility problems and an increased risk of cancer of the testes (Herbst, 1981).

thalidomide A drug once prescribed to relieve morning sickness in pregnant women but discontinued when found to cause serious malformations of the fetus. Current controversy surrounds possible use in treating sysmptoms of such diseases as AIDS, cancer, and leprosy.

Before the full impact of DES was known, another therapeutic tragedy in the early 1960s made the public keenly aware of the often unknown and potentially devastating effects of the use of drugs by pregnant women. **Thalidomide,** an antianxiety and antinausea drug, was prescribed by many physicians to relieve the symptoms of morning sickness. Increasingly, children were born with particularly unusual and often hideous abnormalities that included deformations of the eyes, nose, and ears; cleft palate; facial palsy; and fusing of fingers and toes, as well as dislocations of the hip joint and malformations of the heart and the digestive and genitourinary tracts. The most characteristic and most horrible deformity was something called *phocomelia,* in which limbs are missing and the feet and hands are attached directly to the torso in such a way that to many they resembled flippers (Karnofsky, 1965; Moore & Persaud, 1993). Although there is some controversy, the evidence suggests that thalidomide babies who were reared in a normal home situation and who did not suffer from gross sensory deficits such as blindness or deafness were of normal intelligence (DeCarie, 1961).

The problems in establishing the consequences for offspring of maternal intake of a drug during pregnancy are illustrated clearly in the cases of both DES and thalidomide. The women themselves showed no adverse effects of these drugs, and in the case of thalidomide, only a small percentage of pregnant women produced children with deficits. In some animal studies no adverse effects of the administration of this drug were seen in offspring. Moreover, even when adults have ingested massive quantities of thalidomide in suicide attempts, they have experienced nothing more serious than deep sleep, headaches, and nausea.

Diethylstilbestrol is still on the market today but recommended now only for the alleviation of symptoms in cases of advanced breast and prostate cancer. After being banned entirely from the marketplace in 1962, thalidomide was discovered also to have therapeutic benefit in the treatment of cancer and of other illnesses such as AIDS and leprosy. Although many fear the results of a 1998 announcement by the Food and Drug Administration that it would once again approve the drug, even women of childbearing age who suffer from these illnesses have advocated the drug's return.

DES and thalidomide are probably the best-known therapeutic disasters, but other drugs ingested by the mother may also affect the fetus. For example, if a pregnant woman has malaria and is treated with quinine, her unborn child may be born deaf. In addition, it has recently been found that other drugs that are commonly administered to pregnant women for therapeutic reasons may have deleterious effects. Maternal ingestion of reserpine, a tranquilizer, may lead to respiratory problems in an infant. Some drugs used to combat maternal infections, such as the tetracyclines, may depress infant skeletal growth. There is some evidence that a pregnant woman's intake of certain anticonvulsant drugs may result in her baby's developing the condition of cleft lip and palate as well as failure of the blood to coagulate. Even the common aspirin, if taken in high doses by pregnant women, may produce blood disorders in offspring (Schnoll, 1986; Vorhees & Mollnow, 1987).

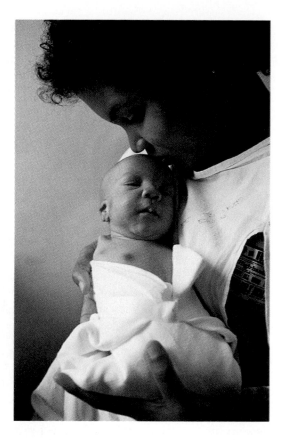

The tragedy of the thalidomide disaster is written on the face of this young Brazilian mother. Her love and her sadness are apparent as she kisses and cradles her newborn son in her arms.

Medications Used in Labor and Delivery

In recent years, researchers have focused concern on the effects of local anesthetics, such as the spinal block, and general anesthetics when these are used to ease pain and to sedate women during labor. Some researchers have found, for example, that the babies of mothers who received large amounts of obstetrical medication during labor showed less responsiveness, less smiling, and more irritability for several days after birth, as well as depression, motoric disorganization, and disruptions in feeding responses (Brackbill, McManus, & Woodward, 1985). Genetic factors, the mother's general health, the length of labor, the size of the baby, and even the mother's attitude may modify the impact of obstetrical medications on the newborn (Horowitz et al., 1977; Lester, Als, & Brazelton, 1982). These medications, especially anesthetics, do cause impaired attention and motor abilities in the infant that are still evident at 1 month of age, but there are often no longer-term effects (Kraemer, Korner, Andes, Jacklin, & Dimiceli, 1985).

In recent years, the use of full anesthesia, which renders the mother unconscious and which has the most deleterious effect on her infant, has declined greatly and, in general, physicians use only modest amounts of drugs in labor and delivery. The *epidural block*, a regional anesthetic that numbs the body from the waist down, is one of the most common forms of pain relief, accounting for 32 percent of anesthetics used in labor and delivery. This type of medication, the least likely of all analgesics to reach the baby, is one of the safest choices. However, even this "safe" pain killer has been criticized recently and may be associated with fever, prolonged labor, and increased risk of cesarean section (Lieberman et al., 1997).

The effects of drugs are difficult to predict. Many drugs that have produced unfortunate effects were tested on animals and on nonpregnant adults and found to be harmless. Unfortunately, however, we cannot make valid generalizations from tests performed on animals and human adults to the rapidly developing fetus; teratogens may affect different species at different stages of development in diverse ways. The difficulties in predicting drug effects are compounded by the wide individual differences among infants and mothers in vulnerability to drug effects. There is as yet little research on the long-term effects of maternal drug intake, and it is clear that physicians must use great caution in prescribing drugs for use in women during pregnancy and labor.

BIRTH AND THE BEGINNINGS OF LIFE

Birth is one of the most dramatic and significant events in the lives of parents and children. For parents, the last few weeks of pregnancy are typically characterized by joyous anticipation and, especially in first births, by apprehension about labor and childbirth, anxiety about whether the child will be normal, and concern about whether the mother will be permanently altered physically by pregnancy and delivery. Although both parents are exhausted by the process of birth, most are exhilarated, even awestruck in seeing and holding their newborn for the first time. One new father said, "When I come up to see my wife . . . I go look at the kid and then I pick her up and put her down . . . I keep going back to the kid. It's like a magnet. That's what I can't get over, the fact that I feel like that" (Greenberg & Morris, 1974, p. 524).

Labor and Delivery

Birth is also a momentous physical and social transition for the infant. The baby moves from the warm, wet, dark environment of the amniotic sac to the dry, cooler, bright environment of an external world full of changing lights, objects, movements, touches, voices, and faces. Even before birth, during pregnancy, the parents and child have established a relationship, and following birth the construction of this relationship becomes more intense and accelerated.

The Three Stages of Childbirth

Birth involves a series of changes in the mother that permit the child to move from the womb out into the external world. Figure 4-5 shows the way the fetus appears and is positioned in the uterus just before labor begins, as well as the three stages in the birth process that we describe next.

The first stage of labor begins as the mother experiences regular uterine contractions that are usually spaced at 10- to 15-minute intervals; these contractions become more intense and frequent as labor progresses. This first stage, which generally lasts between 8 and 14 hours for firstborn children and half that for later-born children, concludes when the cervix is dilated sufficiently to permit the infant's head to pass through it and into the vaginal canal.

In the second stage of labor, which usually lasts less than an hour, the infant descends through the birth canal and is delivered through the vaginal opening.

The third and final stage of birth takes only a few minutes, involving simply the expulsion of the placenta.

Natural Childbirth: Not Such a New Idea

Having a baby in the relatively isolated and unfamiliar setting of a hospital, separated from one's relatives and often from one's husband, was a practice that began in the nineteenth century as a response to a rise in health problems and in infant and maternal mortality associated with rapid urbanization and industrialization. Before that time, women gave birth in their homes, attended by relatives or a midwife.

Currently, 91 percent of U.S. women are still assisted in childbirth by a physician. However, there has been a move to make pregnancy and birth once again a more shared family experience and even to have births occur in the home or in homelike birthing centers. Midwife-assisted births (4.1%) have increased nearly 400

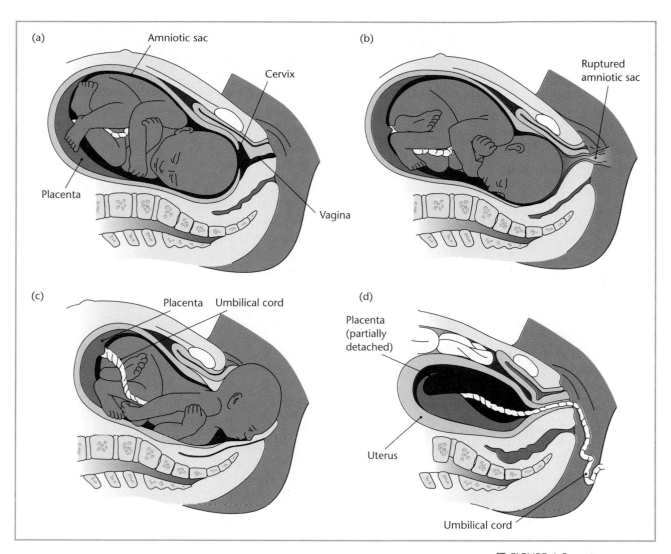

(a) Amniotic sac, Cervix, Vagina, Placenta

(b) Ruptured amniotic sac

(c) Placenta, Umbilical cord

(d) Placenta (partially detached), Uterus, Umbilical cord

■ FIGURE 4-5
The stages of the birth process. With arms and legs folded and head pointed toward the birth canal, the fetus is ready to be born (a). In stage 1, the fetus moves toward the cervix, as it gradually dilates (b). In stage 2, the fetus moves through the vaginal opening (c). In stage 3, the nourishing placenta detaches from the uterine wall preparatory to expulsion (d). *Source:* Adapted from Vander, sherman, & Luciano, 1994.

percent since the early 1970s (Wegman, 1994). Home deliveries by trained personnel or delivery in a birthing center are suitable for normal births; however, between 15 and 25 percent of women who begin labor in such settings are subsequently moved to a hospital because of birth complications (Baruffi, 1982). Not all countries treat childbirth as a medical event. In Holland, for example, 35 percent of the babies are born at home and about 43 percent are delivered by midwives rather than physicians (Treffers, Eskes, Kleiverda, & Van Alten, 1990). Most important, the rates of both infant mortality and postpartum depression are lower for home deliveries, partly because mothers who deliver at home are more likely to have had low-risk pregnancies. It would seem that for uncomplicated births, there's no place like home.

Cesarean Delivery

The **cesarean delivery,** in which a baby is removed from the mother's uterus through an incision in her abdomen, is performed in a variety of situations: Labor may be unusually slow or prolonged, the baby may be in difficulty, there may be vaginal bleeding, or the baby's position may be such that a normal vaginal delivery is impossible (e.g., the baby's feet may be in position to deliver first, or the baby may lie horizontally in the uterus). From the 1960s to the 1980s, the rate at which these deliveries were performed increased from 5 to 23.5 percent of all births (Centers for Disease Control & Prevention, 1993). According to Localio and colleagues (1993), there are several reasons for this increase, including the convenience of physicians (they can schedule this procedure rather than be called to the hospital in the wee

cesarean delivery The surgical delivery of a baby, whereby the baby is removed from the mother's uterus through an incision made in her abdomen and uterus; also known as *cesarean section.*

hours of the morning) and an effort to minimize physician liability associated with the potential complications of vaginal delivery. Concerns have been raised that the rate of *cesarean sections* (another term for this procedure) is unnecessarily high and that these procedures themselves may have unforeseen long-term adverse consequences. The rate at which cesareans are performed leveled out in the late 1980s and began dropping in the 1990s (Van Tuinen & Wolfe, 1993).

Cesarean births place mothers at greater risk of infection and involve longer hospital stays. In addition, cesarean babies are exposed to more maternal medication during delivery; as a result, they have somewhat more trouble breathing and are less responsive and wakeful than other newborns (Trevarthan, 1987). However, short-term studies of cesarean births suggest that this method of delivery has few effects on infants' cognitive or neurological development (Entwisle & Alexander, 1987). Although early mother-child interactions may be adversely affected, by the time the children are 1 year old, these relationships are positive (Reilly, Entwisle, & Doering, 1987). One advantage of cesarean births is that because mothers have a longer recovery period, during which it is often difficult for them to handle all the caretaking of their infants, fathers may become more involved with their babies in the first few months than is usually the case (Parke, 1996; Pedersen, Zaslow, Cain, & Anderson, 1981).

Birth Complications

Although labor and childbirth are normal processes in human development and, in the majority of cases, have no lasting adverse influences, they sometimes do affect an infant in negative ways. We've already discussed the possible passing of sexually transmitted diseases to the infant as it moves through the birth canal. In addition, it has been found that more males than females are born with physical anomalies. This has been attributed in part to the role of the sex chromosomes (see Chapter 3) and in part to the larger size of, and hence greater pressure on, a male's head during birth. The majority of infants do not suffer serious impairment at birth, however. Fewer than 10 percent have any type of abnormality, and many of these difficulties disappear during subsequent development.

anoxia   A lack of oxygen in brain cells.

Important birth factors that are related to developmental deviations and infant mortality are **anoxia** (lack of oxygen in the brain) and prematurity. Severe anoxia, which is usually associated with brain damage and sometimes death, is often found in infants of very low birthweight (Wegman, 1995).

One of the methods frequently used to assess the condition of the newborn infant is the Apgar scoring system (Table 4-3). At 1 minute and 5 minutes after birth, the obstetrician or nurse measures the heart rate, respiratory effort, reflex irritability, muscle tone, and body color of the infant. Each of the five signs is given a score of 0, 1, or 2, and the higher the score attained, the more favorable the baby's condition. A total score of 7 to 10 indicates that the newborn is in good condition, a score below 5 indicates that there may be possible developmental difficulties, and a score of 3 or lower alerts medical staff to possibly life-threatening conditions and the need for immediate emergency procedures.

Prematurity and Low Birthweight

preterm   A term describing a premature baby who is born before its due date and whose weight, though less than that of a full-term infant, may be appropriate to its gestational age.

Premature babies are those born before they have completed the normal or full-term gestational period—on average, 38 weeks from the mother's last menstrual period to delivery—and who are biologically immature in one or more ways. Premature infants are always of low birthweight—that is, they weigh less than 5.5 pounds, compared with the normal full-term baby's average weight of 7.7 pounds—but when their weight is appropriate to the amount of time they have spent in utero, they are considered **preterm** babies (see also Table 4-4). Because some writers have criticized the use only of gestational age and weight as indicators

TABLE 4-3 Apgar Evaluation of the Newborn Infant

	Score		
Sign	0	1	2
Heart rate	Absent	Less than 100 beats per minute	100 to 140 beats per minute
Respiratory effort	No breathing for more than one minute	Slow and irregular	Good respiration with normal crying
Muscle tone	Limp and flaccid	Some flexion of the extremities	Good flexion, active motion
Reflex irritability	No response	Some motion	Vigorous response to stimulation
Color	Blue or pale body and extremities	Body pink with blue extremities	Pink all over

Source: Adapted from Apgar (1953).

TABLE 4-4 Preterm and Small-for-Date Babies

Description	Timing of Delivery	Average Weight at Delivery
Full Term	Average of 38 weeks from conception	7.7 lb (3,500 g)
Premature		
Preterm	Several weeks before due date	Less than 5.5 lb (2,500 g) but weight is often appropriate to time spent in utero
Small for date	Either at about due date or several weeks before	Less than 5.5 lb (2,500 g) and less weight than would be expected for time spent in utero; survival of babies who weigh less than 3.3 lb (about 1,500 g) is severely compromised

of prematurity, investigators are now considering such additional criteria as weight relative to stature of the parent, nutritional condition of the mother, and a variety of skeletal, neurological, and biochemical indexes (Goldberg & DeVitto, 1995).

When premature infants weigh less than 5.5 pounds and their weight is less than would be appropriate to their time in utero, they are called **small-for-date** babies. Note that a small-for-date baby may be born close to its due date (close to full term) but be of low birthweight. Although babies who weigh much less than 3 pounds have many odds against them, modern technology is becoming increasingly successful in enabling very small babies to survive.

Most new parents look forward to holding, cuddling, and feeding their infants soon after birth and to leaving the hospital within two or three days with a healthy, vigorous baby. By 1996, as a result of health insurers' efforts to reduce medical costs, these two or three days had often shrunk to 24 hours for routine vaginal births. The wisdom of such "drive-through deliveries" was questioned by a number of authorities, largely because some problems such as jaundice may not be manifest until a baby is at home. One study found that babies who were sent home within 30 hours of birth were 28 percent more likely than babies kept in hospital

small for date A term describing a premature baby who may be born close to its due date but who weighs significantly less than would be appropriate to its gestational age.

longer to be readmitted within a week and 12 percent more likely to return within a month (Liu, Clemens, Shay, Davis, & Novack, 1997). Another study, however, found few negative effects of early discharge (Edmonson, Stoddard, & Owens, 1997). To be on the safe side, in 1997 the U.S. government passed the Newborns' and Mothers' Health Protection Act, which requires health plans to cover at least 48 hours of hospital care after a routine birth.

Has this solved the problem? Not according to the leaders of the two research teams who, despite their somewhat discrepant findings, argue that inexperienced caregiving, not early discharge, is the real issue. That is, new mothers and fathers need coaching—mothers in nursing and fathers in general infant care. But although the American Academy of Pediatrics recommends that within 48 hours of a short-stay infant's birth a health professional visit the baby in her home, in fact as many as 70 percent of such babies have to wait longer than that (Maisels & Kring, 1997). Nevertheless, although the provisions of the 1997 act may not offer the best solution, they may serve as a stopgap until more efficient programs of postnatal home visits can be put in place.

When a baby is premature, parents may have to endure another stressful change in their plans and lifestyle. Such a baby is generally placed in an *isolette,* a specially constructed crib in which the delicate infant's vital functions can be monitored. Attendants feed, cleanse, and change the baby through side-wall openings, and, if they are allowed in the nursery, parents, too, may touch their infant through these small openings. Because the infant they gaze at—a tiny, fragile-looking creature—is not yet fully developed and has not yet formed a layer of subcutaneous fat, it appears thin, with wrinkled, transparent skin and a disproportionately large head. And perhaps worst of all, mother and father must leave their new baby behind; "preemies" often remain in the care of the hospital staff for several weeks until they are physically mature enough to leave the isolette.

In the United States, African American mothers are twice as likely as European American women to have babies of low birthweight (less than 2,500 grams, or 5.5 pounds) and almost three times as likely to have babies of very low birthweight (less than 1,500 grams, or 3.3 pounds). Among women of Asian and Latino origin, Mexican American women's chances of having such babies are about halfway between black and white women's chances; all others are less likely than Mexican Americans to have low-birthweight babies (U.S. Department of Health and Human Services, 1996).

Extremely low birthweights are often associated with intellectual impairment, but in general, only children who weigh less than 3.5 pounds incur significant impairment in intellectual functioning (Goldberg & DeVitto, 1995; Kopp, 1983). Although most low-birthweight babies catch up in motor and intellectual development by the time they are 4 years old, about 15 percent of those who weigh less than 3.3 pounds (1,500 grams) and about 30 percent of those weighing less than 2 pounds at birth continue to show some kind of cognitive deficit (Goldberg & DeVitto, 1995; Kopp & Kaler, 1989). Problems in academic achievement, hyperactivity, motor skills, and speech and hearing disorders occur more often in very-low-birthweight or premature babies than in maturely born infants (Goldberg & DeVitto, 1995; Landry, 1995). However, in most children the long-term differences are small (Aylward, Pfeiffer, Wright, & Verholst, 1989; Field, 1990).

It is not clear whether the problems enumerated are the consequences of prematurity and low birthweight or the outcome of a number of related factors, such as delivery complications, temporary isolation from most human contact and consequent separation of parents and infant, neonatal anomalies other than prematurity, or the way parents respond to their infants' apparent frailty and small size (Field, 1990; Korner, 1989). We should also keep in mind that many extremely low-birthweight babies would not have survived 15 years ago, before the introduction of neonatal intensive care units with specialized treatment procedures, equipment, and highly trained staff. More very sick infants who require assistance are living, and it is when these high medical risks are compounded by adverse environmental circumstances that long-term developmental deviations may occur (Goldberg & DeVitto, 1995).

In the next two sections we discuss two aspects of these early experiences that have particularly concerned psychologists. First, the preterm infant in the isolette in the early weeks of life may be getting less, and is certainly getting different, sensory and social stimulation than the full-term baby. Second, early parent-child separation may interfere with the formation of affectionate bonds between parent and infant. We conclude this section with a look at the long-term effects of the complications of prematurity.

Stimulation Programs for Premature Babies

Since the 1970s, researchers have experimented with administering extra stimulation to preterm and small-for-date babies and then comparing their development with matched infants who were not given special stimulation. Some experimenters have suggested that stimulation should approximate the conditions experienced by the infant in utero; thus, premature infants have been exposed to tape-recorded heartbeats as heard within the uterus (Barnard & Bee, 1983), to rocking hammocks (Neal, 1968), and to waterbed mattresses (Burns, Deddish, Burns, & Hatcher, 1983) that presumably simulate the rotation, movement, and rhythmic activity experienced by the fetus within the amniotic sac. Other investigators have used stimulation characteristic of the experiences of full-term infants, such as mobiles, tape recordings of the mother's voice, manual rocking, talking and singing, and cuddling and stroking (Field, 1990; Goldberg & DeVitto, 1995). Both prenatal- and postnatal-environment approaches have found that special stimulation can counteract some of the effects of the monotonous stimulation experienced by infants in isolettes (see Box 4-2).

As Figure 4-6 shows, stimulated premature infants have been found to be more advanced in mental development (Field, 1990; Field et al., 1986). They have also been shown to be more advanced than unstimulated premature infants in neurological development, as measured by infant reflexes; in sensorimotor and motor skills; in muscle tonus; and in exploratory behavior (Barnard & Bee, 1983; Burns et al., 1983; Cornell & Gottfried, 1976). In addition, fewer incidents of *apnea* (temporary cessation of breathing, associated with later crib deaths) are found in

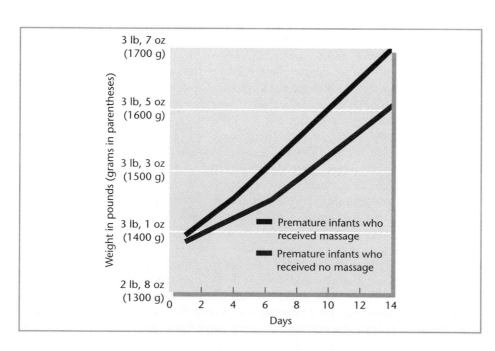

■ FIGURE 4-6
Everyone likes massage, including premature babies. A group of premature infants were given three 15-minute, daily massages for 10 days, while another group received no massage. The infants given extra stimulation averaged 47% more weight gain per day, were awake and active for more of the time, showed more mature behaviors on the Brazelton Neonatal Scale, and were in hospital for six days less than the other infants. Moreover, six to eight months later, the first group weighed more and performed better on the Bayley mental and motor scales than the second group. (*Source:* Adapted from Field, 1990)

BOX 4-2

Child Psychology in Action

Of Babies and Bears and Postnatal Care

Most babies go home from the hospital to brightly decorated rooms and cribs filled with soft squishy animal companions. Now some premature infants in hospital isolettes are sleeping with such companions, too—a teddy bear from whose gentle "breathing" they may derive considerable benefit.

In most programs designed to stimulate premature infants, the stimulation is imposed on the infant, whether she or he wants it or not. Evelyn Thoman (1987) designed a clever study to investigate whether premature infants can actively seek and regulate stimulation, rather than just being its passive recipients, and whether stimulation instigated by the infant will facilitate the infant's developmental progress.

Thoman placed a "breathing" teddy bear in the isolettes of one group of preemies, a nonbreathing teddy bear in the isolettes of another group, and gave a third group no teddy bears. She began her original study when the infants were 32 weeks old (counting from conception), 6 to 8 weeks younger than full term (38-40 weeks) newborns. She continued her intervention for 3 weeks, until the babies were a total of 35 weeks old.

The design of the breathing bear included a pneumatic pump that enabled it to "breathe" at a rate that could be individualized for each infant. Each bear's breathing rate was set at one-half of the infant's quiet-sleep respiration rate (Thoman, Hammond, Affleck, & DeSilva, 1995) on the theory that because premature babies have relatively fast respiration rates (about 60 breaths per minute in quiet sleep), such a rate might be too fast for gentle stimulation.

The breathing of the bear was expected to entrain the more irregular breathing of the premature baby without modifying his or her own endogenous rhythm, and researchers felt that the one-half rate, based as it was on that endogenous rhythm, would be successful in influencing each baby's irregular periods of breathing. Each infant controlled the amount of stimulation it received and the period of time the stimulation continued because it could either stay in contact with the bear or move away from it.

Thoman, in her original study, was interested, first, in the amount of time the infants spent in contact with the breathing and nonbreathing bears and, second, in whether contact with the breathing bear would indeed cause the child's respiration to become more regular. Thoman found that babies spent 63.4 percent of their time in contact with the breathing bear and 13.3 percent of their time with the nonbreathing bear. (Infants who had no bear spent 17.2 percent of their time in the area occupied by bears in the cribs of the two other groups of infants.)

Even these very young, premature babies were able to approach an available and attractive form of stimulation, and they clearly preferred the stimulation offered by the breathing bear to the passivity of the nonbreathing bear. Furthermore, the premature babies with the breathing bear showed more even respiration and more quiet sleep than did infants in the other two groups. Thoman speculates that this is because the additional stimulation may have influenced the organization of brain processes associated with mature sleep patterns. Although physical and sensory maturity are normally associated with more advanced behavior, it may be that stimulating behavior and experiences also advance physical and sensory development.

---

stimulated infants (Korner, 1989). Stimulation clearly has at least a short-term salutary effect on the development of premature infants, although long-term gains are rarely found (Korner, 1989).

Intervention programs facilitate not only the functioning of targeted systems but also of other systems that are about to develop. However, programs must be sensitive to individual differences; not all premature babies benefit from additional stimulation (Goldberg & DeVitto, 1995). Children who are ill, who have intensive medical care routines that disrupt their sleep, or who are being weaned from breathing assistance or other physical support systems may not respond positively or may actually be distressed by added stimulation (Oehler, Eckerman, & Wilson, 1988). In attending to the needs of different children the question is not "whether stimulation for preterm infants is indicated but . . . stimulation for whom, what kind, how much, at what intervals, at what post-conceptual age, and for what purposes" (Korner, 1989, p. 12).

Premature Babies and Parental Contact

It has been suggested that contact between the mother and her newborn in the first few hours of a child's life may facilitate the formation of emotional attachment (Klaus & Kennell, 1982). However, most research findings suggest that although early contact is potentially beneficial, it is not critical (Goldberg, 1983; Goldberg &

Thoman and her colleagues have added more sophisticated measurement techniques in their continuing studies of the effect of the breathing bear in an effort to further support the efficacy of this intervention (Thoman et al., 1995). Introducing a pressure sensor under the baby to record respiration and body movements, they replicated Thoman's earlier findings and also showed that the infants who spent more time with the breathing bear did indeed show a more regular respiratory pattern in quiet sleep. A further enhancement enabled these researchers to show that the breathing bear enabled more quiet sleep not only during the intervention but also several weeks after the intervention ended. They also showed that with practice the premature infants were successful in finding their breathing bears more quickly than the babies who had nonbreathing bears found theirs.

In their most recent study, Thoman and her associates (Thoman et al., 1995) added direct behavioral observation to the respiration recordings. These observations, the researchers assert, are important in recording sleep-related behaviors like startles, small and large movements, and facial expressions, all of which show distinctive patterns of frequencies and have been found to differentiate individual infants. And because newborns spend so much time in sleep, behaviors that occur in sleep serve as communication with the mother as much as do waking behaviors.

Thoman and her colleagues have found that the babies with breathing bears show less waking and more quiet sleep, fewer startles in quiet sleep, and less crying. They were also more likely to smile than grimace during active sleep than babies with nonbreathing bears. The researchers conclude that the breathing bear serves to reinforce instrumental learning as premature babies seek and achieve contact with it. An important area for future research will be the investigation of the neural and physiological correlates of affective expressions of preterm infants during both sleeping and waking, to improve not only our basic understanding of these behaviors but also the clinical care of our most vulnerable infants.

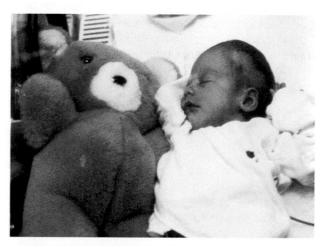

As this newborn snuggles up to a "breathing bear" it seems clear that the baby derives comfort from the bear's presence. This bear was designed by Evelyn Thoman for her studies of premature infants who proved to benefit from the regulatory effects of the simulated breathing sounds. The breathing bear now has many relatives in toy stores across the nation.

DeVitto, 1995); there are many alternative routes to the formation of the parent-infant relationship. The most marked benefit of increased contact seems to be the building of maternal self-confidence, which, particularly for the mother of a premature infant, enhances the sensitivity of her parenting.

Even in modern neonatal intensive care units that encourage parents to spend time with their premature infants, parents still have less early contact with these infants than with full-term babies. How, for example, does purposely increasing the amount of contact that mothers have with their premature infants affect mother-child relations? Some mothers are reluctant to participate. Others who are permitted early physical contact with their premature babies may be more likely to feel self-confident and close to their babies and to cuddle and stimulate their infants than mothers who were only able to look at their infants in the isolette (Barnett, Leiderman, Grobstein, & Klaus, 1970; Seashore, Leifer, Barnett, & Leiderman, 1973). However, unless continued support and training for the mother are available, these effects disappear in a few months.

Some mothers report feelings of guilt, failure, and alienation from their infants and loss of self-esteem, and appear apprehensive about handling and caring for these fragile-appearing infants. When mothers of preemies are eventually able to take their babies home from the hospital, they tend to show less emotional involvement with them than do mothers of full-term babies (Goldberg &

DeVitto, 1995; Lester, Hoffman, & Brazelton, 1985), especially if their infants have been in hospital for more than a month after birth (Corter & Minde, 1987). These effects have been found to last as long as two years after hospital discharge (Barnard, Bee, & Hammond, 1984; Crnic, Greenberg, Ragozin, Robinson, & Basham, 1983).

Some premature infants who fail to gain weight and height normally become battered and failure-to-thrive children. For example, there have been cases in which one twin had to be kept longer in hospital and when finally sent home was abused or returned to the hospital as a failure-to-thrive child. This sort of situation might be attributed to early parent-child separation and lack of emotional bonding, but it might also result from adverse parental responses to characteristics of the low-birthweight child that make the infant unattractive. Premature babies' typical physical appearance, small size, high-pitched cry, feeding difficulties, low responsivity, and failure to smile may make them unappealing and also may increase parental anxiety and frustration. More important than these factors, however, may be the fact that most premature infants are born to mothers who are poor, young, uneducated, and members of a minority group (Bradley et al., 1994; Liaw & Brooks-Gunn, 1994). It is likely that circumstances surrounding poverty, stress, and lack of support are at least as significant contributors to the abuse of a child as its birth-related difficulties.

Long-Term Effects of Prematurity

What are the long-term effects on the family of prematurity and early separation from the infant? As you might expect, disruptions are more marked and enduring for economically deprived families than for middle-income families (Bradley et al., 1994; Lester et al., 1995; Liaw & Brooks-Gunn, 1994; Resnick et al., 1990). When such disruptive effects on parent-child attachment or on the cognitive development of the child do endure they seem to be attributable to a host of factors: the responsiveness of the particular child, the general competence of the mother, the environmental stresses encountered by the family, and the kind of support that is available to the parents from other family members, nursing staff, and self-help groups (Heinicke, Beckwith, & Thompson, 1988; Patterson & Barnard, 1990).

More often than it affects the parent-child relationship, the stress of raising a premature baby may have a negative impact on the relations between the child's parents. Some research has reported a high incidence of marital discord in the first 2 years following the birth of a premature infant (Leiderman, 1983); on the other hand, if a couple perceive that their coping strategies are complementary—that is, if they see that they can usefully share the task of caring for a child with special needs—the challenge may bring them closer together (Affleck, Tennen, & Rowe, 1990). Clearly, to understand the effects of prematurity and early parent-child separation we must focus on the entire family system.

VULNERABILITY AND RESILIENCE IN CHILDREN AT RISK

In this chapter we have discussed a great number of events and conditions that can cause things to go wrong in pregnancy and childbirth. At this point you may be wondering if things ever go right! Indeed they do; most pregnancies proceed without major disruptions, and many couples find the period of waiting and preparing for the arrival of a child one of the happiest times of their lives.

Things do go wrong often enough, however, that scholars have attempted to understand and deal with the cases in which an infant's vulnerability to adverse perinatal influences either is compounded by subsequent conditions of its life or cannot be compensated for by more favorable factors in that life. Starting from the premise that there is a great variety in both the kinds of birth complications and the types of environmental conditions that can cause abnormalities in the child, a number of researchers have tried to uncover the reasons why some vulnerable children develop *resilience,* or the capacity to achieve competence and satisfaction in life despite initially challenging or threatening circumstances.

In the concept of the *continuum of reproductive casualty* Pasamanick and Knoblock (1966) proposed that the kinds of prenatal and perinatal factors that can affect the child negatively vary along a continuum of intensity that ranges from relatively minor perceptual, attentional, intellectual, motor, and behavioral disabilities to gross anomalies. Describing a *continuum of caretaking casualty,* Sameroff and his colleagues (Sameroff & Chandler, 1975; Sameroff & Seifer, 1983) proposed that the environmental, family situation the infant enters also varies along a continuum of intensity, one that stretches from basically healthy (intact family, good caretaking, adequate financial support) to highly adverse (poverty, drug abuse, broken family, violence). Although different groups of researchers have come up with varying specific factors, most agree that the seeds of resilience and the ability to overcome difficulties are sown in the interaction between risk factors and factors of protection or lack of protection (e.g., Lester et al., 1995; Milham, Widmayer, Bauer, & Peterson, 1983; Werner, 1989, 1991, 1993).

In an outstanding longitudinal study of the effects of birth complications on the development of the entire population of 698 children born in 1955 on the Hawaiian island of Kauai, Emmy Werner and her colleagues (Werner, Bierman, & French, 1971; Werner & Smith, 1977, 1982) set out not only to document these complications but to assess their long-term consequences as well as the consequences over time of adverse early rearing conditions. As you can see from Box 4-3, they learned along the way that the effects of adverse perinatal complications—about 10 percent of all children are born with some kind of handicap or anomaly—often lessen in intensity or disappear with age, that this is in large part a function of the particular kind of caretaking environment in which children mature, and that both children's vulnerability to high-risk conditions and their resiliency can change over time.

The Kauai study offered "a more hopeful perspective," according to Werner (1984) than does the general literature on children with problems, and it has been followed by other similarly designed studies that have tended to support its findings. Noting that there are great individual differences in the ways high-risk children respond to their environments, Werner (1993) points out that one of the first choices that must be made in planning intervention programs is to provide greater assistance to some children than others, and that means identifying the degrees of risk for children who have suffered prenatal and perinatal complications and who are born into some form of adversity:

> Intervention programs need to focus on children . . . who appear most vulnerable because they lack some of the essential personal resources and/or social bonds that buffer chronic adversity. Among [these] are the increasing numbers of preterm survivors of neonatal intensive care, . . . children reared by isolated single parents with no roots in a community, and (pre-) adolescents with [behavioral] disorders who have poor reading skills. (p. 267)

More than one study has shown that a close and continuing relationship with another caring person is a highly significant factor in the development of resilience in a young person. Often the caring person is not a parent but a grandparent, an older sibling, a neighbor, a day-care provider, a teacher, a minister, a youth worker, or an elder mentor who can help tilt the balance from vulnerability to resiliency. Such a person can accept children's temperamental idiosyncrasies and allow them some experiences that challenge but do not overwhelm their coping abilities, guide children in developing a sense of responsibility and caring and reward them for

BOX 4-3

Risk and Resilience

What Factors Help Children Overcome Early Adversity?

At the time that Emmy Werner and her colleagues (Werner, Bierman, & French, 1971; Werner & Smith, 1977, 1982) began their now-classic longitudinal study of all children born in 1955 on the Hawaiian island of Kauai there was a considerable literature on children born with serious defects or disorders and the course their lives could be expected to take. However, research on those factors that protect the individual and enable a small percentage of at-risk children to develop a remarkable degree of resilience was still in its infancy (Werner, 1989). Werner's study, which has followed most of its nearly 700 participants for more than 40 years, was one of the first to focus on such questions as: What is *right* with the children who develop this sort of resilience? and, How can we help other children to acquire this same near-invincibility in the face of severe adversity (Werner, 1984)?

When the participants in the Kauai Longitudinal Study were born, 47 percent suffered birth complications, and of these, a third were classified as specifically "at risk." In addition to experiencing moderate to severe birth complications, these children were born into poverty, their mothers had little formal education, and their family environments were characterized by discord, desertion, divorce, alcoholism, and/or mental illness. As we will see, despite these early stresses, fully a third of this at-risk group—10 percent of all participants—developed into confident, competent, and caring young adults.

All the children in this multicultural study—who were of Japanese, Filipino, and Hawaiian descent—were examined not only at birth but at 2, 10, and 18 years of age. At the first follow-up, 12 percent of 2-year-olds were rated deficient in social development, 16 percent were deficient in intellectual functioning, and 14 percent had health problems. The more severe the complications of birth and the more poorly the newborns had performed on various tests, the less adequate was their developmental level. Of particular interest was the relationship the researchers found between perinatal difficulties and environmental factors such as socioeconomic status. Infants who had severe perinatal complications and who were living in unstable fami-

lies of relatively low socioeconomic status, with mothers of low intelligence, achieved lower IQ scores (lower by as much as 37 points) than infants living in the same kinds of conditions who had either no birth complications or only mild ones. By contrast, infants who had experienced severe birth complications but were living in stable family environments of high socioeconomic status, with mothers of high intelligence, obtained IQ scores that differed only slightly from the scores of infants in the same socioeconomic circumstances who had no birth complications. As toddlers, across all groups, the children who matured into resilient young adults were alert, autonomous, and more advanced in communication, self-help, and motor skills. They tended to seek out novel stimuli and had a positive social orientation.

By the age of 10, some two-thirds of the children classified "at risk" had developed serious learning or behavior problems (Werner, 1989). However, the effects of environmental variables had almost obliterated those of perinatal damage: No relationship was found between measures of birth complications and a child's IQ score at this age or later. Instead, the correlation between a child's intellectual performance and his or her parents' IQ scores and socioeconomic status increased as the child grew older; lower-class children showed marked deficits on cognitive measures. In short, the main effects of deviations caused by perinatal complications occurred early in a child's development; after that, development was increasingly influenced by environmental circumstances such as chronic poverty, family instability, and mental health problems.

When the children were 18, Werner and Smith (1982) tried to differentiate between children who had developed problems and a group of "resilient children" who were among the group that had been classified in infancy as "high risk" but who had not developed problems. The resilient children in families of low socioeconomic status seemed to share four personality characteristics: an active, resourceful approach toward solving life's problems; a tendency to perceive even their painful experiences constructively; the ability, from infancy on, to gain other people's positive attention; and a strong ability to use faith to maintain a positive vision of a meaningful life (Werner, 1984). Evidencing cognitive abilities such as effective reading skills

helpfulness and cooperation, and model for children a conviction that life makes sense despite its adversities (Werner, 1984). These ties, Werner (1993) argues, must be encouraged and strengthened, not weakened or displaced by legislative action and social programs.

Because most studies of risk and resiliency have focused on relatively urban, industrialized societies, future research, Werner (1993) proposes, should look at other environments, other physical and social settings in which children live. Child-care customs, gender role socialization, and beliefs about children's needs vary greatly in the parts of the world where five out of every six children are born today: Asia, the Middle East, Africa, and the countries of South, Central, and Middle America.

by the fourth grade served as an additional protective factor (Werner, 1993). Finally, certain features of these children's social environment served as protective buffers: small family size, favorable parental attitudes, a continuous relationship with a caring adult (not necessarily the parent), low levels of family conflict, a smaller load of stressful life experiences, and the availability of counseling and remedial assistance. In addition, in middle childhood or adolescence, high-risk resilient children often assumed responsibility for the care of another person—a sibling, aging grandparent, or ill or incompetent parent. Both such "required helpfulness" and being cared for oneself were critical in buffering these high-risk children from adversity (Werner, 1984, 1989).

Although more high-risk girls than high-risk boys matured into resilient young adults, the periods of stress for each differed. In the first decade of life, boys appeared vulnerable to both biological and environmental stresses, but girls had more difficulty in the second decade of life. By the late elementary school years, boys were more able to cope with their earlier problems—the demands of school achievement and the control of aggression. Adolescent girls, however, confronted social pressures and sexual expectations that led to an increasing rate of mental health problems. The complexity of these interactions demonstrates the difficulty of separating the contributions of prenatal, perinatal, and experiential factors to long-term development.

On follow-up at age 30, three out of four participants had had some college education, almost all were fully employed, and the majority listed career or job success as their primary objective, followed by self-fulfillment. Of the women, 85 percent were married and working, and 75 percent had young children; only 40 percent of the men were married, and only 35 percent had children. Men seemed to have had more difficulty weathering the breakups of relationships than did women and to have become more reluctant to commit to new ones. Among the resilient adults who were parents the primary goals for their children were the acquisition of personal competencies and skills. About three-quarters considered themselves happy and satisfied; a few had divorced, had experienced psychological problems requiring them to seek profes-

sional help, or had drug problems (Werner, 1989). But, again, investigators note that 10 times more of the participants in this study had problems related to the effects of poor environment than to the effects of perinatal stress. Indeed, birth complications, unless they involved serious damage to the central nervous system, were consistently related to impaired physical or psychological development only if they were combined with chronic poverty, parental psychopathology, or persistently poor rearing conditions (Lester et al., 1995; Werner, 1991). Clearly, the environment plays a critical role in helping children overcome a poor beginning.

Thanks to their own resilience, fully a third of the at-risk children studied by Emmy Werner and her colleagues developed into self-confident, successful adults. These children had a positive and active approach to problem-solving, the abilities to see some useful aspects of even painful experiences and to attract positive responses from other people, and a strong tendency to use faith in maintaining an optimistic vision of a fulfilling life.

SUMMARY

Stages of Prenatal Development

- Prenatal development is typically divided into three distinct periods (zygote, embryo, fetus). In reality, these periods represent continuous phases of development during which the organism, protected and sustained by the **amniotic sac,** the **placenta,** the **umbilical cord,** and, after the fifth month, the **lanugo,** undergoes a systematic series of sequential changes to become increasingly complex and differentiated.

- The period of the **zygote,** which lasts about two weeks, extends from fertilization to implantation, when the zygote becomes implanted in the wall of the uterus. The period of the **embryo** begins at that point and lasts until the end of the eighth week. During this period of rapid growth, most of the important organs and physiological systems develop, and the embryo is quite vulnerable to adverse environmental influences.

- The period of the **fetus** extends from the beginning of the third month until birth. Although the major organ systems are well differentiated by this time, the central nervous system continues to develop at a rapid pace, reflexes develop, and regulatory processes and the respiratory system continue to mature. A danger at this time is **respiratory distress syndrome,** and if the child is born before the **age of viability,** or 28 weeks, it may not be developed enough to survive.

The Effects of the Prenatal Environment on Development

- During prenatal development, **teratogens,** agents that produce developmental abnormalities, may affect the growing organism, resulting in physical and mental deviations. Seven general principles summarize the effects of teratogens on prenatal development, indicating that the type, timing, and duration of the teratogen play a role in the outcome as well as the genotypes of the mother and child.

- Mothers who have their first child when they are over 35 or under 15 are likely to experience more problems during pregnancy and difficulties during delivery than women between these ages. In both groups, the risks are related to maternal health. Young adolescents are less likely to eat properly or to get prenatal care; older women are more likely to have hypertension, diabetes, alcoholism, and other problems related to age.

- Deficiencies in maternal diet are related to increased rates of prematurity, stillbirths, infant mortality, physical and neural defects, and small size. The specific form a defect takes is related to the age at which the malnutrition occurs and its duration. Dietary supplements provided during pregnancy and after birth have been successful at reducing some of these effects, but the extent of the reversibility of such damage is not known. Continued ill effects seem to be related to the mother's history of dietary deprivation, the length and severity of the malnutrition, and continuing adverse nutritional, social, and economic factors following birth.

- Maternal emotional disturbance has been related to complications during pregnancy and delivery and to hyperactivity and irritability in infants after birth. It is difficult to discover the causes underlying these relationships because women who are emotionally upset during pregnancy may be poorly adjusted in a variety of ways that affect their caretaking and their infant's adjustment after birth.

- A wide range of maternal diseases and disorders can affect prenatal development, including **Rh factor incompatibility;** high blood pressure; diabetes; rubella; and sexually transmitted diseases such as **gonorrhea, syphilis, chlamydia, genital herpes,** and **acquired immune deficiency syndrome,** or **AIDS.** The effects of maternal diseases are related to the stage of fetal development during which they are contracted, and the length of time that they last.

- Mothers who smoke cigarettes or drink alcohol are more likely to bear premature or low-birthweight babies than women who do not smoke or drink. In addition, maternal drinking is related to **fetal alcohol syndrome,** which results in facial abnormalities, short stature, and mental retardation. Even modest amounts of alcohol and passive smoking have been related to negative effects in the offspring. Moreover, genetic effects of fathers' smoking and drinking may be passed to their offspring.

- In the case of illegal drugs like cocaine or heroin, drug-addicted infants may exhibit symptoms that disrupt parenting and result in long-term adverse outcomes for both child and parent. Drug-using mothers may have particular problems dealing with such infants because of their own troubles.
- Drugs taken by the mother during pregnancy, whether legal or illegal, may have a negative impact on the developing fetus. Sometimes, as in the case of **thalidomide** and **diethylstilbestrol,** the effects of the prescription drug on the infant are not known until much later.
- Some obstetrical medications used to ease pain and sedate women during labor and delivery may affect the newborn's behavior for several days after birth. However, there are often no longer-term effects of such drugs.

Birth and the Beginnings of Life

- Birth involves a series of changes in the mother that permit the child to move from the womb to the outside world. These include uterine contractions during the first stage of labor that allow the cervix to become large enough for the child's head; the child's descent into the birth canal and emergence out of the canal during the second stage; and the expulsion of the placenta during the third stage. If problems arise before or during the delivery, a **cesarean delivery** may be performed by removing the baby through an incision in the mother's abdomen.
- Birth complications occur in only about 10 percent of deliveries. Some important birth factors that are related to developmental deviations and mortality are **anoxia,** or lack of oxygen in the brain, prematurity, and low birthweight. Premature babies may be **preterm** or **small for date.** Anoxia, early birth, and low birthweight have been associated with physical, neurological, cognitive, and emotional deficits. Most of these negative effects diminish with age, except in extreme cases. Stimulation programs have been successful with low-birthweight babies in combating the effects of isolation and separation of infant and parents caused by spending the first weeks of life in an isolette.

Vulnerability and Resilience in Children At Risk

- According to the concepts of the continuum of reproductive casualty and the continuum of caretaking casualty, both birth complications and the environmental situations into which a child is born may vary greatly along continua that stretch from the most favorable to the least favorable conditions for the child's well-being.
- Researchers who have studied the interaction of these continua have found that often early environmental conditions that are more favorable can compensate to some extent for adverse perinatal complications.

Infancy: Sensation, Perception, and Learning

C H A P T E R 5

Joseph's dad played folk songs to his 3-day-old son while rocking him in his cradle; Rebecca's mother started reading Shakespearean sonnets to her when she was 1 month old; Jenny's grandmother bought her picture books and a brightly colored mobile, but she waited to give them to Jenny's mother until she thought Jenny was "ready" for them—at 6 months of age!

Each of these adults had different ideas about a baby's sensory capabilities. As researchers have learned more about the sensory and perceptual world of infants, they have found that babies can hear, see, and respond to interesting sights and sounds at a much earlier age than was once believed. Indeed, we even have some evidence that the fetus can hear its mother's voice and perhaps other sounds. Thus it would seem that the sensory world of a newborn is not the "blooming, buzzing confusion" that psychologist William James once declared it. Newborns are able to organize information and to respond selectively to it even in the first few minutes after birth.

This chapter begins with a look at the newborn's earliest observed behaviors, including its normal reflexes, its time spent in sleep or in wakefulness, its crying and ways of soothing it, and ways of assessing the newborn's health, maturity, and capacities. We then take a look at the infant's growth and development in the use of its sensory and perceptual abilities—auditory, visual, taste, and touch. We conclude with a review of the different kinds of learning we discussed in Chapter 1 as they are evidenced by the infant and with a brief discussion of the baby's memory abilities.

THE NEWBORN

neonate   A newborn baby.

Parents expecting one of those beautiful little creatures we see in ads for baby preparations on television and in the print media are sometimes shocked at the appearance of their newborns, for at the moment of birth and for a little while afterward, most newborns, or **neonates,** are pretty homely little beings. Their noses, ears, and entire heads often bear the marks of the pressures exerted on them as they passed through the birth canal, and their skin is often red, wrinkled, and blotchy, partly as the result of floating for nine months in the amniotic fluid. Their heads are oversized in proportion to their bodies (in fact, from childhood to adulthood the head goes from a quarter to an eighth of total body size), and their little legs appear weak, even useless. But despite these perhaps surprising characteristics—most of which disappear even before the newborn period of three to four weeks is over—most parents welcome their newborns with joy and love. Within a short time these new citizens of the world are as ready for the camera as any infant who models for disposable diapers or baby powder.

A New Baby's Reflexes

Despite their inauspicious looks, newborns are far from totally helpless, passive, nonreactive creatures. Indeed, they are highly competent organisms with surprisingly well-developed reflexes and sensory responses, and they are surprisingly well equipped to begin adapting to their new environments from the very first moments after birth. Nor are their responses random and disorganized; rather, newborns show a capacity to respond in an organized, meaningful way from a much earlier time than scientists had earlier assumed. In sum, babies are born with a repertoire of responses that are "ready to go," that do not require practice to execute, and that help them survive outside the womb.

reflex   A human being's involuntary response to external stimulation.

Some of the first behaviors to appear are **reflexes,** or involuntary responses to external stimuli. Table 5-1 describes the newborn's major reflexes, some of which are permanent (e.g., withdrawal reflexes, such as the knee jerk), others of which disappear during the first year of life. A number of these reflexes have obvious value in helping to ensure the newborn's survival. The rooting and sucking reflexes, for

TABLE 5-1 The Newborn's Major Reflexes

Reflex	Testing the Reflex		Significance of Response	Developmental Course of Reflex
	Method	Baby's Response		
Permanent				
Biceps reflex	Tap on the tendon of the biceps muscle	Baby displays short contraction of muscle	Reflex is absent in depressed babies or those with congenital muscular disease	Brisker in first few days
Eye blink	Flash bright light in baby's eyes	Baby blinks or closes eyes		Relatively unchanging
Patellar tendon reflex ("knee jerk")	Tap on the tendon below the knee cap, or patella	Baby quickly extends or kicks leg	Weak or absent in depressed babies or those with muscular disease; exaggerated in hyperexcitable babies	More pronounced in first 2 days than later
Withdrawal reflex	Prick sole of baby's foot gently with a pin	Baby withdraws foot and pulls leg up, bending knee and hip	Absent when there is damage to the sciatic nerve, the largest nerve of the body	Constantly present during first 10 days; less intense later
Temporary				
Babinski reflex	Stroke bottom of foot from heel to toes	Baby's big toe curves up and other toes fan and curl	Absent in defects of the lower spine	Usually disappears near end of first year; replaced in normal adult by plantar flexion of big toe
Babkin or palmar reflex	With baby lying on his back, apply pressure to both of baby's palms	Baby opens mouth, closes eyes, and moves head to midline position	Inhibited in general depression of the central nervous system	Disappears at 3–4 months
Moro reflex	Allow baby's head to drop back a few inches; lower baby's overall position about 6 inches and suddenly; or make sudden, loud noise	Baby throws arms outward and extends legs; then brings both arms back toward center of body, clenching fists	Absent or consistently weak reflex indicates serious problem in central nervous system	Disappears at 6–7 months
Palmar grasp	Press a finger or cylindrical object against baby's palm	Baby grasps finger or object	Weak or absent in depressed babies	Initially strong; disappears by 3–4 months; replaced by voluntary grasp within a month or so
Plantar or toe grasp	Press on the ball of the baby's foot	Baby curls all toes, as if grasping	Absent in defects of the lower spinal cord	Disappears between 8 and 12 months
Rooting response	Stroke baby's cheek lightly	Baby turns head toward finger, opens its mouth, and tries to suck	Absent in depressed babies	Disappears at about 3–4 months and becomes voluntary
Stepping reflex	Support baby in upright position and move her forward, tilting her slightly to one side	Baby makes rhythmic stepping movements	Absent in depressed infants	Disappears at 3–4 months
Sucking response	Insert finger 1–1.5 inches into baby's mouth	Baby sucks finger rhythmically	Weak, slow, interrupted sucking found in apathetic babies; maternal medication during childbirth may depress sucking	Often less intensive and regular in first 3–4 days; disappears by 6 months

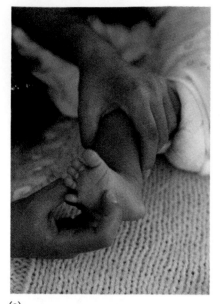

(a)

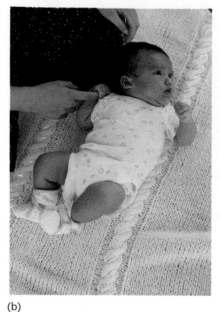

(b)

(c)

Newborns have lots of reflexes (many are described in Table 5-1), some of which they maintain throughout life and others that, though temporary, are important indicators of physical well being. The six-week old's Babinski reflex (a) tells the examiner that the child's lower spine is fully functional; the infant's palmar grasp (b) and rooting response at 4 weeks of age (c) both confirm the absence of harmful depression. A healthy rooting response may also rule out prenatal exposure to cocaine, and it is very useful in helping the newborn locate and obtain food.

example, help the newborn to locate and obtain food, the eye blink helps to shield the eyes from excessively strong light, and the withdrawal reflex helps to protect the baby from painful and possibly harmful stimuli. The functions of other newborn reflexes are less obvious. Researchers speculate that some of them may have bestowed as yet unknown survival benefits on the infants of our early ancestors.

At birth, physicians often specifically test the newborn for certain reflexes to evaluate the soundness of the baby's central nervous system. As we saw in the last chapter, many agents can have negative influences on the fetus during its life within its mother's uterus, and the infant's developing nervous system is particularly susceptible to such attacks. Infants exposed in utero to drugs such as cocaine, for example, show a variety of neurologic deficits that can be assessed by observing the infants' responses to specific kinds of stimulation (Phillips et al., 1996). Babies exposed to cocaine, for example, have been observed to show abnormal patterns in sucking intensity, rooting intensity, and motor abilities such as the ability to stand when supported. Moreover, these babies have performed poorly in assessments of their smiling, irritability, and consolability as well as their self-quieting activities.

Abnormalities in a baby's reflexes during the first days or weeks after birth can be useful in identifying visual and hearing problems, and they can even help predict abnormal functions that don't appear until months or years later (Dubowitz & Dubowitz, 1981; Francis, Self, & Horowitz, 1987). Reflexes that are either weak, absent, or unusually strong can be a sign of brain damage. Moreover, as we have noted, some reflexes normally disappear; their failure to do so may be a sign of neurological problems. As we will see in Chapter 6, the death of some neurons and the pruning of other neurons' connective fibers are part of the developmental process, and when these events do not take place, neurological difficulties surface. However, the nature of the child's caregiving environment is also an important predictor of infant neurodevelopment; a supportive environment can buffer the effects of less optimal neurodevelopment (Black, Schuler, & Nair, 1993).

Infant States

Among the most fascinating aspects of the newborn's behavior are the changes that occur in the baby's state of arousal, that is, its alternating states of sleep and wakefulness. Just as adults have recurring patterns of sleep and wakefulness, so too do babies.

The **infant state,** or this recurring pattern of arousal, ranging from alert, vigorous, wakeful activity to quiet, regular sleep, gives evidence of some important

infant state   A recurring pattern of arousal in the newborn, ranging from alert, vigorous, wakeful activity to quiet, regular sleep.

TABLE 5-2	Newborn Infant States	
State	*Typical Duration*	*Characteristics*
Regular sleep	8–9 hours	Infant's eyes are closed, and body is completely still. Respiration is slow and regular. Baby's face is relaxed, with no grimacing, and eyelids are still.
Irregular sleep	8–9 hours	Baby's eyes are closed, but baby engages in gentle limb movements of various sorts, writhing, and general stirring. Grimaces and other facial expressions are frequent.
Drowsiness	1/2 to 3 hours	Baby's eyes open and close intermittently and display recurrent rapid eye movements. Baby is relatively inactive. Respiration is regular, though faster than in regular sleep.
Alert inactivity	2–3 hours	Infant's eyes are open, have a bright and shining quality, and can pursue moving objects. Baby is relatively inactive; face is relaxed and does not grimace.
Waking activity	2–3 hours	Baby's eyes are open but not alert, and respiration is grossly irregular. Baby frequently engages in diffuse motor activity involving the whole body.
Crying	1–3 hours	Baby makes crying vocalizations and engages in diffuse motor activity.

Sources: Wolff, 1966, 1987.

principles of human behavior (Table 5-2). First, human behavior is *organized* and *predictable.* Rather than occur in a random, haphazard manner, infant states recur in a regular, periodic fashion as part of a larger cycle. Second, human beings are not passive, stirred into action only by outside stimulation. On the contrary, internal forces regulate much of our behavior and account for many changes in our activity levels (Schaffer, 1996). Psychologists who study infants know this all too well. Many have been frustrated when, after attaching an array of electrodes, wires, and recording equipment to an infant participant in an experiment, the infant has burped and happily drifted off to sleep before researchers could begin their formal procedures. This is not to say a baby's states can't be affected by outside forces; our later discussion of soothing techniques attests that they can be. Our point here is simply that internal forces play just as central a role in infant states as they do in adult states.

Evaluations of changes in fetal activity cycles and studies of infants born prematurely tell us that arousal patterns are formed well before birth (Sontag, 1944). In one infant study, even high-risk babies born two months prematurely were seen to exhibit regular changes in state that continued to develop and become more organized as the infants grew older (Holditch-Davis, 1990). As we discussed in Chapter 3, individual differences in state and the ability to regulate one's state of arousal are important components of temperament.

In broadest terms there are two fundamental infant states—waking and sleeping. However, the waking state may be quiet, active, or distressed, as in fussing and crying, and the state of sleeping also includes variations. Here we will focus on sleeping, which we discuss next, and crying behavior.

Sleep
Although babies display individual differences in the amount of time they spend sleeping, in general, as infants grow older they sleep less. The newborn, on average, sleeps about 70 percent of the time in a series of long and short naps that alternate regardless of whether it is night or day. By the time an infant is 4 weeks old her periods of sleep are typically fewer but longer, and by the time she is 8 weeks old she is sleeping more during the night and less during the day (Ferber, 1985; Sostek & Anders, 1981; Whitney & Thoman, 1994). As Figure 5-1 shows, the infant also becomes less fussy as she gains better control over her states of arousal. By the end of the first year, most infants sleep through the night, much to the relief of their parents, who have been trying to steer them toward this goal since their birth.

■ FIGURE 5-1

Infants' sleep patterns.
At 2 weeks of age, infants tend to maintain about the same ratio of total sleep, active sleep, and fussy crying in the morning, afternoon, and at night, but by the time they're 8 weeks old they have begun to spend appreciably more time in quiet sleep during the nighttime hours. (*Source:* Sostek & Anders, 1981)

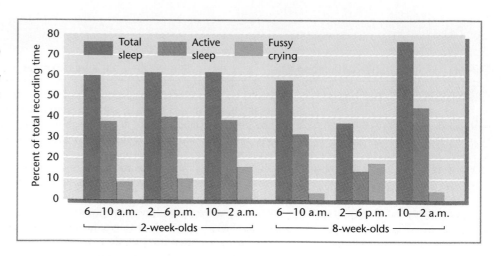

"Establishing a rhythm of diurnal waking and nocturnal sleep is in fact one of the more important developments in early infancy—it makes the baby so much easier to live with!" (Schaffer, 1977, p. 28). This shift to a culturally accepted sleep-wake cycle illustrates how the infant's internal biorhythms become adapted to the demands of the external world.

Not all cultures organize sleep patterns in the same way that U.S. parents do, which serves to remind us that biological rhythms are shaped by cultural practices and beliefs (Harkness & Super, 1995; Morelli, Rogoff, Oppenheim, & Goldsmith, 1992). Among the Kipsigis tribe of rural Kenya, infants are constantly with their mothers and regularly take naps throughout the day. In contrast to American babies, who gradually begin to sleep longer at night and less during the day, Kipsigis babies continue to take shorter and more frequent naps. Although these Kenyan babies eventually sleep through the night, they show this pattern much later than American babies (Super & Harkness, 1981).

Sleeping arrangements differ across cultures as well. In contrast to the U.S. custom of putting babies to sleep alone in their own rooms, many cultures encourage cosleeping arrangements in which parent(s) and infant sleep in the same bed. In a classic study of Japanese cosleeping arrangements, Caudill and Plath (1966) found that children coslept with their parents until they were between 13 and 15 years old—the time at which children usually reach puberty. Kipsigis babies also sleep with their mothers, but arrangements shift when a new child is born. The older sibling still sleeps with the mother, but at the mother's back, an indication that breast feeding and constant carrying is over for the older infant (Harkness & Super, 1995; Super & Harkness, 1981). And some mothers, like Mayan mothers in Guatemala, strongly disapprove of the U.S. custom of separate beds for babies; indeed, they regard it as "tantamount to child neglect" (Morelli et al., 1992, p. 608). Strongly held views like these clearly indicate that customs regarding sleeping arrangements "represent central ideas about family relationships and the proper course of human development" (Harkness & Super, 1995, p. 228). Moreover, as Box 5-1 suggests, cosleeping arrangements may also have specific health benefits for the developing infant (McKenna & Mosko, 1993).

By recording brain activity, investigators have distinguished different phases of sleep. The most important distinction is between **REM sleep** and **non-REM sleep.** REM or rapid-eye-movement sleep, is often identified with dreaming because in adults it is during dreaming that the eyes, under closed eyelids, have been observed to dart around in rapid, jerky movements. (As yet we have no way of knowing if infants dream as well.) REM sleep is characterized also by fluctuating heart rate and blood pressure. Because of these signs of arousal, REM sleep has also been termed *paradoxical sleep;* although we might expect movement of the body during

REM and **non-REM sleep**
REM, or rapid-eye-movement sleep is characterized by rapid jerky movements of the eyes and, in adults, is often associated with dreaming; infants spend 50 percent of their sleep in REM activity, whereas adults spend only about 20 percent. This activity is absent in the remaining, non-REM sleep.

BOX 5-1

Child Psychology in Action

Preventing Sudden Infant Death Syndrome

Each year in the United States about 10,000 babies die in their sleep from unknown causes. These deaths are often classified as **sudden infant death syndrome (SIDS)**, also known as *crib death*.

The prevention of SIDS requires identifying its most likely victims. So far we know that victims are more apt to be low-birthweight male babies who have a history of newborn respiratory problems, who were hospitalized longer than usual after birth, and who have abnormal heart-rate patterns and nighttime sleep disturbances (Mitchell et al., 1993; Rovee-Collier & Lipsitt, 1982; Sadeh, 1996). Their mothers are more likely to be anemic, to smoke or use narcotics, and to have received little prenatal care, although it should be stressed that most babies of women with this history are not affected. Usually, SIDS occurs during sleep in the wintertime, and it often follows a minor respiratory ailment, such as a cold. It is most common between the ages of 2 and 4 months and rarely occurs after 6 months.

The cause of SIDS is still a mystery. It is not due to accidental suffocation, to mucus or fluid in the lungs, or to choking on regurgitated food. Nor has there been any success in isolating a virus associated with it, although this is still a possibility. Another possibility is that *apnea*, the spontaneous interruption of breathing that sometimes occurs during sleep, especially REM sleep, may be a factor in SIDS (Steinschneider, 1975). The brain stem, which controls breathing, may not be well enough developed in these infants to overcome brief cessations in breathing. Researchers are investigating whether babies who have unusually long apnea periods during sleep may be more prone to SIDS.

Parental smoking has also been suggested as a contributing factor to crib death (Haglund, 1993; Mitchell et al., 1993). In addition, SIDS victims may have failed to develop adequate responses to nasal blockage and other threats to breathing (Lipsitt, 1990). Although newborns appear to have built-in defensive reactions to respiratory threats (e.g., when a cloth is placed over a baby's face she will use her hands to try to remove it), between 2 and 4 months of age these reactions may change from reflexive behaviors to voluntary ones. It is during this same age period that crib death is most common. Perhaps failure to make a smooth transition from reflexive to voluntary defenses puts an infant at greater risk for SIDS.

Monitors that sound an alarm to alert parents when an infant's breathing is interrupted may be useful in preventing SIDS. Although some authorities feel that the false alarms these devices occasionally trigger place too much stress on the parents, the evidence suggests that the devices may help to save lives. It can also be helpful to ensure that babies sleep on their backs or sides, not on their stomachs; sleeping in the latter position may depress breathing (Willinger, Hoffman, & Hartford, 1994). Another recommendation is that parents stop smoking, at least in close proximity to their baby (Mitchell et al., 1993). Finally, some researchers have suggested that Western cultures adopt the practices of many Eastern cultures where parent-infant cosleeping is common. Evidence suggests that in countries like Japan and China where this practice is common, rates of SIDS are lower (McKenna & Mosko, 1990). The cosleeping arrangements may aid the baby in breathing regulation, and it does put parents close at hand (McKenna & Mosko, 1993). This proposal is still controversial and needs further study, but maybe we do need to make more room for baby in our Western beds!

REM sleep, this does not happen; the body is relaxed. It may be that if the REM pattern is a reflection specifically of our dreaming, our bodies have been wisely organized so that we cannot act out our dreams. We have yet to discover the true purpose of REM sleep, but we do know that it has some functional value: If people are repeatedly awakened just as they begin REM sleep and thus prevented from obtaining sleep of this type, they tend to be irritable and disorganized during their later waking hours.

The phases of sleep observed in infants change with the child's age (Berg & Berg, 1987). Of particular interest is the change in the percentage of REM versus non-REM sleep. In newborns, 50 percent of sleep is REM sleep, but as children age, the proportion of their sleep characterized by rapid eye movements declines to about 20 percent. By the age of 18 most people are sleeping about eight hours a day, and of that amount, only about an hour and a half to an hour and three-quarters is REM sleep (see Figure 5-2). From there into old age they will continue to spend about the same proportion of time in REM sleep.

An **autostimulation theory** has been proposed to account for the high level of REM sleep in newborns. Researchers have suggested that the mechanism or process that causes REM sleep stimulates higher brain centers and that this in turn

sudden infant death syndrome (SIDS) The sudden, unexplained death of an infant while sleeping; also called "crib death."

autostimulation theory The theory that during REM sleep the infant's brain stimulates itself and that this in turn stimulates early development of the central nervous system.

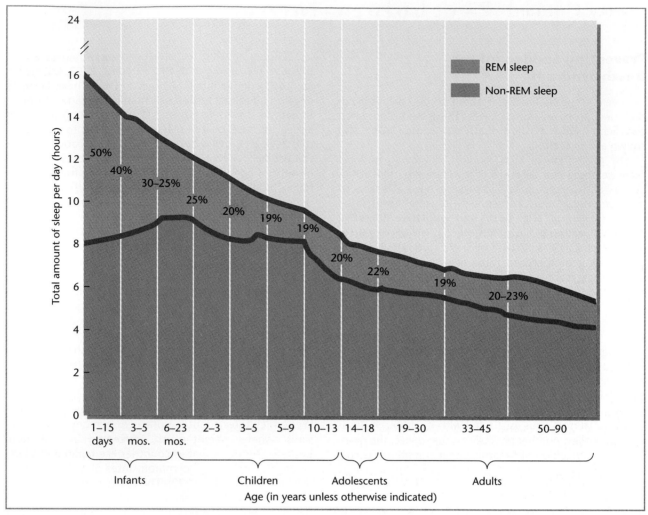

■ FIGURE 5-2
REM and non-REM sleep in infants and children.
Figures in the red area represent the proportion of total sleep time spent in REM sleep during the period depicted. The newborn spends half of her total sleep time in REM sleep, whereas the adolescent, having cut total sleep time almost in half, spends less than a quarter of sleep time in REM sleep. Although total sleep time declines somewhat farther in adulthood, the proportion of REM sleep varies around 20 percent from adolescence on. (*Source:* Adapted from Roffwarg, Muzio, & Dement, 1966, and from a later revision by these authors)

may stimulate early development of the central nervous system (Roffwarg, Muzio, & Dement, 1966). As the infant develops and becomes increasingly alert and capable of processing external stimulation, whether positive or negative in character, this type of built-in stimulation may become less necessary. If this theory is right, the speed with which infants reduce their percentage of REM sleep could depend on how much external stimulation they receive. Some researchers have found, for instance, that male newborns who have been circumcised and thus subjected to a high level of (negative) stimulation spent less time in REM sleep than uncircumcised infants, a finding that is consistent with the autostimulation theory (Emde, Harmon, Metcalf, Koenig, & Wagonfeld, 1971). Presumably, high levels of positive stimulation would yield similar results. The proportion of REM sleep also varies as a function of the amount of physical and social stimulation the child's home and early caretaking provide, as the autostimulation theory would predict. In one study, infants who were encouraged to stay awake and exposed to visual stimuli spent less time in REM sleep than infants in a control condition who were not provided these opportunities (Boismier, 1977).

Crying
At the other end of the continuum of infant states is crying, which, like sleep, is not a simple homogeneous state. Crying is considered important as one of the infant's earliest means of communicating needs to caregivers. Three different patterns of crying have been identified (Schaffer, 1971, p. 61):

Pattern	Characteristics
Basic	Linked to hunger, among other factors. Starts arrhythmically and at low intensity; gradually becomes louder and more rhythmic; sequence is cry-rest-inhale-rest.
Angry	Same as basic pattern except that segments of crying, resting, and inhaling vary in length, and crying segments are longer. Causes include removing a pacifier or toy.
Pain	Sudden in onset, loud from the start, and made up of a long cry followed by a long silence that includes holding of the breath, and then by a series of short, gasping inhalations. Causes include discomfort from soiled diaper, a pin prick or stomachache.

As infant expert Claire Kopp noted, "learning to understand the baby's cries is a little like learning a new language; it's terribly confusing at first" (1994, p. 36). Even so, most mothers can distinguish among these different types of crying but only when listening to the cries of their own babies (Wiesenfeld, Malatesta, & DeLoache, 1981). In general, fathers are less skilled than mothers at distinguishing among types of cries, men are less skilled than women, and nonparents are less skilled than parents (Holden, 1988). These differences are probably related to varying amounts of experience with babies and differences in the amount of time spent caring for them.

In the early months of life, crying is related to the infant's physiology; for example, hunger, hiccups, or digestive problems may disturb his sleep. By the third or fourth month, however, crying becomes less associated with physiological forms of distress and increasingly related to the baby's psychological needs (Kopp, 1994).

Cry patterns are part of a baby's emerging system of communication. Based on home observations of infants, researchers have found that simple crying in the absence of other communicative behavior (looking at, gesturing) decreases over time, and by their first birthday most babies use crying to "tell" caregivers something and get them to respond (Gustafson & Green, 1988). As a way of eliciting a caregiver response, crying often works. In one study, 77 percent of 2,461 episodes of crying studied were followed by some intervention on the mother's part (Moss, 1967). More recently, in a laboratory simulation study, both mothers and nonmothers responded to a crying baby doll by holding, talking to, and soothing the "baby" (Gustafson & Harris, 1990). This intervention becomes an opportunity for social interaction, so the parent is rewarded in two ways: The crying stops and the parent and child engage in a mutually enjoyable exchange (Lester, 1988).

People have been debating the wisdom of *always* responding promptly to a baby's cries for years. In the earlier part of this century, many people believed that rushing to soothe a crying infant would "spoil" the baby and encourage the infant to cry at the least little thing. Then, in the 1970s, research suggested that the opposite might be true: When mothers respond promptly to their crying infants, the frequency and duration of crying may actually *decrease* as the baby

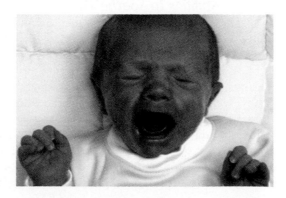

This infant is probably crying because of some form of physiological distress, like hunger, need for a diaper change, or digestive problems. By the time this baby is 3 or 4 months old, its crying—which is a clear form of communication—will often be related to psychological needs, such as the desire to be picked up and loved or played with.

develops the expectation that the mother can be counted on to help (Bell & Ainsworth, 1972).

In a study designed to test the accuracy of this more modern hypothesis, Hubbard and van IJzendoorn (1991) observed infants in their homes over the first 9 months of life. They found that the average duration of crying declined greatly after the first 3 months, probably because the babies were becoming adjusted to life in their new environments. Individual differences in the duration of crying could not be explained by differences in how promptly mothers responded to their babies. However, the researchers did find a correlation between the number of episodes of crying at the end of the first half year and the mother's speed of responding. And to the researchers' surprise, more frequent delays in responding seemed to cause a decrease in the number of crying bouts.

Hubbard and van IJzendoorn concluded that this result makes sense if we differentiate between responding promptly to severe distress on the part of a baby and responding promptly to mild fussing over a minor matter (such as an uncomfortable body position), which through practice the baby might learn to cope with independently. Parents are generally able to distinguish between these levels of distress without difficulty. Delaying a response to this second kind of crying may help to make the baby more self-sufficient in dealing with minor irritations, and so the child fusses less often. The parent, however, must be a good judge of the causes of the baby's cries, for ignoring the cries of a severely distressed infant could have serious consequences.

Sensitivity to differences in cries and their meanings is just as useful for physicians who treat the young as it is for parents. Crying patterns can be a helpful diagnostic tool that alerts pediatricians to possible abnormalities in early development (Lester, 1988). For instance, infants with brain damage and infants with Down syndrome take longer to cry in response to a painful stimulus, require a more intense stimulus to elicit a cry, and produce a less sustained, more arrhythmic, and higher-pitched cry than normal infants (Lester, Corwin, & Golub, 1988). In addition, unusual cries involving extreme variations in pitch have been noted in infants who later became SIDS victims (Lester et al., 1988), and a high-pitched, urgent, "piercing" cry can help to differentiate babies with colic from those who simply cry a great deal (Lester, Boukydis, Garcia-Coll, Hole, & Peucker, 1992). Thus, the infant cry is not only an important communicative signal but also an early warning sign of developmental problems and illness.

How to Soothe an Infant

Developmentalists have long known that as infants grow and mature they are less likely to cry or to engage in other behaviors that appear to signal distress but that don't seem to have specific causes. Nevertheless, researchers have been interested in identifying techniques that may be effective in relieving an infant's agitation and distress.

Infants' Abilities to Soothe Themselves

To some extent, infants can relieve their own distress. One good way is by sucking, a highly organized response in which, even while still in utero, the baby routinely engages. The components of the sucking response, such as the actions of the tongue and lips and the pressure applied to the nipple, are "prepackaged" as a small but elegant and coordinated system that produces sucking behavior—another example of how well prepared the infant is for the world.

After birth, sucking on a pacifier may soothe very young infants more rapidly and completely than almost any other method (Campos, 1989). Although it was long assumed that sucking was effective because of its association with feeding, researchers have found that, immediately after birth and before the baby's first oral feeding, simply sucking on a pacifier reduces a baby's distress (Field & Goldson,

1984; Kessen, Leutzendokff, & Stoutsenberger, 1967; Smith, Fillion, & Blass, 1990). It may be that sucking has a soothing effect because when the baby sucks, its overall body movements are lessened. Recent studies indicate, however, that sucking on certain specific substances more effectively calms infants than sucking on others. For example, sucking on substances with a sweet taste is more effective in calming young infants than sucking plain water (Smith & Blass, 1996). But the soothing techniques that work change as the infant develops. Some researchers have found that sucking on a sweet liquid appeared to be effective in calming a 2-week-old baby but was ineffective in soothing 4-week-olds unless accompanied by eye contact with an adult (Zeifman, Delaney, & Blass, 1996). Even by 4 weeks, it seems, the infant is learning to rely on social contact with caregivers to help regulate his states; as the researchers note, for 4-week-old infants "the eyes have it" (Zeifman et al., 1996, p. 1090).

How Parents Soothe Their Babies

Because infants pay more attention to events in their environment when they are in a calm but alert state, soothing babies and bringing them to a state in which they are neither too drowsy or upset is one of the critical tasks of parenting. To find out how to achieve this optimal state of alertness was the goal of a classic study by Korner and Thoman (1970). These investigators assessed the effectiveness of six different techniques for bringing either a crying or a sleeping newborn into a state of calm alertness. Figure 5-3 shows that clearly the most effective technique was holding the baby on one's shoulder. This position evoked bright-eyed visual scanning in 77.5 percent of the infants. Figure 5-3 also shows that the effect of a certain kind of stimulation depends heavily on the particular state the infant is in to begin with. For example, horizontal movement has a much greater effect on a crying baby than on a sleeping one. A variety of other techniques are effective in soothing a crying infant, including rocking and swaddling. In swaddling, one wraps the baby tightly in a blanket or cloth, thus keeping its arms and legs immobile (Byrne & Horowitz, 1981; Campos, 1989). Swaddling has been used successfully for many years in many cultures; it is common, for example, among the Navajos and Hopis of the American Southwest (Chisholm, 1963; Valsiner, 1989). For some cultural differences in babies' soothability, see Box 5-2.

Evaluating the Newborn's Health and Capabilities

Tests of reflexes (see Table 5-1) may be combined with other assessments to gauge the health, maturity, and capacities of a newborn (look back at the Apgar scoring system displayed in Table 4-3). A variety of scales have been developed to standardize these assessments (Francis et al., 1987). One of the most widely used is the

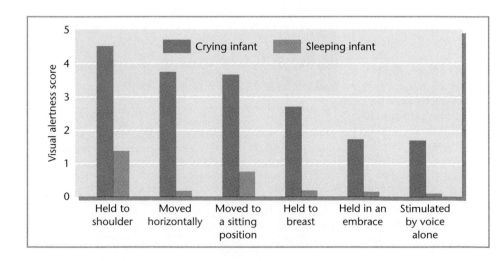

■ FIGURE 5-3
The effects of stimulation on an infant's visual alertness. In a classic study of how to bring an infant into a calm but alert state, holding the baby to one's shoulder was the most effective method. (*Source:* Korner & Thoman, 1970)

BOX 5-2

Perspectives on Diversity

How Culture Affects Soothability

Across cultures and nations there are wide differences in the ease with which babies in distress can be soothed (Bates, 1987; Rothbart & Bates, 1998). As we saw in our discussion of temperament in Chapter 3, some babies are easily calmed and others are really difficult to console; male infants are generally more difficult to pacify than female babies (Moss, 1967).

Of particular interest are the many cross-cultural and subcultural differences in infant soothability. For example, studying infants in the United States, Freedman (1974) found that European American babies shifted more frequently between states of contentment and distress than Chinese American babies. The latter tended to calm themselves more readily when they were upset and were also more easily consoled by caretakers. Moreover, these differences persisted over the first few months of infancy and affected how the infants were treated. Kuchner (1980) found that Chinese American mothers allowed their infants to cry for longer periods before intervening but that Chinese American babies quieted quickly with minimal intervention (e.g., simply hearing their mothers' voices).

Soothability is also greater among babies in some other cultural groups, both within the United States and beyond its borders. Japanese babies, for example, and babies of the Zinacanteco Indian tribe of southern Mexico are more easily quieted than other infants (Nugent et al., 1989). Navajo babies in the American Southwest who, for about the first year of their lives, spend much of the day encased in a cradleboard are also easier to soothe than many other babies.

The *cradleboard*, which is used in other Native North American tribes and in other parts of the world as well, is made up of a wooden back, a hinged footboard, and a hoop that arches over and shields the baby's head and face. These components are held together by leather thongs, and the board itself is cushioned with bedding material and a blanket, the corners of which are tucked in tightly around the baby's body. A laced cover holds the baby and the bedding in place. Newborns and sleeping infants are swaddled from the neck down, but after about three months babies' arms may be left free (Chisholm, 1963).

Although the use of the cradleboard certainly limits a baby's motor actions, it confers another advantage that the bassinet, the crib, and the traditional western carriage do not: it enables the baby to see what is going on around him from a more adult-like perspective (Chisholm, 1963). Because the cradleboard has a rigid back it can be propped up against a wall, a tree, and so on; the board is notched at the top so that it can be securely wedged in this upright position. (Of course, when the child is sleeping, the cradleboard is laid flat.) Toys, beads, feathers, and other objects that interest the baby are often hung from the hoop, and when her arms are free she can reach and bat at these playthings.

Experts disagree on whether to attribute the Navajo infant's greater soothability to the relative motoric restriction of his first year; indeed, some authorities argue that the Navajo newborn is calmer at birth and that this relative quiescence is the reason for the use of the cradleboard (Chisholm, 1963). Some researchers suggest, however, that swaddling has a calming influence on the newborn (see, e.g., Tronick, Thomas, & Daltabuit, 1994). Perhaps simply having more to look at, as the cradleboard baby apparently does, encourages a calm, quiet observational mode.

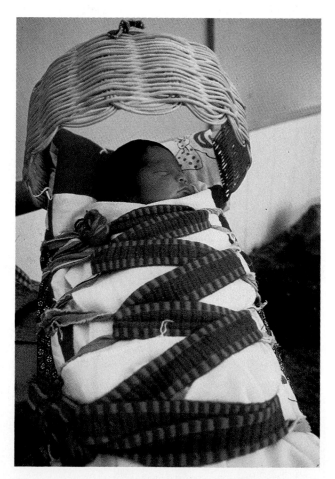

This Havasupai infant is tightly swaddled, providing the baby with a feeling of comfort and security. Like many choices in childrearing, the Native American cradleboard has clear tradeoffs. Although it restricts a baby's movements (until the infant's arms are freed, at about 3 months), because the mother carries it with her and can set it up against a firm backing, it also allows the baby to see and experience many things that the infant who spends most of its time in a crib may miss.

Brazelton Neonatal Assessment Scale (Brazelton, 1984; Brazelton & Nugent, 1995). As you can see from Table 5-3, this assessment device measures many of the capacities that we discuss in this chapter as they interact in the normal, healthy, full-term infant: sensory and perceptual capacities (orientation to sights and sounds, habituation to sensory stimuli); motor development; infant states and the ability to regulate them; and signs that the brain is properly controlling involuntary responses (Brazelton, Nugent, & Lester, 1987).

The Brazelton scale has been used for a variety of purposes. Performance on the scale helps to differentiate infants who are at risk for developmental problems (owing to prematurity or obstetric medication, for example) from healthy infants, and it can aid in diagnosing neurological impairment (Black et al., 1993; Eldredge & Salamy, 1988). For example, a 2-day-old infant was discovered to be blind when an examiner noted the baby's failure to track a bright object, a deficit that had been missed by the medical staff in their routine exams of the baby (Hollies, 1996). (Medical staff routinely evaluate a baby's vision and hearing in the delivery room by noting a simple response, such as movement, to the presentation of a light or a sound.) The Brazelton scale is also useful in predicting later development. For instance, newborns who score high on it tend to score higher on later measures of cognitive, motor, or social development (Bakeman & Brown, 1980; Keefer, Dixon, Tronick, & Brazelton, 1991; Moss, Colombo, Mitchell, & Horowitz, 1988). Finally, the Brazelton scale has been used as an intervention technique, teaching parents about their newborn's capacities either by having them watch a health-care professional administer this test to their baby or by having them try the same tests with their baby themselves. Research has shown that both parental caring and parent-infant interaction can be improved by such demonstrations, although the effects are modest (Britt & Myers, 1994).

In addition, a baby's behavior during the Brazelton assessment is related to later parent-infant interaction during feeding and play. Here the baby's capacities are probably interacting with the kind of parenting environment provided. What the baby is like tends to elicit certain responses on the part of the parents, and how the parents behave, in turn, encourages certain reactions in the child. In this vein, the study by Crockenberg (1981), described in Chapter 3, suggested that both infant temperament and the child-care environment were important predictors of a baby's later social relationships. As we discussed in Chapter 1, contemporary developmentalists increasingly view the interaction between biological, social, and other influences as the basis for human development.

The Brazelton neonatal scale can also detect cross-cultural variations in newborn behavior (Nugent, Lester, & Brazelton, 1991). For example, the superior motor performance of the Gusii, a West African people, in comparison to American babies was related to more vigorous handling by caregivers (Keefer et al., 1991). By 3 months of age, Gusii babies could be lifted by one arm and swung on the mother's back. Clearly the unique characteristics of infants' motor abilities influences the ways in which caregivers treat them and this, in turn, gives them further chances to improve their motor control. These findings underscore as well the value of an interactional or contextual perspective, in which biological capacities are shaped by social environmental factors.

THE INFANT'S SENSORY AND PERCEPTUAL CAPACITIES

As we've already noted, James's view of the newborn as subject to sensory confusion has been supplanted by the realization that the sensory and perceptual world of infants is anything but total chaos. Now that we have found ways to let babies tell us about their **sensations**—that is, what stimuli their sensory receptors detect—and

Brazelton Neonatal Assessment Scale A scale used to measure an infant's sensory and perceptual capabilities, motor development, range of states, and ability to regulate these states. The scale also indicates whether the brain and central nervous system are properly regulating autonomic responsivity.

sensation The detection of stimuli by the sensory receptors.

TABLE 5-3   Brazelton Neonatal Behavioral Assessment Scale

Capacity for Habituation

Habituation, a form of learning in which repeated exposure to a particular stimulus leads to reduced response to that stimulus, enables the infant to conserve energy by remaining alert to things in the environment only so long as they seem to merit attention because they seem either desirable or undesirable. The infant's ability to habituate is also a measure of her capacity for attention to new things in her environment. Tests include habituation to the following:

1. Light
2. Rattle
3. Bell
4. Pinprick

Orientation to Sights and Sounds

The baby's ability to focus on and track various stimuli is measured as an indication of his capacity to see, hear, and orient to things in his physical and social environment:

5. Visual focusing and following an inanimate object
6. Reacting to an inanimate auditory stimulus
7. Visual focusing and following a human face
8. Reacting to the sound of a human voice
9. Reacting to both the sight of a human face and the sound of the person's voice

Motor Development

These tests measure the infant's motor skills:

10. Baby's ability to pull to a sitting position
11. Defensive ability: baby's ability to free himself of light cloth placed over eyes
12. Degree of alertness
13. General tonus
14. Motor maturity
15. Activity

State: Range in Degree of Arousal

Tests measure the variability and intensity of the infant's periods of arousal:

16. Peak excitement
17. Rapidity with which excitement builds
18. Irritability: number of times the baby fusses and things that appear to irritate her are recorded
19. Lability, or variability, of state: frequency and intensity of changes in state are noted

State: Regulation and Self-Regulation

These tests measure the infant's responsiveness to efforts to quiet or soothe her as well as her ability to quiet herself:

20. Cuddliness: A measure of the baby's willingness to be held and to conform to the examiner's body
21. Consolability with intervention: A measure of how long it takes an examiner to quiet a baby who is upset
22. Self-quieting: the baby's own efforts to soothe himself, as by thumb sucking, are measured.
23. Whole hand to mouth

Autonomic Stability

Tests measure the infant's autonomic (uncontrolled) reactivity to various stimuli:

24. Tremors: Severe tremulousness may indicate problems in the central nervous system
25. Startles: The baby's tendency to react to sudden movement, loud sounds, and other strong stimuli with a startle response is measured
26. Skin: Reactivity is assessed by measuring electrical activity on the surface of the skin

Source: Adapted from Brazelton et al., 1987.

TURNING POINTS: The Development of Sensation, Perception, and Early Learning

EARLY WEEKS   Baby can distinguish strong visual contrasts; hears sounds. Demonstrates size constancy and early forms of imitation.

1 MONTH   Baby likes to look at faces; scans visually. Differentiates speech from other sounds. Has learned to tell difference between breast nipple, bottle nipple, thumb, and pacifier.

2 MONTHS   Infant tracks objects visually from side to side. Likes to hear sounds with different intonations. Baby has learned that breast or bottle bring nourishment; she stops crying at the mere sight of either.

3 MONTHS   Baby sees objects clearly, can sustain alertness, begins to localize sounds. Has recognition memory; remembers when cued.

4 MONTHS   Baby looks more alert. Distinguishes colors, shapes, sizes. Can hear and respond to soft sounds; coordinates looking and listening. In immediate anticipation, at sight of bottle opens mouth.

5 MONTHS   Attends to smaller objects; has better depth perception; recognizes a face even if it is upside down. Listens quietly to speech and shows signs of pleasure; takes more interest in sounds. Remembers pictures of faces.

6 MONTHS   Recognizes familiar people easily; visual acuity approximates normal adult vision.

7 MONTHS   Recognizes facial features and distinguishes male and female faces.

8 MONTHS   Shows more interest in distant objects. Becomes quiet when others talk. Distinguishes between questions and declarative statements.

9 MONTHS   More visually aware of tiny objects; if given choice of picking up either large or small object will choose the smaller item. Begins to remember without cues. Uses knowledge to solve problems; aware of cause and effect; recognizes that his own actions may affect outcomes. "Uses" other people to make things happen.

10 MONTHS   Begins to visually group similar objects. Discriminates an object within another: e.g., a cookie inside a jar. Investigates textures, designs, or parts of toys; repeats play sequences with different toys. Peers intently at pictures.

11 MONTHS   Uses props as aids, e.g., uses chair to pull to standing position.

12 MONTHS   Groups toys with like features, such as color or size. Checks own feet when walking. No longer discriminates speech sounds that are not in parents' language(s). Uses imitative learning. Deliberately introduces variations into play sequences. Memory is improved.

15 MONTHS   Makes groupings of objects that go together. Trial and error learning. More aware of functions of objects. Recognizes and uses more cause-and-effect relationships.

18 MONTHS   Differentiates round puzzle pieces from square ones. Recall memory improved. Has primitive idea of what "should be": puts lids on jars; pays attention better; recognizes that others have possessions.

21 MONTHS   Differentiates round, square, and triangular puzzle pieces and puts them in puzzle with help. Has some understanding of past, present, and future, some idea of categories.

24 MONTHS   Tries to copy lines on paper. Elaborate play sequences show recognition of family members' specific roles. Begins to use strategy-like, or planned, behaviors.

Sources: Aslin, Jusczyk, & Pisoni, 1998; Haith & Benson, 1998; Kellman & Banks, 1998; Kopp, 1994.

Note: Developmental events described in this and other Turning Points charts represent overall trends identified in research studies. Individual children vary greatly in the ages at which they achieve these developmental changes.

perception The interpretation of sensations in order to make them meaningful.

their **perceptions**—their interpretations of the stimuli they detect (what they see and hear)—we know that their sensory and perceptual capabilities are quite well organized even at birth, allowing them to begin adapting immediately to their new environments. As this chapter's Turning Points chart (p. 155) shows, at only 1 month a baby enjoys looking at faces and can differentiate speech from other kinds of sounds.

The infant is especially well equipped to respond to his social environment, including human voices, faces, and smells. This suggests that a baby's sensory and perceptual systems may be biologically prepared or programmed to be sensitive to social stimuli. Such programming is clearly adaptive, for a baby's responsiveness to other human beings increases caregivers' interest in the child and so enhances the child's well-being and survival. The infant's inborn sensitivity to social stimuli is one of the themes we will develop in this section of the chapter.

A second theme concerns the interdependence of the various sensory and perceptual systems—vision, hearing, taste, smell, and touch. To present the "facts" about these systems in an orderly way, we have treated each one separately. In the real world, however, these systems develop together, and advances in one may trigger changes in another. Later in this section we will put the developmental pieces together and show how these systems influence each other, all working together to help the infant understand the world.

Of course, perception and action are not independent of each other either. Changes in an infant's physical growth and motor capabilities, such as the emergence of crawling or walking, can have a profound effect on how that child perceives the world. We will look at the interplay of these two developmental domains in the next chapter. The more we know about human development, the more important the principle of interdependence among systems seems to be.

Unlocking the Secrets of Babies' Sensory Capabilities

Because babies guard the secrets of their capabilities very well, it is not easy to study infants' sensations and perceptions. Without language skills, babies can't respond to direct questions as to whether one tone is louder than another or whether they see a difference between two colors. Very young babies even have trouble reaching or pointing toward something that is interesting to them, and crawling in the direction of an interesting stimulus is far beyond their skills. Thus, many of the research methods we use to study sensation and perception in older children and adults are useless in studying infants. What's more, even if we determine that infants possess a certain sensory capability (e.g., distinguishing between the tastes of sweet and sour), how can we be sure that the infants we study define such differences by the same standards we use? Perhaps subjective judgments change with age.

In their efforts to solve these problems, psychologists have used research techniques that capitalize on whatever responses young babies are able to make. In recent years researchers have used the medium of the autonomic nervous system, which controls such functions as heart rate and breathing, to probe an infant's sensory capabilities. For instance, a change in a baby's respiration following a change in the pitch of a sound suggests that the infant heard the pitch change. A newborn's motor responses, although limited, can also give clues to sensory abilities. In fact, one of the earliest means of detecting sensory capabilities was the *stabilimeter,* an apparatus that monitors changes in an infant's movements. Researchers have also used the infant's well-developed sucking pattern as an index of the effect of sensory input. Infants' sucking patterns can change, for example, in intensity or duration of sucking. By noting such changes while presenting a series of stimuli to an infant, researchers can determine that the baby has discriminated or detected a difference between different stimuli presented.

Another commonly used technique of examining infants' abilities to distinguish visual stimuli is the **visual preference method,** in which Robert Fantz (1963) pioneered. In this technique, the examiner presents an infant with two stimuli and measures the amount of time that she spends looking at each. If the infant looks longer at one stimulus than at the other, we can assume not only that she prefers the former but that she can distinguish the two stimuli from each other. The results form an index of the infant's ability to distinguish the two visual stimuli.

Our ability to measure these various responses as indicators of sensory capabilities depends on infants' tendency to **habituate** to a repeatedly presented stimulus, that is, gradually to lessen the intensity of their initial reaction to it until they respond only faintly or not at all (see also Table 5-3). For example, if you shake a rattle near a baby's head, the child may display a *startle* response, thrashing his arms and legs and making general body movements. This response diminishes if you repeat the noise a second time: The infant may give only a brief kick. After a few more times, the infant appears to ignore the sound completely and shows no response at all. Now if you present a different sound, such as a bell, the baby will once again show a reaction, until she habituates to the new noise. This reaction to the new sound tells you that the baby can distinguish between the rattle and the bell. Babies show the same habituation process for stimuli to the other senses—sights, smells, tastes, and tactile sensations. Therefore, habituation is widely used to explore infants' sensory and perceptual capabilities. And in fact this research technique was used to obtain much of the information that we discuss in next few sections on the infant's senses of hearing, vision, smell, taste, and touch.

visual preference method A method of studying infants' abilities to distinguish one stimulus from another by measuring the length of time they spend attending to different stimuli.

habituation The process by which an individual reacts with less and less intensity to a repeatedly presented stimulus, eventually responding only faintly or not at all.

Hearing: The Littlest Pitchers Have Big Ears

Tests administered shortly after birth show that a newborn's hearing is extremely well developed (Aslin et al., 1998). This is not surprising when you consider that the development of the fetus's auditory system is completed well before birth (see Turning Points chart in Chapter 4). One study, in which researchers monitored changes in fetal body movements and heart rates, showed that even before birth, fetuses may hear complex sounds that are presented outside the mother's body (Kisilevsky & Muir, 1991). Such sounds are carried through the amniotic fluid to the fetus as a series of vibrations. Even more interesting is the evidence that infants may learn and remember what is read to them before they were born; as you can see in Box 5-3, fetuses can apparently learn to distinguish not only their mother's voices but the sounds and rhythms of the material their mothers are reading.

It's important to remember, however, that a newborn's hearing is not as well developed as an adult's. For a newborn, a sound must be louder—about 10 to 17 decibels louder—than the sound that an adult can detect (Hecox & Deegan, 1985). (A *decibel* is a measure of sound pressure level, which we perceive as loudness.) Normal conversational speech is generally measured at about 60 decibels, the sound of a train at approximately 100 decibels, and a whisper at around 20 decibels. In addition, compared with adults, babies are less sensitive to low-pitched sounds; they are more likely to hear a sound that is high in pitch (Aslin, et al., 1998). This may help explain why adults so often raise the pitch of their voices when talking to an infant: They know implicitly that a high-pitched voice is more likely to capture the child's attention. Over their first 2 years, however, babies rapidly improve in their ability to discriminate sounds of different pitch, until eventually they reach adult levels of discrimination.

Babies are remarkably sensitive to other differences in the qualities of sounds; for example, they can express a preference for music as opposed to other sounds and for one type of music over another. Even newborns will alter their sucking patterns in one of the ways we've discussed if doing so allows them to hear music instead of

BOX 5-3

Child Psychology in Action

Can Infants Learn Even Before They're Born?

Speculating as to why newborn human babies perceive sound so well, Anthony DeCasper asked himself if perhaps they had already learned to listen in the womb. How could he test such a proposition? With a colleague, DeCasper designed a clever procedure in which babies could suck to control what they heard on a tape recorder: either their mother or a strange woman speaking to them (DeCasper & Fifer, 1980). As you will learn elsewhere in this chapter, newborns can learn to vary their patterns of sucking. In this study, when infants sucked in a pattern of longer and shorter bursts, they activated their mother's voice on the tape recorder; a different sucking pattern activated the stranger's voice. The researchers found that infants sucked to hear their own mother's voice in preference to the voice of the stranger.

It could be argued, of course, that the infants probably heard their mother's voice from the time of birth and thus could have learned to prefer it in their first hours of life. To rule out this familiarity hypothesis, DeCasper and Spence (1986) designed another study in which 16 pregnant women were asked to read Dr. Seuss's famous children's book, *The Cat in the Hat*, to their fetuses twice a day for the last six and a half weeks of pregnancy. Some remarkable results occurred. After birth, when these women's infants could suck in one distinctive pattern to hear their mother's tape-recorded voice read *The Cat in the Hat,* or in another pattern to hear them read *The King, the Mice and the Cheese*, they sucked to hear *The Cat in the Hat*! Because in this test condition, the mothers read not just one of the poems but both of them, it seems pretty clear that what the babies preferred was not their mothers' voices per se but their mothers' voices reading the poem to which the infants had been exposed prenatally.

Although these studies give us evidence that prenatal auditory experiences influence postnatal auditory preferences, we don't have a clear understanding of the exact mechanisms involved in prenatal learning. The sounds babies hear in utero, filtered through the mother's body and the amniotic fluid, must be different from the sounds of their mothers' voices as they hear them after birth. It may be that the component of maternal speech to which

the fetus responds is *prosody*. Prosody includes the rhythm, intonation, and stress of speech and is carried by the sound frequencies that are least altered in the prenatal environment. Because both of the books the mothers in DeCasper's and Spence's studies read to their babies are long poems but of very different meters, the infants may also have been expressing a preference for the familiar prosody.

The evidence that newborns may exhibit a postnatal preference for a specific passage or melody experienced prenatally is accumulating (DeCasper & Spence, 1986; DeCasper & Spence, 1991; Fifer & Moon, 1989). At the same time, despite the claims of marketers and other commercial enterprises, prenatal conditioning has its limits. It is unlikely to produce the supreme benefits claimed by those who want to sell stereo sets for babies, and it's not likely either to raise babies' IQs or radically modify their sociability. That said, there's no reason why expectant mothers shouldn't treat themselves and their unborn infants to their favorite music—a little Bach today, baby?

Reading *The Cat in the Hat* to her unborn baby, this mother may well know that the fetus is sensitive to its mother's voice as heard in the womb. Whether this woman believes that her baby will get a head start on learning language we can't know; however, research has also shown that newborn babies prefer to hear not only their own mothers' voices but the specific pieces of poetry or prose their mothers read to them before they were born!

---

general noise (Butterfield & Siperstein, 1972). By the time they are 2 months old, infants can distinguish among some types of musical sounds, such as those produced by bowing or by plucking the strings of a violin (Jusczyk, Rosner, Cutting, Foard, & Smith, 1977). By the age of 6 months, infants can even distinguish changes in melodies (Chang & Trehub, 1977; Trehub & Trainor, 1993). And infants who are 4 to 6 months old seem to prefer music composed of common chords to music composed of tone combinations not found in common chords (Kagan & Zentner, 1996; Schellenberg & Trehub, 1996). Kagan and Zentner (1996) suggest that "the human infant may possess a biological preparedness" to prefer certain types of music (p. 29).

Several researchers have found that 6-month-old infants are able to distinguish melodies whether they are based on Western musical scales or on Javanese (*pélog*) scales, whereas adult participants did better with the Western scales (Lynch, Eilers, Oller, & Urbano, 1990). "This suggests that in early stages of development infants are equally adept at processing either scale type but that culture-specific experience enhances their ability to process one type of scale over the other" (Aslin et al., 1998, p. 177). As we will see in Chapter 8, research has revealed a similar shift in the infant's response to speech sounds. From initially responding to the speech sounds of many languages, within the first year infants come to respond only to those of the language spoken by those around them.

Babies can also locate where a sound comes from and judge how far away it is. Even newborns will turn their heads toward the sound of a rattle, suggesting that they know what direction the sound came from (Clifton, 1992; Muir & Clifton, 1985; Muir & Field, 1979). Studies also show that 6- to 12-month-old babies are quite good at gauging a sound's distance, particularly when a sound is getting closer (Morrongiello, Hewitt, & Gotowiec, 1991). Because the ability to perceive approaching sounds can have survival value if the source of the sound is on a collision course with the listener, some researchers speculate that the auditory system may be programmed to facilitate this perception.

The human auditory system may also be programmed for special sensitivity to the sound of human voices (Aslin, 1987; Aslin et al., 1998). There seems to be something about a human voice that babies as young as 2 days old prefer to hear, particularly a voice that is high in pitch with exaggerated pitch contours (Aslin et al., 1998; Cooper & Aslin, 1990; Fernald, 1985). Mothers may be aware of these preferences, for when they are with an infant they speak in a high-pitched voice and sing in a high-pitched and melodic fashion (Trehub, Unyk, & Trainor, 1993). Perhaps this accounts in part for the fact that lullabies are sung throughout the world to soothe infants (Trehub & Trainor, 1993). And infants notice: Babies ranging in age from 4 to 7 months prefer infant-directed playsongs and lullabies over non-infant-directed singing (Trainor, 1996).

Babies also learn to discriminate among voices very quickly; as we've seen, even as newborns they can distinguish their mothers' voices from those of other female voices. These abilities, which reflect the contributions of both innate factors and learning, facilitate the development of an emotional bond between parent and child by first channeling babies' attention to other human beings and then helping them single out important adults in their world. Thus, early auditory skills and preferences have functional significance for social development. They also have significance for the development of language, as you will see in Chapter 8.

Vision: How Babies See Their Worlds

Some baby animals, such as kittens, cannot see at all for days after birth, but the eyes of a newborn human being are physiologically ready to begin responding to visual stimuli. Newborn humans can detect changes in brightness, distinguish movement in the visual field, and follow or track a moving object with their eyes (Field, 1990; Kellman & Banks, 1998). In this section we look at several important aspects of visual development.

The Clarity of Infants' Vision

Visual acuity is sharpness of vision, or the clarity with which a person can discern fine details. Since it is harder to see the details of a small object than a big one, acuity and viewing distance are related. If from 20 feet away you can read a letter of the alphabet that people with perfect vision can read from 40 feet, you have 20/40 vision, a relatively small deviation from the optimum of 20/20. The vision of infants under 1 month of age ranges from 20/200 to 20/800 (Courage & Adams, 1990; Dobson & Teller, 1978). This means that most objects not held close to a baby's face

visual acuity Sharpness of vision; the clarity with which fine details can be discerned.

This little girl appears quite fascinated by the patterns displayed in the mobile over her crib. Perhaps this is because, at three months of age, she may be perceiving the patterns in their entirety rather than just the portions of them—such as a corner or periphery—that she perceived at an earlier age.

appear to her as quite blurry and indistinct. Visual acuity improves rapidly over the next few months, however, and seems to be within the normal adult range by the time a child is between 6 months and a year old (Banks & Shannon, 1993; Kellman & Banks, 1998). Figure 5-4 displays the finest black stripes that most 1-week-old infants can discriminate from a gray field when the target is 1 foot away. Babies can discriminate only very coarse outlines at first, but gradually as they develop they can detect more detailed patterns; thus, little by little they are able to detect stripes that are closer together (Kellman & Banks, 1998). To appreciate this ability to see details more clearly, examine Figure 5-5, which shows how well an infant can see at birth and at 1, 2, 3, and 6 months in comparison with what an adult sees.

Babies Do See Colors

By 3 months of age infants can distinguish among most colors and can group colors into basic categories, such as reds, blues, and greens (Teller, 1997; Teller & Bornstein, 1987). For instance, when presented with two shades of blue, a 3-month-old usually responds as if these colors were more similar than one of these shades of blue and a shade of green, even though the three shades are equidistant from each other on the color wheel. Although such findings suggest that both our ability to perceive color and the way we perceive it are probably innate, there is some evidence that infants younger than 7 weeks can't make effective color discriminations (Banks & Shannon, 1993; Kellman & Banks, 1998). The fact that structures and neural pathways important in color discrimination are quite immature during the first weeks of life may account in part for these deficits. In addition, it may be that researchers fail to detect color discrimination in babies because methodological problems in testing young infants confound hue and brightness.

How Babies Perceive Patterns

Psychologists have long debated whether the visual world of a young infant, like that of an adult, is organized into patterns, forms, and unified wholes or whether a baby sees merely unrelated lines, angles, and edges, only gradually learning through experience to perceive larger patterns. The nativist, or hereditary, position supports the first of these two viewpoints, the empiricist, or environmental, position the second. Although there is evidence in favor of both viewpoints, most findings suggest that learning and experience are generally required to see forms and patterns in an adult manner.

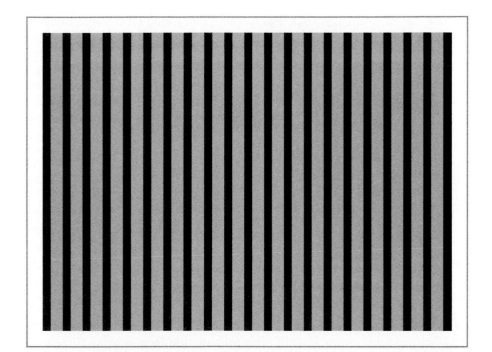

■ FIGURE 5-4

Visual discrimination in infants.

At 1 week of age, infants can discriminate black stripes of this size from a gray field when they are a foot away from the target. This is only about one-thirtieth as fine a discrimination as an adult with normal vision can make, but by the time infants are 8 months old they see about one-fourth as well as adults, and they achieve adult levels by the time they're about 5 years old. (*Source:* Maurer & Maurer, 1988)

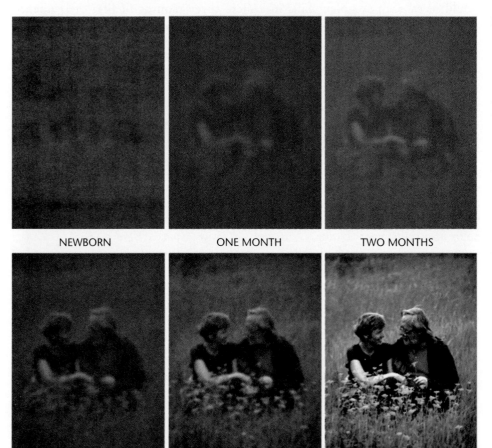

NEWBORN   ONE MONTH   TWO MONTHS

THREE MONTHS   SIX MONTHS   ADULT

■ FIGURE 5-5

How well can infants see?

Newborn infants can perceive motion of large, high-contrast objects, but they probably have no depth perception or color vision and very little if any ability to detect low contrast or fine spatial details (a). At 1 month, babies still show little response to color (b), but 2-month-old babies can begin to see color (c). At 3 months babies' color vision is good, although their depth perception is still poor (d). By 6 months infants see quite well (e), and scientists presume that children's vision continues to improve until it reaches the clarity of the normal adult's sight (f). (*Source*: Teller, 1997)

In one classic study, Salapatek and Kessen (1966) used an infrared camera to determine precisely where on a triangle newborns directed their eyes. They found that a newborn's gaze was not distributed over the whole triangle, as an adult's would be. The typical newborn centered attention on one of the triangle's angles, sometimes, in a limited way, also scanning part of an edge. This suggests that although certain elements of a complex pattern attract a newborn's attention (angles, edges, boundaries), we should not conclude that babies this young perceive whole forms. If they did, they would scan entire forms more completely. The scanning of forms improves quite quickly with age, however. By the age of 2 months, babies visually trace both the edges of a pattern and the internal areas (Aslin, 1987; Kellman & Banks, 1998; Salapatek, 1969). This suggests that they have made some advances in seeing the various parts of a pattern in a unified way.

By 3 months of age, babies are also almost as good as adults at picking unified patterns out of generalized movement (Bertenthal, 1996; Bertenthal & Clifton, 1998). For example, when the amount of the visual information you have about an object, except for information about its motion, is reduced to a minimum, you still automatically see its three-dimensional form. If 10 or 12 points of light are attached to a walking person's head and major joints, adults quickly recognize this moving display as depicting a person. By testing babies 3 to 5 months of age with this same kind of stimulus, researchers have found that even infants this young can extract the same kind of form information from motion (Figure 5-6; Bertenthal, Proffitt, & Cutting, 1984). Inasmuch as it is unlikely that infants could learn such complex skills in a mere three months of life, the evidence strongly suggests that they possess certain inborn motion-processing abilities. Note, however, that although infants 3 and 5 months old can extract a human figure's structure from information about its motion, they don't seem to recognize the form as a person until they are somewhat older—around 9 months of age (Bertenthal, Proffitt, & Kramer, 1987).

A Preference for Faces

The ability to perceive faces is a special kind of pattern perception that seems to develop along with the ability to see other kinds of forms. In the beginning, babies do not seem very good at seeing a face as a whole instead of a collection of parts.

■ FIGURE 5-6
Extracting information about form from movement. Three- to 5-month-old infants are able to detect a form from a moving array of lights but not from a static display. This suggests that motion helps infants understand a form and that this capacity to infer form from movement may be innate or at least develops very early. (*Source*: Bertenthal, Proffitt, & Kramer, 1987)

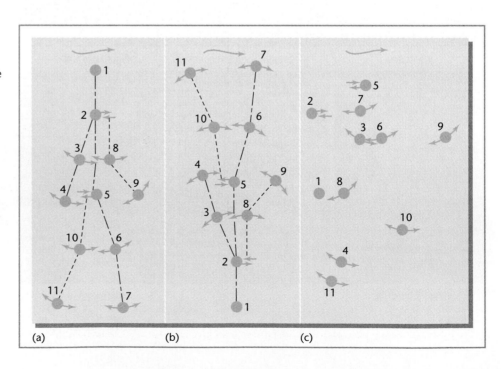

(a) (b) (c)

This is suggested by studies of the way young infants scan faces. As you can see in Figure 5-7, newborns approach a line drawing of a face in the same way they deal with a triangle: They scan only small sections of the outermost contours of the face. Two-month-olds, however, quickly move their eyes to the internal features (Maurer & Salapatek, 1976).

Other researchers, using adult participants' real faces, have documented these same developmental shifts in infants' scanning (Haith, Bergman, & Moore, 1977). These investigators highlighted a finding that can also be seen in Figure 5-7's illustration of the earlier research: Not only did 7-week-old infants spend less time on the contours of real faces, but they also looked at the eyes more than the younger infants did. "It is possible that . . . the eyes . . . become [more] meaningful to the infants as signals of social interaction. Whatever the case, it is highly likely that increased face looking, and especially eye contact, carries special social meaning for the infant's caretakers and plays an important role in the development of the social bond" (Haith et al., 1977, p. 8).

But the fact that internal facial features, especially the eyes, strongly draw the attention of infants by 7 weeks of age does not mean that babies this young are seeing faces as unified wholes. Facial features may simply happen to possess an abundance of perceptual qualities, such as contour, contrast, and movement, that are intrinsically appealing to the infant. Even the discovery that newborns prefer their mothers' faces over the faces of strangers does not necessarily mean that newborns are seeing faces as adults do (Walton, Bower, & Bower, 1992). Instead, the newborn's recognition of and preference for its mother's face may simply reflect the baby's focus on one particular feature of her face. In fact, Pascalis and his colleagues (1995) found that 4-day-old newborns looked longer at their mothers faces than at strangers only when the mother was not wearing a head scarf. This may suggest that the hairline and the outer contour of the face have an integral part to play in the newborn's face recognition. On the other hand, because different investigators have used different methods, it may be premature to draw firm conclusions about the way newborns process facial information. Researchers are still trying to bring the exact features that newborns use into focus!

Other research supports the notion that 7-week-old infants may still be a little too young to perceive whole faces the way adults do (Nelson, 1987). Before they're 2 months old, most babies cannot discriminate a "proper" schematic drawing of a face from a scrambled one (in which the separate features appear in the wrong

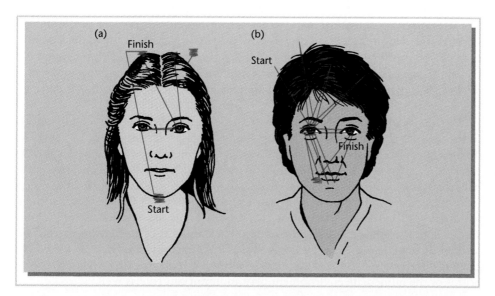

FIGURE 5-7
How infants scan the human face.
(a) A 1-month-old baby sticks pretty much to the outer perimeter of the face, although he shows some interest in the eyes. (b) An infant who is 2 months old focuses particularly on the features of the face, paying a lot of attention to the eyes and mouth. (*Source:* Maurer & Salapatek, 1976)

■ FIGURE 5-8
Evaluating infants'
preferences for faces over
other patterns.
By the time they were 3 months
old, infants clearly preferred the
"best" face (a) to its reverse (b).
Finding that infants had no
preference between patterns (c)
and (d) established that it was
the "naturalness" of the face in
(a) that they liked rather than its
lack of borders. (*Source:*
Dannemiller & Stephens, 1988)

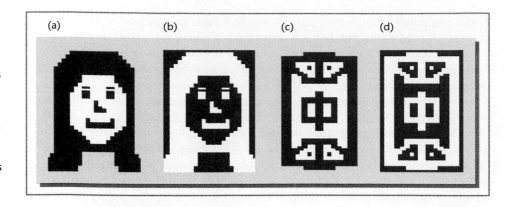

locations; e.g., the nose where the mouth should be). By 3 months of age, however, they show a clear preference for drawings of faces with correctly positioned features. This suggests that at this stage of development, instead of seeing a face as a mere collection of interesting parts, infants now perceive it as a unified whole (Mauer & Mauer, 1988; Olson & Sherman, 1983).

In one experiment that supported this ability of the 3-month-old, researchers showed 1½- and 3-month-old infants the computer-generated stimuli displayed in Figure 5-8 (Dannemiller & Stephens, 1988). Although stimulus (a) looks much more facelike than stimulus (b), the two are identical except that the shading is reversed. At 1½ months, babies showed no preference between these two stimuli, but at 3 months they looked longer at (a), the "better" face. This was not simply because they had a preference for pictures with black borders and white interiors, for they showed no similar preference for stimulus (c) over stimulus (d). These findings suggest that by 3 months of age babies identify faces as faces. The shift from perceiving parts to perceiving whole patterns appears to occur at about the same time for both objects and faces.

Interestingly, babies seem to prefer that faces be not only correctly patterned but attractive. Judy Langlois and her colleagues (1987) showed groups of infants who were 2 to 3 months old and 6 to 8 months old color slides of women's faces. The researchers presented these slides in pairs: One of each pair had been rated attractive by adult judges; the other had been rated unattractive. Both the younger and the older babies looked longer at the "attractive" faces; babies as young as 2 months of age showed a preference for attractiveness. Follow-up studies by Langlois, Roggman, and Reiser-Danner (1990), using both dolls that had been judged attractive or unattractive and adult participants who wore life-like latex masks of theatrical quality that had also been judged either attractive or unattractive, supported these researchers' original findings. One-year-old children played more with the "attractive" doll and clearly preferred to interact with the adults wearing the "attractive" mask, smiling at the adult, laughing, and withdrawing less often from him or her than from the person wearing the "unattractive" mask.

Why do infants prefer attractive faces? Some argue that such faces contain more of the features that the infant's visual system is organized to react to: Infants prefer high contrast, contours, curves, and vertical symmetry, and attractive faces may have more of these characteristics than unattractive faces. Others argue, first, that babies are programmed to respond to social stimuli as guides to their own social behavior, and second, that babies are more sensitive to attractive faces because their features are of a size and proportion that are close to culturally ideal faces. These studies at first seem to challenge the notion that standards of attractiveness must be learned through experience (Langlois et al., 1987). However, in view of the wide-ranging differences in cultural definitions of beauty, it may be that experience with norms of the immediate environment play an important role as well.

Depth Perception

Even when they're only 1 day old, infants can often perceive which objects are closer and which are farther away (Granrud, 1991; Kellman & Banks, 1998), although their ability to perceive depth and distance is not yet as good as that of an older child or an adult. This ability improves with age, as more kinds of cues to depth and distance become available to the infant, and as he hones his use of those cues through experience.

Unlike older children and adults, newborns can make use of some important cues to depth and distance that do not require that both of their eyes work together. Newborns' eyes move in the same direction only about half the time (Mauer & Mauer, 1988; Kellman & Banks, 1998), so young infants must rely on depth and distance cues that are available to each eye independently. Some of these cues involve the motion of objects. For example, as objects approach us they fill more of the visual field, and when we move our heads, the images of close objects move more than the images of distant objects. These kinds of changes associated with movement help babies judge depth.

By 3 to 5 months of age babies can coordinate their two eyes and so can begin to see depth as adults do, using stereoscopic vision (Birch, 1993; Mohn & van Hof-van Duin, 1986). **Stereoscopic vision** is the sense of a third spatial dimension produced by the combination of the images perceived by both eyes, each of which reflects the stimulus from a slightly different angle; it is the brain's fusion of these two images that creates the perception of depth. Proper use of the two eyes together at an early age is necessary for normal stereoscopic vision to develop. Babies born with crossed eyes (a condition called *convergent strabismus*) usually do not develop normal stereoscopic vision unless the eyes are surgically corrected before the age of 2 (Banks, Aslin, & Letson, 1975; Banks & Salapatek, 1983).

The ability to perceive depth normally has much practical value. For example, it helps keep us safe by preventing us from walking off cliffs and other high places. Researchers have wondered how soon a baby becomes cautious of high places as a result of depth perception. To investigate this issue, Gibson and Walk (1960) developed an apparatus called the **visual cliff** (see Figure 5-9). The visual cliff consists of an elevated glass platform with a checkerboard pattern directly beneath the glass on one side (the "shallow" side) and the same pattern several feet below the glass on

stereoscopic vision   The sense of a third spatial dimension produced by the brain's fusion of the separate images contributed by both eyes, each of which reflects the stimulus from a slightly different angle.

visual cliff   An apparatus that tests an infant's depth perception by using patterned materials and an elevated, clear glass platform to make it appear that one side of the platform is several feet lower than the other.

■ FIGURE 5-9
Babies don't take chances. This baby is hesitant to venture beyond the safety of the visual cliff's "shallow" side, despite mom's coaxing. Clearly, the child perceives the "deep" side as threatening.

the other (the "deep" side). Gibson and Walk found that babies 6 to 14 months old would not cross the "deep" side to get to their mothers even when the mother smilingly encouraged the child to do so. Thus, babies this age were fearful enough of heights to avoid them. This fear apparently does not exist in very young infants. When Campos and his associates (Campos, Langer, & Krowitz, 1970) placed 1½-month-old babies first on the shallow side of a visual cliff and then on the deep side, the infants' heart rates *decreased*, which generally indicates interest rather than fear (fear is normally accompanied by an *increase* in heart rate). In contrast, when researchers placed older infants who could crawl on the deep side, these babies showed heart-rate accelerations, suggesting that they had learned to be afraid of cliffs (Campos, Bertenthal, & Kermonian, 1992; Campos, Hiatt, Ramsey, Henderson, & Svejda, 1978).

Apparently, locomotion is involved in the development of a fear of heights. Baby animals that are able to walk shortly after birth avoid the deep side of the visual cliff when they are only 1 day old. And when human infants who are unable to crawl are provided with 30 to 40 hours of experience in wheeled walkers, they begin to show fear of high places (Bertenthal, Campos, & Kermoian, 1994; Campos, Svejda, Bertenthal, Benson, & Schmid, 1981). Note that although 80 to 90 percent of parents use such walkers, these devices are very dangerous; in the early 1990s their use was associated with nearly 30,000 accidents to infants (American Medical Association, 1992; Marcella & McDonald, 1990). Clearly, "infants learn to use the visual information specifying an apparent drop-off to control the consequences of their own locomotion" (Bertenthal & Clifton, 1998).

What is it about locomotion that triggers a fear of heights? Perhaps motion itself in some way helps a baby to judge distances more accurately. Or perhaps locomotion gives the baby an opportunity to fall more often, so that he begins to recognize heights as potentially dangerous. Even when an infant nearly falls, frightening a caregiver, the strong emotional reaction she evidences may prompt the baby to learn vicariously to fear heights (Campos et al., 1992; Lamb & Campos, 1982). Whatever the link, a fear of heights involves an interplay of biology and experience. Infants may be biologically prepared to learn to fear heights, but the experience of moving around on one's own is a necessary condition for that fear to emerge.

Size and Shape Constancy

Regardless of how distant an object is, you can judge its size and shape. For example, even though a truck looks toylike from far away, you still perceive it as a normal-sized vehicle. This ability relies on **size constancy,** the tendency to perceive an object as constant in size regardless of changes in the distance from which you view it and regardless of the corollary changes in the size of the object's image on the retinas of your eyes (see Figure 5-10). Although developmentalists once believed that infants did not achieve size constancy until they were 5 months old (McKenzie, Tootell, & Day, 1980), recent research with newborns suggests that this ability may be present from birth, suggesting again how well prepared newborns are to interact with their perceptual world (Slater, Mattock, & Brown, 1990). Demonstrating that a newborn displays this or any other ability does not mean, of course, that the ability is at its full power. As binocular vision develops, between 4 and 5 months, recognition of size constancy improves (Aslin, 1987; Kellman & Banks, 1998). Although great progress is achieved in the first 12 months, it is not until the child is 10 or 11 years old that this skill matures fully (Kellman & Banks, 1998).

If older babies are able to perceive that a receding object really stays the same in size despite the fact that its image grows smaller, they should also be able to perceive that an image that grows larger is that of an approaching object. It is not surprising, therefore, that by 3 months of age, and perhaps even by 1 month, babies show that they relate image growth to decreasing distance by blinking when the "moving" object seems to be on a collision course with them (Manez, 1987; Yonas,

size constancy The tendency to perceive an object as constant in size regardless of changes in its distance from the viewer and in the image it casts on the retinas of the eyes.

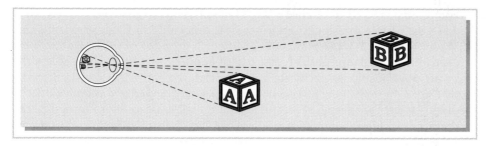

■ FIGURE 5-10
Size constancy.
The two blocks pictured here are exactly the same size and the viewer perceives them as the same size. However, because they are placed at different distances from the viewer, they cast retinal images of different sizes. Four-month-old infants will see the blocks as of different sizes, but by 6 months, babies have grasped the concept of size constancy and see the blocks as the same size.

Arterberry, & Granrud, 1987). The fact that this ability appears earlier than size constancy may reflect the fact that the avoidance of impending collisions has survival value. Alternatively, it may simply be that the perception of an approaching object on the basis of the increasing size of its image is easier to measure than size constancy in very young babies (we have simply to record a blinking response).

Similar to size constancy, **shape constancy** is the ability to perceive an object's shape as remaining constant despite changes in its orientation, and hence the angle from which one views it. The fact that even newborns are capable of shape constancy suggests that this ability may be present at birth, requiring minimal experience with the world (Slater & Morison, 1985).

Perhaps as researchers further improve their techniques for probing infants' visual capacities we will find evidence of even earlier competence in some other areas as well. It is possible that "perceptual constancies in general are an inherent function of the visual system," even though their range and accuracy may be improved by experience (Yonas et al., 1987, p. 7).

shape constancy The ability to perceive an object's shape as remaining constant despite changes in its orientation and the angle from which one views it.

Visual Expectations

Not only do babies begin to perceive colors, forms, depth, and perceptual constancies at quite an early age, but they also soon start to develop expectations about events in their visual worlds (Haith & Benson, 1998). To demonstrate this remarkable ability, Haith and his coworkers (Canfield & Haith, 1991; Haith, Hazen, & Goodman, 1988) presented pictures to babies in either a regular alternating sequence (left, right, left, right) or an unpredictable sequence (left, left, right, left, etc.). When the sequence was predictable, 3-month-olds began to anticipate the location of the next picture by looking to the side on which it was going to appear. And they developed this pattern of expectations in less than a minute! Younger infants did not show this ability to anticipate a picture's location based on a regular sequence. It may be that more cognitive or perhaps biological development is needed for this ability to emerge (Tamis-LeMonda & McLure, 1995). Haith and Benson (1998) suggest that although these simple experiments with pictures will soon be superseded by far more elaborate expectations involving complex sequences of events and much longer time frames, the research to date demonstrates that "expectations are surely important for a range of other future-oriented and cognitive processes" (p. 41). In any case, this study, like others we have discussed, shows that the infant's overall level of visual ability is much greater than had been presumed only a few decades ago.

Smell, Taste, and Touch

Like vision and hearing, smell, taste, and touch are well developed at an early age. For instance, even newborns can discriminate among a variety of odors, and they show "appropriate" facial expressions in response to odors that adults rate as either pleasant or aversive. In one study, infants less than 12 hours old reacted to the odors of strawberry and banana with a look of satisfaction, whereas a whiff of fish or rotten eggs elicited a rejecting look (Steiner, 1979).

Young infants' well-developed sense of smell seems to provide another early guide to the people and things in their world. In a study in England, Macfarlane (1975) showed that 1-week-olds could distinguish the odor of their own mother's breast pad from the odor of the breast pad of another nursing woman. When the two pads were positioned above the infant's head, the baby turned to look at the mother's pad more than the pad of the stranger. This preference was not evident in the first few days of life and seems to depend on babies learning to recognize the mother's special smell. Subsequent studies have shown that it is not just the odor of a mother's breast secretions that is attractive to a breast-fed baby. Breast-fed babies come to learn and prefer the overall scent of their own mothers (Porter, Makin, Davis, & Christensen, 1992).

Newborns also respond selectively to different tastes. In one study, for instance, 2-hour-old infants produced facial expressions in response to sweet, sour, bitter, and salty substances that are characteristic of the faces adults make given these tastes (Rosenstein & Oster, 1988). Because these infants had never been fed anything but milk or formula, it is not unreasonable to assume that taste preferences are innate. Studies of fetal lambs suggest that taste perception may even be present before birth, as may a preference for sweet over bitter substances (Mistretta & Bradley, 1985). However, infant taste preferences can be modified by exposure to different flavors. Mennella and Beauchamp (1996) showed that infants exposed to vanilla-flavored milk were more accepting of the flavor of vanilla later on. Other studies suggest that babies will accept garlic-flavored milk if exposed to garlic during breast-feeding. Although the long-term effects are unclear, animal studies indicate that the more varied the mother's diet, the more likely offspring are to consume novel foods after weaning (Mennella & Beauchamp, 1993). Perhaps one benefit of breast-feeding is that "it provides an opportunity for the infant to become familiar with the flavors of the foods of her or his mother, family and culture" (Mennella & Beauchamp, 1996, p. 19).

The sense of touch is activated long before birth (Field, 1990); indeed, it may be one of the first senses to evolve. As Klaus and colleagues (1995, p. 52) point out, "The skin is the largest sense organ of the body . . . , [and] babies are surrounded and caressed by warm fluid and tissues from the beginning of fetal life. . . . [Moreover,] the lips and hands have the most touch receptors; this may explain why newborns enjoy sucking their fingers." Parents all over the world naturally lift up their newborns and hold, stroke, rock, and walk with them, using other comforting touching acts to soothe their babies, and, according to Klaus and associates, both parents and infants seem prepared to enjoy this activity. Babies are clearly responsive to different types of touch, from the positive quality of gentle stroking to the sometimes negative aspects of changes in temperature, texture, moisture, and pressure and the painful effects of drawing blood for testing.

Although it was once assumed that newborns were indifferent to pain, this is absolutely untrue. It was once standard practice to perform circumcision and other, invasive medical procedures on infants without using any pain-relieving drugs, but advances in our understanding of the newborn's sensitivity to pain have changed this practice. Evidence of the infant's sensitivity to painful procedures comes from studies of infant stress reactions; for example, male infants have shown higher levels of plasma cortisol (a stress marker) after a circumcision than before the surgery (Gunnar, Malone, Vance, & Fisch, 1985). Research has also demonstrated gender differences in pain: females are more sensitive to pain than males.

Not only do babies respond to touch—recall the positive impact that massage had on preterm babies (Field, 1990)—but before the end of their first year they can learn to discriminate among objects using only their sense of touch (Streri & Pecheux, 1986). And babies are not alone in this sensitivity to touch: Mothers can identify their babies not only by smell, as we discussed earlier, but also by touch. After several hours of contact with their newborns, mothers and fathers both can

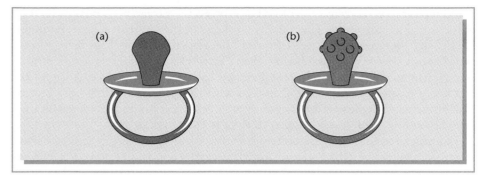

■ FIGURE 5-11
Testing a baby's intermodal perceptual abilities.
Just by looking at these pacifiers, 4-week-old babies knew which one they had sucked earlier, no matter whether it was the smooth (a) or the knobby (b) one. (*Source:* Meltzoff & Borton, 1979)

identify their infants merely by touching the skin on the back of the hand (Kaitz, Meirov, Landman, & Eidelman, 1993; Kaitz, Shiri, Danzinger, Hershko, & Eidelman, 1994). Clearly, parents use multiple sensory means of identifying their own offspring—a skill that probably helps ensure that newborns receive the care and attention they need to thrive and develop.

Intermodal Perception: How Infants Transfer Learning from One Sense to Another

When an infant sees a ball bounce or when her father speaks to her, does she perceive separate visual and auditory events in each case? Or does she match the sight of the moving ball with the sound the ball makes as it hits the floor, and the sight of her father's lip and mouth movements with the voice she hears? **Intermodal perception** is the use of sensory information from more than one modality—in these examples, both vision and hearing—to identify a stimulus and make sense of it. It is also the apprehension of a stimulus that one has already identified by means of one sensory modality by means of a different modality.

Researchers have often explored the question of babies' ability to perceive intermodally by pairing two different sensory systems, such as vision and touch, or vision and hearing. Exploring the first of these pairs, Meltzoff and Borton (1979) designed two different pacifiers, one smooth and one knobby (Figure 5-11), and gave 4-week-old infants a chance to suck one or the other of them. When the researchers let their small subjects look at both pacifiers—but not suck on them—the infants looked longer at the pacifier that they had sucked on earlier than at the unfamiliar one. Pointing out that infants of this age have had little opportunity to simultaneously touch and look at objects, the researchers concluded that "human beings are able to recognize equivalencies in information picked up by different modalities without the need of learned correlations" (Meltzoff, 1981, p. 107).

To rule out the possibility that experience might have played a role in Meltzoff's and Borton's findings—the infants in the study just discussed were a month old—Kaye and Bower (1994) carried out a similar study with newborns who were between 13 and 43 hours old and, because they were breast-fed, had no experience with a pacifier. The finding that these newborns showed a visual preference for the pacifier on which they had been sucking after only 20 seconds of exposure strengthens the argument that infants are probably born with the capacity for intermodal transfer. From an evolutionary perspective, it is not surprising that it is the mouth region, so important for the infants's early feeding and survival, that plays a central role in this type of transfer in the early days of life.

Addressing the link between vision and hearing, Elizabeth Spelke (1987) showed 4-month-old babies two animated films and accompanying soundtracks of a kangaroo and a donkey, each bouncing at a different rate and producing sounds in keeping with its bouncing. Spelke then played one of the sound tracks alone

intermodal perception
The use of sensory information from more than one modality to identify a stimulus; also, the apprehension of a stimulus already identified by one modality by means of another.

from between two screens, one of which showed the bouncing donkey, the other the bouncing kangaroo. The infants looked at the animal whose bouncing "matched" the sounds they were hearing. Because the infants had never seen or heard kangaroos or bouncing before, their reactions were clearly not the result of prior learning. Other studies have shown that babies this age can also "match" the sounds of particular words being spoken with the sight of a face whose lips are synchronized with those sounds, even though the visual stimulus is in one location and the auditory stimulus in another (Spelke & Cortelyou, 1981).

Infants can even match emotions across the visual and auditory modes. Seven-month-old babies who had seen a happy face saying something pleasant and a sad face telling a sad story were later able to match happy or sad voices with the correct faces (Walker, 1980). When tested in a similar fashion with happy and angry faces, pleasant and harsh voices, babies were again able to match the voices alone with the corresponding faces (Soken & Pick, 1992). Intermodal matching can also help infants determine whether an object is approaching or retreating. Pickens (1994) showed 5-month-old infants films of a toy train either approaching the viewers or moving away from them (see Figure 5-12). Infants looked more at the approaching film when the decibel level of the soundtrack increased and more at the retreating train when the sound of the train diminished. Infants did not show evidence of matching in other conditions in which the soundtracks were paired with videos depicting changes in the brightness of the train's image or showing the train moving horizontally with no change in its size. This experiment suggests that infants may be aware of the rules that guide the integration of visual and sound information and that they can use this information to help them judge distance.

The findings we've discussed in this section challenge the commonly held view that babies begin life experiencing unrelated sensations in each sensory system and only gradually learn to put the separate pieces together. Babies as young as 4 months of age appear to experience a world of integrated visual and auditory sensations; perhaps this ability to relate different kinds of sensations to one another will in time be detected in even younger infants (Bahrick & Pickens, 1994). Another important path of study may lead to the discovery of the mechanisms that underlie infants' ability to perceive intermodally (Haith & Benson, 1998).

EARLY LEARNING AND MEMORY

The kind of learning in infants that we have discussed so far is a cognitive kind of learning about the nature of the world, especially about the world's objects and their properties. Such learning stresses the ideas and expectations babies develop as they gradually gain experience interacting with people and things. As you will recall from Chapter 1, psychologists are particularly interested in some other kinds of learning: classical and operant conditioning and learning through imitation. In this section we not only explore these three kinds of learning behavior in infants; we also consider what these and other kinds of learning abilities tell us about a baby's memory capabilities. As you will see, basic learning processes appear to be present very early in life. What changes over the course of development seems to be the nature of the information that babies are capable of learning and, perhaps, the speed and efficiency with which they learn.

Classical Conditioning

For a refresher on the mechanisms of classical conditioning, look at Figure 5-13, in which we diagram the way in which a child might become conditioned to fear his doctor. For years psychologists have debated the issue of how early babies can be classically conditioned, and the controversy is not over (Rovee-Collier, 1987; Rovee-Collier & Shyi, 1992). On the one hand, there is some evidence that new-

(a)

(b)

■ FIGURE 5-12
Combining vision and hearing to detect distance and direction.
Babies can match an engine sound that is becoming louder with the toy train in (a), which is approaching the watching infant, and an engine sound that is growing fainter with the train shown in (b), which is moving away from the infant. (*Source:* Pickens, 1994)

borns can be classically conditioned, especially in biologically meaningful contexts such as feeding. In one study, babies as young as 2 hours old learned to associate a stroke on the head with delivery of a sugar solution to their mouths, until eventually the stroke alone elicited puckering and sucking responses (Blass, Ganchrow, & Steiner, 1984). On the other hand, newborns have much more difficulty learning relationships that involve unpleasant stimuli, such as loud noises or things that are

Stage 1	Stage 2	Stage 3
Conditioned stimulus (CS) elicits no particular reaction	Paired with conditioned stimulus (CS), unconditioned stimulus (US) elicits unconditioned response (UR)	Conditioned stimulus (CS) elicits conditioned response (CR)

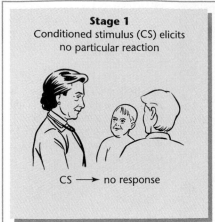
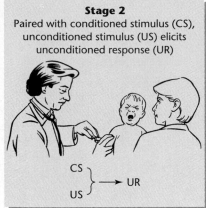
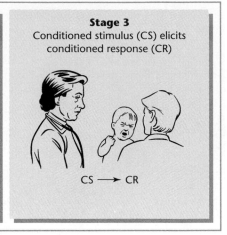

CS ⟶ no response

CS }
US } ⟶ UR

CS ⟶ CR

■ FIGURE 5-13
How a baby may be conditioned to fear a doctor. At their first meeting (Stage 1), the baby may show no particular reaction to the doctor, but when the doctor gives the baby a painful injection that causes the baby to cry (Stage 2), the baby may expect the same pain at his next meeting with the doctor (Stage 3) and cry even if he doesn't see a needle in her hand.

painful, perhaps because they lack the motor skills to escape or avoid them (Rovee-Collier, 1987). Human infants, after all, have parents to protect them, so it may be less critical at an early age to learn the stimuli associated with noxious events. There is also evidence that neurological mechanisms aiding the formation of such associations develop later than neurological mechanisms facilitating positive associations (Rovee-Collier, 1987; Rovee-Collier & Shyi, 1992).

Operant Conditioning

Operant conditioning, you will recall, involves learning to emit (or inhibit) some behavior because of the rewarding (or punishing) consequences it brings. Just as babies can be classically conditioned, they can also learn by operant conditioning (Gewirtz & Peláez-Nogueras, 1992). In the study we described in Box 5-3, DeCasper and Fifer (1980) used operant conditioning to induce sucking in newborns, with the mother's voice as a reward. This research shows not just an early capacity for this kind of learning but also what seems to be a built-in propensity to enjoy contact with other human beings (which is why the sound of the mother's voice could serve as a reward).

As in the case of classical conditioning, successful demonstrations of operant conditioning in newborns typically involve behaviors like sucking or turning the head (related to the rooting reflex), behaviors that are components of feeding and thus of considerable importance to the baby's survival. According to Seligman (1970), the infant has certain biologically *prepared responses* that have been selected through evolution as a result of their ability to protect the infant and help it survive. Organized thus in early life to perform behaviors that are functionally adaptive (Sameroff, 1972, 1983) and possessing limited energy, the infant is often guided in its learning by a principle of energy expenditure; that is, the infant learns just those responses that are most energy efficient (Rovee-Collier & Lipsitt, 1982). Failure to learn a particular response, then, may sometimes be because it costs the baby too much energy to be worthwhile!

Learning through Imitation

Perhaps infants realize that acquiring most of their behaviors through operant conditioning (displaying a behavior, being rewarded, repeating the behavior, being reinforced again, etc.) would be extremely uneconomical in terms of time and energy! Fortunately, they are able to learn a great deal without any overt reward or punishment but simply by observing the behavior of parents, siblings, peers, teachers, and other people. As you learned in Chapter 1, this is observational learning, or learning through imitation.

Imitation begins early in life; it may even be possible in the first few days after birth. Meltzoff and Moore (1983), for example, found that babies between 7 and 72 hours old imitated adults who opened their mouths wide or stuck their tongues out—these movements are, of course, components of the sucking response—and newborns may be able to imitate various lip movements as well (Reissland, 1988). These findings are somewhat controversial because classical developmental theories, such as Piaget's, argue that imitation requires the capacity for symbolic representation,

This woman and her 5-week-old grandchild are playing an age-old game that's fun for grandma and instructive for baby. Imitation may be the sincerest form of flattery, but in newborns it's a basic way of learning!

which is generally not achieved until the end of the second year of life (Chapters 1 and 9). And the infant who sticks its tongue out at the sight of an adult doing the same thing may not be truly imitating another's behavior (Anisfeld, 1991). There is evidence that the sight of any protruding object may cause newborns to stick out their tongues, not in imitation but because they see these objects as suckable!

Babies, however, are soon capable of genuine imitation. Nine-month-olds, for example, can imitate a series of modeled behaviors (such as pushing a set of buttons or picking up and shaking plastic eggs filled with pebbles). What's more, they can carry out these imitations not only immediately after seeing them but after an interval of as much as 24 hours, with no opportunity to practice the behaviors in between (Meltzoff, 1988a; Meltzoff & Moore, 1994). At 14 months of age, infants can delay (or defer) imitation over a period of one week (Meltzoff, 1988b). And between 14 and 18 months they cannot only defer imitation, they can generalize it to new settings. For example, children this age who watched a peer model a new behavior in a day-care setting imitated that behavior two days later when given a chance to do so in their homes (Hanna & Meltzoff, 1993).

Psychologists have wondered what mechanisms underlie the ability of babies, especially younger ones, to imitate behaviors that they see others perform. The answer is still unclear, but the process could be viewed as an example of the ability to engage in active intermodal matching (Meltzoff, 1990). Newborns might form cognitive representations of the behavior they saw a model perform; they would then have to translate these initially visual perceptions into movements and actions that they themselves could perform. This interpretation suggests that babies may be ready for some form of representational thought at a much earlier age than previously believed.

Memory in Babies

Even very young infants can remember what they see and hear over relatively long time spans. Two researchers found that newborns could remember a previously

■ FIGURE 5-14
Memory lessons for babies. Rovee-Collier found that when she taught 3-month-old infants to make a mobile move by attaching the mobile to one of their legs with a ribbon (a) the babies forgot the association between kicking and moving the mobile after about a week. When this researcher gave these infants a "reminder" session, however, during which she removed the ribbon so that they could look at the mobile but couldn't make it move (b), and then reattached the ribbon (as in a), she found that most babies were able to remember the association for as long as four weeks. (*Source:* Rovee-Collier, 1986)

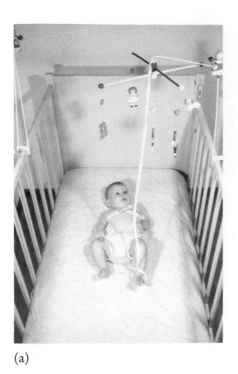

(a)

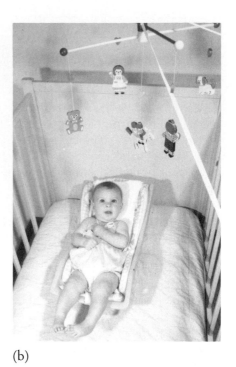

(b)

seen visual event over a 24-hour period (Werner & Siqueland, 1978). The babies in this study altered their sucking patterns when the color and pattern of a visual stimulus changed, even though they had not seen that stimulus for nearly a day. Other studies show that newborns can also remember speech sounds over a similar time period (Swain, Zelazo, & Clifton, 1993; Ungerer, Brody, & Zelazo, 1978). In one study of mothers and their 14-day-old infants, the mothers repeated the words *tinder* and *beguile* to their babies 60 times a day for 13 days (780 exposures); as you may imagine, 2-week-olds rarely hear these particular words. At 14 and 28 hours after this marathon training ended, the researchers tested the babies' memory for the words. The infants showed not only that they remembered the words but that they recognized them better than their own names.

Older babies have even more impressive memory capabilities. In one study, 3-month-old infants first learned to make a mobile move by kicking one of their legs, to which the researcher had attached a long ribbon that was also attached to the mobile suspension bar (see Figure 5-14) (Rovee-Collier, 1986; Rovee-Collier & DuFault, 1991). Usually babies this age will forget the connection between a kick and a bobbing mobile after about eight days. However, with a brief reminder before being tested, these little individuals could remember the connection for as long as four weeks. The reminder, provided about 24 hours before a memory test was given, consisted simply of letting the babies see the mobile bobbing about for 3 minutes. During the reminder session, the babies' legs were not attached to the mobile, so they could not relearn the connection. The visual reminder was enough, however. Babies who had experienced the reminder kicked their legs more often in the testing session (when the ankle ribbon was again attached) than babies who had learned the leg-mobile connection but who had been given no reminder of it in the interim. Apparently, babies can make just as good use of brief reminders in dredging up memories as adults! Another cue that helps babies remember is the context or setting in which the original learning took place. Babies were able to remember better when tested in the same setting in which they originally learned than in a novel context (Shields & Rovee-Collier, 1992).

From the age of 3 months babies' memory powers improve even further. Consider a study in which infants who were about 10 months old saw pictures

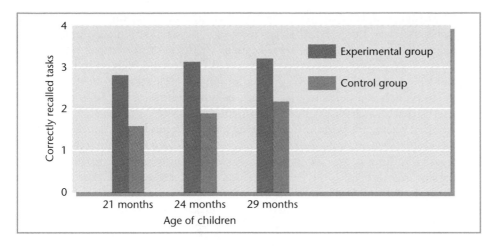

■ FIGURE 5-15
Young children have surprisingly good memories. Bauer and her colleagues tested young children ranging in age from 21 to 29 months on their memory for events in which they'd participated eight months earlier, such as setting up an inclined track and letting a car roll down the track, and found that the youngest group did very nearly as well as the oldest. All three groups recalled significantly more of the tasks than control groups who had had no experience with the tasks. (*Source:* Adapted from Bauer, 1996)

(e.g., a whale), touched objects (e.g., a clothespin), or heard sounds (e.g., a bell, a rattle). Upon returning to the laboratory when they were 3 years old—two years later—the children were more likely to touch the objects and recognize the sounds that they had been exposed to on their earlier visit than were children in a control group who had not had the earlier experience in the lab (Myers, Clifton, & Clarkson, 1987). This study suggests that children have some memory of events that happened to them before they could even walk or talk. Similar evidence comes from recent work of Bauer (1996), who found that 13-month-old infants were able to remember a simple sequence (e.g., putting teddy bear to bed) after an eight-month delay (Figure 5-15). In Chapter 10 we will revisit this issue and examine in more detail the kinds of strategies that children develop to help them remember. Together these studies have led us to reevaluate the widely held belief that infants and children younger than 3 cannot recall the events of their lives. It's time to put that claim aside and realize instead that babies can recall much more of their early lives than we thought possible.

SUMMARY

- Babies can see, hear, and respond to interesting sights, sounds, and other sensory stimuli at a much earlier age than was originally believed.

The Newborn

- The newborn, or **neonate,** has a repertoire of **reflexes,** or involuntary responses to external stimuli. Many of these reflexes, some of which have obvious value in helping the newborn survive, disappear during the first year of life.
- Babies experience predictable changes in state, or recurring patterns of alertness and activity level, ranging from vigorous, wakeful activity to quiet, regular sleep.
- Two significant **infant states** are sleeping and crying. The amount of sleep in which children engage and the nature of their sleep both change gradually until about adolescence, when both parameters conform to a more adult pattern.
- Between the ages of 2 and 4 months babies may fall prey to **sudden infant death syndrome (SIDS).** Although the causes of SIDS are as yet unexplained, this fatal disorder usually occurs in winter and after a cold. Preventive measures include the cessation of parental smoking, preventing infants from sleeping on their stomachs, and parent and infant cosleeping.

- The **autostimulation theory** proposes that infants spend more than twice as much time as adults in **REM sleep** because such sleep stimulates higher brain centers that in turn promote development of the central nervous system. As babies become more able to process external stimulation, they spend more and more time in **non-REM sleep,** approaching the adult level at about the age of 3.
- Crying, which is an effective means of early communication, follows distinct patterns that also change with development.
- Although there are wide differences among individuals, sexes, and races in soothability, certain caregiver techniques, such as holding the baby on the shoulder or swaddling it, are widely successful in helping to calm a distressed baby. Infants can also help to soothe themselves, as when they quiet after starting to suck on a thumb or pacifier.
- Tests of reflexes may be combined with other assessments to gauge the health, maturity, and capacities of a newborn. The **Brazelton Neonatal Assessment Scale** is one widely used assessment tool.

The Infant's Sensory and Perceptual Capacities

- Infants' **sensations** and **perceptions** are no longer completely obscure to researchers, who have learned how to measure infants' sensory and perceptual capacities. In their efforts to understand whether babies can distinguish between one stimulus and another, investigators often make use of the infant's tendency to **habituate,** or become used to, a given stimulus. Another technique is to use the **visual preference method,** in which researchers pinpoint a baby's preference for looking at one of two alternative stimuli.
- At birth, babies are more sensitive to high-pitched sounds than low-pitched ones, and a sound must be slightly louder for them to detect it. Overall, however, a newborn's hearing is very well developed. Newborns can distinguish among different kinds of sounds and tell what direction a sound comes from. They are also predisposed to respond to human voices, which may be significant for later social and language development.
- Although visual capacities continue to develop throughout the first year of life, newborns are sensitive to brightness and can track moving objects. As far as we know, they lack color and depth perception and have poor **visual acuity** at distances beyond close range. During the first three months acuity improves, however, and babies not only begin to distinguish colors but improve their ability to perceive patterns, including the patterning of human faces.
- The accurate perception of distance improves with age as well, as babies begin to coordinate their two eyes and use **stereoscopic vision.** Experiments with the **visual cliff** demonstrate that by the time babies are between 6 months and 14 months old they are capable of depth perception. **Shape constancy** is something that even newborns seem to possess. **Size constancy,** however, appears to be a skill that develops partly through experience.
- Newborns can discriminate among a variety of odors, and by 1 week of age they have learned to distinguish their mother's smells from those of other people. Newborns are also able to discriminate different tastes, and they display a preference for sweet over sour or bitter.
- The sense of touch is activated long before birth, and newborns are clearly responsive to both positive and negative types of touch; contrary to past beliefs, they are highly sensitive to pain. Infants also quickly learn to discriminate among objects based only on their sense of touch.
- From a very early age, using their capacity for **intermodal perception,** babies can integrate information from two different senses, such as the sounds that go with a certain sight. This finding challenges the commonly held view that infants begin life experiencing totally unrelated sensations in each sensory system.

Early Learning and Memory

- Even newborns can be classically conditioned when a previously neutral stimulus is repeatedly paired with a pleasant stimulus that naturally elicits some involuntary response. Eventually, the previously neutral stimulus alone comes to elicit the same reaction. *Classical conditioning* is more difficult in newborns when an aversive stimulus is involved. Young babies don't seem to be biologically prepared to learn such associations easily.

- Newborns can also learn to emit a certain behavior when that behavior is repeatedly rewarded. Successful *operant conditioning* in newborns typically involves a behavior like sucking, which is a component of feeding and of considerable importance to the baby's survival. This suggests that young babies are best organized to learn conditioned responses that are functionally adaptive.

- Although newborns may be capable of some imitation, the basis of the ability to imitate others and the amount of such behavior the child displays change significantly with age. By the early toddler period, at the age of about $1\frac{1}{2}$, children can not only readily imitate others but can defer imitation and generalize imitated behavior to new settings.

- When given adequate retrieval cues for something they have learned, babies can remember information over substantial periods of time. Thus, rather than having poor memories, as many people assume, it appears that infants just need the right reminders to help them access the information they have stored.

The Child's Growth: Brain, Body, Motor Skills, and Sexual Maturation

C H A P T E R 6

Tina's development was rapid from the start. She crawled and walked early, and by her first birthday she was forcing her parents to put their favorite vases on a high shelf out of her reach. When she was 11 years old and in sixth grade she reached sexual maturity, well ahead of her classmates. Jason, in contrast, was a leisurely baby and took his time about everything. As a result the vases were safe in Jason's house until he was 14 months old. This pattern continued into childhood, and Jason was nearly 16 years old when he experienced his pubescent growth spurt.

The differences between these two children are not unusual; they illustrate two common findings. First, rates at which children develop vary enormously among individual children, and second, rates also vary between the genders; at many points in childhood, girls develop more rapidly than boys. In this chapter, we examine the influence of biological and environmental factors on motor development and growth. First, we explore the development of the brain and the way genetic and environmental forces work together to determine brain growth and function. How is information transmitted within the brain? Do the two sides of the brain really control different functions? What happens if one side suffers damage? Next, we explore the motor and growth patterns that infants and children follow. What are the motor achievements of developing infants? What are the factors that speed up or slow down these emerging skills? Then we explore the ways in which children grow. How do biological and environmental factors modify growth patterns? Are children growing taller and if so, why? What are the causes and consequences of being too thin or too fat? What is the role played by nutrition in growth? Can children who are deprived early of such things as proper nutrition "catch up" in growth? Finally, we explore the developmental milestone of puberty, its characteristics, and the factors that influence its course. How is the timing of puberty determined? What are the consequences of reaching sexual maturity earlier or later than other adolescents?

BRAIN DEVELOPMENT IN INFANCY

In the prenatal period, as Figure 6-1 dramatically illustrates, the brain grows very rapidly, and it continues to grow at an amazing pace. Although at birth an infant's brain weighs only about 25 percent as much as a mature brain, by the time the baby is about 6 months old, its brain weighs half what an adult brain weighs, and the brain of the 2-year-old child weighs 75 percent as much as an adult brain (Figure 6-2).

The largest portion of the human brain consists of the two connected hemispheres that make up the **cerebrum,** a mass of tissue that embodies not only attributes particular to humans—such as speech and self-awareness—but also those that we human beings share with other vertebrate animals—such as sensory perception, motor abilities, and memory. The covering layer of the human cerebrum, the **cerebral cortex** (Figure 6-3), is highly convoluted and contains about 90 percent of the brain's cell bodies. Although we do not yet know how these cells control complicated traits, we do know that specific functions, like seeing, hearing, moving, feeling emotion, thinking, and speaking can be traced to specific regions of the cerebral cortex.

As we explore the development and functioning of the infant's brain, we examine the crucial importance of neurons and their interconnections, or synapses, the sequence in which brain functions mature, the topic of hemispheric specialization and, related to this phenomenon, the brain's amazing ability to compensate for damage to one portion or even to an entire hemisphere. The Turning Points chart (pp. 188–189) in this chapter highlights some of the significant milestones in the development of the brain as well as important steps in the child's motor and physical growth; you may find it useful to refer to this chart as you read through this chapter.

cerebrum   The two connected hemispheres of the brain.

cerebral cortex   The covering layer of the cerebrum that contains the cells that control specific functions such as seeing, hearing, moving, and thinking.

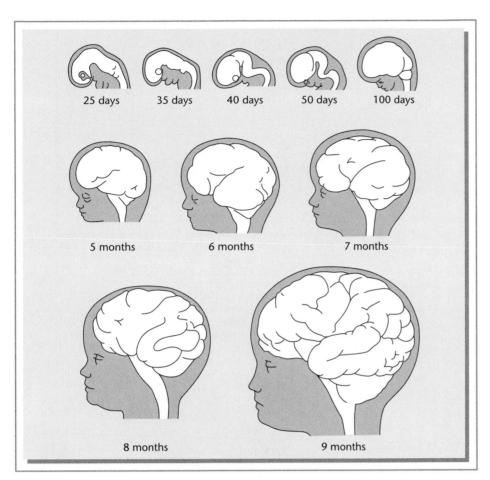

■ **FIGURE 6-1**
Fetal brain development.
As the brain develops, the front
part expands to form the
cerebrum, the large, convoluted
upper mass that in the adult
dominates the upper and side
portions of the brain. The
cerebrum is covered by the
cerebral cortex (Figure 6-3),
specific areas of which are
devoted to particular functions,
such as motor, visual, and
auditory activities. (The first 5 of
the drawings in this figure have
been enlarged to show details.)
(*Source:* From *A Child's World,* 7th
ed. by Restak, p. 172. Copyright
© 1996 The McGraw-Hill
Companies. Reprinted with
permission.)

Neurons and Synapses

Scientists believe that at birth, or even earlier, a baby's brain has most of its **neurons,** or nerve cells—100 to 200 billion of them (Kolb, 1989), as many as there are stars in the Milky Way. In fact, recent estimates suggest that most neurons are present in the brain by the seventh month of gestation (Rakic, 1995). During the embryonic period, neurons multiply at a very rapid pace; in a process called **neuron proliferation,** about 250,000 new neurons are born every minute!

Neurologists and others long assumed that the brain did not grow new neurons after birth, but recent studies (e.g., Gould et al., 1998; Rosenzweig & Breedlove, 1996) have suggested that the adult brain may have the capacity to regenerate nerve cells. Whether or not we grow new neurons, the brain increases in size as existing neurons grow and the connections between them proliferate in great numbers. Brain growth also reflects the growth of **glial cells,** which surround and protect neurons, providing them with structural support, regulating their nutrient concentrations, and repairing neural tissue. Some glial cells are responsible for the important task of **myelination,** in which parts of neurons are covered with layers of a fatty, membranous wrapping called *myelin* (Figure 6-4). This insulation makes the neuron more efficient in transmitting information (Johnson, 1998).

Neurons are "always on the move" (Rosenzweig & Breedlove, 1996, p. 105) as they migrate to their final location. Guided by neurochemical processes, neurons move to a variety of places in the brain. This **neural migration** ensures that all parts of the brain are served by a sufficient number of neurons. The absence of an appropriate number of neurons in their proper locations may be associated with various forms of mental retardation and with disorders such as dyslexia or schizophrenia (Kolb, 1989; Johnson, 1998).

neuron A cell in the body's nervous system, consisting of a cell body, a long projection called an *axon* and several shorter projections called *dendrites*; neurons send and receive neural impulses, or messages, throughout the brain and nervous system.

neuron proliferation The rapid proliferation of neurons in the developing organism's brain.

glial cell A nerve cell that supports and protects neurons and serves to encase them in sheaths of *myelin*.

myelination The process by which glial cells encase neurons in sheaths of the fatty substance *myelin*.

neural migration The movement of neurons within the brain that ensures that all brain areas have a sufficient number of neural connections.

■ **FIGURE 6-2**

How brain weight increases with age.

In this figure the age scale for the early years has been expanded to show this period of rapid growth more clearly. As human beings mature, male brains tend to be heavier than female brains because of men's larger body size. Although scientists are discovering other differences between the brains of women and men, none of these differences have differential effects on either gender's intellectual abilities. (*Source:* Rosenzweig, Leiman, & Breedlove, 1996)

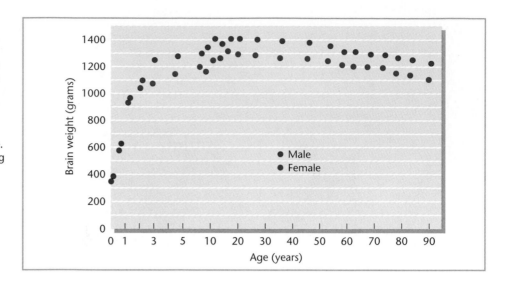

■ **FIGURE 6-3**

The brain's cortex.

The cortex is divided into four *lobes*—frontal, temporal, occipital, and parietal—and specific areas within the lobes tend to specialize in particular functions. The left hemisphere, shown here, is generally associated with the processing of language, whereas the right hemisphere plays a greater role in visual and spatial processing. Because of the brain's plasticity, however, functions lost because of damage to a hemisphere, lobe, or area may be compensated for by another brain region. (*Source:* Postlethwait & Hopson, 1995)

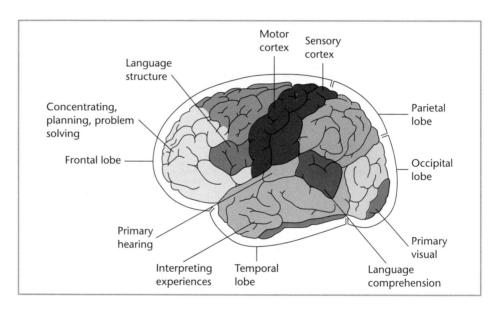

synapse A specialized site of intercellular communication where information is exchanged between nerve cells, usually by means of a chemical *neurotransmitter.*

synaptogenesis The forming of synapses.

Perhaps as essential as neurons themselves are the connections that are formed between neurons, known as **synapses.** It is at these specialized junctions that the extended *axon* of one neuron transmits a message to the projected *dendrites* of another neuron, usually by means of chemicals that cross the small spaces between the neurons (Figure 6-5). This activity is crucial to survival and learning, for as the brain's neurons receive input from the environment—before and after birth—they continue to create new synapses, allowing for increasingly complex communications. **Synaptogenesis,** or the forming of synapses, begins early in prenatal life, as soon as neurons begin to evolve. The brain forms synapses even more rapidly than it forms neurons; for example, at birth, in the brain's visual cortex alone there are 2,500 synapses for every neuron. And synapse formation goes on: In the visual cortex it reaches a peak when the child is about 2, when there are about 15,000 synapses for every neuron (Huttenlocher, 1994). Even if there are fewer synapses per neuron in other parts of the cortex, this still would suggest that there are trillions of synapses in the new young brain!

Are all these neurons and synapses necessary? Do they continue to function throughout life? The answer to both questions is no. The brain is programmed to create more nerve cells and more connections between these cells than are needed.

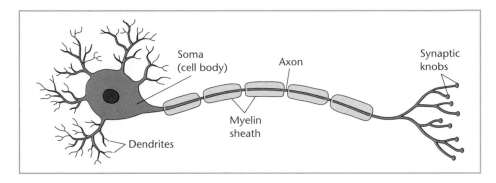

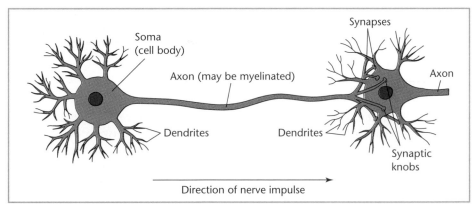

Direction of nerve impulse

■ **FIGURE 6-4**
A myelinated neuron.
The neuron's axon terminates in synaptic knobs that, in synaptic connection with the dendrites of another neuron (Figure 6-5) or with other types of cells, transmit messages through the nervous system. The myelin sheaths that encase much of the axon facilitate the transmission of signals rapidly and efficiently. Neurons are the longest cells in the human body and may reach more than 3 feet in length. (*Source:* From *Fundamentals of Anatomy & Physiology,* 3rd ed. by Martini, figure 12-7b, p. 389. Copyright © 1993 Prentice-Hall, Inc., Upper Saddle River, NJ. Reprinted with permission.)

■ **FIGURE 6-5**
Synaptic connection between two neurons.
Across the small space between one neuron's synaptic knobs and the dendrites or soma of another neuron a chemical substance effects the transfer of information. (*Source:* From *Fundamentals of Anatomy & Physiology,* 3rd ed. by Martini, figure 12-7d, p. 389. Copyright © 1993 Prentice-Hall, Inc., Upper Saddle River, NJ. Reprinted with permission.)

neuronal death The death of some neurons that surround newly formed synaptic connections among other neurons.

synaptic pruning The brain's disposal of the axons and dendrites of a neuron that is not often stimulated.

This excess of neuronal function is designed to ensure that the developing child acquires the information and skills he needs for proper development. Across development, two processes reduce the number of neurons as well as of connecting fibers. When new synapses are formed, in what is called **neuronal death** some surrounding neurons die, apparently to provide more space for these crucial loci of information transmission. And, in **synaptic pruning,** the brain disposes of a neuron's axons and dendrites if that particular neuron is not often stimulated. This, again, frees up space for new synaptic connections. The goals of both neuronal death and synaptic pruning are to increase the speed, efficiency, and complexity of transmissions between neurons and to allow room for new connections that develop as the child encounters new experiences (Huttenlocher, 1994). Brain development is not simply an additive process but one that increases efficiency and specialization. Loss in this case leads to a gain for the developing organism.

By adulthood, each of the brain's approximately 1 trillion neurons makes 100 to 1,000 connections with other neurons. That adds up to about 1 quadrillion synapses in the adult human brain (Huttenlocher, 1994; Lerner, 1984).

Sequential Development of the Brain

There is an orderly sequence to brain development during infancy. By autopsying the brains of infants and young children who die unexpectedly, Huttenlocher (1994) has recorded the development of synapses in the brain and has found that the processes of forming and pruning synapses occur at different times for various parts of the brain. Most interesting is the link between the sequences of synaptic development and the onset in the developing infant of various motor, perceptual, and cognitive skills and abilities.

As the baby moves from mostly reflexive behavior in the early months of life to voluntary control over movements, the motor area of the brain develops most rapidly. When the infant is about 2 months old, motor reflexes like rooting and the startle response (see Chapter 5) drop out, and the motor cortex begins to oversee voluntary movement such as reaching, crawling, and walking. Gradually the infant begins to master purposeful movements such as the effort to make contact with an object, which results at first in a kind of swiping motion.

As we have already noted, in the visual cortex the number of synapses per neuron is multiplied some six times within the first 2 years of life. But even within the first 4 to 12 months the number of connections rises to about 150 percent of those present in the adult brain. As a result of this proliferation, the baby's visual capacities are greatly enhanced; for example, she becomes more skilled at focusing on objects at different distances.

A similar sequence of synaptic and behavioral development characterizes the evolution of the auditory cortex as well as other areas of the brain. The hippocampus, for example, which aids in memory processes, becomes fully functional at about 8 or 9 months. In the prefrontal cortex, which is involved in forethought and logic, synaptic density develops more slowly and does not reach its peak until after the first year.

Hemispheric Specialization

One of the most important organizing features of the brain is its left-right division into two halves or **brain hemispheres.** The left and right hemispheres, which are connected by a set of nerve fibers called the **corpus callosum,** are anatomically different and, in general, control different functions (Best, 1988; Hahn, 1987; Springer & Deutsch, 1993). Studies of people who have suffered damage to one side of the brain caused by such things as head injuries or tumors give us important information about the functions in which each hemisphere normally specializes. At the same time, because a great deal of cross-wiring occurs between the hemispheres the separation is by no means complete. Not only do both hemispheres play some role in most functions but when one side of the brain suffers damage, the other half may take over some functions. Thus the brain has great plasticity and can adapt to adverse circumstances.

Left- and Right-Brain Functions

Hemispheric specialization begins early in life (Hahn, 1987; Molfese & Segalowitz, 1988; Springer & Deutsch, 1993; Turkewitz, 1991). Simple movement is controlled differentially, the left hemisphere of the motor cortex controlling the right side of the body, the right hemisphere controlling the body's left side. Researchers have demonstrated that in full-term and even preterm babies spoken syllables evoke electrical potentials that indicate that these infants' brains process speech syllables faster in the left hemisphere than in the right one (Molfese & Molfese, 1979, 1980). But the brain's division of labor is more complex than this: Each side of the brain tends to specialize in certain perceptual and cognitive tasks. For instance, the right hemisphere is involved in the processing of visual-spatial information, nonspeech sounds like music, and the perception of faces. When damage occurs to the right side of the brain, people may have difficulty attending to a task requiring visual-spatial perception, their drawing skills may deteriorate, they may have trouble following a map or recognizing friends, or they may become spatially disoriented (Bryden, 1982; Carter, Freeman, & Stanton, 1995; McManus & Bryden, 1991).

The right hemisphere is also involved in processing emotional information, as shown by the difficulty people with right-brain damage can have interpreting facial expressions (Bryden & MacRae, 1989; Dawson, 1994; Hahn, 1987). At the same time, right-hemisphere damage can sometimes make people indifferent to or even cheerful about things that would normally upset them. Initially this suggested to some investigators (Springer & Deutsch, 1993) that the right side of the brain might have a special role in expressing negative emotions and inhibiting positive ones, the left side a special role in expressing positive emotions and inhibiting negative ones. This view has since been modified to suggest that the left hemisphere is activated in the

brain hemispheres The two, left and right, halves of the brain's cerebrum.

corpus callosum The band of nerve fibers that connects the two hemispheres of the brain.

hemispheric specialization Differential functioning of the two cerebral hemispheres; for example, the control of speech and language by the left hemisphere and of visual-spatial processing by the right.

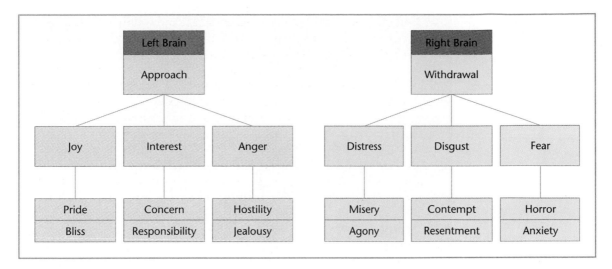

Left Brain				Right Brain		

Left Brain — Approach

Joy	Interest	Anger
Pride	Concern	Hostility
Bliss	Responsibility	Jealousy

Right Brain — Withdrawal

Distress	Disgust	Fear
Misery	Contempt	Horror
Agony	Resentment	Anxiety

■ **FIGURE 6-6**
Emotions associated with left- and right-brain hemisphere activity.
According to a recent theory, both hemispheres are involved in emotional expression, but the left focuses on feelings that trigger approach to the environment, the right on feelings that cause a person to turn away from the environment. (*Source:* Dawson, 1994)

expression of emotions associated with approach to the external environment, such as joy, interest, and anger, whereas the right region is activated in emotional expression that causes the person to turn away or withdraw from that environment, such as distress, disgust, and fear (see Figure 6-6, as well as Fox, 1991; Davidson, 1994).

The left hemisphere of the brain has traditionally been associated with the processing of language, and indeed it has been found that although people with left-hemisphere damage can recognize a familiar song and tell a stranger's face from an old friend's, they may have trouble understanding what is being said to them or in speaking clearly themselves (Springer & Deutsch, 1993). Interestingly, however, in persons who are deaf and use sign language to communicate—a language that involves motor movements of the hands—the right side of the brain takes over language functions. Neville and her colleagues (Mills, Coffey-Corina, & Neville, 1994; Neville, Mills, & Lawson, 1992) studied deaf and hearing adults as they were engaged in language processing and found that electrical activity during this task was greater in the right hemisphere of deaf persons than it was in hearing adults' right brains.

As we will see, these and other findings have suggested that the brain may be even more capable of adapting to external change than we thought. If brain injury occurs in the early years of life, for example, infants and young children often recover their losses (Fox, Calkins, & Bell, 1994; Rakic, 1991). It is probably largely because the young brain is not fully developed and hemispheric specialization is not yet complete that young children enjoy this recovery advantage. For instance, when the left hemisphere is damaged in early infancy, a child can still develop language ability that is close to normal (Bates, 1994). Even in adults, however, there is still a great deal of modifiability, and lost function can often be partially recovered through treatment. Even the old brain can be taught to relearn old tricks and acquire new ones (Kolb, 1989).

Consequences of Brain Lateralization

Researchers have shown that the degree to which a newborn's brain engaged in processing speech sounds is **lateralized,** that is, prone to use one hemisphere rather than the other, is related to the child's language ability three years later (Molfese & Molfese, 1985). In infants who later exhibited better language skills, investigators found that the left hemisphere differentiated among speech sounds and the right hemisphere among nonspeech sounds. It has also been found, however, that a newborn's left-hemisphere dominance for processing language is not as extreme as that of an older child or an adult. In fact, only 70 percent of infants show a left-hemisphere language bias, whereas 90 percent of 3-year-olds do. In children who are 3 years of age and older, researchers find few developmental changes either in

lateralization The process by which each half of the brain becomes specialized for the performance of certain functions.

As this teacher of the hearing impaired demonstrates "I love you" in American Sign Language to her 8th-grade student, it may be the right hemisphere of her brain that is particularly activated. As the text describes, there is evidence that in deaf and hearing-impaired people the right hemisphere may take over language functions.

dyslexia A term for the difficulties experienced by some people in reading or learning to read.

reliance on the left hemisphere for processing verbal information or in the superior ability of the right hemisphere to understand emotional cues (Bryden & Saxby, 1986; Saxby & Bryden, 1984, 1985). Even these findings, however, may be challenged by studies such as that by Molfese, Morse, and Peters (1990), in which it appeared that the brain responses of 14-month-olds to speech and language materials and to matching these with concrete objects were multidimensional and involved a variety of differentiated processes, some of which were lateralized and some of which were not. Clearly, the assignment of brain function between the hemispheres is highly complex and requires continuing study.

One reason we need to know more about this issue is that theories about lateralization underlie current explanations of what is generally called **dyslexia,** or the difficulties some children (and adults) experience in learning to read. In fact, as many as 5 percent of U.S. children experience such problems. Typically, they have difficulty integrating visual and auditory information, for example, in matching written letters or words to the sounds of those letters and words. Some children confuse letters, for example, calling a "d" a "b"; others have difficulty breaking apart the letters and syllables of a word and, treating the word as a whole, have no clues with which to figure it out (Liberman, Shankweiler, Liberman, Fowler, & Fischer, 1976). Kraus and associates (1996) examined the response of children with learning disabilities to different letter sounds by monitoring the electrical activity in their brains. Finding that the children showed no change in brain activity when, for example, the sound /ga/ replaced the sound /da/, these researchers concluded that there may indeed be a biological basis for dyslexia.

This and other similar disorders may have multiple origins, but one possible cause may be abnormal cerebral organization. Some researchers have suggested that poor readers do not show the normal lateralization pattern; that is, they process spatial information on both sides of the brain rather than primarily on the right and, thus, their left hemispheres may become overloaded, leading to deficits in such language skills as reading and understanding verbal information (Baringa, 1996; Witelson, 1977, 1983). This atypical cerebral organization, it is proposed, may be genetically determined or may be caused by environmental factors prenatally or after birth. Although a considerable body of evidence supports this hypothesis (e.g., Bryden, 1988; Corballis, 1983), the view that reading difficulties are caused by faulty lateralization patterns is still controversial.

What about handedness? Like other functions, such as processing verbal information or understanding emotional cues, handedness is lateralized. About 90 percent of adults are right-handed, and a majority even of young infants show right-hand dominance: They use the right hand more than the left for reaching, touching, and grasping (Hawn & Harris, 1983; McCormick & Mauer, 1988). Although young infants tend to shift between right and left hands, handedness is generally fully established by 2 years of age (Bryden & Saxby, 1986; Coren, 1992). The establishment of right-footedness is slower, and it appears to continue to develop until 4 or 5 years of age or even longer (Coren, 1992; Porac & Coren, 1981).

The Brain's Plasticity

As we have seen, the brain continues to develop so rapidly after birth that we cannot hold genes alone responsible for the multitude of neural connections that are formed. Stimulation from the environment clearly plays a crucial role in brain development, strengthening the synapses and modifying brain chemistry to improve the brain's overall efficiency. The human brain's **plasticity,** or the responsiveness of its neural structures and functions to input from the environment, is one of its most remarkable features.

> **plasticity** The capacity of the brain, particularly in its developmental stages, to respond and adapt to input from the external environment.

The importance of the environment in brain development was demonstrated at the turn of the century when A. J. Carlson (1902) showed that in birds the structure of the visual system could be altered by variations in stimulation. Over 40 years later, Austin Riesen (1947) reported his classic experiments on the effects of reduced sensory stimulation on the development of the visual system of the chimpanzee. Riesen found that when chimpanzees were raised in the dark for their first 16 months, their retinas (the light-sensitive areas at the back of the eye) failed to develop properly: The retinas contained fewer *ganglion cells,* or neurons whose fibers form the optic nerve that connects the retina to the brain. When these animals were placed in lighted conditions, their retinas were unable to recover lost ground and they became permanently blind. Other studies have confirmed these original results (Hubel, 1988).

Not only do the structures of the central nervous system need a certain amount of environmental stimulation for proper development, but both brain size and function can be modified by experience (Greenough, Black, & Wallace, 1987). In a series of pioneering studies, Rosenzweig and his colleagues (Benloucif, Bennett, & Rosenzweig, 1995; Rosenzweig et al., 1996) placed young rats from the same litters in two very different environments (Figure 6-7). The enriched environment consisted of large, brightly lit, communal cages with wheels, ladders, platforms, and other toys that were changed daily to ensure that the rats had a steady stream of new learning experiences. In addition, every day the investigators gave the "enriched" rats an opportunity to explore a large obstacle course or maze. In contrast, the researchers placed the remainder of the rats in an "impoverished" environment, in which each was alone in an isolated cage that was totally bare and located in a quiet, dimly lit room. When the researchers compared the brains of the young rats after the rats had spent nearly three months in their respective worlds, they discovered several important differences that apparently resulted from the different rearing environments. (In case you wonder about the relevance of the rat's brain to the human's, the basic neural structures of both brains are very similar.)

For one thing, the weight of the rats' brains was affected, especially the weight of the cerebral cortex, which controls higher-order processes. An enriched rat's cortex weighed about 4 percent more than the cortex of an impoverished rat, and some regions of the cortex were affected more than others. The occipital region, which controls vision, made the greatest gain in weight (6%) whereas the area responsible for touch showed the least gain (only 2%). Other experiments have suggested that the region of the cortex that will be affected by enrichment or

TURNING POINTS: Growth of the Child's Brain, Body, and Motor Skills

AT BIRTH	Infant's brain weighs one-quarter of adult brain weight; it has 100 to 200 billion neurons and 2,500 synapses for every neuron. Baby generally assumes fetal position.	
EARLY INFANCY	Baby shows some evidence of hemispheric specialization. Most infants show right-hand dominance. When baby is held with feet touching flat surface, she makes stepping motions that resemble walking; this response disappears at about 2 months.	
ABOUT 2 MONTHS	Motor cortex of infant brain's begins to control voluntary movement. Baby lifts head and shoulders off mattress.	
3 MONTHS	Within first 3 months baby doubles his weight.	
3–4 MONTHS	Baby looks at and swipes at objects, retains toys put into her hand, but makes no contact with objects on a table. She holds head up for extended time, plays with her fingers, and kicks actively.	
4 MONTHS	Baby sustains head control and rolls from his tummy onto his back; sits with support.	
4–5 MONTHS	Baby contacts toys on table; grasps block precariously.	
5 MONTHS	Baby sits on adult's lap and grasps object; rolls from back to tummy, makes incipient crawling movements.	
5–6 MONTHS	There may be some indication of an inherited tendency to overweight.	
6–7 MONTHS	Baby bangs, shakes, and transfers toys from hand to hand; uses palmar grasp with a block; tries to grasp a raisin with whole hand.	
7 MONTHS	Baby sits alone.	

TURNING POINTS: Growth of the Child's Brain, Body, and Motor Skills *(continued)*

ABOUT 8 MONTHS	Baby uses finger grasp with block, scissors grasp with raisin. Begins creeping; pulls up into unsteady stand but can't get back down; overall body control is better, with fewer unintended movements.
ABOUT 8 OR 9 MONTHS	The brain's hippocampus, which aids in memory processes, becomes fully functional.
ABOUT 9 MONTHS	Baby holds one block in each hand; approaches a raisin with index finger. Easily moves between sitting and lying; sitting is balanced and steady; stands holding furniture.
10 MONTHS	Baby begins cruising (creeping); stands on toes while holding on but stands alone unsteadily; begins to use some implements, such as spoons.
11 MONTHS	Baby is obsessed with learning to walk—walks when led; cruises till exhausted; feeds self with thumb and forefinger. 
11–12 MONTHS	Uses forefinger grasp of block and pincer grasp of raisin.
12–15 MONTHS	Child's brain has about half again as many synapses as adult brain; synaptic pruning gradually reduces this number. Child stands alone and walks without assistance.
18 MONTHS	Child runs and gallops.
2 YEARS	In most children, right-handedness is usually fully established.
3 YEARS	90% of children show left hemisphere bias for language. Children can hop.
4 YEARS	Children who will be obese later in life begin to gain weight at a faster rate than other children.
9 YEARS	Boys catch up with girls in height, but then slow down again until about 14.
10 YEARS	Some young girls succumb to anorexia or bulimia between 10 and the early 20s.
14 YEARS	Girls' height gain slows down considerably while boys' gain takes off; boys' weight gain also shoots up.
16–17 YEARS	Most young people have attained their full height.

Sources: Bertenthal & Clifton, 1998; Kopp, 1994; Shirley, 1931.
Note: Developmental events described in this and other Turning Points charts represent overall trends identified in research studies. Individual children vary greatly in the ages at which they achieve these developmental changes. Milestones in sexual maturation are covered in Table 6-1.

■ **FIGURE 6-7**
Impoverished and enriched
rearing environments.
Impoverished (a) and enriched
(b) environments have differential
effects on the developing brains
of young rats. (*Source:*
Rosenzweig, Leiman, &
Breedlove, 1996)

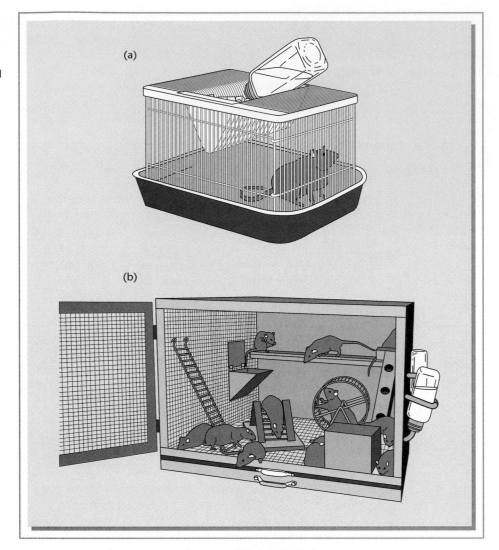

impoverishment is determined by the nature of the enrichment program: Rearing rats in darkness, for example, was found to shrink the visual cortex. The possibility that similar effects may occur in human beings was suggested by the postmortem finding that the brain of a person who had been blind, deaf, and mute showed deficient development of the cortical areas controlling vision, hearing, and speech but normal development of the area controlling skin sensations (Donaldson, 1892 cited by Rosenzweig, 1966).

Early experience can also affect the biochemistry of the brain and the structure of its neurons. An enriched environment tends to increase the complexity of neurons as measured by the number of dendrites they develop (Greenough et al., 1987; Jones & Greenough, 1996), and this proliferation of neural branches may help account for the increase in brain size associated with environmental enrichment. More dendrites per neuron means more synapses formed with other neurons, which in turn means that more information can be sent via these synaptic connections. At the same time, the activity of key chemicals in the brain, especially in the cerebral cortex, increases significantly as a result of an enriched rearing environment. Rosenzweig and Bennett (1970) found that in "enriched" rats the activity of two enzymes—acetylcholinesterase and cholinesterase—that act on acetylcholine, a chemical transmitter that conveys messages from one neuron to the next, was considerably enhanced. It is also possible that the activity of chemical compounds such as cyclic adenosine monophosphate (cyclic AMP), which is involved in energy metabolism, is affected by enriched rearing environments as well. Recent research indicated that young rats reared in such environments performed better than control rats on a test that required the rats to recognize objects to which they had been exposed earlier (Escorihuela et al., 1995).

There is still debate over whether these changes in brain size, complexity, and chemistry result in brighter rats. Mounting evidence suggests, however, that animals from enriched environments may be able to process and remember information more rapidly or efficiently than animals reared in impoverished conditions. Rats raised in environments that offer both social and physical complexity—playmates and a wealth of objects to explore—show an increase in dendritic branching, increased numbers of synapses, and growth in supporting glial cells and capillaries, or small blood vessels (Michel & Moore, 1995). And it may not be just the young who can benefit from enriched experiences. Rosenzweig studied young rats because he assumed that their brains would have their greatest plasticity prior to maturity. But later studies have shown that changes in brain weight, structure, and biochemistry are not restricted to the immature brain. Adult rats exposed to impoverished or enriched environments after being reared in normal laboratory conditions show changes like those we see in young rats (Greenough & Green, 1981). Still, the effects of differential experience may be greater during the earlier periods of life.

Recent research suggests that variations in environmental stimulation can affect the human infant's developing brain as well. As we will explore in detail in Chapter 8, studies of infant language acquisition illustrate the brain's plasticity. Although infants respond to the sounds of all languages at first, over the first year of life they become more selective, responding more to sounds in their own language (Kuhl, Williams, Lacerda, Stevens, & Lindblom, 1992). Kuhl and her colleagues suggest that infant's brains develop "auditory maps," or templates that are designed to respond to certain auditory features and not others. These maps then guide infants in recognizing the language to which they are exposed in their early environment. It is as if different sets of neuronal connections become programmed to respond to particular aspects of speech.

Recent studies have suggested that establishing certain kinds of neural connections can facilitate others. Sarnthein and colleagues (1997), for example, have proposed that the natural harmonies of music may help the brain develop a wiring diagram that can promote the kind of spatial-temporal reasoning that is central to success in math or the game of chess. After six months of weekly piano lessons, 3- and 4-year-olds improved markedly in this kind of reasoning as demonstrated by their ability to look at a disassembled picture of an elephant and to tell the researcher how to put the pieces together. In contrast, children in other groups who received either stimulation such as singing lessons and training with a computer keyboard and mouse or no stimulation showed little improvement. The research suggests that neural circuitry in the brain may be changed by music training, but there is no direct evidence of this, nor is it clear that these young pianists will be either better musicians or better math students in later years.

Just as stimulation can enhance the development of the brain, so can lack of stimulation or exposure to traumatic events damage the brain or cause it to malfunction. Recent studies suggest that in abused children both the cortex and the *limbic system*—centers in the brain that are involved with emotions and infant-parent attachment—are 20 to 30 percent smaller than in other children and that these areas have fewer synapses (Perry, 1997). Investigators have also found that infants raised in high-stress environments, such as a violent, crime-ridden neighborhood, may develop higher levels of cortisol, a natural steroid that increases the activity of the part of the brain involved in vigilance and the control of arousal. Hypothesizing that these children might be more likely to develop hyperactivity and impulsive behavior, Gunnar and her colleagues (Gunnar, 1994; Nachmias,

■ **FIGURE 6-8**
How early deprivation can affect brain activity.
In the brain of a normal child (a), positron emission tomography (PET) reveals many regions of high activity (red), whereas in the brain of an institutionalized Romanian orphan who suffered extreme deprivation from birth (b), there are many fewer such regions and more areas of lesser activity. The degrees of brain activity, from highest to lowest, follow the color sequence red, yellow, green, blue, and black. (*Source:* Begley, 1997).

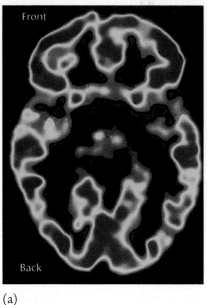

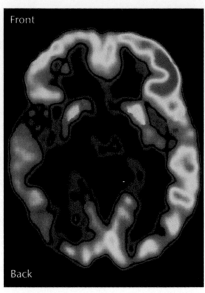

(a)

(b)

Gunnar, Mangelsdorf, Parritz, & Buss, 1996) found that higher cortisol levels were indeed associated with lower inhibitory control. New techniques such as *positron-emission tomography,* or PET, have permitted neuroscientists to track changes in infant brains over development as well as to detect the effects of trauma on the developing brain. PET scans use radioactive tracers to image and analyze such things as the flow of blood through the body's organs and metabolic activity in specific portions of an organ. As Figure 6-8 shows, early deprivation characterized by an unstimulating and unresponsive environment—a Romanian orphanage—can have a profound impact on the developing brain.

MOTOR DEVELOPMENT

What course does the infant's motor development follow? In this section we look first at the way an infant reaches and grasps and at how early she acquires these skills. One of babies' early achievements is the ability to reach, grasp, and pick up objects. These skills are important because they provide another way, in addition to seeing and hearing, that infants can explore and learn about their new world. "Once infants can reach and grasp objects, they no longer have to wait for the world to come to them; their hands now bring objects close enough for exploration" (Bertenthal & Clifton, 1998, p. 38). We also explore infant's first efforts to reach things beyond their immediate grasp—their attempts to crawl to an interesting object and, ultimately, to walk to it. As you will see, cultural practices and other environmental conditions can affect the timing of the emergence of effective locomotion.

Reaching and Grasping

"Manual control ranks as one of the human infant's greatest achievements in the first two years of life" (Bertenthal & Clifton, 1998, p. 58), and the first step the baby takes toward this control is to reach for objects in its view. As we saw in Chapter 5, even newborns display a grasping reflex and a rudimentary form of reaching—called "prereaching"—that involves uncoordinated "swipes" at objects that babies notice. Around 2 months of age these primitive forms of reaching and grasping decline (Bower, 1982; Hofsten & Rönnqvist, 1993). At 3 months, infants initiate a new and more complex and efficient pattern, namely, *directed reaching* (Thelen et al., 1993). By the time they are about 5 months old, normal infants in average environments generally succeed not only in reaching in a directed way for an object but in successfully grasping it.

In early experiments with institutionalized infants whose normal environments were severely restricted, White and his colleagues (White, 1967) showed that enriching such deprived infants' visual world could advance their abilities to attend to objects and to reach for them. Hanging colorful toys over the babies' cribs, providing them with multicolored sheets and bumper pads, and ensuring that the infants were handled more often by their caretakers, the researchers found that the experimental babies exhibited visually directed reaching by the time they were a little over 3 months old and about 40 percent faster than control subjects. At the same time, these infants ignored the new conditions for the first 5 weeks of the experiment and cried more than the other babies during that time. This could suggest that maturation, too, played a role here. Maybe if we want to accelerate a child's development, we need to provide her with new experiences that are paced just ahead of her emerging capacities, but not so far ahead that she can't incorporate these experiences into her repertoire of behavior. On the other hand, yet another factor may have played a role in White's studies: The lack of sensitive caregiving in the institutional environment may have discouraged the infants from exploring—a reminder that contextual and biological factors interact in affecting development.

Maturation alone cannot account for the emergence of the skills of reaching and grasping, however. Although Halverson (1931) proposed an orderly developmental sequence based essentially on maturation of the brain and influenced little if at all by environmental factors, recent research indicates that this view was incorrect. Although there is a strong developmental progression in the frequency and skill with which infants employ various grips (Bertenthal & Clifton, 1998; Siddiqui, 1995) and neurological development undoubtedly sets some limits on infants' abilities to contact and grasp objects, task parameters in the form of object size and shape affect grasping skill at every age (Newell, Scully, McDonald, & Baillargeon, 1990). The baby's grasping system is highly flexible, and there is more room for change in response to the environment than psychologists and others once thought.

Research based on dynamic systems theory (Corbetta & Thelen, 1996) indicates that patterns of specific reaching and grasping behavior reflect coordination tendencies in an infant's general, nonreaching arm movements. If an infant generally tends to move his arms simultaneously, that is, when he is not engaged in reaching for something specific, he may be more likely to reach for an object with both arms. In addition, one of the reasons that infants' early reaching is unskilled, often showing jerky, zigzag movements, is that infants are less able than adults to control their general movement tendencies, which then interfere with their immediate goals (Thelen, Corbetta, & Spencer, 1996). Moreover, the environment exerts its influence: From the perspective of dynamic systems theory, movement is always a product not only of the central nervous system and

Using a finger grasp to pull a peg out of its hole and to hold another in waiting shows some advanced skill on the part of this 7-month-old baby. On average, infants are 8 months old before they can use this type of grasp.

the biomechanical and energetic properties of the body but of "the environmental support and the specific (and sometimes changing) demands of the particular task" (Thelen et al., 1996, p. 1060). For example, babies whose preferred mode was to kick either with one leg only or with alternating legs were induced to shift to kicking both legs simultaneously when researchers gently tied their ankles together (Corbetta & Thelen, 1996).

Another way to illustrate the role that the environment—in this case, the task confronting the infant—plays in the emergence of grasping is to consider how the size and shape of an object alters the infant's grasping behavior. By varying the proportions of the objects they present to 4- and 8-month-old babies, investigators have found that an infant's grasping is actually quite complex. For example, infants vary their grips according to the size and shape of an object as well as the size of their own hands relative to the object's size (Baillargeon, McDonald, Newell, & Scully, 1989; Baillargeon, McDonald, & Newell, 1993). Infants use a grip involving the thumb and index finger (or the thumb, index finger, and middle finger) for small objects, but for large objects they use either all fingers of one hand or both hands. Moreover, these patterns are consistent over time: Both younger and older infants show clear sensitivity to the size and shape of an object relative to the size of their hands. There is an age difference, however, in the way younger and older babies decide how to grasp an object (Newell et al., 1989). Four-month-olds rely more on touch to determine grip configuration, whereas 8-month-olds use vision as a guide; the latter technique is more efficient, of course, because it allows the child to preshape his hand as he reaches for an object (Newell et al., 1990).

Over the course of the first year of life, the infant's progress in controlling his hands is remarkable. Infants not only become highly skilled reachers and graspers (Siddiqui, 1995) but begin to explore the world with their hands, using objects, such as spoons (Connolly & Dalgleish, 1989) as tools. Moreover, as we will see in Chapter 8, they learn the use of gestures in social communication. For example, at about 1 year of age they are able to follow a parent's pointing finger to the target object rather than focus on the finger alone (Butterworth & Grover, 1990), and only a month or so later they can use the pointing gesture themselves to attract other people's attention (Franco & Butterworth, 1996).

Locomotion

According to Thelen and Smith (1994), the development of locomotion consists of three clear phases or transitions. The first of these has long puzzled researchers: When you hold a baby upright and let his feet touch a flat surface, tilting his body slightly from side to side, the baby responds by reflexively moving his legs in a rhythmic stepping motion that resembles walking. But this stepping reflex disappears by the time the infant is about 2 months old. It is not until the second half of the baby's first year that the second transition sees the reappearance of stepping movements. In the third and final transition, infants who are about 1 year old begin to walk without support.

Psychologists have offered various accounts of how independent walking develops. Some maturational theorists believe it depends on the development of the motor cortex (McGraw, 1940). Others view it as a response to cognitive plans or representations that themselves are partly the product of the experience of watching other people walk (Zelazo, 1983). Still others suggest that a motor "program" in the spinal cord guides locomotor development (Forssberg, 1985). None of these explanations, however, have been very successful in accounting for the mysterious disappearance and reappearance of stepping.

A more useful approach may be the dynamic systems view proposed by Thelen (Thelen, 1988; Thelen & Ulrich, 1991), which holds that walking skills are determined by the interplay of a variety of factors: emotional, perceptual, attentional, motivational, postural, and anatomical. According to Thelen, all these

Taking your first steps must be an emotional experience; the joy and excitement mirrored on the faces of both the 11-month-old baby taking those first steps and the child's 7-year-old sister are contagious. Perhaps these positive emotions are also contributing to the baby's slightly advanced ability; on average, children walk alone at about 12 months.

components must be "ready," and the developmental context (in this case, the weight of the baby's body in proportion to the strength of her legs) must be right before walking is evident. On this view, the newborn stepping response disappears for a 10-month interval before true walking emerges, because anatomical factors conspire against the infant as she develops throughout the first year; that is, the baby's size and weight become too much of a load on the emerging motor system, masking the child's stepping capability (Thelen & Fisher, 1982).

If this explanation is right, infants between the ages of 2 months and 12 months should be able to step as long as they're given the stability and postural support necessary to stretch each leg forward and back while in an upright position. Thelen (1986; Thelen & Smith, 1994) tried to provide such support for walking by holding 7-month-old infants on a motorized treadmill. Immediately, they performed alternating stepping movements that were remarkably similar to more mature walking. Subsequently, Thelen and her colleagues found that 7-month-olds could even adjust their walking speed when the treadmill moved at different rates for each leg (Thelen, Ulrich, & Niles, 1987).

In another study based on a dynamic systems approach, Clark and Phillips (1993) investigated the way infants less than a year old learned to coordinate not only their two legs but the two main parts of each leg—the thigh and the shank—and then compared the infants' efforts to walk with adult walking. Weekly, these investigators filmed infants who were able to stand, to observe how walking emerged. They found that stability replaced instability as the infants began to achieve systemic coordination of each leg; that is, the angles at which both thigh and shank moved, the timing of their movements, and the interrelationships of thigh and shank began to resemble adult leg motion. These researchers did not intervene in their young participants' efforts at walking. However, the fact that two of the infants achieved stability in coordinating their leg movements after only 3 months of walking supports the idea that locomotor development may be more advanced in the middle of the first year than was thought. Perhaps infants just need the right conditions, whether specific interventions or simple attention, to be able to "strut their stuff"!

Upright walking is only the beginning, of course, and by the time the average child is 7, she acquires the more complex skills of running, galloping, and hopping (Roberton & Halverson, 1984, 1988). Running, which appears not long after walking, is well established by the time the child is a year and a half old (Forrester, Phillips, & Clark, 1993; Gesell & Amatruda, 1941), and galloping emerges at about the same time (Whitall & Clark, 1994). Hopping, which requires balance and strength, emerges a little later. In one study, only one child among twenty 2-year-olds could hop, but all 3-year-olds were able to hop (Halverson & Williams, 1985). As in the case of walking, a dynamic systems approach provides the best explanation of this developmental progression: These skills depend on improvements in balance and coordination and on the opportunity for practice (Diedrich & Warren, 1995).

How Locomotion May Affect Other Aspects of Development

One important result of locomotor development is the growing degree of independence it provides. Babies who can crawl or walk can explore their environments more fully and initiate more contact with other people. This newfound independence, in turn, changes the way that others respond to the child. No longer can parents place the baby on a blanket in the middle of the floor, expecting that he will be there when they turn around. The baby can now move at will throughout his home, leaving what seems to the pursuing parents like a trail of mayhem—torn magazines, overturned coffee cups, the luscious cherries that filled a favorite bowl squashed and mixed with pottery shards on the living room carpet. Not surprisingly, parents are likely to interrupt the infant's activities by relocating the child, distracting him, prohibiting actions with the ubiquitous "No, no!" or making objects or entire areas inaccessible (Green, Gustafson, & West, 1980). Clearly, not only do parents influence their children; children influence the attitudes and actions of their parents as well.

The onset of locomotion also affects the way babies understand their perceptual world. Babies begin to develop a fear of heights only after they begin crawling (Campos & Bertenthal, 1989; Bertenthal et al., 1994), perhaps partly because at this stage they are better able to solve spatial problems. In one study, researchers compared precrawling infants, belly-crawling infants, and babies who crawled proficiently on hands and knees for their ability to solve a hidden-toy problem. All the babies (who were all the same age) watched while a toy was hidden in one of two containers. Then the researchers rotated each infant 180 degrees and left him or her to find the toy. The fact that good crawlers were more likely to solve the problem than noncrawlers or belly crawlers suggests that locomotion helps infants deal better with changes in spatial orientation. Apparently, motor development and perception should be viewed as interdependent parts of a child's "action system," or the child's system of orienting and moving in his environment.

Another illustration of the links between perception and action is provided by a recent study of the impact of self-produced locomotion on infants' use of visual perceptual information to control their posture (Bertenthal & Bai, 1989). The investigators either moved the room in which their infant participants were situated or moved the walls of the room in such a way that the infants had to make postural adjustments to stay upright. Interestingly, only infants who either were at the crawling stage or had experienced self-produced locomotion in a walker were able to use the perceptual feedback from the distortions of the moving room to adjust their posture. Prelocomotor infants of the same age were unable to use this critical visual feedback to help maintain their posture. Again, self-produced locomotion appears to induce shifts in other developing systems—in this case the visual perception system (Bertenthal & Clifton, 1998; Campos & Bertenthal, 1989). In children who are at risk because of some developmental disability, however, the action system may be in jeopardy; see Box 6-1.

Thus, as we see so often in development, changes in one domain have important implications for changes in another. Recent research has also suggested that early walking may be related both to a greater amount of positive interaction and to more "testing of the wills" between mother and child (Biringen, Emde, Campos, & Appelbaum, 1995); the latter refers to mothers' efforts to stop a particular act by her child. What might be the reason for these correlations? The researchers speculate that either the early walkers may have been strongly predisposed toward walking and at the same time have had more difficult child-parent relationships or that these young hikers may have been trying to achieve independence *because* they confronted such difficult and challenging relationships. Gender turned out to be a variable in this research as well, for the researchers found that mothers tended to perceive their male infants more positively but also, interestingly, to have more confrontations with them. Perhaps future studies will shed some light on the reasons for—and the stability of—this finding.

The Role of Experience and Culture

Although overall limits to motor development may well be set by physical maturation, within those limits the timing of the onset of various skills may be affected by societal and other factors. Studying children in a number of European cities, researchers have found that there are fairly wide variations in the age at which walking begins: Parisian children, for example, walk earlier than their peers in London or Stockholm (Hindley, Filliozat, Klackenberg, Nicolet-Neister, & Sand, 1966). These differences suggest that the onset of walking may be influenced by cultural factors of some sort, perhaps including differences in nutrition and experience as well as differences in biological makeup.

Two related factors that may stimulate children's early motor development are physically handling infants and giving them exercise in various motor skills. As you can see from Box 6-2, although such practices vary among cultures, mothers in developing societies tend to encourage their children's motor development. According to Hopkins (1991), in less-advanced societies there may be more pressure on parents to promote children's physical development simply to ensure their survival. Although it's also possible that families in such societies put special value on physical strength because their local economies are characterized by more jobs that call for motor skills, as Box 6-2 suggests, other factors such as climate and religious and spiritual beliefs also influence infant-rearing styles.

Research in the United States has shown that practice in motor behavior can hasten walking and other skills. Figure 6-9 shows the results of an early study of

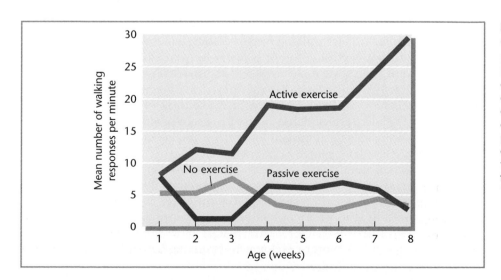

■ **FIGURE 6-9**
Can practice really make perfect?
Newborns given active exercise of the walking reflex showed a clear increase in this response over babies given passive exercise or no exercise at all. The practiced babies also walked earlier than the other children in this experiment. (*Source:* Adapted from Zelazo, Zelazo, & Kolb, 1972)

BOX 6-1

Risk and Resilience

Blind Infants Struggle to "See"

Being unable to see puts an infant at risk for many difficulties. As Figure 6-10 shows, blindness retards motor development considerably, especially the baby's first efforts to raise his body with his arms and his attempts to stand up by holding on to furniture, to walk alone, and to reach for objects (Adelson & Fraiberg, 1974). This limited mobility can have some serious consequences: "It lessens [the blind infant's] ability to explore independently, to discover by himself the objective rules that govern things and events in the external world" (Fraiberg, 1977, p. 270). As we will see, studying the motor development of blind infants not only helps researchers devise ways to help these at-risk children but gives us more information about the interdependence among various sensory and motor systems.

No matter how resilient a blind infant may be, he or she clearly needs help in learning about and functioning in the physical and social environment. On the assumption that blind infants need assistance in learning to associate sound with the information they get from touch, Fraiberg (1977) developed a program that maximizes babies' opportunities to make sound a guide for touch. Parents of blind infants were encouraged to talk to their babies both as they were physically approaching them and during routine activities such as feeding and dressing. Fraiberg's program also called for parents to provide their infants with toys that make sounds and to make sure that these toys were within their infants' easy reach so as to encourage both coordinated two-hand activity and the exploration of objects that make sounds. With the help of these interventions, infants learn to use a combination of sound and touch as a way of identifying people and things. And it does make a difference. In comparison to blind children who do not receive such extra stimulation, stimulated blind babies are less delayed in standing and walking, even though they are still behind sighted infants in the development of motor activities.

Technology is playing a role in building blind infants' motor capabilities. In the 1980s, experimenters in Scotland suggested that an electronic device that produces echoes from nearby objects may help blind babies to "see." The blind infant might learn to use this feedback to judge her distance from an object and even perhaps to assess the object's size and texture. Bower (1979, 1982, 1989) had young, blind infants wear an echo-producing device for several months and found that by using the echo feedback, the babies could judge their distance from objects and even sometimes the objects' sizes and texture. The infants' reaching ability was improved, and they were able to do things more typical of sighted infants.

Because much research in this area has focused on devices that must be carried and manipulated by the user, the so-called electronic travel aids (ETAs) that have been developed are designed for blind adults. Adults have found ETAs, which use laser or sound-wave technologies, to be useful particularly in enabling them to avoid contact with other pedestrians and to detect the presence of nearby objects (Blasch, Long, & Griffin-Shirley, 1989). Two of the newer sensor devices, which provide information to the user in synthesized speech, require that places frequented by the public, such as hotels and public buildings, install special transmitters whose signals can be picked up by the device (Bentzen & Mitchell, 1995). Thus, for example, a transmitter in a hotel lobby might, when activated by a scanning sensor, inform the person that "Elevators are to your right." For the preverbal child perhaps scaled-down versions of ETA might be developed, but it's not beyond imagining that for the child who has acquired good language skills the newer, "talking sign" devices might be adapted to home and school use.

---

the role of specific practice in fostering the onset of walking and other motor skills. Zelazo and colleagues (1972) asked mothers of newborns to give their infants practice in the stepping reflex a few minutes a day. Not only did these two- to eight-week-old babies make more walking responses, but they walked independently at an earlier age than a control group of babies who were given no practice. Even infants who were given passive exercise like that provided by the Jamaican mothers discussed in Box 6-2 walked later than the "practiced" infants or than infants who received no exercise at all. In a later study these investigators found that practice in sitting yielded similar results: Babies who were given practice in sitting for three minutes a day were able to sit upright longer than infants in a no-practice control group (Zelazo, Zelazo, Cohen, & Zelazo, 1988).

But practice apparently does not make perfect. For one thing, the effects of practice are highly specific. Practice in stepping does not affect sitting, and practice in sitting upright does not affect stepping. And the effect of practice on the emergence of motor skills is not enormous; no stepping-trained baby has walked at 3 or 4 months of age (Zelazo et al., 1988). Thus, at least in developed societies, attempting to speed up a child's motor development by giving her specific practice does

One interesting possibility under investigation is a device composed of a camera and a computer contained in eyeglass frames and hooked up to a receiver implanted within the brain that may allow a blind person to "see" actual letters in the form of *phosphenes,* or the colored displays that we all see with our eyes shut (Stone, 1990). Among the drawbacks to this approach is that, at least for now, the device can display only one letter at a time, mak-

ing "reading" for the blind person a very tedious process indeed and, it would seem, hardly preferable to auditory input. There are no miracles in the offing, but if research continues and if blind youngsters and adults can maintain their resilience as they try new techniques that become available, perhaps the difficulties they confront may be lessened in time.

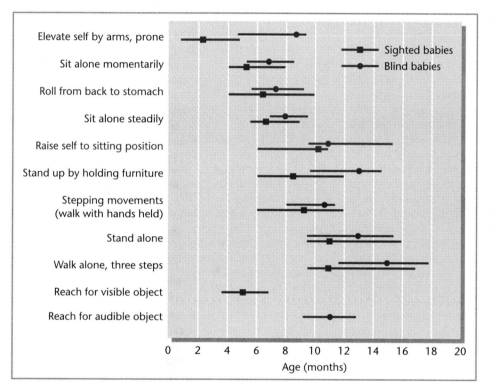

■ **FIGURE 6-10**
Motor development in blind and sighted babies.
Clearly, being sighted helps an infant to develop motorically, but in some movements, such as rolling over and sitting up, blind babies are not so very far behind sighted infants. The squares and circles indicate the average ages at which particular activities emerge in blind and sighted babies; the extent of each line indicates the age range within which babies may begin specific activities. (*Sources:* Adelson & Fraiberg, 1974; Bower, 1979)

not actually accelerate development. Only longitudinal studies could tell us whether such practice might have any long-term effect on a child's general physical and psychological well-being.

PHYSICAL GROWTH

One of the most actively investigated areas of child development, physical growth is guided by two classic principles. First, the human infant is characterized by **cephalocaudal development** (*cephalocaudal* derives from the Latin words for "head" and "tail"); that is, growth in infancy occurs from the head downward. Thus the brain and neck develop earlier than the legs and trunk. Second, growth also follows a **proximal-distal** ("toward the center–away from the center") **pattern.** In other words, development occurs from the center outward; for example, the internal organs develop earlier than the arms and hands.

Height and weight are the two principal measures of overall growth, and both dimensions are of great interest and concern to many, particularly people in the

cephalocaudal development
The notion that human physical growth occurs from head downward, that is, from brain and neck to trunk and legs.

proximal-distal pattern
The tendency for human physical development to occur from the center outward; for example, from internal organs to arms and legs.

BOX 6-2

Perspectives on Diversity

How Infant-Rearing Customs Can Alter Motor Patterns

Cross-cultural studies have provided us with some insights into how specific ways of caring for newborns and infants can alter motor patterns. In general, it seems that when parents or other caretakers give babies special physical attention, including manipulation, massage, exercise, and specific practice of skills, the infants are likely to achieve certain motor milestones somewhat earlier than children who are not given such care and opportunities. As the text suggests, whether such advanced skills are useful to children may depend on the nature of the society in which they live.

In Zambia, a mother carries her new baby with her everywhere in a sling on her back. When the child is able to sit, the mother leaves her sitting alone for considerable periods of time, giving her plenty of opportunity to practice motor skills. Zambian babies, like many African and West Indian infants, show early development of motor skills (Goldberg, 1966; Hopkins & Westra, 1988). A little north of Zambia, in Kenya, Gusii infants are conditioned from birth to vigorous movement; Keefer and her colleagues have observed mothers and other adults handle newborns "with much more vigor than is tolerated with American infants" (Keefer et al., 1991, p. 49). Apparently, such things as being careful not to let a baby's head drop are unknown among the Gusii, who commonly toss their infants into the air after a bath not only to shake off excess water but to help the baby to get over her fright at such treatment! According to these researchers, Gusii children are healthy, robust, and responsive, and, when older, they are among the hardest-working children in the world. They are loved and well cared for, and as adults they maintain strong attachments to their mothers.

Studying mothers and babies in Jamaica, British West Indies, and comparing them with English mothers and children, Hopkins and Westra (1990) found that Jamaican mothers expect their infants to sit and walk alone two or three months earlier than English mothers expect their babies to achieve these skills. Moreover, soon after their babies are born, Jamaican mothers practice what is called "formal handling," in which they regularly massage their infants and stretch their arms and legs. Among Jamaican immigrants in England, mothers also use formal handling, and Hopkins (1991) found that once again children who were handled tended to be more motorically advanced than those who were not. When native Jamaican infants are 2 or 3 months old their mothers begin to give them practice in stepping. Jamaican mothers don't encourage crawling, which they think dangerous and apelike, and instead encourage sitting and then walking, which they consider skills crucial to become a successful adult (Hopkins & Westra, 1990).

Among the Zinacantecos of Mexico, newborns are carried most of the time, tightly swaddled, and even have their faces covered for the first 3 months of life. One reason for this practice is climatic: These Mayan peoples live in the highlands of the state of Chiapas, where the extreme cold could endanger newborns' lives (Greenfield & Childs, 1991). But there may be other, cultural and even economic reasons. For example, Zinacantecos believe that the art of hand-weaving, which not only is traditional in their culture but has become an income-producing activity, must be practiced with calm, quiet, and close attention. Greenfield and Childs (1991) suggest that the early restraint of motor activity may promote the ability to master this kind of endeavor. These researchers, like Brazelton (1972), found that Zinacanteco infants had less-advanced motor skills than babies in the United States but also that the Mexican babies were more alert, observing their surroundings attentively for longer periods than the U.S. infants and not crying or flailing about, "demanding that someone react to them" (Greenfield & Childs, 1991, p. 147).

Swaddling seems to have another purpose for the people who live in fishing towns near Udupi in Karnataka State in southwestern India. Studying families in the coastal lowland village of Malpi, Landers (1989) concluded that swaddling may enable the child to habituate to and to shut out disturbing sounds, movements, or other threatening phenomena. In Malpi babies, however, swaddling and being carried daily did not seem to interfere with motor activity, probably in large part because both mothers and grandmothers typically handled newborns with abrupt and vigorous movements and gave them daily baths that included strong massage. Although mothers did not encourage their infants to explore and master their worlds independently, the fact that in their first 3 months these babies grew 50 percent more than an American sample and performed better on the Bayley Scales of Infant Development suggests the involvement of some other influence. In fact, the Hindu view of the child as a gift of God who should be protected, indulged, and showered with affection may be at work here. Indian mothers cuddle and cater to their babies, responding immediately to the least sign of distress and feeding them on demand, at the breast, sometimes until they are 2 or 3 years old. According to Landers (1989), this immediate response may encourage infants to interact vigorously with their environment, confident that they will succeed in eliciting feedback.

United States. Although no one has ever shown that tall people are brighter, more creative, or superior in any nonphysical way to shorter people, life insurance statistics have demonstrated a positive correlation between height and professional accomplishment! In addition, according to Krogman (1972), in the Great Depression of the 1930s, it was shorter men who were first to be laid off of their jobs, and in U.S. presidential elections, victory has gone to the taller candidate 15 times. (For the record, Abraham Lincoln, at 6' 5", was America's tallest president, and Lyndon Johnson, at 6' 3", ran a close second.) Although taller isn't necessarily better, for some reason Americans tend to think it is, and continue to hope that their children will not be too short.

The regular appearance of books describing innovative diets and frequent openings of new Weight Watchers clubs testify to the concern of adult Americans about weight and weight gain. Infant Americans, however, are encouraged to gain weight; parents and other relatives and friends greet each new pound with delight. According to Lipsitt and Werner (1981), babies grow faster within their first half year of life than ever again. They double their weight in the first 3 months, and until they're 6 months old they continue to gain weight at a rate of about 2 grams, or .07 ounces, every 24 hours! From then on, although infants' growth rate decreases gradually, babies still gain at a rate most adults would not care to imitate: between 6 months and 3 years the average baby adds 2.5 grams, or about an ounce, every week, and from 3 to 6 years she adds 1 gram, or about a half ounce. If a 20-year-old person gained even a half ounce a week, he would be some 44 pounds heavier at the age of 40.

In this section we discuss the various factors that influence the infant's and child's growth in both height and weight, beginning with possible genetic factors and turning next to such environmental factors as nutrition, hygiene and sanitation, and poverty. We then look at the interesting evidence that people—at least in more developed countries—have been growing taller. Our final discussion in this section focuses on the growing problems of obesity and eating disturbance in the United States as well as on methods of preventing and treating these disorders.

Do Genes Affect Height and Weight?

Although both height and weight can be influenced by environmental factors, research suggests that genetic factors strongly influence these physical characteristics (Tanner, 1990). Data from the Colorado Adoption Project, a longitudinal study that compares several hundred adoptive and biological parents, and adopted and natural children, indicate that genetic factors may determine as much as two-thirds of the variance in these characteristics (Cardon, 1994). Using a measure called the body mass index (BMI), a measure of body fat, this study has also found that the tendency to be overweight or obese is also strongly influenced by genetic factors, although this pattern does not stabilize until a child is somewhere between 5½ and 6½. Although people often try to predict a child's future height and weight from his birthweight this is a risky venture. Body mass may not stabilize for a few years, and factors such as a mother's small size may mask a baby's potential for growth. For example, a fetus may grow more slowly during the last few weeks to make childbirth easier for the woman with a small frame. (Some small women do produce future linebackers, however!) On the other hand, it is possible to predict how tall a child will be in adulthood if we know the child's gender, his or her height at the age of 9, and his or her mother's and father's heights (Roche, 1979). Presumably this is because environmental factors, which we discuss shortly, have had their maximal influence by that time.

Gender has a clear effect on height and weight, as you can see from Figure 6-11. Girls tend to be a bit taller than boys from the age of 2 until about the age of 9, when boys catch up. At about 10½ girls experience a growth spurt, shooting well up

Male and female growth in height and weight.
As they approach puberty, girls tend to gain in height and, to a lesser degree, in weight, faster than boys, but by the age of 14 or 15, boys surpass girls on both dimensions. (*Source:* National Center for Health Statistics, 1976)

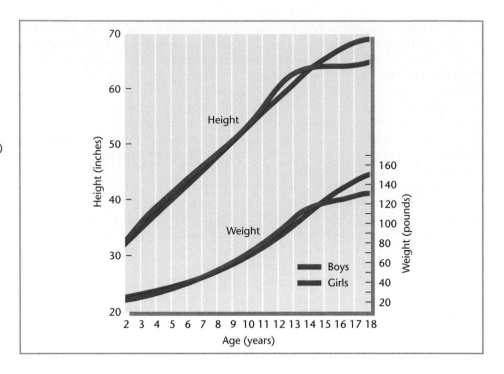

above boys of their own age. At about 14, however, girls' height seems nearly to plateau, whereas boys continue to grow taller until they are about 18. The pattern for weight is not greatly dissimilar, although girls tend to weigh less than boys in the early years and then to exceed them in weight until about 14, when their weight gain slows down while boys' gain continues to accelerate (Tanner, 1990).

It's important to note that there are also wide individual differences in rates of maturation. Because these differences become particularly obvious at adolescence, it is often assumed that they begin only in adolescence. In fact, however, these differences are present at all ages, so that early maturers are always ahead of late-maturing peers. Tanner (1978), an early pioneer in the study of physical growth, coined the term *tempo of growth* to designate this variability in the timing of changes in infants' and children's growth. As Tanner observed, growth is like a musical score: "Some children play out their growth andante, others allegro, a few lentissimo. It seems that heredity plays a large part in setting the metronome, but we do not know the physiological mechanism" (Tanner, 1978, p. 78).

The Influence of Environmental Factors

Growth is determined not only by genetic factors but also by such environmental influences as nutrition, physical and psychological disorders, and climate (Tanner, 1990). When environmental conditions are favorable, individual growth curves tend to be very similar, but in the presence of one or more unfavorable conditions, such as inadequate nutrition, growth rates are often seriously depressed (Pollitt, 1994). Bradley and colleagues (1994) found that among a group of children living in poverty, those few (only about 10%) whose care was more responsive, accepting, stimulating, and organized and who lived in safer, less crowded homes were functioning in the normal range for growth and other important parameters such as cognitive and social skills. Indeed, those children who had fewer than three of these protective aspects of caretaking were very unlikely to develop the resilience to overcome the effects of their unfavorable environments.

Of considerable interest are the variations in growth rates that are attributed to differences in nationality, ethnicity, and socioeconomic class. There are fairly wide variations across regional areas; for example, peoples in northwestern and western European countries, such as Scandinavia, are taller than southern Europeans, such

Being taller than their dance partners is a common experience for girls between the ages of about 11 and 14, for boys their age are typically 2 to 3 inches shorter than they are. These preteens don't seem to mind, though!

as the Mediterranean cultures. Within the continent of Africa and among the countries of Central America there are also substantial variations in height and weight; for example, African Nicotics become 7 feet tall, whereas the Pygmies of Zaire, Ruanda, Burundi, and the western coastal areas are on average only about 4 feet tall. Moreover, people vary in growth within the same country; for example, in Brazil and India people in urban areas where nutrition and standard of living is higher tend to be taller than rural dwellers. In addition, researchers have revealed that in the United States, children in upper-middle-class families are both taller and heavier than children of families living in poverty (Martorell, 1984). Among a number of Hispanic American groups—for example, Puerto Ricans and Mexicans—as many as 39 percent of families with children live in poverty (Children's Defense Fund, 1997). This fact may account for the finding by Martorell and his colleagues (1994) that, aside from gender, poverty was the only variable related to the finding of shorter stature among people in these groups as compared with the general North American population. Reporting similar findings in Sweden, Peck and Lundberg (1995) showed that short stature in adulthood may be a reflection of several adverse childhood conditions, including poverty—which subsumed poor nutrition and substandard housing—and psychological stress within the family.

Nutrition

Research done in a number of countries has revealed that nutrition plays a controlling role in physical growth. Wartime restrictions on food consumption on the home front in order to provide adequate nutrition for fighting forces have proved a useful barometer of change caused by reduced nutrition. In Europe, for example, during World Wars I and II, a general retardation in growth reflected the reductions in nutritional intake caused by such wartime restrictions. In contrast, during the period between these two major wars, from 1920 to 1940, there was a general increase in growth (Tanner, 1990). Interestingly, this increase was seen more in weight than in height and in boys more than in girls. Wartime research also revealed that nutritional factors can affect the age at which children enter puberty; during World War II, girls in occupied France did not achieve menarche (the onset of menstruation) on average until they were 16 years old, which is approximately three years later than the prewar norm (Howe & Schiller, 1952). Probably stress associated with wartime contributed to these outcomes as well.

Studies of people during times of peace have also highlighted the role of nutrition in growth. In a study in Bogota, Colombia, Super and his colleagues (Super, Herrera, & Mora, 1990) demonstrated that the provision of food supplements for entire families from midpregnancy until a child was 3 years old effectively prevented severe growth retardation in children who were at risk for malnutrition. Moreover, the children who received the food supplements remained taller and heavier than control children at 6 years of age, three years after the intervention ceased. Equally impressive are the results of a study by Ahmed and colleagues (1993) in rural Bangladesh which found that changing traditional unhygienic practices by means of educational and supportive interventions improved children's health, their growth rates, and their nutrition. By developing safer methods of food preparation and waste disposal and thus lessening the possibility of food contamination, local people were able to reduce the incidence of diarrhea, which interferes with the absorption of needed minerals and vitamins and depletes the body of these essential substances.

Finally, a survey study of research on the effects of poverty on child development in both the United States and other nations highlighted the importance of providing nutritional supplements and controlling disease among disadvantaged children (Pollitt, 1994). **Iron-deficiency anemia,** a condition in which insufficient iron in the diet causes listlessness and may retard children's physical and intellectual development, is common among poor minority children and children in low-income countries. Supplemental feeding can improve these children's rate of growth and cognitive performance (Pollitt, 1994). For example, a group of studies in Colombia, Guatemala, Jamaica, Taiwan, Indonesia, and the community of Harlem in New York City showed that among children at risk, early supplemental feeding enhanced both motor and mental development during the first two years of life. Researchers found that higher scores on the Bayley Scales of Infant Development (discussed in Chapter 11), and other scales documented improved motor performance during the children's first year.

Catch-Up Growth

In the face of the overwhelming need of millions of children living in poverty around the world, we need to ask not only what we can do to prevent malnutrition and inadequate growth but what, if anything, we can do to help those who are older catch up to their more fortunate peers. As we saw in Chapter 4, human beings have a strong tendency to regain a normal course of development after an early setback such as may be caused by prenatal deficiencies. A similar corrective principle, referred to as **catch-up growth,** operates after birth: Children who have suffered early environmental injury or deprivation are able eventually to catch up to normal physical growth. Tanner (1970) noted that children have growth trajectories that are governed both by genetics and by the energy they absorb from the natural environment: "Deflect the child from its growth trajectory by acute malnutrition or illness, and a restoring force develops so that as soon as the missing food is supplied or the illness terminated the child catches up toward its original curve" (p. 125).

The degree of catch-up growth that a child can achieve will depend on a variety of factors: duration, severity, and timing of the original deprivation she suffered, and the nature of the subsequent treatment or therapy. For example, in a study of the effects of intervention following severe malnutrition Graham (1966) found that malnourished infants who had a 5 percent deficit in height (body length) were able to catch up, but those with a 15 percent deficit remained significantly shorter, benefiting only somewhat from nutritional supplements. And catch-up growth following severe malnutrition may be limited to only some aspects of growth. In a 20-year longitudinal study of severely starved children, even a program of nutritional intervention failed to enable full development in head circumference (and presumably brain development) and produced only some catch-up in height (Stoch, Smyth, Moodie, & Bradshaw, 1982). This impact of malnutrition on brain development may, in part, account for the intellectual and attentional deficits shown by malnourished children (Riciutti, 1993; Sigman, 1995).

Timing is also critical in determining the degree of catch-up growth. For example, pathology and undernutrition early in life can have serious consequences, and

iron-deficiency anemia   A disorder in which inadequate amounts of iron in the diet cause listlessness and may retard a child's physical and intellectual development.

catch-up growth   The tendency for human beings to regain a normal course of physical growth after injury or deprivation.

children starved in utero through some sort of placental imperfection usually show only partial catch-up (Pollitt, Gorman, & Metallinos-Katsaras, 1992; Tanner, 1990). In general, the earlier and more prolonged the malnutrition, the more difficult it is for interventions to be fully effective in achieving the normal level of growth. As we saw earlier in the chapter, a supportive, stimulating, and safe family environment may play a role in catch-up growth as well (Bradley et al., 1994).

People Are Growing Taller

According to British scientists who have measured bones exhumed from gravesites, between the eleventh and fourteenth centuries the average Englishman was about 5 feet 6 inches tall, whereas today the average adult British male is 5 feet 9 inches tall. This kind of change is often called a **secular trend**—a shift that occurs in the normative pattern of a particular characteristic, such as height or weight, over some historical time period, such as a decade or a century (Figure 6-12). Should we keep updating our norms of height on the basis of this sort of gain—about a half inch every hundred years? Yes, probably, but note also that the same increases in height may not occur at every level of society. For example, if we look at the U.S. population from the point of view of socioeconomic status, we find that—at least in the country's current social, nutritional, and medical environment—most people in the upper 75 percent have probably reached their maximum growth potential (Hamill, Drizd, Johnson, Reed, & Roche, 1976). People in other segments of the society do continue to make gains, and in some other countries change is following yet other patterns. In Holland, for instance, people are continuing to gain in height and weight regardless of socioeconomic level, whereas in Japan, England, and Norway increase in stature has apparently come to a halt (Roche, 1979; Tanner, 1990).

Americans are not only growing taller but, as a consequence of their added height, Americans' feet are growing longer too, gaining about a third of an inch in each generation! The average college student's grandfather probably wore a size 7 shoe, whereas today the average American male wears between size 9 and 10. And not only are Americans and their feet increasing in size; Americans are achieving these growth increases at earlier ages than in the past. A hundred years ago, people didn't attain adult height until the early or midtwenties, but today many 16- or 17-year-olds are often as tall as, or taller than, their parents.

There are several possible reasons for these historical trends toward greater height and weight. First, health and nutrition have been improved in many countries of the world. Growth-retarding illnesses have come under control, particularly those that strike in the first 5 years of life, such as *marasmus* (caused by insufficient protein and calories) or *kwashiorkor* (caused by insufficient protein). Children with marasmus are frail, wrinkled, and suffer growth stoppage. Children with kwashiorkor are familiar from news reports: These are the children with bloated stomachs, skin lesions, and thinning hair. In many areas nutritional intake has been improved in terms both of quantity of food consumed and balance among

secular trend   A shift in the normative pattern of a characteristic like height that occurs over a historical time period like a decade or century.

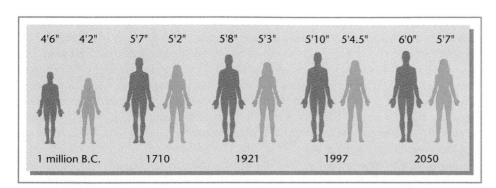

■ **FIGURE 6-12**
Height gains across the centuries and millennia. By 1997, the average American had gained 2.5 to 3 inches in height since the early eighteenth century, and expectations are that both men and women will double this gain by 2050. Compared with prehistoric ancestors, however, by that time we'll have become a foot and a half taller! (*Source*: Richard Steckel, Ohio State University, 1997)

Happiness floods the faces of this Saudi Arabian couple as they pose with their son after his graduation ceremonies at a Texas college. Towering over his parents, the graduate represents the newer generation, who are indeed taller than their parents.

the essential food groups (Tanner, 1990). Medical care and personal health practices have also improved; as we have seen, even in impoverished areas like rural Bangladesh, efforts have been under way to introduce good hygiene and sanitary practices. Second, socioeconomic conditions have generally improved; child labor is less common, and living conditions such as housing and sanitation have improved. Third, the influence of genetic factors has been affected by such things as intermarriage among people of different racial and ethnic backgrounds, which produces increases in height and weight in the offspring of such unions.

Because these trends are largely environmentally determined, if we should experience major changes in the environment such as might be brought about by spectacular medical discoveries, by natural disasters like famine, or by an increase or decrease in environmental pollution levels, the average height of the population could shift again. Clearly, depending on what direction such changes might take, people could again grow taller or they could lose stature.

Are We Growing Heavier? Obesity and Eating Disorders

obesity A condition in which a person's weight is 20 percent or more in excess of average weight for his or her height and frame.

Both children and adults in the United States are growing heavier. **Obesity,** the condition in which a person's weight is 20 percent or more over average weight for his or her height and frame, has been on the rise since the early 1960s (Sallis et al., 1993). This rise has occurred despite the fact that U.S. children are born into a society that reveres youthful, healthy good looks. Although Americans' preference for tall, slender people over short, overweight people may seem narcissistic, the emphasis on losing weight and keeping fit is based partly on realistic concerns about physical health and the avoidance of illness. Unfortunately, the desire to be attractive and physically fit leads many to a near obsession with weight-reduction clubs, magazines about weight and diet, and fad diets, and it is young girls who are most likely to suffer from this preoccupation with weight. Indeed, by midadolescence perhaps 70 to 80 percent of American girls have been on at least one diet (Attie & Brooks-Gunn, 1989; Davis, Best, & Hawkins, 1981). Why? Perhaps because their models have been getting thinner; participants in the Miss America Pageant have continued to weigh less and less (Silverstein, Petersen, & Perdue, 1986). In this section we look at this continuing American struggle to be thin and consider the problems of obesity and of eating disorders such as anorexia and bulimia.

Why Do Children Gain Too Much Weight?

As we've said, both children and adolescents show a tendency to be overweight (Harlan, 1993). One study found that among adults this trend toward obesity was most evident in people of Hispanic and Native American background, whereas in younger groups, prepubescent African American girls were heaviest. Wolf and colleagues (1993) found that among a sample of elementary and high school girls, about half of whom were between the ages of 11 and 14, African Americans tended to be the heaviest; Asian Americans were the least likely to be overweight. Preschool-aged African American children show less tendency toward overweight; this may be partly because African American women tend to bear children at relatively young ages and thus to have smaller babies and to give their children a slower start at weight gain (Kumanyika, 1993).

Genetic factors seem to play a crucial role in obesity. For example, in a longitudinal study Cardon (1994) found considerable stability in body mass index, which is independent of height. Although environmental factors contributed to weight gains at certain ages, overall stability in BMI was explained by genetic mediation. Adoptive and twin studies have also shown a primary effect for inheritance. Stunkard and colleagues (Stunkard, Sorenson, et al., 1986), for instance, found a strong relationship between the weight of adopted children and their biological parents' weight but no relationship between adoptees and their adoptive parents' weights. Similarly, identical twins are twice as likely to resemble each other in weight as are fraternal twins (Stunkard, Foch, & Hrubeck, 1986). And twins reared apart who did not share a common environment have shown marked similarity in weight (Bouchard, Lykken, Segal, & Wilcox, 1986).

Other evidence of the role of inheritance comes from studies of early infant behavior. Milstein (1980) found that newborn infants who had two overweight parents were more responsive to the contrast between a sweet-tasting solution and plain water than were infants of normal-weight parents. The fact that this indication of a preference predicted the children's weight at 3 years of age suggests that the preference for sweet tastes early in life may increase the risk for obesity. It seems fairly likely that babies' sucking patterns are genetically determined, and, interestingly enough, these patterns can help predict later weight (Agras, 1988). Among a group of 2- to 4-week-old infants, the babies who exhibited a more vigorous sucking pattern characterized by higher pressure and shorter breaks between bursts of sucking were found, at 2 years of age, to be heavier.

And what about children who are heavy from infancy on? Are they destined to become overweight adults? Not necessarily; only about a quarter of such infants are overweight adults 20 years later. Predictions made a little later may be more useful, however. Apparently there are at least two critical periods for the development of obesity: the first in infancy and the second when a child is about 4 years old. At that age, children who will be obese later in life begin to gain weight at a faster rate than other children (Agras, 1988; Rolland-Cachera et al., 1984).

All this sounds as though genetic factors dominate the issue of obesity, but wait: Education and income also play a role in obesity. For example, the better educated you are and the more money you earn, the less likely you are to be overweight! Although this may seem facetious, in fact some research with different groups in the United States suggests that socioeconomic factors may be at work. For instance, Kumanyika (1993) reports that among a sample of adults, the scale of overweight ran roughly as follows: Most overweight were the Pima Indians, followed in descending order by Hawaiian Americans, African Americans, Mexican Americans, Puerto Ricans, and Cubans; European Americans were the least overweight. The chances are that among these groups the European Americans had the highest incomes. One factor in their comparative slenderness may have been their ability to pay for such things as health club memberships and foods with fat-reduced content.

There is also evidence that modeling by others strongly affects children's eating behaviors; although we might assume that the fact that obese parents tend to have obese children reflects inheritance, Ray and Klesges (1993) have found that children are very likely to imitate adults' food choices and eating behavior. In addition, Klesges and colleagues (Klesges, Malott, Boschee, & Weber, 1986; Ray & Klesges, 1993) have observed that the parents of children who are obese not only encourage them to eat more than their nonobese siblings (explaining that they're bigger so they need more food!) but also offer such eating prompts nearly two and a half times as often as parents of normal-weight children do. As Box 6-3 shows, teaching children how to recognize when they are hungry and to stop eating when they feel full may help to prevent the development of obesity. Rewarding children for eating everything on their plates, however, may teach them to rely on external instead of internal cues in deciding whether to eat, a practice that for some children may lead to eating whenever food is in sight. It is important to distinguish between reaching the point of being overweight, on the one hand, and becoming and remaining obese for some time, on the other. As we will see in the next section, once overweight is well established a person may have difficulty shedding the pounds.

Obese children and adolescents often suffer from a variety of physical problems, including hypertension and diabetes. They may also run the risk of having high cholesterol levels, which can predispose one to high blood pressure and other cardiovascular problems. But according to recent research, a positive relation between body fat and cholesterol levels may be seen only in boys (Labarthe, 1997). Overweight children suffer psychologically as well, for they have more body-image disturbances than their nonobese peers, and the latter often discriminate against them. Peers tease them more, exclude them from their groups, and choose them last for athletic activities. For their part, because they fear other children will ridicule their bodies, chubby children often seek excuses to avoid gym class and thus get less exercise than they should. Overweight adolescents date less and are less likely to be admitted to prestigious colleges than their thinner classmates. Clearly, the costs of being obese can run very high (Buckmaster & Brownell, 1988).

Treating Overweight Children

Although obesity has been on the rise among children (Sallis et al., 1993), there has also been an unfortunate lack of enthusiasm for treating this disorder—and it *is* a disorder—among physicians and other health personnel (Nader, 1993). Why should health professionals be reluctant to deal with obesity? Most likely, it's because attempts to alter this condition have in the past so often met with failure and high rates of recidivism. Such treatment failures, however, may not reflect solely the strong genetic influences that we've discussed. They may also highlight the fact that we haven't found the right ways to encourage the healthy eating and physical activity habits that can help both children and adults improve their physical and mental health, their physical appearance, and their feeling of well-being.

The studies we review in this section make two principal suggestions for ways of controlling children's weight. First, it appears to be important to involve the family—parents and perhaps siblings as well—in any treatment program. Second, increasing a child's physical expenditure of energy in innovative ways seems to be a useful goal in the effort to achieve ideal weight for height.

Stunkard (1958), a pioneer researcher in the field of obesity, once remarked that few obese people stay in treatment and of those who do, most don't lose weight, and of those who do lose weight, most regain it. However, as Rodin (1981) has reminded us, this seeming inability to learn to control one's weight is not simply a lack of discipline:

> Obesity is unusual because being fat is one of the factors that may keep one fat.... Many an overweight person ... complains, "But I eat so little." Despite the disbelieving and reproachful looks of ... lean friends, the perverse fact is that it often does take fewer calories to keep people fat than it did to get them fat in the first place.... Obesity itself changes the fat cells and body chemistry and alters levels of energy expenditure. Each of these factors operates to maintain obesity once it has developed. (p. 361)

BOX 6-3

Child Psychology in Action

Learning Not to "Clean Your Plate"

Parents play a major role in teaching children about eating. They help children learn about what to eat, when to eat it, and how much to eat (Rozin, 1996). Unfortunately, parents may also teach children to rely more on external cues—such as feedback from them or the mere presence of food—than on cues that come from their own bodies that tell them when they're hungry and when they're not. When a child says, "I'm full" and the parent says, "No, finish what's on your plate," the parent is giving a clear message that it's the external cue that's important.

Birch and colleagues (Birch, McPhee, Shoba, Steinberg, & Krehbeil, 1987) showed that children can learn to rely on either internal or external feedback, depending on adult response to their eating behavior. Twenty-two preschoolers attended a series of special snack sessions over a six-week period. In one group the adult researchers helped the children focus on their sensations of hunger and fullness and stressed how these internal reminders tell us when to eat and when to stop eating. The children felt their stomachs and discussed how eating changes our feelings of hunger. In a second group, external cues were the focus. A bell rang to signal "snack time," and children were rewarded with such things as stickers for cleaning their plates.

Then the groups were combined and everyone was given a yogurt snack to eat, after which they were given a chance to eat another snack of cookies and granola bars. Children in the first group, who had been taught to rely on their internal signals, consumed less of the second snack, but children who had learned to depend on external cues

such as rewards and adult urging ate just as much of the second snack, no matter how full they were. It seems clear that the social context can influence which kinds of cues children learn to rely on in choosing or stopping eating.

Reviewing research on children's eating behavior, Ray and Klesges (1993) find that children can be encouraged to eat more healthily in a number of ways. According to these authors, allowing children to have more control over their food choices and the amounts they consume may result in children knowing more about how foods help us balance energy. In addition, involving children more in food-related activities such as helping to shop and prepare foods may give them more awareness of the importance of good nutrition.

Perhaps the most difficult pill for parents to swallow is the suggestion that they need to model good eating behavior for their children. According to Ray and Klesges, "the major finding to emerge in the research on the influence of adult behavior on the eating behavior of children is that children are more likely to eat a food when they see an adult eating it" (1993, p. 59). In addition, children apparently tend to develop the same food preferences as those of their parents. If parents eat a balanced diet that includes the major food groups, their children are likely to follow suit, but if parents eat large amounts of foods with saturated fatty acid content, children may eat similar amounts of such foods and may eat more of them than peers who eat healthier diets. Perhaps parents should look at this apparent restriction on their behavior as an opportunity rather than a restraint. The need to teach their children healthy eating habits might be just the nudge they need to watch their own diets and keep in shape!

We do not yet know enough about the mechanics of the genetic predisposition to fatness, the ways in which such a predisposition may be compounded by body chemistry, or the ways in which environmental change can affect obesity. But perhaps an increasing awareness of the complexities of this disorder will encourage a more enthusiastic approach on the part of health professionals.

Certainly, behavioral approaches to treatment that recognize the important role of environmental cues for regulating eating behavior look promising. Parents often encourage their children's overeating not only by tying eating to external cues but by their own eating behavior. Researchers like Epstein (Epstein, Valoski, Wing, & McCurley, 1994; Epstein, Wing, Koeske, & Voloski, 1987; Epstein et al., 1995) and Nader (1993) are finding that working with entire families in attempting to reverse these processes may be successful. Other researchers (e.g., Coates & Thoresen, 1976; Israel, 1988) have also found that such things as reducing the likelihood of stressful interactions with family members at mealtime can have good effects.

In one of the first studies by Epstein and his colleagues (Epstein et al., 1987), the most effective weight-reducing program for the obese child included a parent (who was also obese); taught both parent and child to self-monitor, or keep track of their own diet and exercise regimens; taught them to serve as models of good eating and exercise habits for other family members; and formulated a contract between the parent and the child by which the child earned rewards for weight loss. In addition, parents earned refunds from the program for reaching weight-loss goals for themselves and their children. In a second experimental group, researchers targeted only the obese child, teaching him or her to self-monitor, and in a control group, neither parents nor children engaged in self-monitoring activities. All groups showed a similar degree of weight loss at 8 and 21 months, but after five years, the children in the first group had maintained their weight loss, whereas children in group 2 showed no change and children in group 3 were actually heavier. Interestingly, in a "ripple effect," even obese siblings of children in group 1 had a significant weight loss, whereas siblings of children in the other treatment groups gained weight.

Continuing to examine the effects of family behavioral training on obesity reduction, Epstein and his colleagues (Epstein et al., 1994) not only confirmed the significant positive results of including parents in efforts at controlling diet and physical activity (see Figure 6-13) but found that, over the 10-year period of this study, 34 percent of their child participants succeeded in losing 20 percent or more of their overweight poundage and that at the close of the study 30 percent were no longer obese. This longitudinal study is significant also for its finding that encouraging children to engage in either lifestyle exercise (an exercise regimen in which the children themselves may choose among a variety of activities, such as walking, bicycling, skating) or formal aerobics, in combination with diet, was better than diet and only mild exercise (e.g., calisthenics). This finding may reflect the fact that children are still growing physically and thus a healthy diet may serve to channel energy (food) intake to useful body building and exercise rather than to the storage of energy (and thus fat). As always, to "take it off and keep it off" requires not only watching your food choices, but burning off those calories as well.

A study by Epstein and colleagues suggests that choice may be very important in getting children to lose weight (Epstein et al., 1995). These researchers gave children two options: They could spend less time in sedentary behaviors, such as watching TV and playing computer games, or they could increase their physical activity, for example riding an exercise bike or exercising to an aerobics tape. As you can see from Figure 6-14, decreasing sedentary activity was clearly more effective in producing weight loss than were either specific exercise or a combination of the two options. Based on significant improvements in fitness among the children who reduced their sedentary activities, the investigators speculate that these children may have substi-

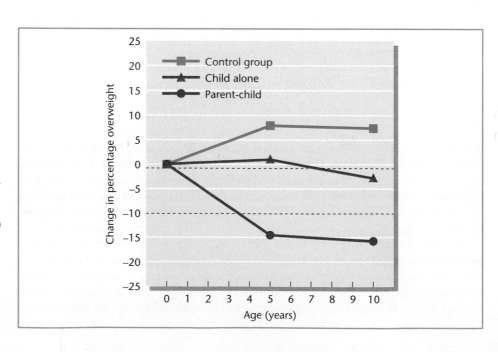

■ **FIGURE 6-13**

Losing weight: Is it better to go it alone or have help? Quite clearly, the experimental condition in which parents and children worked together to help the child lose weight was the most effective. The children who tried to lose weight without help succeeded in losing only minimal amounts of weight, and children in the control group, who neither dieted or exercised, actually gained weight. (*Source:* Epstein, Valoski, Wing, & McCurley, 1994)

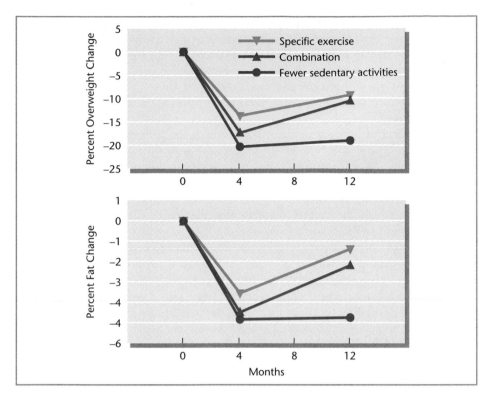

■ **FIGURE 6-14**
Reducing sedentary activities helps reduce weight. Children who spent less time watching TV and playing computer games lost the most weight. Neither a specific exercise regimen nor the combination of exercise and reduction of sedentary activities worked as well! (*Source:* Epstein et al., 1995)

tuted other, higher-energy-expenditure activities of their own choice. Parents had been instructed to make easily available such things as skates and bicycles.

Relatively few studies have been done, however, of the independent effects of exercise on children's weight (Gutin & Manos, 1993), and the topic remains controversial. For example, Sallis and colleagues (Sallis et al., 1993), found a nonsignificant decrease in levels of body fat in a group of fourth-grade children who participated in special physical education activities over a period of two years. Reviewing much of the literature, Gutin and Manos (1993) make an interesting suggestion: "Because children need to ingest sufficient energy and nutrients to assure healthy growth, energy restriction is not the method of choice for prevention of obesity. Shifting from a high fat to a high carbohydrate diet, however, may increase the TEF [the thermic effect of food, i.e., its productive channeling into energy-consuming activity] and [thus] have a subtle long-term preventive effect" (p. 123). These authors suggest that if children are made aware of the importance of a balanced diet, they may be more motivated to maintain their food intake at a constant level when they start an exercise program, and as a result the increased physical activity may gradually reduce fatness.

Eating Disorders in Adolescence

Just as obesity can cause both physical and psychological problems, so being underweight can bring on distressing and even life-threatening conditions. The two most common eating disorders in the United States, anorexia and bulimia, afflict far more women than men and generally strike between the age of 10 and the early twenties. Although there is some indication (Heatherton, Mahamedi, Striepe, Field, & Keel, 1997) that eating difficulties tend to decline in frequency in the transition to adulthood (and after college), a number of women continue to be dissatisfied with their bodies and to indulge in repetitive dieting. Men, on the other hand, who are less affected in adolescence and early adulthood, may begin to gain weight after beginning college and for the first time become concerned with dieting and body image.

People with **anorexia nervosa** have an unaccountable dread of being fat and diet constantly to avoid that state. They see themselves as obese even if they are quite

anorexia nervosa An eating disorder in which the person, usually a young woman, is preoccupied with avoiding obesity, and often diets to the point of starvation.

slender and although they may be preoccupied with food and may even hoard it, they eat less and less. Young women in particular (relatively few young men are anorexic) may lose up to 25 percent of their body weight (some lose even more) and may become so weak that they must be hospitalized to redress fluid and electrolyte imbalances. Without continuing intervention, these skeletal creatures, who often have been attractive, bright, and achieving young women, may die from starvation or suicide.

bulimia nervosa An eating disorder in which people, usually young women, alternate periods of binge eating with vomiting and other means of compensating for the weight gained.

Bulimia nervosa is an eating disorder in which the person—again, typically a young woman in adolescence or early adulthood—goes through recurrent periods of seemingly uncontrollable binge eating followed by either vomiting or the use of laxatives to compensate for the bingeing and to prevent weight gain. Bulimics, like anorexics, risk fluid and electrolyte abnormalities, and the loss of stomach acid through vomiting and the frequent induction of diarrhea can cause other, metabolic problems (American Psychiatric Association, 1994).

Most cases of bulimia emerge during the late teens and early twenties, whereas anorexia may begin at a variety of points throughout adolescence, especially at puberty (Attie & Brooks-Gunn, 1989). Bulimia is thought to affect between 1 and 3 percent of adolescent and young women (American Psychiatric Association, 1994), anorexia probably less than 1 percent. Both disorders are more prevalent in industrialized societies, such as the United States, Canada, Australia, Japan, New Zealand, South Africa, and European countries.

Despite some outward similarities, the two disorders are quite different. Unlike anorexics, young women with bulimia rarely diet to the point of starvation and death; anorexics, however, do sometimes engage in bingeing and purging. In contrast to anorexic young women, who tend to be of normal weight before the illness takes holds of them and to be socially withdrawn, bulimics are sometimes obese before the onset of illness and are typically extraverted and have voracious appetites. Women with both disorders may exhibit depressive symptoms, but whereas bulimics often have poor self-images and low self-esteem, anorexics have a tendency to *obsessive-compulsiveness* (the tendency to have recurrent obsessions or compulsions to do certain things, both of which take up time and may cause marked psychological distress) and a strong need to control their environment (American Psychiatric Association, 1994). It may be that controlling their food intake is, for some anorexics, the only control they feel able to exert over their lives.

Most anorexics and bulimics are of European American descent and relatively high socioeconomic status (Benokraitis, 1996). They often have family histories of eating disorders and/or of substance abuse (alcohol, marijuana, uppers, downers). Anorexic girls often come from families that are high-achieving and protective (Myers, 1992) and may describe their mothers as dominating, intrusive, and overbearing and their fathers as "emotional absentees" (Carson & Butcher, 1992). It's important to remember, however, that family members' behavior often affects other members, and some of these characteristics may represent responses to the behavior of the anorexic girl. According to Fisher and Brone (1991), the families of bulimic adolescents are often chaotic, conflict-ridden, and stressed, and family members have difficulty communicating their feelings.

Treating anorexia may require initial hospitalization and physical intervention. Although in-hospital behavioral modification techniques have succeeded in regularizing anorexics' eating behavior and in achieving weight gain, the effects of this type of therapy seem to be short-lived (Carson & Butcher, 1992). Longer-term psychotherapy that includes the family has had some success (Abraham & Llewellyn-Jones, 1997; Buckroyd, 1996). However, according to one estimate, fewer than half of adolescents with this disorder make a complete recovery (Zerbe, 1993), and 5 to 10 percent die either from starvation or by formal suicide. Treating bulimia is generally more successful than helping adolescents with anorexia. A variety of approaches, including individual and family psychotherapy, support groups, nutrition education, and, in cases where depression is evident, antidepressive medications have been

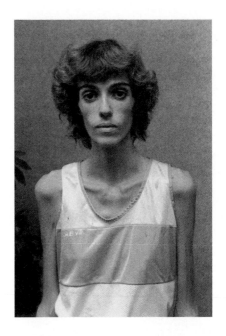 

The treatment of anorexia can achieve remarkably successful changes. From this girl's shocking appearance at diagnosis one might not have believed that she could exude the health and happiness her post-treatment image shows.

successful in treating bulimia (Hsu, 1990; Thakwray, Smith, Bodfish, & Meyers, 1993). Unfortunately, many adolescents never seek treatment for this disorder.

SEXUAL MATURATION

Whereas physical growth. except for one of two growth spurts, is more or less gradual, sexual maturation arrives with rather a flourish. Suddenly, a girl begins to menstruate, a boy has his first ejaculation, and both know or come to know that they are no longer children but young adults, capable both of fully expressing their sexuality and of reproducing their species. **Puberty,** or the attainment of sexual maturity, has long been held as a time of stress for the adolescent, when the intensity of new drives and the social pressures for new behaviors and new responsibilities may cause conflict and confusion. We begin this section by considering the actual changes that occur with puberty, and then explore the question of whether in general young people, just as they seem to be growing taller, are experiencing puberty earlier and earlier. We close the section with a discussion of whether maturing earlier or later than one's peers has a significant effect on a young person.

The Onset of Sexual Maturity

Puberty is marked by a number of growth changes that are triggered when the hypothalamus at the base of the brain stimulates the **pituitary gland** (Figure 6-15), a kind of master *endocrine* (hormone-secreting) gland, to secrete **hormones** that cause the adrenal cortex and the gonads (testes, in males, and ovaries, in females) to initiate a growth spurt. As Table 6-1 shows, in girls this spurt begins with breast development, and in both sexes the appearance of pubic hair is an early sign of puberty. These characteristics, along with voice change in boys, are considered *secondary sex characteristics,* that is, those that are not directly involved in sexual reproduction. *Primary sex characteristics,* which are involved in the reproductive process and which evolve a few years after the first secondary characteristics appear, include, in males, the capability of the testes and associated internal organs to produce sperm-containing ejaculate; this is sometimes referred to as **spermarche.** In females, primary sex characteristics include the changes in the reproductive organs that culminate with **menarche,** or the beginning of *ovulation,* in which each month an egg, released from an ovary, begins its journey through the fallopian tubes to the uterus where, if not fertilized, it is expelled in the menstrual flow.

puberty   The onset of sexual maturity.

pituitary gland   A so-called master gland, located at the base of the brain, that triggers the secretion of hormones by all other hormone-secreting, or endocrine, glands.

hormone   A powerful and highly specialized chemical substance that interacts with cells capable of receiving the hormonal message and responding to it.

spermarche   In males, the first ejaculation of semen-containing ejaculate.

menarche   In females, the beginning of the menstrual cycle.

■ FIGURE 6-15
The pituitary gland.
Cutting through the cerebrum, we can see the location of the pituitary gland, which controls the secretion of important human hormones including those that stimulate cell growth and replication. (*Source:* Adapted from Postlethwait & Hopson, 1995)

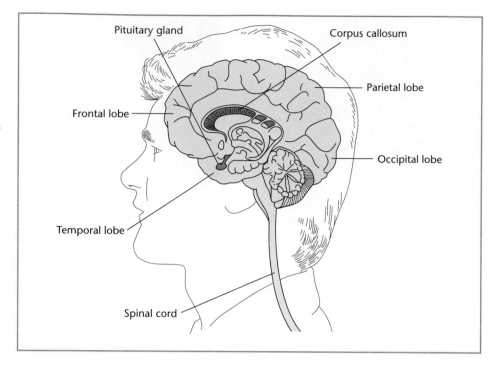

estrogens Hormones that, in the female, are responsible for sexual maturation.

progesterone A hormone that, in females, helps regulate the menstrual cycle and prepares the uterus to receive and nurture a fertilized egg.

testosterone A hormone that, in the male, is responsible for the development of primary and secondary sex characteristics and is essential for the production of sperm.

In both female and male adolescents, the rising concentrations of hormones stimulate the development of both primary and secondary sex characteristics. In females, **estrogens** are crucial to the maturation of the reproductive system, including the ovaries, fallopian tubes, and uterus, and to the onset of ovulation and menstruation. **Progesterone** helps regulate the menstrual cycle and readies the uterus for the reception and nurturing of a fertilized egg. In males, **testosterone,** the most important of several *androgens,* is essential to the maturation of the penis, testes, and other organs of the reproductive system and to the production of sperm. Male sexual motivation is influence by testosterone; female sexual motivation is less dependent on hormonal secretions.

As you can see from Table 6-1, even the attainment of puberty's secondary sex characteristics is rather gradual, with menarche and spermarche occurring two to three years after the beginning of the maturation process. Nevertheless, it is because these two later events signal such a marked change in the person, not only physically and physiologically but psychologically, that they are considered a major turning point. For some women, menarche is the "true" or real onset of puberty (Brooks-Gunn & Ruble, 1984); few accounts of this aspect of maturation are more eloquent or more poignant than the following diary entry written by Anne Frank, not long before she perished at the hands of the Nazis:

> Yesterday I read an article about blushing [that] . . . might have been addressed to me personally. Although I don't blush very easily, the other things in it certainly fit me. [The author] writes that . . . a girl in the years of puberty becomes quiet within and begins to think about the wonders that are happening to her body. . . .
>
> I think what is happening to me is so wonderful, and not only what can be seen on my body, but all that is taking place inside. . . .
>
> Each time I have a period—and that has only been three times—I have the feeling that in spite of all the pain, unpleasantness, and nastiness, I have a sweet secret, and that is why, although it is nothing but a nuisance to me in a way, I always long for the time that I shall feel that secret within me again. (Frank, 1967, cited by Katchadorian, 1977)

In industrialized countries, at least, young women have been reaching puberty at earlier ages than before. In the United States, for example, young women in the

TABLE 6-1	Sexual Maturation: A Timetable	
Average Age of Onset	*Girls*	*Boys*
10	Breasts (breast buds) begin to develop	
11	Pubic hair appears; it is sparse and slightly pigmented	**Testes and scrotum begin to grow**
12		Pubic hair, lightly pigmented, begins to appear
12 to 13	Underarm hair begins to appear	
13	Breasts continue to enlarge; areola and nipple project above contour of breast	**Spermarche: first ejaculation of semen**
13 to 14	**Menarche: beginning of menstruation**	
14	Pubic hair becomes denser, but area covered is smaller than in adult woman	Underarm and facial hair begin to appear
15	Breasts and pubic hair coverage are fully mature	**Penis, testes are fully developed** Pubic hair coverage is complete Mustache and beard hair begin to grow

Sources: Petersen & Taylor, 1980; Tanner, 1978; Turner & Rubinson, 1993.

Note: Primary sex characteristics are in boldface type.

late 1960s tended to experience menarche a year and a half earlier (at 12.9 years) than their mothers had (at 14.4 years) (Damon, Damon, Reed, & Valadian, 1969). As Figure 6-16 shows, in the countries of Finland, Norway, and Sweden, the age of menarche dropped about three and a half years in a little over a century. Some researchers (e.g., Roche, 1979; Wyshak & Frisch, 1982) have suggested that this trend to earlier menarche is slowing down among middle-class girls in the United States, but other investigators (Herman-Giddens et al., 1997; NHLBI, 1992) suggest that among certain groups, for instance African American girls, the onset of menarche is now even earlier—at age 8 or 9. Martorell and colleagues (Martorell et al., 1994) found that young women in the U.S. Puerto Rican community mature a little earlier than Mexican American girls but a little later than girls in the Netherlands. One thing we know for sure is that the reduction in age at menarche has not been uniform around the world. Little change has occurred among Eskimo groups and among only some groups in India (Roche, 1979). Moreover, in certain underdeveloped countries, such as some parts of New Guinea, the median age is very late—17.5 to 18.4 years (Malcolm, 1970).

Is sexual maturation synonymous with sexual attraction? Researchers McClintock and Herdt (1996) say no, arguing that sexual attraction appears first at about the age of 10, four years after the adrenal androgen dehydroepiandrosterone (DHEA) has begun to rise conspicuously (this androgen is said to be a precursor of testosterone and estradiol, sex hormones in men and women). These researchers found that significant numbers of the heterosexual and homosexual young people they studied reported first feelings of sexual attraction at about the age of 10, and they argue for an adjustment in our understanding of puberty so as to accommodate the view of sexuality as a continuous process that begins well before the traditional time of puberty.

■ **FIGURE 6-16**
Decline in the age of menarche.
In the Scandinavian countries represented here, the age of first menstruation declined considerably over a little more than a century and a half. Although the data for the United Kingdom and the United States do not cover the same time period, their trend suggests that the rate of change in menarche onset in all these countries is rather similar. (*Source:* Roche, 1979)

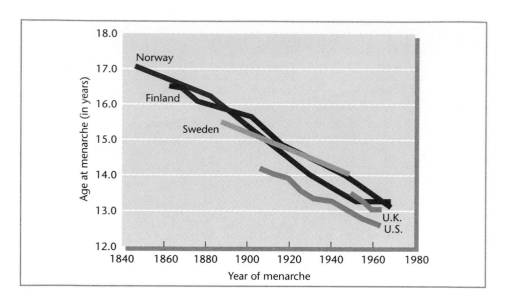

What Determines the Timing of Puberty?

Inheritance seems to play some role in the timing of menarche; girls whose mothers have matured early tend to mature early themselves. But environmental factors have something to say about when this important event occurs also. For example, the choice of a profession can to some degree alter the timing of menarche: Gymnasts, figure skaters, and ballet dancers who practice intensively, perform regularly, and diet to keep fit may delay the onset of menstruation by as much as one year (Brooks-Gunn & Warren, 1985). In fact, of the dancers studied by Brooks-Gunn (1988) only 30 percent were described as either early or "on time," in contrast to 80 percent of a comparison group of girls who were not dancers. And even after girls reach menarche, they may not stay on a regular schedule if they train hard and keep their weight low; for example, runners and gymnasts sometimes stop menstruating, or become *amenorrheic.* Firsch (1984) has found that such girls can literally turn their menstrual cycles on and off by stopping and restarting their training regime.

Parent-child relationships can also alter the timing of sexual maturation. In a longitudinal study of family relationships, Steinberg (1987) found not only that systematic changes in family systems around the time of puberty affected the timing of young people's sexual maturation but that this maturation also affected family relationships. For example, whereas physical maturity was accompanied by decreases in adolescents' closeness with their parents and increases in their desire for autonomy, puberty seemed also to increase conflicts between youth and parent. So far, it seems as if puberty causes a distancing between child and parent. Steinberg also found, however, that the greater the distance between the generations, the earlier young people tended to reach sexual maturity, whereas the closer parent and child were, the slower the process of maturation seemed to be.

Steinberg's findings have been replicated by several other researchers. Moffitt, Caspi, Belsky, and Silva (1992), for example, found that family conflict and father absence from the family scene were correlated with earlier menarche in girls. However, these investigators point out that a genetic inheritance model might equally well explain their results with respect to father absence. Statistics show that women who mature early and have children early are likely to divorce, which leaves these women's children without fathers. Because the female children's genetic inheritance may cause them to mature early, the finding of high correlation between early menarche and father absence would simply be an artifact of the more complex situation. Focusing on family conflict, Wierson, Long, and Forehand (1993) demonstrated that divorce and higher levels of marital conflict predicted the earlier onset of menarche. Because these authors' purpose was to examine whether such factors had any influence at all on the timing of puberty, they did not study factors that bore genetic implications.

Correlations between parent-offspring relationships and the onset of puberty have been reported in still other human studies, as well as in studies of primates (Belsky, Steinberg, & Draper, 1991). It seems clear that future research will have to determine the relative contributions of inheritance and the environment to the timing of sexual maturation.

The Effects of Early and Late Maturation

Do normal individual differences in the rate of maturation make a difference? A set of classic studies carried out at the University of California (Jones & Bayley, 1950) indicate clearly that the timing of physical maturation can affect a child's social and emotional adjustment. However, not only do boys and girls differ in the age at which they reach physical maturity, with girls ahead of boys, but a child's gender determines the advantages and disadvantages of being an early or late maturer. For boys, it is apparently advantageous to mature early but, as you will see, for girls it is less clear whether early or late maturation is to be preferred; the answer may rely on intervening factors such as parental support and the nature of a girl's particular peer group. Moreover, both boys and girls may be strongly affected by challenging environmental transitions, such as changing schools, that occur concurrently with the biological changes they are undergoing.

Pioneering in this area of research, Jones and Bayley (1950) tracked the development of 16 early-maturing and 16 late-maturing public school boys over a six-year period. Independent observers rated the boys who were slower in their physical development lower in physical attractiveness, masculinity, and grooming than their faster-developing peers. The late maturers were also rated as more childish, more eager, and less relaxed, and as generally engaging in more attention-seeking behaviors. Peer evaluations generally confirmed this profile; the late maturer was regarded as restless, bossy, talkative, attention seeking, and less likely to have older friends.

Research has also suggested that later maturers and their parents have lower aspirations and expectations for educational achievement. On the basis of a national study of 493 boys, Duke and coworkers (1982) found that late maturers were less likely to want to complete college and that the parents of these boys did not expect them to graduate from college. Teachers, too, rated later maturers as lower in academic achievement than average or late maturers. And the boys' test scores indicated that these views were not without foundation, for the late maturers scored lower on IQ and achievement tests. The investigators hypothesized that parents and teachers may provide more opportunities for and expect more from early maturers because of their more adultlike physical appearance, but it seems unlikely that this explanation is valid. Because the boys who were destined to be late maturers had lower IQ scores, as early as 8 years of age, their later physical appearance may have had nothing to do with parents' and teachers' interactions with these boys as adolescents. This study raises the intriguing possibility that there are either subtle biological differences between early and late maturers that may elicit differential treatment even before puberty or intrinsic genetic differences that affect not only rate of physical growth but also intellectual capacity. We return to this issue in Chapter 15.

In contrast with boys, girls may not find early maturation advantageous. To begin with, early maturers may not be as prepared for the changes in their bodies and body functions because their development typically occurs before schools offer health classes. And, unfortunately, mothers apparently discuss these changes less often with early-maturing daughters (Brooks-Gunn, 1988). Early-maturing girls tend to have a poorer body image than on-time or late maturers, in part because the weight gains accompanying the onset of maturation violate the cultural ideal of thinness for girls (Brooks-Gunn, 1988; Graber, Petersen, & Brooks-Gunn,

■ **FIGURE 6-17**
Body image in adolescent girls and boys.
For boys, the relation between body image and timing of puberty is a straight line: the sooner the better. Girls tend to have more positive body images the later they mature, but if maturity comes exceedingly late, their body images may suffer. (*Source:* Tobin-Richards, Boxer, & Petersen, 1984)

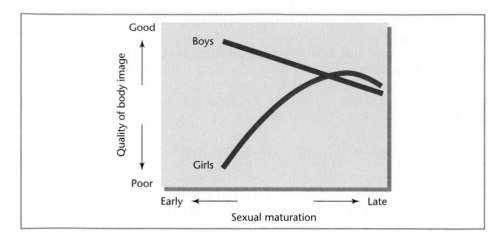

1996). As you can see from Figure 6-17, the trends for positive body image for girls and boys are almost diametrically opposed: Early-maturing boys have a far more positive body image than late-maturing boys; early-maturing girls tend to have negative body images, whereas late-maturing girls have very positive self-images. Notice, however, that like boys who mature late, the latest-maturing girls tend to have some problems with body image.

Early-maturing girls have been found to have more adjustment or behavioral problems, but these kinds of problems may take precedence over early maturation per se. That is, according to Caspi and Moffitt (1991), it may be that girls who have had behavioral problems before reaching puberty are those who are more likely to experience adjustment problems if they mature early. As Caspi and Moffitt put it, "Dispositional factors may be most pronounced when people experience profound discontinuities" in their lives (1991, p. 167), and the stressful effects of early menarche (including being different from most of one's peers) may represent too much of a burden for girls who already have experienced behavioral problems of some sort. Graber and her colleagues (Graber, Brooks-Gunn, and Warren, 1995), on the other hand, believe that psychosocial factors such as presence or absence of parental approval and family conflict may well have a causal effect on age at menarche; these researchers found that conflict and lack of approval and warmth were significantly associated with earlier maturation in middle-class European American girls. Lacković-Grgin, Dekovic, and Opačić (1994) found that late-maturing girls were more likely to have good self-esteem but that healthy relations with the mother were a more important determining factor. Thus early maturers who were close to their mothers often had as good, if not better, self-esteem than late maturers whose relations with their mothers were poor. On the other hand, researchers have also found that early maturers have more difficulty inhibiting impulses and exhibit more depressive affect (Brooks-Gunn & Petersen, 1992; Petersen, Sarigiani, & Kennedy, 1991).

Longitudinal studies in Sweden (Gustafson & Magnusson, 1991; Magnusson, 1988, 1989; Stattin & Magnusson, 1990) have reported that early-maturing girls have a smaller network of close friends and are more likely to engage in "adult behaviors" (such as smoking, drinking, and sexual intercourse) at a younger age than late maturers. Apparently this is because earlier maturers tend to associate with older peers who are closer to them in terms of physical status and appearance. Although many people believe that early sexual maturity leads to early sexual behavior and to unwed teen pregnancy and childbearing, as we will see in Chapter 12, the reasons for adolescent pregnancy and parenting are far more complex than this.

Although early maturation seems to entail some risks for girls, experts (Brooks-Gunn, 1988, 1990) suggest caution in interpreting research results to date. First, individual differences determine that not all early maturers will have a poor body image or will date, smoke, or drink earlier. Second, individuals also differ in terms of whether they perceive early maturation as "on time" (normal) or "off-time" (deviant), depending on such things as the attitudes, beliefs, and behaviors of their particular reference groups. "In the final analysis, a girl's adjustment to the changes of puberty will probably depend more on the kinds of support, encouragement, and guidance she receives from parents, and the values and expectations of her own particular peer group than it will on whether maturation is early, average, or late" (Conger & Petersen, 1984, p. 121).

The impact of the transition to sexual maturity cannot be fully appreciated in isolation from other changes in young people's lives. As we will see in Chapter 13, some adolescents attend junior high school after sixth grade, whereas others stay in elementary school through eighth grade and then go on to high school. Eccles and colleagues (Eccles, Wigfield, & Schiefele, 1998) have found that youth moving through the former type of system experience more adjustment difficulties. In addition, some adolescents date early and others delay this step. Simmons, Blyth, and their colleagues (Simmons & Blyth, 1987; Simmons, Blyth, Van Cleave, & Bush, 1979) found that girls who entered puberty early and at the same time changed schools and started to date had lower self-esteem than other girls. The effects were even more dramatic as the number of life transitions that accompanied puberty in these girls increased. Girls who moved their residences or experienced a major family disruption (divorce, death, remarriage) suffered even more loss in self-esteem and grades, and their participation in extracurricular activities decreased (Simmons, Burgeson, Carlton-Ford, & Blyth, 1987).

The effects of coping with multiple and simultaneous life changes are not limited to girls. Boys for whom sexual maturity is accompanied by a variety of other changes, such as change of school, moving to a new neighborhood, or engaging in early dating, had poorer grades and participated less in extracurricular activities than boys who experienced fewer life transitions (Simmons et al., 1987). These findings underscore the fact that the impact of the timing of puberty can best be understood in the context of other transitions and illustrate the ability of the environmental context to help or hinder children's abilities to cope with biological change.

SUMMARY

Brain Development in Infancy

- The largest portion of the human brain, the **cerebrum,** is covered by a highly convoluted layer called the **cerebral cortex.** The cortex is divided into a number of regions whose cells control specific functions such as seeing, hearing, feeling, moving, and thinking.
- In the developing organism, **neuron proliferation** rapidly increases the brain's nerve cells, or **neurons.** Although all the brain's neurons are present at birth, many subsequent changes take place in the size of neurons, the numbers of connections, or **synapses,** among them, and the production of the surrounding, supportive **glial cells.** These changes, such as **myelination,** increase the speed, efficiency, and complexity of transmissions between neurons.
- **Neural migration** distributes neurons throughout brain regions. The abundance of synapses, formed by **synaptogenesis,** and of neurons is trimmed over time through the processes of **neuronal death** and **synaptic pruning.**
- The human brain is organized in two halves: the two **brain hemispheres** are connected by the **corpus callosum.** The right hemisphere controls the left side of the body and is involved in the processing of visual-spatial information, face

recognition, and interpreting emotional expressions. The left hemisphere controls the right side of the body and is important for understanding and using language. Both **hemispheric specialization** and **lateralization** are evident early in infancy and are well developed by age 3.

- **Dyslexia,** or difficulty in learning to read, may reflect abnormal lateralization patterns, such as the processing of spatial information on both sides of the brain rather than primarily in the right hemisphere, the normal arrangement.

- The environment plays a critical role in brain development. In rats, enriched environments that permit a great deal of activity and exploration are related to increases in brain size, in the number of connections among neurons, and in the activities of key brain chemicals. Apparently, the brain has great **plasticity,** which allows it to compensate for defects or damage in one area or even one hemisphere.

Motor Development

- Research suggests that infants grasp objects in a variety of different ways, depending on the object's size and shape and the relative size of their own hands. This research indicates that the infant motor system is highly flexible and able to adapt to the demands of a situation.

- Research based on dynamic systems theory has shown that patterns of specific reaching and grasping behavior reflect both coordination tendencies in an infant's general, nonreaching arm movements and environmental influences such as task requirements.

- The development of walking follows a U-shaped course, beginning with a stepping reflex at birth that disappears in a few months; that is followed by the emergence of independent, voluntary walking a number of months later, usually around the first birthday.

- A dynamic systems approach to explaining this pattern suggests that the development of walking depends on the combined readiness of a variety of factors, and when the baby's weight becomes too much of a load on the emerging motor system, stepping ability may be temporarily masked. Cross-cultural studies indicate that environmental influences, such as repeated practice of a skill, may either enhance or slow a complex motor skill like independent walking.

- The relations between locomotion, other aspects of development such as perception, social interaction, and problem solving, and environmental forces are complex. In general, the greater a child's motor skills, the more his general development is enhanced; at the same time, negative factors such as conflicted child-parent relations may sometimes promote developmental skills, such as walking.

Physical Growth

- Infants' and children's growth is guided by two basic principles. According to **cephalocaudal development,** growth proceeds from the head downward, and following the **proximal-distal pattern,** development occurs from the center outward. In addition, growth proceeds at different rates during different stages of development. Growth is fastest during the first 6 months of life.

- Adult height is difficult to predict from a baby's size, which tends to be more closely related to the size of the mother. Successful predictions can be made in later childhood based on the child's current height, gender, and parents' heights.

- Inadequate nutrition may result in severely depressed growth rates. During World Wars I and II, height, weight, and age of puberty were affected by lack of adequate nutrition. Other environmental factors that may affect growth rates include illness, disease, and climate.

- Environmental influences such as nutrition and housing interact with other factors to produce a considerable variation in growth rates among people of different nationalities, ethnicities, and socioeconomic class. The effects of poverty may be seen in such disorders as **iron-deficiency anemia,** common in minority children and children in low-income countries.

■ Following environmental injury or deprivation, a strong corrective principle appears to operate in the case of physical growth. The degree of **catch-up growth** will depend on such things as the duration, severity, and timing of the deprivation, in addition to the nature of the subsequent treatment or therapy. In general, the earlier and more prolonged the malnutrition, the more difficult it is to regain a normal level of growth.

■ **Secular trends** in many countries show that across evolution people have become taller. Although in the United States people in the most advantaged groups may have reached their maximum potential in height gain, people in other segments of society continue to grow taller; both genetic and environmental factors influence this growth tendency.

■ Although the problem of **obesity** may begin in infancy and childhood, only about one-quarter of obese infants will remain obese 20 years later. The two critical periods for the development of obesity are during infancy and at about 4 years of age. Recent research indicates that genetic factors may play a role in determining later obesity; however, parents' strategies for getting their children to eat may contribute as well.

■ In addition to physical problems, such as hypertension and diabetes, obese children and adolescents may experience body-image disturbances and may suffer discrimination by peers and adults. Effective diet programs for children have focused on changing the eating patterns and exercise behavior of both the child and other family members.

■ Dieting disorders include **anorexia nervosa,** which may occur early in adolescence and results from reduced intake of calories, and **bulimia nervosa,** which typically occurs in later adolescence and is characterized by food binges and purging through vomiting.

Sexual Maturation

■ **Puberty,** the attainment of sexual maturity, is triggered when the **pituitary gland** stimulates other endocrine glands to secrete **hormones,** including **estrogens** and **progesterone** in females and **testosterone** in males, that initiate a growth spurt. This milestone in growth is marked by changes such as the start of breast development and **menarche** in girls, and the enlargement of the testes and **spermarche** in boys. Girls tend to reach menarche earlier in the more advanced countries, but there is still considerable variation in the onset of menstruation throughout the world.

■ Inheritance is a strong factor in the timing of menarche, although environmental conditions such as conflict within the family and absence of the father may also exert an influence on when a young girl reaches menarche.

■ The timing of physical maturation can affect the child's social and emotional adjustment. Research indicates that the effects for late-maturing boys and early-maturing girls are largely negative. In general, the impact of the timing of puberty is best understood in the context of other transitions, such as school transitions and family disruptions, which may help or hinder the child's ability to cope with biological changes.

■ There are wide individual differences in rates of maturation. However, in general, girls mature earlier than boys; on average, major changes occur two years earlier for girls. Although early maturation is usually seen as advantageous for boys, girls sometimes find early maturation stressful, developing poor body images and engaging in so-called adult behaviors such as drinking and smoking at an early age.

Emotional Development

C H A P T E R 7

Children display a wide range of emotions, even from the time they are infants. Babies communicate their feelings, needs, and desires to others through the expression of emotion. The smiling infant tells others that something is pleasurable to him, and his frown communicates displeasure. Babies also regulate the behavior of other people by their expression of emotions. When a baby smiles, for instance, caregivers are almost sure to approach her, pick her up, talk to her, caress her; when a stranger approaches, on the other hand, her screams are apt to stop the stranger from picking her up. The older child may use smiling as a sign of welcome and express anger as a way of deterring a potential aggressor. In addition to using their own emotions to communicate with and regulate their worlds, children learn to read the emotional signs that other people display. Both processes, the production and the recognition of emotion, are essential to useful interactions with other people, and they enable babies to begin to exert some control over their social world.

We begin this chapter by exploring children's earliest expressions of emotion and their beginning efforts to regulate their own emotions and to recognize emotions in other people. We then explore three of the earliest expressions—smiling, laughter, and fear—in some detail and consider several views of how specific emotions develop. Next we discuss how children learn to identify emotions and to associate them with the right events and situations as well as how children learn and conceptualize complex emotions such as pride and guilt. We then turn to the study of attachment, first reviewing several theories of how attachment relationships form and then tracing the evolution of these relationships between infants and parents, siblings, and others. In the last section of the chapter we explore the nature and quality of attachment relationships, considering such issues as the role of parenting styles in these relationships and the effects of attachment quality on the child's cognitive and social development as well as on her sense of self. We conclude by examining the important question of the effects of day care and multiple caregivers on the child of working parents.

EARLY EMOTIONAL DEVELOPMENT

emotions Subjective reactions to something in the environment that are usually experienced cognitively as either pleasant or unpleasant, that are generally accompanied by physiological changes, and that are often expressed in some form of visible behavior.

What are **emotions**? Emotions, like joy, anger, and fear, have several important aspects: They are subjective reactions to the environment; they are usually experienced cognitively as either pleasant or unpleasant; and they generally are accompanied by some form of physiological arousal. Emotions generally have a fourth aspect, too, that of behavioral expression. Thus, for example, Becky, her family's newest member, may react to the taste of a different formula with disgust, experiencing the new taste as unpleasant, and if we were to measure her heart rate we might find that it had accelerated. Moreover, because Becky has not yet learned to hide her emotions, as adults sometimes do, she would doubtless let her family know in no uncertain terms of her displeasure. Watching her wrinkle up her face, spit up, and cry, Becky's parents could be pretty certain of the source of her unhappiness.

How Babies Express Their Emotions

Most parents pay a great deal of attention to their newborn infants' behaviors and activities, and witnessing displays like Becky's many times over, they are inclined to agree that infants display a wide range of emotions at a very early age. In one study, 99 percent of mothers said that their 1-month-olds clearly displayed interest; 95 percent of mothers observed joy; 85 percent, anger; 74 percent, surprise; 58 percent, fear; and 34 percent, sadness (Johnson, Emde, Pannabecker, Stenberg, & Davis, 1982). These women based their judgments not only on their babies' behavior (facial expressions, vocalizations, body movements) but on the nature of the situations in which those behaviors occurred. For example, a mother who watched her baby staring intently at the mobile above her crib was likely to label the infant's emotion "interest," whereas she might call "joy" the emotion expressed by a gurgling, smiling baby.

But is the human infant really capable of such a broad array of emotions, emotions that are recognizable in terms of adult expression and behavior? Carroll Izard, a pioneer in the study of infant emotion, holds that newborns do express specific emotions (Izard, 1994; Izard, Fantauzzo, Castle, Haynes, & Slomine, 1995; Izard & Malatesta, 1987). According to Izard, the first expressions to appear are *startle, disgust* (as in response to bitter tastes), *distress* (in response to pain), and a *rudimentary smile* that seems unrelated to external events. (The true social smile, with which the baby reacts to specific external stimuli like voices or faces, appears between about 4 and 6 weeks of age.) However, Izard proposes, it is not until babies are about 2½ or 3 months old that they begin reliably to display facial expressions of anger, interest, surprise, and sadness (Izard et al., 1995). For example, although few 1-month-olds show anger expressions when their arms are gently restrained, by the time infants are 4 to 7 months old some 56 percent show clear expressions of anger at this restriction (Stenberg & Campos, 1989). Moreover, Izard and his colleagues (1995) have found considerable stability of emotional expression between 2½ and 9 months of age; that is, both the basic morphology or form of these expressions and their rate of occurrence were stable across the 7-month period. Interest, joy, sadness, and anger dominate the infant's repertoire during this period. Fear expressions enter the infant's emotional repertoire around 7 months (Camras, Malatesta, & Izard, 1991), and shyness comes slightly later, between 6 and 8 months of age. It is not until the second or third year that we see more sophisticated emotions, such as pride, guilt, or contempt, which involve evaluating the self or others according to behavioral standards.

If you are wondering how researchers can distinguish among infants' expressions of all these emotions, the answer is by means of coding systems that pay careful attention to changes in a baby's facial expression and her bodily movements. These systems assign finely differentiated scores to different parts of the face (e.g., lips, eyelids, forehead) and to specific infant movement patterns. Researchers then use these scores to judge whether an infant has displayed a particular emotion. Izard and his associates (e.g., Izard et al., 1995) have developed the most elaborate of the coding systems for infant emotional expressions now in use, the Maximally Discriminative Facial Movement coding system (MAX).

Alan Sroufe (1996), another researcher in the area of emotional development, offers a timetable of development that is quite similar to Izard's (see Table 7-1), although he finds some emotions appearing a bit later than Izard suggests. Sroufe (1996, p. 55) stresses that the evolution of emotions should follow general principles of development; thus, he says, later forms of emotions, although they evolve from earlier forms, should be "more differentiated, more psychologically based . . . and more complexly organized with respect to context." Maturing forms of emotions should thus be more clearly differentiated from one another. They should be responsive to the child's interpretation of the meaning of a situation, rather than simply to general excitation. And children should gradually become able to express and recognize differing emotions in a given context and to relate these feelings to one another. As you continue through this chapter you may find it useful to refer to the Turning Points chart (pp. 228–229), which offers a brief chronology of emotional development.

Other researchers have also found that it is the slightly older infant who displays a variety of emotional expressions. Analyzing videotapes of interactions between 3- and 6-month-old babies and their mothers, Malatesta and Haviland (1982, 1985) observed infant facial expressions that corresponded to adult expressions of anger, pain, interest, surprise, joy, and sadness. Even these observations may not be valid, however, for it is not clear whether the expressions described by the researchers actually reflect the named emotions; babies' facial expressions may not always

		Emerging Emotional Systems		
Period and Age in Months	Developmental Issues	Frustration/Anger	Wariness/Fear	Pleasure/Joy
1 (0–1)	Relative invulnerability to external stimulation	*Distress,* caused by physical restraint or extreme discomfort	*Startle-pain,* caused by sudden change in body position or support or by painful stimulus *Obligatory attention,* in which a stimulus captures an infant's attention and, after a period of unbroken attention, the infant begins to cry	Endogenous *smile,* related to events in central nervous system and/or to REM sleep
2 (2–3)	Relative vulnerability: infant is open to stimulation; beginning coordination of attention and activity; the beginnings of interest, curiosity, and positive emotions			*Turning toward* the environment Reliable social *smile*
3 (4–5)	Positive engagement with external world triggers both positive and negative emotional expressions	*Frustration reaction*	*Wariness*	*Delight*; active *laughter*
4 (6–8)	Active participation, in social games; attempts to initiate social contact; increasing awareness of own emotions	*Anger*		*Joy; surprise*
5 (9–11)	Formation of attachment relationship; caregiver's presence becomes source of security		*Stranger distress*	
6 (12–17)	Active exploration and mastery of the environment	Angry mood; *petulance*	*Anxiety; fear*	*Elation*
7 (18–35)	Awareness of separateness from caregiver; beginning formation of self-concept	*Defiance; rage* Intentional hurting of others	*Shame*	Positive valuation of the self; *affection*
8 (36–54)	Identification with caregivers; development of play and fantasy skills		*Guilt*	*Pride, love*

TABLE 7-1 The Evolution of Emotions in Early Life

Source: Adapted from Sroufe, 1996, Chapter 4 and Tables 4.2, 4.3 (pp. 68–70).

mirror those of adults (Sroufe, 1979, 1996). For example, what looks like anger in a baby may actually represent a generalized state of distress (Camras et al., 1991).

Not unlike adults, infants usually display emotions in response to particular external events (Sroufe, 1996). For example, researchers have evoked anger in 7-month-olds by offering them a teething biscuit and then withdrawing it just before it reaches the baby's mouth (Stenberg, Campos, & Emde, 1983). Two-month-olds respond with a distress expression to being inoculated by a physician, whereas 6-month-old babies respond to the same stimulus with an expression of anger (Izard, Hembree, Dougherty, & Coss, 1983; Izard, Hembree, & Huebner, 1987). It seems that babies respond to emotional provocations in similar and predictable ways at specific ages.

Are there gender differences in infants' emotional expressiveness? Indeed there are (Brody, 1996), and they may surprise you. In one study, 6-month-old boys displayed both more positive (e.g., joy) and more negative (e.g., anger) expressions of emotion than girls (Weinberg, 1992). And another study found that boys cried more in response to frustration and took longer to recover when upset than girls (Kohnstamm, 1989). How can we reconcile these findings with the widely accepted and highly differentiated behaviors considered proper for men and women in U.S. society—lack of emotional expression in men (except, perhaps, for the expression of anger) and often intense emotional expression in women?

According to Brody (1996), this apparent contradiction represents a "developmental shift" that is caused by different ways of socializing girls and boys with respect to the expression of emotions. To begin with, Brody suggests, parents may encourage more emotional expression in their infant daughters for the very reason that their daughters' expressions are less intense and thus perhaps harder for parents to recognize. Brody also proposes that because girls tend to be more verbal at an earlier age than boys, parents may be likely to talk with a girl about emotions, thus heightening the possibility that the child will consider feelings important topics for expression and discussion. Finally, because parents tend to socialize children in accordance with the prevailing notions of what is socially acceptable, they may encourage emotionality in girls and try to suppress it in boys. Do you agree with Brody (1996, p. 141) that these parental behaviors may in some cases produce a "self-fulfilling prophecy"? These observations underscore the importance of the interplay between the child's characteristics and cultural expectations, illustrating once again the value of an ecological viewpoint.

Learning How to Regulate Emotions

Learning how to regulate the expression of their emotions is a major challenge for infants. Often they get their first clue from something they began learning even before they were born: Putting their thumbs in their mouths, they find that this helps soothe them. From this unintentional act of control, infants move to the more deliberate regulation of their emotions. For example, when they encounter a frightening event they may turn away, place their hands over their faces, or distract themselves by some form of play (Bridges & Grolnick, 1995). Children's methods of emotional control continue to change as they grow older. In one study, Mangelsdorf and Shapiro, and Marzolf (1995) found that whereas 6-month-olds who confronted a stranger typically looked away or became fussy, 18-month-olds were more likely to use self-soothing and self-distraction to cope with uncertain or arousing situations.

As infants become toddlers and head toward the preschool years, parents and others start to require them to exert even more control over their emotional expression. Under this pressure, gradually "the intense and unregulated expressions of infancy give way to expressions that are more modulated" (Malatesta, Culver, Tesman, & Shepard, 1989). Several things illustrate this greater self-control over emotions: Emotional expressions become less frequent, less variable and

TURNING POINTS: The Evolution of Emotional Expression and the Sense of Self

EARLY WEEKS	Shows distress by crying
1 MONTH	Generalized distress; may be irritable by late afternoon
2 MONTHS	Shows pleasure; mildly aroused by sight of toy; social smile
3 MONTHS	Excitement and boredom appear; smiles broadly and often; cries when bored; may show wariness and frustration
4 MONTHS	Laughs, especially at certain sounds; crying lessens; gurgles with pleasure; shows beginnings of anger
5 MONTHS	Usually gleeful and pleased but sometime frustrated; shows primitive resistant behaviors; turns head from disliked food; smiles at own image in mirror; some babies may begin to show wariness of strangers
6 MONTHS	Matches emotions to others, e.g., smiles and laughs when mother does; fear and anger may appear now or later
7 MONTHS	Fear and anger; defiance; affection; shyness
8 MONTHS	More individuality in emotional expression; touches and explores body parts
9 MONTHS	Shows negative emotions when restrained; frowns when annoyed; actively seeks others' comfort when tired; nighttime crying may reappear; recognizes self in mirror; most babies display real fear of strangers
10 MONTHS	Intense positive and negative emotions; occasionally testy; uses reflection in mirror—for example, seeing toy in mirror, may move toward toy
11 MONTHS	Greater variability in emotions; individual temperament is more evident; learning to associate names of body parts; may insist on feeding self
12 MONTHS	Becomes distressed when others are distressed; cries when something is not to liking; may show signs of jealousy; laughs often at own cleverness; struts/preens when walking; loves to look at self in mirror; wants to show mastery, and plays on own
15 MONTHS	More mood swings; is more caring to agemates; annoyed by dirty hands; strongly prefers certain clothing; may fret or cry often but usually briefly

more conventionalized, less distinct, and less intense and exaggerated (Demos, 1982; Malatesta, Grigoryev, Lamb, Albin, & Culver, 1986; Malatesta & Izard, 1984; Saarni, 1989). For example, a hungry baby may cry in uncontrollable frustration, whereas an older child whose mealtime is delayed will merely pout and complain.

At the same time, children begin to learn **emotional display rules** that dictate what emotions to show under what circumstances. This often means learning to separate the visible expression of an emotion from its inner experience. Following various social norms, older children (8 to 10 years old) learn to smile even when they feel unhappy, to feign distress that is not really felt, or to mask amusement

emotional display rules
Rules that dictate which emotions one may appropriately display in particular situations.

TURNING POINTS: The Evolution of Emotional Expression and the Sense of Self (*continued*)

18 MONTHS   Can be restless and stubborn; may sometimes have tantrums; sometimes shy; shows shame; uses adjectives to refer to self; uses objects like a blanket or a favorite stuffed animal to soothe self

21 MONTHS   Makes some efforts to control negative emotions; can be finicky and exacting; makes more efforts to control situations; begins to understand parents' values; refers appropriately to self as *good* or *bad*

24 MONTHS   Can be contrary but also appropriately contrite; responds to others moods; very intense; may be overwhelmed by changes; can be upset by dreams; refers to self by name; identifies self by gender; talks about self by using *I* and a verb, such as *hurt* or *need*; keen to experience world on own terms; begins to understand emotional display rules

30 MONTHS   Begins to show shame, embarrassment

36 MONTHS   Shows guilt, pride

48 to 60 MONTHS   Shows increased understanding and use of emotional display rules

72 MONTHS   Begins to understand how two or more emotions can occur simultaneously

Source: Kopp, 1994; Saarni, Mumme, & Campos, 1998; Sroufe, 1996.

Note: Developmental events described in this and other Turning Points charts represent overall trends identified in research studies. Individual children vary greatly in the ages at which they achieve these developmental changes.

when they know they shouldn't laugh (Garner & Power, 1996; Saarni, 1990; Saarni, Mumme, & Campos, 1998). But children as young as 2 may show such understanding of display rules for emotions (Lewis & Michaelson, 1985). In their earliest attempts to follow these rules children typically mirror others' behavior by simply exaggerating or minimizing their emotional displays. Moreover, children acquire knowledge about display rules before they are proficient regulators of their own emotional displays (Saarni, 1990). Learning to follow cultural display rules seems to be an important developmental accomplishment, for competence at implementing these rules is linked with better social relationships with peers (McDowell, O'Neil, & Parke, 1998).

Recognizing Emotions in Others

Another challenge for the developing infant is to learn how to recognize the emotions that other people express. According to Malatesta (1982), between the ages of 3 and 6 months, babies are exposed to others' facial expressions some 32,000 times! Learning to interpret these expressions of emotion presents infants with a formidable task. Nevertheless, during this peak period for face-to-face interaction with parents or other caretakers, facial expressions are an effective way for parents to communicate their feelings and wishes to a child who cannot yet understand speech.

In mother-infant face-to-face interactions, babies tend to recognize positive emotions far more frequently than negative emotions (Izard et al., 1995). More specifically, babies may develop the ability to recognize joy earlier than they can recognize anger. In one study, infants between 4 and 6 months of age looked longer at a face showing an expression of joy than at one showing anger or a neutral expression (La Barbera, Izard, Vietze, & Parisi, 1976). (The researchers used the neutral expression to rule out the possibility that the babies were simply avoiding the anger expression.) And recognizing joy before anger has functional value for a baby:

> Recognition of joy can provide rewarding and self-enhancing experiences for the infant. Such recognition can also strengthen the mother-infant bond and facilitate mutually rewarding experiences, particularly if the joy recognition leads to joy expression. . . . [In contrast], anger recognition is not adaptive in the first half year of life. It seems reasonable that the threat of an anger expression would call for coping responses that are beyond the capacity of the 6 month old. (La Barbera et al., 1976, p. 537)

The joy-anger sequence is also consistent with the course of the infant's own emotional displays. As we will see, smiling and laughter emerge before fear (Camras et al., 1991).

It is probably harder for babies to learn to recognize expressions of emotions in others than it is for them to learn to express emotions accurately themselves. Citing the fact that around the world people use similar facial expressions of emotion, some researchers believe that producing these expressions is at least in part genetically determined (Ekman & Oster, 1979; Izard, 1991, 1994; Izard & Malatesta, 1987). If this were so, it would help to explain why both babies and children are more accurate at producing emotional expressions than at interpreting them (Field, 1990; Field & Walden, 1982a, 1982b). Nevertheless, by the time they are 2 or 3, children show production and recognition skills that are positively correlated: Toddlers who send clear emotional signals also tend to be good at identifying emotions (Magai & McFadden, 1995). Both these abilities continue to improve with age, probably contributing to the older child's ability to participate more often and more successfully in peer group activities as well as to his more sustained and sophisticated social interactions (Denham, 1997; Feldman & Rimé, 1991; Hubbard & Coie, 1994).

THE BEGINNINGS OF SPECIFIC EMOTIONS

With this general overview of early emotional development as a guide, let's turn to some specific examples: the development of smiling, of laughter, and of fear. All three of these show that emotions serve important functions in organizing the ways in which babies interact with others in their social worlds.

Smiling and Laughter: The First Expressions of Pleasure

If you watch closely, you can see smiles even in newborn infants. These **reflex smiles** (Wolff, 1987) are usually spontaneous and appear to depend on the infant's internal state, but the exact nature of the internal stimulus is as yet unknown. The traditional

reflex smile   A newborn infant's smile, which appears to reflect some internal stimulus, such as a change in the infant's level of arousal, rather than an external stimulus such as another person's behavior.

theory, that "gas" was the culprit, has been abandoned. Some investigators argue that these early endogenous smiles result from "oscillating states of excitation of subcortical origin, with the smile occurring as the excitation rises above, then falls below some threshold" (Sroufe, 1996, p. 79). We simply do not know whether early smiling is a response to such fluctuations in arousal or whether it may actually reflect some form of pleasure (Camras et al., 1991). One clue may reside in the fact that babies 3 or 4 weeks old are likely to smile spontaneously when they are either comfortable or in the REM (rapid eye movement) stage of sleep (Emde, Gaensbauer, & Harmon, 1976; Wolff, 1987); as you will recall from Chapter 5, REM sleep periods occur in all human beings and are usually associated with dreaming.

Whether or not researchers can shed light on the origin of the baby's reflex smiles, these smiles serve a good purpose. Most caregivers interpret these smiles as signs of pleasure, and this gives the caregivers pleasure and encourages them to cuddle and talk to the baby. In this sense, these smiles may have adaptive value for the baby, by ensuring critical caregiver attention and stimulation.

Between 3 and 8 weeks of age, infants begin to smile in response not only to internal events but to a wide range of external elicitors, including social stimuli like faces, voices, light touches, and gentle bouncing (Sroufe, 1996). Infants are particularly interested in people and faces, and a high-pitched human voice or a combination of voice and face are reliable elicitors of smiling from the baby who is between 2 and 6 months old. When 3-month-old infants were shown a human face and puppets whose faces varied in their resemblance to a human face, the infants smiled almost exclusively at the human face (Ellsworth, Muir, & Hains, 1993). Babies aren't such gullible little creatures; they know the "real thing" when they see it!

As infants grow older, they tend to smile at different aspects of the human face (Ahrens, 1954). As we saw in Chapter 5 (Figure 5-7), when 4-week old babies look at human faces they tend to focus on the eyes but by the time they're 8 or 9 weeks old they examine the mouth as well. Smiling behavior follows a similar pattern: At first babies smile at the eyes, then the mouth, and finally the entire face and the facial expression. By the time they are about 3 months old, babies also start to smile more selectively at familiar faces (Camras et al., 1991), a fact that lends some support to the notion that smiling has begun to signal pleasure and not just arousal. For example, 3-month-olds show greater increases in smiling when their smiles are reinforced by reciprocal smiles and vocalizations from their mothers than when they are reinforced by equally responsive women who are strangers (Wahler, 1967).

A baby's pleasure at watching a familiar face is revealed in other ways as well. For instance, one study found that 10-month-olds generally reserved a special kind of smile for their mothers, rarely offering it to strangers (Fox & Davidson, 1988). These special smiles, which are called *Duchenne smiles* after Guillaume Duchenne, the French physician and neurologist who noticed this pattern more than 100 years ago, are likely to involve not just an upturned mouth but wrinkles around the eyes as well, making the whole face seem lit up with pleasure. Apparently these seemingly more genuine smiles are signals of the joy the babies feel in interacting with the caregivers to whom they are becoming emotionally attached.

Of course, all babies do not smile with equal frequency at their caregivers. There are individual differences in the amount of smiling a baby does. Some of these differences have to do with the social responsiveness of the baby's environment. For example, as Figure 7-1 shows, Israeli infants reared in a family environment smile more often by the second half year than infants raised in either a kibbutz (a communal living arrangement—see "Styles of Caregiving") or an institution, where the level of social stimulation is presumably lower (Gewirtz, 1967). Gender also seems to affect babies' smiling: In the newborn period, at least, girls generally show more spontaneous smiles than boys do (Korner, 1974). This higher rate of smiling has led some observers to suggest that girls may be genetically better prepared for social interaction than boys, because their greater tendency to smile more often draws others to them (Freedman, 1974). On the other hand, as

■ FIGURE 7-1

Smiling and the environment. Although initially Israeli infants raised either by their families, in a kibbutz, or in an institution smiled at about the same rate, by the time they were 8 or 9 months old they had begun to display the different rates of smiling that were clearly discernible at a year and a half. Kibbutz children smiled more than those who were institutionalized, but children raised at home smiled most of all. (*Source:* Adapted from Gewirtz, 1967)

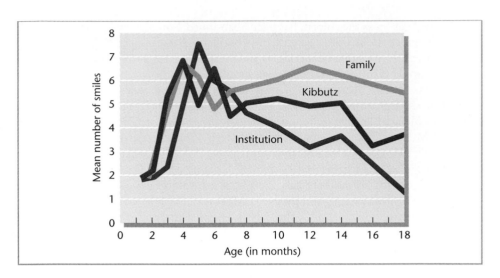

we saw earlier in our discussion of Brody's (1996) work on gender differences in emotional expression, parents generally elicit and expect more emotions from girls than boys, which suggests that both genetic and environmental factors need to be considered.

Infant smiling clearly becomes more discriminating as children develop. However, overall it also increases as a form of social behavior. It plays a central role in the infant's greeting behavior and occurs more frequently when the infant is with other people than when he is alone (Fogel, 1993; Jones, Collins, & Hong, 1991; Sroufe, 1996).

Because smiling has such a magical effect on a baby's caretakers, drawing them to the baby, getting them to smile back and to talk to, cuddle, and play with the baby, it acquires a very clear function for the growing infant. The infant learns that smiling helps keep his caretakers nearby and thus it becomes a means of communication and an aid to survival. And laughing, at which infants become quite skilled by the time they're 4 months old (Sroufe, 1979, 1996), is if anything even more useful in maintaining the baby's well-being (Nwokah, Hsu, Dobrowolska, & Fogel, 1994). If smiling gradually becomes a sign of pleasure, laughter leaves us with little doubt of a baby's positive emotion, and it plays a very important role in caregiver-infant interaction.

What sorts of events elicit laughter across the first year of life? Sroufe and Wunsch (1972), using mothers as their experimental assistants, examined the amount of laughter elicited in babies between 4 and 12 months of age by a wide array of visual, tactile, auditory, and social-behavioral stimuli: for example, a human mask or a disappearing object; bouncing the child on an adult's knee or blowing on the baby's hair; making lip popping, whispering, or horse-whinnying sounds; and playing peek-a-boo, covering the baby's face, or sticking out the tongue.

As Figure 7-2 shows, up to about 7 months there is a clear increase with age in the number of visual, tactile, and social events that elicit laughter, whereas the effect of auditory stimulation remains stable. Note, however, that the nature of the stimuli that elicit laughter changes as the child develops. By the time children are 10 or 12 months old they lose some interest in tactile stimulation. Toward the end of the first year, babies respond more to social games, visual displays, and other activities in which they can participate, such as covering and uncovering the mother's face with a cloth or playing tug-of-war with a blanket. By the end of the first year and throughout the second year, infants increasingly smile and laugh in response to activities that they create themselves (Sroufe, 1996). For example, 9- to 11-month-olds smile and laugh when practicing their motor accomplishments such as pulling themselves to a standing position (Mayes & Zigler, 1992). Or an older infant may repeatedly make a jack-in-the-box pop up

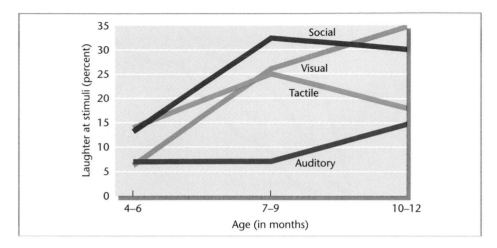

■ FIGURE 7-2
What makes children laugh?
Between the ages of 4 months
and a year, children were most
consistently likely to laugh at
visual and social stimuli, such as a
disappearing object or playing
peek-a-boo. (*Source:* From Sroufe
& Wunsch, 1972)

and laugh uproariously each time. As children grow older, laughing increases and becomes more of a social event. In one study of 3- to 5-year-olds, nearly 95 percent of laughter occurred in the presence of other children and adults (Bainum, Lounsbury, & Pollio, 1984). Acting silly was most often the elicitor of laughter among the nursery school set.

Fear: One of the First Negative Emotions

Timothy, at the age of 8 months, is exploring some toys in his playpen. He looks up and sees a strange woman standing very near, watching him. Timothy turns back to his toys briefly, then again solemnly looks up at the stranger, whimpers, turns away, and begins to cry.

In the continuing search for regularities in early development, few phenomena have captured as much time, effort, and interest as this type of exchange between an infant and a stranger. Apparently, at the same time that babies are beginning to display signs of positive emotions, in smiles and laughter, they are also learning to be fearful of some events and people, especially unfamiliar ones.

Fear of Strangers

The negative emotional response called *fear of strangers* evolves more slowly than the positive emotional expressions we've just discussed. Sroufe (1996) distinguishes two phases in the emergence of fear. At about 3 months of age, Sroufe maintains, infants show *wariness,* in which they respond with distress to an event that includes both familiar and unfamiliar aspects and which they therefore cannot comprehend and assimilate. By the time they are 9 months old, babies show true *fear,* which is an immediate negative reaction to an event that has specific meaning for them, such as the face of a total stranger (e.g., "I don't know what this is, and I don't like it").

Even at 4 months of age, babies smile less at unfamiliar adults than they do at their mothers, showing early signs that they recognize familiar people. But they are not yet distressed by the presence of a stranger. In fact, they show great interest in novel people as well as novel objects. Often they look longer at a stranger than at a familiar person, and if the mother is present, they will frequently look back and forth between her face and the stranger's, as if comparing them. Then, at about 5 months of age, this earlier reaction of perusal and interest starts to be replaced largely by giving a stranger a sober stare. At 6 months, although babies still are most likely to react to strangers with a sober expression, they're also likely to display distress. A distress reaction then gradually increases in frequency over the next half year and by 9 months, the earlier wary reactions give way to clear instances of fear. Figure 7-3 summarizes this progression from interest and exploration to fear over the first year of life.

■ FIGURE 7-3
The onset of stranger distress. At 8 months of age, half of the children studied here were showing distress at the appearance of strangers, and within a month or two this distress reaction was clearly dominant. (*Source:* Adapted from Emde, Gaensbauer, & Harmon, 1976)

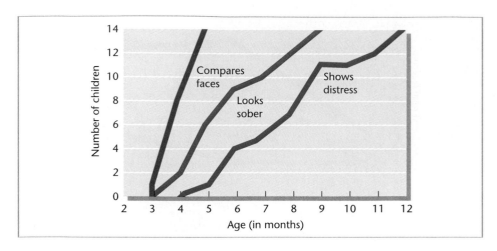

stranger distress   A fear of strangers that typically emerges in infants around the age of 9 months.

Is Stranger Distress Universal?

Fear of strangers, or **stranger distress,** has become enshrined in the psychological literature as a developmental milestone, at one time thought to be both inevitable and universal. Researchers now know that it is neither. Whether or not a baby is fearful of a stranger depends on a host of variables, including who the stranger is, how he or she behaves, the setting in which the person is encountered, and the age of the child (Mangelsdorf, Watkins, & Lehn, 1991). Moreover, babies are not all alike in their reactions to strangers. For some, greeting and smiling may be a frequent reaction, and fear is not typical (Bretherton, Stolberg, & Kreye, 1981; Rheingold & Eckerman, 1973). Let's look at some of the factors that affect infants' reactions to strangers: individual infants' tendencies to fearfulness, the context in which encounters with strangers take place, and characteristics of the strangers themselves.

Individual Differences in Fearfulness.   There are wide individual differences among infants and young children in their reactions to strangers and other potentially fear-arousing people and events. As we saw in Chapter 3, infants and children differ widely in temperament. For instance, Kagan and his colleagues (Kagan, 1994), have identified a subset of children whom they call "behaviorally inhibited." These children tend to be shy, fearful, and introverted, often avoiding even their peers, and they are more anxious and upset by mildly stressful situations than are other children (Kagan, 1989; Kagan, Reznick, & Snidman, 1987). Behaviorally inhibited youngsters tend to show atypical physiological reactions—such as rapid heart rates—in stressful situations, and their fearful responses and shyness tend to endure across time, from toddlerhood on into the start of the school years. According to Kagan (Kagan, Snidman, & Arcus, 1992), inhibitedness may be a stable characteristic of some children; that is, something about the makeup of these youngsters may encourage timidity and fearfulness.

Other evidence that individual makeup partly contributes to a child's level of fearfulness, including fear of strangers, comes from the finding that there is considerable consistency in the way a particular baby reacts to a variety of strangers, regardless of differences in the strangers' personal characteristics (Smith & Sloboda, 1986). And babies who are more sociable, as indicated by their willingness to interact in an outgoing way with a friendly adult, show less wariness in encounters with strangers than less sociable infants (Bohlin & Hagekull, 1993).

The Influence of Context.   Contextual factors also help determine the way an infant will react to a stranger. One such factor is the setting in which the encounter occurs. Ten-month-olds show little fear of strangers whom they meet in their own homes, but nearly 50 percent of youngsters of this age group are fearful when encountering a stranger in the unfamiliar setting of a researcher's lab (Sroufe, Waters, & Matas, 1974). Similarly, babies who sit on their mothers' laps while a stranger approaches rarely show any fear, but when they're placed in infant seats a few feet away from their mothers, they tend to gaze apprehensively, whimper, or cry when a stranger comes near (Bohlin & Hagekull, 1993; Morgan & Ricciuti, 1969). Apparently, it is not just the presence of an unfamiliar person but the degree of security the baby feels in the surrounding context that determines her reaction.

Another situational factor in a baby's response to a stranger is the extent to which the mother's face, voice, and body signal either comfort and serenity or apprehension and alarm. When a baby sees his mother reacting positively to a stranger, he tends to follow suit and responds much more positively, smiling more, approaching the stranger, and offering his toys (Feinman & Lewis, 1983). Conversely, when the mother adopts a worried look in the presence of a stranger, her baby is apt to cry more and smile less (Boccia & Campos, 1989). These studies illustrate **social referencing** in infants—that is, the process of "reading" emotional cues in other people to help determine how to act in an uncertain situation (Mumme, Fernald, & Herrera, 1996). This social referencing undergoes clear changes over time (Walden, 1991; Walden & Ogan, 1988). As infants develop they are more likely to look at the mother's face than at other parts of her body: In one study, babies who were between 14 and 22 months old were clearly more aware that their mother's face was the best source of information than were babies between 6 and 9 months old (Walden, 1991). Infants grow also in their tendency to check with the mother before they act. Younger infants often act first and look later, a strategy that could lead to trouble in a dangerous situation. The fact that even infants learn to use the emotional expressions of others as a guide to their own actions underscores the importance of emotion for regulating social behavior.

A third contextual factor is the degree to which the situation allows the infant some control over the extent and pace of the interaction (Mangelsdorf et al., 1991). When a baby can have an impact on how a stranger acts, he tends to be less apprehensive. In one study researchers presented 12- and 13-month-old infants with an unusual kind of strange event: a toy monkey that clapped cymbals together (Gunnar, 1980). For one group of babies, the monkey remained still except when the child hit a panel that made the cymbals clap. For a second group of infants, the cymbals clapped an equal number of times as for the first group, but the child had no control over when the clapping occurred. The babies who could control the monkey showed less fear of it and more smiling and laughter. The boys, especially, fussed and cried less often when they had control. Another factor that lowered distress in this situation was predictability of the loud noises; in fact, even putting the clapping on a regular, fixed schedule (such as a cycle of four seconds on and four seconds off) was enough to cause a 1-year-old to be less fearful of the toy (Gunnar, Leighton, & Peleaux, 1984).

Characteristics of the Stranger. Babies' emotional reactions to strangers are also affected by a stranger's personal characteristics. In one study, for instance, researchers showed babies between 7 and 19 months of age a strange man, a strange

Somewhere around the age of 7 months children begin to experience fear, especially in response to unfamiliar people or events. This child clearly doesn't want the little Dalmatian puppy anywhere near her.

social referencing The process of "reading" emotional cues in others to help determine how to act in an uncertain situation.

Proximity and age of a stranger affect babies' reactions.
In this study of stranger distress, the gender of a stranger had no effect on infant subjects but age did: The infants did not perceive the 4-year-old stranger as threatening but reacted very negatively to both adults. Distance from the infants had relatively little effect on the way they perceived the young stranger, but the closer the adult strangers got, the more intensely the babies showed their distress. In comparison, the infants reacted quite positively both to their own reflections and to their mothers, and this tendency increased with proximity. (*Source:* Adapted from Lewis & Brooks, 1974)

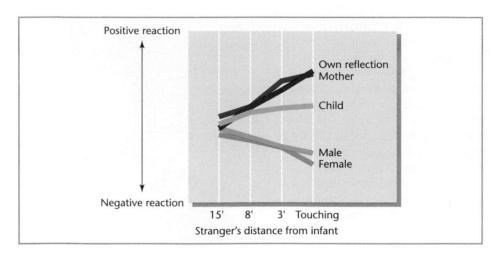

woman, a strange 4-year-old girl, the baby's mother, and the mirror reflection of the baby's own self (Lewis & Brooks, 1974). All the people (and the baby's own mirror image) presented to the babies were positioned at four different distances from them: 15 feet, 8 feet, 3 feet, and actually touching the baby. Two principal findings of this study, as shown in Figure 7-4, were that the babies' reactions to strangers were conditioned by the characteristics of the stranger—the 4-year-old child was apparently less threatening than the adults—and the closeness of the strangers to them—the closer the stranger got, the more negative the child's reaction.

To find out whether it was the size of the stranger or something about the stranger's facial configuration that caused infants to show more apprehensiveness toward adult strangers, Brooks and Lewis showed infants three more strangers: an adult, an adult midget, and a child (1976). The fact that the babies reacted significantly more negatively to the adult midget than to the child suggests that largeness is not the trait that triggers apprehension in them. Probably, it is something about an adult face that seems less benign than a child's. Unfortunately, a "baby-faced" adult was not available to test this hypothesis!

A stranger's behavior also affects the degree of stranger distress that an infant displays (Bretherton et al., 1981; Ross & Goldman, 1977). When confronted by an active, friendly stranger who talks, gestures, smiles, imitates the baby, and offers toys, most 12-month-olds show little fear. In fact, they tend to be highly social and enjoy playing games with the stranger. In contrast, a passive stranger, who looks soberly at the infant, does not elicit this positive reaction. Apprehension, it seems, is elicited as much by behavior that seems threatening as by the simple sight of a stranger's face.

How Do Smiling, Laughter, and Fear Develop?

Few phenomena have a single explanation, and smiling, laughter, and fear are no exceptions. Rather than confuse us, the several perspectives for which there is considerable evidence may well explain different aspects of the child's development at different stages of that development (Campos, Barrett, Lamb, Goldsmith, & Stenberg, 1983; Izard, 1991; Saarni, Mumme, & Campos, 1998). For example, the genetic-maturational view may be more useful than others in explaining fear reactions in the first few months of life. The cognitive perspective may have more relevance after the child is cognitively mature enough to form hypotheses about how things work. Finally, the learning perspective may be particularly useful in explaining the evolution of individual differences. Keep in mind, however, as we examine these three perspectives that all views overlap and may be applicable at any stage of development.

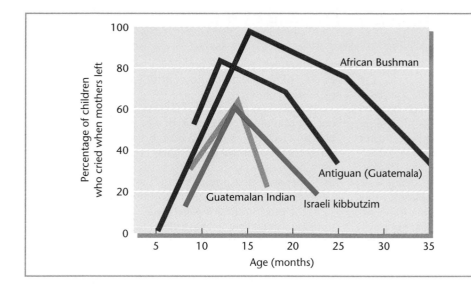

■ FIGURE 7-5
Separation protest.
Although children of the four different cultures depicted here varied considerably in the intensity of their protest at their mothers' departure, they all tended to reach a peak of distress at about the same age, between 13 and 15 months. (*Source:* From *Infancy: Its Place in Human Development* by Kagan, J., Kearsley, R. B., and Zelazo, P. R., p. 107, Figure 2.8. Copyright © 1978 by the President and Fellows of Harvard College. Reprinted by permission of the publisher, Harvard University Press, Cambridge, MA.)

The Genetic-Maturational Perspective

The biological underpinnings for the development of all three early emotions we've discussed is supported by both twin studies and cross-cultural research. Support for the view that smiling and laughter have a strong genetic-maturational component comes from the study of twins. Identical twins show greater similarity than fraternal twins both in the onset of social smiling and in the amount of it (Plomin, 1995; Plomin & DeFries, 1985). Studies of smiling in premature infants also point to the role of genetic-maturational factors in the onset of smiling. The normal *conceptual age* (age since conception) of a newborn human is 40 weeks, and most full-term babies begin to smile at 6 weeks after they are born, or a conceptual age of 46 weeks. Premature infants who are born at 34 weeks often do not smile until 12 weeks after birth, which for them is also 46 weeks since conception (Dittrichova, 1969). Apparently, a certain amount of physical maturation must occur before a baby is ready to start smiling. However, environmental stimulation is necessary as well for smiling to emerge. It is the interplay between genetic factors and the infant's environment that accounts for the timing and form of the behavior.

A genetic-maturational basis for fear is supported by both twin and cross-cultural studies. As we find with smiling and laughter, identical twins are more similar than fraternal twins in their reactions to strangers and their general degree of inhibitedness (Plomin & DeFries, 1985; Robinson, Kagan, Reznick, & Corley, 1993). Moreover, stranger distress emerges at roughly the same age across cultures, despite widely different childrearing practices. For example, babies raised both in Uganda (Ainsworth, 1963) and on a Hopi Indian reservation (Dennis, 1940) show the stranger-distress reaction at approximately 8 months, roughly the same age as Western infants do.

We find cross-cultural similarities as well in the experience of another common childhood fear, that of being separated from one's mother. This fear, called **separation protest,** tends to peak in Western infants at about 15 months and, as Figure 7-5 shows, displays a remarkably similar timetable in such diverse cultures as those of Guatemala and the Kalahari Desert region in Botswana. Although separation anxiety, as this fear is also called, generally becomes less and less common in childhood, it sometimes reappears in other forms: Box 7-1 describes a recent study of homesickness among children at camp and suggests some useful ways of coping with this kind of distress.

Finally, according to Kagan (1983), even young children experience *performance anxiety,* a fear that is generally attributed to older schoolchildren and adults, and they display this fear at about the same age in different cultures. Kagan showed children who were a year and a half to 2 years old an adult model who performed a series of

separation protest An infant's distress reaction to being separated from his or her mother, which typically peaks at about 15 months of age.

BOX 7-1

Child Psychology in Action

Coping with Homesickness

Homesickness, which is common in the middle and later childhood years, usually arises in settings in which children must stay away from their homes for periods of more than a day. Summer camps, boarding schools, college, foster homes, and hospitals are among the sites in which researchers have studied homesickness in children (Thurber & Weisz, 1997). *Homesickness*, which we can define as a longing to be with one's family or regular caretakers, may be expressed in depressive or anxious behavior; in acting out, as in aggressive behavior; or in complaints about physiological problems, such as headache, stomachache, and other pains of an ill-defined nature.

How do children cope with homesickness? According to Thurber and Weisz (1997), a child's beliefs about his ability to exert control over a situation strongly determine his choice of coping mechanism. If a child sent to live with relatives in a neighboring town because of economic distress at home believes he can change his situation, he may exert *primary control* by running away from his aunt's house and returning to his own home. Often, however, a child is unable to change his situation or finds that attempts to do so are unsuccessful and lead only to feelings of helplessness and depression. In this event, a child may instead elect *secondary control*, changing himself or his behavior in adapt to the unwanted situation. Thus a child placed in a boarding school many miles from his home might write letters home every day to feel in touch with his family, or he might join specific activities in which he had participated at home. A third way of dealing with homesickness is to *relinquish control*, or to give up trying to change things and seek solace in expressing sadness through a means such as crying or withdrawing from others.

Because many stressors have elements that are controllable and others that are not, coping is sometimes a mix of primary and secondary measures, the child trying first one and then another. The choice of coping measure depends also on specific constraints of the situation, such as camp rules, as well as on individual characteristics, such as age, perceived ability to control events, and cognitive sophistication.

Thurber and Weisz (1997) chose two summer camps, one for girls and one for boys, at which to study homesickness and found that overall, both boys and girls tended to use secondary control methods to cope with homesickness, most often doing something that was fun in order to forget their negative feelings. Among these youngsters, who ranged in age between 8 and 16 but who were on average 12½, the most homesick were those who were most likely to relinquish control, making little effort to cope with their unhappiness. On the other hand, the least homesick were those who appeared to know how to use different combinations of both primary and secondary methods to cope with whatever unpleasant feelings they had; this group were also the least likely to relinquish control.

Girls were more likely to call upon specific coping devices than were boys. However, there was also a significant gender difference in respect to the use of the primary control device of seeking out "someone who could talk with me and help me feel better, like a leader or one of my friends." Although 8- to 10-year-old boys and girls differed little on this parameter, from 11 on, girls were far more likely than boys to use this social-support approach to solving the problem of homesickness (Figure 7-6). As we've suggested earlier in the book and will discuss at greater length in Chapter 15, girls seem to be more socially oriented from early on.

Thurber and Weisz (1997) conclude that useful intervention in homesickness may involve helping children to understand that homesickness is not just an unhappy emotion but an emotional reaction to circumstances, some of which are controllable and some of which are not; helping them to distinguish these components of the problem; helping them develop specific coping methods at both primary and secondary levels; showing them how to apply each type for maximum benefit; and helping them understand why relinquishing control is not effective.

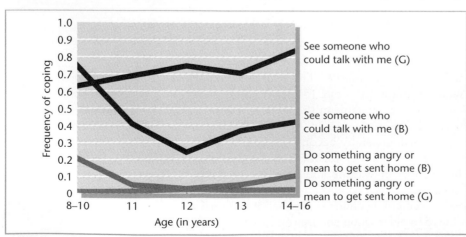

■ FIGURE 7-6
Coping with homesickness. When they were homesick, both girls (G) and boys (B) at camp preferred to talk with someone rather than act out in some way in the hope of being sent home. However, this trend was much stronger in girls than in boys. (*Source:* Adapted from Thurber & Weisz, 1997)

Perhaps if Mom hadn't backed away to take a picture this 1-year old wouldn't have felt so threatened by Santa Claus.

simple actions such as taking some toy animals for a walk and having a doll talk on a toy telephone and then told the children, "Now it's your turn to play." Whether from Vietnam, Fiji, or the United States, the children all showed signs of being upset—clinging, crying, protest, inhibition in play, and requests to go home—and these behaviors peaked at 24 months. According to Kagan, children at this age are beginning to be aware that they may not be able to emulate the model's behavior correctly, a concern that he interprets as the beginning of performance anxiety.

The Cognitive Perspective

The cognitive view focuses on the infant's growing ability to acquire knowledge about the world. This general perspective, which we will discuss at greater length in Chapters 9 and 10, proposes that infants acquire mental representations, or *schemata*, of objects in their world and develop increasing ability to assimilate new stimuli as instances of these representations (Kagan, Kearsley, & Zelazo, 1978). Recall from our introduction to Piaget's theory, in Chapter 1, that assimilation is the process by which we incorporate new events into our existing knowledge base. For instance, if the smiling face of a stranger appears before a baby who is about 2 months old, the child typically will peruse the person soberly for a few moments and then break into a smile (Zelazo, 1972). It is as if the baby suddenly recognizes the face for what it is, "matching" it to a scheme for "face" stored in memory. This recognition gives the child pleasure, hence the smile. According to Sroufe (1996), the baby engages in a tension-relaxation cycle: Confronting a novel event causes a buildup of tension; the infant responds with cognitive effort designed to master the meaning of the event; when the infant is successful, her tension is released and she smiles (Sroufe, 1996).

The cognitive ability to recognize familiar objects and derive pleasure from doing so emerges at around 8 to 10 weeks of age. The model of cognitive processing and tension modulation that we have discussed is clearly useful in explaining the emergence of the true smile, and it helps explain why children of this age start to smile in certain situations that seldom cause such reliable smiling among older children or adults.

Cognitive factors can also help to explain the emergence of fear responses, such as stranger distress. By around 8 months of age, when stranger distress first emerges, a baby is capable of perceiving the difference between a familiar and an unfamiliar person. But, as we have seen, it is not just the perception of someone new that is fear-arousing. Remember that the degree of stranger distress varies with many aspects of the situation, such as the familiarity of the setting, the closeness of the mother, the nearness of the stranger, the degree of friendliness the stranger shows, and how much control the child has over the interaction. Cognitive theorists believe that it is a newfound ability to make a rudimentary evaluation of the threat a stranger poses that explains why babies toward the end of their first year sometimes become upset in the presence of a stranger (Kagan, Kearsley, & Zelazo, 1978; Sroufe, 1996). According to Sroufe (1996, p. 93), the "same stimulus situation can lead to either strong negative or positive affect depending on the infant's context-based evaluation of the incongruity."

The Learning Perspective

A learning perspective is particularly useful in explaining individual differences in emotional expression, that is, the tendency of various emotional expressions to have quite a different onset, frequency, and intensity in different children. For example, the frequency with which children smile and laugh seems to vary with the nature of the environment in which they are raised. Common sense suggests that parents who respond with enthusiastic attention to their smiling infant will tend to encourage him to smile more, and in fact this has been verified in studies that show that when adults, particularly familiar caregivers, respond to a baby's smile with positive stimulation, the child's rate of smiling increases (e.g., Wahler, 1967). Other researchers (e.g., Bloom, 1984) have questioned whether the mechanism here is true reinforcement, as prescribed by learning theory, or the arousal associated with social stimulation, but still others (Poulson, 1984; Rovee-Collier, 1987) provide convincing evidence that social feedback has a clear impact on such infant social responses as smiling and vocalizing.

Learning experiences can also elicit and reinforce fear responses. Recall our example, in Chapter 5, of how a child may become (classically) conditioned to fear his doctor who gave him a painful shot on his first visit. Children may learn other fears through operant conditioning when one of their own behaviors, such as climbing up on a high ladder, is followed by a punishing consequence, such as a painful fall. And they can learn still other fears simply by observing others. For example, a child may watch her mother react fearfully to a bee or to a large dog and later imitate her mother's reaction (Bandura, 1989). In all these cases, the child's particular set of fears depends on what he has learned.

Children not only act on their emotions, but they learn to think about emotions, too. If we understand how children think about feelings, we are in a better position to understand why they act emotionally.

HOW CHILDREN THINK ABOUT EMOTIONS

A child is invited to a birthday party; another child's favorite pet dies; a third child hears a loud, unexpected bang. When are children able to think and talk about the varying emotional reactions that are likely to accompany these very different kinds of events? When can they understand the coexistence of multiple emotions? When can they empathize with another person, predicting how that person will feel in a given situation? And when are they capable of understanding complex emotions like pride and guilt? We will try to answer these questions in this section.

Matching Emotions to Situations: Emotional Scripts

Over time, children not only undergo shifts in the ways they express emotions but also develop a more complete understanding of the meanings of emotion terms and of the situations that evoke different kinds of feelings. According to Lewis (1989), this understanding can be seen as a collection of **emotional scripts,** or complex

emotional script   A complex scheme that enables a child to identify the emotional reaction that is likely to accompany a particular sort of event.

schemes that enable the child to identify the type of emotional reaction that is likely to accompany a particular kind of event.

From quite a young age children possess a number of such emotional scripts. In a classic study, Borke (1971) told 3- and 4-year-old children simple stories about such things as getting lost in the woods or having a fight or going to a party and asked them to tell her the emotions they thought the characters in the different stories would be likely to feel. The children easily identified situations that would lead to happiness, and they were reasonably good at identifying stories that were linked with sadness or anger. Later research (Stein & Trabasso, 1989; Trabasso, Stein, & Johnson, 1981) showed that 3- and 4-year-old children could also describe situations that evoked other emotions, such as excitement, surprise, and being scared. Clearly, young children know which emotions go with which situations.

Children's emotional scripts gain in complexity as they mature. For example, 5-year-olds generally understand only those situations that lead to emotions that have a recognizable facial display (e.g., anger, displayed in frowning) or that lead to a particular kind of behavior (e.g., sadness, displayed in crying or moping about). By the time they are 7, however, children can describe situations that elicit more complicated emotions that have no obvious facial or behavioral expressions, such as pride, jealousy, worry, and guilt. And by the time they reach 10 or 14, children can describe situations that elicit relief and disappointment (Harris, Olthof, Meerum, Terwogt, & Hardman, 1987). A similar developmental sequence is found in a variety of cultures, including Great Britain, the United States, the Netherlands, and Nepal (Harris, 1989).

Another aspect of emotional understanding that develops only gradually is the awareness that one can have more than one feeling at a time and that one can even experience two or more conflicting feelings at the same time. Although toddlers and even young infants show signs of experiencing conflicting feelings, children's ability to understand and express their knowledge of emotions emerges slowly over time and lags well behind their capacity to experience ambivalence and mixed emotions (Arsenio & Kramer, 1992; Wintre & Vallance, 1994). According to Harter (Harter, 1998; Harter & Buddin, 1987), children show a clear developmental sequence in their ability to understand multiple and conflicting feelings. From their study of children between the ages of 4 and 12, Harter and her colleagues (Harter & Buddin, 1987; Whitesell & Harter, 1989) derived the five stages of emotional understanding shown in Table 7-2. As you can see, it is not until the fourth stage, at about the age of 10, that children begin to be able to conceive of opposite feelings existing simultaneously.

As they develop, children learn to consider more and more aspects of an emotion-related situation, such as the desires, goals, and intentions of the people involved in it. Children realize that people's emotional expressions are produced by inner states and are not responsive solely to the characteristics of the situation. For example, young children often get angry when someone thwarts, wrongs, or frustrates them, regardless of whether the wrongful act was intentional, but children 7 years old and up, like adults, tend to reserve their anger for situations in which they think a person intended to upset them (Levine, 1995). A study by Harris and his colleagues (Harris, Johnson, Hutton, Andrews, & Cook, 1989) illustrates how children learn to interpret story characters' reactions to a particular event in terms of the characters' own wishes, desires, and goals. The investigators told 4- and 6-year-old children that one of the characters in a story—a toy elephant—had a preference for either Coke or milk. According to the story, a monkey tricked the elephant by replacing all of the Coke in the cans with milk. Children predicted how the elephant would feel when she found out the real contents by taking a drink from a can. The children adjusted their predictions depending on the elephant's preference; if the elephant liked milk, they said she was happy to discover milk in the can. If she liked Coke, they correctly noted that she would be sad to find milk instead of Coke. It would seem that when children are still quite young, they are able to take into account the desires of another person in judging the emotions that person will feel in a particular situation.

TABLE 7-2 Children's Understanding of Multiple and Conflicting Emotions

Approximate Ages	Children's Capabilities
4 to 6	Conceive of only one emotion at a time: "You can't have two feelings at the same time."
6 to 8	Begin to conceive of two emotions of the same type occurring simultaneously: "I was happy and proud that I hit a home run"; "I was upset and mad when my sister messed up my things."
8 to 9	Describe two distinct emotions in response to different situations at the same time: "I was bored because there was nothing to do and mad because my mom punished me."
10	Describe two opposing feelings where the events are different or different aspects of the same situation: "I was sitting in school worrying about the next soccer game but happy that I got an A in math"; "I was mad at my brother for hitting me but glad my Dad let me hit him back."
11 on	Understand that the same event can cause opposing feelings: "I was happy that I got a present but disappointed that it wasn't what I wanted."

Source: Based on Harter & Buddin, 1987.

Complex Emotions: Pride, Guilt, and Shame

Understanding more complex emotions like pride, guilt, and shame requires the ability to differentiate and integrate the roles of multiple factors in a situation, often including the role of personal responsibility. Often called "self-conscious" emotions because they rely upon the development of the sense of self-awareness (Barrett, 1997; Lewis, 1992; Tangney & Fischer, 1995), these emotions begin to emerge toward the middle of the second year. For example, children show embarrassment by blushing and turning away and express envy or jealousy by pouting when other children receive more desirable toys. When a child is pleased with his accomplishments he shows pride, but when he perceives that someone finds him wanting or deficient—perhaps he has failed an easy task—he gives evidence of shame. The feeling of guilt, which requires the development of the sense of personal responsibility and the internalization of some moral standards, emerges a bit later than pride and shame.

Crucial to distinguishing between children's experience of pride or shame is their emerging sense of the differences between "easy" and "difficult" and between "success" and "failure" (Lewis, 1992). Lewis and his colleagues (Lewis, 1992; Lewis, Alessandri, & Sullivan, 1992) found that by the time they were 3 years old, children had learned that they were more likely to feel pride if they succeeded at difficult tasks rather than easy ones. They had also learned that they were more likely to feel shame if they failed an easy task but to experience little if any shame at failing a difficult task. Solving a problem that was not particularly difficult elicited joy in these youngsters, but succeeding on a difficult task produced pride; failing a difficult task caused sadness, but failing an easy task aroused shame; see also Figure 7-7 (Lewis et al., 1992).

Children's understanding of pride also depends on their ability to entertain multiple emotions—such as pleasure at doing a task well and happiness that others appreciate the accomplishment (Harter & Whitesell, 1989)—and on their sense of personal agency, or effort. To evaluate this understanding, Thompson (1987, 1989) told stories to 7-, 10- and 18-year-olds involving accomplishments that individuals achieved either by their own efforts or by luck and then asked them questions about the stories. The 7-year-olds used the term *proud* in discussing good outcomes regardless of whether the protagonists in the stories had succeeded through their own efforts. More discriminating, the 10- and 18-year-old subjects realized

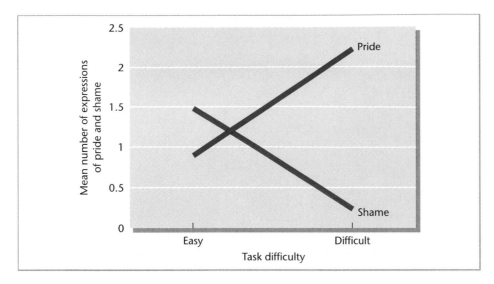

■ FIGURE 7-7
Pride, shame, and task difficulty.
The more difficult the task, the less shame children felt at failing it and the more pride they felt when they succeeded at it. (*Source:* Lewis, Alessandri, & Sullivan, 1992)

that "feeling proud" can occur only when the good outcomes that occur are the result of a person's own effort, not of luck or chance.

It is only gradually that children develop an appreciation of the central role of personal responsibility in their behavior in relation to other people and thus an understanding of guilt. According to Graham, Doubleday, and Guarino (1984), this understanding emerges in middle childhood. Asking 6- and 9-year-old children to describe situations in which they had felt guilty, these researchers found that only the older children had a clear understanding of this emotion and its relation to personal responsibility. For example, even when they had had little control over the outcome of a situation, 6-year-olds often described themselves as feeling guilty: "I felt guilty when my brother and I had boxing gloves on and I hit him too hard . . . sometimes I don't know my own strength." In contrast, 9-year-olds recognized that to feel guilty, it is critical to be responsible for the outcome of a situation: "I felt guilty when I didn't turn in my homework because I was too lazy to do it." Other studies (e.g., Graham, 1988; Thompson, 1989) have reached similar conclusions, namely, that young children focus on simple outcomes, whereas older children, who focus on the role of personal responsibility, understand that unless they themselves caused the outcome they need not feel guilty.

Although we often explore the development of different human capacities such as emotional expression and cognitive competence separately, these capacities clearly are mutually interdependent. For example, as we've seen in this section, it's clear that the development of specific emotions is closely entwined with such cognitive advances as the ability to understand causality and, hence, personal responsibility. In addition, social influences such as variations in the style of family interaction play a role in the way children come to understand emotions both in themselves and in others (Denham, 1997). Children's capacity to experience and show different emotions is closely tied to childrearing history. For example, children who have been abused, particularly girls, are more likely to display shame and less likely to show pride than their nonabused peers; according to Alessandri & Lewis (1996), this reflects the intense and frequent negative feedback these girls receive from their parents. Interactions with siblings also contribute to a child's development of emotional understanding. As Youngblade and Dunn (1995) found, pretend play with siblings, often characterized by conflict and other intense emotional understanding, is associated with increased understanding of other people's feelings and beliefs.

Family styles of interaction also affect a child's ability to understand the emotions of other people. For example, Dunn and her colleagues (Dunn & Brown, 1991; Dunn, Brown, & Beardsall, 1991; Dunn, Brown, & Maguire, 1995) found that 3-year-old children's conversations with their mothers and siblings about feeling states and the

This girl is justly proud of winning a blue ribbon in track and field.

same children's ability, at the age of 6, to understand other peoples' emotions were closely related. Children from families in which there was more discussion of feelings were better able to recognize others' emotions than those raised in families in which feelings were less often discussed. In general, the better a child understands emotions, the more skilled he is at such social behaviors as problem solving and conflict resolution and the more likely he is to be accepted by peers (Cassidy, Parke, Butkovsky, & Braungart, 1992; Garner, 1996; Parke & O'Neil, 1997).

THE DEVELOPMENT OF ATTACHMENT

attachment   A strong emotional bond that forms between infant and caregiver in the second half of the child's first year.

Closely related to emotional development is the development of **attachment,** a strong emotional bond that forms in the second half of the first year between an infant and one or more of the child's regular caregivers. Visible signs of attachment can be seen in the warm greetings the child gives her parents when they approach, smiling broadly, stretching out her arms, and in her active efforts at contact when picked up, such as touching her parent's face, and snuggling close. Attachment can also be seen in a child's efforts to stay near his parents in an unfamiliar situation, crawling or running to their sides, holding on to a leg. And it can be seen in the distress that older babies show when their parents leave them temporarily; its negative counterpart is expressed in the separation protest that we discussed earlier.

The emergence of attachment is one of the developmental milestones in the first year of life. It is of great interest to researchers not only because it is so intense and dramatic but because it is thought to enhance the parents' effectiveness in the later socialization of their children. Children who have developed an attachment to their parents presumably want to maintain their parents' affection and approval and so are motivated to adopt the standards of behavior that the parents set for them.

Attachment is such an important and widely studied topic that we devote the rest of this chapter to it. We begin this section with several theories of why attachment develops, including psychoanalytic theory, learning theory, and ethological theory. We next look how attachment evolves over the first 2 years of life and then consider special characteristics of attachment to fathers and to peers. In the last section of the chapter, we discuss variations in the quality of attachment and in the consequences of such variations.

Theories of Attachment

A variety of theories have been offered to explain the development of attachment, including psychoanalytic, learning, and ethological theory. Each of these positions makes different assumptions about the variables that are important for the development of attachment and about the processes underlying the development of an attachment relationship.

Psychoanalytic Theory

According to Freud's classic **psychoanalytic theory,** babies become attached to their caregivers because the caregivers are associated with gratification of infants' innate drive to obtain pleasure through sucking and other forms of oral stimulation. On this line of thinking, a woman who breast-feeds her baby is particularly important to her child's oral gratification. The baby becomes attached first to the mother's breast and ultimately to the mother herself. Although this argument from traditional psychoanalytic theory has fallen out of favor today, the stress it places on a person's inner needs and feelings and its focus on mother-infant interaction remain important influences in the study of infant attachment.

psychoanalytic theory of attachment The Freudian theory that babies become attached first to the mother's breast and then to the mother herself as a source of oral gratification.

Learning Theory

Like psychoanalytic theory, **learning theory** has traditionally associated the formation of mother-infant attachment with the mother's reduction of the baby's hunger, which is a primary drive. Because the mother provides the infant with food, which is a *primary reinforcer,* she herself becomes a **secondary reinforcer.** Presumably, this ability to satisfy the baby's hunger drive forms the basis for infant attachment to the mother or any other caregiver linked to feeding.

Many studies, however, have challenged the view that feeding is critical for the development of attachment. In what is probably the most famous of these, Harry Harlow (Harlow & Zimmerman, 1959) separated infant monkeys from their real mothers and raised them in the company of two surrogate mothers: one "mother" was made of stiff wire and had a feeding bottle attached to it; the other was made of soft terrycloth but lacked a bottle. Especially in moments of stress, the baby monkeys preferred to cling to the cloth "mother," even though she dispensed no food. Attachment to this surrogate mother clearly didn't require the reduction of hunger.

Research on human beings tells a similar story. Schaffer and Emerson (1964), for example, found that babies formed attachments to their fathers and other frequently seen adults who played little or no role in the child's feeding. These researchers also found that babies who had, on the one hand, relatively unresponsive mothers who tended to avoid contact with their infants except for routine physical care and, on the other, attentive, stimulating fathers tended to form paternal attachments, even though they actually spent more time with their mothers (Schaffer & Emerson, 1964).

The central point of the learning theory explanation is that attachment is not automatic; it develops over time as a result of satisfying interactions with responsive adults. Some learning theorists suggest that the visual, auditory, and tactile stimulation that adults provide in the course of their daily interactions with an infant are the basis for the development of attachment (Gewirtz, 1969). According to this view, babies are initially attracted to their regular caregivers because they are the most important and reliable sources of this type of stimulation. As interactions with these caregivers continue over weeks and months, infants learn to depend on and to value these special adults in their lives, becoming attached to them.

learning theory of attachment The theory that infants become attached to the mother because she provides food, or primary reinforcement, and thus acquires secondary reinforcement properties.

secondary reinforcer A person or other stimulus that acquires reinforcing properties by virtue of repeated association with a primary reinforcer.

Cognitive Developmental Theory

According to the **cognitive developmental view,** before specific attachments can occur, the infant not only must be able to differentiate between her mother and a stranger but also must be aware that people still exist even when she cannot see them. That is, she must have developed what Piaget terms *object permanence,* or the knowledge that objects, including people, have a continuous existence apart from her own interaction with them. As we will see in Chapter 9, there is some evidence that children as young as 3½ months have an awareness of object permanence, although Piaget believed that this awareness did not begin to evolve until about 4 months of age.

cognitive developmental view of attachment The view that to form attachments infants must both differentiate between mother and stranger and must understand that people exist independent of their interaction with them.

Advances in the infant's cognitive development can also account, in part, for the gradual shift in the ways that attachment is expressed. Physical proximity to attachment figures becomes less important as children grow older. Children are now increasingly able to maintain psychological contact with a parent through words, smiles, and looks. In addition, because they are also better able to understand that separations from a parent are sometimes necessary and are usually temporary, they are less upset by separations. Parents can reduce their children's distress over separations further by explaining the reasons for their departures. In one study, for instance, 2-year-olds handled separation from their mothers much better when the mothers gave them clear information ("I'm going out now for just a minute, but I'll be right back") than when the mother left without a word (Weinraub & Lewis, 1977).

Ethological Theory

Another approach that has emphasized the reciprocal nature of the attachment process is John Bowlby's **ethological theory** (1958, 1969, 1973). Influenced by both evolutionary theory and observational studies of animals, Bowlby suggested that attachment has its roots in a set of instinctual infant responses that are important for the protection and survival of the species. The infant responses of crying, smiling, sucking, clinging, and following (visually at first and later motorically) both elicit the parental care and protection that the baby needs and promote contact between the child and the parents. Just as the infant is biologically prepared to respond to the sights, sounds, and nurturance provided by the parents, so the parents are biologically prepared to respond to these eliciting behaviors on the part of the baby. As a result of these biologically programmed responses, both parent and infant develop a mutual attachment.

The value of Bowlby's position lies in its emphasis on the active role of the infant's early social signaling systems, such as smiling and crying, in the formation of attachment. Another attractive feature is the theory's stress on the development of mutual attachment, whereby both partners, not just one, become attached (Belsky & Cassidy, 1994). From this perspective, attachment is a relationship, not simply a behavior of either the infant or the parent (Sroufe & Fleeson, 1986; Sroufe, 1996). More controversial is Bowlby's suggestion that these early behaviors are biologically programmed. As we have seen, for example, there is considerable evidence that smiling has social as well as biological origins.

How Attachment Evolves

Attachment does not develop suddenly and unheralded but rather emerges in a series of steps, moving from a baby's general preference for human beings over inanimate objects to a child's real partnership with its parents. Schaffer (1996) proposes four phases in the development of attachment; these are outlined in Table 7-3. In the first phase, which lasts only a month or two, the baby's social responses are relatively indiscriminate. In the second phase, the baby gradually learns to distinguish familiar from unfamiliar people. As you learned in Chapter 5, even very young infants can distinguish their mothers' faces, voices, and even smells from those of other women. However, although a baby under 6 months of age can make these discriminations between his mother and other caretakers and even prefers them over strangers, he does not yet protest when familiar caregivers depart; he is not yet truly attached to these people.

In the third phase, which begins when the baby is about 7 months old, specific attachments develop. Now the infant actively seeks contact with certain regular caregivers, such as the mother, greeting them happily and often crying when those people temporarily depart. The baby does not show these behaviors to just anyone but only to *specific* attachment figures. When the child passes the 2-year mark and enters toddlerhood (from about 2 to 5), the attachment relationship moves into the final phase—the so-called goal-corrected partnership (Bowlby, 1969). At this point, owing to advances in cognitive development, children become aware of others'

ethological theory of attachment Bowlby's theory that attachment derives from the biological preparation of both infant and parents to respond to each other's behaviors in such a way that parents provide the infant with care and protection.

TABLE 7-3	Phases in the Development of Attachment	
Name	*Age Range (Months)*	*Principal Features*
1 Preattachment	0–2	Indiscriminate social responsiveness
2 Attachment-in-the-making	2–7	Recognition of familiar people
3 Clear-cut attachment	7–24	Separation protest; wariness of strangers; intentional communication
4 Goal-corrected partnership	24 on	Relationships more two-sided: children understand parents' needs

Source: Schaffer, 1996.

feelings, goals, and plans and begin to consider these things in formulating their own actions. As Colin (1996) recently noted, "the child becomes a partner in planning how the dyad will handle separations" (p. 72).

Attachment to Fathers and Others

Infants develop attachments not only to their mothers but to their fathers and to a variety of other persons with whom they regularly interact. When children are a little older, for example, they often develop attachments to siblings or other peers. Moreover, according to several anthropologists (Weisner & Gallimore, 1977; Harkness & Super, 1995), mothers are exclusive caregivers in only about 3 percent of human societies, and in as many as 40 percent of societies, mothers are not even the major caregivers. In addition, as we will see later in this chapter, the quality of attachment relationships can vary greatly (Fox, Kimmerly, & Schafer, 1991; Main & Weston, 1981).

Fathers

Today's American fathers often take a much more active role with their infants than fathers in past generations; just like mothers, fathers develop mutual attachments with their babies (Parke, 1996). Fathers who have the opportunity to interact with their infants in the first few days after infants are born tend to hold, touch, talk to, and kiss them just as much as mothers do (Parke, 1996; Parke & O'Leary, 1976). And later in their first year of life the children of these dads show just as much attachment to their fathers as to their mothers.

In one study, older babies showed equal attachment to their mothers and fathers in a situation in which a friendly but unfamiliar visitor observed the children in their homes with both parents present (Lamb, 1977, 1996). In this nonstressful situation, the babies showed no preference for either parent in terms of their attachment behavior. They were just as likely to touch, approach, and be near their fathers as their mothers. In other, stressful situations, however, babies generally look to their mothers for security and comfort if she is available (Belsky & Cassidy, 1994; Lamb, 1977, 1996). This is probably because it is the mother who has most often served this role in the past.

But although babies can be strongly attached to their fathers, American fathers are usually less involved than mothers in an infant's routine care; this is true also of grandfathers as compared with grandmothers (McGreal, 1985; Tinsley & Parke, 1988). It is significant that American fathers participate more in caregiving when the mother is supportive of the father's involvement and views him as a competent caregiver (Bietel & Parke, 1998). Father involvement in infant care also increases when the mother is less available for such reasons as recovery from a cesarean section delivery (Pederson, Zaslow, Cain, & Anderson, 1980) or employment outside the home (Gottfried, Bathurst, & Gottfried, 1994).

Young American fathers are particularly likely to engage in rough-and-tumble play with their young sons.

In some cultures, particularly hunter-gatherer societies where the search for food and other necessities requires the efforts of both men and women, fathers may be more likely to share in child care. According to Hewlett (1992a, 1992b) fathers among the Aka, who live in the southern part of the Central African Republic and the northern reaches of the Domestic Republic of Congo, provide more direct care to their babies than fathers in any other known society. Among the Efe, however, another African forager society (in Congo), child care is considered a woman's responsibility, and although Efe fathers spend a great deal of time with their infants, a relatively small percentage of that time goes into direct child care (Morelli & Tronick, 1992). Among the Agta, in Cagayan, Philippines, a hunter-gatherer society in which women and men share labor and subsistence activities almost equally, mothers remain the primary caregivers (Griffin & Griffin, 1992).

In many cultures, fathers have a special role in the infant's development—that of playmate. The quality of a father's play with a baby generally differs from a mother's: Fathers engage in more unusual and physically arousing games (especially with their sons), whereas mothers tend to stimulate their babies verbally and to play quieter games such as peek-a-boo (Parke, 1990, 1996; Power & Parke, 1982). Even when fathers have assumed the role of their babies' primary caregiver they tend to display this physically arousing style of interaction (Hwang, 1986; Field, 1978; Lamb, Frodi, Hwang, & Frodi, 1982). Although American fathers as well as fathers in the countries of Australia, Israel, India, Italy, and Japan (Lamb, 1987; Roopnarine, 1992) and among the Aka Pygmies of Central Africa spend four to five times more time playing with their infants than caring for them (Hewlett, 1992a, 1992b), apparently not all fathers engage in rough-and-tumble play with their children. Fathers in India, Central Africa, and Sweden are apparently less likely to engage in this style of play (Hewlett, 1992b; Roopnarine, 1992), and U.S. fathers who enter parenthood at a later age (over 35) tend to be less physical in their play than younger men (Neville & Parke, 1997).

Mothers and fathers continue to show these different styles of play as their children grow older, well into the early childhood years (MacDonald & Parke, 1984, 1986). We don't yet know whether these mother-father differences in play mode are the result of biology or experience, but whatever their cause, infants tend to react more positively to a father's style of play than to a mother's (Field, 1990; Parke, 1996). When given a choice of play partners, 18-month-olds in one study reliably chose their fathers more often than their mothers (Clarke-Stewart, 1978). Probably children like playing with their fathers because they make more exciting and unpredictable playmates.

Other Targets of Attachment

Although infants' most significant attachment relationships are usually with fathers and mothers, as Table 7-4 shows, a variety of other individuals are important in the infant's social world, including peers, siblings, and relatives like grandparents, aunts, and uncles (Dunn, 1992; Parke & O'Neil, 1997; Tinsley & Parke, 1988). Peers can become important attachment figures, even for very young children. For example, one investigator found that in a preschool where some children were

TABLE 7-4 The Breadth of Children's Attachments

Attachment Target	Percentage of Infants Attached	
	Initially	At 18 Months
Mother	95	81
Father	30	75
Grandparent	11	45
Relative other than sibling	8	44
Sibling	2	24
Other child	3	14

Source: Schaffer, 1996.

transferring to new schools, children who were leaving as well as those left behind experienced a variety of reactions, including increased fussiness, activity level, negative effect, and illness, as well as changes in eating and sleeping patterns (Field, 1986). These reactions were viewed as separation stress associated with the loss of familiar peers. For an even more dramatic illustration of the ability of young children to form close attachment relationships with one another see Box 7-2.

THE NATURE AND QUALITY OF ATTACHMENT

Like most aspects of human development, the formation of early attachments is not always uniform from one child to another or from one relationship to the next. Many children form what appear to be highly secure attachments. The important adults in their lives seem to serve as a source of nurturance and affection that gives the youngsters confidence to explore the world and become more independent. For other children, however, attachments seem much less secure and dependable. Researchers describe such variations as differences in the *quality* of attachments.

Before we examine some of the specific factors that may affect the nature and quality of individual child-parent attachments, such as parenting styles and infant temperament, let us consider a classic body of work that has provided a means of characterizing attachment relationships of different qualities. Mary Ainsworth's studies based on her concept of the secure base and using the so-called Strange Situation have been replicated many times and in many parts of the world.

Methods of Assessing Attachment Relationships

Proposing that infants organize their attachment behavior around a particular adult in such a way that they seem to be using the adult as a **secure base** for exploration or a safe haven in the event of distress, Ainsworth made valuable observations of infants' attachment and exploratory behavior at about 1 year of age (Ainsworth, 1973; Waters, Vaughn, Posada, & Kondo-Ikemura, 1995). The striking differences in the infants' behaviors in what is known as the **Strange Situation,** a carefully worked out scenario in which a mother twice leaves her baby alone or with a stranger and returns twice to be reunited with her child (see Table 7-5), enabled Ainsworth to assess the infant-mother relationships and to classify these relationships according to their nature and quality. Subsequent research both expanded on Ainsworth's work and added a longitudinal feature, comparing children's behavior at 1 year old and at 6 years old (Main & Cassidy, 1988).

As we examine Ainsworth's classification system you may find it useful to look at Table 7-6, which summarizes four categories of attachment relationship: secure attachment, insecure-avoidant attachment, insecure-resistant attachment, and insecure-disorganized attachment. Of the white, middle-class children Ainsworth studied, she classified some 60 to 65 percent as displaying **secure attachment** to their

secure base According to Ainsworth, a caregiver to whom an infant has formed an attachment and whom the child uses as a base from which to explore new things and a safe haven in times of stress.

Strange Situation A testing scenario in which mother and child are separated and reunited several times and that enables investigators to assess the nature and quality of a mother-infant attachment relationship.

secure attachment A kind of attachment displayed by babies who are secure enough to explore novel environments, who are minimally disturbed by brief separations from their mothers, and who greet them happily when they return.

BOX 7-2

Risk and Resilience

Peers As Attachment Figures

Anna Freud's classic account (Freud & Dann, 1951) of the behavior of six young German-Jewish orphans brought to England during World War II not only highlights the incredible resilience of these at-risk children, torn from their families and kept in concentration camps from the age of 1 until they were 4, but also illustrates the depth and intensity that peer attachments can have. The children, most of whose parents had died in gas chambers, arrived at Bulldog Banks, a small English country home that had been transformed into a nursery for war children, when they were 4 years old. Quickly, they formed intense, protective attachments to each other while they ignored or were actively hostile to their adult caretakers. Bulldog Banks was the first time any of them had experienced living in a small, intimate setting with adults who offered them kindness rather than cruelty.

In their early days at the nursery these six children were wild and uncontrollable. They destroyed or damaged much of the furniture and all the toys given them within a few days. Most of the time they ignored the adults, but when they were angry, they would bite, spit, or swear at them, often calling them *bloder ochs* ("stupid fools").

The contrast between the children's hostile behavior toward their caretakers and their solicitous, considerate behavior toward one another was surprising. In one case, when a caretaker accidentally knocked over one of the children, two of the other children threw bricks at her and called her names. The children resisted being separated from each other even for special treats like pony rides. When one child was ill, the others wanted to remain with her. They showed little envy, jealousy, rivalry, or competition with each other. The sharing and helping behavior these children showed with each other was remarkable in children of this age.

Here are some typical incidents in the children's first 7 months at Bulldog Banks (Freud & Dann, 1951, pp. 150–168):

- The children were eating cake, and John began to cry when he saw there was no cake left for a second helping. Ruth and Miriam, who had not yet finished their portions, gave him the remainder of their cake and seemed happy just to pet him and comment on his eating the cake.

- In very cold weather one child lost his gloves, and another child loaned his gloves without complaining about his own discomfort.

Even in fearful situations children were able to overcome their trepidation to help others in their group:

- A dog approached the children, who were terrified. Ruth, though badly frightened herself, walked bravely to Peter who was screaming and gave him her toy rabbit to comfort him. She comforted John by lending him her necklace.

- On the beach in Brighton, Ruth was throwing pebbles into the water. Peter, who was afraid of waves, did not dare to approach them. Suddenly, in spite of his fear, he rushed to Ruth, calling out: "Water coming, water coming," and dragged her back to safety.

When, finally, the children began to form positive relations with adults, they made them on the basis of group feelings. Their relationships with their caretakers had none of the demanding, possessive attitudes often shown by young children toward their own mothers. They simply began to include the adults in their group and to treat them, in some ways, as they treated each other. For those children in whom this phase of general attachment was eventually followed by a specific attachment to an individual caretaker, clinging and possessive behaviors did appear. But for all the children throughout their year's stay at Bulldog Banks, the intensity of such attachments to surrogate mothers was never as great as it would have been in normal mother-child relations and the relationships were never as binding as those they maintained with their peers.

These children's circumstances were unusual, and we must therefore interpret this classic work with caution. At the same time, the children's behavior clearly demonstrates not only the intensity of attachments that can develop between young children but the resilience that enabled these children to survive unimaginable risk.

---

insecure-avoidant attachment A type of attachment shown by babies who seem not to be bothered by their mothers' brief absence but specifically avoid them on their return, sometimes becoming visibly upset.

mothers, because they readily sought contact with her after the stress of her departure in an unfamiliar setting and were quickly comforted by her, even if initially quite upset. These babies also felt secure enough to explore a novel environment when the mother was present. They did not whine and cling to her, but actively investigated their surroundings, as if the mother's presence gave them confidence. In familiar situations, such as the home, these children are minimally disturbed by minor separations from the mother, although they greet her happily when she returns.

Ainsworth classified the remaining children she studied as insecure in one of several ways. Exhibiting **insecure-avoidant attachment** were children who typically showed little distress over the mother's absence in the Strange Situation, at least on her first departure. However, these children actively avoided their mothers

TABLE 7-5	The Strange Situation Scenario		
Episode Number	Persons Present	Duration	Brief Description of Actions
1	Mother, baby, and observer	30 seconds	Observer introduces mother and baby to experimental room, then leaves. (Room contains many appealing toys scattered about.)
2	Mother and baby	3 minutes	Mother is nonparticipant while baby explores; if necessary, play is stimulated after 2 minutes.
3	Stranger, mother, and baby	3 minutes	Stranger enters. First minute: stranger silent. Second minute: stranger converses with mother. Third minute: stranger approaches baby. After 3 minutes mother leaves unobtrusively.
4	Stranger and baby	3 minutes or less	First separation episode. Stranger's behavior is geared to that of baby.
5	Mother and baby	3 minutes or more	First reunion episode. Mother greets and/or comforts baby, then tries to settle the baby again in play. Mother then leaves, saying "bye-bye."
6	Baby alone	3 minutes or less	Second separation episode.
7	Stranger and baby	3 minutes or less	Continuation of second separation. Stranger enters and gears behavior to that of baby.
8	Mother and baby	3 minutes	Second reunion episode. Mother enters, greets baby, then picks baby up. Meanwhile stranger leaves unobtrusively.

on their return: They turned away from her, increased their distance from her, and paid her no attention. After the mother's second departure, during which time many of these babies became visibly upset, they again avoided her on her return. Later researchers have found that this first insecure pattern typically characterizes about 20 percent of American samples.

A second type of insecure relationship is called **insecure-resistant attachment.** Researchers have found that infants who display this type of attachment and who make up about 10 to 15 percent of American samples often become extremely upset when the mother leaves them but are oddly ambivalent toward her when she returns. Intermittently they seek contact with her and then angrily push her away.

The third type of insecure relationship, identified by later researchers, is called **insecure-disorganized attachment** (Main & Solomon, 1990). When babies who display this kind of behavior are reunited with their mothers in the Strange Situation scenario, they seem disorganized and disoriented. They look dazed, they freeze often in the middle of their movements, or they engage in repetitive behaviors, such as rocking.

Note that all these attachment classifications reflect the quality of the relationship between the child and the parent, not traits of either the child or the parent. Interestingly, as Table 7-6 shows, similar child-parent relationship patterns can be observed in these children and parents when the children are 6 years old (Main & Cassidy, 1988).

New methods for assessing attachment have been developed in recent years. Relying on the judgments of caregivers who are familiar with the child's behavior, the **Attachment Q Sort (AQS)** (Vaughn & Waters, 1990; Waters & Deane, 1985)

insecure-resistant attachment A kind of attachment shown by babies who tend to become very upset at the departure of their mothers and who exhibit inconsistent behavior on their return, sometimes seeking contact, sometimes pushing their mothers away.

insecure-disorganized attachment A type of attachment shown by babies who seem disorganized and disoriented when reunited with their mothers after a brief separation.

Attachment Q Sort (AQS) An assessment method in which a caregiver or observer judges the quality of a child's attachment based on the child's behavior in naturalistic situations, often including brief separations from parents.

TABLE 7-6 Children's Attachment Behavior in the Strange Situation: A Typology

1 Year Old	6 Years Old
Secure Attachment	
On reunion after brief separation from parents, children seek physical contact, proximity, interaction; often try to maintain physical contact. Readily soothed by parents and return to exploration and play.	On reunion, children initiate conversation and pleasant interaction with parents or are highly responsive to parents' overtures. May subtly move close to or into physical contact with parents, usually with rationale such as seeking a toy. Remain calm throughout.
Insecure-Avoidant Attachment	
Children actively avoid and ignore parents on reunion, looking away and remaining occupied with toys. May move away from parents and ignore their efforts to communicate.	Children minimize and restrict opportunities for interaction with parents on reunion, looking and speaking only as necessary and remaining occupied with toys or activities. May subtly move away with rationale like retrieving a toy.
Insecure-Resistant Attachment	
Although infants seem to want closeness and contact, their parents are not able effectively to alleviate their distress after brief separation. Child may show subtle or overt signs of anger, seeking proximity and then resisting it.	In movements, posture, and tones of voice, children seem to try to exaggerate both intimacy and dependency on parents. They may seek closeness but appear uncomfortable, for example, lying in parent's lap but wriggling and squirming. These children sometimes show subtle signs of hostility.
Insecure-Disorganized Attachment	
Children show signs of disorganization (e.g., crying for parents at door and then running quickly away when door opens; approaching parent with head down) or disorientation (e.g., seeming to "freeze" for a few seconds).	Children seem almost to adopt parental role with parents, trying to control and direct parents' behavior either by embarrassing or humiliating parents or by showing extreme enthusiasm for reunion or overly solicitous behavior toward parents.

Sources: Adapted from Ainsworth, Blehar, Waters, & Wall, 1978; Cassidy & Berlin, 1994; Main & Cassidy, 1988; Main & Hesse, 1990.

calls for the mother or other caregiver to sort a set of cards containing phrases that describe the child's behavior (e.g., "rarely asks for help," "keeps track of mother's location while playing around the house," "quickly greets mother with a big smile when she enters the room") into sets ranging from those that are most descriptive of the child to those that are least descriptive. The method, which is useful for children between the ages of 1 and 5, was designed to facilitate making ratings, in naturalistic settings, of a broad variety of attachment-related behaviors (e.g., secure-base behavior, attachment-exploration balance, and affective responsiveness). As we will see later, other investigators (Main & Cassidy, 1988; Wartner, Grossman, Fremmer-Bombik, & Suess, 1994) have developed later-age assessments of attachment that closely resemble the Strange Situation and permit across-time comparisons between children in infancy and at later ages.

A question that continues to interest researchers is whether Ainsworth's model is equally useful in different cultures both within the United States and in other countries. As Box 7-3 discusses, the model does seem to have considerable applicability, although there are wide differences among the ways children of different cultures organize their secure-base behavior.

The Parents' Role in the Quality of Attachment

We have said that attachment is a *relationship*, developing out of the interaction between infant and parent. Both parents and infants contribute to the nature of the attachment relationship, and we begin, in this section, by considering the parents' input. We look at babies' contribution to the relationship in the section that follows.

Styles of Caregiving

Ainsworth was the first to describe how parents' styles of interacting with their infants are linked with the kinds of attachment relationships that infants and parents develop. Mothers of securely attached infants, for instance, usually permit their babies to play an active role in determining the onset, pacing, and end of feeding early in life. This behavior in and of itself doesn't promote a secure attachment, but it identifies a mother as generally responsive to her baby's needs. The mother of a securely attached infant is also consistently available to her baby; she does not sometimes ignore her baby when he or she signals a genuine need for her (Cassidy & Berlin, 1994). This style of parenting, called **sensitive care,** is widely associated with the formation of secure attachments.

A number of parenting styles are associated with insecure attachments. Cassidy and Berlin (1994), for example, have found that mothers of babies with an insecure-avoidant type of attachment tend to be *unavailable* and *rejecting.* These mothers are generally unresponsive to their infants' signals, rarely have close bodily contact with them, and often interact with them in an angry, irritable way. And the parents of infants with insecure-resistant attachments exhibit an *inconsistently available* parenting style (Cassidy & Berlin, 1994). Mothers who display this style respond to their babies' needs at times, but at other times they do not, and in general they offer little affection and are awkward in their interactions with their infants.

The most deficient forms of parenting are found among parents whose attachment with their infants is of the insecure-disorganized type; these parents often neglect their babies or abuse them physically. The approach/avoidance behavior that infants with this type of attachment display when reunited with their caregivers in the Strange Situation may actually be an adaptive response, for these babies do not know what to expect, given the abuse they have already suffered (Main & Solomon, 1990). Carlson, Cicchetti, Barnett, and Braunwald (1989) found that mistreated infants were significantly more likely to develop insecure-disorganized attachments (82%) than were children who were not mistreated (19%). Another factor often associated with the insecure-disorganized pattern of attachment is maternal depression. Babies of depressed mothers show not only approach/avoidance but sadness upon reunion. Observations of such mothers with their 6-month-old babies have revealed little mutual eye contact and minimal mutual responsiveness; instead, both mother and baby tended to avert their gaze (Field, 1990; Lyons-Ruth, Connell, Gruenbaum, & Botein, 1990). Some researchers have found that depressed mothers are not only detached and unresponsive but often hostile and intrusive as well (Gelfand & Teti, 1991; Teti, Gelfand, Messinger, & Isabella, 1995). The presence of a nondepressed caregiver such as a father can, in part, mitigate the negative effects of maternal depression on infant's development (Hossain et al., 1994).

The beginnings of these different parenting styles and the different kinds of attachment they encourage can be seen even in the earliest months of life. Mothers who are inclined toward sensitive care tend to continually adjust their behavior to their baby's, so that the two are engaged in a kind of synchronous, smooth-flowing dance. Psychiatrist Daniel Stern (1977) has filmed and analyzed such mother-infant interactions, studying the components that create and maintain them. Part of the mother's role is to keep changing her behavior in order to elicit and hold the baby's attention. One technique is to use exaggerated speech. For example, the mother might begin to talk more slowly, using longer vowels: "Hi swee-eet-ee, Hiii, Hi-i-iya, Watcha looking at? Hu-u-uh? O-o-o-o-o-o, yeah, It's mommy ye-e-a-ah" (Stern, 1974, p. 192). In a similar technique, the mother may exaggerate facial expressions, forming them more slowly than normal, and holding them for a longer time. The baby contributes to the interaction largely by control of gaze. When the baby looks at the mother, she takes this as a signal to maintain stimulation or even increase

sensitive care Caregiving that is consistent and responsive and that begins by allowing an infant to play a role in determining when feeding will begin and end and at what pace it will proceed.

BOX 7-3

Perspectives on Diversity

Attachment Types in Different Cultures

Can Ainsworth's Strange Situation be used in cultures other than that of the United States to assess the character of children's relationships with their parents? For example, do *secure, avoidant,* and *resistant* mean the same things in Kenya that they mean in the United States? If mothers and fathers in Norway encourage their young children to develop independence earlier than U.S. parents, how may this affect the interpretation of "avoidant" behavior on a child's reunion with parental figures? A number of researchers have addressed these and other questions relating to the universality of Ainsworth's concepts and have found that although overall the attachment categories seem to have considerable applicability across cultural groups, important variations occur in the way infants of different racial-ethnic groups give expression to secure and insecure attachment relationships.

Another important question is the origin of particular attachment behaviors and relationships. According to Thompson (1998), parental solicitude is affected not only by personality factors and personal belief systems but also by such things as the availability of environmental resources and a parent's degree of freedom to care for a child rather than be stressed or exhausted by the effort to obtain the necessities for survival. On this view, all three major types of attachment can be seen as adaptive responses by infants to parental investment patterns. Thus, in assessing attachment behaviors among parents and children in the resource-poor environments that are found not only in developing countries but in areas within more developed nations, it is important to consider the many factors that may contribute to attachment behavior.

Secure Attachment Relationships
When babies are accustomed to almost constant contact with their mothers, they may react differently to reunion in the Strange Situation, either not seeking contact or failing to be comforted by it, and because behavior at reunion is the primary basis for determining attachment classifications, understanding cultural variations in caretaking is crucial. Secure attachments may be present even when

infants' behavior in the Strange Situation at first seems to indicate otherwise.

For example, the Ganda infants Ainsworth herself studied showed more distress in response to brief separations from their mothers than U.S. babies, but on investigation it was revealed that brief separations are infrequent in this African society: Ganda mothers leave their babies for hours at a time while they work in their gardens, and other relatives look after the children in their absence (Colin, 1996). Thus when they left their babies in the experimental situation, the infants expected a long absence and reacted accordingly.

Gusii infants' reactions to reunion in the Strange Situation also reflect specific cultural practices. Babies in this Kenya tribe are accustomed, until they are as old as 1 year, to being held half the day and, when their mothers are present, to being held by them. In the United States, however, most 1-year-olds are encouraged to play with toys, exercise their motor skills, and to nap alone. And whereas few U.S. parents bring their babies into their own beds, in many parts of the world it is quite common for infants to sleep with their parents. For example, babies in Japan usually sleep in the same bed with their mothers, and even after infancy parents don't hesitate to take a child into their bed when the youngster cries or asks to be fed (Colin, 1996).

Distinctive reactions to the Strange Situation are also found among ethnic groups within the United States. For example, European American mothers tend to stress active, exploratory behavior, personal development, and self-control in their infants, whereas Puerto Rican mothers are more likely to stress close contact, quietness, responsiveness, and respectfulness in their infants (Harwood, 1992). As a result, European American babies may appear to be avoidant in comparison with Puerto Rican infants.

Avoidant Attachment Relationships
In Germany and Sweden, evidence of avoidant relationships is seen more often than in the United States, reflecting the fact that parents in these countries tend to stress early independence somewhat more than American parents do (Colin, 1996). And according to Schaffer (1996), infants in Great Britain are also more likely to evidence avoidant rela-

interactive synchrony A term that characterizes mother-infant interactions in which the mother constantly adjusts her behavior to that of her baby, responding to and respecting his signals as to when he is ready for and wants engagement and interaction.

it. But when the child looks away, the mother stops her input and waits for the baby to signal that he or she is ready for more. In contrast, a mother who is insensitive to her baby's needs does not "read" her child's signals, such as direction of gaze. When the baby looks away, this mother might pursue the interaction by sticking her head in front of the baby's face and continuing stimulation that the baby is not ready for. Soon the baby starts to cry, and the interaction ends unhappily for both.

Some of the parent-infant pairs that fail to achieve early **interactive synchrony** also fail to develop a secure attachment in the baby's second half year of life. Maternal unresponsiveness to infant signals can play an important role in the emergence of an insecure attachment, just as a mother's sensitivity to her baby's needs can help promote secure attachment. This was shown in a longitudinal study

tionships than U.S. babies, though not as likely as German infants. These tendencies are seen even among babies showing secure attachment: For example, secure infants in the Netherlands use their mothers as a secure base while interacting with them across a distance, whereas in the United States secure-base behavior involves close physical contact both initially and on reunion (Colin, 1996).

In contrast, avoidant reactions are uncommon among Japanese babies, partly because children in Japan are socialized to maintain harmonious personal relationships; ignoring or turning away from someone would be considered rude (Colin, 1996). Moreover, in one Japanese study, on reunion, most mothers rushed to pick up their infants before the babies could give any sign that they wanted contact. Presumably these mothers hurried to alleviate the distress that they assumed their babies were experiencing.

Resistant Attachment Relationships

Japanese and Israeli babies seem more likely than American infants to show resistant behavior in both the baby alone episode of the Strange Situation and in the reunion phase. In the case of the Japanese infants, this may well be because they are in close contact with their mothers from the time they are born, including, as we've noted, sharing their parents' beds. For these infants the stress of separation seems much greater than it is for U.S. or European babies.

Babies born and living on Israeli kibbutzim probably show resistant attachment behavior in the Strange Situation for different reasons. Although an infant Israeli "kibbutznik" is usually raised by a hired caretaker (in Hebrew, a *metapelet*), this person is not always highly motivated to engage in infant care and, typically having responsibility for three children, may be unable to respond sensitively to each of them in optimal fashion (Sagi et al., 1995). The child customarily spends only a few hours with her parents, at supper time, and unless she sleeps in her parents' home, she may be watched over at night by a person who must monitor all the babies in the nursery building. As a result, "even secure attachments might be expected often to be tinged with resistance and/or preoccupation with the caregiver, who may often have been unavailable" (Colin, 1996, p. 155).

Can We Rely on the Strange Situation in Cross-Cultural Contexts?

In view of the foregoing findings, we may ask whether the Strange Situation as designed by Ainsworth is truly applicable to assessing attachment relationships in babies of other cultures. Given the cultural practices we've described that either neutralize the effects of separation or make it excessively threatening, it can be argued that this measurement device needs revision or replacement.

Does the fact that children from Germany and Sweden who may be well adjusted in terms of their upbringing nevertheless appear to have avoidant—and thus, by definition, insecure—attachment relationships vitiate the usefulness of the Strange Situation assessment device in those cultures? And what about the charge that the test situation is just too stressful for some infants, for example, Japanese and Israeli babies? With regard to the second issue, several researchers have argued that as long as the experimenter shortens separation episodes for babies who are highly distressed by the scenario, the procedure probably produces valid classifications across cultures. Even within the United States, it's common practice to eliminate the "baby alone" episode and to shorten separations if babies appear excessively distressed (Colin, 1996).

The newer, Attachment Q Sort (AQS) that we discuss in the text allows for more input by infants' caretakers into the assessment process, but even this device may be culture-bound by the nature of the questions it includes. Although Posada and colleagues (1995) found considerable overall cross-cultural consistency in their study of mothers' Q sorts in the countries of China, Colombia, Germany, Israel, Japan, Norway, and the United States, they also report that sociocultural similarity both within and across cultural groups was modest and that there is considerable diversity in the ways that children behave in separation situations. It may be that the issue of multicultural applicability of attachment assessment measures will remain unresolved until researchers undertake multiple naturalistic observations of infant-caregiver dyads in many cultures and social contexts (Colin, 1996; Posada et al., 1995).

in which infants and their mothers were observed in their homes at 1, 3, and 9 months of age in order to assess the mother's general responsiveness to the child (Isabella, 1993; Isabella & Belsky, 1991; Isabella, Belsky, & vonEye, 1989). Then at 12 months, the quality of the mother-infant attachment was assessed in the Strange Situation. Securely attached babies had more synchronous patterns of interaction with the mother (even at 1 and 3 months of age) than did insecurely attached babies. The mother-infant interactions of the insecurely attached children were more one-sided, unresponsive, or intrusive. Mothers of insecure-avoidant infants, for instance, were verbally intrusive. They continued to talk to the baby even when the child signaled a lack of readiness to tolerate more verbal stimulation. Mothers of insecure-resistant infants were generally unresponsive as well as underinvolved.

TABLE 7-7   Attachment in Children Raised in an Israeli Kibbutz[a]

Attachment Type	Children Who Spent the Night		Total Children
	In the Care Center	At Home	
Secure	6 (26)	15 (60)	21 (44)
Insecure-avoidant	0	0	0
Insecure-resistant	7 (30)	2 (8)	9 (19)
Insecure-disorganized	10 (44)	8 (32)	18 (37)

Source: Adapted from Sagi, van IJzendoorn, Aviezer, Donnell, & Mayseless, 1994.
[a]Figures in parentheses are percentages.

What can we learn about attachment from infant-parent interactions in other cultures? An interesting comparison can be drawn between U.S. parenting styles and those of Israeli parents, some of whom live with their families in a *kibbutz,* or communal village, and generally rear their infant children in group-care arrangements. In all *kibbutzim* (plural of *kibbutz*), babies stay in the infant care center during the day, and in some they stay in the center even at night, but in others they spend the night with their families. Sagi and his colleagues (Sagi, van IJzendoorn, Aviezer, Donnell, & Mayseless, 1994), using the kind of natural experimental design we discussed in Chapter 2, examined the effects of these contrasting childrearing arrangements on attachment relationships. Some of their results are summarized in Table 7-7, which shows that infants who slept at home with their families were more likely to develop secure attachments than babies who spent the night in the infant center. As you can see, among the children who spent the night at home, those in the secure and insecure-resistant attachment groups had proportions similar to those of the American groups that we've already mentioned. (Note that no infants were classified as having insecure-avoidant attachments. Babies reared in kibbutzim rarely exhibit such attachments, for kibbutzim caregivers rarely exhibit rejecting behavior or pressure children to act independently; see Sagi, 1990, and Colin, 1996). The differences observed between the sleep-at-home and sleep-at-the-kibbutz babies were not related to any other factors, for the researchers equated their young participants on such things as temperament, early life events, mother-infant interaction in play, quality of day-care environment, and maternal characteristics such as job satisfaction and anxiety about separation from children. The researchers suggest, therefore, that it may have been the mothers' greater opportunity to respond sensitively to their babies' needs during the evening and nighttime hours that increased the mothers' overall sensitivity to their infants (Colin, 1996).

Even more convincing evidence of the impact of maternal sensitivity on the attachment relationship comes from an experimental study in the United States by Anisfield, Casper, Nozyce, and Cunningham (1990). Lower-income inner-city mothers of newborns were divided into two groups: An experimental group received soft baby carriers, and a control group were given rigid carriers of the "car seat" type. The researchers predicted that the soft infant carriers would increase physical contact between infants and mothers and facilitate the development of maternal responsiveness; in fact, the mothers given the soft carriers were indeed more responsive to their infants' vocalizations at 3½ months. Moreover, attachment measured at 13 months was affected as well: 83 percent of the babies in the experimental group were securely attached to their mothers, whereas only 39 percent of the control group babies were securely attached to their mothers.

Of course, relationships between parents and infants do not develop in a vacuum. They are affected by and affect other relationships among family members, as well as relationships outside the home. For example, there is a link between marital adjustment and infant-parent attachment: Secure attachment is more likely when marital adjustment is good (e.g., Goldberg & Easterbrooks, 1984; Howes &

Markman, 1989; Thompson, 1998). Although the birth of a child is generally associated with a decline in marital satisfaction (Cowan & Cowan, 1992), mothers whose infants become securely attached usually report less dissatisfaction with their marriages than mothers whose children are insecurely attached (Belsky & Isabella, 1988). As you will see when we discuss the family, in Chapter 12, marital and parent-child relationships are often closely connected.

Is There Intergenerational Continuity in Attachment?

The kind of care that parents received when they were infants is another influence on the quality of attachment that develops between them and their own children (Bretherton, Ridgeway, & Cassidy, 1990). From our mothers and fathers, we all acquire what Bowlby (1973) calls **internal working models** of the self and parents. According to Bowlby, these models are mental representations about oneself, one's own parents, and the styles of interaction that one experienced as a child. Note that it is not the actual experience of the parent when she was an infant that forms this model but rather how she reconstructs or interprets these early experiences. Because of these internal working models, people tend to re-create their own childhood relationships when they themselves become mothers or fathers. As Bowlby (1973) describes the process,

> Because children tend unwittingly to identify with parents and therefore to adopt, when they become parents, the same patterns of behavior toward children that they themselves have experienced during their own childhood, patterns of interaction are transmitted, more or less faithfully, from one generation to another. (p. 323)

To investigate this notion of intergenerational continuity, Main, Kaplan, and Cassidy (1985) interviewed 40 middle-class mothers about recollections of their own relationships with their mothers during infancy and childhood. Supporting Bowlby's theory, the mothers' patterns of memories did relate to the quality of their current attachment relationships with their own infants. As Table 7-8 shows, Main classified the women into three groups: autonomous, dismissing, and preoccupied. The *autonomous* group, who had developed secure attachment relationships with their infants, revealed in their interviews that although they valued close relationships with their parents and others, they were at the same time objective. They tended not to idealize their own parents but had a clear understanding of their relationships with them and were able to describe both their positive and negative aspects even if the relationship was strong enough to overcome any weaknesses. The *dismissing* group, who had avoidant attachment relationships with their babies, had a different set of memories; they dismissed and devalued attachment and frequently claimed that they

internal working model
According to Bowlby, a person's mental representation of himself as a child, his parents, and the nature of his interaction with his parents, as he reconstructs and interprets that interaction.

TABLE 7-8   Relations between Mothers' and Children's Attachment Status

Attachment Category		Mother-Child Relationship
Mother	Child	
Autonomous	Secure	Mother's mind not taken up with unresolved concerns about her own experience; mother thus able to be sensitive to child's communications
Dismissing	Insecure-Aviodant	Mother reluctant to acknowledge her own attachment needs and thus insensitive and unresponsive to child's needs
Preoccupied	Insecure-Resistant	Mother confused about her attachment history and thus inconsistent in her interactions with her child

Source: Main, Kaplan, & Cassidy, 1985; Schaffer, 1996.

couldn't recall incidents from their childhood. On the other hand, the recollections they did report were often of idealized parents: "I had the world's greatest mom!" The third, *preoccupied* group were the parents of resistant infants. Preoccupied with earlier family attachments, these mothers recalled many conflict-ridden incidents from childhood but couldn't organize them into coherent patterns.

Studies with fathers have yielded similar results (Crowell & Treboux, 1995; van IJzendoorn, 1995). For example, in a longitudinal study, German researchers found that fathers' recollections of their own relationships with their parents during childhood were indeed linked to their relationship with their own children (Grossman & Fremmer-Bombik, 1994). Fathers who viewed their own attachment relationships with their parents as secure were more likely to develop a secure attachment relationship with their own infants, more likely to be present at their children's birth, more likely to participate in infant care, and more likely to be supportive of their wives than men with insecure attachment histories. Moreover, fathers who remembered their childhood attachment experiences, including both positive and negative feelings, and who were open and nondefensive about their recollections, continued to be better fathers as their children developed. They were better play partners to their toddlers and continued to be engaging and tender. They were more sensitive guides in teaching their 6-year-olds, and when their children were 10 years old these men were more accepting of the child's daily concerns and problems. Not all studies of fathers have supported the Bowlby view, however. In one study in the Netherlands, the predictive value of fathers' recollections was less clear than that of mothers, in part because fathers are less active caregivers than mothers (van IJzendoorn & Bakermans-Kranenburg, 1996).

Additional support for intergenerational continuity comes from studies of other racial-ethnic groups and of parents in other countries. When Levine, Tuber, Slade, and Ward (1991) studied a group of largely African American and Hispanic teen mothers, they found these mothers' attachment interview classifications to be reliable predictors of the attachment classification assigned to their relationships with their infants. And in Germany, Klaus and Karin Grossman (1991) found strong links between adult recollections and their attachment relationships with their infants. The validity of the adult attachment interview has been established for parents in the Netherlands and Israel as well (van IJzendoorn, 1995).

Perhaps the most convincing evidence of intergenerational continuity comes from Fonagy, Steele, and Steele (1991), who interviewed pregnant women about their attachment history and then measured infant-mother attachment when these women's babies were 1 year of age. This research design enabled the investigators to rule out the possibility that a parent's current experience with her baby was shaping her memories of her own childhood. Once again, these researchers found strong support for the relations between parental recollections of their own childhood family relationships and the attachment relationship between them and their children.

The Effect of Infant Temperament

As you learned in Chapter 4, some babies are more difficult to interact with and care for than others. Might this affect the quality of attachments that these infants develop? Although the development of attachment is a process of mutual influence, most researchers have neglected the infant's contribution. Some investigators, however, have found a link between certain temperament characteristics in infants and the kinds of relationships they develop with their parents. For instance, newborns who have difficulties orienting to people and to objects may be more apt to develop insecure attachments (Spangler & Grossman, 1993; Waters, Vaughn, & Egeland, 1980). Perhaps these early difficulties reflect underlying problems in adaptive mechanisms that continue to influence a child's behavior and interactions with others as it matures. We must be cautious in drawing such conclusions, however, because many

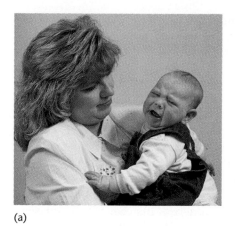

(a)

(b)

Some babies are fussy and difficult no matter how lovingly parents care for them (a), and others are easy-going, right from the start (b).

other researchers have failed to find clear links between early infant temperament and later infant-parent attachment (Bates, 1987; Colin, 1996; Vaughn et al., 1992).

If infant temperament does have some influence on the development of attachment, that influence is probably mediated by many other factors. A "difficult" infant certainly isn't destined to have a poor relationship with his parents. For example, one study found that infants who were judged distress prone were more likely to develop insecure-avoidant or insecure-ambivalent attachment relationships but only when their mothers were highly controlling (Mangelsdorf, Gunnar, Kestenbaum, Lang, & Andreas, 1990). Simply being a distress-prone infant did not predict anxious attachment. Parents who have a difficult or irritable baby can usually cope successfully if they receive help and support from other family members and friends. With adequate social support for the mother, an irritable baby is no more likely to become insecurely attached than a nonirritable one (Crockenberg, 1981). If a mother is socially isolated or has poor relationships with other adults, however, she is more likely to have problems fostering secure attachment in a difficult infant (Levitt, Weber, & Clark, 1986). Thus, the effect of temperament on attachment cannot be separated from the influence of the total social context in which the baby is developing (Bronfenbrenner, 1989; Sroufe, 1996).

Stability in the Quality of Attachment

There is substantial stability in the quality of attachment from one period of time to another. As you saw earlier in the chapter, among infants tested with their mothers in the Strange Situation, the same attachment patterns were detected both at 12 months and at 6 years of age (Main & Cassidy, 1988). Although attachment behavior in these children at different points in time didn't correlate perfectly—for example, 100 percent of the children rated securely attached at 12 months were rated similarly at 6 years of age, but only 66 percent of the children rated insecure-disorganized at 12 months were rated similarly at 6 years of age—the overall findings supported the notion that attachment behavior is highly stable. Lending cross-cultural support to this idea is a German study that found that first-year attachment classifications predicted 78 percent of sixth-year classifications (Wartner, Grossman, Fremmer-Bombik, & Suess, 1994).

But general stability in the quality of parent-child relationships doesn't mean that change is impossible. In the studies just mentioned, substantial minorities of children with insecure attachments as infants did manage to develop better relationships with their parents by school age. This is particularly likely to happen when a child's parents begin to experience less stress in their lives (fewer financial worries, for instance, or less marital tension) and so are able to become more available to their child and to interact in ways that are more responsive to the child's needs (Thompson, Lamb, & Estes, 1982). Alternatively, secure infant-parent attachment relationships can become insecure if the life circumstances of the family deteriorate due to job loss, divorce, or residential mobility (Sroufe, 1996; Thompson, 1998).

Professional intervention can help improve a troubled parent-child relationship. One group of insecurely attached infants whose mothers underwent infant-parent psychotherapy for a year developed more secure attachments than a control group of babies whose mothers received no intervention (Lieberman, Weston, & Paul, 1991). In a study in the Netherlands, mothers who were taught to be more sensitive with their infants developed better attachment relationships with them than did the mothers of a control group of infants, even though the experimental group babies were classified as irritable at birth (van den Boom, 1990). Whereas 68 percent of the experimental group were classified as securely attached at 12 months of age, only 28 percent of the control group were securely attached. Instead, 58 percent were insecure-avoidant and 16 percent were insecure-resistant. Clearly, attachment relationships continue to develop and are responsive to changes in the behavior of both parent and child (Sroufe, 1996; Thompson, 1998).

The Consequences of Attachment Quality

Does the quality of early infant-parent attachments have serious implications for the child's later development? As you will see in this section, early interactions with attachment figures do indeed seem to shape children's continuing development, particularly their development of cognitive and social skills and a sense of self.

Cognitive Development

An early secure attachment appears to be related to more complex exploratory behavior at 2 years of age (Main, 1973). Moreover, as the child continues to develop, this intellectual curiosity is reflected in an intensified interest in and enjoyment of solving problems. This positive approach to problem solving is seldom seen in toddlers who were insecurely attached as infants (Matas, Arend, & Sroufe, 1978; Sroufe, 1983).

Matas and colleagues (1978) found, for example, that securely attached 2-year-olds were more enthusiastic, persistent, cooperative and effective in solving problems than their insecurely attached peers. The former group showed less frustration, less negative affect, less crying and whining, and less aggression toward their mothers. In addition, the securely attached toddlers engaged in more symbolic or pretend play; for example, transforming a block of wood into an imaginary car or a stick into a witch's broom. Slade (1987) also found that 20- to 28-month-old children who were securely attached engaged in more high-level symbolic play than insecurely attached peers. Cognitive development does seem to be facilitated by the kind of mother-infant relationship that is characteristic of a secure infant-mother attachment. In the Slade study, the secure children showed higher-level symbolic play and longer episodes of play when mothers participated in their children's play than when the children played by themselves. In contrast, the insecure children were not able to benefit from their mothers' involvement.

In a longitudinal study in Reykjavik, Iceland, Jacobsen and Hofmann (1997) found that children who at age 7 appeared securely attached, based on their responses to a story about separation, were likely to be more attentive and participative in the classroom at the ages of 9, 12, and 15; to be more secure in their sense of self at these ages; and to maintain higher grade point averages than children judged avoidant, ambivalent, or disorganized in their attachment. Bus and van IJzendoorn (1988) found that during a task in which they asked Dutch mothers to encourage their children in reading, thus promoting their literacy skills, securely attached children were less distractible, paid more attention to the instruction, and required less discipline than insecurely attached children. In turn, the secure children received higher scores on such measures of emerging literacy as letter and word recognition. These studies not only underscore the link between the quality of the parent-child relationship and cognitive development but also point out that the success of adult experts in facilitating children's learning, as proposed by Vygotsky, may at least in part depend on the quality of the attachment relationship. (We introduced Vygotsky's theory and approach in Chapter 1 and will revisit this theory in more detail in Chapter 9.) Finally, it's not only mothers' and fathers' relationships with their child that are important to the child's cognitive development but the child's relations with other significant caregivers as well. A cross-national study in the Netherlands and Israel examined families of employed parents who employed a third primary caregiver for child care (van IJzendoorn, Sagi, & Lambermon, 1992). The quality of the whole attachment network (mother, father, others) in infancy predicted the children's scores on a test of intelligence scores when they were 5 years old; the greater the attachment security, the higher was the test score.

Social Development

A number of studies provide impressive support for the importance of the quality of caregiver-infant relationships for later social development. Studying children from 1 to 3½ years old, Sroufe (1983) found that securely and insecurely attached youngsters developed very different social and emotional patterns. Teachers rated securely attached children as showing more positive emotions and as having greater empathy for others and more ability to initiate, respond to, and sustain interactions with other people. Securely attached children also whined less, were less aggressive, and displayed fewer negative reactions when other children approached them. Not surprisingly, their teachers rated them more socially competent and socially skilled and as having more friends than other children, and their classmates considered them more popular than others (Erickson, Sroufe, & Egeland, 1985; Kestenbaum, Farber, & Sroufe, 1989; Suess, 1987).

A follow-up study at age 11 of the children Sroufe studied suggests that the effects of attachment are not limited to the preschool years (Elicker, Englund, & Sroufe, 1992; Sroufe, Carlson, & Shulman, 1993). Counselors at a summer day camp the children attended rated children with secure attachment histories as having more social competence, self-esteem, and self-confidence and as tending to depend less on adults. The children with secure attachments spent more time with peers and less time alone or with adults. Moreover, these children were more likely to form close friendships than their anxiously attached peers. Attachment history also predicted friendship choices: Children with secure attachment histories were more likely to form friendships with other securely attached peers. Others have found similar links between the quality of early attachment and later school-age peer competence (Cohn, 1990; Erickson et al., 1985; Grossman & Grossman, 1991; Howes & Rodning, 1992) and friendship patterns (Kerns, 1994).

Just as Bowlby argued, the links between attachment and social outcomes are forged by children's internal working models. Cassidy, Kirsch, Scolton, and Parke (1996) found that insecurely attached 5-year-olds are more likely to interpret a neutral event (e.g., being bumped by another child while waiting at the bus stop) as done with harmful intent than children with secure attachments, who tend to interpret such events as accidental. In a similar vein, Lyons-Ruth, Easterbrooks, and Cibelli (1997) found that infants who were judged securely attached at the age of 18 months tended, at age 7, to function well interpersonally in the school setting. Those whose early attachment appeared avoidant, on the other hand, were likely to develop *internalizing* tendencies, such as depression and self-criticism, whereas those who were disorganized in their early attachments were likely to develop *externalizing* tendencies, such as hostile and aggressive behaviors. When internalizing and externalizing tendencies are exaggerated they can lead to serious behavioral problems. These studies illustrate the interplay among attachment, cognitive understanding, and children's social outcomes.

In trying to understand children's later social behavior, it is also important to consider both infant-mother and infant-father attachment relationships. Even very young children often develop distinctly different relationships with each parent. In a study of 1-year-old infants, Main and Weston (1981) classified babies according to whether they were securely attached to both parents, to their mothers but not their fathers, to their fathers but not their mothers, or to neither parent. To determine whether the infants' relationships with their mothers and fathers affected their social responsiveness to other people, Main and Weston then observed the infants' reactions to a friendly clown. The infants who were securely attached to both parents were more responsive to the clown than those who were securely attached to only one parent and insecurely attached to the other, and the babies who were insecurely attached to both parents were the least sociable of all with the clown. These results suggest that a less-than-optimal relationship with one parent can be compensated for by a better relationship with the other parent and that therefore it is not enough to study just mothers or fathers alone. Viewing the parents as part of a family system is the best way to understand their role in child development.

Parents' recollections of their own attachment relationships often combine with such current factors as marital quality and parenting competence to affect the course of their children's development. In a recent study, Cowan, Cohn, Cowan, and Pearson (1996) explored the links between parents' remembered attachment histories and children's social development through preschool and kindergarten. Although fathers' and mothers' own attachment memories were important, an even better understanding of children's behavior in kindergarten emerged when contemporary family relationships were considered as well. For example, fathers with poor attachment histories tended to be in marriages characterized by a great deal of conflict and little satisfaction and to be ineffective parents. They displayed little warmth or responsiveness to their children, and, in completing a task with their children, they failed to communicate adequately or to provide their children with the structure needed to complete the task.

Another finding of this study was that fathers' and mothers' contributions are both important to understanding children's developing behavior and that each makes *unique* contributions to children's social developmental outcomes. In fathers, the three factors of attachment history, current marital relationship, and parenting competence predicted certain behaviors better than these indices in mothers did, and in mothers the same indices predicted other behaviors better than they did in fathers. Two general types of behavior were assessed: Children rated high on externalizing behavior tended often to be off-task, to be unable to sit still, to break rules, to be uncooperative, and to argue, lie, and get into fights; those rated high on internalizing behaviors tended to be judged shy, sad, or nervous or high-strung, as making friends with difficulty, and as preferring solitary activities. Scores for fathers with poor attachment histories, little parenting competence, and marital problems were more predictive of children's externalizing behavior, whereas low scores on these three variables for mothers were more predictive of children's internalizing behavior. Among other things, these findings may reflect the fact that aggressive, externalizing behavior is more likely to define men's personality and roles, whereas internalizing, self-blaming, nonaggressive styles are more characteristic of women. When one parent has the poorer ratings on the three factors of attachment history, marital quality, and parental competence, the parent's gender may determine the effect of these variables on a child's social development.

In summary, a healthy attachment to parents facilitates exploration, curiosity, and mastery of the social and physical environment. Early attachment also increases the child's trust in other social relationships and permits the later development of mature affectional relationships with peers. Longitudinal studies aimed at specifying the links between early parent-infant interaction and later relation-ships in adolescence and adulthood will give us more information about the long-term stability of these positive cognitive and social effects of an early secure attachment. Clearly, developmental history leaves its mark (Sroufe, 1983).

The Sense of Self

The *sense of self,* or the awareness of the self as differentiated from other people, is crucial to the child's development. As this awareness evolves it becomes increas-ingly complicated, incorporating notions like that of the self-concept, self-esteem, self-confidence, and self-respect, all of which partake of cognitive and social as well as emotional factors. Because this growing complexity relies to a considerable extent on advances in cognitive functioning, we will take up the concept of the self again in Chapters 9 and 10 where we consider the child's cognitive development. Our discussions of the self will continue again in Chapters 12 through 16, where our emphasis will often be on the social aspects of the self. Keep in mind, however, that cognitive, social, and emotional factors will play a role in all these discussions, for they overlap in any consideration of the self and its interactions with others.

When do children begin to recognize themselves as different from other people? How does the complex network of feelings and cognitions associated with a per-son's sense of personal identity evolve? Babies as young as 18 weeks of age happily gaze at their reflections in a mirror, but not until they are well past 1 year old do they realize that they are looking at a reflection of themselves. A classic method of examining self-identity in the child has been to allow the child to look into a mir-ror for a bit and then to put a spot of rouge on the child's nose and return her to the mirror (Amsterdam, 1972; Brooks-Gunn & Lewis, 1984; Bullock & Lutkenhaus, 1990; Lewis, 1991). We assume that if the child recognizes that the mirror reflection is of herself, she will be likely to touch her nose. Children under 1 year of age seem to believe that the reflection is another child and sometimes touch it or try to look behind the mirror for the other child, but they don't try to touch their noses (Brooks-Gunn & Lewis, 1984). It is sometime during the second year of life that children begin to recognize their own images, and by the time they are 2 almost all children give evidence of self-recognition, giggling, showing embarrassment, or acting silly at the sight of their rouged noses (Figure 7-8). On average, children are 20 months old before they fairly consistently locate or touch the rouge on their noses. Later, they learn to use self-referent terms such as *I* and *me* and to distin-guish themselves by their age and gender. Table 7-9 presents the stages in the devel-opment of self-awareness in the first 2 years of life.

Although some investigators feel that the mirror exercise is not the definitive test of self-recognition (Hauser, et al., 1995), the method has been used widely and has been adapted by psychologists and others studying the cognitive abilities of infrahuman primates (mostly apes), particularly their ability to learn language. Interestingly, even a type of tamarin monkey has apparently shown itself able to recognize that the creature with paint on its fur that it sees in a mirror is indeed a reflection of itself (Hauser, et al., 1995). But although chimpanzees and bonobos have shown impressive abilities in communicating by means of American Sign Language and computerized programs, the answer to the question of whether apes possess true cognition remains elusive. In any event, the human child and the ape irrevocably part company in this and other areas of achievement when the child begins to verbalize its experience and to speak.

Is it possible that the sense of self develops in human children even earlier than 20 months? Some researchers have suggested that infants as young as 3 months may have some sense of self-awareness (e.g., Case, 1991; Schaffer, 1996), and others have even suggested that a sense of self develops prenatally, citing the behavior of some infrahuman creatures that make clear distinctions between themselves and others (Angier, 1997); still others (e.g., Porges, 1995), however, point out that a

■ **FIGURE 7-8**
Recognizing one's own nose. When experimenters dabbed rouge on their noses, children of different ages in two separate studies showed quite similar behavior. Those less than a year old didn't recognize themselves in the mirror, but by the time they were 2, most children realized images of children with rouge on their noses were images of themselves. (*Source:* Schaffer, 1996; Lewis & Brooks-Wunn, 1979)

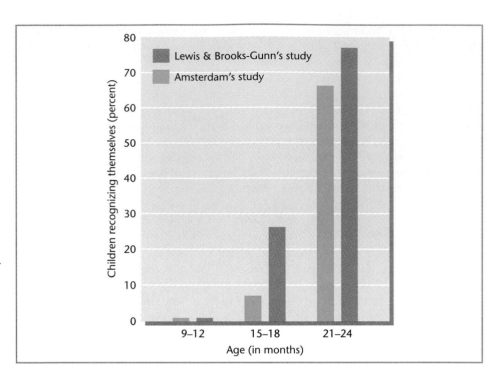

considerable difference exists between survival-adapted tendencies to look out for oneself and a real consciousness of that choice or of one's relationship to others.

However these complicated questions may be answered, we do have some evidence that the quality of the child-parent attachment relationship affects the child's developing self-concept. Pipp, Easterbrooks, and Harmon (1992) examined the links between security of attachment, on the one hand, and children's self-knowledge and knowledge about their mothers. Although there were no differences in self-knowledge (ability to recognize oneself and awareness of one's own gender and name) between securely and insecurely attached 12-month-olds, securely attached children who were 2 and 3 years old showed greater self-knowledge than their less securely attached peers. Moreover, securely attached children were more aware of their mothers' characteristics than were insecure children. Awareness of both self *and* others is clearly linked to attachment history. Moreover, the value that one places on the self varies with the quality of attachment as well. In one study, Cassidy (1988) assessed the attachment relationships of 6-year-olds and then, by having each child participate in a conversation with him as they both manipulated two puppets, attempted to determine the nature of the children's self-concepts. As the experimenters and the children spoke for Bix the frog and Quax the duck, the researcher asked questions designed to find out how the children thought others viewed them. For example, the researcher, as Quax, might ask a child named Misha, operating the Bix puppet, such questions as, "Bix, do you like Misha?" "Do you like Misha the way he is or do you want to make him better?" "Tell me, Bix, do you want Misha to be your friend?"

Children who were securely attached tended to make Bix answer in a positive way about themselves, although they were able to acknowledge their less than perfect qualities. In contrast, insecure-avoidant children tended to present themselves as perfect, while insecure-ambivalent children showed no clear pattern of responses. A group of children classified as insecure-controlling (similar to the disorganized classification discussed earlier) had the puppet make excessively negative comments about themselves. These results strongly suggest that the quality of early attachment is related to the degree to which children view themselves positively and realistically; both of these capacities are important aspects of social adjustment.

TABLE 7-9	The Early Stages of Self-Awareness

Age in Months	Behavioral Indications
0–3	Infant shows interest in social objects but does not distinguish between self and other.
3–8	Child's first signs of self-recognition, based on *contingency clues* (fact that mirror image moves in tandem with child's movements), are tentative and unreliable.
8–12	Notion of self permanence emerges. Child reliably recognizes self based on contingency clues, begins to use *feature clues* (child's own physical features as seen in video or photograph).
12–24	Basic self categories, such as age and gender, are consolidated. Child reliably recognizes self based on feature clues.

Source: Schaffer, 1996.

Multiple Caregivers and Attachment: The Effects of Day Care

The 1994 U.S. Census revealed that more than 20 million American children under the age of 13 had mothers who worked outside the home, and three years later the Children's Defense Fund reported that some 7.7 million children *under the age of 5* were being cared for by someone other than their parents (Children's Defense Fund, 1997). Although many children of working mothers are cared for entirely by their parents, siblings, and other relatives, as many as 59 percent spend many hours a week in some form of day care—that is, care provided by one or more nonfamily members in the child's own home, in the caregiver's home, or in an organized child-care facility (see Figure 7-9) (Children's Defense Fund, 1997).

As we have seen in our discussion of infant-parent attachment, according to John Bowlby, having not only parents but a number of other caregivers share in caring for an infant may impair the quality of infant attachment. This proposition has been central to the controversy surrounding the advantages and disadvantages of day care for the infant's and young child's social development. There is no evidence that being in day care actually prevents the formation of an attachment between infants and their parents. Children who spend time in day care form close relationships with their mother and father, just as children raised at home do (Lamb, 1998). However, some evidence suggests that the amount of time children spend in day care does affect the nature of child-parent relationships (National Institute of Child Health and Human Development Early Child Care Network, 1997). In an extensive study of 1,300 families in 14 different locations in the United States, researchers found that the more time their children spent in day care, the less sensitive mothers were toward their infants at 6 months of age, at 15 months, and at 3 years of age. The study also found that children were less affectionate toward their mothers at 2 and 3 years of age. These associations, however, were relatively weak.

Some earlier studies have suggested that infants who are in day care because their mothers are employed full time—especially babies who begin full-time day care before they're 1 year old—are more likely to be classified as insecurely attached than infants of nonemployed or part-time working mothers (Barglow, Vaughn, & Molitor, 1987; Belsky & Cassidy, 1994; Belsky & Rovine, 1988). Again, however, the correlations were not strong. Moreover, in a review of day-care studies, Clarke-Stewart (1989) found that although on average 36 percent of the infants of full-time working mothers become insecurely attached, 29 percent of the infants of nonemployed or part-time working mothers also develop insecure attachments.

■ **FIGURE 7-9**

Who is caring for our preschoolers?
In 1994, nearly half of all preschoolers whose mothers worked outside the home were cared for by their parents or other relatives. An almost 50 percent increase over the numbers of children cared for by relatives in 1993, this represents primarily families' inability to meet the costs of commercial child care. *Source:* Children's Defense Fund, 1998.

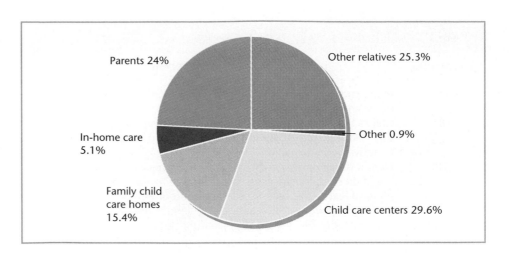

How might we explain why roughly a third of the babies of working mothers, regardless of whether they are in day care or are cared for at home, develop insecure attachments? It is of course possible that day-care babies are somewhat more apt to develop an insecure attachment because their mothers are less available to them or because they interpret her absence as rejection (Barglow et al., 1987; Belsky & Rovine, 1988). However, other explanations are also possible (Clarke-Stewart, 1989, 1993; Hayes, Palmer, & Zazlow, 1990; Lamb, 1998). For instance, it may be that mothers who dislike caring for a baby (and who thus tend to be less sensitive caregivers) are more inclined than other mothers to take full-time jobs. Or it is possible that the stress associated with handling both a baby and work interferes with a working mother's ability to promote secure attachment. These alternative explanations suggest that day care itself may not exert an influence on attachment but rather that something associated with a parent's use of day-care facilities, such as holding a full-time job, may reduce parental effectiveness at being a consistently sensitive and responsive caregiver. As Clarke-Stewart (1989) puts it, it may not be that "40 hours of day care is hard on infants but that 40 hours of work is hard on mothers" (p. 270).

Thus, even with the latest findings on day care and child-parent relationships, it seems unlikely that day care alone is responsible for a lesser degree of security in these relationships. What's more, good day-care providers can sometimes compensate for less than optimal care from parents by giving children an opportunity to form secure attachments outside the home (Howes & Hamilton, 1992; Howes, Hamilton, & Matheson, 1994; Howes, Rodning, Galluzo, & Myers, 1988). Research shows that children with an insecure attachment to their mothers but a secure attachment to a day-care provider tend to be more socially competent than insecurely attached children who have not formed such a strong compensatory relationship outside the family. Interestingly, this positive effect of day care is not restricted to American children; similar findings have been recorded in the Netherlands (Goosens & van IJzendoorn, 1990) and in Israel (Oppenheim, Sagi, & Lamb, 1988).

Stability of staff may be an important determinant of the quality of relationship that emerges between care providers and children in day care. Barnas and Cummings (1994) found that 21-month-old toddlers more frequently sought out caregivers who had been on staff for longer periods of time and who were rarely absent and could thus be relied upon to be there for them. When the children were distressed, these familiar figures were able to soothe them more effectively than were caregivers whose employment records were unstable. Clearly, minimizing turnover of staff is important to provide a stable, predictable environment for child care (Lamb, 1998). It has also been found that a training program aimed at improving the quality of care provided by family day-care providers can have real impact

These infants and toddlers may learn important social and cognitive skills in this multicultural daycare facility. Especially in small centers with favorable staff-child ratios, age-appropriate activities, and responsive caregiving, day care can be a positive and enriching experience for young children.

on the attachment relationships developed between children and nonparental care-givers (Galinsky, Howes, & Kontos, 1995).

It has been found that the higher the level of teacher training staff members have, the more likely are children to develop secure attachment relationships with their caregivers (Howes, Smith, & Galinsky, 1995), and there are other important benefits of such training. Children in high-quality programs are less likely to engage in delinquent and other antisocial behavior as they grow up, and they are less likely to need special education later on or to be retained in a grade (Children's Defense Fund, 1997). Kindergarten teachers have estimated that one in three children enters the classroom unprepared to meet its challenges (Children's Defense Fund, 1997), and inadequate day care for preschoolers may be among the factors responsible for this finding. Another difficulty is that good day care is far more accessible to the affluent than to low-income families (Figure 7-10). This problem may worsen as a result of the 1996 federal welfare law that replaced Aid to Families with Dependent Children (AFDC) with a new program called Temporary Assistance for Needy Families (TANF). The new program requires parents of all but the very youngest children to work and thus will increase the demand for day-care facilities (Children's Defense Fund, 1997). Some states have taken action to fund additional assistance for children. Partnerships among the state, the business community, and parents like those provided for by Florida's Child Care Partnership Act and the Early Childhood Initiative undertaken in Pennsylvania's Allegheny County look promising. Other states, however, have elected less far-sighted programs—for example, licensing child-care providers who lack even a high school diploma or a GED (Children's Defense Fund, 1997).

The large-scale Childcare Consortium Study (1997) research cited earlier found that good-quality day care tended to enhance children's language abilities and cognitive skills, and other studies have found that infants with day-care experience adapt more quickly and explore more in an unfamiliar setting (Belsky, Steinberg, & Walker, 1983; Clarke-Stewart, 1987, 1993). These children play more with peers and are more socially competent, and they exhibit more self-confidence and are less fearful of unfamiliar adults, especially when they have a secure infant-care provider relationship (Howes & Hamilton, 1993; Howes et al., 1994). It's true that day-care children are often reported to be more aggressive and less compliant than their home-reared peers, but their rates of aggression and noncompliance are within normal ranges and do not indicate that day-care children are, in any sense, socially maladjusted (Lamb, 1998; Scarr, Phillips, & McCartney, 1990).

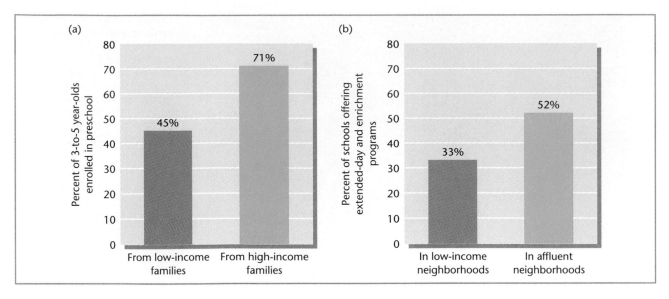

■ FIGURE 7-10
Are child care and
enrichment programs only for
the affluent?
(a) Children from high-income
families are more likely to be
enrolled in preschool than
children from low-income
families, and (b) they are also
more likely to have access to
enrichment and before- and
after-school programs. (*Source:*
Children's Defense Fund, 1997)

Of course, the quality of day care is an important factor in the impact this experience has on children (Lamb, 1998; Phillips, 1991). Optimal social development, as measured by better relationships with teachers and peers, is more likely to be observed in high-quality day care centers, where there are smaller groups, lower staff-to-child ratios, more interaction between staff and children, better caregiver training, more space, and better equipment than in poor-quality centers (Howes, Phillips, & Whitebook, 1992). Moreover, the effects of day-care quality seem to continue even after children reach school age. In one study, high-quality preschool day care was related to less child hostility and better orientation to tasks in kindergarten. Poor quality day care, however, coupled with early entry into day care (before the age of 1) was related to a higher level of destructiveness in kindergarten and less consideration for others (Howes, 1988a, 1988b). In another study, even four years after being enrolled in high-quality day care, children were rated friendlier, more inclined toward positive emotions, more competent, and better at resolving conflicts (Vandell, Henderson, & Wilson, 1988). There seems to be no question that the quality of early day care is associated with children's later social and emotional development.

SUMMARY

■ Through emotional expression infants not only communicate their feelings, needs, and wishes to others but even succeed in regulating other people's behavior.

Early Emotional Development

■ Babies begin expressing their **emotions** quite early in life. Startle, disgust, and distress are among the first true emotions to appear. Next to emerge is the social smile, in which true pleasure is expressed, and this is followed soon thereafter by delight, anger, joy, and surprise. Fear arrives a bit later, and still later come complex emotions like pride and guilt. In general, emotions become more differentiated from one another over time and are more tied to specific situations.

- In infancy, boys are more emotionally expressive than girls, but in a developmental shift caused perhaps by socialization efforts of parents and other caregivers, girls soon begin to express more emotions and boys to restrict emotional expression.
- A major challenge for infants is to learn how to regulate their own emotions, to modify or control them when desirable or needed. By the preschool years, children have generally learned to restrain their emotional expression somewhat. They also begin to follow **emotional display rules,** which dictate what emotions to show under what circumstances.
- Another challenge that infants confront within the first half year of life is that of learning to recognize emotional expressions in others. In general, children are more proficient at producing than at recognizing emotions, but the two abilities are positively related: Children who are skilled at one are typically skilled at the other.

The Beginnings of Specific Emotions

- Smiling in infants follows a general developmental pattern, beginning with the newborn's **reflex smiles,** which depend on the child's internal state. Next, at 3 to 8 weeks of age, come smiles elicited by external events, including social stimuli such as faces and voices. By 12 weeks, infants begin to smile selectively at familiar faces and voices, and their smiles differ depending on the situation. By 4 months, infants begin to laugh, and the number and kinds of events that elicit laughter change with their development. Both laughter and smiling may play a critical role in maintaining the proximity of the caregiver to the baby.
- Although not all infants develop **stranger distress** in their second half year, when they do, the fear emerges gradually. Many factors determine how an infant will react to a particular stranger. Babies tend to be less fearful in a familiar setting and when they feel as if they have some control over the situation. **Social referencing** helps them interpret emotional cues in other people so as to know how to behave in a new situation. They also are less fearful of unfamiliar children than of unfamiliar adults, and they are less likely to be afraid of friendly, outgoing strangers.
- Various explanations for the development of smiling, laughter, and fear of strangers have been offered, including genetic-maturational, learning, and cognitive perspectives. Each of these perspectives may be useful some of the time, depending on the developmental level of the child and the type of emotional reaction being considered. In some cases the appearance of a phenomenon across a range of cultures lends some support to a particular view; for example, the common experience of **separation protest** may suggest the contribution of inherited factors.

How Children Think about Emotions

- As children mature they develop an understanding of the meanings of emotion terms and of the situations that trigger particular feelings; each **emotional script** within this collection helps the child identify the feeling that typically accompanies a given situation. They also learn that they can experience more than one emotion at a time and that two or more such emotions may conflict, and they begin to consider the desires of others in judging emotions that others will experience in particular contexts.
- Learning to differentiate and integrate multiple factors in a situation helps children to understand more complex emotions like pride, guilt, and shame, as do both the ability to understand causal sequences and specific experience in discussing feelings with caretakers and others.

The Development of Attachment

- During the second half of the first year, infants begin to discriminate between familiar and unfamiliar caregivers, and to form **attachments** to the important people in their lives. According to the **psychoanalytic** view, the basis for the mother-infant attachment is oral gratification. The **learning** view stresses the role the mother plays as a **secondary reinforcer.** The **ethological** view stresses the role of instinctual infant responses that elicit the parent's care and protection. According to the **cognitive developmental view,** the infant must be able to differentiate his mother from a stranger and must be aware that his mother continues to exist even when he cannot see her.
- Attachment emerges over the first 6 to 8 months in a consistent series of steps. The first step, which seems to be innate in newborns, is a preference for other humans over inanimate objects. The second step, which begins soon after birth, is learning to discriminate familiar people from unfamiliar ones. Finally, in the third step, babies develop attachments to specific people. These attachments are revealed in the infants' loud protests when attachment figures depart and their joyous greetings of caregivers when reunited with them.
- Infants develop attachment relationships not only with their mothers but with their fathers, siblings, peers, and others. In many cultures fathers have the special role of playmate in the development of their babies; fathers' play with infants tends to be physical, whereas mothers' play is quieter and more verbal.

The Nature and Quality of Attachment

- The quality of an infant's attachment can be assessed in a scenario called the **Strange Situation,** in which the child's interactions with the mother are observed under mildly stressful conditions. This scenario evolved out of the notion that infants use the adult to whom they've become attached as a **secure base.** Typically, some 60 to 65 percent of infants are classified by this method as **securely attached** to their mothers, whereas the rest fall into three categories of insecure attachment: **avoidant, resistant,** or **disorganized.** Attachment classifications generally remain stable over time unless major changes occur in the lives of family members.
- The **Attachment Q Sort (AQS),** a newer method of assessing attachment, makes it possible to rate a broad range of attachment-related behaviors in a naturalistic setting.
- The quality of an infant's attachment to parents is determined by early parent-child interactions. Parents who display **sensitive care,** responding to their infant's needs and giving the baby a sense of control over the environment, seem to have more securely attached infants. **Interactive synchrony** requires that the mother constantly adjust her behavior to her baby's, engaging him when he is ready and backing off when he is not.
- Parents' **internal working models** of their own experience with their parents are likely to influence their attachment relationships with their babies. Both mothers and fathers who have been classified as autonomous, dismissing, and preoccupied have been shown to be more likely to have secure, avoidant, or resistant infants.
- A baby's temperament may play a role in the quality of the infant-parent attachment, but this occurs probably only in combination with other factors, such as the caregiver's behavior.
- Early attachments shape a child's later attitudes and behaviors. Children who were securely attached as infants are more likely than others to see themselves positively, to have high self-esteem, to be intellectually curious and eager to explore, and to have good relationships with peers and others.

- The quality of attachment is relatively stable across time, but changes in the environment may act to improve or lessen that quality, and professional intervention can help improve a troubled attachment relationship.
- Early secure attachment appears to be related to cognitive advancement and to the development of social skills. In addition, the more secure a child's attachment relationship, the more likely she is to develop a positive self-concept.
- Although there is no evidence that having multiple caregivers or spending time in a child-care center prevents the formation of a secure child-parent attachment relationship, some studies have indicated that the amount of time spent in such care is negatively correlated with the sensitivity mothers express toward their children and the affection children show to their mothers.
- Other studies have indicated that infants of working mothers are slightly more likely to be classified insecurely attached than those of nonworking mothers, but the percentage difference is not large. It has been suggested that, rather than the mother's absence, it is the stress of working and also raising a child that interferes with the development of a strong attachment relationship.
- Quality and stability of child-care center staff are important ingredients in the security experienced by children in the care of these part-time caretakers. Where quality of care is good, children may benefit both cognitively and socially. Early attachments shape a child's later attitudes and behaviors. Children who were securely attached as infants are more likely than others to see themselves positively, to have high self-esteem, to be intellectually curious and eager to explore, and to have good relationships with peers and others.

Language and
Communication

C H A P T E R

One of the child's most remarkable developmental achievements is the mastery of language. Language is one of the most complex systems of rules a person ever learns, yet children in a wide range of different environments and cultures learn to understand and use their native languages in a relatively short period. Their ability to do this strongly suggests that human infants are prepared to respond to the language environment and to acquire language skills.

language A communication system in which words and their written symbols combine in various, regulated ways to produce an infinite number of messages.

What is **language**? It is a system of communication in which words and their written symbols combine in various, regulated ways to produce an infinite number of messages. Thus language serves a wide range of purposes for the developing child: It helps him interact with others, communicate information, and express his feelings, wishes, and views. Children can use language to influence other people's behavior, to explore and understand their environment by discussing it with others, and to escape from reality whenever they want through fantasy (Halliday, 1975). Language helps children to organize their perceptions, direct their thinking, control their actions, sharpen their memories, and even to modify their emotions. And, above all, language helps them learn new things.

communicative competence The ability to convey thoughts, feelings, and intentions in an organized, culturally patterned way that sustains and regulates human interactions.

An important part of children's language learning is the development of **communicative competence.** That is, they must acquire the ability to convey their thoughts, feelings, and intentions in an organized and culturally patterned way. This capacity for meaningful and understandable communication helps to maintain and to regulate human interactions (Haslett, 1997; Schaffer, 1974). In addition, communication is by definition a two-way process; we send messages to others and receive messages from them. Thus, language requires us to both produce and receive communication. Not surprisingly, these two aspects of language are often referred to as **productive language** and **receptive language.**

productive language The production of speech.

receptive language Understanding the speech of others.

We start this chapter with an overview of the primary components of language; next we explore the dominant theories of how language develops in the infant and young child. Then we enter the world of words, sentences, grammar, and the rules for the use of language: How, and how well, do children communicate before they are able to use whole words? How does the child's understanding of the meaning of words develop? Do children acquire more complex sentence forms in a systematic fashion? How does the child learn grammar? How similar is grammar in different languages, including the language of the deaf? What skills are necessary to be an effective speaker or listener? After this exploration of how children gain new language skills, we ask how children begin to understand language as a system of rules for communication. Finally, we consider the tasks that confront children who learn two languages at once.

THE COMPONENTS OF LANGUAGE: PHONOLOGY, SEMANTICS, GRAMMAR, AND PRAGMATICS

Children learn about the sounds, meanings, structures, and uses of language in specific contexts, and they learn all these things simultaneously. For purposes of analysis, however, scholars divide the study of language into four main areas: phonology, semantics, grammar, and pragmatics.

phonology The system of sounds that a particular language uses.

phoneme Any of the basic units of a language's phonetic system; phonemes are the smallest sound units that affect meaning.

Phonology, the system of sounds that a particular language uses, includes not only the language's basic units of sound, or **phonemes,** but rules about how we put phonemes together to form words and rules about the proper intonation patterns for phrases and sentences. Phonemes are considered *basic* units of sound because they are the smallest sound units that affect meaning; changing a phoneme changes the meaning of a word. For example, by changing the initial phoneme in the word *bat,* we can make the very different word *cat.* By changing the middle phoneme, we can make yet another word, *bit.* A very important feature of phonologic rules is that they are *generative;* that is, they are applicable beyond the cases on which they are based. A native English speaker, for instance, knows that *kib*, though a nonsense word in English, is a possible sound pattern in the language's system, whereas *bnik* is not possible.

The study of word meanings and word combinations is called **semantics.** Comprehension of written as well as spoken language requires not only a knowledge of specific words and their definitions but an understanding of how we use words and how we combine them in phrases, clauses, and sentences. Thus, as children mature intellectually throughout their school years, their semantic knowledge continues to grow. Even adults continue to expand their vocabularies to encompass new knowledge. For example, a first-year psychology student must learn a whole new vocabulary of psychological terms.

semantics The study of word meanings and word combinations, as in phrases, clauses, and sentences.

Grammar describes the structure of a language and consists of two major parts: morphology and syntax. **Morphology** is the study of a language's smallest units of meaning, called **morphemes**—prefixes, suffixes, and root words—and of how those units are properly combined. Rules for altering root words to produce such things as plurals, past tenses, and inflections are part of a language's morphological system. **Syntax** specifies how words are combined into sentences. For example, each language has syntactic rules for expressing grammatical relations such as negation, interrogation, possession, and juxtaposition of subject and object. The rules of syntax allow us to vary word order so that we are not limited to one way of saying what we mean. For example, we can say "Luis hit a high fly ball that Jake caught," or "Jake caught the high fly ball that Luis hit." Both sentences express the same basic idea but are appropriate in different contexts, depending on whether we want to focus on Luis or on Jake. Syntactic rules offer us great opportunity for linguistic creativity, but if we violate these rules, we will not make sense. Thus, we are free to form the syntactically correct sentence, "After class I went to the library and listened to some music," but the syntactically incorrect sentence, "I listened to some music after class and I went to the library," is ambiguous and unclear.

grammar The structure of a language; made up of *morphology* and *syntax*.

morphology The study of a language's smallest units of meaning, or *morphemes*.

morpheme Any of a language's smallest units of meaning, such as a prefix, a suffix, or a root word.

syntax The subdivision of grammar that prescribes how words are to be combined into phrases, clauses, and sentences.

The fourth component of language, **pragmatics,** consists of rules for the use of appropriate language in particular contexts (Bates, 1976; Shatz, 1983). Thus pragmatics is concerned not only with speaking and writing but with social interaction, and it directly addresses the issue of effective communication. For example, a child learns to speak differently to her younger brother than to her parents, simplifying language for her brother just as her parents initially simplified their language for her. She also learns that she has a better chance of getting what she wants if she asks a schoolmate, "May I have one of your crayons?" rather than demand "Gimme a crayon!" And she learns that she must be more formal in writing than in casual speech but also that written language offers great creative opportunities. Researchers in pragmatics study these and other issues, such as how children learn

pragmatics A set of rules that specify appropriate language for particular social contexts.

Siblings are often good teachers for younger children, encouraging them to look at and manipulate interesting objects and giving names to shapes, colors, and noises that toys make.

to take turns in speaking, to remain silent while others speak, and to speak differently in such different settings as the classroom and the playground.

THEORIES OF LANGUAGE DEVELOPMENT

Among those who study language development in children, as among those in many other subfields of child psychology, advocates of the influence of heredity on development vie with those who hold that learning accounts for the emergence and evolution of language. Most theorists today, however, maintain a more middle ground, recognizing the roles that both genetic and environmental factors play in language development. To gain a full understanding of this interactionist approach, which focuses particularly on the role of early caretakers in the child's acquisition of language, we first explore the environmental and then the nativist views.

The Learning Theory View

As we examine the learning perspective on language development, keep in mind that learning theorists vary widely in the degree to which they adhere to traditional learning principles. At one extreme is the behaviorist B. F. Skinner (1957), who argues that principles of operant conditioning wholly account for language development. At the other extreme are theorists like Albert Bandura (1989), who recognizes the importance of cognitive functioning in his view of the learning process. (Recall our Chapter 1 discussion of the stages of observational learning.)

How Learning Theories Account for Language Development
Traditional learning theorists invoke the principle of *reinforcement* to explain language development. On this view, the parents or other caretakers selectively reinforce each of the child's babbling sounds that is most like adult speech; that is, by giving attention to these sounds and showing approval when their baby utters them, they encourage her to repeat them. She then repeats the sounds, they approve again, and she vocalizes these particular sounds more often. Little by little, by giving their greatest approval to the infant's closest approximations to adult speech sounds, parents shape their child's verbal behavior into what increasingly resembles adult speech.

Other learning theorists (Bandura, 1989; Bullock, 1983) propose that the child learns primarily through *imitation* or observational learning. According to this view, the child picks up words, phrases, and sentences directly by imitating what he hears. Then, through reinforcement and *generalization,* or applying what he has learned to new situations, the child learns when it is appropriate or inappropriate to use particular words and phrases.

Limitations of Learning Theory Accounts
Although learning theory accounts of language acquisition have a contribution to make in the ongoing discussion of how language evolves, they have not fared well as representatives of a sole explanation. First, critics have pointed out that the number of necessary specific connections—that is, linkages between a baby's vocalization and a parent's reinforcing response—to even begin to explain language is so enormous that a child could not acquire all of them in even a lifetime, not to mention a few short years. Second, naturalistic studies of parent-child interaction fail to support the learning theory account. For example, mothers are just as likely to reward their children for statements that are truthful but grammatically incorrect as they are to reinforce the children for grammatically correct utterances (Brown & Hanlon, 1970). After all, parents respond as frequently to a child's meaning as to her grammar, because they are concerned to teach her acceptable behavior as well as correct language. It is difficult to see, then, how adult reinforcement alone might account for the child's learning of grammar (Brown, 1973; Pinker, 1994).

A third argument against learning theory is that it is impossible to predict the vast majority of language utterances from specific utterances by other people. For example, utterances that are closely tied to environmental cues, such as "Hello," "Watch out!" or "You're welcome," are relatively rare. For most sets of circumstances, language affords an enormous degree of creative latitude that, according to nativists, is not accounted for by learning theories. Fourth, learning theory accounts have not explained the regular sequence in which language develops. Children in our culture and other cultures seem to learn the same types of grammatical rules and in the same order. For example, they learn active constructions before passive constructions: They learn to say, "Taisha and Neville prepared the posters for the class presentation" before they learn to say "The posters for the class presentation were prepared by Taisha and Neville." Inasmuch as the passive voice is weaker and less direct, it seems a pity that children ever learn it! Finally, behavioral theories basically portray the child as playing a less active role in language development than the nativist views we discuss next, which argue that the child plays an active and creative role in discovering and applying general rules of language.

Apparently, traditional learning principles are not any more critical for the learning of sign language by the deaf child than they are for the hearing child's acquisition of language rules (Goldin-Meadow & Morford, 1985; Petitto, 1993). Nevertheless, learning principles may play a very important and useful role in modifying language usage and in overcoming language deficits in some people (Whitehurst, Fischel, Caulfield, DeBaryshe, & Valdez-Menchaca, 1989). Some programs based on learning principles, which are available to parents, have been shown to be effective in helping children who are delayed in their language development catch up to their peers (Zelazo, Kearsley, & Ungerer, 1984). And among autistic children, Lovaas (1987; Lovaas & Smith, 1988) has demonstrated the usefulness of imitation and reinforcement principles in at least partially overcoming speech problems. Owing to neurological deficits, however, autistic children still may not reach normal levels of communicative competence.

The Nativist View

Linguist Noam Chomsky (1968), for years the most influential advocate of the nativist position, proposed that children are born with an innate mental structure that guides their acquisition of language and, in particular, grammar. Chomsky termed this structure a **language acquisition device (LAD).** Although not all the specifics of Chomsky's theory of language development have been supported, his influence on the study of language has been revolutionary. His leadership position in the nativist camp has now been taken up by Steven Pinker (1989, 1994), who has continued to build on Chomsky's work. Pinker's book *The Language Instinct* (1994) has become a best-seller, suggesting that the field of language holds great interest for laypeople as well as scholars.

language acquisition device (LAD) Chomsky's proposed mental structure in the human nervous system that incorporates an innate concept of language.

Claims of the Nativist Approach

Nativists assert that certain *universal features* common to all languages are innate. For example, sentences in all languages contain a subject, verb, and object. Nativist theory also claims that children use a set of innate *language hypotheses* to derive rules from the language *data* that they hear. Nativists believe that the normal human child is biologically predisposed to learn any human language with ease. Finally, in contrast to learning perspectives, the nativist approach views language as an abstract system of rules that cannot be acquired by traditional learning principles.

If language ability is an inherited species-specific characteristic, all languages of the species must display universal features, that is, they must share certain basic characteristics. In fact, by examining features such as the sounds used in speaking, the way words are organized in sentences, and how meaning is determined in various languages, investigators have concluded that a set of common principles

BOX 8-1

Perspectives on Diversity

Are Creole Languages Evidence of a Universal First Grammar?

The most striking evidence that children may possess an innate program or template for grammar comes from the work of Derek Bickerton (1983, 1988, 1990), who has studied creole languages around the globe. The **creole language** often arises in a context in which people who speak different languages are thrown together in a single culture. These languages, according to Bickerton, are developed by the children of first-generation immigrants, who often speak a kind of *pidgin* language, and "exhibit the complexity, nuance, and expressive power universally found in the more established languages of the world" (1983, p. 116). In Hawaii, the southeast coast of North America, New Orleans, the Carribbean, the Guyanas, Africa, islands in the Indian Ocean, Indonesia and the Philippines, where peoples from countries of Asia, Africa, Europe, and the Americas came together to form strikingly polyglot societies, all the children in each culture, regardless of their parents' native languages, used a single creole language with a single structure and linguistic system. Moreover, the languages have lived on in succeeding generations and in similar form. How could the children of these different racial and ethnic groups have evolved languages that resemble each other if they did not possess some sort of inner template of a universal grammar?

In these multicultural societies, many of which were made up of immigrants imported to labor on colonial plantations, communication began with workers' development of a pidgin language, a simplified linguistic system created out of two languages that suddenly come into contact with each other. Pidgin adopts the vocabulary of the dominant language, but, as Table 8-1 shows, it lacks grammatical complexity: Its sentences are often no more than strings of nouns, verbs, and adjectives. For this reason and because pidgin is highly individualistic, varying from speaker to speaker, its usefulness is limited. This limitation is probably what leads the children of pidgin speakers to develop the more complex type of communication represented by creole languages.

The language that children in polyglot societies develop is much richer in grammatical structure than pidgin (Bickerton, 1983). And interestingly, creole languages that develop in different places throughout the world are very similar in their structure, no matter what the contributing languages! Even more remarkably, the speech of first-generation creole-speaking children does not differ from that of later generations of speakers, which suggests that the acquisition of this new language happens very rapidly. Together, the uniformity of language across speakers and geographic locales and the speed of language acquisition argue against any simple explanation that children who learn creole are borrowing cafeteria style from one contact language or another.

What are the implications of these observations for theories of language acquisition? According to Bickerton (1983),

> The evidence from creole languages suggests that first-language acquisition is mediated by an innate device . . . the device provides the child with a single and fairly specific grammatical model. It was only in pidgin-speaking communities, where there was no grammatical model that could compete with the child's innate grammar, that the innate grammatical model was not eventually suppressed. The innate grammar

---

creole language A language spoken by children of first-generation, pidgin-language speakers; a language that, in contrast with pidgin, is highly developed and rule governed.

does underlie all human languages (Slobin, 1985, 1992). For instance, speakers of all languages create a vast number of spoken words by combining a relatively small set of particular sounds. Each of the world's languages uses only a limited sample of all the possible vocal sounds human beings can make. Moreover, words are always combined into structured sequences that English calls *sentences*. Finally, all languages have grammars, and nativists claim that these grammars share certain formal properties as well (e.g., the subject-predicate relationship).

In support of their position, nativists make several observations about language acquisition (Maratsos, 1989; Meisel, 1995; Pinker, 1994). Consider, for example, that in many different cultures, normal children acquire language relatively quickly and learn it well. Nativists point out that because children receive such fragmented and incomplete environmental input, this input alone cannot possibly account for the amazing feat of language acquisition. Those about them can give children only a limited number of examples of the tremendous range of complex structures of which language is capable; children have to go beyond these examples and figure out the patterns—a task at which they are very successful. Nativists thus argue that the child must be preset to acquire language. As Box 8-1 suggests, some of the most striking evidence for the possibility of an innate predisposition for language comes from the study of children who speak a creole language.

Another source of support for the nativist view is evidence that human beings learn language far more easily and quickly during a certain critical period of biolog-

was then clothed in whatever vocabulary was locally available and gave rise to the creole languages heard today. (p. 121)

Further support for this argument comes from evidence that the common errors that English-speaking toddlers make are perfectly acceptable creole expressions. For example, between 3½ and 4 years old, children often use double negatives. In "Nobody don't like me," both subject and verb are negative. Although some languages allow the double negative in verb forms (e.g., one may say in French, "*Je ne vais jamais au cinema*," which translates literally as "I no go never to the movies"), creoles are the only languages that allow this doubling up of negatives in both subjects and verbs: "Nothing not have value" is perfectly acceptable in creole tongues. Similarly, when a feature of the local language matches the structure of creole, children avoid making errors that would seem quite natural—further evidence that the structure of

creole may, in fact, be an innate language template. Determining whether we can accept the structure of creole language as the basis of first-language acquisition will require much more research. If it turns out to be true, a biological basis of language would seem to be more than just a possibility.

The case is certainly not closed. Some recent critics like Tomasello (1995) have argued that adult influences may still play a role in the emergence of creole English. Only by observing the language development of first-generation and creole children can we be certain that children are building a language based solely on an internal template and without the assistance of adult models and adult feedback. The interactionist position (see pages 281–285), which suggests that both biological factors and environmental influences provide the best account of language acquisition, may offer a viable alternative explanation for the Hawaiian creole findings.

TABLE 8-1 Some Utterances in Hawaiian Pidgin English

Pidgin:	*Ifu laik meiki, mo beta make time, mani no kaen hapai.*
Direct translation:	If like make, more better die time, money no can carry.
Meaning:	"If you want to build (a temple), you should do it just before you die—you can't take it with you!"
Pidgin:	*Aena tu macha churen, samawl churen, haus mani pei.*
Direct translation:	And too much children, small children, house money pay.
Meaning:	"And I had many children, small children, and I had to pay the rent."

Source: From Bickerton, 1990.

---

ical development. A **critical period** is a time during which a child is sensitive to a particular environmental stimulus that does not have the same effect on him when he encounters it before or after this period. The critical period for language stretches from infancy to puberty. Before puberty, a child may achieve the fluency of a native speaker in any language (or even in two or more languages simultaneously) without special training, but after puberty, it is extremely difficult to learn a first language. Dramatic examples come from several famous case studies. In the winter of 1800, a 12-year-old boy who had lived in the woods near Aveyron, France, was discovered. The boy had no language, and in spite of efforts by Jean Itard at the National Institute for Deaf-Mutes in Paris, the boy was able to learn only a few words. No one knows why. Perhaps the boy was impaired at birth, or perhaps language can only be acquired before puberty (Lane, 1976). In another, modern case, 13-year-old "Genie" was discovered to have been kept locked in a room by her mentally ill father from the time she was 18 months of age (Curtiss, 1977, 1989; Rymer, 1993). Although Genie was more successful in learning to communicate than the wild boy in France, she never acquired normal language. These cases strongly suggest that there is a critical period for language acquisition (Hoff-Ginsberg, 1997). Young children whose speech is disrupted by brain injury often recover their language capacity rapidly and completely, but if the brain damage occurs after puberty, the prognosis for the recovery of language is poorer; there is considerable variation, however, even among adults (Goodglass, 1993; Lenneberg, 1967).

critical period A specific period in children's development when they are sensitive to a particular environmental stimulus that does not have the same effect on them when encountered before or after this period.

Lenneberg (1967) proposed that children not only can achieve fluency in a second language but do so more readily than adults, but the evidence here is mixed. In an early study of English-speaking families who moved to the Netherlands, after one year adolescents and adults had learned more Dutch, and faster, than children between 3 and 11 years old (Snow & Hoefnagel-Hohle, 1978). On the other hand, a more recent study of proficiency in a second language demonstrated by children and adults after a lengthy period of exposure to the language clearly supports the view that there is a sensitive period for learning grammar. Johnson and Newport (1989, 1991) asked native Korean and Chinese speakers between the ages of 3 and 39 to judge the accuracy of the grammar in a variety of English sentences. Participants in the study who had their first exposure to English before reaching puberty had a clear advantage (see Figure 8-1). Deaf people show a similar advantage in learning sign language. Newport (1991) found that those who were exposed early to American Sign Language (ASL) became more competent sign language users as adults. Similarly, in Nicaragua, Senghas (1995) found that deaf children who learned sign language at the age of 4 or 5 acquired a structurally richer language than children who began to learn sign language at older ages. There may also be a critical period for learning the correct accent for a particular language; Krashen (1975) found that accents are hard to modify after puberty, a finding that is consistent with the Lenneberg position. Children often come to sound like native speakers, whereas adults, unless they take up residence in another country, more often do not (Krashen, 1975).

Limitations of Nativist Accounts of Language Development

The nativist view of language development has its limitations as well. First, few theorists agree about the exact nature of the types of grammatical rules that children learn. In fact, several theorists have offered alternative explanations of the early grammar acquisition process that differ from Chomsky's original formulation (Maratsos, 1989, 1998; Slobin, 1985). Moreover, the Chomsky account of grammar itself has been widely discredited as a viable account of how language develops (Pinker, 1994). Second, language learning is a gradual process and is not completed as early as nativist accounts would predict. As we will see later in the chapter, specific aspects of grammar continue to develop in the elementary school years and even beyond.

Third, this perspective makes it very difficult to account for the many languages human beings speak throughout the world. Despite the nativist claim that languages possess universal features, how are we to envision features that produce such different grammatical structures, including many varying forms of syntax? And how can it be that a universal feature of using a set of sounds to express meaning leads to the enormous variety of sound combinations that we find in the

■ FIGURE 8-1
It helps to learn a new language early in life.
On a test of English grammar, native speakers of Chinese and Korean who had immigrated to the United States before they were 7 years old scored as well as native speakers of English. The older immigrants were when they arrived in America the less well they did on the test. (*Source*: Newport, 1990; redrawn from Johnson & Newport, 1989)

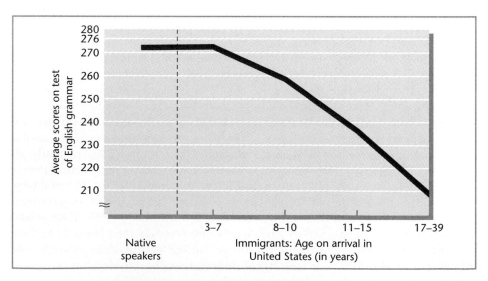

world's languages? Fourth, this view tells us little about the role of pragmatics and communication. Inasmuch as all peoples form societies of one kind or another, why is there not some universal language feature that governs the way language is used in social interaction? The nativist view gives the social context of language little recognition, and we now know that social influences play a much larger role in language development than earlier scholars had thought.

It seems likely that human beings are biologically prepared *in some way* for learning language. However, it seems quite unlikely that biological principles alone can account for all aspects of language development.

The Interactionist View

Most modern theorists of the development of language take the interactionist view, recognizing that language is learned in the context of spoken language but assuming as well that humans are in some way biologically prepared for learning to speak. Interactionists are concerned with the interplay between biological and environmental factors in the acquisition of language. Complementary to the role of socializing agents such as parents in the child's acquisition of language is the child's own very active role in his development of normal speech: "Children are instrumental in the language development process. Not only do they formulate, test, and evaluate hypotheses concerning the rules of their languages, but they also actively compile linguistic information to use in the formulation of hypotheses" (Tagatz, 1976, p. 90; see also Gallaway & Richards, 1994; Morgan, 1990). In the interactionist view, normal language develops as a result of a delicate balance between parent and child understanding; when parents speak to children in a way that recognizes how much the children already know and understand, they increase enormously their children's chance of comprehending a novel message (Bloom, 1998; Ninio & Snow, 1996; Swensen, 1983). You will recall from Chapter 1 that Vygotsky proposed this sort of help from older and more experienced people as necessary to children's learning. We will explore Vygotsky's concepts in greater depth in Chapter 9 (see also Fischer & Bullock, 1984; Rogoff, 1990, 1998; Vygotsky, 1934).

Facilitating Children's Language Development

An advocate of the social interaction view, Jerome Bruner has proposed that the environment provides the language-learning child with a **language acquisition support system,** or **LASS** (Bruner, 1983; Snow, 1989). In contrast to nativists like Chomsky, whose concept of the LAD he parodies, Bruner emphasizes the parents' or primary caretakers' role as facilitators of language acquisition. Of what does Bruner suggest the LASS consists? During children's earliest years, parents support their development of language and their comprehension with several strategies. For example, parents often introduce objects to a child to provide a basis for their mutual play and speak about objects and events that are present and easily visible to the child. They monitor their child's apparent goals or intentions closely, and in general they try to modulate, correct, or elaborate their child's behavior rather than specifically redirect it. "And they construct an internal model of their child's current preferences, skills, and world knowledge, which they continuously update and check" (Fischer & Bullock, 1984, pp. 75–76). Although parents don't usually conceive of these tactics as deliberate teaching techniques but see them rather as natural efforts to carry on conversation with their children, they are very specifically facilitating their children's learning. Again we see how this interactionist view is consistent with Vygotsky's theory.

We turn now to a series of techniques that adults use to facilitate language acquisition in young children. These techniques include playing nonverbal games, using simplified speech, and elaborating on and rewording children's own utterances to help them sharpen their communicative skills.

language acquisition support system (LASS) According to Bruner, a collection of strategies and tactics that environmental influences—intially, a child's parents or primary caretakers—provide the language-learning child.

Playing Nonverbal Games.   Parents make some of their first efforts to "converse" with their children in early nonlinguistic games like peek-a-boo or patty cake. Children learn some structural features of spoken language, such as turn taking, from these games. And because these kinds of games involve regular, repetitive, and thus predictable behaviors, they may also lay a foundation for the systematic rules of language. At first, young babies aren't capable of either initiating or responding in "conversation," to say nothing of taking turns, but parents help them learn this social skill by carrying more than their share of early dialogues and by waiting for pauses in the infant's vocal or motor behavior and then inserting an appropriate response. This supportive activity of parents may contribute not only to later give and take in conversation but also to social turn taking in play and formal games (Garvey, 1990b).

Using Simplified Speech.   Another part of LASS is parents' habit of modifying their speech when they talk to infants and children. Typically, they use a simplified style, called **infant-directed speech** (also called *motherese*), in which they speak in short, simple sentences that refer to concrete objects and events and that often repeat important words and phrases. In this style of speech, parents also talk more slowly and in higher-pitched voices, enunciate more clearly, and often end sentences with a rising intonation (Fernald, 1992; Fernald & Morikawa, 1993). The simplified grammar and syntax may help children learn the relationships between words and objects and may also give them some understanding of the rules of segmentation, that is, how speech is divided into words, phrases, and sentences. The acoustic variations can help highlight important words. For example, in reading to 14-month-olds, mothers consistently positioned a word that identified a picture ("that's a *shirt*" or "that's a *boy*") at the end of a phrase and spoke in exaggerated pitch, thus capturing their infants' attention (Fernald & Kuhl, 1987; Fernald & Mazzie, 1991).

Research has shown that newborns and 4-week-olds prefer to listen to infant-directed speech than to adult-directed talk (Cooper & Aslin, 1990) and that babies are equally responsive to this style of communication whether it is used by men or women (Pegg, Werker, & McLeod, 1992). And infants show a preference for infant-directed speech even when speech is in a nonnative language. For example, even when English-learning infants listened to Cantonese, they still appeared to prefer infant-directed speech (Werker, Pegg, & McLeod, 1994). A recent study of motherese in the United States, Sweden, and Russia has suggested that parents everywhere emphasize three "primary vowels"—*ee*, *ah*, and *oo*—when speaking to

infant-directed speech   A simplified style of speech parents use with young children, in which sentences are short, simple, and often repetitive; the speaker enunciates especially clearly, slowly, and in a higher-pitched voice and often ends with a rising intonation. Also called *motherese*.

Many games parents play with their young children help them learn words as well as pragmatic features of language such as turn taking and the meaning of pauses.

their infants, that these vowels sounds are common to every spoken language in the world, and that hearing these sounds helps babies learn to distinguish major sound differences and makes it easier for them then to learn finer distinctions among vowel sounds (Kuhl, et al. 1997). Perhaps this helps explain why the infants learning English preferred Cantonese motherese!

Exaggerating speech, placing important words at the ends of sentences, and raising pitch and intonation not only help adults gain infants' attention. Simplified speech also tends to elicit more signs of positive emotions in babies, such as more smiles, and may increase the chances that the child will understand the message (Pegg, Werker, & McLeod, 1992; Werker & McLeod, 1989). But does the use of a simplified code actually facilitate children's language learning? In fact, simplified speech may not always be helpful. In one study, children who had progressed beyond the one-word stage were more likely to respond appropriately to an adult form of a command ("Throw me the ball") than to a simplified form ("Throw ball"). As we have seen in other areas of development, a level of complexity that is slightly ahead of children may be most effective in eliciting their attention and may maximize their learning (Hoff-Ginsberg & Shatz, 1982; Sokolov, 1993). When infants or children show signs that they are not comprehending, adults often revert to simpler speech (Bohannon & Warren-Leubecker, 1988). In general, parents adjust their speech to a child's level of linguistic sophistication, using a wider and wider range of words and parts of speech as children mature (Shatz, 1983; Hoff-Ginsberg, 1997).

Other Influence Techniques. Parents facilitate early communication in several other important ways. Consider the following exchanges between a mother and her child:

CHILD: Daddy juice.
ADULT: Daddy drinks juice.
CHILD: Give mama.
ADULT: Give it to mama.

In the technique of **expansion** illustrated here, the adult imitates and expands or adds to the child's statement. Brown (1973) has estimated that among middle-class families, about 30 percent of the time parents' speech to their children is composed of such expansions but that lower-class parents use this technique much less often. Parents are especially likely to use this expansion strategy after a child has made a grammatical error (Bohannon & Stanowicz, 1988).

Although expansion sometimes helps a child's learning, a combination of expansion and recast is more effective. In a **recast** the adult listener renders the child's incomplete sentence in a more complex grammatical form. For example, when the child says, "Kitty eat," the adult may recast the sentence as a question: "What is the kitty eating?" Or a child's "My ball" might become, "Here is your ball." The more grammatical and more complicated speech that children produce spontaneously following such exchanges suggests that they do profit from them (Nelson, Carskadden, & Bonvillian, 1973). Through recasting, children's adult partners are, in effect, both correcting children's utterances and guiding them toward more appropriate grammatical usage. Moreover, some researchers have shown that children whose parents have recast their utterances appear to develop linguistically at a faster rate, using questions and complex verb forms at an earlier age than is common (Nelson, 1977, 1989; Nelson, Welsh, Camarata, Butkovsky, & Camarata, 1995). As we do not know how often parents use recasts, we cannot yet say how powerful a role recasting plays in normal language acquisition.

We do know, however, that children often imitate their parents' expansions and recasts. It is when they are wrong that children are more likely to imitate adult reworkings of their speech; when children's speech is correct, they are unlikely to imitate the adult's speech (Bohannon & Stanowicz, 1988). Perhaps children are more aware of their own mistakes than we recognize! Of particular interest is that children's imitations of their parents' expansions are often grammatically more advanced than their free speech. Table 8-2 displays some of these imitations.

expansion A technique adults use in speaking to young children in which they imitate and expand or add to a child's statement.

recast A technique adults use in speaking to young children in which they render a child's incomplete sentence in a more complex grammatical form.

		Relative Frequency	
Type of Imitation	Example	Adam*	Eve**
Unexpanded	Child: Just like cowboy. Adult: Oh, just like the cowboy's. Child: Just like cowboy.	45	17
Reduced	Child: Play piano. Adult: Playing the piano. Child: Piano.	7	29
Expanded	Child: Pick-mato. Adult: Picking tomatoes up? Child: Pick 'mato up.	48	54

TABLE 8-2   Children's Imitations of Adults' Expansions

Source: From Slobin, 1968.
  *From age of 2 years, 3 months to 2 years, 10 months
**From age of 1 year, 6 months to 2 years, 2 months

Is Social Interaction Crucial to Language Development?

Some theorists hold that although social interaction is necessary to language acquisition, the specific devices of expansion, recasting, and imitation may not be necessary. First, no universal pattern characterizes all parents within a cultural group; some use these methods, others do not (Hoff-Ginsberg, 1997). Indeed, there are impressive individual differences among the linguistic environments that parents within a given cultural group provide their children (Hart & Risley, 1995; Shatz, 1983). Because parents tend to use their own favorite methods very regularly, it may be consistency in the style of interacting rather than the particular style that is most important. In addition, not all cultures use the devices typical of the American middle class (Minami & McCabe, 1995; Peters, 1983). For example, among the Kaluli of New Guinea and in American Samoa, people speak to the very youngest children as if they were adults (Ochs, 1988; Schieffelin & Ochs, 1987), despite the fact that they believe that young children are incapable of communicating intentionally. Evidently there are forms of interaction that we do not yet entirely understand but that nevertheless ensure that children around the world (including American Samoans) develop language at the same general pace.

Nativists, pointing to evidence like that from Samoa, claim that, in general, parents do not correct children's ungrammatical utterances. Children who learn a particular language, however, end up with the same basic grammar. Nativists conclude that if children can learn a language and its grammar without feedback from the social environment, there must be innate constraints on the child's learning for it to proceed as it does. Otherwise, an infinite number of grammars would be consistent with the child's uncorrected utterances.

How can we determine whether parental corrective feedback does play a role in the child's development of language? To determine whether this feedback—called **negative evidence** by language scholars because it shows the child what is *not* correct in her utterances—is a critical and necessary force in language learning, Pinker (1994) has proposed four criteria: Negative evidence must be *present, useful, used,* and *necessary.* To begin with, there is some suggestion that negative evidence may not always be present or, perhaps, may rarely be present. Although most language scholars, especially learning theorists and interactionists, agree that parents correct their children's grammar on occasion, some nativists disagree and, as we have seen, in some societies parents apparently do not offer such correction (Bohannon & Stanowicz, 1988; Morgan, Bonamo, & Travis, 1995).

Second, to be useful, negative evidence needs to be provided in a form that children can process. Many nativists question whether children can use corrective feed-

negative evidence
According to Pinker, corrective feedback that parents may give to young language-learning children.

back, not only because it occurs only a portion of the time but because the parental feedback of which we have evidence is indirect—that is, parents provide it by expanding or recasting rather than by telling a child specifically that what he said is wrong (Pinker, 1989, 1994). One researcher (Marcus, 1993) estimated that a child would have to pronounce an ungrammatical utterance 85 times before he might come to realize that the sentence was ungrammatical—not a very efficient way to learn.

Third, can we show that children actually use this type of feedback to improve their learning of grammar? In a study by Farrar (1992), children were more likely to imitate a recast such as "The dog is running," corrected from "The dog running" —a form of negative evidence—than they were to imitate other forms of feedback like topic continuations, such as "Would you like some water?" in response to "I'm hot." The latter is a facilitative form of feedback but not negative evidence. Although the Farrar study suggests that negative evidence does indeed appear to be particularly helpful in grammar acquisition, others disagree and argue that negative evidence offers no special advantage for learning grammar (Morgan, Bonamo, & Travis, 1995; Morgan & Demuth, 1996).

Finally, if negative evidence were necessary, we would have to show either that all children receive it or that children who do not receive it do not learn language adequately. As we have said, no universal pattern characterizes all parents within a given cultural group, and some children who receive no corrective feedback do learn their language.

The final word on the role of parental influence in language acquisition is not yet in, as nativists and learning theory proponents continue to battle. Those who advocate the interactionist view hold that although the child is probably biologically prepared for learning language, there is also strong support for the role of environmental input in the child's development of language.

THE ANTECEDENTS OF LANGUAGE DEVELOPMENT

Communication is not achieved by words alone. If we restricted our focus to verbal communication only, we could easily underestimate how early in life communication begins. To fully understand the development of human communication, we must consider the many sounds babies make as well as the many looks, movements, and gestures by which they convey meaning before they can begin to approximate adults' vocalizations. These prelinguistic achievements are important precursors of actual language use (Adamson, 1995).

Not by Word Alone: Preverbal Communication

Some of infants' earliest communications take place during interactions with their first caregivers (Fogel, 1993; Uzgiris, 1989). Parent and infant often engage in a kind of dialogue of sounds, movements, smiles, and other facial expressions. Although these may seem at first glance to be "conversations," a closer look suggests that they be described as "pseudo-conversations" or "pseudo-dialogues," because the adult alone is responsible for maintaining their flow (Schaffer, 1977). Babies have only limited control over the timing of their responses, so adults insert their behavior into the infants' cycles of responsiveness and unresponsiveness. For instance, a baby gurgles and her mother replies by smiling and speaking to the infant. She first waits for the child's response, but if none is forthcoming, she may prompt the baby by changing her expression, speaking again, or gently touching the child. The end result, though it often looks like a mutual give and take, is really an early lesson in conversation, one that typically helps the infant to become a true communicative partner by the end of her first year (Schaffer 1977, 1996).

Between 3 and 12 months of age, infants improve greatly in their ability to use gestures to communicate (Fogel, 1993). By at least the time when babies are 3 or 4 months old, adults offer and show things to them, and 6-month-old infants

Gestures such as pointing and touching can help children connect a physical object with the word a parent or other adult is pronouncing.

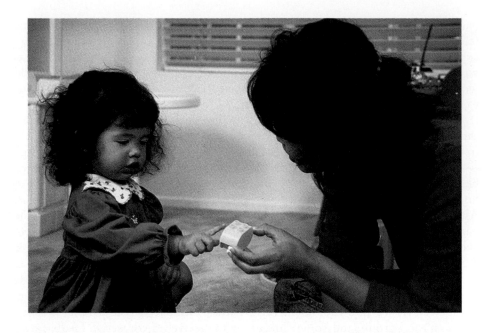

protodeclarative A gesture that an infant uses to make some sort of statement about an object.

protoimperative A gesture that either an infant or a young child may use to get someone to do something she or he wants.

respond with smiles, gestures, movements, and sounds. When babies are 7 or 8 months old, adults begin to point in order to draw their attention to an object or event. Within a few months, infants begin actively to use pointing gestures themselves, and by the time they're 1 year old, they have become highly skilled nonverbal communicators. They can use gestures to make a kind of statement about an object or to bring an object to someone's attention; for example, they may point to the object or hold it up (Adamson, 1995). This kind of preverbal communication has been called a **protodeclarative** (Bates, 1976). Babies can also use gestures to get another person to do something for them; for example, a child may point to a teddy bear on a high shelf in a specific request for help in rescuing it. Older preverbal children use this **protoimperative** form of communication very effectively, often checking to make sure that the listener is looking in the right direction (Bates, 1976, 1987; Bates, Thal, Whitsell, Fenson, & Oakes, 1989). All of us have seen a child tug at the pant leg of a distracted father and point with growing impatience to something she wants. Other common gestures that preverbal children use include reaching, grasping, and staring. Some children develop their own unique gestures, such as waving their hands, jumping up and down, or nodding their heads; others do even more unusual things like looking through their legs or pointing with their feet to attract adult attention to themselves or to an object of interest.

As children learn language, they often combine words and gestures for more effective communication (Adamson, 1995). A toddler may point to an object and then comment verbally or gesture to emphasize the meaning of the words. However, children's ability to use and understand gestures may develop independently of verbal language. It's only in the third year of life that children begin to recognize that gestures and language can be part of the same message and that if they are, they require an integrated response (Bates, 1987; Shatz, 1983). Across time, however, children reduce their use of gestures as they rely increasingly on their verbal skills to communicate their needs and wishes (Adamson, 1995; Bates, 1987).

Early Language Comprehension

The foundations for receptive language skills begin to emerge early. Well before they are able to speak themselves, babies can attend selectively to certain features of others' speech. In fact, newborns prefer listening to speech or to vocal music than to instrumental music or other rhythmic sounds (Butterfield & Siperstein, 1974). As we saw in Chapter 5, infants quickly become skilled listeners. Even 2-day-old infants can distinguish their mother's voice from the voice of an unfamiliar woman. Moreover, like adults, infants respond with different parts of their brain to speech and nonspeech sounds; for example, electrical activity increases in the left half of the brain in response to speech, whereas the right side responds to music (Molfese, 1973; Molfese & Betz, 1988; Neville, 1991).

Categorical Speech Perception

One of the most remarkable discoveries of recent decades is the finding that infants perceive some consonants categorically (Aslin, et al., 1998; Werker & Polka, 1993). Infants hear "one range of acoustic signals all as /p/ and a different range of acoustic signals as /b/ but no acoustic signal is perceived as something in between a /p/ and a /b/" (Hoff-Ginsberg, 1997, p. 50). This phenomenon is known as **categorical speech perception** or, the *phoneme boundary effect*. In a classic study of such discriminatory ability, one group of 5-month-old babies listened to 60 repetitions of the sound *bah*, followed by 10 repetitions of *gah;* a second group listened to 60 repetitions of *gah,* followed by 10 *bah* repetitions; and a third group heard only 70 repetitions of *bah* (Moffitt, 1971). The babies in the first 2 groups showed a marked heart-rate response when the experimenters suddenly presented the new consonant sound, *gah* or *bah,* respectively. Clearly, they perceived the change. This ability to discriminate speech sounds is evident from as early as 1 month of age and holds true for a variety of other consonants, such as *m, n,* and *d* (Aslin, 1987; Aslin et al., 1998; Miller & Eimas, 1994). Infants' discrimination abilities continue to improve, and by the time they are 2 months old, infants can tell the difference between /a / and /i /. Even more remarkable, 2- to 3-month-old infants can recognize the same vowel even when it is spoken by different people and at different pitches (Marean, Werner, & Kuhl, 1992).

> **categorical speech perception** The tendency to perceive a range of sounds that belong to the same phonemic group as the same.

Findings like the foregoing add fuel to the nativist fire, for they seem to suggest that infants are indeed born with some innate mechanism for perceiving oral language. However, although evidence suggests that infants have an innate tendency to look for the boundaries in sound patterns, this tendency is not unique to processing the sounds of speech. Moreover, speech is more easily separable into perceptual categories than are other sound stimuli (Aslin, 1987; Aslin, Pisoni, & Jusczyk, 1983). In addition, Kuhl and Miller's (1975) finding that chinchillas show categorical speech perception and can discriminate between /b/ and /p/ casts further doubt on the notions that this ability is uniquely human and that humans are uniquely prepared for language acquisition! Instead of being a specifically linguistic property of auditory perception, categorical speech perception is thus seen as a property of the mammal's aural system that language simply utilizes (Kuhl, 1997; Miller & Eimas, 1994). In fact, language may have evolved "to take advantage of this pre-existing property of mammalian audition" (Hoff-Ginsberg, 1997, p. 53).

Beyond Categorical Perception

Categorical speech perception is not the only skill that babies exhibit that may help them learn language. In Chapter 5 we discussed a study by DeCasper that suggested that infants may learn some features of language prenatally, and recent evidence suggests that infants can identify key properties of the rhythmic organization of their native language either prenatally or during the first few days of life (Aslin et al., 1998). For example, 4-day-old French babies increased their sucking rate when listening to French speech as opposed to Russian (Mehler et al., 1988). Another study (Mehler, Dupoux, Nazzi, & Dehaene-Lambertz, 1996) suggests that infants respond to the rhythmic properties of speech: French babies were unable to distinguish changes in Japanese speech based on the rhythmic unit around which Japanese utterances are organized, but they could distinguish changes involving the elementary rhythmic unit of French.

Whatever innate abilities infants have for perceiving speech sounds, these abilities constantly interact with experience over the language-learning period. The effects of experience in a certain language environment can be seen even before a baby begins to talk. For instance, newborns whose mothers spoke either Spanish or English preferred recordings in their native language over recordings in the unfamiliar language, a preference that apparently arose simply through exposure to the language spoken in the home (Moon, Cooper, & Fifer, 1993). Other work suggests that as babies develop they lose their ability to distinguish the sounds of languages to which they haven't been exposed (Werker, 1989). For example, one study found that infants of English-speaking parents could distinguish between sounds that are unique to Swedish only until the age of 6 months (Kuhl et al., 1992). Similar findings occur for other languages as well. Jusczyk, Friederici, Wessels, Svenkerud, and Jusczyk (1993) found that by the time American infants were 9 months old, they "tuned out" Dutch words, and Dutch infants were similarly unresponsive to English words. Findings like this certainly underscore the likely dual role of innate and experiential factors in the early recognition of speech sounds.

But even though babies become highly skilled at discriminating the speech sounds of their native language at an early age, it takes time for them to learn to focus on important sound distinctions in everyday speech. As we've seen, 1-month-old infants can detect the differences between the consonant sounds of /bah/ and /gah/. However, one study of children up to 18 months of age showed that these same kinds of distinctions were very difficult to make when the sounds were embedded in words and sentences. The researchers presented the children with two funny toys made up to look like people and given nonsense-syllable names such as *Bok* and *Pok,* chosen so that they differed only by their initial consonants. The experimenters invited the children to do things with each object; for example, "Let Pok take a ride on the wagon" or "Put the hat on Bok." The children had little success in picking out either Bok or Pok correctly (deVilliers & deVilliers, 1979).

The problem here is that part of learning a language is learning which of the many discriminable differences in speech sounds actually signal differences in meanings. Indeed, this task "requires considerable exposure to language and is not complete even at the end of the second year" (deVilliers & deVilliers, 1979, p. 19). Thus, although infants demonstrate many specialized language abilities, including the ability to discriminate among a variety of phonemes, the child faced with recognizing a significant difference between two words, like Bok and Pok, and keeping that difference straight must be able to draw on skills that go beyond discriminating pure sounds—skills at such things as attending to and categorizing phonemic differences.

According to Aslin and colleagues (Aslin et al., 1998),

> Languages differ considerably in the ways words are formed (e.g., what sequences of segments are allowed), in what information is used to mark word boundaries, and in the nature of their inflectional systems (how many they typically allow, what kinds and in what orders). Thus, to be successful in recovering words from fluent speech, infants must learn something about the organization underlying sound patterns in their native language. (p. 41)

Recent evidence suggests that infants can segment fluent speech and recognize words in ongoing speech better and much earlier than we had thought possible—by the end of their first year (Aslin et al., 1998). Moreover, research suggests that infants have the capacity to make the kinds of distinctions that indicate word boundaries (Hohne &

Jusczyk, 1994; Morgan, 1994; Morgan & Saffran, 1995). Infants use a variety of cues such as strong syllables (e.g., *tar* in *guitar*) pitch, pauses, stressed monosyllables (e.g., *cup, dog,* or *bike*), a strong syllable followed by a weak one (e.g., *fowler, turban,* etc.), or rhythmic properties to help define the boundaries of words (Jusczyk et al., 1993; Morgan, 1994). In these studies, words are often presented in strings or lists rather than in sentences, which would be more like normal speech.

According to still other work (Saffran et al., 1996), 8-month-old infants can detect new words in the babble of an unfamiliar artificial language even though they have no idea what the words mean and have no clues to guide them. Researchers had infants listen to two minutes of nonsense syllables mixed with "words" from an artificial language, which the researchers devised to eliminate the possibility that the infants were picking out words based on what they had already learned at home. Using a habituation paradigm, the researchers noted that when the tape was played a second time, the babies did not pay attention to the words—an indication that they had already learned them. This suggests that in the second half of the first year, babies are capable of detecting words in ongoing speech. As the researchers note, "If this is the case, then the massive amount of experience gathered by infants during the first postnatal year may play a greater role in development than has been previously recognized" (Aslin, Woodward, LaMendola, & Bever, 1996, p. 1928). It is a good thing that infants have the ability to detect words in sentences, because this is how most words are introduced to the young language learner. When researchers Woodward and Aslin (1990) asked mothers to teach new words to their 12-month-olds, the mothers presented their infants with most of the words in sentences. They presented only 20 percent of the words as words alone.

Babbling and Other Early Sounds

It is not just receptive language abilities that are rapidly developing in infancy. Babies are actively producing sounds—even though not language—from birth onward. Anyone who has been awakened in the wee hours of the morning by the sound of a baby happily "talking" to herself knows that infants are neither quiet nor passive. They make a great many sounds, as if "gearing up" for their ultimate production of speech.

The production of sounds in the first year of life follows an orderly four-stage sequence that is summarized in Table 8-3. Crying, which begins at birth, is an important way of indicating distress and serves as a rudimentary means of communication. **Cooing,** the production of vowel-like sounds, starts at the end of the first month. Cooing, so named because it often consists of *oo* sounds that resemble the sounds pigeons make, often occurs during social exchanges between infant and caregiver. **Babbling,** or producing strings of consonant-vowel combinations, begins in the middle of the first year. Finally, at the close of the first year, **patterned speech** makes its debut. In this pseudospeech, the child utters strings of "words" that are made up of phonemes in his native language and that sound very much like real speech—including intonation—but are not. These various stages overlap, and even patterned speech and true speech may occur together as the child's first meaningful words begin to appear.

Not only does the early production of sounds follow an orderly sequence but the kinds of sounds made at each of the first 3 stages are quite similar across different language communities. For instance, young Chinese, American, and Ethiopian babies all babble similar consonant-vowel combinations, even though they are exposed to different phonemes in their native languages (Thevenin, Eilers, Oller, & LaVoie, 1985). Even the early babbling of deaf babies sounds similar to the babbling of babies who can hear (Lennenberg, Rebelsky, & Nichols, 1965). Deaf infants born to deaf parents who sign (rather than speak) babble with their hands and fingers at the same age as hearing children babble vocally; moreover, their movements show

cooing A very young infant's production of vowel-like sounds.

babbling An infant's production of strings of consonant-vowel combinations.

patterned speech A form of pseudospeech in which the child utters strings of phonemes that sound very much like real speech but are not.

TABLE 8-3	Stages of Sound Production in the Infant's First Year	
Stage	*Begins*	*Description*
Crying	At birth	Signals of distress
Cooing	At about 1 month	"Oo" sounds that occur during social exchanges with caregiver
Babbling	Middle of first year	Strings of consonant-vowel combinations
Patterned speech	Close of first year	Strings of pseudowords made up of phonemes in native language and that sound like words

similar structure in terms of syllabic and phonetic patterning (Bloom, 1998). These similarities between manual and vocal babbling suggest "a unitary language capacity that underlies human signed and spoken language acquisition" (Petitto & Marenette, 1991, p. 1495). Overall, these findings suggest that the pattern of development of early sounds that infants make is a function of maturational changes in vocal structures and in the parts of the brain that have to do with producing sounds.

In the middle of the second half year, however, cultural differences in the prespeech sounds that babies make begin to emerge. For instance, babies exposed to one of two different native languages, Arabic or French, which contrast significantly in voice quality and pitch, may begin to show differences in their babbling at around 8 months of age (Ingram, 1989). Japanese and French words contain more nasal sounds than Swedish and English words, and in the latter part of the first year, French and Japanese babies' babbling contains more nasal sounds than their Swedish and English counterparts (de Boysson-Bardies et al., 1992). It is as if the babies are now starting to "tune in" to the language they hear spoken around them. This view is supported by the fact that older deaf infants fail to develop the more complex forms of babbling that start to resemble real speech, as infants who can hear do (Oller & Eilers, 1988). It seems that exposure to speech is required for the development of these later, more advanced forms of babbling. Interestingly, the amount of time exposed to language, not just the baby's physical maturation, appears to be an important factor. Babies who are born prematurely, and who are therefore exposed to language earlier (in terms of their gestational age) than full-term babies are, begin complex babbling sooner than the full-term infant (Eilers et al., 1993).

Although historically linguists have argued that there is no relationship between babies' early vocalizations and their later speech (Jakobson, 1968), more recent evidence has challenged this view. Studies of the babblings of infants over their first year have found that babbled syllables resemble the child's first meaningful words in a variety of ways (Elbers & Ton, 1985; Oller, Wieman, Doyle, & Ross, 1976). As one language expert has noted: "Late babbling contains sounds very much like those that are used in early attempts to pronounce words, independent of the language to which the child is exposed. . . . Babbling is indeed relevant to the child's developing linguistic skills" (Sachs, 1985, p. 49). Thus, a child's early vocalizations are not only orderly in their development but also related to later speech. In terms of the foundations for both receptive and productive language skills, the human infant is very well prepared for learning to talk.

SEMANTIC DEVELOPMENT: THE POWER OF WORDS

Despite children's early skills in both receptive and productive language, research suggests that children's understanding of language far exceeds their capacity to express themselves clearly (see Figure 8-2). These findings may help to explain

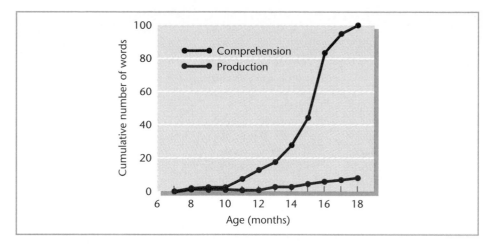

■ FIGURE 8-2
Receptive and productive language in infants.
Children's comprehension outpaces their production of words; on average, children understood nearly 100 words by the time they were 18 months old but could produce only 8 to 10. (*Source*: Huttenlocher, 1974)

the fact that children don't develop their vocabularies in a strictly linear fashion. Like other aspects of development, vocabulary acquisition proceeds in bursts. The **naming explosion,** a term coined by Bloom (Bloom, Lifter, & Broughton, 1985), is the rapid increase in vocabulary that most children begin to show at the age of about a year and a half, when typically they know about 50 words. Children usually utter their first words between 10 and 15 months (Fenson et al., 1994). According to Flavell (Flavell, Miller, & Miller, 1993), this explosion "is a phenomenon that may be all too familiar to the parents of a toddler: The child has discovered that things have names and now—tirelessly, incessantly—demands to know what the names are" (p. 285). In one well-documented case, a 16-month-old learned 44 words in a single week!

By the age of 2, the average child knows approximately 900 root words, and by 6, when he is in either kindergarten or first grade, he knows 8,000! This remarkable growth of vocabulary is a dramatic example of the human capacity for language and communication. How do children learn words? Imagine that you have taken a job in a foreign country, and your first task is to learn the language. A native of the country points to a dog lying on a rug and says, *"Xitf."* How do you know whether *xitf* refers to the dog, the dog's twitching ear, the dog's fur, the fact that the dog is sleeping on the rug, the fact that the dog is the speaker's pet, or indeed, the rug itself? Clearly, the acquisition of object names is no simple matter. Let's look a bit more closely at this issue.

How Children Acquire Words

To learn a word, children must acquire both the appropriate concept and the appropriate phoneme and then link the two, and they do this at an astonishing rate of speed. According to Rice (1989), children may learn new words so quickly by absorbing or "mapping new meanings as they encounter them in conversational interactions" (p. 152). In **fast-mapping,** children learn to link a new word with a concept they already understand (Carey, 1978; deVilliers & deVilliers, 1992; Mervis & Bertrand, 1994). A recent study by Mervis and Bertrand (1994) of 16- to 20-month-olds illustrates this ability. These researchers presented a child with five objects; four were familiar (e.g., ball, cup, shoe, car), and one was unfamiliar (e.g., garlic press). Children were asked to identify the shoe and then asked for the "zib." Children who fast-mapped learned immediately that the garlic press was a zib. Similarly, Rice (1990) found that children could learn meanings for unknown words, especially object names, from a single exposure to these words presented in the context of a video display.

Interestingly, as you can see in Box 8-2, even children with severe retardation may be able to use this method of learning words. As the box discusses, investigators have helped children who are at risk for failure to develop language make use

naming explosion The rapid increase in vocabulary that the child typically shows at about the age of 1½.

fast-mapping A technique by which a child learns to link a new word with a concept that he or she already understands.

BOX 8-2

Risk and Resilience

Children at Risk for Failure to Develop Language

Youth with moderate or severe mental retardation have been considered significantly intellectually impaired, as determined in part by standard intelligence tests (Chapter 11). Generally speaking, these children and young people have other disabilities such as sensory impairments, seizure disorders, cerebral palsy, and other medical conditions, and they often exhibit behaviors that are difficult to control. Such young people typically need extensive and ongoing support in more than one major life activity. One of the most important of such activities is communication. Youth with moderate and severe retardation range from those who do learn to speak, although slowly and often with limited success, to those who are unable to develop spoken communicative skills at all, even with considerable speech and language instruction.

Using one of the methods developed by investigators of nonhuman primate communication, Mary Ann Romski and Rose Sevcik (1996) have shown that youth with moderate and severe retardation who have never developed oral speech can learn to communicate intelligibly with adults and peers. In an approach based on Vygotskian concepts, each of 13 young boys with moderate to severe retardation worked with a partner (a teacher or a parent) who demonstrated and encouraged the child in using a computerized device that enabled them to select a particular symbol on a keyboard to produce a single word or phrase (Figure 8-3). When the child presses a given key, the computer produces a synthesized voicing of the word or phrase and also prints it on a screen. The literature on children with severe retardation had claimed that such children could learn only with continuous prompting. Romski and Sevcik found, however, that a majority of their participants, 12 years old on average, who used the System for Augmenting Language (SAL) device learned rapidly to associate symbols with words and phrases. By the end of the first 2-year experiment, most of the participants could both comprehend and produce a majority of the vocabulary words presented to them in instruction sessions. More than half of the participants even demonstrated the skill of fast-mapping (see this chapter's "How Children Acquire Words"), immediately associating a new name with a new object/symbol.

Romski and Sevcik chose to use arbitrary visual-graphic symbols rather than representational pictures in this work in part because they wanted "to describe the process of learning to communicate symbolically" (p. 61). Hypothesizing that the participants would be able to use symbolic communication, the basis of spoken and written language as we know it, these investigators found that their results supported this hypothesis. They introduced only a small number of symbols at a time to participants, beginning with a set of 12 symbols relevant to mealtime—symbols for specific foods, drinks, and utensils. The next group of words related to leisure time activities—for example, *ball, game, magazine, television*—and the third group of social-regulative words and phrases included *hello, excuse me, I want,* and *thank you.* A final group consisted of words tailored to individual participants' needs; for example, they added the word *work* to the lexicon of a participant who had a part-time job.

By the end of the two-year period, all participants had acquired 53 single words or two-word phrases in the first two categories, 16 words or phrases in the third group, and additional words or phrases in the final category. Moreover, many used their lexicons to engage in independent communication with people in the community. Because people in restaurants and stores, members of church congregations, and coworkers have no experience communicating with someone by means of a computer and synthesized speech, the participants' speech production had to stand on its own. And in many cases participants revealed previously untapped capacities for social exchange.

One youth, classified as severely retarded, went to a mall music store and requested assistance of a clerk by asking "HELP TAPE" and then showing the clerk a photograph of the tape he wanted. With tape in hand the youth then said "THANK YOU." And in an impressive display of social communication, one youth with moderate retardation greeted a new coworker, during a break, by saying, "HELLO." She asked him how he was, and he replied, "FINE." They sat down to have a drink and the coworker said, "Next week we don't work." The youth responded by nodding and saying, "NO WORK" (Romski & Sevcik, 1996, p. 145).

According to Romski and Sevcik, some parents have been reluctant to offer SAL training to their children because they fear that it will impede the children's efforts to learn to speak, and in fact very few data are available on the outcome of the early use of intervention with speech-output communication devices. Clearly, there is room for a great deal more research in this area. Among other things, we need to know what early predictors, such as specific behaviors, may differentiate children who will not develop

of computerized keyboards to select symbols that produce both voiced and printed words and phrases. Many of the children studied were able to learn far more rapidly than anyone expected.

What other factors may contribute to the speed of word acquisition? Recent evidence suggests that the task of acquiring vocabulary may be accelerated by a kind of screening process that enables children to focus on only the most likely of several possibilities. Ellen Markman (1991, 1994; Woodward & Markman, 1998)

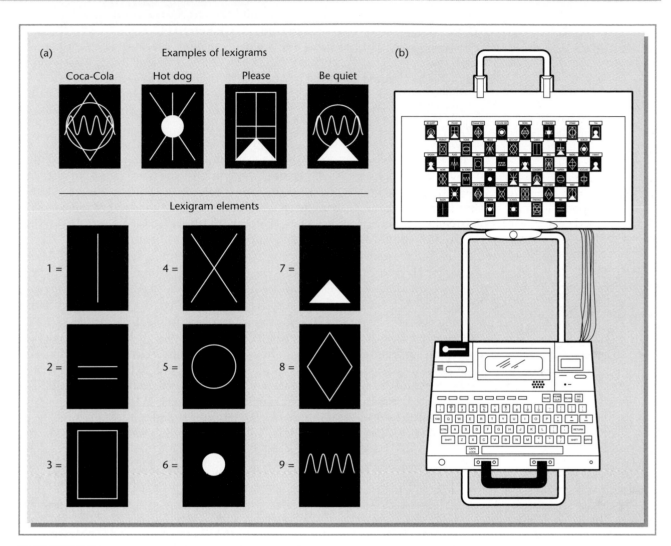

■ FIGURE 8-3

Communicating with a computer and lexigrams.

(a) Lexigrams like these, each made up of some combination of the nine elements shown, appear on the upper keypad of the computerized device (b). When a child presses the key for, say, *hot dog*, the words are sounded in synthetic speech and are also printed on the display screen of the computer (lower portion of b). (*Source*: Adapted from Romski & Sevcik, 1996)

speech from those who will. We also need to determine whether early intervention with SAL could not only help children who are at risk for failure to develop language to communicate but perhaps help provide the cognitive stimulation and trigger the motivation that might facilitate their learning of oral speech. Whatever its ultimate useful-

ness, SAL training has revealed the presence of cognitive capacities in children with mental retardation who, by traditional measures, had been considered only minimally functional. The work suggests that such young people can learn language under the right conditions and can apply it in social interaction and even useful work.

has conceptualized this process as one in which specific and presumably innate *constraints* operate to delimit the areas in which the child hypothesizes. First, the *whole object* constraint involves the assumption, which children as young as 18 months old make, that a new object word refers to the object itself and not to one of its parts or properties. For example, when 2-year-old Jamal visits the zoo and hears the word *anteater* for the first time, he assumes that *anteater* refers to the animal, not to its nose, body, or behavior.

The *taxonomic* constraint reflects an assumption that a new word refers to something related to a known class of things; a *taxonomy* is a system of organizing objects into categories. For example, a child who learns the word *cat* will use it to refer to all types of cats. In an early study, Markman and Hutchinson (1984) taught preschoolers an artificial name for a bluejay, calling the bird a *sud*. When the researchers presented the children with a nest and a duck and asked, Which one is the *sud?*, the children chose the taxonomically correct answer—the duck.

Operating under Markman's *mutual exclusivity* constraint, the child also assumes that every word refers to a distinct referent; that is, each object has one and only one name (Markman, 1989). When children as young as 2½ encounter an unfamiliar word in a context in which the word might refer to either a familiar or an unfamiliar object, they assume that the unfamiliar word refers to the unfamiliar object. For example, 3-year-old Jessica already knows the word *spoon* but does not know the word *tongs;* if she is asked, "Show me the tongs," she will very likely choose the tongs rather than the spoon. Together, these constraints considerably narrow the possible meanings a new word may have and therefore greatly simplify the child's word learning task (Woodward & Markman, 1998).

Critics of the nativist view that provides the underpinning for Markman's theory argue that no clear evidence supports the constraints position. These scholars urge that if we are to acquire a full understanding of the course of semantic development, we must look more closely at the social communicative context in which word learning occurs (Nelson, 1988). Some researchers have found, for example, that parents clearly influence vocabulary growth. In one example, the amount of time parents spent reading to their 2-year-olds was significantly related to the children's language skills when they were 4 years old (Crain-Thoreson & Dale, 1992). Another study found that the more parents talked to their children, the larger the children's vocabularies became (Huttenlocher, Haight, Bryk, Seltzer, & Lyons, 1991).

Some of the strongest support for the environmental approach comes from studies of vocabulary development in children of differing socioeconomic classes. Hart and Risley (1995) studied the language environments of 42 children, ranging in age from 10 months to 3 years, by observing them in their homes. These investigators found that social class, language environment, and children's vocabulary were all highly correlated: The higher the social class, the richer the language environment, and the greater the growth in the child's vocabulary (see Figure 8-4).

Some theorists have advocated a middle ground based on the notion that both constraints and social-communicative context are important for word learning (Hoff-Ginsberg, 1997). Parents and other members of the community provide the input that allows the constraints to operate, according to Behrend (1990), and there may be some regularities in that input that help to drive the child's language-learning apparatus.

What Kinds of Words Do Children Learn First?

Analyzing the kinds of words children acquire and the ways in which they use them can give us important information about children's cognitive development and the degree of sophistication with which they form concepts. Studying the first 50 words learned by a group of 18 young children, Nelson (1973), in a classic study of early word acquisition, classified these words into six categories. Mothers kept diaries of each new word their children produced until the children produced 50 words. On average, children reached the 50-word level by the time they were a year and a half old, but there was a great deal of individual difference. Some infants learned their first 50 words by 15 months whereas others took 24 months. As Figure 8-5 illustrates, about 65 percent of the 50 words were naming, or object words, whereas words denoting action made up only about 14 percent. Schwartz and Leonard (1984) found about the same proportion of action words. Gentner (1982), however, whose

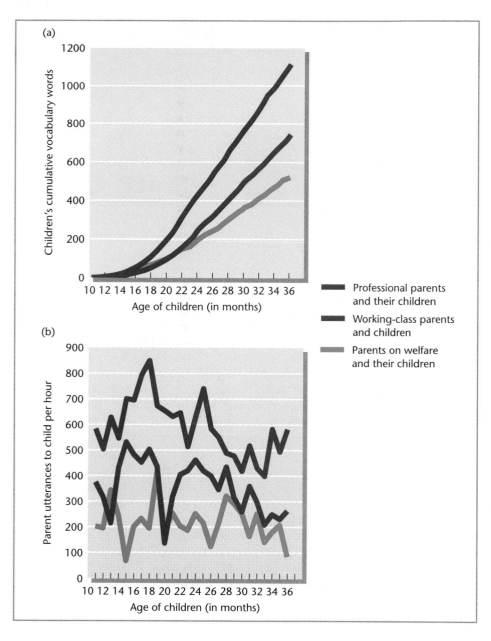

Social class and vocabulary development.
(a) Over a period of a little more than two years, children from working-class families (middle to lower socioeconomic status) built vocabularies about two-thirds as large as those acquired by children from professional families; children from families who were on welfare acquired vocabularies only half as large as those of the children from higher-class families. (b) The frequencies with which parents in each of the three groups talked to their children correlated quite well with children's vocabulary size: Parents in professional families, whose children had the largest vocabularies, talked to their children the most; parents in working-class families, whose children had the next largest vocabularies, talked a good deal less often; and parents in welfare families, whose children had the smallest vocabularies, talked even less. (*Source*: Hart & Risley, 1995)

study encompassed the first 100 words learned by his child participants, found that some children's vocabularies included as many as 30 percent action terms.

Some cross-cultural research found a greater proportion of nouns even among children whose native languages don't emphasize object words in spoken sentences, but studies of Korean children do not find nouns as prominent (Gentner, 1982; Gopnik & Choi, 1995; Slobin, 1985). Similarly, Tardif (1996) found that 21-month-old children learning Mandarin Chinese, used equal numbers of verbs and nouns in their speech. In part, this is because in some Asian languages (e.g., Japanese, Chinese) verbs play a more prominent role in speech and often occur in a prominent place at the end of a sentence (Hoff-Ginsberg, 1997). Moreover, the fact that Japanese mothers spend less time labeling objects than American mothers may account for the less pronounced bias toward noun production among Japanese children (Fernald & Morikawa, 1993). And some U.S. researchers (e.g., Bloom, 1993, 1998) have challenged the assumption that object names predominate in early vocabularies. Studying children who ranged in age from 9 months to 2 years, Bloom found that object words represented only a third of the words the children learned.

■ FIGURE 8-5
Words that children use first. According to the classic work illustrated here, naming or object words make up almost two-thirds of the vocabularies of children between 1 and 2 years old. (*Source*: Based on data from Nelson, 1973)

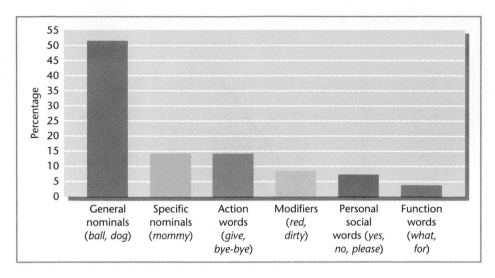

Several researchers have reported that the object words children learn first generally represent objects that they can act on and thereby produce a change or movement. For example, the words *shoes, socks,* and *toys,* all of which children manipulate, are more common than words for things that they cannot move or change in some way, like *table, stove,* or *tree* (Clark, 1983). As we've seen, they tend not to learn as many words for actions themselves. One explanation for these results is that the concepts that object words encode are conceptually simpler than those that action words encode (Gentner, 1982; Huttenlocher & Smiley, 1987). To learn object words, children must match objects with their appropriate linguistic referents (Gentner, 1982), but to learn action words, or verbs, children must also form an understanding of the connections between objects and actions (Huttenlocher & Lui, 1979).

What do these findings tell us about the relative importance of nature and nurture in language development? Studies of children's learning of action words and of words that describe emotions suggest vocabulary acquisition may involve not only the child's maturing ability to form concepts, but her response to parental reinforcement and her imitation of her parents. Huttenlocher and her associates (Huttenlocher, Smiley, & Charney, 1983) found that when children learned action words that require inferences about intentionality, such as *open* and *get,* they applied these words only to themselves and only later extended them to the actions of other people. Recall from Chapter 1 that Piaget described young children as egocentric and less able to take the viewpoints of others than older children.

When Huttenlocher and her colleagues studied children's use of emotional-state words, they discovered that children began to use these words at about the age of 2 and applied them almost exclusively to themselves. When they did use these words to characterize other people, they generally referred to clearly visible behaviors. For example, a child might use the word *sad* to refer to his own inner feeling but use it for another child's crying rather than to describe that child's feelings. When these investigators examined the children's parents' speech, however, they found that the parents also tended to use emotional-state words to describe their children's inner feelings but to use these same words to refer only to outward signs of emotionality in other people. Thus it would appear that the pattern of vocabulary development reflects both maturation in concept formation capabilities and the influence of the social environment.

Errors in Early Word Use

overextension The use, by a young child, of a single word to cover many different things.

Characteristic errors in children's early word use can help illuminate the learning process. Two such errors are overextension and underextension. In **overextension,** children use a single word to cover many different things. For example, everyone

TABLE 8-4   Children's Overextensions: Some Examples

Word	Referents
Ball	Ball, balloon, marble, apple, egg, wool pom-pom, spherical water tank
Cat	Cat, cat's usual location on top of TV even when absent
Moon	Moon, half-moon-shaped lemon slice, circular chrome dial on dishwasher, ball of spinach, wall hanging with pink and purple circles, half a Cheerio, hangnail
Snow	Snow, white tail of a spring horse, white flannel bed pad, white puddle of milk on floor
Baby	Own reflection in mirror, framed photograph of self, framed photographs of others
Shoe	Shoe, sock

Source: Adapted from Hoff-Ginsberg, 1997.

has heard a young child use the word *doggie* for horses, cows, giraffes, and all sorts of four-legged animals. Extensions based on perceptual similarity are common; another example is using the word *ball* for other round things like cakes, pancakes, oranges, the sun, and the moon. Overextension is common; about a third of young children's words are overextended at one time or another (Nelson, 1977). (See Table 8-4 for other examples of children's overextensions.)

Sometimes children's overextensions can be quite elaborate. For example, deVilliers and deVilliers (1992) reported an overextension made by their son, Nicholas, who learned the word *turtle* for a wind-up toy that swam in his bath:

> Within days of its first production, "turtle" was used to refer to other turtles, including ones with wheels, to a real turtle, and to pictured turtles. But other objects were also called "turtle": several toys that shared his bath, including a plastic walrus and a wind-up frog . . . and a pinecone with a stem that stuck out like a turtle's head. . . . Finally, Nicholas's big toe stuck out through a hole (in his pajamas) . . . and he said with delight "turtle." (p. 352)

Evidently, Nicholas had developed the concepts of the texture and/or patterning of the turtle's back and of the movement of the turtle's head. Although children show creativity and ingenuity in their overextensions, as their vocabularies develop and increase they use fewer overextended words (Bloom, 1993; deVilliers & deVilliers, 1992). Interestingly, overextensions in production do not predict overextensions in comprehension, which are infrequent (Naigles & Gelman, 1995).

In **underextension,** a less common type of error, children use a single word in a highly restricted and individualistic way. For example, a child may use the word *car* only when she sees her father's yellow Chevy and call all other automobiles, including her mother's green Ford, *trucks* (Bloom, 1993, 1998).

Parents, who, in speaking with their young children, may not initially give every variant of a class of objects its correct name may actually trigger some word errors. Mervis and Mervis (1982) found that mothers tended to use single nouns to label certain toys and objects; for example, they called both lions and leopards *kitty cats.* Although this may help the child at first, enabling him to pick out a stuffed animal rather than a truck from an array of toys on a shelf, it may lead to overextending categories. Both overextensions and underextensions may reflect children's gradual development (Huttenlocher & Smiley, 1987).

Another explanation for overextension is that as long as the child's vocabulary is limited, she tries to find the relationship between linguistic form and an element of experience; that is, she is not just making an error (Bloom, 1993, 1998). As Bloom notes, "It seems entirely reasonable for the child to use an available word to represent different but related objects—it is almost as if the child were reasoning, 'I know about dogs; that thing is not a dog. I don't know what to call it, but it is like a dog.'"

underextension   The use, by a young child, of a single word in a restricted and individualistic way.

TABLE 8-5 Speech Samples 10 Months Apart	
Child at 28 Months	*Child at 38 Months*
"What dat?"	"Who put dust on my hair?"
"Where birdie go?"	"You got some beads?"
"Read dat?"	"I broke my racing car."
"Have screw . . . "	"It's got a flat tire . . . when it's got flat tire it's need to go . . . to the station."
"Get broom . . . "	"The station will fix it."

Source: Adapted from Brown & Bellugi, 1964; McNeill, 1970.

(1976, p. 23). For the child, applying words in different contexts is a type of hypothesis testing, a process that continues throughout childhood but is particularly evident in the first 3 years when the child begins to relate word forms with objects (Kuczaj, 1982). Gradually, as the child's discriminations improve and her conceptual categories become more stable, her accuracy in the use of words increases.

THE ACQUISITION OF GRAMMAR: FROM WORDS TO SENTENCES

In their early years children achieve an incredible amount of learning about language. From simply crying when in distress to forming complete sentences from a vocabulary base of several thousand words is a great leap, and the rapidity with which children learn the complexities of their languages continues to fascinate developmentalists. As Table 8-5 shows, in just 10 months a child may go from barely intelligible speech to clear communication.

In this section we cover a great deal of this great leap in clarity and sophistication of communication. You may find it helpful to refer to the Turning Points chart on pages 308–309 to keep track of the sequence of development encompassed. We begin with the child's use of single-word utterances and then consider the evolution of two-word sentences, the emergence of modifications such as plurals and possessives, the development of questions and of negating sentences, and learning how to understand the meaning of others' utterances.

Can One Word Express a Complete Thought?

Are first words simply words? Or are they early attempts to express complete thoughts? When a young child points to a toy airplane on a high shelf and says "Down," or when he takes a spoon from his mother and says "Me," is there more to his utterance than meets the ear? In the first case, parents may assume that the child is requesting that the toy be taken down off the shelf; in the second example, they might guess that the child is saying, "I want to do it myself."

Dale (1976) has noted: "First words seem to be more than single words. They appear to be attempts to express complex ideas—ideas that would be expressed in sentences by an adult" (p. 13). The term **holophrase** has been given to such single words that appear to represent a complete thought. Whether or not children are really expressing in these single-word utterances thoughts that could be expressed in sentences—thoughts that include subjects, objects, and actions—remains an unanswered question.

holophrase A single word that appears to represent a complete thought.

Two-Word Sentences

When the child takes his next important step in language development, our uncertainty about what he is communicating is greatly lessened. Somewhere between

TABLE 8-6 Two-Word Sentences in Several Languages

Function of Utterance	Language					
	English	German	Russian	Finnish	Luo	Samoan
Locate, Name	there book	buch der [book there]	Tosya tam [Tosya there]	tuossa Rina [there Rina]	en saa [it clock]	Keith lea [Keith there]
Demand, Desire	more milk	mehr milch [more milk]	yeshchë moloko [more milk]	anna Rina [give Rina]	miya tamtam [give-me candy]	mai pepe [give doll]
Negate	no wet	nicht blasen [not blow]	vody net [water no]	ei susi [not wolf]	beda onge [my-slasher absent]	le' ai [not eat]
Describe event or situation	Bambi go	puppe kommt [doll comes]	mam prua [mama walk]	Seppo putoo [Seppo fall]	odhi skul [he-went school]	pá u pepe [fall doll]
Indicate possession	my shoe	mein ball [my ball]	mami chashka [mama's cup]	täti auto [aunt car]	kom baba [chair father]	lole a'u [candy my]
Modify, Qualify (attributive)	pretty dress	milch heiss [milk hot]	mama khoroshaya [mama good]	rikki auto [broken car]	piypiy kech [pepper hot]	fa'ali'i pepe [headstrong baby]
Question	where ball	wo ball [where ball]	gde papa [where papa]	missä pallo [where ball]		fea Punafu [where Punafu]

Source: Adapted from Slobin, 1979.

Notes: Luo is spoken in Kenya. The order of the two words in each "sentence" is generally fixed in all languages but Finnish, in which children are free to use both orders for some types of utterances.

1½ and 2 years of age the child begins to put two words together in what is often called **telegraphic speech.** Like telegrams, these two-word utterances include only the crucial words that are needed to convey the speaker's intent. Thus, although children generally use nouns, verbs, and adjectives, they are likely to omit other parts of speech such as articles and prepositions. The child's speech is novel and creative and is not merely a copy of adult language. Table 8-6 shows some two-word sentences used by young children speaking either English or one of several other languages (Slobin, 1985). Notice how these two-word phrases resemble one another in terms of the relationships between the words, or the primitive grammar, no matter how different the languages in which they were spoken. Indeed, if you ignore word order, most of these utterances read like direct translations of one another. And this similarity in semantic relations extends to the sign language many deaf people use. As Box 8-3 shows, in acquiring American Sign Language (ASL), deaf children start out with many of the same word combinations that hearing children produce as they acquire oral language.

> **telegraphic speech** Two-word utterances that include only the words that are essential to convey the speaker's intent.

Why are the early utterances of children similar? Language can be viewed as a way of expressing what one knows or understands about the world. The content of what children say is closely related to their cognitive development. As their capacity for understanding events in the world around them continues to grow, they tend to have encounters with similar kinds of situations. Their learning of language is tied to their beginning understanding of such things as the distinction between self and other; the concept of causality; and the notion of object permanence, or the fact that objects that they cannot see continue to exist and can be seen again. Thus wherever they live, in whatever society, children beginning to speak express similar relationships and events, such as agent-action relations, possessives, and disappearance-reappearance. The development of cognitive capacity and the development of language are undoubtedly closely related (Clark, 1983; Carey, 1994).

BOX 8-3

Child Psychology in Action

Language Learning in the Deaf

Deaf children learning American Sign Language (ASL) produce word combinations that are very similar to those that hearing children around the world produce (Meier & Newport, 1990). Compare the examples in Table 8-7 with those in Table 8-6: In both the deaf child's phrases and those uttered by hearing children we see locating and naming, indication of possession, making a demand, and describing-modifying. (For the ASL signs for some of the words in Table 8-7, see Figure 8-6.)

Among deaf children the length of utterances increases steadily, just as it does among hearing children, and like hearing children, those who use sign language tend to overextend (Bellugi, van Hoek, Lillo-Martin, & O'Grady, 1993; Petitto, 1993). Nor are young signing children always accurate; as with the early language of their speaking peers, early signs are not always perfect. For example, intending to point to their mouths in signing (which might indicate "speech" or "speaking"), children may miss and point to their chins (which could mean "preference" or "favorite").

Although the steps that children follow in learning language, whether gestural or spoken, are similar, recent evidence suggests that deaf children may learn sign language faster and earlier than hearing children learn spoken language. In a longitudinal study of 13 infants being reared by deaf parents, Bonvillian and his colleagues (Bonvillian, Orlansky, Novack, & Folven, 1983) found that these children learned signs several months earlier than hearing children learned words. Most hearing children do not utter their first recognizable word before the end of the first year. The signing infants produced their first recognizable sign by the time they were 9 months old. By the age of 17 months, these children began to combine two or more signs; again they were two to three months ahead of hearing children. However, the advantage doesn't appear to last. After 2 years of age, the differences between signers and speakers disappear (Bonvillian, Orlansky, & Folven, 1990). What might account for the early discrepancy? The most plausible explanation is that the motor centers of the brain develop more rapidly than do the speech centers. When the latter catch

■ FIGURE 8-6
Some signs in American Sign Language.
The deaf child whose two-word communications are shown in Table 8-7 might combine the signs in (a) and (b) in her first communication, those in (b) and (d) in her fourth sentence. (*Source*: Adapted from Costello, 1983)

up with the former, language learning may proceed at a similar pace in both deaf and hearing children.

"In spite of these early differences in rate of language acquisition, the really important aspects of language and the really important abilities the child brings to the problem of learning are independent of the modality in which the linguistic system operates. Language is a central process, not a peripheral one. The abilities that children have are so general and so powerful that deaf children proceed through the same milestones of development as do hearing children" (Dale, 1976, p. 59).

TABLE 8-7 Some Two-Word Combinations in a Deaf Child's Signing	
Sign	*Meaning*
Daddy work	"Daddy is at work."
Barry train	"That's Barry's [her brother's] train."
Bed shoes	(Asking where her slippers are)
Daddy shoe	(Attempting to persuade her father to take off his shoes and play in the sand)

Source: Meier & Newport, 1990.

Learning the Rules

One of the most interesting aspects of early grammar acquisition is the way children learn how to modify the meanings of the words they use, an accomplishment that also illustrates the close ties between semantic and grammar development. Roger Brown (1973), in his classic longitudinal study of Adam, Eve, and Sarah, followed these three children from 2 to 4 years of age, and noted, among many other things, that they acquired certain morphemes in a regular order. For example, during this period, the children begin to use qualifiers that indicate plurality or a possessive relationship. Table 8-8 lists the 14 morphemes that Brown studied in the order in which his young participants acquired them. Although Adam, Eve, and Sarah each acquired these morphemes at a different rate of speed, the order in which each child acquired them was the same.

Can we generalize from Brown's work? Fortunately, we don't have to rely on this evidence alone. In a cross-sectional study of 21 children, deVilliers and deVilliers (1973) provided confirmation of Brown's findings. Moreover, Brown's claims have generally been confirmed by later investigators (e.g., Maratsos, 1989, 1998). Notice that the order in which these morphemes are acquired is a sensible one: Simpler morphemes are acquired earlier than more complex ones. For example, plural forms, like -s, are learned before the copula (meaning a linking word) *be*. In the next two chapters we will see that this same general principle of progressing from the simple to the more complex characterizes children's cognitive development as well.

Slobin (1985) suggests that children go through four phases in their application of grammatical rules such as the use of plurals. In phase 1, they try but fail. In phase 2, they succeed in memorizing some of the irregular verbs, such as "broke" and "went," but do not yet acquire a grammatical rule. This kind of learning, of course, is quite inefficient. Imagine how time-consuming it would be if children had to learn separate, specific rules for each new word that they encountered. They might learn, for example, that two dogs is expressed as *dogs,* but they'd have to learn in a

TABLE 8-8   English-Speaking Children's First 14 Morphemes

Form	Meaning	Example
1. Present progressive: -ing	Ongoing process	He is sit*ting* down.
2. Preposition: in	Containment	The mouse is *in* the box.
3. Preposition: on	Support	The book is *on* the table.
4. Plural: -s	Number	The dog*s* ran away.
5. Past irregular: e.g., went	Earlier in time relative to time of speaking	The boy *went* home.
6. Possessive: -'s	Possession	The girl*'s* dog is big.
7. Uncontractible copula be: e.g., are, was	Number; earlier in time	*Are* they boys or girls? *Was* that a dog?
8. Articles: the, a	Definite/indefinite	He has *a* book.
9. Past regular: -ed	Earlier in time	He jump*ed* the stream.
10. Third person regular: -s	Number; earlier in time	She run*s* fast.
11. Third person irregular: e.g., has, does	Number; earlier in time	*Does* the dog bark?
12. Uncontractible auxiliary be: e.g., is, were	Number; earlier in time; ongoing process	*Were* they at home? *Is* he running?
13. Contractible copula be: e.g., -'s, -'re	Number; earlier in time	That*'s* a spaniel.
14. Contractible auxiliary be: e.g., -'s, -'re	Number; earlier in time; ongoing process	They*'re* running very slowly.

Source: Based on Brown, 1973.

separate lesson how to pluralize other words such as *cat* or *house.* In Slobin's third phase, children learn general grammatical rules that can be used with new as well as familiar words. Only in the fourth phase, however, do children—at 7 or 8—finally approach adult usage, recognizing when to apply these rules. A crucial achievement of this last phase is learning when *not* to apply a rule.

Adult language is full of irregularities and other exceptions to the rules. When children are first learning a language, they ignore these irregularities and rigidly apply the rules they learn. In **overregularization** of rules, children apply a rule for forming regularities in cases where the adult form is irregular and does not follow the rule. For instance, a young child may start out using the words *went* and *came* correctly but, after learning that *-ed* forms the past tense for many verbs, he may begin to use this ending for all verbs, producing *goed* and *comed* (Slobin, 1985). Similarly, a child often uses the word *feet* until she learns the regular plural ending; then she may switch to *foots* or sometimes *feets.* Occasionally, after learning that some plurals are formed by adding *-es* (e.g., *boxes*), a child will come up with *footses* for a time.

Children also sometimes create regularized singular words from an irregular plural. For example, a child the authors knew who used the word *clothes* insisted on calling one piece of clothing a *clo.* Another child overregularized a verb form, asking "I'm magic, amn't I?" Overregularization is found not only in the United States but in other countries, including the Soviet Union, where children apply the rules they learn broadly to form novel "regularized" words and phrases that do not occur in adult speech (Slobin, 1982).

Approaching Formal Grammar

In the third year of life "there is a grammatical flowering" (deVilliers & deVilliers, 1992, p. 378). Simple sentences start to become subtle and more complex as children show early signs of understanding the rules of adult grammar (Valian, 1986). Among children's many achievements is the beginning use of auxiliary and modal verbs (deVilliers & deVilliers, 1992). *Mode,* or "mood," is the capacity of verbs to convey factual statements, expressions of possibility (e.g., the subjunctive), or imperatives. For example, a child says, "Daddy *can* run," or he commands, "*Run, Daddy.*" One of the auxiliary verbs children begin to use at this stage is the verb *to be,* which appears in many English sentence structures and thus opens up the possibility of new forms of expression. Children begin to use questions:

overregularization The mistaken application of a principle of regular change to a word that changes irregularly.

Animated conversations like this one are a sign of the "grammatical flowering" that generally characterizes the third year of life.

"Can you run?" and they form simple negative sentences: "No run." They also begin to use tenses other than the present: "I kicked it." And they begin to use pronouns and articles and even begin to create complex sentences: "The teddy and doll are gonna play" (deVilliers & deVilliers, 1992, p. 379). Let us take a closer look at two of these grammatical milestones: questions and negatives.

Questions

To express a question, young children may first use an assertion such as "sit chair" or "see hole," simply raising their voices at the end to indicate that they are asking a question (deVilliers & deVilliers, 1979). For example,

I have some?
You like dis?

In the latter part of the third year children begin to ask "wh" questions—those that start with the words *what, when, who, why,* and *which*—as well as questions that begin with *how.* According to linguists Peter and Jill deVilliers (1979, 1992), the child's first such question is usually some variant of "whatsat," "whasit," "whatsit," "whaddes," "whatisdes." The deVilliers' son, Nicholas, learned these constructions early:

> At the age of 11 months, Nicholas picked up a *whatisdat* as one of his first "words" and pronounced it very accurately. We were trying in vain to keep him under control in a restaurant when he lunged over a neighboring diner's shoulder and demanded loudly, "Whatisdat?" to which the startled woman answered, "Fish!" (deVilliers & deVilliers, 1979, p. 61)

Between 2 and 3, children's "wh" constructions may fail to include the auxiliary verb, and they can be heard to say things like, "Where you going?" A little later they include the auxiliary without inverting it; for example, "Where you are going?" Finally, they incorporate all the rules for producing a "wh" question; for example, "Where are you going?"

An important feature of "wh" questions is that they enable children to exercise their curiosity. "Why" and "how" questions in particular facilitate their learning of new things. Again, we see that language and cognitive development are closely tied, each serving the other and both together promoting the child's overall progress.

Negatives

Research indicates that children use different rules to form different kinds of negatives. Expanding on Bloom's (1970) argument that three distinct types of negation appear in a particular developmental order, Tager-Flusberg (1985) proposed the following categories of negatives in the order of their appearance in young children's speech:

Type of Negation	Explanation	Example
1. Nonexistence	Remark as to the absence of something	"No cake" or "all gone cookie"
2. Rejection	Opposition to something	"No wash hair"
3. Denial	Denial that a statement made or implied by someone else is true	"That not Daddy"

Language researchers have found that these same types of negations appear in the same order in Japanese (Bloom, 1991; Clancy, 1985) as in English.

The development of these two types of speech, questions and negatives, is only a sample of a wide range of grammatical accomplishments during the preschool years. By 3 years of age, children begin to use sentences so complex that they "drive nonlinguists to their descriptive grammar books" (deVilliers & deVilliers, 1992, p. 379). Again, progress is gradual but orderly. At first children tack on relative clauses; for example, "See the ball that I got." It's only later that they interrupt a main clause with a subordinate clause: "The owl who eats the candy runs fast" (Slobin, 1985; Maratsos, 1998). And they ask and answer complex questions: "Where did you say you put my doll?" "These are punk rockers, aren't they?" (deVilliers & deVilliers, 1992, p. 379).

Although most fundamental forms of grammar are acquired by 4½ to 5 years, the process of grammar acquisition is not over during the preschool years. Specific aspects of syntax continue to develop through the elementary school years, as children experience exceptions and try to understand them (Maratsos, 1998). In fact, mastering the intricacies of grammar is, for most of us, a lifelong process!

How Children Make Sense of What They Hear

Children need not only to speak grammatically correct sentences but to understand the meaning of sentences they hear or read. Although we have been discussing language production, it is important to remember that productive and receptive language are closely linked. Several researchers have shown that children are apparently able to use syntactic and semantic cues to help them understand sentences at a very early age, sentences that are more complex than those they can produce. In fact, children seem able to call on a great store of linguistic knowledge to set up expectations about the identity of possible words. Syntax provides clues about the meanings not only of nouns or object words but of verbs or action words as well.

> Verbs can appear in different kinds of sentences. For example, a verb like *hit* means to do something to someone else; and it usually appears in a sentence like "Tom hit Jerry," in which the verb is preceded by one noun, the doer and followed by another noun, the recipient of the deed. In contrast, verbs like *laugh* that refer to an action with no recipient appear in sentences like "Tom laughed" in which there is just one noun, the doer. (Hoff-Ginsberg, 1997, p. 112)

According to Gleitman and her colleagues (Fisher, Gleitman, & Gleitman, 1991; Fisher, Hall, Rakowitz, & Gleitman, 1994; Gleitman, 1990), children use a kind of "syntactic bootstrapping" to figure out word meaning. According to this theory, once children learn how to parse utterances into syntactic units, they use this knowledge to distinguish the meaning of verbs they may not yet understand.

Letitia Naigles (1990, 1995), for example, demonstrated that 2-year-olds can use a verb's appearance in a transitive or intransitive form to decide whether causative or noncausative action is involved. Naigles first read the children the sentence, "The duck is gorping the bunny" and then they saw either a video in which a duck was making a rabbit do something or a video in which the duck and rabbit were both moving about but not directing their action toward each other. The fact that children were more likely to attend to the first video display indicated that they inferred a causal action from the transitive expression ("is gorping the bunny") in the sentence. In contrast, when the toddlers heard, "The duck and bunny are gorping" they looked at the video in which the two actors gestured together, presumably inferring from the intransitive expression that neither actor was making the other do anything.

According to Goodman (1989), even 1½- to 3½-year-old children use semantic and syntactic cues to identify spoken words. In a sentence completion task, Goodman presented children with spoken sentences and asked them to fill in a final missing noun. For example, to the utterance "Mommy feeds the _____," children responded "baby." In a word identification task, children listened to complete sentences and pointed to pictures to identify the final word in each sentence. In one condition of this task, the word called for by the sentence meaning was among those pictured, but the word actually spoken was represented by another picture. For example, children listened to the sentence "Ann drives the duck" and then looked at pictures of a duck, a truck, a dog, and a book; although the word spoken was *duck*, children chose the truck. When the children heard the sentence "The man sees the duck," however, they chose the duck picture.

Does the ability to use semantic and syntactic information improve with age? Entwisle and Frasure (1974) demonstrated that this is very probably so. Using a "noisy telephone" technique, in which background noise was used to make auditory material difficult to hear, these researchers asked groups of children 6, 7, 8, and 9 years old to listen to three sentences. The children were then asked to repeat the sentences as accurately as possible. Because the noise blocked out parts of the sentence, the children had to rely on their knowledge of how sentences are generally formed to fill in the missing words. Here are the sentences:

- Bears steal honey from the hive.
- Trains steal elephants around the house.
- From shoot highways the passengers mothers.

In the first, *meaningful* sentence, both semantics and syntax are correct. The second, *anomalous* sentence is syntactically correct, although it makes no sense. In the last, *scrambled* sentence, both syntax and semantics are jumbled, making this presumably the most difficult sentence for children to reproduce. As you can see from Figure 8-7, the older the child, the more he or she was able to benefit from the available syntactic and semantic clues. At all ages, the more such clues the children had, the better they did; all age groups experienced similar difficulties with the sentence in which these clues were totally absent.

Children's comprehension of many complex constructions remains poorly understood. We still don't know when or how children are able to understand "John was thought by Mary to have been scratched by Sam" or "Whom do you think Mary could ask Sam to talk to about that?" (Maratsos, 1983). It is quite clear that children continue to develop in both their production and understanding of complex syntax well beyond the early school years; a comparison of children's speech at the first- and eighth-grade levels testifies to these developments in production. Moreover, listening to a third-grade English lesson and a college seminar

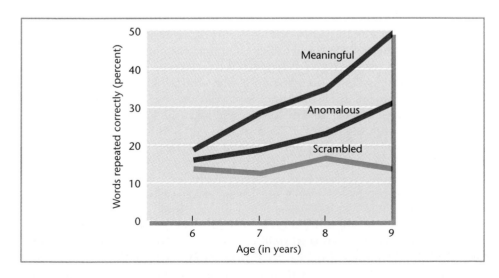

■ FIGURE 8-7
Learning to use semantic and syntactic clues.
The more syntactic and semantic clues offered by sentences heard against background noise, the more successful children were at repeating the sentences. All children had difficulty with the *scrambled* sentence that lacked any clues, but when clues were present, as in the *meaningful* and *anomalous* sentences, older children made better use of them than younger children. (*Source:* Entwisle & Frasure, 1974)

on Shakespearean sonnets clearly indicates that both comprehension and usage continue to develop for many years.

LEARNING THE SOCIAL AND CREATIVE USES OF LANGUAGE

Language, by its very nature, is a social phenomenon; it enables the child to communicate with other people. What becomes very important as children develop, therefore, is the decision as to what words and phrases to use in differing social situations. The rules for this usage, which we have already identified, are known collectively as *pragmatics*. Speakers have a variety of pragmatic intentions, such as getting people to do things for them and thanking people for their help, and they need to know how to express these intentions appropriately, depending on the situation and the other people involved. This focus on the social situation is seen even in the child's early one- and two-word expressions. When these expressions clearly refer to situations or sequences of events rather than to just one object or action, we call these expressions **speech acts.**

Communication becomes **discourse,** or socially based conversation, when children's speech is appropriate to both audience and situation and when children have become able to listen and respond to another's speech. The latter achievement includes the important ability to recognize one's own lack of understanding and to request additional information.

Children also develop the ability to use figurative language at quite young ages. Although we often tend to think of metaphors and the like as they are used in written language, even preschool children can understand such creative devices, and this capacity builds gradually. In this section we begin by looking at some of the rules of pragmatics and then turn to the ways children learn first to communicate and then to be a good listener. The final part of the section examines the evolution of figurative language.

speech acts One- or two-word utterances that clearly refer to situations or to sequences of events.

discourse Socially based conversation.

The Rules of Pragmatics

Even when a child has mastered meaning and syntax, she is not yet fully equipped to be an effective communicator. She must learn another set of rules, namely, when to use what language in what situation. To be an effective speaker requires a complicated set of skills. First, the child must engage the attention of her listeners so they know that she wants to address them and that they should listen. Second, effective speakers have to be sensitive to listeners' feedback. If children don't know when others fail to understand them or don't know how to change their messages to make themselves clear, they are not going to be very successful communicators. Third, speakers must adjust their speech to the characteristics of their listeners, such as age and cultural and social background. For example, the fifth-grade child must learn that in addressing his classmates he can use words and concepts that he can't use when he makes a presentation to the school's kindergartners. Being a good communicator requires that you adapt your message to consider "who the listener is, what the listener already knows, and what the listener needs to know" (Glucksberg, Krauss, & Higgins, 1975, p. 329).

A fourth rule requires that children learn to adjust their speech to suit the situation. Children and adults learn to talk differently on a playground or street than they do in a church or a classroom. A fifth guideline points out that communication is a two-way process. To participate in a conversation, one must be not only an effective speaker but a skilled listener; learning to listen is just as important as learning to speak. A sixth rule underlines the importance of understanding one's own communicative skills; that is, children must learn to evaluate both their own messages and the messages they receive from others for clarity and usefulness. They must also learn to correct their own messages when necessary and to let another speaker know when they do not understand the speaker's communication, often specifying the information that they need from the speaker (Glucksberg et al., 1975).

How early do children acquire these various communication skills? How do they develop? How do they shift across different types of communicative situations? We explore these questions next.

Learning to Adjust Speech to Audience

Speaker skills develop rapidly, and by 2 years of age, children are remarkably adept, both at engaging the attention of a listener and at responding to listener feedback. Videotaping ten 2-year-olds in their day-to-day interactions in a nursery school, Wellman and Lempers (1977) recorded 300 referential communicative interactions in which the communicator's intent was to point out, show, or display a particular object or referent to another child. The results were striking in their demonstration of these children's competence as speakers. The toddlers addressed their listeners when both were either interacting or playing together (82%) or when the listeners were at least not involved with someone else (88%). The children also directed communications to others when they could see each other (97%), when they were physically close to each other (91%), and, to a lesser extent, when the listeners were looking directly at them (41%). Similarly, the children made sure that when they spoke, they were close to the thing they were talking about (92%) and that the listener was also close to the thing referred to (84%), to make it more likely that the listener would understand the message.

In light of these precautions, it is not surprising that these young speakers were very effective in engaging their listeners. In fact, 79 percent of messages met with an adequate response from listeners. Moreover, speakers showed an awareness that certain situations were particularly difficult and adjusted their communications accordingly. They communicated more in difficult situations, as for example when there was an obstacle between the listener and the thing referred to, and used shorter messages in easy situations. Finally, these children were responsive to feedback from their listeners. For example, more than half the time, when the speakers received no response, they repeated their messages in some form, but they repeated messages only 3 percent of the time when they received an adequate response. If the listener either just looked or gave a negative verbal reaction—an indication that the she or he didn't understand—the children always recommunicated. In sum, these 2-year-olds were surprisingly sophisticated speakers.

Children as young as 2 years of age learn to adjust their speech when talking with other children of different ages. In several studies (Dunn, 1988; Dunn & Kendrick, 1982b) 2- and 3-year-olds used more repetitions and more attention-eliciting words (*hey, hello,* and *look*) when talking to their baby brothers and sisters than they did when addressing their mothers. Researchers (Gelman & Shatz, 1977; Shatz, 1983, 1994) have also found that children make the same kinds of adjustments when they speak to people outside the family. Contrast the following statements directed at an adult and a child (Shatz & Gelman, 1973):

> [*Four-year-old to unfamiliar adult*]: You're supposed to put one of these persons in, see? Then, one goes with the other little girl. And then the little boy. He's the little boy and he drives. And then they back up. And then the little girl has marbles. . . .

> [*Four-year-old to unfamiliar, younger child*]: Watch, Perry. Watch this. He backing in here. Now he drives up. Look, Perry, look here. Those are marbles, Perry. Put the men in here. Now I'll do it.

Despite the sophisticated level at which children can often operate, children's communicative competence does face some limitations. Preschoolers, for example, are more effective in a one-to-one conversation; they do less well when they must

TURNING POINTS: Language Milestones from Infancy to Middle Childhood

BIRTH	Crying
	Perception of others' speech
	Preference for human voices

1–6 MONTHS	Decrease in crying
	Makes soft sounds
	Cooing, laughing, gurgling
	Imitates short string of vowel sounds; alternates making sounds with another person
	Making consonant sounds; "says" consonants increasingly often
	Responds to prosodic features of speech (e.g., inflection and pitch)
	Intonations move toward speech patterns heard most often

6–12 MONTHS	Babbling strings of consonant-vowel combinations
	May babble more in familiar than unfamiliar settings
	Sounds resemble speech
	Increasing preference for own language over unfamiliar language
	Produces sound for familiar toy or object; experiments with sounds
	Babbling has sentencelike quality
	May "say" a word—*bah* for *bottle*, *mama* for *mother*
	May say no but doesn't always mean "no"
	May say two or three words; uses same word for category, such as *wah* for both *water* and *milk*

12–18 MONTHS	Sentences usually one word at first
	Tries hard to make self understood
	Symbolic gesturing
	Utterance of first words
	Imitates words; may repeatedly use a new word
	May use a few two-word sentences
	May use adjective to refer to self (*good boy*)
	Understanding of naming processes

compete for their turn with adults and other children. Before they are 4½, according to Ervin-Tripp (1979), children interrupt and are interrupted more often when in a group of other speakers than when talking to another child alone. Children don't track the conversations of two or more people easily, and they have trouble gauging when to enter the conversation and judging when it is their turn. On the other hand, all of us know adults who seem not to have learned these lessons very well either! Children are more competent when speaking about single familiar objects that are present in their immediate environment than when speaking about absent objects (absent in time or space); their own feelings, motivations, and thoughts; or relationships over space and time among people, objects, or situations (Dunn, 1988; Shatz, 1983, 1994). Speaking improves as the child develops, but speaker skills develop at different rates for different kinds of communication tasks.

How do children acquire the ability to converse on an increasingly sophisticated level? Learning language is similar to learning other forms of social behavior; chil-

TURNING POINTS: Language Milestones from Infancy to Middle Childhood *(continued)*

18–24 MONTHS	Beginning of naming explosion; average child goes from 50 to 900 words in about six months) Uses two-word sentences Rapid expansion of understanding
24–36 MONTHS	Decrease in gesturing Disappearance of babbling Increase in use of plurals, past tense, definite and indefinite articles, some prepositions Use of three-word combinations Excellent comprehension Gradually increasing use of sentences to communicate
36–48 MONTHS	Use of *yes/no* questions, *why* questions, negatives, and imperatives Embedding one sentence within another (using clauses) Use of overregularizations Vocabulary increases by about 1,000 words Coordination of simple sentences and use of prepositions
48–60 MONTHS	Increasingly sophisticated use of pragmatic rules of communication Use of humor and metaphor
5 YEARS AND BEYOND	Use of more complex syntax Further expansion of vocabulary (to about 14,000 words) Development of metalinguistic awareness

Source: Kopp, 1994.

Note: Developmental events described in this and other Turning Points charts represent overall trends identified in research studies. Individual children vary greatly in the ages at which they achieve these developmental changes.

dren learn through direct instruction from parents and teachers, and they learn by observing other people who figure in their lives (Bandura, 1989; Dunn, 1988). They also learn by listening to people talk about their own and others' behavior in one kind of situation or another—who said what to whom and how this or that person responded (Miller & Sperry, 1987).

Much of what children learn from parents about the culturally appropriate use of language involves the acquisition of social conventions and moral rules. For example, one of the child's first lessons in formal communication involves learning how to use polite, socially accepted words and phrases, such as *hello, good-bye, please,* and *thank you* (Grief & Gleason, 1980); these simple social routines are common to all cultures (Schieffelin & Ochs, 1987). But children must also learn when, where, and to whom it is appropriate to express negative feelings and thoughts, such as anger. Peggy Miller and Linda Sperry (1987) found that language plays a central role in socializing children into culturally acceptable expressions of emotion. In the working-class community these researchers studied, mothers, in their young children's presence, told stories of encounters they had had in which they and others became angry and used language to express and respond to anger.

An important point to be learned here was that one's anger and aggressiveness must be justified by some instigating remark or act of another person. One mother told of being referred to as a "big-nosed bitch" by another woman and described her own rather inventive retort as, "Well you fat slob you, I put you in a skillet and strip you down to normal size, if you mess with me" (Miller & Sperry, 1987, p. 13). Although mothers in this urban community were concerned to prepare their children to defend themselves against aggression from others, they also made it clear to their children that they needed to apologize when they were at fault and that in such situations anger and aggressive behavior were inappropriate.

Learning to Listen Critically

To learn from a communication, you must be able to recognize when a message sent to you is not clear. Young children are often unaware that they do not understand a message. In one experiment, Markman (1977) gave first and third graders game instructions that left out critical information that was essential to playing the game. The third graders noticed the inadequacy of the instructions more readily than the younger children; indeed, the latter were generally unaware that information was missing and had to be urged to try to play the game before realizing that they didn't know enough to do so. Another group of researchers (Flavell, Speer, Green, & August, 1981) found a similar developmental trend among kindergarten children and second graders: The kindergartners were less likely than the older children to recognize that guides given them for building a toy house were defective.

If the task is simple enough, even 3-year-olds can recognize an ambiguous message when they hear one and can act in appropriate ways to resolve the communication gap. In one study (Revelle, Wellman, & Karabenick, 1985), an adult made a variety of requests of 3- and 4-year-olds during a play session. Sometimes the requests were ambiguous; for example, the investigator might ask for a cup without specifying which of four different cups she or he wanted. Or the adult might yawn in the middle of the request, making it difficult for the child to hear clearly. In other cases, a request was impossible—"Bring me the refrigerator" (the only refrigerator available was a real and very large one)—or the object was unavailable—"Bring me your mother's slippers." Even the 3-year-olds showed clearly that they recognized when a request was problematic, and preschoolers knew how to remedy the communication problem by requesting more information. For example, when asked to bring the refrigerator, more than one 3-year-old asked, "How? It's too heavy." Revelle and associates suggest that the essential skills in monitoring communication are realizing that problems can arise, recognizing problems when they do occur, and knowing how to fix them. Three- and 4-year-olds seem to possess all of these fundamental monitoring skills.

Learning to listen carefully to another's message is an important achievement, and adults can help children learn to attend to objects and events in the environment.

Children can be taught to be more effective listeners, but there may be a minimal age at which children can learn to listen critically. Two studies have shown that when 6- to 10-year-old children were encouraged to ask a speaker questions to clarify his or her communication, they performed more effectively than children who were not given this lesson in listening (Cosgrove & Patterson, 1977; Patterson & Kister, 1981). That 4-year-olds did not benefit from this instruction suggests that this type of listener strategy may be a moderately advanced communication skill.

The Use of Figurative Language

Figurative expressions such as "a seed is like a pregnant woman," "the pillowy clouds," and "he croaked like a frog" are powerful imaginative communications. These expressions communicate something about a concept by comparing it to a similar concept from a different conventional category. When do children begin to produce and comprehend metaphor and other forms of figurative speech? Almost as soon as they start to talk!

According to Winner, McCarthy, Kleinman, and Gardner (1979), an 18-month-old child called a toy car a snake while twisting it up his mother's arm, and a 26-month-old exclaimed "Corn, corn!"' while pointing to a yellow plastic baseball bat. Utterances like these are known as "child metaphors" because, although they are not strictly metaphors, they violate the conventions of naming (they refer to things by a name different from their literal names) or compare two objects that belong to different conventional categories.

Children's comprehension of metaphor is a continuous process that begins very early and develops gradually to encompass a wider and wider range of figurative linguistic input (Gentner & Stuart, 1983; Vosniadou, 1987; Winner, 1988). To understand increasingly complex metaphors, children need to broaden their general knowledge and to hone their linguistic skills (Vosniadou, 1987). Without adequate knowledge, even adults would find it difficult to compare things from widely different frames of reference. In addition, metaphoric expressions can take a variety of linguistic forms, some of which may be easier to understand than others. For example, similes, which are based on nonliteral similarity, make explicit comparisons, using the words *as* or *like* (our first example at the beginning of this section). This makes them easier for children to understand than metaphors, in which the comparison is implied, as in our second example (Vosniadou, 1987).

Very young children can comprehend figurative speech if metaphors are simple and occur in the appropriate context (Winner, 1988). Although the beginnings of metaphor comprehension emerge during the preschool years, development is not complete until the late childhood years, when the child's conceptual and linguistic knowledge approximates that of the adult. Children's ability to produce and comprehend metaphoric language depends critically on what they already know, however, and presenting children with metaphors and encouraging them to think in figurative ways may help to advance and enrich their conceptual development. One kindergarten class, after listening to the teacher read Christina Rossetti's poem "The Clouds," came up with an amazing number of ideas as to why the poet likened clouds to sheep and the sky to a blue hill, including that clouds are "curly." The class went on in subsequent weeks to talk about metaphors in other literature.

Metaphoric competence is based on children's ability to see similarities among objects and events in the world around them, an ability that also plays a fundamental role in categorization. Both categorization and the use of metaphor allow children to use their existing knowledge to understand new things. Metaphors in particular reflect the transfer of knowledge from well-known to less familiar domains and, as such, may serve as important mechanisms in acquiring new knowledge (Vosniadou, 1987).

METALINGUISTIC AWARENESS: KNOWING ABOUT LANGUAGE

One of the crowning achievements in language development, and one of the latest to develop, is the ability not merely to know language in the sense of being able to speak and understand it but to know *about* language. That is, children become aware that they know language and can think and talk about language itself.

metalinguistic awareness The understanding that language is a system of communicating with others that is bound by rules.

Do children understand that words are made up of discrete sounds? Can children tell you what a word is? When can children describe the differences between grammatically correct and incorrect sentences? **Metalinguistic awareness,** the understanding that language is a rule-bound system of communicating with others, includes the ability to talk about the various properties and uses of language. This understanding and ability emerges well after children are proficient producers of sounds and sentences (Bullinger & Chatillon, 1983). Before they are 5 years old, children have trouble recognizing that words are groups of sounds, and they are baffled if you ask them to tell you the first sound in their names. For children, reflecting on sounds is a lot tougher than making them! Nor are words any easier to talk about. Before the age of 8, children confuse words with the objects that they describe. Words are *cats, toys,* and *cars,* but children have trouble articulating the concept that words are elements of language and independent of the objects or events to which they refer (Wetstone, 1977). It is not until children are about 10 years old that they define words as "meaning something" (Berthoud-Papandropoulou, 1978).

To test children's understanding of grammar, we can ask children to judge between grammatical and ungrammatical sentences and acceptable and unacceptable syntax. In one investigation, deVilliers and deVilliers (1972), using the clever technique of asking children to teach a puppet to talk correctly, tested children's ability not only to judge but to correct word order in sentences describing specific actions. Sometimes the puppet spoke in correct word order; for example, "Eat the cake." At other times the puppet reversed word order: "Dog the pat." And at still other times the puppet used correct syntax but described actions that were impossible: "Drink the chair." The children both told the puppet whether it was right or wrong and helped the puppet rephrase the "right way."

The researchers found a clear relationship between the children's level of language development and their metalinguistic awareness; as their ability to produce and comprehend sentences increased, their awareness increased as evidenced by their ability to correct the puppet's "wrong" utterances (deVilliers & deVilliers, 1992). According to Dale (1976), the process of becoming aware of language continues throughout development and "in its highest form, it becomes the basis of aesthetic pleasure in poetry and prose" (p. 128).

BILINGUALISM AND LANGUAGE DEVELOPMENT

bilingual education Teaching children two languages at the same time.

The distribution of ethnic groups in the United States is changing rapidly. By about 2005, in some parts of the United States a majority of children will not speak English as their first language. What are the implications of **bilingual education,** in which children learn two languages simultaneously, for the language acquisition process? Although many experts have expressed concern that the task of learning two languages interferes with children's language learning, this may not be generally the case. Although children who learn two languages may learn both languages more slowly than some of their peers learn one language, the performance gap disappears as

Despite research that suggests a neurological reason why children can learn two languages equally easily and well at the same time (see text), the issue of bilingual education is still highly controversial among both educators and parents.

children develop. Most evidence (Bialystok, 1991; de Houwer, 1995; Hakuta, 1986) suggests that children who are 5 or older when they learn to speak two languages have smaller comprehension vocabularies than monolingual children. In contrast, studies of children between 8 months and 2½ years old found that bilingual and monolingual children had comprehension vocabularies of about the same size (Pearson, Fernández, & Oller, 1993). Although a bilingual child may have in each of her languages a vocabulary that's smaller than a monolingual child's vocabulary, her total production vocabulary—her vocabularies in both languages combined—may be equal in size to the monolingual child's production vocabulary (Pearson et al., 1993).

A recent study (Hirsch & Kim, 1997) has suggested that when children learn two languages simultaneously, from infancy, the languages share the same brain region that is responsible for the execution of speech as well as for some grammatical aspects of language (called *Broca's area*). However, when children learn a second language later in childhood or adulthood, this brain region is divided, with a distinct area reserved for the second language. If these findings are valid, we might speculate that they underlie the apparent greater ease of learning a second language early in childhood. Perhaps future studies will shed more light on this issue.

One important determinant of how well children master each of two languages is how often they are exposed to each one. Very few children, for example, are exposed to equal inputs of Spanish and English. As researchers recently found in Miami, a city that is home to a large Cuban population, children who received less than 25 percent of their language input in Spanish were unlikely to become competent Spanish speakers (Pearson, Fernández, Lewedeg, & Oller, 1997). As in the case of many other kinds of lessons, dosage is an important determinant of how well children will learn.

Learning a second language often has specific benefits. Studies have shown that children who learn two languages are more cognitively advanced, have better concept formation, and are more flexible in their thinking (Diaz, 1983, 1985; Goncz & Kodzopeljic, 1991; Rosenblum & Pinker, 1983). Not only do language and cognitive development benefit from bilingualism but children's social behavior may improve as well. Lambert (1987) studied English-speaking children who participated in a French-language immersion program in Quebec, Canada. In comparison to control pupils, the "immersion" students had less stereotyped attitudes toward French-Canadian peers. Moreover, the immersion experience resulted in more mature and productive "social perspectives." For example, they offered more-sophisticated solutions to solving cultural differences between French and English Canadians. In sum, learning two languages may not be the problem it has been thought but rather an advantage and an opportunity.

SUMMARY

- **Language** serves a variety of purposes for the developing child. It facilitates interpersonal communication, helps organize thinking, and aids in learning. The development of **communicative competence** is an important part of children's language learning.
- Communication requires us to use both **productive language,** transmitting messages to others, and **receptive language,** in which we receive and understand messages others send us.

The Components of Language: Phonology, Semantics, Grammar, and Pragmatics

- The study of language can be divided into four areas. **Phonology** describes a language's systems of sounds, or the way basic sound units, called **phonemes,** are connected to form words. **Semantics** is the study of the meaning of words and sentences. **Grammar,** which describes the structure of a language, includes **syntax** and **morphology; morphemes** are a language's smallest units of meaning. **Pragmatics** consists of rules for the use of appropriate language in particular social settings.

Theories of Language Development

- The traditional learning view explains language development by the principle of reinforcement. Other learning theorists see the child learning language primarily through imitation. Although learning principles seem to be important in modifying language usage, they do not explain how children might acquire the enormous number of reinforcement linkages required to communicate effectively. Neither do they account for the regular sequence of language development, children's creative utterances, or the fact that children learn to speak grammatically even when parents fail to reinforce grammar.
- According to Noam Chomsky's nativist approach to language development, children have an innate **language acquisition device (LAD)** that enables them to learn language early and quickly. Support for this position comes from the finding of certain universal features in all languages, such as the use of a relatively small set of sounds and the combination of words into what in English are called "sentences," as well as from evidence that there may be a **critical period** for learning language. Critics point out that there is little agreement about the exact nature of the early grammatical rules that children learn and argue that language is not acquired as rapidly as nativists once thought. They also point out that the wealth of variant grammatical and syntactic rules around the world argues against any sort of universality and that the nativist view ignores the social context in which language develops.
- Most modern theorists take an interactionist position, recognizing that children are biologically prepared for language but require extensive experience with expressed language for adequate development. According to this view, children play an active role in acquiring language by formulating, testing, and evaluating hypotheses about their languages' rules.

- In proposing a **language acquisition support system (LASS),** Jerome Bruner emphasizes the critical roles of parents and other early caretakers in the child's language development. American middle-class mothers in particular support a child's beginning language by using **infant-directed speech,** or simplified language with their children, by playing nonverbal games with them, by using the technique of **expansion** to expand or add to children's statements, and by **recasting** children's incomplete sentences in grammatical form. Many cultures do not use such specific techniques, nor do they demonstrate that **negative evidence** is a critical force in language learning.

The Antecedents of Language Development

- Infants acquire early training in the give and take of conversation through "pseudo dialogues" with their parents, and by the time they are 1 year old, they are highly skilled at nonverbal communication. Using **protodeclaratives** and **protoimperatives,** young children can make statements about things and get other people to do things for them.
- Infants' capacity for receptive language begins as early as the first month of life, as demonstrated in their **categorical speech perception,** the ability to discriminate among consonant sounds as well as their ability to recognize some vowel sounds by the age of 2 months.
- Initially babies can distinguish sounds in languages other than that of their parents, but as children are exposed to their native languages, their abilities to distinguish and categorize phonemes continue to be refined and specialized for the sounds of their own languages.
- Some evidence indicates that infants may be able to segment speech and to recognize words in the context of ongoing speech earlier than we had thought.
- Precursors to productive language include **cooing, babbling,** and **patterned speech.** Babbling occurs in many cultures, and the babbling of deaf babies is very similar to that of hearing infants. Babbling has also been shown to resemble a child's first meaningful words, a finding that suggests its importance in the development of linguistic skills.

Semantic Development: The Power of Words

- Children's acquisition of vocabulary proceeds in bursts, the first of these occurring at about a year and a half in the **naming explosion.** To build their vocabularies, children use **fast-mapping** to connect a new word with a concept they already understand. Other aids to rapid learning of new words include a number of constraints that allow children to make certain narrowing judgments about a new word, such as that it refers only to an object or that it is entirely different from other words they already know.
- Infants' speed at learning words may be increased by certain kinds of constraints—whole object, taxonomic, and mutual exclusivity—that limit the kinds of hypotheses the child entertains in figuring out the meaning of a new word.
- Children may learn object or naming words first, although some research has suggested that such words make up only a third of early vocabularies. A common error is that of **overextension,** in which a single word covers many different things. In **underextension,** a child may restrict a word to only one representative of a category.

The Acquisition of Grammar: From Words to Sentences

The one-word utterances that children begin to produce from about 1 year on are known as **holophrases** to indicate that these words often appear to represent a complete thought.

■ Somewhere between 1½ and 2, children begin to use **telegraphic speech,** which generally includes only nouns, verbs, and adjectives. Probably because language development and cognitive development go hand in hand, these two-word communications are semantically similar across cultures and languages, including the sign language used by the deaf.

■ Children appear to learn qualifying morphemes in the same order. Typically, they learn simpler morphemes, such as the suffix *-ing* and the plural form *-s,* earlier than more complex ones, such as the contractions *that's* and *they're.* In **over-regularization,** children apply rules for regular formations in all cases, including those where formations are properly irregular.

■ At about the age of 3, children begin to form more complex sentences, showing signs of understanding some of the rules of adult grammar. In the latter part of the third year, the questions they have started to frame begin to include "wh" questions and questions that begin with "how"; these questions facilitate gathering a great deal of new information. Negative statements may express recognition that something is absent or has disappeared or rejection or denial of something.

■ The process of acquiring grammatic forms and achieving grammatic accuracy continues throughout the elementary school years and to some degree is a life-long task.

■ Using a kind of "syntactic bootstrapping," children as young as 1½ or 2 years old use semantic and syntactic cues to help them understand sentences. This ability improves both as a function of an increasing number of cues and with age, but children's comprehension of complex sentence structures continues to develop for many years.

Learning the Social and Creative Uses of Language

■ Because language is a social phenomenon, children must learn **pragmatics,** or the rules for the appropriate use of language in differing social situations. Children must be able to send their own messages to other people as well as receive and understand the messages others send them.

■ To raise their level of communication beyond **speech acts** to true **discourse,** children must learn a complicated set of skills, including how to engage the attention of listeners, how to be sensitive to listeners' feedback, how to adjust speech to characteristics of listeners and to particular situations, how to be good listeners, and how, as listeners, to let others know that their messages are unclear and that they need to provide more information.

■ Even preschoolers are remarkably sophisticated speakers, but because they have difficulty tracking multiple speakers and judging when it is their turn to speak, they are more effective on a one-to-one basis than in a group. Children improve their conversational sophistication through direct instruction and by observing/listening to others speak.

■ Children must learn not only how to express positive thoughts and feelings, through polite linguistic conventions, but how to give expression to such potentially negative things as anger and aggressivenes. They must also learn when expression of the latter is inappropriate and requires apology.

■ Children's ability to recognize that messages directed to them are unclear improves with age. Although children can be taught to be more effective listeners, there may be a minimal age at which they can benefit from such instruction.

- Perhaps as early as a year and a half, children can understand and even produce some forms of figurative speech, although some early efforts, known as "child metaphors," are not true metaphorical expressions. Presenting children with metaphors, along with encouraging their skills at categorization, may facilitate their learning to use existing knowledge in understanding new things.

Metalinguistic Awareness: Knowing About Language

- When children achieve **metalinguistic awareness,** about the age of 10, they can both understand that language is a system of rules for communication and discuss the properties and uses of language. Although they can use many rules at an earlier age, they have difficulty separating words from the object or events they represent and grasping the concept that words are elements of language.

Bilingualism and Language Development

- The evidence indicates that **bilingual education,** in which children learn two languages simultaneously, does not place children at a disadvantage in terms of language proficiency. In fact, learning two languages may have specific benefits, such as advanced cognitive skills, more flexibility of thought, and greater acceptance of peers of other cultural backgrounds.

Cognitive Development: Piaget and Vygotsky

C H A P T E R 9

One of the main tasks that the child confronts is to understand the world. As adults, we take it for granted that an object continues to exist even when we can't see it and that most things that are unsupported or released from a height will fall downward, not float up in the air, and possibly be damaged or broken. We also understand the many symbols people use to communicate with one another, whether by spoken or written language or by gesture. Based on this kind of knowledge, we form expectations about objects, situations, and people. If we put a coat in a closet and shut the closet door, we expect the coat to remain there even though it is out of sight. If we place a fragile glass on the edge of a table so that most of the glass is unsupported, we expect it to topple over, fall to the floor, and break. Spoken language is not just a string of sounds to us, but an organization of meaningful words; the wave of a hand or wink of an eye are not just movements of the body, but gestures that *tell* us something. By contrast, very young babies lack any of this everyday knowledge and must learn it through experience.

The field of cognitive development focuses on how intellectual abilities and knowledge of the world change as a person grows older. **Cognition,** or the mental activity through which human beings acquire and process knowledge, includes the functions of perception, learning, memory, reasoning, and thought. It is such a broadly integrative concept that most of the topics covered in other chapters of this book have relevance for cognitive development. Biological, mental, emotional, and social influences all play a role in how we process information and understand the world.

In this chapter and its companion, Chapter 10, we present several different models of the psychological processes and intellectual structures that underlie cognitive development. In this chapter we consider two models. First, we explore Jean Piaget's monumental theory of cognitive development, which emphasizes developmental changes in the organization or structure of children's thinking processes and the ways that differences in these structures are reflected in children's learning at different ages. In this context we examine a number of the challenges to Piagetian thinking that developmentalists and others have mounted in recent years. Then we consider Lev Vygotsky's sociocultural theory of cognitive development, which suggests that a child's level of cognitive competence interacts with his or her social environment to produce advances in thinking and understanding.

In Chapter 10 we will explore the information-processing view of cognitive development that emerged from a comparison between the workings of the human mind and the workings of the computer. This view, which holds that people use an array of cognitive abilities and strategies to process information, focuses on the role these cognitive operations play in the way people learn about things in their world. In our second cognitive chapter we will also look at a fourth model, sometimes called the neo-Piagetian synthesis, which combines elements of Piaget's theory and the information-processing view. This model proposes that as children grow older, changes in the strategies they use to tackle cognitive tasks bring about structural changes in their thinking processes.

cognition The mental activity through which human beings acquire and process knowledge.

PIAGET'S THEORY OF COGNITIVE DEVELOPMENT

One of the most important yet controversial theories of cognitive development is that of the famous Swiss scientist Jean Piaget (Beilin, 1992). It is at least in part because this theory has stimulated so many other researchers' ideas about cognitive development in children that we explore Piaget's work in considerable depth.

The Evolution of Piaget's Thinking

Piaget began his scientific career in 1907, at the age of 10, when he published his first scholarly article, on a rare albino sparrow, in a natural history journal. As a result of Piaget's subsequent writings on mollusks, the director of the Geneva

Piaget based much of his theory of children's cognitive development on direct observations and interviews with young children. When he traveled to the United States he often visited with children in nursery schools and the early grades.

Museum of Natural History offered Piaget the position of curator of the mollusk collection and was surprised indeed to discover that the creative biologist was still just a schoolboy! (He withdrew his job offer.)

Studying in Paris with Alfred Binet (we discuss Binet's important work on intelligence testing in Chapter 11) shortly after obtaining his degree, Piaget began to focus on the relationship between psychology and biological science, with a particular emphasis on development. As he helped Binet to develop standardized IQ tests for children, Piaget noticed not only that children of the same age made similar errors but that these errors differed from those of older or younger children. Piaget's perspective on cognitive development began to take shape as he perceived that these differences in the types of children's errors seemed to reveal distinct age-related ways of thinking and understanding the world. Thus, for Piaget, children's incorrect responses on tests were often more enlightening than their correct responses, and the study of what children know and do not know became an avenue to understanding changes in how children think.

Piaget's approach to exploring this topic often involved unstructured interviews with children, in which he would present the children with a problem to solve or a question to answer and then ask them to explain their thinking. When he worked with younger children—often his own three infants—he substituted detailed observations for formal interviews. As we will see, it was this subjective nature of his explorations that led others in the field to criticize Piaget, although he did later attempt to test some of his hypotheses with more controlled experiments. In the two decades that followed his work in Paris, Piaget wrote a remarkable series of books on the intellectual development of children; by the time he died, in 1980, he had published more than 40 books and 200 articles.

Although well known in European scientific circles, Piaget did not begin to have an impact on American developmental psychology until the early 1960s. In the United States in the 1930s and 1940s, child psychology was largely a descriptive field that lacked a theoretical focus. Most researchers of the era who were interested in intelligence were concerned with measuring and describing it, not explaining its development. What theory did impinge on the field was mainly the stimulus-response model of learning derived from the behaviorism of John B. Watson (see Chapter 1). Stimulus-response theorists sought to discover general laws of learning that were based on principles of reinforcement, punishment, generalization, and extinction and that applied to all organisms, regardless of age or species. A theory like Piaget's, which saw the human mind as something special and proposed that the developing child evidenced radically different ways of thinking and understanding at different points in development, was contrary to the prevailing view in American psychology.

By the end of the 1950s, however, the influence of behaviorism began to wane. Although learning specialists tried, they failed to produce a satisfactory theory of development, and disenchantment with learning theory itself set in. Piaget's theory was an attractive alternative, for it was a genuine developmental theory derived from direct observations of how children's abilities and limitations change as they grow from infancy to adolescence. Thus, when in 1963 John Flavell published *The Developmental Psychology of Jean Piaget,* a lucid, comprehensive summary and analysis of Piaget's work, the Piagetian perspective emerged as an influential theoretical guide to research on children's cognitive development.

The Child as an Active Seeker of Knowledge

Organizing an understanding of the world is a formidable task. How do children learn about the functions of objects in their environment, such as food, toys, furniture? How do they learn what constitutes stability in their environment? And how do they learn how and why things in their environment change? How do they form expectations based on stability and change? Piaget believed that children play an active role in accomplishing this enormous task; that is, rather than passively wait to take in information from their environment, they continuously and actively seek out information and adapt it to the knowledge they already have. In this way they construct a view of reality from their own experiences, developing cognitive structures and processes that form the basis for comprehension of their environment and response to it. Piaget set out to discover precisely how children at different points in their development think about the world and how systematic changes in their thinking and their understanding of the world come about. Although Piaget was careful to point out that children vary in their achievement of different cognitive advances, he was also careful to provide approximate ages at which these achievements occur. In our Turning Points chart (pp. 324–325) we take account of Piagetian and Vygotskian notions of the milestones of cognitive development as well as those of some contemporary investigators.

Cognitive Structures

Piaget believed that children organize their knowledge of the world into increasingly more complex cognitive structures. A *cognitive structure* is not a physical entity in the brain but an organized group of interrelated memories, thoughts, and strategies that the child uses in trying to understand a situation. Piaget built much of his theory around the concept of the **schema** (plural, **schemata**), a cognitive structure that forms the basis for organizing actions in order to understand and respond to the environment. Children possess many different schemata, which change as they grow older.

Do newborns possess schemata? Yes, they do, but infants' schemata largely take the form of innate reflexes and patterns of physical action that reflect organized ways of relating to and knowing the world. For example, newborns will suck reflexively on anything that touches their lips. This organized sucking behavior in response to a wide range of stimuli is a way of relating to the environment and beginning to learn about it. Thus, newborn babies may be said to possess a sucking schema. Newborns possess many other schema as well, such as grasping, kicking, and looking, all of which are manifested in organized patterns

schema (Plural, *schemata*); a cognitive structure, or an organized group of interrelated memories, thoughts, and strategies that the child uses to try to understand a situation; a schema forms the basis for organizing actions to respond to the environment.

of activities. Although these early schemata are primitive in their reliance on sensory input and physical activity to relate to the environment, they are also organized templates that infants use to respond to the world.

As children grow older and gain experience, they shift gradually from using schemata based on overt physical activities to those based on internal mental activities. Piaget called these mental schemata **operations.** The earliest operations are formed when the physically based schemata of younger babies are internalized and become part of organized mental structures, including strategies, plans, and "rules" for solving problems. Thus, an action-based grasping schema can become part of a complex plan for possessing a desirable object.

Cognitive Processes

Piaget proposed that children use certain innate principles of cognitive processing to continually modify their schemata for learning about and responding to their environment. The most important of these principles are organization and adaptation.

Organization is the predisposition to combine simple mental structures into more complex systems. For example, the infant may initially have a sucking schema, a looking schema, and a grasping schema that function independently, but gradually the three are organized into a more complex system involving the coordination of looking, grasping, and sucking. Now the infant can see an object, inspect it with his eyes, reach for and grasp it, and bring it to his mouth to suck on and explore it.

The second innate principle of cognitive processing is **adaptation,** or the individual's tendency to adjust to environmental demands. Adaptation is composed of two other processes, called assimilation and accommodation, that interact to modify children's schemata. To deal with a new experience, children at first try **assimilation;** that is, applying their existing schemata to the new experience, they try to mold it to fit into their current way of relating to and knowing the world. For example, as babies are confronted with new objects, they try to assimilate those objects to their complex looking-grasping-sucking schema. In most cases they are successful, and object after object gets grasped and placed in the mouth.

What happens when babies encounter an object that is hard to assimilate? A large inflated beach ball, for example, is very difficult to grasp and suck. Now the infant must modify her strategy for exploring objects (her looking-grasping-sucking schema) and adopt a new approach. Using the method of **accommodation,** she may hold the ball in her arms instead of her hands and lick it with her tongue instead of sucking on it. In this way, she has modified an existing schema to fit the characteristics of the new situation. More extreme accommodation is also called for at times, when children must give up old schemas entirely and find a whole different way of relating to a new situation. For example, no matter how hard they try, babies cannot catch hold of a stream of running water, nor can they grasp and draw a beam of light to their mouths. These new experiences demand new strategies for exploration, and new ways of understanding the world, and so babies' organized patterns of thought and behavior expand.

In Piaget's theory, cognitive development is based on modifications to schemata that result from innate predispositions to organize and adapt to new experiences in certain ways. Assimilation and accommodation work together to organize children's knowledge and behavior into increasingly complex structures. These processes are found in all normal children and continue to operate throughout the life span.

operations Schemata based on internal mental activities.

organization The predisposition to combine simple mental structures into more complex systems.

adaptation The individual's tendency to adjust to environmental demands.

assimilation Molding a new experience to fit an existing way of responding to the environment.

accommodation Modifying an existing way of responding to the environment to fit the characteristics of a new experience.

PIAGET'S STAGES OF COGNITIVE DEVELOPMENT

Piaget viewed intellectual growth in terms of progressive changes in children's cognitive structures. These changes manifest themselves in stages of development, each different from the one that precedes it. Although children do not reach these stages

Turning Points: The Child's Cognitive Development from Infancy Through Late Childhood

1 MONTH Becomes more efficient in use of reflexes and can invite stimulation that allows this use; can tell the difference between mother's nipple, the nipple on a bottle, thumb, and a pacifier

2 MONTHS Can anticipate: stops crying at sight of mother's breast or the bottle; expects animate behavior from human beings

3 MONTHS Shows recognition memory; reacts to newness with body stiffening; quiets at sight of interesting toy

4 MONTHS Repeats actions of own body that are pleasurable and satisfying; can reach out and gently probe objects; will search for partially concealed objects and may grasp notion of object permanence; anticipation becomes immediate—opens mouth at sight of bottle; may be capable of simple categorization

5 MONTHS Visually follows an object as it is moved out of direct line of vision; remembers pictures of faces

6 MONTHS Learns behaviors of familiar people; may understand physical causality; reacts to changes in familiar events

7 MONTHS Explores objects by manipulation; drops objects from heights; may understand the notion of physical support; is more attentive when playing

8 MONTHS Likes to make things happen and combines learned behaviors in this effort; searches for completely concealed objects; displays primitive problem-solving abilities; attends to play, shaking, banging, and dangling toys; often mouths toys as a way of exploring

9 MONTHS Begins to remember without cues; uses knowledge to solve problems; is aware of cause and effect; recognizes that own actions may effect outcomes; gets other people to make things happen

10 MONTHS Explores inside and outside surfaces of toys; repeats play sequences with different toys; investigates textures, designs, or parts of toys; may be able to reason about hidden objects; peers intently at pictures

11 MONTHS Uses props as aids (e.g., uses a chair to stand up); is more easily entertained; begins to put knowledge of an "inside" to use (e.g., tries to stack cups)

at exactly the same age, they all pass through the stages in the same order. The attainments of earlier stages are essential for those in later periods to emerge. The changes in children's cognitive abilities across the various stages can sometimes be quite abrupt, but the picture of development as a whole involves gradual and continuous change.

Piaget saw intellectual development as occurring in four main stages: the sensorimotor period, the preoperational period, the period of concrete operations, and the period of formal operations (see Table 9-1). As children pass through these stages, they evolve from infants who are incapable of abstract thought and totally dependent on concrete sensory and motor activities to know the world to emerging young adults capable of great flexibility of thought and abstract reasoning.

Turning Points: The Child's Cognitive Development from Infancy Through Late Childhood (*continued*)

1 YEAR	Searches for objects when they are moved or hidden within sight; actively plans to achieve a goal; comprehensively examines objects; uses imitative learning; deliberately introduces variations into play sequences; recognizes self in mirror
15 MONTHS	Continues to use systematic trial-and-error learning; is more aware of the functions of objects; may use dolls in play; recognizes and uses more cause-and-effect relationships
18 MONTHS	Searches for objects even when they have been moved out of own sight; likes to experiment with the properties of objects; thinks in terms of ideas; has better recall memory; has primitive idea of "what should be" (e.g., puts lids on jars); recognizes that others have possessions
21 MONTHS	To some degree understands past, present, and future; consistently uses scripts to organize activities into episodes; has some understanding of the idea of categories (e.g., colors)
2 YEARS	Can think symbolically and use language symbolically; can store mental representations and replay an action long after observing it; can plan problem solving mentally rather than use trial and error; begins to understand conservation; engages in fantasy play; recognizes that family members have specific roles; shows creative problem solving
3 YEARS	May be able to see the perspectives of others; may grasp conservation of number
4 YEARS	Begins to realize that others have different perspectives from own; may be able to understand part-whole relations
5 YEARS	Can respond to scaffolding in the instructional process
7 YEARS	Can use certain mental operations to solve problems but uses them intuitively, without a clear understanding of how and why they work; has achieved conservation of number, mass, liquid, length; begins to describe self in more abstract terms
8–10 YEARS	Can anticipate and consider the thoughts of others; achieves conservation of weight
11–12 YEARS	Achieves conservation of volume; understands reversibility; begins to think deductively; can form concepts of space and time; can sort things in complicated combinations of attributes
12 AND BEYOND	Thinking becomes logical, more flexible, and capable of abstraction; can apply logic to ideas and problems that violate reality; can entertain many possible solutions of a problem

Sources: Flavell, 1963; Kopp, 1994, Siegler, 1998.

Note: Developmental events described in this and other Turning Points charts represent overall trends identified in reasearch studies. Individual children vary greatly in the ages at which they achieve these developmental changes.

The Sensorimotor Period

Perhaps the most dramatic achievements in children's intellectual development occur during the **sensorimotor period,** which spans approximately the first 2 years of life. By interacting with their environment in active ways, children build what are at first simply reflex responses into the abilities to understand and adapt to the reality about them and to think symbolically. They begin to form mental representations of things and events and, by this means, to develop new behaviors and strategies for attaining goals and solving problems. This increasingly efficient use of

sensorimotor period
Piaget's first stage of cognitive development, during which children move from purely reflexive behavior to the beginnings of symbolic thought and goal-directed behaviors.

TABLE 9-1	Piaget's Stages of Cognitive Development	
	Age Range (Years)	Major Characteristics and Achievements
Sensorimotor period	0–2	Infant differentiates self from other objects; seeks stimulation and prolongs interesting spectacles; grasps concept of object permanence; achieves primitive understanding of causality, time, space; grasps means-end relationships; begins to imitate absent, complex behaviors, engage in imaginative play, and show the beginnings of symbolic thought
Preoperational period	2–7	Child begins to use symbols to represent objects and experiences and to use language symbolically; shows intuitive problem solving. Thinking is characterized by irreversibility, centration, and egocentricity. Child begins to think in terms of classes, see relationships, and grasp concept of conservation of numbers
Period of concrete operations	7–12	Child grasps concepts of the conservation of mass, length, weight, and volume; thinking is now characterized by reversibility, decentration, and the ability to take the role of others; thinking is also logical, enabling child to organize objects into hierarchical classes (classification) and to place objects into ordered series (seriation)
Period of formal operations	12 on	Child acquires flexibility in thinking as well as the capacities for abstraction and mental hypothesis testing; she can consider possible alternatives in complex reasoning and problem solving

symbolic processes leads to the rapid changes in cognitive activity that take place in the second major stage of development, the preoperational period.

One of the child's major achievements during the sensorimotor period is to grasp the concept of object permanence. We discuss Piaget's thinking in respect to this concept in some detail as well as the methods he used to explore how well and at what ages young children attained it. We also examine the thinking and experimentation of some of Piaget's critics, a number of whom have found that children may achieve an understanding of object permanence earlier than Piaget thought. Contemporary investigators have also suggested that children acquire other concepts, such as causality, earlier than Piaget proposed, and we examine these views as well. Before looking at critiques of Piaget's work, however, we need to understand how he saw this earliest period of the child's cognitive development.

Perhaps because the child makes such astonishing advances during his first 2 years, Piaget divided this first, sensorimotor period into six separate stages. Each of these stages is marked by a notable increase in the complexity of the child's cognitive activity.

reflex activity An infant's exercise of and growing proficiency in the use of innate reflexes.

Stage 1: Reflex Activity (0 to 1 Month). In the stage of **reflex activity**, infants become more proficient in the use of their innate reflexes, such as grasping and sucking (recall our discussion of the development of reflexes from Chapter 5). As we've noted, Piaget saw the infant as an active organism, and, consistent with this view, babies literally exercise, or practice, these reflexes as much as possible. They grasp and suck on a variety of objects as a way of providing stimulation for themselves.

primary circular reactions Behaviors in which infants repeat and modify actions focused on their own bodies that are pleasurable and satisfying.

Stage 2: Primary Circular Reactions (1 to 4 Months). During the stage of **primary circular reactions**—repetitive behaviors that are focused on the infant's own body—babies begin to repeat and modify actions that they find pleasurable or satisfying. Often they have initiated these actions quite by chance. For example, a baby may accidentally bring a finger close to her mouth and start sucking on it. Finding this behavior pleasurable, the infant seeks out the finger to suck on it again; if the sucking schema continues to produce satisfying behavior, the baby will tend to repeat it over and over again. Piaget chose the term *reaction* for this sort of behavior because the child is responding to an initiating event. He called these earliest reactions *primary* because they involve basic motor responses of the child's own body, and he termed them *circular* because they occur repeatedly.

Stage 3: Secondary Circular Reactions (4 to 8 Months).

It is not until the infant enters the stage of **secondary circular reactions**—repetitive behaviors that are focused on external objects—that he becomes interested in making things happen outside his own body. During this stage, the child's reactions are still circular; that is, he repeatedly engages in behaviors that please him. For example, the infant may shake a rattle, hear an interesting sound, shake the rattle again, hear the sound once more, and so on, over and over. Notice that the baby now moves from simple schemata, such as sucking, to combinations of schemata, such as grasping and shaking, to produce relatively more complex behavior patterns.

This 7-month-old child seems quite absorbed in shaking his rattle. With its attachments it may make more than just one intriguing sound.

secondary circular reactions Behaviors focused on objects outside the infant's own body that the infant repeatedly engages in because they are pleasurable.

It is tempting to say that at this stage the infant's behavior has become intentional—that is, that the child mentally forms the goal of shaking the rattle to hear the pleasant sound. However, Piaget did not attribute intentionality or the ability to generate specific goals to the child until the fourth stage of the sensorimotor period. Instead he viewed the child's shaking of the rattle as generated by the simple presence of the rattle in his hand. If the rattle were out of the baby's grasp, Piaget said, he would not form the intention of finding the rattle and shaking it.

Stage 4: Coordination of Secondary Schemata (8 to 12 Months).

In the stage called **coordination of secondary schemata**, the child develops more-sophisticated combinations of secondary schemata that do reflect intentionality. At this point in development, Piaget held, the child does plan deliberately for the attainment of a goal. For example, the child will now combine a hitting schema which she developed initially in order to make a mobile move or to strike away a barrier that blocks access to a toy, with reaching and grasping schemata to take possession of a plaything. Notice how the hitting schema is now used not only in a new situation but as an intermediate step in an effort to achieve a specific goal.

coordination of secondary schemata An infant's combination of different schemata to achieve a specific goal.

Stage 5: Tertiary Circular Reactions (12 to 18 Months).

In the stage of **tertiary circular reactions,** children's curiosity leads them to experiment with external objects. Now they use trial-and-error methods to learn more about the properties of objects and how they respond to various actions. For example, children at this age become fascinated by the properties of falling objects and often experiment by deliberately dropping things to see what happens to them. They will vary the way they drop an object, the position and distance of the drop, the place from which they drop it, or the characteristics of the surface on which it lands. This way they may learn, for instance, that whereas a rubber ball bounces *off* the floor, a cup of applesauce spreads nicely all *over* the floor. This exploration is a kind of early problem solving that leads children to accommodate to new aspects of their environment and to assimilate them into their constantly changing schemata.

tertiary circular reactions Behaviors in which infants experiment with the properties of external objects and try to learn how objects respond to various actions.

Stage 6: Inventing New Means by Mental Combination (18 to 24 Months).

It is not until the sixth and last stage of the sensorimotor period, the stage of **inventing new means by mental combination,** that children begin to think symbolically. **Symbolic thought,** or the use of mental images and concepts to represent or symbolize people, objects, and events in the world, is the foundation for the child's beginning use of language in the properational period, but it is

inventing new means by mental combination In this last stage of the sensorimotor period, children begin to combine schemata mentally, thus relying less on physical trial and error.

symbolic thought The use of mental images to represent people, objects, and events.

At 11 months, this child is already beginning to experiment with dropping things to see what happens to them. From this height her toy probably did nothing too startling, but it may have moved in interesting ways.

deferred imitation
Mimicry of an action some time after having observed it; requires that the child have stored a mental image of the action.

object permanence The notion that objects and people continue to exist independent of our seeing or interacting with them.

also reflected in a variety of other behaviors that first emerge in the present stage. For example, drawing relies on symbolic processes; the child creates a series of lines that stand for real objects. Fantasy play involves pretending that things are other than they really are, and **deferred imitation,** in which the child mimics an action some time after observing it, clearly requires that the child have stored a mental representation of what the action entailed.

Symbolic thought also facilitates problem solving, lifting it from a concrete, hands-on level to a more abstract one. Thus the child can now invent ways to attain a goal by *mentally* combining schemata; he is no longer limited to physically exploring, manipulating, and doing things. This newfound ability to think through problems, although still in its primitive stages, leads to the emergence of sudden solutions with little or no overt trial and error. To some extent the child is now able to think before or without acting.

Was Piaget Right About Object Permanence?

Most people find it difficult to conceive of a world in which objects that are not within their perception cease to exist. Even though we can no longer see, hear, or touch an object we generally assume that it continues to exist; that is, we accept the idea of **object permanence,** or the notion that objects and people continue to exist independent of our own interaction with them. According to Piaget, however, young infants do not have a conception of the permanence of objects. For the very young child, when mother goes out of the room or when a favorite toy drops over the edge of the crib, it is not only "out of sight, out of mind" but "out of sight, out of existence" (Flavell, 1985).

According to Piaget, infants learn gradually and in a predictable sequence over the sensorimotor period that objects exist when they are not in direct contact with them (Table 9-2) . In the first stage of the sensorimotor period, from birth to 1

TABLE 9-2 Acquiring the Concept of Object Permanence		

Stage	Age (in months)	Child's Behavior
1 Reflex activity	0 to 1	Focuses only on objects directly in front of him
2 Primary circular reactions	1 to 4	Looks a long time at place where an object disappeared but does not search visually or manually for the object
3 Secondary circular reactions	4 to 8	Searches for partially concealed objects
4 Coordination of secondary schemata	8 to 12	Searches for completely concealed objects
5 Tertiary circular reactions	12 to 18	Searches for objects that have been concealed while she was watching but has difficulty if an object is displaced more than once
6 Inventing new means by mental combination	18 to 24	Searches for an object that has been concealed even if it has been displaced several times

month, infants look only at objects that are directly in front of them. In the second stage, from 1 to 4 months, infants display no comprehension that objects have an existence of their own. When a toy vanishes, they don't look for it. In fact, if the toy drops from a child's hand, he will stare at his hand rather than follow the falling object's path to the floor. Thus when a young infant is not perceiving an object, he behaves as though it does not exist.

At about 4 months of age, in the stage of secondary circular reactions, the infant shows some awareness of the permanence of objects. A child is more likely to search visually for an object if its loss is associated with interruption of her own movements than if another person has hidden it. In addition, a child will now anticipate the path of a moving object, looking at a location where it can be expected to appear. She will search for a partially visible object, but not a covered one, and even if she watches as an object is covered, she will not attempt to retrieve it. For example, if an adult hides a desired toy under a blanket, the infant will not search for the toy, even though she saw it being hidden.

Although marked improvement in the development of object permanence occurs in subsequent stages, these transitions are gradual. In the fourth stage (8 to 12 months), the child's concept of object permanence continues to evolve. That the child now begins to search for completely concealed objects signals her growing realization that objects have a permanent existence. Early in this stage a child will be surprised to see a toy clown disappear behind a screen and then reappear as a brightly colored plastic doughnut, whereas a child in the preceding stage will accept the magical transformation (Gratch, 1982; Meicler & Gratch, 1980).

In the period of tertiary circular reactions (12 to 18 months), the infant is finally able to recognize the permanence of an invisible object. The child will now track an object visually and search for it where it disappeared. But despite this new awareness, Piaget suggests, children in this stage still have difficulty conceiving of more than one displacement of an object. While playing a hiding game with his own son, Laurent, Piaget hid his watch repeatedly behind one of two cushions, alternating the hiding spot between the two. Laurent consistently searched for the watch under the correct cushion. Obtaining the watch was not to be that simple, however. Next, as Laurent observed him, Piaget placed the watch in a box, put the box behind a cushion, and then surreptitiously removed the watch from the box, leaving the watch behind the cushion. He then handed the box to Laurent, who opened it and found it empty. Although he had seen his father place the watch in the box

According to the Piagetian view of object permanence, this 10-month-old child is pretty much on track, searching for an object that was completely concealed. Renée Baillargeon has demonstrated, however, that even 3½ month old infants may be aware that objects exist whether or not they're visible.

and the box behind the cushion, Laurent did not search for the watch behind the cushion. Apparently, the concept of object permanence held for him only when he could observe every displacement of the watch.

It is not until the last stage of the sensorimotor period that children fully aquire the concept of object permanence. When children are between 1½ and 2 years old they are finally able to make inferences about the positions of unseen objects even when the objects have been displaced several times.

Piaget accorded an understanding of object permanence great importance in his account of the developing child; as a result, his claims regarding the acquisition of this concept have undergone a great deal of scrutiny. One common criticism by developmental psychologists and others is that in all the tasks Piaget used to track the development of object permanence, he measured awareness by the child's specific, manual search behavior. Many investigators have wondered whether children may attain object permanence but be unable to reveal it in search activities because of other developmental limitations. For example, might a child be aware that a vanished object still exists but be unable to search effectively for it because of insufficiently developed hand-eye coordination? If this were true, tasks that require children to search manually for an object cannot accurately evaluate their grasp of object permanence.

In an effort to discover whether young infants may understand the permanence of objects, Renée Baillargeon (1986, 1993) designed a clever task that allowed her to investigate this notion by measuring the amount of time infants spent simply looking at a display. Baillargeon presented 6- and 8-month-old infants with what seemed an impossible event: One solid object appeared to move through the space occupied by another solid object. In these experiments, infants sat in front of a large stage on the left side of which there was a long inclined ramp (see Figure 9-1a). At the bottom of the ramp, directly in front of the infant, was a small screen. The infant watched as the screen was raised and then lowered. After the screen had been lowered, a small car rolled down the ramp along a track set in the stage, disappearing behind the screen and reappearing at the other side of the screen. This event was repeated until the infant became habituated to it, that is until he stopped looking at the display.

Next the infant saw one of two test events (Figures 9-1b and 9-1c). Both of these events were identical to the habituation event except that when the screen was raised in each event, the infant saw a box placed behind it and hidden by the lowered screen. The two test events were further differentiated by the precise placement of the box. In the possible event (Figure 9-1b), the box was placed behind the track and well out of the car's trajectory. The car thus rolled behind the screen and out again, as in the habituation event, without a problem. In the impossible event (Figure 9-1c), however, the box was placed on top of the track, directly in the car's path. This time when the car disappeared behind the screen and reappeared at the far side of the screen, it appeared to have rolled right through the box! (During the impossible event, the box was actually removed through a door in the back of the stage.) Based on the finding that infants look longer at surprising events than at events they have come to expect, Baillargeon measured infants' reactions to these two events.

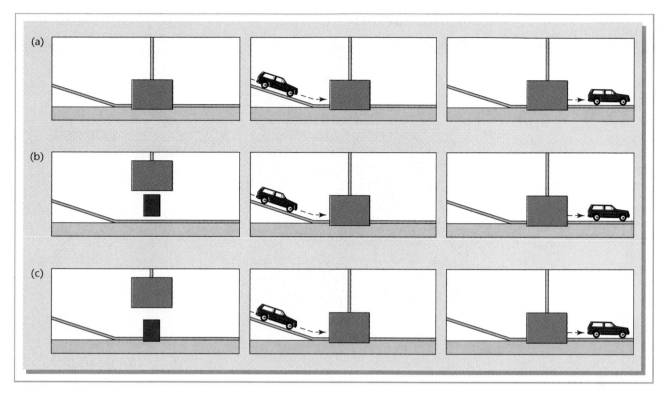

■ FIGURE 9-1
Testing infants' grasp of object permanence.
(a) As 6- to 8-month-old babies watched, a car rolled down a ramp, disappeared behind a screen and reappeared at the other side. (b) After infants saw the box placed *behind* the ramp, the car again rolled down the ramp, disappearing and reappearing once again. (c) After infants saw the box placed *on* the ramp, where it would obstruct the car's passage, the car once again rolled the ramp, disappearing and reappearing as before (the box having been surreptitiously removed from the ramp). By their looking behavior, babies indicated that they found the event in (c) quite surprising. (*Source:* Adapted from Baillargeon, 1986)

If Piaget was correct that infants of this age do not have the concept of object permanence, as soon as the screen covered it, the box should cease to exist for the child. Thus there should be no difference in the infant's response to either the possible or the impossible event: Because the box no longer exists, it cannot stop the movement of the car. If, however, infants do represent the existence of the box even when it is out of sight, they should look longer at the impossible event—which would be surprising—than at the possible event—which is no different from the habituated event. This is in fact what Baillargeon found. The infants looked reliably longer when the box was placed on the track compared with when the box was placed behind the track. In later studies, Baillargeon (1987, 1992, 1995) found that even infants only 3½ months old demonstrated an awareness of object permanence. Moreover, from these and later studies Baillargeon concluded that infants represent not only the existence of hidden objects but their location as well. Both of these findings, which run counter to Piaget's claims, have led to further research that has indicated that infants know a great deal more than Piaget imagined.

More Challenges: The Infant as "Naive Physicist"

The work of Baillargeon and others (see, e.g., Baillargeon, 1993; Spelke, 1991, 1994; Spelke et al., 1994) clearly challenges Piaget's view about the emergence of the concept that hidden objects continue to exist and suggests that children may reach this milestone as much as a year earlier than Piaget thought. But object permanence may not be the only principle of the physical world that children understand earlier than we have thought. Calling infants "naive physicists," Wellman & Gelman (1992) suggest that babies function as amateur physicists, demonstrating a surprisingly rich understanding of the world around them.

Consider some examples. To begin with, babies appear to understand some of the properties of objects. Baillargeon (1987), for example, has found that they can discriminate between a rigid object, like a box, and a soft and compressible object, such as a ball of gauze. Baillargeon and her associates (Baillargeon & Hanko-Summers, 1990; Needham & Baillargeon, 1993) also report that by the time babies are 3 months old, they understand the concept of gravity! According to these

■ FIGURE 9-2
How much physical support do babies think objects need? (a) Both 3-month-old and babies who were between 3 and 6½ months old watched the gloved hand push the box to the edge of the platform with equanimity. (b) When the hand pushed the box until it was 85 percent off the platform, 3-month-old infants had no reaction but the older infants showed by their looking behavior that they found this "impossible" event worth considerable attention. (*Source:* Baillargeon, 1994)

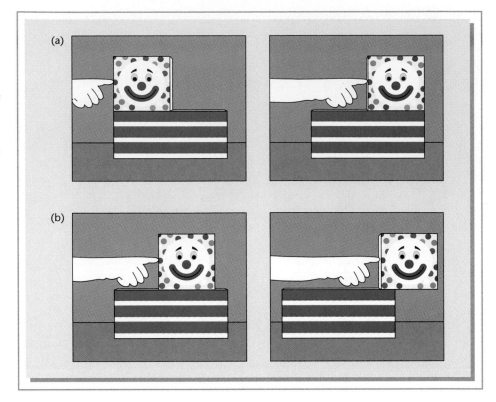

researchers, babies recognize that objects that do not rest on a surface will fall and thus appear to grasp the concept of physical support. However, because others (e.g., Spelke, 1991) have failed to find any evidence that young infants understand gravity, these findings are somewhat controversial. Third, Baillargeon (Baillargeon & DeVos, 1994) has found that infants can reason about hidden objects. Adults know that a lump in a blanket signals the presence of an object beneath the blanket and, conversely, that if the blanket lays flat, no object is underneath; it seems that by the age of 9½ months, babies understand this principle as well!

Evidence of such early achievements does not mean that children do not develop skills gradually over time. As Flavell and colleagues (Flavell et al., 1993, p. 62) point out, it is clear that "very young infants do not know all there is to know"! First, children acquire different skills at different ages; they achieve some skills at about 3 or 4 months of age and others when they're 6 or 7 months old. Second, infants may learn general principles quite early but be unable for some time to grasp the subtleties of applying these principles. For example, in Baillargeon's study of the infant's understanding of physical support, 3-month-old babies expected a box placed on a platform to fall if it was pushed over the platform's edge, but any contact with the platform was sufficient to prevent babies from anticipating that the box would fall (Baillargeon, 1994; see Figure 9-2a,b). Babies who were between 3 and 6½ months of age, however, understood that a significant portion of the box's bottom surface must be in contact with the platform in order for the box not to fall. Baillargeon (1994) suggests the following developmental sequence:

> When learning about the support relation between two objects, infants first form an initial concept centered on a contact/no contact distinction. With further experience this initial concept is progressively revised. Infants identify first a discrete (focus of contact) and later a continuous (amount of contact) variable and incorporate these values into their initial concept, resulting in more successful predictions over time. (p. 4)

This argument proposes that infants are born with highly constrained learning mechanisms that guide the development of their reasoning about objects in the physical world. By "highly constrained" we mean that infants are, in a sense, constrained by the way they are biogically primed to learn certain kinds of principles or laws about their world. As we saw in Chapter 8, it appears very likely that infants are biologically ready to learn certain aspects of language, such as grammar. This theoretical position does not imply that the baby's understanding is innate but rather that infants' biological organization predisposes them to learn some critical features of their environment quite rapidly.

Thus, Baillargeon is suggesting that infants are born biologically prepared to learn about their *physical* world. Other investigators (Leslie, 1994; Spelke, 1991; Spelke & Newport, 1998) have suggested that infants are born with substantive beliefs about objects (e.g., the notion that an object is impenetrable) that in turn direct their interpretations of physical events. To date, the evidence does not allow us to distinguish clearly between these two views, but Baillargeon's learning mechanisms argument is receiving increasing support.

Do Babies Understand Causality?

Research suggests that infants may understand causality by the time they're 6 months old. In one demonstration, babies first watched a film in which a moving object displaced a stationary one—a green brick pushed a red one. Then the babies watched sequences that violated the principle of causality (e.g., the red brick moved even though the green brick didn't reach it, or the red brick moved a second *after* the green brick collided with it). Infants indicated that they understood the principle of a causal sequence by looking longer at violations of this principle than at the original straightforward illustration of the principle (Leslie & Keeble, 1987; Oakes, 1994; Oakes & Cohen, 1994).

As infants develop, their understanding of causality becomes more sophisticated. For example, they learn that the size of a moving object will determine how far it will move a stationary object that it hits (Kotovsky & Baillargeon, 1994). Consider the following situation: A cylinder rolls down a ramp and hits a wheeled toy bug resting at the bottom of the ramp (Figure 9-3). By the time they are 2½ months old, infants already seem to possess clear expectations that the toy bug will remain stationary as long as it is not hit. By the time they're 5½ or 6½ months old, infants judge that the bug will roll farther when hit by a large cylinder than a small cylinder, after they see how far a medium-sized cylinder causes the bug to roll. Infants are apparently able to use this information about the effect of the medium-sized object on the bug "to calibrate their prediction about how far the stationary object will travel with moving objects of different sizes" (Baillargeon, 1994, p. 5).

Although we are still uncertain about specifically how infants attain their physical knowledge and about what form of innate mechanisms or principles equip the infant to demonstrate the remarkable feats we've discussed, clearly we need to revise our views of what infants know and how early they know it. In recent years infants have continued to surprise us with how much they know about their world. Without a doubt, the account of infant cognition outlined in Piaget's six sensorimotor stages is too simple. Moreover, Piaget's use of motor activity as a gauge of the infant's understanding of physical principles and concepts seems clearly to have led him to underestimate the infant's cognitive abilities (Flavell et al., 1993). In spite of his failure to capture the entirety of the young infant's cognitive capacities, however, there is no question but that Piaget pioneered in providing the first truly descriptive mapping of the sequence of how the infant achieves and modifies her cognitive understanding.

The Preoperational Period

The major characteristic of the **preoperational period** is the child's development of the **symbolic function,** or the ability to use symbols, such as words, images, and

preoperational period   In this period, the symbolic function promotes the learning of language; the period is also marked by egocentricity and intuitive behavior, in which the child can solve problems using mental operations but cannot explain how he did so.

symbolic function   The ability to use symbols, such as images, words, and gestures, to represent objects and events in the world.

■ FIGURE 9-3
Babies understand not only causality but the relation between mass, weight, and collision!
(a) A medium-sized cylinder rolls down a ramp, hits a toy bug, and pushes it to the middle of the ramp. (b) This time, a larger cylinder hits the bug, pushing it to the end of the ramp.
(c) Finally, a cylinder smaller than the first one hits the bug—and pushes it to the end of the ramp. Babies between 5½ and 6½ months old found the last event surprising. (*Source:* Baillargeon, 1994)

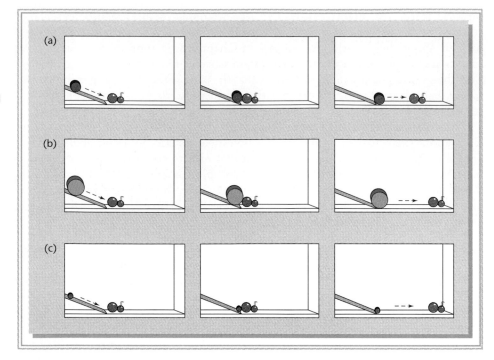

gestures, to represent objects and events in her world. This ability to represent experience symbolically continues to evolve throughout the two stages of this period, the preconceptual and the intuitive stages. In the preconceptual stage, the emergence of the symbolic function is seen in the rapid development of language, in imaginative play, and in the increasing use of deferred imitation. In the intuitive stage, the symbolic function is manifested in changes in thought processes involving such things as new understandings of relationships, numbers, and classifications. All these behaviors suggest that the child can produce mental symbols that mediate his performance.

One of the preoperational child's major accomplishments is the rapid acquisition of language. For Piaget, it is the child's development of the symbolic function that enables her to acquire language proficiency so quickly. Once the child begins to use language symbols, she broadens her problem-solving abilities greatly and becomes able to learn from the verbalizations of other people. The symbolic process in language is also apparent in imaginative play. For example, the child who has seen a train running along a track may push a series of blocks and say "toot toot"; the blocks have become the symbol for a real train.

The first, preconceptual stage of Piaget's preoperational period is characterized particularly by egocentric thinking; the second, intuitive stage is so named because during this period, although they can employ certain mental operations in problem solving, children cannot explain the principles that underlie the operations they have used. After we explore Piaget's descriptions of these substages, we examine his concept of conservation, which children come to understand during the preoperational period. We close this section with an examination of some specific limitations on the preoperational child's thinking.

The Preconceptual Stage (2 to 4 Years).   Notable characteristics of the **preconceptual stage** are animistic thinking and egocentricity. The child who demonstrates **animistic thinking** tends to attribute life to inanimate objects. For example, the child may believe that plants feel pain when he picks their flowers or that the wind talks to his friends, the trees. In the following exchange between Piaget and a preconceptual child, the sun appears quite lifelike indeed:

preconceptual stage   The first substage of Piaget's preoperational period, during which the child's thought is characterized by animistic thinking and egocentricity.

animistic thinking   The attribution of life to inanimate objects.

PIAGET: Does the sun move?

CHILD: Yes, when one walks it follows. When one turns around it turns around too. Doesn't it ever follow you too?

PIAGET: Why does it move?

CHILD: Because when one walks, it goes too.

PIAGET: Why does it go?

CHILD: To hear what we say.

PIAGET: Is it alive?

CHILD: Of course, otherwise it wouldn't follow us, it couldn't shine. (Piaget, 1960, p. 215)

Just as Piaget's claims about the limitations on children's knowledge of object permanence have been questioned, so too has his hypothesis regarding animistic thought. For example, Bullock (1985) and others have pointed out that the objects Piaget used to test the limits of children's animistic thought, such as the sun, the moon, and the wind, are often open to magical interpretations. In contrast, Massey and Gelman (1988) found that when they used simple and familiar objects, children as young as 4 were quite good at deciding whether animate objects, such as mammals, or inanimate objects, such as statues, could move on their own. Dolgin and Behrend (1984) found that even 3-year-olds were unlikely to attribute animate characteristics to cars and trucks (which can move like animate beings) or to stuffed animals (which may look like animate beings).

Piaget's discussion with the preconceptual child about the sun reveals another characteristic of preconceptual thought: **egocentrism.** Children tend to view the world from their own perspective and to have difficulty seeing or to be unable to see things from another person's perspective. In the foregoing dialogue, the sun follows the child, imitates the child's movements, and listens to the child.

To test the child's ability to see things from another person's perspective, Piaget designed what is known as the three-mountain test (see Figure 9-4). Models of three mountains of varying sizes are placed on a square table, and chairs are placed at all four sides of the table. The child is seated in one chair, and the experimenter places a doll in the other three chairs, one at a time, asking the child each time to describe what the doll sees from the three different positions. The child may select one of a set of drawings or use cardboard cutouts of the mountains to construct the doll's views. Piaget found that children could not consistently identify the dolls' view from each of the three locations until they reached the period of concrete operations, when they were 9 or 10 years old.

Piaget's three-mountain task is also open to criticism. First, in his original test he used simple models of mountains that lacked salient characteristics by which one could differentiate one view from the next. Moreover, the task of reconstructing the display, or even of choosing the appropriate drawings, may be beyond the ability of a young child. Making two simple changes in Piaget's design, Borke (1975) obtained very different results: (1) The investigator placed familiar things, such as snowcaps, trees, or houses, on the sides of the mountains to make them more distinctive and (2) asked children to rotate a small model of the display to present the appropriate view rather than reconstruct the display or choose from drawings. Children as young as 3 were then able to identify the correct perspective from each of the three different positions.

The Intuitive Stage (4 to 7 Years).   Piaget called the second stage of the preoperational period "intuitive" because, although the child who is between 4 and 7 years old employs certain mental operations such as ways of classifying, quantifying, or relating objects, she does not seem to be aware of the principles she has used in performing these operations. The child in the **intuitive stage** can solve problems with these operations but can't explain why she solved them in a particular way. The child also engages in semilogical reasoning. For example, when asked, "Why do clouds move?" she might answer "Because they are pulled when people walk."

egocentrism   The tendency to view the world from one's own perspective and to have difficulty seeings things from another's viewpoint.

intuitive stage   The second substage of the preoperational period, during which the child begins to solve problems by means of specific mental operations but cannot explain how she arrives at the solutions.

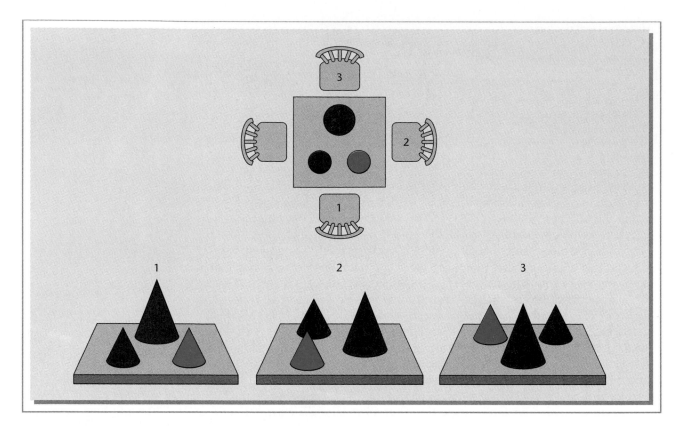

■ FIGURE 9-4
Understanding different perspectives: Piaget's three-mountain test.
We show Piaget's classic test, which used simple cone-shaped figures to represent mountains. As the text discusses, contemporary researchers have found that young children can understand the perspectives of dolls or imaginary people sitting in chairs 1–3 better when the mountains are made more realistic or if they're allowed to rotate small models, such as those shown at the bottom of the figure.

Although the child's symbols are becoming increasingly complex, reasoning and thinking processes have certain characteristic limitations that are manifested in a variety of tasks. For example, the preoperational child cannot perform a *seriation* task, that is, she cannot put a group of objects in order on the basis of a particular dimension, such as length: She cannot place a number of sticks in order from the shortest to the longest. Another limitation affects problems of part-whole relations (also called *class-inclusion* problems). This is vividly illustrated in the following task: A child is given 7 toy dogs and 3 toy cats, for a total of 10 animals. If the child is asked whether there are more dogs or more cats, he can answer correctly that there are more dogs. However, if the child is then asked if there are more dogs than there are animals, the child responds that there are more dogs. Piaget proposes that the child is responding incorrectly because he is unable to focus simultaneously on a part of the set of animals (the set of dogs) and on the whole set of animals, and so assumes that the second question has the same meaning as the first—are there more dogs or more cats?

Again, developmentalists have criticized Piaget's approach and design, suggesting that the way he posed his questions confused his small participants. When Smith (1979) used simpler questions that still addressed children's ability to use part-whole relations, such as "A pug is a kind of dog, but it's not a shepherd. Is a pug an animal?" she found that children as young as 4 displayed knowledge of the part-whole relation between dogs and animals by correctly answering that a pug is an animal. Further research has shown that using collective terms like *family* to describe a whole set (e.g., "Who would have more pets, someone who owned the baby dogs or someone who owned the whole family?") highlighted the part-whole relations between the objects and improved the performance of preschool children (Markman, 1973; Markman & Siebert, 1976).

Understanding Conservation: Limitations on Preoperational Thought
Just as Piaget considered an understanding of object permanence the child's primary accomplishment during the sensorimotor period, he considered an elemen-

tary understanding of conservation the most important acquisition of the preoperational period. To understand **conservation** the child must recognize that even when an object's appearance is altered in some way, the object's basic attributes or properties remain the same. For example, the child must learn that whether a piece of clay is formed into a ball or rolled out to look like a breadstick, it is still the same piece—and the same quantity—of clay.

One test of a preoperational child's knowledge of conservation that is used most often involves changing the containers in which a liquid is held. In this task the experimenter shows a child two short, wide cylindrical glasses, each of which contains the same amount of water. The child then watches as the experimenter pours the water from one of these two glasses into a tall, thin glass. When the experimenter asks the child whether the tall glass contains more, less, or the same amount of water as the remaining short glass of water, the child usually answers that the tall cylinder contains more. Asked if anything was added or taken away from either glass, the child will say no but will still insist that they now contain different amounts of water. The child has thus failed to *conserve* the amount of liquid—he is focusing on the changes that he has observed in the height and width of the water rather than on the constant amount.

This child's decision as to whether the two glasses hold equal amounts of colored water will reveal whether she's attained an understanding of the conservation of liquids.

conservation The notion that altering an object's or a substance's appearance does not change its basic attributes or properties.

What processes may lead the child, who has witnessed the experimenter pouring the same quantity of water from one vessel to another, to make this error in judgment? Piaget proposes that preoperational children's cognitive abilities are characterized by three important limitations that are closely related to the egocentrism that we have already discussed: the inability to grasp the notion of reversibility, the tendency to focus on the end state of an action or a task rather than the means to this end state, and centration. The most important of these limitations, Piaget says, is the child's inability to understand **reversibility,** or the notion that one can mentally reverse or undo a given action. For example, preoperational children presented with the liquid-conservation task that we have outlined do not reason that if the water in the tall, thin glass is poured back into the short, wide glass it will reach the same height it had before. This inability to reverse a series of mental steps manifests itself in many other responses of the child between 2 and 6 years old. For example, an investigator asks a 4-year-old participant,

reversibility The notion that one can reverse or undo a given operation, either physically or mentally.

"Have you a brother?"

The child replies, "Yes."

"What's his name?"

"Jim."

"Does Jim have a brother?"

"No." (Phillips, 1969, p. 61)

Associated with the preoperational child's inability to reverse actions is the tendency to *focus on ends rather than means,* that is, on the end state of a changing event rather than on the process or transformations by which the change occurs. Again, in the liquid-conservation task, the preoperational child ignores both the experimenter's action of pouring the water from one glass to the other and the rising water level in the glass. Instead, the child focuses on the end state of the process; that is, the high water level in the tall container that now appears different from the water level in the short container.

Finally, **centration** in thinking leads preoperational children to center their attention on only one dimension of an object or situation; in our test example, children base their reasons for why they think the amount of water in the containers is no longer equal on either the height of the water or the width of the glass. One child may say that the tall glass contains more because the water level is higher; another child may say that the short glass contains more because it is wider. This tendency to attend to only one attribute of what one observes and to ignore such things as reciprocal changes between aspects of the object or situation—in the present case, to fail to recognize that because the height of one container compensates for its lack of width the amount of water remains the same—prevents the child from grasping the notion of conservation.

Experimenters have studied children's understanding of conservation using many substances other than liquid; as you can see from Figure 9-5, these include the conservation of number, mass, length, area, weight, and volume. Cross-cultural studies have found considerable variation in the age at which children attain conservation (Newman, Riel, & Martin, 1983; Rogoff, 1990), and the age at which they acquire the concept also varies among the substances and qualities they are asked to conserve. In Western societies, in general, children achieve conservation of liquids, mass, and length somewhere between the ages of 6 and 7; they can conserve number a little earlier, by about age 6. Grasping the conservation of weight, area, and volume takes somewhat longer, emerging at about age 9, between 9 and 10, and after age 11, respectively.

It is important to remember that these ages are only approximations. Some children may grasp the conservation of weight by the age of 8 and others by the age of 10. According to Piaget, however, the *order* in which children acquire these concepts remains the same among all children. So regardless of the age at which a child understands the conservation of weight, she will always achieve an understanding of the conservation of area and volume later on. Moreover, this sequence generally holds across different sociocultural groups; only moderate sequential differences in the acquisition of conservation have been found (Newman et al., 1983; Rogoff, 1990).

What may account for the fact that children do not acquire the ability to conserve all types of substances and qualities at the same age? If children develop the logical abilities to perform one type of conservation task, shouldn't they be able to perform all such tasks? Calling this phenomenon **horizontal decalage** (the French word *décalage* can be translated as "time lag"), Piaget proposed that this unevenness in children's cognitive achievements at given ages reflects differing degrees of abstraction required to understand the conservation of particular objects, substances, or qualities. For example, he suggested that conserving mass requires the least abstract operations, whereas conserving volume requires the most; as a result, conservation of mass is acquired earlier. Further, the attainment of the simpler concept is essential for the development of the more abstract one, and thus children must progress over time from one concept to the next.

Can Children Achieve Conservation Earlier Than Piaget Thought?

Many researchers have been dissatisfied with Piaget's description of the evolution of conservation in young children. The concepts underlying conservation seem so basic to daily life that it seems to some developmentalists that children must acquire them earlier than Piaget thought. In a classic series of studies, Rochel Gelman (1972) explored Piaget's claim that children do not conserve number until they're 6 years old. Piaget had shown children two rows of objects, each row containing the same

centration Centering one's attention on only one dimension or characteristic of an object or situation.

horizontal decalage The notion that unevenness in children's cognitive achievements reflects the fact that understanding the conservation of different objects, substances, or qualities requires different levels of the capacity for abstraction.

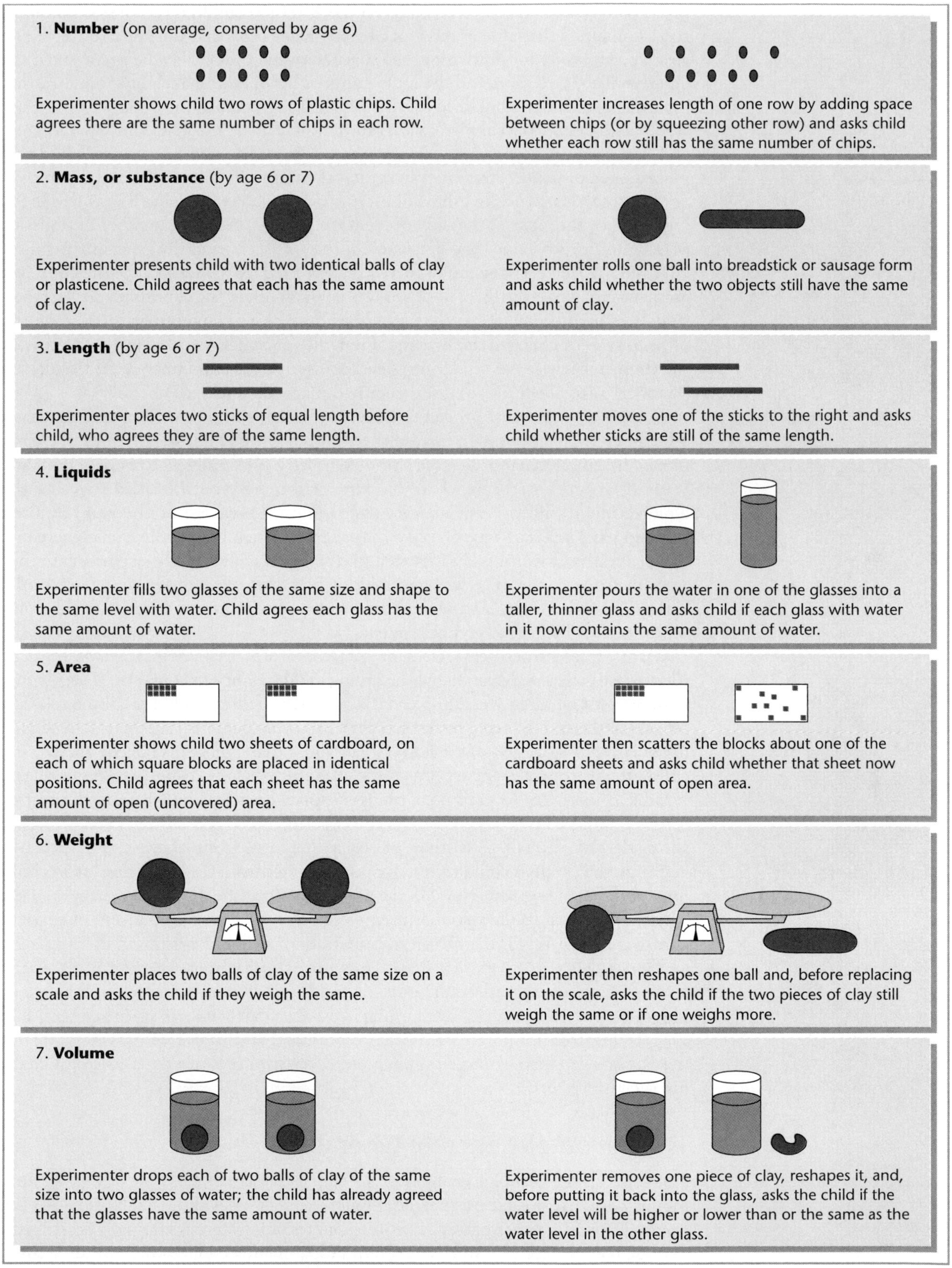

1. **Number** (on average, conserved by age 6)

Experimenter shows child two rows of plastic chips. Child agrees there are the same number of chips in each row.

Experimenter increases length of one row by adding space between chips (or by squeezing other row) and asks child whether each row still has the same number of chips.

2. **Mass, or substance** (by age 6 or 7)

Experimenter presents child with two identical balls of clay or plasticene. Child agrees that each has the same amount of clay.

Experimenter rolls one ball into breadstick or sausage form and asks child whether the two objects still have the same amount of clay.

3. **Length** (by age 6 or 7)

Experimenter places two sticks of equal length before child, who agrees they are of the same length.

Experimenter moves one of the sticks to the right and asks child whether sticks are still of the same length.

4. **Liquids**

Experimenter fills two glasses of the same size and shape to the same level with water. Child agrees each glass has the same amount of water.

Experimenter pours the water in one of the glasses into a taller, thinner glass and asks child if each glass with water in it now contains the same amount of water.

5. **Area**

Experimenter shows child two sheets of cardboard, on each of which square blocks are placed in identical positions. Child agrees that each sheet has the same amount of open (uncovered) area.

Experimenter then scatters the blocks about one of the cardboard sheets and asks child whether that sheet now has the same amount of open area.

6. **Weight**

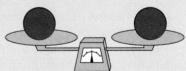

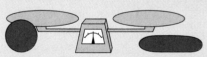

Experimenter places two balls of clay of the same size on a scale and asks the child if they weigh the same.

Experimenter then reshapes one ball and, before replacing it on the scale, asks the child if the two pieces of clay still weigh the same or if one weighs more.

7. **Volume**

Experimenter drops each of two balls of clay of the same size into two glasses of water; the child has already agreed that the glasses have the same amount of water.

Experimenter removes one piece of clay, reshapes it, and, before putting it back into the glass, asks the child if the water level will be higher or lower than or the same as the water level in the other glass.

■ FIGURE 9-5
Some Piagetian tests of conservation.
These tests are discussed at further length in the text. (*Source:* Based on Lefrancois, 1973)

number of objects spaced at equal intervals. After the children responded that both rows contained the same number of objects, Piaget changed the appearance of one row by increasing (or decreasing) the space between the objects; he again asked the children if the two rows had the same number. Preoperational children replied that the transformed row contained more (or fewer) objects than the other.

Gelman designed a simpler conservation task, called "the magic mice paradigm," and tested children younger than 6. In one study she showed a 3-year-old child two plates; one contained three toy mice, the other contained two. Then Gelman covered both plates and asked the child to pick one plate and identify it as either the "winner" or the "loser"; she did not mention number. Across a number of trials the plate with the three mice was consistently the "winner," and the experimenter gave children a prize every time they correctly identified the winner. Once the child had come to recognize the three-mouse plate as the winner, the experimenter surreptitiously altered the winning plate by either decreasing the number of mice on the plate to two, or changed the spacing of the mice to match the two-mouse plate (i.e., the three mice were pushed closer together). When the child uncovered the altered "winner" plate, he found that the mice had magically changed!

Piaget's theory would predict that these children would now be unable to decide which plate was the winner; instead the children would choose purely on the basis of row length or density. Gelman's results directly contradicted this prediction. She found that on those trials where the mice had merely been pushed together the children could still correctly identify the "winning" plate. Not only could children as young as 3 years of age correctly choose the winner, but on the trials where one of the mice had magically disappeared, the children could tell the experimenter not only that one of the mice was missing but how this plate could be made like the earlier "winning" plate, showing that young children can conserve number far younger than Piaget had hypothesized.

Many other studies (e.g., Gelman, 1990; Halford, 1990; Sugarman, 1987) have found that Piaget underestimated the young child's ability to conserve. It seems that if we present children with simpler tasks or teach them to attend to all the relevant aspects of the stimuli being presented, they can often demonstrate their understanding of conservation. To test the notion that failure to conserve may occur because the child attends to irrelevant aspects of the stimulus, such as shape, length, or height, Jerome Bruner (1966) presented preoperational children with a modification of Piaget's liquid conservation task. As the experimenters poured the water from the short glass to the tall glass, they placed a screen in front of the tall glass; thus, although the children could see them pouring water from the short glass, they could not see the changing water level in the tall glass. When the distracting changes in the height and width of the water column were not visible to the children, most were able to conserve, recognizing that the same amount of liquid must be in the container.

The evidence suggests that Piaget was probably right about the timing of the acquisition of conservation for some tasks. However, just as we saw in the case of object permanence, if a task is simplified, children can conserve at earlier ages than Piaget suspected. Children are more precocious than Piaget's theory suggests, but they often need help from a clever experimenter who provides a little help by making the task easier.

The Period of Concrete Operations

concrete operations period
Period in which the child acquires such concepts as conservation and classification and can reason logically.

Piaget described dramatic changes in the characteristics of children's thinking during his **concrete operations period,** which extends from about the age of 7 to the age of 11 or 12. In this period, children's increased understanding of reversibility and decreased tendencies to centration and egocentrism enable them to become more flexible in their thinking. Logic and objectivity increase, and children begin to think deductively. They are able to conserve quantity and number, to form concepts of space and time, and to classify or group things that they experience in everyday life. However, they are still tied to the immediate world and can often solve problems only if the objects necessary for problem solution are physically present. For example, suppose we present three children of varying heights to another child in differently composed pairs. In pair 1, the child sees that Melissa is taller than Zoe, and in pair 2 she sees that Zoe is taller than Fabiana. Without seeing Melissa and Fabiana together, the child can reason that Melissa is taller than both Zoe and Fabiana. If, however, instead of presenting the three girls physically, we present the problem to our participant verbally, as "Melissa is taller than Zoe and Zoe is taller than Fabiana; who is the tallest of the three?" the concrete operational child will have difficulty solving the problem.

Children also make marked advances in the ability to classify objects during the concrete operations period. Between 2 and 7 the child gradually acquires the ability to classify on a consistent basis, such as by size, shape, or color. For example, by the time they are 4 or 5, children can sort a set of large and small blocks into two groups, one of small blocks and the other of large ones. In contrast, the concrete operational child can sort objects according to more complicated combinations of their attributes. For example, the child can sort a group of flowers into a major class and a subclass: yellow roses, yellow tulips, yellow daisies, red roses, red tulips, and red daisies. Concrete operational children become able to understand such multiple classifications even when they involve subtle distinctions on the relevant dimensions, such as different shades of yellow or different types of daisies. Moreover, they are able to ignore irrelevant features such as number of petals or size (Fischer & Roberts, 1986; Frith & Frith, 1978).

Again, developmentalists have questioned whether the solution of such problems is based on the underlying changes in mental operations that Piaget proposed. Some investigators have suggested that in tests of inference, like judging the relative height of three girls based only on a verbal statement, what poses a difficulty for the concrete operational child is not the lack of physical stimuli but the lack of memory capacity. If children could be trained to remember the rather complicated components of this problem, perhaps they could solve it even without the physical presence of the three girls. Bryant and Trabasso (1971) used a task involving judging the different lengths of several sticks to demonstrate that when procedures ensure that children will retain the information they are given, even the very young can make logical inferences. The difference in memory capacity between younger and older children, therefore, is one of the critical factors in the differing levels of performance on tests of logical inference (Harris & Basset, 1975).

Although Piaget held that the ability to classify develops during the preoperational and concrete operational periods, we now have evidence that even infants can place objects into categories based on perceptual similarities. Researchers have shown that babies as young as 3 to 4 months old can form categories of animals that include dogs and cats but exclude birds, or categories that include cats and lions while excluding dogs (Eimas, 1994; Eimas, Quinn, & Cowen, 1994; Haith & Benson, 1998; Quinn, Cummins, Kase, Martin, & Weissman, 1996). In one study, infants who were 3 or 4 months old formed more general categories (Behl-Chadha, in press). Experimenters first showed babies pictures of several different animals (horse, dog, pig). Subsequently, the infants paid more attention to pictures of birds, fish, or furniture but not to pictures of other animals, such as a cow or a lion. This suggests that infants recognize general categories like animals as well as specific members of a class, such as lions and horses. Apparently children can classify objects at a much earlier age and in a more sophisticated fashion than Piaget believed possible.

Finally, we should note that researchers who have undertaken cross-cultural studies of Piagetian concepts—and most such studies have focused on concepts whose acquisition Piaget attributed to this fourth period—have generally underlined the importance of culture in determining what concepts will be learned and when. Box 9-1 not only illuminates this notion but points out that intelligence itself may be defined differently in different societies.

BOX 9-1

Perspectives on Diversity

Different Cognitive Skills in Different Cultures

According to many theorists (e.g., Ceci, 1991; Cole, 1990; Rogoff, 1998), intelligence is culturally relative; that is, any individual's collective cognitive skills must be assessed in the context of the culture in which she or he develops. Moreover, if we define intelligence as adaptation to the environment, as did Piaget, we must expect that paths of cognitive development will diverge in different cultures with different environments. Thus we cannot take the measure of any specific task—such as object permanence or conservation—as indicative of a child's (or adult's) general level of cognitive advancement, for some cultures emphasize the need to learn certain kinds of concepts while others stress other kinds.

Pierre Dasen (1984) has examined the evidence for these claims. Comparing the performance of children of two very different cultures on tasks measuring their understanding of the conservation of liquids and of horizontality (the latter requires the child to understand that when a vessel containing a liquid is tilted at various angles the surface plane of the water will always be horizontal), Dasen found interesting differences. Whereas 90 percent of Inuit children, of Cape Dorset (in Canada's Northwest Territories), understood horizontality by the age of 8 (100% by age 12), only 60 percent grasped the conservation of liquids even by the age of 15 (see Figure 9-6a). In contrast, only 50 percent of Baoulé children, of Ivory Coast, got the idea of horizontality by age 15, but 100 percent had an understanding of the conservation of liquids by the age of 10 (Figure 9-6b). Commenting on these results, Dasen suggests that people value and develop "those skills and concepts that are useful in the daily activities required" by their ecocultural settings. The Inuit, who are nomadic, hunter-gatherers value spatial skills and as a result acquire ideas like horizontality quite quickly, but they have little interest in quantitative comparisons. The Baoulé, on the other hand, are an agricultural people who, because they produce food, store it, and exchange it in the markets, assign considerable value to quantitative concepts.

In further exploration of this notion that cognitive skills or intelligence vary among cultures, Dasen asked Baoulé adults (who were illiterate) to list the skills that they most

valued in their children. The resulting compilation reflected a balance of social skills, on the one hand, and cognitive or more technological skills, on the other. The most important attribute of the intelligent child was the readiness to carry out tasks in the service of the family and the community; this included initiative, or performing a task without being asked, as well as competence, honesty, and responsibility. The second most often mentioned quality embodied respect for elders, politeness, and obedience. Fast learning, observational skills, attention, memory, literacy, school intelligence, and manual dexterity were also included in the list but were apparently seen as valuable only if put into the service of the social group.

In addition to differences in the acquisition of specific concepts and skills, peoples may vary in their overall approach to acquiring knowledge and understanding. Pointing out that the conditions of life that inform human behavior flow from historical-cultural processes that have matured over hundreds of years, Tharp (1994) explored differences between Native American and European American children with respect to the cognitive dimension of wholistic versus analytic thinking: "In wholistic thought, the pieces derive their meaning from the pattern of the whole; in analytic thought, the whole is revealed through the unfolding of the sections" (p. 90). According to Tharp, Native Americans are far more likely to operate wholistically, European Americans to operate analytically. For example, when Yukon elders prepared a 16-week unit plan for teaching children how to make moccasins of caribou skin, they began with preparations for the hunt; moccasins did not appear until the 15th week. To their way of thinking, "it is not possible to understand the moccasin outside the context of the leather, which is not understandable outside the spiritual relationship of the caribou to the land" (Tharp, 1994, p. 90). If European Americans had prepared this unit plan, however, Tharp suggests, they would doubtless have given the children the pattern and the tools to cut the leather in the first 15 minutes.

The wholistic thinker needs to understand the *context* of the thing he is attempting to understand, and this may mean understanding several levels of context. In the preceding example, the moccasin must be seen in the context of the leather of which it is to be made, the leather in the context of the caribou from which it comes, and the

The Period of Formal Operations

formal operations period
Period in which the child becomes capable of flexible and abstract thought, complex reasoning, and hypothesis testing.

In the concrete operations period the child begins to build the foundation of logical thinking that characterizes the adolescent. How do thought processes in the **formal operations period**, which begins at 11 or 12, differ from those typical of the concrete operations period? Perhaps the most significant changes are those in flexibility of thought, in the use of mental hypothesis testing, and in the ability to entertain many possible alternatives for the solution of problems.

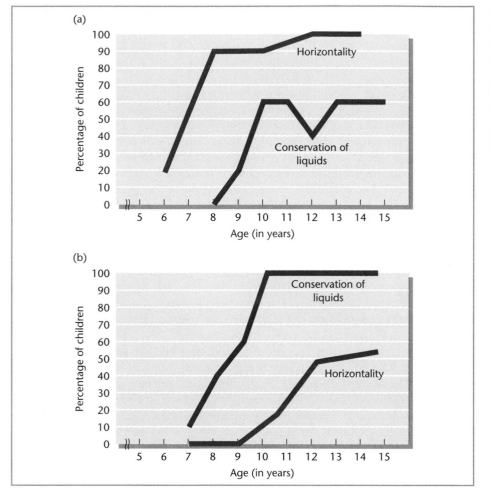

■ FIGURE 9-6
Conservation among Inuit and Baoulé children. Achievement of the concepts of horizontality and the conservation of liquids between the ages of 6 and 15 among (a) Inuit children of the Canadian Northwest Territories and (b) Baoulé children of Ivory Coast. (*Source:* Adapted from Dasen, 1984)

caribou in the context of the land it inhabits and with which it interacts. This approach leads to an emphasis on observational learning and, often, superior visual and spatial skills. It may also lead, however, to difficulties for children raised in one culture when they must attend school and prepare to work and function socially in a culture in which a different cognitive style is dominant.

As these studies suggest, culture alters not only the rate at which children learn but the *ways* in which they learn as well. At the very least, the dominant culture needs to understand the cultural-historical background of the children it seeks to educate, so that no child is considered unintelligent or unteachable because of her cognitive style. But more than this, it may be that teaching methods need to be more flexible—not just for so-called minorities but for all children—if social and community responsibility and an appreciation of the broader context of what children study are as important as analytical and technological skills.

Adolescents can think about fanciful problems not based in reality. They realize that logical rules can be applied to ideas that violate reality. As Siegler observes, "It is no coincidence that many people first acquire a taste for science fiction during adolescence" (1998, p. 43). For example, consider the problem, "If all blue people live in red houses, are all people who live in red houses blue?" The concrete operational child would have difficulty getting beyond the fact that there is no such thing as blue people. In contrast, the child in the formal operations period can move beyond unrealistic content to focus on applying logical solutions to the question posed.

During adolescence the child's thought continues to grow in flexibility and capacity for abstraction. In contrast to the concrete operational child who, under most circumstances, can solve problems only when objects are actually present, the adolescent can solve mentally represented problems. Children in this stage will review several possible alternatives or hypotheses in a problem-solving situation. They will consider alternative organizations of the world, and they will think about and discuss enduring philosophical issues such as truth and justice.

An example from a task used by Inhelder and Piaget (1958) illustrates the differences between children in the two stages. In this task, participants are asked to arrive at a law to explain why some objects float and others do not by experimenting with an assortment of objects and water. What the children are actually being asked is to derive Archimedes' law of floating bodies, which states that an object will float if its weight per unit (or density) is less than that of water. Thus, if two objects are of equal weight, the larger object is more likely to float than the smaller. Concrete operational children may focus on weight or size as a reason why things float or sink; for instance, they may say that the heavier or bigger objects are, the more likely they are to sink. They may even arrive at a double classification that involves the categories large and heavy, large and light, small and heavy, or small and light. However, they always base their solutions on the observable characteristics of size and weight, and they are perplexed when their rules do not fit contradictory observations. They are still unable to consider alternatives not directly observable in the physical world. For example, they cannot predict that a large and heavy piece of wood will float even though it is bigger and heavier than a small lead weight.

In contrast, in the formal operations period, the child can free herself from the obvious cues of weight and size and conceptualize a variety of possible alternatives to arrive at the concept of density. Piaget describes the comments of a child who has just entered the period of formal operations grappling with this kind of problem: "It sinks because it is small, it isn't stretched enough. You would have to have something larger to stay at the surface, something of the same weight and which would have a greater extension" (Inhelder and Piaget, 1958, p. 38).

Developmentalists continue to debate Piaget's notions about cognitive development in this last period and to search for the best ways to describe the child's thinking at this time (Kuhn, 1991; Keating, 1990; Moshman, 1998; Overton & Byrnes, 1991). Actually, not all adolescents or, for that matter, all adults in all societies reach the period of formal operations and achieve the flexibility in problem solving that Piaget associated with this period (Kuhn, 1991, 1998; Niemark, 1981). This is attributable partly to cultural and educational factors and partly to general intellectual level. Unlike concrete operational thought, which seems to be acquired to some degree in all societies, the attainment of formal operations is strongly influenced by culture (Dasen & Heron, 1981; Rogoff, 1990; Schweder et al., 1998). In groups who do not emphasize symbolic skills or in which educational experiences are limited, the stage of formal operations may occur late in development or may even be absent. In addition, admittedly, young people and adults are more likely to achieve the capacity for logical abstract reasoning within their particular areas of interest or expertise than in other domains (DeLisi & Staudt, 1980; Falmagne, 1980). Scientific training in such subjects as physics, chemistry, and the philosophy of logic has been found to be associated with greater ability to use formal operations.

Self and Other: Piagetian Concepts and the Beginning of Social Cognition

Although Piaget was interested in the individual's cognitive development and paid little attention to the child's evolving social awareness and behavior, a number of his important conceptions bear on social cognition and have stimulated research in this area. His concept of object permanence, for example, has relevance for the development of self-recognition—a topic we first discussed in Chapter 7—in that conceiving of the self as an entity distinct from the environment and from others in that environment requires that one grasp the notion of the continuity of existence. And his notions of egocentrism and of the child's growing ability to move away from self-centeredness have clear implications for the development of social cognition. Let's look first at the differentiation of the self and then at the beginnings of one important aspect of social cognition—children's gradual appreciation not only of their own viewpoints, emotions, thoughts, and intentions but the views, feelings, ideas, and purposes of others.

The Self as Distinct from Others

A central process in the development of social cognition is differentiation of the self from the nonself, that is, of the self from the self's environment—from objects, nonhuman beings, and other human beings in that environment (Harter, 1998). This differentiation process has its roots in early infancy: Even young babies seem to expect different responses from people than from objects. For example, if you face a 2-month-old child without moving or speaking, the infant will become distressed (Tronick, 1989). Somehow children know to expect animate behavior from a human being. Babies also learn to expect and use responses from other people to guide their own behavior; they do not expect such guidance from inanimate objects. As we saw in Chapter 7, when a young child encounters an unfamiliar person, he may look to his mother to see how she responds to the stranger; if she appears relaxed and comfortable, the child may respond similarly.

With differentiation comes self-recognition. As we saw in Chapter 7, very young infants will gaze at their reflections in a mirror, but it is generally not until the second year of life that children recognize their own images in a mirror. Because an understanding of the existence and continuity of the self is doubtless a critical part of self-identity, it seems likely that grasping the notion of object permanence is closely related to the development of self-recognition. As we've seen, Piaget held that children achieve a full understanding of object permanence some time between the ages of 1½ and 2 years, about the same time that they first see their mirror images as themselves. The fact that developmentalists have now found evidence of an earlier understanding of object permanence does not necessarily alter the relationship between object permanence and self-recognition; it may be that the former is a prerequisite for the latter.

As we will see in the next section, developmental changes in the child's understanding of her self seem to parallel developments in the way the child begins to view and describe others. The child's view of herself becomes more differentiated and involves more descriptions of values, motives, intentions, and other internal psychological phenomena as she grows older. Preschool children (5 or younger) tend to define themselves mainly by physical attributes, possessions, overt behaviors, or preferred activities (e.g., I'm 4 years old; I have a cat named Twinkie; I like to swim).

At around 7 or 8 (Piaget's period of concrete operations) children become more aware of their private selves and their unique feelings and thoughts, and they begin to describe themselves in more abstract terms. They learn to use trait labels that focus on abilities and interpersonal characteristics, such as *smart* and *dumb*, *nice* and *mean*, and they begin to compare themselves with peers (Harter, 1998; Ruble & Dweck, 1995). It is as if they are trying to build an integrated personality theory that will describe their motives, feelings, and thoughts (Damon & Hart, 1982; Harter, 1998). Children of this age also begin to be concerned with self-control and self-direction. They emphasize intentions, making choices, striving toward long-term goals, and controlling their thoughts and actions: "If I don't like a subject I won't do anything in the subject. . . . On the other hand, in subjects I do like, my science and mathematics, I really work" (Secord & Peevers, 1974, p. 139).

The growing ability to think in the abstract allows the adolescent (from 11 or 12 on) to create a more integrated self view. For example, a young adolescent might conceive of himself as intelligent by combining the qualities of being smart and creative but at the same time think of himself as an "airhead," linking feelings of being ignorant and uncreative. In early adolescence these self-attributions often get compartmentalized as the young person tries to put together his image of himself; thus he may simultaneously think of himself as both intelligent and an "airhead." Ordinarily it is only in late adolescence that the individual develops a coherent or integrated theory of the self; for example, he may reconceptualize the opposing notions of "cheerful" and "depressed" as "moody," thus resolving apparent contradictions in his sense of self (Harter, 1998; Harter & Bresnick, 1996).

Role Taking: Understanding Others' Perspectives

In many ways the changes in social cognition and the processes underlying them parallel changes in nonsocial cognition. Just as children come to recognize that physical objects in the environment continue to exist outside of their own perception and that they themselves have a continuing existence, so they learn that objects in the social environment, that is, other people, have an existence independent of them. Children become less egocentric and more able to understand the thoughts and perspectives of others. And instead of viewing others in terms of attributes and traits that are immediately observable, children come to appreciate people's more abstract characteristics such as emotions, motives, and intentions. A 6- or 7-year-old child, for example, is likely to describe a person in terms of her outward appearance, possessions, or behavior in respect to the child, and any psychological description is likely to be stereotypical or value-laden, like "nice" or "bad": "She is very nice because she gives my friends and me toffee. She lives by the main road. She has fair hair and glasses. . . . She sometimes gives us flowers" (Livesley & Bromley, 1973, p. 214).

As children grow older, they tend to use more psychological statements and more abstractions in describing other people (Livesley & Bromley, 1973; Peevers & Secord, 1973; Shantz, 1983). The biggest increase in such usage occurs around the age of 8; indeed, investigators like Livesley and Bromley (1973) have concluded that "the eighth year is a critical period in the development of person perception" (p. 147). Even so, it is not until adolescence or early adulthood that people become aware of the full complexity of human thoughts, feelings, and intentions or grasp the idea that behavioral characteristics may vary with situations, internal states, or other transitory factors (Flavell & Miller, 1998; Harter, 1998). A 16-year-old boy describes his brother:

> My kid brother . . . loves to be with people. . . . Most of the time he's good natured and a lot of fun . . . but when we play soccer . . . he can't keep up with teenagers [and] he gets mad when he loses the ball. . . . Later I've found him crying in his room. He knows he's made an ass of himself but he gets so frustrated he can't help it. It's tough being the youngest.

It has been suggested that the shift away from an early, egocentric orientation underlies improved communication skills as well as the development of moral standards and empathic understanding of and concern for others (Eisenberg & Fabes, 1998; Harter, 1998). The development of these abilities is basic to the child's socialization, and we will return to this topic in greater detail later in Chapter 16. Here it will be useful to consider the model of role or perspective taking proposed by Selman and his colleagues (Selman, 1980; Selman & Byrne, 1974; Selman & Jacquette, 1978), in which this decentering process evolves through five distinct stages (see Table 9-3). As children move through these stages they learn not only to differentiate between their own perspectives and those of others but to understand others' views and the relations between these views and their own. To explore this

TABLE 9-3 Role Taking: Developing the Ability to Take Different Perspectives

Stage 0 Egocentric Perspective
The child does not distinguish his own perspective from that of others nor recognize that another person may interpret experiences differently.

Stage 1 Differentiated Perspective
The child realizes that she and others may have either the same or a different perspective. Although she is concerned with the uniqueness of each person's cognitions, she can't judge accurately what the other person's perspective may be.

Stage 2 Reciprocal Perspective
Because the child can see himself from another's perspective and knows the other person can do the same thing, he can anticipate and consider another's thoughts and feelings.

Stage 3 Mutual Perspectives
Now the child can view her own perspective, a peer's perspective, and their shared, or mutual perspective, from the viewpoint of a third person. For example, she can think of how a parent, teacher, or other peer might view both her and her friend's perspectives as well as their mutual perspective.

Stage 4 Societal or In-Depth Perspectives
Children (and adults) can see networks of perspectives, such as the societal, Republican, or African American point of view. People understand that these varying perspectives not only exist in awareness but involve deeper, perhaps unconscious representations, such as feelings and values.

Source: Adapted from Selman & Jacquette, 1978.

developmental progression of the capacity for role taking, Selman and associates presented four groups of children—4, 6, 8, and 10 years old—with several filmed stories; here is the description of one of these stories:

> Holly is an 8-year-old girl who likes to climb trees. She is the best tree climber in the neighborhood. One day while climbing down from a tall tree she falls off the bottom branch but does not hurt herself. Her father sees her fall. He is upset and asks her to promise not to climb trees any more. Holly promises.
>
> Later that day, Holly and her friends meet Sean. Sean's kitten is caught up in a tree and cannot get down. Something has to be done right away or the kitten may fall. Holly is the only one who climbs trees well enough to reach the kitten and get it down, but she remembers her promise to her father. (Selman & Byrne, 1974, p. 805)

The researchers then asked the children in each group questions about the thoughts and views of the stories' characters, posing two or three questions to assess role-taking ability at each of four of the stages described in Table 9-3 (Stages 0–3). For example, examining subjective role taking, at Stage 1, the researchers asked, "Does Sean know why Holly cannot decide whether or not to climb the tree? Why or why not?" Again, at the level of Stage 2, one of the questions asked was "Does Holly think her father will understand why she climbed the tree? Why is that?" And at the level of Stage 3 a question posed was "If Holly and her father discussed this situation, what might they decide together? Why is that?"

As you can see from Figure 9-7, the children demonstrated a steady progression in role-taking ability through the four stages. For example, whereas 80 percent of 4-year-olds were at Stage 0, no children in this group functioned at Stages 2 or 3. Conversely, 50 percent or more of children 8 and 10 years old were at Stage 2, and several children in these two groups functioned at Stage 3. Later longitudinal research by Selman and his colleagues (Gurucharri & Selman, 1982) confirmed these findings and demonstrated that role-taking skills emerge in an invariant

■ FIGURE 9-7
Role Taking at Different Ages.
Between the ages of 4 and 6,
children take the enormous step
of moving from egocentricity to a
differentiated perspective. From
here on, progress in appreciating
others' views is less dramatic but
steady. (*Source:* Based on Selman
& Byrne, 1974)

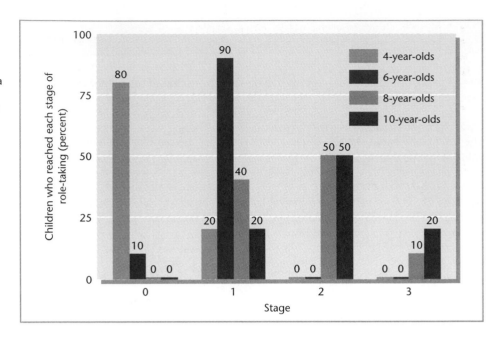

sequence as the child develops; other researchers (e.g., Taylor, 1988) have also confirmed Selman's proposals.

Some people develop greater abilities at social role taking or, as Figure 9-7 indicates, attain these abilities earlier than others. What kinds of factors contribute, or are related to, individual differences in role-taking abilities? Performance on standard intelligence tests shows a modest relation to social role-taking ability (Shantz, 1983), and, as we discuss in Chapter 16, some studies have found positive relations between prosocial behavior, such as helping and sharing, and role-taking skills. For example, observing children's offers of help, offers of support, and responsible suggestions to other children on the playground and in classrooms, Eisenberg and associates (Eisenberg, 1992; Eisenberg & Fabes, 1998) found that laboratory measures of role taking correlated with how often children engaged in such altruistic behaviors.

EVALUATION OF PIAGET'S THEORY

In spite of the towering importance of Piaget's theory as a guide to children's thinking at different points in the child's development, his theory has come under criticism from many developmentalists. We consider the strengths of Piaget's theory and review some specific criticisms before offering an overall assessment.

Strengths of the Theory

As we noted in the first chapter, theories are useful for two reasons: They integrate and give meaning to a wide array of information, and they lead to new research by stimulating hunches and providing direction into new areas of exploration. Piaget's theory achieved both of these goals. With his stage model and his underlying concepts such as schemata and cognitive organization, Piaget integrated a broad spectrum of seemingly diverse issues revolving around children's sense of time, space, and numbers into a single coherent theory. In addition, Piaget's theory has stimulated an enormous amount of research. According to Miller (1993), Piaget offered many heuristic ideas that have both influenced our views of how children develop and served as guides in our efforts to understand children's development. Among these are the following notions:

- Children are active constructors of knowledge.
- Development follows an invariant sequence.
- Children seek knowledge and are not passive recipients of input.
- Errors are informative and may provide important clues about children's thinking as they struggle to understand reality.
- Cognitive development, particularly in the early years, does not depend on language skills; the child's perceptual-motor systems provide important routes to knowledge.

Piaget's theory produced some surprises. Who would have thought that infants believe objects disappear when out of sight? Or that children don't understand that quantities of substances remain the same even when their shapes or appearances are altered? Or that children think about such things as what makes clouds move, where the sun came from, and how a pendulum works? As Miller (1993) suggests, "In a discipline that has few real 'discoveries' [such as] the discovery of a new planet or the structure of DNA Piaget's surprises about cognitive development are refreshing and his observations remarkable. . . . He showed us that developmental descriptions can be profoundly intriguing" (p. 85). And, finally, Piaget's theory is ecologically valid, for it tells us about real children dealing with problems that they encounter in their own world.

Did Piaget Judge the Child's Abilities Accurately?

Focusing on infants' cognitive skills, a great deal of current work has suggested that infants may know a lot more than Piaget thought. Our earlier discussion of infants' remarkable cognitive achievements, such as grasping object permanence at 3½ months and understanding causality at an early age (Baillargeon, 1993), suggests that Piaget may have underestimated the cognitive abilities of infants in a major way. Similarly, the current findings in infant conditionability and perceptual ability discussed in Chapter 5 suggest that the infant may know more than Piaget discerned (Flavell, 1985; Sugarman, 1987).

Piaget also appears to have underestimated the abilities of older children: Many children in the preoperational and concrete operational periods seem to be more cognitively advanced than Piaget's stage theory of development would suggest (Gelman & Baillargeon, 1983; Halford, 1990). For example, preschoolers can use fairly sophisticated biological understanding to distinguish between living and nonliving things (Backscheider, Shatz, & Gelman, 1993). And 3- to 5-year-olds have shown a rudimentary ability to understand conservation of taste and weight, a feat that Piaget clearly thought was too advanced for these young minds. For instance, preschoolers who watched sugar dissolved in a cup of water believed that the water would taste sweet—even though they could not see the sugar—and that it would weigh more as a result of the added sugar (Au, Sidle, & Rollins, 1993). Other studies show that children as young as 4 or 5 years old can take others' perspectives (Newcombe & Huttenlocker, 1992) and that these children's understanding of topological and spatial representation is more advanced than Piaget hypothesized (Liben & Downs, 1993; Miller & Baillargeon, 1990). As Robert Siegler (1998) recently observed, "Discovery of unexpected strengths in infants and young children has been one of *the* leading stories in the recent study of cognitive development" (p. 54).

Does Cognitive Development Proceed in Stages?

According to Piaget's view, children's cognitive development undergoes qualitative shifts from one stage to another, and these stages are presumed to follow each other in an invariant order. Moreover, the child cannot proceed to the next stage until she has mastered the ways of thinking characteristic of the current one.

Recent evidence (Siegler, 1994, 1998) suggests that cognitive development may not occur in the stagelike steps that Piaget portrayed (see Chapter 1 discussion). For example, if we evaluate a child's abilities every 6 months, we may see the changes in these abilities as rapid and discontinuous. However, if we look closely at the changes that occur within a half hour or even across several weeks as a child tries to solve a particular problem, we find that the child's progress appears more gradual and continuous than abrupt and discontinuous. As Siegler wryly notes, "whether children's thinking undergoes qualitative change depends in large part on how closely you look at it" (1998, p. 55).

In addition, the sequence of intellectual growth that Piaget proposes may not be as unvarying as he suggests. The results of cross-cultural studies suggest that growth may be modified by cultural and experiential factors (Dasen, 1984; Rogoff, 1990). As we will see in the section on Vygotsky, culture and historical era are both important determinants of development. In an era of television and computers, it is hard to deny that children's thinking is altered by these technological advances. Moreover, in spite of Piaget's pessimism about the child's ability to proceed more quickly through instruction, the evidence is now clear that active intervention, such as training in problem-solving strategies, can accelerate development (Field, 1987; Gelman & Baillargeon, 1983; Siegler, 1998).

Another criticism is that the child Piaget describes is largely nonsocial and unemotional—quite unlike most children we know. As one researcher put it, the Piaget child "has no fun" (Murray, 1983, p. 231)! Piaget paid little attention to feelings, wishes, and desires and did not investigate social relationships. Except in his theory of children's moral development (Chapter 16), Piaget generally assumed that the same rules that governed cognition applied to emotions and social phenomena, and even this theory was largely cognitive, with no place for feelings like anger, shame, or guilt.

Overall Assessment

Despite these new findings, new hypotheses, and resulting criticisms of Piaget's work, Piaget clearly has had an enormous impact on the study of the child's development of cognitive skills; it is largely to his influence that we can attribute the current concern with cognitive factors in development and the establishment in recent years of so many centers for the study of cognitive psychology throughout the world (Beilin, 1992). Although his theorizing and methodology were sometimes flawed, Piaget asked and answered important questions in an innovative way, and his provocative theory has stimulated a vast amount of research and theorizing by other behavioral scientists. It is inconceivable that our understanding of the child's intellectual development could have advanced to its present stage without the monumental work of Jean Piaget.

VYGOTSKY'S SOCIOCULTURAL THEORY

The important influence of children's social and cultural worlds on their cognitive development is an area of study that Piagetian theory did not address. In contrast, the developmental theory put forth by Lev Vygotsky, whose work we introduced in Chapter 1, focuses specifically on this area of concern. Somewhat ironically, although Vygotsky was greatly influenced in his thinking by the former Soviet Union's communist philosophy, his work was banned in his native land. As a result, his impact on Western developmental theory was delayed. As a result, it is only in recent years that Western psychologists have begun to explore his proposals and concepts (Belmont, 1989; Rogoff, 1990; Wertsch & Tulviste, 1992, 1994).

In his sociocultural theory of development, Vygotsky proposes that children's cognitive development is a function of their interaction with more skilled and more sophisticated partners, who include parents, teachers, older children, and others. The child and her partners solve problems together, and through the assistance that her partners provide, the child gradually learns to function intellectually on her own. As you can see, this overall approach is in marked contrast to that of Piaget, who focused on the individual as the unit of study. Although Vygotsky held that each child is born with a set of innate abilities, such as attention, perception, and memory, he believed that only input from the child's social and cultural worlds, in the form of interactions with more expert adults and peers, could mold these basic abilities into more complex, higher-order cognitive functions. Consistent with this view, Vygotsky held that learning a language, which occurs in social interaction, has a particularly important effect on the child's intellectual development.

As we will see, however, Vygotsky did share some concepts with Piaget; for this reason and because he also shared some concerns with information-processing theorists, our discussion of his work serves in part as a bridge to our second chapter on cognitive development (Chapter 10), in which we focus on information-processing theory. Like Piaget, Vygotsky held that development proceeds through stages, so that change occurs in abrupt shifts rather than in steady quantitative increments. Moreover, Vygotsky had an abiding concern with the processes involved in development; he did not simply observe the end point or products of development. As we mentioned in Chapter 1, Vygotsky accounted for shifts in development by the types of mediation that children rely upon to understand their world. Across development, the emergence of different types of **mediators,** or psychological tools and signs like language, counting, mnemonic devices, algebraic symbols, art, and writing, permit the child to function more effectively in solving problems and understanding his cognitive world.

We begin by discussing Vygotsky's notion of mental functions; here we will see how mediators enable the child to move to new levels of psychological processing. We then examine Vygotsky's concept of the zone of proximal development, which expands on his idea that children learn through social interaction and has given rise to such recent concepts as scaffolding, now used widely in elementary education. We next explore the influence of culture on children's cognitive development, a prime concern of Vygotsky's, and take a side trip into culture's effect on the learning of mathematics. In our final discussion, we examine the effects of culture on children's learning and use of language.

mediators According to Vygotsky, psychological tools and signs like language, counting, mnemonic devices, algebraic symbols, art, and writing.

Elementary and Higher Mental Functions

In Vygotsky's theory, one important transition in children's cognitive development occurs between elementary and higher mental functions. **Elementary mental functions** are those with which the child is endowed by nature and include memory, attention, and perception. These and other "natural" forms of mental functioning are transformed by the child's interaction with his society and culture into higher mental functioning. **Higher mental functions,** such as voluntary attention and logical and abstract thinking, represent a new level of psychological processing for the child. These functions depend on the use of increasingly sophisticated mediators, such as language and other symbol systems, that children develop as they interact with their environment.

Vygotsky's discussion of memory illustrates the difference between these two types of mental function. Vygotksy proposes that the elementary form of memory is constructed of images and impressions of events. This type of memory is very close to perception; it is unanalyzed and is directly influenced by the environment. The higher form of memory, on the other hand, embodies the use of signs to mediate memory functions; for instance, the child begins to use a writing system that enables her to fix in her memory and to transmit to others what she saw, for example, on a trip to the zoo or what happened in a story that her teacher read to her. The

elementary mental functions Functions with which the child is endowed by nature, including attention, perception, and memory.

higher mental functions Functions that rely on *mediators* that have become increasingly sophisticated through the child's interaction with his environment.

child uses a writing system as a sign, or mental tool, to elaborate on the natural functioning of his memory. It is also important to keep in mind the social origins of higher mental functions: It is the child's society that provides him with a writing system and other mediators that enable him to develop better cognitive skills.

The Zone of Proximal Development

In line with his interest in the processes of human development, Vygotsky was much less concerned with children's intellectual abilities at a particular point in time than he was with the child's potential for intellectual growth (Cole, 1985; Wertsch, 1985; Wertsch & Tulviste, 1992). To assess this potential and to understand how intellectual development occurs, Vygotsky proposed the notion of the **zone of proximal development (ZPD)**, defining this zone as the difference between a child's "actual developmental level as determined by independent problem solving" and his "potential development as determined through problem solving under adult guidance or in collaboration with more capable peers" (Vygotsky, 1978, p. 86). The concept of the zone of proximal development is a twofold one. First, it represents an alternative approach to the assessment of intelligence—examining children's intellectual potential under optimal conditions. Second, the zone of proximal development represents a way of understanding how children's intellectual development occurs, namely, through social interaction with more sophisticated partners.

Recently, researchers (Brown, 1994; Brown & Campione, 1990; Rogoff, 1990, 1998) have illustrated the value of this approach in studies of children's learning, by showing that children's planning, problem solving, and memory can indeed be improved when adults or peers who are more skilled provide them with specific help and guidance. According to Vygotsky, working within a child's zone of proximal development—that is, by giving her adult or peer assistance—allows her to respond to her environment in more complex and competent ways and to achieve more than she might alone. Some evidence indicates, however, that adult assistance is superior to that given by peers. In the study described in Box 9-2, the children who were guided in a planning problem by adults demonstrated more efficiency than the children whose partners were same-age peers. It may be that for children to profit significantly from partnering in a learning task, the partners need to be more expert than the children being helped.

Vygotsky's theory has had considerable impact in the field of education in recent years. One form of instruction inspired by Vygotskian thinking is termed scaffolding. **Scaffolding** is an instructional process in which the teacher adjusts to the child's level of development the amount and type of support he or she offers the child. In a classic demonstration, Wood, Bruner, and Ross (1976) taught 3- and 5-year-olds to build a pyramid out of interlocking wooden blocks through both verbal and physical scaffolding. This scaffolding involved modeling the steps, encouraging the child to put the blocks in the right slots, and helping the child by segmenting the task into more easily understood steps. By careful monitoring of each child's progress, the tutor was able to constantly adjust the task to make it manageable and provide assistance when needed. In scaffolding, which has been demonstrated in a variety of tasks by later researchers (Pratt, Kerig, Cowan, & Cowan, 1988; Rogoff, 1990, 1998), as the child becomes more skilled, the teacher or other adult gradually reduces the amount of support he or she provides, so that eventually the child can execute the task in a skilled fashion independently of the partner's help.

One example of the application of this view to the classroom comes from the recent work of Ann Brown and her colleagues (Brown, 1994; Brown & Campione, 1990). In this "community of learners" model of classroom instruction, adults and children work together in shared activities, peers learn from each other, and the teacher serves as an expert guide who facilitates the process by which children learn from both the teacher and each other. Rogoff (1998)

zone of proximal development (ZPD) According to Vygotsky, the difference between the developmental level a child has reached and the level she is potentially capable of reaching with the guidance or collaboration of a more skilled adult or peer.

scaffolding Based on Vygotsky's thought, an instructional process in which the teacher continually adjusts the amount and type of support he offers as the child continues to develop more sophisticated skills.

BOX 9-2

Child Psychology in Action

Adult Partnering Guides Children in Efficient Planning

Do children solve a planning problem more efficiently when given guidance by a more skilled partner? According to Vygotsky, children should do better under these conditions. To find out, Radziszewska and Rogoff (1988) asked 9-year-olds to plan an errand in collaboration with either another 9-year-old or a parent as a partner.

Partners were given a map of an imaginary town (see Figure 9-8) and two lists of errands and were asked to plan a trip to obtain materials for a school play (e.g., to buy uniforms from the theatrical supplies store, paint brushes from the paint shop or the shopping center, and so on). Partners were asked to plan an efficient route to save gas, which required that the participants decide from which stores to purchase the needed supplies and then develop a plan that incorporated all these stores in sequence, without backtracking or other unnecessary travel.

Adult-child dyads were better planners than peer-child dyads. The adult-child couples planned longer sequences of moves (average of 4.9 stores per move) than the peer-child couples (average of 1.3 stores per move). Nearly half

of the adult-child dyads planned the whole route at the onset, whereas none of the peer-child dyads showed this kind of careful planning. Children learned other helpful strategies when they worked with an adult, such as exploring the map of the town before making any moves and marking stores that they wished or did not wish to shop at with different colors. Of great importance was the children's active involvement in the planning decisions, which the adults often verbalized to help the children's understanding. In contrast, peer partners often dominated the decision-making process, ignored their coworkers, and communicated very little.

Not only did children profit more from participation with an adult, but they were able to transfer their learning to later planning tasks that they executed by themselves. In an independent planning test, children who had worked in adult-child dyads in the first test produced more efficient routes (20% shorter) than children who had been in peer-child dyads.

As Vygotsky would have predicted, "children appear to benefit from participation in problem-solving with the guidance of partners who are skilled in accomplishing the task at hand" (Rogoff, 1990, p. 169).

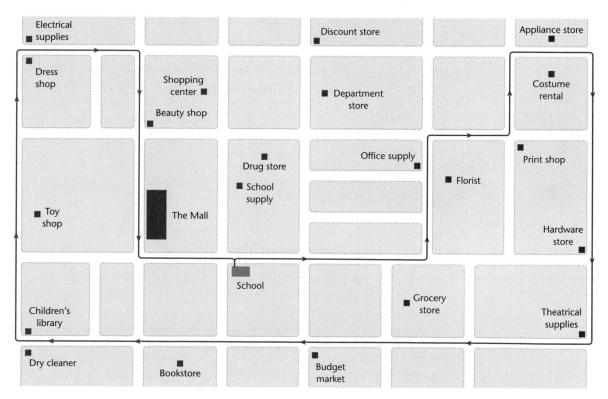

■ FIGURE 9-8

How adult guidance can help children plan efficiently.

This map of an imaginary town shows the efficient route an adult-child pair planned for acquiring all the materials they would need to prepare for and stage a school play. (*Source:* Radziszewska & Rogoff, 1988)

compares this model to traditional apprenticeship learning in trades, in which learning involves both relationships between teacher and apprentice and interactions among apprentices themselves. A similar model has been applied in science education in Japan. Kobayashi (1994) describes a system that involves discussion among students in a classroom, The teacher guides this peer dialogue by defining the central issue, reviewing possible alternatives, and encouraging students to use their informal knowledge and innovative ways of getting further information. The teacher in the community of learners plays two roles—one as a scaffolding agent for the students and the other as a participant in the learning process. The students, who vary in knowledge and ability, help each other learn through their interchanges.

The Role of Culture

An important feature of Vygotsky's approach is his emphasis on the significance of society and culture in accounts of development (Rogoff, 1990, 1998; Wertsch & Kanner, in press). Stressing the importance of considering culture in any effort to understand children's cognitive development, Vygotsky proposed two important principles of cultural influence. First, cultures vary widely in the kinds of institutions and settings they offer to facilitate children's development. Schooling, for example, or the introduction of new economic or occupational activities can significantly alter the ways in which people think. As we saw in Chapter 1, when peoples who had used methods of reasoning and calculation that were based on concrete events in their everyday lives learned to read, to write, and to engage in new and more sophisticated occupational activities they began also to think and to reason quite differently (Luria, 1971; Saxe, 1982; Scribner, 1985).

Sometimes we find that a particular cognitive approach characteristic of a more traditional culture is more precise and useful than one common in industrialized nations. According to Gauvain (1993), the way children learn to organize and encode spatial information also varies according to linguistic and cultural conventions. The Guugu Yamithirr of Australia describe directions and location in absolute rather than relative terms; for example, they will guide a stranger by saying, "turn to the west" rather than "turn to the left." Contrary to what Western people might have thought, these people are more accurate in making spatial judgments than Europeans are because of the very way they organize their understanding of spatial topology.

Vygotsky's second principle of cultural influence states that in any attempt to assess children's cognitive development we must consider cultural contexts; if we ignore the culturally specific nature of children's learning, he claimed, we run the risk of seriously underestimating children's development (Greenfield & Cocking, 1995; Greenfield & Suzuki, 1998; Rogoff, 1990). Indeed, a wide variety of cross-cultural studies have documented that children learn highly sophisticated and complex, culturally important skills through social guidance (e.g., Childs & Greenfield, 1982; Lave, 1977). In the example of the Zinacantecan craft of weaving that we also discussed in Chapter 1, we saw what at first glance appeared to be a method of teaching and learning quite foreign to a U.S.-European style. The apprentice was expected to sit quietly and watch as the master demonstrated the weaving method. Indeed, as Greenfield and Lave (1982) noted, "In the earliest stages of learning the girls spend a bit more than half their time watching the teacher perform the weaving task" (p. 202). However, gradually the young apprentices began to participate cooperatively, much as the Vygotskian notion of social guidance within the zone of proximal development would prescribe.

Several specific teaching methods are involved in this weaving instruction, including developmentally guided scaffolding whereby the teacher provides just the amount of help required for the apprentice weaver to complete the task successfully. In addition, in line with the concept of scaffolding, the teacher intervenes more at the more complicated parts of the learning task, so that task difficulty is always within the learner's ability range. Finally, tasks are carefully sequenced, from the easier to the more difficult aspects of the weaving process.

When we view the Zinacantecan method of teaching the weaving skill not only against a background of the Zinacantecan culture but also through the lens of Vygotsky's sociocultural model for understanding children's learning and development, we may see this "foreign" style differently. Vygotsky's theory leads us to an appreciation of different cultures and their values, which in turn leads us to view the young weaving apprentices as more sophisticated and accomplished than we might originally have thought.

Mathematics and Culture

Children in Western societies often acquire and use rudimentary counting systems before they begin attending school (Saxe, Guberman, & Gearhart, 1987; Wilkinson, 1984), but it is generally in the early elementary grades, from kindergarten on up, that children master the principles underlying counting and acquire more complex numerical concepts. In societies in developing areas of the world or among the less advantaged in wealthier societies, however, children often acquire the ability to solve mathematical problems without the benefit of a formal education. How do they do this? From a Vygotskian perspective, how does the surrounding culture support such children's learning?

Geoffrey Saxe (1988) has studied the acquisition of mathematical concepts in uneducated children, focusing particularly on the young street vendors (10 to 12 years old) in the cities of Brazil. These children make their living by selling candy and fruit to the people riding on buses or walking through the downtown areas of Brazil's major cities. Saxe found that this occupational pursuit had several interesting effects on the children's mathematical abilities. Because of the severe inflation Brazil's economy was experiencing at the time of Saxe's study, these children often dealt successfully with large numerical values in carrying on their daily business. When the researcher asked the children to identify and compare multidigit numbers based on bills and coins, they performed quite well. On the other hand, when they were asked to read multidigit numerical values in written form, the children performed quite poorly. Perhaps because these young vendors often dealt with numbers in the thousands in their daily sales, they found Saxe's small-number comparisons more difficult than comparisons based on large numbers. Or it may be that they could not deal with numbers out of the context of their selling activities.

The findings of several other researchers who have studied the Brazilian street vendors are discussed in Box 9-3. As this box shows, the children's daily interaction with addition and subtraction, as well as their lack of formal schooling, has led them to develop atypical ways of performing mathematical functions, ways that work for them in their daily activities but that constrain their ability to deal with mathematical concepts in an academic setting. If, as Vygotsky insisted, we take culture into account in evaluating such children's cognitive skills, we must recognize the sophistication of their competence, which certainly exceeds what we might have expected. Together, these studies of young street vendors underscore the importance of considering the cultural context in our evaluations of children's cognitive development (Rogoff, 1990).

BOX 9-3

Risk and Resilience

Translating Street Math into Academic Math Isn't So Easy

All of us use mathematics and numerical reasoning every day of our lives. We calculate the costs of items in the supermarket, divide a pizza equally among friends, and balance our checkbooks. In most cases, we have learned the necessary skills in grade school, but not all children or adults have the opportunity to acquire a formal education. How do those without that opportunity perform such daily tasks or, even more demanding, manage to conduct business with some degree of success? Can children learn to function effectively in spite of poverty and lack of opportunity to learn in a formal school setting? As the study we discuss here illustrates, even in the face of hardship and risk, children demonstrate great resilience and an amazing ability to adapt their cognitive functioning.

In a study of young vendors who ply the streets of Brazilian cities, offering coconuts, oranges, and other fruits for sale to pedestrians and riders of public transportation, Carraher, Schliemann, and Carraher (1988) explored the ability of these children to solve common mathematical problems. The experimenters presented five young vendors, who ranged in age from 9 to 15 years old, with either a common commercial transaction between a vendor and a customer—one similar to the transactions the children were accustomed to handle daily—or an exercise in computation framed in academic terms, as it would be presented in a school setting.

The young vendors revealed striking differences in their abilities to perform the two different types of task. When they were tested using the familiar commercial transaction, the children were correct 98 percent of the time, but when the same mathematical problems were presented in the form of an academic exercise, the percentage of cor-rect answers dropped to 37. One notable difference in the children's response to the two tasks lay in method: The young vendors solved the commercial problem mentally but resorted to pencil and paper to solve the school-like problem. Most striking, however, were the differences in mathematical strategies that the children used in the two situations. The following protocol from one of the children illustrates these differences:

Commercial Transaction Problem

CUSTOMER: I'll take two coconuts. (Each coconut costs 40 *cruzados*, and the customer pays with a 500-*cruzado* bill.) What do I get back?

CHILD VENDOR (before reaching for the customer's change): Eighty, ninety, one hundred, four hundred and twenty.

School-type Problem

TEST QUESTION: What is 420 plus 80?

CHILD'S RESPONSE: The child writes 420 plus 80 and obtains 130 as a result. He lowers the zero and then apparently proceeds as follows: He adds the 8 and the 2, carries the 1, and then adds the 8 and the 5, obtaining 13. With the already lowered zero, he gets 130. Note that the child is applying steps from the multiplication algorithm to an addition problem.

The child has approached the same problem (420 + 80) in two distinctly different ways. In the street he uses an "add-on" strategy efficiently to arrive at the correct answer, whereas in the academic setting he applies strategies learned in school incorrectly. As Vygotsky would have predicted, this study underscores the importance of context for understanding cognitive development. It also underlines the resilience of children at risk and their ability to survive and learn despite the lack of opporunity for formal schooling.

The Role of Language

Language played a special role in Vygotsky's social-cognitive theory. Vygotksy believed that the acquisition and use of language is a primary component of children's developing intellectual abilities.

According to Jerome Bruner, Vygotsky was "forever intrigued with the inventive powers that language bestowed on mind—in ordinary speech, in the novels of Tolstoy and the plays of Chekhov . . . , [and] in the play of children" (Bruner, 1987, p. 2; cited by Miller, 1993) For Vygotsky, thought and speech are independent in early development but begin to join together around the second year of life, when children begin to use words to label objects. Within a year, speech assumes two forms: social, or communicative, speech and **egocentric speech** (also called "private speech"). Vygotsky's view of egocentric speech differs markedly from Piaget's concept. For Vygotksy, egocentric speech is a form of self-directed dialogue by which the child instructs herself in solving problems or formulating plans. Egocentric speech becomes a tool for intellectual growth and allows the child to become a more effective and skilled learner. For example, in his efforts to solve a dinosaur puzzle, a

egocentric speech
According to Vygotsky, a form of self-directed dialog by which the child instructs herself in solving problems and formulating plans; as the child matures, becomes internalized as *inner speech.*

child might say, "First I'll put the tail piece here, then the claw goes over here and the head right there." By age 7 or 8, this form of speech goes underground and becomes **inner speech,** as the child thinks in words as a way of guiding his strategies.

For Piaget, egocentric speech was "selfish" speech, because the child made no effort to adapt his speech to make it understandable to others, such as peers. Moreover, Piaget thought that egocentric speech served no useful cognitive function. Finally, Piaget suggested that egocentric speech diminishes at the end of the preoperational period, as the child's perspective-taking abilities improved, whereas Vygotsky thought that this kind of speech simply became internalized.

Who is right? Most of the evidence favors Vygotsky's version. For example, children use more private or self-speech when encountering a difficult cognitive task; as a result, their performance improves, suggesting that children use this form of speech as a cognitive crutch or aid (Berk, 1992). In addition, in a longitudinal study of the developmental sequence of this kind of speech, Bivens and Berk (1990) found that egocentric speech does in fact move from external (audible, self-directed speech) to internal (silent, self-directed speech) between 7 and 10 years of age, supporting Vygotsky's view. Thus, language seems to serve as an aid for regulating cognitive plans and strategies as well as a tool for communicating.

inner speech Internalized *egocentric speech* that continues to direct and regulate intellectual functioning.

How Culture Affects Children's Use of Language

The notion that the culture in which a child is brought up affects his use of language is supported by Blake's (1994) interesting comparison of the language behavior of young African American and European American children. Blake looked at the way children of different ethnic and social-class backgrounds acquired and learned to use language forms in culturally useful ways. Earlier studies had focused on specific differences in language use but had failed to ask whether the particular language forms the child participants used were appropriate to their cultural milieu. Blake's study, however, showed that although each of three groups of children learned the same basic meaning relations in their quite different environments, the emphasis that each group of children put on one or another of these relations reflected their distinctive cultural orientations.

Blake's (1994) method was to describe and compare the semantic-syntactic language development of a group of African American children from working-class homes with two groups of European American children, one from working-class homes, and the other from middle-class homes. The children ranged from about 1½ to a little over 3 years of age. Blake also described how the children's mothers' use of language served as a model for their children's speech patterns. The three groups of children did not differ in either the length of their utterances or in the number of different categories of major semantic-system relations they used. These categories included actions a person took with respect to another person or to an object; statements of intention; labeling or pointing out a particular object; references to the absence of people or objects or to an object's ownership; and references to counting or otherwise identifying an object's features.

There were striking differences among the children, however, in the amounts of their speech that reflected internal states or expressed social messages. Internal states are reflected in verbs like *need, like, know,* and *want* (e.g., "want more Coke"). As Figure 9-9 shows, the difference in expression of internal states seemed to be ethnically based, for working-class African American children expressed such states much more often than European American children of either the middle or the working class. On the other hand, looking at social expressions, such as "Thank you," and "I'm sorry" and vocative expressions (e.g., calling someone's attention), such as "Derek!" or "Hey!" we find quite a different pattern. Here the differences appeared to be based on social class: As Figure 9-10 shows, the two groups of children from working-class families were considerably more likely to use such socially oriented expressions than the one group of middle-class children.

■ FIGURE 9-9
Ethnocultural groups and the expression of internal states. African American children from working-class families expressed internal states in speech three times as often as middle-class European American children and two times as often as working-class European Americans. (*Source:* Blake, 1994)

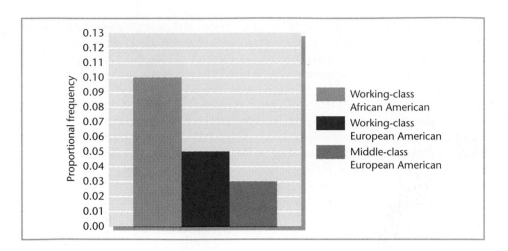

As Blake (1994) notes, "socioemotional reality for . . . African American children is somewhat different from [the same reality] for Euro-American children" (p. 188). Because black culture values socioemotional relationships (Harrison, Wilson, Pine, Chen & Buriel, 1990), it's not surprising that African American speech emphasizes internal states and social meanings. However, the fact that black and white working-class children don't differ in their use of social expressions underscores the important point that both class and ethnicity play important roles in shaping children's development. The "clash of cultures" that often occurs when children first enter school (Chapter 14) undoubtedly contributes to racial-ethnic stresses, but the common denominator of poverty and low-income status may be at least as important a determinant of performance difficulties. Thus improving lower-class families' occupational and income status may help promote children's opportunities to develop needed cognitive and interpersonal skills.

Using the Zone of Proximal Development in Teaching Language

Vygotsky's notion of the zone of proximal development (ZPD) has had considerable impact in the field of elementary education and has formed the basis for the theory of instruction adopted by a well-known educational experiment, the Kamehameha Early Education Program, or KEEP, that is in operation in Hawaii, Arizona, and Los Angeles. In this program, minority public-school children receive language instruction as well as instruction in other subjects, all of this instruction based on the ZPD concept. Findings of the initial study indicated that students taught in the KEEP manner perform at grade level, whereas non-KEEP students typically function below grade level (Tharp, 1994; Tharp & Gallimore, 1988).

The KEEP teacher's instructional repertoire includes the important techniques of modeling, questioning, and feedback, all part of the overall method of scaffolding. For example, the following exchange illustrates teacher modeling with repetition, rewording, and expansion (Tharp & Gallimore, 1988, p. 143):

CHILD: Probably, probably have snow on the . . . stuff and . . . thing, thing was heavy and thing fall.
TEACHER: Oh, you mean there might be so much snow and ice on the plane that it couldn't fly?

Here the teacher questions, offers cognitive structuring (explaining, providing meaning), and gives feedback (Tharp & Gallimore, 1988, pp. 143–144):

TEACHER: What do we put in our mouth underneath our tongue?
CHILD: A temperature . . .
TEACHER: No, that's what we find out. Your temperature goes up. That means your body gets hot.

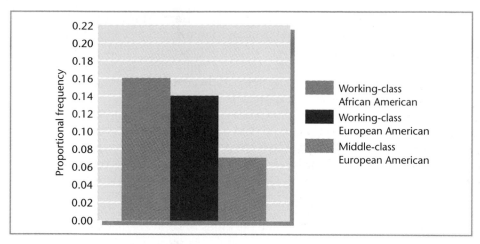

Many KEEP classroom lessons are planned and carried out in such a way that they "teach language without making the children conscious that they are learning language" (Tharp & Gallimore, 1988, p. 139). For example, a teacher may use a joint activity that is guaranteed to engage the energy of all young children as the basis for a lesson:

TEACHER (leading six kindergartners in a rhythmic chant about peanut butter and jelly sandwiches, reaches for a jar of each and a sack of bread slices): We're going to make our peanut butter sandwich. What is the first thing I'm going to need?

CHILD: Get the bread!

TEACHER: I need to get a piece of the bread. What am I going to do with it? . . . .

CHILD: Put the jelly on the sandwich, then that (points to peanut butter) on the sandwich, and then you eat it.

TEACHER: I put the jelly on top of the sandwich? (Places jar of jelly on top of the bread slice)

CHILDREN: No! No! No! (They laugh and smile)

CHILD: You *open* it . . .

TEACHER: Oh! I need to twist the lid off the jar . . .

Through the provisions of models and feedback as in the foregoing examples, children in the KEEP program are enabled to use new language forms and features. Tharp and Gallimore (1988) comment that such lesson transcripts as well as their analyses indicate that it is important for teachers to "maximize interactions in the ZPD of language" (p. 146) but that this kind of teaching is not common in U.S. schools. The researchers believe that minority or other "nonstandard dialect speakers" can benefit greatly from opportunities to converse throughout goal-oriented activities with a responsive yet uncritical teacher who speaks standard English.

EVALUATION OF VYGOTSKY'S THEORY

Vygotsky's approach, emphasizing the socially mediated nature of cognitive processes, offers a fresh perspective from which to view cognitive development and overcomes some of the limitations of Piaget's almost exclusive focus on cognitive development alone. Vygotsky's theory has made us more aware of the importance of the immediate social contexts of learning and cognition, and, particularly through his notion of the zone of proximal development and derivative concepts such as scaffolding, he has pointed the way to new methods of assessing children's cognitive potential and of teaching reading, mathematics, and writing (Belmont, 1989; Brown & Campione, 1990). The KEEP project is a good example of the application of these principles to educational settings. Moreover, Vygotsky has increased our appreciation of the profound importance of cultural variation in development and has made us appreciate the uniqueness of cultural domains. The Vygotskian approach is particularly useful in a multiethnic society like the United States, heightening sensitivity to the range of diversity in the way children of different ethnic and racial traditions approach cognitive tasks.

Although Vygotsky's theory is currently inspiring a great deal of research activity in Western countries, the theory has not yet received the full scrutiny that other cognitive theories, such as Piaget's, have received. However, several weaknesses are evident. First, in contrast to Piaget's view, Vygotsky's approach is not very developmental. Vygotsky simply doesn't provide us with a rich description of how children's development changes across time in various contexts (Miller, 1993). Moreover, he does not tell us how changes in physical, motor, cognitive, perceptual, or social development determine the kinds of contexts that society, through parents and others, makes available to the child. As we will see in Chapter 12, parents often serve as managers of their children's opportunities for cognitive and social experience, such as Little League, violin lessons, or day care. Although decisions about these contexts are determined by a child's developmental level, Vygotsky is relatively silent on this issue.

Vygotsky does not clearly specify the processes that govern development nor does he tell us whether they are the same at all ages. And finally, unlike Piaget, whose object permanence paradigm, conservation tests, and three-mountain problem have served as prototypes or standard tools that others could use, Vygotsky has provided only a general approach, and few standard tasks. In a sense, Vygotksy left developmental psychology a blueprint rather than a fully developed theory, and the task of filling in the details of his theoretical position remains the challenge for the future. His theory does hold great promise, however, as a new way of thinking about cognitive development in context.

SUMMARY

- **Cognition** is the mental activity and behavior that allows us to understand the world. It includes the functions of learning, perception, memory, and thinking, and it is influenced by biological, environmental, experiential, social, and motivational factors. A variety of theories have been proposed to explain the pattern of cognitive development seen in children.

Piaget's Theory of Cognitive Development

- Beginning in the early 1960s, Piaget's theory began to replace behaviorism in America. Unlike behaviorism, this theory was seen as truly developmental because it allowed for the different capacities of children of different ages. Piaget based his theory on observations of his own and other children as they answered questions during unstructured interviews.
- According to Piaget, children actively seek out information and adapt it to the knowledge and conceptions of the world that they already have. Thus, children construct their understanding of reality from their own experiences. Children organize their knowledge into increasingly complex cognitive structures called **schemata.**
- Children possess many different schemata, and these change as the children develop. In the newborn, the schemata take the form of innate reflexes and reaction patterns, like sucking. As the child grows and gains experience, the

schemata shift from motor activities to mental activities called **operations.** These operations become increasingly complex with age.

- Piaget suggested that schemata are modified according to the principles of **organization** and **adaptation,** which continue to operate throughout the life span. Organization is the predisposition to combine simple physical or psychological structures into more complex systems. Adaptation involves the two complementary processes of **assimilation,** or fitting new experiences into current cognitive schemata, and **accommodation,** or adjusting current schemata to fit the new experiences. Most encounters involve both processes.

Piaget's Stages of Cognitive Development

- Piaget divided intellectual development into four unique periods that are indicative of the changes in children's cognitive structures. The attainments of earlier stages are essential for those in later periods of development. All children go through the stages in the same order, although not necessarily at the same ages.
- During the first two years of life, called the **sensorimotor period,** a child makes the transition from relying on reflexes to using internal representation, which is the cornerstone of symbolic thought. Piaget divided this period into six substages, during which the child physically explores the environment, developing abilities such as **symbolic thought** and **deferred imitation.** Throughout these substages, which include **reflex activity, primary circular reactions, secondary circular reactions, coordination of secondary schemata, tertiary circular reactions,** and **inventing new means by mental combination,** children gradually come to understand **object permanence.** Critics of Piaget have suggested that children may acquire this concept as well as other knowledge about the properties of objects and such principles of the physical world as causality earlier than Piaget thought.
- The major developmental milestone during the **preoperational period** is the development of the **symbolic function,** or the ability to use symbols such as words, images, and gestures to represent objects and events. This can be seen in the rapid development of language, in imaginative play, and in an increase in deferred imitation. Piaget divided this stage into the **preconceptual stage** and the **intuitive stage.**
- During the preconceptual period, children's thinking is limited by **animistic thinking,** the tendency to attribute lifelike characteristics to inanimate objects, and by **egocentricity,** an inability to see things from another person's perspective. A shift away from egocentrism may be related to the development of role-taking abilities.
- During the intuitive stage, children are able to use certain mental operations, but they do not seem to be aware of the principles used because they cannot explain them. Limitations in their thinking are still found in problems involving seriation, part-whole relations, and conservation.
- The most important acquisition of the preoperational period is an elementary understanding of the notion of **conservation.** Typically, the child learns to conserve number at the end of this period but cannot yet conserve other characteristics such as mass and volume. The concept of **horizontal decalage** explains this unevenness of children's cognitive achievements. In recent years, however, critics have suggested that children may achieve notions of conservation earlier than Piaget believed.
- Piaget believed that three characteristics of preoperational thought limit children's thinking. The first is the child's inability to understand **reversibility,** or the notion that all logical operations are reversible. The second is the tendency to focus on the end states of a change rather than on the process of transforma-

tion. The third characteristic is **centration**, or focusing on only one dimension of a problem.

- During the **concrete operational period** children acquire the ability to perform most of the tasks that they were unable to master in the preceding stage, including conservation of various substances and characteristics, classification, and seriation.

- Children in the **formal operations period** can use flexible and abstract reasoning, test mental hypotheses, and consider multiple possibilities for the solution to a problem. Not all children or adults attain this stage. The use of symbolic skills and higher education are among the factors associated with formal operations.

- Although Piaget did not emphasize the child's learning to distinguish self from others, his concepts of egocentrism and object permanence have clear implications for this process and the beginnings of social cognition.

Evaluation of Piaget's Theory

- Piaget's theory integrates and illuminates a broad spectrum of diverse issues revolving around children's understanding and use of knowledge, and it has stimulated an enormous amount of research. Among the most significant of Piaget's many heuristic ideas are that children actively construct their knowledge of the world, that the errors they make provide important clues about their thinking, and that cognitive development can be discerned in perceptual-motor behavior as well as in language skills.

- Current evidence indicates that infants and children grasp many concepts, such as object permanence, causality, conservation, and the perspectives of another, considerably earlier than Piaget thought. Research also suggests that the sequence of development may not be invariant as Piaget believed, that it may be modified by cultural experiences, and that development may not occur in the distinct and qualitatively different stages Piaget proposed.

- It is largely thanks to Piaget's work, however, that the field of cognitive development owes its ascendancy. Despite flaws in his theorizing and methods, Piaget asked and proposed answers to important questions in an innovative way, stimulating the work of other investigators.

- Children's ability to distinguish themselves and their own perspectives from others and their views proceeds, according to Selman, through five phases: the stages of egocentric perspective, differentiated perspective, reciprocal perspective, mutual perspectives, and societal or in-depth perspectives.

Vygotsky's Sociocultural Theory

- Vygotsky's theory emphasizes the critical role played by the social world in facilitating the child's development. According to his theory, children generally internalize thought processes that first occur through interaction with others in the social environment. Qualitative transitions between **elementary mental functions** and **higher mental functions** occur because of shifts in the use of **mediators** such as language and other symbols. The acquisition and use of language plays a primary role in children's developing intellectual abilities.

- Vygotsky's interest in the child's potential for intellectual growth led him to develop the concept of the **zone of proximal development.** In recent years this concept has led to the use of **scaffolding,** an instructional process in which the teacher adjusts the amount and type of support offered to the child to suit the child's abilities, withdrawing support as the child becomes more skilled.

- Two principles of cultural influence inform Vygotsky's theory: First, cultures vary widely in the kinds of institutions and settings they offer to facilitate children's development, and second, in assessing children's cognitive development, unless we consider these variations and cultural contexts we may seriously underestimate children's cognitive development.

- Language plays an important role in Vygotskian theory. As children begin to use social speech, **egocentric speech,** and **inner speech,** they learn to communicate and to form thoughts and regulate intellectual functions.

Evaluation of Vygotsky's Theory

- Vygotsky drew attention to the importance of the social context in which learning and the evolution of cognitive skills take place and to the influence of peers and adults on the child's development. He pointed out that the particularities of a given culture determine the nature and manner of functioning of the societal institutions that influence how children think and learn. The resulting research interest in the effect of cultural variation on the child's development has created a focus that is especially useful in multiethnic societies like the United States.

- Vygotsky's theory does not provide the richness of detail that Piaget's approach offers, and he did not provide the kinds of specific tools for research that Piaget's many tests and experiments have given us. Vygotsky's approach offers only a general outline of cognitive development; in its emphasis on the the social and cultural aspects of learning and cognition, however, it challenges future researchers to explore the role of context in greater depth.

Cognitive Development: The Information-Processing Approach

CHAPTER 10

Every day of their lives children encounter cognitive challenges, such as learning to tie their shoes, remembering to bring their homework to school, and figuring out a math problem. This chapter focuses on the cognitive processes with which children address these and other daily challenges as well as on the way children's cognitive skills develop and grow. Although information-processing theory, with which we begin this chapter, shares Piagetian and Vygotskian concerns with how cognitive skills develop over time, it takes quite a different approach to the study of the human mind. Emerging from a comparison between the workings of the mind and the computer, information-processing theory views human beings as possessing an array of cognitive processes and strategies that help them to make use of information. As we will see, when amplified by what is referred to as neo-Piagetian thought, this newer model proposes that structural changes in cognitive processing are brought about by changes in the strategies we use to learn about objects and events in the world, not the other way around.

After examining this third perspective on cognitive development, we explore a number of basic attributes and functions with which children are endowed and which children's developing cognitive skills expand and hone. We begin by describing changes in perception and attention, or the child's growing ability to register and select from the wealth of sensory input confronting her. Next we consider memory and the child's developing competence in storing and retrieving information. We then discuss children's increasing ability to solve various kinds of problems, including their use of logical and numerical reasoning. Finally, we look at children's knowledge of their own mental capabilities and how the kinds of tasks they perform and strategies they apply to these tasks affect this knowledge and their ability to use it.

As you study this chapter, keep in mind that the Piagetian perspective (Chapter 9) also addresses the functions and skills we discuss here. Moreover, because the societies in which children grow and develop affect these skills, we can also study them from a sociocultural, or Vygotskian, perspective.

INFORMATION-PROCESSING THEORY

information-processing approach A perspective on cognition and cognitive development in which the human mind is likened to a computer, processing information from the environment through perception and attention (input), encoding it in memory (storage and retrieval), and applying information to the solution of problems (software).

The **information-processing approach** to the study of cognitive development evolved out of the American experimental tradition in psychology. Psychologists who take this approach are interested in many of the same phenomena that concerned Piaget and his followers, but they tend to use the computer as a metaphor, or model, of human thought. Information-processing theorists propose that, like the computer, the human mind is a system that processes information through the application of logical rules and strategies. Moreover, like the computer, the mind is limited in the amount and nature of information it can process. Finally, just as the computer can be made into a better information processor by changes in its hardware (e.g., circuit boards and microchips) and its software (programming), so do children become more sophisticated thinkers through changes in their brains and sensory systems (hardware) and in the rules and strategies (software) that they learn.

Because viewing the computer as an analog highlights the roles of information input, storage, and retrieval, developmentalists who espouse information-processing theory are interested in the cognitive processes and strategies children of different ages use to make use of information in different situations. In studying children's cognitive processing, investigators often set up such situations as problems to be solved in order to understand how children, through their solutions, modify and refine their mental abilities. These investigators view their task as describing and explaining the changes in children's mental systems that produce changes in children's competence.

Focus of the Information-Processing Approach

According to Siegler (1998), the information-processing approach is characterized by four main beliefs. First, information-processing theorists hold that *thinking is information-processing.* When the individual perceives, encodes, represents, and stores information from the environment in his mind or retrieves that information, he is thinking. Thinking also includes responding to any constraints or limitations on memory processes.

The second tenet of information-processing theory is that the proper focus of study is the role of *change mechanisms* in development. Four critical mechanisms work together to bring about change in children's cognitive skills: encoding, strategy construction, automatization, and generalization. According to Siegler (1998), to solve problems effectively, children must encode critical information about a problem and then use this encoded information and relevant prior knowledge to construct a strategy to deal with the problem. Because new strategies are almost always slow and effortful, children must practice a strategy to make its execution automatic and maximize its effectiveness. And, finally, to gain full benefit from a newly constructed strategy, they must generalize, or apply, it to other problems.

Information-processing theory's third tenet is that development is driven by *self-modification.* Like Piaget's theory of cognitive development, the information-processing approach holds that children play an active role in their own development. Through self-modification, the child uses knowledge and strategies she has acquired from earlier problem solutions to modify her responses to a new situation or problem. In this way, she builds newer and more sophisticated responses from prior knowledge.

The fourth and last tenet of information-processing theory is that investigators must perform *careful task analysis* of the problem situations they present to children. According to this view, not only the child's own level of development but the nature of the task itself constrains the child's performance. Thus a child may possess the basic ability necessary to perform a particular task when it is presented in a simple form, without unnecessary complexities. However, if extra or misleading information is added to that same task, the child may become confused and be unable to perform it.

Nature of the Information-Processing System

Human cognition, according to Siegler (1998), has two primary characteristics. First, our thinking is highly flexible, enabling us to adapt and adjust to myriad changes in circumstances, task requirements, and goals. However, some important constraints: constraints balance this amazing adaptability. We can attend to only a limited amount of information at any one time, and we are limited by how rapidly we can process information. To understand how flexibility and constraints interact in cognitive activity, we focus, in this section, on the structural characteristics of the cognitive system, and in the next section, on the processes that enable us to respond to shifting environmental demands.

By "structural characteristics" we mean the basic organization or the architecture of the cognitive system. The term *structure* does not imply a physical entity, of course, but is a means of organizing important concepts. Like an architectural plan for a building, cognitive structure describes the main characteristics of the system but not its detailed features. Although these features, such as a child's attention to a stimulus, are assumed to function in the same way over time and across cultures, particular individuals may show differences in functioning (Siegler, 1998).

In Atkinson and Shiffrin's (1968) **store model** of the human information-processing system (Figure 10-1), information from the environment that we acquire through our senses enters the system through the **sensory register.** Although the perceptual and attentional processes of the sensory register enable us to store

store model A model of information processing in which information is depicted as moving through a series of processing units—*sensory register, short-term memory,* and *long-term memory*—in each of which it may be stored, either fleetingly or permanently.

sensory register The mental processing unit that receives information from the environment and stores it fleetingly.

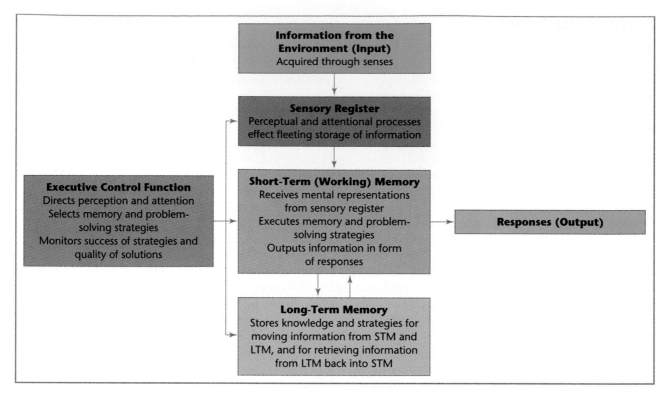

■ FIGURE 10-1
An information-processing model.
The "store" model of information processing represents the way information flows through the cognitive system and is stored, for a brief or longer period, retrieved from storage, and produced in responses to the external world. (*Source*: Based on Atkinson & Shiffrin, 1968)

short-term memory The mental processing unit in which information may be stored temporarily; the "work space" of the mind, where a decision must be made to discard information or to transfer it to permanent storage, in *long-term memory*.

long-term memory The encyclopedic mental processing unit in which information may be stored permanently and from which it may be later retrieved.

information in its original form, that storage is fleeting. For example, according to Sperling (1960), it can store visual sensory information for only one second! The storage capacity of the sensory register appears to be constant across development, for both 5-year-olds and adults apparently have the same time limitations on their ability to store sensory information (Morrison, Holmes, & Haith, 1974).

The store model proposes, next, that an individual may encode information that enters the sensory register, transforming it into mental representations and placing it in **short-term memory,** which can best be thought of as the work space of the mind (in fact, some psychologists prefer to call short-term memory *working memory*). But, because short-term memory itself is limited in the number of meaningful chunks of information on which it can operate at one time, information does not last long here, either. Within 15 to 30 seconds we generally lose it. We can hold on to it a bit longer if we "rehearse" it (repeat it over and over; see the later section on "Rehearsal"). We have evidence of this in the finding that older children have more proficient short-term memory than younger children; the faster you rehearse, the less time will elapse between repetitions of a word and thus the less likely you'll be to forget the word before you rehearse it again (Hitch & Towse, 1995). Figure 10-2 shows how older children's more rapid response enables them to remember more words.

Long-term memory can best be thought of as the mind's encyclopedia, housing memories of objects, events, situations, problems, rules, and problem-solving techniques as well as more general knowledge about the world. In addition, long-term memory stores the strategies for transferring information to it from short-term memory as well as knowledge gained through the processes of encoding and representing the information that is thus stored. According to the store model of information processing, our ability to remember a specific event depends on how we stored the information. If we stored it only in short-term memory, we will be able to recall it only if we respond within a short time; if we transferred the information to long-term memory, we will be able to retrieve it for an indefinite period of time.

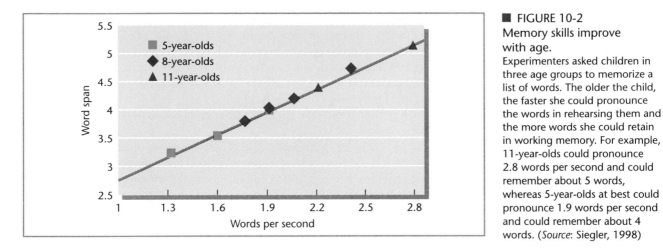

■ FIGURE 10-2
Memory skills improve with age.
Experimenters asked children in three age groups to memorize a list of words. The older the child, the faster she could pronounce the words in rehearsing them and the more words she could retain in working memory. For example, 11-year-olds could pronounce 2.8 words per second and could remember about 5 words, whereas 5-year-olds at best could pronounce 1.9 words per second and could remember about 4 words. (*Source*: Siegler, 1998)

An alternative explanation for why we remember or do not remember things is offered by the **level of processing model** of human information-processing. This model proposes that the *intensity* of processing applied to information, rather than the disposition of the information, determines how long it will be retained (Craik & Lockhart, 1972). If we process information at a superficial level, we will retain it for only a short time. An example of such *shallow processing* would be looking at a page of text and noting its general appearance—whether the words are printed in upper-case or lowercase, whether they are printed in black or red, and so forth. In contrast, if we apply *deep processing* to the information, we will retain it indefinitely. When we read and then think about a passage of text, considering its meaning, the images it calls forth, the relationship between its meaning and other knowledge that we have acquired and stored earlier, we are engaging in deep processing.

level of processing model An information-processing model that proposes that the intensity of processing applied to information determines how long it will be retained.

Information-Handling Processes

The basic structures of the information-processing system do not change with development; rather, the processes by which the system handles information develop and change. As children grow and develop they become more expert at processing information, not because their thought processes change qualitatively but because they become more efficient in using these processes. Although information-processing theorists have proposed many different information-handling processes, we limit ourselves here to four primary ones: encoding and representation, the construction of strategies, automatization, and generalization.

Encoding and Representation. The human information-processing system cannot manage the massive amount of information presented daily to the senses. As a result, rather than try to retain and store every bit of information that impinges on us, we attend to and encode, or change into mental representations, only what we judge to be the relevant features of the environment. If this **encoding** process is efficient, crucial aspects of the stimulus are encoded, but if it is inefficient, critical information is lost. As we will see later, the ability to attend to relevant information often determines what information is retained and what information is lost.

A **mental representation,** a crucial feature of information-processing, is information stored in some form (e.g, verbal, pictorial) after a person has encountered the information in the external environment. Representation depends on the child's understanding that one thing (e.g., a word such as *chair*) can stand for or "represent" something else (e.g., an actual chair). Some developmentalists have proposed that change in the type and complexity of mental representations underlies some aspects of development. Of particular interest to psychologists is the type of representation called the *script*. Scripts, which reflect a particular event or series of events, are based on common experiences of daily life. For example, a child may have a script of a trip to a restaurant that includes the knowledge that you must

encoding The transformation of information from the environment into a lasting mental representation.

mental representation Information stored in some form (e.g., verbal, pictorial) in the cognitive system after the person has encountered it in the environment.

order food before you can eat and that after you receive the food you must pay for it. Scripts are used to understand new events and to generate predictions about how those events will unfold. We discuss scripts in more detail later in this chapter.

Encoding and representation are particularly important in the level of processing model of human cognition. The efficiency with which information is encoded affects the type of processing that can be applied to the information, and the complexity of the representation determines whether an object is processed at a deep or shallow level.

Strategies.   The use of strategies is one of the most important processes proposed by the information-processing approach. **Strategies** are conscious cognitive or behavioral activities that are used to enhance mental performance. Strategies can be applied at all levels of the information-processing system; for example, there are strategies for optimal storage and retrieval of information, for deep processing of information, and for logical problem solving. An example of strategy use can be found in children's counting. When we present younger children with an addition problem like "3 + 14," they will use the *count-all* strategy, counting from 1 up to the first term of the problem (i.e., 3) and then continuing to count the number of the second term (i.e., 14 more) until they arrive at the answer of 17. Older children, in contrast, will use a more efficient strategy, one known as the *min rule*. Using this strategy to solve the problem just described, a child will begin counting from the larger of the two addends (14) and continue upward, adding the amount of the smaller number, thus counting "14, 15, 16, 17" to arrive at the answer (Siegler, 1987).

The main purpose of a strategy is to decrease the load on the child's information-processing system by increasing the efficiency of each process and thus freeing up space for other tasks. Another way to increase the efficiency of the information-processing system is to automatize certain aspects of the solution process.

Automatization.   **Automatization** involves making behaviors that once were conscious and controlled unconscious and automatic. A good example of automatization is an adult's learning to drive a car with a stick shift. At first, every shifting of the gears is slow and strained, the driver concentrating on each aspect of shifting in order to do it right. With practice, however, the driver can shift gears quickly and efficiently, unaware of the individual steps involved and often unaware of shifting altogether. In the same way, the child who has developed a memorization strategy for calculating multiplication problems comes in time to use this strategy without

strategies Conscious cognitive or behavioral activities that are used to enhance mental performance.

automatization The process of transforming conscious, controlled behaviors into unconscious and automatic ones.

Using objects of different shapes, colors, and sizes (sometimes called *manipulables*) can help children in the early grades learn to count, do simple arithmetic problems, and sort objects into categories.

thinking about it (Siegler, 1998). For example, a child who has memorized the mathematic formula that $2 \times 2 = 4$ can use this stored knowledge to answer the question, "What is 2×2?" quickly. In contrast, a child who hasn't memorized the formula may have to stop, think, and perhaps count on his fingers ($[1 + 1] + [1 + 1]$) to figure out the answer.

Generalization.   Initially, the strategies that children develop to solve a given problem tend to be quite specific to the task at hand. Through the process of **generalization,** children apply a strategy learned while solving a problem in one situation to a similar problem in a new situation. Generalization does not happen over night, though, and children may need to gain familiarity with the use of a rule, using it many times over, before they can successfully generalize it to new situations. Suppose, for example, that the child who used the min rule in the earlier addition problem had arrived at this solution in school. Coming home after school he finds that his mother has bought some jelly beans, and he decides to count the jelly beans so that he and his brother will have the same number of candies. Even though he applied the min rule successfully at school, now that he is presented with a set of concrete objects—a different situation—he may revert to the more primitive, count-all strategy. But not for long, especially if his brother is older and faster and gets more of the jelly beans.

> **generalization** The application of a strategy learned while solving a problem in one situation to a similar problem in a new situation.

The Role of Executive Control Processes

All the processes we've discussed are designed to help children increase their efficiency in processing information; crucial to the efficient use of these skills is the ability to know when to use them. For this reason, an *executive process* must be added to any human information-processing model to reflect the child's role in selecting problems and strategies and in monitoring the success of her problem solving. The child's purposes, goals, and motivation will also have a major influence on her performance.

Through the executive process the child directs her intake of information (perception and attention). She can choose what problem she will work on, decide how much effort she will make toward its solution, select the strategies she will apply in this effort, avoid distractions and interruptions that hamper her efforts, and evaluate the quality of her solution. Between the ages of 3 and 12, the child's executive process shows dramatic development. Whereas the preschooler often seems dominated by a task and may apply a single ineffective strategy to a variety of tasks until she is overwhelmed by frustration, the 12-year-old is able to master a wide range of intellectual tasks, orchestrating her strategies to find the best solution to the problem at hand.

Effects of Knowledge on the Information-Processing System

A child's familiarity with the domain of a problem he is trying to solve plays a major role in his abilities to encode and represent information and to use appropriate strategies in solving the problem (Wellman & Gelman, 1998). Research has shown that when children are given problems in an area in which they know a great deal, they will equal, and even surpass, the performance of less knowledgeable adults (Bédard & Chi, 1992; Chi, 1978).

Hypothesizing that adults' apparent superiority over children at recall tasks can be attributed to their greater general knowledge and understanding and not simply to greater memory capacity, Michelene Chi (1978) tested both children and adults on their ability to recall either a set of numbers or specific chess-piece positions. The children were experienced chess players, but the adults had only a basic understanding of the game. Chi found that although the third graders and eighth graders could not remember as many numbers as the adults on immediate recall and needed more

■ FIGURE 10-3
Knowledge and children's memory.
In this test of the hypothesis that amount of knowledge plays a greater role in memory than simple memory capacity, young chess players recalled more chess-piece positions than non-chess-playing adults could (a), and they needed many fewer trials than the adults to reach perfect recall (b). Researchers attributed the adults' superiority in recalling numbers, either for the first time (a) or to perfection (b), to their greater general knowledge and familiarity with number systems. (*Source*: Chi, 1978)

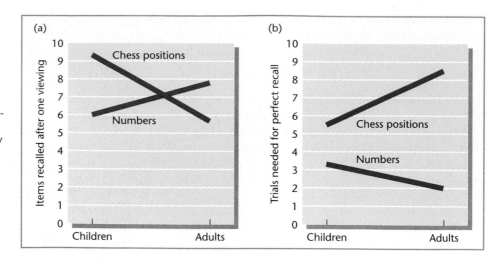

viewings to reach perfect recall, they far outstripped the adults in remembering chess-piece positions, both immediately and with repeated viewings (Figure 10-3). Chi concluded that the children's knowledge of chess played an important role in their memory performance and that the adult's superiority in recalling numbers may have reflected their generally greater familiarity with number systems.

Analyzing Task Performance

Using an information-processing model, the developmental psychologist strives to discover *how the information-processing system changes as the child matures*. Typically, the model assumes that the child's capabilities are more limited than the adult's. The child cannot take in and encode as much information, is less systematic about what information he encodes, and has fewer strategies and less knowledge to apply to an understanding of the problem. Consider an analysis of a very simple task. Imagine that we have asked a preschool child to count a pile of 10 pennies and that he cannot count past 5. There are many possible reasons for the child's difficulty. For example, he may not be able to remember the number words; this would suggest a lack of memory access or possibly a failure to correctly encode numbers from 6 on. Or he may be unable to match numbers with pennies—that is, he may not connect the visual display of 7 pennies with the word *seven;* this may suggest that he lacks counting strategies. Finally, the child quite simply may know how to count to 5, but not to 10; this would reflect a lack of domain knowledge.

Although it is sometimes possible to trace a failure in performance to a short-coming in just one of these components, because they are all interdependent we can often improve a child's performance by decreasing the demands in one area. For example, if we reduce the pile of pennies from 10 to 5 and the child can then complete the task, it may be because now he knows all the numbers he is being asked to provide. His improved performance may also be due to a decrease in memory load; remembering 5 numbers is easier than remembering 10 and thus more effort can be placed on matching numbers to pennies.

The situation of having more pennies than the child can count suggests the developmental psychologist's second major concern within the information-processing approach: *What can we learn about children's cognitive processes and capabilities from problems that they fail to solve* (Roberts, 1981)? You'll recall that Piaget started out with this question. However, whereas Piaget would probably conclude that the child in our example lacked a firm grasp of the number concept, the information-processing theorist would more likely assume that the child understands part of the problem and would set out to discover just what aspects of numbers and counting the child does and does not understand (Siegler, 1998).

Let's return to our penny-counting problem; our preschooler may commit some interesting errors that will tell us what he does understand. Suppose he counts 5 pennies and then says "there are 5 and a bunch more." Clearly he knows there are more than 5, even though he cannot count beyond that number. Now suppose we ask another preschooler to count the 10 pennies and she counts 5, counts another 5, and then concludes that there are "5 and 5 more." She not only knows that there are more than 5 pennies but that the extra pennies add up to 5 also. She may also know that there are fewer pennies than, say, 100. The first child understands that there are more pennies than 5 but he doesn't know how to deal with the larger quantity. The second child uses her "5" strategy over again, providing a more precise answer than "a bunch more." If we noted only that neither child could count to 10 we'd miss the way the two children differ in their knowledge of counting strategies. Clearly we can learn a great deal from a child's answers. The information-processing approach is very much concerned with this form of error analysis, that is, examining incorrect answers for evidence of less sophisticated, yet systematic, strategies that children apply to problems.

Piaget believed that children had to reach the stage of formal operations before they could solve complex problems such as measuring and calculating relative weights. Later researchers, like Robert Siegler, have found that younger children may be able to solve such problems if they have enough information.

Robert Siegler (1983, 1991, 1998) has studied children's solutions, both correct and incorrect, to more complicated problems. In his classic work with Piaget's balance-scale problem, in which children must predict which way a seesaw with different weights placed at different distances from the fulcrum will tilt, Siegler (1978) concluded that memory capacity and knowledge interact to determine children's problem-solving success. As you can see from Figure 10-4, what makes this a difficult problem is the necessity to consider two dimensions: both the number of weights on each side of the seesaw's fulcrum and the distance from the fulcrum at which each set of weights lies. Siegler proposed that children's strategies for solving the problem include rules at four levels of sophistication:

Rule I: The side with more weights is heavier.
Rule II: If weights on both sides are equal, the side whose weights are farther from the fulcrum is heavier.
Rule III: If one side has more weights but the other's weights are farther from the fulcrum, you have to guess at the answer.
Rule IV: Weights x distance from fulcrum equals *torque;* the side with greater torque is the heavier.

Initially, Siegler found that 3-year-olds appeared not to use rules at all; about half of 4-year-olds used Rule I, and all 5-year-olds used Rule I. Among 9-year-olds, about half used Rule II and half used Rule III, and 13- and 17-year-olds almost always used Rule III. Interestingly, although Rule IV embodies the reasoning Piaget attributed to the child in the period of formal operations, only a minority even of college students used it! When Siegler broke the task down to try to discover why young children couldn't solve many of the balance-scale problems, he

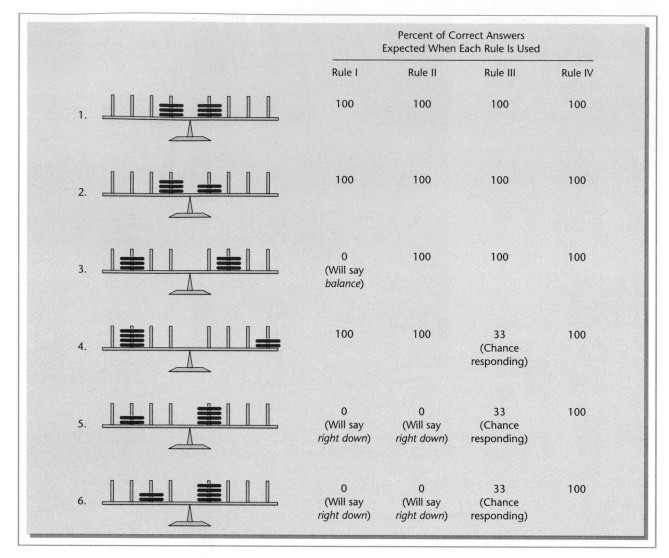

	Percent of Correct Answers Expected When Each Rule Is Used			
	Rule I	Rule II	Rule III	Rule IV
1.	100	100	100	100
2.	100	100	100	100
3.	0 (Will say *balance*)	100	100	100
4.	100	100	33 (Chance responding)	100
5.	0 (Will say *right down*)	0 (Will say *right down*)	33 (Chance responding)	100
6.	0 (Will say *right down*)	0 (Will say *right down*)	33 (Chance responding)	100

■ FIGURE 10-4
Balance-scale problems and strategies for solving them. Using Robert Siegler's Rule IV will get you the correct answers on all these problems. Interestingly, your next best chance to get as many correct answers as possible is to use Rule II. Why might that be? Answers to all problems appear at the end of this caption, upside down. (*Source*: From Children Thinking, 3rd ed. by Siegler, R., table 8.2, p. 256, Copyright © 1998. Reprinted by permission of Prentice-Hall, Upper Saddle River, N.J.) Problems 1 & 6: balance; problems 2–5, left down.

hypothesized that perhaps limited memory and/or lack of knowledge were at fault. But when he allowed children to continue viewing the original balance arrangement (low memory demand) and gave them direct, detailed, and repeated instructions (knowledge), those as young as 5 were often able to solve the problems.

Comparing Piagetian and Information-Processing Approaches

The information-processing approach attempts to provide a quantitative and more systematic analysis of children's cognitive development than Piaget offered. Researchers within the information-processing framework are concerned with the demands different intellectual tasks place on the child's perceptual, attentional, memory, and problem-solving capabilities. They view development as improvement of these capabilities, either through increasing the amount of information that can be handled or by streamlining how children process information.

One of the most troublesome aspects of Piagetian theory is the concept of horizontal decalage. Piaget's argument that certain problems, such as conservation of volume, require a greater degree of abstraction than other problems, such as conservation of length, is, in itself, too abstract to be a useful explanation. In contrast, the information-processing approach can and does account for differences in children's problem solving. By employing a more precise task analysis, researchers have been able to identify the demands specific problems place on children's attention, memory, and problem-solving abilities. Researchers can thus understand children's failures better and make more accurate predictions of their successes.

Horizontal Decalage and Microgenetic Analysis

Siegler (1994, 1998) has used what he calls *microgenetic analysis* to identify the ways in which a child views or understands different tasks, and the factor or factors responsible for this variability. Studying children's ability to solve addition problems, Siegler examined changes in children's use of strategies for addition as the children engaged in problem solving. This approach assumes that developmental strategies emerge slowly over time rather than in a single step after achieving an insight about how to solve a problem. Thus, it is rather like watching action in slow motion: The investigator observes in great detail the way a child arrives at a problem solution.

In a typical study, Siegler (Crowley & Siegler, 1993) tracked children's mastery of various strategies, such as the min rule, over time: before they understood a particular rule, during the time that they grasped it in a rudimentary but incomplete fashion, through the period during which they finally understood the rule completely and applied it consistently. The researchers also asked the children to talk about and explain how and why they chose certain strategies. According to the traditional stagelike view of development, when children have achieved a particular level of understanding they seldom *regress*, or return to less mature levels of skill. The microgenetic method revealed, however, that developmental progress is far less linear than this; children do not use mature strategies exclusively but combine them with less efficient approaches that they learned earlier. Thus, children have lots of strategies available to solve a problem (see Figure 1-1c, in Chapter 1). The strategies compete with one another, however, and it's only gradually that the most efficient strategy becomes dominant. Thus, developmental change is more gradual, more variable, and, overall, "messier" than traditional views would lead us to believe.

From a purely descriptive point of view, Piaget was right about horizontal decalage: Children's cognitive progress is not mapped by a straight line curve but rather by a curve that turns down occasionally, even as over time it moves steadily up. However, Piaget's explanation benefits from the amplification that information-processing theory provides: It is not so much abstraction as complexity that makes some tasks more difficult than others. For example, understanding the conservation of length requires that the child compare objects on only one dimension, whereas understanding the conservation of volume requires that the child understand height of water level, size and shape of clay mass, and the notion that mass can displace liquid (see Figure 9-5). This added complexity increases the load on the information-processing system, thus preventing the child from displaying the ability to conserve even though he may understand the general concept of conservation.

Case's Executive Control Structures

One of several **neo-Piagetians** who have attempted to integrate Piaget's thought with that of information-processing theorists, Robbie Case (1984, 1985, 1992, 1995, 1996) has proposed that developmental change is characterized by increasing sophistication in children's underlying mental structures. Based on concepts developed within the information-processing tradition, such as encoding, strategy use, and generalization, Case has replaced Piaget's assimilation and accommodation with cognitive functions like the ability to set goals, the ability to solve problems, the need to explore, and the use of observation and imitation to acquire new knowledge. Case believes that the stagelike development of children's abilities is based both on improvements in memory capacity—we discuss this notion a bit later—and on the child's formation of what he calls executive control structures.

An **executive control structure,** which is a "mental blueprint or plan for solving a class of problems," has three components (Case, 1984): a representation of the problem situation for which that plan is appropriate; a representation of the objective insolving the problem, or the desired end states; and a representation of

neo-Piagetian theories Theories of cognitie devcelopment that are grounded in Piagetian theory but reinterpret Piaget's concepts in an information-processing context.

executive control structure According to Case, a mental blueprint or plan for solving a class of problems.

■ FIGURE 10-5

How do you make juicier juice?

To demonstrate children's formation of executive control structures, Case presented 3½- to 5-year-olds with four problem situations in which they had to decide whether set A or set B of alternative arrays of glasses of juice and water would produce juicier juice when poured into a pitcher. As the problem situation becomes more complex, the child's executive control structures (shown only for Tasks 1 and 2) must process more information and create additional strategies. (*Source*: Case, 1985)

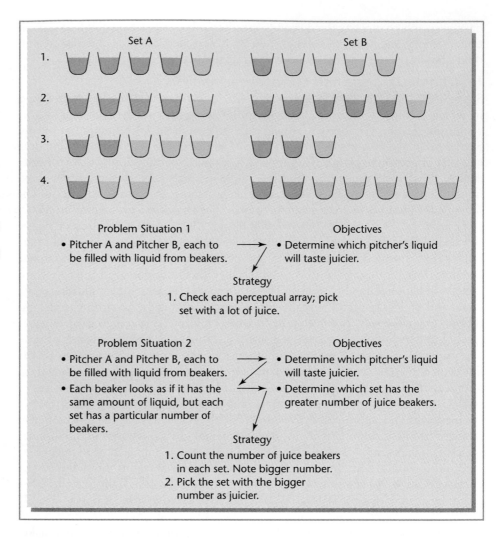

the appropriate strategy, or the actual procedure for moving from the present situation to the stated objective. As Figure 10-5 shows, for each of Case's (1985) four juice-making tasks, the child must form an executive control structure. Notice that each successive task requires the child to make new observations and to use new knowledge in forming strategies capable of solving the increasingly complex problems.

Like Piaget, Case divides development into four stages (Table 10-1). Note that each of these stages is characterized, however, by increasingly sophisticated executive control structures that evolve out of structures of earlier stages. Case's synthesis of Piagetian and information-processing theories can be used to account for many different aspects of development that neither theory can adequately explain. In fact, Case and his colleagues (Case & Griffin, 1990; Case, Okamoto, Henderson, & McKeough, 1993; Okamoto & Case, 1996) have applied this theory to a variety of different tasks and domains, including scientific reasoning (Marini, 1992), music sight reading (Capodilupo, 1992), solving math problems, telling time, and handling money.

STEPS IN INFORMATION-PROCESSING: A CLOSER LOOK

We now examine some important aspects of the information-processing approach. As we noted at the beginning of the chapter, this approach involves a number of specific functions that are activated sequentially as the individual takes in information and processes it. These include perception, attention, memory, planning, and selecting and implementing problem-solving strategies.

TABLE 10-1 Case's Stages of Cognitive Development	
	Examples, of Mental Representations and Operations
Sensorimotor Control Structures (Birth to 1½ Years) Infants' mental representations are linked to their physical movement. Their executive control structures are combinations of physical objects and motor actions.	A child sees a frightening face (sensory) and runs out of the room (motor).
Relational Control Structures (1½ to 5 Years) Children's representations include knowledge of relationships among objects, people, and events. They also include durable concrete internal images, on which they can act. Children's executive control structures now include cause-and-effect statements and explicit goal structures.	The child produces a mental image of the frightening face (representation) he saw the day before and draws a picture of it (action on representation).
Dimensional Control Structures (5 to 11 Years) Children begin to extract significant dimensions from the physical world. They become able to use logical processes in comparing two dimensions, such as distance, number, and weight. They can represent stimuli abstractly and can act on these representations with simple transformations.	A child may realize that two friends don't like each other (abstract representation) and may tell them that they could all have more fun if they were all friends (simple transformation).
Abstract Control Structures (11 to 18½ Years) Building on the dimensional control structures of the preceding stage, children begin to use abstract systems of thought that allow them to perform higher-order reasoning tasks and more complex transformations of information.	The child may realize that such direct attempts to create friendships rarely succeed (abstract representation) and thus may not tell his friends what he proposed but instead plan activities in which they will all engage with the hope that greater familiarity and contact will produce the desired relationships (complex transformation).

Source: Case, 1985, Siegler, 1998.

Perception and Attention

A group of children exposed to the same sensory stimulation do not necessarily take in the same amount and kind of information. Each child's *perception* of the surrounding environment may be the same, but his or her *attention* may be focused on different aspects of that environment. For example, one child in a classroom who is focusing on the teacher will hear and understand the lesson, but another child, more interested in a whispered message from a neighbor, may regard the teacher's voice as no more than an annoying buzz. The effects of the stimulation their surroundings provide will depend on what aspects of the situation the children attend to and what meaning these features have for them.

Perception and attention are tightly interwoven: Perception presupposes the ability to attend, but attention is meaningless unless we glean meaning from what we observe. The child's choice to attend to certain aspects of a situation will determine how the environment's many sights, sounds, smells, touches, and sensations of movement affect her. And as both her perceptual capabilities and attentional strategies develop, they will continue to affect the information she acquires from any particular situation.

How Perception Develops

Two main theories of the way experience affects perceptual learning and development revolve around a basic but unresolved controversy: Do we construct the meaning of a new object by enriching our perception with stored knowledge, or do we become more efficient at detecting and differentiating an object's features?

enrichment theory The notion that the child acquires additional information about an object from each repeated experience with it, further modifying and enriching these data with information in existing schemata.

differentiation theory The notion that the child learns to identify and discriminate the important features of objects and relationships from the rich source of information sensory input provides.

Piaget advocated the first, constructionist viewpoint, whereas Eleanor Gibson advances the second type, a differentiation view that emphasizes perceptual skills.

Piaget's **enrichment theory** proposes that each time a child perceives an object he learns a little more about that object as he integrates the new information with old. For example, the first time a child sees a cat, he may view it as little more than another fuzzy, four-footed animal. The next time he sees the cat he may elaborate his cat schema to include "purrs and likes milk." Yet another time he may try to pick the cat up but find it too heavy. Cats then become fuzzy, four-footed animals that purr, drink milk, and are heavy. According to this theory, the information received from the environment must be modified and enriched by information from existing schemata; as children add new information to an object's schema they also reorganize and elaborate the schema so that it becomes fuller and more detailed.

In contrast, Eleanor Gibson's (1969, 1991, 1992) **differentiation theory** proposes that sensory input is in itself a rich source of information and not in need of enrichment. Instead, the child's task is to learn to identify and discriminate the important features of objects and relationships from the vast flow of sensory information. Gradually, the child learns to attend to the relevant attributes of objects and to make increasingly fine discriminations among objects and events. Gibson terms the relevant attributes of objects or relationships *invariants,* by which she means that these characteristics do not change under different conditions even though their relationships may make them appear to change. For example, a gray cat may appear nearly black in dim light (e.g., indoors, by a table lamp) but nearly white in bright light (e.g., outdoors on a sunny day). But the cat's black collar will always appear darker than its fur, regardless of the amount of light. The relationship between the brightness of the cat and of its collar does not change; an object's brightness relative to other objects in its surroundings is a perceptual invariant.

According to Gibson's theory, it is these invariants to which the perceptual system attends and which uniquely describe objects and relationships despite any changes in distance or orientation (Gibson, 1991, 1992). On this view, perceptual development entails learning to attend to the relevant invariants of objects and finding new differences among similar stimuli. For example, as we saw in Chapter 5, newborns tend to notice the edges and angles of faces but not the internal features such as the nose or mouth. As babies develop, however, they notice and distinguish additional features, such as color, texture, and the central parts as well as the boundaries of an object. Moreover, children learn to ignore an object's irrelevant features and to focus on the important ones. Children also become less distractible. They learn to sit still and pay attention in class more efficiently, and they are less likely to notice the noise from the playground or the construction crew outside the window. Over time they learn to distinguish the friendly neighborhood cat from the tiger in the jungle by noticing differences among each animal's attributes, such as overall size and loudness of cry.

Gibson underscores the interplay between perception and action by noting that we use information about the properties of objects to inform us about action possibilities. For example, we can throw a ball and sit in a chair. These features of objects are called *affordances* because they tell us what actions an object affords us. Gradually, children learn to recognize the properties of objects and their action potentials. For example, one group of researchers found that 14-month-old infants who were just learning to walk were more cautious when confronted by a sloping surface than were crawlers who were only 8½ months old (Adolph, Eppler, & Gibson, 1993). The older children perceived that a slope affords the possibility not only for fast locomotion but for falling!

Gibson's theory has had a major impact on research and has underscored the importance of understanding perceptual processing and its impact on attention (Pick, 1992). The sharp distinction between cognition and perception is becoming increasingly blurry. As the Baillargeon (1993) studies of infants' understanding of the laws of physics that we discussed in Chapter 9 suggest, babies seem not only to detect features but also to impose meaning on their perceptual world. As they develop, infants may be less captives of their perceptions and increasingly active interpreters of events in their environment. In short, both the enrichment and differentiation theories probably play a role in perceptual development.

Attention: Choosing What Is Perceived

When a topic is interesting, attention seems simple and effortless. In fact, however, attention is a very complex process, affected by the perceiver's sophistication and by both the type of information and the way it's presented. Children have difficulty controlling their attention when they are young. As they develop, they face the formidable tasks of learning to attend specifically to what is relevant to them or to a task they must undertake and of learning systematic strategies for planning their attack on a problem they must solve.

Control of Attention.   Very young children can sustain their attention for only short periods, but this ability increases steadily over time (Ruff & Lawson, 1990). Whereas 1-year-olds can attend to a toy for only two seconds, by the time they're 2 children will spend more than eight seconds playing with a single toy. Young children are more easily distracted than older children and adults when watching television: 2- and 3-year-olds will often talk to others, play with toys, and wander around between glances at the screen (Anderson, Lorch, Field, Collins, & Nathan, 1986), whereas older children will attend closely to a TV program. On the other hand, once a program fully engages their attention, children as young as 3 and 5 are less likely to be distracted (Anderson, Choi, & Lorch, 1987). The Turning Points chart in this chapter (page 381) notes these and other advances in children's cognitive skills.

Children are more likely to attend to material that is appropriate to their intellectual level than to other types of information (Anderson, Lorch, Field, & Sanders, 1981). Television programs, for example, that are too complex are of little interest to young children. Interestingly, children are quite sensitive to the importance of information being presented; when questioned about a program they had viewed, 4- and 6-year-old children were more likely to recall important facts from the program than unimportant facts (Lorch, Bellack, & Augsbach, 1987). And, as we have said, the manner of presentation is important; for example, researchers have found that children younger than 6 are more interested in the visual than audio content of programs

Attention is important in learning to read. Children respond best to material that's appropriate to their age level, and at about 3 they begin making marked gains in their ability to focus their attention.

■ FIGURE 10-6
Paying attention to what's important.

All the children in this study initially looked inside every box, finding animals in those with cages on their doors and household items in the boxes that displayed houses. When researchers asked 3-year-olds to recall where animals were they opened "house" doors as well as "cage" ones, but 8-year-olds ignored the irrelevant "house" boxes and checked only the "cage" ones. Maybe the younger children were scared that this lion might jump out at them! (*Source:* Miller & Seier, 1994)

(Hayes, Chemelski, & Bernbaum, 1981). Thus, when watching "Sesame Street," they are more likely to be interested in Big Bird's funny appearance, big feet, awkward movements, and wry facial expressions than in what he is saying.

Learning to Attend to What's Relevant.   As Gibson's theory points out, mere attention is not enough; for the child to learn he must focus on the relevant aspects of a task and ignore the irrelevant features. In fact, as children mature they do acquire these capabilities. Miller and her colleagues (Miller & Weiss, 1981; Miller & Seier, 1994) have shown that children improve markedly in their ability to focus their attention on relevant information.

These researchers presented 7-, 10-, and 13-year-old children with a learning task in which they asked the children to remember the location of a number of toy animals, each of which was hidden behind a different cover. As the experimenters lifted each cover to show the children each target animal, the children also saw a household item, such as a frying pan or an iron. The children's task was to remember the target object (the toy animal) while rejecting the irrelevant object (the household item). Not surprisingly, the older children were much better than the younger ones at recalling the target objects; however, the younger children were better at recalling the irrelevant objects. In fact, the younger children remembered as much about the location of the household objects as they did about the location of the animals.

In another study, investigators (Miller & Seier, 1994) gave children a study period in which they could open up any of the boxes in which objects had been placed to help them remember the location of the target objects (again, animals). There were pictures of cages on the doors to the boxes containing animals and pictures of houses on the doors to the boxes holding household objects (Figure 10-6). Of course, the smart thing for the children to do would be to focus on the first set of boxes and ignore the second, and this is what the oldest children (8-year-olds) did. The youngest children (3-year-olds) looked equally at both kinds of boxes during the study period. Modifying attentional strategies paid off: The older children remembered more than the younger and less selective children. More recently, Davidson (1996) found that older children use more selective search strategies, whereas younger children use more exhaustive methods. It appears that younger children are unable to use clues that will help them avoid a fruitless search.

To investigate how children's attentional and information-search strategies change over time and how these strategies affect both children's acquisition of information for making decisions and the quality of those decisions, Davidson (1996) presented second-, and fifth-grade children with four elaborate visual displays. Each display (called an "information board") provided information on six

TURNING POINTS: Some Cognitive Achievements as Seen from the Information-Processing View

1 YEAR
Has limited attentional capacity; can attend to a toy for only a few seconds

May have a rudimentary understanding of categories

2 YEARS
Has increased attentional capacity; will spend more than eight seconds with a single toy

Can use external supports such as landmarks to find hidden toys

May be able to use basic category labels to help remember things

May be able to draw very simple analogies

Relies on scripts of familiar events

3 YEARS
Can use two rules in combination

Often distracted by other things while watching TV but, when attention is fully engaged, may be quite attentive to a program

May be able to use fairly sophisticated analogies in solving a problem

Understands relationship between scale models and real objects

4 YEARS
With a meaningful context and guidance in using simple strategies, can focus attention on relevant aspects of the environment and apply the information gained to a task

Can combine two or more rules into a higher-order rule

Knows that long lists are harder to remember than short lists

Understands that if you try harder on a more difficult task, you may succeed

5 YEARS
Can memorize four units in a digit-span test

Understands that thinking has content, that it is different from both perception and knowing, and that only people (and perhaps some other animate organisms) can think; can sometimes infer thinking in others if the evidence is strong

6 YEARS
Begins to find audio content of TV programs as interesting as visual content

With enough cues, may be able to plan a very effective strategy of attention

7 YEARS
With training, may score as well on a test of recall as 12-year-olds

10 YEARS
Becomes more selective in searching for information needed to make decisions

11 YEARS
Begins to spend less time processing irrelevant information

12 YEARS
Can memorize six or seven units in a digit-span test

Sources: Flavell, Miller, & Miller, 1993; Siegler, 1998.

Note: Developmental events described in this and other Turning Points charts represent overall trends identified in research studies. Individual children vary greatly in the ages at which they achieve these developmental changes.

TABLE 10-2   Illustration of an Information Board and Its Corresponding Story

Bicycle	Amount of Color on Bicycle	Size of Bicycle	Number of Speeds
Bicycle A	Lots of color	Just right	Some speeds
Bicycle B	Lots of color	Too small	Some speeds
Bicycle C	Some color	Too big	Lots of speeds
Bicycle D	Little color	Just right	No speeds
Bicycle E	Little color	Too big	Some speeds
Bicycle F	Some color	Just right	No speeds

Bicycle	Amount of Rust on Bicycle	Special Features	Number of Your Friends Who Have Bicycle
Bicycle A	No rust	Lots: Horn & light	Some friends
Bicycle B	Some rust	No features	Some friends
Bicycle C	Lots of rust	Lots: Horn & light	No friends
Bicycle D	No rust	Some features	Lots of friends
Bicycle E	Some rust	Lots: Horn & light	Lots of friends
Bicycle F	Lots of rust	No features	No friends

Decision Story:

Sarah (Steve) likes to ride her bicycle, but it is getting old and rusty. Sarah wants to buy a new bicycle with lots of special features like a horn and a light. Sarah's parents took Sarah to the bicycle shop so she could pick out a new bike. The bicycle shop was filled with many beautiful bikes. Sarah knew that she wanted a bike with some speeds and with lots of color. Sarah is having a hard time deciding on a bicycle. Can you find a bicycle that she would like?

Source: Davidson, 1996.

varieties of an item (the four items were bicycles, books, computer games, and kites) and on six dimensions of the items (e.g., color or special features). It also contained a brief "Decision Story" that outlined the problem and the need for a decision (Table 10-2). The experimenter told the children to point to the dimension on which they wanted information and to say when they thought they had enough information to make a decision. For the story illustrated in Table 10-2, the most effective search strategy would be to focus on the dimensions of color and speed, ignoring the rest; narrowing the search to Bicycle A or B, Sarah would choose A because it also has lots of special features.

Once again, Davidson found that the younger children (on average, 8 years old) tended to use exhaustive searches, whereas the older children (11 years old) used more selective search strategies. When she highlighted some of the decision dimensions by placing cards displaying one of the dimensions directly above the appropriate column on the board, however, both second graders and fifth graders

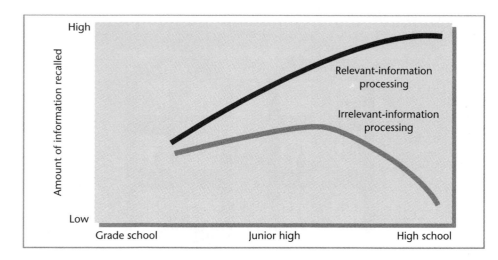

Children's changing attention to relevant and irrelevant information.
Children steadily increase their attention to relevant information, but their concern with irrelevant information weakens and drops off quickly after junior high.

became more selective and thus more efficient in their searching. Even when their performance was facilitated, however, younger and older children clearly differed in their performance. Apparently, some failure to make full use of the information gained in a search prevents younger children from benefiting from an attentional strategy; we will discuss this *utilization deficiency* a bit later (Miller & Seier, 1994).

As Figure 10-7 shows, the processing of relevant information increases steadily throughout the elementary and high school years. Processing of irrelevant information, however, increases slightly until the age of 11 or 12 and then decreases rapidly. This view of children's developing attentional focus fits well with the predictions of the information-processing view of development; that is, it is increasing efficiency in the child's cognitive processing that fuels cognitive development.

Planfulness.   One of the reasons that older children are more adept at deploying attention is that they are able to develop a plan of action to guide their attentional strategies during a problem-solving task. Across time, the child displays a striking change in his ability to attend: He develops systematic strategies for gathering and filtering information needed to solve a problem. Suppose that you were asked to determine whether each pair of houses shown in Figure 10-8 were identical. How might you approach this problem? Probably, you would compare the six pairs of corresponding windows in each pair of houses until you found a pair in which the objects displayed did not match. If all the pairs matched, you would conclude that the houses were identical. When Elaine Vurpillot (1968) administered this task to young children, she found that younger children were far less likely than older children to apply a systematic plan to extract the necessary information. Filming the children's eye movements as they made their comparisons, she found that younger children tended to look at the windows randomly and even made judgments without ever looking at the windows that were different.

Should we conclude from this research that the young child is unable to plan an efficient strategy of attention? Studies in which researchers give children some cues as to how to proceed suggest that this is not the case. Putting a task into a meaningful context and making simple strategies easily available may enable very young children to apply attentional strategies more effectively. Miller & Aloise-Young (1995) gave preschool children (ages 3 to 4) a memory task that required them to open doors to reveal two arrays of pictures and then to determine if the arrays were the same or different. When the task was embedded in a story context the children were able to attend to the appropriate contextual information and to produce the correct selective attention strategy.

These reseachers told the children a story about twins who liked to have the same toys and to put them away in boxes in the same way, that is, so that one twin's toy

■ FIGURE 10-8
A test of children's ability to gather and filter information. How quickly can you perform a task given to young children—to determine which pairs of houses, either pair (a) or pair (b), are identical? (*Source*: Vurpillot, 1968)

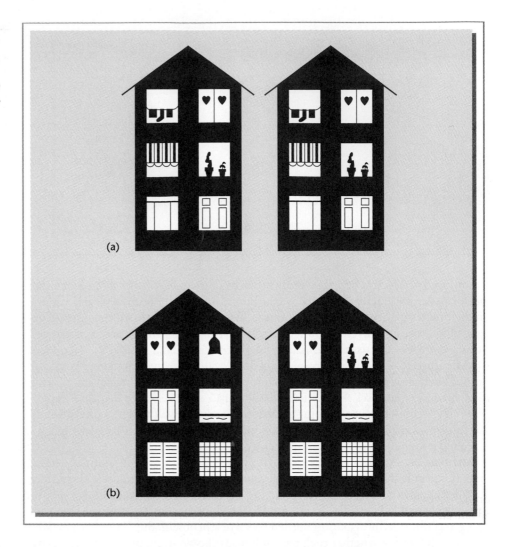

was just above the other twin's toy. During a study period, the children could look behind the doors to try to remember which pair of toys was the same and which was different. Both the older and younger children were strategic in their attention deployment, although they used a variety of strategies in this attention task. Nearly 40 percent of the entire group used the most effective strategy, which involved putting similar toys above one another (referred to as the vertical-pairs strategy. As Figure 10-9 shows, the use of this strategy increased gradually over trials, although progress was cyclic rather than linear. The fact that the children's pattern of correct judgments didn't match the strategic progress suggests that their grasp of the strategy was not firm enough to enable them to use it fully and thus make a correct judgment Although we could interpret these results as an indication that younger children can't use strategies, overall, this study suggests that young children *can* learn to use more effective strategies if a task is presented to them in a meaningful context.

One reason younger children tend not to plan their use of attentional strategies is that they don't understand that a person cannot focus on two things at once. Flavell, Green, and Flavell (1995a) found that 4-year-olds show little understanding that a person who is focusing on a particular task—for example, trying to identify the people in a group photograph—is paying little or no attention to features that have nothing to do with the task—such as the frame around the photo. In contrast, 8-year-olds and to some extent 6-year-olds showed clear understanding of attentional focus; they knew that the person looking at the photo would give little attention to the frame. Perhaps school experiences help children become more aware of their own attentional capabilities, or, as they develop, they begin to understand that the mind is

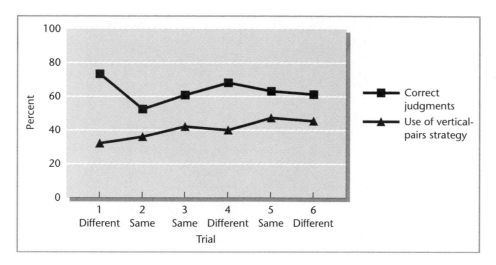

■ FIGURE 10-9
How the strategy of checking analogous factors helps in task performance.
Over six trials, preschoolers made increasing use of the vertical-pairs strategy in attempting to decide whether two arrays of drawings were the same or different, but the correctness of their actual judgments didn't always match their strategy use. (*Source:* Miller & Aloise-Young, 1995)

active and constructive (Lovett & Pillow, 1996). Thus, "attending to things is an active, sometimes effortful process that consumes mental resources rather than a passive process of receiving all the information that is available" (Flavell et al., 1995a, p. 712). Even children know you can't do everything at once!

Planning is often a joint activity. As we saw in Chapter 9, Vygotskian theory reminds us that social and cognitive development are closely linked. In everyday life, parents, older siblings, or other more competent partners such as relatives, friends, and teachers are often available to guide young children in planning more efficiently. Using a model grocery store setting, Gauvain and Rogoff (1989) compared the planning behavior of 5- and 9-year-olds working with a peer, an adult, or alone. The older children were better at planning ahead, and children who planned in advance of action devised more efficient routes. Younger children were more efficient when they worked together than when they worked alone. For older children, however, simply sharing the task was not enough. These children used more advanced planning and were more effective when they held joint responsibility for the task with either a peer or an adult.

Memory

What do we mean when we talk about memory? We mean the ability to remember a phone number from the time we look it up in the directory until we enter it on the telephone keypad. This is the short-term memory that we encountered earlier in the chapter. We also mean the ability to remember what a telephone is, how it works, and how we can use it to call that attractive person whose number we just looked up. This is long-term memory, which holds general information that we have acquired over time. As we discussed in the information-processing section, differing hypotheses explain this difference in memory types, but regardless of whether this difference is due to separate short-term and long-term storage of information or to different levels of processing, the development of these memory abilities is a major accomplishment in children's cognitive development.

The three areas of memory that gain strength and efficiency with time are (1) basic capacity, or the amount of information that can be held in short-term memory; (2) strategies, or actions that enhance the transfer of information from short-term to long-term memory; and (3) world knowledge, the larger context of information into which the child can fit new information. We will discuss each of these aspects in turn.

Before we move on, a word of caution: In practice it is not easy to separate the cognitive functions of memory and problem solving. Think about it. If you couldn't hold things in memory or retrieve them efficiently, you would find it impossible to solve any kind of problem. However, because we need to try to understand pure memory ability, we discuss memory in this major section and problem solving in the next.

If this child is dialing a telephone number from memory, he's probably demonstrating a greater memory span than is common among children his age.

memory span The amount of information one can hold in short-term memory.

Basic Capacities

Suppose I ask you to repeat a sequence of numbers that I recite. I begin with three digits, then progressively add more. Eventually, you will be unable to repeat all the numbers correctly, for I will have exceeded your **memory span** for this kind of information. Digit span is about eight units for college students, six or seven units for 12-year-olds, and four units for 5-year-olds (Brener, 1940; Starr, 1923). Pascual-Leone (1980, 1989) argues that this growing capacity demonstrates that the capacity of working memory increases over time; that is, that actual changes in the brain improve basic memory capability so that the child has more "room" to remember things. Others argue that there is no solid evidence for such changes as children develop (e.g., Dempster, 1985). In fact, young children have been shown to remember more items from lists of things such as children's toys or clothing than adults remember, demonstrating that interest, or motivation, plays a role in remembering (Lindberg, 1980).

Another explanation for older children's and adults' greater ability to remember number sequences is that even on such simple tasks, they apply a different strategy to the task (Chi, 1976). For example, the older person may "chunk" the information into smaller, more easily remembered groups of numbers (Miller, 1956). Thus, whereas the young child may not be able to remember the sequence 1 4 9 2 1 7 7 6 1 9 9 9 because it is too long, the adult can recall the sequence because she "chunks" the numbers into meaningful groups: 1492, 1776, 1999. The first time a child uses this sort of strategy it takes up some space in working memory, but, it is argued, available working memory increases because the application of such strategies becomes automatic. Space in working memory is thus freed to cope with other problems or strategies.

Processing Efficiency. In a similar line of reasoning, Case (1996) proposes that it is the more efficient use of what he calls executive processing space, rather than any increase in basic memory capacity that serves as a major mechanism for development. Case divides *executive processing space*—the space available for cognitive operations— into two distinct components: operating space and short-term storage space. *Operating space* is the amount of space necessary for a particular operation to take place (e.g., identifying a word). *Short-term storage space* refers to the amount of space being devoted to short-term memory storage. Case proposes that, with development, children become more efficient in their execution of operations; consequently, they need less operating space to perform an operation. As Figure 10-10 shows, this decrease in the amount of operating space frees up more short-term storage space. With increased storage space, children can now attempt to solve complex problems that may contain a great deal of information to be remembered.

Case (1985) attributes the child's increasing efficiency to two factors: streamlining of executive control structures (e.g., use of strategies like "chunking") and biological maturation. How does Case suggest these increases in efficiency occur? In

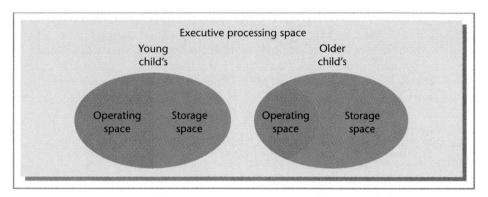

■ FIGURE 10-10
The use of executive
processing space.
According to Robbie Case, as
children learn to process
information more quickly and
efficiently, their lesser need for
operating space frees up more
space for storing information.
(*Source*: Adapted from Case,
1985)

proposing automatization, which we discussed earlier in the chapter, as one contributor, Case draws an interesting analogy: Consider the trunk of your car. Gradually, the longer you own the car, the more the trunk seems to carry—yet its capacity doesn't change. What changes is your experience in packing the trunk. As you acquire efficiency in fitting more and more luggage into the trunk, more and more trunk space seems to materialize! In similar fashion, as children's conceptual structures become more skilled at organizing and accomplishing goals, the limits on children's working memory seem to expand.

With regard to biological maturation, recall from Chapter 6 that as the child grows, the process of myelination coats the axons of neurons in such a way as to increase the efficiency of neuronal firing and, presumably, the efficiency of brain function. Although Case's position on the role of biological maturation in cognitive development has yet to be fully tested (Siegler, 1998), his emphasis on the role of increasing efficiency in the use of memory is well supported. Because the role of memory is so crucial to the cognitive development model that the information-processing approach proposes, researchers have devoted much study to the role of memory capacity and to the use of memory strategies, as we will see shortly.

One study of children's ability to use **prospective memory** strategies asked children to perform a task at a future time and found that, once again, older children (age 14) were more efficient than younger (age 10) ones (Bronfenbrenner & Ceci, 1985). Researchers asked the children either to bake cupcakes or to charge a battery; after a half hour of play activity, they then had to remember to take the cupcakes out of the oven or disconnect the battery from the charger. Older children were more likely than younger ones to use *strategic time monitoring*: At first they checked the clock quite frequently to "synchronize their psychological clocks." Then they focused on their play without checking the clock very often. Finally they began checking the clock again quite frequently as the deadline approached.

prospective memory
Memory for information
that one plans to use at a
given future time.

Another finding of this study was that children performed best when they engaged in these tasks in their own homes; their performance in laboratory settings was less skilled. These results are consistent both with Bronfenbrenner's ecological viewpoint that we discussed in Chapter 1 and with Vygotksy's sociocultural theory that we examined in Chapter 9. Remember, then, that not only memory and memory strategies but *context* as well is critical for cognition!

Processing Speed.   Kail (1991, 1995) has suggested that age-related increases in the speed of information processing are responsible for much of the improvement that occurs in children's cognitive abilities as they develop. According to Kail, processing speed is a global mechanism that affects all aspects of information processing. To determine whether processing speed explains more of the developmental changes in cognitive tasks than do other maturing aspects of thought (such as increased memory capacity or increases in domain-specific knowledge), Kail has studied changes in processing time at a variety of ages and for several different tasks. According to this investigator, the fact that we see developmental changes in processing speeds in many different tasks with widely varying task components and requirements suggests that speed is a fundamental aspect of cognitive development. Kail (1995) showed, for example, that developmental changes in processing speed were similar for tasks that were very different from one another, for example, reading comprehension, mental addition, retrieving names from memory, and visual search. And information-processing speed is not simply a practice effect. According to Siegler (1998), children increase the speed with which they accomplish both tasks that they encounter regularly and those that they rarely encounter (and therefore have little opportunity to practice). Thus speed of processing increases with age, and its effect is evident after practice effects have been taken into account (Kail, 1995; Miller & Vernon, 1997).

Kail's (Kail & Park, 1994) finding of the same relation between processing speed and age in a group of Korean children suggests that this is a universal relation. Moreover, there may be a biological basis for the developmental changes in processing speed. Eaton and Ritchot (1995) recently found that speed of processing increases with physical maturation as measured by gain in height. Although Kail's results do not discount the effects of developmental improvement in other information-processing capacities, they do suggest that increases in processing speed exert a significant influence on children's age-related improvement in task performance.

Memory Strategies

Unless information is processed in some fashion, it is quickly forgotten. If you doubt this, just try to repeat a sentence from the last paragraph. People use a wide range of cognitive activities to increase the likelihood that they will remember needed information at a later time. Some of these strategies involve external supports such as taking notes in lectures or writing appointments on calendars. Even 2-year-olds have been observed to use external memory supports, for example, using furniture as landmarks to find hidden toys (DeLoache, 1989; DeLoache & Brown, 1983; Marzolf & DeLoache, 1994). Other memory supports are purely mental (e.g., repeating that attractive person's name to yourself several times so you can remember to ask a friend about him or her later). Working with children, developmentalists have studied three mental strategies that adults use commonly: rehearsal, semantic organization, and elaboration.

Rehearsal.   One of the simplest strategies for recall is to repeat a number of times, either mentally or out loud, the information to be remembered. Using the strategy of **rehearsal** we may repeat a phone number over and over, for example, en route from directory to telephone. Research has shown (Flavell, Beach, & Chinsky, 1966) that the spontaneous use of verbal rehearsal as a memory strategy clearly increases with age. Young children tend not to rehearse unless explicitly told to do so, and they are less efficient than older children when they do spontaneously rehearse. For example, younger children will repeat the items to be remembered only once or twice when more repetitions are needed, and they are less likely to repeat earlier items (Naus, 1982). However, even young children can employ and

rehearsal A memory strategy in which one repeats a number of times, either mentally or orally, the information one wants to remember.

Competing in a spelling bee usually requires a child to spend a lot of time rehearsing specific words and their spellings. And winning a prize can be a powerful motivator for using such cognitive strategies!

benefit from rehearsal strategies if instructed to use them (Keeney, Cannizzo, & Flavell, 1967).

There are three theories as to why young children fail to use strategies that older children and adults find so useful. First, children may possess a **mediation deficiency**: This suggests that they simply can't make use of strategies for incorporating information into long-term storage. The fact that children can be taught to use such strategies, however, makes this proposal seem unlikely. A second theory proposes that young children have a **production deficiency**: This suggests that although they may know certain strategies for remembering, they are unable to generate and use these strategies spontaneously. Finally, as we've already noted, some suggest that children have a **utilization deficiency** (Bjorklund, Miller, Coyle, & Slawinski, 1997; Miller, 1990; Miller & Seier, 1994). When they are in the early phases of strategy acquisition—for example, when learning how to rehearse—children may produce an appropriate strategy spontaneously but be unable to profit from using it.

In now classic research, John Flavell and his colleagues (Flavell et al., 1966) found support for the production deficiency hypothesis. These investigators showed a series of pictures to a group of children ranging from kindergarteners to fifth graders and asked them to recall the sequence in which an experimenter pointed to a subset of the pictures. Observing the children's lip movements for a sign that they were rehearsing by naming the pictures to themselves, Flavell found first, that the children who used spontaneous verbal rehearsal demonstrated better memory for the pictures and, second, that the use of such rehearsal increased dramatically with age. Whereas only about 10 percent of kindergarten children spontaneously named the common objects in the pictures, more than 60 percent of second graders and about 85 percent of fifth graders did so.

Furthermore, the evidence suggested that the kindergartners' problem was one of production deficiency. Although they did not spontaneously produce verbal mediators, when the experimenter named the objects in the target pictures or instructed the children to name them, the kindergartners' memory was greatly improved. And in further research with a group of first graders, when the investigators asked children who had not spontaneously named the pictures to do so, memory performance differences between children who did and did not spontaneously rehearse were totally eliminated.

The production deficiency theory has been challenged, however, by the findings that, unless given explicit instructions to do so, young children will not use their new knowledge of strategies in new situations (Keeney et al., 1967). Why not? It appears that children's ability to use memory strategies is based not only on a production deficiency but also on an interaction between the costs and benefits of using a particular strategy (Siegler, 1998) when that strategy is a less practiced skill—as it is for younger children as opposed to older children. Consider the way the costs and benefits argument works: For young children, the cost of simply rehearsing a set of numbers is quite high. For example, when researchers asked young children to perform a simple manual task (such as tapping a finger on the table as quickly as possible) while they rehearsed a set of numbers, the children's ability to perform the task declined (Guttentag, 1995, 1985; Kee & Howell, 1988).

Conversely, young children's ability to use strategies increases when the cost of using that strategy is decreased. Ornstein, Medlin, Stone, and Naus (1985) presented second-grade children with a set of words to memorize. They showed half of the children index cards containing the words for five seconds only; for the rest of the children, they left the cards on display throughout the task. The researchers found that the children who could look at the words during the task rehearsed more than the children not given such visual access. Apparently the presence of the stimulus words made it easier to rehearse. In addition, when researchers offered child participants money for successful recall, the children did better on the task (Kunzinger & Witryol, 1984). On the other hand, when the task was more difficult (and thus the cost of using strategies was higher), the children rehearsed less.

mediation deficiency
Inability to use strategies to store information in long-term memory.

production deficiency
Inability spontaneously to generate and use memory strategies that one knows.

utilization deficiency
Inability to use a memory strategy that one knows.

The use of strategies seems to be related to both the costs and the benefits of their use. As children become more adept at strategy use, the costs decrease while the benefits increase. As you will see in the next section, the cost-benefit issue has an impact on children's use of other kinds of strategies as well.

Semantic Organization.   When we store information, we reorganize and reconstruct to make it more meaningful and thus easier to remember. How does the process of actively altering and rebuilding information vary for children of different ages? A good example is found in the use of **semantic organization,** or the process of organizing information to be remembered by means of categories and hierarchical relationships. Recall that according to information-processing theory's level of processing model, deep processing leads to long-term memory storage. Semantic organization is a form of deep processing.

The degree to which children use semantic organization changes over time. For example, as children mature they are more likely to use categories and verbal labels to help them remember. Suppose that we present a series of cards containing pictures of a *sweater, hat, apple, orange, jeans, sandwich, gloves, coat, milk,* and *dress* to children of different ages. Older children would be more likely than younger ones to form the cards into two groups of similar objects: *apple, orange, sandwich,* and *milk* as food items and *sweater, hat, jeans, gloves, coat,* and *dress* as items of clothing (Moely, Olson, Halwes, & Flavell, 1969; Neimark, Slotnick, & Ulrich, 1971). In addition, children who used this strategy would be better able to recall the items in a subsequent test (Best, 1993; Best & Ornstein, 1986) and more likely to argue for the advantages of this organizational strategy when asked to teach a younger child how to remember.

Are we to assume that young children are incapable of learning to use categorization? No, indeed. Recall, from Chapter 9, that partnering by more skilled people such as parents and teachers may enhance a child's cognitive performance; this claim of Vygotsky's has received a good deal of support. Children as young as 2 or 3 years old have been found to use basic category labels to help them learn and remember (Waxman, Shipley, & Shepperson, 1991) and, perhaps more important, researchers have been able to teach children as young as 7 to use organizational strategies like categorization. For example, Ackerman (1996) prompted 7- and 12-year-olds to categorize a set of words (e.g., *horse, pig, cow*) by asking them "Are all of these animals?" Older children generally recalled more than younger ones, but, with training, 7-year-olds did as well as their older peers.

The fact that younger children can use such training to help them retrieve words suggests not only that they can learn to categorize better when they are learning a set of words for the first time but also that the strategy improves their efficiency in retrieving this information at a later time. Another way to help children use a clustering strategy in remembering is to give them a contextual cue. For example, we may give children a set of words to remember (e.g., *horse, pig, goat*) and a place (e.g., *farm*) where they might see these animals. Children who are provided with such a context or place cue do better at recall than children who are not provided with this information. Context reminders are particularly useful when a task is hard; for example, if you've only one word to remember, say *pig,* it's very helpful to have a context cue, like *farm.* Recall from Chapter 5 that even infants can recall better when contextual cues are available.

The relative costs of using a mnemonic strategy affect children's use of semantic organization, just as they affect the use of rehearsal. Presenting third graders with pictures of common objects to be recalled (25 pictures in five categories), Guttentag (1995) explored the effects of intrinsic motivation, success-dependent rewards, and active participation on children's willingness to invest time in a mnemonic strategy. Active participation (being allowed to place the pictures themselves) led all children to use the target categorization strategy and thereby facilitated their recall. Reward for achievement appeared to affect strategy use only in highly motivated children, and these children generally did better at the task than children whose motivation was low.

---

semantic organization
Organizing information to be remembered by means of categorization and hierarchical relationships.

■ FIGURE 10-11
Charlie Brown's elaboration strategy.
Source: Peanuts reprinted by permission of United Feature Syndicate, Inc.

Elaboration.   Using the strategy of **elaboration,** we add to the information we want to remember in order to make it more meaningful and thus easier to place in long-term memory. This is a useful ploy because, despite its seeming addition to the informational burden, we are much more likely to remember something that is meaningful to us (Kee, 1994; Schneider & Bjorklund, 1998). The "Peanuts" cartoon in Figure 10-11 shows how Charlie Brown elaborates the numbers of his locker combination (with major leaguers' player numbers) to provide a meaningful context for three seemingly random numbers.

By training fifth- and sixth-grade children to use a "keyword" strategy, Michael Pressley and colleagues (O'Sullivan & Pressley, 1984; Pressley, Cariglia-Bull, Deane, & Schneider, 1987) were able to improve the children's memory performance greatly. These researchers first prepared a list of 15 real cities in the United States, choosing only cities whose names sounded in part like a concrete object the children would know (e.g., the name Lock Haven contains the word lock). They then showed the children the list of city names, which included the major product of each city. Instructing the children in the keyword method, they told the children to notice the object that appeared in the city's name and to construct an image that linked the object and the city's major product. As an example, they pointed out that Lock Haven's major product is paper and showed the children a picture of a lock attached to a newspaper. Children who learned this keyword strategy recalled many more city-product pairs than children who had not received the keyword training.

Knowledge of the World

As our discussion of elaboration has shown us, what individuals have learned from past experiences—what they know about the world—influences what they understand about a present event and what they will recall about it later. Consider what happens when a fan and a novice attend a basketball game together. The basketball fan will understand more than the novice about the game and will be able to relate more about it to her roommates who could not attend the game because they had

elaboration A memory strategy in which one adds to information to make it more meaningful and thus easier to place in long-term memory.

to study for a child psychology exam. We saw an example of the effects of **world knowledge** on children's memory in our discussion of Michelene Chi's work with child chess experts and adult novices. Chi and others have further documented the differing cognitive performances of novices and experts (Bedard & Chi, 1992; Chase & Simon, 1973; Chi, 1978; Chi & Koeske, 1983; Chi & Slotta, 1993).

Meaningfulness and Goals.   Not only the factual knowledge acquired through instruction or interaction with the environment affects memory processes; information children glean from society and family also influences their memory abilities. Research based on Vygotsky's sociocultural view of development has begun to focus on society's role in children's use of memory strategies and their overall memory performance. Unfortunately, a great deal of cross-cultural research investigating children's memory processes has applied experimental techniques commonly used in Western society to non-Western populations. As a result, members of nonliterate societies are often tested using tasks such as free recall, memory span, or paired associates, tasks that such children often find quite difficult and to which they do not spontaneously apply memory strategies (Cole & Scribner, 1977; Rogoff, 1990, 1998) .

When memory tasks are presented in culturally familiar contexts, however, children in non-Western cultures perform as well as, or better than, children tested in the United States. Rogoff and Waddell (1982) presented 9-year-old Mayan children in Guatemala and a group of 9-year-old U.S. children with a memory reconstruction task. The children watched as 20 familiar objects were placed into a panorama model of a town that contained familiar landmarks (each model was appropriate to the culture of the group being tested). These objects were placed in their culturally appropriate locations; for example, boats on lakes and furniture in houses. The objects were then removed from the display, and after a short delay, the children were asked to re-create the display they had seen prepared. Rogoff and Waddell found that the Mayan children performed slightly better than the North American children.

What led to the Mayan children's advantage? Rogoff speculates that the performance of the American children was hampered by the fact that about a third tried to use the strategy of rehearsal. However, this strategy, which is often taught in U.S. schools, is best suited to memorizing unrelated lists of objects; it may have been only minimally effective in this spatial reconstruction task. In contrast to the U.S. children, the Mayan children appeared to rely on the look of the display; they used the spatial relationships of the objects to organize their memory, which seems to have enhanced their performance (Rogoff, 1990).

In another study designed to explore the role not only of meaning but of goal-oriented activity in children's memory ability, Rogoff (Rogoff & Mistry, 1990) enlisted the help of the parents of a group of 4-year-olds. In a Lab condition, parents presented their children with 10 pictures of lunch-related items: cheese slice, bread, crackers, corn chips, apple juice, grapes, cookies, paper plate, napkin, and plastic bag. After repeating the names of all 10 items, they asked the children to go to the experimenter at the other side of the room and tell her all the items they remembered. After this, the experimenter gave the child a sack lunch containing all the items to take home. Note that this was the first time the term *sack lunch* was mentioned in this condition.

In a Lunch condition, parents told children specifically that they were making a sack lunch and needed all the ingredients from the "grocer" (played by the experimenter). The parent showed the child the pictures of the 10 items, and the child then went to the "grocer" and asked for all the items he or she could recall. The experimenter gave the items to the child in a basket to take to the parent. After the memory test was completed the child kept the sack lunch, which included all the items originally pictured. On average, children in the Lab condition remembered only 2.7 items, whereas children in the Lunch condition remembered 5.3 items. Once again, context was important to children's remembering, as, in this case, were meaningfulness and the motivating force of having a clear goal.

BOX 10-1

Child Psychology in Action

Should Young Children Testify in Court?

How accurate may children be when asked to give testimony in a court of law? Research has indicated that suggestions by others, especially adults, may strongly influence a young child's reporting of past events. Several investigators have explored this issue by having children listen to brief stories and then following the presentation with the introduction of inaccurate information (e.g., Ceci, Ross, & Toglia, 1987; Doris, 1991; Ornstein, Larus, & Clubb, 1992). In general, these researchers have concluded that young children are more often affected by inaccurate information than older children.

Ceci and his colleagues (Ceci & Bruck, 1998; Ceci, Leichtman, & White, 1998) undertook an extensive series of studies to explore these effects of suggestion on children's memory. In one study, the experimenters engaged preschool children in a game similar to "Simon Says." A month later an interviewer talked with each child about the activity. In one condition of the experiment the interviewer was accurately informed about what happened during the activity, and in the other, the interviewer was given false information. When the interviewer was accurately informed, the children's recall was 93 percent accurate. However, when she was misinformed, 34 percent of children 3 to 4 years old and 18 percent of children 5 to 6 years old corroborated false statements about what had happened during the experiment itself. The experimenters concluded that the younger the child, the more likely he or she was to be influenced by false information. Interestingly, although many children seemed at first hesitant to state or corroborate incorrect details, as the incorrectly informed interviewer continued to question them, they abandoned their hesitancy and endorsed the interviewer's erroneous version of what had happened. Moreover, when some time later a second interviewer, basing her questions on the first interviewer's notes, got the children to agree with incorrect statements with even more confidence, the experimenters wondered how far astray the children might have been led if successive interviewers continued to talk with them.

On the premise that children testifying in sexual abuse cases are often exposed to statements such as "X is bad," or "X did bad things," these investigators designed another study to test the effects of such information on children's memories of an event (Leichtman & Ceci, 1995). In the first condition of this study, a stranger named "Sam Stone" spent two minutes with 3- to 6-year-old children at their day-care center. On four later occasions, an interviewer asked the children about Sam's visit, trying to elicit as much detail as possible but taking care not to ask questions that would suggest answers. On a fifth occasion, a new interviewer elicited the same information and then asked specifically about two events that had not occurred during Sam's visit. Only 10 percent of the youngest children confirmed that these events had occurred, and of these, 5 percent said

they had not actually seen or heard these events. Only 2.5 percent insisted on confirming the events when challenged.

In this study's second condition, starting a month before Sam's visit, the experimenters told children specific stories about how clumsy Sam was. After Sam had visited with the children, during which time he showed none of the behaviors that had been described, the children were again interviewed four times; this time, however, on each occasion, the interviewer stated a number of untruths about Sam, such as that he ripped a book during his visit and marked a teddy bear up with a crayon. On a fifth occasion, a new interviewer asked the children for a free narrative about Sam's visit. Among the youngest children, 72 percent reported seeing Sam perform one or more of the misdeeds they'd been told about after the fact. When the interviewer asked if they had actually seen Sam do these things, the percentage dropped to 44. Even when challenged, however, 21 percent maintained that they had seen these events.

Regardless of whether children's testimony is accurate or has been altered by suggestions from others, a jury's perception of a child witness is usually not favorable. Both laypeople and legal scholars believe that children make poor witnesses (Yarmey & Jones, 1983), believing them to be inferior to adults in recall memory. In one study, mock jurors believed that children under 11 could not provide accurate testimony (Leippe & Romanczyck, 1989). At the same time, these same adults believed that children make more *honest* witnesses than adults!

As yet we have an uncertain picture of the child's ability to give an accurate account of past events. As in the case of many other cognitive functions, a variety of factors affect recall. For example, an interviewer who is intimidating and forceful may well affect children's accuracy, but an interviewer who is kind and supportive may elicit accurate information from a child (Goodman, Bottoms, Schwartz-Kenney, & Rudy, 1991). In addition, research has found that when a child has been an active participant in a situation being recalled, rather than merely a spectator, she is less likely to be susceptible to misleading suggestions by others (Rudy & Goodman, 1991).

Research in the 1990s has moved beyond description to focus on the mechanisms that may account for children's ability to recall events accurately. Some cognitive mechanisms include strength of memory, semantic knowledge, knowledge of scripts, and linguistic comprehension. Also playing a role are socioemotional factors like avoiding punishment or embarrassment, keeping promises made to others, eschewing personal gain if it involves being deceitful, and social pressure. As we have repeatedly noted, cognitive and social factors operate together in accounting for the kinds of effects we have discussed here. Finally, this work reminds us that the lines between basic and applied research are often blurred. Although the research reviewed tells us about children's testimony, it also informs us about children's cognitive and social development.

Meaningfulness may not always elicit optimal remembering in children, however. Consider the question of children's reliability as witnesses, an issue that has begun to concern society, as children have increasingly been asked to testify in court. Often the cases in which children serve as witnesses involve domestic conflict or, worse, domestic and/or child abuse that is sometimes of a sexual nature. Although these situations are highly meaningful to children, as Box 10-1 suggests, other factors such as the influence of inaccurate suggestions by others may overrule the elements of context and meaning.

One Strategy or Many Strategies?   Although we have discussed strategies separately, it would be wrong to assume that children use one strategy at a time and progress in a straightforward fashion from less to more efficient strategies across development (Schneider & Bjorkland, 1998; Siegler, 1998). Instead, just as we saw earlier in our discussion of children's acquisition of strategies for solving arithmetic problems, children use multiple strategies and combinations of strategies at any one time. Moreover, as we illustrated in Chapter 1 and in Figure 10-9, progress in the use of a strategy tends to be cyclic. For example, Coyle and Bjorkland (1997) presented second-, third-, and fourth-grade children with sets of words (e.g,. *house, pencil, carrot, bean, dog, book, cat, potato*) that could be organized into categories such as vegetables, animals, or school-related items. The children used not one strategy but many, including sorting items into groups, category naming, rehearsal, and clustering. Although the number of strategies used increased over age (Figure 10-12), even the second graders used a variety of strategies. Children varied their strategies and used one combination of strategies on one trial and a different combination on another one. Note, however, that whereas using more strategies rather than fewer improved older children's memory performance, the more strategies younger children tried to use, the poorer their recall. This is an example of the utilization deficiency we've discussed, whereby young children fail to benefit from the use of a strategy.

This kind of variability or experimenting with different strategies increases learning. "By generating a variety of alternative strategies, children can experiment with different approaches to a problem, discovering what works well, when, and where" (Schneider & Bjorklund, 1998, p. 480).

Problem Solving

Problem solving involves a higher level of information processing than the other functions that we have considered. In fact, problem solving mobilizes perception, attention, and memory in a concerted effort to reach a higher goal: the correct solution to a logical puzzle. As children develop, their problem-solving abilities become more sophisticated as the strategies they possess become better developed and as they acquire new strategies. To illustrate the impact these changes have on children's problem-solving abilities, we examine development in three areas of problem solving: solving problems by analogy, or using information from one problem to solve another; children's use of day-to-day routines, or scripts, in problem solving; and children's use of deductive reasoning in problem solving.

Solving Problems by Analogy

Suppose that you are trying to learn how to use a personal computer and are having difficulty understanding the maze of directories, subdirectories, computer disks, and drives that are part of a computer. In this situation, drawing an analogy between the workings of the computer and that of an office filing system may be helpful: Directories on the computer are the same as filing cabinets, subdirectories are drawers in the filing cabinets, and files are the documents inserted in the drawers.

The use of *analogy*—or the inference that if two or more objects or situations resemble each other in some respects, they are likely to resemble each other in yet other respects—is a powerful problem-solving strategy. The analogic inference drawn between the *source analog*, or the familiar situation, and the *target analog*,

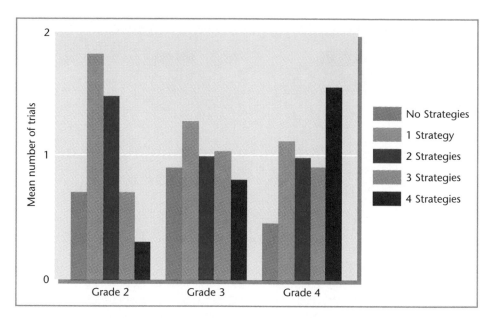

■ FIGURE 10-12
More strategies, more memory.
In a memory task, the oldest children used more strategies and recalled more words. Quite a few of the youngest children used multiple strategies, but their recall was less accurate. (*Source:* Coyle & Bjorklund, 1997)

or the unfamiliar situation, may help deal with the novel situation as well as provide the basis for learning a more general category that encompasses both (Gentner & Holyoak, 1997). Despite the power of this cognitive mechanism, both children and adults often find it difficult either to draw or to make use of analogies (Gick & Holyoak, 1980, 1983). One reason may be that psychological testing has often focused on rather simple analogies (e.g., "foot is to leg as arm is to what?") in which the important relations within each analog may be obscured.

Another reason is that people may confuse analogy and similarity. As Gentner and Markman (1997) point out, analogy involves similarity but only relational similarity, not attribute similarity. Gentner and Markman's (1997) map of "similarity space," seen in Figure 10-13 depicts the relationships among analogy, two kinds of similarity, and metaphor quite clearly. Very young children often appreciate surface similarity, or "mere appearance" correspondence (e.g., they may call the moon "ball"), and this kind of matching, uncorrected, can interfere with learning. On the other hand, "child development is full of . . . moments" that contain the essential characteristics of analogical thinking (Gentner & Markman, 1997, p. 48). For example, a 25-month-old child examined a new toy that had different-colored doors with color-matched keys; when he found an extra, white key he asked his parents where the white door was. And a 2-year-old watched pet ducklings eat, held his arms to his sides, bent up and down as the ducklings did, and then announced that his pets "Have no hands!" He had figured out why they ate differently from him.

Interestingly, in a study of children's ability to solve a problem by drawing an analogy between the problem and one in a story they had been told, it appeared that the children's difficulties stemmed not from inability to reason in this way but, apparently, from failure to recall the details of the story. Brown, Kane, and Echols (1986) asked 3- to 5-year-old children to "help the Easter Bunny move the Easter eggs across the river" and into a basket on the "opposite bank" by using several materials provided by the experimenter: a flat piece of paper, a cardboard tube, a walking cane, tape, scissors, string, and a few other objects. Earlier, the experimenters had told the children a story in which a genie was faced with the problem of moving jewels from one bottle to another. The genie had solved the problem by rolling his magic carpet into a tube and sliding the jewels from the mouth of one bottle to the other through this tube.

The children found it quite difficult to help the Easter Bunny with his problem; however. Very few of the 3-year-olds were able to solve the problem, and even

■ FIGURE 10-13
Similarity space: The relations among analogy, similarity, and metaphor.
Analogy obtains when comparisons have high *relational* similarity but low attribute similarity; for example, "Dan saw the debate as a war and used every weapon at his command, bombarding his opponent with arguments." *Literal* similarity describes matches that share both relational and attribute similarity because they mean the same thing, as in "prison-jail," and *mere-appearance* similarity describes matches that share only attribute similarity, as in "tiger-zebra." Metaphors span the range from relational comparisons, such as "two lovers like twin compasses," to attribute comparisons, such as "a moon like a silver coin." (*Source*: Gentner & Markman, 1997)

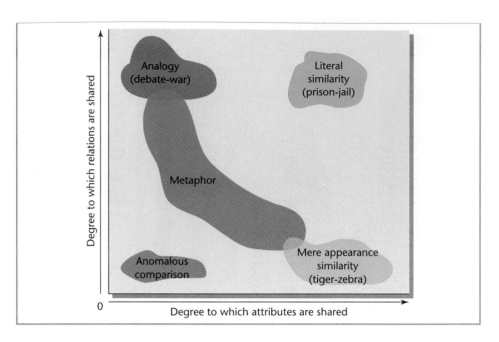

some of the 5-year-olds failed to figure out that they could use the cardboard tube to move the eggs across the river. However, when the experimenter gave the children a hint to help them recall the genie story, their rates of problem solution increased dramatically. This suggests that it was not inability to reason by analogy that kept them from solving the problem but rather inability to recall the details of the analogy-containing story.

Researchers who have replicated this study have found that highlighting the goals of the story's protagonist aids in analogical transfer (Chen & Daehler, 1989), as does giving children multiple examples of the problem solution (Crisafi & Brown, 1986). Other researchers have noted that both children and adults are more likely to draw analogies if there is surface similarity between the situations (e.g., characters' names) in the two problems (Gentner & Rattermann, 1992; Goswami, 1995) or in the deep aspects of the situations (such as goals, obstacles, and potential solutions). For instance, children found it easier to reenact a story about a jealous friend with new characters if the new hero looked something like the original one (Gentner & Toupin, 1986). Children are also likely to find problem solving by analogy more useful when they know a great deal about the topic of the original problem (Inagaki & Hatano, 1987).

Cognitive Tools

If we had to figure out what to do in situations that are repeated day after day (like bathing, dressing, and eating meals) and to find our way to school, work, and other familiar places anew each day, we would have little time or energy to devote to new events and activities. Children quickly become competent in many such routine situations. They learn household routines easily, but it takes them longer to learn how to negotiate their way around the world outside of their homes. Scripts, which we met a little earlier, help children learn daily routines, and mental maps help them learn gradually how to get to friends' homes, school, and other important places.

Scripts.   The 2-year-old not only participates in many activities during the day but also seems to have a good understanding of her "role" in these situations. If you doubt this, just try to deprive a child of the piece of candy she usually gets in the grocery store checkout line. How do children structure information from past experiences to achieve an understanding of the present situation and develop a plan for appropriate behavior? One way to conceptualize this behavior is to assume that

This child's script for her visit to the San Antonio zoo will help her remember the animals she saw and the things she learned about them for a long time after.

people form scripts for many routine activities. **Scripts** provide basic outlines of what one can expect in a particular situation and what one should do in that situation, allowing people to carry out many routine behaviors efficiently and almost automatically (Nelson, 1993; Schank & Ableson, 1977).

Children as young as 20 months know about and rely on the sequences of activities in familiar events such as bedtime, mealtimes, or parties (Bauer & Thal, 1990). You always wash your hands before eating and brush your teeth before you go to bed. And 3- to 4-year-old children can remember a large number of events in the correct order (Fivush, Kuebli, & Clubb, 1992). Even infants and toddlers learn to organize their representations of events along scriptlike lines. Bauer and her colleagues (Bauer & Dow, 1994; Bauer & Mandler, 1992) have shown that by the end of the first year, infants use temporally ordered rules in their recall of a sequence of events. For example, these researchers presented infants with a familiar sequence, such as giving a teddy bear a bath (*put teddy in the tub, "wash" teddy with a sponge, "dry" teddy with the towel*). Not only were babies able to reproduce the familiar sequence with a high degree of accuracy, but they were able to do this with novel events as well (make a rocking horse move with a magnet). Studies by Bauer and associates suggest that the central aspect of the script—that is, the ability to represent events in temporal order—is learned very early in life.

To change such sequences is very confusing and disconcerting for the child; young children are more rigid in their applications of scripts than older children and adults (Wimmer, 1980). In fact, when asked to recall stories, young children will eliminate inconsistent elements of the story to preserve the expected sequence of events (Fivush & Hamond, 1990) or add events that they were expecting to happen in the story but that did not (Myles-Worsley, Cromer, & Dodd, 1986). Moreover, if you present 20-month-olds with an incorrect sequence (e.g., *dry, wash, put teddy bear in tub*), they sometimes correct the order to the real-life script (*wash* before *dry*). When the order of a well understood script is violated, toddlers often say, "That's so silly."

Scripts help children remember over a long period. In one instance, kindergarten children visited a museum, a special event for youngsters. Not only did the children develop and remember a general museum script when questioned six weeks and one year later, but they were able to remember details of their personal museum visit at these times as well (Fivush, Hudson, & Nelson, 1984). Children can distinguish the general from the personal script, and, it seems likely, the general script helps them remember personal experiences better by providing a way to organize specific memories. Moreover, by age 7, children discriminate more clearly between what usually happens (on a trip to McDonald's) and what happened on a specific visit (last Tuesday's dinner at McDonald's) (Farrar & Goodman, 1992).

Mental Maps. Just as children need to be able to negotiate their way through the routine events of the day, so too they must find their way through the spatial

script A mental representation of an event or situation of daily life, including the expected order in which things happen and how one should behave in that event or situation.

TABLE 10-3 Developing an Understanding of Space and Mapping		
Step 1	Using Landmark Knowledge	Children use landmarks, such as the yellow house or the red fire hydrant, to help orient themselves in space.
Step 2	Using Route Knowledge	Children can integrate several landmarks (e.g., yellow house, red hydrant, and blue mailbox) into a sequence that forms a route through space that leads unfailingly to the baseball field or the nearby store.
Step 3	Developing Mental Maps	Children can create an overall mental or cognitive map of a familiar area that incorporates landmarks and routes learned earlier.

mental map   A cognitive representation of the spatial layout of a physical or geographical place.

environment. Even very young children manage to maneuver their way through familiar places, avoiding obstacles and barriers in their paths (Heth & Cornell, 1980). And they do this with the aid of **mental maps,** which are cognitive representations of the spatial layout of, for example, a room, a playground, or a town. But forming maps that make it possible to get to familiar places requires more cognitively complex skills. If someone asked you to draw the route you take to your psychology classroom, you might be able to do this fairly easily, but young children find such a task difficult, even when they are able actually to find their way to a destination (Liben & Downs, 1989; Siegel & White, 1975).

As children mature, they become more skillful at constructing mental and physical maps of places they know (home, school, and neighborhood) and routes they have traveled. According to Siegel and his colleagues (Anooshian & Siegel, 1985; Siegel & White, 1975), children develop the abilities required to form cognitive maps of the spatial environment in three steps (see Table 10-3). In the first step, they learn to recognize specific landmarks, acquiring *landmark knowledge,* and in the second step, they put several landmarks together to form what is called *route knowledge.* In the final step, children acquire the ability to combine routes learned earlier into *mental maps* of entire areas.

Allen and Ondracek (1995) have shown that children's ability to recognize and use spatial landmarks is related generally to age but more specifically to their development of certain cognitive abilities. Studying 5- and 9-year-old children, these researchers found that acquiring needed information about landmarks is related to recognition-in-context memory, or the ability to recognize objects that one has seen before and to distinguish those that are in their original contexts from those that are presented in novel contexts. Further, both landmark knowledge and route knowledge were related to information-processing speed, or the rapidity with which one can recognize and make the necessary judgments of objects.

Young children often interpret the symbols used on maps quite literally. For example, they will assume that the outline of an airplane on a map means that there's a real airplane, rather than an airport, at that location (Downs & Liben, 1986). As children grow, they become better able to use this kind of information accurately to negotiate new surroundings (Anooshian & Siegel, 1985; Scholnick, Fein, & Campbell, 1990).

Symbolic Representation.   As Judy DeLoache (1995) has argued, becoming a proficient symbol user is a universal developmental task, and being able to use symbols is a great aid in solving real-world problems. In this section, we add to scripts and maps symbolic tools such as scale models and pictures. In a classic study of how children use models as representations of actual objects, DeLoache (1987) showed children who were 31 and 39 months old a normal-size living room with furniture and a miniature model of the same room. She also showed them a normal-size doll and a miniature

(a) Hiding toy in model

(b) Finding toy dog in room

(c) Finding toy in model

■ FIGURE 10-14

A room is a room but is it the same room?
In a classic series of experiments, Judy DeLoache has tested the ability of young children to conceive of a model room not only as a representation of a full-size room but as an object in itself. (a) DeLoache hides a small toy dog in a scale-model room while a 3-year-old child watches. (b) The child retrieves a normal-size toy dog from the analogous place in the full-size room. (c) The child retrieves the small toy dog from its hiding place in the scale-model room. (*Source*: Courtesy of Judy S. DeLoache, University of Illinois at Urbana-Champaign)

version of the doll. She hid the tiny doll in the model room while the children watched and then asked the children to find the larger version of the doll in the life-size living room, explaining that it was hidden in the same place in that room as the miniature doll was hidden in the model room. Figure 10-14 shows these steps in another, similar study in which DeLoache used toy dogs instead of toy dolls.

The older children had no problem finding the doll, but the younger children could not do so, although by retrieving the miniature doll from the model room, they showed that they remembered where it had been hidden. DeLoache proposed that the problem for the younger children was their inability to form a *dual representation.* That is, they couldn't conceive of the model room both as an object in its own right and as a representation of the larger, real room. DeLoache tested this hypothesis by giving the younger children a drawing of the real room instead of an actual model, on the theory that they were used to drawings as representations of things in the real world. This time the younger children easily found the large doll in the real room.

In another test of the dual representation hypothesis, DeLoache and her colleagues (DeLoache, Miller, & Rosengren, 1997) presented two groups of children with alternative accounts of the hidden doll problem. To both groups they introduced the full-size room, and hid the large doll in it, as in the original study. They then presented the model room to the first group and hid the miniature doll. To the second group, however, they explained that "a shrinking machine" had shrunk the full-size room and then revealed the small, model room. The 2½-year-old children in this study had no difficulty finding the miniature doll in the "shrunken" room. Describing the task of the first group as symbolic and the task of the second group as nonsymbolic, DeLoache and her colleagues suggest that the second task was easy for the children because it did not require them to represent the (symbolic) *relation* between two objects—the large and small rooms, as the first task did. Instead, they had only to recognize the room in its new, "shrunken" form.

Continuing to explore children's representational abilities, these investigators have found that another source of difficulty may stem from a conflict between viewing something as an interesting object in itself and as a representation of another object. When they allowed children to play with an object—which should increase its salience as an object itself—children were less successful at viewing the object as a representation. But when they put the object in a glass case—which should lessen its salience as object—the children were more successful. According to these researchers, we may also help young children to use a model as a representation if we increase the similarity between the model and the real object, in terms of size, color, shape, and so on (DeLoache, Miller, & Pierroutsakos, 1998).

According to DeLoache and colleagues (DeLoache et al., 1997), the notion that very young children may not be capable of dual representation has several practical implications. For example, it may be that teaching basic mathematic concepts by using blocks of different sizes to represent different numerical quantities may not necessarily be useful with very young children. Similarly, although in a quite different context, using anatomically correct dolls when interviewing young children about possible sexual abuse may not be as effective as psychologists have thought.

Deductive Reasoning

In our discussion of Piaget's cognitive development theory, we noticed that Piaget placed great emphasis on children's ability to perform tasks based on logical reasoning, as evidenced in their understanding of such concepts as conservation and class inclusion. All these skills rely on children's ability to use logic and deductive reasoning. Although we have seen that children's cognitive abilities are far greater than Piaget believed, children do often find tasks based on deductive reasoning quite difficult.

transitive inference The mental arrangement of things along a quantitative dimension.

Transitive Reasoning.   One of Piaget's classic reasoning tasks involves **transitive inference,** or the mental arrangement of things along a quantitative dimension. Recall from Chapter 9 that children younger than 6 or 7 could not deduce that Melissa was taller than Fabiana when given the information "Melissa is taller than Zoe and Zoe is taller than Fabiana." Piaget attributed this failure to an inability to use the logic of transitive inference. An alternative hypothesis, proposed by Halford (1990), is that children do understand transitive inference but use an incorrect strategy to solve this kind of problem. For instance, one strategy young children use is to assume that the most recently mentioned object is also the largest; in this case, the strategy leads them to an incorrect inference. Another strategy is to assume automatically that one of the given objects is longer than the others, regardless of what the experimenter actually said (Brainerd & Reyna, 1990). Both these strategies reduce the child's memory load, which has been shown to be crucial in this type of transitive inference task (Bryant & Trabasso, 1971) but often lead to erroneous conclusions. Children fail to encode, retrieve, and use information correctly and effectively in transitive inference tasks (Rabinowitz, Grant, Howe, & Walsh, 1994).

hierarchical categorization The organization of concepts into levels of abstraction that range from the specific to the general.

Hierarchical Categorization.   Another crucial use of logic can be seen in **hierarchical categorization,** or *class inclusion,* in which concepts are organized into levels of abstraction that range from the specific (e.g., *dog*) to the general (e.g., *animal*). It is one thing to know that there are dogs and there are collies; a much more sophisticated appreciation of categorization is required to understand that a collie is a kind of dog, such that all collies are dogs but not all dogs are collies. Although some studies have suggested that children do not view such class-inclusion problems in the same way as adults and older children, some evidence suggests that even very young children are capable of forming categories based on hierarchical relationships (Haith & Benson, 1998; Klahr & Wallace, 1976; Mandler, 1998; Trabasso et al., 1978).

Mandler and Bauer (1988) studied 12-, 15-, and 20-month-old infants' knowledge of categories using a method called sequential touching, which takes advantage of young children's tendency to touch and manipulate objects within their grasp. These experimenters recorded the order in which an infant reached for and grasped objects that were placed, as a group, within the child's reach. Ensuring that the infants viewed objects from both specific (*dogs* and *cars*) and general (*animals* and *vehicles*) levels, they presented a child with, say, two dogs and a horse, or two cars and a truck and found that children touched sequentially objects that belonged to the same hierarchical category (e.g., all the dogs). This pattern of sequential touch was strongest at the specific level and, to a lesser extent, at more general levels. Thus it appears that even infants have some knowledge of class-inclusion relationships and, further, that they are able to use this information to form categories for familiar objects (Mandler, 1998).

What could infants as young as 1 year use as a basis to form categories? Knowledge of dogs and cars is quite limited at this age. Two factors have been hypothesized to affect children's ability to form hierarchical categories. First, objects that form a category have similarities, and young children may take advantage of this in forming categories (Rosch & Mervis, 1975; Rosch, Mervis, Gray, Johnson, & Boyes-Braem, 1976). For example, most dogs have four legs and a furry coat and they bark. Second, people use labels to denote category membership, which helps children associate words with different objects (Gelman & Markman, 1987; Waxman & Gelman, 1986).

Markman and Hutchinson (1984) gave 2- to 3-year-old children a set of three objects and asked the children to sort the objects "where they belong," sometimes labeling objects and sometimes giving them no labels. When the experimenters did not label an object, for example, a police car, the children put it with either a same-physical-category object (another car) or a same-thematic-category object (a police officer) object, apparently at random. When the experimenters did apply labels to objects, they used nonsense words rather than an object's real name. For example, they referred to the police car as a *daz*. Given this label, most of the children placed the police car with another car, apparently seeing both as having the same category membership. Other researchers have replicated this effect (e.g., Mandler, 1998), and some have reported similar findings using Japanese words instead of nonsense syllables (Waxman & Gelman, 1986).

Children also use category information to determine whether one object shares a quality they've been told another object possesses (Gelman & O'Reilly, 1988). For example, preschool and second-grade children were told that an apple "has auxin inside" (*auxin*, of course, is a nonsense word). Then they were shown an array of objects—some were fruits, some were other kinds of things—and were asked whether any of these other objects would also contain "auxin." The children were quite good at generalizing the possession of auxin only to other fruit; they were unlikely to propose that an object other than fruit contained auxin. Children will also extend common behavioral characteristics based on category membership (Gelman & Markman, 1987). When told that a particular black and white cat can see in the dark, 3- and 4-year-old children said that a brown cat can see in the dark but that a skunk cannot. In summary, children's ability to form hierarchical categories is evident from a very young age.

Numerical Reasoning

Children begin to master some critical principles of counting at an astonishingly early age. Rochel Gelman has studied extensively what preschool children do and do not understand about number systems. Her findings, including her work with 3-year-olds on number conservation (Chapter 9), led Gelman to propose five basic principles of counting that lead to children's competence with numbers (Gelman & Gallistel, 1978):

1. The one-one principle: Each object should be counted once and only once.
2. The stable-order principle: Always assign the numbers in the same order.
3. The cardinal principle: A single number can be used to describe the total of a set.
4. The abstraction principle: The other principles apply to any set of objects.
5. The order-irrelevance principle: The order in which objects are counted is irrelevant.

A simple example will show these principles in action. Suppose we show a child 10 pennies, placed in a row, and ask her to count them. Pointing to each one, she proceeds to count them aloud, "1, 2, 3, 5, a, b, c, 10, 15, 12." When she finishes, we

BOX 10–2

Perspectives on Diversity

It's Easier to Count in Chinese Than in English!

Chinese-speaking children may have an advantage over English-speaking children when it comes to counting. According to Miller and colleagues (Miller, Smith, Zhu, & Zhang, 1995), the Chinese language offers a more consistent "base-10" naming system than the system used in English; this may make it easier for young children to learn to count.

As Miller and associates point out, the base-10 Arabic system of numbering (1, 2, 3 . . . 10, 11, 12 . . . , etc.) is now used throughout the world, but *names* for numbers in different languages reflect older and sometimes more complex number systems. These researchers divided the number-naming systems of both (Mandarin) Chinese and English into four segments of interest: 1 to 10; 11–19, 20–99, and 100 and above. In the first segment, Chinese and English do not differ in difficulty of learning, they propose, for both languages require children to master an unordered sequence of names. There's no way to predict, for example, that *jiŭ* follows *bā* or that *nine* follows *eight*. In the second segment, however, Chinese follows a consistent base-10 rule (e.g., in Mandarin Chinese, the number 11 is called literally "ten-one"), whereas the English system is inconsistent and mixed: The names *eleven* and *twelve* seem to bear no relation to *one* and *two*, and the names for 13 through 19 both place unit values before the tens values and modify the names of both (*thir-teen*, *fif-teen*).

Between 20 and 99, both languages follow a base-10 approach in naming, except that Chinese uses unmodified unit and tens names (e.g., "two-ten-four," for 24) whereas English modifies the first unit name—but not the second—and the tens names (e.g., *twen-ty-four*). Finally, above 100, the naming systems in both languages are fairly consistent in using the base-10 format, with only a few exceptions.

Based on an early study in which they found some differences in mathematical skills favoring Chinese over U.S. children entering school for the first time, Miller and colleagues formulated several hypotheses. If these differences in fact reflected a more easily comprehended number naming system, then (1) Chinese children should show substantial skills advantages after all children begin to learn to count above 10, (2) U.S. children should have more trouble with counting in the teens than Chinese children, and (3) differences should generally be related to the system of number names and not involve other aspects of counting. Engaging 99 Chinese children and 98 U.S. children—all between 3 and 6 years old—in a series of tasks that involved abstract counting, these investigators confirmed their predictions. As you can see from Figure 10-15, there were no substantial differences between the two groups in counting up to 10, but as children began to count in the teens, a significant difference between Chinese and U.S. children emerged. This differential ability was evident until both groups began to count in the 100s, where they again performed similarly. Chinese children were somewhat more successful in counting actual displays of between 14 and 17 objects, but they did not differ from U.S. children in ability to solve simple mathematical problems or to count arrays of 10 or fewer objects. Although this finding might seem to violate the researchers' third prediction, it is consistent with the notion that U.S. children will have the greatest difficulty with number naming in the teens.

ask her to count them again, starting from the other end. Again she counts all 10 of the pennies, counting each one once and only once. "How many pennies are there?" we ask. "Twelve" is her sure reply. We then ask her to count 10 gumballs. She repeats: "1, 2, 3, 5, a, b, c, 10, 15, 12." Again, we ask, "How many?" "Twelve."

Can we say that this child understands numbering and counting? Based on the principles outlined above, the answer is yes. Despite her use of an unconventional number sequence, she does seem to understand the critical principles of counting. She assigned only one number to each of the objects and always assigned the numbers in the same order, showing that she understood the one-one and stable-order principles. She had no problem switching the order in which she counted the objects, nor did she mind counting both pennies and gumballs, demonstrating her command of the order-irrelevance and abstraction principles. Finally, when asked how many objects there were, she replied "Twelve," showing that she understood the cardinal principle.

Children may be competent in some or all of these principles at different points in their development. For example, a 3-year-old may grasp the one-one principle and the cardinal principle. However, he may be able to apply the stable-order principle only to sets with five or fewer members because his numbering becomes unstable after five (e.g., he counts 1, 2, 3, 4, 5, 10, 18, 7 on one occasion and 1, 2, 3, 4, 5, 7, 18, 10 on another). Such a child would be able to solve Gelman's mouse task (Chapter 9) but would fail on more complex number conservation tasks. Through

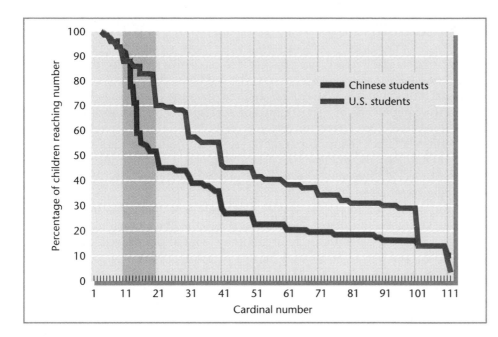

■ FIGURE 10-15
Abstract counting in Chinese and English.
The colored band at the left of the graph highlights the teens (11–19) when Chinese and U.S. children begin to diverge in counting skills, possibly owing to the non-base-10 structure of English names for these numbers. (*Source*: Miller, Smith, Zhu, & Zhang, 1995)

Given that neither the Chinese nor the English language is likely to change its number-naming system, how can we help American children acquire counting skills more efficiently and effectively? According to Miller and colleagues, obstacles that the English system presents can interfere with such math operations as arithmetic carrying and borrowing. Other studies have suggested not only that Chinese children display more sophisticated addition strategies when they first enter school but also that counting strategies for certain kinds of problems predict adult performance on those problems. Although these researchers suggest that it may be important both to familiarize U.S. children with Arabic numerals at an earlier age and to emphasize use of the digits over the use of number words, they also point out that this approach might interfere with other methods used to teach American children the tens-structured addition method. Perhaps the answer lies in both parents and teachers—in the Vygotskian style—encouraging children more to learn math skills.

such a careful analysis of the component skills involved, Gelman has provided a detailed and accurate description of young children's number skills (Gelman, 1978, 1979; Gelman & Gallistel, 1978).

Later studies have suggested that children can count skillfully before they understand counting principles (Siegler, 1998; Wynn, 1992). In addition to Gelman's five basic principles, many different strategies are often useful when trying to count efficiently. Examples of these strategies are counting adjacent objects sequentially, or starting at the end of a linear array (rather than in the middle). Unlike the five principles of counting, these strategies are optional, but young children often overlook the distinction between optional and necessary features of counting (Gelman & Meck, 1983). With 3- to 5-year-old children as an audience, Briars and Siegler (1984) manipulated puppets who, when counting, made two types of errors. In one of these, the puppet counted correctly but did not count adjacent objects sequentially and did not start at the end of an array. In the second type of error, the puppet counted incorrectly, violating the one-one principle. Five-year-olds understood which counting techniques were optional and which were necessary, but 3- and 4-year-old children did not distinguish between the two kinds of techniques.

In recent years, evidence that Asian children display greater mathematical skills than American children has accumulated. As Box 10-2 suggests, as seen in Chinese and U.S. children, this difference may begin to emerge very early in life and may reflect verbal as well as quantitative abilities.

METACOGNITION

metacognition The individual's knowledge and control of cognitive activities.

As cognitive beings, we don't just remember things, solve problems, and form concepts—we have an awareness of the strengths and limitations of our cognitive processing and of the way we control or regulate them to achieve such mental feats. These two components of **metacognition**—knowledge and control of cognitive functioning—are interrelated and act on each other. The child's understanding of her cognitive abilities and processes, of the abilities of others, and of the task situation will influence the strategies she uses in overseeing and monitoring her learning. In turn, her abilities and her experience in planning, monitoring, checking, and modifying cognitive strategies will contribute to her knowledge about cognition and what contributes to her success or failure on intellectual tasks. In this section we look at the child's theory of mind and then examine three other important areas of study within metacognition: children's knowledge about the self, their knowledge of tasks and how to go about them, and their knowledge of specific strategies for learning and remembering.

The Child's Theory of Mind

What do young children understand about their own minds? Henry Wellman (1990) proposes that from the age of 3, children have a "belief-desire" theory about the functioning of their minds: Children believe that a person's internal beliefs and desires lead him or her to action. Although this may appear to be a fairly simple theory of how the human mind works, in fact, it leads to very rich and complex expectations about the beliefs of others, their actions, and the outcome of these actions. Moreover, the theory assumes that children also understand the relationship between their beliefs and desires and those of other people. If any aspect of this relationship is misunderstood, the child's ability to distinguish correctly between his own and other people's actions and desires will suffer (Wellman & Gelman, 1998).

Exploring this theory, Wellman and Bartsch (1988) told 3- and 4-year-old children a story about Jane, who wanted to find her kitten. The kitten was really in the playroom, but Jane thought it was in the kitchen. When the experimenters asked children where Jane would look for her kitten, most 3-year-olds replied that Jane would look in the playroom, disregarding Jane's belief that the kitten was in the kitchen. Wellman (1990) suggests that the children found it difficult to separate their own beliefs regarding the location of the kitten (that it is in the playroom) from the discrepant beliefs of the character in the story. Young children also have difficulty recalling that they once had false beliefs about a situation, once the "truth" of the situation has been revealed (Freeman & Lacohée, 1995, Gopnick & Slaughter, 1991). For example, 3-year old children who discovered that a candy box that they had assumed held candy really contained pencils could not remember ever believing the box had candy in it (Freeman & Lacohée, 1995).

Despite some early difficulties understanding the beliefs and actions of others, children's knowledge of the distinction between thought and reality is quite sophisticated and their knowledge about the process of thinking itself is really quite remarkable. For instance, young children know that it is impossible to touch thoughts, showing that they understand the distinction between objects of the mind and objects of the world (Wellman, 1990). And they understand that their mental image of an object is a representation of something that exists in the world.

From a series of experiments designed to shed further light on what preschool-age children (3 to 5 years old) really know about their own thinking processes, John Flavell and his colleagues (Flavell, Green, & Flavell, 1993; Flavell et al., 1995a, 1995b;

Lyon & Flavell, 1993) have drawn a number of important conclusions. Children understand that only people and perhaps some other animate creatures can think; even 3- to 5-year-olds know that rocks don't think. Children understand that thinking has content and that when you think, you are thinking about *something* or something related to some other thing. However, even young children recognize that the content of our thinking can be a product of our own imagination. They can even distinguish thinking from such perceptual-motor activities as seeing, moving, and feeling. Even more remarkable, they can tell the difference between knowing and thinking; for example, they understand that you can know about something (the goodies in your lunch box) but not be thinking about it at the moment.

Young children's understanding of thinking has limitations, however (Table 10-4). For example, young children have a poor understanding of the concept of a "stream of consciousness," or of the fact that people continually experience mental content of one kind or another. In one series of studies, experimenters tested children's assumptions about a person's mental state in several different conditions (Flavell et al., 1993). In two conditions, while three groups of children of different ages (3-, 4-, and 6- to 7-year-olds) and a group of college students observed, one experimenter asked the other to look at a particular picture or to respond to a question such as, "How did the ship get into the little bottle?" While the second experimenter looked or considered her answer (remarking, "Hmm—let me see—give me a moment"), the first experimenter asked the observers to say whether they thought her colleague was "having thoughts" or whether her mind was empty of thoughts. Under these conditions, a majority even of 3-year-olds attributed thoughts and ideas to the experimenter's colleague (Figure 10-16). However, in two other conditions, when the experimenter asked her colleague to simply sit and wait and then asked the observers about her colleague's mental state, only 12 percent of 3-year-olds and fewer than half of the 4-year-olds thought the colleague was having thoughts and ideas. Even though we have emphasized how insightful young children are about their own cognitive processes, there is still plenty of room for developmental advance.

Knowledge About the Self

Every student burning the midnight oil and studying for a critical test has asked the question "Do I need to go through these notes once more in order to ace the exam?" Younger children are less able to assess whether they have studied material well enough to remember it than are older children (Flavell, Friedricks, & Hoyt, 1970).

Older children have a more realistic and accurate picture of their own memory abilities and those of others than do younger children (Flavell, 1985; Flavell et al., 1970; Yussen & Berman, 1981). Younger children, for example, will greatly overestimate the number of items they can remember from a brief viewing. Further, older children are more likely to appreciate that one's memory ability varies from occasion to occasion and that memory ability may vary among individuals in any age group. An older child recognizes, for example, that he doesn't learn well when tired or anxious and that whereas his sister may be a whiz at math, he is better at French. Young children do recognize that older children are better at remembering (Wellman, 1978), but unlike their older peers, they fail to attribute this difference to study strategies (Kreutzer, Leonard, & Flavell, 1975).

Knowledge About the Task

The ability to monitor one's comprehension is critical for a wide range of problem-solving and communication tasks. Do I understand the directions to get to the party tomorrow? Do I understand the instructions for this week's science project? What is the teacher saying about the test tomorrow? To be an effective processor of information, the child has to be sensitive to her present state of knowledge so that she can seek out the information she needs to further her understanding.

TABLE 10-4   Limitations on Young Children's Metacognition

Young Children

- Underestimate the amount of thinking they and others do.
- Don't understand the concept of a "stream of consciousness."
- Fail to appreciate that someone sitting quietly and not obviously "doing" something might be engaging in mental activity.
- Don't understand that activities such as looking, listening, or reading involve thinking. When someone is engaged in such an activity, preschoolers do not automatically understand that the person's mind is active. Similarly, they don't recognize that *they* have been thinking when engaging in these kinds of activities.
- Cannot infer what another person might be thinking about, even when they realize the person is thinking.
- Fail to understand that when you focus attention on one thing, you are often not able to think about other things.
- Have difficulty saying, when asked, whether they were thinking or what they were thinking about, even when their responses are prompted and facilitated.
- Tend to understand thinking in terms of its products rather than in terms of the process of thinking itself.

Source: Flavell, Green, & Flavell, 1995b.

Markman (1977, 1979) assessed children's ability to monitor their comprehension of task instructions. In one study, Markman (1977) gave first, second, and third graders inadequate instructions for playing a card game. The experimenter dealt each child four cards, which had letters on them, and explained the game:

We each put our cards in a pile. We both turn over the top card in our pile. We look at cards to see who has the special card. Then we turn over the next card in our pile to see who has the special card this time. In the end, the person with the most cards wins the game. How would you like to try to play this game with these instructions?

The experimenter made no mention either of what the "special card" might be or of how one acquired more cards. The first graders were far less likely to realize the inadequacy of the instructions than the second and third graders, who asked for more instructions before attempting to play the game. One-quarter of the first graders never asked a question, and most recognized that a problem existed only when they were asked to repeat the instructions or when they began to flounder in playing the game. It was because these children had failed to execute the instructions mentally that they did not notice the problem.

Do children realize that some things are harder to learn than others? Apparently, yes. Even 4-year-olds know that a long list of objects is harder to remember than a very short list and that success on the harder task is more likely if one makes a greater effort (Wellman, 1978; Wellman, Collins, & Glieberman, 1981). Many kindergartners and first graders know that it would be easier to relearn information (e.g., a list of birds) that one had forgotten than to learn it for the first time. Further, even young children realize that it is easier to recognize items than recall them (Speer & Flavell, 1979). Of course, younger children are not aware of some aspects of memory; for example, only older children appreciate that it is easier to retell a story in their own words than to repeat it verbatim (Kurtz & Borkowski, 1987).

Knowledge About Strategies

Children know a great deal more about using strategies to help in memorizing than we might think. They seem particularly sensitive to the value of external

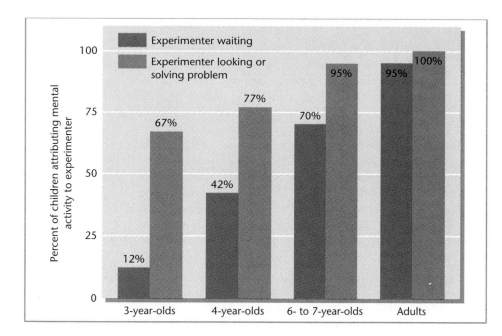

■ FIGURE 10-16
The child's notion of mental activity.
Although even very young children realize that a person who is looking at something or trying to solve a problem is thinking, they find it difficult to conceive that the person may also be thinking when she is just sitting and waiting. (*Source*: Flavell, Green, & Flavell, 1993)

aids to memory: for example, leaving your books where you will see them in the morning and writing notes to yourself. According to Lovett and Pillow (1995), even children who were not yet literate suggested the latter ploy! Children are also aware of the value of associations in memory (e.g., remembering your mother's age by adding 30 to your own) and develop an understanding of the use of "mental searches" for information (Wellman, 1977). As children grow older, their understanding of what strategy is appropriate increases (O'Sullivan, 1996), and sometimes they reveal a rather sophisticated understanding of memory strategies. When asked how she would remember a phone number, a third grader responded:

> "Say the number is 633-8854. Then what I'd do is—say that my number is 633, so I won't have to remember that, really. And then I would think, now I've got to remember 88. Now I'm 8 years old, so I can remember, say, my age two times. Then I say how old my brother is, and how old he was last year. And that's how I'd usually remember that phone number."

> "Is that how you would most often remember a phone number?" the experimenter asked.

> "Well, usually I write it down." (Kreutzer et al., 1975, p. 11)

Can we define the relationship between metacognition and performance on cognitive tasks? Unfortunately, this relationship is not straightforward (Miller & Weiss, 1981). Some situations, for example, are more likely to engage the child's metacognitive activity than others. Carr and Jessup (1995) found that first graders to third graders who understood which strategy they were using employed some strategies more correctly when solving math problems. If children understand that a strategy like rehearsal is useful, do they actually use it in situations in which it would help them remember things? And, conversely, can children articulate all the cognitive strategies and techniques they use? Can they tell how they solved an arithmetic problem and why they did it that way? Again, the answer is, not always. But even adults don't always apply strategies they "know" to be effective in situations where they would be useful. It would be unrealistic to expect the child always to act at an optimal level of cognitive functioning.

Metacognition and School Performance

One reason for developmentalists' intense interest in metacognition is the relevance of this issue to problems in the field of education such as poor reading ability. Poor readers have been shown to have metacognitive deficits in many aspects of reading (Baker, 1982). They are less likely than better readers to spend more time on difficult passages, less likely to review passages that they've learned least well, and less likely to adapt their reading methods to the demands and goals of the reading task (Brown, Bransford, Ferrara, & Campione, 1983). Moreover, they tend not to refocus their efforts and try new methods over time.

If many children are lacking the metacognitive skills necessary for effective school learning, can we modify school curricula to train them in these skills? Several investigators have initiated school-based programs to train children in the metacognitive skills involved in effective reading comprehension (Brown, 1994; Brown & Campione, 1990; Palincsar & Brown, 1984, 1987). These efforts, based on principles derived from Vygotsky's sociocognitive approach to learning (Belmont, 1989; Brown & Campione, 1996), involve a method of instruction called **reciprocal teaching,** in which a teacher and a small group of students take turns leading discussions about the content of a text passage (Heilman, Blair, & Rupley, 1994). With the goal of gradually encouraging the student to take responsibility for thinking while reading, the method uses comprehension and monitoring techniques to aid in reading. The teacher instructs students in using four cognitive strategies: predicting, questioning, summarizing, and clarifying. *Predicting* requires students to activate their background knowledge to predict what they will find in a text, what will happen next, how a situation will be resolved, and so on. In *questioning,* students learn what a good question is, how to ask questions, and how to read to answer questions. *Summarizing* requires students to identify the important content in a text passage. And in *clarifying,* students address things in the text that may be difficult to understand, such as new vocabulary and new concepts.

Using the reciprocal teaching method and enlisting the help of more skilled fellow students or specially trained classroom teachers, Palincsar and Brown (1984, 1987) found that the reading ability of seventh graders who were reading below grade level improved over the course of the training. The investigators also found that when students understood the benefits of the four cognitive strategies discussed, they were more likely to use them even without being prompted; this resulted in improvements not only in their reading but also in their studying and academic problem-solving skills. In fact, three months after the intervention, the reciprocal teaching group showed an average gain of 15 months in reading comprehension grade level.

reciprocal teaching A method of instruction in which a teacher and a small group of students take turns leading discussions of text passages and which makes use of four specific cognitive strategies: predicting, questioning, summarizing, and clarifying.

SUMMARY

The Information-Processing Approach

- The **information-processing approach** views the human mind as a system that processes information according to a set of logical rules and limitations similar to those with which a computer is programmed. Research using this perspective tries to describe and explain changes in the processes and strategies that lead to greater cognitive competence as children develop.
- The **store model** of human information processing proposes that information enters the system through the **sensory register** and is encoded and stored in either **short-term memory** or **long-term memory**. The **level of processing model** proposes that memory is based on the depth and intensity applied to the information stored rather than on the way or the location in which it is stored.

- The basic structures of the information-processing system do not change with development; instead, development occurs through changes in the efficiency of the processes applied to the information. Four important processes considered to be important in development are **encoding** and **representation, strategies, automatization,** and **generalization**. Most theorists also add an *executive function* that develops in order to monitor, select, and organize the processes that are applied to the information. In addition. knowledge plays a critical role in children's abilities to encode and represent information.

- Researchers using the information-processing perspective often use task analysis to examine children's incorrect answers for evidence of systematic errors. Although this approach is somewhat similar to Piaget's concern with error analysis, more precise task analyses lead to a more complete understanding of cognitive development.

- Through *microgenetic analysis*, Robert Siegler has shown that developmental change is more gradual, more variable, and "messier" than traditional views had suggested. This kind of analysis shows that it is not so much abstraction, as Piaget believed, as complexity that makes some tasks more difficult than others.

- In his **neo-Piagetian theory,** Robbie Case has elaborated the concept of executive function, proposing that children develop an **executive control structure** for each set of problems that they must solve. Each task in a series requires children to make new observations, use new knowledge in forming new strategies, and create a new structure for solving increasingly complex problems.

Steps in Information Processing: A Closer Look

- Although every child may perceive the same things in a particular environment, each child's attention may be concentrated on different aspects of that environment. Perception and attention are tightly interwoven, so that perception depends on how well we attend.

- Two main theories describe how experience affects perceptual learning. Piaget's **enrichment theory** proposed that children add information to existing schemata over repeated contacts with an object, elaborating or enriching a schema until they can distinguish among different objects. In contrast, Gibson proposed a **differentiation theory**, in which children gradually learn to attend to, identify, and make increasingly fine discriminations among objects and events.

- As children mature they can control and focus their attention for greater periods. In addition, older children are better than younger children at modifying their attention to fit task requirements. Older children also implement more systematic plans to focus their attention when gathering needed information, although younger children can make use of attention-focusing strategies when these are provided to them.

- Our **memory span**, or the amount of information we can hold in short-term memory, improves between infancy and adulthood. Some researchers suggest that this is due to the development of increased capacity based on changes in the brain. Case suggests that the difference is due to greater efficiency in the use of *executive processing space*, or to the development of better strategies for organizing or "chunking" the information.

- Children employ a wide range of cognitive activities, such as **prospective memory** strategies, that increase the likelihood that they will remember information at a later time. Some of these are external, such as taking notes, but many are mental strategies.

- The spontaneous use of verbal **rehearsal** as a memory strategy clearly increases with age. Although even young children can use rehearsal as a strategy if instructed to do so, they fail typically to generalize the strategy to new tasks.

Research suggests that this failure probably results not so much from a **mediation deficiency** or a **utilization deficiency** as from a **production deficiency** which may in turn spring from an interaction between the costs and benefits of using a particular strategy. As children become more adept at strategy use, costs decrease and benefits increase.

- Another strategy that improves with age is **semantic organization** in which children use categorization and hierarchical relationships to process and store information. As is the case with rehearsal, young children can successfully learn to use this strategy if instructed to do so; partnering, in the Vygotskian sense, can help them to do this.

- **Elaboration**, a strategy that involves adding to information to make it more meaningful and thus easier to remember, appears to aid children's retention. The fact that elaboration improves recall, despite the increase in informational load that it involves, underlines the importance of meaning in memory.

- **World knowledge**, or what a person has learned about the world from past experiences, influences what the person will understand and remember about a present event. Evidence for the role of world knowledge comes from studies indicating that experts remember more than novices, and that when memory tasks are presented in culturally familiar contexts, children in Western and non-Western cultures perform equally well.

- One important application of developmental research on memory is in children's eyewitness testimony. Recent studies suggest that children may not be reliable witnesses because they are susceptible to suggestions by others. However, children are more resistant to misleading questions when an interviewer is supportive and when they have been actively involved in the recalled event.

- Problem solving involves a high level of information processing because it mobilizes perception, attention, and memory to reach a solution. Although analogy is a powerful tool in problem solving, young children and even adults often have difficulty recognizing and using analogies. This may be in part because they fail to understand that the correspondence between relations that obtain within both source and target analogies is far more important than similarity of analogies' features. With guidance in drawing analogies, multiple examples of problem solution, surface similarity between the problems, and experience with the problem's domain, children can often succeed in reasoning by analogy.

- **Scripts** of routine activities provide children with basic outlines of how events occur in many familiar situations so that their behaviors in those situations become almost automatic. Children as young as 3 know about and use scripts to guide their actions. Children also use **mental maps** and physical maps to negotiate their way through their surroundings. Very young children, however, cannot draw a reasonable map of familiar territory even though they may be good at finding their way through it. Age interacts with the abilities to recognize objects that one has seen, as well as their original context, and to do this quickly.

- Children use deductive reasoning skills, such as **transitive inference** and **hierarchical categorization** to solve problems. Even young children may understand transitive inference, but they employ poor strategies when using it. One-year-olds can form categories based on the similarity between objects, and slightly older children can use labels to form hierarchical categories.

- Children's competence with numbers is based on five basic principles of counting that develop during the preschool years. Children also learn other strategies for counting and, over time, become able to distinguish between optional and necessary features of counting. Counting skills may to some degree reflect the number-naming system of a child's native language; it may be that systems that are inconsistent in reflecting the base-10 concept make it more difficult for children to learn to count above 10.

Metacognition

- **Metacognition** refers to the individual's knowledge and control of cognitive activities. Metacognitive knowledge includes the child's knowledge about the self, his theory of mind, and his knowledge about the task and about specific strategies. Metacognitive control involves using strategies to plan, monitor, check, and modify current strategies to maximize performance.

- Flavell and his associates have articulated a number of important understandings that preschool-age children have about their own minds as well as a number of limitations on such young children's thinking. In particular, young children have difficulty conceiving of continuous mental content. They are likely to say that a person sitting quietly is not "having thoughts."

- Although young children understand the importance of some task parameters for memory, even first graders are not good at monitoring their comprehension of information about a task. Young children are aware of the importance of memory strategies, and they are particularly sensitive to the use of external memory cues. However, older children have a more accurate and realistic view of their own memory abilities, and they are able to separate their own beliefs and desires from reality.

- Researchers who have applied the concept of metacognition to reading performance have found that better readers have more metacognitive knowledge. Some school-based interventions aimed at teaching metacognitive skills, such as **reciprocal teaching**, have resulted in improved reading, studying, and academic problem solving.

Intelligence

C H A P T E R 11

In this third chapter on cognitive functioning we take a slightly different perspective. In Chapters 9 and 10 we were concerned with cognition and cognitive processes in general; as a result, we were more concerned with similarities among people than with their differences. Now, however, we want to know how people use their cognitive skills and find ourselves confronting the fact that people differ in terms of the intelligence they demonstrate. Are such differences caused by genetic factors, by environmental influences, or by both? Are these differences found only among individuals, or are there group differences in intelligence? And are these differences permanent, or can they be changed? You may be familiar with the federally supported Head Start programs, begun in the 1960s and designed to give early, extra help in learning to children considered disadvantaged by virtue of lower socioeconomic status or membership in an ethnic minority group. Have these programs worked? Can they do better? In this chapter we ask in what way it is useful to measure individual differences in intelligence. For example, what may such measured differences predict about children's responses to enrichment programs like Head Start? What may they predict about peoples' behavior and performance in varying situations? How best can we devise and use such measures?

Although, as we have seen, developmentalists and other psychologists have become increasingly interested in the *processes* that contribute to intellectual functioning, the study and testing of intelligence has traditionally focused on its *products*, that is, on the specific knowledge and skills that people taking intelligence tests display. On the basis of such tests researchers have developed the **intelligence quotient (IQ)**, an index of the way a person performs on a standardized intelligence test relative to the way others her or his age perform. Much research on the development of intellectual abilities has come from the IQ testing tradition.

Although the term IQ is widely used, it is often misconstrued; some people think IQ is as innate and unchanging as long, slender fingers or "the family nose." In fact, IQ can vary over the life span, and it can be modified by experience. It depends, at least to some extent, on the type of test from which it is derived, on factors in the test taker's past experience, on his emotional state at the time of the test, and on other circumstances of the testing situation. In discussing intelligence and intelligence testing, it is important to remember that we can only *infer* intellectual capacity from the results of an IQ test; we cannot measure capacity directly. Although we assume that capacity and performance are correlated—this is the rationale for any test—we cannot prove it. This distinction between capacity and performance will be crucial to your understanding of much of the controversy about IQ and IQ testing that we review in this chapter.

intelligence quotient (IQ) An index of the way a person performs on a standardized intelligence test relative to the way others his or her age perform.

A LAY DEFINITION OF INTELLIGENCE

What do you think intelligence is? Most of us judge others' intelligence every day and consider ourselves quite competent to do so. Moreover, we make these judgments—in the classroom, the workplace, and in social situations—far more often than people take formal IQ tests. Robert Sternberg and his colleagues (Sternberg, Conway, Ketron, & Bernstein, 1981) were interested in what the average person believes about intelligence and the ways it is manifested. In a classic study, they asked people in New Haven, Connecticut, to list the behaviors they saw as characteristic of intelligence. A wide variety of people—commuters waiting in a train station, shoppers in supermarkets, people studying in the Yale library—described behaviors that the researchers ultimately classified into three primary categories: practical problem-solving ability, verbal ability, and social competence (Table 11-1). In the second phase of their study, Sternberg and his associates asked psychologists who specialized in the study of intelligence to examine the original participants' responses and to indicate the degree to which the psychologists themselves thought

TABLE 11-1 What Is Intelligence?	
Problem-solving ability	Reasoning logically; identifying connections among ideas; seeing all aspects of a problem
Verbal ability	Speaking articulately; reading widely; writing well
Social competence	Making fair judgments; showing sensitivity to other people's needs; admitting one's own mistakes

Source: Based on Sternberg, Conway, Ketron, & Bernstein, 1981.

the behaviors cited were characteristic of intelligence. Interestingly, these experts agreed that the same three components—problem-solving ability, verbal ability, and social competence—were central to intelligence.

If both laypeople and investigators who specialize in the study of intelligence are in basic agreement as to what composes intelligence, have we a definition? No, we have not. From a scientific point of view we need to specify more than just how intelligence appears to affect observable behavior. For example, we need to determine how we may best measure intelligence; how useful such measurement can be in predicting behavior, particularly academic performance; what factors affect intelligence; and to what degree these factors can be modified to improve intelligent behavior.

THEORIES OF INTELLIGENCE

In attempting to formulate useful theories of intelligence, scientists have focused on three primary issues: whether intelligence is unitary or multifaceted; whether it is determined by genetic or environmental factors; and whether it is more important in predicting academic success or other real-life factors. Although the first of these questions was hotly debated in the early years of the twentieth century, most theorists today would agree that intelligence is composed of many varied factors and skills. If intelligence were a generalized function, an intelligent child should perform well across a variety of intellectual tasks, but if intelligence is composed of independent factors or skills, the child might excel on some cognitive tasks and do poorly on others. In fact, the latter is what we generally find. As we will see, although David Wechsler (1958) defined intelligence as "the aggregate or global capacity of the individual to act purposefully, to think rationally and to deal effectively with his environment" (p. 7), the tests he devised—the Wechsler Scales, which we describe later—clearly tap a number of separate abilities.

Like the first question, the second question—whether intelligence is determined primarily by genetic factors or by environmental influences—has largely been answered, although the answer has led to more difficult questions. Generally agreeing that both heredity and the environment are implicated in the development of intelligence, investigators now confront such questions as to what extent each factor is involved; that is, is heredity more influential than the environment or the other way around, and to what degree may intelligence be changed by environmental conditions?

The third and last question is closest to the concerns of Sternberg's lay folk: How important is intelligence as measured by IQ tests in predicting how well people succeed in real-life situations? Is it useful primarily in predicting academic success? Or is it substantially linked to important life factors like obedience to the law, economic success, job stability, and general good health and adjustment? Throughout the chapter we will find some answers to the questions we've raised about intelligence, but we'll also raise more questions. Let's look now at several ways of understanding this elusive concept.

The Factor Analytic Approach

To many people it may seem obvious that intelligence has many components. Think, for example, of the molecular biologist who'd be lost without a calculator, or the auto mechanic who repairs today's computer-driven cars yet cannot write a simple letter, or the corporate lawyer who can't balance a checkbook. All these people are intelligent and competent in their chosen areas; can we then assume that they have more of certain kinds of intelligence than others? The answer is pretty much yes. As we will see, there is support for both views, namely, that a general factor accounts for intelligent functioning (Carroll, 1997) but the fact that people specialize and are "smarter" in some domains than others supports the multifaceted character of intelligence (Gardner, Krenchevsky, Sternberg, & Okagaki, 1994). The debate, however, is far from settled.

In the belief that intelligence is unitary, or a single ability, early investigators asserted that a general factor of ability permeates or connects all a person's multiple abilities. Researchers have tested this theory by performing **factor analysis,** a statistical procedure that can be used to determine which of several factors, or scores, are closely related to one another and relatively independent of other groups of factors or scores. An early factor analyst, Charles Spearman (1927), proposed that intelligence is composed of a **general factor (g)** and a number of **specific factors (s)**. Spearman regarded g as general mental energy, or ability that was involved in all cognitive tasks, and he saw s factors as factors unique to particular tasks. A person with a high g would be expected to do generally well on all tasks, and any variations in her performance on different tasks could be attributed to her possession of varying amounts of s factors.

Interest in g and the notion of a unitary concept of intelligence was challenged decades ago by Lewis Thurstone (1938), who proposed that seven primary skills comprise intelligence. Thurstone constructed tests to measure each of these skills: verbal meaning, perceptual speed, reasoning, number, rote memory, word fluency, and spatial visualization. Still later, J. P. Guilford (1966) postulated 120 separate factors of intelligence; to date he has devised tests for about 75 of these factors. Modern intelligence specialists like Carroll (1993, 1997) have confirmed the existence of a general factor of cognitive ability. It seems that people who do well on one kind of cognitive test (e.g., reading comprehension) are likely to do well on other such tests (e.g., listening comprehension or folding paper into specific shapes, as in Japanese *origami*). At the same time, intelligence researchers recognize that individuals vary in their competence across different domains. Carroll (1993, 1997), for example, proposes a hierarchically organized model involving both a general, g, factor and more narrowly defined abilities, such as vocabulary knowledge in one's native language, basic mathematic skills, or the ability to discriminate musical pitch. According to this model, children vary both in overall level of intellectual power and in how proficient they are in specific aspects of cognitive functioning. This "middle ground" position nicely characterizes the current view of modern approaches to the study of intelligence.

The Information-Processing Approach: Sternberg's Triarchic Theory

The interest of information-processing researchers in the processes involved in intellectual activity has led to a new approach to intelligence testing. As we will see, many skills that intelligence tests have attempted to measure, such as memory, general knowledge, use of analogy, and general comprehension, presaged tasks and cognitive skills that information-processing researchers examine. Information-processing specialists believe, however, that to truly understand intelligence, we must supplement traditional IQ tests with procedures that assess the components

factor analysis   A statistical procedure used to determine which of a number of factors or scores are both closely related to each other and relatively independent of other groups of factors or scores.

general factor (g)   General mental energy or ability that is involved in all cognitive tasks.

specific factors (s)   Factors that are unique to particular cognitive tasks.

of information processing, such as the strategies people use in performing intellectual tasks (Sternberg, 1985).

Sternberg's (1985, 1989) **triarchic theory of intelligence** is an important example of the new, information-processing approach. As this theory's name implies, it proposes three major components of intelligent behavior: information-processing skills, experience with a given task or situation, and ability to tailor one's behavior to the demands of a context. *Information-processing skills* are required to encode, combine, and compare varying kinds of information. These skills make use of a wide range of cognitive processes that the person may bring to bear on a variety of tasks, ranging from attention and memory to analogical reasoning and metacognition.

As an example of *experience*, the very important second component of Sternberg's model, consider a situation in which we ask two children to solve a long-division problem. Meilin has never studied long division; Kenji has studied it for several years. If Meilin solves the problem but Kenji fails to solve it, we will probably make quite different judgments about these children's relative intelligence (Sternberg, Wagner, & Okagaki, 1993). On the one hand, if a person who lacks experience in a particular area can use her experience in other areas to cope successfully with a novel task, we will judge her intelligent. On the other hand, if a person has had considerable experience with a task, he should be able to sail through it smoothly; if he does not, we will judge his performance as rather poor.

Context, Sternberg's third component, recognizes that intelligence cannot be separated from the sociocultural context in which it is exercised. Because people must function effectively in many different environments they must be able both to adapt to the requirements of an environment and to select and shape others to their own needs (Sternberg, 1985). With experience, an intelligent person can learn to adjust the ways he processes information in the different contexts in which he operates. Thus one dimension on which the intelligence of a particular behavior can be measured is its suitability and effectiveness in the context in which it is exercised (Ceci, 1990; Ceci & Hembrooke, 1995; Sternberg & Wagner, 1994; Vygotsky, 1978). For example, consider how the young Brazilian street vendors we discussed in Chapter 9 were able to adapt their functioning to the requirements of their trade. Societal norms in China offer another illustration of how culture can affect definitions of intelligence: In China, cooperation and group achievement are valued over individual prowess. In this culture, therefore, the person who helped all group members discover the right answer would be considered more intelligent than the person who jumped up quickly with that answer before anyone else. Historical views of intelligence have changed as well. For example, computer literacy is now a valued form of intelligence in industrialized societies, whereas planting and harvesting skills are still adaptive in the agrarian society.

According to Sternberg (Sternberg & Wagner, 1993) traditional IQ tests do a poor job of measuring the kind of intelligence that is important for success in the real world, as in an occupation or career. Sternberg asserts that for many real-world challenges, IQ is less critical than *tacit knowledge*, defined as "the practical know-how one needs for success on the job" (Sternberg & Wagner, 1993, p. 2). This kind of commonsense intelligence includes the ability to manage both one's own activity and that of other people. Practical knowledge of this sort is not often taught directly, as are academic skills, but is learned by observing others perform their daily routines. Table 11-2 displays examples of test items that Sternberg and his colleagues use to measure tacit knowledge, or the ability to make sensible choices, in two domains: academic psychology and college study. As you can see, this kind of assessment measure taps very different aspects of intelligence than those elicited by more traditional IQ tests. As Sternberg would predict, "tacit knowledge is relatively independent of IQ scores but this practical intelligence does predict job performance" (Sternberg, Wagner, Williams, & Horvath, 1995).

triarchic theory of intelligence A theory that proposes three major components of intelligent behavior: information-processing skills, experience with a particular situation, and ability to adapt to the demands of a context.

TABLE 11-2 Tacit Knowledge: Some Sample Test Questions

Academic Psychology

It is your second year as assistant professor in a prestigious psychology department. This past year you published two unrelated empirical articles in established journals. You don't, however, believe there is yet a research area that can be identified as your own. You believe yourself to be about as productive as others. The feedback about your first year of teaching has been generally good. You have yet to serve on a university committee. There is one graduate student who has chosen to work with you. You have no external source of funding, nor have you applied for any.

Your goals are to become one of the top people in your field and to get tenure in your department. The following is a list of things you are considering doing in the next two months. You obviously cannot do them all. Rate the importance of each by its priority as a means of reaching your goals.

____ Improve the quality of your teaching.

____ Write a grant proposal.

____ Begin a long-term research project that may lead to a major theoretical article.

____ Concentrate on recruiting more students.

____ Begin several related short-term research projects, each of which may lead to an empirical article.

____ Participate in a series of panel discussions to be shown on the local public television station.

College Student Life

You are enrolled in a large introductory lecture course. Requirements consist of three exams and a final. Please indicate how characteristic (on a scale of 1 to 5, from least to most characteristic) it would be of your behavior to spend time doing each of the following if your goal were to receive an A in the course.

____ Attend class regularly.

____ Attend optional weekly review sections with the teaching fellow.

____ Read assigned text chapters thoroughly.

____ Take comprehensive class notes.

____ Speak with the professor after class and during office hours.

Source: Adapted from Sternberg & Wagner, 1993.

Gardner's Theory of Multiple Intelligences

theory of multiple intelligences Gardner's multifactorial theory that proposes seven distinct types of intelligence.

Like Thurstone, Howard Gardner (1983, 1998; Gardner, Kornhaber, & Wake, 1996) has suggested separate types of intelligence but a much more limited set. Gardner's **theory of multiple intelligences,** a multifactorial approach to the notion of intelligence, proposes that there are linguistic, logical-mathematical, spatial, musical, bodily-kinesthetic, intrapersonal, and interpersonal types of intelligence (see Table 11-3). The first three types are clearly similar to the kinds of abilities assessed in traditional intelligence tests. The remaining four have been much less widely studied, yet, according to Gardner, they are equally important to human functioning. For example, interpersonal intelligence may be particularly important to a parent, a nurse's aide, a teacher; bodily-kinesthetic intelligence may be important to athletes, sports medicine professionals, and dancers.

Each type of intelligence, Gardner proposes, has its own developmental path and is guided by its own forms of perception, learning, and memory. For example, linguistic intelligence generally develops throughout years of educational experience, whereas bodily-kinesthetic intelligence may manifest itself quite early in life. In addition, Gardner suggests, a single individual can display different combinations of these intelligences. Albert Einstein, for instance, had high levels of both logical-mathematical and spatial intelligence; he demonstrated the latter particu-

TABLE 11-3 Gardner's Theory of Multiple Intelligences	
Type of Intelligence/Description	*Examples*
Linguistic: Sensitivity to word meanings; mastery of syntax; appreciation of the ways language can be used	Poet, teacher
Logical-mathematical: Understanding of objects, symbols, the actions that can be performed on them, and the interrelations among these actions; ability to operate in the abstract and to identify problems and seek explanations	Mathematician, scientist
Spatial: Accurate perception of visual world; ability to transform perceptions and mentally re-create visual experience; sensitivity to tension, balance, and composition; ability to detect similar patterns	Artist, engineer, chess player
Musical: Sensitivity to musical tones and phrases; ability to combine tones and phrases into larger rhythms and structures; awareness of music's emotional aspects	Musician, composer
Bodily-kinesthetic: Skilled and graceful use of one's body for expressive or goal-directed purposes; ability to handle objects skillfully	Dancer, athlete, actor
Intrapersonal: Access to one's own feeling life; ability to draw on one's emotions to guide and understand behavior	Novelist, psychotherapist, actor
Interpersonal: Ability to notice and distinguish among others' moods, temperaments, motives, and intentions; ability to act on this knowledge	Political or religious leader, parent, teacher, psychotherapist

Source: Gardner, 1983.

larly in his *gedanken experiments* (experiments performed in the mind only; from the German *Gedanke*, meaning "thought"), intensely visual experiences that led to many of his greatest insights. Gardner has been working on the development of tests to measure his seven areas of intelligence, and he has created educational programs to train children in all these areas (Gardner, 1993, 1998; Winn, 1990).

Gardner's theory has its critics. For example, based on a considerable body of literature that suggests a hierarchical organization of intellectual skills, some investigators have pointed out that Gardner's intelligences may not all be separate entities; that is, some may be subsets of others (e.g., Weinberg, 1989). Other authors dispute the kinds of evidence with which Gardner supports his theory. For example, Gardner claims that the **idiot savant** (from the French, meaning "learned idiot"), a mentally retarded person who typically shows a remarkable talent in a single area of knowledge, is proof that human beings possess many separate types of intelligence. Critics, however, note that idiot savants typically function at much lower levels than filmmakers would have us believe. According to these critics, the character of Raymond, played by Dustin Hoffman in the 1988 film *Rain Man*, was far more able to cope in the everyday world than most people with his difficulties. (According to Carson & Butcher, 1992, Raymond was an autistic savant.) Moreover, some writers point out, even the special, isolated skills of the idiot savant are more limited than those of true experts in an area (Gleitman, 1991; Hill, 1978). Finally, there have been relatively few efforts at rigorous evaluation of the theory, using standard assessment techniques, or to develop tests based directly on the theory (Benbow & Lubinski, 1996; Sternberg & Wagner, 1994).

idiot savant A mentally retarded or sometimes autistic person who shows a remarkable talent in one particular area of knowledge, such as the ability to predict day of the week and date many years in the future.

(a)

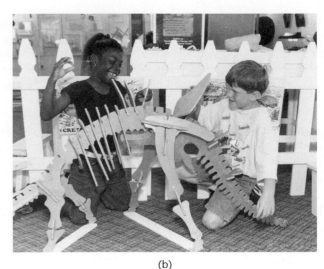

(b)

Playing an indigenous xylophone, (a) these Anang youngsters (in Nigeria) illustrate Howard Gardner's musical intelligence. The American children (b), in constructing their dinosaur model, demonstrate Gardner's spatial intelligence.

Despite these and other criticisms, Gardner's theory has caused psychologists and educators to broaden their understanding of intelligence and to recognize that existing intelligence tests tap a rather limited set of abilities. The theory also informs the continuing debate as to whether IQ tests can properly assess the intelligence of people of different nations, cultures, and subcultures. According to Gardner, different cultures value different intelligences. North Americans, for example, prize logical-mathematical intelligence, whereas the Anang of Nigeria place a high value on musical and bodily-kinesthetic intelligences. By the age of 5, an Anang child is expected to be able to sing hundreds of songs , play several musical instruments, and perform intricate dances. Researchers' increasing attention to abilities that have not traditionally been recognized as reflecting intelligence per se represents a promising new direction in intelligence research.

TESTING INTELLIGENCE: PURPOSES AND METHODS

Although, as we have seen, theorists and researchers are still working on a definition of intelligence, psychologists, educators, and others who face a very real need to measure intelligence in some way continue to study existing tests and to explore ways to improve their ability to provide us with useful information. Why do we need to measure intelligence? There are three primary purposes in intelligence testing: predicting academic performance, predicting performance on the job, and assessing general adjustment and health.

The earliest intelligence tests were designed to meet the first of these goals, and most existing intelligence tests, such as the Binet and Wechsler scales, predict performance in school better than they predict anything else. Predicting how well a person will succeed at a job is the second goal of intelligence testing, and according to Gottfredson (1997), such measures are the most powerful predictors of overall work performance. A third use of intelligence testing is in assessing people's general adjustment and health. The Binet and Wechsler tests that we discuss in this section can detect signs of neurological problems, mental retardation, and emotional distress in children as well as adults, and the Bayley scales and other infant tests are useful in assessing developmental progress in infants as well as neurological disorders or mental retardation.

Unfortunately, traditional tests do not make predictions as accurately for some groups in our society as for others. Many critics, for example, have pointed out that these tests often require knowledge that children with fewer advantages are unlikely to have and that, thus, traditional tests may unfairly classify some people as less intelligent than they actually are. For some years researchers have been attempting to develop what are known as **culture-fair tests,** that is, tests that attempt to exclude or minimize the presence of culturally biased content that could prejudice test takers' responses. The Raven Progressive Matrices test, which requires people to identify, distinguish, and match patterns of varying complexity, and the Kaufman test we discuss shortly are such tests.

We begin this section with a brief discussion of the Bayley scales and then examine the two most widely used sets of traditional tests—the Stanford-Binet tests and the Wechsler scales. Neither of these tests is culture-fair, and both tests measure the products of intelligence, that is, actual information. Next we examine the relatively new, Kaufman assessment measure, which attempts both to be culture-fair and to measure the processes by which people acquire information and solve problems. We then turn to the methodology of test construction, including the ways in which psychologists develop norms for test scoring and the kinds of procedures they adopt to ensure the validity and reliability of their tests. We conclude the section by considering the relative stability of intelligence as well as what factors may effect changes in intelligence over time.

Measuring Infant Intelligence

The **Bayley Scales of Infant Development** (Bayley, 1969, 1993) are probably the best known and most widely used of all infant development tests. Because these tests were designed to be used with the very young, their nonverbal test items were chosen for their ability to measure specific developmental milestones. The Bayley scales are used with infants and children between 1 and 3½ years of age, and they are generally used to assess children who are suspected to be at risk for abnormal development. For example, the Bayley *mental* scale includes such things as looking for a hidden object and naming pictures, whereas the *motor* scale includes such items as grasping ability and jumping skills. In a third part of the test, the examiner observes the child's behavior, making notes about such things as sociability and displays of fear.

The growing emphasis on the processes of intelligence has led some investigators to explore ways of assessing processing skills in the very young as well as to devise measures that are culture-fair. Box 11-1 discusses one of these newer tests, the Fagan Test of Infant Intelligence, which is capable not only of assessing process but of eliciting similar performance from infants of different cultures. The test also correlates well with measures of intelligence in children of older ages. Such predictive value not only can tell us something about the relative stability of intelligence, a topic we discuss later in this section, but also can serve a diagnostic purpose, indicating the need for special assistance for a child at risk for less than adequate cognitive development (Fagan, 1992).

The Stanford-Binet Test

Widely used by psychologists both in schools and in health settings, the **Stanford-Binet Test** is the modern version of the test devised in the early 1900s by Binet and Simon at the request of the Paris school system. At that time, because of new compulsory education laws, the city's schools were overcrowded, and school administrators wanted to identify children who were unable to learn in traditional classroom settings. Fearing that teachers might judge these children unfairly, school officials proposed giving them the opportunity for special education.

Binet and Simon, who believed that intelligence was malleable and that children's academic performance could be improved with special programs, took an innovative approach to the construction of their test (Binet, 1909/1973; Siegler, 1992). Critical of earlier psychologists, who had tried to assess intelligence by measuring simple sensory or motor responses, Binet and Simon asserted that to differentiate among individuals, one had to sample higher mental functions such as

culture-fair test A test that attempts to minimize cultural biases in content that might influence the test taker's responses.

Bayley Scales of Infant Development A set of nonverbal tests that measure specific developmental milestones and that are generally used with children who are thought to be at risk for abnormal development.

Stanford-Binet Test The modern version of the first major intelligence test; emphasizes verbal and mathematical skills.

Child Psychology in Action

The Fagan Test of Infant Intelligence

All mothers and fathers know that their babies are destined to win Nobel Prizes or to become great leaders, but is it really possible to test intelligence in very young children? The Fagan Test of Infant Intelligence was built on the notion that infants display their intelligence in their capable use of such processes as encoding the attributes of objects, seeing similarities and differences between objects, forming mental representations, and retrieving those representations (Fagan, 1992). Of course we cannot see an infant's selective attention to novelty, the primary basis of the Fagan test, but we can infer it from infants' behavior. Suppose, for example, that we show a 5-month-old a red diamond shape; next we show the infant a green diamond and a green square. Typically, the infant will show a preference for the square, indicating that she has processed the element of form from the original color-form compound and is now interested in the new form. (Remember our discussion in Chapter 5 of habituation and the infant's tendency to attend to what is novel in her environment.)

The Fagan test estimates an infant's intelligence by measuring the amount of time the infant spends looking at a new object compared with the time he spends looking at a familiar object (Fagan et al., 1991). Using a set of 20 photographs of human faces, arranged in pairs, the examiner begins by showing a baby one photograph of the first pair, for 20 seconds. Then the examiner pairs that photograph with its mate, showing the baby the two photos together for 5 seconds, and then again for another 5 seconds, this time reversing the two photos left to right (to avoid any tendency for the infant to "choose" one side). The score the infant receives is made up of the total time he spends looking at the novel photograph throughout presentation of all the 10 pairs.

To determine whether infants from different cultures would be equally adept at this task, Fagan and his colleagues administered the test to groups of European American and African American babies in the United States, a group of infants in Bahrain (bordering Saudi Arabia), and a group of infants in Kampala, Uganda. Within each cultural group, infants of four ages—6, 8, 18, and 24 months—were tested. The researchers found that there were practically no differences between the average scores obtained by the nearly 200 infants in these groups: European American babies scored an average of 58.8, African Americans 59.1, Bahrainians 59.6, and Ugandans 58.4. According to Fagan (1992), "The most parsimonious explanation for these findings is that differences in IQ between blacks and whites spring from differences in cultural exposure to information [that] influences scores in the domain of cultural knowledge tested" (p. 85).

Interestingly, among these infants, 54 percent of European Americans, 49 percent of African Americans, and 26 percent of Bahrainians were considered to be physically at risk—that is, they had spent five or more days in a neonatal intensive care unit. Moreover, among the Ugandan babies, 62 percent had mothers who were HIV positive. The presence of these potentially negative influences may add significance to the authors' statement that there appeared to be no differences in intelligence among the four groups.

Fagan and his associates (Fagan, 1984) have demonstrated the Fagan test's ability to predict intelligence scores at a later age, a quality that greatly enhances the potential usefulness of the test (see also text discussion of the predictive value of infant testing). In fact, a primary goal of the test is to differentiate normal from cognitively deficient infants. According to Fagan (1992), the test has been shown highly sensitive to later evidence of mental retardation, identifying some 85 percent of children who later obtained low IQ scores.

comprehension, reasoning, and judgment. They developed an array of intellectual tasks involving such things as the ability to attend to something and the ability to recognize logical absurdities. They also included tests of skills taught in school, such as recalling details of a story read aloud, naming the days of the week, and counting coins. In addition, they recognized and built into their test the chronology of children's learning, that is, the fact that as children grow they become able to solve increasingly complex problems (Siegler, 1992). You'll recall that it was when Piaget worked in Binet's laboratory that he first began to think in terms of children's gradual development of cognitive skills.

In refining their tests, Binet and Simon administered large numbers of items to groups of children whose teachers had identified them as either bright or dull, retaining items that discriminated between these two groups. In later revisions, based on the criterion that any test item must effectively sort children by age, Binet and Simon selected items to reflect children's competence at different age levels. For example, they assumed that the average 6-year-old's knowledge was accurately reflected by a test item on which 60 percent of 6-year-olds, substantially fewer 5-year-olds, and significantly more 7-year-olds were successful.

Binet originated the concept of **mental age,** which is an index of a child's actual performance level as contrasted with her true age. Thus, if a 6-year-old child gets as many items correct as the average 7-year-old, the 6-year-old's mental age is 7; she performs as well as a child 7 years old. The mental age concept was later superseded by the intelligence quotient, for which the German psychologist William Stern devised the following formula:

$$IQ = \frac{MA}{CA} \times 100,$$

where IQ equals mental age (MA) divided by chronological age (CA), multiplied by 100. Thus, if a child's mental age equaled her chronological age, she would be performing like an average child of her true age, and her IQ would be 100. If her performance were superior to other children her age, her IQ would be above 100: If it were inferior, her IQ would be less than 100.

Today's Stanford-Binet test, a revision of the Binet-Simon measure, has been designed to include items that tap other than language and math skills, such as putting together jigsaw puzzles and making designs with blocks, but the extent to which academic experience influences the latter types of tasks is not completely clear. As we will see next, the Wechsler scales have placed more emphasis on tests that assess so-called performance skills.

The Wechsler Scales

The **Wechsler Intelligence Scales,** developed by David Wechsler (1952, 1958), include the Wechsler Adult Intelligence Scale (WAIS), the Wechsler Intelligence Scale for Children (WISC), and the Wechsler Preschool and Primary Scale of Intelligence (WPPSI). Although these tests show the influence of Binet's tests, Wechsler designed them specifically to yield separate verbal and performance IQ scores as well as a combined, full-scale IQ score. The descriptions of the WISC subtests shown in Table 11-4 highlight that performance items are somewhat less likely to be influenced by formal education or cultural factors. As a result, a child who has a specific learning problem such as a difficulty with language may do quite well on these items, even if he performs poorly on the verbal subtests. Children who come from homes that lack some of the advantages other children enjoy may also be more successful on these performance tests.

Rather than use mental age as a basis for estimating intelligence, Wechsler created the **deviation IQ,** which is a number that reflects the higher, lower, or similar position of the test taker's score in relation to the score obtained by an average child of the test taker's age. How is this different from the concept of mental age? The deviation IQ scoring system, which like the Binet IQ takes 100 as an average score, is based on extensive testing of people of different ages in many parts of the United States and on the statistical computation of mean scores for each age group. In computing these average scores, psychologists use a statistic called the *standard deviation* to signal the extent to which nonaverage scores deviate from the norm. As a result, an individual's score may be at the mean, or it may be one or more standard deviations above or below the mean.

The Kaufman Assessment Battery for Children

The first test to include a specific focus on processing skills, the **Kaufman Assessment Battery for Children (K-ABC),** is based directly on cognitive development research (Kaufman & Kaufman, 1983). The test measures several types of information-processing skills grouped into two categories: *sequential processing* (solving problems in a step-by-step fashion) and *simultaneous processing* (examining and integrating a wide variety of materials in the solution of a problem). The test also assesses achievement in academic subjects, like vocabulary and arithmetic, yet

mental age An index of a child's actual performance on an intelligence test as compared with his true age.

Wechsler Intelligence Scales Three intelligence tests for infants, children, and adults that yield separate scores for verbal and performance IQ as well as a combined IQ score.

deviation IQ An IQ score that indicates the extent to which a person's performance on a test deviates from age-mates' average performance.

Kaufman Assessment Battery for Children (K-ABC) An intelligence test designed to measure several types of information-processing skills as well as achievement in some academic subjects.

TABLE 11-4 The Wechsler Intelligence Scale for Children (WISC)*

Subtest/Description	Some Examples	Skills Thought to Tap
Verbal Scale		
General Information: Questions that ask for information most children will have	Where does the sun rise? How many weeks are there in a year?	Factual knowledge; long-term memory; intellectual interest
General comprehension: Questions that ask child to explain why certain actions or practices are desirable	Why should we not waste fuel? What should you do if you lose a friend's toy?	Judgment; social judgment
Arithmetic: Child is asked to perform arithmetic operations ranging from simple counting to more involved mental computation and reasoning		Mathematic skills; problem solving; concentration
Similarities: Child is asked to tell how paired words are alike	How are a shoe and a slipper alike? How are a boat and a car alike?	Concept formation; categorization
Vocabulary: Child is asked to define a list of increasingly difficult words		Concept formation; long-term memory; vocabulary
Digit span: Examiner says several series of numbers, each longer than the preceding one, and child must repeat them in either the same or reverse order		Attention; short-term memory
Performace Scale		
Picture completion: Child must tell which part is missing in each of 12 pictures of common objects	A car with a wheel missing A rabbit with an ear missing	Visual organization; concentration
Picture arrangement: Child must arrange sets of cartoon-type pictures so that they tell a story		Visual organization; reasoning; knowledge of scripts
Block design: Child must reproduce pictured red and white designs using a set of wooden blocks whose sides are red, white, or half red and half white		Visual-motor coordination; concept formation; pattern recognition; spatial ability
Object assembly: Child must assemble jigsaw-like parts into whole object	A chair A foot	Visual-motor coordination
Coding: Child must match a series of symbols with numbers on the basis of a code: □/2, </5, etc.		Visual-motor coordination; concentration; motor speed
Mazes: Child must trace correct route from a starting point to home in a series of mazes		Spatial ability; memory; concentration

*Examples are similar but not identical to actual questions on the WISC.

its test items (many nonverbal) are intended to be culture-fair. In fact, the designers of this test used a wide and representative sample of many American cultural and socioeconomic groups in establishing norms for the test.

An interesting innovation is that if a child fails early items on a subscale, K-ABC examiners teach the child how to complete these items before they administer the rest of the subtest. According to the designers of the test, this ensures that no child who is capable of learning an unfamiliar task receives a failing score on it. The Kaufman test has been criticized for offering only a limited range of items that tap information-processing functions, such as short-term memory (Conoley, 1990;

Sternberg, 1985). Critics have argued that the test should focus more on problem-solving strategies, a central component of the information-processing approach to intelligence. Nevertheless, the Kaufman test is a creative approach to the measurement of intelligence that applies important insights from the information-processing approach to the study of intelligence and intelligence testing.

Constructing Measures of Intelligence

Devising an intelligence test depends first and foremost on the model of intelligence held by the **psychometrician,** or test constructor. For example, if the model emphasizes the products of intelligence, the test will include many subtests that ask for specific information. A test based on the information-processing model, on the other hand, will include items designed to tap the strategies by which a person attempts to resolve a problem. Certain goals and principles, however, are shared by all constructors of intelligence tests, and it is to these issues that we now turn. We look first at how norms for a test are established and at how the test is standardized; then we consider the important issues of establishing a test's validity and reliability.

Development of Norms and Standards

A person's performance on an intelligence test is always described by his position relative to the performance on the same test of others in a specified group; the person is thus considered either average, above average, or below average in relation to other group members. The establishment of **test norms,** which are values or sets of values that describe the typical test performance of a specific group of people, gives us the basis for this description of a single individual's test performance.

As you may imagine, determining the critical similarities among the members of a comparison group is fundamental to establishing the norms for a particular test. Age is probably the single most important dimension on which we base similarity of comparison group members, and it is a particularly critical factor when setting norms for children's test performance. Although children generally improve their test performance as they grow older, each year giving more correct answers than they did the year before, their position relative to other children of their age continues to be the significant factor in the evaluation of their intellectual development.

Psychometricians do not agree on whether comparison groups in intelligence testing should be equated on such factors as level of education, socioeconomic class, or gender. Nevertheless, in evaluating test performance we should always consider how closely the attributes and experiences of the person being tested approximate those of the normative group. For example, it would be inappropriate to use the same set of norms in evaluating the performance of children raised in an isolated New Guinea tribe without access to formal schooling as the set we might use to evaluate the performance of white, middle-class North American children. And as we will discuss later, norms for the latter group may not be appropriate even for the children of minority groups within North America.

The conditions under which a given test is administered may vary widely; in different locations and at different times, the examiners, the setting, and the examinees themselves may vary. Thus it is extremely important that we subject a test to **standardization,** in which test constructors attempt to ensure that on every testing occasion the procedures that examiners follow, the instructions they give to examinees, and test scoring are identical.

Ascertaining Validity and Reliability

Psychometricians have two ways of ensuring the quality of a test. First, they ascertain its **validity;** that is, they determine whether the test actually measures what it claims to measure. For example, does a test of the ability to recognize and form analogies actually measure this capacity? In establishing the validity of an intelligence test, psychometricians most often correlate performance on the test with

---

psychometrician A psychologist who specializes in the construction and use of tests designed to measure various psychological constructs such as intelligence, motivation, achievement orientation, and personality characteristics.

test norm Values or sets of values that describe the typical performance of a specific group of people.

standardization The process by which test constructors ensure that testing procedures, instructions, and scoring are identical on every testing occasion.

validity The extent to which a test actually measures what it claims to measure.

some criterion measure that is believed to reflect the capacity being tested. The most frequently used criteria are achievement test scores, grades in school, teachers' ratings of cognitive ability, and performance on other intelligence tests. These criteria restrict not only the range of skills that can be tested but also the psychometrician's view of what constitutes intelligent behavior. It comes as no surprise that intelligence tests are much more successful in predicting school performance than in predicting things like unusual creativity or adaptive ability in social situations. Even within school performance, intelligence test scores are more closely related to mathematical problem solving and reading comprehension than to expressed ability in drama, art, or music.

The second measure of test quality is **reliability**—the extent to which a test yields consistent results over time or administrations. To be useful, a test's scores must not fluctuate unpredictably from one administration to another; thus we can assess reliability by correlating the test scores of the same people on repeated administrations. We can also assess internal consistency by taking the scores from a single administration and correlating the scores on even-numbered items with the scores on items that are odd numbered.

reliability The degree to which a test yields consistent results over successive administrations.

Stability of Measured Intelligence

Is intelligence an absolute quality that remains stable over time, or can it change as a function of experience? To answer this question we need to understand the limitations of intelligence measures. At least in part because studies of IQ stability have traditionally used tests like the Binet and Wechsler scales, which focus on the products of intelligence and measure current performance, researchers have generally found that IQ scores do fluctuate. As investigators have begun to use newer tests that focus on the processes of intelligent functioning, however, the evidence for stability has been mounting.

The stability issue has several interesting aspects. The first and most obvious is the question of whether an *individual's* level of intellectual functioning remains essentially the same over time. In the present section, our concern with this question will lead us to review a considerable body of research that has generally taken the form of longitudinal studies in which children have been tested repeatedly over long periods. In concluding the section, we will address a second, corollary question, that of whether average intelligence levels within a population are stable across time.

As we will see, the evidence to date suggests that there is both stability and change in intellectual functioning over time. This finding highlights a third question: Can intelligence be changed by purposeful effort and if so, how? Throughout the rest of the chapter, we explore the many ramifications of this important issue.

Predictive Value of Infant Testing

Most of our information on the consistency of performance on intelligence tests derives from longitudinal studies in which children—in some cases as young as 1 month old—have been repeatedly tested over time. Some of these studies are the Berkeley Guidance Study, the Berkeley Growth Study, and the Fels Longitudinal Study. The Berkeley studies followed one group of participants for more than 50 years (from the late 1920s to the 1980s). Because the Fels study enrolled individuals yearly, it followed different groups of people for different periods of time—for example, some for 20 years, some for 30 years. These and other early research studies found no significant relationship between intelligence test scores attained in infancy and later in childhood or even adulthood (Figure 11-1; see also Honzik, 1983; Lewis, 1983; McCall, Hogarty, & Hurlburt, 1972).

It is important to note, however, that the early studies compared infants' performance on tasks involving primarily sensorimotor skills, like reaching and grasping an object or visually following a moving object, with the performance of the same children at later ages on tasks that tapped problem-solving abilities and verbal skills. It may be that these two kinds of tasks correlated little, if at all. Early

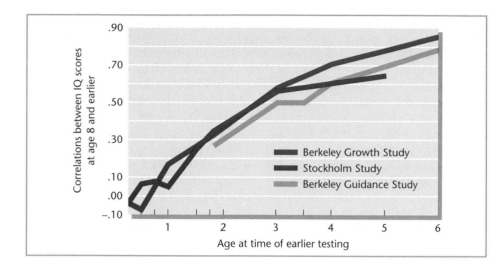

■ **FIGURE 11-1**
Predicting IQ scores.
The height of each curve
represents the degree to which
children's early intelligence test
scores were correlated with their
Stanford-Binet IQ scores when
they were 8 years old. The longer
the time lapse between earlier
and later testing, the less
predictive value the earlier score
had. Notice that in the Berkeley
Growth and Stockholm studies
the earliest scores were actually
negatively correlated with later
ones. (*Source*: Honzik, 1976,
1983)

researchers also found that scores toddlers (about 18 months old) achieved on the kinds of tasks that appear on older children's tests were much more predictive of later performance (Golden & Birns, 1983; Honzik, 1983).

In recent years, however, research using quite different measures has shown that infant test scores may indeed predict later childhood performance (e.g., Rose & Feldman, 1995). Beginning in the 1980s, several investigators attempted to devise new ways of measuring infant intelligence and predicting children's later intellectual performance. Reflecting the rising interest in the information-processing approach to intelligence, these researchers have focused on some of the attentional processes that we described in Chapter 5, particularly habituation and recovery. Investigators have focused on the infant's ability to habituate—recall that this means to discontinue attending to a stimulus after several presentations—interpreting this behavior as the ability to familiarize oneself quickly with new material. In addition, studying the process called **recovery**, researchers have measured infants' ability to recognize a totally new stimulus as novel and to direct their attention to it in preference to a stimulus with which they're already familiar.

What kinds of correlations are found between measures of infant attentional processes and later IQ scores? As we saw in Box 11-1, Joseph Fagan and his colleagues found significant correlations between infants' visual preferences at 7 months of age and their later cognitive development. They tested 36 infants for their preference for looking at a novel or a familiar visual stimulus and then retested the same children later at 3 and 5 years on intellectual functioning. These researchers found that the more the 7-month-olds had indicated a preference for novel stimuli, the higher these children's later IQ scores were. Interestingly, the same kinds of attentional measures enabled Montie and Fagan (1988) to predict lowered IQ scores at 3 years of age among infants who were at risk because of such conditions as prematurity or maternal diabetes. Bornstein and Sigman (1986) also found at least moderate correlations between attentional measures in infants 2 to 7 months of age and the scores these children achieved on traditional tests of intelligence at ages 3 to 6. Rose, Feldman, Wallach, and McCarton (1989) reported that infant preference for novelty was a better predictor of later intelligence scores than were standard infant intelligence measures such as the Bayley test, and DiLalla et al. (1990) have offered evidence to suggest that infant novelty preferences as well as other measures of infant visual processing are related to estimates of adult intelligence.

In recent work, Rose and Feldman (1995) have successfully predicted IQ scores in middle childhood on the basis of two measures in infancy: *visual recognition memory* and *cross-modal transfer*. Using the first of these measures, the researchers showed 7-month-old infants such stimuli as pictures of faces, abstract patterns, and three-dimensional geometric forms. Each pair of stimuli consisted of one that

recovery The ability to recognize a new stimulus as novel and to direct attention to it in preference to a familiar stimulus.

was familiar and one that was novel, and the researchers measured the attention the babies paid to each member of the pair. Measuring cross-modal transfer, the investigators allowed infants to feel and manipulate something that they couldn't see (hidden by a screen) and then showed them a pair of stimuli that included the item the babies had felt (familiar stimulus) and one they had had no contact with (unfamiliar), again measuring the attention they paid to each stimulus. Both infant measures of time spent attending to the novel stimulus were significantly and positively correlated with the children's WISC IQ scores at 11 years of age, as well as with such specific cognitive skills as verbal and spatial ability and perceptual speed.

According to Rose and Feldman, tests of perceptual speed and speeded tests of verbal and spatial abilities that were administered to 11-year-olds, showed the highest correlations with information-processing measures in infants. This suggested to the researchers that *speed of processing* is a crucial component of cognitive advancement or even of intelligence. Citing McCall and Mash (1994), however, these researchers draw attention to the possibility that *inhibition* may be equally important; that is, to devote attention to a novel stimulus, the infant must be able to inhibit her attention to familiar—and thus irrelevant—stimuli. The ability to concentrate one's attention on a task at hand is another, more familiar description of this capacity.

Changes in Children's IQ Over Time

The correlations between infant testing and later measures of intelligence, though often significant, are moderate, and there is room for change as a child develops (Bornstein & Sigman, 1986). Although we may be tempted to conclude that early individual differences in habituation and response to novelty reflect genetic predispositions, it's important to recognize that a child's environment has the opportunity to affect her attentional processing probably from birth. In fact, one study indicated that attentional processing in 5-month-olds was related to the infants' mothers' responsivity (Bornstein & Tamis, 1986). Another study found a correlation between 4-month-olds' attention to the environment and the infants' mothers' encouragement of such attention. Specific parental behaviors may well have a significant impact on infant intelligence.

What does happen as children grow older? To what degree is the child likely to demonstrate a change in his IQ score over time? Most research suggests that from the middle years of childhood onward, intelligence tests are fairly reliable predictors of later performance on such tests. For example, Honzik, MacFarlane, and Allen (1948) found a correlation of .70 between children's IQs at ages 8 and 18. Note, however, that these researchers studied 250 children; the larger the sample studied, the higher a correlation may be. There is also evidence of considerable variability in children's IQs. Many of the 140 children tested in the Fels study, mentioned earlier, shifted considerably upward in IQ scores between the ages of 2½ and 17 (McCall, Appelbaum, & Hogarty, 1973): One of every three children scored higher by some 30 points, and one in seven shifted upward more than 40 points. On rare occasions, individuals have improved their IQ performance as much as 74 points. Investigators have also observed that high-IQ children are likely to show greater amounts of change than low-IQ children.

Some of the variability demonstrated in IQ scores reflects the fact that different children develop cognitively at different rates of speed, just as they experience physical growth in spurts and at different ages (Chapter 6). These variations in cognitive development affect the reliability of IQ scores. Interestingly, studies suggest that most changes in IQ are most likely to occur at the ages of 6 and 10. Some researchers have proposed that a change at the age of 6 may be associated with the shift about that age to higher levels of abstract reasoning and conceptual ability that Piaget and his followers have described. Reasons for the shift at the age of 10 are less clear.

Stressful life events such as parental divorce or death or a geographical move or shift in schools can cause at least temporary disruptions in cognitive performance.

Indeed, children who show the most dramatic changes in IQ over time have often experienced major changes in their life circumstances, such as foster home placement or a serious illness (Honzik, 1983).

As we said at the beginning of this section, IQ scores for groups of people are of course based on individual scores, and if the latter change, we may expect the former to change as well. We've seen that intelligence is relatively stable over time but that IQ scores can and do shift. The records for North Americans as a population suggest that average IQ increased by nearly 14 points between 1932 and 1978 (Flynn, 1984). What might be the cause of this rise in mean IQ among U.S. people? We'll look for some answers to this question in the next two sections of the chapter.

WHY DO PEOPLE DIFFER IN MEASURED INTELLIGENCE?

Closely related to the question of the stability of intelligence is one of the most controversial issues in the study of human intellectual functioning: how individual differences in intelligence develop. The modern controversy on this issue was touched off nearly 30 years ago when educational psychologist Arthur Jensen (1969) claimed that as much as 80 percent of differences in IQ among people were attributable to genetic, or inherited factors, and only a small proportion of differences to social-environmental factors. What was so shocking about Jensen's 1969 paper was his charge that the differences he recorded between IQ scores attained by African Americans and European Americans were attributable to inheritance, and that they demonstrated that blacks were inherently less intelligent than whites.

Undoubtedly individuals differ in level of intelligence; few would argue this point. But Jensen was in effect consigning an entire group to a lower level of functioning and, on top of that, he was asserting that these differences were immutable. Although some have supported Jensen's view, many more theorists and researchers have opposed it, in general asserting that social and environmental factors have as much influence on intelligence as inherited factors. Those taking the latter view have been among the strongest advocates of culture-fair testing to offer those children whose environments have not given them optimal nurturing a fair chance to demonstrate their abilities.

In this section we review some of the research on the side of heredity and then examine the evidence for the role of social and environmental factors in intelligence. Because the issue of the effects of racial, ethnic, and social-class differences on intelligence is so important we have reserved much of our discussion of this topic for the next major section of the chapter.

How Much of Intelligence Is Inherited?

As we saw in our Chapter 3 discussions of the relative roles of heredity and environment in the development of many human characteristics, there is considerable support for the importance of heredity in intelligence. Most estimates of the heritability of intelligence—that is, the proportion of the variability in intelligence that's attributable to genetic factors—have supported a figure of about 40 to 50 percent for middle-class European Americans (McGue & Bouchard, 1987; Plomin, 1989, 1990a; Plomin & Petrill, 1997). This suggests that the remaining 50 to 60 percent of the variability is a function of environmental factors, both social (family, peers, school) and nonsocial (dietary and disease factors, toxins, pollutants). For many educated laypeople today these data have a certain appeal; common sense suggests that probably both heredity and environment play a role in all human characteristics.

Many psychologists disagree with this more or less 50-50 proposition, however. Some, like Stephen Ceci (1990), hold that the estimates of the heritability of intelligence are too high; others, like Jensen, insist that they are too low. The 1994 publication of Richard Herrnstein and Charles Murray's *The Bell Curve,* which argued that intelligence is in part genetically based, rekindled this argument among students of intelligence. (The book's title refers to the bell-shaped curve that, for psychometricians, represents the tendency of scores or measures of a given characteristic to cluster in the middle of a range, with extreme highs and lows at either end). The book also aroused the concern of many laypeople who, to at least some degree led by the media, understood the book not only to attribute most of the variability in IQ to inheritance but to suggest that IQ is relatively unchangeable.

In an effort to correct these and other misunderstandings of theory and research on intelligence, a number of investigators endeavored, in a special issue of the journal *Intelligence,* both to state the "mainstream" view of the issues surrounding this area of study and to encourage researchers in the field to become more sensitive to and concerned with the practical implications of their work (Gottfredson, 1997). Among the views expressed in this journal issue was that although most estimates of the heritability of intelligence allot greater strength to genetic than environmental factors, this does not mean that intelligence is not affected by the environment.

Although present knowledge suggests that intelligence stabilizes during childhood and changes little from then on, this is not proof that people are born with immutable levels of intelligence. As we will see in this chapter, a considerable body of research has shown that environmental manipulations are indeed capable of creating changes in measured intelligence. The problem is that while some studies of early cognitive intervention have found early gains in measured intelligence maintained through adolescence (Lazar & Darlington, 1982; Ramey, Campbell, & Blair, in press), others, such as those of Head Start programs, have found that early gains tended to disappear by the second year in school (McKey et al., 1985). Clearly, we must determine why some studies have shown permanent gains but others unstable ones.

It is important also to remember that the measures of intelligence used in many of the studies that we discuss in this chapter are based on traditional views of intellectual functioning and do not necessarily reflect some of the more recent thinking about multiple views of intelligence. In addition, you should keep in mind that behavior genetic research gathers information on what is true *on average;* such data do not tell us anything about the capacities of a particular individual. Finally, as Gottfredson (1997) points out, genetic research necessarily describes "what is," not what can or should be.

Jensen's Types of Learning

Arthur Jensen (1969, 1993), who has been the most articulate exponent of the genetic position, proposes two types of learning, both inherited but each clearly distinct from the other. **Associative learning** (*level I* learning) involves short-term memory, rote learning, attention, and simple associative skills. For example, we might ask a child to look at a group of familiar objects and then later to recall these objects or to memorize a list of numbers and then to recall them. **Cognitive learning** (*level II* learning) involves abstract thinking, symbolic processes, conceptual learning, and the use of language in problem solving. An example of cognitive learning is the ability to answer questions like the following:

What should be the next number in the following series?
2, 3, 5, 8, 12, 17, . . .
How are an apple and a banana alike?

Most intelligence tests measure predominantly cognitive abilities, although they may include a subtest or two of associative ability. According to Jensen, only cognitive intelligence as measured by IQ tests predicts school achievement. Further, Jensen suggests that associative abilities are equally distributed across all people but that cognitive abilities are more concentrated in middle-class and European

associative learning
According to Jensen, lower-level learning tapped in tests of such things as short-term memorization and recall, attention, rote learning, and simple associative skills. Also called *level I* learning.

cognitive learning
According to Jensen, higher-level learning tapped in tests of such things as abstract thinking, the use of symbolic processes, conceptual learning, and the use of language in problem solving. Also called *level II* learning.

American groups than in working-class or African American groups. In other words, Jensen is saying that we all have associative learning abilities but that the genes or gene patterns responsible for cognitive learning abilities have somehow been restricted to certain ethnic and racial groups. And, some scholars claim, because people tend to marry within their own groups, the differences between cognitive learning abilities across populations, as measured in IQ tests, will tend to increase over time (Herrnstein, 1971; Herrnstein & Murray, 1994).

Williams and Ceci (1997) have challenged this argument by showing that the trend is in the opposite direction; that is, that the IQ gap between racial groups has been closing. Moreover, as we discuss later in the chapter, the social-class gap in intellectual performance has also been narrowing, perhaps reflecting in part the upward movement of African Americans and other minority groups. Further complicating these issues is the fact that, at least in the United States and other highly multicultural nations, many people have mixed ancestries. Clearly, this issue is far from settled, and we will need to revisit it repeatedly as our society changes and opportunities and challenges for different groups shift.

Culture and Inheritance

In evaluating the findings of studies of intelligence, it is important to distinguish between estimates of heritability that are based on members of a particular group and estimates that are based on a broader sample of people. When we estimate heritability based on people within a group, our estimates are going to be higher because these people, by definition, share some characteristics that may be both inherited and environmental. Let's take as an example the issue of height, a physical characteristic of human beings that, when children have good nutrition and are immunized against serious diseases, is essentially the result of inheritance (Kagan, 1969). Because the majority of North Americans are well nourished, the genes associated with height express themselves fairly directly in the actual height of the American child. However, height is *not* primarily determined by inheritance in cultures where extremely adverse health and/or nutritional factors overwhelm and thus minimize genetic contributions to physical stature. Most starving children, if they live to adulthood, remain small of stature, regardless of the typical height of the ethnic-racial groups to which they belong. The Tutsi (Watusi) of central Africa are a very tall people. How do you suppose a Tutsi child, if she were undernourished and seriously ill as an infant, might as an adult compare in height with the average adult in her society?

Because heritability may contribute to height differentially in two different cultures, it would be inappropriate to apply the same heritability indexes to both groups. In similar fashion, many argue, it is inappropriate to use estimates of the heritability of intelligence obtained from one group in interpreting findings based on the study of another group. Thus heritability measures for middle-class white North American families with reasonably similar backgrounds and life circumstances may be quite different from such measures for minority or working-class groups whose circumstances may differ dramatically from those of the former group. Genes depend on the environment for their expression. Poor nutrition, disease, and stress due to myriad factors—for example, economic deprivation, overcrowded living quarters, homelessness, lack of sleep, lack of adequate or appropriate clothing, neglect, abuse—may, like poor nutrition in our example of height, overwhelm and thus minimize the genetic contribution to intelligence and intellectual performance (Garcia Coll, 1990; Goldstein, 1990; Huston, McLloyd, & Garcia Coll, 1994). On this view, the heritability estimates calculated for middle-class European American families simply do not apply to individuals from other, less advantaged groups.

The Malleability of Inherited Characteristics

Whatever the precise contribution of genetic inheritance in IQ, clearly the environment affects some significant portion of the child's developing intellectual skills.

When we consider whether intelligence levels can be changed, we must keep in mind that many investigators in the field of intelligence whose work has been widely publicized are scientists who seek to describe and explain what is real at a particular point in time and in a particular group of people. Such researchers have not traditionally been concerned with the implications of their findings for such issues as whether or in what way these findings illuminate the situation of a particular individual or whether changing the situation they have identified is desirable or feasible. According to Carroll (1997), an estimate of heritability is a statistic that applies to a specific population (which is the focus of a particular study); it does not apply to individual members of that population. Finding evidence for genetic influence in such a population does not suggest that differences among individuals are unchangeable any more than finding that training can produce impressive skills contradicts the notion of genetic influence in the population (Plomin & Petrill, 1997). Thus, an estimate that heritability accounts for 50 percent of the variation in intelligence (or 40 or 80 percent) applies *on the average*; in a particular individual who for one reason or another has suffered disadvantages in opportunities to learn, the effect of the environment might be large and the genetic influence small (Carroll, 1997).

Let us consider some other kinds of developmental differences that we know to be influenced by genetic factors, such as blindness and deafness. The fact that these conditions are often genetically induced hasn't interfered with the ability of special education programs to help affected children. And as we noted earlier in this chapter, probably the most persuasive evidence that the black-white IQ difference has a strong environmental component is that this very difference has been declining over the last several decades (Brody, 1992; Neisser et al., 1995). Scores on tests of achievement in mathematics and reading show similar trends (Williams & Ceci, 1997). Over a period of about 15 years, (from the early 1970s to the late 1980s) the scores of black students narrowed the gap with those of white students by between a third to a half (Figure 11-2). This convergence of test scores stopped in the late 1980s, but although data for the early 1990s suggest a slight increase in the divergence between black and white students' scores, the differences were not statistically reliable. If and when psychologists achieve an understanding of precisely how nature and nurture interact in these matters, they will be able to design intervention programs that will be more effective than those already tried (Scarr & Weinberg, 1983). We will have more to say about such programs in the last major section of the chapter.

In an interesting line of research, investigators have explored the possibilities that experience influences some intellectual abilities more than others. In a classic study Bayley (1970) speculated that certain characteristics that are probably genetically based, like people's thresholds of physiological arousal and their characteristic levels of activity, might interact either positively or negatively with cognitive development. In a longitudinal study "low-intensity" infants—babies who were relatively undisturbed by interfering stimuli—were found to be more advanced, at 2½ years of age, than other children in such things as speech development and manipulative skills (Bell, Weller, & Waldrop, 1971). Other researchers have found similar relationships between temperament and intellectual development. However, temperament alone seems to be less predictive of intellectual development than the goodness-of-fit between the child's temperament and the needs and expectations of his parents and teachers (Lerner & Lerner, 1983; Wachs, 1992). This finding would suggest that both genetic and environmental influences are at work. In the next section we look at specific environmental factors that may interact with, shape, and modify the effects of genetic predispositions.

Environmental Factors

Even the most hidebound advocates of the genetic source of human characteristics will admit that children are brought up in circumstances that range from the most

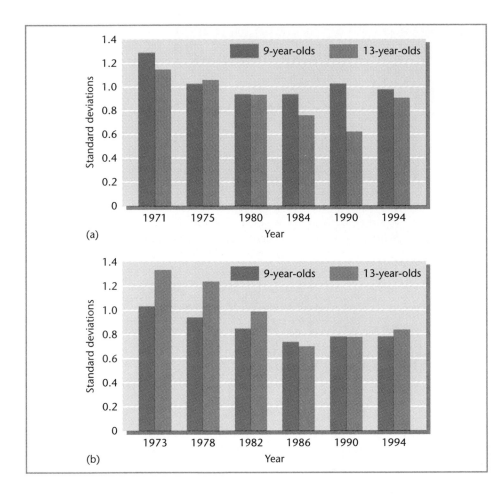

(a)

(b)

■ **FIGURE 11-2**

Narrowing the gap. Between the early 1970s and the late 1980s the racial "gap" of one standard deviation (15-16 points) that had separated the IQ scores of European and African Americans narrowed considerably. The bars in this graph represent the extent of these point "gaps" in (a) reading and (b) math scores of two groups of black students, 9- and 13-year olds. The gaps between these students' scores and those of European American classmates decreased over the 15-year period by as much as 40 percent in reading and 50 percent in math. As you can see, in the early 1990s the "gaps" widened slightly, but the changes were not significant. Moreover, although some categories (age groups combined with subject areas) showed divergence, others showed further convergence. Thus for the moment, at least, the most parsimonious conclusion is that the convergence in black and white scores achieved is holding. (*Source:* Williams & Ceci, 1997).

favorable to the most destructive. Most proponents of heritability recognize that the quality, amount, and patterning of stimulation offered to children in these varying conditions strongly affect their cognitive and intellectual development. In this section we consider some of the factors that can affect the child's cognitive abilities before or during its birth; in addition we explore the important influences of the family, the school and peer culture, and the community.

Pregnancy and Birth

As we pointed out in Chapter 4, such factors as poor maternal nutrition can have highly influential and lasting effects on a child. Moreover, an extensive body of research details the negative effects on intellectual development of such things as maternal disease, such as AIDS, or a mother's alcoholism or addiction to other drugs. In addition, events attending the process of birth, like oxygen deprivation, can have destructive effects on a child's mental functioning. Deficits or defects traced to such factors are considered **congenital,** meaning that they occur during gestation or at birth. Rather than genetic in origin, they are either transmitted directly from the mother to the fetus or result from events during the birth process.

The Family

The child's first environment has important influences on her intellectual functioning. Studies have found that across social classes several very specific aspects of family interaction are related to differences in measured intelligence. For example, a supportive, warm home environment that encourages a child to become self-reliant, to express her curiosity, and to explore has been linked to higher intellectual functioning (Gottfried & Gottfried, 1984). Parents who are emotionally and verbally

congenital Describing deficits or defects that the child incurs in the womb or during the birth process.

This mother is using marbles and printed numbers to encourage her son in learning to match number symbols and names with quantities of actual objects.

responsive to their children, who provide appropriate play and reading materials, who encourage their children's interest in and efforts at learning, and who provide their children with a variety of learning experiences tend to have children with higher IQ scores (Bradley et al., 1989; Gottfried & Gottfried, 1984; Wachs, 1992). It's important to note, however, that such family environments do not uniformly produce high-achieving children. Recall from Chapter 3 that even though children in the same family have many shared environmental influences, they are also subject to nonshared environmental stimuli that may counteract other influences and affect their intellectual development (Rowe, 1994; Scarr, 1992). In addition, some scholars (e.g., Ogbu, 1988) think that the focus on family interaction patterns as influencing children's academic achievement is overly narrow; they suggest that we look more closely at the educational, societal, and economic factors that constrain families' options. We discuss one study that does this in the section "Social-Class Factors and Cumulative Risk."

Schools and Peer Groups

As an essentially middle-class institution espousing middle-class values and often staffed by middle-class teachers, the school can put the child who comes from a different social class or cultural background at a disadvantage from the outset. He may experience this setting as so different from his home environment as to seem alien (Comer, 1988, 1991). Studies that have compared the attitudes of white and black teachers have suggested that African American teachers see lower-class students in a much more positive light than do European American teachers (e.g., Gottlieb, 1966). Negative attitudes can translate into differential treatment that, in turn, can lead to lower-class children's failure to meet classroom and school standards. For example, in one study, in both preschool and first-grade settings, teachers were observed to make significantly more negative comments to African American students than to European American students (Cadmus, 1974; Quay and Jarrett, 1986).

Negative attitudes and comments are not the worst of it. Teachers are more likely to judge minority children as not ready for formal learning and, as a result, these children are more likely to be retained in kindergarten. According to Meisels (1992), we may see the long-term result of this in preadolescence. Meisels found that among African American 13-year-olds, nearly half the boys and more than a third of the girls were below grade level. By contrast, among European American 13-year-olds, only 29 percent of the boys and 21 percent of the girls were below grade level. The consequences of differential treatment may be that lower-income students learn less: "If pupils of low socioeconomic status come to school with patterns of behavior that the teacher dislikes and responds to with negative affect, a *vicious circle* is created that makes it difficult for such pupils to learn" (Soar & Soar, 1979). It is not surprising that nearly twice as many lower-class as middle-class students drop out before completing high school, especially among African American and Latino youth (Children's Defense Fund, 1997).

Peer culture plays an enormously important role in children's attitudes toward, and success in, academic work. For example, one study found that peer groups of Asian Americans supported each others' academic pursuits and participated in education-related activities such as studying together (Steinberg, Dornbush, & Brown, 1992). In another study, Asian American students as well as students in Taiwan and Japan were more likely to see their peers as having high academic standards than were European American students (Chen & Stevenson, 1995). The same investigators also found that dating and general socializing—activities that often interfere with studying—were less common among Asian American students than among European American peers (Chen & Stevenson, 1995).

Some researchers have reported a different pattern of behavior among African American students (Steinberg et al., 1992). Often African American peer groups express antiacademic attitudes, ridiculing and isolating students who try to succeed in school (Ogbu, 1988). Because of the strong adolescent need to belong in a peer culture, many low-income black children face a tough choice, and the effect of negative feedback from their peers may often outweigh parental encouragement of academic achievement (Steinberg et al., 1992). Often, children who succeed in school choose strategies to hide or camouflage their true attitudes toward schoolwork and their actual efforts to achieve academic success (Fordham & Ogbu, 1986). For example, a student may excel in athletics or take on a role such as class comedian to disguise her intellectual pursuits.

The Community

The community as a cultural unit may have significant effects on a child's cognitive and intellectual development. For example, studies have shown that children living in isolated circumstances, such as rural areas, score lower on IQ tests than children in nearby villages or in metropolitan areas (Kennedy, 1969; Sherman & Key, 1932). Similarly, economically disadvantaged areas of modern cities are often associated with slowed intellectual development. The poor diets, unsafe housing, and high levels of community violence and unemployment that characterize impoverished areas may all contribute to less adequate cognitive functioning (Bronfenbrenner, McClelland, Wethington, Moen, & Ceci, 1996; Garbarino, 1995; Pollitt, 1994). It's important to note, however, that in some cases environments stimulate and help children to develop abilities that are highly adaptive in their specific circumstances. Children living in remote communities in Newfoundland, for example, were found to have highly developed perceptual and motor abilities that were useful in their setting, although their verbal and reasoning skills—less important in that setting—were below average (Burnett, Beach, & Sullivan, 1963).

The Pulawat islanders, who have little formal education or technology, have developed an amazing navigational system that reveals their clear understanding of navigational rules and of the relationship among directions, winds, tides, and currents and enables them to sail long distances out of the sight of land. Nevertheless, these skilled navigators would not perform well either on a standard test of intelligence or on Piagetian tasks of formal operations, despite the fact that their navigational skills evidence formal operational functioning and even though they demonstrate highly advanced deductive reasoning on culturally relevant problems. Observations like these show us how important it is to analyze intellectual performance within the natural cultural context in which it occurs (Ceci, 1990; Christenson, Abery, & Weinberg, 1986).

ETHNIC, RACIAL, AND SOCIAL-CLASS FACTORS IN INTELLECTUAL PERFORMANCE

Ethnicity, race, and social class are important correlates of measured intelligence and intellectual performance. *Social class* is a broad term that includes such variables as education, occupation, income, lifestyle, housing, possessions, and use of leisure time. The term *socioeconomic status (SES)*, which refers to education, occupation, and income, is often used as an index of social class because these three variables are generally reliable and valid measures of social class, they are more easily quantified than other variables, and data on them (from U.S. government sources) are readily available (Benokraitis, 1998). Because these factors are also frequently associated with each other, researchers have generally explored them together. Unfortunately, there's a catch-22 factor here: Because these parameters are so closely associated, researchers often find it very difficult to disentangle the effects of being a member of a minority group from simply being poor.

Another issue that confounds research in this area is the tendency of researchers to lump subcultures together; thus a study of "Asians" or "Asian Americans" may mask important differences among such distinct racial, ethnic, and cultural groups as Chinese, Filipinos, Indians, Japanese, Koreans, and Vietnamese. And, finally, a very disturbing problem is that researchers' assumptions may shape the kinds of questions they ask and the way they ask them. For example, many studies of Asian Americans ask why these children are successful in school, whereas many studies of African Americans ask why these children perform poorly. Researchers studying minority groups must avoid such self-fulfilling-prophecy techniques and instead look specifically at each group's strengths as well as at the areas in which each could improve (Fisher et al., 1998).

With these constraints on existing research in mind, let's look at three main sets of explanations for the differences in IQ and intellectual performance that have been observed among different racial, ethnic, and socioeconomic groups. The first set proposes that existing standardized tests are inappropriate for lower-class and minority children. The second set of explanations attempts to focus specifically on the role socioeconomic factors play in intellectual performance. The third set explores how parent-child interactions may differ among social classes and racial and ethnic groups.

Are Intelligence Tests Biased Against Minority Groups?

Those who argue that existing tests of intelligence are biased against a sizable group of the American population point out that the most widely used tests were standardized on European American middle-class people; thus, they maintain that test items do not accurately measure adaptive or problem-solving abilities appropriate to the circumstances in which low-income groups and some members of racial and ethnic groups live. These tests, their detractors insist, draw on white middle-class language, vocabulary, experience, and values. For example, the vocabulary used on traditional IQ tests often differs from the dialect or even language some children use every day. On this view, some researchers have argued that minority children's lower verbal scores may reflect cultural bias, not lack of intelligence. Consider also the implications of an item on a recent version of the Stanford-Binet scale. The correct responses to the item "What's the thing for you to do if another boy hits you without meaning to do it?" include such statements as "I'd say, 'That's all right. I know it was an accident,' and walk away." In some minority communities, a child must fight to survive; if he took such a chance he might risk a later problem with the other child (Fisher et al., 1998; Williams, 1970).

Tests like the Kaufman Battery that claim to be culture-fair aim at minimizing cultural bias, and in fact, there's much less difference between the scores of African American and European American children on the Kaufman test than on standard IQ tests. However, on the Raven Progressive Matrices Test, another presumably culture-fair test that bases its scores on a test taker's ability to detect, evaluate, and match graphic patterns, the more educated test takers are, the better they do (Anastasi, 1988). This suggests that even a test of the ability to discriminate visual patterns from each other is tapping some store of knowledge not available to people who have fewer advantages in society.

Racial and Ethnic Groups May Excel in Different Areas

Do you think standard IQ tests measure the ability to cope with the everyday activities and problems of life? Consider the results of a classic work by Mercer (1971), who studied a large group of children and young adults whose IQ scores had classified them as mentally retarded. Mercer's test of adaptive ability assessed these young people's abilities to perform skills required for such things as self-care (e.g., dressing), household tasks (e.g., shopping, cooking), holding a job, and traveling alone to and from their jobs. The results were amazing: 90 percent of the African American children and 60 percent of the Hispanic children who had IQs below 70 (i.e., these children scored in the lowest range of measured intelligence, the bottom 3%, traditionally labeled "mentally defective") *passed* Mercer's test, but every European American child with an IQ below 70 *failed* it! The disturbing implications of these findings were that minority children are far more likely than white children to be inappropriately classified as mentally retarded—a label that will have a pervasive effect on their life experiences and on others' expectations of them—and that intelligence tests are incapable of accurately assessing the competencies of minority children.

Jensen (1973) found that in poor areas of the rural south, African American children did less well than European Americans on both verbal and performance tests and that this difference increased as the children grew older (from 5 to 18 years of age). Interestingly, among children raised in better circumstances, blacks and whites showed no appreciable difference on performance tests; on verbal tests, however, black children did less well than white children, and these differences tended to increase with age. These and other findings (e.g., Neisser et al., 1995) have led some investigators to reason that it may be more useful to look at achievement levels on different kinds of cognitive skills than at overall IQ levels; recall Gardner's and others' theories that there are many different types of intelligence.

On the theory that members of different groups may show different patterns of abilities on tests of such things as verbal skills, reasoning, number, facility, and spatial ability, a classic study examined these parameters among middle- and lower-class African American, Chinese American, Jewish, and Puerto Rican children between about 6 and 7 years of age (Lesser, Fifer, & Clark, 1965). Lesser and his

This 6-year-old child is studying the WISC Picture Arrangement task, which requires her to put an array of picture cards in order so that "they tell a story."

colleagues found that these four groups did indeed have different profiles of ability scores. In general, Jewish American and Chinese American children scored higher on these tests than African American and Puerto Rican children, although black children showed greater verbal abilities than Chinese children. The latter, like the Puerto Rican children, were handicapped by language difficulties. African American children scored better on reasoning than Puerto Rican children, but the latter scored slightly above African Americans on numerical and spatial abilities. Chinese American children scored the highest of all on spatial ability. Social class clearly influenced score levels for all groups. Race and ethnicity affected both score levels and patterns of scores among the different ability tests, but social class had no effect on these patterns. Moreover, differences in score level attributed to socioeconomic factors were greatest for African Americans, suggesting that social class disadvantages had relatively greater impact on black children.

The Effect of Context on Intellectual Performance

Not only may traditional intelligence tests be biased in their content and approach, but the conditions under which they are administered to minority children of lower socioeconomic status may have interfered with these children's ability to perform. Recall that the newer, information-processing approaches to intelligence testing have pointed to the importance of context in children's intellectual performance. Theorizing that children from minority and low-income groups may be made uncomfortable by European American examiners and that such children may become anxious in unfamiliar testing situations, especially when pressed to respond within rigid time limits, some researchers have attempted to raise children's performance levels (Golden & Birns, 1971; Zigler & Seitz, 1982). They have tried to familiarize children with the test environment and test materials, to encourage them specifically on various tasks, and to use material rewards, such as candy, to motivate performance. They have been successful in this effort with some low-income and minority group children. That such efforts have been significantly more successful with economically deprived children than with middle-class children (Zigler, Abelson, Trickett, & Seitz, 1982) supports the notion that intelligence tests do not measure the competencies of low-income black children as well as they measure the abilities of white middle-class children. Here again we draw the distinction between capacity and performance: The research cited suggests that lower-class children may be equally competent but that they have been unable to perform under the conditions set for them.

Social-Class Influences on Intellectual Performance

The task of separating the closely interwoven influences on intelligence and academic performance of class, race, and ethnicity is enormously challenging. Yet, if estimates that nongenetic factors control about 50 percent of the variation in IQ scores and intellectual performance turn out to be right, it is a task of increasing importance. Moreover, as we will see in this section, those who study cultural contributions to intellectual performance have produced some surprising and potentially disturbing data. For example, a study that combined both cross-cultural (between or among nations) and multicultural (between or among cultural groups within the same nation) comparisons confirms recent expressions of concern that North America's so-called Protestant work ethic is on the decline (Chen, Stevenson, Hayward, & Burgess, 1995). According to these researchers, many American students believe that it is innate ability rather than hard work that ensures success.

In this section we look first at some efforts to isolate North American social-class factors in intellectual development and performance. We then explore research that has compared intellectual performance among various ethnic and racial groups within the United States and that has also compared United States students' performance with that of students in China and Japan.

Social-Class Factors and Cumulative Risk

The influence of social class on intellectual performance has begun to receive more research attention. The narrowing of the performance gap between black and white children on reading achievement tests and on Scholastic Aptitude Test (SAT) verbal and mathematics subtests that has been occurring in recent years (Brody, 1992; Neisser et al., 1995; Williams & Ceci, 1997) has been interpreted as indicating that more and more African American families have been entering the middle class. Indeed, social-class differences in IQ have been declining, although some (e.g., Flynn, 1998) have suggested that this trend has slowed in recent years.

Several investigators have described differences in performance on standardized intelligence tests among children from various social-class, ethnic, and racial groups (Brody, 1992; Neisser et al., 1995), although cultural differences and influences appear to be less marked among children under 18 months of age (Golden & Birns, 1983). In general, children in the lower socioeconomic classes score 10 to 15 IQ points below middle-class children, and black children on average score 20 IQ points below white children (Brody, 1992). These differences are generally observed by first grade and remain consistent throughout the school years (Kennedy, 1969; Moffitt, Caspi, Harkness, & Silva, 1993).

In one study that controlled for race and ethnicity, social-class differences alone were found to affect cognitive measures that involve language as early as 18 months of age (Golden & Birns, 1983). In addition, these researchers found that beginning at about the age of 2, these same measures were highly correlated with performance on standardized intelligence tests.

The concept of **cumulative risk** may help us understand the significance of the effects of socioeconomic factors on intelligence and intellectual performance. If in the life circumstances of a given child only one of the many negative aspects of poverty is present—say, being too poor to have appropriate clothing for school—many other factors in that child's environment may outweigh the risk that one factor poses for her. However, as more and more poverty factors are added to the child's life experience, her risk of poor academic performance will increase. To test this notion, Sameroff and colleagues (Sameroff, Seifer, Baldwin, & Baldwin, 1993; Sameroff, Seifer, Barocas, Zax, & Greenspan, 1987) identified specific environmental factors likely to present risks to children's cognitive development (Table 11-5) and then, among 215 4-year-old African American, European American, and Puerto Rican children, examined the links between these risks and WPPSI IQ scores.

cumulative risk The notion that risk factors in children's life circumstances have cumulative negative effects on their intellectual performance.

TABLE 11-5 Major Risk Factors That Endanger Children's Cognitive Development

Poor maternal mental health
High maternal anxiety
Low maternal education
Head of household either unemployed or in unskilled occupation
Father absent from family
Minority-group membership
Family in which there were more than four children
High incidence of stressful events such as illness, job loss, or death in the family

Source: Sameroff, Seifer, Baldwin, & Baldwin, 1993.

As you can see in Figure 11-3, the findings were striking. Children with only one risk factor had verbal IQ scores well above average; an IQ of 115 is considered "bright normal." As the number of environmental risk factors increased, however, IQ scores dropped, and children whose life circumstances included 7 or 8 of the risk factors had IQs 30 points lower, putting them in the "dull normal" range.

Social class did not appreciably affect these findings: The presence of several risk factors was associated with low IQs in families of both low and high socioeconomic status. At the same time, any one of these factors was more likely to be present in low-income families than in families with more financial advantages. A follow-up study (Sameroff et al., 1993) of 152 of the same families when the children were 13 years old revealed a similar pattern: a 30- to 35-point IQ difference between the children whose risks were few and those who confronted many risk factors.

These findings argue for the notion that there are forces in the lives of children who confront multiple risk factors that contribute to declines in their performance on intelligence tests. The findings also allow us to hypothesize that in the absence of such risk factors children should achieve higher test scores. How can we test this hypothesis? In fact, psychologists have tested it; Scarr and Weinberg (1976) asked what would happen if African American children were adopted by European American parents who could offer them the economic advantages and intellectual climate that the typical white middle-class child enjoys. If the racial and social-class differences that have appeared in IQ scores of blacks and whites were attributable to such experiential differences, then the IQs of white-adopted black children should more closely resemble those of white middle-class children. In fact, that is what these researchers found. As you can see from Figure 11-4, adopted African American children achieved scores some 20 points above the national average for black children, and the younger they were at adoption, the higher their scores were.

In a 10-year follow-up study, when the children were 17 years old, Weinberg, Scarr, and Waldman (1992) found that there were no differences between the transracial adoptees and the biological offspring of the adoptive parents in IQ change from time 1 to time 2. Like other adoption studies (e.g., Capron & Duyme, 1989), this study demonstrated not only strong effects of a rearing environment on IQ but the maintenance of these effects over a lengthy period, in this case into late adolescence.

Social Class and Parent-Child Interactions

Several investigators have suggested that maternal behavior differs across social classes and may differentially affect children's intellectual performance in the school setting. Studies have shown that middle- and lower-class mothers tend to differ most in their use of language. Middle-class mothers were more likely than lower-class mothers to speak in response to their babies' vocalizations (Hart & Risley, 1995; Lewis & Wilson, 1972; Tulkin & Kagan, 1972), and their infants tended to stop vocalizing and listen when their mothers spoke. In contrast, lower-class children were more likely to continue vocalizing when their mothers were

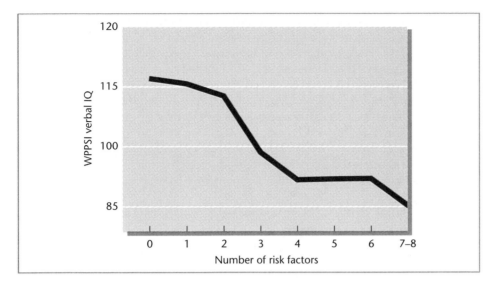

■ **FIGURE 11-3**
Risk and intellectual performance.
This graph dramatically illustrates the relationship between risk factors associated with poverty and intellectual performance. The more risk factors such as hunger, poor clothing, and family stress in the lives of these 4-year-olds, the lower were their scores on the Wechsler Preschool and Primary Scale of Intelligence. (*Source*: Sameroff, Seifer, Baldwin, & Baldwin, 1993)

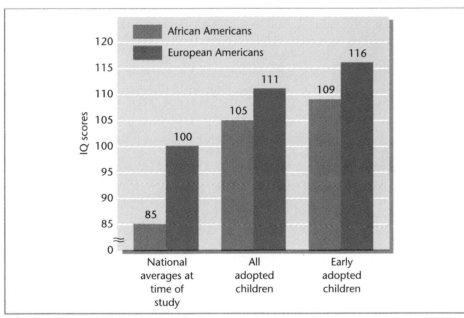

■ **FIGURE 11-4**
How do children adopted into European American homes fare?
Both African and European American children adopted into middle-class European American homes obtained IQ scores that were substantially above the national averages for their respective groups. We don't know why the European Americans fared somewhat better than the African Americans. (*Source*: Adapted from Scarr & Weinberg, 1976)

speaking (Lewis & Freedle, 1973). Some scholars have suggested that these early differences in the way infants attend to their mothers' speech may be related to later differences in the ease with which children learn from verbal information (Golden & Birns, 1983; Hoff-Ginsberg & Tardif, 1995).

Barnard, Bee, and Hammond (1984) found that mothers who had gone beyond a high school education were more highly involved with their infants than mothers who had not finished high school; these differences, measured at several intervals before the children reached age 2, were significantly related to the children's IQ scores at age 4. Many researchers have argued that stress, presumably more commonly experienced by lower-class parents than by middle-class parents, may directly influence parental styles of interaction, for example, leading parents to be more concerned with discipline than with positive emotional communication (Goldstein, 1990; McLloyd, Jayaratne, Ceballo, & Borguez, 1994).

Studying the interactions among maternal control techniques, teaching styles, language, and children's cognitive development, Robert Hess and Virginia Shipman (1967) found a number of differences between middle-class and lower-class African American mothers. The former were more responsive to their children's feelings, provided them with more rational and complex reasons for rules and guidelines, and generally encouraged their children to become aware of the complexities of the social and physical environment and to attend to relevant cues in problem-solving situations. In contrast, lower-class mothers' communications with their children were more restricted and generic; they were less likely to respond to specific questions or statements offered by their children. Hess and Shipman concluded that the lower-class mothers' communicative style was less likely to help their children learn to make the kinds of discriminations necessary to develop effective problem-solving skills.

In China, where there are relatively small differences in income across groups who vary in education, Tardif (1993) found that less educated parents used more imperatives with their toddlers than better-educated mothers. This style of interaction is likely to be associated with poorer cognitive development.

Multicultural and Cross-Cultural Factors in Intellectual Performance.

In recent years, both scholarly and lay publications have documented a trend in North American students' academic performance that is disturbing to many. These reports have warned that in math and science and even in the language arts, American students are falling behind students in other countries, particularly countries in Asia. The Perspectives on Diversity box in this section (Box 11-2) recounts a series of studies by Harold Stevenson, Chuansheng Chen, and their colleagues that have followed groups of North American, Chinese (Beijing, China, and Taipei, Taiwan), and Japanese (Sendai, Japan) students from the first through the eleventh grades and that demonstrate the importance of differing family influences on cognitive development in these children. The findings of these longitudinal studies raise several provocative questions about American education practices and policies (Chen et al., 1995; Stevenson & Stigler, 1992).

One question is whether patterns of interaction in Asian American families can explain the high levels of performance frequently shown by Asian American children. African American and Hispanic American parents appear also to value education highly and in fact to be more likely to believe that it is important for their children to do well in school than European American parents (Chen et al. 1995). However, African Americans and Hispanic Americans may be constrained in their support of their children's schooling by beliefs that are based on their social and economic positions relative to the European American majority. For example, some may believe that European Americans cannot be trusted, that they will prevent others from improving their status in society, and that discrimination against non–European Americans will not end.

Asian American families, on the other hand, appear to strongly support their children's academic achievement. They hold high expectations for their children's education and also tend to convey the idea that achievement is part of children's duty to parents. Asian American families often strictly monitor the time their children spend in homework and in free play. In addition, they frequently profess the belief that effort will be rewarded (Slaughter-Defoe, Nakagawa, Takanishi, & Johnson, 1990). However, the critical family factors that determine the different patterns of achievement across diverse ethnic groups are not yet fully understood.

COGNITIVE INTERVENTION STUDIES

We have seen that a really quite enormous number of factors contribute to a child's intellectual functioning. When some of these factors are negative and stand ready to impede or halt children's intellectual development as well as their ability and motivation to use their intellectual powers to grow and prosper, can we alter them and improve a child's intellectual functioning? Cognitive intervention studies are designed to address this question.

BOX 11-2

Perspectives on Diversity

Making the Grade in Japan, Taiwan, and the United States

The declining school achievement of U.S. children decried by the media has often been attributed to failures of the North American school system. Teachers and educators who, particularly in inner-city schools, have struggled to help children from varying backgrounds and life circumstances learn to read, write, do math, and, most important, enjoy learning, have felt deeply wronged by these reports. Longitudinal studies by Harold Stevenson and his associates (Chen et al., 1995; Stevenson, Chen, & Lee, 1993; Stevenson, Chen, & Uttal, 1990) have now provided evidence that in the earliest months of first grade, children in the United States already lag behind other children in academic achievement. Thus, although differences in academic performance may well reflect varying educational systems, that these differences appear when children have as yet had little exposure to formal education suggests that more is involved than inadequate educational practices.

Over a 10-year period, Stevenson and colleagues administered tests of reading and mathematic ability to groups of first, fifth, and eleventh graders in classrooms in two U.S. metropolitan areas (Minneapolis, Minnesota, and Fairfax

County, Virginia), in two East Asian cities (Beijing, China, and Taipei, Taiwan), and in Japan (Sendai). The U.S. students included four cultural groups—European, Chinese, African, and Hispanic Americans, although not all these groups were represented in every study. To the degree possible, the investigators retested the same students at different ages and in all studies; over the 10-year span, Stevenson and his associates tested several thousand children. In each study the researchers interviewed teachers, students, and students' mothers on a variety of topics, such as the value of education, beliefs about learning, attitudes toward school, and family involvement in children's schoolwork.

Some of the findings of these studies have been quite startling. In one study, although American children tended to dominate both the best and the worst groups of readers at the first-grade level, by the time children had reached fifth grade, the number of poor readers among Americans had increased markedly. The deficits in mathematics shown by U.S. children as compared with Chinese and Japanese students were even more distressing: In the same study, U.S. first graders made up 58 percent of the lowest-scoring students from all three countries, and this proportion rose to 67 percent among U.S. fifth graders. Conversely, only 15 per-

(continued)

■ **FIGURE 11-5**

Reading scores in China, Japan, and the United States. Overall, across both first and fifth grades, Chinese and Japanese students tended to do better in reading than any of the U.S. cultural groups. In first grade, Asian American students ran second to Japanese students but, for some reason, dropped down by fifth grade. In the fifth grade, Chinese students still took top honors, but European Americans, Japanese, and Asian Americans, ranking in that order, all had very close scores. The relations among European, African, and Hispanic American students remained fairly stable from 1st to 5th grade; these groups scored from higher to lower, respectively. (*Source*: Adapted from Chen, Stevenson, Hayward, & Burgess, 1995)

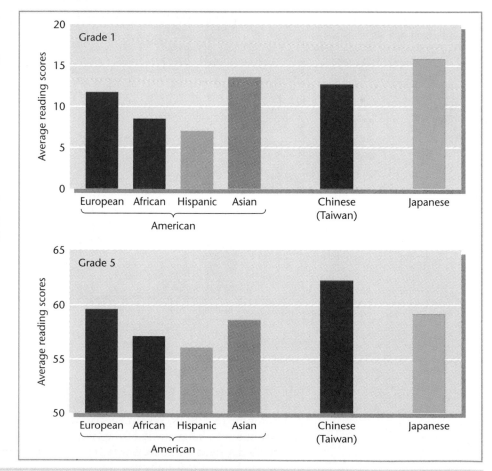

BOX 11-2

Perspectives on Diversity (*continued*)

cent of students with the highest scores were American first graders, and only 1 percent were American fifth graders.

In another study, there were noticeable differences in reading test scores among seven groups of students even in the first grade (Figure 11-5). In first grade, Japanese students scored highest, followed fairly closely by Asian American, Taiwanese, and European American students; African American and Hispanic American students scored the lowest. By fifth grade Taiwanese and European American students had jumped ahead of Japanese and Asian Americans. Once again, American students scored considerably below others on a mathematics test, and between first and fifth grade these differences became more pronounced (Figure 11-6): At both times Chinese, (Beijing, Taiwan), and Japanese students had the highest scores, Asian Americans following close behind.

What could be contributing to these results? Stevenson and his colleagues found no evidence that the American children had lower intellectual levels, and parental education levels argued, if anything, in favor of European American students. However, there were marked differences in parents' beliefs, their reported activities with their children, and the evaluations they made of their children and their educational systems. Chinese and Japanese mothers generally viewed academic achievement as the child's most important pursuit. Once children entered school, Chinese and Japanese families mobilized to help their children and to provide an environment conducive to achievement. Japanese mothers in particular were likely to see themselves as *kyoiku mamas,* that is, "education moms" responsible for assisting, directing, and supervising their children's learning.

■ **FIGURE 11-6**
Mathematic skills in China, Japan, and the United States. As in reading, Chinese and Japanese students outscored U.S. students in math. Although the differences were small in Grade 1, they were large in Grade 5, and Asian American students clearly led their American peers. (*Source*: Adapted from Chen, Stevenson, Hayward, & Burgess, 1995)

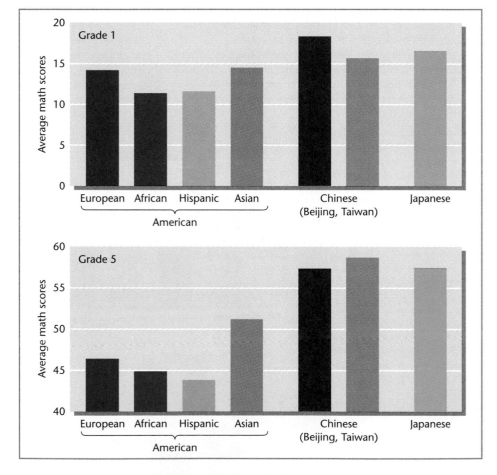

Head Start and Similar Programs

Beginning in the 1960s, researchers and policymakers have implemented a great many programs aimed at modifying the development of learning-disabled or economically deprived children. Some *preventive* programs were designed to prevent the decline in cognitive skills that was theorized to occur in preschool children who

American mothers were less likely to be actively involved in helping their children with homework than mothers in other groups. They tended to put more emphasis on the role of innate ability in school performance and less on the role of effort. Mothers in all three countries viewed their children's academic performance as above average but, as Figure 11-7 shows, American mothers voiced the most positive views about their children's scholastic achievement and experience, even though they were aware of the country's low rank in comparative studies of children's performance.

American children spend significantly less time on homework and reading for pleasure and more time playing and doing chores than Japanese or Taiwanese children. Differences with Taiwanese families may be especially notable. In one study, only 17 percent of first-grade and 28 percent of fifth-grade Taiwanese children did chores, in contrast to 90 and 95 percent of American first and fifth graders, respectively. When researchers asked one Taiwanese mother why she did not assign her children chores she replied, "It would break my heart. Doing chores would consume time that the child should devote to studying."

American mothers appeared to be more interested in their children's general cognitive development than in their academic achievement per se, attempting to provide the children with experiences that fostered cognitive growth (Stevenson et al., 1990). These mothers reported reading more frequently to their young children, taking them on excursions, and accompanying them to more cultural events than did Chinese or Japanese parents (Stevenson et al., 1993). The fact that most of these enriched out-of-school experiences took place before children entered first grade was reflected in American kinder-gartners' and first graders' clear superiority to other cultural groups on a test of general information, which asked questions like "What are two things a plant needs in order to grow?" Although the extent of this superiority diminished by 11th grade, Americans still led other groups in knowledge acquired through everyday experience, answering questions such as "What do we mean by inflation when we talk about a country's economy?"

Even some differences between schools in China, Japan, and the United States seemed attributable to home factors. For example, American teachers complained that often they had to forego the goal of teaching to spend time in roles irrelevant to that goal (such as counselor, family therapist, and surrogate parent). In addition, teachers had to devote more time to classroom management than to teaching because American schoolchildren had not been trained to be attentive and disciplined and spent much more time in inappropriate and uncontrolled activities than did their Japanese and Taiwanese peers.

What might Americans do to improve U.S. students' competitive status? Some school districts have moved toward lengthening the academic year, which has traditionally been much shorter than the school year in Asian countries. The shorter U.S. school day may also contribute to the fact that American students spend more time than Asian students in extracurricular pursuits, including sports activities, socializing, and dating. But if Stevenson and his colleagues are right, intervention needs to begin earlier and at home. Helping children build self-esteem and learn to interact effectively and cooperatively with others are certainly important parental functions, but perhaps American families need to rediscover the work ethic that built a multicultural nation.

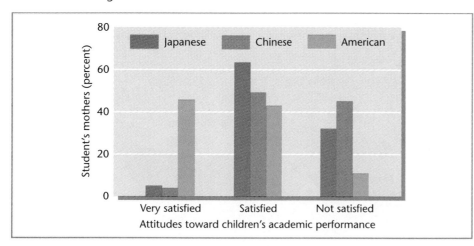

■ **FIGURE 11-7**
Mothers' attitudes toward their children's academic performance.
In 1990, more Japanese and Chinese mothers than U.S. mothers were "satisfied" with their children's academic performance. However, more than 40 percent of American mothers but fewer than 5 percent of Chinese and Japanese mothers were "very satisfied," and many of the latter said they were specifically not satisfied with their children's achievements. (*Source*: Stevenson, Chen, & Lee, 1993)

were relatively disadvantaged in society; other *interventionist*, or remedial, programs focused on school-age children who already had demonstrated learning difficulties. Some programs emphasized the teaching of specific skills such as counting or vocabulary, and others focused on teaching general problem-solving strategies, communication patterns, and principles of logical thought. Still others tried to alter such things as self-concept and achievement motivation. One of the most well known cognitive

Head Start A federally funded program that provides disadvantaged young children with preschool experience, social services, and medical and nutritional assistance.

intervention programs is **Head Start,** a federally funded program for severely economically deprived preschoolers begun in 1965. The program provides children with an intensive preschool experience, combined with social services and medical and nutritional interventions, for one or two years before they enter kindergarten.

Almost all programs of this sort, whether preventive or interventionist, have been able to produce at least short-term gains in children's academic performance. According to several studies, when Head Start children reached kindergarten, they were more advanced than others on a number of measures of cognitive and social development, and when they reached the first grade they continued to show cognitive gains (Brooks-Gunn, 1995; Lee, Brooks-Gunn, & Schnur, 1988; Lee, Brooks-Gunn, Schnur, & Liaw, 1990).

The long-term effects of the Head Start intervention programs have been examined as well. A survey of 14 long-term follow-up studies of children who were involved in preschool intervention projects in the 1960s indicates that some positive effects of intervention may not appear for a while (Lazar & Darlington, 1982). When these children were in later elementary grades or junior high school, they scored higher on arithmetic and reading achievement tests and on IQ tests than children from similar backgrounds who did not participate in intervention projects. In addition, the intervention children were less likely to have been retained in a grade or to have been assigned to special education classes. The latter findings were among the positive results of the Carolina Early Intervention Program, one of the most successful programs of this type (Box 11-3). Children who participated in intervention programs also saw themselves as more competent when they were adolescents. Fewer of them dropped out of school and more went to college. Several other follow-up studies have supported this pattern of findings (Seitz, 1990; Seitz, Rosenbaum, & Apfel, 1985; Smith, 1995).

Characteristics of Successful Intervention Programs

The earlier intervention programs start and the longer they continue, the more successful they are likely to be (Ramey & Ramey, 1992). Thus, such programs need to begin within the first two years of life and to continue at least until children enter kindergarten. Table 11-6 lists seven principles on which the most effective intervention programs have been based. In fact, children from impoverished settings who are not given early intervention efforts suffer a significant loss in both cognitive and

These children in a Head Start program seem totally involved in what the teacher is saying and showing them.

TABLE 11-6   Seven Principles of Successful Early Intervention Programs

Principle	Description
I. Timing	Interventions should begin during the first two years of life and continue at least until children enter kindergarten, and they should engage families earlier rather than later. If in such two-generation programs assistance to the family requires a long period of time, the child must continue to receive the supports critical for learning and social development during that time.
2. Intensity	The more intensive the intervention, that is, the greater the number of hours per day, days per week, and weeks per year during which intervention activities take place, the more positive the program's effects, particularly in families in which parents have the lowest education levels and during the first five years of the child's life. Intensive early intervention is as important as other services such as health, housing, and employment.
3. Direct provision of learning experiences	Intervention programs that offer services directly to the child rather than through an intermediary, such as a parent or a home visitor, are more successful than others. Home visits can be useful but only if made at least three times a week.
4. Breadth	The broader the spectrum of services provided and the more routes used to enhance children's development, the more successful the program. Not every family needs a full range of all available services, and the program must judge the proper combination for each family.
5. Recognition of individual differences	Programs must recognize the varying needs of individuals. In the lives of poor families, myriad reasons may account for one individual's failure to do well; thus, individualization of treatment interventions is very important.
6. Environmental maintenance of development	Unless poor or at-risk children are supported in multiple domains of development beyond the preschool years, they will not develop the skills, motivation, health, and resources needed to succeed in school settings. Two-generation programs may, by helping parents, create the support system children need to make academic progress.
7. Cultural appropriateness and relevance of intervention strategies	To be valued, used, and incorporated into participants' everyday lives, interventions must be culturally relevant and welcome to family and child. Because individuals within cultures vary greatly, stereotyping cultures will lead to failure.

Source: Based on Ramey, Ramey, Gaines, & Blair, 1995.

social-emotional development during the second and third years of life (Blair, Ramey, & Hardin, 1995). Moreover, it is not very likely that children can ever achieve a complete catch-up in these areas of development, although later intervention programs can effect some gains.

Intervention endeavors that focus on improving both the parent-child relationship and the family's natural support systems and that place the child in an educationally stimulating program are among the most successful (Slaughter, 1988; Smith, 1995). Almost as successful are programs that involve low-income parents actively in their children's education. In some cases, mothers are employed as teaching aides in preschool centers; in others, program staff visit mothers in their homes and instruct and support them in their educational activities with their children.

Sometimes the family ecology may need to be altered. Parents whose children are at the greatest risk for cognitive problems are often unable to benefit from parent-training interventions. Severely stressed and economically disadvantaged, such people may be spending all their time and energy on simply surviving. There are too many adverse factors in their lives, such as crowded or inadequate housing, lack of money, or unemployment, to make concerns like improving child-care practices seem important (Horowitz & Paden, 1973; Stipek & McCroskey, 1989). Thus, the most successful, **two-generation programs** have extended help to parents as well as

two-generation program
A program of early cognitive intervention that extends help to parents as well as to their children.

BOX 11-3

Risk and Resilience

Early Intervention with Children at Risk

One of the most successful intervention efforts yet undertaken, the Carolina Early Intervention Program involves both day care and parent education (Ramey, Lee, & Burchinal, 1989; Ramey & Ramey, 1992, in press; Ramey, Ramey, Gaines, & Blair, 1995). The Carolina program is a structured, cognitively and socially stimulating day-care program that focuses on developing children's communication skills as well as on intensive parent education. In one study within this program, a group of high-risk chil-

dren began attending the preschool center, most by the age of 3 months, while a second, control group received no intervention. As Figure 11-8 shows, by the time the children in both groups were 12 months old their cognitive performances had already begun to diverge. By the time the children were 4 years old the IQ scores of those in the combined day-care plus parent-education (preschool intervention) group were some 13 points higher than the scores of those in the nontreated high-risk (control) group (Ramey, Campbell, & Blair, in press).

When the children were between the ages of 2 and 4,

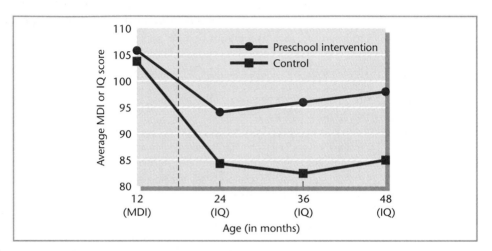

■ FIGURE 11-8

Early cognitive intervention works.
The preschool, two-generation Carolina Intervention Program has produced significant gains in intellectual performance. At 12 months of age the children in both the intervention and control groups received rather similar Mental Development Index scores on the Bayley Scales, but their subsequent Stanford-Binet IQ scores were significantly different. When the two groups of children were 4 years old, the intervention group's average IQ score was some 13 points above the score for the control group, almost a full standard deviation. (The vertical dashed line marks the transition from Bayley Scales to Stanford-Binet assessment measures.) (*Source:* Adapted from Ramey, Campbell, & Blair, in press)

children, enabling the former to take advantage of community resources in furthering their own education, getting job training and finding work, or strengthening family relationships and family functioning through supportive social relationships (Slaughter, 1988; Smith, 1995). Of course, placing a young child in a nursery school setting may free parents to pursue these aims and relieve their stress while it also gives the child cognitive and social stimulation.

BEYOND THE NORMS: GIFTEDNESS AND MENTAL RETARDATION

intellectual giftedness A characteristic defined by an IQ score of 130 or over; gifted children learn faster than others and may show early exceptional talents in certain areas.

Children vary greatly in the rate and manner in which they learn. Some children are exceptionally talented, learning much faster than classmates, whereas others function at significantly lower intellectual levels than their peers. Traditionally, specialists in intelligence testing have held that an IQ score above 130 signals **intellectual**

the researchers classified some 40 percent of control-group children as mentally retarded (IQ 84 or below) but found that only 8 percent of the intervention-group children had IQs this low. The combined treatment program had prevented the deterioration in intellectual skills that ordinarily occurs by this age in such economically deprived, high-risk populations. Ramey and his colleagues note that their data support the notion that Jensen's (1969) 15-point IQ difference favoring European over African Americans "can be effectively eliminated during the preschool years and that high-risk, socially disadvantaged children can perform at least at the national average on standardized tests of intelligence if they and their families are provided additional educational and family support services" (Ramey, Bryant, Campbell, Sparling, & Wasik, 1988, p. 17).

The effects of the Carolina program were long lasting. As you can see from Figure 11-9, the positive effects of the preschool intervention continued to be evident when the children were 15 years old. Children who had been in the preschool intervention group had made better school progress than the children who had been in the control group; the intervention children were less often retained in a grade and less often assigned to special education programs.

The Carolina project has reported the most durable positive effects of an early educational program that have been reported to date. The results are particularly meaningful because the intervention was a true experiment, in which children were randomly assigned to treatment and control conditions. The project clearly underscores the malleability of children's intellectual performance.

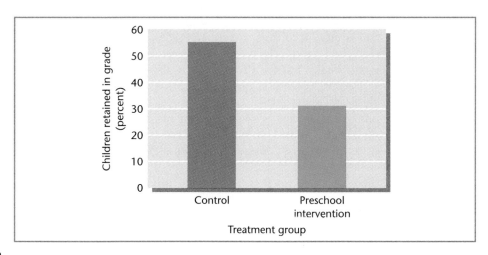

■ **FIGURE 11-9**
Early cognitive intervention has longlasting effects.
When the children in the original Carolina program reached 15 years of age, those who had been in the preschool intervention group were much less likely to have been retained in a grade than the control group of children—only 30 percent versus 55 percent.
(*Source:* Adapted from Ramey, Campbell, & Blair, in press)

giftedness; a score below 70, coupled with a person's difficulty in coping with age-appropriate activities of everyday life, indicates **mental retardation.** What do these terms mean for the individuals—not more than 3 percent of the population—whom they describe? How are gifted children different from those who fall within the average range of intelligence, and how can their unique talents be realized? And how should children termed retarded be taught and encouraged to develop to their best potential? Must we accept their apparent limitations or may their level of functioning, like that of other children who are a bit slower than their peers, be raised? We look first at the evidence on giftedness and then at the contemporary view of retardation and the prospects for fulfilling lives for those who fall into this category.

mental retardation A characteristic defined by an IQ score below 70 and the inability to cope adequately with age-appropriate activities of everyday life.

The Intellectually Gifted

Do children who are intellectually gifted burst upon society, speaking when they're only a year old, solving problems in calculus at the age of 2? Not usually. Often, however, gifted children show special interests and talents quite early, and they apply themselves to these interests with enthusiasm and perseverance (Feldman & Goldsmith, 1991). And sometimes a child's exceptional intelligence does break through without warning:

> I was standing at the front of the room explaining how the earth revolves and how, because of its huge size, it is difficult for us to realize that it is actually round. All of a sudden, Spencer blurted out, "The earth isn't round." I curtly replied, "Ha, do you think it's flat?" He matter-of-factly said, "No, it's a truncated sphere." (Payne, Kauffman, Brown, & DeMott, 1974, p. 94)

The question of how to educate and encourage exceptionally bright and talented children is controversial (Sternberg, 1988; Tomlinson-Keasey, 1990). Should these children be permitted to begin school early? Should they skip grades? Graduate ahead of their age-mates? Some argue that these sorts of steps are necessary to maintain an exceedingly bright child's interest and motivation. Critics retort, however, that if we adopt such an approach, we may meet the child's intellectual needs at the expense of her social and emotional development. Placing such a child with older peers, critics claim, may cause her to be socially isolated. Opposing this view is the fact that very bright children often seek out the company of older children and adults. According to Terman (1954), one of the earliest leaders in the study of the gifted child, bright children are usually far ahead of their age-mates, not just intellectually, but socially and physically as well.

Recent evidence suggests that Terman was probably right! Apparently, bright children aren't viewed as "nerds" or rejected by their peers, nor do they confront unusual problems of social adjustment. Richardson and Benbow (1990) assessed social development among 1,247 gifted children in accelerated education programs, comparing these young people with a group of gifted peers who were in regular classrooms. All of these children were identified between the ages of 12 and 14 and then evaluated for social-emotional adjustment at 18 and again at 23. Among 18-year-olds there was little evidence that academic acceleration had altered their sense of self-esteem; only 5 percent felt that being moved ahead had affected them negatively. By age 23 only 3.3 percent of the students felt that their social-emotional adjustment had been hindered by being moved ahead rapidly in school.

Are gifted children unique? Veronica Dark and Camilla Benbow (1993) suggest that the processes that underlie the cognitive feats of gifted children are not unique—it's simply that such children use their cognitive skills more efficiently than the rest of us. For example, gifted children seem to be able to process information more rapidly than others; you'll recall that we've discussed the role that processing speed may play in cognition and intelligence earlier in this chapter and in Chapters 5 and 10. In their study, Dark and Benbow found, for example, that gifted children could distinguish two numbers or words faster than their less gifted peers. Not surprisingly, the children who were mathematically talented were outstanding on the number task and the verbally gifted excelled on the word task.

Further support for the practice of academic acceleration comes from a program at Johns Hopkins University called "Study of Mathematically Precocious Youth" (Brody & Benbow, 1987; Stanley & Benbow, 1983). In this ongoing program, seventh and eighth graders with exceptional talent for mathematics are identified and then helped, through a variety of special programs, to move ahead in mathematics at an accelerated pace. The results have been spectacular. By 1982 approximately 35,000 mathematically talented youth had been identified, and the program continues to identify about 2,200 more students every year. The participants in the program either take college courses or enter college early, and a number have graduated from college before their 18th birthdays. One of the earliest graduates, barely 17, obtained his bachelor's degree in mathematical sciences after only five college semesters and one year each in junior and senior high school (Stanley, 1976). As the program shows dramatically, talented children can be advanced rapidly in school and succeed extremely well (Southern, Jones, & Stanley, 1994).

Other education alternatives for gifted children include enrichment programs, which attempt to provide these children with extra stimulation without advancing them to higher grade levels. In one of these types of programs, teachers give the gifted child additional, extra work but at the same level of difficulty. One critic termed this form of enrichment "busywork" (Stanley, 1976). In a second type of program, the school sets up a special subject or activity meant to enrich the educational lives of a group of intellectually talented students. For example, a special class in science or social studies might be arranged as a supplement for bored high-IQ students. Yet a third, "cultural" type of enrichment program offers gifted students instruction in creative writing or foreign languages or opportunities for study in the arts, including painting, sculpture, drama, and dance. Critics argue that the "enrichment" offered by this type of program is often unrelated to the area of a particular child's talent, thus failing to encourage the child's development of that talent.

Under the influence of Gardner's argument that children display multiple intelligences, more schools have begun to offer programs to nurture the specific talents of children who are gifted in particular ways (Gardner, 1993). As we noted earlier, whether or not these programs have succeeded in their goals of increasing children's specific talents remains a hope rather than an established fact (Lubinski & Benbow, 1995).

Children with Intellectual Deficits

We first encountered the problem of mental retardation in Chapter 3, where we discussed three specific disorders that are accompanied by serious intellectual deficits: Down syndrome, phenylketonuria (PKU), and fragile X syndrome. Down and fragile X syndromes, you'll recall, are chromosomal disorders, whereas the cause of PKU is lack of a specific enzyme for processing phenylalanine. Mental retardation that results from such genetic or other factors that are clearly biological is referred to as *organic* retardation (Hodapp, 1995). Intellectual deficits that derive from factors surrounding the birth process (such as lack of sufficient oxygen) and those that are the result of conditions of infancy or childhood (such as infections, traumas, or lack of nurturance) are considered *familial* retardation. In some 30 to 40 percent of cases it is not possible to determine the etiology of mental retardation; about 35 percent of cases appear to be organic, and 30 to 35 percent are considered familial (American Psychiatric Association, 1994). In general, organic retardation is more severe than familial retardation.

Mental retardation is diagnosed by two basic measures: assessments of the child's mental functioning and of his or her adaptive behavior (American Psychiatric Association, 1994). Traditionally, an IQ score below 70, together with adaptive behavior deficits, has indicated mental retardation. Each of four IQ score ranges reflect an increasingly serious degree of retardation: mild mental retardation, IQ 50–55 to 70; moderate retaration, IQ 35–40 to 50–55; severe retardation, IQ 20–25 to 35–40; and profound retardation, IQ below 20 or 25. In addition, according to the guidelines of the American Association on Mental Retardation, to be classified as mentally retarded children must show deficits in their ability to function in the real world. Young children who can dress themselves, find their way around the neighborhood, and use the telephone, for example, are less likely to be identified as mentally retarded than children with the same IQs who do not exhibit these practical competencies.

By far the majority of mentally retarded people—some 95 percent—can learn and hold jobs of more or less complexity and can live in the community. Children with mild retardation (about 85% of all retarded children) usually acquire social and communicative skills during preschool years and may be indistinguishable from other children until they reach their teens, at which time they may begin having difficulty with more advanced academic work. Children who are moderately retarded (about 10%) generally acquire communication skills in early childhood, and although they can benefit from vocational training, they are limited in their grasp of academic subjects. Young people in both of these groups may join the workforce and live in supervised settings or, in some cases, independently.

The severely retarded (3% to 4% of all retarded children) may learn to speak and communicate but have rarely progressed beyond reading a few words. Finally, profoundly retarded children (1% to 2%) require close supervision in sheltered settings. Such children may learn communicative skills and some self-care. Both of the latter groups can learn to do some simple tasks with close supervision; at present, young people in both these groups must live in supervised settings.

Whether the competencies of any or all of these groups of mentally retarded children can be improved is yet to be determined. As you will recall from Chapter 8, researchers at the Language Research Center in Georgia have succeeded in enabling nonspeaking severely and moderately retarded youngsters to communicate intelligibly with adults and peers for the first time using a computerized keyboard device and have begun to explore the use of this device with 1½- to 3½-year-old children at risk for failure to develop language. And, as we mentioned in Chapter 3, with caring parenting that includes extra stimulation and training, many children with Down syndrome can lead very productive lives (Hodapp, 1995).

CREATIVITY

The nature of creativity and its relationship to intelligence have long been of interest to psychologists. In recent years, however, researchers have devoted more attention to intelligence. Some investigators, like Robert Sternberg, see intelligence and creativity as intertwined, but others, like Howard Gardner, see clear distinctions between the two. In this section we look first at some efforts at definitions and theories of creativity and then at some evidence on the distinctions between creativity and intelligence. We then consider children's creative behaviors and conclude with some thoughts on how to encourage creativity in children.

Definitions and Theories

Defining creativity is just about as hard as defining intelligence; both are multifaceted qualities that vary as a function of personal characteristics (which are both inherited and learned), the context in which they are exercised, the risk factors that may inhibit them, and the environmental supports that may encourage and sustain them. The key to creativity is the notion of *uniqueness.* Most people—including most psychologists—would agree that the creative product is novel. In some way, it is unlike anything else in its class. But most authorities also agree that a truly creative idea or product must be characterized by *usefulness.* It must be of benefit in some area of life, whether that be astrophysics, the visual arts (e.g., painting, sculpture), household products, literature, microbiology, music, or another field of human endeavor.

creativity The ability to solve problems, create products, or pose questions in a way that is novel or unique; also, the ability to envision new problems not yet recognized by others and to come up with their solutions.

According to Howard Gardner (1998), **creativity** is the ability to solve problems, create products, or pose questions in a way that is different (novel, unique) from the approaches that most other people use. It is also, he says, the ability to fashion new problems—that is, to look at some event or situation and to envision problems that the situation may engender that no one else has thought of—and then to come up with a solution to the problem. For example, kitty litter was invented when someone complained about having to take smelly, messy, torn-up newspaper used by his cat out with the garbage. The proverbial lightbulb went on over the head of an auto mechanic who for years had used clay-based granules to sop up oil in his shop.

Sternberg and Lubart (1992, 1995) have offered an "investment theory" of creativity, in which they propose that "to be creative is to invest one's abilities and efforts in ideas that are novel and of high quality, and to be creative, one must, like any good investor, " 'buy low and sell high' " (1992, p. 2). That is, the creative person must formulate ideas that appear to be out of sync with current fashions (the investment analogy is to underrated stocks) but that have the potential to be accepted by others eventually (the analogy is to stocks that will rise in value). But how does the person *know* that her currently underrated idea will take off? According to Sternberg and Lubart (1992), knowledge is one of six resources required by creativity: "Advancing knowledge beyond where it is requires knowing where it is" (p. 3). The other five essential resources are intelligence, thinking style (e.g., taking on challenges, using a macro versus a micro approach to an issue), certain personality characteristics (e.g., willingness to overcome obstacles and to take sensible risks), motivation, and a supportive environment. Keegan (1996) agrees that knowledge is crucial, illustrating this point with the work of Charles Darwin, who amassed an enormous body of knowledge of natural history before he offered his theories to the world. Keegan, who also finds that motivation (his term is *purpose*) is crucial to the creative endeavor, adds affect, or emotional involvement—a love for what one is doing.

Relationship between Creativity and Intelligence

According to Gardner (1998), psychologists and others once thought that creativity and intelligence were closely related, but others (e.g., Wallach & Kogan, 1965) have shown that IQ and creativity are relatively independent of each other. These researchers administered WISC subtests and other intelligence tests as well as a set of tasks designed to tap creative modes of thinking to a group of fifth graders, half girls and half boys. The researchers found only minimal correlations between "correct" answers on the intelligence tests and answers judged creative on the more freewheeling tasks. In addition, they found no gender differences in the responses of these 10- to 11-year-old children.

According to Gardner (1998), this research showed "enduring differences" between intelligence and creativity. The results suggested that the intelligent person excels at *convergent thinking*, or thinking with the goal of recognizing or remembering specific information or solving traditional problems for the correct answers, and the creative person at *divergent thinking*, or thinking that is imaginative and seeks variety, novelty, and uniqueness. Although highly creative people tend to be above average in intelligence, "above an IQ level of 120 (1.33 standard deviations above the norm) greater psychometric intelligence [i.e., intelligence as measured on a standard intelligence test] does not predict greater psychometric creativity" (Gardner, 1998, p. 437).

Others disagree, however, that these two phenomena can be so neatly separated. Indeed, Sternberg and Lubart (1992) consider the early "psychometric" approaches such as that of Wallach and Kogan to focus on "individual differences in creative production . . . of a fairly minor kind" (p. 2). Proposing intelligence as one of the resources required for creative endeavors, they include within the category of intelligence several abilities that others have used to define creativity! For example, they suggest that intelligence includes the capacity to reconceptualize problems in new ways by "seeing novel aspects in everyday experience . . . putting these aspects together in significant and nonobvious ways . . . and seeing significant, nonobvious connections between a current problem and past knowledge" (Sternberg & Lubart, 1992, p. 3).

Clearly, the true relationship between creativity and intelligence is yet to be determined. One thing people do agree on, however, is that both are desirable characteristics.

Are Children Creative?

When your kindergartner proudly shows you the painting he worked on at every free moment of the day (according to his beaming teacher), can you doubt that he's creative? It displays an utterly unique view of the world (his view). It is useful because it gives both of you a sense of pleasure and pride in his accomplishment. You know he's intelligent (and that's what his test scores say). He's always sought to get around obstacles, literally and figuratively, and he's often taken risks you wish he wouldn't. His motivation and emotional involvement with the work seem clear. And his environment (his teacher) obviously supported his endeavor. But what about his knowledge?

Keegan (1996) argues that children are indeed capable of gathering significant bodies of knowledge. He describes, for example, the child who can tell you not only the names of different dinosaurs but in what geological period they lived, what led to their extinction, and where the crater formed by that meteorite is located. On the other hand, Albert (1996) and Runco (1996) hold that it is not only knowledge of a subject area but knowledge of the self that one needs to make the judgments and decisions required to evaluate one's own creative effort. Runco adds that because young children often cannot distinguish between reality and fantasy, they cannot be truly creative until they reach preadolescence.

Still, according to Russ (1996), although young children don't have the knowledge base or technical mastery to make such contributions, "they do have good and novel ideas and productions that are creative for their age group" (p. 31), and they often engage in creative acts and creative problem solving. Thurstone (1952) said that if a person creates something that is new to him it qualifies as a creative act, whether or not someone else somewhere at some time has created the same thing. In addition, play—especially fantasy, or pretend, play—gives children a chance to practice the kind of divergent thinking that can lead them some day to invent better widgets or build great museums and centers of learning (Russ, 1996).

Vygotsky thought that play facilitated creativity and viewed creativity as a developmental process: "The child's play activity is not simply a recollection of past experience but a creative reworking that combines impressions and construct-forming new realities addressing the needs of the child" (1930 [1967], p. 7). According to Vygotsky, through play children develop *combinatory imagination*, the ability to combine elements of experience into new situations and new behaviors, and this ability is part of artistic and scientific creativity (Russ, 1996).

How Can We Encourage Creativity in Children?

Formal school instruction tends to be focused on learning specific content, passing tests and exams, advancing in grade, and, ultimately, getting into college. Indeed, according to Albert (1996), a number of researchers have identified a period in middle childhood through preadolescence when early signs of creativity seem to disappear as children concentrate on well-organized (and thus well-controlled) learning skills. Divergent thinking simply does not enjoy great popularity in the schoolroom. In addition, as Gardner (1998) points out, concern with creativity and use of creativity tests have not been widespread, probably because of a "lack of consensus on whether tests of creativity are actually tapping the forms of originality or inventiveness" that societies most value (Gardner, 1998, p. 437).

The findings on stability of creative tendencies are contradictory, with researchers like Russ reporting evidence of stability but investigators like Albert asserting that there is a qualitative difference between childhood creativity and the creativity of the adolescent and young adult. Certainly this is an area that warrants further study. In the meantime, it cannot do any harm for parents to encourage their children's creative impulses. "Developing programs that help children learn to play . . . would be a good investment in the creative futures of our children" (Russ,

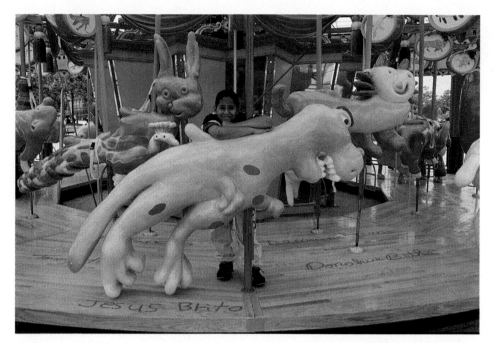

Jesus Brito smiles proudly above his lunging Tyrannosaurus Rex, one of the Totally Kid Carousel's marvelous steeds that were all created by children. Mike Mottola, designer of the carousel, turned 36 of the 1,000 drawings submitted by first and second graders in New York City schools into mounts for this merry-go-round in the city's Riverbank State Park. Encouraging children's creative expression clearly can produce things that are unique and useful!

1996). According to Russ, we need to determine what kinds of environments are optimal to facilitate the processes that are important in creative behavior and to explore how these creative processes interact with other processes important for such areas of development as social skills and values.

SUMMARY

- Interest in intelligence has traditionally centered on the products of intelligence rather than on the processes of intellectual endeavor. Specialists in intelligence testing have generally described intelligence by means of an **intelligence quotient (IQ).** However, it is important to remember that what is measured on an IQ test is performance; capacity cannot be directly measured.

A Lay Definition of Intelligence

- Although a number of experts have agreed with laypeople that intelligence has three central aspects—practical problem-solving ability, verbal ability, and social competence—a satisfactory definition of intelligence must consider additional factors, such as the predictive value of intelligence for behavior and the degree to which various factors that affect intelligence may be modified.

Theories of Intelligence

- It is generally agreed that intelligence is composed of multiple abilities and is not a single, general construct. **Factor analysis** has been instrumental in research leading to this view. However, contemporary intelligence specialists have confirmed the existence of a general factor of cognitive ability, derived from Spearman's original **general factor (g).** This modern middle-ground position, which also recognizes Spearman's concept of **specific factors (s),** holds that children may vary both in overall intellectual power and in their proficiency in specific aspects of cognitive functioning.

- An information-processing approach to intelligence, Sternberg's **triarchic theory of intelligence** holds that intelligent behavior is built on information-processing skills, experience with particular kinds of tasks and problems, and the abilities to adapt to a particular context, or environment, and to shape others to one's needs.
- Gardner's **theory of multiple intelligences** suggests that each of seven kinds of intelligence has its own developmental path and is guided by different forms of perception, learning, and memory. Each type of intelligence is likely to characterize individuals and cultures with particular interests and endeavors, and a single individual may possess one or more types. The **idiot savant** may or may not be an example of a person with only one specialized type of intelligence.

Testing Intelligence: Purposes and Methods

- Intelligence tests have three primary purposes: predicting academic performance, predicting performance on the job, and assessing general adjustment and health. Although traditional tests predict school performance better than anything else, they have been criticized as unfair to minority groups, and efforts have been made to develop **culture-fair tests**.
- The widely used **Bayley Scales of Infant Development,** designed for infants and very young children, measure certain developmental milestones and are generally used with children who are thought to be at risk of abnormal development. The newer Fagan Test of Infant Intelligence is designed not only to measure processing skills but to be culture-fair.
- The intelligence test developed by French scientists Alfred Binet and Theophile Simon focused on verbal and problem-solving abilities. The **Stanford-Binet Test** is an American adaptation of Binet's test.
- Binet developed the concept of **mental age,** an index of a child's performance level as compared with her true age. Stern combined chronological age with mental age to create the intelligence quotient.
- The **Wechsler Intelligence Scales**—the Wechsler Adult Intelligence Scale, Intelligence Scale for Children, and Preschool and Primary Scale of Intelligence—are probably the most commonly used intelligence tests today, in part because they include a substantial performance section. Their scoring is based on a **deviation IQ,** or the relation between an individual's score and the distribution of scores for the group of which she is a member.
- Emphasizing the processes of intelligence, the **Kaufman Assessment Battery for Children** also attempts to be culture-fair. Examiners teach a child who fails an item how to solve it before moving on to the next item.
- **Psychometricians** establish **test norms** by administering a test to groups having particular characteristics, such as age. The stimuli, instructions, and scoring of test items are also carefully **standardized** so that the test procedures will be the same when administered by different people.
- Intelligence tests must have both **validity** and **reliability.** Test constructors may examine for these characteristics by splitting a test's items and comparing each half with the other or by comparing the results of one administration with those of another on another date.
- IQ scores can and do fluctuate, because they measure current performance rather than underlying ability. Early studies indicated that scores on intelligence tests during infancy did not predict to later childhood or adulthood, but recent research suggests that measures of infant attention may be related to IQ scores during early childhood. The study of infants' skill at **recovery** has contributed to our ability to measure intelligence and predict from it. Other factors in the development of cognitive skills include visual recognition memory, cross-modal transfer, and speed of processing.

- After about age 8, prediction of intelligence becomes more accurate. The rate of mental growth varies among children, however, so that IQ scores are more stable for some than others. Children develop cognitively at different rates of speed, and major stresses or changes in life circumstances may temporarily disrupt cognitive performance.

Why Do People Differ in Measured Intelligence?

- Most estimates of the heritability of intelligence have indicated that 40 to 50 percent of the variability in intelligence among middle-class white Americans is due to genetic factors. In addition, other genetically determined behaviors such as temperament or personality may affect intellectual performance.
- Many psychologists continue to debate the heritability of intelligence, some holding that it is less than 50 percent, others that it is more. Arthur Jensen, the most extreme representative of the latter group, proposes two types of learning, both inherited—**associative learning** and **cognitive learning.** According to Jensen, all people share the first type of learning, but the second type is more prevalent among certain racial-ethnic groups.
- Although contemporary specialists believe that intelligence generally stabilizes in middle childhood, they also acknowledge that researchers have not yet determined how to manipulate the environment to raise IQ levels permanently.
- When we estimate heritability among people within a specific cultural or ethnic group our estimates of heritability will be higher because such people by definition share some characteristics that are both inherited and environmental. Conversely, it is inappropriate to apply heritability indexes based on one group to members of another. In addition, because heritability estimates are based on specific groups of people, they yield average numbers; thus they do not necessarily apply to an individual member of such a group.
- Because differences in group average IQ scores have been declining, the continuing effort to determine precisely how nature and nurture work together to affect intelligence will be important, particularly as new knowledge may affect intervention programs designed to improve cognitive functioning.
- Significant environmental factors that affect the child's intellectual functioning include events during pregnancy and the child's birth that can result in **congenital** defects as well as the interpersonal relationships that the child develops with family members, teachers, peers, and members of the community at large.

Ethnic, Racial, and Social-Class Factors in Intellectual Performance

- According to those who hold that intelligence tests are biased against members of minority groups, the content of standard IQ tests is drawn from white middle-class language, vocabulary, experience, and values and thus is inappropriate for other groups. Although more tests that attempt to be culture-fair are now available, on even some of these the more educated and advantaged child appears to do better.
- Context is an important factor in children's intellectual performance. Testing conditions, such as unfamiliar surroundings and all-European-American examiners, may be deleterious to the performance of lower-class and minority children.
- Researchers have found that children from different racial-ethnic backgrounds may do better in different areas of knowledge and expertise than in others. However, social-class factors may compound such findings. The concept of **cumulative risk** suggests that the more negative aspects of poverty and deprivation, such as poor

nutrition and homelessness, that constrain the life of a child, the more likely he is to score poorly on a test of intellectual skills.

■ Varying styles of parent-child interactions in different social classes may influence a child's development of verbal and cognitive skills. Studies indicate that early differences in mothers' use of language and infants' attention to their mothers' speech may account for later differences in the use of verbal information.

■ Research indicates that multicultural and cross-cultural differences in parents' attitudes and enthusiasm for education may affect children's performance on academic tasks. Chinese and Japanese students have been found to perform at a higher intellectual level, particularly in mathematics, than Asian American students who, in turn, score higher than European American, African American, and Hispanic American students.

Cognitive Intervention Studies

■ Since the 1960s educationists and government offices have launched many programs aimed at modifying the development of learning-disabled or economically deprived children. One of the most well known and successful is **Head Start,** a federally funded program for severely economically deprived preschool children. The findings with respect to maintenance of gains achieved in initial years in this and other programs are mixed. Almost all programs, whether preventive or interventionist, have reported short-term gains in academic performance, but some others have reported a loss over time of the initial advances.

■ Keys to long-term success may be involving children in these programs within the first two years of their lives, continuing intervention efforts at least until children enter kindergarten, and offering **two-generation programs,** in which educational, occupational, health, and counseling services are provided to the children's parents at the same time as intervention efforts proceed with the children themselves.

Beyond the Norms: Giftedness and Mental Retardation

■ Whether or not to advance children who display **intellectual giftedness** to higher grades in school remains controversial, although some such programs have shown considerable success. Although some voice concerns that advancement to sometimes much older peer groups will isolate gifted young children socially, others hold that such children are generally advanced socially as well as intellectually.

■ Some 95 percent of children with **mental retardation** can pursue academic studies to a greater or lesser degree, hold jobs, and as adults live either independently or in supervised settings. Only 4 to 6 percent of children afflicted with mental retardation must live under close supervision throughout their lives. We do not yet know to what degree the intellectual competencies of any of these children can be improved, although some studies (discussed in Chapter 8) have shown that mentally retarded children who do not speak can learn to communicate through the computerized use of visual symbols.

Creativity

■ The defining features of **creativity** are uniqueness and usefulness. The creative person asks questions, proposes solutions, and creates products that are novel and that are useful in some area of human life. The relationship between creativity and intelligence continues to be debated, but a current theory suggests that the sources of creativity lie in intelligence and motivation as well as a willingness to meet challenges, overcome obstacles, and take risks.

■ Because children lack the knowledge base required to evaluate true creative efforts, some psychologists believe that creativity begins only in preadolescence. Others, however, hold that young children have novel ideas, engage in creative acts, and use play to practice divergent thinking. These psychologists believe that encouraging imaginative play in children may promote future creativity.

The Family

C H A P T E R 12

The family is both the earliest and the most sustained source of social contact for the child. Even though many contemporary families have new and different structures, family relationships remain the most intense and enduring of all interpersonal and social bonds. Family members share not only their memories of the past but their expectations of future shared events and experiences. It is largely this continuity over time that makes the family relationship qualitatively different from the shorter-lived relationships children have with playmates and friends, teachers, neighbors, and ultimately coworkers and others. Children carry their memories of past family interactions in their perceptions and feelings about family members and in the standards they hold not only for family behavior but for the behavior of people in general.

In the child's earliest years, his sole interpersonal relationships may be with his parents, and parents generally present cultural beliefs, values, and attitudes to their children in a highly personalized and selective fashion. Yet even though parents' own personalities, family backgrounds, attitudes, values, education, religious beliefs, socioeconomic status, and gender influence the way they socialize their children, their role in this **socialization** process—ensuring that their child's standards of behavior, attitudes, skills, and motives conform as closely as possible to those regarded as desirable and appropriate to her role in society—is crucial. We will see in the next several chapters that peers, school, churches, the media, and other forces also contribute importantly to a child's socialization. From the moment of birth, however, "whether the child is wrapped in a pink or blue blanket, swaddled and placed on a cradleboard . . . , nestled in a mobile-festooned bassinet, indulged by a tender mother, or left to cry it out by a mother who fears spoiling the child, socialization has begun" (Hetherington & Morris, 1978, p. 3).

We begin this chapter by examining the family system from the ecological systems perspective that we described in Chapter 1. We explore the several subsystems of the family—including the relationships between and among marital partners, parents and children, and siblings—and examine how the family as a whole contributes to the child's socialization. We look then at the effects of social class, socioeconomic status, and ethnicity on the family and its role as socializing agent. In addition, we explore some of the major changes in the structure and functioning of the American family that have occurred in recent decades. In a majority of families today, both parents work outside the home, a change that can have important effects on the child's development. In addition, there is enormous diversity in the way modern families are structured—some families are headed by a single and/or divorced parent, some families are blended by divorce and remarriage, and still other families are headed by gay or lesbian parents. In some families, partners are becoming parents at later ages; in other families, parents cherish adopted children. We also consider the development of children born to teenage parents or unwed mothers. Our discussion of child abuse crosses all of the aforementioned categories of families, and we conclude with a brief look at the effect on children of living with war and political violence.

THE FAMILY SYSTEM

It's not uncommon for people to see socialization as a process by which parents modify children's behavior, but it would be more accurate to think of this phenomenon as a process of mutual shaping. That is, parents do indeed influence and direct their children, but their children also influence them and, in fact, play an active role in their own socialization (Bronfenbrenner & Morris, 1998; Bugental & Goodnow, 1998). In a complex system in which members are interdependent, changes in structure or the altered behavior of a single family member can affect the functioning of the entire system. Moreover, families do not function in isolation; they are influenced by the larger physical, cultural, social, and historical settings

---

socialization The process by which parents and others ensure that a child's standards of behavior, attitudes, skills, and motives conform closely to those deemed appropriate to his or her role in society.

and events about them. And families are not static; they change over time. Every family member, from the youngest infant to the oldest adult, is changing all the time, and these changes are reflected in family relationships.

The Ecological Systems Perspective

The view of the family as an interdependent system that functions as a whole has two principal origins: the realization by psychotherapists that to change the behavior of a troubled child one usually must change the family system as well (Minuchin, 1985; Reiss & Klein, 1987; Steinglass, 1987), and the work of psychologists like Urie Bronfenbrenner. You will recall from Chapter 1 that Bronfenbrenner's ecological theory is concerned both with the relationships between the child and the many, nested systems within which she lives, interacts with others, and develops as well as with the relationships among these systems themselves, from the familiar microsystem to the larger social and cultural setting of the macrosystem (Bronfenbrenner & Morris, 1998).

To refresh your memory, look back at Table 1-4 (Chapter 1), which used the family system to illustrate several important principles of systems theory. We learned there that a system is *complex* and *organized;* that it has an ongoing *identity* of its own; and that although it maintains a certain *stability* over time, it must also be capable of *morphogenesis,* adapting to changes both within the system and outside of it. In addition, a system demonstrates *equifinality* as time goes by, developing many similarities with other systems like it, even though such systems (e.g., families in different cultures) may express these similarities in different ways.

Before we discuss the family's major subsystems we need to consider one or two other principles that govern system functioning. *Interdependency* explains why the functioning of the family system is not always smooth: Because each family member and family subsystem influences and is influenced by each other member and subsystem, both cooperative behavior and behavior that is hostile or antisocial may have widespread effects on the system as a whole. Parents who have a good relationship with each other are more likely than not to be caring and supportive with their children, and in turn the latter are likely to be cooperative and responsible. On the other hand, parents whose marriages are unhappy may become irritable with their children, and the latter may exhibit antisocial behavior that may in turn intensify problems in the parents' relationship.

Families tend to attain equilibrium, or *homeostasis,* in their functioning and to become resistant to forces that might alter this balance. This can be useful, when routines and rituals help establish a sense of family history, identity, and tradition, making interactions easier and more comfortable. On the other hand, adaptability is the central criterion of a well-functioning family; when family members are unbending in the face of parental

This family is clearly having fun building their snowman. Such shared activities can reinforce family members' interdependency and increase positive and supportive feelings among them.

dissension or family distress over an aggressive child, routines can solidify and intensify negative patterns of interaction (Katz & Gottman, 1997; Patterson, 1982). In these circumstances, members may make no effort to communicate rationally, defuse anger, protect others, or solve problems and may become locked into a pattern of interaction that promotes or sustains maladaptive behavior in one or more family members. Resistance to change can prevent parents or other family members from recognizing problems and can cause members to blame all family difficulties on one child, who becomes the scapegoat for everyone else.

Finally, families have *boundaries* that vary in how permeable or vulnerable they are to outside influences. A well-functioning family tends to have permeable boundaries that allow members to maintain satisfying relationships both within and outside of the family itself. If families are too rigidly bounded, members may have difficulty disengaging appropriately from the family as, for example, in adolescence, starting college, marrying, or, in time of need, making use of resources outside of the family. Such families may have few positive community contacts and social supports and may be more likely than others to perceive their children negatively and to be punitive and inconsistent with them (Dumas & Wahler, 1985; Wahler & Dumas, 1987). On the other hand, families whose boundaries are too permeable can be vulnerable to disruptions by external forces such as intrusive in-laws or peer groups whose behavior is at odds with the family's own standards.

The Marital System

Both partners in a marriage, or other form of committed relationship, make up the marital system, the first and indeed the founding subsystem within the family system. Although developmentalists sometimes tend to downplay the significance of the marital system, the nature of the partners' relationship with one another unquestionably has a clear impact on their children. Indeed, a satisfying marital relationship is often regarded as the cornerstone of good family functioning. Directly or indirectly, it facilitates good parenting, good sibling relationships, and the healthy development of all the family's children.

How Does the Marital Relationship Affect Children?

It is important to remember that parents have a relationship with each other as well as with their children. When a couple offer each other emotional and physical support and comfort, the likelihood that they will provide the same kind of support and caring to their children is greatly increased. Research has shown that when partners are mutually supportive, they are more involved with their children and that their relationships with their children demonstrate affection, sensitivity, and competent childrearing practices (Cowan & Cowan, 1992; Katz & Gottman, 1997).

Couples who share child care and household chores have more time for playful and pleasurable interactions with their children and increase their chances of witnessing developmental milestones like a child's first words or staggering steps. Moreover, children's academic, social, and athletic successes are more fun if involved partners share them. Couples who cooperate in caring for their children also help each other shoulder some of the special burdens new parents experience, such as 2 A.M. feedings, changing dirty diapers, and soothing a crying or sick child.

Conflict between partners, however, can have seriously negative effects on both parents and children (Dix, 1991; Erel & Burman, 1995; Hetherington & Clingempeel, 1992). For example, Katz and Gottman (1993, 1996) found that not only level of conflict but the way it's managed can have deleterious effects on a couple's children. Within families whose marital partners typically confronted conflicts with hostility, belligerence, and contempt, children tended to display more aggressive and acting-out behavior than other children. In addition, fathers who had an angry and withdrawn style of dealing with marital disputes had children who were more likely to be depressed than others.

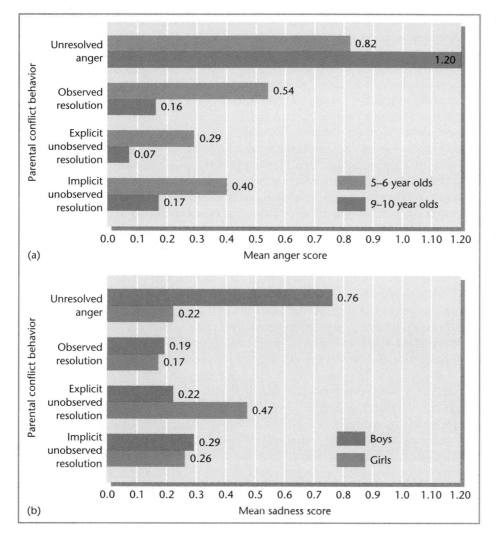

(a)

(b)

■ FIGURE 12-1
How children respond to
parental conflict.
(a) Parents' failure to resolve an
angry conflict was the most likely
behavior to arouse children's
anger and caused the most
displays of anger in older
children. (b) Such a failure was
also more likely to trigger sadness
in boys, but girls were more likely
to be sad when parents resolved
a conflict out of their presence
and made only a brief reference
to it later (explicit, unobserved
resolution). (*Source:* Adapted
from Cummings, Simpson, &
Wilson, 1993)

The effect of marital conflict on children takes two pathways: direct and indirect (Fincham, 1994; Parke & O'Neil, 1997). Children may be affected by such conflict *indirectly* when parents change their childrearing practices. In the Katz and Gottman (1997) work, parents in conflicted marriages had a poor parenting style that was characterized as cold, unresponsive, angry, and deficient in providing structure and setting limits; the children of these couples tended to display a lot of anger and noncompliance in interacting with their parents. Children may also be affected *directly* by marital conflict when they are actual witnesses to arguments and fights. In a series of studies, Mark Cummings and his colleagues have shown children real or videotaped interactions between adult actors behaving like two parents in a home setting. For example, the actors might disagree about which movie to see or argue about who will wash the dishes. The more frequent and violent the conflict and the more often the arguments were about something a child had done or said, the more likely the children were to show distress, shame, and self-blame (Davies & Cummings, 1994; Grych & Fincham, 1993). Moreover, when the actors failed to settle their dispute, the children expressed more anger and distress than when the actors resolved a conflict (Figure 12-1; Cummings, Simpson, & Wilson, 1993). Fighting in front of the kids has never been a good idea.

Mothers and fathers may influence their children's outcomes in different ways. Kahen, Katz, and Gottman (1994) found that when both parents were hostile toward each other, fathers were more likely to be intrusive—that is, physically interfering with children's actions—and children were more likely to express anger during a parent-child interaction task. Fathers' intrusiveness also predicted more negative peer play and more aggressive play with a best friend. Interestingly, these researchers also discovered that one parent's style of handling conflict may be related to the quality of his or her partner's relationships with the children. When fathers were angry and withdrawn in a conflict resolution task, mothers were more critical and intrusive in their interactions with their children, and, in turn, the children tended to be unresponsive or to "tune out" their mothers. In addition, the children's teachers rated them as tending to *internalize* problems, that is, to be shy and withdrawn, a finding that Cowan, Cowan, Schulz, and Heming (1994) replicated. Both these groups of researchers also found that hostile interaction between parents predicted children's tendency to *externalize,* or to exhibit aggressive and antisocial behaviors. Typically, in response to parents' marital difficulties, boys tend to display more externalizing behavior and girls to show more internalizing behavior.

Boys are much more susceptible to the negative effects of family disharmony than girls (Rutter & Rutter, 1993). Why should this be so? It seems that boys are more likely to be directly exposed to parental bickering and physical abuse than are girls (Hetherington, Cox, & Cox, 1982). Parents quarrel more often and their quarrels are longer in the presence of their sons. If parents begin to disagree when daughters are present, they are more likely to raise their eyebrows, nod in the direction of the child, and mutter "we'll talk about this later." Parents are simply more protective of daughters than sons.

Impact of a New Baby on the Marital System

Just as the relationship between marital partners affects their response to their children, the presence and behavior of a child influences the marital relationship. The most immediate effect—especially after the birth of a couple's first child—is a shift toward a more traditional division of labor between husband and wife, even when the initial role arrangement was egalitarian (Cowan & Cowan, 1992). Despite the changes that have occurred in gender roles in recent years, an implicit assumption seems to be that the role of the mother with young children is in child care and homemaking, the role of the father in providing for the family (Parke, 1996). Rarely, a father will take time from his job to be with his wife and newborn, but that time hardly ever exceeds two weeks. In families where both partners have worked outside the home, the wife is most likely to give up her job. Thus, not surprisingly, marital satisfaction declines more markedly in women than men after the birth of a couple's first child (Belsky, Long, & Rovine, 1985; Cowan, Cowan, Heming, & Miller, 1991). Fathers' marital satisfaction also takes a dive but more slowly; it may be only gradually that men become aware of the restrictions a baby imposes on their lives and realize that they are no longer the central focus of their wives' attention. In general, mothers get more of the responsibilities of raising a child, but they also often have more of the pleasures (Wilkie & Ames, 1986).

Children can influence the relationship between their parents in other ways. For example, children who are temperamentally difficult or handicapped in some way often are the cause of heightened family stress that may be translated into marital conflict. Couples who were satisfied with their relationship before the child's birth weather such pressures reasonably well, and their relationships show fewer disruptions than those of couples who were experiencing dissension before a child's arrival. Thus although the presence of a difficult child may be enough to fragment a fragile marriage (Bristol, Gallagher, & Shopler, 1988; Hodapp, 1995), the birth of a child rarely destroys a good marriage. However, because becoming parents does pose risks to a young family, intervention programs like that described in Box 12-1 have been designed to strengthen couple relationships and reduce the adverse consequences of the transition to parenthood.

BOX 12-1

Child Psychology in Action

Helping New Parents Cope with Becoming a Family

Although the Becoming a Family Project didn't succeed in immunizing young families forever from adversity and marital problems, this intervention effort did get 24 expectant couples and their new babies through at least five years of pretty healthy growth and development. Reviewing their results, the researchers who undertook this program concluded that to sustain the good family functioning that the project facilitated it might be necessary to give "booster shoots" from time to time over the family life cycle (Cowan & Cowan, 1992; Cowan et al., 1991).

From a group of 72 couples who were expecting their first babies and 24 other couples who had not yet decided whether to become parents, the researchers selected a third of the expectant couples to participate in a six-month group intervention that concluded three months after the birth of the couples' babies. In weekly sessions a clinically trained married couple encouraged the participants to raise any issues they were grappling with. Both wives and husbands described their dreams of creating an ideal family and talked about the families they grew up in and about the impending birth. Interestingly, everyone had trouble imagining what would happen after the baby was born.

As each couple's baby was born the couples began bringing their infants to the group. It was only then that partners began to try to find their way through the common changes, problems, and conflicts people encounter in becoming a family. Who could give up what? Who would take responsibility for what? How could they keep the marital relationship fulfilling while dealing with the incessant demands of the child? The researchers assessed family functioning, the quality of the marital relationship, parenting effectiveness, and parents' and children's adjustment in late pregnancy and when the baby was 6 months, 18 months, 3 years, and 5 years old.

At the 18-month follow-up, the effects of the intervention were encouraging. Compared with fathers in the nonintervention group, fathers in the intervention group were more involved and satisfied in parenting and reported less negative change in marital satisfaction, sexual relations, and social supports. In comparison to mothers in the nonintervention group, mothers in the intervention group saw their nonfamily roles—for example, as worker or student—as more important. Intervention mothers were more satisfied with the division of labor between themselves and their husbands and with their marriages overall; they were happier with their sexual relations, and they seemed better able to balance life stresses and social supports. In addition, at the 18-month and 3-year follow-ups, significantly fewer of the intervention couples were separated or divorced.

By the time the couples' children were in kindergarten, however, the positive effects of the early intervention had waned. Marital satisfaction was beginning to decline, and there were few differences between the intervention and nonintervention groups in either parenting style or children's adaptation. Early interventions clearly do not last forever. However, later findings from this research project indicated that another intervention (e.g., parent training to deal with problems unique to rearing toddlers) when the child was 2 could address some of the issues that led to later declines in marital satisfaction, to disruptions in family functioning, and to children's behavior problems. As new changes and challenges arise over the family life cycle, continued intermittent intervention focusing on new issues may be necessary to sustain good family functioning. Some family therapists have even suggested that, just as we go for regular medical checkups, we should go for regular checkups of family well-being to identify family problems and prevent them from escalating.

The Parent-Child System

Most parents have some beliefs about the qualities they would like to see their children develop and the childrearing methods that ought to encourage them. There are many paths to the development of positive as well as negative social behaviors, however, and there is no magic childrearing formula. Parents have to try to adapt their methods to each child's temperament and needs and to the demands of the culture, but it's important to keep in mind that individual children may develop very differently within the same family situation. It is also important to remember that, as we saw in Chapter 4 (Box 4-3), even in adverse environments some children seem to be relatively resilient (Cicchetti & Toth, 1998; Hetherington, 1989, 1991b; Werner, 1991).

Ways in Which Parents Socialize Children

Attachment between parent and infant, as we discussed in Chapter 7, forms the foundation for later family relationships. Although socialization begins at birth, it seems to become more conscious and systematic as the child achieves greater mobility and begins to use formal language. Parents cuddle and pet the child and praise her for all sorts of achievements that parents and society regard as desirable, such as learning to use a spoon, naming objects, and repeating new words. On the other hand, whereas up to now parents have accepted and even indulged a number of "cute" behaviors, all of a sudden the air rings with "No!" "Don't!" and "Stop!" as children climb out of their cribs, totter to the head of the stairs, and discover the grand fun that can be had with the pots and pans so conveniently stored in cabinets at their own level. Practicing their newfound motor skills and exploring the world about them becomes a real trial when exploration is restrained by playpen bars and parents make serious attempts at toilet training.

In teaching their children social rules and roles, parents rely on several of the learning principles we discussed earlier. For example, they use *reinforcement* when they explain acceptable standards of behavior and then praise or discipline their children according to whether they conform to or violate these rules. Parents also teach their children by *modeling* behaviors they want the children to adopt. An important difference between these two approaches is that whereas parents knowingly use reinforcement techniques, observational learning may occur by chance. As a result, the modeled behavior may not always be what they want to produce. Suppose a child sees a churchgoing, platitude-spouting, moralizing parent lie about his golf score, cheat on his income tax, bully his children, and pay substandard wages to his help. Do you think the child will emulate his parent's hypocritical words or his actual behavior? The "do as I say, not as I do" approach to socialization doesn't work.

Parents also manage aspects of their children's environment that will influence their social development. They choose the neighborhoods and home in which the child lives, decorate the child's room in a masculine or feminine style, provide the child with toys and books, and expose the child to television viewing. They also promote the child's social life and activities by arranging social events and enrolling the child in activities such as sports, art, music, and other social and skill enhancement programs (Ladd & LeSieur, 1995; Parke, Burks, Carson, Neville, & Boyum, 1994; Parke, MacDonald, Beitel, & Bhavnagri, 1988).

Dimensions of Parental Behavior

Parenting patterns and styles tend to reflect two primary dimensions of behavior. The first revolves around emotionality: Parents may be warm, responsive, and child-centered in their approach to their children, or they may be rejecting, unresponsive, and essentially uninvolved with their children and more focused on their own needs and wishes. The second dimension concerns the issue of control: Parents may be very demanding of their children, restricting their behavior, or they may be permissive and undemanding, pretty much allowing the child to do as he wishes. We discuss some aspects of these two dimensions and then consider four parental patterns of behavior to which they contribute.

Emotionality.   Parental warmth is important in the socialization process. When a parent is warm and loving, the child is likely to want to maintain the parent's approval and to be distressed at any prospect of losing the parent's love (Baumrind, 1991a; Maccoby & Martin, 1983). If a parent is cold and rejecting, however, the threat of withdrawal of love is unlikely to be an effective mechanism of socialization. From such a parent, what has the child to lose? Physical punishment too is more effective in the hands of warm parents, again probably because the child wants to conform to his parents' standards. But also the child knows from experience that his parents are involved and concerned with his well-being and that they will give him information about alternative behaviors that are socially acceptable. The child with rejecting parents has no such expectation. It is easier to learn the rules of the game if someone not only tells you what they are but explains why you should play that way (Holden, 1997).

Warm and loving parents tend to have children who are secure, feel good about themselves, and return their parents' affection.

Warmth and nurturance are likely to be associated with parental responsiveness to the child's needs. Loving parents make children feel good about themselves, dispelling anxiety and building their sense of security and their self-esteem. Children with such parents are more likely to learn and to accept and internalize parental standards than children of rejecting parents (Crockenberg & Litman, 1990). The high levels of tension and anxiety that are likely to be associated with hostile parents and frequent physical punishment may make it very difficult for the child to learn the social rules the parent is attempting to teach.

Control.   The goal of socialization is to enable the child eventually to regulate her own behavior and to choose socially responsible alternatives. Although the process of socialization does involve mutual influence between parents and children, the parent usually has more control than the child in their interactions. Indeed, if parents are not in charge, the family is likely to be dysfunctional (Baumrind, 1991a, 1993). When, rather than issue unexplained ultimatums, parents use suggestions and reasoning and present possible alternative courses of action, the child is more likely to comply with their wishes. Moreover, if parents are consistent in their discipline, use the minimum amount of pressure necessary to change the child's behavior, and encourage the child to view his compliance as self-initiated, children are more likely to cooperate and to adopt or internalize their parents' standards (Crockenberg & Litman, 1990; Holden, 1997).

As you might expect, warm, responsive parents are generally better at exercising control than hostile, rejecting parents. If parents use *power-assertive* methods of discipline that rely heavily on the superior power of the parent or are demeaning to the child, such as physical punishment, threats, or humiliation, children may come to view themselves as helpless or unworthy. Furthermore, although such techniques may enable a parent to gain immediate control of a child's behavior, in the long run they are likely to be deleterious. For example, suppose a hostile parent tries to control a child's aggressive behavior through physical punishment. By frustrating the child the parent may make her angry, and by offering an aggressive model to the child the parent may encourage the very behavior she is trying to eliminate. Moreover, the child may now try to avoid contact with the punishing parent, which gives the parent less opportunity to socialize the child, and may displace her aggressive urges to people outside the family of whose retaliation she is less certain. Again, the parent's method of discipline has simply intensified the behavior she was trying to get rid of.

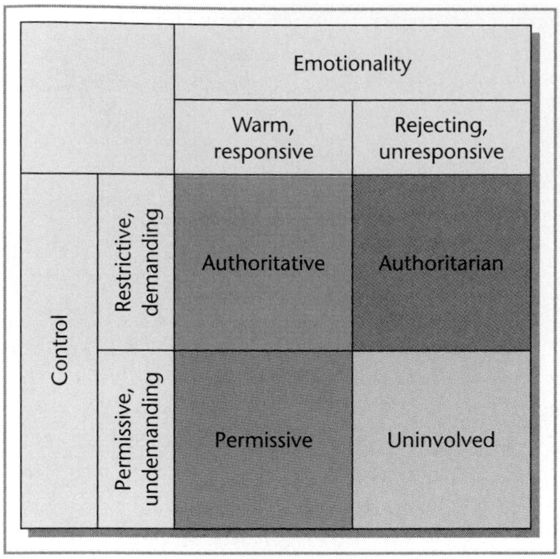

■ FIGURE 12-2
Parenting styles.
Although recent multicultural and cross-cultural studies suggest that these four parenting styles are not universally applicable, the essential characteristics and qualities on which they were based remain valid measures of behavior in many settings. New research may further refine these categories and add qualifying information based on cultural variations. (*Source:* From *Handbook of Child Psychology, 4* (E.M. Hetherington, Ed.) by Maccoby, E.E. and Martin, J.A., "Socialization in the context of the family: Parent-child interaction." Copyright © 1983 John Wiley & Sons Limited. Reprinted with permission.

Age plays an important role in children's responses to discipline. As children grow older they resist being controlled and manipulated by others, and self-reinforcement for appropriate social behavior becomes increasingly important. Even older preschool children try to negotiate with their parents:

CHILD: "I'll do it after I finish my painting. All right?"
PARENT: "How about if you and I do it together?"

As the child gains in social and cognitive competence and becomes more autonomous, parents rely increasingly on reasoning, and the child engages more and more in active bargaining (Kuczynski, Marshall, & Schell, 1997). This gradual shift from control by parents and others to self-control becomes critical for the child as he moves out of the home. Parents' opportunities to monitor and control the child's activities directly decline markedly in the elementary school years and even more in adolescence (Steinberg, 1990).

It is fortunate that over the school years children become more able to substitute long-term rewards for immediate gratification and more oriented toward the welfare of others. Older children's more efficient information-processing skills improve their ability to interpret events, to consider their motives and those of others, and to weigh alternative outcomes. For this reason, using immediate rewards or punishments to control behavior is much more effective with younger than with older children (Maccoby & Martin, 1983). Parents' effectiveness as agents of socialization is determined ultimately by a mix of factors: their emotional relationship with the child, the types of controls they try to use, and the appropriateness of these controls to the child's age and personality and the demands of the particular situation.

Parenting Styles

Family systems theorists would argue that what is important in a child's socialization is not any particular parental dimension of behavior but the overall combination of these behaviors. The four parenting styles shown in Figure 12-2—authoritative, authoritarian, permissive, and uninvolved—are composed of different combinations of the warm-responsive/rejecting-unresponsive and the restrictive-demanding/permissive-undemanding dimensions that we've discussed. They also reflect research that has explored the relationships between each parenting style and children's emotional, social, and cognitive development. In a now-classic study, Baumrind (1967) linked the first 3 of these styles with specific and quite distinctive patterns of children's interactions with their parents. Maccoby and Martin (1983) extended the

Baumrind typology, adding the fourth, "uninvolved" parenting style. We discuss Baumrind's work first and then examine this fourth parenting style.

Baumrind (1967) began by observing nursery-school children in their daily activities for 14 weeks. Gradually she was able to identify three groups of children who had widely varying patterns of behavior: energetic-friendly children, conflicted-irritable children, and impulsive-aggressive children. Baumrind then interviewed each of the children's parents and observed them interacting with their children both at home and in the laboratory, finding that three of the parenting styles displayed in Figure 12-2 were related to the three patterns of child behavior that she observed.

Authoritative parenting was correlated with the behavior of the energetic-friendly children, who exhibited positive emotional, social, and cognitive development. Authoritative parents were not intrusive and permitted their children considerable freedom. At the same time, they were quite willing to impose restrictions in areas in which they had greater knowledge or insight, and they were firm in resisting children's efforts to get them to acquiesce to their demands. In general, warmth and moderate restrictiveness, with the parents expecting appropriately mature behavior from their children, setting reasonable limits but also being responsive and attentive to their children's needs, were associated with the children's development of self-esteem, adaptability, competence, internalized control, popularity with peers, and low levels of antisocial behavior. Such discipline gives children the opportunity to explore their environment and gain interpersonal competence without the anxiety and neurotic inhibition associated with hostile, restrictive, power-assertive discipline practices, or the difficulty in adapting to the demands and needs of others associated with extreme permissiveness.

In contrast, **authoritarian parenting** was linked with the behavior of conflicted-irritable children, who tended to be fearful, moody, and vulnerable to stressors. These parents were rigid, power-assertive, harsh, and unresponsive to their children's needs. In these families, children had little control over their environment and received little gratification. Baumrind proposed that these children often felt trapped and angry but also fearful of asserting themselves in a hostile environment.

Finally, **permissive parenting**, although it appeared to have produced reasonably affectionate relationships between parents and children, tended to be correlated with children's impulsive-aggressive behavior. Excessively lax and inconsistent discipline and encouragement of children's free expression of their impulses were associated with the development of uncontrolled, noncompliant, and aggressive behavior in children. Baumrind found that both authoritarian and permissive parents viewed their children as dominated by primitive self-centered impulses over which they had little control. However, the permissive parents thought that free expression of these impulses was healthy and desirable, whereas the authoritarian parents perceived impulses as something to be suppressed or stamped out. Figure 12-3 summarizes Baumrind's findings on some major dimensions of parents' behaviors; parents of the energetic-friendly children scored highest on all these dimensions during both home and lab observations.

The fourth type of **uninvolved parenting**, identified by Maccoby and Martin (1983), characterized parents who were indifferent to or actively neglected their children and were "motivated to do whatever is necessary to minimize the costs in time and effort of interaction with the child." Uninvolved parents are parent centered, rather than child centered; they focus on their own needs. Particularly when a child is older, these parents fail to monitor the child's activity or to know where she is, what she's doing, or who her companions are. This parenting pattern is sometimes found in mothers who are depressed (Egeland & Sroufe, 1981a, 1981b). In depression, people tend to focus on themselves and may find it difficult to respond to others, even their own children (Kochanska, 1991). The pattern may also characterize people under the stress of such things as marital discord or

authoritative parenting Parenting that is warm, responsive, and involved yet unintrusive, and in which parents set reasonable limits and expect appropriately mature behavior from their children.

authoritarian parenting Parenting that is harsh, unresponsive, and rigid, and in which parents tend to use power-assertive methods of control.

permissive parenting Parenting that is lax and in which parents exercise inconsistent discipline and encourage children to express their impulses freely.

uninvolved parenting Parenting that is indifferent and neglectful and in which parents focus on their own needs rather than their children's needs.

■ FIGURE 12-3
Dimensions of parental behavior and children's characteristics.
Not only did the parents of energetic-friendly children get higher scores on all four dimensions measured—control, demands for mature behavior, communication, and nurturance—but the scores of these parents were more consistent within each child group and across two observational settings, one at home and one in the laboratory. (*Source:* Adapted from Baumrind, 1967)

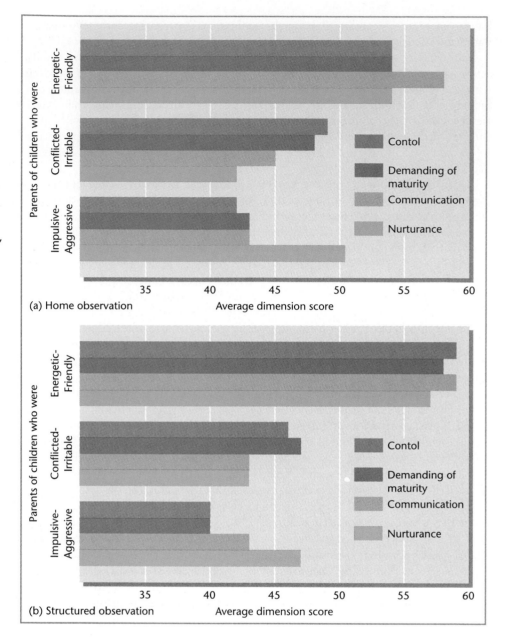

(a) Home observation

(b) Structured observation

divorce. Their own anxiety and emotional neediness may drive some parents to pursue self-gratification at the expense and neglect of their children's welfare (Patterson & Capaldi, 1991). Table 12-1 summarizes the characteristics of parents who display the four parenting styles as well as the kinds of behaviors the children of each group of parents manifest.

Parental involvement plays a crucial role in the development of both social and cognitive competence in children. In infants, lack of parental involvement is associated with disruptions in attachment (Thompson, 1998), and in older children it is associated with impulsivity, aggression, noncompliance, moodiness, and low self-esteem (Baumrind, 1991a). In a kind of "double whammy," children of uninvolved parents tend not only to be socially incompetent, irresponsible, immature, and alienated from their families but to show disruptions in cognitive development, achievement, and school performance (Baumrind, 1991; Hetherington & Clingempeel, 1992). Adolescents and young adults whose parents are uninvolved are likely to be truant, to spend time on the streets with friends whom the parents

TABLE 12-1 Relation between Parenting Styles and Children's Characteristics	
Parenting Style	*Children's Characteristics*
Authoritative Parent Warm, involved, responsive; shows pleasure and support of child's constructive behavior; considers child's wishes and solicits her opinions; offers alternatives Sets standards, communicates them clearly, and enforces them firmly; does not yield to child's coercion; shows displeasure at bad behavior; confronts disobedient child Expects mature, independent, age-appropriate behavior Plans cultural events and joint activities	**Energetic-Friendly Child** Cheerful Self-controlled and self-reliant Purposive, achievement oriented Shows interest and curiosity in novel situations Has high energy level Maintains friendly relations with peers Cooperates with adults; is tractable Copes well with stress
Authoritarian Parent Shows little warmth or positive involvement Does not solicit or consider child's desires or opinions Enforces rules rigidly but doesn't explain them clearly Shows anger and displeasure; confronts child regarding bad behavior and uses harsh, punitive discipline Views child as dominated by antisocial impulses	**Conflicted-Irritable Child** Moody, unhappy, aimless Fearful, apprehensive; easily annoyed Passively hostile and deceitful Alternates between aggressive behavior and sulky withdrawal Vulnerable to stress
Permissive Parent Moderately warm Glorifies free expression of impulses and desires Does not communicate rules clearly or enforce them; ignores or accepts bad behavior; disciplines inconsistently; yields to coercion and whining; hides impatience, anger Makes few demands for mature, independent behavior	**Impulsive-Aggressive Child** Aggressive, domineering, resistant, noncompliant Quick to anger but fast to recover cheerful mood Lacks self-control and displays little self-reliance Impulsive Shows little achievement orientation Aimless; has few goal-directed activities
Uninvolved Parent Self-centered, generally unresponsive, neglectful Pursues self-gratification at expense of child's welfare Tries to minimize costs (time, effort) of interaction with child Fails to monitor child's activity, whereabouts, companions May be depressive, anxious, emotionally needy Vulnerable to marital discord, divorce	**Neglected Child** Moody, insecurely attached, impulsive, aggressive, non-compliant, irresponsible Low self-esteem, immature, alienated from family Lacks skills for social and academic pursuits Truancy, association with troubled peers, delinquency and arrests, precocious sexuality

Sources: Baumrind, 1967, 1991a; Hetherington & Clingempeel, 1992; Maccoby & Martin, 1983.

dislike, to be precociously sexually active, to have drinking problems, and to have a record of delinquent behavior and arrests (Baumrind, 1991a; Patterson, Reid, & Dishion, 1992).

In a longitudinal study, Baumrind (1991a) followed her original authoritarian, authoritative, and permissive parents and their children through adolescence. Authoritative parenting continued to be associated with positive outcomes for adolescents as it was with younger children; responsive, firm parent-child relationships were especially important in the development of competence in sons. Moreover, authoritarian childrearing had more negative long-term outcomes for boys than for girls. Sons of authoritarian parents were low in both cognitive and social competence. Their academic and intellectual performance was poor. In addition, they were unfriendly and lacked self-confidence, initiative, and leadership in their relations with peers.

Other investigators have challenged the parenting style approach, asserting that more research is needed on several fronts. First, some have suggested that we need to identify more clearly the components of each style that contribute to its relative effectiveness or ineffectiveness in respect to the child's development. Second, some authorities propose giving greater attention to how much the child's temperament and behavior influences the parent's style (Kochanska, 1993b, 1995). Finally, recent work has raised serious questions about the generalizability of these styles across either socioeconomic or ethnic/cultural groups (Baldwin, Baldwin, & Cole, 1990; Chao, 1994). There are two primary issues: First, do all groups use the parenting styles we've identified to the same degree, and, second, are the advantages and disadvantages of each style for the child's development similar across groups? The answer to both of these questions seems to be no.

For one thing, neighborhoods make a difference in children's development, not only by confronting them with physical and social challenges that may or may not be beneficial but by determining the kinds of socialization strategies their parents adopt. For example, although an authoritative childrearing style may promote social and academic competence in children living in low-risk environments (Baumrind, 1991a; Steinberg et al., 1992), it may not work in other situations. Several studies have found that poor minority parents who used more authoritarian childrearing practices, especially those who lived in dangerous neighborhoods, had better-adjusted children than those who relied on authoritative strategies (Baldwin et al., 1990; Furstenberg, 1993; Parke & O'Neil, 1997). Parental social integration into the neighborhood may also be an important predictor of more adequate parenting practices (Furstenberg 1993; Steinberg, Darling, & Fletcher, 1995; Wilson 1995). The more socially integrated the parents, the more vigilant they may be about their children's behavior, although this probably holds true only when families reside in neighborhoods where "good parenting" is the norm.

In Chinese families, a style of childrearing that may appear to be authoritarian is quite common, but some have argued that there are major differences between the U.S. and Chinese conception of *authoritarian* and that the application of such a style to Chinese parents may be ethnocentric and misleading (Box 12-2). According to Ruth Chao (1994), the childrearing styles described here reflect a U.S. perspective that emphasizes an individualistic view of childhood socialization and development; we revisit Chao's views in the section on cultural patterns in childrearing. In summary, it is important that in developing new concepts of parenting styles we consider contextual and cultural issues.

The Emerging Self and Parental Socialization

According to Kopp, the challenge of socializing young children is "not trivial." Parents need to induce young children to comply with family and cultural conventions because "children's self-regulatory activities have implications [not only] for contemporaneous family relationships and other social interactions [but] for long-term social abilities, emotional well being, and educational attainments" (Kopp & Wyer, 1994, p. 33). Yet parents can't force children's compliance, and young children are not inherently motivated to follow rules and regulations. Parent-child relationships that meet children's emotional needs, however, can provide children with incentives for meeting the first goal of socialization, or **compliance**—going along with a specific request. As we have seen, secure attachment between child and parent leads the child to want to please the parent and thus to maintain the good relationship. In addition, secure attachment is associated with a more positive view of the self (Chapter 7) and thus presumably with the child's confidence that he can do the things the parent asks him to do.

The child also acquires incentives for compliance when her cognitive development encompasses an awareness of her self as differentiated from others. Recognizing that, like other family members, she is a person and has existence over time (Chapter 9) gives her a feeling of equality and reinforces her sense of capability. The second goal of socialization is **self-regulation,** or the child's ability to reg-

compliance Going along with a specific request or rule.

self-regulation The child's ability to regulate his behavior on his own, without parental reminder.

BOX 12-2

Perspectives on Diversity

Parental Childrearing Styles Carry Different Meanings in Different Cultures

There may be more than one explanation of why Asian American students outstrip European American and other cultural groups in academic performance. As we dicuss later in the text (pages 485–486), Steinberg and his colleagues (1991, 1992) have proposed that the character of the peer groups with whom Asian and other students identify and socialize makes the difference, Asian students on average being more supportive of academic achievement. According to Ruth Chao (1994, 1995, 1996), however, other, much earlier factors in children's lives may also be at work. It seems likely that the supportive Asian peer group is reflecting a kind of childrearing that has no real U.S. equivalent.

In response to the finding that Chinese parents score high on U.S. psychologists' "authoritarian" scales, Chao points out that *authoritarian* does not mean in Chinese what it means in English. Thus, when Chinese parents get such high scores, they may be expressing behavior patterns that are quite different from the U.S. patterns that illustrate this concept. Moreover, this culturally based difference may hold for parents from other Asian cultures who espouse such Confucian principles as family unity and respect for elders and may help explain why Asian students typically do better in school than other U.S. students. (Confucius was a Chinese philosopher of the sixth to fifth centuries B.C. whose system of ethical precepts informs modern-day Confucianism.)

Whereas the American concept of authoritarianism subsumes many quite negative beliefs, attitudes, and behaviors (see Table 12-1), the Chinese style of parenting characterized by the concepts of *chiao shun* ("training") and *guan* ("to govern") requires a high degree of involvement with the child, physical closeness to the child, and devotion—mainly by the mother—of a great amount of time and effort. These concepts subsume teaching or educating children, focusing particularly on children's performance in school (for it is the Chinese belief that education is the key to success) and also connote "loving"

and "caring for" the children. In this sense, these notions are antithetical to the concept of authoritarianism as it is defined in Western society. As Chao (1994) suggests, the seemingly restrictive behaviors that cause Asian parents to get high scores on Western scales may be equated with parental concern, caring, and involvement, and Asian parental control may reflect a more organizational effort designed to keep the family running smoothly and to foster family harmony.

It seems likely that the Chinese concepts of *chiao shun* and *guan* may actually resemble authoritativeness more than authoritarianism. The major difference between Chinese and Western concepts is the U.S. emphasis on soliciting the child's opinions, considering her wishes, and offering her alternatives (Table 12-1). As Chao (1995) points out, the Chinese notion of the self does not emphasize independence and autonomy, as the Western notion does. Instead, it derives from the Confucian notion of *jen* ("humanity" or "humankindness"), which holds that human beings are bound to one another and defined by their relationships with one another. For Chinese—and many other Asian—parents, adhering to social rules of conduct and interaction and developing a sensitive knowledge of others and their expectations are more crucial than focusing on the free expression of internal attitudes, feelings, and thoughts. Whereas the Western child is socialized to achieve according to some internalized standards of excellence, the Chinese child is encouraged to achieve according to family and social norms and expectations (Chao, 1995). These studies underscore the importance of recognizing how different cultures interpret various childrearing practices.

To return to the suggestion by Steinberg and his colleagues that it is support of young people by their Asian peer groups that explains Asian students excelling in school, despite their "authoritarian" upbringing, it is just possible that the peer groups are reflecting the *chiao shun* and *guan* that these peers have received from their parents. In effect, then, they support a given child's motivation and endeavor to achieve because they have the same motivation and belief in hard work.

---

ulate her behavior *on her own*, without parental reminder. Self-regulation develops as the child's self system begins to emerge. The **self system** depends on expanding cognitive abilities. It includes not only self-awareness and the distinction between self and other but such things as access to stored memories of experiences related to the self, the understanding that others may judge one's actions and behaviors for their appropriateness to a given situation, and the capacity for self-evaluation (Kopp & Wyer, 1994). Self-regulation requires that the child recognize and understand her own responsibility for behaviors within the rule system that her parents have established. Evidence indicates that by about age 1½ children can make judgments about the goodness or badness of events or even of their own actions, although they are unlikely to fully appreciate their role in wrongdoing before the age of 3 (Kopp & Wyer, 1994).

> **self system** The sense of self as distinct from others, combined with such things as stored knowledge of past experiences related to the self, awareness of being judged by others, and the capacity for self-evaluation.

■ FIGURE 12-4
Compliance and
self-regulation.
The child's developing
characteristics and capabilities
(shown in left-hand boxes) lead
him gradually to comply with
expressed parental wishes in
various specific situations and
ultimately to regulate his own
behavior in these and other
circumstances. The arrows
running between each set of
characteristics or capabilities
indicate that each set probably
affects others. (*Source:* Adapted
from Kopp & Wyer, 1994)

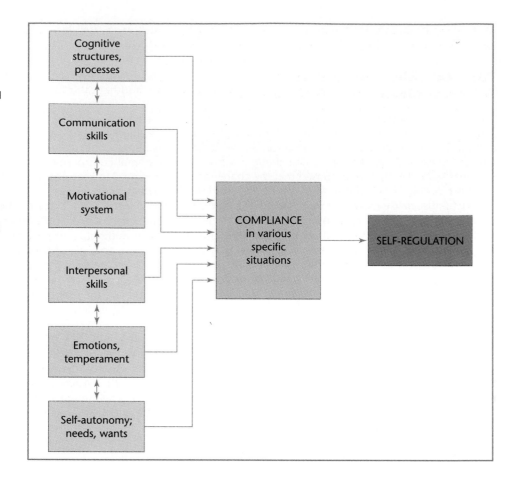

Figure 12-4 summarizes the characteristics and capabilities that underlie the child's path to compliance and self-regulation. According to Kopp and Wyer, 1994, these processes seem to be essential for self-regulation, but just how all of them work, both separately and together, has not yet been determined. In any event, it seems likely that the child's acquisition of self-regulation springs both from a maturing of specific capabilities and the experience she gains from complying with parental reminders in specific situations.

The Sibling System

Over 80 percent of U.S. families have more than one child, and the number, gender, spacing, and relations among a family's children affects the functioning of the entire family unit. These factors affect not only parent-child interactions but the relations among siblings, or sisters and brothers. In fact, most children probably spend more time in direct interaction with their siblings than with their parents or other people significant in their lives (Dunn, 1994; Larson & Richards, 1994). Interactions between siblings provide plenty of opportunities for learning about positive and negative behaviors, and the emotional intensity of these exchanges may be greater than that of exchanges with other family members and friends (Katz, Kramer, & Gottman, 1992).

How Are Siblings Affected by Birth Order?
A child's position in the family—that is, whether he is the firstborn or a later-born child—affects him, his siblings, his parents, and the interactions among all family members. Each child's experience is different, but the experience of the firstborn child is unique. He is the only child who reigns supreme in the love and attention of his parents until he is displaced by the birth of a new baby, with whom he now

must share his parents' affection. The only child, of course, enjoys his parents' exclusive attention all his life. Firstborn children are generally more adult-oriented, helpful, and self-controlled than their siblings, and they also tend to be more studious, conscientious, and serious and to excel in academic and professional achievement (Zajonc & Mullally, 1997; Zajonc, Marcus, & Marcus, 1979). Indeed, firstborns are overrepresented in *Who's Who* and among Rhodes scholars and eminent Americans in the fields of letters and science!

Interestingly, however, research has found that it is secondborn sons who support innovative theories in major scientific controversies related to such issues as evolution, whereas firstborn sons support the status quo (Sulloway, 1995). It may be that the greater expectations and demands that parents typically place on their firstborns are responsible for some other, less desirable characteristics of firstborns. For example, they tend to be more fearful and anxious than their siblings, to experience more guilt, to have more difficulty coping alone with stressful situations, to be admitted more often to child guidance clinics, and to have less self-confidence and social poise.

Although the only child has sometimes been called a "spoiled brat," research findings suggest that in many ways the only child has advantages over other children, especially children in families with three or more siblings. An only child is exposed to the same high level of parental demands as other firstborns, but does not have to adapt to displacement and competition with siblings. Like firstborns, the only child tends to be a high achiever, sustained by her close relationship with her parents, but she tends to be less anxious and to show more personal control, maturity, and leadership (Falbo & Polit, 1986). In social relations both outside and inside the home, only children seem to make more positive adjustments than children who are involved in sibling rivalry.

Birth Order and Parent-Child Interactions

How distressing the firstborn child finds the changes wrought by the arrival of a sibling depends to a great extent on the parents. If a mother continues to be responsive to the needs of the older child and helps him to understand the feelings of the younger child, intense sibling rivalry is unlikely to occur (Howe & Ross, 1990). And if a father becomes increasingly involved with his firstborn child, this too can counter the child's feelings of displacement and jealousy. In fact, one positive effect of the birth of a second child may be that a father participates more in child care (Parke, 1996; Stewart, Mobley, Van Tuyl, & Salvador, 1987). Friends, too, can serve as buffers in this potentially stressful transition. Kramer and Gottman (1992) found that preschoolers who had good friendships showed less upset than children who did not get along well with friends. Moreover, these preschoolers were more accepting and behaved more positively toward their new sibling.

On the other hand, the birth of a new baby usually decreases the amount of interaction both between spouses and between mothers and older children, and firstborn boys are especially likely to show emotional and behavioral problems (Dunn, 1993). Children of depressed mothers and children who have difficult temperaments also have more trouble adjusting to this change in the family situation (McCoy, Brody, & Stoneman, 1994; Stocker & Dunn, 1990). Many of these problems seem to be traceable to changes specifically in the mother-child interaction. After the birth of a second child, mothers tend to become more coercive with their firstborns and to engage in fewer playful interactions with them (Dunn, 1993; Dunn & Kendrick, 1982a).

A new infant or younger child needs more attention and care from parents than an older child and usually gets it, but parents and firstborn children seem to maintain an especially intense involvement throughout life. Parents have higher expectations of their firstborns. They put more pressure on them to take responsibility and to achieve, and they interfere more with the activities of their eldest children

(Sulloway, 1995). Parents are also likely to administer more physical punishment to their firstborns, and these children tend to experience greater disciplinary friction with their parents than the other children in the family. Parents are more consistent and relaxed about discipline with later-born children, probably as a result of experience. In a sense, the firstborn is the "practice baby" with whom the parent, through trial and error, learns parenting skills.

Older siblings in large families are often assigned the supervisory and disciplinary roles that in smaller families parents play. According to Edwards and Whiting (1993) girls are more likely than boys to fulfill such roles; a firstborn 12-year-old girl in a large family may warm bottles, burp babies, change diapers, and soothe a squalling infant with the alacrity and skill of a young mother. In some cultures, such as Polynesia, sibling caretakers are common (Whiting & Edwards, 1988; Wiesner, 1993), and in others, for example, Mexico, siblings rather than parents are the major play partners (Farver, 1993).

Sibling Interactions and Birth Order

Position in the family also affects a child's interactions with his siblings. The eldest child is often expected to assume some responsibility for the younger sibling who has displaced her. Older siblings may function as tutors, managers, or supervisors of their younger siblings' behavior during social interactions and may also act as gatekeepers who extend or limit siblings' opportunities to interact with other children outside of the family (Edwards & Whiting, 1993; Parke & O'Neil, 1997). Parents are likely to restrain or punish the eldest child for showing signs of jealousy or hostility toward a younger sibling and to protect and defend the younger child. On the other hand, the eldest child is dominant and more competent and can either bully or help and teach younger offspring. Thus it is not surprising that older

When older children are secure in their parents' affection they often make good teachers and guides for their younger siblings.

children tend to show both more antagonistic behavior, such as hitting, kicking, and biting, and more nurturant, prosocial behavior toward their younger siblings (Dunn, 1994).

Eldest children focus on parents as their main sources of social learning, whereas younger children use both parents and older siblings as models and teachers (Dunn, 1994). Younger siblings, even infants as young as a year old, tend to watch, follow, and imitate their older siblings; the fact that they adopt older brothers' and sisters' recently abandoned toys suggests that older siblings play an important role in facilitating the younger child's mastery over the environment (Pepler, Corter, & Abramovitch, 1982). When children enter school, the older child's teaching role may become more formalized; 70 percent of children report getting help with homework from siblings, especially from older sisters (Cicirelli, 1976).

Siblings may also serve as resources in times of stress (Conger, 1992; Conger & Elder, 1994; Hetherington & Clingempeel, 1992). Children are most likely to turn to each other when a supportive adult is not available. For example, East and Rook (1993) found that children who had few peer relationships were buffered from adjustment problems when they had positive relationships with a favorite sibling. Boys are less likely to obtain support from siblings and tend to "go it alone" in times of family crises, whereas female siblings may become mutually protective.

Sibling relationships change with age. In adolescence, some of the early overt sibling rivalry and ambivalence may diminish and a special intimacy may arise in which a sibling serves as the most trusted confidant and source of emotional support. In concerns about appearance, peer relations, social problems, and sexual feelings and activities, siblings may be able to communicate more openly with each other than with peers or parents (Dunn, 1994). Female siblings often become increasingly close over the life span.

The sibling relationship may provide an important opportunity for practicing behaviors before trying them out with others outside the family (Dunn, 1988, 1993). For example, mild conflict may be a helpful way to learn to resolve disputes in the relatively safe context of the home. According to Katz and colleagues, "The sibling relationship may be a prime context for learning to oppose another and how to tolerate negative affect. Because conflict is not a threat to the continuance of a relationship with a sibling, children may be freer to explore . . . in this context" (Katz et al., 1992, p. 134). A sibling is also a less threatening target for aggression than a parent. Of course, there is no simple "carryover effect" of behavior with siblings to other relationships such as those with friends or peers; many other factors, including a child's temperament and the nature of the nonfamily relationship, will determine whether this kind of home study can be applied elsewhere (Dunn, 1993).

The Family Unit as an Agent of Children's Socialization

Consideration of marital, parent-child, and sibling influences on children's socialization alone fails to recognize the important role the family unit itself plays as an agent of socialization (Parke, 1988). As systems theory emphasizes, the properties, functions, and effects of the family unit cannot necessarily be inferred by analyzing only family subsystems (Minuchin, 1985; Sameroff, 1994). Indeed, as Figure 12-5 suggests, the family unit plays an equally important role with the marital, parent-child, and sibling systems in socializing the family's children. Families as units change across development and develop distinct "climates," "styles" of responding to events, and "boundaries," all of which provide differing socialization contexts for the developing child (Cowan & McHale, 1997; Sameroff, 1994). They also develop stories and rituals that help transmit family values and roles and that reinforce the uniqueness of the family as a unit. According to Reiss (1989), through *coordinated practices*—activities in which all family members share—the family unit as a whole regulates the child's socialization through stories and rituals.

■ FIGURE 12-5
Family systems and children's socialization. This model indicates hypothesized relations among family subsystems and the outcome of children's socialization. (*Source:* From *Handbook of Personal Relationships,* 2nd ed. (S. Duck, Ed.) by Parke, R.D., and O'Neil, R., p. 56. Copyright © 1998 John Wiley & Sons Limited. Reprinted with permission.)

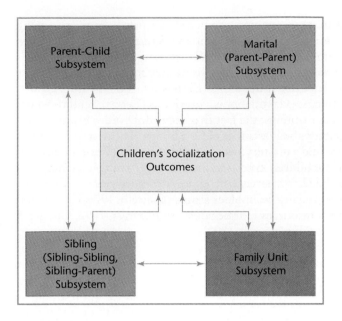

Family Stories

People often use *family stories* to transmit family values and teach family roles. In general, parents and other family members recount stories in naturalistic contexts and when children are present. For example, Miller and Sperry (1987) found that mothers told informal stories in the presence of their children about events in which someone became angry or responded with verbal or nonverbal aggression. Through these stories children learn to distinguish between justified and unjustified anger.

Family members may transmit family-of-origin experiences across generations by telling stories and sharing memories, in this way shaping contemporary interaction between family members. Fiese (1990), for example, found that mothers who told stories of their own childhood that emphasized affiliative, nurturant, and playful themes engaged in more turn taking and reciprocal interactions with their children. On the other hand, mothers who told stories of either achievement or rejection were less engaged and when they interacted with their children were more intrusive and directive. Parents may also tell stories designed both to compensate for their childhood difficulties and to try to ensure that their children do not suffer the same problems. Putallaz, Costanzo, and Smith (1991) found that mothers with predominantly anxious/lonely recollections of their own childhood experiences with peers took an active role in their children's social development and had more socially competent children than mothers without such backgrounds.

Family Rituals

People have recognized the importance of *family rituals* in family life for decades, but the socialization function of these rituals has only recently become apparent (Fiese, 1995; Fiese & Kline, 1993). According to Sameroff (1994), family rituals range from formal and intricate religious observances, such as a first communion or a bas or bar mitzvah, to less-articulated daily interaction patterns like the kind of greeting family members give to someone returning home.

Central to the concept of ritual is its provision of meaning to the notion that we are a unique family unit. Wolin and Bennett (1984) have identified several types of family rituals: *celebrations,* such as special holidays; *rites of passage,* such as weddings; *traditions,* such as special ways of celebrating birthdays, or family vacations at a particular spot; and *patterned routines,* such as the family having dinner together, bedtime routines like reading to the children, or typical weekend activities like going to the park.

Rituals serve an important protective function (Cicchetti & Toth, 1998; Garmezy & Rutter, 1983). Researchers have found, for example, that children who came from families who were able to preserve family rituals such as dinner and holiday routines were less likely to become alcoholic as adults and that adolescents from families who attach more meaning to their rituals tend to have higher self-esteem than other children (Fiese, 1995; Wolin, Bennett, & Jacobs, 1988). In sum, rituals offer a powerful clue to the nature and quality of family functioning and have clear protective advantages for the child.

In sum, these examples of stories and rituals illustrate how families function not just as collections of individuals but as true systems. Moreover, families differ from one another in special ways, much the way individuals differ from each other. In a sense, just as each individual develops a unique personality, so families develop ways of interacting that give them a unique signature or identity.

SOCIAL CLASS, ETHNICITY, AND SOCIALIZATION

No culture is entirely homogeneous. Subgroups within a culture may have different values, attitudes, and beliefs as well as different problems to cope with. Any or all of these differences may be reflected in unique goals of socialization and methods for achieving it.

Poverty and Powerlessness

Both scholarly and lay writers have focused much attention, in recent years, on the differences between the life situations of families of the lower and middle social classes in the American culture. Of particular importance is the prevalence of children living in poverty and under extremely unfavorable circumstances (Table 12-2). Since the early 1970s the percentage of U.S. children under 18 living in poverty has risen by more than 60 percent. In 1996, nearly 15 million children (over 20% of America's children) were living in poverty (Figure 12-6). Although the most obvious differences between the lower and middle classes are seen in the indicators of socioeconomic status—income, education, and occupation—and in the general regard in which members of these classes are held, other related and pervasive features of the lives of the lower and middle classes may be more directly relevant to the socialization process (e.g., dangerous neighborhoods, chronic stress).

Economic Misery
Powerlessness is a basic problem of the poor. The poor have less influence over the society in which they live and are less likely than members of the middle class to be treated adequately and with appropriate concern by social organizations. The poor receive fewer health and public services, and their lack of power, information, and

TABLE 12-2 Some Facts about U.S. Children and Their Families: 1997

1 in 2	Lives with a single parent at some point during childhood
1 in 3	Is born to unmarried parents
1 in 4	Is born poor
1 in 5	Lives in a family receiving food stamps
1 in 7	Lives in a family in which one adult works but family is still poor
1 in 8	Is born to a teenage mother
1 in 11	Is born into a family living at less than half the poverty level
1 in 24	Is born to a mother who received late or no prenatal care
1 in 25	Lives with neither parent

Source: Adapted from Children's Defense Fund, 1998.

■ FIGURE 12-6
Children living below the poverty line, 1996.
Whereas the percentages of European and Asian American children living below the poverty line are lower than the average figure for all U.S. children, the percentages of Native, African, and Hispanic American children far exceed the average. (*Source:* Based on Children's Defense Fund, 1997)

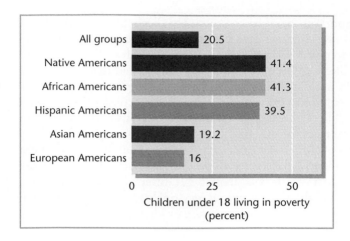

educational and economic resources restrict the options available to them. The poor have little choice of occupations or housing and little contact with other social groups; they are vulnerable to job loss, financial stress, and illness and subject to impersonal bureaucratic decisions in the legal system and in social institutions like welfare agencies. Agents of the law, social workers, educators, and others are more likely to violate their individual rights than those of middle class people.

According to McLoyd and her colleagues (McLoyd, 1990; McLoyd et al., 1994), in view of the multiple stresses, few resources, and little social power possessed by poor parents, it is not surprising that many experience considerable psychological distress, feel helpless, insecure, and controlled by external forces, and are unable to support and nurture their children adequately (Figure 12-7). Nor is it only poor families who suffer in this way. As Conger and Elder (1994) have shown, families at a variety of income levels who suffer economic stress of any kind are more likely than nonstressed families to experience depression and marital conflict and to be harsh with their children.

Only the phenomenon of mutual assistance and support among the poor themselves relieves this dismal picture. Perhaps the very stresses that highlight their powerlessness lead working-class families to form extensive support networks of kin, friends, and neighbors; such networks are particularly common among economically deprived black families (Brody, Stoneman, & Flor, 1996; McLoyd, 1990; Wilson, 1989). These systems provide families not only with emotional support but with unpaid services that could not be purchased. Families and friends render each other mutual assistance in fulfilling emergency needs in times of unemployment, childbirth, illness, and death, as well as the day-to-day needs of family life (McLoyd et al., 1994; Pearson, Hunter, Ensminger, & Kellam, 1990).

Cycles of Disadvantage

The poor get involved in *cycles of disadvantage*. That is, the economic disadvantages they suffer lead them into successive failures that tend to spiral downward in such a way that they not only cannot acquire more resources but tend to lose the ones they have. Consider, for example, the situation of the teenage girl who becomes pregnant, often out of wedlock. She is likely not only to drop out of school but to fail to catch up educationally after her baby is born; if she has already left school she is unlikely to return. Without education, she is limited in the kinds of jobs she can secure, and her earning power is low. She can rarely afford child care and, unless relatives or others can care for her child, she may give up her job and go on welfare. Without money or education, or the opportunity to acquire either, she may find herself in a recurring cycle of low educational attainment, few skills, economic dependence, and poverty. Happily, as we will see later in the chapter, some teenage

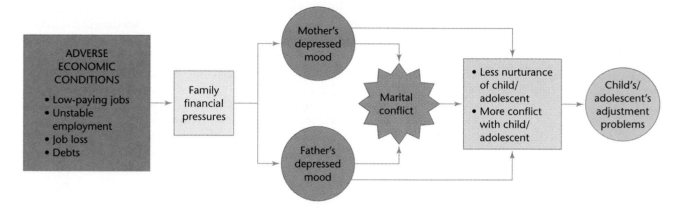

■ FIGURE 12-7
How economic stress can lead to children's adjustment problems.
Adverse economic conditions may combine with personal financial stressors to create worry and insecurity in parents, which can lead to family conflict that may interfere with children's and adolescents' healthy adjustment. (*Source:* Adapted from Conger, Conger, Elder, Lorenz, Simons, & Whitbeck, 1992)

mothers can pull themselves out of this swamp and into better lives for themselves and their children.

Family poverty, whether caused by an unplanned birth, catastrophic illness, company layoffs, or simple inability to find work, is often characterized by a downward spiraling of everything that's crucial to healthy family life, to say nothing of the ordinary pleasures that reassure people that they can actually enjoy life. The task of raising children in this kind of setting is always difficult and sometimes overwhelming.

How Social Class Affects Childrearing

The discrepancy in life circumstances between the poor and the more economically privileged is so great that it is a wonder that we don't find more differences between these groups in values and methods of childrearing. We can best conceptualize the few differences there are in terms of two dimensions: power and self-direction versus helplessness and obedience to the demands of others. Lower-class parents emphasize the development of respectability and obedience to authority in their children; middle-class parents encourage their children to develop curiosity, internal controls, the ability to delay gratification and to work for distant goals, and sensitivity in relations with others (Holden, 1997).

We do find social-class differences in the nature of the restrictions that parents place on children (Hart & Risley, 1995; Kelley, Sanchez-Hycies, & Walter, 1993). Kagan and his colleagues (1978) found that working-class mothers uttered a prohibition—e.g., "no, no" or "don't do that"—every five minutes when interacting with their preschool children at home, whereas middle-class mothers restrained their children only about half as often. In addition, lower-class mothers were less likely than middle-class mothers to offer reasons for their punishments or restrictions, and, perhaps partly because of this, lower-class children were less likely to evidence internalized control systems than middle-class children.

Social class affects childrearing practices through parents' experience at work. For example, working-class fathers tend to have jobs that offer them little scope for self-determination; as a result, they are likely to demand obedience, conformity, and service from their wives and children. They are also more willing to use physical punishment to attain these goals. Middle-class fathers, whose work is more likely to be self-directed, generally value and promote self-control, initiative, and independence in their children (Kohn & Schooler, 1983).

The effects on children's development of the kinds of jobs their parents have are more complex, however, than the foregoing might lead us to believe. For example, when fathers have complex, stimulating, and challenging jobs, boys seem to benefit much more than girls. Greenberger and O'Neil (1991) found that fathers whose jobs were characterized by teaching or mentoring junior employees rather than serving under others spent more time with their sons, particularly in developing their academic, athletic, and other skills; however, this was not the case for daughters. In fact, fathers with daughters spent more time in work and work-related activities. These fathers tended to behave more warmly and responsively with their sons and to control them less strictly, but to exert firm, albeit flexible, control over daughters. Fathers whose jobs were characterized by a high level of challenge (e.g., constant problem solving, decision making) also devoted more time to their sons. The strong father-son link found in this study is consistent with earlier work that suggested that fathers tend to be more involved with their sons than with their daughters.

In contrast, fathers with time-urgent jobs (that require one to work fast most of the day, with few breaks) spent more time on work activities, less time interacting with children, and were more lax in controlling their daughters. Greenberger and O'Neil (1991) suggest that "spillover of positive mood" may account for the relationship between good fathering and jobs that are stimulating and challenging and that "complexity of work with people may increase fathers' intellectual and emotional flexibility in dealing with their sons" (p. 13).

Although mothers' job characteristics are generally less predictive of their parenting styles, where there is a link, boys seem to reap similar benefits and to benefit more than girls. The fact that mothers tend to make a clearer distinction between their work and home responsibilities may, in part, explain the lesser link between mothers' job characteristics and their behavior with their children. Mothers may view boys as more vulnerable and prone to problem behaviors and, as a result, attend more to son's concerns than the concerns of daughters.

Cultural Patterns in Childrearing

In general, social-class differences in family relations are more marked than variations based on race or ethnicity (Parke & Buriel, 1998; Zill, 1986). However, because race and social class do tend to be related, separating these factors has often been difficult; minorities are overrepresented in poorer and less educated families. Unfortunately, investigators have often treated ethnic groups as if they were homogeneous rather than recognize the great variability within such groups. For example, in the United States there are many distinct Hispanic groups—Mexicans, Puerto Ricans, Cubans, Spanish, Colombians, Chileans, and Dominicans, to name only a few. Spanish-speaking people from these and other ethnic groups have quite different socioeconomic, cultural, and linguistic characteristics and within each subgroup there is of course great individual variation.

Parents' and children's behavior must always be understood in the context of the meanings and values of the individual's particular socioculture (Harrison, Wilson, Pine, Chan, & Buriel, 1990; McLoyd, 1990; Parke & Buriel, 1998). For example, in socializing their children many ethnic minorities place greater emphasis than the European American majority on continuity of ethnic values and worldviews and on social interdependence, as seen in the importance of the **extended family**—the family inclusive of grandparents, aunts, uncles, nieces, and nephews— in many groups (Harrison et al., 1990). This emphasis on interdependence is also reflected in a concern with cooperation, obligation, sharing, and reciprocity, which contrasts with North American ideals of self-reliance and competition. On the other hand, Chinese American parents and parents in other Asian American subcultures, who also emphasize family cooperation and obligation, encourage self-sufficiency and achievement even more than do European American parents. Once again, we must always know what group we're talking about when we make general statements.

Ogbu (1981, 1994) has argued that childrearing within subcultures is oriented toward the development of the competencies required for adult political, economic, and social roles. These competencies and the childrearing practices necessary to

extended family Typically, a family that many relatives, including such as grandparents, aunts, uncles, nieces, and nephews, within the basic family unit of parents and children.

Both the nuclear and the extended family are important in most Hispanic cultures, who emphasize sharing and cooperation in both good times and bad.

develop them differ for the white middle class and for minority groups such as urban ghetto blacks. Ogbu speculates that for ghetto African Americans, although adult categories of success include conventional jobs, they also include such "survival strategies" as sports, entertainment, protest activities, hustling, and preaching. Success among ghetto inhabitants, Ogbu suggests, includes the same goals as success for the white middle class—money, power, social acceptance, and self-esteem—but each group has different means for attaining these goals. Long barred from white schools, blacks learned other techniques of developing functional competencies. In addition, Ogbu (1994) theorizes, some childrearing practices common among African Americans, such as verbal rebuffs and physical punishment, may have been designed to promote such things as self-reliance, resourcefulness, ability to manipulate people and situations, wariness of people in authority, and the ability to "fight back."

Different parenting styles are found among many U.S. subcultural groups, but the effects of these styles seem to vary among some groups. Studying more than 20,000 high school students who were from varying ethnic and class backgrounds, Steinberg and colleagues (1992) found that in European American, African American, and Asian American families, authoritative parenting had similar benefits in promoting better psychosocial adjustment and minimizing depression and delinquency in adolescents. However, these researchers found that the relations specifically between authoritative parenting and school performance were less consistent for African American and Asian American adolescents than for European American and Hispanic American adolescents (Steinberg et al., 1995; Steinberg, Mounts, Lamborn, & Dornbusch, 1991). European and Hispanic American adolescents were more likely to benefit academically from authoritative parenting than were African American or Asian American adolescents. Within African American and Asian American groups, adolescents with authoritative parents did not show greater academic achievement than those with nonauthoritative parents. How can these findings be explained?

Research has often shown that African American and Hispanic American students earn lower grades, drop out more often, and attain less education than non-Hispanic white students, whereas the academic performance of Asian American students exceeds that of the other three groups (Fuligni, 1997; Mickelson, 1990; Sue & Okazaki, 1990). Moreover, even when such factors as socioeconomic status and family structure are controlled for, these ethnic differences in achievement appear. In their study, Steinberg and his colleagues concluded that differences in achievement in students of different ethnic backgrounds may well reflect the nature of the peer groups with whom students associate. Mapping the social structure of these groups across the students' schools, these investigators found that students from one ethnic group rarely knew or associated with students from other ethnic groups. Even more interesting was their finding that across all ethnic groups, children performed best when both their parents and their peer groups supported achievement. They did less well, however, with support from only one of these sources, and least well when neither their parents nor their peers supported achievement.

European American and Asian American adolescents were more likely to belong to peer groups that encouraged engagement in school activities and academic achievement. In Steinberg's study, both Hispanic American and Asian American parents tended to be authoritarian, a parenting style that has been associated with low achievement. The researchers postulated that it was the Asian American students' access to supportive peer groups that enabled them to perform better. Recall our discussion of this issue in Box 12-2, however, which suggests that this parenting style, at least among Chinese parents, may encourage achievement (Chao, 1994) and, moreover, that same-culture peer groups are likely to reflect same-parental training.

Supportive, achievement-oriented peer groups were less available to African American adolescents—even to those with authoritative parents. According to Fordham and Ogbu (1986), African American children often view achievement as giving in to the system, or as "white" behavior, and thus they often find themselves torn between the wish to be popular and the wish to perform well in school. As a result, high-achieving African American students often do cross ethnic lines, associating with students from other cultural groups (Liederman, Landsman, & Clark, 1990).

THE CHANGING AMERICAN FAMILY

The American family has been changing for some years now, and although some have predicted the demise of the family, it seems more accurate to say that family forms and family members' roles are becoming more varied. Most children still live in families with two parents who have been married only to each other. However, the proportion of **traditional nuclear families**—composed of two parents and children, with the father as the sole breadwinner—is declining. What are some of the main changes in family structure and functioning that are occurring?

The average household size has decreased to 2.6 people. The average number of children in a family is now slightly less than two, and there are a greater number of single-adult households. This is attributable, in part, to delays in marriage, declines in birth rates and in remarriages, and an increase in the number of elderly people living alone.

There are more single-parent households today, primarily because of the rising divorce rate and secondarily because more unmarried women are having children. The divorce rate doubled between 1960 and 1985; it is estimated that 40 to 50 percent of marriages today will end in divorce, and that 60 percent of these divorces will involve children. In 1996, nearly 28 percent of children under 18 lived with a single parent, but this figure was much higher for some ethnic groups (Figure 12-8). One-third of children will experience the remarriage of one or both of their parents, and 62 percent of remarriages end in divorce. Thus more parents and children are undergoing multiple marital transitions and rearrangements in family relationships.

traditional nuclear family The traditional family form, composed of two parents and one or more children, in which the father is the breadwinner and the mother the homemaker.

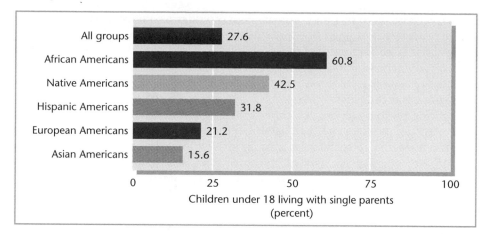

■ FIGURE 12-8
Children living with single
parents, 1996.
Like children living in poverty
(see Figure 12-6), children living
with a single parent are much
more likely to be African, Native,
or Hispanic American than
European or Asian American.
(*Source:* Based on Children's
Defense Fund, 1997)

There also has been a marked increase in out-of-wedlock births, from 4 percent in 1950 to 33 percent in 1994 (Children's Defense Fund, 1997). Among African American women, 70 percent bore babies out of wedlock, among Native Americans the percentage was 57, among Hispanics 43, among European Americans 25, and among Asians and Pacific Islanders it was 16 (Children's Defense Fund, 1997). Contrary to popular wisdom, more than twice as many unmarried mothers are women over the age of 20 as are teenagers. Among European Americans, 54 percent of teen pregnancies and births are out of wedlock.

The number of working mothers has increased. In 1996, 57 percent of mothers with children under the age of 18 were in the labor force (Children's Defense Fund, 1997). Young mothers, poor mothers, and mothers from single-parent families are most likely to enter the labor force because of economic need. Two-thirds of mothers in single-parent families work outside the home, and another 20 percent are seeking employment. Eighty-six percent of black mother-headed households and 38 percent of white mother-headed households fall below the poverty line, in contrast to 46 percent and 16 percent, respectively, of two-parent households.

We look first, in this section, at changes in the family that are associated with maternal employment, and then at the kinds of changes that unwed single parenting, divorce, and remarriage bring about. As we will see, although many children of divorce continue to live with their mothers, joint custody arrangements have become somewhat more common.

Maternal Employment and Child Development

Since the 1970s increasing numbers of mothers, particularly of preschool children, have been entering the labor market. As mothers spend more time on the job and less in the home, family roles and patterns of functioning are changing. What are some of the changes that have already occurred, and how do they influence children's behavior?

Role Models

One shift may be a growing similarity between the roles of the mother and father. When children more often see both of their parents as providing for the family and as participating actively in family and childrearing tasks, the stereotypical roles of the breadwinner father and the homemaking mother may begin to fade away (Pleck, 1984, 1993). Note, however, that although father participation increases in dual-career families, currently mothers are still doing most of the child care and housework (Biernat & Wortman, 1991; Ferree, 1991; Robinson, 1988; Shelton, 1992; Thompson & Walker, 1989). According to one recent estimate, since about 1970 men's contributions to inside housework have roughly doubled, whereas women's contributions have decreased by about a third (Coltrane, 1995). Of course, because up to that time women were shouldering almost all the homemaking, they were still doing two-thirds of this work. In the late 1980s, men were doing about 20 to 25 percent of the inside chores (Coltrane, 1996), but, rather than an absolute increase in the amount of time men devote to household tasks, this apparent change may reflect a reduction in the amount of time wives devote to housework and child care.

Working mothers report that time is their scarcest and most valued resource. Both working mothers and their school-age children complain that the mothers have too little time to spend with their children. However, greater father involvement may compensate for some of these problems. In both dual-earner and single-earner families, high father involvement is associated with children's higher IQ and achievement test scores as well as with greater social maturity (Gottfried, Bathurst, & Gottfried, 1994).

The role model working mothers provide not only has pronounced effects on daughters but alters sons' perceptions of men and women as well. Children of working mothers have more egalitarian views of gender roles (Hoffman, 1989), and children in middle-class families whose mothers are employed have higher educational and occupational goals. Daughters are less likely to display traditional feminine interests and characteristics and more often perceive the woman's role as involving freedom of choice, satisfaction, and competence; daughters themselves are career- and achievement-oriented, independent and assertive, and high in self-esteem (Hoffman, 1989). The sons of working mothers, in contrast to sons of unemployed mothers, not only perceive women as more competent but view men as warmer and more expressive.

Researchers in this area have just begun to look at possible delayed effects of maternal employment on children's development. In a recent longitudinal study, Gottfried et al. (1994) found no relationship between maternal employment and children's development from infancy to the age of 12 and concluded that no sleeper effects were associated with mothers' working outside the home. These investigators found that the children of both mothers who were full-time homemakers and mothers who worked outside the home were similar in cognitive, socioemotional, academic, motivational, and behavioral domains from infancy through adolescence. Supporting this conclusion was the researchers' finding that the home environments and parenting of all the children in the study were very similar in terms of nurturing, intellectual stimulation, parent-child interactions, and family climate.

Individual differences among mothers seem likely to be more significant for children's development than whether mothers are employees outside the home or full-time homemakers. For example, research has shown that such factors as parental involvement and the quality of the home environment were clearly linked to children's development, regardless of mothers' occupations (Bradley, Caldwell, & Rock, 1988; Gottfried et al., 1994; Parke & Buriel, 1998).

Parental Attitudes

The attitudes of both parents toward the dual-earner arrangement and the mother's satisfaction with her work will modify the effects of maternal employment on children. If the working mother obtains personal satisfaction from employment, if she does not experience excessive guilt about being away from her children, and if she has adequate household arrangements to prevent her from being stressed by dual-role demands, she may be as good a mother or better than a homemaking mother (Greenberger & Goldberg, 1989).

Mothers who derive a sense of satisfaction and self-efficacy from their homemaking role and working mothers who enjoy their employment both show more positive relations with their husbands and with their children than unhappy homemakers who would like to be employed (Hoffman, 1989; Schultz, 1991). However, mothers and fathers both display more negative feelings and behavior toward their children when their attitudes toward maternal employment and the wife's work status are not congruent (Hoffman, 1989).

Parent-Child Relations

Some evidence indicates that the childrearing practices of working mothers may differ from those of homemaking mothers, particularly in the area of independence training. Unless they feel guilty about leaving their children in order to work, employed mothers encourage their children to become self-sufficient and independent, and to assume responsibility for household tasks at an earlier age (Hock, 1978). This early independence training may lead children to have high achievement motivation and to perform at a high level of competence (Woods, 1972). However, maternal employment in some families is also associated with less supervision and monitoring of school-age children (Crouter & MacDermid, 1991). Lack of monitoring appears to have particularly adverse consequences for boys—lower school performance, more behavior problems, and an increase in mother-child conflict (Crouter & MacDermid, 1991). For both boys and girls, lack of supervision is associated with earlier dating behavior, precocious sexuality, and greater susceptibility to peer pressures (Dornbusch et al., 1983).

In spite of many predictions to the contrary, studies have indicated that with adequate alternative child care, maternal employment does not usually have detrimental effects on children. In fact, it typically has positive consequences, especially for girls. It is important, however, that in evaluating the effects of maternal employment we consider all relevant factors, such as the mother's reasons for working outside the home, her level of job satisfaction, the demands her employment may place on other family members, the attitudes of these family members toward her employment, and the quality of the substitute care and supervision provided for the children.

Marital Transitions

We need to view divorce and remarriage not as discrete events but as steps in a transition that will modify the lives and development of parents and children. Children's experiences in earlier family situations will modify their response to this transition. The response of family members to divorce and to life in a single-parent family is generally a function of the quality of family life that preceded the separation and divorce; response to remarriage will be shaped by experiences in the earlier marriage and the subsequent, single-parent household. Both divorce and remarriage force a restructuring of the household and changes in family roles and relationships.

Although divorce is sometimes a positive solution to destructive family functioning, for many family members the transition period following separation and divorce is highly stressful. Some evidence indicates that during the first year after a divorce, parents' feelings of distress and unhappiness, troubled parent-child relationships, and children's social and emotional adjustment actually get worse (Hetherington et al., 1982). In the second year, however, when families are adapting to their new single-head-of-household status, many parents experience a dramatic improvement in the sense of personal well-being, interpersonal functioning, and family relations. In the long run, children in stable, well-functioning single-parent households are better adjusted than children in conflict-ridden nuclear families.

Some researchers have suggested that when parents delay divorcing—sometimes in the hope of protecting their children—those children show behavior problems long before the divorce finally takes place; moreover, these problems may be greater than those of children whose parents have some difficulties but remain in their marriage (Block, Block, & Gjerde, 1986; Cherlin et al., 1991). It is possible that children respond adversely to the acrimony and conflict in a stressed marriage, particularly when it is suppressed; or behavior problems in children may exacerbate difficulties in a troubled marriage and help to precipitate a divorce.

Divorce and the Single-Parent Household

What are the most important effects of divorce on children? When divorce leads, as it usually does, to children living in single-parent households, how does the family's lifestyle and functioning differ? What kinds of stresses are single-parent households more likely than nuclear families to encounter? Can a single parent cope with all that two parents have handled up to now? Has she or he time to be a parent?

When divorced parents and their children do not experience additional stresses following divorce, by the second or third year after a divorce, most are coping reasonably well. However, one-parent mother-headed households are at increased risk of encountering multiple stresses that make it difficult to raise children successfully, and, in fact, a period of diminished parenting often follows divorce (Hetherington et al., 1982; Hetherington & Stanley-Hagan, 1995). Custodial mothers may become self-involved, erratic, uncommunicative, nonsupportive, and inconsistently punitive in dealing with their children. They may also fail to control and monitor their children's behavior adequately. Not uncommonly, children reciprocate in the immediate aftermath of divorce by being demanding, noncompliant, and aggressive or by whining and being overly dependent. Not a very winning combination!

Disciplining children can present mothers in single-parent households with troublesome problems. Children tend to view fathers as more powerful and threatening than mothers. In nuclear families, children exhibit less noncompliant and deviant behavior toward their fathers than toward their mothers, and when children do misbehave, fathers can terminate such behavior more readily than mothers (Hetherington et al., 1982). Some researchers have suggested that children's healthy development depends particularly on the presence of their same-gender parents. Some evidence suggests that preadolescent sons adapt better in father-custody homes, whereas preadolescent daughters may develop better in mother-custody homes (Zill, 1988). On the other hand, there is also some evidence that adolescent children living with their fathers may exhibit more deviant and antisocial behavior, perhaps because fathers are less persistent in monitoring their children's activities, friends, and whereabouts (Buchanan, Maccoby, & Dornbusch, 1992).

Divorced mothers and sons are particularly likely to engage in escalating, mutually coercive exchanges. Some desperate divorced mothers have described their relationships with their children right after a divorce as "declared war," a "struggle for survival," "the old Chinese water torture," or "like getting bitten to death by ducks." Although inept parenting is most marked in the first year following divorce and improves markedly in the second year, it is more likely to be sustained with sons—especially temperamentally difficult sons—than with daughters. Divorced mothers and their daughters are likely eventually to form exceptionally close relationships, although mothers may have to weather their daughters' acting-out behavior in adolescence (Hetherington, 1991a; Hetherington & Clingempeel, 1992; Hetherington & Stanley-Hagan, 1995).

In most single-parent households, particularly where the father has custody, parents expect older children to be more autonomous, to participate more actively in family decision making, and to assume greater household and child-care responsibilities than children in two-parent households. Some parents may make inappropriate emotional demands on their children, elevating the older child to the level of a confidant. For many children the increased practical and emotional responsibilities accelerate their development of self-sufficiency and maturity, but if the parent's demands for maturity are excessive, the child may experience feelings of incompetence and resentment.

Both mothers and fathers are at risk for psychological and health problems immediately following divorce (Dura & Kiecolt-Glaser, 1991; Hetherington, Bridges, & Insabella, 1998). And because a custodial parent in a single-parent household is likely to become particularly salient in a child's development, if both parent and child are suffering serious psychological distress or if the parent is incompetent or dysfunctional, the child may suffer. Moreover, negative effects may go both ways: A depressed, preoccupied, or ill parent and a confused, angry, demanding child may be able to give each other little support, and each may exacerbate the other's problems (Hetherington, 1989).

Single parents also face some very practical problems. Mothers in particular suffer from task overload, attempting to deal with family tasks and responsibilities that are considered a full-time job for two adults (Hetherington et al., 1982; Hetherington, Stanley-Hagan, & Anderson, 1989). Money is another major problem: Far more single parents are custodial mothers, and women suffer marked declines in income following divorce (Zill, 1991). Custodial fathers are luckier; they typically have greater economic resources and can hire someone to assist in child care and housekeeping tasks, and they're also more likely to receive help from friends. Social isolation is also a problem for many mothers in single-parent households. A divorced mother's main source of social and emotional support is her family, especially her mother. About one-third of divorced mothers spend some time living in their family of origin after a divorce.

Although we have emphasized the increasing salience of the custodial parent in the child's development, noncustodial parents can continue to play a significant role in their children's development. When divorced parents agree on childrearing methods and maintain a reasonably friendly attitude toward each other, frequent visits between the children and the noncustodial parent may be associated with positive adjustment and self-control in the children. When the mother has custody, such visits are particularly helpful for sons. When there is continued conflict between parents, however, especially conflict where the child feels caught in the middle or when the parent is a nonauthoritative parent or is poorly adjusted, frequent contact between the noncustodial parent and the child may be associated with disruptions in the child's behavior (Buchanan, Maccoby, & Dornbusch, 1991; Camara & Resnick, 1988). Clearly what counts is the quality of the contact with a noncustodial parent and the exposure of the child to conflict and stress.

Family Interaction in Remarried Families

Family members' experience in their original family setting greatly affects their response to remarriage. For divorced women, remarriage is the most common route out of poverty, and a new partner may give a custodial mother not only economic but emotional support as well as help in childrearing.

Children sometimes resist the arrival of a stepparent, creating stress in the new marital relationship. Sons, who have often been involved in coercive relationships with their custodial mothers, may have little to lose and much to gain from a relationship with a caring stepfather. Daughters, on the other hand, may feel the intrusion of stepfathers into their close relationships with their mothers as more threatening and disruptive. Among preadolescent children, divorce seems to have more adverse consequences for boys, and remarriage seems to be more difficult for girls; in adolescence, however, such gender differences are rarely found (Cherlin et al., 1991; Hetherington, 1991b; Hetherington & Clingempeel, 1992).

In general, neither stepmothers nor stepfathers take as active a role in parenting as biological parents (Bray, 1988; Hetherington, 1991a; Hetherington & Clingempeel, 1992). Even after they've been in the family for two years, stepfathers are likely to exhibit an uninvolved parenting style. Indeed, many stepfathers are rather like polite strangers with their stepchildren, hesitating to become involved in controlling or disciplining them. Biological fathers are more likely to praise children for good behavior, be affectionate and interested in their children's activities, set limits, and criticize children for undesirable behavior—for not cleaning up their rooms, not getting their homework done, or for fighting with a younger sibling. Stepmothers, who walk into the maternal role, are forced to take a more active role in discipline than are stepfathers (Cherlin & Furstenberg, 1994; Santrock & Sitterle,

1987). This may in part explain the finding that children are more resistant and have poorer adjustment in stepmother families (Cherlin & Furstenberg, 1994; Hetherington et al., 1998). In addition, a child's age at the time of a parent's remarriage will affect both the child's attitude toward the new marriage and the likelihood that he or she will develop any kind of problem behavior. Adolescents have a particularly difficult time accepting a parent's remarriage (Hetherington, 1991a; Hetherington & Clingempeel, 1992).

Although we have been focusing on the effects of divorce and remarriage on parent-child relations, sibling relations also are often disrupted. More antagonistic, nonsupportive relations are found among siblings in divorced and remarried families than among those in nondivorced families (Conger & Conger, 1996; Hetherington et al., 1998; Hetherington & Clingempeel, 1992). These adverse effects are most marked for male siblings, whereas some pairs of female siblings serve as mutual supports in coping with their parents' marital transitions.

Children in Divorced and Remarried Families

Over time, most boys and girls adjust reasonably well to their parents' marital transitions. Exhibiting remarkable resiliency, some children actually become stronger through coping with divorce and remarriage. In fact, only about 25 percent have long-term problems. Authoritative parenting is associated with more positive adjustment in children in divorced and remarried families, just as it is in nondivorced families. If divorce reduces stress and conflict and leads to better functioning on the part of the custodial parent or if the child's loss of an uninvolved or incompetent father eventually results in the acquisition of a more accessible, responsive father figure, the child often benefits in the long run from divorce and remarriage. Preadolescent boys in particular may benefit from a close, caring relationship with a stepfather.

Behavioral disruptions and emotional upheavals are common, however, in the early weeks and months. Children often express anger, resentment, anxiety, and depression, and some suffer sustained developmental delays or disruptions. Others appear to adapt well in the early stages of family reorganization but show delayed effects that emerge at a later time, especially adolescence. The most commonly reported sustained problem behaviors found in children of divorced and remarried families are aggressive, noncompliant, antisocial behavior; a decline in prosocial behaviors; and disruptions in peer relations (Hetherington et al., 1998; Hetherington & Clingempeel, 1992). Adolescence seems to trigger behavior problems in both boys and girls in divorced and remarried families, even in some who have previously been functioning well. Depression is common, and substance abuse and precocious sexual activity are found in both boys and girls in mother-headed one-parent families (Hetherington, 1991a; Hetherington & Clingempeel, 1992; Newcomer & Udry, 1987). Problems in academic achievement, school adjustment, and school dropout are greater for boys than girls in divorced families.

As children mature, girls continue to do somewhat better than boys. Following up on an initial study, Hetherington (1989) found that six years after divorce and in families in which the mother was still single, girls who were relatively well adjusted after two years remained so. These girls had more responsibility and more power within the family and had close relationships with their mothers. Among girls, adjustment problems are more evident at the onset of adolescence. During the teen years, girls of divorce may show increased conflict with their mothers, increased noncompliance, antisocial behavior, emotional disturbance, loss in self-esteem, and problems in heterosexual relations and sexual behavior (Chase-Lansdale & Hetherington, 1990; Hetherington, 1998; Newcomber & Udry, 1987). Being an early maturer increased the likelihood that a girl would become alienated from her family, although girls are also likely to manifest a "sleeper effect." The risk of being a teenage mother increased three times as a result of divorce, from 11 percent in intact families to 33 percent in divorced families. Hetherington also found that

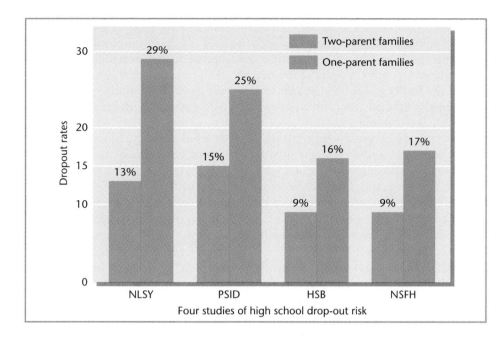

■ FIGURE 12-9
Education and one-parent families.
As measured in four distinct survey studies, the risk of dropping out of high school was twice as high for children living in one-parent families (including stepfamilies) as for those living with two parents (NLSY=National Longitudinal Survey of Youth; PSID=Panel Study of Income Dynamics; HSB=High School and Beyond Study; NSFH=National Survey of Families and Households.) (*Source*: From *Growing Up with a Single Parent* by McLanahan, S. and Sandefur, G., "The risk of dropping out of high school," p. 41. Copyright © 1994 by the President and Fellows of Harvard College. Adapted by permission of the publisher, Harvard University Press, Cambridge, MA.)

these young women were more likely to have married at a young age, to have been pregnant before marriage, and to have selected husbands who were more psychologically unstable and less educated and economically secure than women in intact or widowed families (Hetherington, 1988a, 1998). Survey studies of nationally representative samples confirm the increased difficulties in heterosexual relationships for young women whose parents divorce (Cherlin & Furstenberg, 1991). Adult women from divorced families were more likely than those from nondivorced families to have higher rates of divorce themselves (Hetherington, 1987).

Over the long haul, boys continue to experience major problems. Hetherington (1988a, 1993), found that divorced mothers continued to spend less time with their sons than mothers in nondivorced families. Mothers continued to be ineffective in their control efforts and to engage in coercive interactions with their sons. Monitoring of boys' activities was lower in divorced non-remarried households, and the boys engaged in more antisocial behavior and spent more time away from home with peers.

What are the long-term effects of divorce and remarriage on a family's children? National survey studies suggest that divorce is related to several negative outcomes (McLanahan & Sandefur, 1994). The risk of dropping out of high school was twice as high for children of divorced families as it was for children in intact families (Figure 12-9). This outcome has serious long-term implications and may reduce future employment and educational opportunities.

Perhaps the most dramatic evidence of the long-term effects of divorce comes from a recent study of the predictors of longevity (Freidman et al., 1995). In a follow-up investigation of a group of gifted children originally studied by Lewis Terman in the 1920s, individuals who experienced parental divorce during childhood were likely to die sooner than those whose parents stayed married. Although these individuals were more likely themselves to divorce as adults, even after taking this into account, parental divorce was still a predictor of premature death. Clearly divorce has long-term consequences, although the mechanisms by which divorce alters longevity are still not clearly understood.

Joint Custody
In view of the changes that increasing maternal employment has brought about, especially the realization that fathers not only can be highly competent caregivers but can derive pleasure from being with their children, it is not surprising that the

traditional doctrine of sole custody has been reexamined. Perhaps children and ex-spouses would all benefit if joint custody was always an option in divorce cases involving children: "At its best, joint custody presents the possibility that each family member can 'win' in post divorce life" (Thompson, 1994, p. 17). Neither mother nor father is identified as a better or worse parent, and mothers and fathers each win a significant future role in the lives of their children. Perhaps even more important, the children win.

Joint custody takes two main forms. In **joint legal custody**, both mother and father retain and share responsibility for decisions concerning their children's lives, but the children usually reside with one parent. Under a **joint physical custody** arrangement, the children live with each parent for certain periods throughout the year. Although the length and timing of these periods vary, it is expected that children will have physical access to both parents on a regular basis. To examine the impact of joint custody on children, Maccoby and Mnookin (1992) followed 1,100 families for three and a half years, beginning with the married couples' separation, and found that nearly 80 percent of the families had joint legal custody. Mothers received sole physical custody in more than 67 percent of the cases, whereas fathers received sole physical custody less than 10 percent of the time. Even when joint physical custody was the legal decision, only about half of the children actually lived in dual residence arrangements, and a third lived with their mothers. Overall, more than two-thirds of the families opted for a mother residence arrangement and continued with this residence plan for the period of the study. However, boys were more likely to live with their fathers or in dual residence than girls, who more often lived with their mothers. Moreover, older children were more likely to live with their fathers and children between 3 and 8 in dual residence arrangements. Finally, arrangements were not static; many children changed their residential arrangements over the course of the study. More than one-quarter (28%) of the children had changed houses during the three and a half years of the study. Moreover, nearly half (45%) of the children in mother-residence families changed—either increased or decreased—the amount of contact that they had with their fathers.

To understand the impact of differing custody arrangements on children, we first need to consider parenting patterns. Buchanan, Maccoby, and Dornbusch (1996) found that only about a quarter of families were able to cooperate. Another 25 to 30 percent of the parents were conflicted. The largest group (30% to 40%) were uninvolved, with the parents avoiding contact with each other and practicing "parallel" uncoordinated parenting in the two residences. Over time, conflicted parenting decreased and disengagement increased. In a follow-up, four and a half years after separation, researchers interviewed adolescents to assess their feelings about their parenting arrangements and their own adjustment. "Feeling caught" between parents, measured by items such as "Parents ask children to carry messages," and "Parents ask questions you wish they wouldn't ask," was more likely to occur in high-conflict/low-cooperation families. Adolescents of parents who had disengaged from each other were less likely to feel this way than adolescents whose parents were still "at war" but more likely to "feel caught" than adolescent children of parents who were cooperating. Dual residence arrangements are particularly harmful when parents continue to be in conflict. Older adolescents and girls were more likely to feel caught in the between-parent squeeze. Adolescents with higher feelings of "being caught" were more likely to experience depression and anxiety and to engage in more deviant behavior (e.g., smoking, drug use, fighting, cheating, stealing) than adolescents who experienced more interparental cooperation.

This pattern of findings is consistent with earlier, smaller-scale studies, which found that the degree of parental conflict rather than custody arrangements themselves seems to be the best predictor of children's adjustment (Goodman, Emery, &

joint legal custody A form of child custody in which both parents retain and share responsibility for decisions regarding the child's life but which generally provides for the child to reside with one parent.

joint physical custody As in *joint legal custody,* parents make decisions together regarding their child's life, but they also share physical custody, the child living with each parent for a portion of the year.

Haugaard, 1998). Joint custody is clearly not a panacea for divorced families or for divorced fathers in particular. Fathers' influence and contact with their children seems less governed by custody arrangements than by other factors, such as geographic distance and relationships with their ex-spouses. In the long run, the advantage of joint custody may be its "symbolic value to parents and children" (Emery, 1988)—a sign to fathers that they retain some rights and obligations as a parent and a message to their children that their fathers are still part of their larger family and a significant figure in their lives. At the same time it is evident that joint custody is not a problem-free solution, especially if interparental conflict continues after divorce. Evaluations of the long-term impact of differing types of custody arrangements on children as well as on their parents are needed.

Parenting after Thirty

People are not only marrying later today than in earlier times (three or four years later than they did in the 1950s) but are becoming first-time parents at later ages. Although there may be many reasons for later parenthood, important factors are doubtless widespread maternal employment, more flexibility in gender roles for both men and women, and greater availability of support services such as child care. In addition, by the time a couple are in their thirties, they have usually completed their education and are fairly well established in their careers.

Both mothers and fathers who delay parenting seem to interact differently with their infants. Mothers may not only feel more responsibility in caretaking but also enjoy it more and express more positive affect with their infants (Ragozin, Bashman, Crnic, Greenberg, & Robinson, 1982). In addition, older mothers tend to spend more social time with their babies and to be more successful in eliciting vocal and imitative responses from them, perhaps because these mothers have gained more social and cognitive teaching skills.

The older father, with more flexibility and freedom in balancing the demands of work and family, is three times as likely as a younger father to have regular responsibility for some part of a preschool child's daily care (Daniels & Weingarten, 1988). Moreover, the older father may be generally more involved in the parental role and may experience more positive affect associated with childrearing (Cooney, Pedersen, Indelicato, & Palkovitz, 1993). The fact that younger fathers tend to engage in more strenuous physical play with their children and older fathers to use more cognitive mechanisms in their play may reflect less stereotypical views of men's and women's roles in parenting as much as a lessening of physical energy (Neville & Parke, 1997; Parke & Neville, 1995).

As family systems theory would predict, greater participation by fathers in caring for and playing with their children may help facilitate the more enjoyable and productive relations that older mothers enjoy with their children. It seems clear that the timing of first parenthood is a powerful organizer of both maternal and paternal roles. Future investigations of marital and parenting interaction patterns need to consider this timing as well as other factors.

Gay and Lesbian Parents

Another recent change in the American family is the greater numbers of lesbian and gay parents. Although we have only estimates at the moment, most authorities believe that there are somewhere between 1 and 5 million lesbian mothers and between 1 and 3 million gay fathers and that gay or lesbian parents are rearing between 6 and 14 million children (Patterson, 1995b).

Homosexual families are diverse. The largest group of children with gay or lesbian parents are children who were born to one of the homosexual partners before they established their relationship and in the context of a heterosexual relationship or marriage. Within this group there are two primary variations: When one of a child's biological parents declares his or her same-gender sexual preference and the

Lesbian partners who choose to
become parents tend to share
childrearing and homemaking
tasks more equally than
heterosexual couples.

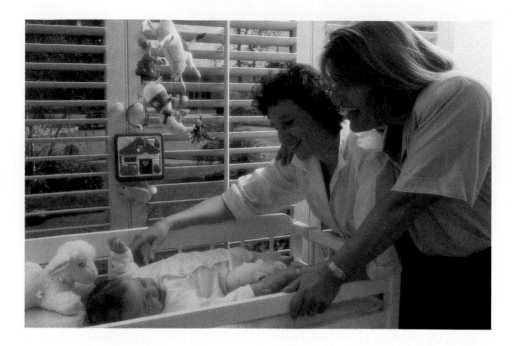

couple divorce, the gay or lesbian parent may then form a new, homosexual relationship in which these partners together care for the child. In another arrangement, a gay or a lesbian couple who do not have children from previous
relationships may choose to become parents. One partner in a lesbian relationship
may choose to bear a child through donor insemination. Or either gay or lesbian
couples may adopt children.

Research suggests that heterosexual mothers and lesbian mothers who have
divorced their heterosexual partners differ little in terms of self-concept, general
happiness, overall adjustment, or presence of psychiatric problems (Patterson,
1995b). We know less about divorced gay fathers because only a small minority of
these men are granted custody of their children or live with them (Bigner & Bozett,
1990). Most of our knowledge of gay and lesbian parenting comes from studies of
couples who, after establishing their relationship, chose to become parents (Hand,
1991; Osterweil, 1991; Patterson, 1995a,b). Research that compared these couples'
households with heterosexual households found that both gay and lesbian couples
tended to share household duties more equally (McPherson, 1993). Among lesbian
partners, biological mothers appeared to be more involved in child care and nonbiological mothers to spend longer hours in paid employment (Figure 12-10;
Patterson, 1995a). At the same time, children in lesbian families, like those in heterosexual families, were likely to be better adjusted when both partners shared
child care more or less equally, and lesbian parents were also likely to be more satisfied (Patterson, 1995a).

What about the children? According to Patterson (1995b), the evidence suggests that "children of lesbian mothers are developing in a normal fashion"
(p. 265). We have no evidence that these children have any greater emotional or
social problems—including peer relationships and relationships with adults—than
other children, nor is there any appreciable evidence of altered gender roles among
lesbian parents' children (see also Chapter 15). In similar fashion, the great majority of gay fathers' children grow up to be heterosexual adults. There is no evidence
that these children are victims of sexual abuse nor that they are at any significant
disadvantage in comparison with children of heterosexual fathers. Moreover,
although gay fathers undoubtedly face prejudice and discrimination, children have
described their relationships with gay fathers as warm and supportive (Patterson
& Chan, 1997).

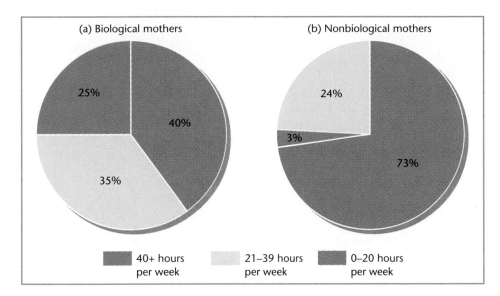

Lesbian mothers and paid employment.
Not surprisingly, among lesbian parents, (a) biological mothers spent less time in paid employment (only 40% worked a full week) and more time in child care whereas (b) nearly three-quarters of nonbiological mothers were engaged in full-time employment. (*Source:* Adapted from Patterson, 1995a)

Teenage Pregnancy: Children Having Children

Why do teenagers have babies out of wedlock? The immediate causes include the facts that young people among all major cultural groups in the United States are initiating sexual behavior earlier and that, as we've noted, people generally are marrying later. The underlying causes are complicated and difficult to combat. Poverty, being socially and economically disadvantaged, having models (parents and other adults) who also have children out of wedlock, and growing up too soon—that is, not having the luxury of an adolescence during which one can devote oneself to self-understanding and academic achievement—play particularly important roles in early teen pregnancy (Brooks-Gunn & Chase-Lansdale, 1995; Burton, 1990).

What is the magnitude of this problem? Slightly over half of the one million American teenage girls who become pregnant each year give birth (the others miscarry or have abortions), and among these more than 70 percent are unmarried (Figure 12-11; Children's Defense Fund, 1998). Minority teens are 1½ to 2 times as likely as European teens to bear children, and all together, American teenagers have almost twice as many babies as United Kingdom adolescents, more than five times as many babies as teens in several European countries, and more than thirteen times as many babies as are born to teenagers in Japan (Children's Defense Fund, 1998). Although almost a quarter of teenage mothers are married and another third have fairly stable relationships with the fathers of their babies, more than half face personal, economic, and social problems that make it very difficult for them to support and care for their children (Children's Defense Fund, 1998). As a result, these half million babies have poor prospects, largely because of the economic constraints most teen mothers confront, and the younger the mother the greater the risk:

> During the preschool years, signs of delays in cognitive development begin to emerge and tend to grow more evident as the children age. Preschool children of teen mothers also tend to display higher levels of aggression and less ability to control impulsive behavior. By adolescence, children of teen mothers have, on the whole, higher rates of grade failure and more delinquency. . . . They also become sexually active earlier [and have] a greater likelihood of pregnancy before age 20 (Children's Defense Fund, 1998, p. 98).

Teen parents and their children pay huge prices, and over time the society as a whole pays in lost productivity and the need of disadvantaged children for public care and services.

■ FIGURE 12-11

Changes in percentage of births to adolescent girls, 15 to 19 years old, that were to unmarried teens.
Births to unmarried teens account for a growing proportion of all births to adolescent girls. In 1995, more than 70 percent of teens having babies were unmarried, compared with only about 15 percent in 1960. (Source: Children's Defense Fund, 1998; figure 7.1, p. 94)

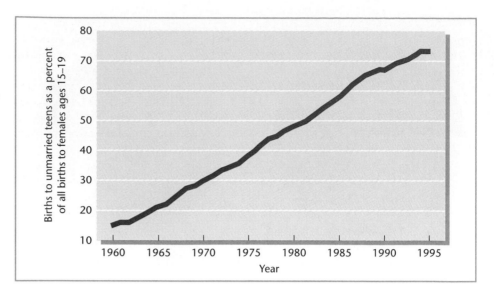

Women who have their first child as teenagers tend to drop out of school and subsequently do not catch up educationally; those already out of school at the time of birth tend not to return to school (Furstenberg, Brooks-Gunn, & Chase-Lansdale, 1989; Hetherington, 1998). In addition, young mothers have more children over time, which in turn limits their freedom to work. The lack of education, work skills, and available work time tends to be associated with continued poverty.

Cultural factors contribute to some differences among subcultural groups. Teenage pregnancy is most common among African Americans, somewhat less common among Hispanic women, and least likely among European Americans (Sullivan, 1993). African Americans tend to initiate sexual behavior earlier than European Americans or Hispanics, to be less likely to use contraceptive methods, and to be less likely to marry before the birth of their babies. Beginning in the early 1990s, the birth rate for unmarried African American teens began to decline; the rate for Hispanic adolescents rose a little, and the rate for European American teenagers remained stable.

In this section we begin by examining the effects, on both teenage mothers and their children, of out-of-wedlock birth and of being raised by a single parent, the most common scenario. We discuss the role of the teenage father briefly and look at the quality of parenting teenagers can provide their children. We conclude with a discussion of factors that can operate to protect unwed teenagers from conceiving children as well as factors that can enable an unmarried teenage parent to break out of the cycle of poverty and social disadvantage and achieve a reasonable degree of comfort for herself and her child.

Effects of Teen Pregnancy on Young Parents and Children

In a sense, the effects of teenage pregnancy complete a cyclical process: Unwed teen pregnancy takes place largely in a context of poverty and deprivation, and the results of such pregnancy often increase a mother's poverty and socioeconomic disadvantage (e.g., Sullivan, 1993). In general, unwed pregnancies lead teens into greater economic problems, academic problems, and, often, welfare (Hetherington, 1998; Sullivan, 1993). In the United States, at least, the effects of unwed teen births tend to vary among different subcultural groups; for example, economic problems tend to be worse for African Americans (Cherlin, 1996). On the other hand, some teen mothers who get help and support from family and other sources later return to school and, even though this sometimes takes as much as 20 years, are eventually successful in jobs that enable them to support a family (Cherlin, 1996).

Although teenagers account for more than a quarter of all abortions in the United States, the decision to abort the child one is carrying is more common among people of higher socioeconomic status (Hetherington, 1998). Religion also plays a role in such a decision: Hispanic teenagers, mostly Roman Catholic, are less likely than African Americans or European Americans to choose abortion (Sullivan, 1993). In a recent study, Hispanic unwed teenage fathers often described abortion as "murder," and "a sin" (Sullivan, 1993, p. 302). Nevertheless, when viewed across all groups, poverty is a more powerful predictor of the outcome of pregnancy than are either race or ethnicity.

What determines whether unwed teenage parents will marry? Again, there seem to be cultural differences. Among African Americans, marriage is unlikely, although teenage fathers often keep in contact with their babies and contribute to their support. Hispanic teen fathers often marry the mothers of their babies but, in a recent study, they were found to marry only after the baby was born, and common-law marriage is not uncommon among Hispanic youth (Sullivan, 1993). European American fathers were likely to marry the mothers of their babies before the latter were born. One reason for these differences may be that European Americans are generally in more favorable financial circumstances, whereas minority couples often face the problem of securing Temporary Assistance for Needy Families (TANF) assistance; mothers may be more successful in obtaining this government help if they are without partners.

How do the children of unwed teenage mothers fare? Apparently the younger the teenage mother, the more likely her child will have deficits in cognitive and academic functioning (Hetherington, 1998). Even when the mother's age is controlled, however, mothers and children are troubled by such things as early health problems and increased frequency of premature birth, both associated with poor nutrition and prenatal care in the mothers. Children, especially boys during the preschool and elementary school years, tend to show deficits in cognitive functioning, academic performance, and self-regulation. In one study, 3-year-old children of adolescent mothers achieved lower IQ scores (84, on average) than would be expected and in general displayed intellectual, linguistic, and emotional delays in development (Sommer et al., 1995). When such children reach high school age, they tend more often to experience misbehavior, learning problems, retention in a grade, truancy, school drop out, and idleness. In addition they show less self-control and more antisocial behavior, such as drug abuse and delinquency (Nord, Moore, Morrison, Brown, & Myers, 1991). These effects are likely to be related to the environment of economic disadvantage, family instability, and high stress encountered by both the teenaged mothers and their children.

Teen Parenting and the Father's Role

Largely because of personal problems and a lack of resources, teenage parents are thought to be less competent caregivers (Brooks-Gunn & Chase-Lansdale, 1995). Teenage mothers may be less warm and nurturing than older mothers and less likely to stimulate their babies verbally and cognitively, reading to them less and being less involved in their school activities. Young unwed mothers may also have lower educational aspirations for their children, and there is some suggestion that these mothers may more often engage in aggressive behavior with their children and abuse or neglect them (Brooks-Gunn & Chase-Lansdale, 1995). As Hetherington (1998) puts it, "Many of the personal and socioeconomic factors that put very young teenagers at risk for childbearing also create stresses that may erode nurturant, responsive and authoritative childrearing."

Although society tends to fault teenage fathers for their failure to support their babies and the babies' mothers, two-thirds of European American fathers and nearly as many Hispanic fathers were found to marry the mothers of their babies (Sullivan, 1993). Among the African American fathers, only 23 percent married, but job opportunities were least favorable for these young men. According to Cherlin (1996), male partners in unwed teenage pregnancy and parenting contribute little support for several reasons. First, most teenage boys lack the earning power to help much; second, the mothers' parents may try to keep the young father out, assuming that his support is unlikely anyway; third, some teen fathers simply don't want the responsibility. Some teenage fathers do support their children, but the determinants of father involvement are still unclear.

Prevention and Intervention

Teenagers whose parents not only are educated and reasonably comfortable financially but who are warm and responsive to their children have a better chance at avoiding teen pregnancy (Hetherington, 1998). A family's religion also is a protective factor that can help avoid early sexual activity and childbearing among the family's children. Most studies indicate that the denomination, or particular religion to which the family adheres, makes no difference; it is the family's active involvement with religious beliefs and practices that acts as a preventive device.

The use of contraceptives by teenagers who have initiated sexual activity can of course prevent pregnancy as well as serious and life-threatening sexual diseases. According to Cherlin (1996), although the rate at which teenagers use contraceptives has been increasing, so far this rate of increased protection has just managed to keep up with the increase in numbers of young people who are sexually active.

Once an unwed teen has carried a pregnancy to term and has become a parent, what are her options for avoiding some of the negative effects we've discussed and for escaping poverty and socioeconomic disadvantage? According to Cherlin (1996), marriage is one of the most important routes out of poverty, largely because of the male worker's income it brings, but marriage is also a difficult route. The majority of marriages entered into by the teenage mothers that Cherlin (1996) studied had ended by the 22-year reinterview or earlier, leading Cherlin to speculate that one factor may be immaturity in these marriages and the inability to judge who will make a good life partner.

According to Hetherington (1998), getting a good education and limiting future births are other important ways for a teenage mother to improve her lot. In addition, when the children of unwed mothers have good quality relationships with their fathers, they tend to achieve higher educational levels and to be less subject to depression and less likely to be imprisoned for misbehaviors or crimes (Hetherington, 1998). Particularly for African American children, having a stepfather join the family seems to have positive effects, increasing the likelihood that the children will be successful in life.

The negative impact of the conditions under which teenage mothers and their children live is greater for the children than for the mothers. This may be because the children have always lived under these conditions, whereas some of the mothers at least may have known better. In any event, evidence indicates that if the mother's situation changes for the better, and particularly if she moves off welfare, becomes economically independent, acquires more education, or enters a stable marriage before her child becomes an adolescent, the child's adjustment and academic performance may be enhanced (Brooks-Gunn & Chase-Lansdale, 1995).

CHILD ABUSE WITHIN THE FAMILY

Although it is difficult to obtain precise figures on how many children in the United States are abused, it is estimated that every year between 1 and 3 million children are physically or psychologically abused and that the majority of these children are abused by family members (National Committee to Prevent Child Abuse, 1997). In 1996, Child Protective Services received reports of 3.1 million cases of child abuse, about 31 percent of which were substantiated (Goodman et al,

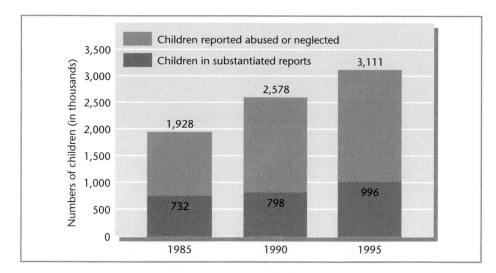

■ FIGURE 12-12
Rising incidence of child abuse and neglect, 1985–1995.
A 36 percent increase in substantiated reports of child abuse and neglect within one decade is frightening, to say nothing of the 61 percent increase in total reports. Moreover, because many cases of abuse are never reported, the problem may be even more devastating. (*Source:* Children's Defense Fund, 1997)

1998; National Committee to Prevent Child Abuse, 1997). Of these children, nearly 20 percent were infants or toddlers (Children's Defense Fund, 1997). What is more, child abuse in the United States is rising: Between 1985 and 1995, reports of abuse increased by 61 percent, and substantiated cases increased by 36 percent (Figure 12-12). Because many instances of child abuse are not even reported or are discovered only after abuse has continued for a long time or the child is dead, these figures are conservative. Children are subjected to verbal abuse; they are starved, beaten, burned, cut, chained, isolated, left unbathed and to lie in their own excrement, or sexually molested, and not a small number are murdered. In 1996 in the United States, more than 1,000 children died as a result of child abuse—about 3 children a day (National Committee to Prevent Child Abuse, 1997).

What can possibly lead to this inhuman treatment of children? Some of the contributing risk factors lie in the characteristics of parents and their abused children, some are attributable to ecological factors such as the quality of the neighborhood and available support systems, and still others are related to the life experiences and stresses family members encounter. Abuse is unlikely to occur when only one risk factor is present. It is the occurrence and interaction among multiple risk factors, especially in the face of few protective factors such as a supportive marital relationship, social network, and community resources, high intelligence and education, good health and adaptability, that is likely to lead to abuse (Cicchetti & Toth, 1998).

Abused Children and Their Parents

Most students reading this book probably think that no one they know would ever abuse a child or that only someone who is really mentally ill would inflict grievous physical harm on defenseless children. However, although chronic maltreatment is most likely to occur in economically deprived, poorly educated families, child abusers are found in all social classes and all religious, racial, and ethnic groups. In addition, there is little evidence of severe mental illness or specific personality traits that consistently distinguish abusive from nonabusive parents. Rather, abusive parents are enmeshed in a multiproblem family with deficits that include a wide range of dysfunctions in family members and in their relationships with each other. Differences between maltreating and nonmaltreating parents are most likely to be found in their self-involvement, that is, their inability to take the role of others and to understand the child's needs, capabilities, and responses in relation to the parent's specific situation or demands (Pianta, Egeland, & Erickson, 1989). It is an understatement to say that abusive parents are less concerned about social conformity and the needs of others than are nonabusive parents (Cicchetti & Toth, 1998).

Two factors most commonly associated with abusive behavior by parents are a distressed, often sexually unsatisfying marriage and the abuse of one or both marital partners by his or her own parents. Accumulating evidence indicates that both competent, loving parenting and incompetent, abusive parenting may to some extent be transmitted across generations (Grusec, Covell, & Paucha, 1991). This does not mean that young parents are locked into their own parents' style of parenting. Only about a third of parents who were abused when they were young abuse their own children (Cicchetti & Toth, 1998; Kaufman & Zigler, 1987). Mothers who break this intergenerational cycle are more likely to have had a warm, caring adult in their background, to have established a close marital relationship, and at some time to have received therapy (Egeland, Jacobvitz, & Sroufe, 1988).

Certain characteristics of the child and family also are associated with maltreatment of children. Child abuse is more likely to occur in large families and to children under the age of 3. A higher-than-normal incidence of birth anomalies, physical and intellectual deviations, irritability, negativism, and other behaviors that exasperate the parents are found in many of these children. These factors may all contribute to the parents' feeling antagonistic to the child and feeling that the child is somehow different. Abusive parents frequently feel that the child is abusing them. These characteristics are not found in all abused children; it is just that they are found more often in abused than nonabused children. These factors alone do not lead to abuse; however, such problems in children may be enough to tip the balance in already stressed or dysfunctional families.

Parents in these families often have conflicts with each other and are socially isolated (Belsky, 1993; Trickett & Susman, 1988). They seem to have fewer friends, relatives, or neighbors they can turn to in times of stress. The isolation may contribute, in part, to the fact that these parents frequently do not seem to recognize the seriousness of their behavior and blame the child rather than themselves for what is occurring. They may even justify their behavior by saying they are doing it for the child's good or that harsh discipline is necessary if children are to be taught what is right. Shocking as it may seem, mothers are frequently the persons who abuse children. Some mothers feel locked into a stressful family situation, and mothers spend more time with a child than do other family members (Cicchetti & Toth, 1998).

In addition, abusive parents seem to have unrealistic beliefs about parent-child relationships and respond less appropriately to their children's behavior than do nonabusive parents. They often expect their children to perform in an impossibly developmentally advanced way or to exhibit levels of independence and self-control that are unlikely in children of their age (Trickett, Aber, Carlson, & Cicchetti, 1991). Abusive parents frequently think their child should act as a caregiver for the parent, and role reversals where the child appears to be the more nurturant member of the dyad often occur in these families (Dean, Malik, Richards, & Stringer, 1986).

Physical violence does not suddenly emerge in usually well-controlled parents. Child abuse is preceded by an escalating cycle of other forms of verbal and physical aggression (Straus & Donnelly, 1994). Abusive mothers show fewer positive behaviors (Cicchetti & Toth, 1998) and more severe negative behaviors, such as threatening commands, criticism, and physical punishment toward their children, than do nonabusive mothers (Trickett & Kuczynski, 1986). In addition, in comparison to nonabusive parents, the behavior of abusive parents is unpredictable and less contingent on the type of behavior the child exhibits (Mash, Johnson, & Kovitz, 1982). A mother's response may not distinguish between a tantrum or a task well done. This failure of maltreating mothers to discriminate between desirable and undesirable children's behavior is also reflected in physiological measures. Abusive mothers, in contrast to nonabusive mothers, show a similar pattern of autonomic arousal in response to either a smiling or a crying baby (Frodi & Lamb,

TABLE 12-3 Words Can Hurt, Too	
Category of Verbal Abuse	*Example*
1. Rejection or withdrawal of love	"Nobody could love you."
2. Verbal put-downs	"You dummy."
3. Demands for perfection	"How come you came in second?"
4. Negative predictions	"You're never going to amount to anything."
5. Negative comparison	"Why can't you be like your sister?"
6. Scapegoating	"You're the reason your mother and I are getting a divorce."
7. Shaming	"Look, everybody, at what a baby Tom is."
8. Cursing or swearing	"Go to hell."
9. Threats	"I'm going to kill you."
10. Inducing guilt	"How could you do that after all I've done for you?"

Source: Based on Schaefer, 1997.

1980). They seem to be experiencing both the crying baby and the pleasant, happy baby as emotionally aversive. We have spoken earlier of the importance of parents' accurately reading and responding to children's cues. This distorted perception of the child's behavior must greatly increase the stress and confusion in already disturbed parent-child relationships. Intervention programs that have been successful in lowering rates of abuse have focused on educating parents about child development and childrearing and on providing support networks and raising parents' self-esteem (Garbarino, 1989; Sedlack, 1989).

Although abusive parents usually use verbal abuse along with physical forms of maltreatment, even verbal abuse alone can be devastating to a child. In an effort to define what constitutes such abuse, Schaefer (1997) asked mental health professionals and parents to rate categories of verbal abuse that abusing parents had heaped on their children. Table 12-3 shows the 10 categories of abuse that the participants rated "never acceptable."

The Ecology of Child Abuse

Individuals and families do not operate in a social vacuum but are embedded in a variety of important social contexts outside the family (Belsky, 1993; Cicchetti & Toth, 1998). The recognition of this linkage between families and other institutions has profoundly altered how we understand both the causes of and the solutions to the problem. This level of analysis—Bronfenbrenner's exosystem—includes neighborhoods and communities as well as schools, workplaces, peer groups, and religious institutions. Research has clearly shown that the social support and guidance that these contexts provide can alter parental attitudes, knowledge, and their child-rearing practices, which in turn may modify the likelihood of abuse.

First, poverty makes a difference. As we've already pointed out, the poverty rate of families with children has been rising steadily. Although violence against children occurs in all social classes, it is higher in poor families. However, we know much more about the fact that it occurs in poor families than we do about the reasons for the link between abuse and poverty. Several candidates have been suggested: Among them are the stressors associated with being poor, the higher number of single-parent families, the violence that often pervades poor neighborhoods, and limited access to social services. All these factors may be part of the explanation for this tragic link.

Poverty is a national disgrace; it is also a costly one that takes a toll in a variety of ways on the developing child—abuse is simply one of a variety of consequences of living in poverty for young children (Petersen, 1993). Although physical abuse and neglect both have been linked with poverty, sexual abuse is not. In fact, according to some experts, sexual abuse appears to be more common in middle-class families. However, studies are often biased, for middle-class families have more access to services for the treatment of sexual abuse problems in the family.

Closely linked with poverty as a factor in abuse is unemployment. Several studies have clearly shown that unemployment is related to rates of child abuse. Steinberg, Catalano, and Dooley (1981) found that occurrences of child abuse rose following a period of high job loss. Fathers are especially likely to be affected by job loss. Again we are more certain of this link than we are about the processes that account for the relationship. As many have argued, stress, frustration, and increased contact between parents and children may all contribute to the potential link between job loss and child abuse.

Neighborhoods matter, and neighborhoods differ considerably in abuse rates, even after holding poverty level constant. Some neighborhoods serve a protective or buffering function against abuse, whereas others seem to exacerbate or increase the family's risk for abuse. Protective or low-risk neighborhoods have more social resources, and the families tend to use these resources—especially informal sources such as friends, neighbors, and relatives—for advice, guidance, and physical and financial assistance in a balanced and reciprocal fashion. They tend to use resources such as youth groups and community centers in a regular ongoing fashion that presumably serves a preventive and protective function. They place a higher value on their neighborhood and view their neighborhood as permitting a higher quality of life than families in high-risk neighborhoods. High-risk neighborhoods, on the other hand, are less friendly places; people rely on each other for guidance and support less often and tend to exploit each other more when they do exchange goods and services (Steinberg et al., 1995).

What neighborhood factors might be associated with child abuse? To answer this question, James Garbarino and Deborah Sherman (1980) identified two neighborhoods that were similar in racial and socioeconomic composition but had markedly different rates of child maltreatment. The high-risk neighborhood had a rate of 130 cases of child abuse per thousand families, compared with only 15 cases per thousand in the low-risk neighborhood. How did these neighborhoods differ? The high-risk neighborhood was physically run-down, uncared for, and unstable (much movement in and out); there was less adequate child care and less exchange among families; there were more **latchkey children** (children who come home from school to an empty house); and people were generally less self-sufficient. Residents perceived themselves as more stressed and in more need of support yet as having less support; they were less likely to use the community services that were available to them and tended to seek family services only when crises struck. It does appear that the interaction between family characteristics and neighborhood characteristics, rather than either alone, produces abuse.

People in high-risk neighborhoods tend to be more socially isolated—a feature that has long been associated with higher rates of abuse (Thompson, 1995). Some early studies even found that abusive parents were more likely to have unlisted phone numbers. And it is not just adults who are more isolated; children who are abused are often restricted by their parents from maintaining contact with other children. This may explain, in part, why children who experience abuse have more difficulties with their peers and are less well accepted by their age-mates (Howe, Tepper, & Parke, 1998). As a recent report from the National Research Council stressed, "Research attention needs to be directed toward maladaptive qualities of [support] networks. Abusive parents may select [maladaptive] networks, thereby increasing the likelihood of continued abuse rather than acting as a protective factor" (Petersen, 1993, p. 24). It is important to recognize also that abuse is often the manifestation of a wide range of family problems,

latchkey children
Children who must let themselves into their homes after school because a parent or both parents are working outside the home.

One reason some schoolchildren come home to empty houses— estimates of the numbers of latchkey children have run as high as 10 million—is the lack of sufficient childcare and after-school programs.

including lack of education, unemployment, drug abuse, poverty, and living amid filth and danger.

Families are embedded not just in communities, but in a set of cultural and societal contexts that shape their values, attitudes, and practices. Broad cultural changes in American society may play a role in the emergence of abusive patterns. For example, increased divorce rates, increased mobility, limited availability of day care, lack of medical coverage, and lack of paid leave at the birth of a child may increase stress that may, in turn, contribute to abuse. In addition, societal attitudes with regard to both the privacy of the family and the issue of children's versus parents' rights may also play a role (Petersen, 1993). Finally, a widespread indifference to violence or even acceptance of violence as a solution to social problems may contribute to the rise in child abuse in the American society (Straus & Donnelly, 1994). As we will see in Chapter 14, children's exposure to an enormous amount of violence in television and films may help set the stage for later violence in their own lives.

Some social scientists have suggested that the high incidence of child abuse in the United States may owe something to the American culture's general acceptance of the physical punishment of children (Christoffel, 1990; Straus & Donnelly, 1994). Battered children are rare in cultures like that of the Chinese, who do not punish children physically. Thus, the cultural approval of violence such as spanking in childrearing may sometimes combine with caretakers' lack of social, economic, and emotional resources to produce child abuse.

In summary, no single factor leads to child abuse. It involves complex interactions among dysfunctional family relationships, multiple stressful experiences, a disorganized or nonsupportive environment, and cultural values that tolerate or justify aggression and physical punishment.

Consequences of Abuse

The consequences of abuse are, in a word, devastating. As we have said, more than 1,000 children die each year; 65 percent of these children die as a direct result of physical abuse, and another 36 percent die from the consequences of neglect. If abused or neglected children do not die, they may suffer brain dysfunction, neuro-motor handicaps, physical defects, stunted growth, and mental retardation. Abuse can slow intellectual development and cause psychosocial problems as well.

BOX 12-3

Risk and Resilience

Surviving War and Living with Violence

Whether children experience a single, acute episode of warfare or many experiences of violence occurring over an extended period, they are likely to exhibit a variety of behaviors that range from mild distress to severe trauma (Garbarino & Kostelny, 1996). It is amazing that children are able to recover from such stress and lead normal lives, but with sufficient support from caring others, many do.

Thousands of children involved in the civil war in Mozambique during the 1980s were exposed to violence, physical and sexual abuse, torture, and abduction not only as observers but as victims and even as forced instigators. Neil Boothby (1991) described the experience of 6-year-old Franisse who was kidnapped by the Renamo (the Mozambique National Resistance). Franisse was forced to set his family's hut ablaze and watch as his parents were decapitated and dismembered and their heads were impaled on stakes. He was then taken back to a Renamo camp where he went through a brutal and systematic indoctrination program to transform the kidnapped children into combat soldiers and cold-blooded killers.

What happens to children who go through a dehumanizing experience like this, in which violence is not only approved but required? Are their social and moral values permanently damaged and their behavior patterns irreversibly altered? Boothby studied the adjustment of 42 boys between the ages of 6 and 16 after they had been recovered from the Renamo and taken to a government refugee center where staff attempted to establish regular daily routines and safe codes of behavior. Rather than the boys' amount of direct involvement in violence, it was the length of time they had spent in a Renamo camp that was related to their later ability to behave in a socially responsible fashion. Boys who had been in a camp less than six months tended to define themselves as victims. Although they were unusually aggressive and distrustful of adults, they rapidly showed appropriate feelings of remorse over previous acts of violence and decreases in antisocial behav-

ior. In contrast, the boys who had been in camp longer than six months seemed to have crossed some kind of identity threshold; they identified with their captors and viewed themselves as members of Renamo. Most of these boys eventually gained control over their aggressive feelings and became able to express remorse, but these changes occurred very slowly. The acceptance of these children, the recognition that they were victims, and the forgiveness of families, teachers, and community members played a major role in many boys' remarkable recovery.

Studying Palestinian mothers and children living amid the *Intifada*, or Palestinian uprising, Garbarino and Kostelny (1996) found that children exposed to the full range of war-related risks, such as personal injury and witnessing a violent political event or the arrest of a family member, generally were well adjusted if they faced these risks in the context of a functional and supportive family system. On the other hand, if these children experienced family problems as well as war risks, they were more likely to suffer serious psychological distress that required professional intervention, termed "clinical-range" problems.

The Intifada, or Palestinian uprising, began formally in 1987 in the Gaza Strip but had its roots in the ongoing political violence that had engulfed that area and the West Bank since before 1948. Thus, it became a condition of life for most Palestinian children. By 1989, when the researchers began their work, 159 Palestinian children had died from gunshot wounds, tear gas, and beatings, 6,500 to 8,500 had been injured, and more than 25,000 required some form of medical treatment. Overall, it is estimated that as many as 63,000 Palestinian children and youth were injured in the first two years of the Intifada, or about 7 percent of the total youth population.

Among Garbarino's and Kostelny's findings was the fact that boys and younger children were more likely than girls and older children to display problems in the "clinical range," that is, of sufficient severity to merit formal intervention (Figure 12-13). In addition, the accumulation of multiple risks appeared to have a more devastating effect

Even as infants, abused children show less secure attachment and more noncompliant, resistant, and avoidant behavior toward their mothers (Cicchetti & Toth, 1995; Lyons-Ruth, Repacholi, McLeod, & Silva, 1991). Moreover, problems in emotional regulation and the transmission of aggressive behavior can be seen in the social interactions of abused children outside of their homes (Cicchetti & Toth, 1998). Carol George and Mary Main (1979) observed that abused toddlers in a day-care center not only were more aggressive with their peers but also were more ambivalent toward their caregivers. They threatened to attack or did attack caregivers, behaviors that never occurred in nonabused children. In addition, they showed great wariness in response to friendly behavior by the caregivers. They seemed both to have learned not to trust adults and to have acquired their parents' aggressive responses. Such attitudes and behaviors would seem likely to lead to difficulties in childrearing when the abused children themselves become parents.

As abused children advanced through the school year, they not only continued to show problems in relations with peers, teachers, and caregivers, they also had

on boys than on girls. The researchers speculate that recent changes in women's status in Palestinian society as well as families' tendencies to assign girls more responsibilities, such as caring for younger children during curfew hours, enhanced girls' feelings of independence and resilience. Younger children of course have fewer physiological and cognitive resources for coping with stress and, in addition, older children may have experienced more "normal" times than younger ones.

Garbarino and Kostelny confirm the crucial importance of family support and parental well-being to a child's ability to deal with stress and underline the threat posed to such support by dysfunction and violence within the family. They point out not only that the Palestinian children most vulnerable to the stresses of the Intifada were young boys in dysfunctional families but that these families were most often in a low-income stratum. As we have seen often in this book, it is children of lower socioeconomic status who are least likely to receive the support and services they need to combat unfavorable circumstances.

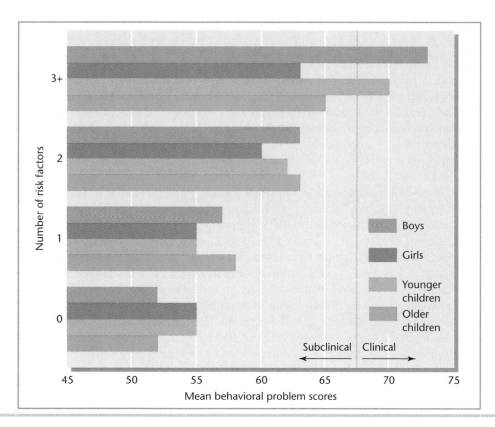

■ FIGURE 12-13
Palestinian children under stress.
Although all children showed more behavioral problems the more risk factors they confronted, only boys' and younger children's scores reached the clinical level when risk factors rose beyond 3. (*Source:* Adapted from Garbarino & Kostelny, 1996)

academic problems and low self-esteem, exhibited behavior problems, and, not surprisingly, were depressed and withdrawn (Cicchetti & Toth, 1998; Howe et al., 1998). Of course, most abused children do not become delinquents or violent offenders. Long-term effects of abuse are most likely to be found if children remain in low-income socioeconomic environments with multiple stresses and few supports available (Cicchetti & Lynch, 1995; Malinosky-Rummell & Hansen, 1993). For sexually abused children, inappropriate sexual behavior directed toward themselves or other children and adults and play and fantasy with sexual content are commonly reported (Trickett & Putnam, 1998). Higher rates of fears, nightmares, aggressive behavior, behavior problems, and self-injurious behavior have also been found (Cicchetti & Toth, 1998; Trickett, 1997).

CHILDREN, FAMILIES, AND POLITICAL VIOLENCE

One event that has modified the experiences of many families and the adjustment of their children is war (see Box 12-3). Families and children in the United States have not directly experienced wartime violence and deprivation for more than 100 years, but the effects of war and political violence on children's psychological well-being can be and is often devastating. In context of armed combat children witness, experience, or participate in violent acts. They see the destruction of social networks and social institutions, and experience hunger, homelessness, and the disruption or loss of their families (Goldson, 1993). Children compose three-quarters of the populations of refugee camps in warring developing nations (Green, Asrat, Maurs, & Morgan, 1989).

Research on the effects of war on families and children began in World War II. Much of this research indicated that the long-term psychological effects of war and air raids on children were less severe than might have been expected. In addition, continuity in social networks and support from family, friends, and neighbors played a major role in buffering children from the adverse consequences of war. If children were separated from their parents or if parents showed anxiety, the children exhibited more psychological disturbance than those who remained with their families or who had parents who were able to maintain a responsive, stable caretaking regime (Burbury, 1941; Freud & Burlingham, 1943). When separations from parents did occur, continuity of contact with other family members or familiar adults and neighbors were a benefit to the children.

More recently, many children in Bosnia, Israel, Cambodia, Ruwanda and Burundi, Iraq, Ireland, and South Africa have experienced violence and deprivation and yet have demonstrated considerable resiliency following such traumatic experiences. For example, only 20 percent of children exposed to political violence in South Africa (Straker, Mendelsohn, Moosa, & Tudin, 1996) or Palestine (Garbarino & Kostelny, 1996) showed stress-related outcomes in the clinical range. Even children exposed to sustained conflict in Belfast and the violence generated by the "troubles" in Northern Ireland have maintained conventional moral standards and have shown no increases in juvenile delinquency, antisocial behavior, or school absenteeism (Cairns, 1991, 1996).

As we have seen (Chapter 4), resiliency is related to family support and to the continuity and availability of social networks and ethnic and cultural practices. In Box 12-3 we see the effects of such support on children who lived through the civil war in Mozambique and children who have experienced the risks of living amid the Palestinian uprising referred to as the *Intifada*. In general, boys and younger children suffer most. Similar findings have been reported in the United States: Children who experience both community violence and family violence are most likely to suffer severe behavioral problems (Richters & Martinez, 1993). In circumstances of peace or war, of tranquillity or stress, of poverty or affluence, of transition or stability, but especially in adversity, a well-functioning family and a supportive social environment can serve to protect children and promote children's psychological well-being.

SUMMARY

- The family is both the earliest and most sustained source of social contact for the child. The beliefs and values of the culture are filtered through the parents, and their interpretation is influenced by the parents' personalities, religion, social class, education, and gender. Although rearrangements in family ties are increasingly common, family relationships remain the most intense and enduring bonds.
- **Socialization** is the process by which an individual's standards, skills, motives, attitudes, and behaviors are shaped to conform to those regarded as appropriate

for the society. Parents, siblings, peers, and teachers are major agents of socialization. They may influence the child by directly teaching standards, rules, and values; by providing role models; by making attributions about the child; and by creating the environment in which the child lives.

The Family System

- The family is a complex system involving interdependent members whose functioning may be altered by changes in the behavior of one member, or relationships among family members, and by changes over time. In addition, family functioning is influenced by the larger physical, cultural, and social setting in which the family lives.

- Family processes involve mutual influences among family members and adaptation to changes in family members and their relationships as well as to circumstances external to the family. In addition to the systems theory principles discussed in Chapter 1, the family system is governed by the principles of interdependency and homeostasis and by the types of boundaries it establishes.

- The functioning of the marital system, parent-child system, and sibling system are interrelated and influence children's adjustment. A satisfying marital relationship is often regarded as the basis of good family functioning, which directly or indirectly affects the interactions with the children. Increased parent-child involvement and positive parent-child relationships have been found when spouses are mutually supportive.

- Marital conflict, which can affect children either directly or indirectly, is associated with negative feelings and behaviors directed toward the children and with disruptions in children's social and cognitive competence. Particularly when conflicts are unresolved, children are likely to react with anger, sadness, or other negative emotions. Boys are more susceptible to the negative effects of family disharmony than girls because they are more likely to be directly exposed to family conflict whereas girls are more likely to be protected from it.

- Children have an impact on the marital relationship. Pregnancy and the birth of a first child are associated with a shift toward more traditional masculine and feminine roles, so that the woman does more of the child care. Both mothers and fathers report declines in marital satisfaction following the birth of their first child, but fathers are slower to express such declines than mothers. In addition, temperamentally difficult, deviant, or handicapped children place additional strain on the marriage and may be enough to destroy an already fragile marriage.

- Parents typically begin to consciously and systematically socialize their child during the second year by saying "no" to some behaviors and by praising other behaviors. They also teach social rules directly, serve as models with whom the child may identify or imitate, and choose the environment and social life that their child will experience.

- Parents' relationships with their children have frequently been categorized along the dimensions of emotionality and control. Parental warmth and responsiveness are regarded as important to socialization, and some degree of parental control is necessary for positive social development. The goal should be the child's learning of self-regulation rather than continuing external control by the parents. Thus, discipline strategies that present alternatives and rely on reasoning and attributions about the child's positive intentions are the most effective.

- The interaction of the dimensions of warmth and responsiveness with those of permissiveness and control creates a four-way typology: **authoritative, authoritarian, permissive,** and **uninvolved parenting.** In a classic study Baumrind found that distinctive types of parental behavior were related to specific patterns of child behavior. She found that authoritative parenting involving high-warmth responsiveness and communication, but also consistent and firm control and high-maturity demands, led to the most positive emotional, social, and cognitive development in children and adolescents.

- Critics of this typology have cited the need to identify more clearly the components of each style that contribute to its effects on the child's development, the need to pay more attention to the role played by the child's temperament and behavior, and the question of the generalizability across cultures of the original findings. As one example, the most effective Chinese style of parenting may fall somewhere between authoritative and authoritarian. In addition, the relative emphasis, in China and many other Asian countries, on the relation of the self to the group is quite different from the emphasis on the individual self common in the United States and other Western nations.

- The first goal of socialization is **compliance**, and as children meet this goal at their parents' specific requests and reminders in many specific situations, they begin to acquire the capacity for **self-regulation.** Learning compliance and self-regulation is part of the evolution of the **self system.**

- Most families in the United States have more than one child. The functioning of the family is affected by the number, gender, and spacing of the children. These factors influence both parent-child interaction and sibling interaction. As family size increases, parents and children have less opportunity for extensive contact, but siblings experience more contact. This may result in greater independence but lower self-esteem and academic achievement in children from large families.

- Variations in interactions with parents and siblings have been associated with birth order. Firstborn children often show emotional and behavioral problems after the birth of a sibling, but the outcome is mediated by the mother's reaction and efforts to include the firstborn and by the father's involvement. In general, parents tend to stay highly involved with firstborn children throughout their lives, often having higher expectations, exerting greater pressure for achievement, and requiring the acceptance of more responsibility.

- Different characteristics have been related to firstborn and later-born children. Firstborns are more adult-oriented, helpful, self-controlled, conforming, and anxious than their siblings, and they tend to excel in academic and professional achievement. Although only children experience many of the same parental demands of firstborns, they do not have to compete with siblings. Thus, they tend to be high in achievement, but lower in anxiety, and make more positive adjustments in social relations both within and outside of the home.

- Birth order is associated with variations in sibling relations. Eldest children are typically expected to assume some responsibility for and self-control toward the younger children. This leads both to antagonistic behavior and to more nurturant behavior toward younger siblings. Eldest children tend to focus on parents as sources of social learning, whereas younger children use both parents and older siblings as models and teachers.

- The family as a unit is as much a family subsystem as are the marital, parent-child, and sibling subsystems. The family unit is particularly responsible for the development and perpetuation of family stories and rituals, which transmit values, teach family roles, and reinforce the family's uniqueness.

Social Class, Ethnicity, and Socialization

- Subgroups within our culture have both divergent values and different problems with which to cope. These may have an impact on the goals and methods of socialization parents choose.

- In addition to obvious differences in income, education, and occupation, lower-class and middle-class families may differ in other ways. Poor families generally experience little power within all of the systems (e.g., education, health) that they encounter, leading them to feel helpless, insecure, and controlled by external forces. In addition, they may be involved in cycles of disadvantage, associated with accumulating risk factors that make childrearing difficult and lead to adverse outcomes in the next generation. However, the stresses experienced by poor families often result in the formation of extensive support networks which involve both emotional support and services that cannot be purchased.

- Social class, ethnicity, race, and culture have been related to differences in childrearing. Among these four, race is probably the least significant factor. Among other things, childrearing may differ according to whether a given cultural group emphasizes the **traditional nuclear family** or the **extended family**; the former is likely to be found among people who stress individualism, the latter among those who stress the importance of the relationships between the individual and the group. Specific differences in styles of childrearing and their effect on children are also influenced by other systems—for example, the workplace, the neighborhood, peers, and the school—that in turn are influenced by culture and society.

The Changing American Family

- In recent years family roles and forms have become more varied. As the number of working mothers has increased, the average size of households has decreased. Single-parent households have increased greatly in number due largely to rising divorce rates and increases in out-of-wedlock births.

- The effects of maternal employment have been related to the mother's reason for working, the mother's satisfaction with her role, the demands placed on other family members, the attitudes of the other family members, and the quality of substitute care provided for the children. If each of these is positive, maternal employment not only has no detrimental effects on children but instead may have specific positive effects, especially for girls.

- Divorce, life in a one-parent family, and remarriage should be viewed as part of a series of transitions that modify family roles and relationships and the lives of parents and children. In the first year following divorce, the children in single-parent households tend to be more disturbed, but in the long run most are able to adapt to their parents' divorce. However, single, custodial mothers suffer from task overload, a marked decline in income, and a lack of social support.

- Family interactions immediately following divorce are characterized by inept parenting on the part of custodial parents—usually mothers—and distressed, demanding, noncompliant behavior on the part of children. These effects seem to last longer and to be more negative for preadolescent sons than for daughters.

- Children's responses to remarriage vary depending on the previous family experience, but, the age at which the remarriage occurs is associated with the child's acceptance of the new parent. It is particularly difficult for adolescents to cope with a parent's—or both parents'—remarriage. Antisocial behavior, depression and anxiety, school problems, and disruptions in peer relations have been associated with divorce and remarriage. In preadolescence, boys show the most negative responses to divorce and girls the most lasting resistance to remarriage; however, gender differences are rarely found in adolescence.

- Although in nearly 75 percent of divorce and custody cases the children reside with the mother, a divorced couple may select either **joint legal custody** and

joint physical custody arrangements. Even when parents choose the latter, however, close to half of children live full-time with their mothers.

- The timing of first parenthood is a powerful organizer of parental roles. People are marrying and becoming parents later today than in earlier years, and there are some positive aspects to later parenthood, such as being better established in careers, feeling more responsibility, and being more flexible about family roles.

- Gay and lesbian families are becoming increasingly common, whether composed of children from former heterosexual marriages or of children adopted or conceived by various assisted reproductive techniques. The evidence suggests that the children of gay and lesbian couples develop as children of heterosexual marriages do, that they generally adopt heterosexual lifestyles, and that their concepts of gender roles do not differ from those of children of heterosexual parents.

- Although births to teenage parents have declined somewhat, births to unwed adolescent mothers more than tripled between the 1960s and the 1990s. Largely because of economic constraints on unmarried mothers, the children of teen mothers are at particular risk. The younger the mother, the more likely the child is to experience cognitive and eventual academic deficits. Children of teen mothers are more likely to have behavior problems, to have less self-control, and to show more antisocial behavior, such as the misuse of drugs and delinquency.

- Education, a comfortable economic situation, and religious faith can help to prevent teenage pregnancy, as of course can the proper use of contraceptives. Once an unmarried teenager has had a child, getting an education, limiting future births, and forming a stable marriage may help her pull herself out of poverty and give her child a chance for good adjustment and academic performance.

Child Abuse within the Family

- In 1996 nearly a million cases of child abuse or neglect were substantiated, another 2 million cases were reported, and the number of unreported incidents was unknown. The severe abuse of children is most likely to occur in the presence of multiple risk factors and the absence of protective factors such as community resources, good health, high intelligence, education, and a supportive social network.

- Child abuse is more likely to occur in large families, to children under age 3, and to children with physical and intellectual deficits or excessive fussiness and crying. Parents in abusive families often are socially isolated and have unrealistic beliefs about young children's abilities and about the parent-child relationship. Child abuse is preceded by escalating verbal and physical aggression that is often unpredictable and not contingent on the child's actual behaviors.

- Parents who abuse their children are frequently involved in a distressed marriage, have been abused by their own parents, and are unemployed, poorly educated, and economically deprived. No single factor leads to abuse. It is a product of the interactions among family characteristics, nonsupportive environments, and cultural values that tolerate aggression and physical punishment as well as poverty, unemployment, and high-risk, dangerous neighborhoods. The latter sort of neighborhood may promote insecurity, feelings of helplessness and vulnerability, and children are often left to fend for themselves, as the prevalence of **latchkey children** attests.

- The devastating consequences of child abuse include less secure attachment in infants; problems with emotional regulation and aggressive behavior in toddlers; poor relations with peers and adults, academic problems, and low self-esteem as children get older; brain dysfunction; mental retardation, neuromotor deficits, physical handicaps—and death.

Children, Families, and Political Violence

- Research indicates that many children are able to survive the disruptions and violence associated with war without long-term adverse psychological effects. Resiliency is associated with continuity in social networks and social support but especially with sustained supportive family relationships.

Peers and Friends

C H A P T E R 13

EARLY PEER INTERACTIONS
Infancy and Toddlerhood
The Early School Years

THE ROLE OF PEERS IN CHILDREN'S SOCIALIZATION
Peers as Reinforcers of Desired Behaviors
Peers as Models
Peers and the Development of the Self
Peers as Guides and Instructors

PLAY AND ITS FUNCTIONS
Play, Fantasy, and Social Competence
Play, Peers, and Pathology

PEER ACCEPTANCE
Assessing Peer Status
Consequences of Being Unpopular
■ BOX 13-1 *Child Psychology in Action:*
What Happens to Shy Children—Thirty Years Later?
■ BOX 13-2 *Risk and Resilience:*
Victimization by Peers: It Helps to Have Friends

DEVELOPING FRIENDSHIPS
What Is a Friend?
How Children Make Friends

THE FORMATION OF GROUPS
Dominance Hierarchies
Cliques and Crowds

PEER AND ADULT INFLUENCES ON THE CHILD AND ADOLESCENT

PEER GROUPS IN DIFFERENT CULTURES
■ BOX 13-3 *Perspectives on Diversity:*
Cross-Cultural Variations in Children's Peer Relationships

SUMMARY

In recent years, observers have begun to recognize the importance of individuals outside the family in the socialization process. With the rise in maternal employment and the increase in the availability of preschool education, the roles of peers and teachers have been brought into sharp focus. This chapter and the next focus on the contributions of the peer group and the school to childhood socialization.

Peers play a special role in children's development. Although children's relationships with their parents are more intense and enduring than relations with peers, interactions among age-mates are more free and egalitarian. The greater fluidity of peer relationships offers children the opportunity for a new kind of interpersonal experimentation and exploration. In particular it stimulates a new sensitivity that forms a cornerstone for the development of social competence, a sense of social justice, and the capacity to form relationships with others outside the family.

We begin by exploring the child's first interactions with peers, which begin in early infancy. We then examine the special roles peers play in children's socialization and of the ways play and fantasy contribute to development. Next we consider the many factors that go into peer acceptance, the kinds of problems that children can face in peer relationships, and how children develop friendships. We examine the formation of cliques and of hierarchical relationships in groups and explore the special influence of peers in preadolescence and the teen years. Finally, we look at cross-cultural differences in peer relationships. Our Turning Points chart (p. 525) will help you track the progession of these changes in children's relations with their peers.

EARLY PEER INTERACTIONS

Interactions with peers begin to shape children's behavior at an early age. Before they're more than a few months old babies begin to react to each other, and when children make their first forays into spoken language, social interaction really gets under way. Contact with peers continues to grow, and somewhere between the ages of 2 and 3 children begin to prefer interaction with peers to that with adults.

Infancy and Toddlerhood

Infants are sometimes surprisingly responsive to their peers. Babies in the first 6 months of life touch and look at each other and even cry in response to each other's crying. However, it is unlikely that these early responses are really social in the sense of the infant's seeking and expecting a social response from the other child. It is not until the second half of the first year that truly social behaviors begin to appear and infants begin to recognize the peer as a social partner (Brownell, 1990; Howes, 1987). Between 6 and 12 months they begin to attempt to influence their partner, by vocalizing, looking, touching, and waving at the other baby. Although they may engage in a little hitting or pushing as well (Bronson, 1981; Rubin, Bukowski, & Parker, 1998), a considerable amount of social behavior among the baby crowd is friendly (Eckerman & Didow, 1988). Here's a classic example:

> Larry sits on the floor and Bernie turns and looks toward him. Bernie waves his hand and says "da," still looking at Larry. He repeats the vocalization three more times before Larry laughs. Bernie vocalizes again and Larry laughs again. Then, the same sequence of one child saying "da" and the other laughing is repeated twelve more times before Bernie turns away from Larry and walks off. Bernie and Larry become distracted at times during the interchange. Yet, when this happens, the partner reattracts attention either by repeating his socially directed action or by modifying it, as when Bernie both waves and says "da," reengaging Larry. (Mueller & Lucas, 1975, p. 241)

During the second year of life children make gains in locomotion and language, and these gains make social exchange more complex (Rubin et al., 1998). In the early toddler period (13 to 24 months), peers develop the capacity to engage in social interaction that has a complementary structure (Howes, 1987). That is, partners exchange both turns and roles, so that we see complementary role relationships, such as "chaser" and "chased," "hider" and "seeker," or "giver" and "receiver." Peers begin to imitate one another's activity, and they show awareness that they're being imitated (Eckerman, 1993). Now when children engage in positive social interactions, they are more likely to smile or laugh or display other kinds of appropriate positive affect (Mueller & Brenner, 1977). And interactions last longer (Ross & Conant, 1992).

In the late toddler period (25 to 36 months), the child's main social achievement is the ability to share meaning with a social partner (Mueller, 1989). "When children communicate meanings, they know how to play a particular game, for example, being pulled in or pulling a wagon, the signal or invitation to begin the game (eye gaze, plus run to wagon), the signal to switch roles ('my turn' plus a tug) and how to communicate that they share this knowledge . . . children's communication of meaning makes possible a wider range of games and variations on the themes of games, as well as early forms of pretend play" (Howes, 1987, p. 260).

As children develop, negative exchanges and conflict increase also (Hay & Ross, 1982; Rubin et al., 1998). In fact, being sociable and getting into conflicts seem to go together. As Brown and Brownell (1990) found, toddlers who frequently initiated conflicts with agemates were also the most sociable and the most likely to initiate interactions. It is only later that these outgoing toddlers learn how to manage their social interchanges effectively.

As children become familiar with each other their early peer interactions tend to develop into relationships. By **relationship** we mean a succession of interactions between two people who know each other (Rubin et al., 1998). Moreover, because the people know each other, not only their history of past interactions but their expectations of future interactions influence the nature and course of each encounter. Hildy Ross and her colleagues (Ross, Conant, Cheyne, & Alevizos, 1992), have found that toddlers develop reciprocal relationships based on both positive and negative exchanges. Young as they are, these familiar peers display the beginnings of friendship in their simple exchanges. As Rubin and colleagues note, however, "it is doubtful that they carry the same strength of psychological meaning as the friendships of older children" (1998, p. 634)—a topic we explore later in greater detail.

relationship A succession of interactions between two people who know each other that are altered by their shared past interactions and that also affect their future interactions.

As children develop competence in interacting with peers, they shift toward increased social play and exhibit a clear preference for playing with peers rather than adults. In a classic study of social play in children between 10 months and 2 years of age, Eckerman, Whatley, and Kutz (1975) found that although solitary play changed very little from the youngest to the oldest group of children, older children engaged in significantly more social play than younger ones. In addition, the older children were less interested than the younger children in playing with their mothers and much more interested in playing with peers (Figure 13-1).

Social exchanges with mothers differ from those with other infants (Rubin et al., 1998; Vandell & Wilson, 1987). Mothers are more reliable and respond more often than infant peers. Exchanges with mothers are longer and more sustained, but the interchanges may be a bit one-sided. Mothers tend to bear the larger responsibility for maintaining the interaction. In exchanges between infant peers, the two partners contribute more equally. Mothers make it easy; peers make you work for your social life!

The Early School Years

Trends toward increased peer interactions continue throughout the preschool and elementary school years. In one study, investigators observed more than 400 children in social interaction at home or outdoors (Ellis, Rogoff, & Cromer, 1981). With whom do children of various ages (from 1 to 12 years old) spend time? These

■ FIGURE 13-1
The development of
social play.
In this study, (a) the oldest
children were twice as likely to
engage in social play as the
youngest ones, and (b) they were
also about twice as likely to play
with peers. (*Source:* Eckerman,
Whatley, & Kutz, 1975)

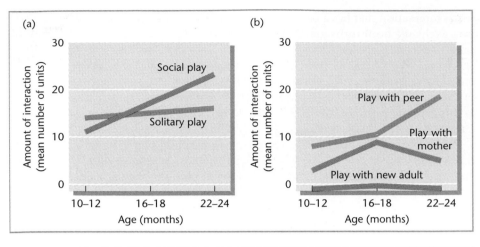

■ FIGURE 13-2
Getting to like you, getting to
hope you like me.
At about the age of 2½ children
begin to prefer other children as
companions over adults. The
difference in companionship
choice widens rapidly over time.
(*Source:* Ellis, Rogoff, Cromer,
1981)

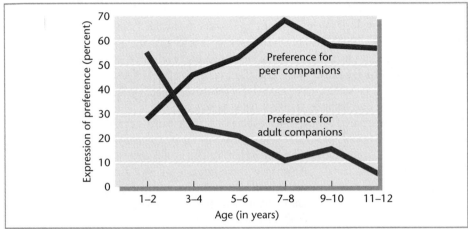

children from a middle-class neighborhood were alone 26 percent of the time, with
other children in 46 percent of the observations, and with both adults and peers 15
percent of the time. As Figure 13-2 shows, across development, children spend less
time with adults and more time with child companions. These trends continue into
adolescence, when children continue to spend less time with family and more time
either alone or with friends (Larson, 1997; Larson & Richards, 1994). Moreover,
the kinds of peers children choose to spend time with change also. For example,
companionship with same-age peers increases with age. However, although children are just as likely to choose an opposite-gender companion up to age 7, after
this age, boys choose boys and girls choose girls more than opposite-gender play
partners. Adolescence, of course, heralds a reversal, as cross-gender friendships
begin to blossom once again (Parker & Gottman, 1989; Rubin et al., 1998).

THE ROLE OF PEERS IN CHILDREN'S SOCIALIZATION

We have described socialization as learning to play by the rules of the social game.
Peers are a source of information about these rules and about how well the child is
playing the game. They offer a different perspective than that offered by the family—
the perspective of equals who have common problems, goals, statuses, and abilities.
How does the peer group influence the development of the child? In many of the
same ways that parents do—through reinforcement, modeling, and social comparison and by providing opportunities for socializing and learning.

Peers as Reinforcers of Desired Behaviors

As children grow older, the salience of peers as reinforcing agents and as models increases. Many parents, particularly of adolescents, bemoan the fact that their children ignore their wise advice but listen to, and emulate, their peers. Even throughout the preschool years, the frequency with which peers reinforce each other increases. Four-year-olds praise, attend to, or share with their peers more than 3-year-olds (Charlesworth & Hartup, 1967). Even among nursery schoolers, reciprocity is common: Children tend to reinforce the same peers who reinforce them (Hartup, 1983). There is no doubt that peer reinforcement in the form of attention and approval affects the behavior patterns of a child. Numerous studies have documented that when adults instruct a child's peers to attend only to certain of his behaviors (e.g., helpful, cooperative ones) and to ignore other behaviors (e.g., nasty, aggressive ones), this schedule of reinforcement may produce significant changes in the classmate's behavior. (Furman & Gavin, 1989; Furman & Masters, 1980; Rubin et al., 1998).

Peers as Models

Peers also influence each other by serving as social models. Children acquire a wide range of knowledge and a variety of responses by observing the behavior of their peers. Imagine the situation of the new child at school. Through observation, he may rapidly learn that the children are expected to stand when the teacher enters the room, that it is risky to shoot spitballs, that the game of marbles is played with different rules in this school, and that he should avoid contact with the big redheaded kid in the corner because he is the class bully. Children also learn new social skills through imitation, modeling the dominant and (presumably socially skilled) member of the group (Grusec & Abramovitch, 1982). Children also imitate older, more powerful, and more prestigious peer models (Bandura, 1989; Rubin et al., 1998). As children develop and internalize the rules, the need to rely on others decreases and they imitate others less often (Grusec & Abramovitch, 1982). However, rule learning may not be the only function of imitation. Because most often a child's imitation of another is followed by continuing or increased social interaction, imitation may indeed be an important way of maintaining such interaction. As Eckerman (1989, 1993) has shown, even in 2-year-olds imitation sustains joint play between partners and leads to more sophisticated forms of play, such as social games.

As we will see, in many cultures siblings are primary caregivers for infants and toddlers, which allows the young child to learn from peers of different age groups. It is interesting to speculate on how the rigid age grading of many Western institutions, like schools and sports organizations, may alter or at least limit children's opportunities to learn from other children who are both older and younger than themselves.

Peers and the Development of the Self

Peers may play an important role in helping a child develop a self-image and self-esteem, through serving as standards against which children evaluate themselves. Because there are few objective ways in which children can rate their own characteristics, values, and abilities, they turn to other people, particularly to peers. Through **social comparison** they use others as a yardstick with which to measure themselves.

To whom do we turn when we engage in social comparison? If a child wants to know how good a fighter he is, for example, he probably doesn't think about how he'd do against Mike Tyson but rather how he's done in neighborhood scuffles and how tough his peers think he is. Similarly, a child isn't likely to judge her reading ability by how many more words her mother can read or how much faster her teacher reads than she does but by how well other children in her class read. In matters of self-definition, the peer group is unequaled.

social comparison The process of evaluating one's characteristics, abilities, values, and other qualities by comparing oneself with others, usually one's peers.

Children build self-esteem in part by comparing their own characteristics, abilities, and skills with those of their peers.

Research has shown that in the early elementary school years children display a marked increase in their use of social comparison, with the peer group as a means of self-evaluation (Harter, 1990, 1998; Ruble, 1987; Zarbatany, Hartmann, & Rankin, 1990). The child's self-image and self-acceptance are closely associated with how he is received by peers.

Peers as Guides and Instructors

Peers provide opportunities for socializing and developing relationships and a sense of belonging (Zarbatany et al., 1990). These functions increase in importance as the child begins increasingly to spend more time with peers than family (Larson & Richards, 1994). Peers also offer a context for instruction and learning (Zarbatany et al., 1990). This is evident in Western cultures, where children acquire skills in games and sports with peers or in tutorial relationships in schools (see also Chapter 14); it is even more dramatic in some other cultures, such as India and many countries of Africa, where older siblings and peers care for and instruct young children (Whiting & Edwards, 1988).

PLAY AND ITS FUNCTIONS

play Activity that is intrinsically motivated, concerned more often with means than with ends, free from external rules, nonserious, and highly engaging.

Most social interchanges with peers occur in play settings, and children spend more of their time outside of school playing with friends than they spend in any other activity. What is **play**? We would all agree that when children are chasing each other around the school grounds, swinging on swings, climbing trees, or engaging in a game of chess, Monopoly, or baseball, they are playing. What distinguishes play from other types of activity? It seems to be intrinsically motivated rather than imposed or directed by others, it is concerned with means not ends, it is free from external rules, and it is nonserious and highly engaging (Rubin, Fein, & Vandenberg, 1983).

What functions does play serve in the development of children's competence? First, play facilitates cognitive development. It permits children to explore their environment, learn about things in that environment, and solve problems (Garvey, 1990b; Howes & Matheson, 1992). Second, play advances the child's social development. Particularly in fantasy play, through acting out roles, children learn to understand others and to practice roles they will assume as they grow older

(Haight & Miller, 1993). Finally, play permits children to solve some of their emotional problems and to learn to cope with anxiety and inner conflicts in a non-threatening situation.

Play, Fantasy, and Social Competence

In play, children can discover the world without risk. For example, in make-believe, they can experiment with dominant and submissive roles with few adverse consequences. Children learn not only to make use of their own fantasies but to act them out and to act in fantasies of their peers. Moreover, in just one play session a child can take a variety of roles, ranging from cowhand to lion to baby. Children can learn behaviors that are appropriate to each play situation in a relatively risk-free setting. Without fear, they can test the limits of what's acceptable. Testing or flouting social conventions later in life can be costly (Fein, 1978).

Pretend play—which we discussed briefly in the Chapter 11 section on "Creativity"—seems particularly important in the development of social competence. It permits children to practice their own future roles as well as to experience the roles and feelings of others in a playful context. Play teaches children to function as part of the social group and to coordinate their activities and roles with those of other children.

Pretend play initially appears about halfway through the second year, although some children begin as early as 12 months of age (Haight & Miller, 1993). Although it was once thought that pretend play was solitary at first, research has shown that it is often social. In the early years, pretend play is usually with the mother or siblings; as the child develops and gains opportunities to meet peers, other age-mates become common pretend-play partners (Dunn, 1988; Haight & Miller, 1993). Pretend-play partners vary across cultures as well. Mothers are usually the most frequent play partners in the United States, but in Mexican villages mother-child pretend play is rare; instead, siblings and other young relatives are the child's primary partners for pretend play (Farver, 1992; Zukow, 1989). In the United States, pretend play usually involves symbolic activities such as feeding a doll with make-believe food. In other cultures, such as in the Marquesas Islands, pretend play often focuses on adult behavior that is part of everyday responsibilities, such as paddling canoes or hunting and fishing (Martini, 1994).

Not only themes but the amount and style of pretend play differ across cultures. JoAnn Farver and her colleagues (Farver, Kim, & Lee, 1995; Farver & Shin, 1997) found that pretend play is less frequent among Korean American than European American children. This is consistent with the emphasis that Korean families, like Chinese and other Asian families, place on academic skills. And the style of play is different, too, again reflecting some of the Asian-American differences we've discussed. In the Korean culture, where harmonious relationships are valued, communication is rarely direct or confrontational.

pretend play A form of play, usually social, in which children often use symbolic meanings to act out their fantasies and by so doing learn social roles and how to interact with others. Also called imaginative and fantasy play.

U.S. children may play *at* real-life but tend to do so symbolically, as this little girl pretends to feed her doll. Play for children in some other cultures *is* real life; children often practice adult behaviors like hunting or fishing.

■ FIGURE 13-3
Preferred play themes among European and Korean American children.
The clear differences between Korean American and European American children's play preferences may reflect a variety of factors, including the Korean culture's emphasis on harmony and sharing in interpersonal relationships and the American culture's promotion of independence and pursuit of one's own interests. (*Source:* Adapted from Farver & Shin, 1997)

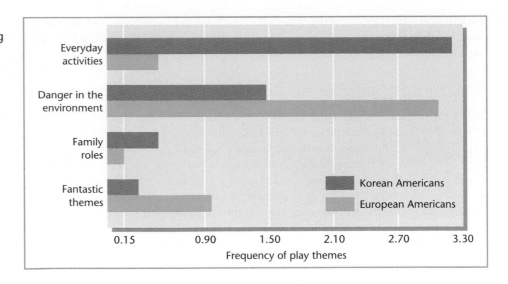

Moreover, Koreans emphasize the "we" of things, that is, relatedness and interdependence among individuals, whereas European Americans focus on the "I" of things, or the individuated self. These differing cultural values were reflected in the pretend play of groups of Korean and European American preschoolers studied by Farver and Shin (1997). As Figure 13-3 shows, the Korean American children stressed themes that revolved around everyday activities, whereas European American children put much more emphasis on themes of danger in the environment. In communicating with each other, Korean American children used more polite requests, were more likely to describe their partner's actions, used more statements of agreement, and were more likely to ask for confirmation of their own actions (e.g., "ok?" "right?"). The European American children used more directive statements in which they told their partners what to do, were more likely to describe their own actions and to add elements to a partner's statement, and were more likely to refuse or ignore a partner's suggestion, refuse to share toys, or prohibit a partner from taking part in the play (Table 13-1).

By age 3, children's prentend play becomes more complex, cooperative, and dramatic play in which children share symbolic meanings (Fein, 1989; Garvey, 1990b; Haight & Miller, 1993; Howes & Matheson, 1992.); Goncu (1993) refers to the ability to share meaning as "intersubjectivity" and shows that it increases with age. In contrast to 3-year-olds, 4½-year-olds have longer play sequences and more easily negotiate roles, rules, and themes of their pretend play. All the 3-year-olds want to be Batman, but the 4½-year-olds will accept the role of Robin or the Joker more readily, recognizing that their turn as Batman will come later. In aggressive play, children may have slow-motion fistfights and gun battles or prolonged, staggering, agonized death throes that would do credit to a diva at the Metropolitan Opera. The gestures are broad caricatures, and the mock blows are telegraphed. Pretend play peaks around 6 years of age when it involves highly coordinated fantasies, rapid transitions between multiple roles, and unique transformations of objects and situations (MacDonald, 1993).

Domestic fantasy play begins to decline in the school years as children play more structured games (Fein, 1981). Other types of fantasy, such as adventure fantasies, actually increase through preadolescence (Gottman & Parker, 1986), and even adults daydream, read, and enjoy space-adventure movies. Fantasy doesn't disappear but is expressed in different ways as children develop. In fact, fantasy play may help children learn to master fear. In their pretend play, they select something to be afraid of, rehearse the fear in a milder form, and then master the fear, often pretending to be or to conquer the feared object.

TABLE 13-1 Korean and European American Children's Communicative Strategies in Play

Strategies	Frequency of Strategy's Use (times per minute)	
	Korean American Children	*European American Children*
Making a polite request	13.80	2.56
Issuing a directive to partner	1.13	5.28
Describing a partner's action	9.32	4.36
Describing one's own action	2.91	4.82
Making a statement of agreement with partner	6.30	1.45
Adding elements to a partner's statement	9.52	4.56
Asking for confirmation	2.28	.41
Rejecting partner's suggestions or play	2.71	4.23
Using intonation and pitch to mark fantasy and animation	5.59	5.95
Calling attention ("Hey!" "Look!")	1.98	2.02

Source: Adapted from Farver & Shin, 1997.

A 4-year-old girl who was afraid of the dark and slept with a night-light often played a game involving dolls being afraid of the dark. With the lights off, the little girl would pretend to be the doll, would scream, and then, as mommy, would comfort the doll. After a few months, she announced to her parents that she no longer needed the night-light, and the theme of being afraid of the dark disappeared from her fantasy play. Both the girl and the doll were cured. (Gottman, 1986, pp. 26-27)

Boys and girls may differ in how they cope with fear (Gottman, 1986). Girls more often overcome fears by the use of emotional support, and they love to comfort, soothe, and ease the fear. Boys tend to use humor or a strategy of mastery and involvement in which they pretend to be the thing they are afraid of or pretend to conquer it.

Play, Peers, and Pathology

Peer interactions provide a critical opportunity for children to acquire certain social competencies. They also play an important role in the child's development of self-control and in his ability to work through or modify problem behavior (Berndt & Ladd, 1989; Rubin et al., 1998).

Imaginativeness in play is associated not only with self-control, low impulsivity, and low aggression, but also with sharing, cooperativeness, independence, and social maturity (Rubin et al., 1983). In addition, children who show spontaneous imaginativeness in play are likely to show a broader range of emotions and more positive emotions than less imaginative children. They are more likely to smile, to be curious and interested in new experiences, and to express joy in play and in peer relations (Singer & Singer, 1980).

Emotionally troubled children, on the other hand, tend to be rigid in their play patterns and to show disruptions in their play. That is, because these children often have trouble maintaining a theme or idea for an extended period, their pretend play may be choppy and discontinuous. Investigators have consistently found that children who experience anxiety and other emotional disturbance tend to engage in play that is age inappropriate and to be unpopular with peers (Singer, 1977). Imaginative play seems to be particularly vulnerable to the effects of psychological stress; indeed, some researchers have even suggested that children's failure to develop imaginative play is indicative of serious pathology, particularly of an aggressive, acting-out, impulsive nature. Children who are experiencing psychological stress, such as those whose parents have recently gone through a divorce, show a marked rigidity in imaginative play (Hetherington, Cox, & Cox, 1979). These children's fantasies involve fewer different characters, they're less likely to make different uses of the same objects in play, and they're more bound to objects in play. They are less able to free themselves from reality and rarely fantasize completely imaginary objects or people. For example, they need a stick to be a sword or a chair to be a castle. They also show less reversibility in play. Once a stick is a sword, they can't later transform it into a witch's broomstick or a magic wand or a horse. In addition, such children show less diversity in both themes and affect; that is, they tend to replay the same themes and to restrict the characters in their fantasies to one emotion, such as everybody is angry and fighting or everyone is afraid.

PEER ACCEPTANCE

Few things are more important to children than acceptance by their peers. Getting along with peers is the child's first experience of interaction with the world at large. Good experiences can lay the foundation for healthy adult social interactions, but bad ones can lay a heavy burden on the developing child. In this section, we look first at the way psychologists measure children's status among their peers and at some of the factors that go into peers' judgments of a child's standing. Next, we consider the effects on children of not being popular among their peers and then discuss some ways of helping children whose relationships with peers are unsatisfying. Finally, we look at what parents can do to promote their children's healthy social interactions with peers.

Assessing Peer Status

A common way of studying peer acceptance is to assess the status of children in a specific peer group. Using the **sociometric technique**, investigators ask children to identify a number of peers "you especially like" and those "you don't like very much." Or researchers may ask each child in the group to rate every other child in the class on likeability or desirability as a companion. Using peers—rather than teachers or others—as raters has several advantages. First, as "insiders," peers can identify children's behaviors and characteristics better than adults, for the latter see only a limited range of relevant behaviors. Second, peers have had extended and varied experience with one another. Third, peer assessments represent the perspectives of many raters with whom each child has had experience. No single child's view is likely to sway the vote when a range of individuals—generally all a child's classmates—rate a child.

Investigators derive various measures of social status from these simple procedures. **Popular children** are those who receive the greatest "most like" scores and the fewest "like least" scores. **Average children** receive some nominations (liked and disliked) but are neither as well liked as popular peers nor as disliked as rejected classmates. **Controversial children** are liked by many classmates but also disliked by many. **Neglected children**, or isolated peers, are friendless but not necessarily disliked by their classmates. **Rejected children**, on the other hand, tend to elicit many "like least" nominations. Researchers have distinguished two categories of rejected children—aggressive and nonaggressive (Bierman, Smoot, & Aumiller, 1993; French, 1988; Parkhurst & Asher, 1992). The **aggressive rejected** children are characterized by high levels of aggression, low self-control, and behavior problems. The **nonaggressive rejected** group are withdrawn, anxious, and socially unskilled (Crick & Ladd, 1993; French, 1990; Parkhurst & Asher, 1992). Children are probably rejected for different reasons but they probably also respond to rejection in different ways.

Children have expectations about how other children should behave, but are these expectations the main basis for acceptance or rejection by the peer group? Let

sociometric technique A procedure for determining children's status within their peer group in which children nominate others whom they like best or least or rate each child in the group for his likeability or desirability as a companion.

popular children Children who are liked by many peers and disliked by very few.

average children Children who have some friends but are not as well liked as *popular children*.

controversial children Children who are liked by many peers but also disliked by many.

neglected children Children who tend to be socially isolated and, though they have few friends, are not necessarily disliked by others.

rejected children Children who are disliked by many peers and liked by very few.

aggressive rejected children *Rejected* children who are characterized by high levels of aggressive behavior, have low self-control, and exhibit behavior problems.

nonaggressive rejected children *Rejected* children who tend to be withdrawn, anxious, and socially unskilled.

TURNING POINTS: Peer Relationships and Social Interaction

0–6 MONTHS	Touches and looks at another infant and cries in response to the other's crying
6–12 MONTHS	Tries to influence another baby by looking, touching, vocalizing, laughing, or waving Interactions with other infants are generally friendly, but may sometimes hit or push another
13–24 MONTHS	Begins to adopt complementary behavior, taking turns, and exchanging roles Social play increases throughout this period Begins to engage in imaginative play
25–36 MONTHS	In play and other social interaction, begins to communicate meaning, such as inviting another to play or signaling that it's time to switch roles Begins to prefer peer over adult companions
3 YEARS	Begins to engage in complex cooperative and dramatic play
4 YEARS	Shares more with peers than 3-year-olds May engage in fantasy play that's designed to master specific fears
4½ YEARS	Begins to have longer play sequences and is more willing to accept roles other than the protagonist
6 YEARS	Reaches a peak in imaginative play
3–7 YEARS	Main friendship goal is coordinated and successful play
7 YEARS	Begins to choose same-gender playmates
7–9 YEARS	Expects friends to share activities, offer help, be physically nearby
8–12 YEARS	Main goal of friendship is to be accepted by one's same-gender peers
9–11 YEARS	Expects friends to accept and admire her and to be loyal and committed to the relationship; is likely to build friendships on the basis of earlier interactions
11–13 YEARS	Expects genuineness, intimacy, self-disclosure, common interests, and similar attitudes and values in friends
13–17 YEARS	Important goal of friendship is understanding of the self
16–17 YEARS	Expects friends to provide emotional support

Sources: Hartup, 1983; Rubin, Bukowski, & Parker, 1998.
Note: Developmental events described in this and other Turning Points charts represent overall trends identified in research studies. Individual children vary greatly in the ages at which they achieve these developmental changes.

us examine some of the personal characteristics and social skills associated with being well received by peers. It would be pleasant to believe that children base their judgments of a child's acceptability on his possession or lack of desirable personal attributes such as altruism, honesty, and sensitivity. However, several characteristics associated with peer acceptance not only have little to do with the personal merits of the individual child but are enduring and difficult to change. Children cannot readily modify their appearance, race, gender, age, or name, but these attributes are correlated with how well their peers accept them.

First Impressions: Name and Appearance.

Children often form first impressions of others based on surface characteristics, such as names and physical appearance. Children seem to respond adversely to names that are unfamiliar or seem strange to them. Of course, fashions in given names change over time. Someone born in the 1920s, for example, might have been called Horace or Myrtle, but in the 1990s names like Zachary and Jennifer became popular. Thus peer groups today are likely to greet a child with a familiar name, such as Maria or Sam, more cordially than a child with an unusual name, such as Darcy or Lana (Asher, Oden, & Gottman, 1976; McDavid & Harari, 1966; Rubin et al., 1998). A person's name, of course, is only one of the many variables that influence social acceptance. In this century, the United States has had presidents named Theodore, Woodrow, Warren, Calvin, Herbert, Franklin, Dwight, Lyndon, and Gerald, and vice presidents named Alben, Hubert, and Spiro. Names are apparently not everything.

Although everyone has heard the maxim "Beauty is only skin deep," physical attractiveness plays an important role in both children's and adults' responses to and evaluations of others. Children as young as 3 or 5 can differentiate attractive from unattractive children and seem to make their judgments on the basis of the same physical attributes that adults use (Langlois, 1985). (As we saw in Chapter 5, this ability to distinguish attractive and unattractive faces may even be evident in infancy.)

Both children and adults attribute more desirable characteristics to attractive than to unattractive people. Children regard aggressive, antisocial behavior and meanness as more characteristic of unattractive children, and attribute behaviors such as independence, fearlessness, friendliness, sharing, and self-sufficiency to attractive children. Peers prefer good-looking partners and view unattractive ones as unacceptable (Langlois & Stephan, 1981). Moreover, attractiveness is more important to a girl's being accepted than to a boy's acceptance by others (Vaughn & Langlois, 1983). Thus, the prevailing perception appears to be that what is beautiful is good.

Are these negative views of unattractive children all in the eye of the beholder, or are they based on behavioral reality? Langlois and Downs (1979) found no difference in the social behavior of attractive and unattractive 3-year-olds. However, unattractive 5-year-olds, in contrast to attractive peers, were more likely to be aggressive, to hit other children, to play in an active, boisterous manner, and to prefer masculine toys. This age trend suggests that the aggressive behavior may be a response to being perceived negatively by others and that a self-fulfilling prophecy is at work. Perhaps the negative expectations and perceptions peers and adults have of unattractive children foster the emergence of the very characteristics they attribute to these children.

Age and Peer Acceptance.

Particularly among small children, groups in Western societies tend to be age-graded. In the United States, for example, children play less than a third of the time with cross-age companions who are 2 or more years older; they spend most of their time with same-age peers (Ellis et al., 1981). In many cultures, however, such as India and African countries, older children not only care for and teach younger ones but also engage in play with them. (Edwards, 1992; Whiting & Edwards, 1988).

Older and younger peers serve different functions, and even young children seem to understand these variations among peers of differing ages. Children attribute helping, assisting functions to older peers and expect play behavior from age-mates and younger peers (Edwards & Lewis, 1979). Observations of children across three continents (the Indian subcontinent, Africa, and North America) indicate that in fact most children understand the different functions of peers of various ages (Edwards, 1992; Whiting & Edwards, 1988).

For children who are socially isolated or poorly adjusted, association with younger peers may provide an opportunity to acquire caretaking or social skills. Children with emotional or social problems may actually be driven out of their same-age peer groups and find acceptance easier to gain with younger children (Hetherington et al., 1979). In addition, younger children may be less threatening and may exhibit social skills at a level more comparable to that of a disturbed or socially immature child. Interaction with younger peers may actually play a therapeutic role. In Harlow's studies (Chapter 7), the negative social effects of prolonged isolation on rhesus monkeys were reversed by a program of sustained contact with younger monkeys (Suomi & Harlow, 1972). Subsequently, Furman, Rahe, and Hartup (1979) found that providing contact with younger peers could improve the sociability of socially withdrawn 4- and 5-year-old children.

In spite of the contributions of older and younger peers, the preference for same-age peers serves a very special role in social development. Age-grading would occur even if our schools were not age-graded and children were left alone to determine the composition of their own societies. After all, children share interests most closely with others of their own age, who are at similar points in their cognitive, emotional, social, and physical development.

Gender and Peer Acceptance.

A child's gender has a marked effect on playmate choices. Although, as we've said, up to the age of 7 children are relatively willing to choose playmates of either gender, same-gender peers still tend to play together. This tendency is evident as early as the preschool years and increases throughout the elementary school years (Maccoby, 1988, 1990). In early adolescence, when dating begins, children once again become willing to choose companions of the opposite gender. Consider this exchange among preschoolers:

> (Jake and Danny are on the big swing together.)
> LAURA (running up, excited): Can I get on?
> JAKE (emphatically): No!
> DANNY (even more emphatically): No!!
> JAKE: We don't want you on here. We only want boys on here. (After Laura leaves, I ask Jake why he said that.)
> JAKE: Because we like boys—we like to have boys.
> (Rubin, 1980, p. 102)

Similar attitudes may be expressed in junior high school:

> The chairs in Mr. Socker's room are arranged in the shape of a wide, shallow U. As the first few kids come into the room, Harry says to John, who is starting to sit down in an empty section of the room along one side of the U, "Don't sit there, that's where all the girls sit." Harry and John sit elsewhere. . . . (Schofield, 1981, p. 62)

There are exceptions, of course, but cross-gender friendships across the elementary school years often operate underground. A boy and girl might remain friends outside of school; for example, they may associate at church or in their neighborhood but generally keep their friendship a secret from their classmates (Gottman, 1986; Thorne, 1986). Some commentators see this low level of cross-gender interaction as unfortunate, for cross-gender play "can expose boys and girls to a wider range of behavioral styles and activities, expand their pool of potential friends and help to give them a fuller appreciation of the qualities that are in fact shared by the two sexes" (Rubin, 1980, p. 104).

One reason children in the elementary school years tend to choose same-gender playmates is the traditional difference in preferred activities. Boys spend a lot of time playing team sports, whereas girls may prefer less organized activities, such as walking and talking. As girls' participation in team sports continues to grow, however, perhaps playmate choices will change too.

What might be causing this self-imposed segregation and lack of acceptance between boys and girls? It seems to be related to differences in the interests and play patterns of girls and boys. In a study of boys and girls in elementary school, Thorne (1986) found marked differences in the play styles of the two sexes. Girls tend to play in low-energy games in small groups near the school building and close to adult supervision. Boys occupy nearly 10 times the space of girls and play high-energy run-and-chase games when they are young and organized rule-oriented games when they become older. As they develop, girls prefer unstructured, unorganized activities such as talking and walking in contrast to structured group activities (Savin-Williams, 1987). Moreover, young boys are involved in boisterous, rough-and-tumble play or play with blocks and cars (DiPietro, 1981; MacDonald & Parke, 1984), whereas girls prefer art, books, and dolls (Eisenberg, Murray, & Hite, 1982). Even the nature of pretend play differs; boys are more likely to enact superhero roles, while girls portray familial characters (Garvey, 1990b; Haight & Miller, 1993). Play doesn't go well when Batman and Robin meet Mom and her little baby! It seems possible that as traditional gender roles break down, more shared interests will emerge, and boys and girls will accept and interact with one another more. We return to this issue in Chapter 15.

Social Skills and Peer Social Acceptance.

Children of various social status differ in their goals, strategies, and behaviors in social encounters with their peers (Chung & Asher, 1996; Crick & Dodge, 1994). First, not all children have the same goals. Renshaw and Asher (1983) presented third to sixth graders with a hypothetical social situation and then asked the children to choose an appropriate goal. Here are two of the situations:

Your parents have moved to a new town. This is your first day at a new school. As recess begins, the children go out to play.
You ask a child who is new to the neighborhood to watch cartoons one Saturday morning. After about 10 minutes, the child changes the channel without asking.

Children of high status, in contrast to low-status children, focused on wanting to be outgoing, sociable, and sympathetic toward other children (e.g., "I'd want to start making friends with them"). Similarly, older children, in contrast to younger children, were more likely to suggest these types of positive, outgoing goals as well as more positive, accommodating goals, which focus on wanting to be friendly but in a more cautious manner ("I just like making friends slowly"). On the other hand, younger children suggested more hostile goals ("I'd want to get back at that kid").

As Crick and Dodge (1994) suggest, both the goals and the behavioral strategies of children of different social status vary. When children indicated what they

Joining a group of peers who are already friends with one another is often difficult. Self confidence, persistence, and the ability to adopt a new strategy when another hasn't worked are all helpful.

would do in these situations, it was clear that children differed in their strategies. High-status children offered more direct and friendly strategies (e.g., "I'd say, 'Can you play with me?' ") than low-status peers. Older low-status children, however, were likely to avoid the situation ("I'd probably just go play outside by myself"). As Chung and Asher (1996) recently found, goals and strategies operate together in social problem-solving situations. For example, children with *relationship* goals were more likely to use prosocial than hostile and coercive strategies, whereas children with *control* goals were more hostile in a conflict situation.

Social skills, such as reinforcing others and being able to initiate interactions effectively and communicate well, play an important role in social acceptance (Coie, Dodge, & Kupersmidt, 1990). The new child in school who tries to initiate a relationship by hovering silently or making aggressive or inappropriate responses is behind before he gets started. In contrast, the young child who asks for information (e.g., "Where do you live?"), gives information (e.g., "My favorite sport is basketball"), or tries to include the other child in a mutual activity (e.g., "Wanna help me build this sand castle?") is well on the way to being accepted by the group (Putallaz & Gottman, 1981).

Persistence and flexibility help, too. Many children are rebuffed or ignored when they first try to interact with their peers, but most children eventually succeed in being accepted. The ability to adopt alternative strategies when initial attempts fail is important in successful peer interaction. Variations in children's willingness to persist is due, in part, to their differing perceptions of "what happened" when their initial tries fail. Goetz and Dweck (1980) examined the explanations of elementary school children when their attempts to begin a new relationship with a peer were rebuffed. Some thought the problem was due to lack of effort or misunderstanding—a temporary problem that can be remedied. Others saw their failure as due to their own lack of ability ("It happened because it is hard for me to make friends"). In contrast to the former children, the latter children were less likely to continue to try to make friends. We will see a repeat of these contrasting views of lack of effort and lack of ability when we discuss achievement motivation and behavior in Chapter 14.

Erdley, Loomis, Cain, and Dumas-Hines (1997) found that focusing on a learning goal (emphasizing the learning opportunities of a task) was more socially adaptive than focusing on performance goals (stressing the evaluative nature of the task). In their study, these researchers told child participants that they were trying out for membership in a pen-pal club. To the children in the learning-goal condition they explained, "The important thing is, this will give you a chance to practice and improve your ways of making friends. So think of it as a chance to work on your skills and maybe learn some new ones" (Erdley et al., 1997, p. 266). The researchers told the children in the performance-goal condition, "The important thing is we'd like to see how good you are at making friends. Think of it as a chance for you [too] to see how good you are at making friends" (p. 266).

Erdley and colleagues found that the children who focused on the learning goal displayed a more mastery-oriented response, whereas those who were given a performance goal showed more helplessness. They also found that children's implicit theories about personality affect their responses to social challenges. The children who believed that personality is nonmalleable were more likely to endorse performance goals than those who viewed personality as malleable. These studies suggest that children's goals in social situations often reflect their responses to social failure and are also predicted by their implicit theories of personality.

Research suggests that the categories of children's social status derived by the sociometric technique that we discussed earlier—popular, average, rejected, and neglected—are linked with particular kinds of social behaviors (Coie et al., 1990; Newcomb, Bukowski, & Pattee, 1993; Rubin et al., 1998). One study found that popular boys who engaged in more prosocial behavior were rarely aggressive and helped set the rules and norms for their group (Newcomb et al., 1993). Popular children tend to be assertive but not disruptive. When entering an ongoing play situation, they do so in a way that allows the ongoing interaction to continue—an index of their communicative competence (Black & Hazen, 1990). Rejected boys are aversive, aggressive, and active, whereas neglected boys are less aggressive, less talkative, and more withdrawn. However, aggressive children who are competent at developing a social network are unlikely to be rejected (Cairns, Cairns, Neckerman, & Gest, 1988).

Often children who are unpopular have multiple cognitive and behavioral deficits, and this combination of problems leads them to be unsuccessful with their peers. To succeed in forming and maintaining good relationships with other children requires that the child understand the behavior of the other child and make the appropriate responses to the partner's behavior. This is not a simple task; the child must make a series of decisions to evaluate the situation and respond according to his assessment. In the belief that children's effectiveness in making these decisions strongly influences their success with peers, Crick and Dodge (1994) have proposed the six decision-making steps that are outlined in Figure 13-4. At each stage of the decision-making chain, the child can make a decision that will be either helpful or misleading. The arrows with dotted lines indicate feedback and its possible effect in changing one's interpretation or decision.

Let us suppose that Vimala, a socially competent 7-year-old, encounters two children playing a board game. She carefully surveys the situation and notices that one of the children smiles at her in a friendly way (step 1—encoding of cues). Next she interprets this cue to mean that the girl wants her to play too (step 2—interpretation of cues). (If Vimala had interpreted the other girl's smile as one of amusement at her, however, she might have encoded the smile as *un*friendly.) In the third step, Vimala selects a goal or desired outcome for the situation or continues with a preexisting goal. Children bring goal orientation to a situation, or they may reverse and construct new goals in response to immediate social stimuli. In this case, Vimala decides that she would like to make friends with the other children. In the fourth step, Vimala thinks about what she could do, that is, what sort of response she might make to access her goal, for example, smile back, ask to join in, or make a positive comment. She next considers the likely reaction that each response would elicit from the girls and, in the fifth step, decides to make a friendly comment about the game. (If she had decided to smile back and the girls just kept on playing, she would have to go back to step 4 and consider other possible responses.) In the sixth step, the smiling girl looks up again and Vimala smiles back and says, "Looks like fun." The pair of girls invite her to play the next game.

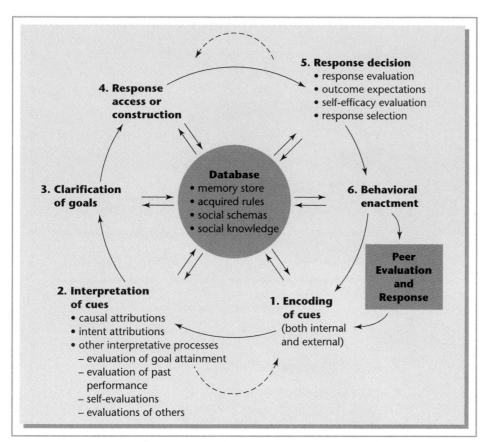

■ FIGURE 13-4
An information-processing model of children's social behavior.
This model outlines the steps children go through in evaluating a social situation, deciding what they would like to achieve in the situation, choosing a behavior that they think likely to accomplish that goal, and acting on their decisions. For an example of how the model works, see the text discussion. (*Source:* Crick & Dodge, 1994)

When Christopher—a not very socially competent 6-year-old—surveys two boys playing, he fails to notice the friendly look from one boy and instead notices their sneakers. At the next stage, because he failed to see the friendly look, he decides that the boys are unfriendly. At the third stage Christopher thinks about what he might do but can think only of mean things ("Why are you so unfriendly?" "It's not nice not to let me play"). He decides that these strategies will work and finally blurts out, "You two are really selfish not to let me play." And it is no great surprise that they didn't invite him to play!

Using these models, Dodge (1986) and coworkers compared 5- to 7-year-old children who were rated either socially competent or socially incompetent by their teachers and peers. They presented children with a videotape of situations similar to the ones just described where a child is trying to join the play of two other children and asked their participants about what they would do in each of five stages (the researchers omitted stage 3 in this study). Predicting that children of different levels of competence would respond differently, the researchers found just that. The incompetent children were less likely to notice and interpret the cues correctly, generated fewer competent responses, chose less appropriate responses, and in the next phase of the experiment, were less skilled at actually enacting or carrying out the behavior. The researchers then asked the children to participate in an actual peer-group entry task with two peers from their classroom. Measures of each of the five stages in the model predicted children's competence and success at this task; children who understood what to do were better at the real task of gaining entry into the peer group (see Figure 13-5*a*). In a related study, well-adjusted children as well as aggressive 8- to 10-year-olds were presented with a situation involving their response to a peer's provocation (e.g., a peer knocks over a child's block tower—in an ambiguous way so the child can't tell if it was accidental or not). Figure 13-5*b* shows that aggressive children showed more deficits at each of the processing steps. In addition, children's processing ability successfully predicted how children responded when another child actually provoked them. These studies provide

■ FIGURE 13-5
Social competence, tendency toward aggression, and skills in processing social cues. Children who were more socially competent (a) and who were nonaggressive and better adjusted (b) displayed fewer deficits in their ability to process cues and other information in social situations than socially incompetent and aggressive children. (*Source:* Adapted from Dodge, et al., 1987)

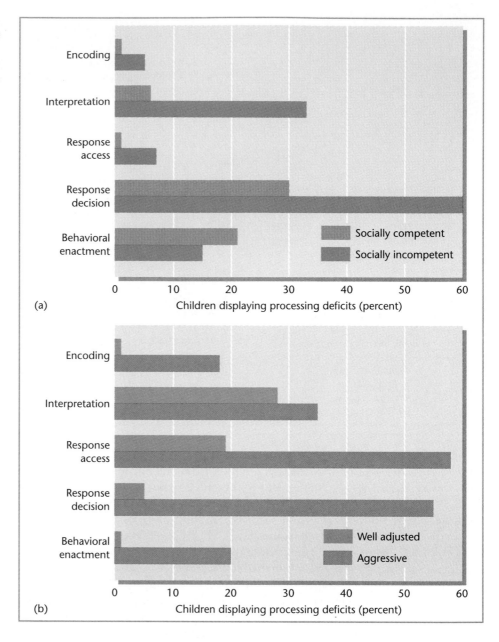

(a) Children displaying processing deficits (percent)

(b) Children displaying processing deficits (percent)

strong support for the role of cognitive factors in understanding children's social relationships with peers. Deficits in social understanding can lead to poor social relationships. In this case, thought and action are clearly linked.

Consequences of Being Unpopular

Being unpopular among peers can lead to both short-term and long-term problems. First, children feel differently if they have friends than if they are not accepted by their peers. Unpopular children report feeling lonely and socially dissatisfied (Asher & Hopmeyer, in press; Asher, Hymel, & Renshaw, 1984; Cassidy & Asher, 1992). Table 13-2 displays some moving descriptions by children of how it feels to be lonely. Neglected children seem to be no more lonely than average children, but rejected children are especially likely to feel lonely (Figure 13-6). Moreover, nonaggressive rejected children feel lonelier than aggressive rejected children (Parkhurst & Asher, 1992). Being actively disliked by many of one's peers, not simply lacking friends in a class, leads to strong feelings of social isolation and alienation. Moreover, as social relationships change, feelings of loneliness change as well. Renshaw and Brown (1993) tracked

TABLE 13-2   Some Children's Loneliness Narratives

Girl, Grade 6

"Today everybody's going to Mary Ann's party in the group. I'm sort of the one that gets left behind. I'm not invited to the party so I won't do anything on the weekend. Anywhere the whole group goes, I don't."

(Why did that make you feel lonely?) "I'm just the person that gets left back. Maybe they don't realize that I get left, that I'm there, but it happens all the time."

Boy, Grade 5

"I was living in Greenvalley. It was a Sunday. All the stores were closed, I had no money. Jason, a friend, had to go to his aunt's. I decided to call on Jamie, but no one was home. I went to turn on the TV and only church stuff was on. I went upstairs to play with my toys, but it was so boring. The dog was behind the couch so I didn't want to bother him. Mom was sleeping. My sister was babysitting. It wasn't my day."

(Why did that make you feel lonely?) "There was no one to talk to or play with, nothing to listen to."

Girl, Grade 8

"Last year, at the beginning of the year, I had a friend, Sandy. Then she went with another group of people who didn't like me. They would walk away when I'd go over to Sandy. They started spreading rumors about me to make everyone hate me. Sandy also didn't hang around me 'cause her other friends didn't like me."

(Why did that make you feel lonely?) "I didn't have any friends. They didn't want to be near me."

Source: Hayden, Turulli, & Hymel, 1988.

a group of third–sixth-grade Australian children over a year. Children who became less accepted by their peers, lost friends, and made more statements about being poor at developing friendships (e.g., "It's hard for me to make friends at school") showed gains in loneliness across time. Finally, being verbally and physically victimized by peers is associated with higher levels of loneliness even among kindergarten children (Kochenderfer & Ladd, 1996b). However, having a friend helps. Rejected children who have a stable friendship with at least one other child feel less lonely than rejected and friendless children (Parker & Asher, 1992; Sanderson & Siegal, 1991).

What are the long-term consequences for a child of being accepted by only a few of his peers? Poor peer relationships in childhood do have implications for later adjustment. Parker and Asher (1987) found that children who were poorly accepted by their peers were more likely to drop out of school and to develop patterns of criminal activity than well-accepted children. As Box 13-1 shows, even children who are shy and withdrawn follow a different life-course pattern than less shy children.

Unfortunately for socially unpopular children, social standing tends to remain stable across time and in different situations. Across a five-year span, Coie and Dodge (1983) found modest stability for popular children and neglected children. In the fourth through the seventh grade, popular children sometimes lost their high status and neglected children occasionally became more socially accepted. However, children who were once rejected had a higher chance of maintaining this status across a wide time span. Even as early as

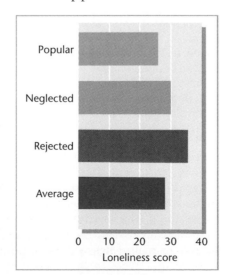

■ FIGURE 13-6
Loneliness and peer status. Popular and average children attained the lowest loneliness scores and rejected children the highest. Being neglected didn't seem to trigger much more loneliness that being average or popular. (*Source:* Asher et al., 1984)

BOX 13-1

Child Psychology in Action

What Happens to Shy Children—Thirty Years Later?

What happens to shy children as they grow up? To find out, Caspi, Elder, and Bem (1988) traced the developmental patterns of children whom teachers rated on shyness when they were between 8 and 10 years old. On the basis of two measures, these researchers defined shyness as both social anxiety and inhibited social behavior. Teachers rated the children on a shyness scale that ranged from high (acutely uncomfortable to the point of panic in social situations) to low (enjoys meeting new people), as well as on a measure of social reserve. On this scale, children who scored high were so emotionally inhibited that other people reported feelings of strain and awkwardness when in their company, whereas children who scored low were "spontaneous and uninhibited in their expression of feelings." The teachers who rated the children found the shy boys and girls to be less friendly, less sociable, more reserved, more withdrawn, and to be followers rather than leaders.

Twenty and 30 years later, researchers reinterviewed their former participants, who were now adults. Boys rated shy in childhood were delayed in marrying, becoming fathers, and establishing stable careers (see Figure 13-7). Moreover, as adults these men achieved less occupationally than their less shy peers. "Men who were reluctant to enter social settings as children appear to have become adults who are more generally reluctant to enter the new and unfamiliar social settings required by the important life course transitions into marriage, parenthood and career" (Caspi et al., 1988, p. 827).

Shy girls, on the other hand, were more likely than their peers to follow a conventional pattern of marriage, childbearing, and homemaking. The majority (56%) of women with a childhood history of shyness were more likely either to have no history of outside employment or to terminate employment at marriage or childbirth and not to reenter the labor force. In contrast, only 36 percent of their more outgoing peers followed this more traditional pattern. In addition, women with a history of childhood shyness were married to men who had higher occupational status at midlife than husbands of other women.

Clearly the life course of these men and women was shaped, in part, by cultural gender-role prescriptions. Although shyness in men has never been thought desirable, at the time this group were growing up, shyness in women was widely considered a positive attribute, suited to the wife-mother-homemaker role many deemed appropriate for women.

Shy children, regardless of their gender, have probably never thought that shyness was a good thing, and interventions designed to help such children gain poise and self-confidence can begin early. One kindergarten teacher had her class draw pictures about things that had happened in their lives and then, one by one, display their drawings and briefly describe the events pictured to the rest of the class. In the first presentation session many children looked down and spoke in whispers or not at all, but after a few such sessions even the shyest child was looking around coolly at his audience, making sure that he had everyone's attention, and then clearly and calmly presenting his work.

Psychologists have developed a variety of programs to help shy and withdrawn children become more socially outgoing (Rubin et al., 1998). Although shyness seems to have a genetic component, temperament is not destiny (Kagan, 1994; Goleman, 1995). Children can, to some extent, overcome their shyness through coaching, modeling, and instruction (see the text section on "Helping Children with Peer Problems").

■ FIGURE 13-7

Shyness may retard developmental transitions.
Boys who displayed shyness late in childhood were likely to establish their careers later, marry later, and father children later than boys who weren't shy. (*Source:* Caspi et al., 1988)

kindergarten, the status of rejected children is more stable across time than other peer statuses (Parke et al., 1997). In part, the stability is due to *reputational bias*, or the tendency of children to interpret the behavior of their peers based on their past encounters with and feelings about these children (Hymel, Wagner, & Butler, 1990). When judging the negative behavior of previously disliked or liked peers, children are more likely to deny or minimize actor responsibility for the negative behavior in the case of a liked than a disliked peer. Liked peers are given the "benefit of the

TABLE 13-3   Coaching a Child in Group Participation

COACH: Okay, I have some ideas about what makes a game fun to play with another person. There are a couple of things that are important to do. You should cooperate with the other person. Do you know what cooperation is? Can you tell me in your own words?

CHILD: Ahh . . . sharing.

COACH: Yes, sharing. Okay, let's say you and I are playing the game you played last time. What was it again?

CHILD: Drawing a picture.

COACH: Okay, tell me then, what would be an example of sharing when playing the picture-drawing game?

CHILD: I'd let you use some pens, too.

COACH: Right. You would share the pens with me. That's an example of cooperation. Now let's say you and I are doing the picture-drawing game. Can you also give me an example of what would not be cooperating?

CHILD: Taking all the pens.

COACH: Would taking all the pens make the game fun to play?

CHILD: No.

COACH: So you wouldn't take all the pens. Instead, you'd cooperate by sharing them with me. Can you think of some more examples of cooperation? (The coach waited for a response.) Okay, how about taking turns. . . . Let's say you and I . . . (etc.). Okay, I'd like you to try out some of these ideas when you play [name of new game] with [other child]. Let's go and get [other child], and after you play, I'll talk to you again for a minute or so and you can tell me if these things seem to be good ideas for having fun at a game with someone.

Source: Oden & Asher; 1977.

doubt"; disliked peers are not. Thus, reputations color the way children interpret peer actions and help account for the stability of behavior across time (Hymel, 1986).

Reputation, however, is not the only thing that accounts for the stability of peer ratings of rejected children. The behavior of these children matters, too. Interestingly, when the composition of peer groups changes, and rejected children interact with new and different peers, they tend to retain the social rank they've already been assigned (Coie et al., 1990). When unfamiliar boys of differing social status were brought together in play groups once a week for six weeks, within three weeks their social status in these new groups was very similar to their social status in their classrooms. Boys who were rejected in school were similarly shunned by their peers in the new group, just as the popular boys in school retained their high social rank in the new setting (Coie & Kupersmidt, 1983). In view of the difficulties that rejected children encounter, it is important to find ways to help them.

Helping Children with Peer Problems.

What can we do to help socially isolated and rejected children become more accepted and perhaps less lonely? Shaping socially desirable behavior through reinforcement or modeling and directly coaching children in social skills can increase social acceptance (Mize & Ladd, 1990). Coaching involves teaching a general concept or strategy, usually through providing examples of successful approaches (Table 13-3). Ladd (1981) coached unpopular third graders on three communication skills: asking positive questions, offering useful suggestions or directions, and offering supportive statements. Children participated in eight 40- to-50-minute sessions over a three-week period. During these sessions, the adult "coach" verbally instructed children in the concepts; guided them through rehearsals of the ideas, letting the children practice on their own while playing with a classmate; and reviewed the concepts following the practice session. The review phase involved teaching the

■ FIGURE 13-8
How parents help their children develop peer relationships.
Children learn how to interact socially by practicing with their parents and modeling their parents' actions. In addition, parents coach and educate their children in ways of relating to others. And parents are the gatekeepers for their children's social behavior, providing and monitoring children's opportunities for social interaction with peers. The upper arrow indicates that parent-child interactions can affect parents' decisions about social opportunities for the children and that, in turn, choices and decisions about such opportunities inform parents' interactions with their children. Finally, children's relative success in peer interactions can provide useful feedback, helping parents and children make any necessary adjustments in social interaction patterns.

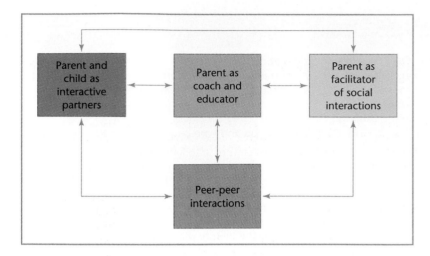

children to evaluate their own behavior in relation to what they had learned about successful social interaction. Assessments immediately after the training program and again four weeks later indicated that the coached children's classroom behavior improved and their popularity increased. The control group, who received no coaching, showed no improvement. And coaching can help even young children: Mize and Ladd (1990) were able to improve the social relationships of neglected and rejected preschool children with similar types of interventions.

Do all unpopular children need help? As we noted earlier, unpopularity can assume a variety of forms, and not every unpopular child should be changed. For example, neglected children, who have often been the focus of intervention, probably are not at such high risk for later problems. As Coie and Dodge (1983) found in their longitudinal study, many neglected children are quite likely to become more socially accepted and competent. And there are many kinds of lone play that are not related to indices of social competence, such as solitary constructive play—artwork, puzzles, block construction—a frequent kind of play among preschoolers. Moreover, some forms of solitary activity, such as constructive play in which children sit around a table and individually put together Lego sets or practice their artistic skills as budding Picassos, are highly predictive of social competence. It's important to keep in mind that there may be nothing wrong with solitary play. Indeed, the preschooler with a passion for puzzles may turn out to be the college computer whiz!

On the other hand, Rubin (1982; Rubin & LeMare, 1990) has found that preschoolers who play simple repetitive games such as banging on the table whether they're alone or close to other children tend to be less socially competent. Similarly, children who engage in dramatic play—for example, pretending to be Batman—by themselves are not very socially skilled. At greatest risk for later problems of social adjustment are rejected children who appear to retain their outcast status; it is these children who can clearly benefit from intervention. Box 13-2 considers some reasons certain children are repeatedly victimized by their peers as well as some factors that can support an at-risk child's resiliency.

Parents as Peer Promoters.

Parents influence their children's peer relationships in a variety of ways. Figure 13-8 illustrates three common ways in which parents contribute to their children's developing peer relationships (Parke & O'Neil, 1996). First, they serve as partners with whom the child may acquire skills that help her to interact successfully with other children. As we saw in Chapter 7, infants who developed secure attachments to their mothers became socially competent preadolescents (Elicker et al., 1992). In addition, the way parents are currently interacting with their children is related to the children's social behavior with peers. Mothers of higher-status first graders were found

BOX 13-2

Risk and Resilience

Victimization by Peers: It Helps to Have Friends

Some children are the regular targets of other children's wrath. Although it is possible to identify these victims of other's aggression early, unfortunately they often remain as victims over the school years (Khatri, Kupersmidt, & Patterson, 1994). Who are these children that peers target to pick on, tease, or attack? They are children who may even invite attack by sending implicit signals that they are unlikely to defend themselves or retaliate. Some of these children exhibit *internalizing* problems: They cry easily; they exhibit anxiety; they lack humor, self-confidence, and self-esteem; and they use ineffectual persuasion tactics. And they often encourage their attackers by giving in to the bully's demands, being submissive, or surrendering possessions (Perry, Williard, & Perry, 1990; Schwartz, Dodge, & Coie, 1993).

Other children who suffer others' aggression exhibit *externalizing* problems: They disrupt, argue, and attack but not very effectively. Instead, they somehow provoke and irritate other children without threatening them or giving the impression that they will follow through on their hostile displays. One investigator (Olweus, 1993) has termed these children "provocative victims." Not surprisingly, victimized children are also physically weak (Olweus, 1993). The school fullback could provoke others, but even bullies will leave him alone.

Victimization takes its toll on children. They are more likely to be lonely, avoid school, and show increasing depression across time (Hodges, Malone, & Perry, 1997; Kochenderfer & Ladd, 1996a). Young adolescents who have been abused by peers report elevated depression and low self-esteem 10 years later, in early adulthood (Olweus, 1992).

What factors protect or buffer children from being victimized? Hodges, Malone, and Perry (1997) recently tested the notion that children at risk of being attacked or bullied will be more likely to become victims if they lack friends or are rejected by their peers. Indeed, the children who were at risk were less likely to be victimized as their number of friends increased. Not just any friend will do; the qualities of the friend are important. When children's friends possessed qualities that served a protective function (e.g., physical strength, aggressiveness) children at risk were less likely to be victimized.

Rejection by a peer group is another social risk factor related to increased victimization for children at risk. In other words, the link between each behavioral risk factor (e.g., physical weakness, showing anxiety, low self-confidence) and victimization was greater for peer-rejected children than for better-accepted children.

These findings support the notion that the expression of an individual's vulnerabilities often depends on social context factors (Hodges et al., 1997). Having friends—the right kind of friends—can serve to buffer the at-risk child from victimization.

---

to interact in a more positive and agreeable manner with their children and to be more concerned with feelings, both their own and those of their children, than mothers of lower-status first-grade children; in contrast, mothers of lower-status children were found to exhibit more negative and controlling behavior with their children than did mothers of higher-status children (Puttallaz, 1987; Puttallaz & Heflin, 1990). Similar findings have been documented for fathers as well (Parke & O'Neil, 1996, 1998).

A second way in which parents influence their children's peer relationships is through their roles as coaches or educators (Bhavnagri & Parke, 1991; Lollis & Ross, 1992; Pettit & Mize, 1993). They can give advice, support, and directions about the most helpful strategies their children can use in interactions with their peers. In a comparison of parents of popular and unpopular children, Australian researchers (Finnie & Russell, 1988; Russell & Finnie, 1990) found differences in the advice and guidance that mothers would give when their children encountered a problem with a peer (e.g., how the child can reduce conflict after another child has thrown sand at him during play in the sand box, or how the child should gain entry to a group after being told to go away). Mothers of children of high social status suggested more positive-direct approaches (e.g., a positive alternative action) and more rule-oriented strategies (tell the other child that they can take turns). In contrast, mothers of low-status children used more avoidance strategies (don't bother about it if another child throws sand) or vague-nonspecific tactics (the child should "look friendly" or "get to know the children"). Not only did the mothers differ in knowledge, but they behaved differently when assisting their children in joining in and playing with two unfamiliar peers. Mothers of high-social-status children used more skillful strategies (e.g., they encouraged communications and helped their own child join in a dyad's conversation), whereas mothers of low-social-status children used less skillful strategies (e.g., took control of the game, disrupted play patterns of the children) or avoided active supervision of the children. Parents can clearly be helpful, but some ways seem more effective than others.

A third way in which parents influence their children's peer relationships is through their role as providers of opportunities for peer interaction (Ladd & LeSieur, 1995; Ladd, Muth, & Hart, 1992). This can assume a variety of forms. Parents can set the stage through their choice of a neighborhood that may increase or limit the children's opportunities to find suitable playmates. As one parent put it: "Just look at this street—kids, swing sets, swimming pools everywhere. It's a kid's paradise. That's one of the main reasons we moved. Before, we were in another section of town. We had a beautiful house, but there weren't many kids to play with" (Rubin & Sloman, 1984, p. 231). Indeed, choosing a neighborhood in which to live can have a serious impact on the nature of children's friendships. In a study of 12-year-olds' social relationships, Medrich and his colleagues (Berg & Medrich, 1980; Medrich, 1981) discovered wide variations in friendship patterns across neighborhoods. In one affluent California neighborhood, friends often lived far apart. This made it hard for them to see one another on their own, and parents typically chauffeured their children to preplanned social events. In contrast, in a low-income black inner-city neighborhood, friends were abundant and nearby, and play tended to be more extensive and spontaneous. In the first neighborhood, children were unusually selective in their friendships; many had only one or two friends whom they chose because they had "something in common." In the second neighborhood, children typically had four or five close friends and moved in large groups. Clearly, economic and ethnic and economic factors may have accounted for some of these differences, but the physical environment of the two neighborhoods was probably responsible as well.

Especially in the case of young children, parents play an important role as "social arrangers." Two-year-olds generally have trouble finding age-mates without help from a parent. Parents facilitate their children's peer contacts by scheduling visits between young friends, enrolling children in organized activities, and of course fetching, carrying, and chauffeuring them from one house or social event to another (Rubin & Sloman, 1984). And arranging makes a difference. Children of parents who tended to arrange peer contacts had a larger range of playmates and more frequent play companions outside of school than children of parents who were less active in initiating peer contacts. In the school context, boys with parents who initiated peer contacts were better liked and less rejected by their classmates than were boys with noninitiating parents; girls did not differ in their acceptance by their classmates as a function of parental initiation activities (Ladd & Golter, 1988; Ladd & LeSieur, 1995; Ladd et al., 1992).

Parents play an important role in promoting children's peer relations, but children's peer relations may influence parents as well. For example, the parents of a child's playmates may become friends with the child's parents, too. As in most domains of development, bidirectional influences are common.

DEVELOPING FRIENDSHIPS

In our exploration of peers, we have focused largely on how well children are accepted by their classmates or peer group. Although this group perspective is an important one, children also develop close dyadic relationships with a few peers that we commonly refer to as friendships. The essentials of a **friendship**, according to Hartup (1989), are reciprocity and commitment between people who see themselves more or less as equals.

friendship A reciprocal commitment between two people who see themselves as relative equals.

What Is a Friend?

As the following exchange indicates, young children don't always find it easy to define a friend. What is a friend? Here is one child's answer:

INTERVIEWER: Why is Caleb your friend?
TONY: Because I like him.
INTERVIEWER: And why do you like him?
TONY: Because he's my friend.
INTERVIEWER: And why is he your friend?
TONY (with mild disgust): Because—I—choosed—him—for—my—friend. (Rubin, 1980)

Children do seem, however, to have certain expectations about relationships with friends that appear across different kinds of peer groups (Keller & Wood, 1989). In addition, these expectations about friends seem to progress over time in three stages. The expectations that emerge at each stage do not disappear with the next stage; in fact, those shown in italics tend to increase with age (Bigelow, 1977; Bigelow & LaGaipa, 1975).

1. **Reward-cost stage (Grades 2–3)**: Children expect friends to *offer help*, *share common activities*, provide stimulating ideas, be able to join in organized play, *offer judgments*, *be physically nearby*, and be demographically similar to them.
2. **Normative stage (Grades 4–5)**: Children now expect friends to *accept* and *admire* them, to bring *loyalty and commitment* to a friendship, and to express similar values and attitudes toward rules and sanctions.
3. **Empathic stage (Grades 6–7)**: Children begin to expect *genuineness* and the *potential for intimacy* in their friends; they expect friends to understand them and to be willing to engage in **self-disclosure**; they want friends to accept their help, to share *common interests*, and to hold similar attitudes and values. This is the relationship that Sullivan (1953) has so poignantly described as "chumship" and that represents a unique kind of intimacy in children's development.

> **self-disclosure** The honest sharing of information of a very personal nature, often with a focus on problem solving; a central means by which adolescents develop friendships.

The obligations of friendship change as well. Youniss and his colleagues (Smollar & Youniss, 1982; Youniss, 1980) have examined 10- to 17-year-olds and find that friendship obligations undergo marked shifts over adolescence. Although 80 percent of the 10- to 11-year-olds thought friends should "be nice to one another and help each other," only 11 percent of the 16- to 17-year-olds indicated that this was a central obligation. In contrast, 62 percent of the 16- to 17-year-olds thought that providing emotional support was important, but only 5 percent of the 10- to 11-year-olds agreed. The reasons change also. Young children view obligations as important "so he'll be nice to you too" or "to keep the relation going good." Obligations are important to older children because they would benefit the other person ("because she'll be happier if you do") or because it defines the relationship ("That's what friends are supposed to do"). Gender matters: Females at all ages are more likely than males to be concerned with emotional assistance and to stress reasons based on benefiting the other person (Rubin et al., 1998).

Unfortunately, there is no clear evidence that these expectations always translate into action! What children say and expect and what they do are not highly related. Nor are friendships always smooth and everlasting. Fights often occur, friends can and do hurt each other, and friendships do end. In the next section, we explore how children make friends and how they behave with their friends.

How Children Make Friends

In spite of many decades of studying children's peer relations, it is still difficult to answer a simple question, "How do children become friends?" Gottman and his colleagues (Gottman, 1983; Gottman & Parker, 1986; Parker & Gottman, 1989)

TABLE 13-4 The Social Processes of Friendship Formation

Process	Definition	Example
Communication clarity and connectedness	Request for message clarification followed by appropriate clarification of the message.	Child A: Give it to me. Child B: Which one? Child A: The purple one with yellow ears.
Information exchange	Asking questions and eliciting revelant information.	Where do you live? What color is your crayon?
Establishing common ground	Finding something to do together and/or exploring their similarities and differences.	Let's play trucks. I like tea parties, do you?
Self-disclosure of feelings	Questions about feelings by one child are followed by expression of feeling by the partner.	I'm really scared of the dark and snakes, too.
Positive reciprocity	One partner responds to another's positive behavior or serves to extend or lengthen a positive exchange: usually involves joking, gossip, or fantasy.	Child A: Did you hear what happened to Mary's sister? Child B: No, tell me and then I'll tell you another thing about Mary.
Conflict resolution	The extent to which play partners resolve disputes and disagreements successfully.	Child A: I want the blue truck. Child B: No, I'm playing with it. Child A: I want it. Child B: OK let's play with it together.

Source: Adapted from Gottman, 1983.

have set out to try to provide an answer. Children ranging in age from 3 to 9 years participated in a series of studies. Gottman sent a tape recorder into the children's homes and listened to children while they played together. Some children played with their best friends; others played with strangers. Eighteen unacquainted peers played in their homes for three sessions, while the researchers tracked how much children progressed toward being friends as they became more familiar with each other. One of this study's achievements was the discovery of a set of social processes that successfully distinguished between the play patterns of friends and strangers (Table 13-4). Friends communicated more clearly, disclosed themselves more, had more positive exchanges, established common ground more easily, exchanged more information, and were able to resolve conflict more effectively than strangers. Moreover, unacquainted children who got along well and who were rated as more likely to become friends scored higher on these dimensions.

Other studies confirm many of these findings with other samples of children at different ages. Not surprisingly, children spend more time with friends and express more positive affect than with nonfriends (Hartup, 1989). They share more with their friends (Jones, 1985), although friends are sometimes tough competitors, which may decrease their sharing with each other (Berndt, 1986). Being friends does not mean never disagreeing (Hartup, 1992; 1996; Laursen, Hartup, & Koplas, 1996). In fact, friends disagree more than nonfriends but engage in less heated conflicts and are more likely to stay in contact after the disagreement than nonfriends (Hartup, Laursen, Stewart, & Eastenson, 1988). Friends are more likely to resolve conflicts in an equitable way and to ensure that the resolution preserves the friendship (Hartup, 1996; Laursen et al., 1996). And friends, of course, are more intimate and self-disclosing with each other than acquaintances (Berndt & Perry, 1990). In turn, they are more knowledgeable about each other than nonfriends—they know each other's strengths and secrets as well as their wishes and weaknesses (Ladd & Emerson, 1984). As someone once said, "A friend is one who knows our faults but doesn't give a damn!"

How do friendship patterns change across development? Parker and Gottman (1989) suggest that the goals and central processes involved in successful friendship formation shift across age. For young children (ages 3 to 7 years), the goal of peer interaction is coordinated play with all the social processes organized to promote successful play. In the second developmental phase—the 8- to 12-year period—the goal changes from playful interaction to a concern with being accepted by one's same-gender peers. Children are concerned with the norms of the group, figuring out which actions will lead to acceptance and inclusion, and which to exclusion and rejection. The most salient social process in middle childhood is **negative gossip**, which involves sharing some negative nugget about another child. When it works well, the partner responds with interest, more negative gossip, and even feelings of solidarity. Both boys and girls engage in gossip, ritual insults, and teasing during this period. It reaches organized levels in some cases. One study found, for example, that in some schools, girls kept "slam books" in which nasty things were written by each girl about other girls (Giese-Davis, cited by Gottman, 1986). Here is an example of two children, Erica and Mikaila, gossiping about another girl, Katie.

> ERICA: Katie does lots of weird things. Like every time she, we make a mistake, she says, "Well, *sorry.*" (Sarcastic tone)
> MIKAILA: I know.
> ERICA: And stuff like that.
> MIKAILA: She's mean. She beat me up once. (Laughs) I could hardly breathe she hit me in the stomach so hard.
> ERICA: She acts like . . .
> MIKAILA: She's the boss. (Gottman, 1986)

> **negative gossip** Sharing with a peer some negative information about another child.

Often gossip is used as a way of establishing the norms for the group; in this case it is important not to be too aggressive or bossy.

In the third developmental period (ages 13 to 17 years), the focus shifts to the understanding of self. The salient social processes are self-exploration and self-disclosure, with a heavy emphasis on problem solving and intense honesty; self-disclosure is the most central process. Table 13-5 summarizes these developmental periods.

Gottman and Mettetal (1986), who listened to the conversations of friends at three age levels—6- to 7-year-olds, 11- to 12-year-olds, and 16- to 17-year-olds—have confirmed that the focus of friendship changes across age. As expected, coordinated play is highest for the youngest group and declines rapidly for the middle and adolescent groups. Similarly, gossip shifts across age. It first becomes important in middle childhood and remains important into adolescence. Beginning in middle childhood, negative gossip about someone children know is especially important. Finally, self-disclosure, a vehicle for self-exploration, increases across age and is most important and frequent during adolescence.

THE FORMATION OF GROUPS

Children not only develop friendships and acquaintanceships with individuals but they also form groups that possess common goals and aims and rules of conduct. In addition, groups usually develop a hierarchical organization or structure that identifies each member's relationship to other members of the group and facilitates the interaction among its members. Some group members are identified as dominant, or as leaders, and their roles are quite different from those of the less dominant children in the group.

Dominance Hierarchies

Groups are not organized in a random fashion; instead, children form "pecking orders," or **dominance hierarchies**, even in the preschool years. Although

> **dominance hierarchy** An ordering of individuals in a group from most to least dominant; a "pecking order."

TABLE 13-5	Characteristics of Friendships in Three Developmental Periods		
	Early Childhood (3 to 7 years old)	Middle Childhood (8 to 12 years old)	Adolescence (13 to 17 years old)
Underlying theme of concern	Maximization of excitement, entertainment, and affect levels in play	Inclusion by peers, avoidance of rejection; self-presentation	Self-exploration; self-definition
Salient conversational processes in friendship	Processes of play coordination: activity talk, play escalation, play de-escalation, conflict resolution	Negative evaluation gossip	Self-disclosure; problem solving
Affective developments	Management of arousal in interaction	Acquisition of affect display and feeling rules; rejection of sentiment	Fusion of logic and emotion: understanding of implications of affect for relationships

Source: Adapted from Gottman & Mettetal, 1986.

preschool children may tend to perceive their own positions of relative dominance as rather higher in the pecking order than they really are, they become increasingly accurate at judging their own status in the early school years (Strayer, 1984). For example, if we ask a preschool child, "Who is the toughest?" he will often respond "me." In contrast, by second grade, children are in more than 70 percent agreement on the relative toughness of students in their class (Edelman & Omark, 1973). Although preschool children's dominance hierarchies are simpler and more loosely differentiated than those of older children, older preschool children show considerable agreement in identifying group status structures (Sluckin & Smith, 1977; Strayer & Strayer, 1976). Moreover, recent evidence suggests that dominance hierarchies emerge very quickly (Pettit, Bakshi, Dodge, & Coie, 1990). In the first 45 minutes of contact, unacquainted first- and third-grade boys began to develop a coherently organized social structure.

Children's ability to order their peers from highest to lowest in dominance seems to be related to their ability to perform cognitive seriation tasks. Children who are able to do such things as order a series of sticks of varying length from the shortest to the longest are also able to order peers in terms of dominance (Omark, Strayer, & Freedman, 1980). Again, we see the close relationship between the child's cognitive and social development. Moreover, dominance ratings among children who stay together are surprisingly stable across time. Children who were rated by their classmates as high in toughness in 1st and 2nd grade are viewed as high in dominance, athletic ability, popularity, leadership, and self-confidence in the 12th grade (Weisfeld, Muczenski, Weisfeld, & Omark, 1987). At the same time, the criteria for determining dominance changes across age. Young children seem to differentiate the status of peers on the basis of toughness, the ability to direct the behavior of others, leadership in play, and physical coercion. In contrast, status structures in older children are more likely to be based on appearance, leadership skills, pubertal development, athletic prowess, and academic performance (Savin-Williams, 1987).

Dominance and status affect social interaction as well. A number of researchers, observing nursery school children in free play, found that dominant children are looked at and imitated more than nondominant children (Strayer, 1980; Vaughn & Waters, 1981). In addition, children are more likely to conform to the opinions and behavior of high-status peers (Rubin et al., 1998).

What functions do hierarchies serve? First, they reduce aggression among the group members, who establish nonaggressive means of resolving conflict. For example, a high-ranking member may use a threat gesture to keep a lower-ranking group member in line. In fact, aggression is rarely seen in a group with a well-established hierarchy (Strayer, 1984). A second purpose is to help divide up the tasks and labor of the group, with worker roles being assumed by the lower-status members and leadership roles going to the more dominant members. Third, dominance hierarchies determine the allocation of resources—especially limited resources (Charlesworth, 1988). Whether it is among the nursery school set (Charlesworth & Dzur, 1987) or among adolescent summer campers (Savin-Williams, 1987), rank has its privileges. In a study of adolescents at a summer camp, Savin-Williams (1987) found that the dominant campers "frequently ate the bigger piece of cake at mealtimes, sat where they wanted to during discussions and slept in the preferred sleeping sites during camp-outs (near the fire)—all scarce resources at summer camp" (p. 934). Clearly, dominance hierarchies play important roles in regulating interaction, but as is often the case, the ones at the top of the hierarchy seem to benefit most.

Cliques and Crowds

In middle childhood, children begin to form cliques (Brown, 1990; Eder, 1985). **Cliques** are voluntary groups based on friendship, unlike activity or work groups to which adults may assign children (Rubin et al., 1998). Cliques range in size from three to nine children and members usually are of the same gender and same race (Kindermann, McCollam, & Gibson, 1995). By the time children are 11, most of their interaction with peers is in the context of the clique. Membership in cliques enhances children's psychological well-being and ability to cope with stress (Hansell, 1981; Rubin et al., 1998), just as social acceptance and friendship are buffers against loneliness.

clique A voluntary group formed on the basis of friendship.

Cliques are evident in adolescence as well but decline across the high school years (Shrum & Cheek, 1987), where they are superseded by crowds. A **crowd** is a collection of people based on shared attitudes or activities that define a particular stereotype—for example, *jocks, brains, eggheads, loners, burnouts, druggies, populars, nerds,* and *greasers*—and who may or may not spend much time together (Brown, 1990; Brown & Huang, 1995). Crowd affiliation is assigned by consensus of the peer group; adolescents don't select it themselves (Rubin et al., 1998). The salience of crowds probably peaks in the early years of high school and decreases through the end of high school (Brown, 1990; Brown & Huang, 1995).

crowd A collection of people whose shared attitudes or activities have been designated by a stereotypical term, such as *populars* or *nerds*.

PEER AND ADULT INFLUENCES ON THE CHILD AND ADOLESCENT

Many behavioral scientists view preadolescence and adolescence as particularly stressful periods during which the child is being pulled and buffeted by the often conflicting standards of parents and peers. However, other authors have argued that the conflict between these two sets of standards is not as extreme as is believed and that there is often remarkable agreement between the values of peers and adults (Brown & Huang, 1995; Cooper & Cooper, 1992; Douvan & Adelson, 1966). A better question than whether peers or adults are more influential is, "Under what conditions and with what behaviors are peers or adults influential?"

Peers and parents each have their own areas of expertise; while peers may not be the best advisers on occupational choices, parents are not the best source for the latest word on video music. Peers exert more influence in friendship choices, interpersonal behavior, entertainment, and fashion standards, whereas parents are more influential in job preferences, academic choices, and future aspirations (Hartup, 1996). Moreover, when adolescents are with parents and peers they engage in very different types of activities—work and task activities with parents, recreation and conversation with peers (Larson & Richards, 1994).

In most cases, a child's behavior is a result of both peer and parental influence (Brown & Huang, 1995; Simons, Conger, & Whitbeck, 1988). Studying the use of marijuana, Kandel (1973) found that among teenagers whose best friends were

■ FIGURE 13-9
Hanging out and peer pressure.
The adolescent sons of parents rated low on authoritativeness were more susceptible to peer pressure, even when at home, than the sons of parents rated high on authoritativeness. Daughters of such parents were much more likely to conform when they were at home but were somewhat more susceptible to peer pressure when hanging out. Among children of highly authoritative parents, boys showed little difference in vulnerability to peer pressure whether at home or with peers, but these girls showed a little more susceptibility when with their peers than at home. (*Source:* Steinberg, 1986)

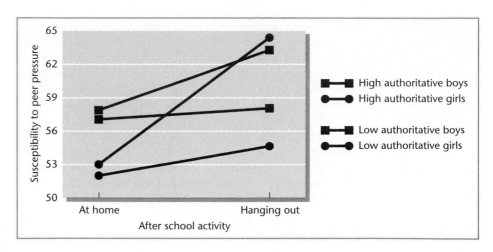

nonusers but whose parents were users, only 17 percent smoked marijuana. If friends used drugs, however, and parents did not, 56 percent of adolescents reported using marijuana. When both parents and peers were users, 67 percent of the adolescents used marijuana. Thus, drug usage by parents and peers had a combined impact on adolescents' use of marijuana. Similar findings have been reported for alcohol, tobacco, and other forms of illegal drugs, and for early and risky sexual behavior (Dishion, French, & Patterson, 1995; Mounts & Steinberg, 1995; Steinberg, Darling, & Fletcher, 1995).

Family relations play an important part in children's susceptibility to peer pressure. When families are warm and supportive and neither highly punitive nor highly permissive—where parents are what in Chapter 12 we called "authoritative"—children are less likely to succumb to peer influence. Steinberg (1986) studied 865 adolescents who had different kinds of after-school supervision. Some were at home after school or at a friend's house, whereas others described themselves as "hanging out," with little adult supervision. As Figure 13-9 shows, supervision matters, and children are more likely to be open to peer pressure when "hanging out" than when they're at home. However, being reared authoritatively can buffer children and make them less susceptible to peer influence even when adult supervision is lax. Being reared by authoritative parents helps to minimize adverse outcomes, but it also helps if children's friends are reared in authoritative homes as well. In a recent study of more than 4,000 high school students, Fletcher, Darling, Steinberg, and Dornbusch (1995) found that adolescents whose friends described their parents as authoritative were less likely to use drugs and run afoul of the law than adolescents whose friends had authoritarian parents. Significantly, the effects of a friend's family's childrearing style was evident even after considering the adolescent's own family influence. Perhaps well-adjusted adolescents seek out similar peers as friends, or maybe parents encourage them to associate with these kinds of friends. Together these studies suggest that parenting style clearly carries over to peer settings and can help children avoid being swayed by their peers.

Parental influence depends on the type of group that the adolescent joins. Brown and Huang (1995) assessed four dimensions of parenting: *warmth, demandingness, psychological autonomy granting*, and *parental encouragement of education*. They found that adolescents in maladaptive crowds (e.g., druggies, outsiders) did less homework and were more likely to use drugs if their parents were *inhibitive*, that is, low on one of the four dimensions. In contrast, if parents were *facilitative*, that is, high on one of the dimensions, adolescents did more homework and were less likely to use drugs even if they were in a maladaptive crowd. Even if adolescents joined an adaptive crowd (e.g., nerds, brains), they adjusted better if their parents were authoritative rather than authoritarian.

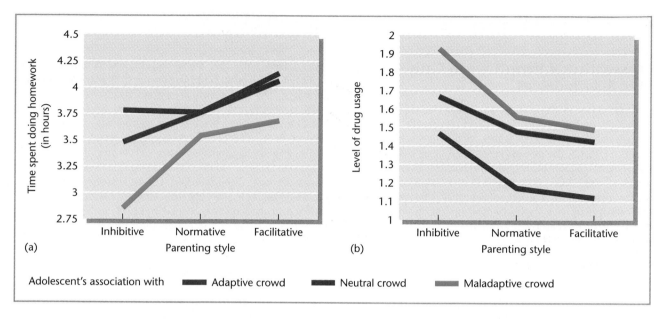

(a)   Parenting style

(b)   Parenting style

Adolescent's association with   ■ Adaptive crowd   ■ Neutral crowd   ■ Maladaptive crowd

As these findings suggest, parental influences are "filtered" through adolescents' experiences in peer contexts. In this study, the extent to which positive parenting led to prosocial outcomes or problematic parenting to antisocial outcomes depended on the type of peer crowd that an adolescent associated with. The belief that parenting is over by adolescence is simply wrong; parents' influence may diminish, but both parents and peers play a significant role in determining adolescent adjustment. As Figure 13-10 shows, children of facilitative parents tended to do considerably more homework and to engage in less use of drugs than children of inhibitive parents, no matter which of three crowds they associated with. Children of the normative parenting group (who scored average on all four of Brown and Huang's dimensions) fell between the two extremes.

■ FIGURE 13-10
Parenting style, crowd type, academic effort, and drug use. The more facilitative adolescents' parents were and the more adaptive the crowd with whom teenagers associated, the more likely teens were to do their homework (a) and the less likely they were to engage in drug use (b). (*Source:* Brown & Huang, 1995)

PEER GROUPS IN DIFFERENT CULTURES

Are peers equally important in all cultures or in all parts of one culture? Is America a uniquely peer-oriented culture? Even within cultures, patterns of peer interaction may differ; for example, comparison of urban and rural peers indicates that Israeli children reared in rural kibbutzim are more cooperative and supportive than city-reared children (Auger, Bronfenbrenner, & Henderson, 1977). (For another view of cooperativeness and sharing among peers see Box 13-3.) Therefore, it is not surprising that there are cross-cultural variations that deviate in both directions from the American pattern. In some countries, peers play an even more influential role, while in others the family and adult agents are more important. For example, in Hispanic cultures, children are more family oriented and less influenced by peers (DeRosier & Kupersmidt, 1991). In Mexico and Central America, for example, parents often maintain this family orientation by directly discouraging peer interaction (Holtzman, Diaz-Guerrero, & Schwartz, 1975).

SUMMARY

■ Children's interactions with peers are freer and more egalitarian than their interactions with their parents. They allow for more interpersonal experimentation, and children take on a new kind of interpersonal sensitivity to the feelings of others.

BOX 13-3

Perspectives on Diversity

Cross-Cultural Variations in Children's Peer Relationships

Cultures differ in the degree to which they focus on the individual or the group. In individual-oriented societies, like Canada, the United States, and many countries of Western Europe, the person's identity is largely determined by personal accomplishments. In contrast, in collective societies, like China, Japan, and Native American tribes, a greater proportion of a person's identity is related to his or her membership in the larger group (Schneider, Smith, Poisson, & Kwan, 1997; Triandis, 1990). Just as adult relationships are shaped by these cultural orientations, so are children's peer relationships.

Studying children's peer relationships in China and Canada, Orlick, Zhou, and Partington (1990) found several differences in the tendencies to be cooperative, to share, to engage in prosocial behavior; to get involved in conflict, and to be aggressive. Among 5-year-olds, 85 percent of Chinese children were cooperative with one another and more likely to help and to share than Canadian children. On the other hand, 78 percent of the "individualistic" Canadian children were involved in conflict of one kind or another.

Across these two cultures, the behavioral correlates of peer acceptance showed both similarities and differences. In both China and Canada, sociable and prosocial behaviors were positively related to social acceptance, and aggression was linked with low social acceptance (Chen & Rubin, 1994). On the other hand, among 7- to 9-year-old Canadian children, shy and sensitive characteristics were associated with peer rejection, while the same characteristics in a group of Chinese children were linked to peer acceptance (Chen, Rubin, & Sun, 1992). Interestingly, however, these perceptions appear to change across development; among 12-year-old Chinese children shyness-sensitivity was related to peer rejection (Chen & Rubin, 1994). This shift is due in part to the changes in pressure from Chinese parents for achievement and academic excellence in the 11- to 13-year-old age group as well as to the expectation that as children grow older, they must become more assertive.

In a recent study in Canada, among Chinese Canadian children, those who were competitive in academic tasks were well liked, whereas those who were competitive in physical or athletic activities were disliked (Udvari, Schneider, Labovitz, & Tassi, 1995). In contrast, non–Asian Canadian children who were competitive in athletics were well liked, and among these children academic competition was unrelated to peer acceptance. These findings highlight the value that Chinese people place on educational attainment (recall our Chapter 11 discussion of cross-national studies of achievement by Stevenson and his colleagues). Clearly, in our efforts to understand peer relationships we need to recognize the broader cultural contexts in which these relationships develop.

Children in all cultures spend time with peers, but the nature of their interactions may differ. Chinese children, for example, are less aggressive and more cooperative than U.S. children.

Early Peer Interactions

- During the second half of the first year, infants begin to recognize peers as social partners and attempt to influence one another by vocalizing, looking, touching, and waving.

- In the early toddler period, peers begin to exchange both turns and roles during social interactions; in the late toddler period, a major achievement is the ability to share meaning with a social partner. As children's competence with peers develops, they begin to form true **relationships**. They shift toward increased social play and a preference for playing with peers rather than adults, a trend that continues throughout the preschool and elementary years.
- After about age 7, children are more likely to choose same-gender rather than opposite-gender play partners; this remains the case until adolescence, when interest in the opposite gender begins.

The Role of Peers in Children's Socialization

- The peer group influences the development of the child in many of the same ways that parents do, including reinforcement and modeling. Peers reinforce one another with increasing frequency throughout the preschool years, with reinforcement commonly reciprocated by those who receive it.
- In addition to the effects of reinforcement, children acquire a wide range of knowledge and a variety of responses by observing and imitating the behavior of their peers. Imitation may serve as a way both to learn social rules and maintain social interaction.
- Peers also serve as standards against which children evaluate themselves. Research indicates that the use of **social comparison** with the peer group as a means of self-evaluation increases dramatically in the early elementary school years. The process of self-comparison is one basis of the child's self-image and self-esteem. In addition, peers provide opportunities for socializing and forming relationships as well as the development of a sense of belonging.

Play and Its Functions

- The functions of **play** are to facilitate cognitive development, advance social development, and provide a nonthreatening situation for coping with emotional problems.
- Pretend or make-believe play appears as early as 12 months, usually involving symbolic activities about routine events (e.g., cooking, shopping). By age 3, pretend play has become complex, cooperative dramatic play with partners; peaking around age 6, pretend play involves highly coordinated fantasies, multiple roles, and transformations of objects and situations. There are cultural differences in the themes children choose for their pretend play and in their communicative styles. In some cultures children emphasize familiar, everyday activities whereas others choose fantastic and danger-laden themes.
- Domestic fantasy play declines in the school years and is replaced by more structured games, but adventure fantasies continue into preadolescence. Imaginative play allows the child to experiment with multiple roles and learn to coordinate activities with other children in relatively risk-free situations. Fantasy play also may be used to master fears when children practice conquering the fear, comforting someone who is fearful, or even becoming the feared object.
- Disruptions and rigidity in the play patterns of emotionally disturbed children have been noted. Failure to develop imaginative play may indicate serious pathology, and children who are undergoing stress show less reversibility, less diversity, and more aggression in play. Imaginativeness in play is associated with self-control, less impulsivity, independence, and social maturity.

Peer Acceptance

- Peer status is typically assessed in research by using **sociometric techniques**, in which children identify peers whom they "especially like" and those whom they "don't like very much." On the basis of these nominations, children have been classified as **popular** (those who receive many positive but few negative nominations), **rejected** (those who receive many negative but few positive nominations), **neglected** (those who receive few nominations in either direction), and **average** (those who have some friends but not as many as the popular group). **Controversial** children are liked by some peers and disliked by others. Rejection occurs for a variety of reasons: **nonaggressive rejected** children tend to be withdrawn and to lack social skills; **aggressive rejected** children have low self-control and exhibit aggressive and other problem behaviors.

- Children often form first impressions based on names and appearance. Children respond adversely to unfamiliar names and to unattractive children. By age 3, children distinguish attractive from unattractive children on the same basis that adults do, and they attribute more negative characteristics to children judged to be unattractive. Some evidence indicates that unattractive children tend to behave in more aggressive ways than other children, but this may be a result of being perceived more negatively by others.

- In general, children prefer spending time with peers of the same age and the same gender. Although age preferences may be due to the age-grading of many institutions in our society, some research suggests that children would choose same-age playmates on their own. Segregation by gender is clearly self-imposed, and it seems to be related to differences in the interests and play patterns of girls and boys.

- Although children may have different goals, strategies, and behaviors when playing with peers, social skills such as reinforcing others, being able to initiate interactions effectively, and communicating well play important roles in achieving social acceptance. Popular children engage in more prosocial behavior and help set the norms for a group, while rejected children are often aggressive, aversive, and socially unskilled. Neglected children are less talkative and more withdrawn.

- Children may use a cognitive decision-making process in approaching and engaging in social interactions with their peers. In the six stages of this model, children must evaluate a social situation, assess other children's behavior, decide what their own goals in a situation are and how they may best achieve them, decide on certain actions, and act on their decisions. Children who show social competence and are not overly aggressive use this process most successfully.

- Being unpopular among peers can lead to both short-term and long-term problems. Unpopular children (especially rejected ones) feel lonely and socially dissatisfied, and they are more likely to drop out of school and develop criminal behavior patterns. Social standing tends to remain stable across time and situations, showing the most stability for rejected children. Some programs to help these children by shaping socially desirable behavior through reinforcement and coaching in social skills have proved beneficial. Although not all unpopular children need help in peer interactions, rejected children clearly can benefit from intervention.

- Parents play an important role in promoting a child's peer relations. They serve as partners with whom the child acquires social skills that help them interact with other children. They also act as coaches or educators by giving advice and support, reinforcing useful behaviors, and modeling strategies for conduct with peers. Finally, they provide opportunities for peer interaction through their choice of neighborhood and their willingness to schedule visits with friends (especially for preschoolers).

Developing Friendships

- Children develop **friendships** with only a few peers. Expectations about what a friend is change during the elementary school years from simply someone who shares activities to someone who can also be told secrets and will be understanding.

- Studies indicate that friends interact differently with each other than do unacquainted peers and that the goals of friendship appear to change with development. For young children (ages 3 to 7) the goal is coordinated play, while for older children (ages 8 to 12) the goal is establishing group norms and being accepted by peers. During this period, **self-disclosure** becomes important. By adolescence (ages 13 to 17) the focus shifts to understanding the self, making self-disclosure a critical component of friendship.

- Although children who are friends often disagree and fight, they tend to communicate more clearly, disclose themselves more, exchange more information, establish more common ground, and become able to resolve conflicts more effectively than strangers. They also share more and express more positive affect toward each other.

- As children become concerned with acceptance into peer groups and figuring out what actions will promote this and what actions will not, they may engage in **negative gossip** about other children. This may result in more bonding between those who share the gossip.

The Formation of Groups

- In addition to friendships, children form groups that possess common goals and rules of conduct. Such groups are usually hierarchically organized to identify members' relationships with one another and to facilitate interaction. **Dominance hierarchies** within groups are apparent even among preschoolers, and a "pecking order" appears to develop within a short time of first contact. The criteria for establishing dominance changes with age from physical toughness to leadership abilities and academic performance.

- Within groups of children, hierarchies serve the purposes of resolving conflict, dividing up tasks, and allocating resources. A child's position in a hierarchy will affect the degree to which other children associate with her and imitate her.

- In middle childhood, children may form **cliques**, which enhance their well-being and ability to cope with stress. Later children may be assigned by their peers to **crowds**, whose salience decreases by the end of high school.

Peer and Adult Influences on the Child and Adolescent

- Peers and parents both exert some influence on children, with peers exerting more influence during the preadolescent and adolescent periods. However, peers and parents each have their own areas of expertise. Parents are more likely to be consulted about academic and career decisions, while peers are more likely to influence entertainment, fashion, and friendship choices. In most cases, both parents and peers influence adolescents' choices. Children from homes with authoritative parents are less susceptible to negative peer pressure.

- Parents who are warm yet demanding and who grant psychological autonomy to their children and encourage them in education tend to counteract the negative influences of adolescents' association with less adaptive crowds. Teenagers whose parents are low on these characteristics may be particularly susceptible to negative peer influence.

Peer Groups in Different Cultures

- Within and between cultures, patterns of peer interaction differ. Due to different socialization practices, peers have more or less influence. In Mexico and in Central American countries, for example, family influences remain strong throughout adolescence. Latino parents often directly discourage peer interaction.

Schools, Technology, and Television

C H A P T E R 14

THE SCHOOL'S ROLE IN LEARNING AND SOCIALIZATION

Schools and the mass media join the family and the peer group in the child's social-ization. In many families in many parts of the world, television is part of children's lives from early on. Thus the effects on children of watching TV are particularly important. By the time children are 4 or 5, school begins to fill an increasingly large portion of their lives, becoming a highly significant factor in both their cognitive development and their socialization. Even outside of school hours, the school affects children's daily activities, through homework assignments, social obliga-tions, and participation in clubs and other extracurricular activities. But does school replace television in the child's life? No indeed! Together, school and tele-vision fill a large chunk of children's waking hours, and both exert a strong influ-ence over their development.

In this chapter, we focus particularly on how schooling and the media con-tribute to the child's socialization. We begin by examining the important role of the school, and consider factors that make up the school's environment—school and class size, age groupings, and classroom organization. We then look at the role of the teacher, considering such elements as teacher expectations, classroom disci-pline, and variations in teaching styles. Next, we examine teaching methodology, including the character of textbooks and the ways that computer technology has changed learning styles and peer interaction within the classroom. We then con-sider the important topic of achievement motivation, examining various factors that affect children's interest and motivation to excel in school. Next we explore some of the issues raised by social class and cultural diversity. Then we review the way schools provide instruction for children with special needs such as learning disabilities and mental retardation. And finally, we discuss the effect on children of television viewing, focusing particularly on what programs children watch and how they understand them, the positive and negative effects on children of heavy TV viewing, and ways in which parents can modify these effects.

THE SCHOOL'S ROLE IN LEARNING AND SOCIALIZATION

Children in the United States today spend more time in school—more hours each day, more days each year—than did preceding generations. Children now go to school an average of five hours a day, 180 days a year. In 1880 the average pupil attended school about 80 days each year. Not only are children attending school more often and for longer periods, but a larger proportion of the population actually goes to school than in the nineteenth century. In addition, children typically begin their school careers ear-lier, in preschool, and stay in school longer, often through graduate school.

The primary purpose of the school is to instruct and thus to influence children's cognitive development. Some early critics, however, questioned whether schools make a difference in children's developing cognitive skills independently of family and socioeconomic background (e.g., Coleman et al., 1966; Jencks et al., 1972). Recent evidence indicates that schooling does indeed influence pupil achieve-ment—even when we consider variations in children's achievement levels at the time of school entry (Epstein, 1990; Rutter, 1983). Moreover, as cross-cultural studies have demonstrated, schooling has a major influence on the way children organize their thoughts and cognitions (Farnham-Diggory, 1990; Rogoff, 1990, 1998). Schooling helps children acquire an abstract symbolic orientation to the world, an orientation that allows them to develop the capacity to think in terms of general concepts, rules, and hypothetical situations. Schools do not simply teach children knowledge; schools teach children to think about the world in different ways. These diverse impacts of schooling underline the important and unique role that the school plays in modifying children's social and cognitive development.

How does the school contribute to children's socialization? Evidence of the important socializing force that schools exert come from studies of school's effect

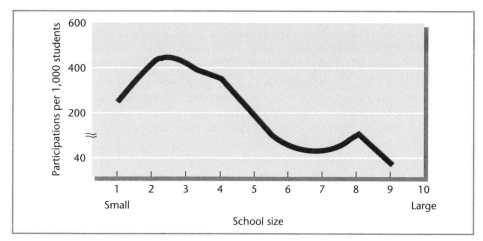

■ FIGURE 14-1
Extracurricular participation.
In a classic study, researchers
found that the smaller the school,
the more likely students were to
participate in extracurricular
activities. (*Source:* Barker &
Gump, 1964)

on children's values and aspirations. These studies show that schools, along with the family and the peer group, can influence children's moral-value orientation and political views as well as their motivation to achieve and their occupational aspirations (Epstein, 1990; Greenfield & Suzuki, 1998).

SCHOOL ENVIRONMENTS

The school environment's structural features can have important influences on children's social and cognitive development. Does the size of the school that a child attends make any difference? Do such factors as class size affect the child's scholastic achievement, her attitudes toward school, or the degree to which she actively participates in class and in extracurricular functions? Research has given us the answers to some of these questions.

School Size

From an outsider's point of view, the large school may seem to have great authority. Its exterior dimensions, its long halls and myriad rooms, and its crowds of students suggest strength and influence. The small school, on the other hand, with its modest building, short halls, few rooms, and smaller groups of students may seem less impressive. But appearances are often deceiving. How do schools of different sizes look from the standpoint of the students? Does the extent of student participation in extracurricular functions vary in small and large schools?

It is clear that much of the schools' influence in transmitting social and cultural values comes through these extracurricular functions—a reminder that much school learning takes place outside of the classroom. In a classic study of school size, Barker and Gump (1964) found that participation rates in extracurricular activities were higher in small schools than large schools (Figure 14-1). Although the largest school had 20 times as many students as the smallest school, it had only 5 times as many extracurricular activities. More important, the large and small schools in this study did not differ greatly in terms of the variety of activities they offered. The small school had low enrollment but was not necessarily limited in opportunities for activity and participation.

In the small-school setting, students felt more obligation and responsibility to play an active role in their school functions, and they felt that their peers expected them to participate more. This greater sense of identification and involvement of even marginal students in the smaller school may be partly why dropout rates tend to be lower in small schools. It is noteworthy that in one recent study, children at risk for such problems as dropping out of school, substance abuse, teenage pregnancy, suicide, and depression were also less likely to be involved in school and extracurricular activities (Dusek, 1991).

Although it is difficult to change school size, educators have argued for greater flexibility in the organization of schools (Farnham-Diggory, 1990; Sizer, 1984). Some recommend an organizational structure in which smaller units designed to achieve a closer match with the needs of students would function simultaneously within the large unit. These "schools within schools result in the creation of additional behavior settings or niches in which students can develop a sense of identity and belonging that may prevent them from dropping out of school and [that may] enhance the likelihood of positive academic and socioemotional outcomes" (Linney & Seidman, 1989, p. 338).

Age Groupings: What About Junior High?

In addition to school size, the way the different grades, from kindergarten through grade 12, are organized can have important effects on children's well-being and school performance (Eccles, Lord, & Roeser, 1996). Traditionally, the first 8 years of elementary school (or, including kindergarten) and the four years of high school have been arranged in two separate segments, but other organizational schemes have emerged in recent years. In the alternative that's most often seen today, the first 6 years of elementary school are grouped together, followed by three years of junior high or "middle" school (grades 7–9), followed by three years of high school (grades 10–12). Recent research suggests that such organizational variations make a difference. Simmons, Blyth, and McKinney (1984) compared students moving from the sixth to the seventh grade, either in a regular eight-year elementary school or in a junior high school, where this transition involved moving to a new school. For preadolescents who may be undergoing other transitions as well, the added burden of shifting to a new school often has a negative impact. In comparison to the seventh graders who stayed in elementary school, the junior high schoolers had lower self-concepts, were less involved in activities and clubs, and perceived themselves as less integrated into their school and peer groups (Eccles et al., 1996).

For preadolescents and adolescents, the onset of puberty, the start of dating, a change in residence, or some disruption in family life may make the burden of shifting to a new school especially heavy. In a later study, Simmons, Burgeson, Carlson-Ford, and Blyth (1987) found that children, especially girls, who were undergoing three or more transitions had lower self-esteem and that they participated less in extracurricular activities and had lower grade-point averages as well. The implications seem clear:

> If change comes too suddenly, or if change is too early given children's cognitive and emotional states, or if it occurs in too many areas of life at once, . . . individuals may experience considerable discomfort. . . . [Children] do better both in terms of self-esteem and behavioral coping if there is some "arena of comfort" in their lives. (Simmons et al., 1987, p. 1231)

On the other hand, it is also clear that no single age grouping system will be ideal for all children. Think back for example, to the individual differences among adolescents in the timing of puberty and in their reactions to this transition, which we discussed in Chapter 6.

Class Size

The debate as to whether there is an optimal class size for maximal academic achievement has continued for more than half a century. Although classes that range in size from 20 to 40 children may show few differences in achievement, below that range investigators have found that having fewer pupils in a class has a positive effect. In a word, smaller does seem to be better.

In one early study, Dawe (1934) found that in kindergarten classes ranging in size from 15 to 46 children, total amount of class discussion increased as class size decreased, and more children participated in the discussions. And evidence suggesting that the educational experience is different in small and large classes continues to accumulate. Small classes seem to promote individualization, more group activity, and more positive student attitudes, and to discourage misbehavior. They may be particularly advantageous in the learning of reading and mathematics in the early grades and may also facilitate the academic progress of handicapped or disadvantaged pupils (Rutter, 1983). Not surprisingly, teachers are more satisfied in smaller classes (Minuchin & Shapiro, 1983).

In a major study of class size, children were assigned to small-size classes (15–20 students) or to regular-size classes (22–25 pupils) from kindergarten through the third grade (Finn & Achilles, 1990; Achilles, Nye, Zaharias, & Fulton, 1993). Children in the smaller classes did better in math and reading not only while the experiment continued but after it had ended, in the 4th and 5th grades. Although teachers' aides are often helpful in the classroom, in this study their presence did not compensate for the advantage of having a smaller class.

Classroom Organization

The teacher can organize the classroom in many ways. For example, she can arrange to have students participate in decision making, she can organize the class into small groups, she can arrange for students to help one another, or she can organize classroom activities in the traditional manner. In this section we focus on the consequences of different types of classroom organization.

Originally developed in Great Britain, the concept of the **open classroom** was based on the assumption that children learn best by getting involved and participating actively in their own learning rather than passively receiving knowledge from the teacher. In the typical open classroom, groups of children are usually engaged in different activities. Two children might be stretched out on a rug reading books chosen from the classroom library. The teacher might be at the math table, showing a small group of children how to use a set of scales to learn about relative weights. And other children might be working either alone or in small groups at desks or tables.

Do children benefit from the open-classroom arrangement? Socially there are clear benefits: "[Elementary school] children in open environments have more varied social contacts, positive attitudes toward school and show both self-reliant and cooperative behavior in learning situations. Students in less . . . [strictly] organized high schools participate more in school activities, have more varied social relationships and create fewer disciplinary problems than students in traditionally organized schools" (Minuchin & Shapiro, 1983, p. 67). The academic benefits are less clear. Some investigators find no differences in the achievement test scores of children in open and conventional classrooms, whereas others report that children learn more math and read better in structured classes (Minuchin & Shapiro, 1983).

The open classroom is a mixed success. The arrangement seems to help most children socially; however, the bottom line seems to be that some children do best in a **traditional classroom,** in which all students sit facing the teacher, who normally presents one subject at a time to the entire group, and others fare better in alternative kinds of classroom organization (see Box 14-1). In the final analysis, the effect of classroom organization on schoolchildren is determined to a great extent by those who manage the classroom and the school day, and with rare exception these are the children's teachers. Let's look now at the teacher's impact on children's social and academic progress.

TEACHERS: THEIR IMPACT ON CHILDREN'S DEVELOPMENT

Teachers are by far the most important influences on schoolchildren. In this section we examine what teachers do and how they influence their pupils' academic progress and social and emotional adjustment. Teachers play several roles in the

open classroom A relatively unstructured classroom organization, in which different areas of the room are devoted to particular activities and children work simultaneously, either alone or in small groups, at these activities under the teacher's supervision.

traditional classroom A structured classroom arrangement, in which the teacher presents one subject at a time to the entire student body, who sit in rows, facing the teacher.

BOX 14-1

Perspectives on Diversity

Suiting Classroom Organization to Cultural Values and Practices

Some cultures stress individual learning, whereas other cultures encourage cooperative and collaborative approaches to learning. Awareness of students' cultural backgrounds is critical in designing classroom organization, because students learn best when the social structure matches their cultural orientations and values.

The typical North American classroom still uses primarily whole-class organization, with rank and file seating and a teacher-leader who instructs and demonstrates to the entire group at once. The teacher follows this presentation with some form of individual practice for each child and teacher-organized assessment of each child (Tharp, 1989).

But does this social structure work well for students from all cultures? For students from European American cultures, which stress individual learning, the system may work well. For others, however, such as children from the Hawaiian culture, which values cooperative approaches to learning, it works less well. In a traditional European American classroom structure, Hawaiian American children

are likely to pay rather minimal attention to teachers and classwork and instead to seek a lot of attention from peers (Tharp, 1989). Although many teachers might regard this problem as a lack of motivation and interest on the part of the students, it is much more likely the result of the imposition of an alien social organization.

As we discussed in Chapter 9, an innovative project in Hawaii, called the Kamehameha Early Education Program (KEEP) has developed a culturally compatible program for kindergarten through third grade for children of Hawaiian ancestry. Taking into account the emphasis the traditional Hawaiian culture places on collaboration, cooperation, and assisted performance, as well as on sibling caretaking, the KEEP program designed an alternative social organization for the classroom. Hawaiian children do much better academically in this small-group classroom organization in which the children work in independent groups of four to five students and the teacher moves from group to group to offer intensive instruction. Adjusting classroom organization to make it more suitable to the cultural backgrounds of the students has led to the children learning more! Classroom social organization needs to match the cultural experiences of the pupils.

classroom—instructor, social model, evaluator, and disciplinarian, to name just a few. How the teacher manages each role can affect the pupils in a variety of ways.

Teacher Expectations and Academic Success

Although many teachers would probably deny it, early in the school year most teachers form impressions about the probable performance of their new students. These expectations come from a variety of sources, such as the pupil's past academic record and classroom conduct, achievement test scores, family background, and appearance. Do these prejudgments of the child's performance affect the child's actual scholastic success or failure? In a classic experiment, Rosenthal and Jacobsen (1968) planted certain expectations about specific children in the minds of some elementary school teachers. They told these teachers that 20 percent of their students—the experimenters chose these students randomly—were "intellectual bloomers who would show unusual intellectual gains during the academic year" (Rosenthal & Jacobsen, 1968, p. 66). Before the experiment actually began, the researchers gave all the children an IQ test. They repeated this test after the children had had eight months' experience in the classrooms of the teachers in whose expectations they had manipulated.

Can you guess the result of this manipulation? The children the teachers had been led to expect would make great intellectual strides showed a significantly greater increase in IQ scores than the other students in the school. Moreover, the "intellectual bloomers" did better than their classmates in reading, and their teachers rated them as higher in "intellectual curiosity" than the control children. Because these gains were most marked in younger children—indeed, the lower the grade level, the greater the effect—the experimenters concluded that it may be easier to modify teacher expectations in the lower grades.

Rosenthal's results, dubbed the **Pygmalion effect,** were an impressive demonstration of the self-fulfilling prophecy. (In Greek mythology, after Pygmalion

Pygmalion effect The tendency of a teacher's expectation about a child's academic performance to become a self-fulfilling prophecy.

endowed the statue of a woman that he sculpted with characteristics he considered ideal the statue came to life.) Believing that certain students were exceptionally bright, the teachers *saw* these students as brighter than others and *treated* them differently. They gave them more chances to participate in class and more time to answer questions; they praised them more often for correct answers and criticized them less frequently for wrong ones. By giving these children special treatment, the teachers reinforced and sustained the patterns they expected (Brophy, 1986). And with so much attention, reinforcement, and feedback, how could these children not do well? On the other hand, the teachers provided the other children, whom they expected to do less well, with less opportunity and encouragement for good performance (Minuchin & Shapiro, 1983).

Researchers have criticized Rosenthal's work for methodological flaws (e.g., Snow, 1995), and many who have tried to repeat his results have failed. Parenthetically, we may also question the ethics of this study—see Chapter 2. Other investigators, however, have corroborated the central findings. Studies of Head Start children, mentally retarded children, and institutionalized adolescent female offenders as well as of children in regular classrooms have found the same self-fulfilling prophecy at work (e.g., Goldenberg, 1996a; Jussim & Eccles, 1992; Raudenbusch, 1984; Rosenthal, 1994). In the light of these findings, what role do you think teacher expectations might play in determining how low-achieving, minority students will perform in the classroom?

Classroom Discipline and Operant Reinforcement

Teachers spend much of their time as disciplinarians. How effective are different teacher-control techniques in achieving and maintaining classroom order, and what effect do teacher tactics have on children's motivation? How important are classmates in achieving classroom control? Can the teacher harness the power of the peer group to achieve more effective discipline?

Attempts to apply operant reinforcement principles to classroom control have been very successful (Kazdin, 1982). Teachers have learned to use social reinforcement in the form of verbal approval, systematically praising appropriate behavior and ignoring disruptive behavior. Another technique that has proved effective is to combine social reinforcements with material rewards. More than 1,300 years ago clergy offered children a baked treat for learning their prayers (O'Leary & O'Leary, 1977). Called a *pretiola* (Latin for "little reward"), this treat was made of bread dough formed into a twisted loop to represent the folded arms of children in prayer.

By now, numerous studies have demonstrated the effectiveness of this approach for controlling children in classrooms (Kazdin, 1982). Today, children accumulate points or tokens for good behavior, which they can then exchange for material rewards such as candy or toys. In addition, children may pool their rewards for special treats such as parties or trips to museums or the zoo. Such group rewards can exert considerable pressure on rebellious students to improve their behavior. Not many classroom cutups are eager to deprive their peers of a Halloween party!

But token rewards may not always be necessary, and under some circumstances they may undermine children's interest in their school activities. Activities that are intrinsically interesting may lose their appeal if children are rewarded for engaging in them. Studies by Lepper and his colleagues (Lepper, Greene, & Nisbett, 1973; Lepper & Hoddell, 1988) found that rewarding children for completing tasks that were unappealing, however, like learning multiplication tables, did increase the children's interest in these tasks. Rewards can also undermine artistic creativity. Amabile and Hennessey (1988) found that children were more creative when they did not anticipate any prize and less creative when they did expect a reward. On the other hand, if children think that they are being rewarded for performing especially well on a task, they will not necessarily lose interest in it (Boggiano & Ruble, 1979).

Receiving a reward contingent on superior performance tells a person that she is doing well at an activity, and this information is likely to enhance her interest.

Token programs have a place in the classroom, but teachers need to exercise care in choosing the target activities and in applying the reward system. Using rewards in a consistent, immediate, and clear manner increases their effectiveness, but teachers who have as many as 30 or 40 children in a class often find it difficult to manage reward programs in such an ideal manner. In the next section we look at some issues that focus on academic learning itself.

TEACHING METHODS AND TECHNIQUES

Teaching methods in elementary school classrooms have changed over the years, moving from the traditional to the open classroom, increasingly making use of cooperative and other innovative learning arrangements, putting more emphasis on the use of quality literature in the teaching of reading, and incorporating computer technology into the learning situation. At the same time, many innovations have been controversial, and the best instructional approaches are still under debate.

Cooperative Learning

cooperative learning   A teaching technique in which small groups of students work together to master material to be learned.

Cooperative learning involves small groups of students who work together to master learning material. Often the group is heterogeneous, with children of different gender, abilities, and ethnic backgrounds working together on common problems. No one is obviously more knowledgeable at the outset or singled out to lead the group. "The goal is to maximize the learning of all students and to increase the mutuality of their relationships with children different from themselves" (Minuchin & Shapiro, 1983, p. 114).

Most studies of cooperative learning environments have found that this teaching technique has a positive impact on children's self-esteem, their feelings about their peers and their mutual concern for one another, their tendency to help and cooperate with each other, and their general attitudes toward school and learning (Minuchin & Shapiro, 1983). Slavin and his colleagues (Slavin, 1995, 1996) have also reported that students in cooperative classrooms achieve greater improvement in their math skills, have higher self-esteem, and enjoy school more than children in control classroom arrangements.

peer collaboration   A kind of *cooperative learning*, in which two students work together to master a task that neither has mastered before.

Another form of cooperative learning is **peer collaboration** in which two students work together to solve a task that neither could master before. Damon and Phelps (1989) found that even when teachers provided no instruction to such pairs of students, the children in these programs made substantially greater progress in solving math problems than control children.

Peers as Teachers

peer tutoring   A method of instruction in which an older, more experienced student tutors a younger, less experienced child.

Teachers can sometimes help both older and younger children to learn simultaneously through the method of **peer tutoring,** a technique often combined with other approaches, including cooperative learning (Slavin, 1996). Although the older children usually gain more from this arrangement, in which an older, more experienced student tutors a younger, less experienced child, both tutor and pupil can benefit in a variety of ways (Dansereau, 1987). Older children learn more for several reasons: They gain in self-esteem and in status, they are forced to clarify—both for themselves and for their pupils—some of the principles that they teach, and they derive satisfaction from helping others.

An example of combining peer tutoring with cooperative learning is the *jigsaw method* developed by Aronson and his colleagues (Aronson, Stephan, Sikes, Blaney, & Snapp, 1978). Using this technique, the teacher divides the class into small groups and the material to be learned into segments and assigns each segment to one member of each small group. Each child who is responsible for a particular

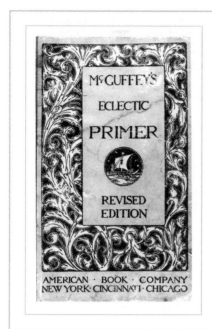

■ FIGURE 14-2
How children learned to read in 1896.
In this "primer," designed for use in the first year of school, the publishers endeavored to help the teacher "pursue the Phonic Method, the Word Method, the Alphabet Method, or any combination" thereof. In Lesson I (not shown), the student learned the words *a*, *and*, *cat*, and *rat*. Lesson II continues to emphasize words with the short sound of /a/ but offers them this time in complete sentences—and in action! (*Source:* McGuffey's Eclectic Primer, 1896)

segment works with the members of the other groups who are responsible for the same segment. Pupils then teach the other members of their original group the material they have mastered. Students are interdependent for their learning, but each student is responsible for all parts of the "jigsaw" and is tested individually. The teams neither compete with other teams nor produce a group product. This technique promotes greater achievement in children than individualistic and competitive learning modes do, and it improves ethnic relations and reduces racial conflict (Aronson et al., 1978; Renninger, 1998).

Assuming the role of assistant teacher and guiding younger children is a big responsibility for older students. Schools generally provide such peer helpers with instruction sessions in which they learn techniques of relating to and teaching younger children. In addition, these student assistants often meet periodically with the teachers of the children they're helping so as to coordinate their work with the younger child's regular classroom experience. Many students including low achievers of all ethnic and racial backgrounds and children with psychological disturbances, can benefit from these peer tutoring experiences (Allen & Feldman, 1976; Cochran, Feng, & Gwendolyn, 1993).

Textbooks and Basic Skills

The first American textbooks, the nineteenth-century *McGuffey's Primers*, took a basicallly alphabetic-phonetic approach to reading and offered a limited vocabulary, at least for the earliest grades (Figure 14-2). The language of these beginning readers was choppy and uninteresting, and content was often aimed at teaching religious, moral, and patriotic precepts (Heilman, Blair, & Rupley, 1994). The "Dick and Jane" series readers that appeared in the mid-1900s, named familiarly for their two principal child characters, put somewhat less emphasis on phonics and more on narrative writing but, like their predecessors, offered a controlled vocabulary. Both series' readers offered lessons and stories that dealt with white, middle-class families living in suburban areas. Needless to say, in both these classic reader series, gender stereotypes were rampant.

In recent years textbook publishers have tried to correct social class and gender biases in their books, but the African American or Native American child is still far less likely than the European American child to see herself in the material presented. Boys are still portrayed as more achieving than girls and girls as more in need of help than boys (Purcell & Stewart, 1990; Turner-Bowker, 1996). Today, the widely used *basal reader*—an organized set of reading materials sequenced by skill level—puts even more emphasis on narrative writing. Basal readers also add a host of aids for both teacher and student, such as suggested lesson plans, classroom and homework projects, and multiple-choice, fill-in-the-blank, and "critical thinking" questions. However, these texts still lag in providing children with narratives and stories that represent the best in children's literature and that reflect a variety of cultural backgrounds and heritages.

Children attending school for the first time vary enormously in their prior experience with books and reading. For those who have had little encouragement to read and thus do not yet appreciate the rewards of reading, it is particularly important that textbooks present content that is interesting to them and written in a lively and appealing way. For example, multicultural studies have suggested that Navajo and Hawaiian children show higher levels of interest and participation when textual material is related to their own personal experiences (Greenfield & Suzuki, 1998; Tharp, 1989). In general, children seem to understand more of high-interest reading material than of low-interest material; for example, when fifth-grade boys read stories about airplanes and astronauts, they read much better than when they read less interesting stories (Asher, 1980; Asher & Markell, 1974).

Growing in large part out of the concern to improve children's motivation to read, the *whole-language* approach has stressed the use of quality children's literature in teaching children to read and, often, has de-emphasized the learning of phonics (essentially a word-identification strategy that uses letter-sound relationships to arrive at the pronunciations of unknown words). A large body of literature has grown up in the latter half of this century that, added to some of the older children's classics, provides a rich source of reading material for children from preschool on up. The rise of the whole-language school of thought, however, has engendered one of the hottest debates in education in recent years (Adams, Trieman, & Pressley, 1998; Smith, 1992; Stanovich, 1994). Educators who believe that children must learn not only the alphabet but the system of phonics in order to be able to read and write have vociferously opposed the proponents of whole language on the grounds that children will not be able to benefit from good literature if they can't read the words.

In fact, most whole-language proponents agree that children need phonics instruction, but they do not yet agree on just how this instruction should be interwoven with the reading of literature. For this and other reasons, the whole-language approach places a considerable burden on the teacher. Partly because it is so new but partly because by definition the approach calls for original books and other reading materials, whole language has not generated any standardized teaching materials. Without such materials or instruction in this new approach, the California school system's substitution of whole language for phonics in the 1990s presented teachers with great difficulties. In view of the evidence that phonemic awareness and phonological processing abilities are related to reading abilities, it was not surprising that, without an emphasis on phonics, students' reading scores suffered (Adams et al., 1998; Hansen & Bowey, 1994).

New trends, such as a *literature-based* approach, are emphasizing both the basics of phonics and reading literature and are trying to avoid teaching phonics in a rote fashion, which is often of limited success (Hatcher, Hulme, & Ellis, 1994). Instead, to motivate students, schools are placing a new emphasis on collaborative group work in which the teacher is a facilitator who establishes an agenda for discussion: "Typically a problem is posed, students work in small groups to address it, and then the class reconvenes in order to sort through their understanding of what they still need to know" (Renninger, 1998, p. 247).

The literature-based or whole-language classroom is typically an open one, and cross-disciplinary exercises are also common. For example, students may read (or have read to them) a story and then write their account of some related event in their own experience. Or they may read a story about science and then perform a simple experiment and, using number or arithmetic skills, graph its results (Brown & Campione, 1994). In these classrooms, teachers often do not prepare traditional report cards but instead collect children's work in *portfolios,* which they then, on a regular basis, evaluate and discuss both with the child and with his parents (Meisels, 1996).

The children in the foreground are using a school computer to learn about some interesting phenomena in space. "Gaseous pillars" are said to be columns of gas and dust that are incubators for new stars.

This approach to teaching is not only demanding of teachers but requires a lot of reading materials and other supplies and relies on interested and cooperative parents. In less than affluent neighborhoods where school populations are likely to be heavily lower class, school funding does not always support the teacher time and effort, teacher's aides, books and materials, and classroom equipment that can make this kind of program effective. Moreover, blue-collar, dual-earner families may be less able to participate in parent-oriented programs than more affluent families in other areas. Educators continue to face difficult questions and difficult choices.

Computer Technology

Although technological advances are not likely to replace teachers, computers, software, and access to the Internet have become important aids to children's learning (Greenfield & Suzuki, 1998; Schofield, 1997). Computer technology has also contributed to the use of such alternative teaching techniques as cooperative learning. For example, where schools haven't enough computers for students to work individually, teachers may have students work together in small groups to carry out a project, such as graphing the outcomes of a recent presidential election or the results of a science experiment.

The computer can be used in the classroom in three primary ways: as a personal tutor, as a medium for experiential learning, and as a multipurpose tool (Lepper & Gurtner, 1989; Lepper, Woolverton, Mumme, & Gurtner, 1993). When a child uses the *computer as a personal tutor* his learning can be individualized and tailored to his particular needs and capabilities. For example, in **computer-assisted instruction,** software programs designed to facilitate children's learning typically pose questions or problems, give the student a chance to respond, and then tell him if he is correct. Thus students can proceed at their own pace and receive immediate and personal feedback as well as help if they need it. This kind of instruction can be a useful supplement to traditional teaching and can free a teacher for other activities. Researchers have found that children who use a computer for such drill and practice do better in a variety of subjects than children who do not use the computer (Niemiec & Walberg, 1987; Schofield, 1997). One advantage of computer-assisted instruction is that it lowers both the real and the psychological costs of error. "Many negative patterns of behavior in school grow out of fear of error and fear of failure" (Greenfield, 1984, pp. 131–132).

computer-assisted instruction A form of instruction embodied in computer software programs that typically pose questions or problems, give the student a chance to respond, and then tell her if she is correct.

The computer serves as a *medium for experiential learning* when it enables children to do such things as experiment with physical laws like gravity and observe the results or perform experiments that would be too complex or dangerous to try in the real world. Through software that simulates scientific laboratories or other real-world situations, children can engage in more open-ended, exploratory learning than might be possible in their particular school environments (Lepper & Gurtner,

1989). For example, the effects of weightlessness on objects in space is often difficult to grasp. A trip in a spaceship would probably enable students to acquire this kind of understanding, but such a trip is unlikely to be a common classroom exercise any time soon! With the aid of a computer, children can see the effects of weightlessness on different objects right on their monitors. Transfer to noncomputer tasks is sometimes limited (Salomon & Perkins, 1987), although more recent studies appear to be more successful in achieving successful generalization to regular classroom environments (Schofield, 1997; Strommen, 1994).

As a *multipurpose tool* in the classroom the computer can help children expand their learning in many ways. For example, children learn to write better with the help of a good word processor. Revision, a key element in the writing process, requires care and patience, and word processing programs not only make revision easier but provide the writer with instant feedback as to whether her revision has improved her work (Collins, Brown, & Newman, 1990; Schofield, 1997). Kleiman and Humphrey (1982) found that learning-disabled children between the ages of 7 and 16, many of whom had refused to do any kind of writing, began writing more, editing more, and producing better compositions when permitted to use a word processor.

Software programs for graphic design can foster creativity, enabling children to create pictures and to produce animations and special visual effects. Other programs can help children record and graph findings in various subject-matter fields. And music composition programs make it possible to explore musical structure and theory even for those who do not know how to play an instrument (Kleiman, 1984; Schofield, 1995).

The value of computers as learning aids is clearly very great, and computers are being used for homework, especially on topics that require information searches. For many students CD-ROMs and the Internet supplement the encyclopedia and the local public library as sources of new information, both at home and in the classroom (Schofield, 1995). Although some educators have warned that computer use will lead to social isolation, research suggests that the opposite is true. In one study, observers watched children as they worked with computers and engaged in more traditional classroom activities, at both times free to interact with one another. Researchers found that the children talked more and interacted more—verbally and physically—when they worked with computers than when they engaged in noncomputer activities (Hawkins, Sheingold, Gearhart, & Berger, 1982; see also Schofield, 1995). Apparently computers promote rather than reduce social interaction—at least in the school setting. A problem for many schools, especially in poor districts, is that too few computers are available to allow children to use them to full advantage.

ACHIEVEMENT MOTIVATION

Children's academic performance is affected not only by their school environments, teachers, and the instructional methods and techniques that teachers use but by their own **achievement motivation,** that is, their tendency to strive for successful performance, to evaluate their performance against specific standards of excellence, and to experience pleasure as a result of having performed successfully (Eccles et al., 1998). Variations in achievement motivation and performance are often related to a child's emotions and opinions of himself as a person and a learner—in short, to self-esteem.

How Emotions, Beliefs, and Self-Esteem Affect Achievement Motivation

Some children have negative feelings about specific learning tasks and may be convinced of their inability to learn in certain areas. For example, mathematics is a par-

achievement motivation
A person's tendency to strive for successful performance, to evaluate her performance against standards of excellence, and to feel pleasure at having performed successfully.

ticularly troublesome area for some people. Sometimes a child's feelings and beliefs about his ability to succeed are sufficiently negative that they distract the learner from the task itself and may prevent him from learning (Brown et al., 1983).

Researchers have identified two contrasting response patterns that are particularly likely to appear when children are working on a task that is challenging and thus holds the possibility of failure (Burhans & Dweck, 1995; Dweck & Leggett, 1988; Nicholls, 1984). In an early study, fifth- and sixth-grade children attempted to solve a series of difficult hypothesis-testing problems that somewhat resembled a complex game of Twenty Questions (Diener & Dweck, 1978). At first the children were able to solve the problems, but then the experimenter presented several problems that they failed. Some children, whom the researchers called *mastery-oriented*, maintained or even improved their level of performance despite failure on some problems. In contrast, other children, whom the researchers labeled *helpless*, tended to give up easily or to show marked performance deterioration when working on challenging problems. Once these children failed a difficult task they often began to use inefficient strategies of the sort more often seen in kindergartners.

Mastery-oriented children expressed neutral or even positive emotions at failure; one boy, working on a problem and failing to solve it, leaned forward, smacked his lips, and said, "You know, I was hoping this would be informative." In addition, when mastery-oriented children performed poorly they attributed their failure to insufficient effort rather than to lack of ability, and they maintained high expectations for future success. Helpless children, on the other hand, expressed negative emotions like frustration, blamed their own lack of ability for their performance, and expressed low expectations for future performance.

What might cause different children to react so differently to the same task? Helpless and mastery-oriented children do not differ in their actual levels of ability levels; rather, they *think* differently about ability and achievement (Dweck, 1991; Dweck & Leggett, 1988). Mastery-oriented children tend to have *learning goals*. In other words, they are more concerned with improving their skills and learning new things than they are with specific judgments of their ability. Children who show the helpless pattern, on the other hand, tend to have *performance goals*—that is, they are concerned with "looking smart," obtaining positive judgments, and avoiding negative judgments of their ability. Dweck and her colleagues have proposed that these different goals are associated with different beliefs about the nature of ability itself. That is, mastery-oriented children tend to hold an *incremental* theory of intelligence, viewing intelligence as a malleable body of skills and knowledge that can be increased with effort. In contrast, helpless children tend to hold an *entity* theory of intelligence, believing, if implicitly, that intelligence is a fixed and unchangeable entity that people possess in varying degrees.

Dweck suggests that the two theories of intelligence and the two goals orient children to react very differently to achievement tasks. As Table 14-1 illustrates, when children are successful at tasks, they do not appear to differ in their behavior; even children with an entity theory and performance goals are likely to show the mastery-oriented pattern. It may be that in this situation children believe that their good performance indicates high ability. However, when children fail at a task, their different theories of intelligence and types of goals find expression in either mastery-oriented or helpless behavior. Under these circumstances, mastery-oriented children may interpret their failure as an indication that they must work harder to learn more, whereas helpless children may see failure as evidence of their lack of ability and give up. According to Dweck and Bempechat (1983), if we ask children who hold entity and incremental theories, "Sometimes kids feel smart in school, sometimes not. When do you feel smart?" we may get responses like the following:

TABLE 14-1   Theories of Intelligence, Goal Orientations, and Behavior Patterns

Theory of Intelligence	Goal Orientation	Present Performance Level	Behavior Pattern
Entity (intelligence is fixed)	**Performance** (to gain positive, avoid negative judgments of competence)	High	**Mastery oriented** (seeking challenge, persistence)
		Low	**Helpless** (avoiding challenge, low persistence)
Incremental (intelligence is malleable)	**Learning** (to increase competence)	High	**Mastery oriented** (seeking challenge that fosters learning, persistence)
		Low	**Mastery oriented** (seeking challenge that fosters learning, persistence)

Source: Dweck & Leggett, 1988.

Children Holding Incremental Theory	*Children Holding Entity Theory*
When I don't know how to do it, and it's pretty hard, and I figure it out without anybody telling me.	When I don't do mistakes.
When I'm doing school work because I want to learn how to get smart.	When I turn in my papers first.
When I'm reading a hard book.	When I get easy work.

Of course, different situations can elicit different responses, and mastery-oriented children may occasionally show helpless responses when examiners or others put a lot of stress on performance goals (Dweck, 1991).

Moreover, although an incremental theory is usually more advantageous than an entity theory, sometimes this may not be the case. Many teachers may foster a classroom "entity" environment where the emphasis is on success and evaluation and little other encouragement is given for engaging in learning activities. In such a setting, children may learn lessons to please the teacher, not for their own value or interest. However, as the academic and professional environment changes to encourage independent choice, perseverance, and long-term outcomes, the incremental theorist will have an advantage. For example, many children with entity theories begin to receive lower grades when they start junior high school, perhaps because the new school and the more challenging course materials make them feel doubtful about their abilities (Henderson & Dweck, 1990). In addition, research on high school students (Boyum, Dweck, & Hill, 1990) suggests that children with entity theories may be less likely to seek out challenging courses when they are allowed to select their own classes.

In this connection, recall our Chapter 11 discussion of the intellectual performance of Asian, Asian American, and other cultural groups. Chen and colleagues (Chen & Stevenson, 1995) found some differences in the ways these students from varied ethnic backgrounds thought about learning and academic achievement. For example, these researchers found that European American students tended to endorse "having a good teacher" as the most important factor in their performance in mathematics, whereas the Asian American students thought that "studying hard" was the most important factor (Figure 14-3). Relying on someone else to provide instruction could reflect a somewhat entity theory of intelligence; working hard oneself to learn material would seem to reflect a more incremental theory. Of

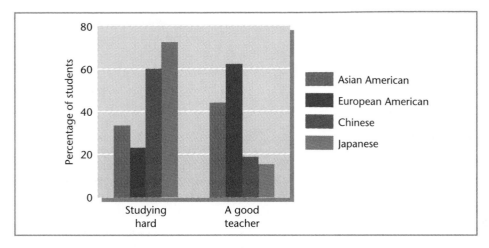

■ FIGURE 14-3
To study hard, or to be taught well—is there a question?
When researchers asked Chinese and Japanese high school students in their own countries and Asian and European American students in the United States to choose among several factors that may influence students' academic performance, the majority chose either "studying hard" or "having a good teacher." Within these choices, the Japanese and Chinese students were far more likely to choose the first of these factors, whereas U.S. high school students were much more likely to choose the second. (*Source:* Chen & Stevenson, 1995)

course, this is only one study, and it's also important to remember that this research focuses on cultural, or group, differences. Within each culture individual children differ greatly in motivational orientation.

How early do children's achievement motivation patterns develop? One set of answers to this question looks at developmental changes within the child. Many researchers in this field have argued that children younger than 9 or 10 do not fully understand the concept of ability, do not view achievement tasks in the same ways as older children, and therefore cannot show the helpless pattern of deteriorating performance and self-blame when failing at a task (e.g., Nicholls & Miller, 1983; Stipek 1993, 1996). However, recent research suggests that this picture of development is not entirely accurate. Several studies have found that some 4-, 5-, and 6-year-old children show a response pattern that closely resembles the helpless pattern found in older children (Burhans & Dweck, 1995; Cain, 1991; Heyman, Dweck, & Cain, 1992). For example, Patricia Smiley (1989) asked 4- and 5-year-old preschoolers to complete four wooden puzzles, three of which could not be solved by the children. Afterward, children were asked which puzzle they would like to do again. Children who chose to repeat the easy puzzle rather than try to solve one of the difficult puzzles were classified as nonpersisters (42% of the sample). In comparison to other children, the nonpersisters expressed more negative emotion and self-doubts about their abilities during the puzzle task, were less likely to believe their performance would improve if they had another chance, and had lower expectations for success on an entirely different task (building with blocks).

Can Social Class Affect Motivation to Achieve?

Examining the ways in which middle- and lower-class African American mothers introduced their children to school, Hess and Shipman (1967) found that lower-class mothers tended to give their children simple commands about how to behave, such as "don't holler," and "mind the teacher." In contrast, the middle-class mothers tended to offer their children explanations, such as, "You shouldn't talk in school because the teacher can't teach so well and you won't learn your lessons properly." According to these researchers, these different approaches may lead lower-class children to view the school as a rigid, authoritarian institution governed by inflexible and unexplained rules. They may also be more likely to accept absolute answers and to refrain from asking questions and becoming interested and involved. In contrast, these authors suggest, middle-class children will be more likely to expect and to inquire for the reasons that underlie teachers' answers, thus pleasing the teachers and promoting the children's progress in school.

Although Hess and Shipman did find a clear relationship between mothers' orientations and children's academic performance—lower-class mothers' typical

Having Mom's help with homework not only can be enjoyable for a child but may significantly improve her academic performance.

approach was associated with children's poorer performance—it is unlikely that these kinds of school performance are always closely linked with social class. There can be other reasons for children to play either an active or a passive role in school and for teachers' differential responses to them. Differences in the cultural and social-class backgrounds of teachers and students sometimes lead to mutual misunderstanding (Greenfield & Suzuki, 1998; Steinberg, 1996). Minority parents are often less knowledgeable about schools and how they work, and they are less likely to participate in school-related activities such as parent-teacher associations. Evidence indicates that when minority parents do get involved in school activities, their children do better academically (Connell, Spencer, & Aber, 1994; Steinberg, 1996).

These findings do not imply that lower-class or minority-group parents place little importance on their children's education and intellectual development. Indeed, in a recent study of African, Hispanic, and European American mothers and their first-, third-, and fifth-grade children, African American and Hispanic American mothers placed a higher value on their children's education and saw homework as more important for improving children's education than European American mothers (Steinberg et al., 1992). A study of nearly 8,000 San Francisco Bay area adolescents and 3,000 parents (Ritter, Mont-Reynaud, & Dornbush, 1990) reported similar findings: African American parents evidenced clear concern about and involvement in their children's education. Hispanic parents surveyed were also concerned about their children's education, although, perhaps because of language barriers, they were less directly involved.

Academic Context and Achievement

Changes in the contexts in which children perform intellectual tasks are important in achievement. As children grow older, schools increasingly emphasize competition and provide less praise and individual support. These contextual changes may make it increasingly likely that some children will worry about their abilities and show motivational difficulties (Eccles & Midgley, 1989).

Recent research has examined the changes that occur in children's environments when they enter junior high school (Eccles & Midgley, 1989; Eccles, Lord, & Midgley, 1991; Henderson & Dweck, 1990). On entering junior high, children frequently experience declines in self-confidence, motivation, school interest, and grades. At the same time, children become more likely to worry about performance rather than about learning (moving away from a mastery and toward a helpless orientation). They tend also to show test anxiety and to be more likely to stay away from school (truancy). Eccles and colleagues believe that there is a developmental mismatch between the characteristics of junior high schools and young adolescents' needs (Eccles et al., 1991; 1996, 1998). These researchers conducted a two-year longitudinal study of 1,350 students making the transition from elementary school (sixth grade) to junior high school (seventh grade). The children's teachers completed questionnaires, and the researchers supplemented these survey results with systematic classroom observations. The study revealed that seventh-grade junior high school teachers are more likely than sixth-grade teachers to emphasize classroom control and discipline, and to see children as untrustworthy. Teachers in seventh grade were also apt to feel less confidence in their ability to influence students' learning. Observers and students saw seventh-grade teachers as less supportive, less friendly, and less fair than sixth-grade teachers. Moreover, in seventh-grade classes, teachers were more likely to group students by ability, and the students were more likely to compare grades with one another. In addition, teachers offered less individualized instruction.

How did these contextual changes affect students? After children made the transition from a sixth-grade teacher who felt effective to a seventh-grade teacher who felt less effective, they had lower expectancies for their own performance and evaluated their performance more negatively. When junior high school teachers were less supportive and more controlling than elementary school teachers, the students' interest in the subject matter declined. Unfortunately, both sets of effects were more pronounced for low-achieving students. Finally, when seventh-grade teachers exerted more classroom control than sixth-grade teachers and allowed children less freedom in decision making, student interest in the subject area declined. Eccles and her colleagues argue that adolescence is a time when children need emotional support and opportunities to make independent decisions, and that many junior-high schools are less likely to meet these needs than are elementary schools. Together, the many changes we discussed in Chapter 6 that adolescents experience during this period—physical, social, and cognitive—probably account for these effects. A mismatch between children's needs and the contexts in which they must perform may very likely contribute to declines in achievement motivation.

CULTURE, CLASS, AND RACE

Why has the Children's Defense Fund (1997) estimated that schools have a cumulative and negative effect on lower-class children, many of whom not only are far behind their middle-class peers academically but are candidates for dropping out by the time they're in high school? We've seen that lower-class families may not prepare children as thoroughly as middle-class families for the intellectual give and take of the school environment. And in Chapter 11 we discussed the differential effects of such factors as parent-child interaction styles, peer contexts, and teacher behavior on the cognitive development of children from lower- and middle-class homes and of differing ethnic backgrounds. Because those differences are present and detectable before children even reach the schoolroom, we may conclude that lower-class children's lesser performance is not entirely the schools' fault. Nevertheless, the aim of education is to teach children regardless of their background. Various societal strategies have been developed to achieve these aims, some

Participation in sports events like this San Antonio, Texas, regional high school track meet—we are looking at the girls' 800-meter race—can go a long way toward improving interracial relations.

of which we touched on in Chapter 11. Since the mid-1950s *desegregation* and *affirmative action* have assumed a prominent place in U.S. efforts to make not only education but jobs and housing equally accessible and relevant to all children and adults, regardless of demographic or cultural background.

Few topics have generated as much public concern in recent years as the desegregation of American schools. In 1954 the United States Supreme Court mandated an end to segregated education, asserting that "separate educational facilities are inherently unequal" (*Brown v. Board of Education*, 1954). Desegregation was expected to improve African American students' self-esteem and raise their levels of academic achievement; it was also expected to lead both African Americans and European Americans to view one another in a more positive light. The evidence regarding the achievement of these goals to date, however, is mixed (Wells, 1995). Although there have been some reports of increased self-esteem and higher levels of academic achievement among disadvantaged children, other studies have found either no change or declines. Moreover, relationships among children of different racial and ethnic groups have not necessarily improved (Grant, 1990; Wells, 1995). In fact, as Asher, Singleton, and Taylor (1982) discovered, children may actually make fewer cross-race friendships as they move from the earlier to the later grades.

Why might this be? For one thing, varying curricula and minimal time spent together in classes may work against cross-race friendships, particularly because black and white students generally come from different neighborhoods and are often of different social classes; thus they are unlikely to have much after-school contact. What might help to improve interracial relations in schools? For elementary school children, active learning programs, curricula embracing concepts of equal racial status, and integrated work groups can help promote positive interracial attitudes and friendships (Epstein, 1980; Hallinan & Teixeira, 1987). At the high school level, assigning students to work together or encouraging them to participate in multiethnic sports teams seems to have a positive effect on race relations (Minuchin & Shapiro, 1983; Slavin & Madden, 1979). It also helps if the numbers of black and white children in a school are equal. According to Stephan and Rosenfield (1982), "contact that is intimate, equal status, cooperative and sanctioned by authority promotes favorable relations between groups"; this recipe clearly requires more effort than just putting children with different backgrounds together and expecting changes to happen on their own.

In the 1990s, disenchantment with desegregation increased as a function of conservative Supreme Court decisions, the withdrawal of federal involvement in education, continuing patterns of segregation in housing, and growing opposition among middle-class whites as well as decreasing consensus among blacks as to the value of desegregated schools (Armor, 1995; Tauber, 1990). Moreover, racial and ethnic balance in schools is now a much broader issue, for a wide range of groups— for example, Hispanic, Asian, Native American, African American—are seeking to secure their rights in schools and other social institutions (Goldberg, 1996). In California, for example, it is estimated that Hispanic Americans will constitute 27 percent of the population in 2000, and Asian Americans 12 percent by the turn of the century. For a discussion of a recent and successful effort to facilitate learning and achievement among Hispanic American youth in that state, see Box 14-2.

In the context of education, although *affirmative action* does not affect public schools, it does affect private schools at the elementary and high school level, and of course it affects both public and private colleges and universities. In 1996 the University of California Board of Regents voted to discontinue the practice of giving preferential treatment to minority members in college admissions, a decision that engendered a great deal of controversy across the country. Some social scientists have presented data to show that African Americans and Hispanic Americans have made far greater social and economic progress than had been thought; others believe that we still have far to go before we can dispense with special support for

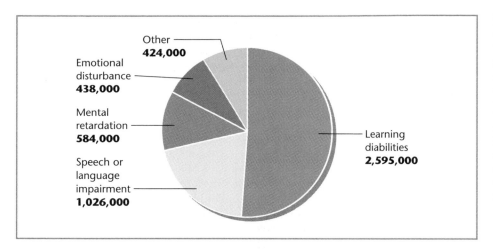

Children with disabilities. The two largest groups of schoolchildren classified as disabled, those with learning disabilities such as dyslexia and those with speech or language impairments, are generally those who can most easily profit from intervention, whether this takes place within the regular classroom or in special sessions. (*Source:* U.S. Department of Education, 1997)

peoples who have long been disadvantaged in our society (Fisher et al., 1998). The issue has sparked interest not only in minority education issues but also in the education of girls (Ruble & Martin, 1998). The rise of all-girl schools is one of the outcomes of this new awareness, which early evidence suggests may benefit girls' achievement and self-esteem.

The complexities of these issues require investigation of many factors, including attitudes and values of families and teachers, voluntary and mandatory integration, desirable ethnic ratios, and busing (Wells, 1995). Among the many questions we may need to ask is, *Under what circumstances* are integration and segregation desirable, appropriate, useful, or necessary?

SPECIAL CHILDREN: THE POLICY OF INCLUSION

Not all children learn at the same pace or in the same way. Some learn faster than their classmates, as we saw in Chapter 11, but others, some of whom have various mental, emotional, and physical handicaps, learn more slowly. As Figure 14-4 shows, of the more than 5 million U.S. children classified as disabled (about 11% of all students), a little more than 50 percent are considered learning disabled, about 20 percent have speech or language difficulties, almost 12 percent are mentally retarded, about 9 percent are emotionally disturbed, and another 8 percent have various other kinds of handicaps (Terman, Larner, Stevenson, & Behrman, 1996; U.S. Department of Education, 1997). A major question in recent years has been whether these "special" children should be placed in separate classes or integrated into regular classrooms. Currently, in 44 percent of the United States, more than half of disabled students spend most of their school days in regular classrooms, whereas in 56 percent of the states, more than half are generally relegated to "special education" classes (U.S. Department of Education, 1997).

In 1975 the U.S. Congress passed the Education for All Handicapped Children Act, which required that school districts across the nation provide, for children with special needs, an educational experience

A school policy of inclusion can support the need of the child with a disability to belong, and it can also encourage peers to accept such a child as just another member of their group.

BOX 14-2

Risk and Resilience

Helping Hispanic American Children to Achieve

In 1990 Claude Goldenberg and his colleagues (Goldenberg, 1996a,b; Goldenberg & Sullivan, 1994) undertook a challenge: how to improve average achievement in a largely Hispanic Southern California school in which the students scored between the 7th and 15th percentiles on statewide tests of reading, writing, and mathematics. More than 95 percent of the students were first-generation Hispanic Americans whose parents were immigrants from Mexico or from Central American countries. The families were poor—89 percent of the children qualified for free school meals—and the children were clearly at risk for failure.

Underlying Goldenberg's work was a four-element change model "aimed at providing overall coherence to the school's effort to change, something that is often missing in the current patchwork of attempts to reform or 'restructure' schools" (Goldenberg, 1996a, p. 17). As you can see in Figure 14-5, the four change elements proposed to affect teachers' attitudes and behaviors and, thereby, student outcomes were goals, indicators, assistance, and leadership. Setting shared *goals* was judged to help in altering behavior. *Indicators* that measured success were designed to complement goals by reinforcing their importance and helping gauge progress. *Assistance* stressed presenting new information, creating settings that encouraged discussion, and analyzing teaching practices. Finally, *leadership* that both supports and exerts pressure on the teaching staff was deemed critical to promote change and make the schools more successful.

To implement this program an Academic Expectations Committee made up of teachers, administrators, and a researcher met together to devise and implement a literacy curriculum with reading and writing goals and expectations. And parents were given a chance to react. One parent said she felt "our standards are a lot lower" than they should be and that "we really need to push our children." At the urging of parents, the committee wrote "parent-friendly" versions of the literacy curriculum and made these available to parents.

And the program worked: At the outset, only 31 percent of first graders were reading at grade level; by third grade, 61 percent were at or above grade level (compared with 49% for the rest of the school district). Whereas the school's students performed below state and district levels before the project began, they now outperformed students in the rest of the district. Their voluntary reading went up too: from 5.3 books and magazines within the school year to 13 publications in that period.

As this project suggests, effective instruction, schoolwide curriculum organization, and home-school collaboration can have substantial positive effects on Spanish-speaking children's academic achievement. And as these children do better, society benefits. As Goldenberg wisely notes, "education is cheaper than ignorance."

Finally, this program represents the importance of several theoretical views on development. First, a systems theory approach that recognizes the interplay across different levels of the school organization—the students and teachers (individual level), classroom (group level), and school climate (organizational level)—is important for understanding this project. Second, the project illustrates Bronfenbrenner's ecological theory (Chapter 1) by showing the interplay between the school and the family—an example of the mesosystem in action. Finally, this project illustrates how social institutions like our schools can foster resiliency among children who are at risk for academic failure and school drop out (Zimmerman & Arunkumar, 1994). In this case, the school served as a buffer or protection against the risks associated with being poor and a first-generation minority.

---

comparable to that provided nonhandicapped children. A 1986 amendment of that act specified that such educational experience must also be given to children between the ages of 3 and 5, thus providing for early intervention. And in 1997, further amendments required that all states adopt school financing plans that offer no financial incentive to place disabled children outside their home schools. All this legislation has brought about a continuing debate over the best method of accomplishing these various mandates. Many schools have adopted the approach of **inclusion** (also called *integration* or *mainstreaming*), in which children of all ability levels are included in the same classroom. Other schools have placed children thought to be mentally retarded, as well as children with learning disabilities, physical handicaps, and other special learning needs, in separate, special education classes (Farnham-Diggory, 1992).

Supporters of this legislation cite some powerful arguments. First, they argue that inclusion will result in disabled children reaching higher levels of achievement, both academically and socially. Second, they suggest that this move to a regular school setting gives children with special needs more help in adjusting to and cop-

inclusion A policy by which children of all ability levels, whether learning disabled, physically handicapped, or mentally retarded, are included in the same classroom.

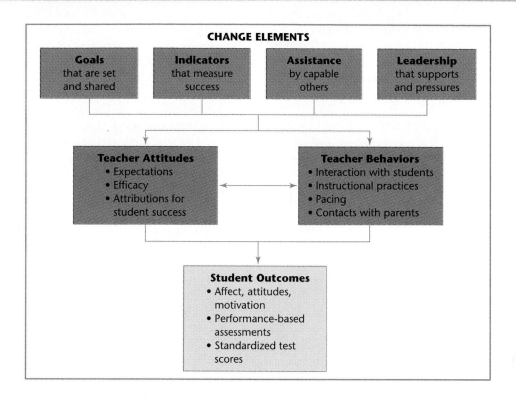

CHANGE ELEMENTS

| Goals
that are set
and shared | Indicators
that measure
success | Assistance
by capable
others | Leadership
that supports
and pressures |

Teacher Attitudes
- Expectations
- Efficacy
- Attributions for
  student success

Teacher Behaviors
- Interaction with students
- Instructional practices
- Pacing
- Contacts with parents

Student Outcomes
- Affect, attitudes,
  motivation
- Performance-based
  assessments
- Standardized test
  scores

■ FIGURE 14-5

A model for improving student achievement.

The striking improvements in students' skills achieved in the project for which this model was devised demonstrated the potential of a unified plan carried out by teamwork and with strong leadership. The change elements were crucial to the effort. Some *goals* were that kindergartners should know the letters and sounds of the alphabet, begin to write or dictate narratives, and be able to ask and answer questions about favorite books, and that fifth graders should read for pleasure books and other materials, compose stories with conflicts and resolutions, and keep daily journals. *Indicators* included the grade level of the reader a child was using and yearly assessments of reading and writing skills. A variety of modes of *assistance* included regular workgroups in which teachers could discuss and refine strategies for improving teaching and learning. *Leadership* was provided by the principal, who was so skilled at balancing pressure on teachers with support that teachers generally perceived her as concerned primarily with support of their efforts. (*Source:* Adapted from Goldenberg, 1996a)

ing with the world in which they will live as adults. Third, they assert that children who function normally will benefit from coming to know and understand people who function at other levels and that they will be less likely to stereotype or shun such people in future.

Has the policy of inclusion accomplished these goals? Sometimes yes but, unfortunately, more often no. First, researchers have found relatively small differences in academic achievement between students who have been included in regular classrooms and pupils in special classrooms (Buysse & Bailey, 1993; MacMillan, Keogh, & Jones, 1986). Second, integration of children with mild retardation into regular classrooms can lead to increased rather than decreased social rejection (Taylor et al., 1987; Weissberg & Greenberg, 1998). Although the causes of this rejection may vary—for example, some mildly retarded children are shy and avoidant whereas others are aggressive and disruptive—it certainly doesn't go unnoticed, and the children who are rejected are more lonely and more dissatisfied and anxious about their peer relationships than other children (Taylor et al., 1987).

Interventions designed to improve social acceptance of children with retardation in schools that have adopted the policy of inclusion have had some success, though such children are still not as well accepted as their classmates (Gottlieb & Leyser, 1981; Gresham & Reschly, 1988). Among recent interventions, the PATHS Curriculum ("PATHS" is an acronym for Promoting Alternative Thinking Strategies), which holds that emotional recognition and emotional regulation are necessary processes for effective coping in classrooms, has met with impressive success (Greenberg, Kusche, Cook, & Quamma, 1995). Under this multiyear intervention program, 300 special needs children in the second and third grades increased their emotional understanding and social cognitive skills, reported less depression, and improved in general social competence. Moreover, the children maintained these gains over a two-year period.

TELEVISION: HARMFUL OR HELPFUL?

There is no doubt that television is a pervasive influence on children, from a very early age, nor that it will continue to affect children's cognitive and social development (Huston et al., 1992; Liebert & Sprafkin, 1988). How much time do children spend watching TV? A lot. By the age of 16 the average American child has spent more time in this activity than attending school!

Television can be educational and beneficial (see Box 1-1 in Chapter 1), but its negative aspects, such as the amount of aggressive and violent activity it displays daily, have concerned parents and educators around the world. Whether and how we will manage to control the harmful effects of television and harness its potential for the good of children is the subject of ongoing debate. In this section we ask such questions as, Do children's viewing patterns change with age? What kinds of programs do children watch? How much of the content of TV programs do children actually understand? Do children read fewer books as a result of watching TV? What are the major effects of TV viewing on children's behavior, and are they primarily positive or negative? Finally, what can parents do to modify the effects of television on their children?

How Much TV and What Programs Do Children Watch?

TV viewing starts even in infancy. The typical 6-month-old spends an hour and a half every day in front of a TV set (Hollenbeck & Slaby, 1982). Children do not generally become consistent viewers, however, until they're about 2½ to 3 years old; even then they don't watch the set constantly. For example, one study found that 3- to 5-year-olds watching "Sesame Street" looked away about 215 times an hour (Anderson & Field, 1991). When they did look, nearly 75 percent of their glances at the set were brief, lasting just six seconds!

Children's TV viewing patterns are affected not only by program content but by the "formal features" of television, such as animation, high action, loud music, and visual and auditory special effects. These formal features, which help to recruit as well as maintain children's attention, are, to some degree, independent of program content, and they are important for younger and older children alike (Huston et al., 1992; Huston & Wright, 1998). Children increase their viewing time gradually until, in preadolescence, they are watching TV almost four hours a day (Figure 14-6). Although this sounds like a lot, adults, especially people who are retired and over 65, watch even more TV than children (Gunter & McAleer, 1990). This pattern of TV viewing may be near universal, for similar trends have been found across Europe, Canada, and Australia (Comstock, 1991; Liebert & Sprafkin, 1988). Children between 2 and 11 decreased their TV viewing time over the 10 years between 1984 and 1994: They watched 26 hours a week in 1984 and 22 hours a week 10 years later—still a lot of "tube time" (Fabrikant, 1996).

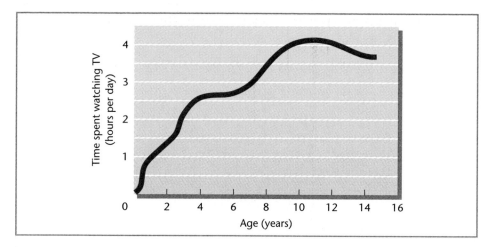

■ FIGURE 14-6
How much television do children watch?
In 1987, research indicated that the amount of time American children spend watching TV each day increases fairly steadily throughout childhood, peaking at a little more that four hours in preadolescence.

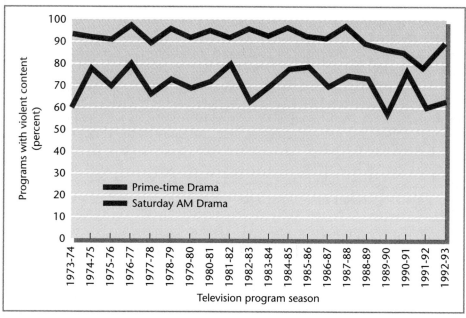

■ FIGURE 14-7
Violence on TV.
Over the 20-year period surveyed, there was very little change in the amount of violent material in television programs. Prime-time shows dropped from 95 percent violence to 89 percent, but Saturday morning shows—watched mostly by children—stayed the same, at 60 percent. (Source: Gerbner, Morgan, & Signorielli, 1993)

What about content—what do children watch? They watch a variety of programs, including cartoons, situation comedies, family-oriented programs, and educational shows like "Sesame Street," but a majority of what they watch is violence. American TV programming contains an enormous amount of violence: As Figure 14-7 shows, on average over 91 percent of prime-time programs sampled from 1973 through 1993 contained violence, and 70 percent of Saturday morning programs—watched principally by children—contained some violence. Weekend cartoons that are typically designed for children had an even higher rate: 95 percent of these programs contained violence, and violent acts were presented at a rate of 21 per hour. By late adolescence the average American child has witnessed 13,000 violent murders on TV (Waters & Malamud, 1975). In spite of claims to the contrary, these rates remained remarkably stable from the late 1960s to the mid-1990s, especially for Saturday-morning fare directed at children (Gerbner, Gross, Morgan, & Signorielli, 1994). These figures are discouraging in view of the policy debates and frequent legislative proposals aimed at curbing the amount of television violence (Huston & Wright, 1998). As we discuss later, the "V" chip and more parental vigilance may be helpful in reducing children's exposure—in spite of the continuing proliferation of aggressive and violent content in TV programming.

There are some gender-based differences in choice of programs. Boys watch more action-adventure and sports programs, whereas girls prefer social dramas like soap operas. However, as children develop, both girls and boys watch fewer children's programs and more general-audience fare (Wright & Huston, 1995).

Do Children Understand What They Watch?

magic window thinking
The tendency of very young children to believe that TV images are as real as the people and things about them.

To understand reasonably accurately what they see on television, children need, first, to be able to distinguish between fantasy and reality. Displaying what has been called **magic window thinking,** the very youngest children are likely to believe that TV images are as real as the people and things about them (Huston & Wright, 1998). Some time between the ages of 2 and 4, however, children come to understand that the characters and objects they see on TV are not actually present, inside the set (Flavell, Flavell, Green, & Korfmacher, 1990).

Studying preschoolers, Nikken and Peters (1988) found evidence for three kinds of magic window thinking: First, the children thought that Sesame Street was a real place where people live; second, they believed that when TV characters like Big Bird appeared on the screen they could see and hear the children who were watching them; and third, the children thought that everything they saw on the screen actually existed, just as they saw it, inside the TV set. As children grow and their cognitive skills continue to improve, their ability to distinguish fantasy from reality improves as well. Another study found that older children understood that shows are made up, scripted, and rehearsed (Wright, Huston, Reitz, & Piemyat, 1994).

A child's perception of a television program affects his ability to understand it. For example, researchers found that third and fourth graders who understood a TV story as real recalled more complex content and more of the characters' psychological and emotional states than children who accepted the story as fictional or made up (Huston et al., 1995). Children clearly are more motivated to process and remember real events, which they assume have relevance for their own lives.

Children's developing cognitive skills also help them to understand cause-and-effect relationships (Chapter 9). Researchers have found that this ability to connect action with consequence may protect children from being unduly influenced by what they see on TV, especially content of an aggressive or violent nature. Researching children's reactions to modeled aggressive behavior, numerous studies have found that if a model was punished for his or her aggressive acts, children were less likely to imitate those acts (e.g., Huston & Wright, 1998; Parke & Slaby, 1983). However, because the complex plots of television shows often separate a character's aggressive or violent action and the punishment for that action, young viewers may have difficulty linking the crime with the punishment (Collins, 1983). To evaluate this hypothesis, Collins (1983) showed 3rd, 6th, and 10th-grade children an aggressive TV sequence. Then they showed one group of children a sequence in which the characters in the first sequence were punished and showed another group a commercial before showing them the punishment sequence. Third graders who saw the commercial indicated that they would behave more aggressively than classmates who saw the violent sequence followed immediately by the punishment. Collins found, however, that the commercial break had little effect on 6th and 10th graders; they were as likely to endorse aggressive behavior whether they viewed the punishment sequence alone or after the commercial.

The inability of young children to link actions and outcomes in regular TV programming may contribute to the heightened effect of TV aggression on young viewers (Huston & Wright, 1998). On the other hand, as Box 14-3 shows, young children can be taught to draw a distinction between what they see on television and what is acceptable in the real world.

Usefulness of TV: Its Educational Benefits

Television clearly has a positive side, and it is important to underscore its benefits for the developing child. As you'll recall from our first chapter, "Sesame Street" is a vivid

BOX 14-3

Child Psychology in Action

Teaching Children to Distinguish between Television and Reality

Can we reduce the impact of violent television on young children by helping them distinguish between what they see on the screen and what actually occurs in real life and is acceptable to society? It appears that some of the negative effects of watching TV may in fact be reduced by a program of helping children understand that the world of TV and the everyday world are different.

Rowell Huesmann and his colleagues (Huesmann, Eron, Lefkowitz, & Walder, 1984) conducted a two-year study with more than 170 children, 6 to 8 years old, who were heavy consumers of violent TV programs. Children in the treatment group participated in five small-group discussion sessions over a two-year period. Researchers focused these group discussions on three specific messages:

1. Television is an unrealistic portrayal of the real world.
2. Aggressive behaviors are not as universal in the real world as they appear to be on television, nor are they acceptable to society.
3. It is not good to behave like the aggressive characters on TV.

Children in the control group also met in small groups over the same period but discussed neutral topics.

When, after two years, researchers asked peers to rate the children in both groups for their aggressiveness, the children in the experimental group were rated as less aggressive than those in the control group. Moreover, whereas researchers continued to see a positive relation between television violence viewing and aggression in the control group children, they found no evidence of such a link in the children who had been taught to interpret media aggression differently.

Perhaps if these girls, like the children in Huesmann's study, discuss the program they're watching they'll draw some of the same negative conclusions about aggressive and violent behaviors.

illustration of television's educational potential. "The Electric Company," which ran from 1971 to 1985 on American TV, was designed to help second graders learn to read, and evaluations indicated that children in the first through the fourth grade who watched the program in school did achieve higher reading scores than children who did not watch this program (Ball & Bogatz, 1972). Later studies modified these findings, suggesting that "The Electric Company" was indeed effective but only when watched with teacher guidance (Corder-Bolz, 1980). Similar findings have emerged from recent entries into the educational TV arena, such as "Barney and Friends." Preschool children who viewed the Barney program improved in counting skills and vocabulary but mostly when teachers accompanied the viewing with related activities (Singer & Singer, 1994). In this study, viewing alone was of limited value. We do not yet know what the impact of home viewing may be. These programs and more recent shows like "Reading Rainbow," "Storytime," and "Ghostwriter" may serve to increase children's motivation and interest in reading as well as help them improve their reading skills (Huston & Wright, 1998).

Recent math and science programs like "Square One," which aims to teach math and problem-solving skills, have been successful in improving these skills in fifth graders (Hall, Esty, & Fisch, 1990). The availability of these educational TV offerings means that children have increased viewing options. Clearly, children's development is better served when there is more to watch than cartoons, comedies, soaps, and shoot-outs.

Finally, as we explore in Chapter 16, television can have a positive impact on children's social and emotional development as well. For example, programs such as "Mr. Rogers' Neighborhood" can have beneficial effects on children's helping and sharing activities (Huston & Wright, 1998).

Negative Effects of TV

Because children spend so much time watching TV, it would be surprising if their attitudes and behaviors were not altered by this influence. For example, television is a powerful source of children's knowledge about other people. George Gerbner, a prominent TV researcher, has remarked that "the more time one spends 'living' in the world of television, the more likely one is to report perceptions of social reality [that] can be traced to television's representations of life and society" (Gerbner, Gross, Morgan, & Signorielli, 1980, p. 14). Gerbner has found that heavy TV viewers tend to overestimate the degree of danger and crime in the world and to underestimate the trustworthiness and helpfulness of others (Gerbner et al., 1994).

Singer and Singer (1981) traced children's TV viewing patterns and reading achievement scores from age 3 to age 8. Heavy viewing had a clearly adverse impact on reading. Children who were early and heavy viewers remained high consumers of TV at age 8, and their reading scores were significantly lower than those of children who watched less TV. A recent Dutch study found similar results: The more time 8- to 10-year-old children spent viewing TV, the poorer was their reading comprehension (Koolstra, van der Voort, & van der Kamp, 1997). However, some researchers suggest that socioeconomic and family factors may account for these links between TV and reading ability (Huston & Wright, 1998). Other research has shown that attitudes toward racial groups, gender roles, sexual relationships, and aggressive sexual behavior are also affected by the way television represents these issues (Truglio, 1990). In this section we consider television's displacement of other, perhaps more useful activities; the tendency of the medium to stereotype minority groups; its pervasive display of aggression and violence; and the effect of advertising on children.

Television Displaces Other Activities

TV viewing takes time and may displace other activities, such as sports, reading, or even talking with others. To find out whether TV displaces other pursuits is not easy, for nearly 99 percent of households have a TV set. A study in Canada helped provide an answer by comparing towns that had either no TV reception, only one channel, or four channels (Williams & Handford, 1986). The results were clear: People's involvement in community activities was greatest in the no-TV town and least in the town with four TV channels. Once television became available, children's attendance at dances, supper parties, and even sports declined (Figure 14-8). Similar results were found in a South African study (Mutz, Roberts, & van Vuuren, 1993), which revealed that heavy TV consumers spent less time with friends, got less sleep, and were less likely to participate in organized sports and other activities outside the home.

Many children learn to watch TV while doing other things—such as eating dinner or even doing homework (Kubey & Csikszentmihalyi, 1990). In a British study, about half of a group of children between the ages of 7 and 15 watched TV while doing their homework (Wober, 1992). Watching television at dinner, however, may prevent family members from conversing with one another, and we may well wonder about the quality of homework done while watching TV!

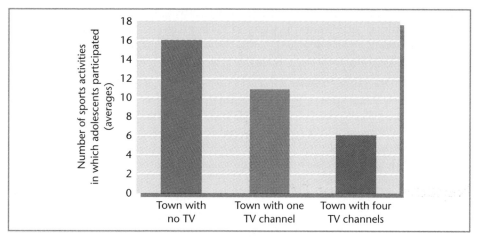

■ FIGURE 14-8
Television and sports activity participation.
The more opportunity adolescents (grades 7 through 12) in three Canadian towns had to watch TV, the less likely they were to participate in various sports activities. (*Source:* Williams, 1986)

TV Stereotypes Minority Groups

Children's attitudes toward minority groups can be influenced by television portrayals of members of these groups. Some progress has been made in this area, although white men are still the most common characters on TV. The proportion of African Americans in television programs has risen since the 1970s; by the 1990s, 11 percent of prime-time characters were African American. However, only 3 percent of characters on children's Saturday TV programs were black (Greenberg & Brand, 1994).

Improvement in TV's representation of minority groups has not been uniform. Hispanic, Asian, and Native American characters, for example, are still rarely seen on regular TV shows. Educational TV has done better: 38 percent of PBS educational programs portray minority characters, whereas 27 percent of commercial shows feature minorities (Neapolitan & Huston, 1994).

The roles of African Americans on TV shows represent a range of characters in a variety of occupations. The highly popular Bill Cosby series in which the lead character was a successful physician in a upper-middle-class environment (now off the air) represented a significant improvement over earlier distorted pictures of blacks as poor, dangerous, or silly. However, this change may be deceptive (Greenberg & Brand, 1994; Liebert & Sprafkin, 1988), for blacks and whites are still often segregated on TV. Even children's programs and cartoons are segregated; in 82 percent of programs surveyed, white and African American children didn't appear together (Barcus, 1983; Greenberg & Brand, 1994).

Do these portrayals affect children's racial attitudes? The evidence is mixed. An early study suggested that white children who watched a cartoon depicting blacks in a poor light (inept, destructive, lazy, and powerless) developed more negative attitudes toward blacks, whereas positive portrayals of blacks as competent, trustworthy, and hardworking had a positive impact on white children's racial attitudes (Graves, 1975). More recent evidence suggests that when minorities are cast in a favorable light, children's attitudes and behavior (e.g., their forming of more minority friendships) change in a positive direction (Graves, 1993). Other long-term studies of the impact of TV viewing on racial attitudes suggest that people's prior attitudes have a considerable impact on the way TV depictions affect their views (Atkin, Greenberg, & McDermott, 1978). Rather than produce dramatic changes, TV may, instead, strengthen existing attitudes. Thus even if TV doesn't necessarily produce bigotry, if it reinforces existing prejudice, we still have plenty of reason for concern.

Children may not get very appealing portraits of older people from television shows, either. Despite their growing numbers, old people are underrepresented on TV, especially older women (Huston & Wright, 1998; Liebert & Sprafkin, 1988), and their portrayals are not very flattering. Typically, they are depicted as unhappy, negative, helpless, and rarely romantic. The TV program "The Golden Girls," in which older women were depicted positively as fun loving and capable, was a step in the right direction, but it is no longer on the air.

Aggression and Violence Are Pervasive

As we have seen, exposure to aggressive models on TV can increase children's subsequent aggressive behavior (Huston & Wright, 1998; Paik & Comstock, 1994), and aggressive and violent behavior are endemic in the medium. Heavy doses of TV violence can affect both attitudes and behavior, leading children to view violence as an acceptable and effective way to solve interpersonal conflict (Thomas & Drabman, 1977). Children learn a lesson from TV that "violence works, for both the good guys and the bad guys; it gets things done" (Dominick & Greenberg, 1972, p. 331). Moreover, the effect of TV violence on aggression is not a strictly American phenomenon. Cross-cultural studies indicate that children in Australia, Finland, Great Britain, Israel, the Netherlands, and Poland show similar reactions to violent TV fare (Huesmann & Miller, 1994; Wiegman, Kuttschreuter, & Baarda, 1992).

There are other outcomes. For example, frequent viewers may become immune to violence; they show less emotional reaction when viewing televised aggression (Cantor, 1994; Cline, Croft, & Courier, 1973). Children who watch televised violence may also become indifferent to real-life violence (Drabman & Thomas, 1976). However, exposure to TV violence affects children differently at different ages, due to shifts in children's cognitive abilities. As we've said, children who can distinguish between fantasy and reality and between what is acceptable and unacceptable may react differently from those who cannot make these distinctions. Children who were told that a violent film clip was real (i.e., a newsreel of an actual riot) later reacted more aggressively than children who believed that the film was a Hollywood production (Atkin, 1983). As children develop and are able to make this fiction-reality distinction, many TV programs may have less impact (Huston et al., 1995).

Advertising Influences Children's Choices

Not only the programs children watch but the commercials and advertising that accompany these programs affect children's development (Huston & Wright, 1998). On average, children watch nearly 20,000 TV commercials each year! Parents and developmental psychologists are understandably concerned because so many ads advocate foods and fads that may impede children's healthy development (Tinsley, 1992). Sugary cereals, fast-food snacks, and expensive and sometimes silly or even dangerous toys are frequently the subjects of TV advertising directed at children.

But do kids pay attention to these ads? Probably not as much as advertisers would like. Children's attention wanes when commercials appear, and this tendency increases with age. Even so, according to Gaines and Esserman (1981), 90 percent of 4- and 5-year-olds and 100 percent of 6- to 8-year-olds could correctly distinguish a commercial from the program itself. On the other hand, only 1 percent of 4- to 5-year-olds and 28 percent of 6- to 8-year-olds realized that the goal of the ad was "to try to make you buy things."

Despite children's limited understanding of the purpose of commercials, TV ads are effective in influencing their preferences. Gorn and Goldberg (1982) exposed 5- to 8-year-olds to one of several different commercials. Some saw sweetened snack food commercials (candy bars, Crackerjacks, Kool-Aid), while others saw fruit ads (orange juice, grape juice) or a public service message emphasizing a balanced diet. Children in the control group saw no commercials. The researchers then offered the children their choice of orange juice, Kool-Aid, fruit, and candy bars. The children who had watched the ad for sweetened snacks were the least likely of the four groups to select orange juice or fruit. In view of one researcher's finding that 34 percent of commercials were for sweetened cereals, 29 percent for candies and

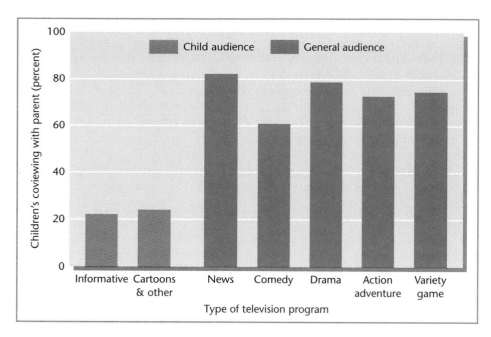

■ FIGURE 14-9
Children's television
coviewing with parents.
Apparently, children watch
general or adult TV fare more
than half the time with their
parents. If parents interpret
programs for their children, they
may help them learn how to
evaluate what they see on
television. This may be
particularly important with
respect to news stories, dramas,
and "action adventure"
programs. Note that parents
relatively rarely watch child-
addressed programs. Because
cartoons can be extremely
violent, it might not be a bad
idea for Dad or Mom to do a little
interpreting here as well! (*Source:*
Adapted from St. Peters, Fitch,
Huston, Wright, & Eakins, 1991)

sweets, and 15 percent for fast-food chains, parents have reason to be alarmed! Although few 5-year-olds make independent trips to the supermarket, children often try to influence their parents' consumer choices. In one study, 85 percent of children indicated that they had asked their parents to buy them something that they had seen on a TV ad (Greenberg, Fazel, & Weber, 1986), and a majority of children indicated that they were successful in influencing their parents (Kunkel & Roberts, 1991). Parents beware!

How Can Parents Modify the Effects of TV on Their Children?

Parents can help diminish the negative impact of TV by helping children interpret and evaluate the programs that they are watching (Huston & Wright, 1998). Family members frequently chat while watching television; adults might use such conversations to help younger children make the important connection between actions and their consequences. When adults help children make this connection, younger children's subsequent understanding of TV plots is just as good as that of older children (Collins, Sobol, & Westby, 1981). Moreover, children whose parents explain events and clarify information tend to be more imaginative, less aggressive, and less hyperactive, and to understand the plots of shows better, especially if they have relatively light TV viewing habits (Singer, Singer, Desmond, Hirsch, & Nicol, 1988).Unfortunately, the evidence suggests that parents rarely explain content, discuss values, or interpret the meaning of TV programs for their children (Comstock, 1991; Huston & Wright, 1998).

Coviewing in which parents or other adults clearly disapprove of violence or other undesirable aspects of TV shows can help children sort out their reactions. As Figure 14-9 suggests, children are likely to watch programs intended for an adult or general audience with their parents. For example, to assess the impact on children of adult reactions to a violent TV show, Grusec (1973) had an adult either approve ("Boy, he really landed a good one"; "Terrific") or disapprove ("That's awful; he's really hurting him") of the program. Children who heard the disapproving remarks were less likely to behave aggressively than the children who watched with an adult who condoned the televised violence. Coviewing can also help a child cope with fear produced by a scary program. In fact, children say "sit by mom or dad" is their most common strategy to reduce fear of a TV show (Wilson, Hoffner, & Cantor, 1987). In an experimental study of preschoolers in which they watched a scary show alone or with an older sibling, the children were less upset and liked the show better when with their sibling (Wilson & Weiss, 1993).

Beyond coviewing and discussing TV program content with their children, parents may actively manage the children's TV viewing. However, it is not clear how common this practice may be (Comstock, 1991; Wright, St. Peters, & Huston, 1990). When approximately 5,000 parents were asked if they controlled the kinds of TV programs their children watched, 85 percent reported that the children themselves controlled the channel selector. Only 10 percent reported that they engaged in "positive guidance," telling their children what they "should" or "must" watch on TV (Mohr, 1979).

Perhaps the 1996 Telecommunications Act, which requires TV manufacturers to incorporate a "V chip" into their sets, will help parents regulate their children's viewing. The chip permits a parent to block programs that have been assigned particular ratings, similar to the ratings used in the movie industry. However, there are still disagreements about how to define these ratings (Huston & Wright, 1996). In addition, making some programs forbidden may simply increase their attractiveness, and a recent survey supports this concern, at least for boys (Cantor & Harrison, 1996). Direct, personal, parental control is still probably the simplest and most effective solution to the problem of regulating children's TV program choices.

SUMMARY

- Schools and the media consume a great portion of children's daily lives and exert strong influences over their development.

The School's Role in Learning and Socialization

- Schools help children acquire an abstract, symbolic orientation to the world. They alter children's moral-value orientations and political views, as well as their achievement motivation and their occupational aspirations.

School Environments

- School size determines the extent of children's involvement in extracurricular activities; students in small schools are more likely to participate. Although there are fewer dropouts from small schools, academic achievement is unaffected by school size.
- The way grade levels are combined can affect children's social and academic learning and achievement. The widespread use of three-year junior highs and three-year senior highs has had a negative impact on some preadolescents.
- Class size may determine the extent to which children participate in classroom activities; participation is higher in smaller classrooms.
- Studies of classroom organizations found that students generally prefer group-centered or **open classrooms** that allow them some opportunity to participate in decision making. Children in open classrooms are more cooperative, more self-reliant, and better behaved. The academic benefits are less clear, however, and some children do better in the more structured, **traditional classroom**.

Teachers: Their Impact on Children's Development

- Teachers' early impressions and expectations of a pupil's probable success can affect the child's academic progress. A self-fulfilling prophecy, or **Pygmalion effect**, is evident: Children succeed when teachers believe they will do well and perform poorly when teachers expect them to fail.
- Behavior modification techniques have sometimes been successful in controlling children's classroom behavior, especially when they used material or token reinforcers for shaping appropriate behavior. External rewards may, however, undermine children's intrinsic interest in school activities.

Teaching Methods and Techniques

- In **cooperative learning,** small groups of students work together to master material. This method often enhances children's self-esteem. Two students may work in **peer collaboration,** a technique that allows students to complete tasks that they could not complete alone. In the jigsaw method, members of several small groups learn segments of a task and then teach what they've learned to the other members of their groups.
- Peers may function as assistant teachers in **peer tutoring,** which is often combined with other techniques, such as cooperative learning. Both the tutor and the other child can benefit from this arrangement. Peer tutors generally receive instruction and assistance from teachers.
- Textbook publishers have made efforts to present material in an unbiased fashion, but girls and minority group members are still often inaccurately represented. The whole-language versus the phonics approach to reading continues to be debated in many school districts, but a middle-of-the road, literature-based approach is gaining adherents. Classrooms that use this approach are often open, and teachers emphasize collaborative group work.
- Computers are now found in most classrooms, although there are rarely enough for every child to use a computer for a substantial task. Children benefit by being able to practice previously learned material with **computer-assisted instruction.** Simulating such things as scientific laboratories and outer space, computers can contribute to science learning. Word processing programs aid children's writing skills, and graphics programs can foster artistic creativity. Students are also using computers for homework and research. Contrary to expectations, computers increase rather than decrease social interaction among children in the classroom.

Achievement Motivation

- Children's intellectual performance is influenced by their own **achievement motivation,** the emotions they associate with learning tasks, the ways they view themselves and their abilities, and their responses to success and failure.
- In one approach to understanding motivation, children seen as helpless tend to give up easily or show deterioration when working on hard problems. Other, mastery-oriented children use failure feedback to maintain or improve their performance. Helpless children may hold an entity theory of intelligence, whereas mastery-oriented children may hold an incremental theory of intelligence. Research indicates that these kinds of motivational differences may characterize even young, preschool children.
- Parents of different social classes may exhibit parenting styles and behaviors that encourage or inhibit their children's approach to schooling and their motivation

to excel. Lack of knowledge about school systems as well as language barriers may prevent many lower-social-class parents from helping their children achieve as they would like them to do.

- Changes in the contexts in which children perform are just as important as the other factors discussed. For example, the change in school context that occurs during the transition from elementary school to junior high tends to result in motivational declines for most students. This may be due to a mismatch between children's needs and the contexts in which they must perform.

Culture, Class, and Race

- Several factors mitigate against the success of the lower-class child in school, including parental attitudes and behavior, peer contexts, and teacher attitudes and behavior.
- Desegregation has not always improved race relations, and ethnic cleavages increase across grades, partly as a result of varying curricula and the lack of opportunity for children of different racial and ethnic groups to spend time together. Multiethnic activities such as team sports may have a modest positive impact.
- Trends toward desertion of affirmative action policies may reflect some current theorizing that African Americans have made greater social progress than has been thought. Other thinkers believe that U.S. society has still a long way to go toward true equal opportunity for all.
- Complex issues confront social scientists and others, who must ask such questions as, When are integrated programs most helpful and when are segregated methods of instruction more useful for children?

Special Children: The Policy of Inclusion

- Special children, such as those who are mentally retarded, often require special assistance. The controversy over the policy of **inclusion** continues, although there are some indications that programs designed especially for such children may be of considerable benefit.

Television: Harmful or Helpful?

- The role that television plays in socializing children is very great. TV viewing starts early in life, and viewing time gradually increases until adolescence.
- Children watch a variety of programs. Boys prefer action-adventure and sports programs, and girls prefer human social dramas. Many TV programs, however, especially children's cartoons, contain considerable aggressive and violent content.
- Although the very youngest children often display **magic window thinking**, children's cognitive skills develop gradually, and they become increasingly able to comprehend what they watch—to understand cause and effect relationships and to distinguish fantasy from reality.
- TV has beneficial effects, as indicated by the positive impact of educational programs such as "Sesame Street" or "The Electric Company" on children's cognitive development. Such programs are especially useful when children view them in a supportive home or school environment.

- Television viewing has many negative effects. Heavy viewing is correlated with poorer reading comprehension. It tends to displace other activities, such as participation in sports and other forms of recreation and social and community events. Minorities are only beginning to be fairly represented on TV, and TV programs still often serve to strengthen existing racial stereotypes. Exposure to aggressive and violent action on television may lead to aggressive behavior in children, and consumers who have heavy TV viewing habits may become immune to real-life violence.
- Advertising often engenders children's preferences for foods and toys that are not healthy and that may even be dangerous.
- Parents can modify the effects of TV by serving as interpreters of TV messages and managers of program selection.

Gender Roles and Gender Differences

C H A P T E R 15

GENDER-ROLE STANDARDS AND STEREOTYPES

GENDER DIFFERENCES IN DEVELOPMENT
Developmental Patterns of Gender Typing
Stability of Gender Typing
■ **BOX 15-1** *Child Psychology in Action:*
Will We Let Computers Widen the Gender Gap?

BIOLOGICAL FACTORS IN GENDER DIFFERENCES
Hormones and Social Behavior
Hormones and Cognitive Skills
Brain Lateralization and Gender Differences
Biology and Cultural Expectations

COGNITIVE FACTORS IN GENDER TYPING
Kohlberg's Cognitive Developmental Theory
Gender-Schema Theory: An Information-Processing Approach
A Comparison of Cognitive Developmental and Gender-Schema
    Theories

INFLUENCE OF THE FAMILY ON GENDER TYPING
Parents' Influence on Children's Gender-Typed Choices
Parental Behavior toward Girls and Boys
Modeling Parents' Characteristics
Parental Absence or Unavailability
Gender Roles in Children of Gay and Lesbian Parents

EXTRAFAMILIAL INFLUENCES ON GENDER ROLES
Books and Television
Peers, Gender Roles, and Self-Esteem
Schools and Teachers

ANDROGYNY
■ **BOX 15-2** *Perspectives on Diversity:*
Childrearing in Countercultural Families

SUMMARY

In most societies, males and females behave differently, are viewed and treated differently by others, and play distinctive roles. At the same time, there are many occasions and situations in which the two genders behave alike or nearly so, receive equal treatment from others, and play very similar roles. The challenge to developmental psychologists is to determine the nature of these differences and similarities and to articulate the varied processes that contribute to gender-specific patterns of similarities and differences.

Four primary theories have sought to explain these patterns. Freud's psychoanalytic theory proposed that the child, through a process of **identification,** acquired either feminine or masculine traits and behaviors by identifying with a same-sex parent. Because this process was not completed until the child had resolved his or her Oedipus or Electra complex (see Chapter 1), the child presumably did not identify with either gender until the age of 5 or 6. Cognitive social learning theory, which we introduced in Chapter 1, holds that children acquire gender identification both through direct guidance and encouragement from parents and by imitating parents and others about them. According to this view, children understand gender quite early, for as we will see, parents behave differently toward their male and female babies from the moment of birth. Gender-schema theory, an information-processing approach, proposes that children as young as 2½ begin to develop their own naive theories about gender differences and gender-appropriate behaviors. Finally, Lawrence Kohlberg's cognitive developmental theory asserts that children categorize themselves as male or female on the basis of physical and behavioral clues and then proceed to behave in gender-appropriate ways. According to Kohlberg, it's not until children are about 6 or 7 that they make true gender-typed choices.

But let's not forget some even more basic influences: Biological factors affect gender-based behaviors, too! Specific hormones and levels of those hormones as well as male-female differences in brain lateralization contribute to differences in male and female attitudes and behaviors. As we've stressed throughout this book, most human characteristics are products of both genetic and environmental forces, and gender behavior is no different.

We begin this chapter by examining some standards of female and male behavior common to the American culture and take a brief look at some quite different cross-cultural behaviors. We then consider some actual patterns of gender differences and ask how stable these patterns are over the life course. With at least a rudimentary understanding of what we're talking about in this chapter, we turn to the issue of biological influences in gender behavior. Next we explore cognitive factors, focusing on Kohlberg's approach and gender-schema theory. The balance of the chapter is devoted to considering the influences on gender behavior of parental teaching, reinforcement, and modeling and of the social forces represented by peer groups, schools, and the media. Essentially, these sections on family and extrafamilial influences illuminate the cognitive social learning approach, but they also incorporate concepts from the other cognitive theories we discuss in this chapter. We conclude with a brief look at androgyny, the quality of possessing within oneself both masculine and feminine psychological characteristics.

Before we move into the world of the child as male or female, we need to define some of the terms that guide research and thinking in the area of gender differences. To begin with, we use the terms *gender* and *sex* more or less interchangeably, for both refer to identity as either female or male. Traditionally, *gender* has been used to refer to cognitive and social issues and *sex* to biological and physiological matters, but it is often very difficult to separate these issues. Of course, we use the term *sex* solely when discussing either primary or secondary sex characteristics or specifically sexual behavior.

The process by which children acquire the values, motives, and behaviors viewed as appropriate to their gender in a specific culture, referred to as **gender typing,** is a multidimensional concept (Huston, 1983; Ruble & Martin, 1998). Children begin by developing **gender-based beliefs,** or ideas and expectations about what behaviors are

identification The Freudian notion that children acquire gender identity by identifying with and imitating their same-sex parents.

gender typing The process by which children acquire the values, motives, and behaviors considered appropriate for their gender in their particular culture.

gender-based beliefs Ideas and expectations about what is appropriate behavior for males and females.

appropiate for males and females. These beliefs are derived largely from **gender stereotypes,** which are the beliefs that members of an entire culture hold about the attitudes and behaviors that are acceptable and appropriate for each sex. These stereotypes prescribe the way males and females *should* be and *should* act. For example, in America, boys are expected to be sports oriented and aggressive, whereas girls are expected to be nonaggressive and to like caring for others. **Gender roles** are composites of the distinctive behaviors that males and females in a culture actually exhibit and thus are essentially the reflections of a culture's gender stereotypes. Early in life, children develop a **gender identity,** or a perception of themselves as either masculine or feminine and as having characteristics and interests that are gender typed. And finally, children develop **gender-role preferences**, or desires to possess certain gender-typed characteristics. Children's choices of toys and of play partners reflect these preferences. Later in the chapter we will encounter two other important terms, *gender stability* and *gender constancy,* and will define them at that time.

GENDER-ROLE STANDARDS AND STEREOTYPES

When children are still young infants, parents and other agents of socialization attempt systematically to teach them standards for behavior that are gender based and to shape different behaviors in boys and girls (Bandura, 1969). In fact, this process starts immediately after a baby's birth, when parents give the baby a name and bring her or him home to a nursery often decorated in gender-typed ways—flowered bumper pads and pale, beribboned lampshades or bright-colored curtains with sports or space themes. Parents dress male and female children in distinctive clothes, style their hair in different ways, select toys and activities for them that they deem gender appropriate, promote children's association with same-gender playmates, and often react negatively when children behave in ways they consider gender inappropriate.

One investigator who was studying gender differences in infancy and did not want her observers to know whether they were watching boys or girls complained that, even in the first few days of life, some parents brought their infant girls to the laboratory with pink bows tied to their wisps of hair or taped to their little bald heads. Later, when she tried again to conceal the children's gender by asking mothers to dress their infants in overalls, girls appeared in pink overalls and boys in blue ones! The frustrated experimenter commented to a colleague, "And would you believe, overalls with *ruffles?*"

In Western cultures particularly, the women's movement and the rise of feminism have led us to revise our ways of thinking about gender differences and gender roles. However, these topics remain highly controversial. In this chapter's discussions you will find two major threads. One is social scientists' continuing challenge to the traditional view that apparent differences between males and females—such as women's superior abilities at verbal tasks and men's superior performance on mathematical problems—are fixed for all time. The other thread is modern scientists' consistent focus, in their theorizing about gender behavior and roles, on the multiple influences that shape our gender roles, including biological, cognitive, and social factors.

Cultures are internally quite consistent with regard to their standards of "appropriate" gender-role behavior. In this chapter, unless we are specifically referring to people in another country, when we talk about culturally defined behavior as either masculine or feminine we will be talking about the U.S. culture. Keep in mind, however, that within the U.S. culture, gender roles and stereotypes vary as a function of a person's ethnic and social-class background. It is also important to note that we do not use the term *appropriate* to mean "desirable"; we mean, instead, what people in general *think* is appropriate—what is typical and generally accepted. Finally, although some of the gender-role standards we discuss may seem outdated to you, just remember that according to a considerable body of research, few gender stereotypes have changed since the 1970s!

gender stereotypes Beliefs that members of a culture hold about how females and males ought to behave; that is, what behaviors are acceptable and appropriate for each.

gender roles Composites of the behaviors actually exhibited by a typical male or female in a given culture; the reflection of a *gender stereotype* in everyday life.

gender identity The perception of oneself as either masculine or feminine.

gender-role preferences Desires to possess certain gender-typed characteristics.

In American society, the male role is stereotypically oriented toward controlling and manipulating the environment. Males are expected to be independent, assertive, dominant, and competitive in social and sexual relations. Females are expected to be relatively passive, loving, sensitive, and supportive in social relationships, especially in their family roles as wife and mother. In general, people regard the expression of warmth in personal relationships, the display of anxiety under pressure, and the suppression of overt aggression and sexuality as more appropriate for women than for men (Broverman, Vogel, Broverman, Clarkson, & Rosenkrantz, 1972). Despite the concern with gender equality that has grown over nearly 30 years, a recent comparison of gender stereotypes expressed in 1972 and 1988 by college students found no evidence of shifts over the intervening 16 years (Bergen & Williams, 1991; Liben & Bigler, 1987; McHale, Bartko, Crouter, & Perry-Jenkins, 1990). Moreover, cross-cultural studies have found these stereotypical roles widespread not only in the American culture but in a wide range of societies; in 25 countries from the American continents, Europe, Africa, Asia, and Oceania, a similar pattern of gender stereotypes appeared (Whiting & Edwards, 1988; Williams & Best, 1990).

There is, however, some variation in culturally accepted gender-role standards both within the United States and across cultures. Within the United States, gender-role standards vary with ethnicity, age, education, and occupation. For example, African American families are more likely to socialize children without strict boy-girl gender-role distinctions. These families value early independence for both boys and girls, and they make fewer gender distinctions in deciding who is to carry out which family roles and which family tasks (Gibbs, 1989; Peters, 1981). Moreover, African American families encourage girls to be aggressive and assertive and boys to express emotion and nurturance (Allen & Majidi-Abi, 1989; Basow, 1992). Among Mexican Americans, however, gender-role socialization standards for boys and girls are much more clearly differentiated (Ramirez, 1989). In this subculture, boys are expected to show independence earlier than females.

Age and education alters gender-role expectations as well. Young children are especially rigid in their gender stereotyping (Golombok & Fivush, 1994), and children between 3 and 6 years old are more gender stereotyped than adults (Signorella, Bigler, & Liben, 1993). This sense of absolutism about rules is common among young children. As they develop, children become more differentiated and flexible in their attitudes about a variety of concepts, including gender issues.

In the United States, female students and college-educated women between the ages of 18 and 35 are more likely than older or less educated females to perceive the feminine role as involving greater independence and achievement striving. Children with mothers who are employed in skilled occupations and professions also regard female educational and professional aspirations and the assumption of housekeep-

Despite the changes that have occurred in recent years in men's and women's roles in society, gender stereotypical roles are still widespread. In Japan, some women continue to teach their daughters to perform the formal and highly ritualized tea ceremony, and in the Philippines, some men train their sons in traditional male skills—here, a young boy learns the blacksmith trade.

ing and child-care tasks by males as more appropriate than do children whose mothers are fulltime homemakers. At the same time, men, even young educated men, maintain more stereotyped gender-role standards than do women (Basow, 1992; Golombok & Fivush, 1994). Moreover, single-earner fathers are more traditional in their gender-typed attitudes than fathers from dual-earner families, while mothers, whether working within or outside the home, did not differ in their gender-typed attitudes (McHale et al., 1990).

Adult men and women differ in the way they view gender typing in children. For example, one study found that men were more likely than women to rate the behaviors of 18-month-old toddlers as gender typed (Fagot, 1973). Perhaps these men saw what they expected to see. It is common to find fathers more concerned than mothers that their children maintain behaviors appropriate to their gender, and fathers have been seen to play a more important role in children's gender typing than mothers (Block, 1983; Siegel, 1987). However, researchers have recently challenged this view, suggesting that in view of recent shifts in male and female roles, mothers and fathers may play more similar roles in gender typing than previously thought (Fagot & Hagan, 1991; Lytton & Romney, 1991). It is interesting that in spite of some variations in gender-role standards among groups in the United States, almost all groups, regardless of gender, social class, and education, still view aggression as more characteristic of men and interpersonal sensitivity as more common in women (Basow, 1992). Note, however, that even within groups there are important individual differences in the *strength* with which people endorse these and other gender stereotypes (Beal, 1994).

One of the most frequently cited reports of divergence among cultures in gender-role standards and behavior is Margaret Mead's study of social roles in three primitive tribes: the Arapesh, the Mundugumor, and the Tchambuli (Mead, 1935). Little gender-role differentiation was prescribed by the Mundugumor and the Arapesh. However, the Arapesh men and women exhibited behaviors that in many societies would be regarded as feminine while the Mundugumor displayed behaviors traditionally thought of as masculine. The Arapesh were passive, cooperative, and unassertive, whereas both men and women in the Mundugumor tribe were hostile, aggressive, cruel, and restrictive. Both Arapesh mothers and fathers were actively involved in raising infants. In fact, Mead remarks, "If one comments upon a middle-aged Arapesh man as good-looking, the people answer: 'Good looking? Ye-e-e-s? But you should have seen him before he bore all those children!'" (Mead, 1935, p. 56).

Among the Tchambuli, Mead found a reversal of traditional gender roles. The men were dependent, socially sensitive and concerned with the feelings of others, and interested in arts and crafts. The women were independent and aggressive and played the controlling role in decision making. Although around the world the gender roles Western society labels traditional seem to be the most common, there is enough variability within and across cultures to suggest considerable plasticity in the development of masculine and feminine behaviors. If there are actually genetically based social and cognitive differences between males and females, apparently these differences can be considerably modified by cultural forces.

GENDER DIFFERENCES IN DEVELOPMENT

How accurately do gender stereotypes reflect differences in the actual gender role behaviors of males and females? As Table 15-1 shows, although clear gender differences have been found in some characteristics, many others that have been considered gender linked seem only questionably so, and still others are wholly mythical. Because gender differences that are not always observed are, by definition, suggestive only, we need more research in order to draw definite conclusions. Moreover, as children develop into adulthood, many differences emerge among adult men and women in terms of employment and work opportunities; power and status in the workplace;

TABLE 15-1   Gender Differences: Real, Only Occasional, or Completely Mythical?

SOME GENDER DIFFERENCES ARE REAL . . .

Physical, Motor, and Sensory Development
At birth, girls are physically and neurologically more advanced. They walk earlier, and they attain puberty earlier. Boys have more mature muscular development and larger lungs and heart, and at birth they are less sensitive to pain. With increasing age, boys become superior at activities involving strength and gross motor skills. On the other hand, male fetuses are more likely to be miscarried, and boys have a higher rate of infant mortality and are more vulnerable to many hereditary anomalies, malnutrition, disease. In terms of physical and physiological vulnerability, females are clearly not the weaker sex.

Cognitive Development
From infancy through the early school years, girls display superior verbal abilities, including vocabulary, reading comprehension, and verbal creativity. During middle childhood and adolescence, gender differences are either nonexistent or very small. From about age 10, boys display greater visual-spatial ability, which is involved in such tasks as manipulating objects in two- or three-dimensional space, reading maps, or aiming at a target. Beginning at about age 12, boys excel in mathematics, especially mathematical reasoning.

Social and Emotional Development
Even in early social play, boys are more often the aggressors and the victims of aggression, particularly physical aggression. Girls tend to use more indirect forms of aggression, such as excluding another child from social interaction. As early as age 2, girls are more likely to comply with the demands of parents and other adults. Boys are more variable in their responses to adult direction. We don't find gender differences in compliance consistently in peer relations, although preschool boys are less likely to comply with girls' demands than with boys' demands, and less likely to comply than girls are with partners of either gender. Girls are more nurturant toward younger children.

Atypical Development
Boys are more likely to have genetic defects, physical disabilities, mental retardation, reading disabilities, speech defects, and school and emotional problems.

OTHERS MAY BE FOUND ONLY SOMETIMES . . .

Activity Level
Many studies find no gender differences in activity level. When they do find differences, it is usually boys who are more active than girls.

Dependency
Younger children do not display gender differences in dependency. Older girls and women tend to rate themselves as more dependent, but this is probably changing.

Fear, Timidity, and Anxiety
Again, young children do not exhibit consistent gender differences in timidity. Older girls and women report themselves as being more fearful, and males are more likely to involve themselves in physically risky recreations and occupations. On the other hand, many women today are in dangerous occupations (e.g., firefighting, high-steel construction) and enjoy risky sports (e.g., mountain climbing, hang gliding).

homemaking, child-care, and family obligations; sexual experiences and concerns; and, of course, reproductive experiences that shape and regulate our lives (Beal, 1994; Ruble & Martin, 1998; Tavris, 1992).

In examining Table 15-1 and studying our discussions of gender differences, keep in mind that the characteristics of males and females overlap considerably. Some males are more compliant, verbal, and interested in the arts than some females. Similarly, although males generally are physically designed for greater strength and thus are better adapted for successful aggressive interactions, some women are pretty hardy types, as witnessed not only by their greater health and longevity but by their growing success in team sports like basketball and hockey. In addition, in the area of intellectual and occupational achievement there are outstanding women architects, mathematicians, engineers, and scientists. Unfortunately, males still get more encouragement in these areas.

TABLE 15-1   Gender Differences: Real, Only Occasional, or Completely Mythical? *(concluded)*

Exploratory Activity

Studies do not find consistent gender differences in exploratory activity. A number of studies of early exploratory activity have found boys to be more venturesome and curious and more likely to attack barriers intervening between themselves and a desirable object.

Vulnerability to Stress

Findings over the last decade suggest that males may be more vulnerable to family disharmony and interpersonal stress, as evidenced by an overrepresentation of boys in child guidance clinics. However, we need further research to draw firm conclusions.

Orientation to Social Stimuli

Some evidence indicates that infant girls may orient to faces more than boys and may recognize their mother's faces at an earlier age.

AND STILL OTHERS ARE WHOLLY MYTHICAL . . .

Sociability

Boys and girls are equally social; they spend as much time with others and are equally responsive to others. There's no gender difference in the need for love and attachment. Males and females are equally capable of nurturance, although girls and women do more of the actual care of children, relatives, and friends.

Suggestibility and Conformity

Girls and boys do not differ in suggestibility or in the tendency to conform to standards of a peer group or to imitate the responses of others.

Learning Style

Boys and girls are equally good at rote learning and simple repetitive tasks. They also display similar skills in tasks involving the inhibition of previously learned responses and in complex cognitive tasks. Girls and boys are equally responsive to visual and auditory stimuli.

Achievement

Girls and boys generally display equal levels of achievement motivation. Under neutral conditions girls are often more achievement-oriented than boys, but in a competitive situation, boys are more likely to exhibit enhanced achievement motivation than girls.

Self-Esteem

Boys and girls do not differ in self-esteem. However, girls rate themselves as more competent in social skills, and boys view themselves as stronger and more powerful.

Verbal Aggressiveness and Hostility

Girls and boys engage equally in verbal aggression but use different approaches: Girls tend to gossip and exclude others; boys are more directly verbally assaultive.

Sources: Crick et al., 1998; Hyde & Linn, 1988; Hyde & Plant, 1995; Linn & Hyde, 1989; Maccoby & Jacklin, 1974; Tavris, 1992.

Developmental Patterns of Gender Typing

Children develop gender-typed behavior patterns at an early age (Beal, 1994; Ruble & Martin, 1998). As Figure 15-1 shows, 15- to 36-month-old toddlers in a day-care center had already developed clear preferences for toys that were gender appropriate (O'Brien, Huston, & Risley, 1983). Note, however, that girls were more likely than boys to choose gender-inappropriate toys. Why do you suppose girls are more likely to play with a truck than boys are to cuddle a doll? Let's look at some reasons.

Western culture is basically male oriented, according greater esteem, privileges, and status to the masculine role. The male role is more clearly defined, and there is greater pressure for boys than for girls to conform to narrow gender-appropriate standards. Although the situation is gradually changing, boys shy away from things that are "for girls," fearing derision from other boys, whereas girls may want to do things that are regarded as higher status. In short, although we tolerate

■ FIGURE 15-1
Choosing boys', girls', or
unisex toys.
Preschool boys clearly preferred
toys considered appropriate for
boys, but the girls were more
eclectic in their choices. (*Source:*
O'Brien, Risley, and Huston,
1983)

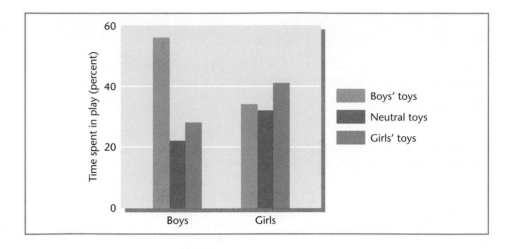

■ FIGURE 15-1
Choosing boys', girls', or unisex toys.
Preschool boys clearly preferred toys considered appropriate for boys, but the girls were more eclectic in their choices. (*Source:* O'Brien, Risley, and Huston, 1983)

tomboys, we reject sissies. Parents and peers condemn boys for crying, retreating in the face of aggression, wearing feminine apparel, or playing with dolls. In contrast, we tend to accept a girl's occasional temper tantrum, rough-and-tumble play, wearing of jeans, or playing with trucks.

Boys and girls do develop distinctive patterns of interest that are consistent with gender stereotypes. In a national survey of more than 2,000 children between the ages of 7 and 11, Zill (1986) found that boys liked guns, boxing, wrestling and karate, team sports, and fixing and making things more than girls did. In contrast, girls preferred dolls, sewing, cooking, dancing, and looking after younger children more than boys did. Parents and others encourage these patterns of interest in a variety of ways, including assigning household tasks. Even in the 1990s, girls are more likely to make beds, clean, prepare meals, wash dishes, and do laundry. Boys are more likely to fix things, take out the garbage, and mow lawns (Goodnow, 1988, 1996; McHale et al., 1990). Unfortunately, as Box 15-1 suggests, parents and others in society also differentially encourage and discourage certain academic interests in boys and girls, which may be detrimental to children in the long run.

Remember that families differ, and some boys wash dishes and some girls fix cars! Nevertheless, a great many "old" stereotypes still persist in contemporary roles for boys and girls.

Stability of Gender Typing

Masculinity or femininity not only appears to develop early but is a stable personality characteristic. The longitudinal Fels Institute Study, which examined the development of a group of middle-class children from birth to adulthood, found that adult heterosexual behavior could be predicted from gender-typed interests in elementary school (Kagan & Moss, 1962). Figure 15-2 presents a summary of the relationship between some selected child behaviors and similar adult behaviors. Boys who were interested in competitive games, activities that required gross motor skills, and such things as mechanics, and girls who were interested in cooking, sewing, reading, and noncompetitive games were involved in similar gender-typed activities in adulthood.

The stability of many of the personality characteristics investigated was related to cultural acceptance. That is, when a characteristic conflicted with gender-role standards, it led in adulthood to some more socially acceptable behavior (e.g., dependence in a boy might lead to entrepreneurial endeavors in an adult). When a characteristic was congruent with such standards, however, it tended to remain stable from childhood to maturity (e.g., dependence in a girl might lead to a preference for a less aggressive role in business in an adult). In some cases, however, stability appeared to be related to gender: In males, but not in females, childhood sexuality and aggression were predictive of adult sexuality and anger. In females, but not in males, childhood

BOX 15-1

Child Psychology in Action

Will We Let Computers Widen the Gender Gap?

Computers are becoming commonplace in classrooms, but do boys and girls benefit equally from this technological revolution? Studying many types of computer activities that are available to children—elective courses in school, summer camps and after-school clubs—as well as the use of computers at home, Mark Lepper (1985; Lepper & Gurtner, 1989) found large gender differences in girls' and boys' use of these opportunities. In formal computer programs there were as many as 5 to 10 boys for every girl, and this difference in participation rates increased as activities became more costly and more effortful. In California schools, boys outnumbered girls in introductory programming classes by a 2 to 1 ratio, but in advanced programming classes, the ratio was as high as 10 to 15 boys for each girl.

What may be the reasons for this gender gap? The computer field—like the fields of math and science—has long been dominated by males, in large part because of the myth that males are more capable than females in technical subjects. Thus the computer science field has few female role models. On the basis of similarly faulty reasoning, parents are more likely to buy a computer for a son than for a daughter. In his study, Lepper found that families with only boys were twice as likely to own a computer as families with only girls. Computer labs in schools are often competitive, noisy, and high-activity environments in which boys may feel more comfortable than girls.

The kinds of programs that are often used to introduce students to computers seem also to have been written for boys (Schofield, 1995). The two most common themes of games are war and violence and male-gender-typed sports like football. Even the titles of specifically educational games may turn girls off: Alien Addition, Demolition Division, Spelling Baseball. It's not surprising, therefore, to find that boys play electronic games more often than girls and that they tend to make more gender distinctions about the acceptability of these games for either boys or girls. According to Funk and Buchman (1996), although most fourth and fifth graders of both genders thought both girls and boys could play video games, boys were considerably more likely than girls to say that playing video games was not an acceptable activity for girls. Boys clearly spent more time at such games, and they were a good deal more likely than girls to describe video game playing as their favorite activity. A number of boys also said that girls who spent a lot of time playing video games were not popular and that if girls wanted to be popular they ought not play such games, especially "the fighting games." Few girls agreed with these statements; as many as a third held that fighting games were okay for girls.

Funk and Buchman concluded that boys tended to be more gender stereotyped in their attitudes toward electronic game playing. This finding is consistent with other research which suggests that females are more flexible than males in their attitudes toward gender roles.

In spite of the fact that computers have many varied uses, including word processing and graphic design, schools typically present computers as mathematical tools. Computer labs are usually found in the math department and math teachers supervise their use. In addition, credits for computer courses often count toward math requirements. Inasmuch as girls have long been brainwashed into believing that they can't do math as well as boys, this arrangement both keeps girls away from computers and reinforces the myth. As Lepper (1985) notes, the ultimate result is to turn girls ever further away from careers in math and science.

When girls and boys learn that they are equally apt at math and science, boys' edge being confined to the area of spatial visualization, perhaps they will be equally interested in using computers as learning aids and in other ways. It seems clear that if we don't ensure that children understand their capabilities early on, we may instead ensure that the gender gap will widen.

---

passivity was predictive of similar adult behaviors. However, this study was conducted several decades ago, and less stability may be evident in the 1990s.

In both genders, behaviors that are deemed gender inappropriate and that are thus likely to be eliminated through socialization often do emerge in adulthood but in altered forms. For example, girlhood anger and tantrums may evolve in adult women as intellectual competitiveness, masculine interests, and conflict over dependency needs. Passivity in boys, on the other hand, may be related in adult men to social apprehension, noncompetitiveness, and sexual anxiety. Even in adulthood there is evidence of stability: In one study that spanned a 10-year period, researchers found that 54 percent of adults continued to be rated similarly in terms of masculinity or femininity (Hyde, Krajnik, & Skuldt-Neiderberger, 1991).

However, not all adults maintain the same gender roles over their life course. Gender roles fluctuate as adults change to meet the demands of new situations and circumstances. One of the most important transitions—parenthood—is associated

■ FIGURE 15-2
Relationships between childhood and adult behaviors.
The highest correlations between male behaviors in childhood and adulthood were obtained for achievement orientation and intellectual concerns and for gender-typed activities. For females, achievement-intellectual concerns tied with passivity-withdrawal for highest correlation, and gender-typed activity was a close third. Note that, in general, childhood-adulthood correlations for males were higher than those for females, with the exception of passivity-withdrawal and dependence. (*Source:* Kagan and Moss, 1962)

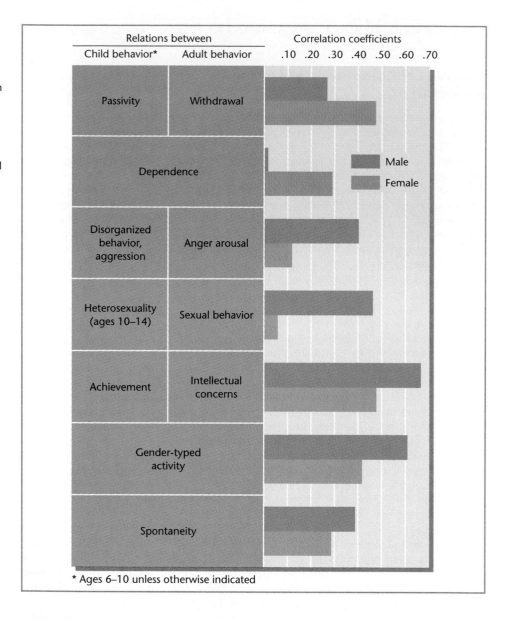

expressive characteristics
Presumably typical of females, these characteristics include nurturance and concern with feelings.

instrumental characteristics
Presumably typical of males, these characteristics include task and occupation orientation.

with a sharp divergence of gender roles. Even among egalitarian couples who are committed to equal sharing of household tasks, the onset of parenthood generally heralds a return to traditional gender roles (Cowan & Cowan, 1992; Parke, 1996). In these roles, women are seen as having more **expressive characteristics**—they are more nurturant, concerned with feelings, and child oriented. Men, on the other hand, are thought to have more **instrumental characteristics**—they are more task and occupation oriented. Self-perceptions of gender roles shift as well. As they age, men tend to become more expressive and nurturant, especially in old age. Women tend to become more autonomous as they develop, but return to a more feminine gender-role orientation in old age, perhaps in part because as one becomes less self-sufficient, one has a greater need for help (Hyde et al., 1991). Thus, gender typing is best viewed as an ongoing and changing process; development in this area clearly continues across the years of adulthood.

BIOLOGICAL FACTORS IN GENDER DIFFERENCES

Most research on the influence of biological factors on gender-role typing has focused on two principal areas: hormonal function and cerebral lateralization. In this section we begin by exploring how hormones influence gender typing, both in social behavior and in the development of cognitive skills. We then examine how the lateralization of brain function affects gender differences in development and discover that females are more bilateral than males. Finally, we consider the ways in which biology and cultural notions of gender-appropriate behaviors interact to influence gender typing.

Hormones and Social Behavior

Hormones are powerful and highly specialized chemical substances that interact with cells programmed to receive hormonal messages and to respond to them. Hormones associated with sexual characteristics and with reproductive functions are found in differing concentrations in males and females from infancy through adulthood. Women have small amounts of the "male" hormone testosterone and men have small amounts of "female" hormones like estrogen and progesterone. The differences in the concentrations of these hormones in prepubertal boys and girls of preschool and elementary-school age are not great, but they become quite prominent in adolescents and adults.

Both the prenatal and pubertal periods may be critical periods in terms of the effect of hormonal action on the development of human beings (Hines, 1993; Hoyenga & Hoyenga, 1993). In the prenatal period, hormones organize the biological and psychological predispositions to be masculine or feminine, and the surge in hormonal function during puberty (Chapter 6) activates these early predispositions.

Hormonal differences experienced prenatally or during the subsequent course of development may contribute to differences in social behavior between the sexes and among people of the same sex. When Young, Goy, and Phoenix (1967) injected pregnant monkeys with testosterone during the second quarter of pregnancy, the monkeys' offspring were pseudohermaphroditic females who exhibited not only physical changes in their genitalia but also social behavior patterns that are characteristic of male monkeys. These infant female monkeys manifested masculine behaviors such as more threatening gestures, less withdrawal from approach or threat by other animals, more mounting behavior, and more rough-and-tumble play.

Subsequent studies have found that if male hormones are injected into normal female monkeys after birth but preceding puberty, these females also become more assertive, sometimes even attaining prime dominance status in their monkey troop. They may restrict sexual behavior and rough-and-tumble play between males and demand more restrained and docile behavior from their followers.

The relation between testosterone and aggression is useful in demonstrating the complexities of interactions between biological and environmental factors, some of which may be reciprocal. For example, in one study, not only were testosterone levels in young adult male monkeys associated with aggression, but subjecting a male to stress and repeated defeats, and making it impossible for the male to become dominant caused a drop in the animal's testosterone levels (Hood, Draper, Crockett, & Petersen, 1987). Thus testosterone may cause social responses, but social experiences may alter testosterone levels as well.

A dramatic example of the way social experience can modify the effects of hormonal factors is demonstrated in the classic studies of John Money and his colleagues (Ehrhardt, 1987; Money, 1987; Money & Annecillo, 1987; Money & Ehrhardt, 1972). These investigators studied prenatal hormonal anomalies, such as high levels of androgen in a female fetus, which result in masculinizing the female child and causing mistaken sexual identity. Many of the participants in these studies were female infants who had normal internal female reproductive organs but an enlarged clitoris that resembled a penis and labial folds that were often fused, resembling a scrotum. Money found that if such a child were reassigned to her correct feminine gender role after the first few years of life, her gender typing was inadequate, and she made a poor psychological adjustment. If reassignment were early,

TURNING POINTS: Development of Gender Roles and Gender Typing

FROM BIRTH	Father typically greets male infant with something like "Hey, Tiger"/female infant with "Hello, little darlin'" or some such expression
	Parents typically set stage for gender typing by dressing baby and decorating nursery in pink or blue
	Parents select gender-appropriate toys, promote contact with same-gender playmates, react disapprovingly when child displays behavior that's "inappropriate" for gender
	Other adults describe boys as "strong," "active" and girls as "sweet," "cuddly"
1 YEAR	Child may recognize male and female faces as belonging to two distinct categories
18 MONTHS OR YOUNGER	Fathers are more likely to gender-type children than mothers
2 YEARS	Child can correctly label own gender but has limited understanding of gender identity and its wider implications
	As they approach 3 years of age, children begin to grasp concept of gender identity
3 YEARS	Children understand that they themselves, along with other children, belong to a gender *class*
	They've developed clear preferences for gender-appropriate toys by this time
3–6 YEARS	Children of this age range are more gender stereotyped than adults
4 YEARS	Children who grasped gender identity early (before 27 months) have greater knowledge of gender-role stereotypes
4–5 YEARS	Children begin to understand the concept of gender stability but do not grasp it fully until about the age of 7
	Children 4 and younger tend to rely more on gender schemas than do children 5 and older
	By 4½ children spend three times as much time with same-gender playmates as with other-gender peers
	Girls interact more with babies and in a more active way than boys do
5 YEARS	Few children this age show knowledge of traits
4–6 YEARS	Boys are more likely than girls to congregate in same-gender groups
6½ YEARS	Children spend 11 times as much time with same-gender playmates as with other-gender children
6–7 YEARS	Children now understand gender stability and also grasp gender constancy
7–11 YEARS	Children develop distinct patterns of interest in activities that are consistent with cultural gender stereotypes
8 YEARS	Most children display knowledge of gender-typed traits
6–13 YEARS	Studies of children in this age range suggest that female brains may be more bilaterally organized than male brains

Sources: Beal, 1994; Golombok & Fivush, 1994; Huston, 1993; Ruble & Martin, 1998.
Note: Developmental events described in this and other Turning Points charts represent overall trends identified in research studies. Individual children vary greatly in the ages at which they achieve these developmental changes.

however, most girls experienced normal psychosexual development. The authors concluded that there is a "critical period" for the establishment of gender role between birth and the age of 3.

Money found that 25 fetally androgenized girls who were raised as girls—and given corrective surgery if necessary—were characterized by tomboyishness. These girls enjoyed vigorous athletic activities, like ball games. They showed little interest in such things as playing with dolls or baby-sitting or caring for younger children. They also preferred simple utilitarian clothing, such as slacks and shorts, and showed little concern with cosmetics, jewelry, or hairstyles. Not only were these girls' play and grooming interests more like those of boys, but their assertiveness and attitudes toward sexuality and achievement were also more like male behavior.

Later studies (Berenbaum & Snyder, 1995; Hines & Kaufman, 1994) confirmed some of Money's classic findings, including preference for boys' toys and for boys as playmates. It seems clear that biology alone does not determine gender roles. Shaping these roles may well involve an interplay between biological factors and environmental influences (Ruble, 1988).

Hormones and Cognitive Skills

Researchers have suggested that at a critical period in prenatal development sex hormones may determine a fetus's potentials for brain organization and hemispheric lateralization and that these events may, in turn, lead to gender differences in males' and females' verbal and spatial skills. Studies suggest, for example, that prenatal hormones may sensitize female brains to process verbal information more effectively and male brains to process spatial information more accurately. To date, however, research relating early hormonal levels to later abilities has yielded mixed findings.

In one study, girls whose blood at birth showed high-normal levels of androgens (testosterone and androstanedione) had lower scores on tests of spatial ability when they entered school than girls whose blood at birth showed low-normal androgen levels (Jacklin, Wilcox, & Maccoby, 1988). Similarly, a later study (Finegan, Niccols, & Sitarenios, 1992) found that female fetuses with higher levels of androgens later showed lesser spatial and numerical abilities than other girls. However, in non-normal samples, where prenatal androgen levels in female fetuses are exceptionally high, these effects may be reversed. Resnick, Berenbaum, Gottesman & Bouchard (1986) found that in adolescence, such girls had better visual-spatial skills than other girls. Perhaps the "masculine" behavior of these girls led to differential encouragement of pursuits, like team sports, that facilitated their spatial abilities.

Some evidence of gender differences in spatial abilities comes from studies of children's understanding of horizontals and verticals in the physical world. Consider the following situations. A glass of water is tipped from an upright position to an angle of 50 degrees. What would the water level in the glass look like? Or how would a lightbulb suspended by a cord hanging from the ceiling of a van look if the van drove up a hill inclined at 50 degrees? As Figure 15-3 shows, boys and girls in grades 3 to 11 answer differently. Boys are more likely to make correct judgments about both the water level and the position of the lightbulb and cord (Liben, 1991; Liben & Golbeck, 1980). Although males and females continue to differ in these kinds of judgments at all ages, both girls and boys improve in their judgments as they become older. This suggests that genetically based differences can be modified by environmental experiences, just as we saw in Chapter 4.

Study of male superiority at spatial processing has helped to explode the myth that males are superior to females in math (Benbow, 1988; Casey, 1996). Why? Because, according to Hyde, Fennema, and Lamon (1990), male superiority in math is found *only* in performance on problems in geometry, a form of mathematics that requires spatial visualization skills! In fact, girls do better in computational skills than boys, and there are no gender differences in girls' and boys' performance

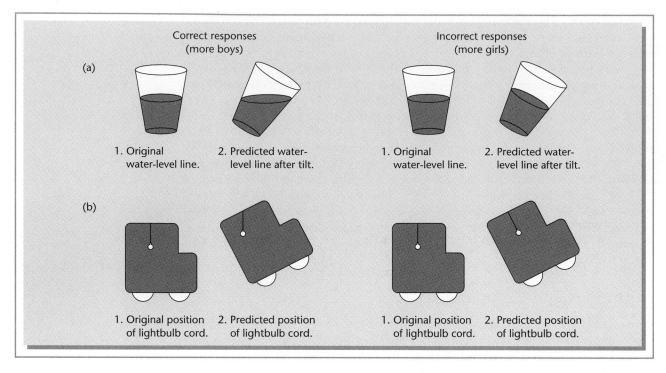

■ FIGURE 15-3
Boys' and girls' understanding of horizontal and vertical relations. Between the ages of about 8 or 9 to about 16 or 17, boys tend to make correct predictions of changes in horizontals and verticals following tilt, whereas girls are more likely to predict the results incorrectly. In general, boys seem to be more skilled at visual-spatial tasks. (*Source:* Liben & Golbeck, 1980)

on tests either of basic math knowledge or on algebra—which is less reliant on spatial ability than geometry (Hyde et al., 1990).

Spatial reasoning ability may depend in part on participation in physical activities in which one must understand one's body position vis-à-vis one's teammates and have the ability to judge size and distance (e.g., hit a home run or drop a ball in the basket). According to Beal (1994), girls' greater participation in sports in recent years may have something to do with the fact that their performance on spatial reasoning has also improved (Feingold, 1988). We still have a long way to go on this issue, for even in today's schools, girls rarely have the opportunity to participate in a full range of sports.

It is very important to note not only that the demonstrated difference between males and females in spatial ability is relatively small but also that even if researchers established a clearly biological basis for this gender difference, it would not mean that spatial abilities are not culturally influenced and environmentally modifiable (Linn & Hyde, 1989; Petersen & Gitelson, 1984; Ruble & Martin, 1998). For example, it has been suggested that boys are encouraged more often than girls to play with toys—such as building sets—that involve spatial abilities and to undertake mathematical and scientific endeavors (Beal, 1994; Kimball, 1989; Sherman, 1980). Moreover, U.S. researchers have found that mothers of first-grade children *believe* that boys are better at mathematics and girls at reading (recall our discussion of the Pygmalion effect, in Chapter 13). Investigators in other countries—for example, Japan and Taiwan—have found the same thing (Lummis & Stevenson, 1990). Perhaps it is in part because of the faulty assumptions people make about girls' math abilities that girls enroll in increasingly fewer mathematics and science courses over the high school and college years. Indeed, it becomes more difficult to interest even those girls who have displayed superior mathematical abilities to remain involved in the subject (Eccles, 1985). For example, in a study of California schools between 1983 and 1987, girls made up only about 38 percent of physics classes, 34 percent of advanced physics classes, and 42 percent of chemistry classes (Linn & Hyde, 1991). Fortunately, recent evidence suggests that this particular gender gap is narrowing (Feingold, 1988; Hyde et al., 1990). Perhaps changing gender-role standards are beginning to have some effects.

Brain Lateralization and Gender Differences

Behavior is determined to some extent by the organization of the two cerebral hemispheres, and brain functioning becomes increasingly specialized and lateralized with age. As we discussed in Chapter 6, in most people the right hemisphere is more involved in processing spatial information and the left hemisphere in processing verbal information.

There is some evidence that men's brains are more lateralized that women's (Halpern, 1992; Springer & Deutsch, 1989). For example, women whose left hemispheres suffer damage are less likely than men with similar damage to experience verbal deficits, and right-hemisphere-damaged women show fewer spatial deficits than do men (Halpern, 1992; Witelson & Swallow, 1987). Also supporting the notion that women are more bilateral than men are the results of a study in which boys and girls between the ages of 6 and 13 had to recognize shapes merely by handling them. Boys were more accurate in recognizing shapes with their left hands, but girls were just as accurate in perceiving shapes with their right as with their left hands (Witelson, 1978). Moreover, studies of spatial tasks have yielded similar evidence of lesser lateralization in females (Reite et al., 1993).

Recent studies using brain-imaging techniques that detect blood flow in the brain as people perform different cognitive tasks have confirmed this greater bilaterality among females. In a task in which men and women participants were asked to decide if nonsense words rhymed, both left and right sides of women's brains were activated; in men, however, only the left hemisphere was activated (Shaywitz, Shaywitz, Pugh, & Constable, 1995). Recall from Chapter 6 that even infants show this gender difference in patterns of brain activation in a word comprehension task.

Biology and Cultural Expectations

Researchers have asked what role people's physical bodies play in shaping gender-role standards and gender typing. For example, are the female's abilities to carry a fetus to term and to breast-feed her child related to some kind of biological programming that causes her to be more responsive than a male to the sights and signals of infants and children? Investigators have found that by the age of 4 or 5, girls interact more with babies and in a more active way than boys do. When asked to care for a baby, boys are inclined to watch the baby passively, whereas girls are more likely to engage actively in taking care of the baby (Berman, 1987; Reid, Tate, & Berman, 1989).

These behavioral tendencies, however, could as easily be due to cultural expectations and training as to biological differences (Parke, 1996). Interestingly, in adolescents and adults, such gender-based differential behavior is less apparent under conditions of privacy than in situations where people know that someone is observing them (Berman, 1987). And when experimenters have used subtle measures of responsiveness to an infant's crying, such as changes in blood pressure, electrical skin conductance, or other responses of the autonomic nervous system, they have not detected any differences in mothers' and fathers' responses to the child (Frodi, Lamb, Leavitt, & Donovan, 1978). Indeed, factors other than gender may determine responsiveness to a child. For example, research has shown that young mothers are more responsive to babies than are childless women (Nash & Feldman, 1981). It seems very likely that men's and women's responses to babies are to a considerable extent conditioned by culturally sanctioned gender roles. Biological programming notwithstanding, culture may have considerable impact on behavior.

COGNITIVE FACTORS IN GENDER TYPING

Biology and social influences are not the only determinants of gender typing. Children's own understanding of gender roles and rules may contribute to the developmental process of gender-role acquisition. Two related questions are central to understanding the role of cognition in the development of gender differences. First, when do children acquire different types of gender information? (As you study this section and the rest of the chapter you may find it useful to refer to our Turning Points chart on page 596, which offers some chronological information about children's development of gender concepts.) Second, does knowledge modify children's gender-role activities and behavior? In this section we explore two cognitive approaches to gender typing: Kohlberg's cognitive developmental theory and an information-processing-based approach called gender-schema theory. Both theories share the assumption that human beings take an active role in perceiving and interpreting information from the environment—that we are not passively shaped by environmental forces. Cognitively oriented scientists assume that people use implicit theories to interpret environmental information and that in so doing they create environments that will support their theories (Martin, 1992). For example, our views of appropriate gender roles may lead us to select activities and social partners consistent with these views.

Kohlberg's Cognitive Developmental Theory

cognitive developmental theory of gender typing Kohlberg's theory that children use physical and behavioral clues to differentiate gender roles and to gender-type themselves very early in life.

Lawrence Kohlberg's (1966) provocative **cognitive developmental theory of gender typing** proposes that children's differentiation of gender roles and their perception of themselves as more like same-gender than opposite-gender models begins very early, before the Freudian process of identification and without the reinforcement or modeling hypothesized by cognitive social learning theory. According to Kohlberg, the child, using physical and behavioral clues such as hairstyle or occupation, categorizes himself or herself as male or female; the child then finds it rewarding to behave in a gender-appropriate manner and to imitate same-gender models. For example, the girl's thinking goes something like this: "I am a girl because I am more like my mother and other girls than like boys; therefore I want to dress like a girl, play girl games, and feel and think like a girl." Consistency between children's actual gender, the way they see themselves, and their behaviors and values is critical in sustaining their self-esteem.

Kohlberg thinks all children go through three phases in gaining an understanding of gender. First, as we have just seen, the child acquires basic gender identity, recognizing that she or he is a girl or a boy, which in turn serves to organize incoming information and attitudes (Huston, 1983). Children acquire gender identity, according to Kohlberg, between the ages of 2 and 3. Second, the child acquires the concept of **gender stability:** By the age of 4 or 5 the child accepts that males remain male and females remain female. The little boy no longer thinks he might grow up to be a mommy, and the little girl gives up

gender stability The notion that gender does not change; males remain male and females remain female.

These children don't seem worried that either rock-climbing, a more stereotypically male activity, or sewing, more traditionally a female task, will alter their gender; they have grasped the notion of gender constancy.

her heady hopes of becoming Batman. And, third, by about 6 or 7 the child acquires the notion of **gender constancy**, recognizing that superficial changes in appearance or activities do not alter gender. Even when a girl wears jeans or plays football, or when a boy wears long hair or has a burning interest in needlepoint, she or he recognizes—and peers recognize, too—that gender remains constant. This achievement is important because Kohlberg argues that gender constancy should influence sex-typed choices.

What is the evidence for Kohlberg's developmental progression? Researchers who have tested his theory have confirmed that both boys and girls acquire gender identity first, an understanding of stability next, and finally an appreciation of constancy (Martin & Little, 1990; Slaby & Frey, 1975). Moreover, children in other cultures (Belize, Kenya, Nepal, and American Samoa) show a similar progression in their understanding of gender (Munroe, Shimmin, & Munroe, 1984). Working-class children and children in nonindustrialized cultures, however, reach these milestones approximately a year later than middle-class U.S. children (Frey & Ruble, 1992).

Some researchers have suggested that the process by which children come to recognize males and females as distinct categories probably has its origins in early infancy—well before babies can understand labels and language. In one study, 75 percent of 12-month-old infants were able to recognize male and female faces as belonging to distinctive categories (Leinbach & Fagot, 1992). This is not the same thing as recognizing that you yourself belong to one of these categories, but it does suggest that the process of understanding of gender begins earlier than Kohlberg originally thought.

The ability to understand gender labels such as *boy* and *girl* is not far behind. By the time they're 2 years old, children can correctly label their own gender, but they still have a very limited understanding of gender identity (Fagot & Leinbach, 1992). Young children have some understanding of gender words such as *man* and *woman* and recognize that some activities and objects are associated with each gender. For example, they recognize that men wear neckties and women don't and that women sometimes wear skirts but men never do, but it's not until they're about 3 years old that they grasp the concept that they themselves, along with other children, belong to a *gender class* or *group*.

We think now that children begin to grasp the notions of gender stability and constancy around the age of 5, but that they do not fully appreciate the meaning of these concepts until they are about 7. Consider the following exchange between two 4-year-old boys. A boy named Jeremy who wore a barrette to nursery school was accused by another boy of being a girl because "only girls wear barrettes." Jeremy pulled down his pants to show that he really was a boy. His young classmate replied, "Everyone has a penis; only girls wear barrettes" (Bem, 1983, p. 607). Clearly he did not yet understand gender constancy.

Genital knowledge is an important determinant of gender constancy. Bem (1989, 1993) showed nursery schoolers anatomically correct photos of a nude boy and a nude girl and then showed the youngsters pictures of the same children dressed in either clothing appropriate to their own gender or clothing appropriate to the opposite gender. Even when boys wore dresses or girls wore pants, nearly 40 percent of the children correctly identified the gender of the child in spite of the opposite-gender clothing. When Bem then tested the preschoolers' understanding of genital differences between the sexes, she found that nearly 60 percent of the children who possessed genital knowledge had shown gender constancy on the photo test, whereas only 10 percent of children who lacked genital knowledge had displayed gender constancy.

When gender constancy applies to children themselves they seem to understand it earlier than when it applies to others (Eaton & VonBargen, 1981; Wehren & DeLisi, 1983). Preschoolers (ages 2½ to 6) could label their own gender before the gender of other children (95% versus 90%), showed better understanding of their own gender stability than the gender stability of others (87% versus 82%), and showed a similar

gender constancy The awareness that superficial alterations in appearance or activity do not alter gender.

pattern for gender constancy (30% versus 20%). Children achieved gender constancy by 4½ years of age when considering themselves but did not understand that this concept applied to other children until they were 5½ years old. Young children are certain that no matter how much they might want to be transformed into a member of the opposite gender, this could not happen, but they are not so sure about that kid down the street! In addition, as you might expect, gender constancy is related to a child's level of cognitive functioning and to performance on Piagetian tasks of physical conservation (Chapter 9). The ability to conserve requires that a child recognize the constancy of physical objects in spite of the appearance of superficial transformations (Brown & Pipp, 1991; Marcus & Overton, 1978).

Gender-Schema Theory: An Information-Processing Approach

gender-schema theory
The notion that children develop schemas, or naive theories, that help them organize and structure their experience related to gender differences and gender roles.

Another cognitive approach to sex typing, **gender-schema theory,** derives from modern information-processing perspectives (Bem, 1981, 1993; Martin, 1993; Martin & Halverson, 1981, 1983). According to this viewpoint, children develop *schemas,* or naive theories, that help them organize and structure experience related to gender differences and gender roles. These schemas tell the child the kinds of information to look for in the environment and how to interpret such information. In Chapter 14 we discussed how children's theories about intelligence may cause them to perceive and respond to achievement situations and to success and failure in different ways. In a similar manner, according to Martin and Halverson (1981), children's beliefs about gender stereotypes are important because they are relevant to their emerging self-concepts and because they are salient in their everyday worlds.

Do gender-role schemas affect the way children see things? To find out, Martin and Halverson (1983) showed 5- and 6-year-olds pictures of males and females involved in activities that were either gender-consistent (e.g., a boy playing with a train) or gender-inconsistent (e.g., a girl sawing wood). A week later the researchers asked the children to recall the pictures. Recalling the gender-inconsistent pictures, children tended to distort information by changing the gender of the actor; when they recalled gender-consistent pictures, they were more confident of their memory. A variety of studies report similar findings; for example, girls and boys remember feminine and masculine toys and objects, respectively, more easily, and both also remember more about same-gender peers and activities (Martin, 1993; Signorella et al., 1993). Moreover, children's memory for schema-consistent information grows stronger as they grow older (Ruble, 1994; Stangor & Ruble, 1989).

The degree to which children rely on gender schemas in interpreting their social world varies among individual children and across age (Martin, 1993). Young children (4 years or younger) appear to rely relatively more on gender schemas than older children (5 years or older). This is partly because older children not only have more complete and elaborate knowledge of gender roles but attach less importance to these roles and are less rigid in applying their knowledge (Levy, 1989, 1994). Similarly, children vary in the extent to which they have well-formed gender schemas (Signorella et al., 1993). Some children are "gender schematic" and highly sensitive to gender notions, whereas other children are "gender aschematic" and focus more on nongender aspects of information in their environment. Not surprisingly, gender-schematic children display better memories for gender-consistent information and are more likely to distort gender-inconsistent information than less gender-schematic children (Levy, 1989, 1994). Part of their ability to remember may be due to differential attention to same-gender information. In a naturalistic study of TV viewing, Luecke-Aleksa, Anderson, Collins, and Schmitt (1995) found that boys who had a better grasp of gender constancy watched male characters more and programs that featured a greater number of males than did boys who had not yet fully achieved gender constancy (Figure 15-4). Gender-constant girls also watched same-gender characters more than did girls whose constancy was not yet secure. Interestingly, gender-constant girls also

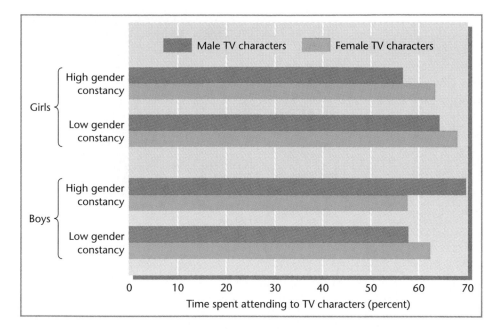

■ FIGURE 15-4
Gender constancy and attention to TV characters. Grasping the concept of gender constancy led both boys and girls to pay more attention to same-gender characters on TV. Because both girls and boys who haven't yet grasped this concept tend to pay more attention to female characters, constancy did not alter girls' viewing pattern very much, although it reversed the boys' pattern. (*Source:* Based on Luecke-Aleska, Anderson, Collins, and Schmitt, 1995)

watched more action programs; the researchers hypothesized that this may be the result of women's having more glamorous and key roles in such programs, even though they are still subordinate to the men's roles. These studies remind us that it is important to consider individual as well as developmental differences in understanding cognitive approaches to gender typing. In short, gender-role schemas clearly alter the ways in which children process social information and either recall it accurately or distort it to suit their prior concepts.

A Comparison of the Cognitive Developmental and Gender-Schema Theories

Does increasingly sophisticated gender-typed knowledge influence children's gender-role activities and behavior? Kohlberg's cognitive developmental theory and gender-schema theory provide different answers (Martin, 1993). Kohlberg's theory predicts that the achievement of gender constancy should influence children's gender-typed choices. Therefore, prior to the 5- to 7-year age period, there should be little preference for gender-appropriate activities. Gender-schema theory, on the other hand, suggests that children may need only basic information about gender, such as identification of the sexes (Martin, 1993). According to this theory, merely labeling the genders is sufficient for children to begin to form rules concerning gender.

Apparently the gender-schema theorists are correct. Contrary to Kohlberg's proposals, gender labeling is sufficient to affect gender-typed activity preferences—an achievement that occurs well before the child develops a stable concept of gender constancy (Martin, 1993; Martin & Little, 1990). As Fagot and Leinbach (1989) found, children who developed gender identity early (before 27 months) engaged in more gender-typed play than children who gained gender identity later in development. In short, the early boys were more likely to be playing with trucks and trains, while the early girls were more likely to be found in the doll corner! Moreover, at age 4, the early gender-role identifiers possessed greater knowledge of gender-role stereotypes as well. Children even respond to novel toys based on gender labels. As Martin, Eisenbud, and Rose (1995) found, even when novel toys were very attractive, children showed a "hot potato" effect: They quickly lost interest in toys after being told that they were for the opposite gender (Figure 15-5).

Another kind of basic gender category information that is important in organizing gender-typed preferences is children's recognition of their membership in a gender class or group (Maccoby, 1988). Recognition of their gender membership as

■ FIGURE 15-5
Toys for the other gender are "hot potatoes."
For preschoolers, the attractiveness of a toy increased its likability, particularly if experimenters described it as a toy either children of the same gender or all children really liked. Children liked a toy a lot less if it was described as something that other-gender children really liked, treating these toys like "hot potatoes." (*Source:* Martin, Eisenbud, and Rose, 1995)

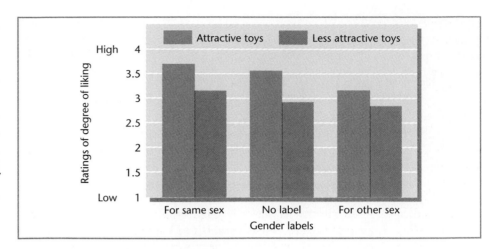

male or female is related to children's gender-typed preferences and to their gender-role knowledge (Martin & Little, 1990).

Gender-typed play such as choosing trucks or dolls as the appropriate gender-role choices does not seem to depend on the achievement of gender stability or gender constancy. Instead, the first stage—the acquisition of basic gender identity—seems sufficient for the emergence of gender-typed play. However, according to Smetana and Letourneau (1984), choice of playmate may depend on the level of gender understanding. In these researchers' study, girls who had acquired gender stability chose to play with other girls more than did girls who had acquired only gender identity. "Lacking the certainty that gender is invariant across contexts and situations, females may actively seek the presence of same sex peers to affirm their conceptions of themselves as females" (1984, p. 695). Once girls acquire gender constancy and their gender concepts are firmly established, they are less rigid in their choice of playmates and play with both boys and girls. Girls at the highest level of gender understanding are confident that play with boys will not alter their gender. Cognitive understanding, in this case, brings increased freedom of social choice. Together, these studies suggest that the link between the acquisition of gender concepts and behavior varies across both the stage of gender understanding and the kind of behavior.

INFLUENCE OF THE FAMILY ON GENDER TYPING

Parents have an enormous impact on children's gender-role behaviors and gender typing. They speak differently to male and female babies, they hold and move them differently, and, as we've said, they tend to choose clothing, room decor, and toys that are considered appropriate for either girls or boys. As children grow, parents encourage them in gender-appropriate activities, and they disapprove or reinforce their children's behaviors according to whether they are gender appropriate or inappropriate. And by their own behaviors and lifestyles parents sometimes, although not always, provide models for their children's behavior.

Cognitive social learning theory would predict that parents should play an important role as encouraging and reinforcing agents and as models in shaping children's gender-role behaviors and attitudes, and it seems likely that they do. Parents are the first people children observe, and they're also the first people who try to teach children or shape their behavior. As we will see, there is considerable evidence of the influence of social factors in children's gender typing.

Parents' Influence on Children's Gender-Typed Choices

Well before children are making lists of toys they'd like to receive for their birthdays or holidays, parents are actively shaping their children's tastes and preferences. Have you ever compared the bedrooms of girls and boys? This is exactly what several researchers did. Carefully and systematically they recorded the kinds of toys, decorations, furniture, and even the curtains and bedspreads that adorned the bedrooms of boys and girls between 1 month and 6 years old (Pomerleau, Bolduc, Malcuit, & Cossette, 1990; Rheingold & Cook, 1975). Boys' rooms contained more vehicles, machines, army equipment, soldiers, and sports equipment. In contrast, girls' rooms were more likely to house dolls and floral-patterned and ruffled furnishings (e.g., floral curtains with lace). The toys of boys were more action oriented; girls' toys were less action oriented and more family focused. Of particular interest was the finding that there was little difference between the results of studies conducted in 1975 and 1990; the times they may be a-changin', but not children's rooms!

Parents often announce the gender of their offspring to the world by the way they dress their children, subtly shaping their children toward "appropriate" gender roles. When a group of researchers watched 1- to 13-month-olds in a shopping center, they found baby girls in pink, puffed sleeves, ruffles, and lace. Boys wore blue or maybe red, but few bows, barrettes, or ribbons (Shakin, Shakin, & Sternglanz, 1985). According to Fagot and Leinbach (1987), gender-typed clothing serves very well not only to announce a child's gender but to ensure that even strangers will respond to the child in ways that are appropriate to his or her gender.

Parents' Behavior toward Girls and Boys

Parents tend to behave differently with their male and female babies, but mothers are more likely than fathers to treat girls and boys in an egalitarian manner. Fathers show a preference for sons, perhaps partly because they feel free to talk and play with them in a more rough-and-tumble way. As children grow older, however, both parents tend to encourage their children in play and other activities that the culture sees as gender appropriate.

Infants and Toddlers

From earliest infancy, parents are likely to view their sons and daughters differently. Parents are more likely to describe their newborn daughters as smaller, softer, less attentive, cuter, more delicate, and finer featured than their sons. And fathers, even if they have only seen and not yet handled their infants, are more extreme than mothers in emphasizing the size, strength, coordination, and alertness of sons versus the fragility and beauty of daughters (Rubin, Provenzano, & Luria,

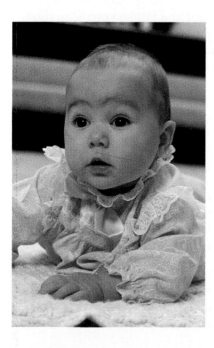

When we meet an infant for the first time we often use clothing to judge the child's gender. If the beruffled infant in pink and the baby in the sailor outfit changed clothes, would you be just as likely to judge the first a girl and the second a boy?

1974; Stern & Karraker, 1989). In view of such differences in parents' perceptions of their male and female infants, it is not surprising that, from the earliest days of life, boys and girls are treated differently and that this differential treatment is most marked among fathers (Stern & Karraker, 1989). Researchers have also found that adults will play in more masculine ways with a baby they have been led to believe is a boy and in a gentler fashion with an infant they think is a girl, regardless of the infant's actual gender! Gender-role stereotypes clearly serve to shape our treatment of children—even in infancy.

From the time women learn they are pregnant, fathers-to-be generally show a strong preference for sons (Hoffman, 1977). And after children are born fathers are more likely to play and talk with sons than with daughters, especially when the new babies are firstborns (Parke, 1996). As children grow older, fathers spend more time in play with male toddlers, and they watch and touch their infants more. They indulge in rough-and-tumble antics with male infants and may talk with them in a kind of macho way, saying things like "Hello, Tiger!" (Jacklin, DiPietro, & Maccoby, 1984; Parke, 1996). Fathers are more likely to cuddle their infant daughters gently than to engage in active play with them. In contrast, mothers tend to treat female and male babies pretty much the same way (Lytton & Romney, 1991; Siegel, 1987). Both parents, however, are more verbally responsive to girls; they talk to them more, and they use more supportive and directive speech with daughters than they do with sons (Leaper, Anderson, & Sanders, 1998).

This pattern of differences in mothers' and fathers' interactions with sons and daughters suggests that the social forces involved in gender-role typing may begin almost at birth and that fathers, through their more markedly different treatment of boys and girls, may play a more important role in the gender-typing process than do mothers. As Ruble and Martin (1998) point out, however, parents today may be making conscious efforts to encourage egalitarian behaviors in both boys and girls, although they may tend to do this more often with older than with younger children. Perhaps the twenty-first century may see more equal roles for moms and dads in the gender-typing process.

Older Children

As children grow older, do parents actively encourage and reinforce them for behaving in a gender-stereotypic manner? If the environment has anything to do with gender behavior, social learning theory would predict that both reinforcement and modeling should play important roles, and it seems likely that they do. Langlois and Downs (1980) observed how mothers and fathers reacted to their 3- and 5-year-old girls' and boys' play, purposely manipulating the children's choices of toys. Both "masculine" toys, such as soldiers and a gas station, and "feminine" toys, such as a dollhouse and kitchen utensils, were available to the children, but the researchers told the children specifically to play with either gender-appropriate or cross-gender toys. They then recorded parents' reactions to their children's choices of toys, mothers in one session, and fathers in another.

Fathers consistently exerted pressure on their children—both boys and girls—to play with gender-typed toys. They were also quite consistent in rewarding both sons and daughters for play with gender-appropriate toys and punishing them for play with cross-gender toys. With daughters, mothers took the same approach, but their responses to their sons were inconsistent: They sometimes punished and sometimes rewarded them for playing with cross-gender toys. Other studies found that when children are engaged in same rather than in other-gender behaviors, parents are more responsive and supportive (Leaper, Leve, Strasser, & Schwartz, 1995).

These findings are consistent with other evidence that men are more likely to gender-type toys and to purchase such toys than women are, especially playthings for boys (Fisher-Thompson, 1990; Thompson, Molison, & Elliott, 1988). The findings are also consistent with the view that the father is the principal agent of gender-role socialization and that the mother plays a less influential role in this process.

In general, parents seem to be more protective of daughters' than of sons' physical well-being. Parents tend to encourage dependency and close family ties in girls and to put more emphasis on independence, early exploration, achievement, and competition in boys. Whereas parents typically display similar expectations for boys' and girls' independence and maturity in relation to such safe activities as tidying up rooms, putting away toys or clothes, or getting dressed, they treat boys and girls differently in areas where there are greater risks. Parents generally think boys should be able to play away from home without telling parents where they are, run errands in the neighborhood, cross the street alone, use sharp scissors, and indulge in other venturesome activities at an earlier age than girls. Parents are also less likely to pick up or supervise boys after school (Hoffman, 1977; Ruble & Martin, 1998). Moreover, parents often communicate these messages quite directly: Pomerantz and Ruble (in press) found that parents were more likely to tell sons specifically that they were free to do certain activities than they were to grant such freedom to daughters.

Not all cultural groups make these kinds of gender-based distinctions. As we saw earlier, African American parents treat boys and girls more similarly than do European American parents. Many psychologists are concerned, however, that among those groups that do tend to gender-type their children along traditional lines, girls may suffer. Restricting girls' freedom more than boys' may lead girls to lack feelings of self-efficacy and to discourage them from exploring their worlds and taking intellectual and creative risks. Under these conditions, girls may continue to be much more likely than boys to conform to cultural norms and values; clearly, this may sometimes be useful, but it may also be highly detrimental (Allen & Majidi-Abi, 1989; Ruble, 1988).

Parents' gender-differentiated behaviors often seem to be associated with achievement. Fathers, who are particularly prone to differentiate among boys and girls in this regard, are more likely to stress the importance of a career or occupational success for sons than for daughters (Block, 1983; Hoffman, 1977). Differential treatment of boys and girls is particularly marked in the area of mathematical achievement (Eccles et al., 1993). In a variety of cultures, including Japan, Taiwan, and the United States, parents still believe boys are better in math than girls, while girls are superior readers (Lummis & Stevenson, 1990). In both teaching and problem-solving situations, fathers of boys are more attuned to achievement and to the cognitive aspects of the situation. Fathers of girls seem to be less concerned with performance and more concerned with interpersonal interactions with their daughters (Block, 1983). When reading bedtime stories, even mothers teach their boys more than their girls. They supply unfamiliar names for sons ("Look, here's a giraffe. Can you say *giraffe*?"), while with daughters they emphasize enjoying the time spent with them (Weitzman, Birns, & Friend, 1985). And these parental behaviors are not lost on children. Eccles and colleagues (1993) found that parents who held stronger stereotyped beliefs about boys' and girls' skills in English, math, and sports had matching expectations about their own children's abilities in these areas. Moreover, even controlling for their children's actual levels of skill in these areas, the children's performance and their perceptions of their own competence matched their parents' expectations.

Modeling Parents' Characteristics

To what degree does children's imitation of a parent's characteristics explain the development of gender typing? Although a warm and nurturant parent may by example encourage children of her or his own gender to learn the roles she or he has adopted, for boys especially parental power has an even greater impact on gender typing. In boys' masculine identification, the combination of a dominant mother and a passive father is particularly destructive, whereas this combination has no particular effect on girls' femininity. A boy with a weak father and a powerful mother is likely to exhibit feminine characteristics. Fathers who are dominant and decisive in setting limits and dispensing rewards and punishments, however,

Modeling a parent is one of the most important ways a child learns social roles and the behaviors and skills judged appropriate to those roles.

are likely to have very masculine sons (Hetherington, 1967).

Turner and Gervai (1995) have recently confirmed the role of parent characteristics in children's gender typing. Parents who are highly traditional in their gender roles have children who are also highly gender typed, especially in terms of their knowledge of gender stereotypes, but who don't necessarily give expression to this knowledge in their actual behavior. This was particularly true with regard to children's choice of same- or other-gender play partners. Both sons and daughters of very "masculine" fathers were more assertive and less emotionally expressive than children of men judged less masculine (Hetherington, 1967).

The roles parents play within the family—whether traditional or nontraditional—have a strong impact on children's gender-typed preferences and behavior (Ruble & Martin, 1998). In less traditional families where mothers are employed outside the home both boys and girls may have less stereotyped concepts of gender-appropriate behavior, and girls may display fewer gender-typed behaviors (Huston & Alvarez, 1990; Lerner, 1994). However, maternal employment is now so prevalent that children's gender concepts may be affected just by the presence of women in the workplace; it doesn't seem to matter whether their own mothers work outside the home (Ruble & Martin, 1998; Serbin, Polwishta, & Gulko, 1993). As we discussed in Chapter 1, secular trends affect children's development; as the social contexts of children's lives change, the critical socialization influences will change as well.

The ways in which parents divide up household tasks also influence gender typing. An egalitarian division of labor is linked to less traditional occupational choices, and fathers who modeled nontraditional behaviors had children with less advanced knowledge of gender distinctions (Serbin et al., 1993; Turner & Gervai, 1995). In a unique longitudinal study of families in which fathers were the primary caregivers during children's preschool years, the children, when they became adolescents, endorsed nontraditional employment and childrearing roles (Williams, Radin, & Allegro, 1992).

Parental Absence or Unavailability

Particularly because the father plays such an important role in gender typing, we might expect that children from homes in which the father is either permanently absent or away for long periods would show disruptions in gender typing. When there is no father in the home, the mother must, of necessity, assume a more decisive role in rearing her children. The absence of a male model and the lack of opportunity for children to interact with a father may contribute both to children's difficulties in developing gender identity and gender typing in such homes (Hetherington, 1989).

When fathers are permanently gone owing to divorce or death, when they are temporarily absent or unavailable because of occupational demands or wartime service, and when they simply show little interest in their children, young boys especially may have problems with gender identity and gender role (Huston, 1983; Ruble & Martin, 1998). Disruptions in gender roles are most apparent in preadolescent boys and are most severe when the separation has occurred before the child was 5 (Hetherington, 1966). As the child grows older and has wider social contacts, other models such as peers, siblings, surrogate fathers, teachers, and people in the mass media can partially mitigate the effects of father absence on gender-role adoption (Huston, 1983).

The effects of parental absence on preadolescent girls appear to be minimal. However, studies of adolescents suggest that parental absence may have a delayed effect on girls' gender typing. Father absence may cause adolescent daughters to have difficulties relating to other males; these difficulties may take different forms for daughters of widows and of divorcees. In some studies, adolescent girls from divorced homes appeared to be more sexually precocious and assertive with males, whereas those whose mothers were widowed were characterized as excessively anxious about sexuality and as shy and uncomfortable around males (Hetherington, 1972, 1991a; Newcomer & Udry, 1987).

Daughters learn to feel competent and to value and acquire the social skills necessary for effective heterosexual interactions by interacting with warm, responsive, masculine fathers who reward and enjoy their daughters' femininity. Studies of paternal absence again indicate the important role of the father in girls' social development. Mothers can moderate the effects of father absence on their daughters, however. Women who cast their former husbands and their relationships with them in a positive light and who themselves demonstrate emotional stability can lessen the deleterious effects of father absence.

Gender Roles in Children of Gay and Lesbian Parents

Recent studies of children who grow up in a gay or lesbian household have challenged the importance of the father's contribution to gender typing. Children reared in lesbian families do not differ in gender-role behavior from children reared in heterosexual households. The choices boys and girls in lesbian homes make of toys, activities, and friends are traditional. Nor is there any evidence that children reared in lesbian households are likely to develop a gay or a lesbian sexual orientation (Patterson, 1992, 1995b).

Similarly, recent evidence suggests that boys raised by gay fathers are largely heterosexual in their sexual orientations and that this is so regardless of how long sons lived with their gay fathers (Bailey, Bebrow, Wolfe, & Mikach, 1995). As we discussed in Chapter 12, the socioemotional adjustment of children in homosexual households seems very similar to that of children reared in traditional families. Research in this area has raised important questions about the role of environmental and biological influences on the development of gender-related orientations and behaviors. Although fathers do appear to be influential in gender-role typing, these studies suggest that children can learn gender roles in a variety of family arrangements.

EXTRAFAMILIAL INFLUENCES ON GENDER ROLES

Families are the first among the many social forces that play a role in shaping our gender-linked behaviors, but they are not the only influences. Moreover, as children grow older, influences outside the family become increasingly important in shaping gender typing. Among the earliest of these forces are the books that parents read to children and the television programming that children watch. Peers and peer groups have considerable impact on a child's assumption of a gender identity and gender roles, as does the child's own understanding of what is appropriate and inappropriate behavior for her gender. And, as we will see, the schools and teachers with whom children spend so much of their time have great influence on gender typing, both for good and for ill. Once again, we review research results that support cognitive social learning theory.

In this section we explore some of the forces that may contribute to children's amazingly clear distinctions about what's gender appropriate and inappropriate. Asked to rate various activities (e.g., reading or doing math, art, or mechanical tasks) as to how "boyish" or "girlish" they were, how important accomplishment in each was, how well they thought they would perform in each activity, and with what minimum standard of performance they would be satisfied, sixth and ninth graders drew very clear gender-based distinctions (Huston, 1983; see also Ruble & Martin, 1998). They attached more importance to achievement in activities they viewed as appropriate to their own gender, set higher minimum standards for these tasks, and expected to do better on them than on activities they considered inappropriate for their gender.

Books and Television

Male and female roles are portrayed in similarly gender-stereotyped ways in children's stories and on television. Although there has been pressure within educational circles for more egalitarian treatment of boys and girls as well as of different cultural groups, children's literature and schoolbooks still contain many gender stereotypes. A comparative study of elementary school children's readers over a period of some 15 years offered some hopeful signs: Girls appeared as often as boys did in the books surveyed in 1989 and in a wider range of activities than they enjoyed in 1975 books (Purcell & Stewart, 1990). Nevertheless, books continue often to show females as more passive, dependent, and engaged in a narrower range of occupations than men and to show males as more assertive and action oriented (Turner-Bowker, 1996).

Males on television are more likely than females to be depicted as aggressive, decisive, professionally competent, rational, stable, powerful, and tolerant. In contrast, females tend to be portrayed as warmer, more sociable, more emotional, and happier but also unemployed or involved in housework and child care. When women on television are aggressive, they are usually inept or unsuccessful aggressors, and women are more likely to be shown as victims than as initiators of violence. There are exceptions, of course, such as "Xena: Warrior Princess" and cartoon characters like Catwoman. Females are less likely to be leading characters and are more likely to be in comedy roles, to be married or about to be married, and to be younger than males (Huston et al., 1992; Signorielli, 1993), although there is a trend, as in books, toward depicting women in a wider range of occupational roles (Allan & Coltrane, 1996). Even in television commercials, males are more often portrayed as the authorities and are used in the voice-over comments about the merits of products. Women are more likely to play the role of the consumer, displaying interest in demonstrations of a product's superiority (Loudal, 1989). When women are shown as experts, they are likely to be discussing food products, laundry, soap, or beauty aids. These trends have been identified in the United States as well as other countries (Best & Williams, 1993; Williams, Baron, Phillips, Travis, & Jackson, 1986).

The likelihood that these stereotypical presentations of male and female roles have a real impact on children is underscored by findings that children who are heavy TV viewers are more likely to have stereotypical notions of gender and race and to show conformity to culturally accepted gender-role typing (Huston et al., 1992). When television was first introduced in a small town in Canada (see the section on natural experiments in Chapter 2), analysts recorded marked increases in traditional gender attitudes two years later (Kimball, 1986).

Television can also be used to change children's gender-role stereotypes. In one study, 5- and 6-year-olds who were shown a cartoon in which the characters played nontraditional roles (girls helping boys build a clubhouse) developed less conventional gender-role attitudes (Davidson, Yasuna, & Tower, 1979). Similarly, "Freestyle," a television series that tries to counteract children's gender and ethnic stereotypes, has been moderately successful in increasing acceptance of boys and girls who exhibit nontraditional gender-typed behaviors. For example, 9- to

12-year-old viewers were more accepting of girls who participated in athletics and mechanical activities and of boys who engaged in nurturant activities (Johnston & Ettema, 1982). However, the effects of most TV-based interventions have been relatively modest and short-lived (Liben & Bigler, 1987; Matteson, 1991). It is likely that it will take much more change in books, television, and many other spheres of life to change gender-role stereotypes and attitudes.

Peers, Gender Roles, and Self-Esteem

Peers often serve as enforcers of society's gender-role standards, and they may also help to define them. In these roles, peers may also help the individual child to define himself or herself and to solidify a gender identity. The importance of forging a clear gender identity stems from its link with self-esteem. Researchers have found that children who were masculine or androgynous (combining both masculine and feminine characteristics) had higher self-esteem than those who had a feminine gender identity (Boldizar, 1991; Ruble & Martin, 1998). As the feminine role becomes more equal to the male role this link with self-esteem is likely to change, but girls and women still suffer more discrimination than men in many spheres of society.

Observing 200 preschoolers at play over several months' time, Fagot (1985a) found that peers displayed marked reactions when children violated appropriate gender-role behavior patterns. Boys who play with dolls rather than trucks have a tough time; their classmates criticize them five to six times more often than they heckle children who conform. On the other hand, peers aren't as harsh in their treatment of girls who would rather play firefighter than nurse; they tend to ignore rather than criticize such girls. And this kind of feedback makes a difference in children's behavior. Researchers have found that peer punishment was an effective way to stop children's cross-gender activity (Lamb, Easterbrooks, & Holden, 1980; Lamb & Roopnarine, 1979).

When peers rewarded children for appropriate gender-role behavior, the children tended to persist longer in the rewarded type of activity. However, the source of the reinforcement makes a difference, too. For example, Fagot (1985a) found that children respond more to feedback from a same-gender child. That is, boys respond to feedback from boys, but not from girls, while girls are more receptive to feedback from other girls. This pattern of responsiveness can lead to gender segregation which, in turn, may provide additional opportunities to learn accepted gender roles.

On any school playground you can see that children have a very strong tendency to associate and play with other children of their same gender. In preschool, when children are 4½ years old, they spend nearly three times as much time with same-gender play partners as with children of the other gender. By age 6½, the effect is even stronger: Children spend 11 times as much time with same-gender as with opposite-gender partners (Maccoby & Jacklin, 1987). And between 4 and 6 years of age, boys tend even more than girls to congregate in same-gender groups (Benenson, Apostoleris, & Parnass, 1997).

What actually goes on in same-gender peer groups? Maccoby (1990) has summarized the differences:

> The two [genders] engage in fairly different kinds of activities and games. . . . Boys play in somewhat larger groups on the average and their play is rougher . . . and takes up more space. Boys more often play in the streets and other public places; girls more often congregate in private homes and yards. Girls tend to form close, intimate friendships with one or two other girls, and these friendships are marked by sharing of confidences. . . . Boys' friendships, on the other hand, are more oriented around mutual interests in activities. . . . The breakup of girls' friendships is usually attended by more intense emotional reactions than in the case of boys. . . . In male groups there is more concern with issues of dominance. (p. 516)

These stylistic differences in boys' and girls' groups have led Maccoby to suggest several reasons for gender segregation. First, girls view the rough-and-tumble play style of boys and their competition-dominance orientation as aversive; as a result, girls avoid interactions with boys. Second, girls find it difficult to influence boys. They influence one another successfully, using their preferred method, that of making polite suggestions. These tactics are not very effective with boys, who prefer to make more direct demands. "Girls find it aversive to try to interact with someone who is unresponsive, and they begin to avoid such partners" (Maccoby, 1990, p. 515).

This phenomenon is evident across many cultures, ranging from the United States, to India, to the countries of Africa, and it occurs without specific adult encouragement, guidance, or pressure. Although earlier parental influence may play a role in setting the process in motion, children spontaneously choose same-gender play partners. Although individual children may differ in terms of how masculine or feminine they are or in their grasp of such concepts as gender stability and gender constancy, they all show the same preference for same-gender playmates (Powlishta, 1989). Thus, from preschool onward, children choose to live in segregated play worlds that, in turn, nurture and encourage separate styles of interaction that are distinctly male and female. This **self-socialization,** or children's spontaneous adoption of gender-appropriate behavior, may be another powerful way in which gender roles are learned and maintained. Thus children themselves and children's peer groups play an important role in children's gender-role socialization.

self-socialization The child's spontaneous adoption of gender-appropriate behavior.

Schools and Teachers

Teachers and the schools themselves deliver a number of gender-related messages to children (Ruble & Martin, 1998). To begin with, the structure of the school system is predominantly male—men hold many more of the positions of power, such as principal and superintendent—whereas the teaching staff is predominantly female. This mirrors the power structure in the traditional family and in society at large. In addition, as we discussed in Chapter 14, teachers sometimes structure classroom activities by gender and provide differential reinforcements and punishments to boys and girls. In this section we consider the differential impact of the school culture and environment on girls and boys, and we explore some specific effects of teachers' attitudes and practices.

The School Culture

Although, as we've already learned, teachers in individual classrooms often seem to pay more attention to boys than to girls, the general culture of the school may in

Teachers often resort to segregating a child from the rest of the class for a period of time as a way of controlling unruly behavior. Many more boys than girls get the "time out" treatment.

some ways favor girls. The school system often frowns upon the independent, assertive, competitive, and boisterous qualities that the culture has encouraged in boys since they were infants. In contrast, the more verbally oriented girls, who are generally better behaved and follow rules more readily than boys, may find more acceptance from teachers who—at least in the early grades—are likely to be females. Is it surprising, then, that from the start girls tend to like school more than boys and to perform better in their academic work? For many boys, school may not be a happy place. Boys may feel that their teachers like them less than girls and may have more difficulty adjusting to school routines; they may create more problems for teachers and elicit more criticism from them; and, most important, they may perform not only at a lower level than their female classmates but well below their own abilities (Ben Tsvi-Mayer, Hertz-Lazarowitz, & Safir, 1989; Dweck & Goetz, 1977; Ruble & Martin, 1998).

What might be the implications of young boys' perception of school as a gender-inappropriate institution? Clearly, one potential effect is that boys may be less likely to be as motivated and interested in school-related activities than girls, who are likely to view school as consistent with their own gender-role identity. Girls outperform their male peers in the early grades, especially in reading skills; some surveys have found that boys are between three and six times as likely as girls to experience problems in learning to read (Halpern, 1992; Lummis & Stevenson, 1990). On the other hand, the school environment and culture as we've described them do not explain the often greater eventual achievement of boys and men in the late high school and college years.

It seems that although girls may have an advantage in the early grades, this jump start, as it were, has a short-lived effect. Girls' achievement levels decline as they grow older, and by college, the proportion of female underachievers exceeds the proportion of male underachievers (Eccles et al., 1993; Eccles et al., 1998). The kinds of conforming and dependent behaviors that schools encourage in girls may, in the long run, be detrimental to them. Dependency is negatively related to intellectual achievement. Independence, assertiveness, and nonconformity are much more likely to lead to creative thinking and problem solving and to high levels of achievement in both girls and boys (Dweck, 1991; Dweck & Leggett, 1988). The many conflicting messages that girls receive in the school years can put them at risk, if not for failure, for less than satisfying lives.

Over the years, psychologists have found that public achievement, particularly in competitive activities, is often threatening to girls and women. Some girls cope with their conflict about achievement by concealing their abilities, particularly from boys (Huston, 1983; Ruble & Martin, 1998). For example, a girl may tell a male peer that she received lower grades than she actually did in a course they both attend. Or she may lower her effort, intentionally performing below her capabilities. And even women who are highly successful professionals sometimes seek to disguise their achievement striving by appearing superfeminine—they may try not only to be super career women but super wives, super mothers, and super volunteers. What boy or man would try to hide his ambition and his accomplishments from others?

Impact of Teacher Attitudes and Behaviors

Even in the preschool years, teachers respond differently to boys and girls, often reacting to boys and girls in gender-stereotypic ways (Fagot (1985a). Researchers have found that teachers interrupt girls more frequently than boys during conversations and pay more attention to boys' assertive behavior than to girls' pushing and shoving (Hendrick & Stange, 1991). On the other hand, teachers respond to girls' social initiatives, such as talking and gesturing, more than to these same behaviors in boys. Moreover, although teachers may encourage boys to engage in quiet activities rather than aggressive and rough-and-tumble play, both teachers and peers criticize boys for cross-gender behaviors (e.g., dressing up or playing with dolls) whereas they are much less likely to criticize girls for cross-gender play (Fagot, 1985a).

Not surprisingly, differential teacher attention has an impact. Fagot (1985a) found that nine months after her initial observations of preschoolers, there were clear gender differences. Girls talked to the teacher more, and boys exhibited a higher level of assertiveness. Although educators once believed that increasing the number of male teachers would counteract female teachers' apparently differential treatment of boys and girls, Fagot (1985b) discovered that both male and female teachers reacted more positively to children involved in stereotypical female gender-role behaviors, such as art activities and helping others, no matter what the individual child's gender! At the same time, some evidence indicates that male teachers may have more nontraditional gender beliefs and preferences as well as nontraditional views of the teacher's role (Koblinsky & Sugawara, 1984; Mancus, 1992).

As we have seen, boys and girls have traditionally differed in their performance on verbal and quantitative tasks, girls doing better in English and boys in mathematics (Eccles et al., 1998). We have also discussed the finding, however, that girls' lower math achievement is apparently caused, in part, by their often lesser ability to deal with geometry and that this, in turn, is related to boys' superior abilities in spatial relations. In fact, we said, girls are better at computational skills and do not differ from boys in respect either to basic mathematical knowledge or knowledge of algebra. Why, then, do enrollments in school courses, selections of college majors and fields of college degrees, and adult career choices continue to reflect the old idea that boys and men are better at math?

For one thing, teachers and others who continue to encourage boys more than girls in mathematical pursuits may be unaware of these findings (Eccles et al., 1998; Shepardson & Pizzini, 1992). And if people in general are unaware of researchers' data, males may continue to perceive themselves as more competent in mathematics, and females may continue to view mathematics as a male-achievement domain, which would then make the study of math inconsistent with their gender-role identity. Eccles (1985) found that 668 children in the 5th through the 12th grades thought boys were better at math and could make more use of it than girls, despite the fact that these children displayed no gender differences in their actual mathematics performance!

Interestingly, as they grew older, girls expressed a decreasing liking for mathematics and more enjoyment of English, but boys' attitudes toward both subjects remained fairly stable. Lacking any positive reinforcement for studying math, more girls than boys dropped math during their high school years. In contrast, boys' course enrollment decisions reflected their past performance; if they had done well in math, they continued to take math courses. It seems that educators may need further education about children's educational skills and potential capabilities!

ANDROGYNY

Many psychologists believe that traditional ideas of masculinity and femininity have been socially and psychologically destructive. To speak and act as if each individual person is either "masculine" or "feminine" in his or her interests, attitudes, and behaviors makes little sense when we know that in reality most people possess a combination of characteristics that we have traditionally viewed as masculine or feminine. Any person, male or female, can be tender and nurturant with children, professionally successful, fiercely competitive on the tennis court, and an excellent cook. Many people are **androgynous;** that is, they possess both masculine and feminine psychological characteristics (Bem, 1974, 1981, 1993; Spence, 1985).

androgynous Possessing both feminine and masculine psychological characteristics.

Children, as well as adults, can be androgynous; such children are less likely to make stereotyped choices of play and activities (Boldizar, 1991). And, as we noted earlier, gender-oriented interests and concerns tend to change with age. Women may become more feminine and men more androgynous; thus, each gender may become more feminine with age. Of course, the increase in femininity in later life may also reflect the increased dependency both genders may experience as a result of the lack of employment after retirement age and a disadvantaged financial position (Hyde et al., 1991).

It is important to recognize that not only do gender-related traits such as expressiveness, nurturance, instrumentality, or assertiveness vary across individual males and females but individual people will display one or another of these characteristics

BOX 15-2

Perspectives on Diversity

Childrearing in Countercultural Families

One of the most powerful demonstrations of the plasticity or modifiability of gender roles can be seen in the lifestyles of families who deliberately choose to emphasize gender-role equality in their overall lifestyle. These countercultural families often show a high commitment to questioning conventional cultural dictates and institutions. Often a product of the 1960s cultural rebellion, these parents frequently endorse more egalitarian attitudes toward gender roles.

Beginning in the mid-1970s, the Family Lifestyles Project followed a group of more than 200 of these non-traditional families, studying the relationship between family lifestyle and child development and focusing particularly on the variables that affected the socialization of children (Eiduson, Kornfein, Zimmerman, & Weisner, 1988). All families were European American. Some were composed of single parents, some of common-law (living together but not legally married) couples, and some of traditionally married couples. Other families lived in communes or similar group living arrangements.

Interested in the way parents put their gender egalitarian values into practice in raising their children, Thomas Weisner and Jane Wilson-Mitchell (1990) brought the children and their parents to a southern California university center for a daylong visit when the children were about 6 years old—in kindergarten, first, and second grade. These researchers interviewed the parents on several issues and assessed the children's gender typing in several specific areas: appearance, activities and interests, personal-social attributes (e.g., "adventurous," "considerate," "outgoing," "calm"), and gender-based social relationships.

In comparison with children reared by conventional married couples, these countercultural children were less gender typed in a variety of ways. They were more androgynous in their chosen activities and interests and more likely to assume that girls could be engineers or firefighters and boys could be librarians or nursery school teachers. Indeed, more than 70 percent of these children gave non-gender-typed answers to questions about appropriate occupations for boys and girls, whereas only 40 per-

cent of the children in the comparison group gave such answers.

It is important to note that these countercultural children were very like other children in a variety of ways. In their play preferences and in their basic knowledge of the way familiar play objects (e.g., dishes, trucks, dolls, racing cars) are culturally gender typed, they were similar to conventionally reared children. All children acquired the normative cultural schemas for gender typing, regardless of their family lifestyle; they were not counter stereotyped. Instead, these children tended to be **multischematic:** They displayed either conventional or more egalitarian gender-typing schemas depending on the situation or the domain. "These children have more than one cultural schema available for responding to their world and have developed selective criteria for when to recognize and use either [a] conventional or [an] egalitarian schema" (Weisner & Wilson-Mitchell, 1990, p. 19).

This capacity to be flexible and multischematic is part of a more general pattern that characterizes the kinds of families multischematic children come from. These families regularly "engage in negotiations and conversation regarding all kinds of cultural standards, reflexively debate and question these standards and include children in these negotiations. When focused on [gender] typing schemas and [gender] roles, this process encourages children to think about and question beliefs rather than to always adopt either conventional or alternative beliefs. . . . Overall [these children] have acquired the ability to think about situations, and to [purposefully] select the type of schema best suited for [a particular] situation" (Weisner & Wilson-Mitchell, 1990, p. 20).

Some family styles, however, can make children even more rigidly gender typed. Investigators found that children reared in devotional communes that strongly emphasized culturally conventional gender typing were even less likely to be androgynous than children in conventionally married families (Weisner & Wilson-Mitchell, 1990). Socializing institutions such as families and schools can modify children's gender roles, but the form that these shifts assume clearly depends on the value system of the social agent.

---

in different situations, settings, and tasks (Spence, 1985). Facilitating the development of desirable characteristics such as social sensitivity, nurturance, open expression of positive feelings, appropriate assertiveness, and independence in both males and females would seem to be constructive.

Can children's gender-role stereotypes be modified? Can children be taught to be more androgynous? Can children learn that fashion models and firefighters can be either males or females? The study we discuss in Box 15-2 suggests that they can but, as the following exchange illustrates, the task may not be easy.

A psychologist overheard her 4-year-old son trying to explain her occupation to a young friend:

multischematic
Possessing more than one cultural schema for responding to the environment as well as criteria for deciding what schema to use in a particular situation.

SON: My mother helps people. She's a doctor.
FRIEND: You mean a nurse.
SON: No. She's not that kind of doctor. She's a psychologist. She's a doctor of psychology.
FRIEND: I see. She's a nurse of psychology.

Work by Bigler and Liben (1990) does suggest that children can learn to use fewer stereotypes. Using 10 occupations that children view as typically masculine (e.g., dentist, farmer, construction worker) or feminine (e.g., beautician, flight attendant, librarian), these researchers tried to lessen children's stereotyping of these work roles. They taught the children, first, that gender is irrelevant and then focused on two other ways of conceptualizing these jobs: liking a job, and having the skills needed for the job. For example, construction workers must like to build things, and they must acquire the skill to drive big machines. The investigators gave the children practice problems and, when the children based their answers on gender, gave them corrective feedback. In contrast, children in a control group participated in a group discussion about the roles of specific occupations within the community, with no emphasis on gender stereotyping. Children in the experimental group later gave more nonstereotyped answers not only for the occupations involved in the "lessons" but for a range of other occupations as well. For instance, when they were asked who could do various specific activities, such as police work and nursing, they gave more "Both men and women" responses. Children in the control group, however, still argued that "girls can't be firefighters!"

Consistent with the theory of gender schemas that we discussed earlier, these investigators found that children in the experimental intervention showed better recall of counterstereotypic information in a later memory test. Although children in both the experimental and control groups remembered stories about Frank the firefighter and Betty the beautician, children who were in the experimental group remembered stories about Larry the librarian and Ann the astronaut far better than did children in the control group. These findings suggest that even children's ways of thinking about gender roles can be modified.

Some parents and schools are working toward the goal of reducing gender typing. In open preschools, where the staff consciously attempts to minimize gender stereotyping, children spend more time in mixed-gender groups and less time in conventional gender-typed activities than children in traditional schools. In nontraditional preschools, children of both genders are likely to be playing house and gassing up their toy trucks (Bianchi & Bakeman, 1983). It is clear that gender roles and attitudes are modifiable. Attitudes toward gender roles are slowly changing, but there is no single formula for what may be appropriate behaviors for males and females. Individuals, families, and cultures vary widely, and no single script for gender roles will suit these many variations.

SUMMARY

- In addition to the influence on gender behaviors of biological factors, there are four principal psychological explanations of gender-linked behavior patterns: Freudian theory's process of **identification**, cognitive social learning theory, gender-schema theory, and Kohlberg's cognitive developmental theory.
- The process by which children acquire the values, motives, and behaviors viewed as appropriate for males and females within a culture is called **gender typing.** Children develop **gender-based beliefs,** largely on the basis of **gender stereotypes;** the latter are reflected in **gender roles.** Children adopt a **gender identity** early in life and develop **gender-role preferences** as well.

Gender-Role Standards and Stereotypes

- Both within and across different cultures we find great consistency in standards of desirable gender-role behavior. Males are expected to be independent, assertive, and competitive; females are expected to be more passive, sensitive, and supportive. These beliefs have changed little over the past 20 years within the United States, and apparently around the world as well.
- There is some variation in cultural gender-role standards both within the United States and across cultures, however. Within the United States, standards vary depending on ethnicity, age, education, and occupation. For example, African American families are less likely to adhere to strict gender-role distinctions when socializing their children, whereas Mexican-American families are more likely to highlight gender differences.
- Divergence between cultures is also clearly seen in Margaret Mead's classic study of three primitive tribes. In two tribes both men and women displayed what the Western world considers to be either feminine or masculine characteristics. In a third tribe the genders reversed the traditional Western roles. However, even within groups, individual differences in the strength of stereotypes often outweigh group characteristics.

Gender Differences in Development

- Of the many presumed differences between the behaviors of males and females, some are real, some are found only inconsistently, and some are wholly mythical.
- Girls are more physically and neurologically advanced at birth. Boys have more mature muscular development but are more vulnerable to disease and hereditary anomalies. Girls excel early in verbal skills, but boys excel in visual-spatial and math skills. Boys' superior mathematic abilities reflect only a better grasp of geometry, however, which depends on visual-spatial abilities. Boys are more aggressive, and girls more nurturant. Boys have more reading, speech, and emotional problems than girls.
- More equivocal are gender differences in activity level, dependency, timidity, exploratory activity, and vulnerability to stress. There are no gender differences in sociability, conformity, achievement, self-esteem, or verbal hostility.
- Although differences exist, it is important to remember that the overlap between the distributions is always greater than the differences between them. In addition, noting the existence of the differences does not tell us why they exist. It is clear that girls and boys have many different experiences and opportunities as they develop, which may lead to divergent outcomes or highlight existing differences.
- Children develop gender-typed patterns of behavior and preferences as early as age 15 to 36 months. Girls tend to conform less strictly to gender-role stereotypes than do boys, possibly because parents and teachers exert greater pressure on boys to adhere to the masculine role. Girls may also imitate the male role because it has greater status and privilege in our culture. Although some boys and girls receive support for cross-gender behavior, most are encouraged to behave according to traditional stereotypes.
- A longitudinal study found that adult heterosexual behavior could be predicted from gender-typed interests in elementary school. Greater stability was found when a characteristic was related to culturally accepted standards; culturally nontraditional childhood behaviors tended to emerge in divergent forms in adulthood. Thus gender-typed interests tended to remain stable from childhood to maturity.
- Research indicates that gender roles fluctuate across the life course as adults change to meet the demands of new situations and circumstances, such as childrearing. Whatever their roles up to this point, women tend to show more **expressive characteristics** in parenthood and men more **instrumental characteristics.**

Biological Factors in Gender Differences

- Biological factors that are thought to shape gender differences include hormones and lateralization of brain function. Hormones may organize a biological predisposition to be masculine or feminine during the prenatal period, and the increase in hormones during puberty may activate that predisposition. In addition, social experiences may alter the levels of hormones, such as testosterone. Gender differences in the brain's organization may be reflected in the greater lateralization of brain functioning in males, which may help explain male success at spatial and math tasks. It may also explain female tendencies to be more flexible than males and to withstand injury to the brain more effectively.
- Androgenized female fetuses may become girls whose behavior and interests are more traditionally male. Exceptionally high prenatal or perinatal androgen levels in females may be correlated with greater visuo-spatial skills later on, but the evidence is mixed. Environmental factors also influence both sexes' development of traditional and nontraditional gender-based abilities and interests.

Cognitive Factors in Gender Differences

- Cognitive factors in children's understanding of gender and gender stereotypes may contribute to their acquisition of gender roles. Two cognitive approaches to gender typing have looked at when children acquire different types of gender information and how such information modifies their gender-role activities and behaviors. Kohlberg's three-stage **cognitive developmental theory of gender typing** suggests that children begin by categorizing themselves as male or female, then feel rewarded by behaving in gender-consistent ways. To do this, they must develop gender identity, **gender stability,** and **gender constancy.**
- **Gender-schema theory** suggests that children develop naive mental schemas that help them organize their experiences in such a way that they will know what to attend to and how to interpret new information. According to this theory, we should expect individual differences in how gender-schematic children will be.
- According to cognitive developmental theory, we should not see gender-typed behavior until a child has achieved gender constancy (around age 6). However, children express gender-typed toy and activity preferences much earlier, whereas they do not choose same-sex playmates until later. These findings suggest that the link between the acquisition of gender concepts and behavior varies depending on gender understanding and kind of behavior.

Influence of the Family on Gender Typing

- Families play an active role in gender-role socialization in the way they organize their children's environment. They dress boys and girls differently, give them different toys to play with, and furnish their bedrooms differently. In addition, parents—especially fathers—treat girls and boys differently. Parents tend to see boys as stronger, even at birth, and to treat them more roughly and play with them more actively than with girls. As children grow older, parents protect girls more and allow them less autonomy than boys. Parents also expect boys to achieve more in the areas of mathematics and careers than girls.
- As predicted by cognitive social learning theory, parents influence children's gender typing through role modeling. Parental power has a great impact on gender typing in boys, but not in girls. Femininity in girls, however, is related to the father's masculinity, his approval of the mother as a model, and his reinforcement of his daughter's participation in feminine activities.
- Because the father plays such a critical role in the development of children's gender roles, his absence has been related to disruptions in gender typing in preado-

lescent boys and to problems in relationships with peers of the opposite sex for adolescent females. Studies show that the effects of a father's absence on his daughter's interactions with men are long lasting, extending to marital choices.
- There is no evidence of differences in the gender roles of boys and girls raised in gay or lesbian families. Most children of such families grow up to have heterosexual sexual orientataions.

Extrafamilial Influences on Gender Roles

- Many extrafamilial influences affect gender-role typing. Male and female roles are portrayed in gender-stereotypic ways in many childrens' books and on television. Males are more likely than females to be portrayed as aggressive, competent, rational, and powerful in the workforce. Females are more often portrayed as involved primarily in housework or caring for children.
- Females are less likely to be leading characters on TV, and male characters are overrepresented in children's books—although some change toward greater equality has occurred in recent years. Children who are heavy TV viewers hold more gender-stereotyped views; however, this may be due to their interpretations of what they see based on previously held stereotypes. A few attempts to use television to change gender stereotypes have been successful, but the effects typically have been modest and short-lived.
- Peers also serve as an important source of gender-role standards. Children who have masculine or androgynous characteristics are likely to have higher self-esteem than those who have traditionally feminine characteristics.
- Children are likely to react when other children violate gender-typical behaviors, and boys' cross-gender behaviors are more likely to meet with negative reactions from peers. Reactions from peers typically result in changes in behavior, particularly if the feedback is from a child of the same sex. This pattern of responsiveness may lead to gender segregation, which, in turn, provides opportunities to learn gender-typical roles. In **self-socialization**, children often spontaneously adopt gender-appropriate behavior.
- Teachers also treat girls and boys differently. Schools emphasize quiet and conformity to rules. Girls tend to like school better and perform better than boys in the early grades. Even in preschool, teachers, who often react to children in gender-stereotypic ways, tend to criticize boys more than girls. If young boys perceive school as gender inappropriate they may be less motivated to participate in school activities. This may in part explain the higher rate of learning problems found in boys in the early grades.
- The kinds of conforming and dependent behaviors encouraged in girls may be detrimental to their later academic success. The lack of public awareness of research findings, such as that in most areas of math girls do as well as boys, may prevent parents and others from encouraging girls to excel in these areas.

Androgyny

- Most people are not strictly feminine or masculine but possess both masculine and feminine characteristics. Children who are more **androgynous** make less stereotyped play and activity choices.
- Research interventions and the experience of nontraditional preschools indicate that children's gender stereotypes can be reduced. Similarly, children of nonconventional parents who place a high value on gender egalitarianism are less gender typed in their beliefs about possible occupations for males and females, although they are no different from other children on play preferences and knowledge of cultural sex typing. In other words, they are **multischematic**, holding more than one gender schema for responding to the world.

Morality, Altruism, and Aggression

C H A P T E R 16

Anyone who spends time observing children in the classroom or on the playground must be impressed by the great diversity of children's behaviors. Some children engage in cooperative play, in helping or sharing with others, or in soothing a classmate who has a broken toy or a scraped knee. Other children are involved in one altercation after another—successive bouts of name calling, quarreling, shoving, and pushing, with occasional bursts of more violent physical fighting. And watch children during an exam—some are whispering or peeking surreptitiously at a neighbor's exam paper or stealthily slipping out crib notes concealed in their desks. Others sit with their brows furrowed in focused attention, trying to solve the problems on the exam.

What contributes to such marked variations in children's behavior toward one another and in their apparent attitudes toward ethical issues? How do moral values and behaviors develop in the young child? How does the child become capable of self-control, resistance to temptation, and personal sacrifices for the welfare of others? This chapter traces the course of moral development, the evolution of prosocial and altruistic behaviors, and the development and control of aggressive behaviors. We begin by discussing two of the most important theories of moral development, those of Jean Piaget and Lawrence Kohlberg. We examine the relationship of moral judgment and moral behavior, and the consistency of these attributes across situations and over time. We then explore the development of prosocial and altruistic behaviors, asking how early these behaviors begin, how they change, and what role parents play in their emergence in the child. Finally, we consider the topic of aggression, raising a number of issues: How does aggression develop? How does it change in form and frequency? How do biological and environmental factors, such as the family, influence the development of aggressive behaviors? And how can we control aggression most effectively?

AN OVERVIEW OF MORAL DEVELOPMENT

In every culture, one of socialization's most basic tasks is communicating ethical standards and shaping and enforcing the practice of "good" behaviors in the developing child. Although the specific values and behaviors regarded as desirable vary among cultures, every society has a system of rules about the rightness and wrongness of certain behaviors. Adults expect children to learn these rules and to experience satisfaction when conforming to them and emotional discomfort or guilt when violating them.

Initially, parents control the young child's behavior largely through immediate external factors, such as their displeasure or the child's fear of punishment. As children mature, however, they begin to regulate their own behavior by means of internalized standards of conduct. They become able, in the absence of external restraints, to exert self-control. As we've discussed earlier in the book, it is through *internalization* that children incorporate others' ideas and beliefs into their own concepts of themselves, thus developing personal standards of conduct. Many psychologists believe that internalization is the fundamental and essential process in the development of morality.

Psychological research has focused on the development of three basic components of morality—the cognitive component, the behavioral component, and the emotional component—and the relationships among these three factors and their roles in the process of internalization. The cognitive component involves the knowledge of ethical rules and judgments of the "goodness" or "badness" of various acts. The behavioral component has to do with people's actual behavior in situations that invoke ethical considerations, and the emotional component focuses on people's feelings about situations and behaviors that involve moral and ethical decisions. As we will see, these same three components can help us understand the development of altruism and of aggression.

In general, studies of moral behavior in children have investigated activities that most adults consider wrong, such as cheating or lying, being unable to delay gratification, and failing to resist temptation or to control aggressive behavior. Recently, however, researchers have begun to study positive behaviors, such as sharing, helping, cooperating, and performing prosocial or altruistic acts. Studies of the emotional dimension of morality have also traditionally focused on negative aspects, such as feelings of guilt after a transgression, but recent work has focused on positive emotions such as empathy for other people's misfortunes or distress (Eisenberg & Fabes, 1998). The particular theory a researcher embraces generally determines the specific aspect of moral development she or he explores. Cognitive theories drive investigations of moral judgments, learning theories provide the underpinning for studies of ethical behaviors, and psychoanalytic theories underlie examinations of the affective components of morality.

COGNITIVE THEORIES OF MORAL DEVELOPMENT

Jean Piaget and Lawrence Kohlberg have offered alternative explanations for the acceptance and development of moral standards. As you will see, Piaget's theory of moral development involves many of his principles and processes of cognitive growth that we discussed in Chapter 9. Indeed, both Piaget and Kohlberg consider moral development essentially an aspect of cognitive development as this development bears on the specific topic of ethics and morality.

Jean Piaget's Cognitive Theory of Moral Development

Piaget proposes a cognitive developmental theory of moral development in which the child's moral concepts evolve in an unvarying sequence through three stages. The first, *premoral stage* runs from birth to the age of 5; the *stage of moral realism* runs from 6 to 10 years of age; and the third stage of *morality of reciprocity,* or *autonomous morality,* runs from 11 onward. One cannot reach the stage of moral reciprocity without first passing through the stage of moral realism. According to Piaget, mature morality includes both an understanding and acceptance of social rules and a concern for equality and reciprocity in human relationships; these qualities form the basis of justice. Piaget investigated children's developing moral judgment in two main ways: by noting how children change their attitudes toward rules in common games and how they change their judgments of the seriousness of transgressions over time.

Learning the Rules of Moral Behavior

The preschool child is in the **premoral stage;** she shows little concern for, or awareness of, rules. In games like marbles, children don't try to play systematically with the intention of winning but seem rather to gain satisfaction from manipulating the marbles and finding out how they can be used in different ways. By the time children are 5, however, they begin to develop great concern and respect for rules as they move into the stage of **moral realism.** They see rules as coming from authority, usually their parents, and they see rules as immutable—unchanging through time, and never to be questioned. In this stage, what Piaget calls *moral absolutism* prevails. If we ask children of this age if children in other countries could play marbles with different rules, they will assure us that they could not. We see a similar rigidity in the way children approach social interactions, frequently falling back on a "my mommy says" ploy to solve disputes.

In addition, young children subscribe to the notion of **immanent justice:** They see any deviation from the rules as inevitably resulting in punishment. Someone or something is going to get you, one way or another! Such retribution might take the form of accidents or mishaps controlled by inanimate objects or by God. A child

premoral stage Piaget's first stage of moral development, in which the child shows little concern for rules.

moral realism Piaget's second stage of moral development, in which the child shows great respect for rules but applies them quite inflexibly.

immanent justice The notion that any deviation from rules will inevitably result in punishment or retribution.

Starting to play formal games is one of the ways children, like these Moroccan boys, learn the meaning of rules. However, rules may vary across different cultures.

who has lied to his mother may later fall off his bike, skin his knees, and think, "That's what I get for lying to mother." In this stage, children also evaluate the seriousness of an act solely in terms of its consequences; they don't take the perpetrator's intentions into account. The two factors that contribute to young children's moral realism are their egocentrism, that is, their inability to subordinate their own experiences and to perceive situations as others might, and their immature way of thinking, which leads them to confuse external reality with their own thought processes and subjective experiences.

morality of reciprocity
Piaget's third stage of moral development, in which the child recognizes that rules may be questioned and altered, considers the feelings and views of others, and believes in equal justice for all.

Piaget believes that a **morality of reciprocity** begins to emerge in older children at about the age of 11. The child's moral judgments are now characterized by his recognition that social rules are arbitrary agreements that can be questioned and changed. He realizes that obedience to authority is neither necessary nor always desirable and that violations of rules are not always wrong, nor inevitably punished. In judging another's behavior, the child considers the other's feelings and viewpoint. In this stage, children believe that if behavior is to be punished, the punishment should be related to both the wrongdoer's intentions and the nature of the transgression. The punishment, the child thinks, should also be of such a nature that it somehow makes up for the harm done or helps teach the wrongdoer to behave better in the future. Children in this stage also believe in "equalitarianism"—that is, they believe that there should be equal justice for all.

Some of the shifts in attitude from the stage of moral realism to the stage of moral reciprocity are vividly illustrated in Piaget's account of his investigations, *The Moral Judgment of the Child* (1932). Piaget would read paired stories to a child and then ask the child if the children in each story were equally guilty, which child was the naughtier, and why.

> *Story I.* A little boy who is called John is in his room. He is called to dinner. He goes into the dining room. But behind the door there [is] a chair, and on the chair there [is] a tray with 15 cups on it. John couldn't have known that there was all this behind the door. He goes in, the door knocks against the tray, "bang" to the 15 cups and they all get broken!
>
> *Story II.* Once there was a little boy whose name was Henry. One day when his mother was out he tried to get some jam out of the cupboard. He climbed up on a chair and stretched out his arm. But the jam was too high up and he couldn't reach it and have any. But while he was trying to get it, he knocked over a cup. The cup fell down and broke. (Piaget, 1932, p. 122)

A characteristic response for a child in the stage of moral realism is given by a 6-year-old:

"What did the first boy do?"

"He broke 15 cups."

"And the second one?"

"He broke a cup by moving roughly."

"Is one of the boys naughtier than the other?"

"The first one is because he knocked over 15 cups."

"If you were the daddy, which one would you punish most?"

"The one who broke 15 cups."

"Why did he break them?"

"The door shut too hard and knocked them over. He didn't do it on purpose."

"And why did the other boy break a cup?"

"Because he was clumsy. When he was getting the jam the cup fell down."

"Why did he want to get the jam?"

"Because he was alone. Because his mother wasn't there." (Piaget, 1932, p. 129)

Although Henry tried to deceive his mother, the child in the stage of moral realism regards John as less ethical because he broke more cups, even though John's act was an accident and unintentional. In contrast, René, who is 10, shows signs that he's reached the stage of moral reciprocity when he responds that the child who wanted to take the jam was the naughtier. When asked if it makes any difference that the other child broke more cups, René replies: "No, because the one who broke 15 cups didn't do it on purpose" (Piaget, 1932, p. 130).

Evaluation of Piaget's Theory

How well has Piaget's theory fared after nearly 70 years? Most cognitive theories of moral development hold that people progress from one level of moral judgment to another in a fixed and invariant sequence, and Piaget's developmental progression from moral realism to moral reciprocity has been supported (Ferguson & Rule, 1982). In industrialized Western countries such as the United States, Great Britain, France, and Switzerland, across a wide range of populations and social classes, and among both genders, investigators find regular age trends in the development of moral judgment. However, the findings in other cross-cultural studies are less consistent. For example, Havinghurst and Neugarten (1955) found that among the people of 10 Native American tribes, the belief in immanent justice increased rather than decreased over time. Also, only 2 of the 10 groups showed the predicted shift toward greater flexibility in the conception of rules with age.

Although research on moral development lends support to the general developmental sequence, it also suggests that Piaget underestimated the cognitive capacities of young children. In judging the behavior of others, even 6-year-old children are able to consider an actor's intentions when the situation is described in a way that they can comprehend. For example, when Chandler, Greenspan, and Barenboim (1973) presented stories to 6-year-olds by videotape, rather than orally, the children responded to the intentions of the actors as well as older children did. As the authors noted, "The medium is the message!"

Another methodological shortcoming in Piaget's early studies may help account for his underestimation of young children's ability to make moral judgments. Piaget always mixed action outcome with actor intention. Thus he invariably required children to judge whether a child who causes a small amount of damage in the service of bad intentions is "worse" than a child who causes a large amount of damage but has good intentions. When researchers present stories in which good and bad intentions can be evaluated separately from good and bad outcomes, even elementary-school-age children can use intentions as a basis for judgment (Bussey, 1992; Feldman, Klosson, Parsons, Rholes, & Ruble, 1976; Yuill & Perner, 1988). For example, if the case of the broken cups is presented with a focus on intention (i.e., the child breaks cups *in trying to help his mother* or *in trying to sneak a cookie*), but the outcome is the same for all stories (i.e., the child breaks 6 cups), children have no trouble understanding the role of intention. In this kind of presentation, they are not confused by the variation in the relativity of the bad outcomes (e.g., 1 broken cup versus 15 broken cups). By cleverly creating variations on these basic stories, researchers have been able to isolate factors that affect moral judgments. Just as in real life, many issues influence our judgments about rightness and wrongness.

James Rest (1983), an expert on moral development, describes some of these additional considerations. In isolating these issues, researchers use combinations of these factors in building their stories—and of course do not use them all at once—to avoid the problems that plagued Piaget's original studies. And they do continue to use Piagetian stories to isolate the factors that influence moral judgments (Grueneich, 1982; Jose, 1990; Turiel, 1998). As Rest (1983) describes this approach,

> Instead of having only two factors (intentions and consequences), some studies have shown the influence of a multitude of factors: (1) whether the consequences are negative or positive, (2) the extent or degree of the consequences, (3) whether the object of the consequence is an inanimate object, animal, or person, and if a person, (4) whether the effects of the action were physical or psychological, (5) whether the consequences were intended, or happened accidentally or through carelessness or recklessness, and if intended, (6) whether the person was provoked, forced or pressured, or whether the consequences were willful and premeditated, (7) whether the specific activity was part of an overall plan to be helpful, or malicious and selfish, or part of no plan at all . . . and so on. (p. 119)

The "simple" tasks that Piaget devised more than half a century ago have become much more complicated today! Clearly there are many more factors to consider in understanding moral reasoning than simply intentions and consequences. In the next section we will see that Kohlberg has offered a more complex approach to the study of moral judgment.

Lawrence Kohlberg's Cognitive Theory of Moral Development

Lawrence Kohlberg (1963a, 1963b, 1969, 1985) has based his theory of moral development on Piget's theory, but he has modified the latter greatly. Although Kohlberg has retained Piaget's notion of stages of development, he has refined and expanded these stages and extended the age periods covered. Like Piaget, Kohlberg believes that the child's cognitive capabilities determine the evolution of her moral reasoning. Thus, moral development builds on concepts grasped in preceding stages, much as in Piaget's general theory of cognitive development the attainments of each stage build on the achievements of earlier stages.

To test his theory, Kohlberg began by interviewing boys between the ages of 10 and 16, presenting them with a series of moral dilemmas in which they had to choose either to obey rules and authority or to ignore such regulatory forces and instead to respond to the needs and welfare of other people. Here is a representative story presented to Kohlberg's young participants:

> Heinz needs a particular expensive drug to help his dying wife. The pharmacist who discovered and controls the supply of the drug has refused Heinz's offer to give him all the money he now has, which would be about half the necessary sum, and to pay the rest later. Heinz must now decide whether or not to steal the drug to save his wife; that is,

whether to obey the rules and laws of society or to violate them to respond to the needs of his wife. What should Heinz do, and why?

On the basis of his findings, Kohlberg formulated a series of three broad levels of moral development and subdivided these into six stages. Each stage was based not only on participants' choices of either an obedient or a need-serving act but on the reasons participants gave and on the ways they justified their choices. Table 16-1 presents these levels and stages of moral development. Kohlberg believes that although the sequence of all six stages is fixed—that is, all people pass through the

---

TABLE 16-1   Kohlberg's Theory of Moral Development

Level I Preconventional Morality

Stage 1

Obedience and punishment orientation	To avoid punishment, the child defers to prestigious or powerful people, usually the parents. The morality of an act is defined by its physical consequences.

Stage 2

| Naive hedonistic and instrumental orientation | The child conforms to gain rewards. The child understands reciprocity and sharing, but this reciprocity is manipulative and self-serving rather than based on a true sense of justice, generosity, sympathy, or compassion. It is a kind of bartering: "I'll lend you my bike if I can play with your wagon." "I'll do my homework now if I can watch the late night movie." |

Level II Conventional Morality: Conventional Rules and Conformity

Stage 3

| Good boy morality | The child's good behavior is designed to maintain approval and good relations with others. Although the child is still basing judgments of right and wrong on others' responses, he is concerned with their approval and disapproval rather than their physical power. It is to maintain goodwill that he conforms to families' and friends' standards. However, the child is starting to accept others' social regulations and to judge the goodness or badness of behavior in terms of a person's intent to violate these rules. |

Stage 4

| Authority and morality that maintain the social order | The person blindly accepts social conventions and rules and believes that if society accepts these rules, they should be maintained to avoid censure. He now conforms not just to other individuals' standards but to the social order. This is the epitome of "law and order" morality, involving unquestioning acceptance of social regulations. The person judges behavior as good according to whether it conforms to a rigid set of rules. According to Kohlberg, many people never go beyond this conventional level of morality. |

Level III Postconventional Morality: Self-Accepted Moral Principles

Stage 5

| Morality of contract, individual rights, and democratically accepted law | People now have a flexibility of moral beliefs they lacked in earlier stages. Morality is based on an agreement among individuals to conform to norms that appear necessary to maintain the social order and the rights of others. However, because this is a social contract, it can be modified when people within a society rationally discuss alternatives that might be more advantageous to more members of the society. |

Stage 6

| Morality of individual principles and conscience | People conform both to social standards and to internalized ideals. Their intent is to avoid self-condemnation rather than criticism by others. People base their decisions on abstract principles involving justice, compassion, and equality. This is a morality based on a respect for others. People who have attained this level of development will have highly individualistic moral beliefs that may at times conflict with rules accepted by the majority of a society. According to Kohlberg, among the nonviolent, activist students who demonstrated in the mid to late 1960s against the Vietnam War, more had attained the postconventional level of morality than had nonactivist students. |

Source: Kohlberg, 1963a.

stages in the same order—they may occur in different people at different ages. Moreover, many people may never attain the highest level of moral judgment, and even some adults continue to think in immature terms.

Kohlberg agrees with Piaget that the young child is oriented toward obedience, but he cites different reasons. Whereas Piaget regarded this early conformity as based on the young child's dependency and respect for authority, Kohlberg sees behavior at the **preconventional level** as based on the desire to avoid punishment and gain rewards (see Table 16-1, Level I). At Level II, the **conventional level,** although the child identifies with his parents and conforms to what they regard as right and wrong, what he has internalized is the motive to conform, not the notion of ethical standards. It is only at Level III, the **postconventional level,** that moral judgment is rational and internalized and that conduct is controlled by an internalized ethical code that is relatively independent of others' approval or castigation. At this level, moral conflict is resolved in terms of broad ethical principles, and violating these principles results in guilt and self-condemnation.

In Kohlberg's original and later studies (Colby & Kohlberg, 1987; Kohlberg, 1963a, 1985), young children gave more preconventional (Level I) responses and older children gave more postconventional responses (Figure 16-1). Although as we've said, Kohlberg predicts no specific level of response at any specific age, the general sequence of stages is followed in these participants' responding. The sequence should be invariant across cultures, Kohlberg asserts, although the ultimate level attained may vary among cultures and for individuals within the same society. Once a person has attained a high level of moral cognition, especially Stage 6, he will not regress and go back to earlier stages.

Moral Development in Girls and Women

Have you perhaps missed something so far in our account of Kohlberg's theory of moral development? Did you notice that the participants in his studies were boys and male adolescents? A lot of women have! Feminists contend that Kohlberg's theory is biased against females. Carol Gilligan, the foremost spokesperson for this view, argued eloquently in her book *In a Different Voice* (1982) that Kohlberg failed to take account of possible differences in the moral orientations of females and males. Citing the fact that women usually score lower than men on Kohlberg's tests, Gilligan (1982) points out that "the very traits that traditionally have defined the 'goodness' of women are those that mark them as deficient in moral development" (p. 18). Researchers have rated most women's moral judgments on these tests at Stage 3, the stage in which morality is conceived in terms of goodness and badness. In this stage the person is motivated primarily to maintain the goodwill and approval of others, although she or he is beginning to accept the notion of social regulations and to judge behaviors in terms of whether people conform to or violate these rules.

Because Kohlberg derived his levels and stages largely from his study of boys and men, Gilligan argues, women may appear to score lower on moral reasoning simply because they have a different moral orientation. Women may take a more caring and interpersonal approach to moral dilemmas, whereas men tend to emphasize such less clearly personal values as individual rights and principles of justice. Consider how two children—a boy and a girl—responded to the question, Should Heinz steal the drug to save his wife's life?

Jake, age 11:

For one thing, a human life is worth more than money, and if the druggist only makes $1,000, he is still going to live, but if Heinz doesn't steal the drug, his wife is going to die. [Why is life worth more than money?] Because the druggist can get a thousand dollars from rich people with cancer, but Heinz can't get his wife again. [Why not?] Because people are all different and so you couldn't get Heinz's wife again. (Gilligan, 1982, p. 26)

Jake's response emphasizes logic and the balance between life and property rights, according to Gilligan, a masculine orientation.

---

preconventional level
Kohlberg's first level of moral development, in which he sees the child's behavior as based on the desire to avoid punishment and gain rewards.

conventional level
Kohlberg's second level of moral development, in which the child's behavior is designed to solicit others' approval and maintain good relations with them. The child accepts societal regulations unquestioningly and judges behavior as good if it conforms to these rules.

postconventional level
Kohlberg's third level of moral development, in which the child's judgments are rational and his conduct is controlled by an internalized ethical code that is relatively independent of the approval or disapproval of others.

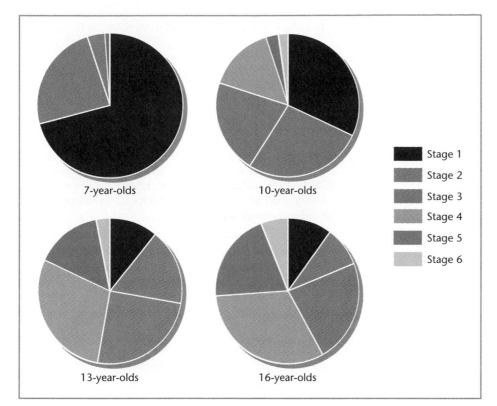

■ FIGURE 16-1
Use of Kohlberg's six stages of moral reasoning and judgment.
Most 7-year-olds responded at Level I (Stages 1 and 2), although a very few offered some Level III (Stages 5 and 6) responses. the 10-year-olds showed the most regular pattern: In descending order of frequency, they gave Stages 1, 2, 3, 4, 5, and 6 responses! Among 16-year-olds, the most common responses were at Level II (Stages 3 and 4). Quite a few participants responded at Level III (Stages 5 and 6), but there were also some Level I responses. (*Source:* Adapted from Kohlberg, 1963a)

Amy, age 11:

Well, I don't think so. I think there might be other ways besides stealing it, like if he could borrow the money or make a loan or something, but he really shouldn't steal the drug—but his wife shouldn't die either. If he stole the drug, he might save his wife then, but if he did, he might have to go to jail, and then his wife might get sicker again, and he couldn't get more of the drug, and it might not be good. So, they should really just talk it out and find some other way to make the money. (Gilligan, 1982, p. 28)

Instead of focusing on the issues of property or law, Amy focuses on the impact the theft might have on Heinz, his wife, his wife's condition, and their relationship—an interpersonal orientation to morality.

Others have found support for Gilligan's claim of separate moral orientations for males and females. Walker, deVries, and Trevethan (1987) found that when they asked adults to recall real-life dilemmas (e.g., birth control, abortion, the preservation of life, the inequitability of a will), women were more likely to express a caring orientation whereas men more often adopted a "rights" orientation. Women were also more likely to recall dilemmas that concerned personal relationships, whereas men recalled more impersonal kinds of dilemmas. Interestingly, when men and women were asked to respond to similar real-life dilemmas, the gender differences disappeared (Walker et al., 1987). Other studies using both hypothetical and real-life situations have yielded no clear pattern of gender differences (Turiel, 1998; Walker, Pitts, Hennig, & Matsuba, 1995).

Although there is some basis for Gilligan's contention that there may be different orientations to morality, we have little evidence of a gender bias in moral reasoning. Reviewing data from more than 10,000 research participants, Walker (1988) found little support for the notion that females and males differ in the levels of their moral judgments. At the same time, Gilligan (1991, 1993) argues that the caring and interpersonal perspective should be added to the understanding of moral reasoning in all people, and this view has received some support from cross-cultural studies. Consider, for example, the research described in Box 16-1. The case is not closed, and the debate continues.

BOX 16-1

Perspectives on Diversity

Justice versus Interpersonal Obligations: India and the United States

The debate about the significance of a caring and interpersonal perspective for a model of moral reasoning may have broader implications than Gilligan foresaw when she first challenged Kohlberg's model of moral development. Cross-cultural research that has pitted interpersonal obligations against justice obligations has revealed significant differences between the choices American and Hindu Indian children and adults make in the face of moral dilemmas. Miller and Bersoff (1992) found that whereas more than 80 percent of Indian schoolchildren and adults endorsed interpersonal considerations in judging these issues, little more than a third of U.S. schoolchildren and adults endorsed such considerations.

According to Miler and Bersoff (1992), Kohlberg's model is based on a philosophical tradition (Kantian) that sees "beneficence" obligations (obligations to care for others) as subordinate to justice obligations. The latter are based on "fairness, rights [and] the Golden Rule" (Kohlberg, 1973, quoted in Miller & Bersoff, 1992, p. 431). In contrast, concerns for the welfare of others that subsume such things as caring, prosocial behavior, loyalty, and charity are matters of either beneficence or interpersonal responsibility. According to Miller and Bersoff, Americans attribute a personal moral status to such interpersonal responsibilities and assume that personal choice rather than rules of justice apply. These researchers find that "American children believe that only justice obligations, and not helping behavior, should be rule governed" (1992, p. 542). On the other hand, Hindu Indian children and adults apparently see helping others as fully moral, that is, as involving "a sense of objective obligation and as being within the scope of legitimate regulation" (p. 542).

Comparing groups of third- and seventh-grade children and college-age adults in New Haven, Connecticut, and in Mysore, a city in southern India, Miller and Bersoff asked their participants first to rate the undesirability of single incidents in which people were described as breaching either justice or interpersonal obligations. In this phase of the study

the researchers endeavored to adjust their examples so as to ensure that participants considered all incidents of the same or nearly the same degree of importance. In the second phase of the study, the researchers presented participants with fully described conflict situations in which the respondents could fulfill one kind of behavioral obligation (justice or interpersonal) only by violating the other (interpersonal or justice). In the following example, personal names, names of cities, and other details were altered for the stories presented to Indian participants:

> Ben was in Los Angeles on business. When his meetings were over . . . Ben planned to travel to San Francisco . . . to attend [his best friend's wedding]. He needed to catch the very next train if he was to be on time for the ceremony, as he had to deliver the wedding rings.
>
> However, Ben's wallet was stolen in the train station. He lost all of his money as well as his ticket to San Francisco. . . . He approached several officials as well as passengers . . . and asked them to loan him money to buy a new ticket. But . . . no one was willing to lend him the money he needed.
>
> While Ben was sitting on a bench trying to decide what to do next, a well-dressed man sitting next to him walked away for a minute. . . . Ben noticed that the man had left his coat unattended. Sticking out of the man's coat pocket was a train ticket to San Francisco. Ben knew that he could take the ticket and use it to travel to San Francisco on the next train. He also saw that the man had more than enough money in his coat pocket to buy another train ticket.

In this example, participants were asked to decide which of the following two alternative actions Ben should choose. Note that both the purpose that would be fulfilled and the obligation that would be violated by each choice was clearly stated:

1. *Ben should not take the ticket from the man's coat pocket*—even though it means not getting to San Francisco in time to deliver the wedding rings to his best friend.

2. *Ben should go to San Francisco to deliver the wedding rings to his best friend*—even though it means taking the train ticket from the other man's coat pocket.

Relation of Moral Judgments to Other Cognitive Measures

It is not surprising that general cognitive maturity has been found to be related to moral maturity. A child needs to have achieved a high level of abstract thinking to evaluate her own or others' intent and to have developed generalized and rational ethical standards, as well as sensitivity to the roles, perceptions, and feelings of others. In one study (Tomlinson-Keasey & Keasey, 1974), college women who reasoned at the postconventional level (Stages 5 and 6) also showed formal operational thinking. However, not all who reasoned at the formal operations level reached the postconventional levels of moral development. This evidence suggests that formal operations are a necessary, but not sufficient, condition for advanced levels of moral judgment. In addition, measures of role-taking skills correlate with

As Figure 16-2 shows, Indian participants at all age levels were more than twice as likely to decide in favor of the interpersonal alternatives than were American participants. The more serious the breach of an obligation, the more likely Hindu Indians were to switch to a justice choice, but even in these circumstances Indians clearly preferred the interpersonal alternatives. Indians also tended to categorize their recommendations as moral imperatives whether they opted for justice or interpersonal alternatives. Americans, however, tended to describe an interpersonal alternative as a personal-moral or personal-choice decision. Interestingly, when Americans and Indians considered life-threatening situations, they both viewed helping others as moral issues; they disagreed, however, when the dilemmas were less extreme. It seems that Indians tend to view helping others in fully moral terms no matter how minor the issue, a view more compatible with the view of morality Gilligan originally proposed as more "feminine."

Kohlberg's model specifies that at Stage 6, "individuals conform both to social standards and to internalized ideals [and] . . . make decisions that are based on abstract principles that include compassion . . . [evidencing] a morality that is based upon a respect for others" (Table 16-1). This formulation certainly does not seem to rule out so-called interpersonal concerns. Moreover, as we have noted in the text, many researchers who have used Kohlberg's model have failed to find the gender differences that early research detected. The Hindu religion holds that all life is sacred, and Hindu Indian culture emphasizes "social duties as the starting point of society" (Miller & Bersoff, 1992, p. 552). These views are not greatly different from those many in Western society have attributed to a "feminine" perspective. It seems likely that caring and interpersonal moral reasoning is not feminine but rather a view of morality that differs from a moral perspective based on the concept of justice and individual rights.

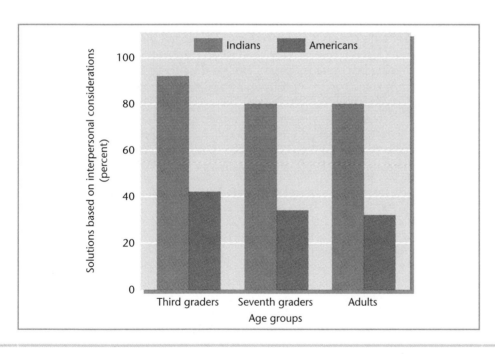

■ FIGURE 16-2
Moral dilemmas and interpersonal versus justice considerations.
In every age group, Indians were far more likely than Americans to cite interpersonal considerations in deciding on solutions to moral dilemmas (*Source:* Based on Miller & Bersoff, 1992)

Kohlberg's levels of moral judgment; that is, increases in role-taking ability precede shifts to higher levels of moral development (Rest, 1983; Turiel, 1998).

Effects of Social Interactions on Moral Development

Kohlberg has emphasized the importance for the child's moral development of social interactions that involve role-taking opportunities. Children who participate in more social activities are more often elected group leaders, are rated by their peers and teachers as more popular; in addition, these socially active children have been rated more mature in moral judgments (Enright & Sutterfield, 1980). In contrast, researchers have found that children in restricted social environments (e.g., isolated communities or schools that offered little opportunity for role-taking experience) tended to give relatively simplistic descriptions of social roles, a finding that might well be accompanied by limitations in these children's role-taking abilities, which are basic to moral judgment (Rest, 1983; Turiel, 1998).

Researchers have devised educational programs to foster the development of moral judgment based on Kohlberg's theory. Designed for classroom use, these programs usually focus on peer discussion of controversial moral issues. Practice in exploring possible solutions to moral dilemmas and in negotiating with others are key ingredients in these programs, which explore the relationship between social interactions and moral development and also provide a way of evaluating Kohlberg's theory. Although we have some evidence that these educational interventions foster moral judgment and promote closer links between judgments and behavior (Higgins, 1991; Higgins, Power, & Kohlberg, 1984), they are still controversial. Some programs fail to meet their goals, and it is still unclear what specific teaching tactics or curriculum materials are most effective in helping children develop their moral reasoning (Damon, 1988).

Kohlberg argues that parents do not play a crucial role in moral development. However, other researchers have found that the cognitive structuring involved in parental discipline does affect moral judgments. When parents use consistent disciplinary techniques that involve reasoning and explanation, initiate discussion of the feelings of others, and promote a democratic family-discussion style, children evidence more mature moral judgments and more self-controlled behavior (Aronfreed, 1976; Edwards, 1980; Hoffman, 1984; Parke, 1977). And in fact, children's understanding of moral rules may begin at a very early age. Observing the natural interactions among young children and members of their families, Judy Dunn (1987, 1989) and her colleagues found that the children showed not only the beginnings of moral understanding but rapid increases between the ages of 2 and 3. They showed clear awareness of rules, for example, looking at their mothers and laughing when carrying out a forbidden act or pointing out the consequences of the rule violation, like a broken object. As early as 16 months, mothers and children engaged in "moral dialogues" about rules, with children often nodding, shaking their heads, or providing verbal answers to their mothers' inquiries about rules. Interestingly, children at a young age commented on their own responsibility for transgressions.

> ELLA (21 months): [At table, throws toy to floor, a previously forbidden act. Looks at mother.]
> MOTHER: No! What's Ella?
> CHILD: Bad bad baba.
> MOTHER: A bad bad baba.

Children also joined in conversations between mother and siblings to comment on the transgressions of others.

> SIBLING: [shows mother that she has drawn on a piece of jigsaw puzzle.] Look.
> MOTHER [to sibling]: You're not supposed to draw on them, Caroline. You should know better. You only draw on pieces of paper. You don't draw on puzzles.
> CHILD (24 months): [to mother] Why?
> MOTHER [to child]: Because they aren't pieces of paper.
> CHILD: Naughty.
> MOTHER: Yes, that is a naughty thing to do.

As children develop, they learn to justify their actions. By 36 months, in nearly a third of their disputes with mothers and siblings, children produced justifications, which were often in terms of their own wants, needs, or feelings. (For example, one child said, "But, I need that" as a sibling tried to take the child's spoon); "That doesn't belong to you," in reference to social rules; "Rachel will be cross if you do that," referring to the feelings of another; and "You'll break it if you do that," indicating the material consequences of actions. Children emerge at an early age as budding moral philosophers.

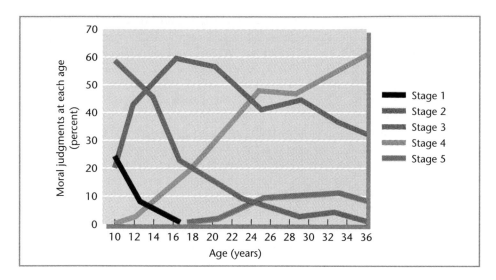

Evaluation of Kohlberg's Theory

Kohlberg's theory of moral judgment maintains more current support than Piaget's, but there are critics as well as defenders (Snarey, 1987; Turiel, 1998). The notion that children proceed through the stages of moral judgment in an invariant fashion has received general support (Rest, 1983; Turiel 1988; Walker, 1988, 1989). The most impressive evidence comes from a longitudinal study of 58 males (Colby, Kohlberg, Gibbs, & Lieberman, 1983). The participants were 10, 13, and 16 years old at the start of the study and gave their judgments of nine hypothetical moral dilemmas five times over a 20-year period, at three- and four-year intervals. All but two participants moved to higher stages over the course of the study, and no one skipped stages. Although the vast majority stopped at Stage 4, a few continued to develop their moral reasoning in their twenties, reaching Stage 5 in young adulthood (Figure 16-3). Role-playing and modeling studies that have attempted to learn whether people can be induced to shift their moral reasoning to another level have generally found that it is easier to advance a person's moral judgment to a higher stage than to a lower one (Rest, 1979, 1983; Turiel, 1966). Moreover, participants who are exposed to a model's reasoning about a moral dilemma at a stage above or a stage below their own stage of moral development prefer the more advanced to the less advanced stage (Rest, 1983; Turiel, 1998). These findings are generally consistent with both Piaget's and Kohlberg's views that progress should be toward higher rather than lower stages.

The research we've discussed, however, also underscores a possible major flaw in Kohlberg's theory. The dominant pattern of moral reasoning in most adults appears to be conventional (Level II, or Stages 3 and 4). Notice in Figure 16-3 that no adults reached Stage 6, and fewer than 10 percent reached Stage 5. Even Kohlberg has expressed doubts about the practical value of scoring stories for Stage 6 responses and has dropped this final stage from the most recent form of the scoring system (Colby & Kohlberg, 1987). There may be fewer Gandhis among us than Kohlberg originally imagined!

How does the theory fare in cross-cultural studies? A three-year longitudinal study in the Bahamas that began with children ranging between 8 and 17 confirmed the general pattern of progression from lower to higher stages of moral reasoning (White, Bushnell, & Regnemer, 1978). And studies in Turkey (Nisan & Kohlberg, 1982), Taiwan (Lei & Cheng, 1989), and Israel (Snarey, Reimer, & Kohlberg, 1985) have supported the proposal that individuals, regardless of their cultural background, would develop through the stage sequence in the same manner. In addition, in this study few participants skipped or regressed to lower stages. On the other hand, some research evidence suggests the possibility of cultural bias. For example, in New Guinea, people place community obligations over individual rights, whereas in India, people emphasize the sacredness of all forms of life. As Box 16-1 suggests, Kohlberg's focus on individual rights and obligations may lead to underestimates of moral development in other cultures or may exclude some culturally unique domains of morality (Shweder & Haidt, 1993; Shweder & Much, 1987; Snarey 1987).

Events in history often shape people's views of morality as they develop, just as the life span perspective (Chapter 1) would predict. The Watergate political crisis, the Vietnam War, the Midwest farm crisis, and the women's movement shaped a generation of people, perhaps sensitizing them to issues of fairness and justice. People who grew up in other eras (e.g., the Great Depression of the 1930s) may have different understandings of moral issues. Changes in moral judgment, in short, may be affected by the sociopolitical context of the times that we live in (Rest, Davison, & Robbins, 1978; Turiel, 1998).

In spite of criticisms and limitations, Kohlberg's pioneering work revolutionized the way that we think about moral development. Due to his influence, cognitive judgment and understanding are central concerns of a contemporary approach to the issue of morality.

Distinguishing Moral Judgments from Other Social Rules

social-convention rules Socially based rules about everyday conduct.

Children must learn many rules for behavior. At the same time that they learn moral strictures against cheating, lying, and stealing they learn many other nonmoral, **social-convention rules** about everyday conduct: table manners, kinds of dress, modes of greeting, forms of address, and other rules of social etiquette. According to Elliot Turiel (1983, 1998), children make clear distinctions between reasoning about moral issues and reasoning about social conventions. In one study of nursery-school-age children (Nucci & Turiel, 1978), researchers asked children how wrong it would be to hit someone, lie, or steal (violate moral rules), and how wrong to address teachers by their first names, for a boy to enter a girl's bathroom, or to eat lunch with one's fingers (violate rules of social convention). In support of Turiel's argument that morality and social conventions represent independent domains, children and adolescents from second grade to college consistently viewed the moral violations as more wrong than the violations of social convention.

Even children as young as 3 can distinguish moral from social-convention issues (Smetana & Braeges, 1990). However, young children can generally make this distinction only with respect to familiar situations. When children reach the ages of 9 or 10, they can apply the distinction to both familiar and unfamiliar issues (Smetana, 1995; Turiel, 1998). Children view moral violations as more wrong because they result in harm to another and violate norms of justice and others' rights, whereas they see deviations from social conventions as being impolite or disruptive and as violations of social rules and traditions (Turiel, 1998).

personal domain An area of rules and conventions distinct from moral rules; involves issues such as choice of friends and styles of dress.

Children also learn to distinguish issues that involve morality and social convention from those that touch on the **personal domain** (Nucci, 1996). The latter include such issues as friendship choices, personal conversations, personal diaries, and choices of such things as hairstyle and clothing. Even in cultures that have a more collectivist than individualistic orientation, children and adolescents distinguish moral and social-convention issues from personal ones. In Brazil and Hong Kong, for example, children made this distinction increasingly over time (Nucci, Camino, & Milnitsky-Sapiro, 1996; Yau & Smetana, 1996). This domain is seen as essential for children's development of individuality and for their construction of a self-concept and personal identity (Erikson, 1970; Nucci, 1996).

Children agree with the notion that although moral issues are fixed, absolute, and invariant across cultures, social conventions are arbitrary and relative and vary across communities and cultures (Helwig, 1995; Turiel, Killen, & Helwig, 1988). When asked if it would be acceptable to steal in a country that had no laws against stealing, children as young as 6 thought it was wrong to steal. On the other hand, children thought that people in different countries could play games by different rules (Turiel et al., 1988). In many countries, including Brazil, India, Indonesia, Korea, Nigeria, and Zambia, children and adolescents judge moral issues (such as welfare and justice) differently from social-convention issues (such as eating and bathing) (Bersoff & Miller, 1993; Turiel, 1998).

How do children learn to make these distinctions between moral and social-convention transgressions? Probably parents and other family members help children learn these distinctions (Nucci & Weber, 1995). Children learn from their parents at a very early age that eating your spaghetti with your hands or spilling your milk has different consequences than taking your brother's toy or pulling your kid sister's pigtail. Mothers of 24- to 26-month-olds responded to social-convention violations with rules about social order and social regulation that focused on the disorder that the act created ("Look at the mess that you made!"). In contrast, mothers' responses to moral transgressions focused on the consequences of the acts for other's rights and welfare or by perspective-taking requests ("Think about how you would feel if you were hit!") (Smetana, 1989, 1995). Moreover, mothers tend to allow children much more choice and freedom around personal issues (Nucci & Weber, 1995).

Parents influence adolescents as well as young children. Even teenagers understand and accept that parents may legitimately regulate and enforce moral behavior (Smetana, 1995; Smetana & Asquith, 1994). Adolescents even agree with parents on parental regulation of social-convention matters; however, adolescents view parental regulation of moral issues as more legitimate (Smetana & Asquith, 1994). Adolescents do not agree, however, that parents have a right to regulate personal matters (e.g., appearance, friendship choices, spending decisions); conflicts most often arise in this area and they arise increasingly, as the adolescent grows older. Conflicts that mix social-convention and personal issues—for example, cleaning one's own room affects the entire home—are more intense.

Other socializing agents, including teachers and peers, play a part, too. In day-care centers, adults respond differently to the moral and social-convention transgressions of 12-month-old toddlers than those of 36-month-old toddlers (Smetana, 1984, 1995, 1997). Even other children react differently to these different kinds of violations: Smetana found that 2- and 3-year-olds reacted more emotionally and retaliated more often in the face of moral transgressions than they did when they confronted social-convention transgressions. Not surprisingly, children become more sophisticated in their responses as they develop. For example, the 3-year-olds displayed more adult responses than the 2-year-olds. The older children were more likely to make statements about rights (e.g., "That's not fair," or "The rules say that you can't do that"), a major accomplishment for a 3-year-old! In sum, children can distinguish different kinds of violations and can do so at a surprisingly early point in development. As in other areas of development—perception, cognition, language, emotion—we're learning that children are more competent at earlier ages than previous generations of developmental psychologists believed.

Do Moral Judgments Always Lead to Moral Behavior?

Knowledge of the maturity of a child's moral judgments does not necessarily predict how a child will actually behave in a situation where she must choose between ethically desirable and undesirable behavior. Moral judgments and moral behavior are often unrelated, especially in young children (Blasi, 1983; Straughtan, 1986). Much behavior is impulsive and not guided by rational and deliberate thought (Burton, 1984). A child may have reached Kohlberg's Stage 3, the level of "good girl morality," where she is concerned with maintaining parental approval. However, when her younger brother breaks her favorite toys, she may kick him even if the parent is present to disapprove of her action. Later, the child may even be able to offer mature reasoning that it is wrong to hit young children because they do not really know what they're doing. Thought does not always guide action!

We do have some evidence, however, that in older children, moral judgments and moral behavior may be linked. People who have reached Kohlberg's Level III (Stages 5 and 6) are less likely to cheat than those at earlier levels, less likely to inflict pain on others, and more likely to endorse free speech and due process and to oppose capital punishment (Kohlberg & Candee, 1984; Leming, 1978; Rest, 1986). Nevertheless, as we noted earlier, relatively few people may reach Stage 6 in Kohlberg's moral scheme. Thus although moral judgments may relate to behavior among older children, the link between moral cognition and action among young children is very weak.

Although it's convenient to divide the world of morality into separate parts—cognitive, emotional, and behavioral—in real life these different aspects often operate together in determining how a child will act when faced with the need for a moral decision. Rest (1983) proposes a four-step process in executing a moral action (this process is reminiscent of Dodge's information-processing approach to social interaction that we considered in Chapter 13). When faced with a situation that requires such action, in Step 1 the child first interprets the situation in terms of how other people's welfare could be affected by his or her possible actions. Then, in Step 2, the child must figure out what the ideally moral course of action would be, given the possibilities presented in Step 1. In Step 3 the child must decide what she or he actually intends to do, and finally, in Step 4, the child actually performs the action chosen. So far we have considered Steps 1 and 2; in the next section we'll be exploring Steps 3 and 4.

THE BEHAVIORAL SIDE OF MORAL DEVELOPMENT

People don't just think about actions, they act, and to differing degrees in moral ways. In this section we focus on the action, or behavioral, component of moral judgment—deciding what to do and doing it.

Self-Regulation and the Delay of Gratification

As we learned in Chapter 12, one goal in socializing the child is to help her achieve *self-regulation,* or the ability to control her behavior on her own, without reminders from others. In the context of moral development, the child must also learn to inhibit or direct her actions to conform to social or moral rules. Life is full of temptations, traps, and tugs that try to pull the young child away from socially acceptable courses of action. Children's ability to resist these forces is a consequence of both their own emerging cognitive and representational capacities as well as the guidance parents, siblings, and other socializing agents provide.

How does this capacity to monitor and regulate one's own behavior develop? According to Kopp (1982, 1987), the child proceeds through several phases. In the **control phase** (12 to 18 months) "children show awareness of social and task demands that have been defined by caregivers and initiate, maintain, modulate or cease acts accordingly upon demand . . . In [this] phase, children are highly dependent upon the caregiver for reminder signals about acceptable behaviors" (Kopp, 1987, p. 38). And, in fact, children do begin to show compliance to caregiver demands during this period (Kaler & Kopp, 1990). In the next, **self-control phase** the child gains the ability to comply with caregiver expectations in the absence of external monitors. Kopp suggests that development of representational thinking and recall memory permits the child to remember family rules and routines involved in common activities such as eating, dressing, and playing. At last, in the **self-regulation phase,** children become able to use strategies and plans to direct their behavior and to aid them in resisting temptation and in the **delay of gratification.** For example, Vaughn, Kopp,

---

control phase According to Kopp, the first phase in learning self-regulation, when children are highly dependent on caregivers to remind them about acceptable behaviors.

self-control phase According to Kopp, the second phase in learning self-regulation, when the child becomes able to comply with caregiver expectations in the absence of the caregiver.

self-regulation phase According to Kopp, the third phase in learning self-regulation, when children become able to use strategies and plans in directing their own behavior and capable of delaying gratification.

delay of gratification Putting off until another time possessing or doing something that gives one pleasure.

and Krakow (1984) displayed attractive objects such as a toy telephone, an attractively wrapped gift, or a raisin under a cup to 18-, 24-, and 30-month-olds and then told the children not to touch the objects right away. Whereas the 18-month-olds were able to wait only 20 seconds, the 24-months-olds waited 70 seconds, and the 30-month-olds waited nearly 100 seconds before touching the attractive but forbidden objects!

Other research confirms the progression in self-control over the preschool period (Kopp, 1992; Kuczynski & Kochanska, 1990). For example, children can learn how to resist temptation and how to give themselves explicit instructions that help keep them focused. Charlotte Patterson and Walter Mischel (Mischel & Patterson, 1978; Patterson, 1982) promised children attractive prizes

This boy may be trying to guess what's in the packages or just itching to start tearing off the paper—or both! Learning to delay gratification is a significant part of self-regulation.

for completing the task of copying letters of the alphabet onto a page, and then made the children's task harder by attempting to distract them with a talking clown who invited the children to look at him and play with him. The researchers provided some children with a specific plan to help them resist the clown (say, "No, I can't. I'm working") but gave others no verbal plan for resisting the clown's invitation. The preschoolers who had the verbal plan were less distracted by the clown than were the classmates without a plan.

Apparently some plans are better than others, though. A verbal plan that focuses on the specific temptation ("When Mr. Clown says to look at him . . . you can just not look at him and say, 'I'm not going to look at Mr. Clown'") is more effective than a task-formulating plan ("You can just look at your work and say to yourself, 'I'm going to look at my work'"). Children who were provided with the temptation-inhibiting plan spent less time attending to the clown, worked longer, and completed more work than did either the children with the task-oriented plan or those with no plan. And children become more skilled at using plans for delaying gratification. A nonspecific plan—that is, one offering general instructions but no specific script—doesn't help young children very much, but older children, who are capable of filling in appropriate details when they need them, can use generalized plans to help achieve self-control. Why do most young children fail to come up with their own specific, verbal plans? This may be partly because preschoolers' knowledge about the effectiveness of different strategies is limited. As they develop, children not only learn to use self-control strategies more efficiently but become more aware of which ones work best. Gradually, they learn to use a range of techniques including self-distraction (e.g., looking away, sitting on their hands), self-instructions (e.g., "No, no; don't touch"), or redefinition of the object (e.g., thinking about marshmallows as puffy clouds to reduce their appeal) (Kopp, 1987; Shoda, Mischel, & Peake, 1990).

The development of self-control is influenced not only by the child's own efforts but by the actions of parents and other caregivers as well. Various kinds of parental disciplinary practices, such as consistent and carefully timed punishment as well as the provision of a rationale for compliance, help increase resistance to temptation (Kuczynski, 1983; Kuczynski, Marshall, & Shell, 1997; Parke, 1977). Moreover, as children age, mothers shift their control strategies from physical to verbal modalities; explanations, bargaining, and reprimands increase as the child grows older, and distraction techniques decrease (Kuczynski, Kochanska, Radke-Yarrow, & Girnius-Brown, 1987). This suggests that parents shift their strategies to match the increasingly sophisticated quality of the child's cognitive and language capacities. In turn, these types of parental input aid the child's own abilities to use verbally based control strategies (Kopp, 1987, 1992). In addition, models who follow the rules, such as siblings and peers, are often effective in reducing cheating in young children (Bandura, 1989; Grusec, Kuczynski, Rushton, & Simutis, 1979). Models are particularly effective if they display alternative acceptable behavior at the same time that they resist breaking the rules (Bussey & Perry, 1977).

Self-control may also be affected by temperament. According to Kochanska (1993a,b, 1995), the process of internalization through which children develop self-regulatory capabilities involves two particular aspects of temperament: the passive and active inhibition systems. The *passive inhibition system* is driven primarily by fear and anxiety and often operates outside of awareness. The *active inhibition system,* on the other hand, is expressed in conscious, effortful control, by which the person regulates his or her behavior, particularly when desirable behavior requires giving up or postponing pleasurable outcomes (Rothbart, 1989; Kochanska et al., 1997). Researchers assess these aspects of temperament by measuring how a child slows down motor activity, makes a clear effort to attend, and suppresses or initiates activity in response to a specific signal. For example, Kochanska (1995) found that fearful toddlers who responded with distress and withdrawal in laboratory situations when researchers presented them with novel or mildly risky events were more likely to inhibit prohibited behavior than less fearful children.

Children who are high in effortful control show more internalization of rules of conduct than children who display little control of this sort than children who are low on this kind of control. Moreover, these links between effortful control and measures of internalization are evident both cross-sectionally and longitudinally. Kochanska has also found that effortful control increases with age and is a stable individual difference among children (Kochanska, Murray, & Coy, 1997; Kochanska & Thompson, 1997).

Because children differ in temperament, it is not surprising that varying parental disciplinary strategies are effective with different children. And indeed, Kochanska's findings suggest that there are different routes to the emergence of **conscience**—internalized values and standards of behavior—and children's control of their actions. Kochanska (1995, 1997) has found that for children who were relatively fearful as 2-year-olds, mothers' gentle discipline that deemphasized power was correlated with strong evidence of conscience at toddler and preschool ages. In contrast, with relatively fearless children, low-key maternal discipline did not work; instead, parental strategies that focused on positive motivation promoted higher levels of self-control. Overall, a mother-child relationship that was positive, responsive, and cooperative was linked with strong conscience development in young children. This work illustrates the important interplay between children's temperamental characteristics and parental child-rearing practices. As they say, "Different strokes for different folks."

conscience The child's internalized values and standards of behavior.

Consistency across Situations and Time

Are children consistent in their moral behavior across situations? To answer this question, we turn to the most extensive investigation of moral behavior in children ever attempted. In their project, Hartshorne and May (1928) studied the responses of 11,000 school-age children who were given the opportunity to cheat, steal, and lie in a wide variety of situations: athletics, social events, the school, the home, alone, or with peers. Some years after the close of this study, Burton (1963, 1984) analyzed the measures that were proved reliable from Hartshorne's and May's studies in deceit and found strong evidence for a general factor of moral behavior. Burton concluded that every child does have a different general predisposition to behave morally or immorally in a variety of situations. The more similar the situations, the greater the consistency in self-control; the less the situations resemble each other, the less likely the child's response will be the same on each occasion. For example, measures of cheating on achievement tests in the classroom correlated more highly with each other than they did with measures of cheating on games in the home. Such findings underscore the importance of situational variables, such as fear of detection, peer support for deviant behavior, and the instigation of other powerful motivational factors, such as the temptation to cheat on an exam to get a better grade. Because these measures also showed considerable variability among individual children, however, they also suggest that some children are more likely than others to yield to situational demands.

Are children consistent in their moral behavior over time? There is evidence to suggest that children who are able to delay gratification in early life are able to cope better socially and academically as adolescents (Mischel, Shoda, & Peake, 1988; Shoda, Mischel, & Peake, 1990). Researchers gave 4-year-olds a simple test of self-control to evaluate their ability to wait for an attractive reward (a toy or candy). They gave the children the option of obtaining a small reward immediately or a much larger and more attractive one later. Some children were very poor at waiting; others were able to delay taking their prize for a considerable period. Ten years later, when these children were adolescents, Mischel asked the parents to rate their children on a variety of traits. Parents rated the children who had been able to delay gratification in nursery school as more socially and cognitively competent. They were playful, resourceful, skillful, attentive, and able to deal with frustration and stress—a cluster of traits that are important ingredients in successful coping with the academic and social demands of adolescence. In sum, the early ability to inhibit impulses and delay gratification may have been an important antecedent of these children's later competence.

THE EVOLUTION OF PROSOCIAL AND ALTRUISTIC BEHAVIORS

As we will see later in this chapter, psychologists and others have spent many years studying the causes and consequences of antisocial behavior as well as ways of controlling aggression and violence. The influence of Freudian theory, with its strong emphasis on the dark side of human development (e.g., the forces of the id, the aggressive drive, and the punitive superego) led to this situation. As the grip of Freudian thinking on developmental psychology gradually loosened, some of the more positive aspects of development emerged as topics of investigation. Researchers did not begin in earnest to explore the more positive aspects of social behavior, such as helping others, until the 1970s. As a result, we know much less about these kinds of behaviors than we know about aggression.

Prosocial behavior is voluntary behavior that is intended to benefit another. It may be performed for a variety of motives, including egoistic, other-oriented, and practical concerns (Eisenberg & Fabes, 1998). **Altruism** is an unselfish concern for the welfare of other people. Altruistic behavior, like prosocial behavior, is voluntary behavior that is designed to help someone else. However, what distinguishes **altruistic behavior** from prosocial behavior is essentially the willingness to help another without any thought of recompense. Altruistic acts are motivated by "internalized values, goals, and self-rewards rather than by the expectation of concrete or social rewards" (Eisenberg & Fabes, 1998, p. 702). People may act prosocially, sharing and cooperating with others, helping or caring for them, sympathizing and comforting others in times of distress and need, and performing acts of kindness toward others. Prosocial behavior can also encompass actions designed to help groups of people, societies, nations, even the world. When people

prosocial behavior
Behavior that is designed to help or benefit other people.

altruism An unselfish concern for the welfare of others.

altruistic behavior
Intrinsically motivated behavior that is intended to help others without expectation of acknowledgment or concrete reward.

act altruistically, however, they do so without thought for their own immediate welfare, without expectation of reciprocity or acknowledgment (often acting anonymously), and sometimes even at the sacrifice of their own longer-term needs and wishes. According to Eisenberg & Fabes (1998), we see the beginnings of prosocial behavior in quite young children, whereas truly altruistic behavior, seen as a refinement of prosocial behavior, arises later on.

In this section we explore how prosocial behavior evolves and changes. We consider both biological and environmental determinants of prosocial behavior and then examine the influence of the child's evolving cognitive capabilities on prosocial reasoning and activity. Our concluding discussion examines the child's ability to understand and empathize with others' feelings and circumstances.

How Prosocial Behavior Evolves

As the Turning Points on chart p. 641 shows, prosocial behavior may begin even before an infant is 6 months old. For example, when children point out or show things to others or share toys, they are engaging in prosocial behavior (Hay, 1994). As we noted in Chapter 8, even before the end of the first year, children learn to use such gestures as pointing to communicate with those about them; this gesturing can be seen as a way of sharing interesting sights and objects with others. Rheingold and her colleagues have found that among 12- to 18-month-old children, showing and giving toys to a variety of adults (mothers, fathers, and strangers) is very common (Hay, 1979, 1994; Rheingold, Hay, & West, 1976). Moreover, children engage in these early sharing activities without prompting or direction and without being reinforced by praise. According to these authors, such behaviors as holding an object up for others to see and offering an object to another person represent developmental milestones. "That children so young share contradicts the egocentricity so often ascribed to them and reveals them instead as already contributors to social life" (Rheingold et al., 1976, p. 1157).

Changes in Prosocial Behaviors

Sharing and showing are not the only ways in which young children reveal their capacity for prosocial action. From an early age, children engage in a variety of other behaviors such as caregiving, helping adults with housework, or comforting another in distress—striking evidence that prosocial behavior begins very early in life (Rheingold, 1982). Children between 10 and 12 months old typically become agitated or cry in response to another child's distress, but they make little effort to help the other child. By the time they're 13 or 14 months old, however, they will often approach and comfort another child in distress. This comforting, though, is often general and not specific to the source of distress. When children are a year and a half old, they will not only approach a distressed person but offer specific kinds of help. For example, they may offer a toy to a child with a broken toy or a Band-Aid to a mother with a cut finger. And by the age of 2 children engage in a wide range of prosocial actions, including verbal advice ("Be careful"), indirect helping (getting their mother to retrieve the baby's rattle), sharing (giving food to a sister), distraction (closing a picture book that has made their mother sad), and protection/defense (trying to prevent another from being injured, distressed, or attacked). As Box 16-2 discusses, when young children begin to react to the distress of another, parents can encourage their emerging sense of altruism.

Children's altruistic behavior changes in form and expression as children develop. Children do not always show prosocial reactions to others' distress and indeed, they sometimes laugh or behave aggressively or even become distressed themselves (Radke-Yarrow & Zahn-Waxler, 1983; Zahn-Waxler, Radke-Yarrow, Wagner, & Chapman, 1992). However, based on a recent meta-analysis (a large-scale review of relevant studies), Eisenberg and Fabes (1998) found clear evidence that as children grow older they are generally more likely to engage in prosocial behaviors. This may be in part because over time, children become increasingly

TURNING POINTS: Prosocial and Altruistic Behavior

BIRTH–6 MONTHS	Responds positively to others (smiles, laughs with others) Participates in social games (e.g., peek-a-boo) Reacts emotionally to others' distress (crying or general upset)
6–12 MONTHS	Takes an active role in social games Exhibits sharing behaviors Displays affection to familiar persons
12–24 MONTHS	Refines ability to point with index finger Complies with simple requests Indicates knowledge of rules of cooperative games Shows knowledge of caregiving skills Comforts people in distress Participates in adults' work, household tasks Shows and gives toys to adults
24–36 MONTHS	Draws person's attention to objects with words as well as gestures Exhibits increasingly planful caregiving and helping behaviors Verbally expresses own intentions to help and knowledge of tasks Gives helpful verbal advice Tries to protect others
3–ABOUT 7 YEARS	Is hedonistically motivated to perform prosocial acts
3–11 YEARS	Recognizes others' needs even when they conflict with own
6–17 YEARS	Justifies prosocial or nonprosocial behavior by reference to stereotypical notions of good and bad and considerations of approval and acceptance from others
10–17 YEARS	Empathizes with others and feels pride or guilt about consequences of own actions
14–17 YEARS	May justify helping or not helping by internalized values and by concern with rights and dignity of others May believe in individual and social obligations, the equality of all individuals, and may base self-respect on living up to own values and accepted norms

Sources: Based on Eisenberg & Fabes, 1998; Eisenberg & Roth, 1983; Hay & Rheingold, 1983.

Note: Developmental events described in this and other Turning Points charts represent overall trends identified in research studies. Individual children vary greatly in the ages at which they achieve these developmental changes.

able to detect subtle cues that someone needs help (Eisenberg & Fabes, 1998). Presenting 4- and 8-year-old children with a series of vignettes in which the explicitness of distress cues varied (from a slight frown to a full-blown cry), Pearl (1985) found that the children were equally likely to note distress when the cues were explicit. However, when cues were subtle, 4-year-olds were less likely to see a problem or to suggest help. Naturalistic studies have shown similar results. Radke-Yarrow, Zahn-Waxler, and Chapman (1983) found that after 2- and 7-year-old children viewed a TV report of a family killed in a fire the 7-year-olds were better able to deal with subtle cues and more abstract kinds of distress and to consider

Child Psychology in Action

How Parents Can Teach Children Prosocial Behavior

To find out how children learn to react in helpful ways when they have caused distress in another person or when they see another person suffering, Carolyn Zahn-Waxler and her colleagues (Zahn-Waxler, Radke-Yarrow, Wagner, & Chapman, 1979, 1992) devised a clever scheme. They trained mothers of 18-month-olds to tape-record their children's reactions to others' distress that the children themselves either caused or witnessed. The mothers recorded both the child's and their own behavior over a nine-month period, during which observers occasionally visited the home to check on the accuracy of the mothers' records. The researchers also asked the mothers to simulate distress from time to time: For example, mothers might pretend to be sad (sobbing for five to ten seconds), to be in pain (bumping their feet or heads, saying "Ouch," and rubbing the injured parts), or to suffer respiratory distress (coughing/choking).

How did the children respond to others' distress? Overall, whether they had hurt someone else or merely witnessed another person's distress, they reacted in a helpful fashion about a third of the time. However, some children responded in most distress situations (between 60% and 70%), whereas some failed to respond at all.

Zahn-Waxler's research also revealed that mothers' reactions to their own children's harmful behavior toward others as well as to the sight of another person's distress can influence their children's development of helpful behavior in distress situations. Some mothers linked a child's behavior with its consequences for the child's victim; the children of these mothers were more likely to respond in a

helpful way when they caused harm to someone. These mothers might say, for example, in a clear but objective manner, "Tom's crying because you pushed him." Other mothers' discussions of distress situations had strong emotional overtones, and these explanations appeared to be even more effective. The children of these mothers were more likely to intervene in bystander situations where they did not cause any harm but saw that someone else was upset. These mothers might say something like, "You must never poke anyone's eyes," or "When you hurt me, I don't want to be near you. I am going away from you."

Other studies have confirmed these findings. For example, Denham, Renwick-DeBardi, and Hewes (1994) found that the children of mothers who pointed out a peer's personal distress in an affectively charged manner reacted in a sad fashion. On the other hand, some maternal tactics were ineffective in encouraging prosocial behavior. For example, physical restraint (simply moving away from the child or moving her away from a victim), physical punishment (a mother might have reported, "I swatted him a good one"), or unexplained prohibitions ("Stop that!") may even interfere with the development of prosocial behavior. These researchers also found that when mothers showed anger as they delivered their disciplinary reasoning and tried to induce guilt in children, preschoolers were unlikely to engage in parent-directed prosocial actions.

Prosocial and altruistic behavior can begin early, and parents play an important role. They can facilitate and encourage the child's emerging altruistic behaviors by helping children make connections between their own actions and other people's emotional states. Altruism truly does begin at home!

---

feelings other than those expressed in the immediate situation. For example, one child said, "I hope that those children weren't so young, so they had a chance to have some life before having to die."

Stability in Styles of Prosocial Behavior

Does knowledge of children's early prosocial tendencies help predict their helpful behavior at later ages? In a classic study, Baumrind (1971) measured nursery school children's nurturant and sympathetic behaviors toward their peers, their thoughtfulness, and their understanding of other children's viewpoints and then assessed these characteristics in the same children five or six years later. Between the two points in time she found that the characteristics showed moderate stability. A more recent, longitudinal study tells a similar story. Studying children's tendencies to donate to needy children and to assist an adult (e.g., by helping pick up paper clips), researchers found that both donating and helping behaviors were consistent between 10 and 12 years of age. Children who were highly prosocial at one age were likely to remain so at later ages (Eisenberg et al., 1987). It seems likely that there is a fair amount of consistency or stability in children's prosocial behavior across time.

We can look at the issue of stability from other angles. Radke-Yarrow and Zahn-Waxler (1983), found that children showed their prosocial tendencies in

Donating to a school food drive to help people less fortunate than themselves is an important lesson in prosocial behavior for young children.

different ways: Their prosocial responses varied in both frequency and quality. Consider the reactions of Althea, Jenny, Talia, and Kim—all 2-year-olds—when their mothers cry after reading a sad story in the newspaper. Althea begins to tense up and fights back her tears. Jenny shows little emotion but asks, "What's wrong, Mommy?" Talia tears up the newspaper that makes her mother cry, while Kim covers her ears and turns the other way. As these very different reactions illustrate, infants and children develop their own styles of dealing with others' distress. Some children are very emotional, like Althea, and show a great deal of upset. Other youngsters, like Jenny, are cool and reflective and appear to approach the situation more cognitively, by inspecting, exploring, and asking questions. Still others, like Talia, show an aggressive, defensive prosocial approach; for example, "hit the person who made the baby cry." Finally, some children, like Kim, try to "shut out" signals of distress and turn or run away.

These researchers, who observed their young participants first when they were 2 years old and again when they were 7, found stability in style of reaction in about two-thirds of the children. The same style of reacting to others' upset and discomfort was evident both in infancy and five years later. Similarly, the pattern of intense, empathic, affective prosocial attempts made by certain toddlers was still evident at age 7, and the combative responders, the problem-solvers, and the anxious-guilty types were still exhibiting their characteristic styles 5 years later. Of course, not all children responded similarly across time and for some, "development meant change" (Radke-Yarrow & Zahn-Waxler, 1983, p. 16).

Are Girls More Prosocial than Boys?

Based on our discussions in Chapter 15, we might expect to find that girls are more responsive, empathic, and prosocial than boys. Although girls tend to be more generally oriented toward helping others than boys, the reality is more complex. According to a recent meta-analysis of a large number of studies (Eisenberg & Fabes, 1998; Fabes & Eisenberg, 1996), gender differences vary depending on what type of prosocial behavior we're looking at. Differences are largest for kindness and consideration. Girls are apparently also higher in instrumental helping, comforting, sharing, and donating, but gender differences on these behaviors were less dramatic.

Interestingly, gender differences are most pronounced in data derived from self-reports and reports of others (family members, peers) than in data gathered by observational techniques. This may suggest that some gender differences "reflect people's conceptions of what boys and girls are *supposed* to be like rather than how they actually behave" (Eisenberg & Fabes, 1998, p. 754). Parents stress the importance of politeness and prosocial behavior more for daughters than for sons (Power & Parke, 1986; Power & Shanks, 1989). When girls behave prosocially, parents attribute such behaviors to inborn tendencies, whereas they attribute boys' prosocial behaviors to the influences of the environment and socialization. These findings do not mean that gender differences are *only* in the eye of (the self or) the beholder but that these cultural stereotypes and beliefs may contribute to the gender differences that researchers have found.

> **empathy** The capacity to experience the same emotion that someone else is experiencing.

Closely related are gender differences in **empathy,** the capacity to experience the emotions that others feel. Girls are clearly more empathic than boys, and the gender difference becomes greater as children develop (Eisenberg & Fabes, 1998; Fabes & Eisenberg, 1996). Again, self-report measures have shown the greatest gender differences. According to Eisenberg and Fabes (1998), gender differences in empathy may increase as children become more aware of gender stereotypes and expectations and perhaps more likely to internalize these in their self-images.

Determinants of Prosocial Development

> **prosocial reasoning** Thinking and making judgments about prosocial issues.

Like most behaviors, prosocial behavior and **prosocial reasoning**—thinking about and judging prosocial issues—may have both genetic and environmental determinants. So far, however, the evidence for a biological contribution is modest, so our discussions in this section emphasize environmental influences such as parental behavior—both teaching and modeling—cultural customs and practices, and the media, particularly, television programming.

Biological Influences

Some argue that human beings have a biological predisposition to respond with empathy and that we are biologically prepared to engage in prosocial behavior. In his book *Sociobiology* (1975), the evolutionary biologist E. O. Wilson cites evidence of helping and sharing among infrahuman animals and argues that evolution has prepared us for such behavior. Research supports this view as well. Some theorists have claimed that the fact that newborn infants cry in response to the cries of other infants is evidence of our biological predisposition to behave in an empathic fashion (Hoffman, 1981).

Some researchers have proposed that individual differences in prosocial behavior may have a genetic basis. Identical twins have been found more alike in respect to prosocial behavior than fraternal twins (Davis, Luce, & Kraus, 1994; Rushton, Fulker, Neale, Nias, & Eysenck, 1986), but other research has provided only limited support to the notion that prosocial behavior may be inherited (Zahn-Waxler et al., 1992). In a study of 2-year-olds, identical and nonidentical twins did not differ in their observed prosocial behaviors, but the researchers found modest evidence for the heritability of empathic concern for a victim in (simulated) distress (Zahn-Waxler et al., 1998). Temperament may play a role in sympathetic responding and prosocial behaviors, just as it appears to influence children's ability to inhibit undesirable responses, as we saw in the section "Self-Regulation and the Delay of Gratification" (Eisenberg & Fabes, 1998).

Prosocial children are generally better at regulating their emotions and impulses than other children. For example, comforting behavior has been associated with physiological self-regulation, as indexed by measures of heart rate (Eisenberg, Fabes, Guthrie, & Murphy, 1996).

Environmental Influences

Whatever the biological contribution to prosocial behavior may be, environmental factors including the family, mass media, and culture clearly make a difference.

Laboratory studies in which children see others donate to others or share with them as well as real-life situations in which parents, peers, and others model prosocial and altruistic behaviors support this social-learning notion of the acquisition of prosocial behavior (Eisenberg & Fabes, 1998; Hart & Fegley, 1995). Interestingly, Rosenhan (1972) showed, in a now-classic study, that civil rights activists came from families in which parents were committed to altruistic and humanitarian causes.

Parents may act as models, or they may directly encourage, elicit, and shape prosocial behaviors in their children (Eisenberg, 1992; Eisenberg & Fabes, 1998; Grusec & Dix, 1986). As the study in Box 16-2 shows, mothers' childrearing practices do contribute to children's reactions to distress in others. Parents who use power-assertive techniques (such as physical punishment) and little reasoning and who show little warmth are unlikely to have altruistic children. In a study in the Netherlands, Dekovic and Janssens (1992) found that democratic parenting (warm, supportive, demanding, and providing guidance and positive feedback) was linked to more prosocial behavior in children as rated by both teachers and peers. In the United States, Biringen, Robinson, and Emde, (1994) supported these results, finding that mothers who were negative and controlling had children who showed increasingly less empathic tendencies between 14 and 20 months of age.

Most of the time, however, children probably acquire prosocial concepts and behavior through modeling and imitation rather than direct teaching. For example, parents may show things to their infants, thus encouraging the infants to imitate these actions, and at other times parents may request things of their infants—things that belong to the babies. "Such experiences inform infants about situations in which certain actions are socially appropriate and offer them opportunities for practicing and refining the actions" (Hay & Rheingold, 1983, pp. 28–29).

Parents who explicitly model prosocial behavior and at the same time provide opportunities for children to perform these actions may be particularly successful in promoting altruism (Eisenberg & Fabes, 1998). A common way parents provide opportunities for learning prosocial behavior is by assigning children responsibility for household tasks. Even children as young as 2 will spontaneously help adults in a variety of household tasks such as sweeping, cleaning, and setting tables (Rheingold, 1982). And allowing children to help in these ways may be important for their prosocial development. As Rheingold wryly notes, [parents'] "efficient execution of chores makes for inefficient teaching of the young" (1982, p. 124).

TV and Prosocial Behavior   Models of prosocial behavior are not confined to the family. Television is another source for learning prosocial behaviors. A variety of studies have assessed the impact on young children's prosocial behavior of watching segments from "Mister Rogers' Neighborhood," a program focusing on understanding the feelings of others, expressing sympathy, and helping. The children who watched "Mister Rogers' Neighborhood" not only learned the specific prosocial content of the program but were able to apply that learning to other situations involving peers. In comparison to children who watched shows with neutral content, the children who saw the prosocial programs learned some generalized rules about prosocial behavior (Friedrich & Stein, 1973; Huston et al., 1992; Huston & Wright, 1998). Television may be an important learning medium for such behavior.

Cross-Cultural Perspectives   In contrast to U.S. children, children in other cultures often are given the responsibility to take care of siblings and other children as well as to perform household tasks (Eisenberg & Fabes, 1998). What effect does this have? Cross-cultural studies of children from a wide range of cultures—Mexico, the Philippines, Okinawa, India, and Africa—suggest that "children who perform more domestic chores, help more with economic tasks and spend more time caring for their infant brothers, sisters, and cousins, score high on the altruistic dimension" (Whiting & Edwards, 1988; Whiting & Whiting, 1975). Researchers have made similar findings in other cultures that stress prosocial and communal values, such as the Aitutaki of Polynesia or the Papago tribe in Arizona (Eisenberg & Fabes, 1998). On the other hand, prosocial behaviors are rare and hostility and cruelty are the norms in cultures such as the Ik of Uganda (Eisenberg, 1992; Eisenberg & Fabes, 1998; Goody, 1991). Further evidence of both the role of culture and the modifiability of prosocial behavior comes from studies of children raised in Israeli kibbutzim, which stress prosocial and cooperative values, as you will recall from our discussion of attachment in kibbutz children in Chapter 7. Researchers found children reared in these communal settings more prosocial than city-reared peers (Aviezer, Van Ijzendoorn, Sagi, & Schuengel, 1994).

The Influence of Cognitive Development

We've said that prosocial behavior shifts in form and expression across development. These changes reflect alterations in prosocial reasoning, and these alterations, in turn, reflect changes in children's cognitive development. As you can see in Table 16-2, Nancy Eisenberg and her colleagues (Eisenberg, Lennon, & Roth, 1983; Eisenberg et al., 1987) have proposed a model of the development of prosocial reasoning that is in some ways similar to the Kohlberg model of the development of moral reasoning. To test the model's depiction of how children's thinking about prosocial acts changes across development, Eisenberg devised a number of accounts of hypothetical interpersonal or social dilemmas. Here is a sample:

> One day a girl (boy) named Mary (Eric) was going to a friend's birthday party. On her (his) way she (he) saw a girl (boy) who had fallen down and hurt her (his) leg. The girl (boy) asked Mary (Eric) to go to her (his) house and tell her (his) parents so the parents could come and take her (him) to the doctor. But if Mary (Eric) did run and get the child's parents, she (he) would be late to the birthday party and miss the ice cream, cake, and all the games. What should Mary (Eric) do? Why?

Eisenberg and her colleagues tested groups of children when they were 4½ and again when they were 11½ years old. As the children matured they became less egocentric and more other oriented, as well as more abstract in their reasoning about prosocial dilemmas. The first level of reasoning shown in Table 16-2, **hedonistic reasoning**, in which the child bases his decision to perform a prosocial act on the promise of material reward, decreased with age. The second level, **needs-oriented reasoning**—a relatively simple type of reasoning in which children express concern for the needs of others even though these needs may conflict with their own—peaked in midchildhood and then leveled off. However, the third, fourth, and fifth levels of reasoning described in the table—all of which fall under the rubric of prosocial reasoning—all increased with age. The gender differences we've discussed emerged as well; in early adolescence, girls made more use of empathic reasoning than boys. Predictably, sharing and empathy were both negatively related to hedonistic reasoning, and needs-oriented reasoning was positively related to prosocial behavior (Carlo, Koller, Eisenberg, Pacheco, & Loquercio, in press). Moreover, prosocial moral reasoning is more likely to be linked with prosocial behaviors when the behaviors require some cognitive reflection, rather than a simple, low-cost, prosocial action, such as helping someone pick up books that he dropped (Eisenberg & Shell, 1986; Miller, Eisenberg, Fabes, & Shell, 1996).

Assessing the possible relationships between children's levels of prosocial and moral reasoning, Eisenberg and her colleagues found only modest correlations. It may be that children's development within these two domains follows parallel but more or less independent paths. On the other hand, if helping behavior involves an important value or principle—for example, helping support or defeat legislative action to "save the trees"—a person's level of prosocial reasoning is likely to be relevant. As Eisenberg and Fabes (1998) note, "Moral reasoning is more likely to be associated with children's prosocial behavior in situations involving a cost because

hedonistic reasoning Basing one's decision to perform a prosocial act on the basis of expected material reward.

needs-oriented reasoning Reasoning in which children express concern for others' needs even though their own needs may conflict with those needs.

Level	Age Group	Orientation	Mode of Prosocial Reasoning
		TABLE 16-2 Evolution of Prosocial Reasoning	
1	Preschoolers and younger elementary school children	Hedonistic, self-focused	Child is concerned with self-oriented consequences rather than moral considerations. Decision to help or not help another is based on consideration of direct gain to self, future reciprocity, and concern for people to whom the child is bound by affectional ties
2	Preschoolers and elementary school children	Recognition of needs of others	Child expresses concern for the physical, material, and psychological needs of others even if these needs conflict with her own. Concern is expressed in the simplest terms, without verbal expressions of sympathy, evidence of self-reflective role taking, or reference to internalized affect such as guilt.
3	Elementary and high school students	Seeking others' approval and acceptance	Child uses stereotyped images of good and bad persons and behaviors and considerations of others' approval and acceptance in justifying prosocial or nonhelping behaviors.
4	Older elementary school and high school students	(a) Empathic	Child's judgments include evidence of sympathetic responding, self-reflective role taking, concern with the other's humanness, and guilt or positive affect related to the consequences of her actions.
	Minority of high-school-age children	(b) Transitional (empathic and internalized)	Child's justifications for helping or not helping involve internalized values, norms, duties, or responsibilities, and may refer to the necessity of protecting the rights and dignity of other persons. These ideas, however, are not clearly stated.
5	Only a small minority of high school students and virtually no elementary school children	Strongly internalized	Child's justifications for helping or not helping are based on internalized values, norms, or responsibilities, the desire to maintain individual and societal contractual obligations, and the belief in the dignity, rights, and equality of all individuals. Child also construes her self-respect as based on living up to her own values and accepted norms

Source: Adapted from Eisenberg, Lennon, & Roth, 1983.

consideration of the cost [will probably] evoke cognitive conflict and morally relevant decision making" (p. 732).

Making cross-cultural comparisons of children's (and adults') moral and prosocial thinking and behavior is difficult, for cultural norms relevant to the issue of social responsibility vary widely, and cultures differ in the ways they value specific kinds of prosocial actions (Eisenberg & Fabes, 1998). In general, there are relatively few differences in prosocial moral reasoning among children of industrialized Western cultures but quite a considerable difference between the way these children reason and the children of non-Western, developing nations think. In cultures such as that of Hindu India, for example, people tend to have a more stringent, duty-based view of social responsibility than do most people in the United States, where interpersonal responsiveness and caring is more of a personal choice (Miller, Bersoff, & Harwood, 1990; see also Box 16-1).

Beliefs about morality and appropriate behavior toward others are grounded in bodies of religious and philosophical thought that have deep roots in the histories of many cultures. For example, as we've discussed earlier, many people in Asian countries take a more collective approach to social and interpersonal behavior than do people in Western nations, placing the emphasis on the welfare of the group or nation rather than the individual. And indeed, some researchers argue that the norms that characterize the American culture are more linked with an emphasis on individual rights (Miller & Bersoff, 1992). When people live in communal fashion, as in traditional societies or developing nations, where people are more interdependent in their daily existence, or in the modern Israeli kibbutzim, ties of responsibility and reciprocity may be more binding.

Investigators have found that in Germany and Israel, school-age children were more likely then American children to emphasize direct reciprocity, whereby children expect to receive similar payback for their prosocial actions (Eisenberg, Boehnke, Schuler, & Sibereisen, 1985), and Brazilian urban adolescents were less likely to use higher-level prosocial reasoning than U.S. teens (Carlo et al., in press). Clearly, as we saw earlier, cultural experiences and values not only shape prosocial behaviors but organize the ways in which people think about their prosocial obligations to others.

Empathy, Perspective Taking, and Altruism

Two important determinants of altruism are empathy, and perspective-taking ability, or the capacity to understand another's point of view (Eisenberg, 1992; Hoffman, 1987). According to Hoffman, children have the capacity to feel or empathize with another person's emotional states. Another child's distress can elicit a similar emotion in an observer, just as a child can experience another person's joy or happiness. This empathic ability often motivates children to engage in prosocial actions that relieve not only another person's distress but also their own emotional upset. In turn, prosocial acts that result in positive affective feelings can vicariously produce similar positive emotions in the helping child. Evidence supports the expectation that children who are more empathic behave in a more prosocial manner (Eisenberg & Fabes, 1998; Eisenberg et al., 1990). Moreover, the daughters of mothers who are sensitive to their children's emotions (i.e., try to find out why children feel bad and listen to them when they are anxious and upset) display more prosocial behavior; for example, they will comfort an infant in distress (Eisenberg et al., 1993). The way that mothers talk about emotions matters, too. Preschoolers whose mothers explain their own sadness display more prosocial behavior (Denham & Grout, 1992).

Researchers have found clear links between perspective taking and altruism (Eisenberg & Fabes, 1998; Strayer & Roberts, 1988). However, perspective-taking ability alone may not be enough to produce prosocial behavior if a child doesn't have the motivation or the social assertiveness necessary to act prosocially. Several researchers have found that children who demonstrated ability in perspective taking and who were also either socially assertive or sympathetic were more prosocial than children good at perspective taking alone (Denham & Couchoud, 1991; Knight, Johnson, Carlo, & Eisenberg, 1994). In one study, children who donated money to help a child who was burned in a fire were those who were sympathetic, had perspective-taking ability, and understood units and value of money (Knight et. al., 1994).

Altruism is expressed in a complex and multiply determined set of behaviors. Although we are gradually learning more about prosocial action, we are not yet in a position to write a prescription for raising a helpful and caring child. Perhaps that ultimate prescription will include the prevention of the very troublesome aspect of social development to which we now turn—aggression.

THE DEVELOPMENT OF AGGRESSION

Altruism is a behavior that parents, peers, and teachers view positively; aggression, on the other hand, is seen as an unwelcome but common occurrence. For decades, psychologists have puzzled over the knotty problem of aggression. Why do some children—and adults—attack others? Do patterns of aggression change over time and how? What roles do families, peers, and the mass media play in the development of aggression? Finally, how can we control aggression in our children?

What Is Aggression?

Aggression is usually defined as behavior that intentionally harms other people by inflicting pain or injury on them. We use the term *intentionally* to distinguish aggression from the acts of doctors, dentists, surgeons, and other medical personnel or even of parents. Such individuals may, in fact, inflict pain on others, but that is not the intent or goal of their actions.

> **aggression** Behavior that intentionally harms other people by inflicting pain or injury on them.

How Aggressive Behavior Develops in Children

A visit to a nursery school and a stopover at an elementary school playground reveal some striking age differences in the form and frequency of aggressive behavior. (Our Turning Points chart on page 650 offers a brief outline of how aggression changes over time.) The nursery school children display aggression, but they are more likely to quarrel and fight over toys and possessions; that is they demonstrate **instrumental aggression.** In contrast, in the older children (6- and 7-year-olds) we see **hostile aggression,** or more personally oriented aggressive acts in which a child criticizes, ridicules, tattles on, and calls others names (Coie & Dodge, 1998; Hartup, 1974). This shift from fighting over things to fighting over human characteristics and behaviors may occur as older children acquire a greater ability to infer the intentions and motives of others (Ferguson & Rule, 1980). Thus, when older children recognize that another person wants to hurt them, they are more likely to retaliate by a direct assault on the tormentor rather than by an indirect attack on the aggressor's possessions.

> **instrumental aggression** Quarreling and fighting over toys and possessions.
>
> **hostile aggression** Aggressive behavior directed at another person, including criticizing, ridiculing, and name-calling.

Despite children's gradually improved ability to infer intent, individual children differ in how accurately they can "read" another person's intentions. Some children, especially those who are highly aggressive, have more difficulty in judging the intentions of their peers. Again, recall our discussion in Chapter 13 of the information-processing model of social behavior. We can apply this model to understanding aggressive behavior as well (Crick & Dodge, 1994; Dodge, 1985). According to Dodge, this is especially true in ambiguous situations, where the intentions are not clearly either aggressive or prosocial. In such situations, boys who are rated by their classmates as aggressive are likely to react in a hostile way—as if the other person intended to be aggressive. Aggressive boys see the world as a threatening and hostile place. They perceive the actions of others differently and see more anger and aggression in others than do less aggressive boys. Dodge and Frame (1982) found that aggressive boys not only committed more unprovoked aggressive acts but were the targets of more aggressive attacks than nonaggressive boys. They thus concluded that "the biased attributions of aggressive boys may have a basis in their experience. Their collective expectancy that peers will be biased in aggressing toward them is consistent with their experience" (Dodge & Frame, 1982, p. 28). Researchers have found this bias toward hostile attribution in a variety of samples, including European American, African American, and Latino

TURNING POINTS: The Development of Aggressive Behavior

INFANCY: 0–2 YEARS
Infants express anger and frustration.

They show some early signs of aggression (pushing, shoving).

Temperamental differences in irritability predict later aggression.

PRESCHOOL YEARS: 2–5 OR 6 YEARS
Children encouraged by family members in antisocial behavior may later begin to display seriously aggressive behavior.

Children in this age group tend to display instrumental aggression, fighting over toys and possessions, and to rely on the physical expression of aggression.

Even in the preschool period, girls exhibit more verbal and relational aggression, excluding and gossiping about others, whereas boys are more physical.

6–7 YEARS
Children display hostile aggression, using criticism, ridicule, name-calling, and tattling, as they begin to infer and to judge the intentions of others.

Instrumental aggression decreases.

ELEMENTARY SCHOOL AGE: 7–10 YEARS
The difference between boys' reliance on physical aggression and girls' reliance on relational aggression becomes more marked.

However, in both boys and girls, physical aggression gradually declines and verbal aggression becomes more common.

Aggressive children may begin to do poorly in school and to be rejected by peers.

In the fourth or fifth grade parental monitoring becomes particularly important, to deter delinquency and vandalism.

ADOLESCENCE
Aggressive children select aggressive and deviant peer groups.

Among some youths, vandalism, use of guns, and delinquency increase.

Gender differences are marked: rates of delinquency and violent behavior are much higher among boys than girls.

Hormonal changes, such as rising levels of testosterone, are associated with increases in reactive aggression in boys. Individual differences in hormonal levels are important determinants of the levels of aggression.

Sources: Coie & Dodge 98; Crick et al., 1998; Parke & Slaby, 83.
Note: Developmental events described in this and other Turning Points charts represent overall trends identified in research studies. Patterns of aggressive behavior vary greatly among individual children (see especially "The Family As a Training Center for Aggression").

American children (Graham & Hudley, 1994; Graham, Hudley, & Williams, 1992; Guerra & Slaby, 1989).

reactive aggression
Aggressive behavior that is responsive to attack, threat, or frustration.

proactive aggression The use of force to dominate another person or to bully or threaten others.

The kind of aggression a child displays can be characterized in yet another way. Some children act aggressively only in response to being attacked, threatened, or frustrated, displaying **reactive aggression.** In contrast, other children show **proactive aggression,** using force to dominate another person or to bully or threaten others to gain a prized object or possession. According to Dodge and Coie (1987), boys who display reactive aggression are more likely to misinterpret others' intentions, whereas those who are proactively aggressive—like the playground bully—are less likely to misread another's intent. Like instrumental aggression, proactive aggression decreases across development.

The way children express aggression also changes over development. Whereas toddlers rely more on physical attacks, older children, with their improved language and communication skills, are more likely to aggress verbally than physically (Coie & Dodge, 1998). These developmental shifts in the style of expressing aggression are due not only to increased verbal skills but to changes in adult expectations and rules. Most parents and teachers become less tolerant of physical aggression as children mature, while they are more likely to ignore a "battle of words" even among older children. On the other hand, different measures of aggression may reflect the same underlying pattern at different ages. For example, fighting at age 8, vandalism at age 12, and homicide at age 18 may all be indices of aggression, a reminder that the same disposition or trait is expressed differently at different ages (Farrington, 1993).

How stable is aggression over time? Does the level of aggression fluctuate across development? For both males and females, aggression appears to be moderately stable (Cairns & Cairns, 1994; Coie & Dodge, 1998; Olweus, 1979, 1982). In fact, aggression is as stable as intelligence. For both genders, stability is more pronounced across shorter spans of time; as the time between assessment points stretches out, the degree of stability decreases. Earlier research such as the Fels Longitudinal Study that we've mentioned before found greater stability of aggression for boys (Kagan & Moss, 1962). Perhaps owing to changing societal values, girls are beginning to show greater stability in assertive and aggressive behaviors. Even more important, if we distinguish between the kinds of aggression displayed by males (more physical) and females (more indirect) we find that aggression is stable for both (Cairns & Cairns, 1994; Lagerspetz & Bjorkqvist, 1994). Even across a 22-year span, aggression shows a moderate degree of consistency. In a follow-up study of more than 600 individuals who were originally seen at 8 years of age, Huesmann and his colleagues (1984) found that the more aggressive 8-year-olds were still more aggressive than their peers at age 30. The boys who were rated by their peers in childhood as aggressive were more likely as adults to have more moving traffic violations, to have been arrested for drunk driving, and to have abused their wives. Moreover, both males and females who were rated aggressive as children were more likely to have criminal convictions by the age of 30 (Figure 16-4).

Early aggression may have rather similar long-term consequences for males and females. Men who were rated ill-tempered as 8- to 10-year-old boys at age 40 had experienced erratic work lives, held poorer jobs than their parents, and were more likely to divorce than their even-tempered peers (Caspi et al., 1987). Ill-tempered girls married men with lower occupational mobility; were less adequate and more ill-tempered mothers; and were also more likely to divorce (Caspi et al., 1987). Clearly, an early pattern of aggressive behavior leaves its mark.

Gender Differences in Aggression

One of the most striking aspects of these developmental trends is the markedly divergent courses that boys and girls follow. Although there are few gender differences in infancy, toddlerhood, and the preschool years, even then boys are more likely than girls to instigate and be involved in aggressive incidents (Loeber & Hay, 1993; Maccoby & Jacklin, 1980). This gender difference is evident not only across U.S. socioeconomic groups but across cultures including Britain, Switzerland, Ethiopia, Kenya, India, the Philippines, Mexico, and Okinawa (Coie & Dodge, 1998; Whiting & Whiting, 1975). Boys' and girls' aggressive patterns differ in other important ways. Boys are more likely than girls to retaliate after being attacked (Darvill & Cheyne, 1981), and they are more likely to attack a male than a female (Barrett, 1979). Boys are more physically confrontational, they are less likely than girls to anticipate negative self-evaluation and parental disapproval

■ FIGURE 16-4
Childhood aggression and criminal behavior in adulthood.
Among males, the correlation between highly aggressive behavior in childhood and number of criminal convictions in later life was .75, which is extremely high. The correlations with adult criminal behavior for boys who showed little or only moderate aggressiveness in childhood were much lower, as were all the correlations for females between aggressiveness in childhood and criminal convictions in adulthood. (*Source:* Adapted from Huesmann, Eron, Lefkowitz, & Walder, 1984)

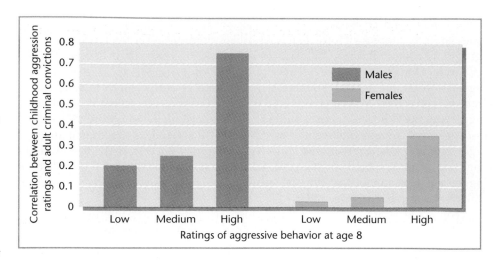

relational aggression
Damaging or destroying interpersonal relationships by such means as excluding another, or gossiping about or soiling another's reputation.

for acting aggressively, and they are also more likely to approve of aggression (Huesmann, Guerra, Zelli, & Miller, 1992; Perry, Perry, & Weiss, 1989).

In attempting to resolve conflicts, girls tend to use such strategies as verbal objection and negotiation, methods that may limit the escalation of a quarrel into overt aggression (Eisenberg, Fabes, Nyman, Bernzweig, & Pinuelas, 1994). This does not mean that girls are not aggressive, but rather that they use different tactics in achieving their goals. Especially in the elementary school years, girls often use what is called **relational aggression,** or the damaging or destruction of interpersonal relationships (Crick et al., 1998). In this mode, according to Coie and Dodge (1998), girls may attempt "to exclude peers from group participation, besmirch another's reputation, and gossip about another's negative attributes" (p. 791). For example, some researchers have found that seventh-grade girls may use social ostracism to harm others rather than direct confrontation. Other investigators have found that as girls entered adolescence they tended to make increasing use of the aggressive strategy of excluding others from social cliques (Cairns, Cairns, Neckerman, Ferguson, & Gariepy, 1989).

Although relational aggression becomes more common in elementary school grades, even preschool girls show significantly more relational aggression and are less overtly aggressive than preschool boys (Crick, Casas, & Mosher, 1997). Moreover, relational aggression is significantly related to social and psychological maladjustment; boys or girls who engage in this type of aggression are more likely to be rejected by their peers, both in the United States and in Italy (Crick, 1997; Crick et al., 1997; Tomada & Schneider, 1997). Although this kind of aggression may be less overt, other children don't fail to notice it, and, in turn, they ostracize those who engage in it. More girls than boys view this type of aggression as hurtful, even though they tend to use it themselves, and indeed view both relational and physical aggression as equally hurtful (Galen & Underwood, 1997). Boys, on the other hand, tend to view physical aggression as more hurtful than relational aggression. Table 16-3 and Figure 16-5 illustrate some of the differences between these two types of aggression and between girls' and boys' use of these behaviors.

Thus the preschool gender differences are not only perpetuated but become more salient as children develop. Marked male-female differences in aggressive behavior are evident in adolescence and adulthood. Approximately five times as many adolescent boys as girls are arrested for violent crimes (e.g., robbery, aggravated assault, criminal homicide), although in recent years the number of females found guilty of violent crimes has increased (Cairns & Cairns, 1994; Schlossman & Cairns, 1993). Figure 16-6 displays data on violent criminal behavior among young people in 1994.

TABLE 16-3	Some Characteristics of Overt and Relational Aggression in School Children	
Overt Aggressors	*Relational Aggressors*	
Hit, kick, punch other children	Try to make other children dislike a certain child by spreading rumors about her or him	
Say mean things to insult others or put them down	When angry, get over it by excluding another person from group of friends	
Tell other children that they will beat them up unless the children do what they say	Tell friends that they will stop liking them unless the friends do what they say	
Push and shove others	When angry at a person, ignore the person or stop talking to them	
Call other children mean names	Try to keep certain people out of their own group during activity or play time	

Source: Based on Crick, 1997.

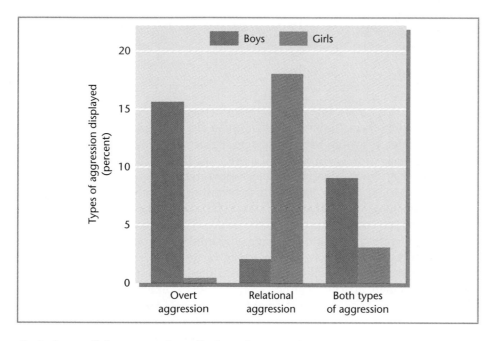

■ FIGURE 16-5
Aggression in boys and girls. Boys and girls do not differ greatly in the amount of aggression they express, but they express it in quite different ways. (*Source:* Based on Crick & Grotpeter, 1995)

Origins of Aggressive Behavior

The theme of biological versus environmental influences reappears once again, as we explore the possible causes of aggressive behavior. As we will see, there is some evidence for the influence of biological factors, at least as they act in concert with environmental influences. Probably more impressive, however, is the evidence for the effects of the child's early learning within the family and, later in development, the influence of the peer group on the emergence of aggression.

The Role of Biology

Does aggression have a biological basis? Let's look at the physiological evidence first. Biology's impact on aggression may be seen rather clearly in adolescence, when, as we saw in Chapter 6, hormone levels are rising (Archer, 1994). A study of 15- to 17-year-old boys in Sweden (Olweus, Mattson, Schalling, & Low, 1988) found a link between testosterone and aggression. Boys whose blood showed higher levels of testosterone rated themselves as more likely to respond aggressively to provocations

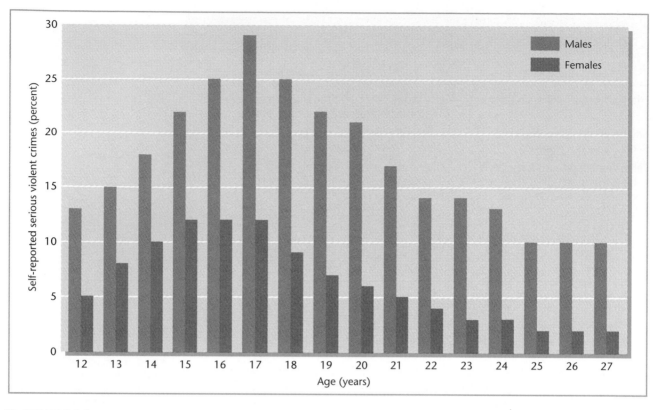

■ FIGURE 16-6

Serious violent crime among adolescents and young adults: Self-reports.
Serious violent offenses (SVOs), which include aggravated assault (assault with intent to commit a crime), robbery, and rape, rise sharply between the ages of 12 and 17. Although more males than females commit violent offenses, girls are likely to get involved in criminal behavior when they are about two years younger than boys (14 versus 16). (*Source:* Coie & Dodge, 1998)

and threats from others. In this case the hormone would seem to have a direct effect on the aggressive behavior. A second finding suggested an indirect effect: Boys with high blood levels of testosterone were more impatient or irritable, which in turn increased their readiness to engage in unprovoked and destructive kinds of aggressive behavior (e.g., to start fights or say rude or hostile things without being provoked). The effect this time was construed as indirect inasmuch as the hormone affected the level of irritation, which in turn altered the tendency to aggression.

Although temperament and the kinds of childrearing practices a boy's parents use are important contributing factors in aggression, even when researchers controlled for these factors, the hormonal effects held. Interestingly, later work has suggested that there may be reciprocal effects; that is, dominance or success in conflict may lead to a rise in testosterone levels (Schaal, Tremblay, Soussignan, & Susman, 1996). Boys rated as tough and social leaders had the highest testosterone levels, although they were not necessarily higher in aggression on a routine basis. Tough, dominant boys, however, may be more likely to respond aggressively to provocation by lower status peers. Hormones may affect aggression in girls as well. In one study, levels of hormones, especially estradiol, that increase during puberty were positively linked with adolescent girls' expressions of anger and aggression during interactions with their parents (Inoff-Germain et al., 1988).

Recently research has examined the links between aggression and neurotransmitters, chemical compounds that can facilitate and inhibit the transmission of neural impulses within the central nervous system. For example, a two-year study found a negative relationship between levels of the neurotransmitter serotonin and the severity of children's physically aggressive behavior; the lower a child's level of serotonin, the higher was his level of aggression (Kruesi et al., 1992). *Serotonin,* which is involved in regulating the activity of the endocrine glands (see Chapter 6), can affect attention and emotional states and may also be involved in depression.

Twin studies have given some support to a role for genetic factors in aggressive behavior (Gottesman & Goldsmith, 1994; Rushton et al., 1986). Responding to a questionnaire about aggression that contained such items as, "Some people think that I have a violent temper," same-sex identical twins rated themselves as more similar than did nonidentical twins (Gottesman & Goldsmith, 1994). Researchers in the Netherlands obtained similar results when they asked teachers and parents to rate aggression in 3-year-old twins (Van Den Oord, Verhulst, & Boomsma, 1992).

Temperament may also be linked with tendencies toward aggressive behavior. As you'll recall from Chapters 3 and 5, infants differ in temperament. Some babies are difficult and others are easygoing. Recent evidence suggests that difficult babies—those who are irritable, whiny, unpredictable, hard to soothe, and prone to negative affect—may be more likely to develop aggressive behavior patterns at later ages. At 3 years of age, infants who had been rated difficult at 6, 13, and 24 months were rated higher in anxiety, hyperactivity, and hostility (Bates, 1987; Rothbart & Bates, 1998).

Biological factors like hormone and neurotransmitter levels and temperamental predisposition don't act independently of the social environment, of course; rather, they interact with it. It may be that hormones are more influential at certain points in development, such as adolescence, and under certain conditions, such as provoking and threatening situations (Carey, 1994; Coie & Dodge, 1998). For example, although some individuals may be more likely than others to be aggressive because of their biological makeup, they may be even more likely to engage in aggressive acts if they live in a high-risk and conflict-ridden environment. In a Swedish study of adopted males, if both the biological and adoptive parents were criminals, 40 percent of adopted males were likely to engage in criminal acts. If only the biological parent was a criminal, the percentage declined to 12; if only the adoptive parent was a criminal, it declined to 7 percent. If neither parent was a criminal, the proportion of adopted males who engaged in criminal acts dropped to 3 percent (Cloninger, Sigvardsson, Bohman, & van Knoring, 1982). A similar gene-environment interaction has been reported for females (Cloninger, Christiansen, Reich, & Gottesman, 1978).

The Family as a Training Center for Aggression

The family, as we have said, is the child's first social environment. Do parents play a role in children's tendencies to be aggressive or nonaggressive? They do indeed; a child's early relationships with his parents matter, especially when the family faces external stressors. Although some evidence indicates that insecure forms of attachment (especially disorganized attachment) are linked to aggressive behavior at 5 and 7 years of age (Lyons-Ruth, Alpern, & Repacholi, 1993; Lyons-Ruth, Easterbrooks, & Davidson, 1995), other research suggests that it is when insecure attachment combines with other risk factors that the child is in danger of developing aggression-related problems. For example, in a study of more than 4,000 males in Denmark, a combination of birth complications and early rejection by the mother (unwanted pregnancy, abortion attempts) predicted that adolescents would be involved in violent crime by the time they were between 17 and 19 years old. Among the young offenders who had experienced both risk factors, 40 percent became violent, whereas only 20 percent of those who experienced only one risk factor committed violent crimes (Raine, Brennan, & Mednick, 1994).

Although some parents may deliberately teach their children, especially boys, to "defend" themselves or to "be a man," most parents do not view themselves as giving aggression tutorials. As we saw in our earlier discussion of gender roles (Chapter 15), cultural groups differ: African American families, for example, are more likely than are European American families to encourage daughters to be more assertive and to defend themselves. However, as we saw in Chapter 12, when parents argue or fight with another and, especially, fail to resolve their conflicts in useful ways, they may well be giving implicit instruction to their children. In addition, parents' typical control tactics may contribute to their children's aggression.

Whether her parents have spanked her or spanked a sibling in her presence, this little girl has clearly got the message that misbehavior is to be punished and severely.

Parents who use physical punishment, especially on an inconsistent basis, are likely to have aggressive, hostile children, and this is true whether their children are playground bullies or juvenile delinquents (Cohen & Brook, 1995; Eron & Huesmann, 1984; Patterson et al., 1992). Physical punishment is especially likely to lead to aggressive behavior in a child when the parent-child relationship is lacking in warmth and otherwise unsatisfying (Deater-Deckard, Dodge, Bates, & Pettit, 1996; Deater-Deckard & Dodge, 1997).

In considering the effect of the family environment on the development of aggressive tendencies in children, the work of Gerald Patterson (Patterson, 1982, 1995; Patterson et al., 1992) is of particular importance. Since the 1970s Patterson's Social Learning Center in Eugene, Oregon, has been one of the world's leading research institutions devoted to understanding the origins of aggressive behavior, the developmental pathways that children follow toward delinquent and criminal behavior, and ways of treating and changing children who have problems with aggression. Patterson has based his conclusions on actual observations of families of aggressive and nonaggressive children, especially boys, in their home environments. Schools and clinical agencies refer aggressive children to the center for treatment of their excessive antisocial, aggressive behavior. In carrying out its research, the center regularly recruits nonaggressive children from the same ethnic or socioeconomic community from which the aggressive children come for purposes of comparison.

Patterson (1982, 1995) has found that the family environments of aggressive and nonaggressive children are strikingly different. Aggressive children's families tended to be erratic and inconsistent in their use of punishment for deviant behaviors and ineffective in rewarding their children for prosocial behaviors. Moreover, these families not only punished their boys more often but punished them even when the children were behaving appropriately! Such inept parenting practices often lead to cycles of mutually coercive behavior. (Recall our Chapter 12 discussion of coercive interactions between child and parent, especially in the single-parent family following a divorce.) As Patterson notes, children are not passive victims in this sort of process; they often develop behavior patterns in which they quite purposely use aversive behaviors—such as whining and being difficult or committing directly aggressive acts—to coerce parents into giving them what they want. Children learn that such coercive behaviors can help them control other family members' behavior. As a result, the most appropriate model of discipline is a bidirectional one, which recognizes that parent and child influence each other, and that both contribute to the development of aggressive behavior patterns.

Families not only contribute directly to their children's aggressive tendencies through the control tactics they use but also shape the development of aggression indirectly. For example, their monitoring or lack of monitoring of their children's whereabouts, activities, and social contacts can be an important determinant of whether children will develop aggressive behavior. Some parents are fully aware of their children's activities, problems, and successes and can report accurately what their children are doing, whom they're with, and where they are. Other parents are largely oblivious to their children's lives. They don't know if their children are hanging around on street corners or are at a school dance, whether they are habit-

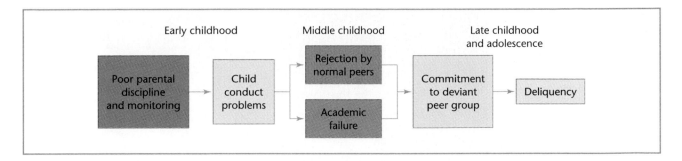

Early childhood   Middle childhood   Late childhood and adolescence

Poor parental discipline and monitoring → Child conduct problems → Rejection by normal peers / Academic failure → Commitment to deviant peer group → Deliquency

ual truants or involved students, or whether their child is the friendly neighborhood drug dealer. Patterson and colleagues have found that lack of parental monitoring is associated, among seventh and tenth graders, with high rates of delinquency, attacks against property, and poorer relations with peers and teachers (Patterson, 1995; Patterson & Stouthamer-Loeber, 1984). To understand the development of aggression in the home, we must view the family unit not only as a social system in which all the interrelations among family members are important but as a gatekeeper in respect to external influences. Children's development of aggressive behaviors may depend as much on parents' awareness of activities in the surrounding community and their efforts to control negative aspects of these activities as on direct parental childrearing practices. Training parents to use more effective disciplinary techniques and to increase their monitoring of their children's activities may help reduce aggressive behavior (Kazdin, 1993).

Patterson, DeBarshyshe, and Ramsey (1989) have shown how children may progress from conduct problems in early childhood to full-fledged delinquency in adolescence as a consequence of the early experience of poor parental disciplinary practices and lack of monitoring. As you can see from Figure 16-7, when such children enter school, two things typically happen: Their peer group rejects them, and they experience academic failure. In late childhood and early adolescence, these now antisocial children may seek out deviant peers who, in turn, provide further training in antisocial behavior and opportunities for delinquent activities. Antisocial youth are more likely to be school dropouts, to be employed only sporadically, to experience marital problems, and to end up in jail (Patterson & Bank, 1989). Interestingly, it matters a great deal whether the child starts along a deviant path early or later in development. If the family environment is already encouraging antisocial behavior before age 5 or 6, the child is more likely to develop serious and persistent delinquent behavior than if the child starts on the deviancy road at a later age—in middle to late adolescence (Moffitt, 1993; Patterson & Bank, 1989). The late starter may have avoided the social rejection and school failure that is common among early starters. Clearly, the developmental timing of earlier experience makes an important difference in determining whether childhood aggression results in serious delinquent behaviors.

Peers, Gangs, and Neighborhoods

As we saw in Chapter 13, peers, especially deviant peers, can encourage other children's aggressive tendencies. One study found that if a child's friends engaged in disruptive behavior (e.g., disobedience or truancy), the child was more likely to engage in either overt (e.g., fighting) or covert (e.g., stealing) delinquent behavior both concurrently and a year later (Keenan, Loeber, Zhang, Stouthamer-Loeber, & Van Kammen, 1995). Similarly, association with gangs is likely to increase violent activity: Individuals in a gang are three times more likely to engage in violent offenses than those not in a gang (Spergel, Ross, Curry, & Chance, 1989). Joining a gang increases a child's illegal and violent activity, and leaving one decreases these activities (Thornberry, Krohn, Lizotte, & Chard-Wierschem, 1993).

Other environmental conditions such as living in a poor, high-crime neighborhood will increase aggression, but these effects are generally due to changes in family

■ FIGURE 16-7
Evolution and progression of antisocial behavior.
Note that parents, peers, and school all play a role in the evolution of antisocial behavior but at different stages in the child's development. (*Source:* Adapted from Patterson, DeBarshyshe, & Ramsey, 1989)

In many juvenile gangs violence is common, both within gangs as a way of controlling their members and between gangs to protect their "turf."

functioning that are associated with poverty or unemployment. Several researchers (Guerra, Huesmann, Tolan, Van Acker, & Eron, 1995; McLoyd, 1990) have found that poor African American mothers who experienced stress and lack of social support were more likely to display ineffective and coercive parenting; this in turn led to aggressive behavior in their children.

Control of Aggression

How can we control aggression in our children? One of the most commonly offered solutions, and yet one whose beneficial effects have been seriously questioned, is the notion of *catharsis,* popularly known as letting off steam. We look at the myth of catharsis first and then turn to cognitive modification strategies, in which parents and others may attempt to explain the consequences of aggression and to teach alternative problem-solving behaviors. Finally we explore the possibilities of altering a child's environment to reduce incitement to aggression and violence.

The Catharsis Myth

catharsis Presumably, discharging aggressive impulses by engaging in actual or symbolic aggressive acts that do not impinge on another person.

One of the most persistent beliefs about aggression is that if people have ample opportunity to engage in aggressive acts, whether in actuality or symbolically, a process known as **catharsis,** they will be less likely to act on hostile aggressive urges. The catharsis doctrine asserts that aggressive urges build up in an individual and unless this accumulating reservoir of aggressive energies is drained, a violent outburst will occur. The implications are clear: Provide people with a safe opportunity to behave aggressively and the likelihood of antisocial aggression will be lessened. In clinical circles there is widespread belief in catharsis. People are often encouraged to express aggression in group-therapy sessions. There are punching bags on many wards in mental hospitals, and Bobo dolls, pounding boards, and toy guns and knives in many play-therapy rooms.

Advice columnists in the media have sometimes propagated a similar view. For example, Ann Landers once advised a reader that "Hostile feelings must be released" and went on to recommend that children be taught to vent their anger against furniture rather than against other people. Another reader replied: "I was shocked at your advice to the mother whose 3-year-old had temper tantrums. . . . My younger brother used to kick the furniture when he got mad. . . . He's 32 years old now and still kicking the furniture. . . . He is also kicking his wife, the cat, the kids, and anything else that gets in his way. . . . Why don't you tell mothers that children must be taught to control their anger? This is what separates civilized human beings from savages."

The research evidence on the value of catharsis tends to support the reader's position. Most studies suggest that aggressive experiences may promote rather than "drain off" aggressive urges. In a classic test of the issue, Mallick and McCandless (1966) allowed third-grade children to shoot a toy gun after being frustrated by a peer who interfered with a task they were working on. Another group of children were allowed to work on arithmetic problems after the peer upset them. Then all the children were given a chance to express their aggression toward the peer who had upset them. The researchers used a rigged procedure in which children thought they were delivering a shock to the other child; in reality, of course, they were not delivering shocks to anyone. Whether the children, after being frustrated by the peer, had shot the toy gun or worked on math problems made little difference in their delivery of "shocks." Thus catharsis appeared to be insufficient to reduce aggression.

Cognitive Modification Strategies

According to the social information-processing approach to aggression, aggressive children may behave in a hostile and inappropriate fashion because they are **socially unskilled**—that is, they're not very skilled at solving interpersonal problems (Coie & Dodge, 1998; Crick & Dodge, 1994). In several studies (Crick & Dodge, 1994; Slaby & Guerra, 1988), researchers who asked children and adolescents to come up with solutions to conflict problems in social situations found that aggressive participants in the studies offered fewer solutions than their nonaggressive peers. Moreover, the proposals aggressive children and adolescents made for resolving social disputes were generally less effective than the solutions less aggressive individuals offered.

socially unskilled Being unskilled at solving interpersonal problems.

Making aggressive children and adolescents aware of the negative consequences of aggression for themselves and others through modeling and explanations can reduce aggression, and teaching and encouraging children to use alternative problem-solving behaviors such as cooperation or turn taking have also been found to reduce aggression (Chittenden, 1942; Guerra & Slaby, 1990). One study found that teaching children how to read another person's behavior more accurately—especially helping them to reduce if not wholly give up their biases toward making hostile attributions about other people and their behavior—led to a decrease in aggression among African American boys (Hudley & Graham 1993). This approach will be especially effective with reactively aggressive children, who are poor at reading other people's intentions. Empathy also plays an important role in the control of aggression. Several studies have found that training children and adolescents to be more empathic and sensitive to the views and feelings of other individuals can be an effective way of controlling aggression (Chandler, 1973; Guerra & Slaby, 1990).

Another approach to aggression control is to elicit alternative responses that are incompatible with the expression of aggression, such as cooperation and humor. Brown and Elliot (1965) decreased aggression among nursery school children by guiding teachers in ignoring aggression and rewarding cooperative and peaceful behaviors. Laughing and having fun may be incompatible with aggression and, thus, making someone laugh may be an effective way to control aggressive behavior. Indeed, watching a humorous cartoon decreased aggression in angry college students (Parke & Slaby, 1983).

Some psychologists are putting these findings into practical use. Curricula have been developed to improve the social problem-solving skills of aggressive children, and some success has been reported in studies in both the United States and Sweden (Guerra & Slaby, 1990; Weissberg, Caplan, & Sivo, 1989; Weissberg & Greenberg, 1998). Box 16-3 describes a Swedish example of a successful school-based intervention program.

Altering the Environment

Aggression is to some extent under environmental control, and alterations in the organization of children's social and physical worlds often can affect the level of

Child Psychology in Action

Reducing Aggression in Scandinavian Schools

Aggression is a worldwide problem. In Norway and Sweden nearly 9 percent of children in the first nine grades of school are victims of aggression. To help these 150,000 students, Dan Olweus (1989, 1993), in cooperation with the Ministry of Education, launched a nationwide campaign to reduce the amount of aggression in the schools. The program enunciated four primary goals:

1. Increase awareness of the problem of aggression among the general public and provide schools with information to increase their knowledge about aggressive behavior

2. Get teachers and parents actively involved in the program

3. Develop clear classroom rules to combat aggressive behavior, such as the following:
   We will not bully others.
   We will help students who suffer bullying by others.
   We will include students who have been excluded.

4. Provide support and protection for the victims of aggression

Because it is well known that parents, teachers, and children themselves may all contribute to the levels and kinds of aggressive behavior children display, the program was designed to target all three groups. The program's main components were as follows:

- A booklet was prepared for school personnel that described the nature and scope of aggression in the schools and that offered practical suggestions about what teachers and other school personnel could do to control or prevent aggressive behavior. For example, the booklet stressed the importance of increasing not only teachers' awareness of their responsibility to control interpersonal aggression in school but the awareness of other adult personnel as well and the importance to everyone of providing more adequate supervision of students during recess times. The booklet

encouraged teachers to intervene in bullying situations, and to give students the clear message that, "Aggression is not acceptable in our school." In addition, the booklet's guidelines advised teachers to initiate serious talks with victims, their aggressors, and the children's parents if aggressive attacks persisted.

- A four-page folder was designed to address all parents, giving them basic information and in particular offering assistance to parents of both victims and aggressors.

- A videocassette was prepared, showing episodes from the everyday lives of two children who were victims of aggressive attacks.

- Students were asked to fill out a short questionnaire anonymously, providing information about the frequency of aggressor/victim problems in the school and describing the ways teachers and parents had responded, including how aware they were of the problem and how ready to take action to deal with it.

Although the program was made available to all schools in Norway and Sweden, the researchers based their detailed evaluation of its effectiveness on data from about 2,500 students in 112 fourth-grade to seventh-grade classes in 42 primary and junior high schools in Bergen, Norway. Did this multilevel cross-national campaign aimed at reducing aggression work? The answer was clearly yes.

Both 8 and 20 months after the intervention program was initiated, the levels of aggressive behavior the researchers reported were markedly reduced. Fewer children reported being attacked by others, and fewer children reported that they themselves had acted aggressively. Peer ratings told a similar story: Classmates reported that both the "number of students being bullied in the class" and "the number of students bullying others" showed a marked drop. In addition, general antisocial behavior such as vandalism, theft, and truancy declined significantly, and student satisfaction with school life rose appreciably. Although we can't be sure just which aspect of this program (class rules, teacher awareness, parental intervention) was most important in achieving these effects, it is clear that intervention can make a difference!

---

aggression. Stress, crowding, and competition for inadequate resources can increase aggression. If the population of a nursery school that has only a modest number of toys and types of playground equipment suddenly doubles, aggression is likely to increase as well. On the other hand, if the school can add more toys, slides, swings, and other items, even the greater number of children may not cause any increase in aggression (Smith & Connolly, 1980).

Not only the number of toys but the kinds of toys that are available to children may alter the amount of aggressive behavior. Thus another way to control aggression is to reduce exposure to aggressive toys (Berkowitz, 1993; Goldstein, 1994). For example, researchers have found that preschoolers behave less aggressively toward other children in the presence of nonaggressive toys like airplanes than when aggressive playthings like toy guns are available (Turner & Goldsmith, 1976). Although research has demonstrated that aggression can be controlled in multiple ways, it is still unclear which tactics are most effective for which children. Children's personalities vary, and their everyday experiences with a wide range of situations outside both the home and the school vary also; we do not yet know just how these multiple factors interact.

SUMMARY

An Overview of Moral Development

- The socialization of moral beliefs and behavior is one of the main tasks in all cultures. Psychological research has focused on the three basic components of morality—the cognitive, the behavioral, and the emotional components.
- Research, which has in the past focused mostly on nonmoral, nonethical behaviors, is beginning to give more attention to other aspects of moral behavior such as sharing, helping, and cooperating with others.

Cognitive Theories of Moral Development

- Jean Piaget and Lawrence Kohlberg have both proposed theories involving invariant sequences of stages of moral development through which children progress as their cognitive capacities become increasingly sophisticated.
- Piaget proposed a three-stage approach; the **premoral stage,** the stage of **moral realism,** and the stage ruled by a **morality of reciprocity,** also called *autonomous morality.* Moral absolutism and a belief in **immanent justice** and objective responsibility, characterize moral realism. In contrast, children in the stage of reciprocity recognize the arbitrariness of social rules and intentionality in their moral judgments.
- Later research has shown that young children can distinguish between intentions and consequences if material is presented to them in a less complex manner. Many other factors affect children's judgments.
- Kohlberg proposed a theory of the development of moral judgment in which each of three levels contains two stages. The order of development is fixed and invariant, and movement is generally from lower levels—the **preconventional** and **conventional levels**—toward higher ones. Moral judgments continue to develop into adulthood, but few individuals reach the most advanced, **postconventional level** (Stages 5 and 6).
- Gilligan has proposed that Kohlberg's model emphasizes a more masculine orientation, focusing on rights and logic, whereas an interpersonal and caring orientation may more accurately describe women's moral reasoning and judgments.
- Piaget emphasized the role of peers and Kohlberg emphasizes the importance of varied opportunities for role taking in the development of moral judgments. Both views tend to minimize the influence of parents in the development of moral judgments. There is evidence, however, that consistent discipline involving reasoning and explanation and concern with the feelings of others leads to both more mature moral judgments and more self-control and that maturity of moral reasoning is related to cognitive maturity. Educational programs in which students explore possible solutions to moral dilemmas may be useful in developing moral reasoning.
- Kohlberg's theory may be flawed in some ways. The theory's third level is controversial; relatively few people reach this level, in particular, the sixth stage of

moral reasoning. In addition, cross-cultural research suggests that Kohlberg's theory is culture-bound.

- Rules of **social convention,** such as table manners and forms of address, are distinct from moral rules and follow a different developmental course, although children learn quite early to distinguish these kinds of rules from each other. Children also distinguish issues of morality and of social convention from those that belong to the **personal domain.**
- Moral judgments do not always lead to moral behavior, particularly among very young children.

The Behavioral Side of Moral Development

- **Self-regulation,** the ability to inhibit one's impulses and to behave in accord with social or moral rules, proceeds through three stages—the **control phase,** the **self-control phase,** and the **self-regulation phase.** In the latter phase, children become capable of **delaying gratification.**
- Children can learn to use strategies and plans to help them postpone rewards and attend to a task at hand. Specific verbal plans are more useful to children than general directions.
- Self-control or moral behavior is strongly influenced by situational factors. As the elements of situations and types of behavior assessed become more similar, moral conduct becomes more consistent. The development of **conscience** is linked with children's achievement of self-regulatory capacities. Both self-regulation and the development of conscience are linked with mother-child relationships that are positive, responsive, and cooperative.
- Some evidence indicates that children's early ability to regulate their behavior is related to later social and cognitive competence.

The Evolution of Prosocial and Altruistic Behaviors

- **Prosocial behavior** begins very early; helping, sharing, and exhibiting emotional reactions to the distress of others occur in the first and second years of life. **Altruism** may also appear quite early.
- Parents influence the emergence of **altruistic behavior** by their direct teaching in "distress" situations, by providing models, and by arranging for opportunities to behave in prosocial ways. Opportunities for children to take responsibility appear to lead to increased altruistic behavior. Similarly, role playing and **empathy** both contribute to the development of altruism and helping behavior.
- Girls tend to be more prosocial than boys, but gender differences depend on the type of prosocial behavior being expressed. Such differences are largest for expressions of kindness and consideration.
- Evidence of helping and sharing behavior in infrahuman animals leads some scientists to believe that evolution has prepared both humans and animals for prosocial behavior.
- Environmental factors, including the family, the mass media, and general cultural influences influence prosocial and altruistic behaviors, but children probably learn such behaviors most often from modeling parental behaviors.
- Children's prosocial reasoning evolves over time through a number of stages including **hedonistic reasoning** and **needs-oriented reasoning,** as values and norms become increasingly internalized.
- Both empathy and perspective taking contribute to the child's capacity for altruistic behavior.

The Development of Aggression

- **Aggression** undergoes important developmental shifts: Younger children show more **instrumental aggression,** while older children display more person-oriented or **hostile aggression.** Children's ability to correctly infer intent in others—which varies among individual children—may account, in part, for these shifts. **Proactive aggression,** which is used to dominate another person, decreases across development more than **reactive aggression,** which occurs in response to being attacked.
- The expression of aggression changes over time, becoming more verbal as children mature, but the amount and quality of aggression remain fairly stable. Clear gender differences in aggression are evident, with boys instigating and retaliating more than girls. Girls are more likely to use **relational aggression** than boys, who are more likely to use physical aggression. Aggression is moderately stable over age for both sexes.
- Certain parental disciplinary practices, especially ineffectual and erratic physical punishment, contribute to high levels of aggression in children. Lack of parental monitoring of children is another contributor to later aggressive behavior or even serious delinquency.
- Biological influences on aggression include genetic, temperamental, and hormonal factors. All of these factors find expression in interaction with the environment.
- Association with deviant peers can increase the possibility that a child will engage in aggressive or delinquent activities. Poverty and high-crime neighborhoods can also promote aggressive behavior.
- **Catharsis** theory, the belief that behaving aggressively against a safe target can reduce aggression has been seriously challenged by research evidence. Strategies that involve cognitive modification may be more successful. Some aggressive children who are **socially unskilled** may be helped to learn more prosocial behaviors through teaching them how to read others' behavior more accurately and encouraging them to be more sensitive to the views and feelings of others.
- Increasing children's awareness of the harmful effects of aggression is an effective control technique, as are eliciting cooperation and the enjoyment of humor. Altering the environment by reducing crowding, providing adequate numbers of toys and playthings and toys that are nonaggressive in nature may also reduce aggression.

Epilogue

Throughout this book we have reviewed the results of many studies of children's development. We have described and critiqued a variety of theories—including those we introduced in Chapter 1—that attempt to explain and interpret the detailed and highly complex information amassed by theorists and researchers in their effort to understand child development. And we have identified and discussed the themes of development that we also introduced to readers in Chapter 1. Neither data nor the many theories advanced are final answers in our continuing attempt to unravel the many puzzles of development. As in any field of science, our information is constantly expanding and changing. As a consequence, in this fifth edition of our book we have replaced or further elaborated many findings that we highlighted in earlier editions.

Recognizing that many of the "facts" discussed in this volume will change, we have nevertheless identified some broad principles that characterize, first, our general views about child development and, second, our views of the field's needs in respect both to theory building and to the conduct of research. The first group of principles (1–12) expand and add to the six themes we introduced in Chapter 1. As you study our discussion in this closing statement, you'll find it useful to refer to Table E–1, which helps link these principles with our original themes. The second group of principles (13–17) focus on the roles of theory and research in advancing our knowledge about children's development as well as in finding ways to improve development for all children. We outlined these methodological principles in Chapter 2 and have illustrated them with research examples throughout the book. The last principle (18) reminds us that people continue to develop and change throughout their lives and that as they do, both children and adults participate in each other's development.

1. *The child is competent.* Recent years have seen a dramatic change in our view of the infant and young child. Although scientists once viewed infants and young children as more or less helpless, passive creatures who had limited sensory, perceptual, and social capacities and who were simply awaiting the imprint of the adult world, child psychologists now view children as competent and active beings who from an early age possess a wide range of perceptual, motoric, cognitive, and social capacities.

2. *The child's behavior is organized.* Organization is evident in the child's behavior, from infancy on. Behaviors such as sucking and looking are not just disorganized reflexes or reactions but highly structured response patterns.

3. *The domains of childhood are interdependent.* Although we often study social, emotional, physical, linguistic, and cognitive development as separate domains, these areas overlap and mutually influence one another.

4. *The child's behavior has multiple causes.* Current views stress that development is the outcome of the interaction among biological, environmental, and experiential factors.

5. *The child's development is the outcome of an interaction between factors of both risk and resilience.* Risk factors—biological, social, demographic—may

TABLE E-1   Linking the Themes and Principles of Child Development

Themes

Principles	Biological vs. Environmental Influences	Active vs. Passive Child	Continuity vs. Discontinuity	Situational Influences vs. Individual Characteristics	Cultural Universals vs. Cultural Relativism	Risk & Resilience
1. The child is competent.	X	X		X		X
2. The child's behavior is organized.		X				X
3. The domains of childhood are interdependent.	X				X	X
4. The child's behavior has multiple causes.	X			X	X	X
5. The child's development is the outcome of an interaction between factors of risk and resilience.		X		X		X
6. There is no single pathway to normal or abnormal development.	X		X	X	X	X
7. The child's development is generally continuous but marked by periods of more rapid and dramatic change.			X			
8. The child influences the responses of other people.		X		X	X	X
9. The child's behavior varies across situations and settings.	X		X	X	X	X
10. The child's behavior is influenced by social systems.	X			X	X	X
11. The child's behavior is culture-bound.	X		X	X	X	X
12. The child's behavior is time-bound.	X			X	X	X

alter a developmental trajectory. A range of buffering or protective factors may modify an individual child's resilience in the face of risk. These factors include individual strengths, support from others, and institutions that, all together, can help keep development on a healthy pathway.

6. *There is no single pathway to normal or abnormal development.* Children may take alternative routes to normal development. No single pathway is necessarily the "best" one to follow, for socially and intellectually competent

adults often have reached their goals by very different routes. Different kinds of experiences have profound influences on children's development, as does the timing of these experiences. Children may confront a risk at one time or another with greater or lesser resilience. The same principles hold true with respect to less than ideal development; children whose lives become dysfunctional to one degree or another may reach this state by a variety of pathways.

7. *The child's development is generally continuous but marked by periods of more rapid and dramatic change.* These periods mark the onset of biological and social changes, such as puberty and school transitions, or unexpected or nonnormative events such as loss of a parent or of a friendship. In addition, the characterization of development as continuous or discontinuous depends, in part, on how closely we look. A detailed examination reveals that developmental progress is gradual but marked by periods of developmental advance as well as of temporary regressions.

8. *The child influences the responses of other people.* Just as adults influence children, so children may alter adult behavior. Even in infancy, children play an active role in modifying the behaviors of parents and others. Now widely accepted, this bidirectional view of child development also sees children as playing an influential part in all aspects of their own development.

9. *The child's behavior varies across situations and settings.* The same child may behave in a very different manner in different situations or with different people—in the home, the laboratory, the school, or the peer play group. Thus, we need to study children in multiple settings and to exercise caution in generalizing children's behaviors from one situation to another.

10. *The child's behavior is influenced by social systems.* The child is embedded in a variety of systems and settings, the members of which shape one another's behavior. Systems range from the smaller and more immediate—such as the family or the peer group—in which the child has considerable influence, to the larger and more remote—such as the school, community, or greater society—in which the child has less control. The stresses and supports children encounter in their interactions with these systems will influence their development.

11. *The child's behavior is culture-bound.* No single picture of development is accurate for all cultures, social classes, or racial and ethnic groups. Children develop different skills and competencies in different cultural milieus. We need to take both intracultural and cross-cultural perspectives, paying careful attention both to cultural and ethnic variations within our own society and to differences between that society and other cultures around the globe. We cannot make generalizations about any child's development without first specifying the child's cultural background and current cultural milieu.

12. *The child's behavior is time-bound.* Knowledge about children is time-bound. As social conditions shift, children and families undergo changes that alter their behavior. The experiences of children growing up in the Great Depression of the 1930s were different from the experiences of children who have grown up in the 1990s. Changing gender roles for women and men are altering family lifestyles. When both parents work outside the home and household labor is divided differently, children's lives are altered, too. Legal demands for ethnic integration have markedly altered the school experience for many children. One of the aims of child psychology is to monitor these and other changes on a continuing basis to determine how such shifts affect children's behavior.

13. *Child psychologists need to employ multiple research methods.* No single research method is adequate for understanding the complex and multifaceted aspects of children's development. A wide variety of methods, includ-

ing naturalistic observations of children, formal experiments, self-reports, clinical studies, and standardized tests provide us with different types of information about children. In addition, different reporters, including parents, peers, teachers, and objective observers, each provide unique perspectives and together provide a more complete understanding of the developing child.

14. *Child psychologists need to select multiple samples.* To fully understand how children grow and develop, we need multiple samples to capture the cultural and ethnic richness—the diversity—of children's development. Developmental psychologists are beginning to use research designs that compare small samples, in which they can make an intensive study of a process or issue in a particular region or ethnic group, with national samples that are representative of all the groups found in a diverse society.

15. *Child psychologists need multiple theories of development.* Just as we have multiple methods, we have multiple theories. Although grand theoretical schemes that attempt to provide a full and comprehensive account of development, such as those of Piaget, Freud, and Vygotsky, have inspired a great deal of useful research, contemporary psychologists believe that the complex and multidetermined nature of development requires that we explain smaller pieces of the developmental puzzle before we attempt to assemble an all-embracing theory. Thus today developmental psychologists are more likely to advance theories of such phenomena as gender typing, memory function, aggression, and language development than to present elaborate theories aimed at explaining all of social or cognitive development.

16. *Child psychologists need the contributions of multiple disciplines.* Many disciplines besides child psychology contribute in important ways to our understanding of children. For example, anthropology provides a cross-cultural perspective, sociology offers a societal viewpoint, pediatrics illuminates the role of physical health in the child's development, clinical psychology and psychiatry offer an understanding of deviant and abnormal development, and history views children's development against the changing panorama of time. Multidisciplinary approaches are increasingly common in studies of children's development.

17. *Child development research influences, and is influenced by, social policy.* As this book has stressed, there is a close link between basic research in child development and the application of research findings. For example, just as basic research on the importance of children's early environment for their development stimulated government efforts like Head Start and day-care programs, so, in turn, child psychologists have become more actively involved in issues of concern to society and government, such as problems of family breakdown, poverty, schooling that accommodates different cultural styles of learning, and the influence of violent content in television and other media.

18. *Development is a lifelong process.* Although this book focuses on development from conception through the adolescent years, development—social, emotional, cognitive, language, and physical—continues throughout adulthood. People respond to, and are modified by, experiences throughout their life spans. Thus, to understand children, we must recognize that parents are also developing and that this process can provide a changing context for their children's development. Teenage parents provide a different context for children than do parents who begin parenthood in their late thirties. A life-course view of development helps us appreciate the interdependence of adult lives and children's development.

Glossary

ABAB design A technique in which an experimental treatment is administered, withdrawn, and readministered in order to measure its effects. Also called a *reversal* design.

accommodation Modifying an existing way of responding to the environment to fit the characteristics of a new experience.

achievement motivation A person's tendency to strive for successful performance, to evaluate her performance against standards of excellence, and to feel pleasure at having performed successfully.

acquired immune deficiency syndrome (AIDS) A viral disease that attacks the body's immune systems; transmitted to a fetus or newborn in the form of the *human immunodeficiency virus (HIV)*, this disorder weakens the child's immune system and may ultimately cause its death.

adaptation The individual's tendency to adjust to environmental demands.

age cohort People born within the same generation.

age of viability The age of 28 weeks from conception, by which point the fetus's physical systems are well enough advanced that it has a chance at survival if born prematurely.

aggression Behavior that intentionally harms other people by inflicting pain or injury on them.

aggressive rejected children *Rejected* children who are characterized by high levels of aggressive behavior, have low self-control, and exhibit behavior problems.

allele An alternate form of a gene; typically, a gene has two alleles, one inherited from the individual's mother and one from the father.

alphafetoprotein assay (AFP) A blood test performed prenatally to detect such problems as Down syndrome, the presence of multiple embryos, and defects of the central nervous system.

altruism An unselfish concern for the welfare of others.

altruistic behavior Intrinsically motivated behavior that is intended to help others without expectation of acknowledgment or concrete reward.

amniocentesis A technique for sampling and assessing fetal cells for indications of abnormalities in the developing fetus; performed by inserting a needle through the abdominal wall and into the amniotic sac and withdrawing a small amount of the amniotic fluid.

amniotic sac A membrane containing a watery fluid that encloses the developing organism, protecting it from physical shocks and temperature changes.

androgynous Possessing both feminine and masculine psychological characteristics.

animistic thinking The attribution of life to inanimate objects.

anorexia nervosa An eating disorder in which the person (usually a young woman) is preoccupied with avoiding obesity and often diets to the point of starvation.

anoxia A lack of oxygen in brain cells.

assimilation Molding a new experience to fit an existing way of responding to the environment.

associative learning According to Jensen, lower-level learning tapped in tests of such things as short-term memorization and recall, attention, rote learning, and simple associative skills. Also called *level I* learning.

attachment A strong emotional bond that forms between an infant and a caregiver in the second half of the child's first year.

Attachment Q Sort (AQS) An assessment method in which a caregiver or observer judges the quality of a child's attachment based on the child's behavior in naturalistic situations, often including brief separations from parents.

attention deficit/hyperactivity disorder (ADHD) A childhood disorder characterized by a persistent pattern of inattention and hyperactivity or impulsivity that is far in excess of such behaviors observed in children at comparable levels of development.

authoritarian parenting Parenting that is harsh, unresponsive, and rigid, and in which parents tend to use power-assertive methods of control.

authoritative parenting Parenting that is warm, responsive, and involved yet unintrusive, and in which parents set reasonable limits and expect appropriately mature behavior from their children.

autistic disorder A disorder in which children's ability to communicate and interact socially is seriously impaired; autistic children have specific language deficiencies, demonstrate a need for sameness in their environment, and often engage in repetitive and stereotyped kinds of behaviors.

automatization The process of transforming conscious, controlled behaviors into unconscious and automatic ones.

autosomes The 22 paired non-sex chromosomes in males and females that determine the development of most body structures and attributes.

autostimulation theory The theory that during REM sleep the infant's brain stimulates itself and that this in turn stimulates early development of the central nervous system.

average children Children who have some friends but are not as well liked as *popular children*.

babbling An infant's production of strings of consonant-vowel combinations.

Bayley Scales of Infant Development A set of nonverbal tests that measure specific developmental milestones and that are most often used with children who are thought to be at risk for abnormal development.

behavior therapy A psychological form of treatment, often used in treating conduct disorders, that is based on such learning principles as reinforcement and social learning.

behaviorism A school of psychology that holds that theories of behavior must be based on direct observations of actual behavior and not on speculations about such unobservable things as human motives.

bilingual education Teaching children two languages at the same time.

brain hemispheres The two, left and right halves of the brain's cerebrum.

Brazelton Neonatal Assessment Scale A scale used to measure an infant's sensory and perceptual capabilities, motor development, range of states, and ability to regulate these states. The scale also indicates whether the brain and central nervous system are properly regulating autonomic responsivity.

bulimia nervosa An eating disorder in which people, usually young women, alternate periods of binge eating with vomiting and other means of compensating for the weight gained.

canalization The genetic restriction of a phenotype to a small number of developmental outcomes, permitting environmental influences to play only a small role in these outcomes.

case study method A form of research in which investigators study individual persons.

catch-up growth The tendency for human beings to regain a normal course of physical growth after injury or deprivation.

categorical speech perception The tendency to perceive a range of sounds that belong to the same phonemic group as the same.

catharsis Presumably, discharging aggressive impulses by engaging in actual or symbolic aggressive acts that do not impinge on another person.

centration Centering one's attention on only one dimension or characteristic of an object or situation.

cephalocaudal development The notion that human physical growth occurs from head downward, that is, from brain and neck to trunk and legs.

cerebral cortex The covering layer of the cerebrum that contains the cells that control specific functions such as seeing, hearing, moving, and thinking.

cerebrum The two connected hemispheres of the brain.

cesarean delivery The surgical delivery of a baby, whereby the baby is removed from the mother's uterus through an incision made in her abdomen and uterus; also known as *cesarean section*.

child development A field of study that seeks to account for the gradual evolution of the child's cognitive, social, and other capacities first by describing changes in the child's observed behaviors and then by uncovering the processes and strategies that underlie these changes.

chlamydia Probably the most widespread bacterial sexually transmitted disease; can cause pneumonia or a form of conjunctivitis in a pregnant woman's baby.

chorionic villi sampling A technique for sampling and assessing cells withdrawn from the chorionic villi, projections from the chorion that surrounds the amniotic sac; cells are withdrawn either through a tube inserted into the uterus through a tube inserted into the uterus through the vagina or through a needle inserted through the abdominal wall.

chromosomes Threadlike structures, located in the central portion, or nucleus, of a cell, that carry genetic information to help direct development.

chronosystem In Bronfenbrenner's ecological theory, the time-based dimension that can alter the operation of all other levels, from *microsystem* through *macrosystem*.

classical conditioning A type of learning in which individuals learn to respond to unfamiliar stimuli in the same way they are accustomed to respond to familiar stimuli if the two stimuli are repeatedly presented together.

clique A voluntary group formed on the basis of friendship.

codominance A genetic pattern in which heterozygous alleles express the variants of the trait for which they code simultaneously and with equal force.

cognition The mental activity through which human beings acquire and process knowledge.

cognitive behavior therapy A group therapy technique particularly useful in treating depression in adolescents. Therapeutic goals include reducing self-consciousness and feelings of being different and teaching strategies for dealing with depressive moods and for acquiring a more positive outlook and improving social interactions.

cognitive developmental theory of gender typing Kohlberg's theory that children use physical and behavioral clues to differentiate gender roles and to gender-type themselves very early in life.

cognitive developmental view of attachment The view that to form attachments infants must differentiate between their mothers and strangers and must understand that people exist independent of their interaction with them.

cognitive learning According to Jensen, higher-level learning tapped in tests of such things as abstract thinking, the use of symbolic processes, conceptual learning, and the use of language in problem solving. Also called *level II* learning.

cognitive social learning theory A learning theory that stresses learning by observation and imitation mediated by cognitive processes and skills.

communicative competence The ability to convey thoughts, feelings, and intentions in an organized, culturally patterned way that sustains and regulates human interactions.

community psychology A form of social and psychological intervention in which psychologists try to change general social conditions that play a role in children's—and adults'—psychological problems as well as to treat such problems.

compliance Going along with a specific request or rule.

computer-assisted instruction A form of instruction embodied in computer software programs that typically pose questions or problems, give the student a chance to respond, and then tell her if she is correct.

concordance rate The percentage of cases in which a characteristic or trait exhibited by one member of a twin pair is also exhibited by the other twin.

concrete operations period Period in which the child acquires such concepts as conservation and classification and can reason logically.

conduct disorder A disorder characterized by a repetitive and persistent pattern of behavior in which a young person violates the basic rights of others or major age-appropriate societal norms or rules.

congenital Describing deficits or defects that the child incurs in the womb or during the birth process.

conscience The child's internalized values and standards of behavior.

conservation The notion that altering an object's or a substance's appearance does not change its basic attributes or properties.

control group In a formal experiment, the group that is not exposed to the treatment.

control phase According to Kopp, the first phase in learning self-regulation, when children are highly dependent on caregivers to remind them about acceptable behaviors.

controversial children Children who are liked by many peers but also disliked by many.

conventional level Kohlberg's second level of moral development, in which the child's behavior is designed to solicit others' approval and maintain good relations with them. The child accepts societal regulations unquestioningly and judges behavior as good if it conforms to these rules.

cooing A very young infant's production of vowel-like sounds.

cooperative learning A teaching technique in which small groups of students work together to master material to be learned.

coordination of secondary schemata An infant's combination of different schemata to achieve a specific goal.

corpus callosum The band of nerve fibers that connects the two hemispheres of the brain.

correlation coefficient A numerical measure of how closely two factors are related to each other.

correlational method A research design that permits investigators to establish relationships among variables as well as the strength of those relationships.

creativity The ability to solve problems, create products, or pose questions in a way that is novel or unique; also, the ability to envision new problems not yet recognized by others and to come up with their solutions.

creole language A language spoken by children of first-generation, pidgin-language speakers; a language that, in contrast with pidgin, is highly developed and rule governed.

criminal offense Behavior that is illegal.

critical period A specific period in children's development when they are sensitive to a particular environmental stimulus that does not have the same effect on them when encountered before or after this period.

crossing over The process by which equivalent sections of homologous chromosomes switch places randomly, shuffling the genetic information each carries.

cross-sectional method A method of research in which researchers compare groups of individuals of different age levels at approximately the same point in time.

crowd A collection of people whose shared attitudes or activities have been designated by a stereotypical term, such as *populars* or *nerds.*

culture-fair test A test that attempts to minimize cultural biases in content that might influence the test taker's responses.

cumulative continuity The tendency to seek out experience and environments that support or reinforce maladaptive predispositions. *Transactional stressors,* such as irritability, fuel a cycle in which irritability leads to job loss, which heightens irritability.

cumulative risk The notion that risk factors in children's life circumstances have cumulative negative effects on their intellectual performance.

deferred imitation Mimicry of an action some time after observing it; requires that the child have stored a mental image of the action.

delay of gratification Putting off until another time possessing or doing something that gives one pleasure.

delinquency Juvenile behavior in violation of the law.

deoxyribonucleic acid (DNA) A ladderlike molecule that stores genetic information in cells and transmits it during reproduction.

dependent variable The variable, or factor, that researchers expect to change as a function of change in the independent variable.

depression in childhood Like adult depression, often manifested in a depressed mood and loss of interest in familiar activities, but also likely to be expressed as irritability and crankiness. Difficulty concentrating or focusing on tasks and concomitant drops in school grades are not uncommon, and depressed children often complain of physical problems such as headache.

developmental psychopathology The investigation of the origins, course, changes, and continuities in disordered or maladaptive behavior over a person's life span.

deviation IQ An IQ score that indicates the extent to which a person's performance on a test deviates from age-mates' average performance.

diagnosis The identification of a physical or mental disorder on the basis of symptoms and of knowledge of the cause or causes of the disorder and its common course. A diagnosis may also include information about effective forms of treatment.

diagnostic reliability A measure of how often two or more clinicians arrive independently at the same diagnosis of a particular disorder.

diethylstilbestrol (DES) A synthetic hormone once prescribed for pregnant women to prevent miscarriage but discontinued when cancer and precancerous conditions were detected in the children of such women.

differentiation theory The notion that the child learns to identify and discriminate the important features of objects and relationships from the rich source of information sensory input provides.

direct observation A method of observation in which researchers go into settings in the natural world to observe behaviors of interest.

discourse Socially based conversation.

dizygotic Characterizing *fraternal* twins, who have developed from two separate fertilized eggs.

dominance hierarchy An ordering of individuals in a group from most to least dominant; a "pecking order."

dominant Describing the more powerful of two alleles in a heterozygous combination.

Down syndrome A form of chromosome abnormality in which the person suffers disabling physical and mental development and is highly susceptible to such illnesses as leukemia, heart disorders, and respiratory infections.

dynamic systems theory A theory that proposes that individuals develop and function within systems and that studies the relationships among individuals and systems and the processes by which these relationships operate.

dyslexia A term for the difficulties experienced by some people in reading or learning to read.

echolalia Repeating word for word what is said by another rather than responding to a question or making a statement of one's own; a common problem in autistic children.

ecological theory A theory of development that stresses the importance of understanding not only the relationships between the organism and various environmental systems but the relations between such systems themselves.

ecological validity The degree to which a research study accurately represents events and processes that occur in the natural world.

ego In Freudian theory, the rational, controlling component of the personality, which tries to satisfy needs through appropriate, socially acceptable behaviors.

egocentric speech According to Vygotsky, a form of self-directed dialog by which the child instructs herself in solving problems and formulating plans; as the child matures, becomes internalized, as *inner speech.*

egocentrism The tendency to view the world from one's own perspective and to have difficulty seeing things from another's viewpoint.

elaboration A memory strategy in which one adds to information to make it more meaningful and thus easier to place in long-term memory.

Electra complex A primary dynamic of the *phallic* stage of Freudian development theory in which a girl resents her mother for having deprived her of a penis, and transfers her affections to her father.

elementary mental functions Functions with which the child is endowed by nature, including attention, perception, and memory.

embryo The developing organism between the second and eighth week of gestation; the period of the embryo comprises the differentiation of the major physiological structures and systems.

emotional display rules Rules that dictate the emotions that it is appropriate to display in particular situations.

emotional script A complex scheme that enables a child to identify the emotional reaction that is likely to accompany a particular sort of event.

emotions Subjective reactions to something in the environment that are usually experienced cognitively as either pleasant or unpleasant, that are generally accompanied by physiological changes, and that are often expressed in some form of visible behavior.

empathy The capacity to experience the same emotion that someone else is experiencing.

encoding The transformation of information from the environment into a lasting mental representation.

enrichment theory The notion that the child acquires additional information about an object from each repeated experience with it, further modifying and enriching these data with information in existing schemata.

estrogens Hormones that, in the female, are responsible for sexual maturation.

ethological theory A theory that holds that behavior must be viewed and understood as occurring in a particular context and as having adaptive or survival value.

ethological theory of attachment Bowlby's theory that attachment derives from the biological preparation of both infant and parents to respond to each other's behaviors in such a way that parents provide the infant with care and protection.

etiology In medicine and psychiatry, the cause or causes of a specific disorder.

event sampling An observational technique in which investigators record participants' behavior only when an event of particular interest occurs, not at other times.

executive control structure According to Case, a mental blueprint or plan for solving a class of problems.

exosystem In Bronfenbrenner's ecological theory, the collection of settings that impinge on a child's development but in which the child does not play a direct role.

expansion A technique adults use in speaking to young children in which they imitate and expand or add to a child's statement.

experimental group In a formal experiment, the group that is exposed to the treatment.

expressive characteristics Presumably typical of females, these characteristics include nurturance and concern with feelings.

extended family Typically, a family that includes many relatives, such as grandparents, aunts, uncles, nieces, and nephews, within the basic family unit of parents and children.

factor analysis A statistical procedure used to determine which of a number of factors or scores are both closely related to each other and relatively independent of other groups of factors or scores.

family therapy A form of psychotherapy in which all family members join to find solutions to a child's problem behaviors.

fast-mapping A technique in which a child learns to link a new word with a concept that he or she already understands.

fetal alcohol syndrome A disorder exhibited by infants of alcoholic mothers and characterized by stunted growth, a number of physical and physiological abnormalities and, often, mental retardation.

fetus The developing organism from the third month of gestation through delivery; during the fetal period development of bodily structures and systems becomes complete.

field experiment An experiment in which researchers deliberately create a change in a real-world setting and then measure the outcome of their manipulation.

formal operations period Period in which the child becomes capable of flexibility and abstract thought, complex reasoning, and hypothesis testing.

fragile X syndrome A form of chromosome abnormality, more common in males, than in females, in which an X chromosome is narrowed in some areas, causing it to be fragile and leading to a variety of physical, psychological, and social problems.

friendship A reciprocal commitment between two people who see themselves as relative equals.

gender-based beliefs Ideas and expectations about what is appropriate behavior for males and females.

gender constancy The awareness that superficial alterations in appearance or activity do not alter gender.

gender identity The perception of oneself as either masculine or feminine.

gender-role preferences Desires to possess certain gender-typed characteristics.

gender roles Composites of the behaviors actually exhibited by a typical male or female in a given culture; the reflection of a *gender stereotype* in everyday life.

gender-schema theory The notion that children develop schemas, or naive theories, that help them organize and structure their experience related to gender differences and gender roles.

gender stability The notion that gender does not change; males remain male and females remain female.

gender stereotypes Beliefs that members of a culture hold about how females and males ought to behave, that is, what behaviors are acceptable and appropriate for each.

gender typing The process by which children acquire the values, motives, and behaviors considered appropriate for their gender in their particular culture.

gene A portion of DNA that is located at a particular site on a chromosome and that codes for the production of certain kinds of proteins.

general factor (*g*) General mental energy or ability that is involved in all cognitive tasks.

generalization The application of a strategy learned while solving a problem in one situation to a similar problem in a new situation.

genital herpes A common viral infection spread through sexual contact; if contracted by an infant during birth can cause blindness, motor abnormalities, mental retardation, and a wide range of neurological disorders.

genotype The particular set of genes that a person inherits from his or her parents.

glial cell A nerve cell that supports and protects neurons and serves to encase them in sheaths of *myelin*.

gonorrhea A sexually transmitted bacterial infection that, in a pregnant woman, can cause blindness in her infant; normally treatable with antibiotics.

grammar The structure of a language, made up of *morphology* and *syntax*.

habituation The process by which an individual reacts with less and less intensity to a repeatedly presented stimulus, eventually responding only faintly or not at all.

Head Start A federally funded program that provides disadvantaged young children with preschool experience, social services, and medical and nutritional assistance.

hedonistic reasoning Basing one's decision to perform a prosocial act on the basis of expected material reward.

hemispheric specialization Differential functioning of the two cerebral hemispheres; for example, the control of speech and language by the left hemisphere and of visual-spatial processing by the right.

hemophilia A disorder caused by an X-linked recessive gene in which the blood fails to clot; found more often in males than in females.

heritability factor A statistical estimate of the contribution made by heredity to a particular trait or ability.

heterozygous Describing the state of an individual whose *alleles* for a particular trait from each parent are different.

hierarchical categorization The organization of concepts into levels of abstraction that range from the specific to the general.

higher mental functions Functions that rely on *mediators* that have become increasingly sophisticated through the child's interaction with his environment.

holophrase A single word that appears to represent a complete thought.

homozygous Describing the state of an individual whose *alleles* for a particular trait from each parent are the same.

horizontal decalage The notion that unevenness in children's cognitive achievements reflects the fact that understanding the conservation of different objects or substances requires differing levels of abstraction.

hormone A powerful and highly specialized chemical substance that interacts with cells capable of receiving the hormonal message and responding to it.

hostile aggression Aggressive behavior directed at another person, including criticizing, ridiculing, and name-calling.

human behavior genetics The study of the relative influences of heredity and environmental forces on the evolution of individual differences in traits and abilities.

Huntington disease A genetically caused, fatal disorder of the nervous system that begins in midadulthood and is manifested chiefly in uncontrollable, spasmodic, movements of the body and limbs and eventual mental deterioration.

id In Freudian theory, the person's instinctual drives; the first component of the personality to evolve, the id operates on the basis of the *pleasure principle*.

identification The Freudian notion that children acquire gender identity by identifying with and imitating their same-sex parents.

idiot savant A mentally retarded or sometimes autistic person who shows a remarkable talent in one particularized area of knowledge, such as the ability to predict the date and the day of the week many years in the future.

immanent justice The notion that any deviation from rules will inevitably result in punishment or retribution.

inclusion A policy by which children of all ability levels, whether learning disabled, physically handicapped, or mentally retarded, are included in the same classroom.

independent variable The variable, or factor, that researchers deliberately manipulate in a formal experiment.

infant state A recurring pattern of arousal in the newborn, ranging from alert, vigorous, wakeful activity to quiet, regular sleep.

infant-directed speech A simplified style of speech parents use with young children, in which sentences are short, simple, and often repetitive; the speaker enunciates especially clearly, slowly, and in a higher-pitched voice and often ends with a rising intonation. Also called *motherese*.

information-processing approach A perspective on cognition and cognitive development in which the human mind is likened to a computer, processing information from the environment through perception and attention (input), encoding it in memory (storage and retrieval), and applying information to the solution of problems (software).

information-processing theories Theories of development that focus on the flow of information through the child's cognitive system and that are particularly interested in the specific operations the child performs between input and output phases.

informed consent Agreement to participate in a research study that is based on a clear and full understanding of the purposes and procedures of that study.

inner speech Internalized *egocentric speech* that continues to direct and regulate intellectual function.

insecure-avoidant attachment A type of attachment shown by babies who seem not to be bothered by their mothers' brief absence but specifically avoid them on their return, sometimes becoming visibly upset.

insecure-disorganized attachment A type of attachment shown by babies who seem disorganized and disoriented when reunited with their mothers after a brief separation.

insecure-resistant attachment A kind of attachment shown by babies who tend to become very upset at the departure of their mothers and who exhibit inconsistent behavior on their return, sometimes seeking contact, sometimes pushing their mothers away.

instrumental aggression Quarreling and fighting over toys and possessions.

instrumental characteristics Presumably typical of males, these characteristics include task and occupation orientation.

intellectual giftedness A characteristic defined by an IQ score of 130 or over; gifted children learn faster than others and may show early exceptional talents in certain areas.

intelligence quotient (IQ) An index of the way a person performs on a standardized intelligence test relative to the way others his or her age perform.

interactional continuity The tendency for negative temperamental or personality characteristics to evoke negative responses from others, which reinforce the negative characteristics.

interactive synchrony A term that characterizes mother-infant interactions in which the mother constantly adjusts her behavior to that of her baby, responding to and respecting his signals as to when he is ready for and wants engagement and interaction.

intermodal perception The use of sensory information from more than one sensory modality to identify a stimulus; also, the apprehension of a stimulus already identified by one modality by means of another.

internal working model According to Bowlby, a person's mental representation of himself, his parents, and the style of his interaction with his parents, as he reconstructs and interprets that interaction.

intuitive stage The second substage of the preoperational period, during which the child begins to solve problems by means of specific mental operations but cannot yet explain how she arrives at the solutions.

inventing new means by mental combination In this last stage of the sensorimotor period, children begin to combine schemata mentally, relying less on physical trial and error.

iron-deficiency anemia A disorder in which inadequate amounts of iron in the diet cause listlessness and may retard a child's physical and intellectual development.

joint legal custody A form of child custody in which both parents retain and share responsibility for decisions regarding the child's life but which generally provides for the child to reside with one parent.

joint physical custody As in *joint legal custody*, parents make decisions together regarding their child's life but they also share physical custody, the child living with each parent for a portion of the year.

Kaufman Assessment Battery for Children (K-ABC) An intelligence test designed to measure several types of information-processing skills as well as achievement in some academic subjects.

Klinefelter's syndrome A form of chromosome abnormality in which a male inherits an extra X sex chromosome, resulting in the XXY pattern, and has many feminine physical characteristics as well as language deficits and, sometimes, mental retardation.

laboratory analogue experiment An experiment in which investigators try to duplicate in the laboratory features or events of everyday life.

laboratory experiment A research design that allows investigators, through controlling variables and treatments and assigning participants randomly to treatments, to determine cause and effect.

language A communication system in which words and their written symbols combine in various, regulated ways to produce an infinite number of messages.

language acquisition device (LAD) Chomsky's proposed mental structure in the human nervous system that incorporates an innate concept of language.

language acquisition support system (LASS) According to Bruner, a collection of strategies and tactics that environmental influences—initially, a child's parents or primary caretakers—provide the language-learning child.

lanugo A fine, soft hair that covers the fetus's body from about the fifth month of gestation on; may be shed before birth or after.

latchkey children Children who must let themselves into their homes after school because a parent or both parents are working outside the home.

lateralization The process by which each half of the brain becomes specialized for the performance of certain functions.

learned helplessness A kind of behavior that results from the belief that one is helpless to control the events in one's world.

learning theory of attachment The theory that infants become attached to the mother because she provides food, or primary reinforcement, and thus acquires secondary reinforcement properties.

level of processing model An information-processing model that proposes that the intensity of processing applied to information determines how long it will be retained.

life span theory A theory that sees development as a process that continues throughout the life cycle, from infancy through adulthood and old age.

longitudinal method A method of research in which investigators study the same people repeatedly at various times in the participants' lives.

long-term memory The encyclopedic mental processing unit in which information may be stored permanently and from which it may be later retrieved.

macrosystem In Bronfenbrenner's ecological theory, the system that surrounds the *microsystem, mesosystem,* and *exosystem,* and that represents the values, ideologies, and laws of the society or culture.

magic window thinking The tendency of very young children to believe that TV images are as real as the people and things about them.

maturation A genetically determined process of growth that unfolds naturally over a period of time.

mediation deficiency Inability to use strategies to store information in long-term memory.

mediators According to Vygotsky, psychological tools and signs like language, counting, mnemonic devices, algebraic symbols, art, and writing.

meiosis The process by which a germ cell divides to produce new germ cells with only half the normal complement of chromosomes; male and female germ cells (sperm and ovum) each contain only 23 chromosomes so that when they unite the new organism they form will have 46 chromosomes, half from each parent.

memory span The amount of information one can hold in short-term memory.

menarche In females, the beginning of the menstrual cycle.

mental age An index of a child's actual performance on an intelligence test as compared with his true age.

mental map A cognitive representation of the spatial layout of a physical or geographical place.

mental representation Information stored in some form (e.g., verbal, pictorial) in the cognitive system after the person has encountered it in the environment.

mental retardation A characteristic defined by an IQ score below 70 and the inability to cope adequately with age-appropriate activities in everyday life.

mesosystem In Bronfenbrenner's ecological theory, the interrelations that obtain among the components of the *microsystem,* such as home and school, with which the child interacts.

metacognition The individual's knowledge and control of cognitive activities.

metalinguistic awareness The understanding that language is a system of communicating with others that is bound by rules.

microsystem In Bronfenbrenner's ecological theory, the context in which the child lives and interacts with the people and institutions closest to her, such as parents, peers, and school.

mitosis The process in which a body cell divides in two, first duplicating its chromosomes so that the new, daughter cells each contain the usual 46 chromosomes.

modifier genes Genes that exert their influence indirectly, by affecting the expression of still other genes.

monozygotic Characterizing *identical* twins, who have developed from a single fertilized egg.

moral realism Piaget's second stage of moral development, in which the child shows great respect for rules but applies them quite inflexibly.

morality of reciprocity Piaget's third stage of moral development, in which the child recognizes that rules may be questioned and altered, considers the feelings and views of others, and believes in equal justice for all.

morpheme Any of a language's smallest units of meaning, such as a prefix, a suffix, or a root word.

morphology The study of a language's smallest units of meaning, or *morphemes.*

multischematic Possessing more than one cultural schema for responding to the environment as well as criteria for deciding what schema to use in a particular situation.

myelination The process by which glial cells encase neurons in sheaths of the fatty substance *myelin.*

naming explosion The rapid increase in vocabulary that the child typically shows at about the age of one and a half.

national survey A method of sampling in which a very large, nationally representative group of people are selected for a particular study.

natural experiment An experiment in which researchers measure the results of things that occur naturally in the real world.

needs-oriented reasoning Reasoning in which children express concern for others' needs even though their own needs may conflict with those needs.

negative evidence According to Pinker, corrective feedback that parents may give to young language-learning children.

negative gossip Sharing with a peer some negative information about another child.

neglected children Children who tend to be socially isolated and, though they have few friends, are not necessarily disliked by others.

neonate A newborn baby.

neo-Piagetian theories Theories of cognitive development that are grounded in Piagetian theory but reinterpret Piaget's concepts in and information-processing context.

neuron A cell in the body's nervous system, consisting of a cell body, a long projection called an *axon* and several shorter projections called *dendrites;* neurons send and receive neural impulses, or messages, throughout the brain and nervous system.

neuron proliferation The rapid proliferation of neurons in the developing organism's brain.

neuronal death The death of some neurons that surround newly formed synaptic connections among other neurons.

neuronal migration The movement of neurons within the brain that ensures that all brain areas have a sufficient number of neural connections.

niche picking Seeking out or creating environments that are compatible with one's own (genetically based) predispositions.

nonaggressive rejected children *Rejected* children who tend to be withdrawn, anxious, and socially unskilled.

nonshared environment A set of conditions or activities that is experienced by one child in a family and not shared with another child in the same family.

nucleotide A compound containing a nitrogen base, a simple sugar, and a phosphate group.

obesity A condition in which a person's weight is 20 percent or more in excess of the average weight for his or her height and frame.

object permanence The notion that objects and people continue to exist independent of our seeing or interacting with them.

observer bias The tendency of researcher-observers to be influenced in their judgments by their knowledge of the hypotheses guiding the research.

obsessive self-stimulatory behavior Behavior common in autistic children in which they engage in repetitive actions that have no apparent purpose.

Oedipus complex A primary dynamic of the *phallic* stage of Freudian development theory in which the boy is sexually attracted to his mother, sees himself as his father's rival, and fears his father's retribution.

open classroom A relatively unstructured classroom organization, in which different areas of the room are devoted to particular activities and children work simultaneously, either alone or in small groups, at these activities under the teacher's supervision.

operant behavior therapy A form of behavior therapy in which behavior is carefully monitored and consistently rewarded with such things as food.

operant conditioning A type of learning that depends on the consequences of behavior; rewards increase the likelihood that a behavior will recur, whereas punishment decreases that likelihood.

operations Schemata based on internal mental activities.

organization The predisposition to combine simple mental structures into more complex systems.

overcontrolled disorders A group of psychological disturbances in which a child appears overly controlled, withdrawing from others, lacking spontaneity, and generally appearing to be not a happy child.

overextension The use, by a young child, of a single word to cover many different things.

overregularization The mistaken application of a principle of regular change to a word that changes irregularly.

ovum The female germ cell, or egg.

patterned speech A form of pseudospeech in which the child utters strings of phonemes that sound very much like real speech but are not.

peer collaboration A kind of *cooperative learning*, in which two students work together to master a task that neither has mastered before.

peer tutoring A method of instruction in which an older, more experienced student tutors a younger, less experienced child.

perception The interpretation of sensations in order to make them meaningful.

permissive parenting Parenting that is lax and in which parents exercise inconsistent discipline and encourage children to express their impulses freely.

personal domain An area of rules and conventions distinct from moral rules; involves issues such as choice of friends and styles of dress.

pervasive developmental disorders Childhood disorders characterized by gross deficits in many areas of cognitive, emotional, and social development that are linked with severe and pervasive impairment of social interaction and communication skills.

phenotype Created by the interaction of a person's genetic makeup with the environment; the visible expression of the person's particular physical and behavioral characteristics.

phenylketonuria (PKU) A disease caused by a recessive allele that fails to produce an enzyme necessary to metabolize the protein phenylalanine; if untreated immediately at birth, damages the nervous system and causes mental retardation.

phoneme Any of the basic units of a language's phonetic system; phonemes are the smallest sound units that affect meaning.

phonology The system of sounds that a particular language uses.

pituitary gland A so-called master gland, located at the base of the brain, that triggers the secretion of hormones by all other hormone-secreting, or endocrine, glands.

placenta A fleshy, disclike structure formed by cells from the lining of the uterus and from the *zygote,* and that, together with the *umbilical cord*, serves to protect and sustain the life of the growing organism.

plasticity The capacity of the brain, particularly in its developmental stages, to respond and adapt to input from the external environment.

play Activity that is intrinsically motivated, concerned more often with means than with ends, free from external rules, nonserious, and highly engaging.

play therapy A form of psychotherapy in which therapists encourage children in free play with dolls and toys on the premise that such play will reveal a child's unconscious conflicts and concerns.

popular children Children who are liked by many peers and disliked by very few.

postconventional level Kohlberg's third level of moral development, in which the child's judgments are rational and his conduct is controlled by an internalized ethical code that is relatively independent of the approval or disapproval of others.

pragmatics A set of rules that specify appropriate language for particular social contexts.

preconceptual stage The first substage of Piaget's preoperational period, during which the child's thought is characterized by animistic thinking and egocentricity.

preconventional level Kohlberg's first level of moral development, in which he sees the child's behavior as based on the desire to avoid punishment and gain rewards.

premoral stage Piaget's first stage of moral development, in which the child shows little concern for rules.

preoperational period In this period, the *symbolic function* promotes the learning of language; period is also marked by egocentricity and intuitive behavior, in which the child can solve problems using mental operations but cannot explain how he does so.

preterm A term describing a premature baby who is born before its due date and whose weight, though less than that of a full-term infant, may be appropriate to its gestational age.

primary circular reactions Behaviors in which infants repeat and modify actions that focus on their own bodies and that are pleasurable and satisfying.

primary prevention A form of *community psychology* in which mental health professionals attempt to alter social conditions, such as changing school curricula and teaching childrearing skills to new parents.

proactive aggression The use of force to dominate another person or to bully or threaten others.

production deficiency Inability spontaneously to generate and use memory strategies that one knows.

productive language The production of speech.

progesterone A hormone that, in females, helps regulate the menstrual cycle and prepares the uterus to receive and nurture a fertilized egg.

prosocial behavior Behavior that is designed to help or benefit other people.

prosocial reasoning Thinking and making judgments about prosocial issues.

prospective memory Memory for information that one plans to use at a given future time.

protodeclarative A gesture that an infant uses to make some sort of statement about an object.

protoimperative A gesture that an infant or a young child may use to get someone to do something she wants.

proximal-distal pattern The tendency for human physical development to occur from the center outward; for example, from internal organs to arms and legs.

psychoactive medications Medications that are designed to alter mood and/or thinking processes.

psychoanalytic theory of attachment The Freudian theory that babies become attached first to the mother's breast and then to the mother herself as a source of oral gratification.

psychoanalytic theory of development Freud's theory that development which proceeds in discrete stages, is determined largely by biologically based drives shaped by encounters with the environment and through the interaction of three components of personality—*id*, *ego*, and *superego*.

psychometrician A psychologist who specializes in the construction and use of tests designed to measure various psychological constructs such as intelligence, motivation, achievement orientation, and personality characteristics.

psychopathology Psychological and behavioral dysfunction as it occurs in various types of mental disorder.

psychosocial theory Erikson's theory of development that sees the child developing through a series of stages largely through accomplishing tasks that involve her in interaction with her social environment.

psychostimulant medications Drugs, such as amphetamines and caffeine, that increase alertness and attention as well as psychomotor activity.

puberty The onset of sexual maturity.

Pygmalion effect The tendency of a teacher's expectation about a child's academic performance to become a self-fulfilling prophecy.

random assignment The technique by which researchers assign individuals randomly to either an experimental or a control group in a formal experiment.

range of reaction The notion that the human being's genetic makeup establishes a range of possible developmental outcomes, within which environmental forces largely determine how the person actually develops.

reactive aggression Aggressive behavior that is responsive to attack, threat, or frustration.

recast A technique adults use in speaking to young children in which they render a child's incomplete sentence in a more complex grammatical form.

receptive language Understanding the speech of others.

recessive Describing the weaker of two *alleles* in a heterozygous combination.

reciprocal teaching A method of instruction in which a teacher and a small group of students take turns leading discussions of text passages and which makes use of four specific cognitive strategies: predicting, questioning, summarizing, and clarifying.

recovery The ability to recognize a new stimulus as novel and to direct attention to it in preference to a familiar stimulus.

reflex A human being's involuntary response to external stimulation.

reflex activity An infant's exercise of and growing proficiency in the use of innate reflexes.

reflex smile A newborn infant's smile, which appears to reflect some internal stimulus, such as a change in the infant's level of arousal, rather than an external stimulus such as another person's behavior.

rehearsal A memory strategy in which one repeats a number of times, either mentally or orally, the information one wants to remember.

rejected children Children who are disliked by many peers and liked by very few.

relational aggression Damaging or destroying interpersonal relationships by such means as excluding another or gossiping about or soiling another's reputation.

relationship A succession of interactions between two people who know each other that are altered by their shared, past interactions and that also affect their future interactions.

reliability The degree to which a test yields consistent results over successive administrations.

REM and non-REM sleep REM, or rapid-eye-movement sleep is characterized by rapid, jerky movements of the eyes and, in adults, is often associated with dreaming; infants spend 50 percent of their sleep in REM activity, whereas adults spend only about 20 percent. This activity is absent in the remaining, non-REM sleep.

representativeness The degree to which a sample actually possesses the characteristics of the larger population it represents.

respiratory distress syndrome A condition of the newborn marked by labored breathing and a bluish discoloration of the skin or mucous membranes and which often leads to death.

reversibility The notion that one can reverse or undo a given operation, either physically or mentally.

Rh factor incompatibility A condition in which an infant's Rh negative blood opposes its mother's Rh positive blood, and threatens fetuses in later births, when the mother's body has had time to produce antibodies that will attack fetal blood cells.

sample A group of individuals who are representative of a larger population.

scaffolding Based on Vygotsky's thought, an instructional process in which the teacher continually adjusts the amount and type of support he offers as the child continues to develop more sophisticated skills.

schema (Plural, *schemata*); a cognitive structure, or an organized group of interrelated memories, thoughts, and strategies that the child uses to try to understand a situation; a schema forms the basis for organizing actions to respond to the environment.

scientific method The use of measurable and replicable techniques in framing hypotheses and collecting and analyzing data to test a theory's usefulness.

script A mental representation of an event or situation of daily life, including the expected order in which things happen and how one should behave in that event or situation.

secondary circular reactions Behaviors focused on objects outside the infant's own body that the infant repeatedly engages in because they are pleasurable.

secondary prevention A form of *community psychology* in which mental health professionals try to identify people's problems at the outset and to undertake interventions to prevent disorders in those who are at risk.

secondary reinforcer A person or other stimulus that acquires reinforcing properties by virtue of repeated association with a primary reinforcer.

secular trend A shift in the normative pattern of a characteristic, like height, that occurs over a historical period, like a decade or century.

secure attachment A kind of attachment displayed by babies who are secure enough to explore novel environments, who are minimally disturbed by brief separations from their mothers, and who greet them happily when they return.

secure base According to Ainsworth, a caregiver to whom an infant has formed an attachment and whom the child uses as a base from which to explore new things and as a safe haven in times of stress.

self-control phase According to Kopp, the second phase in learning *self-regulation,* when the child becomes able to comply with caregiver expectations in the absence of the caregiver.

self-disclosure The honest sharing of information of a very personal nature, often with a focus on problem solving; a central means by which adolescents develop friendships.

self-regulation The child's ability to regulate his behavior on his own, without parental reminder (Chapter 12). Also his ability to inhibit or direct his actions to conform to social and moral rules (Chapter 16).

self-regulation phase According to Kopp, the third phase in learning *self-regulation,* when children become able to use strategies and plans in directing their own behavior and capable of delaying gratification.

self-report Information that people provide about themselves, either in a direct interview or in some written form, such as a questionnaire.

self-socialization The child's spontaneous adoption of gender-appropriate behavior.

self system The sense of self as distinct from others combined with such things as stored knowledge of past experiences related to the self, awareness of being judged by others, and the capacity for self evaluation.

semantic organization Organizing information to be remembered by means of categorization and hierarchical relationships.

semantics The study of word meanings and word combinations, as in phrases, clauses, and sentences.

sensation Detection of stimuli by the sensory receptors.

sensitive care Caregiving that is consistent and responsive and that begins by allowing an infant to play a role in determining when feeding will begin and end and at what pace it will proceed.

sensorimotor period Piaget's first stage of cognitive development, during which children move from purely reflexive behavior to the beginnings of symbolic thought and goal-directed behaviors.

sensory register The mental processing unit that receives information from the environment and stores it fleetingly.

separation protest An infant's distress reaction to being separated from his or her mother, which typically peaks at about 15 months of age.

sequential method A research method that combines features of both the cross-sectional and the longitudinal methods.

sex chromosomes In both males and females, the 23rd pair of chromosomes, which determine the individual's sex and

are responsible for sex-related characteristics; in females, this pair normally comprises two X chromosomes, in males an X and a Y chromosome.

shape constancy The ability to perceive an object's shape as remaining constant despite changes in its orientation and the angle from which one views it.

shared environment A set of conditions or experiences that is shared by children raised in the same family with each other; a parameter commonly examined in studies of individual differences.

short-term memory The mental processing unit in which information may be stored temporarily; the "work space" of the mind, where a decision must be made to discard information or to transfer it to permanent storage, in *long-term memory.*

sickle-cell anemia A disorder, caused by a recessive gene, in which the red blood cells become distorted when low in oxygen, causing fatigue, shortness of breath, and severe pain and posing a threat to life from blockage of crucial blood vessels.

size constancy The tendency to perceive an object as constant in size regardless of changes in its distance from the viewer and in the image it casts on the retinas of the eyes.

small for date A term describing a premature baby who may be born close to its due date but who weighs significantly less than would be appropriate to its gestational age.

social comparison The process of evaluating one's characteristics, abilities, values, and other qualities by comparing oneself with others, usually one's peers.

social referencing The process of "reading" emotional cues in others to help determine how to act in an uncertain situation.

social-convention rules Socially based rules about everyday conduct.

socialization The process by which parents and others ensure that a child's standards of behavior, attitudes, skills, and motives conform closely to those deemed appropriate to his or her role in society.

socially unskilled Being unskilled at solving interpersonal problems.

sociocultural theory A theory of development, proposed by Lev Vygotsky, that sees development as evolving out of children's interactions with more-skilled others in their social environment.

sociometric technique A procedure for determining children's status within their peer group in which children nominate others whom they like best or least or rate each child in the group for his likeability or desirability as a companion.

specific factors (s) Factors that are unique to particular cognitive tasks.

specimen record An observational technique in which researchers record everything a person does within a given period of time.

speech acts One- or two-word utterances that clearly refer to situations or to sequences of events.

sperm The male germ cell.

spermarche In males, the first ejaculation of semen-containing ejaculate.

standardization The process by which test constructors ensure that testing procedures, instructions, and scoring are identical on every testing occasion.

Stanford-Binet Test The modern version of the first major intelligence test; emphasizes verbal and mathematical skills.

status offense Illegal behavior in an under-age offender.

stereoscopic vision The sense of a third spatial dimension produced by the brain's fusion of the separate images contributed by both eyes, each of which reflects the stimulus from a slightly different angle.

store model A model of information processing in which information is depicted as moving through a series of processing units—*sensory register, short-term memory,* and *long-term memory*—in each of which it may be stored, either fleetingly or permanently.

Strange Situation A testing scenario in which mother and child are separated and reunited several times and that enables investigators to assess the nature and quality of a mother-infant attachment relationship.

stranger distress A fear of strangers that typically emerges in infants around the age of 9 months.

strategies Conscious cognitive or behavioral activities that are used to enhance mental performance.

structured observation A form of observation in which researchers structure a situation so that behaviors they wish to study are more likely to occur.

substance abuse The excessive use of legal or illegal drugs in such a way as to interfere seriously with one or more important areas of functioning in life: work, intimacy with another, or general interpersonal and social relationships.

sudden infant death syndrome (SIDS) The sudden, unexplained death of an infant while sleeping, also called "crib death."

superego In Freudian theory, the personality component that is the repository of the child's internalization of parental or societal values, morals, and roles.

symbolic function The ability to use symbols, such as images, words, gestures, to represent object and events in the world.

symbolic thought The use of mental images to represent people, objects, and events.

synapse A specialized site of intercellular communication where information is exchanged between nerve cells, usually by means of a chemical *neurotransmitter*.

synaptic pruning The brain's disposal of the axon and dendrites of a neuron that is not often stimulated.

synaptogenesis. The forming of synapses.

syntax The subdivision of grammar that prescribes how words are to be combined into phrases, clauses, and sentences.

syphilis A sexually transmitted bacterial disease that today can usually be treated with antibiotics but that untreated in the pregnant woman can lead to miscarriage or blindness, mental retardation, or other physical abnormalities in her baby.

telegraphic speech Two-word utterances that include only the words that are essential to convey the speaker's intent.

temperament The individual's typical mode of response to the environment, including such things as activity level, emotional intensity, and attention span; used particularly to describe infants' and children's behavior.

teratogen An environmental agent, such as a drug, medication, dietary imbalance, or polluting substance, that may cause developmental deviations in a growing human organism; most threatening in the embryonic stage but capable of causing abnormalities in the fetal stage as well.

tertiary circular reactions Behaviors in which infants experiment with the properties of external objects and try to learn how objects respond to various actions.

tertiary prevention A form of *community psychology* in which mental health professionals provide treatment to children and families who are suffering various psychological problems.

test norm Values or sets of values that describe the typical performance of a specific group of people.

testosterone A hormone that, in the male, is responsible for the development of primary and secondary sex characteristics and is essential for the production of sperm.

thalidomide A drug once prescribed to relieve morning sickness in pregnant women but discontinued when found to cause serious malformations of the fetus. Current controversy surrounds possible use in treating symptoms of such diseases as AIDS, cancer, and leprosy.

theory of multiple intelligences Gardner's multifactorial theory that proposes seven distinct types of intelligence.

time out Removal of a child from a situation or context in which she or he is acting inappropriately until the child is able and ready to act appropriately.

time sampling An observational technique in which researchers record any of a set of predetermined behaviors that occur within a specified time period.

traditional classroom A structured classroom arrangement, in which the teacher presents one subject at a time to the entire student body, who sit in rows, facing the teacher.

traditional nuclear family The traditional family form, composed of two parents and one or more children, in which the father is the breadwinner and the mother the homemaker.

transitive inference The mental arrangement of things along a quantitative dimension.

triarchic theory of intelligence A theory that proposes three major components of intelligent behavior: information-processing skills, experience with a particular situation, and ability to adapt to the demands of a context.

Turner syndrome A form of chromosome abnormality found in females, in which secondary sex characteristics develop only if female hormones are administered and in which abnormal formation of internal reproductive organs leads to permanent sterility.

two-generation program A program of early cognitive intervention that extends help to parents as well as to their children.

ultrasound A technique that uses sound waves to visualize deep body structures; commonly used to reveal the size and structure of a developing fetus. Also called *ultrasonography*.

umbilical cord A tube that contains blood vessels going between the growing organism and its mother by way of the *placenta*; carries oxygen and nutrients to the growing infant and removes carbon dioxide and waste products.

undercontrolled disorders A group of psychological disturbances in which a child appears to lack self-control and to act out in a variety of ways, through such behaviors as noncompliance, disobedience, and aggression.

underextension The use, by a young child, of a single word in a restricted and individualistic way.

uninvolved parenting Parenting that is indifferent and neglectful and in which parents focus on their own needs rather than their children's needs.

utilization deficiency Inability to use an attentional strategy that one knows.

validity The extent to which a test actually measures what it claims to measure.

visual acuity Sharpness of vision; the clarity with which fine details can be discerned.

visual cliff An apparatus that tests an infant's depth perception by using patterned materials and an elevated, clear glass platform to make it appear that one side of the platform is several feet lower than the other.

visual preference method A method of studying infants' abilities to distinguish one stimulus from another.

Wechsler Intelligence Scales Three intelligence tests for infants, children, and adults that yield separate scores for verbal and performance IQ as well as a combined IQ score.

world knowledge What a child has learned from experience and knows about the world in general.

X-linked genes Genes that are carried on the X chromosome and that, in males, may have no analogous genes on the Y chromosome.

zone of proximal development (ZPD) According to Vygotsky, the difference between the developmental level a child has reached and the level she is potentially capable of reaching with the guidance or collaboration of a more skilled adult or peer.

zygote The developing organism from the time of the union of sperm and egg to about the second week of gestation; the period of the zygote comprises the implantation of the fertilized egg in the wall of the uterus.

References

Aaronson, L. S., & MacNee, C. L. (1989). Tobacco, alcohol, and caffeine use during pregnancy. *Journal of Obstetrics, Gynecology and Neonatal Nursing, 18*, 279–287.

Abraham, S., & Llewellyn-Jones, D. (1997). *Eating disorders: The facts* (4th ed.). Oxford, England: Oxford University Press.

Abramowitz, A., & O'Leary, S. G. (1991). Behavioral interventions for the classroom: Implications for students with ADHD. *School Psychology Review, 20*, 220–234.

Achenbach, T. M. (1990). Conceptualization of developmental psychopathology. In M. Lewis & S. Miller (Eds.), *Handbook of developmental psychopathology* (pp. 3–14). New York: Plenum.

Achenbach, T. M. (1990). What is "developmental" about developmental psychopathology? In J. Rolf, A. Masten, D. Cicchetti, K. Nuechterlein, & S. Weintraub (Eds.), *Risk and protective factors in the development of psychopathology* (pp. 29–48). New York: Cambridge University Press.

Achenbach, T. M., & Edelbrock, C. S. (1978). The classification of child psychopathology: A review and analysis of empirical efforts. *Psychological Bulletin, 85*, 1275–1301.

Achilles, C. M., Nye, B. A., Zaharias, J. B., & Fulton, B. D. (1993). *The lasting benefits study (LBS) in grades 4 and 5 (1990–91): A legacy from Tennessee's four year (K-3) class size study, Project STAR.* Paper presented at the North Carolina Association for Research in Education. Greensboro, NC.

Ackerman, B. P. (1996). Induction of a memory retrieval strategy by young children. *Journal of Experimental Child Psychology, 62*, 243–271.

Adams, M. J., Trieman, R., & Pressley, M. (1998). Reading, writing, and literacy. In W. Damon (Gen. Ed.), I. Sigel, & K. A. Renninger (Vol. Eds.). *Handbook of child psychology: Vol. 4. Child psychology in practice* (pp. 275–355). New York: Wiley.

Adamson, L. B. (1995). *Communication development during infancy.* Madison, WI: Brown & Benchmark.

Adelson, E., & Fraiberg, S. (1974). Gross motor development in infants blind from birth. *Child Development, 45*, 114–126.

Adler, A. (1990). Cocaine babies' reactions explored. *APA Monitor*, p. 8.

Adolph, K. E., Eppler, M. A., & Gibson, E. J. (1993). Crawling versus walking infants' perception of affordances for locomotion over sloping surfaces. Special Section: Developmental biodynamics: Brain, body, behavior connections. *Child Development, 64*, 1158–1174.

Affleck, G., Tennen, H., & Rowe, J. (1990). Mothers, fathers and the crisis of newborn intensive care. *Infant Medical Health Journal, 11*, 12–25.

Agras, W. S. (1988). Does early eating behavior influence later adiposity? In N. A. Krasnegor, G. D. Grave, & N. Kretchmer (Eds.), *Childhood obesity: A biobehavioral perspective* (pp. 49–66). Caldwell, NJ: Telford Press.

Ahmed, N. U., Zeitlin, M. F., Beiser, A. S., Super, C. M., & Gershoff, S. N. (1993). A longitudinal study of the impact of behavioural change intervention on cleanliness, diarrhoeal morbidity and growth of children in rural Bangladesh. *Social Science and Medicine, 37*, 159–171.

Ahrens, R. (1954). *Beitrag zur entwicklun des physionomie und mimikerkennens. A. F. Exp. U. Angew, Psychol., 2*, 599–633.

Ainsworth, M. D. (1963). The development of infant-mother interaction among the Ganda. In D. M. Foss (Ed.), *Determinants of infant behavior* (Vol. 2, pp 67–104). New York: Wiley.

Ainsworth, M. D. (1973). The development of infant-mother attachment. In B. Caldwell & H. Ricciuti (Eds.), *Review of child development research* (Vol. 3). Chicago: University of Chicago Press.

Ainsworth, M. D., Blehar, M., Waters, E., & Wall, S. (1978). *Patterns of attachment.* Hillsdale, NJ: Erlbaum.

Albert, R. S. (1996, Summer). Some reasons why childhood creativity often fails to make it past puberty into the real world. In M. A. Runco (Ed.), *Creativity from childhood through adulthood: The developmental issues* [Special issue]. *New Directions for Child Development*, No. 72, 43–56.

Alessandri, S. M., & Lewis, M. (1996). Differences in pride and shame in maltreated and nonmaltreated preschoolers. *Child Development, 67*, 1857–1869.

Allan, K., & Coltrane, S. (1996). Gender displaying television commercials: A comparative study of television commercials in the 1950s and 1980s. *Sex Roles, 35*, 185–203.

Allen, G. L., & Ondracek, P. J. (1995). Age-sensitive cognitive abilities related to children's acquisition of spatial knowledge. *Developmental Psychology, 31*, 934–945.

Allen, L., & Majidi-Abi, S. (1989). Black American children. In J. T. Gibbs & L. N. Huang (Eds.), *Children of color.* San Francisco: Jossey-Bass.

Allen, V. L., & Feldman, R. S. (1976). *Children as teachers: Theory and research on tutoring.* New York: Academic.

Amabile, T. M., & Hennessey, B. A. (1988). The motivation for creativity in children. In A. K. Boggiani & T. Pittman (Eds.), *Achievement and motivation: A social developmental perspective.* New York: Cambridge University Press.

A man's drinking may harm his offspring. (1975). *Science News, 107*(8), 116.

American Medical Association. (1992, December). *Report to the Consumer Product Safety Commission on infant walkers.* Nashville, TN: American Medical Association.

American Psychiatric Association. (1994). *Diagnostic and statistical manual of mental disorders* (4th ed.). Washington, DC: Author.

American Psychological Association. (1992). Ethical principles of psychologists: Code of conduct. *American Psychologist, 44*, 1597–1611.

Amsterdam, B. (1972). Mirror self-image reactions before age two. *Developmental Psychobiology, 5*, 297–305.

Anastasi, A. (1988). *Psychological testing* (6th ed.). New York: Macmillan.

Anastopoulos, A. D., & Barkley, R. A. (1988). Biological factors in attention deficit-hyperactivity disorder. *Behavior Therapist, 11*, 47–53.

Anderson, D. R., Choi, H. P., & Lorch, E. P. (1987). Attentional inertia reduces distractability during young children's TV viewing. *Child Development, 58*, 798–806.

Anderson, D. R., & Field, D. E. (1991). Online and offline assessment of the television audience. In J. Bryant & D. Zillmann (Eds.), *Responding to the screen: Reception and reaction processes* (pp. 199–216). Hillsdale, NJ: Erlbaum.

Anderson, D. R., Lorch, E. P., Field, D. E., Collins, P., & Nathan, J. (1986). Television viewing at home: Age trends in visual attention and time with TV. *Child Development, 57*, 1024–1033.

Anderson, D. R., Lorch, E. P., Field, D. E., & Sanders, J. (1981). The effects of TV program comprehensibility on preschool children's visual attention to television. *Child Development, 52*, 151–157.

Anderson, W. F. (1995). Gene therapy. *Scientific American, 273*, 124–128.

Andrews, J. A., & Lewinsohn, P. M. (1992). Suicidal attempts among older adolescents: Prevalence and co-occurrence with psychiatric disorders. *Journal of American Academy of Child and Adolescent Psychiatry, 31*, 655–662.

Angier, N. (1997). Evolutionary necessity or glorious accident? Biologists ponder the self. *The New York Times,* April 22, p. C1.

Anisfeld, E., Casper, V., Nosyce, M., & Cunningham, N. (1990). Does infant carrying promote attachment? An experimental study of the effects of increased physical contact on the development of attachment. *Child Development, 61,* 1617–1627.

Anisfeld, M. (1991). Neonatal imitation. *Developmental Review, 11,* 60–97.

Anooshian, L. J., & Siegel, A. W. (1985). From cognitive to procedural mapping. In C. J. Brainard & M. Pressley (Eds.), *Basic process in memory development.* New York: Springer-Verlag.

Antonarakis, S. E., & Down Syndrome Collaborative Group. (1991). Parental origin of the extra chromosome in trisomy 21 as indicated by analysis of DNA polymorphisms. *New England Journal of Medicine, 324,* 872–876.

Apgar, V. A. (1953). A proposal for a new method of evaluation of the newborn infant. *Current Research in Anesthesia and Analgesia, 32,* 260–267.

Archer, J. (1994). Testosterone and aggression. *Journal of Offender Rehabilitation, 21,* 3–39.

Armor, D. J. (1995). *Forced justice: School desegregation and the law.* New York: Oxford University Press.

Aronfreed, J. (1976). Moral development from the standpoint of a general psychological theory. In T. Lickona (Ed.), *Moral development and behavior.* New York: Holt.

Aronson, E., Stephan, C., Sikes, J., Blaney, N., & Snapp, M. (1978). *The jigsaw classroom.* Beverly Hills, CA: Sage.

Arsenio, W. F., & Kramer, R. (1992). Victimizers and their victims: Children's conceptions of mixed emotional consequences of moral transgressions. *Child Development, 63,* 915–927.

Asher, J. R., & Hopmeyer, A. (in press). Loneliness in childhood. In G. Bear, K. Minke, & A. Thomas (Eds.), *Children's needs II: Psychological perspectives.* Silver Spring, MD: National Association of School Psychologists.

Asher, S. R. (1980). Topic interest and children's reading comprehension. In R. Spiro, B. Bruce, & W. Brewer (Eds.), *Theoretical issues in reading comprehension* (pp. 525–534). Hillsdale, NJ: Erlbaum.

Asher, S. R., Hymel, S., & Renshaw, P. D. (1984). Loneliness in children. *Child Development, 55,* 1456–1464.

Asher, S. R., & Markell, R. A. (1974). Sex differences in comprehension of high and low interest reading material. *Journal of Educational Psychology, 66,* 680–687.

Asher, S. R., Oden, S. L., & Gottman, J. M. (1976). Children's friendships in school settings. *Quarterly Review of Early Childhood Education, 1,* 1–17.

Asher, S. R., Oden, S. L., & Gottman, J. M. (1977). Children's friendships in school settings. In L. G. Katz (Ed.), *Current topics in early childhood education* (Vol. 1). Norwood, NJ: Ablex.

Asher, S. R., Singleton, L. C., & Taylor, A. R. (1982). *Acceptance versus friendship: A longitudinal study of racial integration.* Paper presented at the American Educational Research Association Meeting, New York.

Aslin, R. (1987). Visual and auditory development in infancy. In J. Osofsky (Ed.), *Handbook of infant development* (2nd ed.). New York: Wiley.

Aslin, R. N., Jusczyk, P. W., & Pisoni, D. B. (1983). Auditory development and speech perception in infancy. In P. Mussen (Ed.), *Handbook of child psychology* (Vol. 2). New York: Wiley.

Aslin, R. N., Jurczyk, P. W., & Pisoni, D. B. (1998). Speech and auditory processing during infancy: Constraints on and precursors to language. In W. Damon (Gen. Ed.), D. Kuhn, & R. Siegler (Vol. Eds.), *Handbook of child psychology: Vol. 2. Cognition, perception and language.* New York: Wiley.

Aslin, R. N., Woodward, J. Z., LaMendola, N. P., & Bever, T. G. (1996). Models of work segmentation in fluent maternal speech to infants. In J. L. Morgan & K. Dermuth (Eds.), *Signal to syntax.* Hillsdale, NJ: Erlbaum.

Atkin, C. (1983). Effects of realistic TV violence vs. fictional violence on aggression. *Journalism Quarterly, 60,* 615–621.

Atkin, C. K., Greenberg, B. S., & McDermott, S. (1978). *Television and racial socialization.* Paper presented at meeting of the Association for Education in Journalism, Seattle, WA.

Atkins, W. T. (1988). Cocaine: The drug of choice. In I. J. Chasnoff (Ed.), *Drugs, alcohol, pregnancy and parenting.* Boston: Kluwer Academic.

Atkinson, R. C., & Shiffrin, R. M. (1968). Human memory: A proposed system and its control processes. In K. W. Spence & J. Spence (Eds.), *Advances in the psychology of learning and motivation: research and theory* (Vol. 2). New York: Academic.

Attie, I., & Brooks-Gunn, J. (1989). Development of eating problems in adolescent girls: A longitudinal study. *Developmental Psychology, 25,* 70–79.

Attwood, A., Frith, W., & Hermelin, B. (1988). The understanding and use of interpersonal gestures by autistic and Down's syndrome children. *Journal of Autism and Developmental Disorders, 18,* 241–257.

Au, T. K., Sidle, A. L., & Rollins, K. B. (1993). Developing intuitive understanding of conservation and contamination: Invisible particles of a plausible mechanism. *Developmental Psychology, 29,* 286–289.

Auger, A., Bronfenbrenner, U., & Henderson, C. R. (1977). Socialization practices of parents, teachers and peers in Israel: Kibbutz, Moshav, and city. *Child Development, 48,* 1219–1227.

Aviezer, O., Van Ijzendoorn, M. H., Sagi, A., & Schuengel, C. (1994). "Children of the dream" revisited: 70 years of collective early child care in Israeli Kibbutzim. *Psychological Bulletin, 116,* 99–116.

Aylward, G. P., Pfeiffer, S. I., Wright, A., Verholst, S. J. (1989). Outcome studies of low birth weight infants published in the last decade: A meta-analysis. *Journal of Pediatrics, 115,* 515–520.

Babson, S. G., Pernoll, M. C., Benda, G. I., & Simpson, K. (1980). *Diagnosis and management of the fetus and neonate at risk: A guide for team care* (4th ed.). St. Louis: Mosby.

Backscheider, A. G., Shatz, M., & Gelman, S. A. (1993). Preschooler's ability to distinguish living things as a function of regrowth. *Child Development, 64,* 1242–1257.

Bahrick, L. E., & Pickens, J. N. (1994). Amodal relations: The basis for intermodal perception and learning in infancy. In D. J. Lewkowicz & R. Lickliter (Eds.), *The development of intersensory perception: Comparative perspectives* (pp. 205–233). Hillsdale, NJ: Erlbaum.

Bai, D. L., & Bertenthal, B. I. (1989). *The role of self-produced locomotion in the development of object localization skills.* Unpublished manuscript, University of Virginia.

Bailey, A. J. (1993). The biology of autism. *Psychological Medicine, 23,* 7–11.

Bailey, J., Bobrow, D., Wolfe, M., & Mikach, S. (1995). Sexual orientation of adult sons of gay fathers. Special Issue: Sexual orientation and human development. *Developmental Psychology, 31,* 124–129.

Baillargeon, R. (1986). Representing the existence and the location of hidden objects: Object permanence in 6- and 8-month-old infants. *Cognition, 23,* 21–41.

Baillargeon, R. (1987). Object permanence in 3.5 and 4.5 month-old infants. *Developmental Psychology, 23,* 655–664.

Baillargeon, R. (1993). The object concept revisited: New directions in the investigation of infants' physical knowledge. In C. E. Granrud (Ed.), *Visual perception and cognition in infancy.* Hillsdale, NJ: Erlbaum.

Baillargeon, R. (1994). How do infants learn about the physical world? *Current Directions in Psychological Science, 3,* 133–140.

Baillargeon, R. (1995). A model of physical reasoning in infancy. In C. Rovee-Collier & L. Lipsitt (Eds.), *Advances in infancy research* (Vol. 9). Norwood, NJ: Ablex.

Baillargeon, R., & DeVos, J. (1994). *Qualitative and quantitative inferences about hidden objects.* Unpublished manuscript. University of Illinois, Champaign-Urbana.

Baillargeon, R., & Hanko-Summers, S. (1990). Is the top object adequately supported by the bottom object? Young infants' understanding of support relations. *Cognitive Development, 5,* 29–53.

Bainum, C. K., Lounsbury, K. R., & Pollio, H. R. (1984). The development of laughing and smiling in nursery school children. *Child Development, 55,* 1946–1957.

Bakeman, R., & Brown, J. V. (1980). Early intervention: Consequences for social and mental development at three years. *Child Development, 51,* 437–447.

Bakeman, R., & Gottman, J. (1986). *Observing behavior.* New York: Cambridge University Press.

Bakeman, R., & Gottman, J. (1997). *Observing Behavior* (2nd ed.). New York: Cambridge University Press.

Baker, L. (1982). An evaluation of the role of metacognitive deficits in learning disabilities. *Topics in Learning and Learning Disabilities, 2,* 27–35.

Baldwin, A., Baldwin, C., & Cole, R. E. (1990). Stress-resistant families and stress-resistant children. In J. E. Rolf, A. S. Masten, D. Cicchetti, K. N. Wechterlein, & S. Weintraub (Eds.), *Risk and protective factors in the development of psychopathology* (pp. 257–280). New York: Cambridge University Press.

Ball, S., & Bogatz, J. (1972). Summative research of Sesame Street: Implications for the study of preschool children. In A. D. Pick (Ed.), *Minnesota symposia on child psychology* (Vol. 6). Minneapolis: University of Minnesota Press.

Baltes, P. B. (1987). Theoretical propositions of life span developmental psychology: On the dynamics between growth and decline. *Developmental Psychology, 23,* 611–626.

Baltes, P. B., Lindenberg, U., & Staudinger, U. M. (1998). Life span theory in developmental psychology. In W. Damon (Gen. Ed.) & R. M. Lerner (Vol. Ed.), *Handbook of child psychology: Vol. 1. Theoretical models of human development* (pp. 1029–1144). New York: Wiley.

Bandura, A. (1969). Social learning theory and identifactory processes. In D. A. Goslin (Ed.), *Handbook of socialization theory and research* (pp. 213–262). Chicago: Rand McNally.

Bandura, A. (1989). Social cognitive theory. In R. Vasta (Ed.), *Annals of child development: Six theories of child development* (Vol. 6). Greenwich, CT: JAI Press.

Banks, M. S., Aslin, R. N., & Letson, R. D. (1975). Sensitive period for the development of human binocular vision. *Science, 190,* 675–677.

Banks, M. S., & Salapatek, P. (1983). Infant visual perception. In M. H. & J. Campos (Eds.), *Handbook of child psychology; biology and infancy.* New York: Wiley.

Banks, M. S., & Shannon, E. (1993). Spatial and chromatic visual efficiency in human neonates. In C. Granrud (Ed.), *Visual perception and cognition in infancy* (pp. 1–46). Hillsdale, NJ: Erlbaum.

Barcus, F. E. (1983). *Images of life on children's television.* New York: Praeger.

Barglow, P., Vaughn, B. E., & Molitor, N. (1987). Effects of maternal absence due to employment on the quality of infant-mother attachment in a low-risk sample. *Child Development, 58,* 945–954.

Baringa, M. (1996). Learning defect identified in the brain. *Science, 273,* 867–868.

Barker, R. G., & Gump, P. V. (1964). *Big school, small school.* Stanford, CA: Stanford University Press.

Barkley, R. A. (1990). Attention deficit disorders. In M. Lewis & S. Miller (Eds.), *Handbook of developmental psychopathology.* New York: Plenum.

Barkley, R. A. (1995). *Taking charge of ADHD: The complete, authoritative guide for parents.* New York: Guilford.

Barkley, R. A. (1997). *ADHD and the nature of self-control.* New York: Guilford.

Barkley, R. A., & Ullman, D. G. (1975). A comparison of objective measures of activity and distractibility in hyperactive and nonhyperactive children. *Journal of Abnormal Child Psychology, 3,* 231–244.

Barnard, K., Bee, H., & Hammond, M. A. (1984). Development of changes in maternal interactions with term and preterm infants. *Infant Behavior and Development, 7,* 101–113.

Barnard, K. E., & Bee, H. L. (1983). The impact of temporally patterned stimulation on the development of preterm infants. *Child Development, 54,* 1156–1167.

Barnard, K. E., Bee, H. L., & Hammond, M. A. (1984). Home environment and cognitive development in a healthy, low-risk sample:

The Seattle study. In A. W. Gottfried (Ed.), *Home environment and early cognitive development* (pp. 117–149). Orlando, FL: Academic.

Barnas, M. V., & Cummings, E. M. (1994). Caregiver stability and toddlers attachment-related behavior towards caregivers in day care. *Infant Behavior and Development, 17,* 141–147.

Barnes, D. M. (1989). "Fragile X" syndrome and its puzzling genetics. *Science, 243,* 171–172.

Barnett, C. R., Leiderman, P. H., Grobstein, K., & Klaus, M. (1970). Neonatal separation: The maternal side of interactional deprivation. *Pediatrics, 45,* 197–205.

Baron-Cohen, S. (1988). Social and pragmatic deficits in autism: Cognitive or affective? *Journal of Autism and Developmental Disorders, 18,* 379–397.

Baron-Cohen, S. (1995). *Mindblindness: An essay on autism and theory of mind.* Cambridge, MA: MIT Press.

Barr, H. M., Streissguth, A. P., Darby, B. L., & Sampson, P. D. (1990). Prenatal exposure to alcohol, caffeine, tobacco and aspirin: Effects on fine and gross motor performance in 4-year-old children. *Developmental Psychology, 26,* 339–348.

Barrett, D. E. (1979). A naturalistic study of sex differences in children's aggression. *Merrill-Palmer Quarterly, 25,* 193–203.

Barrett, D. E., Radke-Yarrow, M., & Klein, R. E. (1982). Chronic malnutrition and child behavior: Effects of early caloric supplementation on social and emotional functioning at school age. *Developmental Psychology, 18,* 541–556.

Barrett, K. C. (1997). The self and relationship development. In S. Duck (Ed.), *Handbook of personal relationships* (2nd ed., pp. 61–97). New York: Wiley.

Baruffi, G. (1982). *Review of the safety of maternity care in different birth locations.* In Committee on Assessing Alternative Birth Settings, Research Issues in the Assessment of Birth Settings. National Research Council, Commission on Life Sciences. Washington, DC: National Academy Press.

Basow, S. A. (1992). *Gender stereotypes and roles.* Pacific Grove, CA: Brooks/Cole.

Bates, D., Thal, D., Whitsell, K., Fenson, L., & Oakes, L. (1989). Integrating language and gesture in infancy. *Developmental Psychology, 25,* 1004–1019.

Bates, E. (1976). *Language and context: The acquisition of pragmatics.* New York: Academic.

Bates, E. (1994). Language development in children after early focal injury. *Infant Behavior and Development, 17,* 426.

Bates, J. E. (1987). Temperament in infancy. In J. D. Osofsky (Ed.), *Handbook of infant development* (2nd ed.). New York: Wiley.

Bauer, P. J. (1996). What do infants recall of their lives? *American Psychologist, 51,* 29–41.

Bauer, P. J., & Dow, G. A. (1994). Episodic memory in 16- and 20-month-old children: Specifics are generalized but not forgotten. *Developmental Psychology, 30,* 403–417.

Bauer, P. J., & Mandler, J. M. (1992). Putting the horse before the cart: The use of temporal order in recall of events by one-year-old children. *Developmental Psychology, 28,* 441–452.

Bauer, P. J., & Thal, D. J. (1990). Scripts or scraps: Reconsidering the development of sequential understanding. *Journal of Experimental Child Psychology, 50,* 287–304.

Bauer, W. D., & Twentyman, C. T. (1985). Abusing, neglecting, and comparison mothers' responses to child-related and non-child-related stressors. *Journal of Consulting and Clinical Psychology, 53,* 335–343.

Baumeister, A. A. (1967). The effects of dietary control on intelligence in phenylketonuria. *American Journal of Mental Deficiency, 71,* 840–847.

Baumrind, D. (1967). Child care practices anteceding three patterns of preschool behavior. *Genetic Psychology Monographs, 75,* 43–88.

Baumrind, D. (1971). Current patterns of parental authority. *Developmental Psychology Monographs, 1,* 1–103.

Baumrind, D. (1991a). Effective parenting during the early adolescent transition. In P. A. Cowan & E. M. Hetherington (Eds.), *Family transitions* (pp. 111–164). Hillsdale, NJ: Erlbaum.

Baumrind, D. (1991b). To nurture nature. *Behavioral and Brain Sciences, 14,* 386–387.

Baumrind, D. (1993). The average expectable environment is not good enough: A response to Scarr. *Child Development, 64,* 1299–1317.

Bayley, N. (1969). *Bayley scales of infant development.* New York: Psychological Corporation.

Bayley, N. (1970). Development of mental abilities. In P. H. Mussen (Ed.), *Carmichael's manual of child psychology* (Vol. 1, pp. 1163–1210). New York: Wiley.

Bayley, N. (1993). *Bayley scales of infant development* (revised ed.). New York: Psychological Corporation.

Beal, C. R. (1994). *Boys and girls: The development of gender roles.* New York: McGraw-Hill.

Beardslee, W. R., Bemporad, J., Keller, M. B., & Klerman, G. L. (1983). Children of parents with major affective disorder: A review. *American Journal of Psychiatry, 140,* 825–832.

Beckwith, L. (1979). Prediction of emotional and social behavior. In J. D. Osofsky (Ed.), *Handbook of infant development.* New York: Wiley.

Bédard, J., & Chi, M. T. H. (1992). Expertise. *Current Directions in Psychological Science, 1,* 135–139.

Begley, S. (1997). How to build a baby's brain. *Newsweek Special Issue.* Spring/Summer, 28–32.

Behl-Chadha, G. (in press). Superordinate-like categorical representation in early infancy. *Cognition.*

Behrend, D. A. (1990). Constraints and development: A reply to Nelson (1988). *Cognitive Development, 5,* 313–330.

Beilin, H. (1992). Piaget's enduring contribution to developmental psychology. *Developmental Psychology, 28,* 191–204.

Beitel, A., & Parke, R. D. (in press). Paternal involvement in infancy: The role of maternal & paternal attitudes, *Journal of Family Psychology.*

Bell, R. Q. (1968). A reinterpretation of the direction of effects in studies of socialization. *Psychological Reveiw, 75,* 81–95.

Bell, R. Q., Weller, G. M., & Waldrop, M. F. (1971). Newborn and preschooler: Organization of behavior and relations between periods. *Monographs of the Society for Research in Child Development, 36-4,* Serial No. 142), 1–145.

Bell, S., & Ainsworth, M. D. (1972). Infant crying and maternal responsiveness. *Child Development, 43,* 1171–1190.

Bellinger, D. C., Sloman, J., Leviton, A., Rabinowitz, M., Needleman, H. L., & Waternaux, C. (1991). Low-level lead exposure and children's cognitive function in the preschool years. *Pediatrics, 87,* 215–227.

Bellugi, U., Van Hoek, K., Lillo-Martin D., & O'Grady, L. (1993). The acquisition of syntax and space in young deaf signers. In D. Bishop & K. Mogford (Eds.), *Language development in exceptional children* (pp. 132–149). Hove, England: Erlbaum.

Belmont, J. M. (1989). Cognitive strategies and strategic learning: The socio-instructional approach. *American Psychologist, 44,* 142–148.

Belsky, J. (1993). Etiology of child maltreatment: A developmental-ecological analysis. *Psychological Bulletin, 114,* 413–434.

Belsky, J., & Cassidy, J. (1994). Attachment: Theory and evidence. In M. Rutter, D. Hay, & S. Baron-Cohen (Eds.), *Developmental principles and clinical issues in psychology and psychiatry.* Oxford: Blackwell.

Belsky, J., & Isabella, R. (1988). Maternal, infant, and social-contextual determinants of attachment security. In J. Belsky & T. Nezworski (Eds.), *Clinical implications of attachment: Child psychology* (pp. 41–94). Hillsdale, NJ: Erlbaum.

Belsky, J., Long, M. E., & Rovine, M. (1985). Stability and change in marriage across the transition to parenthood: A second study. *Journal of Marriage and the Family, 47,* 855–865.

Belsky, J., & Rovine, M. (1988). Nonmaternal care in the first year of life and infant-parent attachment security. *Child Development, 57,* 1224–1231.

Belsky, J., Steinberg, L., & Draper, P. (1991). Childhood experience, interpersonal development, and reproductive strategy: An evolutionary theory of socialization. *Child Development, 62,* 647–670.

Belsky, J., Steinberg, L. D., & Walker, A. (1983). The ecology of day care. In M. E. Lamb (Ed.), *Nontraditional families.* Hillsdale, NJ: Erlbaum.

Bem, S. L. (1974). The measurement of psychological androgyny. *Journal of Clinical and Consulting Psychology, 42,* 155–162.

Bem, S. L. (1981). Gender schema theory: A cognitive account of sex typing. *Psychological Review, 88,* 354–364.

Bem, S. L. (1983). Gender schema theory and its implications for child development: Raising gender-aschematic children in a gender-schematic society. *Signs: Journal of Women in Culture and Society, 8,* 598–616.

Bem, S. L. (1989). Genital knowledge and gender constancy in preschool children. *Child Development, 60,* 649–662.

Bem, S. L. (1993). *The lenses of gender: Transforming the debate on sexual inequality.* New Haven, CT: Yale University Press.

Ben Tsvi-Mayer, S., Hertz-Lazarowitz, R., & Safir, M. P. (1989). Teacher's selections of boys and girls as prominent pupils. *Sex Roles, 21,* 231–245.

Benbow, C. P. (1988). Sex differences in mathematical reasoning ability in intellectually talented preadolescents: Their nature, effects and possible causes. *Behavioral and Brain Sciences, 11,* 169–232.

Benbow, C. P., & Lubinski, D. J. (Eds.) (1996). Intellectual talent: Psychometric and social issues. Baltimore, MD: Johns Hopkins University Press.

Bender, B. C., Linden, M. G., & Robinson, A. (1987). Environment and developmental risk in children with sex chromosome abnormalities. *Journal of the Academy of Child and Adolescent Psychiatry, 26,* 499–503.

Benenson, J. F., Apostoleris, N. H., & Parnass, J. (1997). Age and sex differences in dyadic and group interaction. *Developmental Psychology, 33,* 538–543.

Benloucif, S., Bennett, E. L., & Rosenzweig, M. R. (1995). Norepinephrine and neural plasticity: The effects of Xylamine on experience-induced changes in brain weight, memory and behavior. *Neurobiology of Learning and Memory, 63,* 33–42.

Bennett, W. J. (1994). *The index of leading cultural indications: Facts & figures on the state of American society.* New York: Simon & Schuster.

Benokraitis, N. V. (1996). *Marriages and families: Changes, choices, and constraints* (2nd ed.). Upper Saddle River, NJ: Prentice Hall.

Benokraitis, N. V. (1998). Personal communication.

Bentley, D. B. (1996). Genomic sequence information should be released immediately and freely in the public domain. *Science, 274,* 533–534.

Bentur, Y., & Koren, G. (1991). The three most common occupational exposures reported by pregnant women: An update. *American Journal of Obstetrics and Gynecology, 165,* 429–437.

Bentzen, B. L., & Mitchell, P. A. (1995). Audible signage as a way-finding aid: Verbal landmark versus talking signs. *Journal of Visual Impairment & Blindness, 88,* 494–505.

Berenbaum, S. A., & Snyder, E. (1995). Early hormonal influences on childhood sex-typed activity and playmate preferences: Implications for the development of sexual orientation. *Developmental Psychology, 31,* 31–42.

Berg, M., & Medrich, E. A. (1980). Children in four neighborhoods: The physical environment and its effects on play and play patterns. *Environment and Behavior, 12,* 320–348.

Berg, W. K., & Berg, K. M. (1987). Psychophysiologic development in infancy: State, startle and attention. In J. Osofsky (Ed.), *Handbook of infancy* (2nd ed.). New York: Wiley.

Bergen, D. J., & Williams, J. E. (1991). Sex stereotypes in the United States revisited: 1972–1988. *Sex Roles, 24,* 413–423.

Berk, L. E. (1992). Children's private speech: An overview of theory and the status of research. In R. M. Diaz & L. E. Berk (Eds.), *Private speech: From social interaction to self-regulation* (pp. 17–53). Hillsdale, NJ: Erlbaum.

Berkowitz, L. (1993). *Aggression: Its causes, consequences, and control.* New York: McGraw-Hill.

Berman, P. W. (1987). Children caring for babies: Age and sex differences in response to infant signals and to the social context. In N. Eisenberg (Ed.), *Contemporary topics in developmental psychology.* New York: Wiley.

Berndt, T. J. (1986). Sharing between friends: Contexts and consequences. In E. C. Mueller & C. R. Cooper (Eds.), *Process and outcome in peer relationships.* New York: Academic.

Berndt, T. J., & Ladd, G. W. (1989). (Eds.) *Peer relationships in child development.* New York: Wiley.

Berndt, T. J., & Perry, T. B. (1990). Distinctive features and effects of adolescent friendships. In R. Montemeyer, G. R. Adams, & T. P. Gullotta (Eds.), *From childhood to adolescence: A transition period?* London: Sage.

Bersoff, D. M., & Miller, J. (1993). Culture, context, and the development of moral accountability judgments. *Developmental Psychology, 29,* 664–676.

Bertenthal, B., & Bai, D. L. (1989). Infants' sensitivity to optical flow for controlling posture. *Developmental Psychology, 25,* 936–945

Bertenthal, B. I. (1996). Origins and early development of perception, action and representation. *Annual Review of Psychology, 47,* 431–459.

Bertenthal, B. I., Campos, J. J., & Kermoian, R. (1994). An epigenetic perspective on the development of self-produced locomotion and its consequences. *Current Directions in Psychological Science, 3,* 140–145.

Bertenthal, B. I., & Clifton, R. K. (1998). Perception and action. In W. Damon (Gen. Ed.), D. Kuhn, & R. Siegler (Vol. Eds.), *Handbook of child psychology: Vol. 2. Cognition, perception and language* (pp. 51–102). New York: Wiley.

Bertenthal, B. I., Proffitt, D. R., & Cutting, J. E. (1984). Infant sensitivity to figural coherence in biomechanical motions. *Journal of Experimental Child Psychology, 37,* 213–230.

Bertenthal, B. I., Proffitt, D. R., & Kramer, S. J. (1987). The perception of biomechanical motions. Implementation of various processing constraints. *Journal of Experimental Psychology. Human Perception and Performance, 13,* 577–585.

Berthoud-Papandropoulou, I. (1978). An experimental study of children's ideas about language. In A. Sinclair, R. J. Jarvella, & W. J. M. Levelt (Eds.), *The child's conception of language* (Vol. 2). Heidelberg: Springer.

Best, C. T. (1988). The emergence of cerebral asymmetries in early human development: A literature review and a neuroembryological model. In D. L. Molfese & S. J. Segalowitz (Eds.), *Brain lateralization in children* (pp. 5–35). New York: Guilford Press.

Best, D. L. (1993). Inducing children to generate mnemonic organizational strategies: An examination of long-term retention and materials. *Developmental Psychology, 29,* 324–336.

Best, D. L., & Ornstein, P. A. (1986). Children's generation and communication of mnemonic organizational strategies. *Developmental Psychology, 22,* 845–853.

Best, D. L., & Williams, J. E. (1993). A cross-cultural viewpoint. In A. E. Beall & R. J. Sternberg (Eds.), *The psychology of gender.* (pp. 215–248). New York: Guilford Press.

Bhavnagri, N., & Parke, R. D. (1991). Parents as direct facilitators of children's peer relationships: Effects of age of child and sex of parent. *Journal of Social and Personal Relationships, 8,* 423–440.

Bialystok, E. (1991). *Language processing in bilingual children.* Cambridge, MA: Cambridge University Press.

Bianchi, B. D., & Bakeman, R. (1983). Patterns of sex typing in an open school. In M. B. Liss (Ed.), *Social and cognitive skills: Sex roles and children's play.* New York: Academic.

Bickerton, D. (1983). Creole languages. *Scientific American, 249,* 116–122.

Bickerton, D. (1988). Creole languages and the bioprogram. In F. J. Newmeyer (Ed.), *Linguistics: The Cambridge survey: Vol. II* (pp. 268–284). Cambridge: Cambridge University Press.

Bickerton, D. (1990). *Language and species.* Chicago, IL: University of Chicago Press.

Bierman, K. L., Smoot, D. L., & Aumiller, K. (1993). Characteristics of aggressive-rejected, aggressive (nonrejected), and rejected (nonaggressive) boys. *Child Development, 64,* 139–151.

Biernat, M., & Wortman, C. (1991). Sharing of home responsibilities between professionally employed women and their husbands. *Journal of Personality and Social Psychology, 60,* 844–860.

Bigelow, B. J. (1977). Children's friendship expectations: A cognitive-developmental study. *Child Development, 48,* 246–253.

Bigelow, B. J., & LaGaipa, J. J. (1975). Children's written descriptions of friendship: A multidimensional analysis. *Developmental Psychology, 11,* 857–858.

Bigler, R. S., & Liben, L. S. (1990). The role of attitudes and interventions in gender-schematic processing. *Child Development, 61,* 1440–1452.

Bigner, J. J., & Bozett, F. W. (1990). Parenting by gay fathers. In F. W. Bozett & M. B. Sussman (Eds.), *Homosexuality and family relations* (pp. 155–176). New York: Harrington Park Press.

Binet, A. (1909/1973). *Les idées modernes sur les enfants.* Paris: Flammarion.

Birch, E. E. (1993). Stereopsis in infants and its developmental relation to visual acuity. In K. Simons (Ed.), *Early visual development: Normal and abnormal* (pp. 224–236). New York: Oxford University Press.

Birch, L. L., McPhee, L., Shoba, B. C., Steinberg, L., & Krehbeil, R. (1987). "Clean up your plate." Effects of child feeding practices on the conditioning of meal size. *Learning & Motivation, 18,* 301–317.

Biringen, Z., Emde, R. N., Campos, J. J., & Appelbaum, M. I. (1995). Affective reorganization in the infant, the mother, and the dad: The role of upright locomotion and its timing. *Child Development, 66,* 499–514.

Biringen, Z., Robinson, J. L., & Emde, R. N. (1994). Maternal sensitivity in the second year: Gender-based relations in the dyadic balance of control. *American Journal of Orthopsychiatry, 64,* 78–90.

Bivens, J. A., & Berk, L. E. (1990). A longitudinal study of the development of elementary school children's private speech. *Merrill-Palmer Quarterly, 36,* 443–463.

Bjorklund, D. F., Miller, P. H., Coyle, T. R., & Slawinski, J. L. (1997). Instructing children to use memory strategies: Evidence of utilization deficiencies in memory training studies. In D. F. Bjorklund & P. H. Miller (Eds.), *New themes in strategy development.*

Black, B., & Hazen, N. (1990). Social status and patterns of communication in acquainted and unacquainted preschool children. *Developmental Psychology, 26,* 379–387.

Black, M., Schuler, M., & Nair, P. (1993). Prenatal drug exposure: Neurodevelopmental outcome and parenting environment. *Journal of Pediatric Psychology, 18,* 605–620.

Blair, C., Ramey, C. T., & Hardin, M. (1995). Early intervention for low birthweight premature infants: Participation and intellectual development. *American Journal of Mental Retardation, 99,* 542–554.

Blake, I. K. (1994). Language development and socialization in young African-American children. In P. M. Greenfield & R. R. Cocking (Eds.), *Cross-cultural roots of minority child development.* Hillsdale, NJ: Erlbaum.

Blasch, B. B., Long, R. G. & Griffin-Shirley, N. (1989). Results of a national survey of electronic travel aid use. *Journal of Visual Impairment & Blindness, 82,* 449–453.

Blasi, A. (1983). Moral cognition and moral action: A theoretical perspective. *Developmental Review, 3,* 178–210.

Blass, E., Ganchrow, J. R., & Steiner, J. E. (1984). Classical conditioning in newborn humans 2–48 hours of age. *Infant Behavior and Development, 7,* 223–234.

Block, J. H. (1983). Differential premises arising from differential socialization of the sexes: Some conjectures. *Child Development, 54,* 1335–1354.

Block, J. H., Block, J., & Gjerde, P. F. (1986). The personality of children prior to divorce: A prospective study. *Child Development, 57,* 827–840.

Block, J., Bock, J. H., & Keyes, S. (1988). Longitudinally foretelling drug usage in adolescents: Early childhood personality and environmental precursors. *Child Development, 59,* 336–355.

Bloom, K. (1984). Distinguishing between social reinforcement and social education. *Journal of Experimental Child Psychology, 38,* 93–102.

Bloom, L. (1970). *Language development: Form and function in emerging grammars.* Cambridge, MA: MIT Press.

Bloom, L. (1976). *An interactive perspective on language development.* Keynote address, Child Language Research Forum, Stanford University.

Bloom, L. (1991). *Language development from two to three.* New York: Cambridge University Press.

Bloom, L. (1993). *The transition from infancy to language.* New York: Cambridge University Press.

Bloom, L. (1998). Language acquisition in its developmental context. In W. Damon (Gen. Ed.), R. Siegler, & D. Kuhn (Vol. Eds.), *Handbook of child psychology: Vol. 2. Cognition, perception, and language* (5th ed., pp. 309–370). New York: Wiley.

Bloom, L., Lifter, K., & Broughton, J. (1985). The convergence of early cognition and language in the second year of life: Problems in conceptualization and measurement. In M. Barrett (Ed.), *Single word speech.* London: Wiley.

Boccia, M., & Campos, J. (1989). Maternal emotional signals, social referencing, and infants' reactions to strangers. In N. Eisenberg (Ed.), *Empathy and related emotional responses: New directions for child development* (pp. 25–49). San Francisco: Jossey-Bass.

Boggiano, A. K., & Ruble, D. N. (1979). Perception of competence and the overjustification effect: A developmental study. *Journal of Personality and Social Psychology, 37,* 1462–1468.

Bohannon, J. N., III, & Stanowicz, L. (1988). The issue of negative evidence: Adult responses to children's language errors. *Developmental Psychology, 24,* 684–689.

Bohannon, J. N., III, & Warren-Leubecker, A. (1988). Recent developments in child-directed speech: We've come a long way, baby talk. *Language Sciences, 10,* 89–110.

Bohlin, G., & Hagekull, B. (1993). Stranger wariness and sociability in the early years. *Infant Behavior and Development, 16,* 53–67.

Boismier, J. D. (1977). Visual stimulation and wake-sleep behavior in human neonates. *Developmental Psychobiology, 10,* 219–227.

Boldizar, J. P. (1991). Assessing sex typing and androgyny in children: The children's sex role inventory. *Developmental Psychology, 27,* 505–515.

Bonvillian, J. D., Orlansky, M. D., & Folven, R. J. (1990). Early acquisition: Implications for theories of language acquisition. In V. Volterra & C. J. Erting (Eds.), *From gesture to language in hearing and deaf children.* Heidelberg: Springer-Verlag.

Bonvillian, J. D., Orlansky, M. D., Novack, L. I., & Folven, R. J. (1983). Early sign language acquisition and cognitive development. In D. R. Rogers & J. A. Sloboda (Eds.), *The acquisition of symbolic skills.* New York: Plenum.

Boothby, N. (1991). *Children of war: Survival as a collective act.* Paper presented at the meeting on vulnerability and resiliency in children and families: Focus on children with disabilities. Baltimore, MD.

Borduin, C. M., & Henggeler, S. W. (1990). A multisystemic approach to the treatment of serious delinquent behavior. In R. J. McMahon & R. D. Peters (Eds.), *Behavior disorders of adolescence: Research, intervention, and policy in clinical and school settings* (pp. 63–80). New York: Plenum Press.

Borke, H. (1971). Interpersonal perception of young children: Egocentrism or empathy. *Developmental Psychology, 5,* 263–269.

Borke, H. (1975). Piaget's mountains revisited: Changes in the egocentric landscape. *Developmental Psychology, 11,* 240–243.

Bornstein, M. H., & Sigman, M. D. (1986). Continuity in mental development from infancy. *Child Development, 57,* 251–274.

Bornstein, M. H., & Tamis, C. (1986). *Origins of cognitive skills in infants.* Paper presented at the International Conference on Infant Studies, Los Angeles.

Bouchard, T. T., Lykken, D. T., Segal, N. L., & Wilcox, K. J. (1986). Development in twins reared apart: A test of the chronogenetic hypothesis. In A. Demirijian (Ed.), *Human growth: A multidisciplinary review* (pp. 299–310). London: Taylor & Francis.

Bower, T. G. R. (1979). Visual development in the blind child. In V. Smith & J. Keen (Eds.), *Visual handicap in children.* Clinics in Development Medicine, No. 73. London: Lippincott.

Bower, T. G. R. (1982). *Development in infancy.* New York: W. H. Freeman.

Bower, T. G. R. (1989). *The rational infant: Learning in infancy.* San Francisco: Freedman.

Bowlby, J. (1958). The nature of the child's tie to his mother. *International Journal of Psychoanalysis, 39,* 350–373.

Bowlby, J. (1960). Grief and mourning in infancy and early childhood. *The Psychoanalytic Study of the Child, 15.*

Bowlby, J. (1969). *Attachment and loss: Vol. 1. Attachment.* New York: Basic Books.

Bowlby, J. (1973). *Separation and loss.* New York: Basic Books.

Boyum, L. A., Dweck, C. S., & Hill, K. T. (1990, March). *Students' conceptions of their intelligence: Impact on academic course choice.* Poster presented at the biennial meeting of the Society for Research on Adolescence, Atlanta.

Boyum, L., & Parke, R. D. (1995). Family emotional expressiveness and children's social competence. *Journal of Marriage and Family, 57,* 593–608.

Brackbill, Y., McManus, K., & Woodward, L. (1985). *Medication in maternity: Infant exposure and maternal information.* Ann Arbor, MI: University of Michigan Press.

Bradley, R. H., Caldwell, B. M., & Rock, S. L. (1988). Home environment and school performance: A ten-year follow-up and examination of three models of environmental action. *Child Development, 59,* 852–867.

Bradley, R. H., Caldwell, B. M., Rock, S. L., Barnard, K. E., Gray, C., Hammon, M. A., Mitchell, S., Siegel, L., Ramey, C. T., Gottfried, A. W., & Johnson, D. L. (1989). Home environment and cognitive development in the first 3 years of life: A collaborative study involving six sites and three ethnic groups in North America. *Developmental Psychology, 25,* 217–235.

Bradley, R. H., Whiteside, L., Mundfrom, D. J., Casey, P. H., Kelleher, K. J., & Pope, S. K. (1994). Early indications of resilience and their relation to experiences in the home environments of low birthweight, premature infants living in poverty. *Child Development, 65,* 346–360.

Brainerd, C. J., & Reyna, V. F. (1990). Inclusion illusions: Fuzzy trace theory and perceptual salience effects in cognitive development. *Developmental Review, 10,* 365–403.

Bray, J. H. (1988). Children's development during early remarriage. In E. M. Hetherington & J. D. Arasten (Eds.), *Impact of divorce, single parenting and step parenting on children* (pp. 279–298). Hillsdale, NJ: Erlbaum.

Brazelton, T. B. (1972). Implications of infant development among the Mayan Indians of Mexico. *Human Development, 15,* 90–111.

Brazelton, T. B. (1984). *Neonatal behavioral assessment scale.* Philadelphia: Lippincott.

Brazelton, T. B., & Nugent, J. K. (1995). *Neonatal behavioral assessment scale* (3rd ed.) London, England: MacKeith Press.

Brazelton, T. B., Nugent, J. K., & Lester, B. M. (1987). Neonatal behavioral assessment scale. In J. Osofsky (Ed.), *Handbook of infancy* (2nd ed.). New York: Wiley.

Brederode-Santos, M. E. (1993). *Learning with television: The secret of Rua Sésamo.* [English translation of Portuguese, Brederode-Santos, M. E. (1991). *Com a Televisão o Segredo da Rua Sésamo.* Lisbon: TV Guia Editora.] Unpublished translation, Children's Television Workshop, New York, NY.

Brendt, T. J., & Bulleit, T. N. (1985). Effects of sibling relationships on preschoolers' behavior at home and at school. *Developmental Psychology, 21,* 761–767.

Brener, R. (1940). An experimental investigation of memory span. *Journal of Experimental Psychology, 33,* 1–19.

Brenton, M. (1974). Mainstreaming the handicapped. *Today's Education, 63,* 20–25.

Bretherton, I., Ridgeway, D., & Cassidy, J. (1990). Assessing internal working models of the attachment relationship: An attachment story completion task for 3-year-olds. In M. T. Greenber, D. Cicchetti, & E. M. Cummings (Eds.), *Attachment in the preschool years: Theory, research, and intervention* (pp. 273–308). Chicago, IL: University of Chicago Press.

Bretherton, I., Stolberg, U., & Kreye, M. (1981). Engaging strangers in proximal interaction: Infants' social initiative. *Developmental Psychology, 17,* 746–755.

Briars, D., & Siegler, R. S. (1984). A featural analysis of preschoolers' counting knowledge. *Developmental Psychology, 20,* 607–618.

Bridges, L. J., & Grolnick, W. S. (1995). The development of emotional self-regulation in infancy and early childhood. In N. Eisenberg (Ed.), *Social development. Review of personality and social psychology* (pp. 185–211). Thousand Oaks, CA: Sage.

Bristol, M., Gallagher, J., & Shopler, E. (1988). Mothers and fathers of young developmentally disabled and nondisabled boys: Adaptation and spousal support. *Developmental Psychology, 24,* 441–451.

Britt, G. C., & Myers, B. J. (1994). The effects of Brazelton intervention: A review. *Infant Mental Health Journal, 15,* 278–292.

Brody, G. H., Stoneman, Z., & Flor, D. (1996). Parental religiosity, family processes, and youth competence in rural, two-parent African American families. *Developmental Psychology, 32,* 696–706.

Brody, L. E., & Benbow, C. P. (1987). Accelerative strategies: How effective are they for the gifted? *Gifted Child Quarterly, 3,* 105–110.

Brody, L. R. (1996). Gender, emotional expression, and parent-child boundaries. In R. D. Kavanaugh, B. Zimmerberg, & S. Fein (Eds.), *Emotion: Interdisciplinary perspectives.* Hillsdale, NJ: Erlbaum.

Brody, N. (1992). *Intelligence* (2nd ed.). San Diego, CA: Academic Press.

Bronfenbrenner, U. (1979). *The ecology of human development.* Cambridge, MA: Harvard University Press.

Bronfenbrenner, U. (1986). Ecology of the family as a context for human development: Research perspectives. *Developmental Psychology, 22,* 723–742.

Bronfenbrenner, U. (1989). Ecological systems theory. In R. Vasta (Ed.), *Six theories of child development.* Greenwich, CT: JAI Press.

Bronfenbrenner, U., & Ceci, S. J. (1985). "Don't forget to take the cupcakes out of the oven." Prospective memory, strategic time-monitoring, and context. *Child Development, 56,* 152–164.

Bronfenbrenner, U., McClelland, P., Wethington, E., Moen, P., & Ceci, S. J. (1996). *The state of Americans: This generation and the next.* New York: Free Press.

Bronfenbrenner, U., & Morris, P. A. (1998). The ecology of developmental processes. In W. Damon (Gen. Ed.), & R. M. Lerner (Vol. Ed.), *Handbook of child psychology: Vol. 1. Theoretical models of human development* (pp. 993–1028). New York: Wiley.

Bronson, G. W. (1968). The development of fear in man and other animals. *Child Development, 39,* 409–431.

Bronson, W. (1981). Toddlers' behaviors with age mates; Issues of interaction, cognition and affect. *Monographs on Infancy, 1,* 127.

Brooks, J., & Lewis, M. (1976). Infants' responses to strangers: Midget, adult, and child. *Child Development, 47,* 323–332.

Brooks-Gunn, J. (1988). Antecedents and consequences of variations in girls' maturational timing. *Journal of Adolescent Health Care, 9,* 1–9.

Brooks-Gunn, J. (1990). Barriers and impediments to conducting research with young adolescents. *Journal of Youth and Adolescence, 19,* 425–440.

Brooks-Gunn, J. (1995). Children in families in communities: Risk and intervention in the Bronfenbrenner tradition. In P. Moen, G. H. Elder, & K. Lüscher (Eds.), *Examining lives in context* (pp. 467–519). Washington, D.C.: American Psychological Association.

Brooks-Gunn, J., Boyer, B., & Hein, K. (1988). Preventing HIV infection and AIDS in children and adolescents. *American Psychologist, 43,* 958–964.

Brooks-Gunn, J., & Chase-Landsdale, P. L. (1995). Adolescent parenthood. In M. H. Bornstein (Ed.), *Handbook of parenting: Vol 3. Status and social conditions of parenting* (pp. 113–149). Mahwah, NJ: Erlbaum.

Brooks-Gunn, J., & Lewis, M. (1984). The development of early visual self-recognition. *Developmental Review, 4,* 215–239.

Brooks-Gunn, J., & Petersen, A. C. (1991). Studying the emergence of depression and depressive symptons during adolescence. *Journal of Youth and Adolescence, 20,* 115–119.

Brooks-Gunn, J., & Reiter, E. O. (1990). The role of pubertal processes in the early adolescent transition. In S. Feldman & G. Elliott (Eds.), *At the threshold: The developing adolescent.* Cambridge, MA: Harvard University Press.

Brooks-Gunn, J., & Ruble, D. N. (1984). The experience of menarche from a developmental perspective. In J. Brooks-Gunn & A. C.

Petersen (Eds.), *Girls at puberty: Biological, psychological and social perspectives.* New York: Plenum.

Brooks-Gunn, J., & Warren, W. P. (1985). The effects of delayed menarche in different contexts: Dance and nondance students. *Journal of Youth and Adolescence, 14,* 285–300.

Brophy, J. (1986). Teacher influences on student achievement. *American Psychologist, 41,* 1069–1077.

Broverman, I. K., Vogel, S. R., Broverman, D. M., Clarkson, F. E., & Rosenkrantz, P. S. (1972). Sex-role stereotypes: A current appraisal. *Journal of Social Issues, 28,* 59–78.

Brown v. Board of Education of Topeka, 347 U.S. 483 (1954).

Brown, A., & Campione, J. (1994). Guided discovery in a community of learners. In K. McGilly (Ed.), *Classroom lessons integrating cognitive theory and classroom practice* (pp. 229–272). Cambridge, MA: MIT Press.

Brown, A. L. (1994). The advancement of learning. *Educational Researcher, 23,* 4–12.

Brown, A. L., Bransford, T. D., Ferrara, R. A., & Campione, J. C. (1983). Learning, remembering and understanding. In J. H. Flavell & E. M. Markman (Eds.), *Handbook of child psychology: Vol. 3. Cognitive development.* New York: Wiley.

Brown, A. L., & Campione, J. (1990). Communities of learning and thinking, or a context by any other name. In D. Kuhn (Ed.), *Developmental perspectives on teaching and learning thinking skills: Contributions in human development* (Vol. 21, pp. 108–126). Basel: Karger.

Brown, A. L., & Campione, J. C. (1996). Psychological theory and the design of innovative learning environments: On procedures, principles, and systems. In R. Glasser & L. Schauble (Eds.), *Innovations in learning: New environments for education* (pp. 289–325). Mahwah, NJ: Erlbaum.

Brown, A. L., Kane, M. J., & Echols, C. H. (1986). Young children's mental models determine analogical transfer across problems with a common goal structure. *Cognitive Development, 1,* 103–121.

Brown, B. B. (1990). Peer groups and peer cultures. In S. S. Feldman & G. R. Elliott (Eds.), *At the threshold* (pp. 171–196). Cambridge, MA: Harvard University Press.

Brown, B. B., & Huang, B. (1995). Examining parenting practices in different peer contexts: Implications for adolescent trajectories. In L. J. Crockett & A. C. Crouter (Eds.), *Pathways through adolescence: Individual development in relation to social contexts.* Mahwah, NJ: Erlbaum.

Brown, E., & Brownell, C. (1990). *Individual differences in toddlers' interaction styles.* Paper presented at International Conference on Infant Studies, Montreal.

Brown, P., & Elliot, R. (1965). Control of aggression in a nursery school class. *Journal of Experimental Child Psychology, 2,* 103–107.

Brown, R. (1973). *A first language: The early stages.* Cambridge, MA: Harvard University Press.

Brown, R., & Bellugi, U. (1964). Three processes in the child's acquisition of syntax. In E. G. Lenneberg (Ed.), *New directions in the study of language.* Cambridge, MA: MIT Press.

Brown, R., & Hanlon, C. (1970). Derivational complexity and order of acquisition in child speech. In J. Hayes (Ed.), *Cognition and the development of language* (pp. 11–54). New York: Wiley.

Brown, S. R., & Pipp, S. (1991). *The role of the appearance-reality distinction and the genital basis of gender in the development of gender constancy.* Paper presented at the biennial meeting of the Society for Research in Child Development. Seattle, WA.

Brownell, C. A. (1990). Peer social skills in toddlers: Competencies and constraints illustrated by same age and mixed-age interaction. *Child Development, 61,* 838–848.

Bruner, J. (1983). *Children's talk.* New York: Norton.

Bruner, J. (1987). The transactional self. In J. Bruner & H. Haste (Eds.), *Making sense: The child's construction of the world.* London: Methuen.

Bruner, J. S. (1966). On cognitive growth. In J. S. Bruner, R. R. Olver, & P. M. Greenfield (Eds.), *Studies in cognitive growth.* New York: Wiley.

Bryant, P. E., & Trabasso, J. (1971). Transitive inferences and memory in young children. *Nature, 232,* 456–458.

Bryden, M. P. (1982). *Laterality.* New York: Academic.

Bryden, M. P. (1988). Does laterality make any difference? Thoughts on the relation between asymmetry and reading. In D. L. Molfese & S. J. Segalowitz (Eds.), *Brain lateralization in children* (pp. 509–525). New York: Guilford Press.

Bryden, M. P., & MacRae, L. (1989). Dichotic laterality effects obtained with emotional words. *Neuropsychiatry, Neuropsychology & Behavioral Neurology, 1,* 171–176.

Bryden, M. P., & Saxby, L. (1986). Developmental aspects of cerebral lateralization. In J. E. Obrzat & G. W. Hynd (Eds.), *Child neuropsychology: Vol. 1. Theory and research.* Orlando, FL: Academic.

Buchanan, C. M., Maccoby, E. E., & Dornbusch, S. M. (1991). Caught between parents: Adolescents' experience in divorced families. *Child Development, 62,* 1008–1029.

Buchanan, C. M., Maccoby, E. E., & Dornbusch, S. M. (1992). Adolescents and their families after divorce: Three residential arrangements compared. *Journal of Research on Adolescence, 2*(3), 261–291.

Buchanan, C. M., Maccoby, E. E., & Dornbusch, S. M. (1996). *Adolescents after divorce.* Cambridge, MA: Harvard University Press.

Buck, R. W. (1984). *The communication of emotion.* New York: Guilford.

Buckmaster, L., & Brownell, K. D. (1988). The social and psychological world of the obese child. In V. A. Krasnagor, G. D. Grave, & N. Kretchmer (Eds.), *Childhood obesity: A biobehavioral perspective* (pp. 9–28). Caldwell, NJ: Telford Press.

Buckroyd, J. (1994). Eating disorders as psychosomatic illness: The implications for treatment. *Psychodynamic Counseling, 1,* 106–118.

Bugental, D. B., & Goodnow, J. J. (1998). Socialization processes. In W. Damon (Gen. Ed.) & N. Eisenberg (Vol. Ed.), *Handbook of child psychology: Vol. 3. Social, emotional, and personality development* (pp. 389–462). New York: Wiley.

Bullinger, A., & Chatillon, J. (1983). Recent theory and research of the Genevan school. In P. H. Mussen (Ed.), *Handbook of child psychology* (Vol. 3). New York: Wiley.

Bullock, D. (1983). Seeking relations between cognitive and social-interactive transitions. In K. W. Fischer (Ed.), *Levels and transitions in children's development: New directions in child development.* San Francisco: Jossey-Bass.

Bullock, D., & Merrill, L. (1980). The impact of personal preference on consistency through time: The case of childhood aggression. *Child Development, 51,* 808–814.

Bullock, M. (1985). Animism in childhood thinking: A new look at an old question. *Developmental Psychology, 21,* 217–225.

Bullock, M., & Lutkenhaus, P. (1990). Who am I? Self-understanding in toddlers. *Merrill-Palmer Quarterly, 36,* 217–238.

Burbury, W. M. (1941). The effects of evacuation and of air-raids on city children. *British Medical Journal, 2,* 361–396.

Burhans, K. K., & Dweck, C. S. (1995). Helplessness in early childhood: The role of contingent worth. *Child Development, 66,* 1719–1738.

Burke, P., & Puig-Antioch, J. (1990). Psycho-biology of childhood depression. In M. Lewis & S. Miller (Eds.), *Handbook of developmental psychopathology* (pp. 327–339). New York: Plenum.

Burks, B. S. (1928). The relative influence of nature and nurture upon mental development: A comparative study of foster parent-foster child resemblance and true parent-true child resemblance. *27th Yearbook of the National Society for the Study of Education* (Pt. 1, pp. 219–316). Chicago: University of Chicago Press.

Burnett, A., Beach, H. D., & Sullivan, A. M. (1963). Intelligence in a restricted environment. *Canadian Psychologist, 4,* 126–136.

Burns, B., & Lipsitt, L. P. (1991). Behavioral factors in crib death: Toward an understanding of the sudden infant death syndrome. *Journal of Applied Developmental Psychology, 12,* 159–184.

Burns, G. W., & Bottino, P. J. (1989). *The science of genetics* (6th ed.). New York: Macmillan.

Burns, K. A., Deddish, R. B., Burns, K., & Hatcher, R. P. (1983). Use of oscillating waterbeds and rhythmic sounds for premature infant stimulation. *Developmental Psychology, 19,* 746–751.

Burton, L. M. (1990). Teenage childbearing as an alternative life-course strategy in multigeneration Black families. *Human Nature, 1,* 123–143.

Burton, R. V. (1963). The generality of honesty reconsidered. *Psychological Review, 70,* 481–499.

Burton, R. V. (1984). A paradox in theories and research in moral development. In W. M. Kurtines & J. L. Gewirtz (Eds.), *Morality, moral behavior, and moral development.* New York: Wiley.

Bus, A. G., & Van Ijzendoorn, M. H. (1988). Mother-child interactions, attachment and emergent literacy: A cross-sectional study. *Child Development, 59,* 1262–1272.

Bussey, K. (1992). Lying and truthfulness: Children's definitions, standards and evaluative reactions. *Child Development, 63,* 129–137.

Bussey, K., & Perry, D. G. (1977). The imitation of resistance to deviation: Conclusive evidence for an elusive effect. *Developmental Psychology, 13,* 438–443.

Butterfield, E. C., & Siperstein, G. N. (1972). Influence of contingent auditory stimulation upon non-nutritional suckle. In J. F. Bosoma (Ed.), *Third symposium on oral sensation and perception: The mouth of the infant.* Springfield, IL: Charles C Thomas.

Butterfield, E. C., & Siperstein, G. N. (1974). Influence of contingent auditory stimulation upon non-nutritional suckle. In *Proceedings of the Third Symposium on Oral Sensation and Perception: The Mouth of the Infant.* Springfield, IL: Charles C Thomas.

Butterworth, G., & Grover, L. (1990). Joint visual attention manual pointing and preverbal communication in human infancy. In M. Jeannerod (Ed.), *Attention and performance XIII.* Hillsdale, NJ: Erlbaum.

Buysse, V., & Bailey, D. B. (1993). Behavioral and developmental outcomes in young children with disabilities in integrated and segregated settings: A review of comparative studies. *Journal of Special Education, 26,* 434–461.

Byrne, J. M., & Horowitz, F. D. (1981). Rocking as a soothing intervention: The influence of direction and type of movement. *Infant Behavior and Development, 4,* 207–218.

Byrnes, J. P. (1988). Formal operations: A systematic reformulation. *Developmental Review, 8,* 66–87.

Cadmus, H. (1974). *The behavioral and structural dynamics of social stratification as manifested in a racially integrated first grade classroom.* Doctoral dissertation, College of Education, University of Florida, Gainesville.

Cain, K. M. (1991, April). The relationship between conceptions of intelligence and motivational patterns: A developmental analysis. In C. S. Dweck & K. M. Cain (Chairs), *Self-conceptions and motivational development.* Symposium presented at the biennial meeting of the Society for Research in Child Development, Seattle.

Cairns, E. (1996). *Children and political violence.* Oxford, England: Blackwell.

Cairns, R. B., & Cairns, B. D. (1994). *Lifelines and risks: Pathways of youth in our time.* Cambridge, England: Cambridge University Press.

Cairns, R. B., Cairns, B. D., Neckerman, H., Fergusen, L. L., & Gariepy, J. L. (1989). Growth and aggression: Childhood to early adolescence. *Developmental Psychology, 25,* 320–330.

Cairns, R. B., Cairns, B. D., Neckerman, H. J. & Gest, S. D. (1988). Social networks and aggressive behavior: Peer support or peer rejection? *Developmental Psychology, 24,* 815–823.

Caldera, Y. M., Huston, A. C., & O'Brien, M. (1989). Social interactions and play patterns of parents and toddlers with feminine, masculine and neutral toys. *Child Development, 60,* 70–76.

Camara, K. A., & Resnick, G. (1988). Interparental conflict and cooperation: Factors moderating children's post-divorce adjustment. In E. M. Hetherington & J. D.

Arasten (Eds.), *Impact of divorce, single parenting and step parenting on children* (pp. 169–195). Hillsdale, NJ: Erlbaum.

Campbell, S., Cohn, J., & Meyers, T. (1995). Depression in first-time mothers: Mother-infant interaction and depression chronicity. *Developmental Psychology, 31,* 349–357.

Campos, J. J., & Bertenthal, B. I. (1989). Locomotion and psychological development in infancy. In F. Morrison, C. Lord, & D. Keating (Eds.), *Applied developmental psychology* (Vol. 3). New York: Academic.

Campos, J. J., Barrett, K. C., Lamb, M. E., Goldsmith, H. A., & Stenberg, C. (1983). Socioemotional development. In P. H. Mussen (Gen. Ed.), *Handbook of child psychology* (4th ed.); M. M. Haith & J. J. Campos (Vol. Eds.), *Infancy and developmental psychobiology.* New York: Wiley.

Campos, J. J., Bertenthal, B., & Kermonian, R. (1992). Early experience and emotional development: The emergence of wariness of heights. *Psychological Science, 3,* 61–64.

Campos, J. J., Langer, A., & Krowitz, A. (1970). Cardiac responses on the visual cliff in prelocomotor human infants. *Science, 170,* 196–197.

Campos, J. J., Svejda, M., Bertenthal, B., Benson, N., & Schmid, D. (1981, April). *Self-produced locomotion and wariness of heights: New evidence from training studies.* Paper presented at the meeting of the Society for Research in Child Development, Boston.

Campos, J., Barrett, K., Lamb, M., Goldsmith, H., & Stenberg, C. (1983). Socioemotional development. In M. M. Harth & J. J. Campos (Eds.), *Infancy and development psychobiology: Vol. 2. Handbook of child psychology.* New York: Wiley.

Campos, J., Hiatt, S., Ramsey, D., Henderson, C., & Svejda, M. (1978). The emergence of fear on the visual cliff. In M. Lewis & L. Rosenblum (Eds.), *The origins of affect.* New York: Plenum.

Campos, R. P. (1989). Soothing-pain elicited distress in infants with swaddling and pacifiers. *Child Development, 60,* 781–792.

Camras, L. A., Malatesta, C., & Izard, C. (1991). The development of facial expressions in infancy. In R. Feldman & B. Rime (Eds.), *Fundamentals of nonverbal behavior.* New York: Cambridge University Press.

Canfield, R. L., & Haith, M. M. (1991). Young infants' visual expectations for symmetrical and asymmetrical sequences. *Developmental Psychology, 27,* 198–208.

Cantor, J. (1994). Fright reactions to mass media. In J. Bryant & D. Zillmann (Eds.), *Media effects: Advances in theory and research* (pp. 213–245). Hillsdale, NJ: Erlbaum.

Cantor, J., & Harrison, K. (1996). Ratings and advisories for television programming: University of Wisconsin, Madison study. In *National television violence study: Scientific papers, 1994–1995.* Los Angeles: Mediascope.

Cantwell, D. P. (1990). Depression across the early life span. In M. Lewis & S. Miller (Eds.), *Handbook of developmental psychopathology* (pp. 293–309). New York: Plenum.

Cantwell, D. P., Baker, L., & Rutter, M. (1978). Family factors. In M. Rutter & E. Schopier (Eds.), *Autism: A reappraisal*

of concepts and treatment. New York: Plenum.

Cantwell, D. P., Russell, A. T., Mattison, R., & Will, L. A. (1979). A comparison of DSM-II and DSM-III in the diagnosis of childhood psychiatric disorders. *Archives of General Psychiatry, 36,* 1208–1228.

Capaldi, D. M., & Rothbart, M. K. (1992). Development and validation of an early adolescent temperament measure. *Journal of Early Adolescence, 12,* 153–173.

Capodilupo, A. M. (1992). A neostructural analysis of children's response to instruction in the sight-reading of musical notation. In R. Case (Ed.), *The mind's staircase: Exploring the conceptual underpinnings of children's thought and knowledge* (pp. 99–115). Hillsdale, NJ: Erlbaum.

Capron, C., & Duyme, M. (1989). Assessment of effects of socioeconomic status on IQ in a cross-fostering study. *Nature, 340,* 552–554.

Capute, A. J., Shapiro, B. K., & Palmer, F. B. (1987). Marking the milestones of language development. *Contemporary Pediatrics, 4,* 24.

Cardon, L. R. (1994). Height, weight, and obesity. In J. C. DeFries, R. Plomin, & D. W. Fulker (Eds.), *Nature and nurture during middle childhood.* Oxford: Blackwell.

Carey, G. (1994). Genetics and violence. In A. J. Reis, K. A. Miczek, & J. A. Roth (Eds.), *Understanding and preventing violence* (pp. 21–58). Washington, DC: National Academy Press.

Carey, S. (1978). The child as word learner. In M. Halle, J. Bresnan, & G. Miller (Eds.), *Linguistic theory and psychological reality* (pp. 264–293). Cambridge, MA: M.I.T. Press.

Carey, S. (1994). Does learning a language require the child to reconceptualize the world? In L. Gleitman & B. Landau (Eds.), *The acquisition of the lexicon* (pp. 143–168). Cambridge, MA: Elsevier/MIT Press.

Carlo, G., Koller, S., Eisenberg, N., Pacheco, P., & Loquercio, A. (in press). Prosocial cognitions, emotions, and behaviors: A cross-cultural study of adolescents from Brazil and the United States. *Developmental Psychology, 34.*

Carlson, A. J. (1902). Changes in Nissl's substance of the ganglion and the bipolar cells of the retinal of the brandt cormorant phalacrocorax pencillaturs during prolonged normal stimulation. *American Journal of Anatomy, 2,* 341–347.

Carlson, V., Cicchetti, D., Barnett, D., & Braunwald, K. (1989). Disorganized/disoriented attachment relationships in maltreated infants. *Developmental Psychology, 25,* 525–531.

Carr, M., & Jessup, D. L. (1995). Cognitive and metacognitive predictors of mathematics strategy use. *Learning and Individual Differences, 7,* 235–247.

Carraher, T. N., Schliemann, A. D., & Carraher, D. W. (1988). Mathematical concepts in everyday life. *New Directions for Child Development, 41,* 71–87.

Carroll, J. B. (1993). *Human cognitive abilities: A survey of factor analytic studies.* New York: Cambridge University Press.

Carroll, J. B. (1997). Psychometrics, intelligence, and public perception. *Intelligence, 24,* 25–52.

Carson, R. C. (1991). Dilemmas in the pathway of the DSM-IV. *Journal of Abnormal Psychology, 100,* 302–307.

Carson, R. C., & Butcher, J. N. (1992). *Abnormal psychology and modern life* (9th ed.). New York: HarperCollins.

Carter, C. S., Freeman, J. H., & Stanton, M. E. (1995). Neonatal medial prefrontal lesions and recovery of spatial delayed alternation in the rat: Effects of delay interval. *Developmental Psychobiology, 28,* 269–279.

Case, R. (1984). The process of stage transition: A neo-Piagetian view. In R. Sternberg (Ed.), *Mechanisms of cognitive development.* New York: Freeman.

Case, R. (1985). *Intellectual development: Birth to adulthood.* New York: Academic.

Case, R. (1991). Stages in the development of the young child's sense of self. *Developmental Review, 11,* 210–230.

Case, R. (1992). Neo-Piagetian theories of child development. In R. J. Sternberg & C. A. Berg (Eds.), *Intellectual development,* (pp. 161–196). New York: Cambridge University Press.

Case, R. (1995). Capacity-based explanations of working memory growth: A brief history and reevaluation. In F. E. Weinert & W. Schneider (Eds.), *Memory performance and competencies: Issues in growth and development* (pp. 23–44). Mahway, NJ: Erlbaum.

Case, R. (1996). Modeling the dynamic interplay between general and specific change in children's conceptual understanding. In R. Case & Y. Okamoto (Eds.), The role of central conceptual structures in the development of children's thought. *Monographs of the Society for Research in Child Development, 61,* Serial No. 246 Nos. 1 & 2, 156–188.

Case, R., & Griffin, (1990). Child cognitive development. The role of central conceptual structures in the development of scientific and social thought. In C. A. Hauert (Ed.), *Developmental psychology: Cognitive, percetuo-motor and neuropsychological perspectives.* Amsterdam: North Holland.

Case, R., Okamoto, Y., Henderson, B., & McKeough, A. (1993). Individual variability and consistency in cognitive development: New evidence for the existence of central conceptual structures. In R. Case & W. Edelstein (Eds.), *The new structuralism in cognitive development: Theory and research on individual pathways.* Basel: Karger.

Casey, M. B. (1996). Understanding individual differences in spatial ability in females: A nature/nurture interaction framework. *Developmental Review, 16,* 241–260.

Casper, L. M., & Hogan, D. P. (1990). Family networks in prenatal and postnatal health. *Social Biology, 37*(1–2), 84–101.

Caspi, A. (1998). Personality development across the life course. In W. Damon (Gen. Ed.) & N. Eisenberg (Vol. Ed.), *Handbook of child psychology: Vol. 3. Social, emotional, and personality development* (pp. 311–388). New York: Wiley.

Caspi, A., Elder, G. H., & Bem, D. J. (1987). Moving against the world: Life course patterns of explosive children. *Developmental Psychology, 23,* 308–313.

Caspi, A., Elder, G. H., & Bem, D. J. (1988). Moving away from the world: Life-course

patterns of shy children. *Developmental Psychology, 24,* 824–831.

Caspi, A., & Moffitt, T. E. (1991). Individual differences are accentuated during periods of social change: The sample case of girls at puberty. *Journal of Personality and Social Psychology, 61,* 157–168.

Cassidy, J. (1988). Child-mother attachment and the self in six-year-olds. *Child Development, 59,* 121–135.

Cassidy, J., & Asher, S. R. (1992). Loneliness and sociometric status among young children. *Children Development, 63,* 350–365.

Cassidy, J., & Berlin, L. J. (1994). The insecure/ambivalent pattern of attachment: Theory and research. *Child Development, 65,* 971–991.

Cassidy, J., Kirsh, S. J., Scolton, K. L., & Parke, R. D. (1996). Attachment and representations of peer relationships. *Developmental Psychology, 32,* 892–904.

Cassidy, J., Parke, R. D., Butkovsky, L., & Braungart, J. M. (1992). Family-peer connections: The roles of emotional expressiveness within the family and children's understanding of emotion. *Child Development, 63,* 603–618.

Catalano, R. F., Hawkins, J. D., Krenz, C., & Gilmore, M. (1993). Using research to guide culturally appropriate drug abuse prevention. *Journal of Consulting & Clinical Psychology, 61,* 804–811.

Caudill, W., & Plath, D. W. (1966). Who sleeps with whom? Parent-child involvement in urban Japanese families. *Psychiatry, 25,* 344–366.

Ceci, S. (1990). *On intelligence: A bioecological treatise on intellectual development* (Expanded ed.). Cambridge, MA: Harvard University Press.

Ceci, S. J. (1991). How much does schooling influence general intelligence and its cognitive components? A reassessment of the evidence. *Developmental Psychology, 27,* 703–720.

Ceci, S. J., & Bruck, M. (1998). Children's testimony: Applied and basic issues. In W. Damon (Gen. Ed.), I. Sigel, & K. A. Renninger (Vol. Eds.), *Handbook of child psychology: Vol. 4* (pp. 713–774). New York: Wiley.

Ceci, S. J., & Hembrooke, H. A. (1995). A bioecological model of intellectual development. In P. Moen, G. H. Elder, & K. Luscher (Eds.), *Examining lives in context.* Washington, DC: American Psychological Association Press.

Ceci, S. J., Leichtman, M. D., & White, T. (1998). Interviewing preschoolers rememberance of things planted. In D. P. Peters (Ed.), *The child witness in context cognitive, social and legal perspectives.* Holland: Kluwer.

Ceci, S. J., Ross, D. F., & Toglia, M. P. (1987). Suggestibility of children's memory: Psycholegal implications. *Journal of Experimental Psychology: General, 116,* 38–49.

Centers for Disease Control. (1996). Summary of notifiable diseases, United States, 1996. *Morbidity and Mortality Weekly Report, 46.*

Centers for Disease Control and Prevention (CDC). (1993). Rates of cesarean delivery—United States, 1991. *Morbidity and Mortality Weekly Report, 42,* 285–289.

Centers for Disease Control and Prevention. (1998). Tobacco use among high school

students—United States, 1997. *Morbidity and Mortality Weekly Report, 47,* April 3, 229–233.

Chandler, M. J. (1973). Egocentrism and antisocial behavior: The assessment and training of social perspective taking skills. *Developmental Psychology, 9,* 326–332.

Chandler, M. J., Greenspan, S., & Barenboim, C. (1973). Judgments of intentionality in response to videotaped and verbally presented moral dilemmas: The medium is the message. *Child Development, 44,* 315–320.

Chang, H. W., & Trehub, S. E. (1977). Infants' perception of grouping in auditory patterns. *Child Development, 48,* 1666–1670.

Chao, R. K. (1994). Beyond parental control and authoritarian parenting style: Understanding Chinese parenting through the cultural notion of training. *Child Development, 65,* 1111–1119.

Chao, R. K. (1995). Chinese and European American cultural models of the self reflected in mothers' childrearing beliefs. *Ethos, 23*(3), 328–354.

Chao, R. K. (1996). Chinese and European American mothers' beliefs about the role of parenting in children's school success. *Journal of Cross-Cultural Psychology, 27*(4), 403–423.

Charlesworth, R., & Hartup, W. W. (1967). Positive social reinforcement in the nursery school peer group. *Child Development, 38,* 993–1002.

Charlesworth, W. (1988). Resources and resource acquisition during ontogeny. In K. MacDonald (Ed.), *Sociobiological perspectives on human development.* New York: Springer-Verlag.

Charlesworth, W., & Dzur, C. (1987). Gender comparison of preschoolers' behavior and resource utilization. *Child Development, 58,* 191–200.

Charlton, A. (1994). Children and passive smoking: a review. *Journal of Family Practice, 38,* 267–277.

Chase, W. G., & Simon, H. A. (1973). The mind's eye in chess. In W. G. Chase (Ed.), *Visual information processing.* New York: Academic.

Chase-Lansdale, P. L., & Hetherington, E. M. (1990). The impact of divorce on life-span development: Short and long-term effects. In D. Featherman & R. M. Lerner (Eds.), *Life span development and behavior* (Vol. 10, pp. 105–150). Orlando, FL: Academic Press.

Chase-Lansdale, P. L., Mott, F. L., Brooks-Gunn, J., & Phillips, D. A. (1991). Children of the National Longitudinal Study of Youth: A unique research opportunity. *Developmental Psychology, 27,* 918–931.

Chasnoff, I. J., & Griffith, D. R. (1991). Maternal cocaine use: Neonatal outcome. In H. E. Fitzgerald, B. M. Lester & M. W. Yogman (Eds.), *Theory and research in behavioral pediatrics,* Vol. 5. (pp. 1–17). New York: Plenum Press.

Chasnoff, I. J., Griffith, D. R., MacGregor, S., Dirkes, B. M., & Burns, K. A. (1989). Temporal patterns of cocaine use in pregnancy. *Journal of the American Medical Association, 261,* 1741–1744.

Chen, C., & Stevenson, H. W. (1995). Motivation and mathematics achievement: A comparative study of Asian-American, Caucasian-American and East Asian high school students. *Child Development, 66,* 1215–1234.

Chen, C., Stevenson, H. W., Hayward, C., & Burgess, S. (1995). Culture and academic achievement: Ethnic and cross-national differences. In P. Pintrich & M. Maehr (Eds.), *Advances in motivation and achievement: Vol. 9. Culture, race, ethnicity, and motivation.* New York: Plenum.

Chen, M. (1996). Six myths about television and children. In T. M. MacBeth (Ed.), *Tuning into young viewers: Social science perspectives on television.* Thousand Oaks, CA: Sage.

Chen, X., & Rubin, K. H. (1994). Family conditions, parental acceptance, and social competence and aggression in Chinese children. *Social Development, 3,* 269–290.

Chen, X., Rubin, K. H., & Sun, Y. (1992). Social reputation and peer relationships in Chinese and Canadian children: A cross-cultural study. *Child Development, 63,* 1336–1343.

Chen, Z., & Daehler, M. W. (1989). Positive and negative transfer in analogical problem solving by 6 year old children. *Cognitive Development, 4,* 327–344.

Cherlin, A. (1996). *Sociology of the family.* Englewood Cliffs, NJ: Prentice-Hall.

Cherlin, A. J., Chase-Lansdale, P. L., Furstenberg, F. F. Jr., Kiernan, K. E., Robins, P. K., Morrison, D. R., & Teitler, J. O. (1991, April). *How much of the effects of divorce on children occurs before the separation? Longitudinal evidence from Great Britain and the United States.* Paper presented at meetings of the Society for Research in Child Development. Seattle, WA.

Cherlin, A. J., & Furstenberg, F. F. (1991). *Divided families.* Cambridge, MA: Harvard University Press.

Cherlin, A. J., & Furstenberg, F. F. (1994). Stepfamilies in the United States: A reconsideration. *Annual Review of Sociology, 20,* 359–381.

Cherlin, A. J., Furstenberg, F. F., Chase-Lansdale, P. L., Kiernan, K. E., et al. (1991). Longitudinal studies of effects of divorce on children in Great Britain and the United States. *Science, 252,* 1386–1389.

Chi, M. T. H. (1976). Short term memory limitations in children: Capacity or processing deficits? *Memory and Cognition, 4,* 559–572.

Chi, M. T. H. (1978). Knowledge structures and memory development. In R. S. Siegler (Ed.), *Children's thinking: What develops?* Hillsdale, NJ: Erlbaum.

Chi, M. T. H., & Koeske, R. D. (1983). Network representation of a child's dinosaur knowledge. *Developmental Psychology, 19,* 29–39.

Chi, M. T. H., & Slotta, J. D. (1993). The ontological coherence of intuitive physics. *Cognition & Instruction, 10,* 249–260.

Children's Defense Fund. (1997). *The state of America's children: Yearbook 1997.* Washington, DC: Children's Defense Fund.

Children's Defense Fund. (1998). The state of *American's children: Yearbook 1998.* Washington, D. C., author.

Childs, C. P. & Greenfield, P. M. (1982). Informal modes of learning and teaching: The case of Zinacenteco weaving. In N. Warren (Ed.), *Advances in cross-cultural psychology* (Vol. 2). London: Academic.

Chisholm, J. S. (1963). *Navajo infancy: An ethological study of child development.* New York: Aldine.

Chittenden, G. E. (1942). An experimental study in measuring and modifying assertive behavior in young children. *Monographs of the Society for Research in Child Development, 7* (Serial No. 31).

Chomsky, C. (1969). *The acquisition of syntax in children from 5 to 10.* Cambridge, MA: M.I.T. Press.

Chomsky, N. (1968). *Language and mind.* New York: Harcourt, Brace & World.

Christenson, S., Abery, B., & Weinberg, R. (1986). An alternative model for the delivery of psychology in the school community. In S. N. Elliott & J. C. Witt (Eds.), *The delivery of psychological services in schools: concepts, processes, and issues* (pp. 349–391). Hillsdale, NJ: Erlbaum.

Christoffel, K. K. (1990). Violent death and injury in U.S. children and adolescents. *American Journal of Disease Control, 144,* 697–706.

Chung, T., & Asher, J. R. (1996). Children's goals and strategies in peer conflict situations. *Merrill Palmer Quarterly, 42,* 125–147.

Cicchetti, D. (1990). A historical perspective on the discipline of developmental psychopathology. In J. Rolf, A. S. Masten, D. Cicchetti, D. Nuechterlein, & S. Weintraub (Eds.), *Risk and protective factors in human development.* New York: Cambridge University Press.

Cicchetti, D., & Rogosch, F. (1996). Equifinality and multifinality in developmental psychopathology. *Development and Psychopathology, 8,* 597–600.

Cicchetti, D., & Toth, S. L. (1995). Child maltreatment and attachment organization: Implications for intervention. In S. Goldberg, R. Muir, & J. Kerr (Eds.), *Attachment theory: Social, developmental, and clinical perspectives* (pp. 279–308). Hillsdale, NJ: Analytic Press.

Cicchetti, D., & Toth, S. L. (1998). Perspectives on research and practice in developmental psychopathology. In W. Damon (Gen. Ed.), I. E. Sigel, & K. A. Renninger (Vol. Eds.), *Handbook of child psychology: Vol. 4. Child psychology in practice* (pp. 479–583). New York: John Wiley.

Cicchetti, D., Toth, S. L., & Lynch, M. (1995). Bowlby's dream comes full circle: The application of attachment theory to risk and psychopathology. In T. Ollendick & R. Prinz (Eds.), *Advances in clinical child psychology* (Vol. 17, pp. 1–75). New York: Plenum Press.

Cicero, T. J. (1994). Effects of paternal exposure to alcohol on offspring development. *Alcohol Health and Research World, 18,* 37–41.

Cicirelli, V. G. (1976). Siblings helping siblings. In V. L. Allen (Ed.), *Children as tutors.* New York: Academic.

Clancy, P. (1985). Acquisition of Japanese. In D. I. Slobin (Ed.), *The cross-linguistic study of language acquisition: Vol. 1. The data* (pp. 323–524). Hillsdale, NJ: Erlbaum.

Clark, E. V. (1983). Meanings and concepts. In P. H. Mussen (Eds.), *Handbook of child psychology* (Vol. 3). New York: Wiley.

Clark, J. E., & Phillips, S. J. (1993). A longitudinal study of intralimb coordination in the first year of independent walking: A dynamical systems analysis. *Child Development, 64,* 1143–1157.

Clarke, D. C. (1993). Suicidal behavior in childhood and adolescence: Recent studies and clinical implications. *Psychiatric Annals, 23,* 271–283.

Clarke, G., Hops, H., Lewinsohn, P. M., & Andrews, J. (1992). Cognitive-behavioral group treatment of adolescent depression: Prediction of outcome. *Behavior Therapy, 23,* 341–354.

Clarke-Stewart, K. A. (1978). And daddy makes three: The father's impact on mother and young child. *Child Development, 49,* 466–478.

Clarke-Stewart, K. A. (1987). Predicting child development from day care forms and features: The Chicago study. In D. A. Phillips (Ed.), Quality in child care: What does research tell us? *Research Monographs of the National Association for the Education of Young Children* (Vol. 1, pp. 21–42). Washington, DC: National Association for the Education of Young Children.

Clarke-Stewart, K. A. (1989). Infant day care: Maligned or malignant? *American Psychologist, 44,* 266–273.

Clarke-Stewart, K. A. (1993). *Daycare* (rev. ed.). Cambridge, MA: Harvard University Press.

Clegg, D. J. (1971). Teratology. *Annual Review of Pharmacology,* pp. 409–423.

Clifton, R. K. (1992). The development of spatial hearing in human infants. In L. A. Werner & E. W. Rubel (Eds.), *Develop mental psychoacoustics* (pp. 135–157). Washington, DC: American Psychological Association.

Cline, V. B., Croft, R. G., & Courier, S. (1973). Desensitization of children to television violence. *Journal of Personality and Social Psychology, 27,* 360–365.

Cloninger, C. R., Christiansen, K. O., Reich, T., & Gottesman, I. I. (1978). Implications of sex differences in the prevalences of antisocial personality, alcoholism, and criminality for familial transmission. *Archives of General Psychiatry, 35,* 941–951.

Cloninger, C. R., Sigvardsson, S., Bohman, M., & van Knoring, A. L. (1982). Predisposition to petty criminality in Swedish adoptees: II. Cross-fostering analyses of gene-environmental interactions. *Archives of General Psychiatry, 39,* 1242–1247.

Coates, T. J., & Thoresen, C. E. (1976). *Treating obesity in children and adolescents: A review.* Unpublished manuscript. Stanford University, Stanford, CA.

Cochi, S. L., Edmonds, L. E., Dyer, K., Grooves, W. L., Marks, J. S., Rovira, E. Z., Preblud, S. R., & Orenstein, W. A. (1989). Congenital rubella syndrome in the United States, 1970–1985: On the verge of elimination. *American Journal of Epidemiology, 129,* 349–361.

Cochran, L., Feng, H., Cartledge, G., & Hamilton, S. (1993). The effects of cross-age tutoring on the academic achievement, social behaviors, and self-perceptions of low-achieving African-American males with behavioral disorders. *Behavioral Disorders, 18,* 292–302.

Cohen, D. J., Volma, F, Anderson, G. M., & Klin, A. (1993). Integrating biological and behavioral perspectives in the study and care of autistic individuals: The future. *Israel Journal of Psychiatry and Related Sciences, 30,* 15–32.

Cohen, P., & Brook, J. S. (1995). The reciprocal influence of punishment and child behavior disorder. In J. McCord (Ed.), *Coercion and punishment in long-term perspectives* (pp. 154–164). New York: Cambridge University Press.

Cohn, D. A. (1990). Child-mother attachment in six-year-olds and social competence at school. *Child Development, 61,* 152–162.

Cohn, J., & Campbell, S. (1992). Influences of maternal depression on infant affect regulation. In D. Cicchetti & S. Toth (Eds.), *Rochester Symposium on Developmental Psychopathology: Vol. 4. A developmental approach to affective disorder* (pp. 103–130). Rochester, NY: University of Rochester Press.

Coie, J. D., & Dodge, K. A. (1983). Continuities and changes in children's social status: A five-year longitudinal study. *Merrill-Palmer Quarterly, 29,* 261–282.

Coie, J. D., & Dodge, K. A. (1988). Multiple sources of data on social behavior and social status in school: A cross-age comparison. *Child Development, 57,* 815–829.

Coie, J. D., & Dodge, K. A. (1998). Aggression and antisocial behavior. In W. Damon (Gen. Ed.), & N. Eisenberg (Vol. Ed.), *Handbook of child psychology: Social, emotional, and personal development* (Vol. 3, pp. 779–862). Wiley: New York.

Coie, J. D., Dodge, K. A., & Kupersmidt, J. (1990). Peer group behavior and social status. In S. R. Asher & J. D. Coie (Eds.), *Peer rejection in childhood.* New York: Cambridge University Press.

Coie, J. D., & Kupersmidt, J. B. (1983). A behavioral analysis of emerging social status in boys' groups. *Child Development, 54,* 1400–1416.

Colby, A., & Kohlberg, L. (1987). *The measurement of moral judgment* (Vols. 1–2). New York: Cambridge University Press.

Colby, A., Kohlberg, L., Gibbs, J., & Lieberman, M. (1983). A longitudinal study of moral judgment. *Monographs of the Society for Research in Child Development, 48* (Serial No. 200).

Cole, C. F., & Richman, B. A. (1997). Sesame Street around the world. *Research Roundup, 7,* 4–5.

Cole, M. (1985). The zone of proximal development: Where culture and cognition create each other. In J. V. Wertsch (Ed.), *Culture, communication and cognitive: Vygotskian perspectives.* Cambridge: Cambridge University Press.

Cole, M. (1990). Cognitive development and formal schooling: The evidence from cross-cultural research. In L. C. Moll (Ed.), *Vygotsky and education* (pp. 89–110). Cambridge, England: Cambridge University Press.

Cole, M., & Scribner, S. (1977). Cross-cultural studies of memory and cognition. In R. V. Kail, Jr., & J. W. Hagen (Eds.), *Perspectives on the development of memory and cognition.* Hillsdale, NJ: Erlbaum.

Cole, P. M. (1985). Display roles and the socialization of affective displays. In G. Zivin (Ed.), *The development of expressive behavior: Biology-environment interaction* (pp. 269–290). New York: Academic.

Coleman, J. S., Campbell, E. Q., Hobson, C. J., McPartland, J., Mood, A. M., Weinfeld, F. D., & York, R. L. (1966). *Equality of educational opportunity.* Washington, DC: Government Printing Office.

Colin, V. L. (1996). *Human attachment.* New York: McGraw-Hill.

Collins, A., Brown, J. S., & Newman, S. E. (1990). The new apprenticeship: Teaching students the craft of reading, writing and mathematics. In L. B. Resnick (Ed.), *Cognition and instruction: Issues and agendas.* Hillsdale, NJ: Erlbaum.

Collins, F., & Galas, D. (1993). A new five-year plan for the U.S. Human Genome Project. *Science, 262,* 43–46.

Collins, W. A. (1983). Interpretation and inference in children's television viewing. In J. Bryant & D. C. Anderson (Eds.), *Children's understanding of television: Research on attention and comprehension.* New York: Academic.

Collins, W. A., Sobol, S. K., & Westby, S. (1981). Effects of adult commentary on children's comprehension and inferences about a televised aggressive portrayal. *Child Development, 52,* 158–163.

Coltrane, S. (1995). The future of fatherhood: Social, demographic, and economic influences on men's family involvements. In W. Marsiglio (Ed.), *Fatherhood: Contemporary theory, research* (pp. 255–274). Thousand Oaks, CA: Sage.

Coltrane, S. (1996). *Family man: Fatherhood, housework, and gender equity.* New York: Oxford University Press.

Comer, J. (1988). The education of low-income black children. *Scientific American, 259,* 42–48.

Comer, J. (1991). The black child in school. In M. Lewis (Ed.), *Child and adolescent psychology: A comprehensive textbook.* Baltimore: Williams & Watkins.

Compas, B. E., & Hammen, C. L. (1992, May). *Child and adolescent depression: Covariation and comorbidity in development.* Paper presented at the Grant Foundation Conference on Risk, Resiliency, and Development, Kiawah Island, SC.

Comstock, G. (1991). *Television and the American child.* Orlando, FL: Academic Press.

Conduct Problems Prevention Research Group. (1992). A developmental and clinical model for the prevention of conduct disorder: The FAST track program. *Development & Psychopathology, 4,* 504–527.

Conger, J. J., & Petersen, A. C. (1984). *Adolescence & youth* (3rd ed.). New York: Harper & Row.

Conger, K. J. (1992, March). *Sibling relationship quality as a mediator and moderator of the relationship between parental mood and behavior and adolescent self esteem.* Paper presented at the meetings of the Society for Research in Adolescence. Washington, DC.

Conger, R. D., & Conger, K. J. (1996). Sibling relationships. In R. L. Simons et al., (Ed.), *Understanding differences between divorced and intact families* (pp. 104–124). Thousand Oaks, CA: Sage.

Conger, R. D., Conger, K. J., Elder, G. J., Jr., Lorenz, F. O., Simons, R. L., & Whitbeck, L. B. (1992). A family process model of economic hardship and adjustment of early adolescent boys. *Child Development, 63,* 526–541.

Conger, R. D., & Elder, G. H. (Eds.). (1994). *Families in troubled times: Adapting to change in rural America.* New York: Aldine.

Connell, J. P., Spencer, M. B., & Aber, J. L. (1994). Educational risk and resilience in African-American youth: Context, self, action, and outcomes in school. *Child Development, 65,* 493–506.

Conners, C. K., & Werry, J. S. (1979). Pharmacotherapy. In H. C. Quay & J. S. Werry (Eds.), *Psychopathological disorders of childhood* (2nd ed.). New York: Wiley.

Connolly, K. J., & Dalgleish, M. (1989). The emergence of tool using skill in infancy. *Developmental Psychology, 25,* 894–912.

Connor, E. M., Sperling, R. S., Gelber, R., Kiselev, P., Scott, G., O'Sullivan, M. J., Van Dyke, R., Bey, M., Shearer, W., & Jacobsen, R. L. (1994). Reduction of maternal-infant transmission of human immunodeficiency virus type 1 with treatment. Pediatric AIDS Clinical Trial Group Protocol 076 Study Group. *New England Journal of Medicine, 331,* 1173–1180.

Conoley, J. C. (1990). Review of the K-ABC: Reflecting the unobservable. Conference on Intelligence: Theories and practice (1990, Memphis, TN). *Journal of Psychoeducational Assessment, 8,* 369–375.

Cooney, R. S., Pedersen, F. A., Indelicato, S., & Palkowitz, R. (1993). Timing of fatherhood: Is "on time" optimal? *Journal of Marriage and the Family, 44,* 621–631.

Cooper, C. R., & Cooper, R. G. (1992). Links between adolescents' relationships with their parents and peers: Models, evidence and mechanisms. In R. D. Parke & G. W. Ladd (Eds.), *Family-peer relationships: Modes of linkage.* Hillsdale, NJ: Erlbaum.

Cooper, R. P., & Aslin, R. N. (1990). Preference for infant-directed speech in the first month after birth. *Child Development, 61,* 1584–1595.

Corballis, M. C. (1983). *Human laterality.* New York: Academic.

Corbetta, D., & Thelen, E. (1996). The developmental origins of bimanual coordination: A dynamic perspective. *Journal of Experimental Psychology: Human Perception and Performance, 22,* 502–522.

Corder-Bolz, C. R. (1980). Mediation: The role of significant others. *Journal of Communication, 30,* 106–118.

Coren, S. (1992). *The left-hander syndrome: The causes and consequences of left-handedness.* New York: Free Press.

Cornell, E. H., & Gottfried, A. W. (1976). Intervention with premature human infants. *Child Development, 47,* 32–39.

Corner, G. W. (1961). *Congenital malformations: The problem and the task* (pp. 7–17). Papers and discussions presented at the First International Conference on Congenital Malformations. Philadelphia: Lippincott.

Corter, C. M., & Minde, K. K. (1987). Impact of infant prematurity on family systems. In M. Wolbraich (Ed.), *Advances in developmental and behavioral pediatrics* (Vol. 8). Greenwich, CT: JAI Press.

Cosgrove, J. M., & Patterson, C. J. (1977). Plans and the development of listener skills. *Developmental Psychology, 13,* 557–564.

Costello, E. (1983). *Signing: How to speak with your hands.* New York: Bantam.

Council on Scientific Affairs. (1991). Hispanic health in the United States. *Journal of the American Medical Association,* January 9, 265(2), 248–252.

Courage, M. L., & Adams, R. J. (1990). Visual acuity assessment from birth to three years using the acuity card procedures: Cross-longitudinal samples. *Optometry and vision science, 67,* 713–718.

Cowan, C. P., & Cowan, P. A. (1992). *When partners become parents: The big life change for couples.* New York: Basic Books.

Cowan, C. P., Cowan, P. A., Heming, G., & Miller, N. B. (1991). Becoming a family: Marriage, parenting and child development. In P. A. Cowan & E. M. Hetherington (Eds.), *Family transitions.* Hillsdale, NJ: Erlbaum.

Cowan, P., & McHale, J. (1997). Coparenting in a family context: Emerging achievements, current dilemmas, and future directions. In J. McHale & P. Cowan (Eds.), *Understanding how family-level dynamics affect children's development: Studies of two-parent families: Vol. 74. New directions in child development* (pp. 93–106). San Francisco: Jossey-Bass.

Cowan, P. A., Cohn, D. A., Cowan, C. P., & Pearson, J. L. (1996). Parents' attachment histories and children's internalizing and externalizing behavior: Exploring family systems models of linkage. *Journal of Consulting & Clinical Psychology, 64,* 1–11.

Cowan, P. A., Cowan, C. P., Schulz, M. C., & Heming, G. (1994). Prebirth to preschool family factors in children's adaptation to kindergarten. In R. D. Parke & S. Kellam (Eds.), *Exploring family relationships with other social contexts* (pp. 75–114). Hillsdale, NJ: Erlbaum.

Cowen, E. (1985). Primary prevention in mental health: Past, present, and future. In R. Felner, L. Jason, N. Mortsuger, & S. Farber (Eds.), *Preventive psychology.* New York: Pergamon.

Cowen, E. L. (1994). The enhancement of psychological wellness: Challenges and opportunities. *American Journal of Community Psychology, 22,* 149–179.

Coyle, T. R., & Bjorklund, D. F. (1997). Age differences in, and consequences of, multiple and variable-strategy use on a multitrial sort-recall task. *Developmental Psychology, 33,* 372–380.

Craik, F. I. M., & Lockhart, R. S. (1972). Levels of processing: A framework for memory research. *Journal of Verbal Learning and Verbal Behavior, 12,* 599–607.

Crain-Thoreson, C., & Dale, P. S. (1992). Do early talkers become early readers? Linguistic precocity, preschool language and emergent literacy. *Developmental Psychology, 28,* 421–429.

Crawley, S. B., & Spiker, D. (1983). Mother-child interactions involving two-year-olds with Down syndrome: A look at individual differences. *Child Development, 54,* 1312–1323.

Crick, N. R. (1997). Engagement in gender normative versus nonnormative forms of aggression: Links to social-psychological adjustment. *Developmental Psychology, 33,* 610–617.

Crick, N. R., Casas, J. F., & Mosher, M. (1997). Relational and overt aggression in preshcool. *Developmental Psychology, 33,* 579–588.

Crick, N. R., & Dodge, K. A. (1994). A review and reformulation of social information processing mechanisms in children's social adjustment. *Psychological Bulletin, 115,* 74–101.

Crick, N. R., & Grotpeter, J. K. (1995). Relational aggression, gender, and social-psychological adjustment. *Child Development, 66,* 710–722.

Crick, N. R., & Ladd, G. W. (1993). Children's perceptions of their peer experiences: Attributions, loneliness, social anxiety, and social avoidance. *Developmental Psychology, 29,* 244–254.

Crick, N. R., Wellman, N. E., Casas, J. F., O'Brien, K. M., Nelson, D. A., Grotpeter, J. K., & Markon, K. (1998). Childhood aggression and gender: A new look at an old problem. In D. Bernstein (Ed.), *Nebraska symposium on motivation* (Vol. 44). Lincoln: University of Nebraska Press.

Crisafi, M., & Brown, A. L. (1986). Analogical transfer in very young children: Combining two separately learned solutions to reach a goal. *Child Development, 57,* 953–968.

Crnic, K. A., Greenberg, M. T., Ragozin, A. A., Robinson, N. M., & Basham, R. (1983). Effects of stress and social support on mothers and premature and full-term infants. *Child Development, 54,* 209–217.

Crockenberg, S., & Litman, D. (1990). Autonomy as competence in 2-year-olds: Maternal correlates of child defiance, compliance and self assertion. *Developmental Psychology, 26,* 916–971.

Crockenberg, S. B. (1981). Infant irritability, mother responsiveness and social support influences on the security of infant-mother attachment. *Child Development, 52,* 857–865.

Crouter, A. C., & MacDermid, S. M. (1991). *A longitudinal study of parental monitoring in dual and single-earner families.* Paper presented at the meetings of the Society for Research in Child Development. Seattle, WA.

Crowell, J., & Treboux, D. (1995). A review of adult attachment measures: Implications for theory and research. *Social Development, 4,* 294–327.

Crowley, K., & Siegler, R. S. (1993). Flexible strategy use in young children's tic-tac-toe. *Cognitivie Science, 17,* 531–561.

Cummings, E. M., & Davies, P. (1994). *Children and marital conflict.* New York: Guilford Press.

Cummings, E. M., Simpson, K. S., & Wilson, A. (1993). Children's responses to interadult anger as a function of information about resolution. *Developmental Psychology, 29,* 978–985.

Cummings, J. S., Pelligrini, D. S., Notarius, C. I., & Cummings, E. M. (1989). Children's responses to angry adult behavior as a function of marital distress and history of interparent hostility. *Child Development, 60,* 1035–1043.

Curtiss, S. (1977). *Genie: A psycholinguistic study of a modern day "wild child."* New York: Academic Press.

Curtiss, S. (1989). The independence and task-specificity of language. In M. H. Bornstein & J. S. Bruner (Eds.), *Interaction in human development* (pp. 105–138). Hillsdale, NJ: Erlbaum.

Dale, P. S. (1976). *Language development: Structure and function* (2nd ed.). New York: Holt.

Damon, A., Damon, S. T., Reed, R. B., & Valadian, I. (1969). Age at menarche of mothers and daughters, with a note on accuracy of recall. *Human Biology, 41,* 161–175.

Damon, W. (1988). Socialization and individuation. In G. Handel (Ed.), *Childhood socialization* (pp. 3–10) New York: Hawthorne.

Damon, W., & Hart, D. (1982). The development of self-understanding from infancy through adolescence. *Child Development, 53,* 841–864.

Damon, W., & Phelps, E. (1989). Strategic uses of peer learning in children's education. In T. Berndt & G. Ladd (Eds.), *Peer relationships in child development.* New York: Wiley.

Daniels, P., & Weingarten, K. (1988). The fatherhood click: The timing of parenthood in men's lives. In P. Bronstein & C. P. Cowan (Eds.), *Fatherhood today: Men's changing role in the family* (pp. 36–52). New York: Wiley.

Dannemiller, J. L., & Stephens, B. R. (1988). A critical test of infant pattern perception models. *Child Development, 59,* 210–216.

Dansereau, D. F. (1987). Transfer from cooperative to individual studying. *Journal of Reading, 30,* 614–619.

Dark, V. J., & Benbow, S. P. (1993). Cognitive differences among the gifted: A review and new data. In D. K. Detterman (Ed.). *Current topics in human intelligence,* Vol. 3. Norwood, NJ: Ablex.

Darvill, D., & Cheyne, J. A. (1981). *Sequential analysis of response to aggression: Age and sex effects.* Paper presented at the biennial meeting of the Society for Research in Child Development, Boston.

Darwin, C. (1872). *The expression of emotions in man and animals.* London: John Murray.

Dasen, P. E., & Heron, A. (1981). Cross-cultural tests of Piaget's theory. In H. C. Triandis & A. Heron (Eds.), *Handbook of cross-cultural psychology: Developmental psychology* (Vol. 4). Boston: Allyn & Bacon.

Dasen, P. R. (1984). The cross-cultural study of intelligence: Piaget and the Baoulé. *International Journal of Psychology, 19,* 407–434.

Davidson, D. (1996). The effects of decision characteristics on children's selective search of predecisional information. *Acta Psychologica, 92,* 263–281.

Davidson, E. S., Yasuna, A., & Tower, A. (1979). The effects of television cartoons on sex role stereotyping in young girls. *Child Development, 50,* 597–600.

Davidson, R. J. (1994). Temperament, affective style, and frontal lobe asymmetry. In G. Dawson & K. W. Fischer (Eds.), *Human behavior and the developing brain.* New York: Guilford Press.

Davies, P. T., & Cummings, E. M. (1994). Marital conflict and child adjustment: An emotional security hypothesis. *Psychological Bulletin, 116,* 387–411.

Davis, M. H., Luce, C., & Kraus, S. J. (1994). The heritability of characteristics associated with dispositional empathy. *Journal of Personality, 62,* 369–391.

Davis, S. W., Best, D. L., & Hawkins, R. C. (1981). *Sex stereotypes, weight, and body image in childhood and adolescence.* Paper presented at the biennial meeting of the Society for Research in Child Development, Boston.

Dawe, H. C. (1934). The influence of size of kindergarten group upon performance. *Child Development, 5,* 295–303.

Dawson, G. (1994). Development of emotional expression and regulation in infancy. In G. Dawson & K. W. Fischer (Eds.), *Human behavior and the developing brain.* New York: Guilford Press.

Day, N. L., & Richardson, G. A. (1991). Prenatal alcohol exposure: A continuum of effects. *Seminars in, 15,* 271–279.

Day, N. L., & Richardson, G. A. (1994). Comparative teratogenicity of alcohol and other durgs. *Alcohol Health and Research World, 18,* 42–48.

Dean A., Malik, M., Richards, W., & Stringer, S. A. (1986). Effects of parental maltreatment on children's conceptions of interpersonal relationships. *Developmental Psychology, 22,* 617–626.

Deater-Deckard, K., & Dodge, K. A. (1997). Externalizing behavior problems and discipline revisited: Nonlinear effects and variation by culture, context, and gender. *Psychological Inquiry, 8,* 161–175.

Deater-Deckard, K., Dodge, K. A., Bates, J. E., & Pettit, G. S. (1996). Physical discipline among African American and European American mothers: Links to children's externalizing behaviors. *Developmental Psychology, 32,* 1065–1072.

De Boysson-Bardies, B., Vihman, M., Roug-Hellichius, L., Durand, C., Landberg, I., & Arao, F. (1992). Material evidence of infant selection from target language: A cross-linguistic study. In C. A. Ferguson, L. Menn, & C. Stoel Gammon (Eds.), *Phonological development* (pp. 369–391). Timonium, MD: York Press.

DeCarie, T. C. (1961). A study of the mental and emotional development of the thalidomide child. In B. Foss (Ed.), *Determinants of infant behavior* (Vol. 4). London: Methuen.

DeCasper, A., & Fifer, W. (1980). Of human bonding: Newborns prefer their mothers' voices. *Science, 12,* 305–317.

DeCasper, A., & Spence, M. (1991). Auditory mediated behavior during the perinatal period. A cognitive view. In M. Weiss & P. Zelazo (Eds.), *Newborn attention* Norwood, NJ: Ablex.

DeCasper, A. J., & Spence, M. (1986). Newborns prefer a familiar story over an unfamiliar one. *Infant Behavior and Development, 9,* 133–150.

de Houwer, A. (1995). Bilingual language acquisition. In P. Fletcher & B. MacWhinney (Eds.), *The handbook of child language* (pp. 219–250). Oxford: Basil Blackwell.

Dekovic, M., & Janssens, J. M. (1992). Parents' child-rearing style and child's sociometric status. *Developmental Psychology, 28,* 925–932.

DeLisi, R., & Staudt, J. (1980). Individual differences in college students' performance on formal operations tasks. *Journal of Applied Developmental Psychology, 1,* 201–208.

DeLoache, J. S., (1987). Rapid change in symbolic functioning of very young children. *Science, 238,* 1556–1557.

DeLoache, J. S. (1989). The development of representation in young children. In H. W. Reese (Ed.), *Advances in child development and behavior* (Vol. 22, pp. 1–39). New York: Academic Press.

DeLoache, J. S. (1995). Early understanding and use of symbols: The model model. *Current Directions in Psychological Science, 4,* 109–113.

DeLoache, J. S., & Brown, A. L. (1983). Very young children's memory for the location of objects in a large-scale environment. *Child Development, 54,* 888–897.

DeLoache, J. S., Miller, K., & Rosengren, K. (1997). The credible shrinking room: Very young children's performance in symbolic and non-symbolic tasks. *Psychological Science, 8,* 308–314.

DeLoache, J. S., Miller, K. F., & Pierroutsakos, S. L. (1998). Reasoning and problem solving. In W. Damon (Gen. Ed.), D. Kuhn, & R. S. Siegler (Vol. Eds.), *Handbook of child psychology, Vol. 2. Cognition, perception, and language* (pp. 801–850). New York: Wiley.

Demos, V. (1982). Facial expressions of infants and toddlers. In T. Field & A. Fogel (Eds.), *Emotion and early interaction* (pp. 127–160). Hillsdale, NJ: Erlbaum.

Dempster, F. N. (1985). Proactive interference in sentence recall: Topic similarity effects and individual differences. *Memory and Cognition, 13,* 81–89.

DeMulder, E., Tarullo, L., Klimes-Dougan, B., Free, K., & Radke-Yarrow, M. (1995). Personality disorders of affectively ill mothers: Links to maternal behavior. *Journal of Personality Disorders, 9,* 199–212.

Denham, S. A. (1997). ``When I have a bad dream, mommy holds me": Preschoolers' conceptions of emotions, parental socialization, and emotional competence. *International Journal of Behavioral Development, 20,* 301–320.

Denham, S. A., & Couchoud, E. A. (1991). Social-emotional predictors of preschoolers' responses to adult negative emotion. *Journal of Child Psychology and Psychiatry, 32,* 595–608.

Denham, S. A., & Grout, L. (1992). Mothers' emotional expressiveness and coping: Relations with preschoolers' social-emotional competence. *Genetic, Social, and General Psychology Monographs, 118,* 73–101.

Denham, S. A., Renwick-DeBardi, S., & Hewes, S. (1994). Emotional communication between mothers and preschoolers: Relations with emotional competence. *Merrill-Palmer Quarterly, 40,* 488–508.

Dennis, W. (1940). Does culture appreciably affect patterns of infant behavior? *Journal of Social Psychology, 12,* 305–317.

DeRosier, M., & Kupersmidt, J. B. (1991). Costa Rican children's perceptions of their social networks. *Developmental Psychology, 27,* 656–662.

Derryberry, D., & Rothbart, M. K. (1988). Arousal, affect, and attention as components of temperament. *Journal of Personality and Social Psychology, 55,* 958–966.

Desai, S., Chase-Lansdale, P. L., & Michael, R. T. (1989). Mother or market: Effects of maternal employment on intellectual abilities of four-year-old children. *Demography, 26,* 545–561.

Desai, S., Michael, R. T., & Chase-Lansdale, P. L. (1990). *The home environment: A mechanism through which maternal employment affects children.* Unpublished manuscript.

deVilliers, J. G., & deVilliers, P. A. (1973). A cross-sectional study of the acquisition of grammatical morphemes in child speech. *Journal of Psycholinguistic Research, 2,* 267–278.

deVilliers, P. A., & deVilliers, J. G. (1972). Early judgments of semantic and syntactic acceptability by children. *Journal of Psycholinguistic Research, 1,* 299–310.

deVilliers, P. A., & deVilliers, J. G. (1979). *Early language.* Cambridge, MA: Harvard University Press.

deVilliers, P. A., & deVilliers, J. G. (1992). Language Development. In M. E. Lamb & M. H. Bornstein (Eds.), *Developmental psychology: An advanced textbook* (3rd ed.). Hillsdale, NJ: Erlbaum.

DeVries, M., & Sameroff, A. J. (1984). Culture and temperament: Influences on temperament in three East African Societies. *American Journal of Orthopsychiatry, 54,* 83–96.

Diaz, R. M. (1985). Bilingual cognitive development: Addressing three gaps in current research. *Child Development, 56,* 1376–1388.

Diedrich, F. T., & Warren, W. H., Jr. (1995). Why change gaits? Dynamics of the walk-run transition. *Journal of Experimental Psychology: Human Perception & Performance, 21,* 183–202.

Diener, C. I., & Dweck, C. S. (1978). An analysis of learned helplessness: Continuous changes in performance, strategy and achievement cognitions following failure. *Journal of Personality and Social Psychology, 36,* 451–462.

Dietrich, K. N., Berger, O. G., Succop, P. A., Hammond, P. B., & Bornschein, R. L. (1993). The developmental consequences of low to moderate prenatal and postnatal lead exposure: Intellectual attainment in the Cincinnati Lead Study cohort following school entry. *Neurotoxicology and Teratology, 13,* 37–44.

DiLalla, L. F., Thompson, L. A., Plomin, R., Phillips, K., Faga, J. F., Haith, M. M., Cyphers, L. H., & Fulker, D. W. (1990). Infant predictors of preschool and adult IQ: A study of infant twins and their parents. *Developmental Psychology, 26,* 759–769.

DiPietro, J. A. (1981). Rough and tumble play: A function of gender. *Developmental Psychology, 17,* 50–58.

Dishion, T. J., French, D. C., & Patterson, G. R. (1995). The development and ecology of antisocial behavior. In D. Cicchetti & D. J. Cohen (Eds.), *Developmental psychopathology: Vol. 2. Risk, disorder, and adaptation* (pp. 421–471). New York: Wiley.

Dittrichova, J. (1969). The development of premature infants. In R. J. Robinson (Ed.), *Brain and early development.* London: Academic.

Dix, T. (1991). The affective organization of parenting: Adaptive and maladaptive processes. *Psychological Bulletin, 110(1),* 3–25.

Dobson, V., & Teller, D. Y. (1978). Visual acuity in human infants: A review and comparison of behavioral and electrophysiological studies. *Vision Research, 18,* 1469–1483.

Dodge, K. A. (1985). A social information processing model of social competence in children. In M. Perlmutter (Ed.), *Minnesota symposia on child psychology* (Vol. 18, pp. 77–126). Hillsdale, NJ: Erlbaum.

Dodge, K. A. (1985). Attributional bias in aggressive children. In Philip C. Kendall (Ed.), *Advances in cognitive-behavioral research and therapy, Vol. 4.* (pp. 73–110). Orlando, FL: Academic Press.

Dodge, K. A., & Coie, J. D. (1987). Social information-processing factors in reactive and proactive aggression in children's peer groups. *Journal of Personality and Social Psychology, 53,* 1146–1158.

Dodge, K. A., & Feldman, E. (1990). Issues in social cognition and sociometric status. In S. R. Asher & J. D. Coie (Eds.), *Peer rejection: Origins, consequences and intervention.* New York: Cambridge University Press.

Dodge, K. A., & Frame, C. L. (1982). Social cognitive biases and deficits in aggressive boys. *Child Development, 53,* 620–635.

Dodge, K. A., Pettit, G. S., McClaskey, C. L., & Brown, M. M. (1987). Social competence in children. *Monographs of the Society for Research in Child Development, 51,* (2, Serial No. 213).

Dolgin, K. G., & Behrend, D. A. (1984). Children's knowledge about animates and inanimates. *Child Development, 55,* 1646–1650.

Dominick, J. R., & Greenberg, B. S. (1972). Attitudes toward violence: The interaction of television exposure, family attitudes, and social class. In G. A. Comstock & E. A. Rubenstein (Eds.), *Television and social behavior: Television and adolescent aggressiveness* (Vol. 3, pp. 314–335). Washington, DC: Government Printing Office.

Doris, J. (Ed.). (1991). *The suggestibility of children's recollections.* Washington, DC: American Psychological Association.

Dornbusch, S. M., Carlsmith, J. M., Bushwall, S. J., Leiderman, H., Hfastorf, A. H., Gross, R. T., & Rutter, P. (1983, April). *Single parents, extended households, and the control of adolescents.* Paper presented at the Pacific Sociological Meetings, San Jose, CA.

Douvan, E., & Adelson, J. (1966). *The adolescent experience.* New York, Wiley.

Downey, G., & Coyne, J. C. (1990). Children of depressed parents: An integrative review. *Psychological Bulletin, 108,* 50–76.

Downs, R. M., & Liben, L. S. (1986). Children's understanding of maps. In P. Ellen & C. Thinus-Blanc (Eds.), *Cognitive processes and spatial orientation in animal and man: Vol. 1. Neurophysiology of spatial knowledge and developmental aspects.* Dordrecht, Holland: Martinius Nijhoff.

Drabman, R. S., & Thomas, M. H. (1976). Does watching violence on television cause apathy? *Pediatrics, 52,* 329–331.

Dreher, M. C., Nugent, K., & Hudgins, R. (1994). Prenatal marijuana exposure and neonatal outcomes in Jamaica: An ethnographic study. *Pediatrics, 93,* 254–260.

Drew, C. J., Hardman, M. L., & Logan, D. R. (1996). *Mental retardation: A life cycle approach* (6th ed.). New York: Macmillan.

Dryfoos, J. (1994). *Full Service Schools: A revolution in health and social services for children, youth and families.* San Francisco, CA: Jossey-Bass, Inc.

Dubowitz, L., & Dubowtiz, V. (1981). *The neurological assessment of the preterm and full-term newborn infant.* Philadelphia: Lippincott.

Duke, P. M., Carlsmith, J. M., Jennings, D., Martin, J. A., Dornbusch, S. M., Siegel-Gorelick, B., & Gross, R. T. (1982). Educational correlates of early and late sexual maturation in adolescence. *Journal of Pediatrics, 100,* 633.

Dumas, J. E., & Wahler, R. G. (1985). Indiscriminate mothering as a contextual factor in aggressive oppositional child behavior. *Journal of Abnormal Child Psychology, 13,* 1–17.

Dunn, J. (1987). The beginning of moral understanding. In J. Kagan and S. Lamb (Eds.), *The emergence of morality in young children.* Chicago: University of Chicago Press.

Dunn, J. (1988). *The beginnings of social understanding.* Cambridge, MA: Harvard University Press.

Dunn, J. (1989). *The beginnings of social understanding.* Cambridge, MA: Harvard University Press.

Dunn, J. (1992). *Fights and fantasies: Siblings and their separate lives.* Invited address at the fourth annual convention of the American Psychological Society. San Diego, CA.

Dunn, J. (1993). *Young children's close relationships.* Newbury Park, CA: Sage.

Dunn, J. (1994). Changing minds and changing relationships. In C. Lewis & P. Mitchell (Eds.), *Children's early understanding of mind: Origins and development* (pp. 297–310). Hove, England: Erlbaum.

Dunn, J., & Brown, J. (1991). Relationships, talk about feelings, and the development of affect regulation in early childhood. In J. Garber & K. Dodge (Eds.), *The development of emotional regulation and dysregulation.* New York: Cambridge University Press.

Dunn, J., Brown, J., & Beardsall, L. (1991). Family talk about feeling states and children's later understanding of others' emotions. *Developmental Psychology, 27,* 448–455.

Dunn, J., Brown, J. R., & Maguire, M. (1995). The development of children's moral sensibility: Individual differences and emotional understanding. *Developmental Psychology, 31,* 649–659.

Dunn, J., & Kendrick, C. (1982a). Interaction between young siblings: Association with the interaction between mother and firstborn. *Developmental Psychology, 17,* 336–343.

Dunn, J., & Kendrick, C. (1982b). The speech of two- and three-year-olds to infant siblings: "Baby talk" and the context of communication. *Journal of Child Language, 9,* 579–595.

Dunn, J., & Plomin, R. (1991). Why are siblings so different? The significance of differences in sibling experiences within the family. *Family Process, 30,* 271–283.

Dunn, J., Stocker, C., & Plomin, R. (1990). Nonshared experiences within the family: Correlates of behavioral problems in middle childhood. *Development and Psychopathology, 2,* 113–126.

DuPaul, G. J., & Barkley, R. A. (1990). Medication therapy. In R. A. Barkley, *Attention-deficit hyperactivity disorder: A handbook for diagnosis and treatment* (pp. 573–612). New York: Guilford.

DuPaul, G. J., Barkley, R. A., & McMurray, M. B. (1991). Therapeutic effects of medication on ADHD: Implications for school psychologists. *School Psychology Review, 20,* 213–219.

Dura, J. R., & Kiecolt-Glaser, J. K. (1991). Family transitions, stress and health. In P. A. Cowan & E. M. Hetherington (Eds.), *Family transitions.* Hillsdale, NJ: Erlbaum.

Dusek, J. B. (1991). *Adolescent development and behavior* (2nd ed.). Englewood Cliffs, NJ: Prentice-Hall.

Duyme, M. (1988). School success and social class: An adoption study. *Developmental psychology, 24,* 203–209.

Dweck, C. S. (1991). Self-theories and goals. Their role in motivation, personality, and development. In D. Dienstbier (Ed.), *Nebraska symposium on motivation* (Vol. 36, pp. 199–255). Lincoln: University of Nebraska Press.

Dweck, C. S., & Bempechat, J. (1983). Children's theories of intelligence: Consequences for learning. In S. G. Paris, G. M. Olson, & H. W. Stevenson (Eds.), *Learning and motivation in the classroom.* Hillsdale, NJ: Erlbaum.

Dweck, C. S., & Goetz, T. E. (1977). Attributions and learned helplessness. In J. H. Harvey, W. Ickes, & R. F. Kidd (Eds.), *New directions in attribution research* (Vol. 2). Hillsdale, NJ: Erlbaum.

Dweck, C. S., & Leggett, E. L. (1988). A social-cognitive approach to motivation and personality. *Psychological Review, 95,* 256–273.

East, P. L., & Rook, K. S. (1993). Compensatory patterns of support among children's peer relationships: A test using school friends, nonschool friends, and siblings. *Developmental Psychology, 28,* 163–172.

Eaton, W., & VonBargen, D. (1981). Asynchronous development of gender understanding in preschool children. *Child Development, 52,* 1020–1027.

Eaton, W. O., & Ritchot, K. F. (1995). Physical maturation and information-processing speed in middle childhood. *Developmental Psychology, 31,* 967–972.

Eccles, J. S. (1985). Sex differences in achievement patterns. In T. Sonderegger (Ed.), *Nebraska symposium on motivation.* Lincoln: University of Nebraska Press.

Eccles, J. S., Jacobs, J., Harold, R., Yoon, K. S., Abreton, A., & Freedman-Doan, C. (1993). Parents' and gender-role socialization during the middle childhood and adolescent years. In S. Oskamp & M. Costanzo (Eds.), *Gender issues in contemporary society* (pp. 59–83). Newbury Park, CA: Sage.

Eccles, J. S., Lord, S., & Midgley, C. (1991). What are we doing to early adolescents? The impact of educational contexts on early adolescents. *American Journal of Education, 99,* 521–542.

Eccles, J. S., Lord, S. E., & Roeser, R. W. (1996). Round holes, square pegs, rocky roads and sore feet: The impact of stage-environment fit on young adolescents' experiences in schools and families. In D. Cicchetti & S. L. Toth (Eds.), *Adolescence: Opportunities and challenges. Rochester symposium on developmental psychopathology* (Vol. 7, pp. 47–92). Rochester, NY: University of Rochester Press.

Eccles, J. S., & Midgley, C. (1989). Stage/environment fit: Developmentally appropriate classrooms for early adolescents. In R. E. Ames & C. Ames (Eds.), *Research on motivation in education* (Vol. 3). New York: Academic.

Eccles, J. S., Wigfield, A., & Schiefele, U. (1998). Motivation to succeed. In W. Damon (Gen. Ed.) & N. Eisenberg (Vol. Ed.), *Handbook of child psychology: Vol. 3 Social, emotional, and personality development* (5th ed.). New York: Wiley.

Eckerman, C. O. (1989). *Imitation and the achievement of coordinated action.* Paper presented at the biennial meeting of the Society for Research in Child Development, Kansas City, KS.

Eckerman, C. O. (1993). Imitation and toddlers' achievement of co-ordinated action with others. In J. Nadel & L. Camaioni (Eds.), *New perspectives in early communicative development* (pp. 116–156). New York: Routledge.

Eckerman, C. O., & Didow, S. M. (1988). Lessons drawn from observing young peers together. *Acta Paeditrica Scandinavica, 77* (Suppl. 344), 55–70.

Eckerman, C. O., Whatley, J. L., & Kutz, S. L. (1975). Growth of social play with peers during the second year of life. *Developmental Psychology, 11,* 42–49.

Edelman, M. S., & Omark, D. R. (1973). Dominance hierarchies in young children. *Social Science Information, 12,* 1.

Eder, D. (1985). The cycle of popularity: Interpersonal relations among female adolescents. *Sociology of Education, 58,* 154–165.

Edmondson, R. (1994). Drug use and pregnancy. In R. J. Simeonsson (Ed.), *Risk, resilience and prevention: Promoting the well being of all children.* Baltimore, MD: Brooks.

Edmonson, M. B., Stoddard, J. J., & Owens, L. M. (1997). Hospital readmission with feeding-related problems after early postpartum discharge of normal newborns. *The Journal of the American Medical Association, 278,* 299–303.

Edwards, C. P. (1980). The comparative study of the development of moral judgment and reasoning. In R. L. Munroe, R. Munroe, & B. B. Whiting (Eds.), *Handbook of cross-cultural human development.* New York: Garland.

Edwards, C. P. (1992). Cross-cultural perspectives on family-peer relations. In R. D. Parke & G. W. Ladd (Eds.), *Family-peer relationships: Modes of linkage* (pp. 285–316). Hillsdale, NJ: Erlbaum.

Edwards, C. P., & Lewis, M. (1979). Young children's concepts of social relations: Social functions and social objects. In M. Lewis & L. A. Rosenblum (Eds.), *The child and its family: Genesis of behavior* (Vol. 1). New York: Plenum.

Edwards, C. P., & Whiting, B. B. (1993). "Mother, older sibling, and me": The overlapping roles of caregivers and companions in the social world of two- and three-year-olds in Ngeca, Kenya. In K. MacDonald (Ed.), *Parent-child play: Descriptions and implications* (pp. 305–329). Albany, NY: State University of New York Press.

Egeland, B., Jacobvitz, D., & Sroufe, L. A. (1988). Breaking the cycle of abuse. *Child Development, 59,* 1080–1088.

Egeland, B., & Sroufe, L. A. (1981a). Attachment and early maltreatment. *Child Development, 52,* 44–52.

Egeland, B., & Sroufe, L. A. (1981b). Developmental sequelae of maltreatment in infancy. *New Directions for Child Development, 11,* 77–92.

Ehrhardt, A. A. (1987). A transactional perspective on the development of gender differences. In J. M. Reinisch, L. A. Rosenblum, & S. A. Sanders (Eds.), *Masculinity/femininity: Basic perspectives.* New York: Oxford University Press.

Eiduson, B. T., Kornfein, M., Zimmerman, I. L., & Weisner, T. S. (1988). Comparative socialization practices in traditional and alternative families. In G. Handel (Ed.), *Childhood socialization* (pp. 73–101). Hawthorne, NY: Aldine de Gruyter.

Eilers, R. E., Oller, D. K., Levine, S., Basinger, D., Lynch, M. P., & Urbano, C. (1993). The role of prematurity and socioeconomic status in the onset of canonical babbling in infants. *Infant Behavior & Development, 16,* 297–315.

Eimas, P. D. (1994). Categorization in early infancy and the continuity of development. *Cognition, 50,* 83–93.

Eimas, P. D., Quinn, P. C., & Cowan, P. (1994). Development of exclusivity in perceptually based categories of young infants. *Journal of Experimental Child Psychology, 58,* 418–431.

Eisenberg, N. (1992). *The caring child.* Cambridge, MA: Harvard University Press.

Eisenberg, N., Boehnke, K., Schuhler, P., & Silbereisen, R. K. (1985). The development of prosocial behavior and cognitions in German children. *Journal of Cross-Cultural Psychology, 16,* 69–82.

Eisenberg, N., & Fabes, R. A. (1998). Prosocial development. In W. Damon (Gen. Ed.) & N. Eisenberg (Vol. Ed.), *Handbook of child psychology: Vol. 3. Social, emotional, and personality development.* 9th ed. (pp. 701–778). New York: Wiley.

Eisenberg, N., Fabes, R. A., Carlo, G., Speer, A. L., Switzer, G., Karbon, M., & Troyer, D. (1993). The relations of empathy-related emotions and maternal practices to children's comforting behavior. *Journal of Experimental Child Psychology, 55,* 131–150.

Eisenberg, N., Fabes, R. A., Guthrie, I. K., & Murphy, B. C. (1996). The relations of regulation and emotionality to problem behavior in elementary school children. *Development & Psychopathology, 8,* 141–162.

Eisenberg, N., Fabes, R. A., Miller, P. A., Shell, C., Shea, R., & May-Plumlee, T. (1990). Preschoolers' vicarious emotional responding and their situational and dispositional prosocial behavior. *Merrill-Palmer Quarterly, 36,* 507–529.

Eisenberg, N., Fabes, R. A., Nyman, M., Bernzweig, J., & Pinuelas, A. (1994). The relations of emotionality and regulation to children's anger-related reactions. *Child Development, 65,* 109–128.

Eisenberg, N., Lennon, R., & Roth, K. (1983). Prosocial development: A longitudinal study. *Developmental Psychology, 19,* 846–855.

Eisenberg, N., Murray, E., & Hite, T. (1982). Children's reasoning regarding sex-typed toy choices. *Child Development, 49,* 500–504.

Eisenberg, N., & Shell, R. (1986). Prosocial moral judgment and behavior in children: The mediating role of cost. *Personality & Social Psychology Bulletin, 12*(4), 426–433.

Eisenberg, N., Shell, R., Pasternack, J., Lennon, R., Beller, R., & Mathy, R. M. (1987). Prosocial development in middle childhood: A longitudinal study. *Developmental Psychology, 23,* 712–718.

Ekman, P. (1972). Universal and cultural differences in facial expressions of emotion. In K. Cole (Ed.), *Nebraska symposium on motivation.* Lincoln: University of Nebraska Press.

Ekman, P. (1994). Antecedent events and emotion metaphors. In P. Ekman & R. J. Davidson (Eds.), *The nature of emotion* (pp. 146–149). New York: Oxford University Press.

Ekman, P., Friesen, W. V., O'Sullivan, M., Chan, A., Diacoyanni-Tarlatzis, I., Heider, K., Krauss, R., LeCompte, W. A., Pitcairn, T., Ricci Bilti, P. E., Scherer, K., Tomita, M., & Tzavaras, A. (1987). Universals and cultural differences in the judgements of facial expressions of emotion. *Journal of Personality and Social Psychology, 52,* 712–717.

Ekman, P., & Oster, H. (1979). Facial expressions of emotion. *Annual Review of Psychology, 30,* 527–554.

Elbers, L., & Ton, J. (1985). Playpen monologues: The interplay of words & babbles in the first words period. *Journal of Child Language, 12,* 551–565.

Elder, G. (1984). Parent-child behavior in hard times and the life course: A multi-generational perspective. In P. B. Baltes & O. G. Brim, Jr. (Eds.), *Life-span development and behavior.* New York: Academic.

Elder, G. (1998). The life course and human development. In W. Damon (Gen. Ed.) & R. M. Lerner (Vol. Ed.), *Handbook of child psychology: Vol. 1. Theoretical models of human development.* New York: Wiley.

Elder, G. H. (1974). *Children of the Great Depression.* Chicago: University of Chicago Press.

Eldredge, L., & Salamy, A. (1988). Neurobehavioral and neurophysiological assessment of healthy and "at risk" full-term infants. *Child Development, 59,* 186–192.

Elia, M., Musumeci, S. A., Ferri, R., & Bergonzi, P. (1995). Clinical and neurophysiological aspects of epilepsy in subjects with autism and mental retardation. *American Journal on Mental Retardation, 100,* 6–16.

Elicker, J., Egeland, B., & Sroufe, L. A. (1992). Predicting peer competence and peer relationships from early parent-child relationships. In R. D. Parke & G. W. Ladd (Eds.), *Family-Peer relationships: Modes of linkage.* Hillsdale, NJ: Erlbaum.

Ellis, S., Rogoff, B., & Cromer, C. (1981). Age segregation in children's social interactions. *Developmental Psychology, 17,* 399–407.

Ellsworth, C. P., Muir, D. W., & Hains, S. M. J. (1993). Social competence and person-object differentiation. An analysis of the still face effect. *Developmental Psychology, 29,* 63–73.

Emde, R. N., Gaensbauer, T. J., & Harmon, R. J. (1976). Emotional expression in infancy: A biobehavioral study. *Psychological Issues* (Vol. 10, No. 37). New York: International Universities Press.

Emde, R. N., Harmon, R. J., Metcalf, D., Koenig, K. L., & Wagonfeld, S. (1971). Stress and neonatal sleep. *Psychosomatic Medicine, 33,* 491–497.

Emery, R. E. (Ed.). (1988). *Marriage, divorce and children's adjustment.* Newbury Park, CA: Sage.

Enright, R. D., & Sutterfield, S. J. (1980). An ecological validation of social cognitive development. *Child Development, 51,* 156–161.

Entwisle, D. R., & Alexander, K. L. (1987). Long-term effects of cesarean delivery on parents' beliefs and children's schooling. *Developmental Psychology, 23,* 676–682.

Entwisle, D. R., & Doering, S. G. (1981). *The first birth.* Baltimore, MD: Johns Hopkins University Press.

Entwisle, D. R., & Frasure, N. E. (1974). A contradiction resolved: Children's processing of syntactic cues. *Developmental Psychology, 10,* 852–857.

Epstein, J. L. (1980). *After the bus arrives: Resegregation in desegregated schools.* Paper presented at the meeting of the American Educational Research Association, Boston.

Epstein, J. L. (1990). School and family connections: Theory, research, & implications for integrating sociologies of education and family. *Marriage & Family Review, 15,* 99–126.

Epstein, L. H., Valoski, A. M., Vara, S., McCurley, J., Wisniewski, L., Kalarchian, M. A., Klein, K. R., & Shrager, L. R. (1995). Effects of decreasing sedentary behavior and increasing activity on weight change in obese children. *Health Psychology, 14,* 109–115.

Epstein, L. H., Wing, R. R., Koeske, R., & Valoski, A. (1987). Long-term effects of family-based treatment of childhood obesity. *Journal of Counsulting and Clinical Psychology, 55,* 91–95.

Epstein, L. R., Valoski, A., Wing, R. R., & McCurley, J. (1994). Ten-year outcomes of behavioral family-based treatment for childhood obesity. *Health Psychology, 13,* 373–383.

Erdley, C. A., Loomis, C. C., Cain, K. M., & Dumas-Hines, F. (1997). Relations among children's social goals, implicit personality theories, and responses to social failure. *Developmental Psychology, 33,* 263–272.

Erel, O., & Burman, B. (1995). Interrelatedness of marital relations and parent-child relations: A meta-analytic review. *Psychological Bulletin, 118,* 108–132.

Erickson, M. F., Sroufe, L. A., & Egeland, B. (1985). The relationship between quality of attachment and behavior problems in preschool in a high risk sample. In I. Bretherton & E. Waters (Eds.), Growing points of attachment theory and research. *Monographs of the Society for Research in Child Development, 50* (1–2, Serial No. 109).

Erikson, E. H. (1970). Reflections on the dissent of contemporary youth. *International Journal of Psycho-Analysis, 51,* 11–22.

Eriksson, M., Catz, C. S., & Yaffe, S. J. (1973). Drugs and pregnancy. In H. Osofsky (Ed.), *Clinical obstetrics and gynecology: High-risk pregnancy with emphases upon maternal and fetal well being* (Vol. 16, pp. 192–224). New York: Harper & Row.

Eron, L. D., & Huesmann, L. R. (1984). The control of aggressive behavior by changes in attitudes, values and the conditions of learning. In R. J. Blanchard & C. Blanchard (Eds.), *Advances in the study of aggression* (Vol. 2). New York: Academic.

Ervin-Tripp, S. (1979). Children's verb turn taking. In E. Ochs & B. Schieffelin (Eds.), *Developmental pragmatics.* New York: Academic.

Escorihuela, R. M., Fernandez-Teruel, A., Tobena, A., Vivas, N. M., Marmol, F., Badia, A., & Dierssen, M. (1995). Early environmental stimulation produces long-lasting changes on beta-adrenoceptor transduction system. *Neurobiology of Learning and Memory, 64,* 49–57.

Everett, C. A., & Volgy, S. S. (1993). Treating the child in systemic family therapy. In T. Kratochwill & R. Morris (Eds.), *Handbook of psychotherapy with children and adolescents* (pp. 247–257). Boston: Allyn & Bacon.

Fabes, R. A., & Eisenberg, N. (1996). *An examination of age and sex differences in prosocial behavior and empathy.* Unpublished data, Arizona State University.

Fabrikant, G. (1996, April 8). The young and restless audience. Computers and videos cut into children's time for watching TV and ads. *New York Times,* p. C1.

Fagan, J. F. (1984). The relationship of novelty preferences during infancy to later intelligence and later recognition memory. *Intelligence, 8,* 339–346.

Fagan, J. F., III. (1992). Intelligence: A theoretical viewpoint. *Current Directions in Psychological Science, 1,* 82–86.

Fagan, J. F., III, Drotar, D., Berkoff, K., Peterson, N., Kiziri-Mayengo, R., Guay, L., Ndugwa, C., & Zaidan, S. (1991). The Fagan Test of Infant Intelligence: Cross-cultural and racial comparisons. *Journal of Developmental and Behavioral Pediatrics, 12,* 168.

Fagot, B. I. (1973). Sex-related stereotyping of toddlers' behaviors. *Developmental Psychology, 9,* 429.

Fagot, B. I. (1985a). Beyond the reinforcement principle: Another step toward understanding sex role development. *Developmental Psychology, 21,* 1097–1104.

Fagot, B. I. (1985b). Changes in thinking about early sex role development. *Developmental Review, 5,* 83–98.

Fagot, B. I., & Hagan, R. (1991). Observations of parent reactions to sex-stereotyped behaviors: Age and sex effects. *Child Development, 62,* 617–628.

Fagot, B. I., & Leinbach, M. D. (1987). Socialization of sex roles within the family. In D. B. Carter (Ed.), *Current conceptions of sex roles and sex typing: Theory and research* (pp. 89–100). New York: Praeger.

Fagot, B. I., & Leinbach, M. D. (1989). The young child's gender schema: Environmental input, internal organization. *Child Development, 60,* 663–672.

Fagot, B. I., & Leinbach, M. D. (1992). Gender-role development in young children: From discrimination to labeling. *Developmental Review, 13,* 205–224.

Fagot, B. I., Leinbach, M. D., & Hagan, R. (1986). Gender labeling and the adoption of sex typed behaviors. *Developmental Psychology, 22,* 440–443.

Falbo, T., & Polit, D. F. (1986). Quantitative review of the only child literature: Research evidence and theory development, *Psychological Bulletin, 100,* 176–189.

Falmagne, R. (1980). The development of logical competence: A psycholinguistic perspective. In R. M. Kluovie & H. Spade (Eds.), *Developmental models of thinking.* New York: Academic.

Fantz, R. (1963). Pattern vision in newborn infants. *Science, 140,* 296–297.

Farnham-Diggory, S. (1990). *Schooling.* Cambridge, MA: Harvard University Press.

Farrar, M. J. (1992). Negative evidence and grammatical morpheme acquisition. *Developmental Psychology, 28,* 90–98.

Farrar, M. J., & Goodman, G. S. (1992). Developmental changes in event memory. *Child Development, 63,* 173–187.

Farrell, A. D., & Danish, S. T. (1993). Peer drug associations and emotional restraint: Causes or consequences of adolescents' drug use? *Journal of Consulting & Clinical Psychology, 61,* 327–334.

Farrington, D. P. (1993). The challenge of teenage antisocial behavior. In M. Rutter (Ed.), *Psychosocial disturbances in young people.* Cambridge: Cambridge University Press.

Farver, J. A. M. (1993). Cultural differences in scaffolding pretend play: A comparison of American and Mexican mother-child and sibling-child pairs. In K. MacDonald (Ed.), *Parent-child play: Descriptions and implications* (pp. 349–366). Albany, NY: State University of New York Press.

Farver, J. M. (1992). Cultural differences in scaffolding pretend play: A comparison of American and Mexican mother-child and sibling-child pairs. In K. B. MacDonald (Ed.), *Parents and children at play.* Albany, NY: SUNY Press.

Farver, J., & Howes, C. (1993). Cultural differences in American and Mexican mother-child pretend play. *Merrill-Palmer Quarterly, 39,* 344–358.

Farver, J., & Shin, Y. L. (1997). Social pretend play in Korean and Anglo-American preschoolers. *Child Development, 68,* 544–556.

Farver, J., Kim, Y. K., & Lee, Y. (1995). Cultural differences in Korean- and Anglo-American preschoolers social interaction and play behaviors. *Child Development, 66,* 1088–1099.

Federal Bureau of Investigation, U.S. Department of Justice. (1989). *Uniform crime reports.* Washington, DC.

Federal Interagency Forum on Child and Family Statistics. (1997). Washington, DC: U.S. Government Printing Office.

Fein, G. (1978). *Child development.* Englewood Cliffs, NJ: Prentice-Hall.

Fein, G. (1981). Pretend play: An integrative review. *Child Development, 52,* 1095–1118.

Fein, G. (1989). Mind, meaning and affect: Proposals for a theory of pretense. *Developmental Review, 9,* 345–363.

Feingold, A. (1988). Cognitive gender differences are disappearing. *American Psychologist, 43,* 95–103.

Feinman, S., & Lewis, M. (1983). Social referencing at ten months: A second-order effect on infants' responses to strangers. *Child Development, 54,* 878–887.

Feiring, C., & Lewis, M. (1987). The ecology of some middle class families at dinner. *International Journal of Behavioral Development, 10,* 377–390.

Feldman, D. H., & Goldsmith, L. T. (1991). *Nature's gambit.* New York: Teachers College Press.

Feldman, N. S., Klosson, E. C., Parsons, J. E., Rholes, W. S., & Ruble, D. N. (1976). Order of information presentation and children's moral judgments. *Child Development, 47,* 556–559.

Feldman, R. S., & Rimé, B. (Eds.). (1991). *Fundamentals of nonverbal behavior.* New York: Cambridge University Press.

Fenson, L., Dale, P. S., Reznick, J. S., Bates, E., Thal, D. J., & Pethick, S. J. (1994). Variability in early communicative development. *Monographs of the Society for Research in Child Development, 59,* (Serial No. 242).

Ferber, R. (1985). *Solve your child's sleep problems.* New York: Simon & Schuster.

Ferguson, T. J., & Rule, B. G. (1980). Effects of inferential sex, outcome severity and basis of responsibility on children's evaluations of aggressive acts. *Developmental Psychology, 16,* 141–146.

Ferguson, T. J., & Rule, B. G. (1982). Influences of inferential set, outcome intent and outcome severity on children's moral judgments. *Developmental Psychology, 18,* 843–851.

Fernald, A. (1985). Four-month-olds prefer to listen to motherese. *Infant Behavior and Development, 8,* 181–196.

Fernald, A. (1992). Meaningful melodies in mothers' speech to infants. In H. Papousek, U. Jurgens, & M. Papousek (Eds.), *Nonverbal communication: Comparative and developmental approaches.* Cambridge, England: Cambridge University Press.

Fernald, A., & Kuhl, P. K. (1987). Acoustical determinants of infant preference for motherese speech. *Infant Behavior and Development, 10,* 279–293.

Fernald, A., & Mazzie, C. (1991). Prosody and focus in speech to infants and adults. *Developmental Psychology, 27,* 209–221.

Fernald, A., & Morikawa, H. (1993). Common themes and cultural variations in Japanese and American mothers' speech to infants. *Child Development, 64,* 636–637.

Ferree, M. M. (1991). The gender division of labor in two-earner marriages: dimensions of variability and change. *Journal of Family Issues, 12,* 158–180.

Field, D. (1987). A review of preschool conservation training: An analysis of analyses. *Developmental Review, 7,* 210–251.

Field, T., & Goldson, E. (1984). Pacifying effects of nonnutritive sucking on term and preterm neonates during heelstick procedures. *Pediatrics, 74,* 1012–1015.

Field, T., Sandberg, D., Quetal, T. A., Garcia, R., & Rosario, M. (1985). Effects of ultrasound feedback on pregnancy, anxiety, fetal activity and neonate outcome. *Obstetrics and Gynecology, 66,* 525–528.

Field, T. M. (1978). Interaction behaviors of primary versus secondary caretaker fathers. *Developmental Psychology, 14,* 183–184.

Field, T. M. (1986). Affective responses to separation. In T. B. Brazelton & M. W. Yogman (Eds.), *Affective development in infancy.* Norwood, NJ: Ablex.

Field, T. M. (1990). *Infancy.* Cambridge, MA: Harvard University Press.

Field, T. M. (1992). Infants of depressed mothers. *Development and Psychopathology, 4,* 49–66.

Field, T. M., Schanberg, S. M., Schafedi, F., Bauer, C. R., Vega-Lahr, N., Garcia, R., Nystrom, J., & Kuhn, C. M. (1986). Effects of tactile/kinesthetic stimulation on preterm neonates. *Pediatrics, 77,* 654–658.

Field, T. M., & Walden, T. A. (1982a). Perception and production of facial expressions in infancy and early childhood. In H. W. Reese & L. P. Lipsitt (Eds.), *Advances in child development and behavior* (Vol. 16). New York: Academic Press.

Field, T. M., & Walden, T. A. (1982b). Production and discrimination of facial expressions by preschool children. *Child Development, 53,* 1299–1311.

Fiese, B. H. (1990). Playful relationships: A contextual analysis of mother-toddler interaction and symbolic play. *Child Development, 61,* 1648–1656.

Fiese, B. H. (1995). Family rituals. In D. Levinson (Ed.), *Encyclopedia of marriage and the family* (pp. 275–278). New York: Macmillan.

Fiese, B. H., & Kline, C. A. (1993). Development of the Family Ritual Questionnaire (FRQ): Initial reliability and validation studies. *Journal of Family Psychology, 6,* 290–299.

Fifer, W. P., & Moon, C. (1989). Auditory experience in the fetus. In W. P. Smotherman & S. R. Robinson (Eds.), *Behavior of the fetus* (pp. 175–187). Caldwell, NJ: Telford Press.

Fincham, F. D. (1994). Understanding the association between marital conflict and child adjustment: Overview. *Journal of Family Psychology, 8,* 123–127.

Finegan, J. K., Niccols, G. A., & Sitarenios, G. (1992). Relations between prenatal testosterone levels and cognitive abilities at 4 years. *Developmental Psychology, 28*(6), 1075–1089.

Finn, J. D., & Achilles, C. M. (1990). Answers and questions about class size: A statewide experiment. *American Educational Research Journal, 27,* 557–577.

Finnie, V., & Russell, A. (1988). Preschool children's social status and their mothers' behavior and knowledge in the supervisory role. *Developmental Psychology, 24,* 789–801.

Firsch, R. E. (1984). Fatness, puberty, and fertility. In J. Brooks-Gunn & A. C. Petersen (Eds.), *Girls at puberty: Biological, psychological, and social perspectives.* New York: Plenum.

Fischer, K. W., & Bullock, D. (1984). Cognitive development in middle childhood: Conclusions and new directions. In W. A. Collins & K. Heller (Eds.), *The elementary school years: Understanding development during middle childhood.* Washington, DC: National Academic Press.

Fischer, K. W., & Lazerson, A. (1984). A summary of parental development. In K. W. Fischer & A. Lazerson, *Human development* (p. 117). New York: Freeman.

Fischer, K. W., & Roberts, R. J. (1986). A developmental sequence of classification skills and errors in preschool children. Unpublished manuscript, Harvard University.

Fisher, C., Gleitman, H., & Gleitman, L. (1991). On the semantic content of subcategorization frames. *Cognitive Psychology, 23,* 331–392.

Fisher, C., Hall, D. G., Rakowitz, S., & Gleitman, L. (1994). When it is better to receive than to give: Syntactic and conceptual contraints on vocabulary growth. In L. Gleitman & B. Landau (Eds.), *The acquisition of lexicon* (pp. 333–376). Cambridge, MA: MIT Press/Elsevier.

Fisher, C. B., & Brone, R. J. (1991). Eating disorders in adolescence. In R. M. Lerner, A. C. Petersen, & J. Brooks-Gunn (Eds.), *Encyclopedia of Adolescence* (Vol. 1). New York: Garland.

Fisher, C. B., Jackson, J. F., & Villaruel, F. A. (1998). The study of ethnic minority children and youth in the United States. In W. Damon (Gen. Ed.) & R. M. Lerner (Vol. Ed.), *Handbook of child psychology: Vol. 1. Theoretical models of human development.* New York: Wiley.

Fisher-Thompson, D. (1990). Adult gender typing of children's toys. *Sex Roles, 23,* 291–303.

Fisher-Thompson, D. (1993). Adult toy purchase for children: Factors affecting sex-typed toy selection. *Journal of Applied Developmental Psychology, 14,* 385–406.

Fivush, R., & Hamond, N. R. (1990). Autobiographical memory across the preschool years: Toward reconceptualizing childhood amnesia. In R. Fivush & J. A. Hudson (Eds.), *Knowing and remembering in young children* (pp. 233–248). Cambridge, England: Cambridge University Press.

Fivush, R., Hudson, J., & Nelson, K. (1984). Children's long-term memory for a novel event: An exploratory study. *Merrill-Palmer Quarterly, 30,* 303–316.

Fivush, R., Kuebli, J., & Clubb, P. A. (1992). The structure of events and event representations: A developmental analysis. *Child Development, 63,* 188–201.

Flake, A. W., Roncarolo, M. G., Puck, J. M., Almeida-Porada, G., Evans, M. I., Johnson, M. P., Abella, E. M., Harrison, D. D., & Zanjani, E. D. (1996). Treatment of X-linked severe combined immunodeficiency by in utero transplantation of paternal bone marrow. *New England Journal of Medicine, 335,* 1806–1810.

Flavell, J. H. (1963). *The developmental psychology of Jean Piaget.* Princeton, NJ: Van Nostrand.

Flavell, J. H. (1985). *Cognitive development.* Englewood Cliffs, NJ: Prentice-Hall.

Flavell, J. H., Beach, D. R., & Chinsky, J. M. (1966). Spontaneous verbal rehearsal in a memory task as a function of age. *Child Development, 37,* 283–299.

Flavell, J. H., Flavell, E. R., Green, F. L., & Korfmacher, J. E. (1990). Do young children think of television images as pictures or real objects? *Journal of Broadcasting and Electronic Media, 34,* 399–419.

Flavell, J. H., Friedricks, A. G., & Hoyt, J. D. (1970). Developmental changes in memorization processes. *Cognitive Psychology, 1,* 324–340.

Flavell, J. H., Green, F. L., & Flavell, E. R. (1993). Children's understanding of the stream of consciousness. *Child Development, 64,* 387–398.

Flavell, J. H., Green, F. L., & Flavell, E. R. (1995a) The development of children's knowledge about attentional focus. *Developmental Psychology, 31,* 706–712.

Flavell, J. H., Green, F. L., & Flavell, E. R. (1995b) Young children's knowledge about thinking. *Monographs of the Society for Research in Child Development, 60,* 243–256.

Flavell, J. H., & Miller, P. H. (1998). Social cognition. In W. Damon (Gen. Ed.), D. Kuhn, & R. S. Siegler (Vol. Eds.), *Handbook of child psychology: Vol. 2. Cognition, perception, and language.* New York: Wiley.

Flavell, J. H., Miller, P. H., & Miller, S. A. (1993). *Cognitive development* (3rd ed.). Englewood Cliffs, NJ: Prentice-Hall.

Flavell, J. H., Speer, J. R., Green, F. L., & August, D. L. (1981). The development of comprehension monitoring and knowledge about communication. *Monographs of the Society for Research in Child Development, 46* (5, Serial No. 192).

Fletcher, A. C., Darling, N. E., Steinberg, L., & Dornbusch, S. (1995). The company they keep: Relation of adolescents' adjustment and behavior to their friends' perceptions of authoritative parenting in the social network. *Developmental Psychology, 31,* 300–310.

Flynn, J. R. (1984). The mean IQ of Americans: Massive gains 1932 to 1978. *Psychological Bulletin, 95,* 29–51.

Flynn, J. R. (1998). IQ trends over time: Intelligence, race, and meritocracy. In S. Durlauf, K. Arrow, & S. Bowles (Eds.), *Meritocracy and equality.* Princeton, NJ: Princeton University Press.

Foa, E. B., & Kozak, M. J. (1995). DSM-IV field trial: Obsessive-compulsive disorder. *American Journal of Psychiatry, 152,* 90–96.

Fogel, A. (1993). *Developing through relationships: Origins of communication, self, and culture.* Chicago: University of Chicago Press.

Folstein, S. E., & Rutter, M. L. (1988). Autism: Familial aggregation and genetic implications. *Journal of Autism and Developmental Disorders, 18,* 3–30.

Fombonne, E., & du Mazaubrun, C. (1992). Prevalence of infantile autism in four French regions. *Social Psychiatry & Psychiatric Epidemiology, 27,* 203–210.

Fonagy, P., Steele, H., & Steele, M. (1991). Maternal representations of attachment during pregnancy predict organization of infant-mother attachment at one year of age. *Child Development, 62,* 891–905.

Fordham, S., & Ogbu, J. V. (1986). Black students' school success: Coping with the burden of acting white. *Urban Review, 18,* 176–206.

Forrester, L. W., Phillips, S. J., & Clark, J. E. (1993). Locomotor co-ordination in infancy: The transition from walking to running. In G. J. P. Savelsbergh (Ed.), *The development of*

coordination in infancy* (pp. 359–393). Amsterdam: Elsevier.

Forssberg, H. (1985). Ontogeny of human locomotor control: I. Infant stepping, supported locomotion and the transition to independent locomotion. *Experimental Brain Research, 57,* 480–493.

Fox, H. E., Steinbrecher, M., Pessel, D., Inglis, J., Medvid, L., & Angel, E. (1978). Maternal ethanol ingestion and the occurrence of human fetal breathing movements. *American Journal of Obstetrics and Gynecology, 132,* 354–358.

Fox, N. A. (1991). If it's not left, it's right: Electroencephalograph asymmetry and the development of emotion. *American Psychologist, 46,* 863–872.

Fox, N. A., Calkins, S. D., & Bell, M. A. (1994). Neural plasticity and development in the first two years of life: Evidence from cognitive and socioemotional domains. *Development and Psychopathology, 6,* 677–696.

Fox, N. A., & Davidson, R. J. (1988). Patterns of brain electrical activity during facial signs of emotion in 10-month-old infants. *Developmental Psychology, 24,* 230–236.

Fox, N., Kimmerly, N. L., & Schafer, W. D. (1991). Attachment to mother/attachment to father: A meta-analysis. *Developmental Psychology, 62,* 210–225.

Fraiberg, S. (1977). *Insights from the blind.* New York: Basic Books.

Fraiberg, S., Lieberman, A., Pekarsky, J., & Pawl, J. (1981). Treatment and outcome in an infant psychiatry program. *Journal of Prevention Psychiatry, 1,* 143–167.

Francis, P. L., Self, P. A., & Horowitz, F. D. (1987). The behavioral assessment of the neonate: An overview. In J. Osofsky (Ed.), *Handbook of infancy* (2nd ed.). New York: Wiley.

Franco, F., & Butterworth, G. (1996). Pointing and social awareness: Declaring and requesting in the second year. *Journal of Child Language, 23,* 307–336.

Frank, A. (1967). *Anne Frank: The diary of a young girl* (translated from Dutch by B. M. Mooyaart-Doubleday). Garden City, NY: Doubleday.

Freedman, D. G. (1974). *Human infancy: An evolutionary perspective.* Hillsdale, NJ: Erlbaum.

Freedman, D. G. (1976). Infancy, biology, and culture. In L. P. Lipsitt (Ed.), *Developmental psychobiology: The significance of infancy.* Hillsdale, NJ: Erlbaum.

Freeman, N. H., & Lacohée, H. (1995). Making explicit 3-year-olds' implicit competence with their own false beliefs. *Cognition, 56,* 31–60.

Freidman, H. S., Tucker, J. S., Schwartz, J. E., Tomlinson-Keasey, C., Martin, L. R., Wingard, D. L., & Criqui, M. H. (1995). Psychosocial and behavioral predictors of longevity. *American Psychologist, 50,* 69–78.

French, D. C. (1988). Heterogeneity of peer-rejected boys: Aggressive and nonaggressive subtypes. *Child Development, 53,* 976–985.

French, D. C. (1990). Heterogeneity of peer rejected girls. *Child Development, 61,* 2028–2031.

Freud, A., & Burlingham, D. (1943). *Children and war.* New York: Basic Books.

Freud, A., & Dann, S. (1951). An experiment in group upbringing. In *The psychoanalytic study*

of the child (Vol. 6). New York: International Universities Press.

Frey, K. S., & Ruble, D. N. (1992). Gender constancy and the "cost" of sex-typed behavior: A test of the conflict hypothesis. *Developmental Psychology, 28,* 714–721.

Friedrich, L. K., & Stein, A. H. (1973). Aggressive and prosocial television programs and the natural behavior of preschool children. *Monographs of the Society for Research in Child Development, 38* (Serial No. 151).

Frith, C., & Frith, U. (1978). Feature selection and classification: A developmental study. *Journal of Experimental Child Psychology, 25,* 413–428.

Frodi, A. M., & Lamb, M. E. (1980). Child abusers' responses to infant smiles and cries. *Child Development, 51,* 238–241.

Frodi, A. M., Lamb, M. E., Leavitt, L. A., & Donovan, W. K. (1978). Father's and mother's responses to infant smiles and cries. *Infant Behavior and Development, 1,* 187–198.

Fuligni, A. J. (1997). The academic achievement of adolescents from immigrant families: The roles of family background, attitudes, and behavior. *Child Development, 68,* 351–363.

Furman, W., & Gavin, L. A. (1989). Peers influence on adjustment and development. In T. J. Berndt & G. W. Ladd (Eds.), *Peer relationships in child development.* New York: Wiley.

Furman, W., & Masters, J. C. (1980). Affective consequences of social reinforcement, punishment, and neutral behavior. *Developmental Psychology, 16,* 100–104.

Furman, W., Rahe, D., & Hartup, W. W. (1979). Social rehabilitation of low-interactive preschool children by peer intervention. *Child Development, 50,* 915–922.

Furstenberg, F. F. (1993). How families manage risk and opportunity in dangerous neighborhoods. In W. J. Wilson (Ed.), *Sociology and the public agenda* (pp. 231–258). Newbury Park, CA: Sage.

Furstenberg, F. F., Jr., Brooks-Gunn, J., & Chase-Lansdale, L. (1989). Teenaged pregnancy and child bearing. *American Psychologist, 44,* 313–320.

Furstenberg, F. F., Jr., & Cherlin, A. J. (1991). *Divided families: What happens to children when parents part.* Cambridge, MA: Harvard University Press.

Gadow, K. D. (1991). Clinical issues in child and adolescent psychopharmacology. *Journal of Consulting & Clinical Psychology, 59,* 842–852.

Gaines, L., & Esserman, J. (1981). A quantitative study of young children's comprehension of television programs and commercials. In J. F. Esserman (Ed.), *Television advertising and children: Issues, research and findings.* New York: Child Research Service.

Galen, B. R., & Underwood, M. K. (1997). A developmental investigation of social aggression among children. *Developmental Psychology, 33,* 589–600.

Galinsky, E., Howes, C., & Kontos, S. (1995). *The family child care training study.* New York: Families and Work Institute.

Gallaway, C., & Richards, B. J. (1994). *Input and interaction in language acquisition.* Cambridge: Cambridge University Press.

Galler, J. R., Ramsey, F., & Solimano, G. (1985). A follow-up study of effects of early malnutrition on subsequent development to fine motor skills in adolescence. *Pediatric Research, 19*, 524–527.

Garbarino, J. (1982). Sociocultural risk: Dangers to competence. In C. Kopp & J. Krakow (Eds.), *Child development in a social context* (pp. 630–685). Reading, MA: Addison-Wesley.

Garbarino, J. (1989). The psychologically battered child. San Francisco: Jossey-Bass.

Garbarino, J. (1995). *Raising children in a socially toxic environment.* San Francisco: Jossey-Bass.

Garbarino, J., & Kostelny, K. (1996). The effects of political violence on Palestinian children's behavior problems: A risk accumulation model. *Child Development, 67*, 33–45.

Garbarino, J., & Sherman, D. (1980). High-risk neighborhoods and high-risk families: The human ecology of child maltreatment. *Child Development, 51*, 188–198.

Garcia Coll, C. T. (1990). Developmental outcome of minority infants: A process-oriented look into our beginnings. *Child Development, 61*, 270–289.

Gardner, H. (1983). *Frames of mind: The theory of multiple intelligences.* New York: Basic Books.

Gardner, H. (1993). *Multiple intelligences: The theory in practice.* New York: Basic Books.

Gardner, H. (1998). Extraordinary cognitive achievements (ECA): A symbol systems approach. In W. Damon (Gen. Ed.), and R. M. Lerner (Vol. Ed.), *Handbook of child psychology: Vol. 1. Theoretical models of human development* (5th ed., pp. 415–466). New York: Wiley.

Gardner, H., Kornhaber, M., & Wake, W. (1996). *Intelligence: Multiple perspectives.* Fort Worth, TX: Harcourt Brace.

Gardner, H., Krechevsky, M., Sternberg, R. J., & Okagaki, L. (1994). Intelligence in context: Enhancing students' practical intelligence for school. In K. McGilly (Ed.), *Classroom lessons: Integrating cognitive theory and classroom practice* (pp. 105–127). Cambridge, MA: MIT Press.

Garmezy, N., & Masten, A. S. (1994). Chronic adversities. In M. Rutter, E. Taylor, & L. Hersov (Eds.), *Child and adolescent psychiatry: Modern approaches* (3rd ed., pp. 191–208). London: Blackwell.

Garmezy, N., & Rutter, M. (1983). *Stress, coping and development in children.* Baltimore, MD: Johns Hopkins University Press.

Garner, P. W. (1996). The relations of emotional role taking, affective/moral attributions, and emotional display rule knowledge to low-income school-age children's social competence. *Journal of Applied Developmental Psychology, 17*, 19–36.

Garner, P. W., & Power, T. G. (1996). Preschoolers emotional control in the disappointment paradigm and its relation to temperament, emotional knowledge and family expressiveness. *Child Development, 67*, 1406–1429.

Garvey, C. (1990a). *Children's talk.* Cambridge, MA: Harvard University Press.

Garvey, C. (1990b). *Play.* Cambridge, MA: Harvard University Press.

Gaulden, M. E. (1992). Maternal age effect: The enigma of Down Syndrome and other trisomic conditions. *Mutation Research, 296*, 69–88.

Gauvain, M. (1993). Spatial thinking and its development in sociocultural context. *Annals of Child Development, 9*, 67–102.

Gauvain, M., & Rogoff, B. (1989). Collaborative problem solving and children's planning skills. *Developmental Psychology, 25*, 139–151.

Gelfand, D., & Teti, D. (1991). The effects of maternal depression on children. *Clinical Psychology Review, 10*, 329–353.

Gelfand, D. M., Jensen, W. R., & Drew, C. J. (1982). *Understanding child behavior disorders.* New York: Holt, Rinehart, and Winston.

Gelfand, D. M., Jensen, W. R., & Drew, C. J. (1997). *Understanding child behavior disorders* (3rd ed.). Fort Worth TX: Harcourt Brace.

Gelman, R. (1972). Logical capacity of very young children: Number invariance rules. *Child Development, 43*, 75–90.

Gelman, R. (1978). Cognitive development. *Annual Review of Psychology, 29*, 297–332.

Gelman, R. (1979). Preschool thought. *American Psychologist, 34*, 900–905.

Gelman, R. (1990). First principles organize attention to and learning about relevant data: Number and the animate-inanimate distinction as examples. *Cognitive Science, 14*, 79–106.

Gelman, R., & Baillargeon, R. (1983). A review of some Piagetian concepts. In J. H. Falvell & E. M. Markman (Eds.), *Handbook of child psychology: Cognitive development* (Vol. 3). New York: Wiley.

Gelman, R., & Gallistel, C. R. (1978). *The child's understanding of number.* Cambridge, MA: Harvard University Press.

Gelman, R., & Meck, E. (1983). Preschoolers' counting: Principles before skill. *Cognition, 13*, 343–359.

Gelman, R., & Shatz, M. (1977). Appropriate sppech adjustments: The operation of conversational restraints on talk to two year olds. In M. Lewis & L. Rosenblum (Eds.), *Interaction, conversation and the development of language.* New York: Wiley.

Gelman, S. A., & Markman, E. M. (1987). Young children's inductions from natural kinds: The role of categories and appearances. *Child Development, 58*, 1532–1541.

Gelman, S. A., & O'Reilly, A. W. (1988). Children's inductive inferences within superordinate categories: The role of language and category structure. *Child Development, 59*, 876–886.

Gentner, D. (1982). Why nouns are learned before verbs: Linguistic relativity versus natural partitioning. In S. A. Kuczaj II (Ed.), *Language development: Vol. 2. Language, thought, and culture* (pp. 301–332). Hillsdale, NJ: Erlbaum.

Gentner, D., & Holyoak, K. J. (1997). Reasoning and learning by analogy: Introduction. *American Psychologist, 52*, 32–34.

Gentner, D., & Markman, A. B. (1997). Structure mapping in analogy and similarity. *American Psychologist, 52*, 45–56.

Gentner, D., & Rattermann, M. J. (1992). *Analogy and similarity: Determinants of accessibility and inferential soundness.* Unpublished manuscript, Northwestern University.

Gentner, D., & Stuart, P. (1983, April). *Metaphor as structure mapping: What develops?* Paper presented at the biennial meeting of the Society for Research in Child Development, Detroit.

Gentner, D., & Toupin, C. (1986). Systematicity and surface similarity in the development of analogy. *Cognitive Science, 10*, 277–300.

George, C., & Main, M. (1979). Social interaction of young abused children: Approach, avoidance and aggression. *Child Development, 50*, 306–318.

Gerbner, G., Gross, L., Morgan, M., & Signorielli, N. (1980). The "mainstreaming" of America: Violence profile No. 11. *Journal of Communication, 30*, 10–29.

Gerbner, G., Gross, L., Morgan, M., & Signorielli, N. (1994). Growing up with television: The cultivation perspective. In J. Bryant & D. Zillmann (Eds.), *Media effects: Advances in theory and research* (pp. 17–42). Hillsdale, NJ: Erlbaum.

Gesell, A., & Amatruda, C. S. (1941). *Developmental diagnosis: Normal and abnormal child development.* New York: Paul B. Hoeber.

Gesell, A., L. (1928). *Infancy and human growth.* New York: Macmillan.

Gewirtz, J. L. (1967). The course of infant smiling in four child-rearing environments in Israel. In B. M. Foss (Ed.), *Determinants of infant behavior* (Vol. 3, pp. 105–248). London: Methuen.

Gewirtz, J. L. (1969). Mechanisms of social learning: Some roles of stimulation and behavior in early human development. In D. A. Goslin (Ed.), *Handbook of socialization theory and research.* Chicago: Rand McNally.

Gewirtz, J. L., & Peláez-Nogueras, B. F. (1992). Skinner's legacy to human infant behavior and development. *American Psychologist, 47*, 1411–1422.

Gibbons, D. C. (1970). *Delinquent behavior.* Englewood Cliffs, NJ: Prentice-Hall.

Gibbs, J. T. (1989). Black American adolescents. In J. T. Gibbs & L. N. Huang (Eds.), *Children of color.* San Francisco: Jossey-Bass.

Gibson, D., & Harris, A. (1988). Aggregated early intervention effects for Down syndrome persons. *Journal of Mental Deficiency Research, 32*, 1–7.

Gibson, E. J. (1969). *Principles of perceptual learning and development.* New York: Appleton-Century-Crofts.

Gibson, E. J. (1991). *An odyssey in learning and perception.* Cambridge, MA: MIT Press.

Gibson, E. J. (1992). How to think about perceptual learning: Twenty-five years later. In H. L. Pick, P. Van den Broek, & D. C. Knoll (Eds.), *Cognitive psychology: Conceptual and methodological issues* (pp. 215–237). Washington, DC: American Psychological Association.

Gibson, E. J., & Walk, R. D. (1960). The "visual cliff." *Scientific American, 202*, 64.

Gick, M. L., & Holyoak, K. J. (1980). Analogical problem solving. *Cognitive Psychology, 12*, 306–355.

Gick, M. L., & Holyoak, K. J. (1983). Schema induction and analogical transfer. *Cognitive Psychology, 15*, 1–38.

Gillham, J. E., Reivich, K. J., Jaycox, L. H., & Seligman, M. E. (1995). Prevention of depressive symptoms in schoolchildren: Two-year follow-up. *Psychological Science, 6,* 343–351.

Gilligan, C. (1982). *In a different voice.* Cambridge, MA: Harvard University Press.

Gilligan, C. (1991, April). *Psychology and the good: How should we talk about development?* Symposium at the biennial meeting of the Society for Research in Child Development.

Gilligan, C. (1993). Woman's place in man's life cycle. In A. Dobrin (Ed.), *Being good and doing right: Readings in moral development* (pp. 37–54). Lanham, MD: University Press of America.

Ginsburg, H. J., Pollman, V. A., & Wauson, M. S. (1977). An ethological analysis of nonverbal inhibitors of aggressive behavior in male elementary school children. *Developmental Psychology, 13,* 417–418.

Gittleman, R., Abikoff, H., Pollack, E., Klein, D. F., Katz, S., & Mattes, J. (1980). A controlled trial of behavior modification and methylphenidate in hyperactive children. In C. K. Whalen & B. Henker (Eds.), *Hyperactive children.* New York: Academic.

Glasberg, R., & Aboud, F. (1982). Keeping one's distance from sadness: Children's self-reports of emotional experience. *Developmental Psychology, 18,* 287–293.

Gleitman, H. (1991). *Psychology* (3rd ed.). New York: Norton.

Gleitman, L. (1990). The structural sources of verb meanings. *Language acquisition, 1,* 3–55.

Glucksberg, S., Krauss, R., & Higgins, E. T. (1975). The development of referential communication skills. In F. D. Horowitz (Eds.), *Review of child development research* (Vol. 4). Chicago: University of Chicago Press.

Goddard, H. H. (1912). How shall we educate mental defectives? *Traeniey School Bulletin, 9,* 43.

Goetz, T. E., & Dweck, C. S. (1980). Learned helplessness in social situations. *Journal of Personality and Social Psychology, 39,* 246–255.

Goldberg, S. (1966). Infant care and growth in urban Zambia. *Human Development, 15,* 77–89.

Goldberg, S. (1983). Parent-infant bonding: Another look. *Child Development, 54,* 1355–1382.

Goldberg, S., & DeVitto, B. (1995). Parenting children born preterm. In M. Bornstein (Ed.), *Handbook of parenting* (Vol. 1). Hillsdale, NJ: Erlbaum.

Goldberg, W. A., & Easterbrooks, M. A. (1984). The role of marital quality in toddler development. *Developmental Psychology, 20,* 504–514.

Golden, M., & Birns, B. (1971). Social class, intelligence, and cognitive style in infancy. *Child Development, 42,* 2114–2116.

Golden, M., & Birns, B. (1983). Social class and infant intelligence. In M. Lewis (Ed.), *Origins of intelligence: Infancy and early childhood* (2nd ed., pp. 347–398). New York: Plenum.

Goldenberg, C. (1996a). Latin American immigration and U.S. schools. *Social Policy Report, 10,* 1–31.

Goldenberg, C. (1996b). Schools, children at risk, and successful interventions. In A. Booth & J. Dunn (Eds.), *Family-school links: How do they affect educational outcomes?* (pp. 115–124). Mahwah, NJ: Erlbaum.

Goldenberg, C., & Sullivan, J. (1994). *Making change happen in a language-minority school: A search for coherence* (EPR #13). Washington, DC: Center for Applied Linguistics.

Goldin-Meadow, S., & Morford, L. (1985). Gesture in early language: Studies of deaf and hearing children. *Merrill-Palmer Quarterly, 31,* 145–176.

Goldsmith, H. H. (1983). Genetic influences on personality from infancy to adulthood. *Child Development, 54,* 331–355.

Goldsmith, H. H. (in press). Studying temperament via construction of the Toddler Behavior Assessment Questionnaire. *Child Development, 68.*

Goldson, E. (1993). War is not good for children. In L. A. Leavitt & N. A. Fox (Eds.), *The psychological effects of war and violence on children* (pp. 3–22). Hillsdale, NJ: Erlbaum.

Goldstein, J. H. (Ed.). (1994). *Toys, play, and child development.* New York: Cambridge University Press.

Goldstein, N. (1990, January). *Explaining socioeconomic differences in children's cognitive test scores.* Unpublished manuscript, Malcolm Weiner Center for Social Policy, J. F. Kennedy School of Government, Harvard University.

Golombok, S., & Fivush, R. (1994). *Gender development.* New York: Cambridge University Press.

Goncu, A. (1993). Development of intersubjectivity in the dyadic play of preschoolers. *Early Childhood Research Quarterly, 8,* 99–116.

Goncz, L., & Kodzopeljic, J. (1991). Exposure to two languages in the preschool period: Metalinguistic development and the acquisition of reading. *Journal of Multilingual and Multicultural Development, 12,* 137–142.

Gonzalez, N. M., & Campbell, M. (1994). Cocaine babies: Does prenatal exposure to cocaine affect development? *Journal of the American Academy of Child & Adolescent Psychiatry, 33,* 16–19.

Goodglass, H. (1993). *Understanding aphasia.* New York: Academic Press.

Goodman, G. S., Bottoms, B. L., Schwartz-Kenney, B. M., & Rudy, L. (1991). Children's testimony for a stressful event: Improving children's reports. *Journal of Narrative and Life History, 1,* 69–99.

Goodman, G. S., Emery, R. E., & Haugaard, J. J. (1998). Developmental psychology and law: Divorce, child maltreatment, foster care, and adoption. In W. Damon (Gen. Ed.), I. E. Sigel, & K. A. Renninger (Vol. Eds.), *Handbook of child psychology: Vol. 4. Child psychology in practice* (pp. 775–874). New York: Wiley.

Goodman, J. C. (1989). *The development of context effects of spoken word recognition.* Doctoral dissertation. The University of Chicago.

Goodman, J. R., & Stevenson, J. (1989). A twin study of hyperactivity: II. The ateiological role of genes, family relationships, and perinatal adversity. *Journal of Child Psychology and Psychiatry, 30,* 691–709.

Goodnow, J. (1988). Children's household work: Its nature and functions. *Psychological Bulletin, 103,* 5–26.

Goodnow, J., & Collins, A. (1991). *Ideas according to parents.* Hillsdale, NJ: Erlbaum.

Goodnow, J. J. (1996). From household practices to parents' ideas about work and interpersonal relationships. In S. Harkness & C. Super (Eds.), *Parents' cultural belief systems* (pp. 313–344). NY: Guilford Press.

Goody, E. (1991). The learning of prosocial behavior in small-scale egalitarian societies: An anthropological view. In R. A. Hinde & J. Groebel (Eds.), *Cooperation and prosocial behavior* (pp. 106–128). Cambridge, England: Cambridge University Press.

Goosens, F., & Van IJzendoorn, M. (1990). Quality of infants' attachment to professional caregivers. *Child Development, 61,* 832–837.

Gopnik, A., & Choi, S. (1995). Names, relational words, and cognitive development in English and Korean speakers: Nouns are not always learned before verbs. In M. Tomasello & W. E. Merriman (Eds.), *Beyond names for things: Young children's acquisition of verbs* (pp. 83–90). Hillsdale, NJ: Erlbaum.

Gopnik, A., & Slaughter, V. (1991). Young children's understanding of changes in their mental states. *Child Development, 62,* 98–110.

Gorn, G. J., & Goldberg, M. E. (1982). Behavioral evidence of the effects of televised food messages on children. *Journal of Consumer Research, 9,* 200–205.

Goswami, U. (1995). Transitive relational mappings in 3- and 4-year-olds: The analogy of Goldilocks and the Three Bears. *Child Development, 66,* 877–892.

Gottesman, I. I. (1963). Genetic aspects of intelligent behavior. In N. Ellis (Ed.), *Handbook of mental deficiency: Psychological theory and research.* New York: McGraw-Hill.

Gottesman, I. I. (1993). Origins of schizophrenia: Past as prologue. In R. Plomin & G. E. McClearn (Eds.), *Nature, nurture and psychology.* Washington, DC: American Psychological Association.

Gottesman, I. I., & Goldsmith, H. H. (1994). Developmental psychopathology of antisocial behavior: Inserting genes into its ontogenesis and epigenesis. In C. A. Nelson (Ed.), *Threats to optimal development: Integrating biological, psychological, and social risk factors* (pp. 69–104). Hillsdale, NJ: Erlbaum.

Gottesman, I. I., & Shields, J. (1982). *Schizophrenia: The epigenetic puzzle.* Cambridge: Cambridge University Press.

Gottfredson, L. S. (Ed.). (1997). Intelligence and social policy [Special issue]. *Intelligence, 24,* 1–320.

Gottfried, A. E., Bathurst, K., & Gottfried, A. W. (1994). Role of maternal and dual-earner employment status in children's development: A longitudinal study from infancy through early adolescence. In A. E. Gottfried & A. W. Gottfried (Eds.), *Redefining families: Implications for children's development* (pp. 55–97). New York: Plenum Press.

Gottfried, A. W., & Gottfried, A. E. (1984). Home environment and cognitive development in young children of middle-socioeconomic-status families. In A. W. Gottfried (Ed.), *Home environment and early cognitive development* (pp. 57–115). Orlando, FL: Academic.

Gottlieb, D. (1966). Teaching and students: The view of Negro and white teachers. *Sociology of Education, 37,* 345–353.

Gottlieb, G. (1991). Experiential canalization of behavioral development theory. *Developmental Psychology, 27,* 4–13.

Gottlieb, G. (1992). *Individual development and evolution: The genesis of novel behavior.* New York: Oxford University Press.

Gottlieb, G., Wahlsten, D., & Lickliter, R. (1998). The significance of biology for human development: A developmental psychobiological systems view. In W. Damon (Gen. Ed.) & R. M. Lerner (Vol. Ed.), *Handbook of child psychology: Vol. 1. Theoretical models of human development* (pp. 233–273). New York: Wiley.

Gottlieb, J., & Leyser, Y. (1981). Friendship between mentally retarded and non-retarded children. In S. R. Asher & J. M. Gottman, *The development of children's friendships.* New York: Cambridge University Press.

Gottman, J. M. (1983). How children become friends. *Monographs of the Society for Research in Child Development, 48* (Serial No. 201).

Gottman, J. M. (1986). The world of coordinated play: Same and cross-sex friendship in young children. In J. M. Gottman & J. G. Parker (Eds.), *The conversations of friends.* New York: Cambridge University Press.

Gottman, J. M., & Mettetal, G. (1986). Speculations on social and affective development: Friendship and acquaintanceship through adolescence. In J. M. Gottman & J. G. Parker (Eds.), *The conversations of friends.* New York: Cambridge University Press.

Gottman, J. M., & Parker, J. G. (Eds.). (1986). *The conversations of friends.* New York: Cambridge University Press.

Gould, E., Tanapat, P., McEwen, B. S., Flügge, G., & Fuchs, E., (1998). Proliferation of granule cell precursors in the dentate gyrus of adult monkeys is diminished by stress. *Proceedings of the National Academy of Sciences, U.S.A., 95,* 3168–3171.

Graber, J. A., Brooks-Gunn, J., & Warren, M. P. (1995). The antecedents of menarcheal age: Heredity, family environment, and stressful life events. *Child Development, 66,* 346–359.

Graber, J. A., Petersen, A. C., & Brooks-Gunn, J. (1996). Pubertal processes: Methods, measures and models. In J. A. Graber, J. Brooks-Gunn, & A. C. Petersen (Eds.), *Transitions through adolescence.* Mahwah, NJ: Erlbaum.

Graham, G. G. (1966). Growth during recovery from infantile malnutrition. *Journal of the American Medical Women's Association, 21,* 737–742.

Graham, S. (1988). Children's developing understanding of the motivational role of affect: An attributable analysis. *Cognitive Development, 3,* 71–88.

Graham, S. (1992). Most of the subjects were white and middle class: Trends in published research on African-Americans in selected APA journals, 1970–1989. *American Psychologist, 47,* 629–639.

Graham, S., Doubleday, C., & Guarino, P. A. (1984). The development of relations between perceived controllability and the emotions of pity, anger and guilt. *Child Development, 55,* 561–565.

Graham, S., & Hudley, C. (1994). Attributions of aggressive and nonaggressive African-American male early adolescents: A study of construct accessibility. *Developmental Psychology, 30,* 365–373.

Graham, S., Hudley, C., & Williams, E. (1992). Attributional and emotional determinants of aggression among African-American and Latino young adolescents. *Developmental Psychology, 28,* 731–740.

Granrud, C. E. (1991). Visual size constancy in newborns. In C. E. Granrud (Ed.), *Visual perception and cognition in infants.* Hillsdale, NJ: Erlbaum.

Grant, C. A. (1990, September). Desegregation, racial attitudes and intergroup contact: A discussion of change. *Phi Delta Kappan,* pp. 25–32.

Grant, J. P. (1993). *The state of the world's children.* New York: UNICEF and Oxford University Press.

Grantham-McGregor, S., Powell, C., Walker, S., & Chang, S. (1994). The long-term follow up of severely malnourished children who participated in an intervention program. *Child Development, 65,* 428–439.

Grantham-McGregor, S. M., Powell, C. A., Walker, S. P., & Hines, J. H. (1991). Nutritional supplementation, psychological stimulation and mental development of stunted children: The Jamaican study. *Lancet, 338,* 1–5.

Gratch, G. (1982). Responses to hidden persons and things by 5-, 9-, and 16-month-old infants in a visual tracking situation. *Developmental Psychology, 18,* 232–237.

Graves, S. B. (1993). Television, the portrayal of African-Americans, and the development of children's attitudes. In G. L. Berry & J. K. Asamen (Eds.), *Children and television: Images in a changing socio-cultural world* (pp. 179–190). Newbury Park, CA: Sage.

Graves, S. N. (1975). *How to encourage positive racial attitudes.* Paper presented at the Society for Research in Child Development, Denver, CO.

Green, J. A., Gustafson, G. E., & West, M. J. (1980). Effects of infant development on mother-infant interactions. *Child Development, 51,* 199–207.

Green, R. H., Asrat, D., Maurs, M., & Morgan, R. (1989). Children in Southern Africa. In United Nations Children's Fund (Ed.), *Children on the front line* (pp. 9–42). New York: United Nations.

Greenberg, B. S. & Brand, J. E. (1994). Minorities and the mass media: 1970s to 1990s. In J. Bryant & D. Zillman (Eds.), *Media effects: Advances in theory and research* (pp. 273–314). Hillsdale, NJ: Erlbaum.

Greenberg, B. S., Fazel, S., & Weber, M. (1986). *Children's view on advertising.* Independent Broadcasting Authority Research Report, New York, NY.

Greenberg, M., & Morris, N. (1974). Engrossment: The newborn's impact upon the father. *American Journal of Orthopsychiatry, 44,* 520–531.

Greenberg, M. T., Kushce, C. A., Cook, E. T., & Quamma, J. P. (1995). Promoting emotional competence in school-aged children: The effects of the PATHS curriculum. *Development & Psychopathology, 7,* 117–136.

Greenberger, E., & Goldberg, W. A. (1989). Work, parenting and the socialization of children. *Developmental Psychology, 25,* 22–35.

Greenberger, E., & O'Neil, R. (1991, April). *Characteristics of fathers' and mothers' jobs: Implications for parenting and children's social development.* Paper presented at the biennial meeting of the capital Society for Research in Child Development, Seattle, WA.

Greenbough, W. T., & Black, J. E. (1992). Induction of brain structure by experience: Substrates for cognitive development. In M. Gunnar & C. A. Nelson (Eds.), *Behavioral developmental neuroscience: Vol. 24. Minnesota symposium on child psychology.* NJ: Erlbaum.

Greenfield, P., & Cocking, R. (Eds.). (1995). *Cross-cultural perspectives on child development.* Hillsdale, NJ: Erlbaum.

Greenfield, P. M. (1984). *Mind and media: The effects of television, video games and computers.* Cambridge, MA: Harvard University Press.

Greenfield, P. M., & Childs, C. P. (1991). Developmental continuity in biocultural context. In R. Cohen & A. W. Siegel (Eds.), *Context and development.* Hillsdale, NJ: Erlbaum.

Greenfield, P. M., & Lave, J. (1982). Cognitive aspects of informal education. In D. A. Wagner & H. W. Stevenson (Eds.), *Cultural perspectives on child development.* San Francisco: Freeman.

Greenfield, P. M., & Suzuki, L. K. (1998). Culture and human development: Implications for parenting, education, pediatrics and mental health. In W. Damon (Gen. Ed.) & I. Sigel (Vol. Ed.), *Handbook of child psychology* (Vol. 4). New York: Wiley.

Greenough, W. T., Black, J. E., & Wallace, C. S. (1987). Experience and brain development. *Child Development, 58,* 539–559.

Greenough, W. T., & Green, E. J. (1981). Experience and the aging brain. In J. L. McGaugh, J. G. March, & S. B. Kiesler (Eds.), *Aging: Biology and behavior.* New York: Academic Press.

Gresham, F. M., & Reschly, D. (1988). Social skills and peer acceptance in the mildly handicapped. In T. R. Kratochwill (Ed.), *Advances in school psychology* (Vol. 6, pp. 203–247). Hillsdale, NJ: Erlbaum.

Grief, E. B., & Gleason, J. B. (1980). Hi, thanks, and goodbye: More routine information. *Language in Society, 9,* 159–166.

Griffin, P. B., & Griffin, M. B. (1992). Fathers and childcare among the Cagayan Agta. In B. Hewlett (Ed.), *Father-child relations: Cultural and biosocial contexts* (pp. 297–320). New York: Aldine de Gruyther.

Grossman, K., & Fremmer-Bombik, E. (June, 1994). Father's attachment representations and the quality of their interactions with their children in infancy and early childhood. Poster presented at the meeting of the International Society for the Study of Behavioral Development, Amsterdam.

Grossman, K. E., & Grossman, K. (1991). Attachment quality as an organizer of emotional and behavioral responses in a longitudinal perspective. In C. M. Parkes,

J. Stevenson-Hinde, & P. Marris (Eds.), *Attachment across the life cycle* (pp. 93–114). London: Tavistock/Routledge.

Grotevant, H. (1986). Assessment of identity development: Current issues and future directions. *Journal of Adolescent Research, 1,* 175–181.

Grueneich, R. (1982). The development of children's integration rules for making moral judgments. *Child Development, 53,* 887–894.

Grusec, J. (1973). Effects of co-observer evaluations on limitation: A developmental study. *Developmental Psychology, 8,* 144–148.

Grusec, J., & Walters, G. (1991). Psychological abuse and childrearing belief systems. In R. H. Starr & D. A. Wolfe (Eds.), *The effects of child abuse and neglect: Issues and research* (pp. 100–128). New York: Guilford Press.

Grusec, J. E., & Abramovitch, R. (1982). Imitation of peers and adults in a natural setting: A functional analysis. *Child Development, 53,* 636–642.

Grusec, J. E., Covell, K., & Paucha, P. (1991). *Intergenerational transmission of discipline styles and associated belief systems.* Paper presented at the meetings of the Society for Research in Child Development. Seattle, WA.

Grusec, J. E., & Dix, T. (1986). The socialization of prosocial behavior: Theory and reality. In C. Zahn-Waxler, E. M. Cummings, & R. Ioannotti (Eds.), *Altruism and aggression.* New York: Cambridge University Press.

Grusec, J. E., Kuczynski, L., Rushton, P., & Simutis, Z. M. (1979). Learning resistance to temptation through observation. *Developmental Psychology, 15,* 233–240.

Grych, J., & Fincham, F. D. (1993). Children's appraisals of marital conflict: Initial investigations of the cognitive-contextual framework. *Child Development, 64,* 215–230.

Grych, J. H., & Fincham, F. D. (1990). Marital conflict and children's adjustment: A cognitive-contextual framework. *Psychological Bulletin, 108,* 267–282.

Guerra, N. G., Huesmann, L. R., Tolan, P. H., Van Acker, R., & Eron, L. D. (1995). *Correlates of environmental risk for aggression among inner-city children: Implications for preventive interventions.* Unpublished manuscript. University of Illinois at Chicago.

Guerra, N. G., & Slaby, R. G. (1989). Evaluative factors in social problem solving by aggressive boys. *Journal of Abnormal Child Psychology, 17,* 277–289.

Guerra, N. G., & Slaby, R. G. (1990). Cognitive mediators of aggression in adolescent offenders: 2. Intervention. *Developmental Psychology, 26,* 269–277.

Guilford, J. P. (1966). Intelligence: 1965 model. *American Psychologist, 21,* 20–26.

Gunnar, M. (1980). Control, warning signals and distress in infancy. *Developmental Psychology, 16,* 281–289.

Gunnar, M. (1994). Psychoendocrine studies of temperament and stress in early childhood: Expanding current models. In J. Bates & T. Wachs (Eds.), *Temperament: Individual differences at the interface of biology and behavior.* New York: APA Press.

Gunnar, M., Leighton, K., & Peleaux, R. (1984). *The effects of temporal predictability on year-old infants' reactions to potentially frightening*

toys. Unpublished manuscript, University of Minnesota, Minneapolis.

Gunnar, M. R., Malone, S. M., Vance, G., & Fisch, R. O. (1985). Coping with aversive stimulation in the neonatal period: Quiet sleep and plasma cortisol levels during recovery from circumcision. *Child Development, 56,* 824–834.

Gunter, B., & McAleer, J. L. (1990). *Children and television: The one-eye monster?* London: Routledge.

Gurman, A. S., & Kniskern, D. P. (Eds.). (1980). *Handbook of family therapy.* New York: Brunner/Mazel.

Gurucharri, C., & Selman, R. L. (1982). The development of interpersonal understanding during childhood, preadolescence, and adolescence: A longitudinal follow-up study. *Child Development, 53,* 924–927.

Gusella, J. F., Wexler, N. S., Conneally, P. M., Naylor, S. L. Anderson, M. A., & Tanzi, R. E. (1983). A polymorphic DNA marker genetically linked to Huntington's disease. *Nature, 306,* 234–238.

Gustafson, G. E., & Green, J. A. (1988, April). *A role of crying in the development of prelinguistic communicative competence.* Paper presented at the International Conference on Infant Studies, Washington, DC.

Gustafson, G. E., & Harris, K. L. (1990). Women's responses to young infants' cries. *Developmental Psychology, 26,* 144–152.

Gustafson, S. B., & Magnusson, D. (1991). *Female life careers: A pattern approach* (Vol. 3). Hillsdale, NJ: Erlbaum.

Gutin, B., & Manos, T. M. (1993). Physical activity in the prevention of childhood obesity. In C. L. Williams & S. Y. S. Kimm (Eds.), *Prevention and treatment of childhood obesity* (pp. 115–126). Annals of the New York Academy of Sciences, Vol. 699. New York: The New York Academy of Sciences.

Guttentag, R. E. (1985). A developmental study of attention to auditory and visual signals. *Journal of Experimental Child Psychology, 39,* 546–561.

Guttentag, R. E. (1995). Mental effort and motivation: Influences on children's memory strategy use. In F. E. Weinert & W. Schneider (Eds.), *Memory performance and competencies: Issues in growth and development* (pp. 207–224). Mahwah, NJ: Erlbaum.

Hagerman, R. J., & Sobesky, W. E. (1989). Psychopathology in fragile X syndrome. *American Journal of Orthopsychiatry, 59,* 142–152.

Haglund, B. (1993). Cigarette smoking and sudden infant death syndrome: Some salient points in the debate. *Acta Paediatrica, 389* (Suppl.), 37–39.

Hahn, W. K. (1987). Cerebral lateralization of function: From infancy through childhood. *Psychological Bulletin, 101,* 376–392.

Haight, W., & Miller, P. (1993). *The ecology and development of pretend play.* Albany: State University of New York Press.

Haith, M. M., & Benson, J. (1998). Infant cognition. In W. Damon (Gen. Ed.), D. Kuhn, & R. Siegler (Vol. Ed.), *Handbook of child psychology: Vol. 2. Cognition, perception and language.* New York: Wiley.

Haith, M. M., Bergman, T., & Moore, M. J. (1977). *Eye contact and face scanning in early*

infancy. Unpublished manuscript, University of Denver. Denver, Colorado.

Haith, M. M., Hazen, C., & Goodman, G. S. (1988). Expectation and anticipation of dynamic visual events by 3.5-month-old-babies. *Child Development, 59,* 467–479.

Hakuta, K. (1986). *Mirror of language: The debate on bilingualism.* New York: Basic Books.

Halford, G. S. (1990). Is children's reasoning logical or analogical? Further comments on Piagetian cognitive developmental psychology. *Human Development, 33,* 356–361.

Hall, E. R., Esty, E. T., & Fisch, S. M. (1990). Television and children's problem-solving behavior: A synopsis of an evaluation of the effects of Square One TV. *Journal of Mathematical Behavior, 9,* 161–174.

Halliday, M. A. K. (1975). *Learning how to mean: Exploration in the development of language.* London: Arnold.

Hallinan, M. T., & Teixeira, R. A. (1987). Opportunities and constraints: Black-white differences in the formation of interracial friendships. *Child Development, 58,* 1358–1371.

Halpern, D. (1992). *Sex differences in cognitive ability* (2nd ed.). Hillsdale, NJ: Erlbaum.

Halverson, H. M. (1931). An experimental study of prehension in infants by means of systematic cinema records. *Genetic Psychology Monographs, 10*(2–3), 107–286.

Halverson, L. E., & Williams, K. (1985). Developmental sequences for hopping over distance: A prelongitudinal screening. *Research Quarterly for Exercise and Sport, 56,* 37–44.

Hamill, P., Drizd, T. A., Johnson, C. L., Reed, R. B., & Roche, A. F. (1976). HCHS growth charts. *Monthly Vital Statistics Report, 25* (Suppl. HRA), 76–112.

Hammen, C. (1992). Cognitive, life stress, and interpersonal approaches to a developmental psychopathology model of depression. *Development and Psychopathology, 4,* 189–206.

Hammen, C. (1992). The family-environmental context of depression: A perspective on children's risk. In D. Cicchetti & S. L. Toth (Eds.), *Rochester symposium on developmental psychopathology: Vol. 4. Developmental perspectives on depression* (pp. 252–282). Rochester, NY: University of Rochester Press.

Hammen, C. (1997). *Depression.* Washington, DC: Brunner/Mazel.

Hammen, C., & Rudolph, K. D. (1996). Childhood depression. In E. J. Mash & R. A. Barkley (Eds.), *Child Psychopathology* (pp. 153–195). New York: Guilford Press.

Hampe, E., Noble, H., Miller, L. C., & Barrett, C. L. (1973). Phobic children one and two years post-treatment. *Journal of Abnormal Psychology, 82,* 446–453.

Hand, S. I. (1991). *The lesbian parenting couple.* Unpublished doctoral dissertation. The Professional School of Psychology, San Francisco.

Hanna, E., & Meltzoff, A. N. (1993). Peer imitation by toddlers in laboratory, home, and day-care contexts: Implications for social learning and memory. *Developmental Psychology, 29,* 701–710.

Hansell, S. (1981). Ego development and peer friendship networks. *Sociology of Education, 54,* 51–63.

Hansen, J., & Bowey, J. A. (1994). Phonological analysis skills, verbal working memory and reading ability in second-grade children. *Child Development, 65,* 938–950.

Hanser, Marc D. (1996). *The evolution of communication.* Cambridge, MA: MIT Press.

Hardman, M. L., Drew, C. J., & Egan, M. W. (1996). *Human exceptionality: Society, school, and family* (5th ed.) Boston: Allyn & Bacon.

Harkness, S., & Super, C. (1995). Culture and parenting. In M. Bornstein (Ed.), *Handbook of parenting* (Vol. 2, pp. 211–234). Hillsdale, NJ: Erlbaum.

Harlan, W. R. (1993). Epidemiology of childhood obesity: A national perspective. In C. L. Williams & S. Y. S. Kimm (Eds.), *Prevention and treatment of childhood obesity* (pp. 1–5). Annals of the New York Academy of Sciences, Vol. 699. New York: The New York Academy of Sciences.

Harlow, H. F., & Zimmerman, R. R. (1959). Affectional responses in the infant monkey. *Science, 130,* 421–432.

Harris, P. L. (1989). *Children and emotion.* New York: Basil Blackwell.

Harris, P. L., & Bassett, E. (1975). Transitive inferences by 4-year-old children? *Developmental Psychology, 11,* 875–876.

Harris, P. L., Johnson, C. N., Hutton, D., Andrews, G., & Cook, T. (1989). Young children's theory of mind and emotion. *Cognition and Emotion, 3,* 379–400.

Harris, P. L., Olthof, T., Terwogt, M., & Hardman, C. E. (1987). Children's knowledge of the situations that provide emotions. *International Journal of Behavioral Development, 10,* 319–343.

Harrison, A. O., Wilson, M. N., Pine, C. J., Chon, S. Q., & Buriel, R. (1990). Family ecologies of ethnic minority children. *Child Development, 61,* 347–362.

Hart, B., & Risley, T. R. (1995). *Meaningful differences in the everyday experience of young American children.* Baltimore, MD: Brookes.

Hart, D., & Fegley, S. (1995). Prosocial behavior and caring in adolescence: Relations to self-understanding and social judgment. *Child Development, 66,* 1346–1359.

Harter, S. (1990). Issues in the assessment of the self-concept of children and adolescents. In A. M. LaGrecca (Ed.), *Through the eyes of the child.* Boston: Allyn and Bacon.

Harter, S. (1998). The development of self-representations. In W. Damon (Gen. Ed.) & N. Eisenberg (Vol. Ed.), *Handbook of child psychology: Vol. 3. Social, emotional & personality development* (pp. 553–618). New York: Wiley.

Harter, S., & Bresnick, S. (1996). *Developmental and gender differences in role-related opposing attributes within the adolescent self-portrait.* Unpublished manuscript. University of Denver, Denver, CO.

Harter, S., & Buddin, B. J. (1987). Children's understanding of the simultaneity of two emotions: A five-stage developmental acquisition sequence. *Developmental Psychology, 23,* 388–399.

Harter, S., & Whitesell, N. (1989). Developmental changes in children's emotion concepts. In C. Saarni & P. L. Harris (Eds.), *Children's understanding of emotions.* New York: Cambridge University Press.

Hartshorne, H., & May, M. S. (1928). *Moral studies in the nature of character: Vol. 1. Studies in deceit; Vol. 2. Studies in self-control; Vol. 3. Studies in the organization of character.* New York: Macmillan.

Hartup, W. W. (1974). Aggression in childhood: Developmental perspectives. *American Psychologist, 29,* 336–341.

Hartup, W. W. (1983). Peer relations. In P. H. Mussen (Ed.), *Handbook of child psychology* (Vol. 4). New York: Wiley.

Hartup, W. W. (1989). Social relationships and their developmental significance. *American Psychologist, 44,* 120–126.

Hartup, W. W. (1992, August). *Friendships and their developmental significance.* Invited address, American Psychological Association Annual Meeting, Washington, DC.

Hartup, W. W. (1996). The company they keep: Friendships and their developmental significance. *Child Development, 67,* 1–13.

Hartup, W. W., Laursen, B., Stewart, M. I., & Eastenson, A. (1988). Conflict and the friendship relations of young children. *Child Development, 59,* 1590–1600.

Harwood, R. L. (1992). The influence of culturally derived values on Anglo and Puerto Rican mothers' perceptions of attachment behavior. *Child Development, 63,* 822–839.

Haslett, B. B. (1997). Basic concepts: Communication, cognition, and language. In B. B. Haslett & W. Samter (Eds.), *Children communicating: The first five years.* Mahwah, NJ: Erlbaum.

Hatcher, P. J., Hulme, C., & Ellis, A. W. (1994). Ameliorating early reading failure by integrating the teaching of reading and phonological skills: The phonological linkage hypothesis. *Child Development, 65,* 41–57.

Hauser, M. D., Kralik, J., Botto, M. C., Garrett, M., & Oser, J. (1995). Self-recognition in primates: Phylogeny and the salience of species-typical features. *Proceedings of the National Academy of Sciences, U.S.A., 92,* 10811–10814.

Havinghurst, R. F., & Neugarten, B. L. (1995). *American Indian and white children.* Chicago: University of Chicago Press.

Hawkins, A. J., & Dollahite, D. E. (Eds.). (1997). *Generative fathering.* Thousand Oaks, CA: Sage.

Hawkins, J., Sheingold, K., Gearhart, M., & Berger, C. (1982). Microcomputers in schools: Impact on the social life of elementary classrooms. *Journal of Applied Developmental Psychology, 3,* 361–373.

Hawley, T. L., & Disney, E. R. (1992). Crack's children: The consequences of maternal cocaine abuse. Society for Research in Child Development. *Social Policy Report, 6,* 1–23.

Hawn, P. R., & Harris, L. J. (1983). Laterality in manipulative and cognitive related activity. In G. Young, S. Segalowitz, C. Corter, & S. Trehub (Eds.), *Manual specialization and the developing brain.* New York: Academic.

Hay, D. F. (1979). Cooperative interactions and sharing between young children and their parents. *Developmental Psychology, 15,* 647–653.

Hay, D. F. (1994). Prosocial development. *Journal of Child Psychology & Psychiatry & Allied Disciplines, 35,* 29–71.

Hay, D. F., & Rheingold, H. L. (1983). *The early appearance of some valued social behaviors.* Unpublished manuscript, State University of New York at Stony Brook.

Hay, D. F., & Ross, H. S. (1982). The social nature of early conflict. *Child Development, 53,* 105–113.

Hayden, L., Turulli, D., & Hymel, S. (1988, May). *Children talk about loneliness.* Paper presented at the biennial meeting of the University of Waterloo Conference on Child Development, Waterloo, Ontario, Canada.

Hayes, A., & Batshaw, M. L. (1993). Down Syndrome. *Pediatric Clinics of North America, 40,* 523–535.

Hayes, C. D., Palmer, J. L., & Zazlow, M. (Eds.). (1990). *Who cares for America's children? Child care policy for the 1990's.* Washington, DC: National Academy Press.

Hayes, D. S., Chemelski, B. E., & Birnbaum, D. W. (1981). Young children's incidental and intentional retention of televised events. *Developmental Psychology, 17,* 230–232.

Hayes, K. J. (1962). Genes, drives and intellect. *Psychological Reports, 10,* 299–342.

Hazebrigg, M. D., Cooper, H. M., & Borduin, C. M. (1987). Evaluating the effectiveness of family therapies: An integrative review and analysis. *Psychological Bulletin, 101,* 428–442.

Healy, B. (1995). *A new perspective for women's health.* New York: Viking.

Heatherton, T. F., Mahamedi, F., Striepe, M., Field, A. E., & Keel, P. (1997). A 10-year longitudinal study of body weight, dieting, and eating disorder symptoms. *Journal of Abnormal Psychology, 106,* 117–125.

Hecox, K., & Deegan, D. M. (1985). Methodological issues in the study of auditory development. In G. Gottlieb & N. A. Krasnegor (Eds.), *Measurement of audition and vision in the first year of postnatal life: A methodological overview.* Norwood, NJ: Ablex.

Heilman, A. W., Blair, T. R., & Rupley, W. H. (1994). *Principles and practices of teaching reading* (8th ed.). New York: Merrill/Macmillan.

Heinicke, C., Beckwith, L., & Thompson, A. (1988). Early intervention in the family system: A framework and review. *Infant Mental Health Journal, 9,* 111–141.

Helwig, C. C. (1995). Adolescents' and young adults' conceptions of civil liberties: Freedom of speech and religion. *Child Development, 66,* 152–166.

Henderson, V. L., & Dweck, C. S. (1990). Motivation and achievement. In S. Feldman & G. Elder (Eds.), *Adolescence: At the threshold* (pp. 308–329). Cambridge, MA: Harvard University Press.

Hendrick, J., & Stange, T. (1991). Do actions speak louder than words? An effect of the functional use of language on dominant sex role behavior in boys and girls. *Early Childhood Research Quarterly, 6,* 565–576.

Henggeler, S. W. (1989). *Delinquency in adolescence.* Newbury Park, CA: Sage.

Henggeler, S. W., Melton, G. B., & Rodrigues, J. R. (1992). *Pediatric and adolescent AIDS.* Newbury Park, CA: Sage.

Henggeler, S. W., Melton, G. B., & Smith, L. A. (in press). Multisystemic treatment of serious juvenile offenders: An effective alternative to incarceration. *Journal of Consulting and Clinical Psychology.*

Henneborn, W. J., & Cogan, R. (1975). The effect of husband participation on reported pain and the probability of medication during labor and birth. *Journal of Psychosomatic Research, 19,* 215–222.

Herbst, A. L. (1981). Diethylstilbestrol and other hormones during pregnancy. *Obstetrics and Gynecology, 58,* 355–405.

Herman-Giddens, M. E., Slora, E. J., Wasserman, A. C., Bourdony, C. J., Bhapkar, M. V., Koch, G. G., & Hasemeie, C. M. (1997). Secondary sexual characteristics and menses in young girls seen in office practice: A study from the pediatric research in office settings network. *Pediatrics, 99,* 505–512.

Herrnstein, R. (1971). I. Q. *Atlantic, 228,* 44–64.

Herrnstein, R., & Murray, C. (1994). *The bell curve: Intelligence and class structure in American life.* New York: Basic Books.

Hess, R. D., & Shipman, V. (1967). Cognitive elements in maternal behavior. In J. Hill (Ed.), *Minnesota symposia on child psychology* (pp. 57–81). Minneapolis: University of Minnesota Press.

Heston, L. (1966). Psychiatric disorders in foster-home reared children of schizophrenic mothers. *British Journal of Psychiatry, 112,* 819–825.

Heth, C. D., & Cornell, E. H. (1980). Three experiences affecting spatial discrimination learning by ambulatory children. *Journal of Experimental Child Psychology, 30,* 246–264.

Hetherington, E. M. (1966). Effects of paternal absence on sex-typed behaviors in Negro and white preadolescent males. *Journal of Personality and Social Psychology, 4,* 87–91.

Hetherington, E. M. (1967). The effects of familial variables on sex typing, on parent-child similarity and on imitation in children. In J. P. Hill (Ed.), *Minnesota symposia on child psychology* (Vol. 1, pp. 82–107). Minneapolis: University of Minnesota Press.

Hetherington, E. M. (1972). Effects of father absence on personality development in adolescent daughters. *Developmental Psychology, 7,* 313–326.

Hetherington, E. M. (1987). *Long-term impact of divorce on children's marital stability.* Unpublished manuscript, University of Virginia, Charlottesville.

Hetherington, E. M. (1988a). *The impact of the experience of divorce during childhood on women's adult adjustment.* Unpublished manuscript, University of Virginia, Charlottesville.

Hetherington, E. M. (1988b). Parents, children and siblings six years after divorce. In R. Hinde & J. Stevenson-Hinde (Eds.), *Relationships within families* (pp. 311–331). Cambridge, MA: Cambridge University Press.

Hetherington, E. M. (1989). Coping with family transitions: Winners, losers and survivors. *Child Development, 60,* 1–14.

Hetherington, E. M. (1991a). Families, lies and videotapes. *Journal of Adolescent Research, 1*(4), 323–348.

Hetherington, E. M. (1991b). The role of individual differences and family relationships in children's coping with divorce and remarriage. In P. A. Cowan & E. M. Hetherington (Eds.), *Family transitions* (pp. 165–194). Hillsdale, NJ: Erlbaum.

Hetherington, E. M. (1993). An overview of the Virginia longitudinal study of divorce and remarriage with a focus on early adolescence. *Journal of Family Psychology, 7,* 39–56.

Hetherington, E. M. (1998). Social capital and the development of youth from nondivorced, divorced, and remarried families. In A. Collins (Ed.), *Relationships as developmental contexts: The 29th Minnesota symposium on child psychology.* Hillsdale, NJ: Erlbaum.

Hetherington, E. M., Bridges, M., & Insabella, G. M. (1998). Five perspectives on the association between divorce and remarriage and children's adjustment. *American Psychologist.*

Hetherington, E. M., & Clingempeel, W. G. (1992).Coping with marital transitions: A family systems perspective. *Monographs of the Society for Research in Child Development, 57,* (2, 3, Serial No. 227).

Hetherington, E. M., Cox, M., & Cox, R. (1979). Play and social interaction in children following divorce. *Journal of Social Issues, 35,* 26–49.

Hetherington, E. M., Cox, M. J., & Cox, R. (1982). Effects of divorce on parents and children. In M. E. Lamb (Ed.), *Nontraditional families.* Hillsdale, NJ: Erlbaum.

Hetherington, E. M., & Morris, W. N. (1978). The family and primary groups. In W. H. Holtzman (Ed.), *Introductory psychology in depth: Developmental topics.* New York: Harper & Row.

Hetherington, E. M., & Stanley-Hagen, M. (1995). Parenting in divorced and remarried families. In M. H. Bornstein (Ed.), *Handbook of parenting: Vol. 3. Status and social conditions of parenting.* Mahwah, NJ: Erlbaum.

Hetherington, E. M., Stanley-Hagan, M., & Anderson, E. R. (1989). Marital transitions: A child's perspective. *American Psychologist, 44,* 303–312.

Hewlett, B. S. (1992a). Husband-wife reciprocity and the father-infant relationship among Aka pygmies. In B. Hewlett (Ed.), *Father-child relations: Cultural and biosocial contexts* (pp. 153–176). New York: Aldine de Gruyther.

Hewlett, B. S. (1992b). The parent-infant relationships and socio-emotional development among Aka pygmies. In J. Roopnarine & D. B. Carter (Eds.), *Parent-child socialization in diverse cultures.* Norwood, NJ: Ablex.

Heyman, G. D., Dweck, C. S., & Cain, K. M. (1992). Young children's vulnerability to self-blame and helplessness: Relationship to beliefs about goodness. *Child Development, 63,* 401–415.

Higgins, A. (1991). Lawrence Kohlberg: The vocation of an educator, part II. In W. M. Kurtines & J. Gewirtz (Eds.), *Moral behavior and development* (Vol. 1). Hillsdale, NJ: Erlbaum.

Higgins, A., Power, C., & Kohlberg, L. (1984). The relationship of moral atmosphere to judgments of responsibility. In W. M. Kurtines & J. L. Gewirtz (Eds.), *Morality, moral behavior and moral development.* New York: Wiley.

Hill, A. L. (1978). Savants: Mentally retarded individuals with specific skills. In N. R. Ellis (Ed.), *International review of research in mental retardation* (Vol. 9). New York: Academic.

Hinde, R. A. (1987). *Individuals, relationships and culture.* New York: Cambridge University Press.

Hinde, R. A. (1989). Ethological and relationships approaches. In R. Vasta (Ed.), *Six theories of child development.* Greenwich, CT: JAI Press.

Hinde, R. A. (1994). Developmental psychology in the context of the other behavioral sciences. In R. D. Parke, P. Ornstein, J. Reisen, & C. Zahn-Waxler (Eds.), *A century of developmental psychology.* Washington, DC: American Psychological Association.

Hindley, C. B., Filliozat, A. M., Klackenberg, G., Nicolet-Neister, D., & Sand, E. A. (1966). Differences in age of walking for five European longitudinal samples. *Human Biology, 38,* 264–379.

Hines, M. (1993). Hormonal and neural correlates of sex-typed behavioral development in human beings. In M. Haug, R. E. Whalen, C. Aron, & K. L. Olsen (Eds.), *The development of sex differences and similarities in behavior.* Boston: Kluwer.

Hines, M., & Kaufman, F. R. (1994). Androgen and the development of human sex-typical behavior: Rough-and-tumble play and sex of preferred playmates in children with congenital adrenal hyperplasia (CAH). *Child Development, 65,* 1042–1053.

Hinshaw, S. P. (1992). Externalizing behavior problems and academic under-achievement in childhood and adolescence: Casual relationships and underlying mechanisms. *Psychological Bulletin, 111,* 127–155.

Hirsch, J., & Kim, K. (1997). New views of early language. *Nature, 103,* 1141–1143.

Hitch, G. J., & Towse, J. N. (1995). Working memory: What develops? In F. E. Weinert & W. Schneider (Eds.), *Memory performance and competencies: Issues in growth and development* (pp. 3–21). Mahwah, NJ: Erlbaum.

Hobbs, N. (1975). *The futures of children.* San Francisco: Jossey-Bass.

Hobson, R. P. (1989). Beyond cognition: A theory of autism. In G. Dawson (Ed.), *Autism: Nature, diagnosis, and treatment.* New York: Guilford.

Hock, E. (1978).Working and nonworking mothers with infants: Perceptions of their careers, their infants' needs, and satisfaction with mothering. *Developmental Psychology, 4,* 37–43.

Hodapp, R. M. (1995). Parenting children with Down syndrome and other types of mental retardation. In M. H. Bornstein (Ed.), *Handbook of parenting: Vol. 1. Children and parenting* (pp. 233–253). Mahwah, NJ: Lawrence Erlbaum.

Hodges, E. V. E., Malone, M. J., & Perry, D. G. (1997). Individual risk and social risk as interacting determinants of victimization in the peer group. *Developmental Psychology, 33,* 1032–1039.

Hoff-Ginsberg, E. (1997). *Language development.* Pacific Grove, CA: Brooks-Cole.

Hoff-Ginsberg, E., & Shatz, M. (1982). Linguistic input and the child's acquisition of language. *Psychological Bulletin, 92,* 3–26.

Hoff-Ginsberg, E., & Tardiff, T. (1995). Socioeconomic status and parenting. In M. H. Bornstein (Ed.), *Handbook of parenting: Vol. 2. Biology and ecology of parenting* (pp. 161–188). Mahwah, NJ: Erlbaum.

Hoffman, L. W. (1977). Changes in family roles, socialization and sex differences. *American Psychologist, 32,* 644–657.

Hoffman, L. W. (1989). Effects of maternal employment in the two-parent family. *American Psychologist, 44,* 283–292.

Hoffman, L. W. (1991). The influence of the family environment on personality: Accounting for sibling differences. *Psychological Bulletin, 110,* 187–203.

Hoffman, M. L. (1981). Is altruism part of human nature? *Journal of Personality and Social Psychology, 40,* 121–137.

Hoffman, M. L. (1984). Empathy, its limitations, and its role in a comprehensive moral theory. In W. M. Kurtines & J. L. Gewirtz (Eds.), *Morality, moral behavior and moral development.* New York: Wiley.

Hoffman, M. L. (1987). The contribution of empathy to justice and moral judgment. In N. Eisenberg & J. Strayer (Eds.), *Empathy and its development.* New York: Cambridge University Press.

Hofsten, C. von, & Rönnqvist, L. (1993). The structuring of neonatal arm movement. *Child Development, 64,* 1046–1057.

Hohne, E. A., & Jusczyk, P. W. (1994). Two-month old infants sensitivity to allophonic differences. *Perception and Psychophysics, 56,* 613–623.

Holden, G. W. (1997). *Parents and the dynamics of child rearing.* Boulder, CO: Westview Press.

Holden, G. W. (1997). *Parents and the dynamics of child rearing.* Boulder, CO: Westview Press.

Holden, G. W., & Edwards, L. A. (1989). Parental attitudes toward child rearing: Instruments, issues & implications. *Psychological Bulletin, 106,* 29–58.

Holditch-Davis, D. (1990). The development of sleeping and waking states in high-risk preterm infants. *Infant Behavior and Development, 13,* 513–531.

Hollenbeck, A. R., & Slaby, R. G. (1982). Influence of a television model's vocalization pattern on infants. *Journal of Applied Developmental Psychology, 3,* 57–65.

Hollies, A. (1996). Motor development in infancy. *Perceptual-Motor Skills, 84,* 113–119.

Holtzman, W. H., Diaz-Guerrero, R., & Schwartz, J. D. (1975). *Personality development in two cultures: Cross-cultural and longitudinal study of school children in Mexico and the United States.* Austin: University of Texas Press.

Honzik, M. (1983). Measuring mental abilities in infancy: The value and limitations. In M. Lewis (Ed.), *Origins of intelligence: Infancy and early childhood* (2nd ed.) (pp. 67–105). New York: Plenum.

Honzik, M. P. (1976). Value and limitations of infant tests: An overview. In M. Lewis (Ed.), *Origins of intelligence.* New York: Plenum.

Honzik, M. P., Macfarlane, J. W., & Allen, L. (1948). The stability of mental test performance between two and eighteen years. *Journal of Experimental Education, 17,* 309–324.

Hood, K. E., Draper, P., Crockett, L. J., Petersen, A. C. (1987). The ontogeny and phylogeny of sex differences in development: A biosocial synthesis. In D. B. Carter (Ed.), *Current conceptions of sex roles and sex-typing: Theory and research.* New York: Praeger.

Hook, E. B. (1982). Epidemiology of Down syndrome. In S. M. Pueschel & J. E. Rynders (Eds.), *Down syndrome: Advances in biomedicine and the behavioral sciences.* Cambridge, MA: Ware Press.

Hopkins, B. (1991). Facilitating early motor development: An intracultural study of West Indian mothers and their infants living in Britain. In J. K. Nugent, B. M. Lester, & T. B. Brazelton (Eds.), *The cultural context of infancy: Vol. 2. Multicultural and interdisciplinary approaches to parent-infant relations* (pp. 93–143). Norwood, NJ: Ablex.

Hopkins, B., & Westra, T. (1988). Maternal handling and motor development: An intracultural study. *Genetic Psychology Monographs, 14,* 377–420.

Hopkins, B., & Westra, T. (1990). Motor development, maternal expectations, and the role of handling. *Infant Behavior and Development, 13,* 117–122.

Horney, K. (1945). *Our inner conflicts.* New York: Norton.

Horowitz, F. D., Ashton, J., Culp, R., Gaddis, E., Leven, S., & Reichmann, B. (1977). The effects of obstetrical medication on the behavior of Israeli newborn infants and some comparisons with Uruguayan and American infants. *Child Development, 48,* 1607–1623.

Horowitz, F. D., & Paden, L. Y. (1973). The effectiveness of environmental intervention programs. In B. Caldwell & H. Riccuiti (Eds.), *Review of child development research* (Vol. 3, pp. 331–402). Chicago: University of Chicago Press.

Hossain, Z., Field, T., Gonzalez, J., Malphurs, J., De Valle, C., & Pickens, J. (1994). Infants of depressed mothers interact better with their non-depressed fathers. *Infant Mental Health Journal, 15,* 348–357.

Howe, N., & Ross, H. S. (1990). Socialization perspective taking and the sibling relationship. *Developmental Psychology, 26,* 160–165.

Howe, P. E., & Schiller, M. (1952). Growth responses of the school child to changes in diet and environment factors. *Journal of Applied Physiology, 5,* 51–61.

Howe, S. C., & Hamilton, C. E. (1992). Children's relationships with caregivers: Mothers and child care teachers. *Child Development, 63,* 859–866.

Howe, T., Tepper, F., & Parke, R. D. (1998). The emotional understanding and peer relationships of abused children in residential treatment. *Residential Treatment for Children and Youth, 15,* 69–82.

Howes, C. (1987). Social competence with peers in young children. Developmental sequences. *Developmental Review, 7,* 252–272.

Howes, C. (1988a, April). *Can age of entry and the quality of infant care predict behaviors in kindergarten?* Paper presented at the International Conference of Infant Studies, Washington, DC.

Howes, C. (1988b). Relations between early child care and schooling. *Developmental Psychology, 24,* 53–57.

Howes, C., & Hamilton, C. E. (1993). The changing experience of child care: Changes in teachers and in teacher-child relationships and children's social competence with peers. *Early Childhood Research Quarterly, 8,* 15–32.

Howes, C., & Matheson, C. C. (1992). Sequences in the development of competent play with peers: Social and social-pretend play. *Developmental Psychology, 28,* 961–974.

Howes, C., Matheson, C. C., & Hamilton, C. E. (1994). Maternal, teacher, and child care history correlates of children's relationships with peers. *Child Development, 65,* 264–273.

Howes, C., Phillips, D., & Whitebook, M. (1992). Thresholds of quality: Implications for the social development of children in center-based child care. *Child Development, 63,* 449–460.

Howes, C., & Rodning, C. (1992). Attachment security and social pretend play negotiation. In C. Howes, O. A. Unger, & C. C. Matheson (Eds.), *The collaboration construction of pretend: Social pretend play functions.* Albany: State University of New York Press.

Howes, C., Rodning, C., Galluzo, D. C., Myers, L. (1988). Attachment and child care: Relationships with mother and caregiver. *Early Childhood Research Quarterly, 3,* 403–406.

Howes, C., Smith, E., & Galinsky, E. (1995). *The Florida Child Care Quality Improvement Study.* New York: Families and Work Institute.

Howes, P., & Markman, H. J. (1989). Marital quality and child functioning: A longitudinal investigation. *Child Development, 60,* 1044–1051.

Hoyenga, K. B., & Hoyenga, K. T. (1993). *Gender related differences: Origins and outcomes.* Needham Heights, MA: Allyn & Bacon.

Hubbard, F. O. A., & van IJzendoorn, M. H. (1991). Maternal unresponsiveness and infant crying across the first 9 months: A naturalistic longitudinal study. *Infant Behavior and Development, 14,* 299–312.

Hubbard, J. A., & Coie, J. D. (1994). Emotional correlates of social competence in children's peer relationships. *Merrill-Palmer Quarterly, 40,* 1–20.

Hubel, D. H. (1988). *Eye, brain and vision.* New York: Scientific American Library.

Hudley, C., & Graham, S. (1993). An attributional intervention to reduce peer-directed aggression among African-American boys. *Child Development, 64,* 124–138.

Huesmann, L. R., Eron, L. D., Klein, R., Brice, P., & Fischer, P. (1983). Mitigating the initiation of aggressive behaviors by changing children's attitudes about media violence. *Journal of Personality and Social Psychology, 44,* 899–910.

Huesmann, L. R., Eron, L. D., Lefkowitz, M. M., & Walder, L. O. (1984). The stability of aggression over time and generations. *Developmental Psychology, 20,* 1120–1134.

Huesmann, L. R., Guerra, N. G., Zelli, A., & Miller, L. (1992). Differing normative beliefs about aggression for boys and girls. In K. Bjorkquist & P. Niemele (Eds.), *Of mice and women: Aspects of female aggression.* Orlando, FL: Academic.

Huesmann, L. R., & Miller, L. S. (1994). Long-term effects of repeated exposure to media violence in childhood. In L. R. Huesmann (Ed.), *Aggressive behavior: Current perspectives* (pp. 153–186). New York: Plenum Press.

Humphries, T., Kinsbourne, M., & Swanson, J. (1978). Stimulant effects on cooperation and social interaction between hyperactive children and their mothers. *Journal of Child Psychology and Psychiatry, 19,* 13–22.

Huston, A. C. (1983). Sex-typing. In P. H. Mussen (Ed.), *Handbook of child psychology* (Vol. 4). New York: Wiley.

Huston, A. C., & Alvarez, M. M. (1990). The socialization context of gender role development in early adolescence. In P. Montemayor, G. R. Adams, & T. P. Gullotta (Eds.), *From childhood to adolescence: A transitional period?* (pp. 156–179). Newbury Park, CA: Sage.

Huston, A. C., Donnerstein, E., Fairchild, H., Feshbach, N. D., Katz, P. A., Murray, J. P., Rubinstein, E. A., Wilcox, B. L., & Zuckerman, D. (1992). *Big world, small screen.* Lincoln: University of Nebraska Press.

Huston, A. C., McLloyd, V., & Garcia Coll, C. (1994). Children and poverty: Issues in contemporary research. *Child Development, 65,* 275–282.

Huston, A. C., & Wright, J. C. (1996). Television and socialization of young children. In T. M. MacBeth (Ed.), *Tuning into young viewers: Social science perspectives on television.* Thousand Oaks, CA: Sage.

Huston, A. C., & Wright, J. C. (1998). Mass media and children's development. In W. Damon (Gen. Ed.), I. E. Sigel, & K. A. Renninger (Vol. Eds.), *Handbook of child psychology: Vol. 4. Child psychology in practice* (pp. 999–1058). New York: Wiley.

Huston, A. C., Wright, J. C., Alvarez, M., Truglio, R., Fitch, M., & Piemyat, S. (1995). Perceived television reality and children's emotional and cognitive responses to its social content. *Journal of Applied Developmental Psychology, 16,* 231–251.

Huttenlocher, J. (1974). The origins of language comprehension. In R. L. Solso (Ed.), *Theories in cognitive psychology.* Hillsdale, NJ: Erlbaum.

Huttenlocher, J., Haight, W., Bryk, A., Seltzer, M., & Lyons, T. (1991). Early vocabulary growth: Relation to language impact and gender. *Developmental Psychology, 27,* 236–248.

Huttenlocher, J., & Lui, F. (1979). The semantic organization of some simple nouns and verbs. *Journal of Verbal Learning and Verbal Behavior, 18,* 141–162.

Huttenlocher, J., & Smiley, P. (1987). Early word meanings: The case of object names. *Cognitive Psychology, 19,* 63–89.

Huttenlocher, J., Smiley, P., & Charnery, R. (1983). Emergence of action categories in the child: Evidence from verb meanings. *Psychological Review, 90*(2), 72–93.

Huttenlocher, P. R. (1994). Synaptogenesis, synapse elimination, and neural plasticity in human cerebral cortex. In C. A. Nelson (Ed.), *Threats to optimal development. The Minnesota symposia on child psychology* (Vol. 27, pp. 35–54). Hillsdale, NJ: Erlbaum.

Hwang, C. P. (1986). Behavior of Swedish primary and secondary caretaking fathers in relation to mothers' presence. *Developmental Psychology, 22,* 749–751.

Hyde, J. S., Fennema, E., & Lamon, S. J. (1990). Gender differences in mathematics performance: A meta-analysis. *Psychological Bulletin, 107,* 139–155.

Hyde, J. S., Krajnik, M., & Skuldt-Neiderberger, K. (1991). Androgyny across the life span: A replication and longitudinal follow-up. *Developmental Psychology, 27,* 516–519.

Hyde, J. S., & Linn, M. C. (1988). Gender differences in verbal ability: A meta-analysis. *Psychological Bulletin, 104,* 53–69.

Hyde, J. S., & Plant, E. A. (1995). Magnitude of psychological gender differences. *American Psychologist, 50,* 159–161.

Hymel, S. (1986). Interpretations of peer behavior: Affective bias in childhood and adolescence. *Child Development, 57,* 431–445.

Hymel, S., Wagner, E., & Butler, L. (1990). Reputational bias: View from the peer group. In S. R. Asher & J. D. Coie (Eds.), *Peer rejection in childhood.* New York: Cambridge University Press.

Inagaki, K., & Hatano, G. (1987). Young children's spontaneous personification as analogy. *Child Development, 58,* 1013–1020.

Ingram, D. (1989). *First language acquisition.* New York: Cambridge University Press.

Inhelder, B., & Piaget, J. (1958). *The growth of logical thinking from childhood to adolescence.* New York: Basic Books.

Inoff-Germain, G., Arnold, G. S., Nottleman, E. D., Susman, E. J., Cutler, G. B., & Chrousos, G. P. (1988). Relations between hormone levels and observational measures of aggressive behavior of young adolescents in family interactions. *Developmental Psychology, 24,* 129–139.

Isabella R. (1993). Origins of attachment: Maternal interactive behavior across the first year. *Child Development, 64,* 605–621.

Isabella, R. A., & Belsky, J. (1991). Interactional synchrony and the origins of infant-mother attachment: A replication study. *Child Development, 62,* 373–384.

Isabella, R. A., Belsky, J., & vonEye, A. (1989). Origins of infant-mother attachment: An examination of interactional synchrony during the infant's first year. *Developmental Psychology, 25,* 12–21.

Israel, A. C. (1988). Parental and family influences in the etiology and treatment of childhood obesity. In N. A. Krasnegor, G. D. Grave, & N. Kretchmer (Eds.), *Childhood obesity: A behavioral perspective.* Caldwell, NJ: Telford Press.

Izard, C. E. (1991). *The psychology of emotions.* New York: Plenum.

Izard, C. E. (1994). Innate and universal facial expressions: Evidence from developmental and cross-cultural research. *Psychological Bulletin, 115,* 288–299.

Izard, C. E., Fantauzzo, C. A., Castle, J. M., Haynes, O. M., & Slomine, B. S. (1995). *The morphological stability and social validity of infants' facial expressions.* Unpublished manuscript, University of Delaware.

Izard, C. E., Hembree, E. A., Dougherty, L. M., & Coss, C. L. (1983). Changes in two- to nineteen-month-old infants' facial expressions following acute pain. *Developmental Psychology, 19,* 418–426.

Izard, C. E., Hembree, E., & Huebner, R. (1987). Infants' emotional expressions to acute pain: Developmental changes and stability of individual differences. *Developmental Psychology, 23,* 105–113.

Izard, C. E., & Malatesta, C. Z. (1987). Perspectives on emotional development I. Differential emotions theory of early emotional development. In J. D. Osofsky (Ed.), *Handbook of infant development* (2nd ed., pp. 494–554). New York: Wiley.

Jacklin, C. N., DiPietro, J. A., & Maccoby, E. E. (1984). Sex-typing behavior and sex-typing pressure in child-parent interaction. *Sex Roles, 13,* 413–425.

Jacklin, C. N., Wilcox, K. T., & Maccoby, E. E. (1988). Neonatal sex steroid hormones and intellectual abilities of six year old boys and girls. *Developmental Psychobiology, 21,* 567–574.

Jacob, T., & Johnson, S. L. (1997). Parent-child interaction among depressed fathers and mothers: Impact on child functioning. *Journal of Family Psychology, 11,* 391–409.

Jacob, T., Tennenbaum, D., Seilhamer, R. A., Bargiel, K., & Sharon, T. (1994). Reactivity effects during naturalistic observation of distressed and nondistressed families. *Journal of Family Psychology, 8,* 354–363.

Jacobs, P. A. (1991). The fragile X syndrome. *Journal of Human Genetics, 28,* 809–810.

Jacobsen, T., & Hofmann, V. (1997). Children's attachment representations: Longitudinal relations to school behavior and academic competency in middle childhood and adolescence. *Developmental Psychology, 33,* 703–710.

Jacobson, J. L., & Jacobson, S. W. (1996). Prospective longitudinal assessment of developmental neurotoxicity. *Environmental Health Perspectives, 104,* 275–283.

Jacobson, J. L., Jacobson, S. W., Fein, G. G., Schwartz, P. M., & Dowler, J. K. (1984). Prenatal exposure to an environmental toxin: A test of the multiple effects model. *Developmental Psychology, 20,* 523–532.

Jacobson, J. L., Jacobson, S. W., Padgett, R. J., Brumitt, G. A., & Billings, R. L. (1992). Effects of prenatal PCB exposure on cognitive processing efficiency and sustained attention. *Developmental Psychology, 28,* 297–306.

Jacobson, S. W., & Jacobson, J. L. (1992). Early exposure to PCBs and other suspected teratogens: Assessment of confounding. In C. Greenbaum & J. Auerbach (Eds.), *Longitudinal studies of infants born at psychological risk* (pp. 135–154). Norwood, NJ: Ablex.

Jacobson, S. W., Jacobson, J. L., Sokol, R. J., Martier, S. S., & Ager, J. W. (1993). Prenatal alcohol exposure and information processing ability. *Child Development, 64,* 1706–1721.

Jacobvitz, D., Sroufe, L. A., Stewart, M., & Leffert, N. (1990). Treatment of attentional and hyperactivity problems in children with sympathomimetic drugs: A comprehensive review. *Journal of the American Academy of Child and Adolescent Psychiatry, 29,* 677–688.

Jakobson, R. (1968). *Child Language, aphasic, and phonological universals.* The Hague: Mouton.

Jencks, C. S., Smith, M., Acland, H., Bane, M. J., Cohen, D., Gintis, H., Heynes, B., & Michelson, S. (1972). *Inequality: A reassessment of the effects of family and schooling in America.* New York: Basic Books.

Jensen, A. R. (1969). How much can we boost IQ and scholastic achievement? *Harvard Educational Review, 39,* 1–123.

Jensen, A. R. (1973). *Genetic, educability, and subpopulation differences.* London: Methuen.

Jensen, A. R. (1981). *Straight talk about mental tests.* New York: The Free Press.

Jensen, A. R. (1993). Test validity: "g" versus "tacit knowledge." *Current Directions in Psychological Science, 2,* 9–109.

Jessor, R. (1992). Risk behavior in adolescence: A psychosocial framework for understanding and action. *Developmental Review, 12,* 374–390.

Johnson, J. S., & Newport, E. L. (1989). Critical period effects in second language learning: The influence of maturational state on the acquisition of English as a second language. *Cognitive Psychology, 21,* 60–99.

Johnson, J. S., & Newport, E. L. (1991). Critical period effects on universal properties of language: The status of subjacency in the acquisition of a second language. *Cognition, 39,* 215–258.

Johnson, M. J. (1998). The neural basis of cognitive development. In W. Damon (Ed.), *Handbook of child psychology* (5th ed.). New York: Wiley.

Johnson, S. L., & Jacob, T. (1997). Marital interactions of depressed men and women. *Journal of Consulting & Clinical Psychology, 65,* 15–23.

Johnson, S. M., & Bolsted, O. D. (1973). Methodological issues in naturalistic observation: Some problems and solutions for field research. In L. A. Hamerlynck, L. C. Handy, & E. J. Mash (Eds.), *Behavior change: Methodology, concepts and practice.* Champaign, IL: Research Press.

Johnson, W., Emde, R. N., Pannabecker, B., Stenberg, C., & Davis, M. (1982). Maternal perception of infant emotion from birth through 18 months. *Infant Behavior and Development, 5,* 313–322.

Johnston, J., & Ettema, J. S. (1982). *Positive images: Breaking stereotypes with children's television.* Beverly Hills, CA: Sage.

Johnston, L. D., O'Malley, P. M., & Bachman, J. G. (1997). National Survey Results on drug use from the monitoring the future study, 1975–1995. Rockville, MD: National Institutes of Health.

Jones, D. C. (1985). Persuasive appeals and responses to appeals among friends and acquaintances. *Child Development, 56,* 757–763.

Jones, M. C., & Bayley, N. (1950). Physical maturing among boys as related to behavior. *Journal of Educational Psychology, 41,* 129–148.

Jones, S. S., Collins, K., & Hong, H. W. (1991). An audience effect on smile production in 10-month-old infants. *Psychological Science, 2,* 45–49.

Jones, T. A., & Greenough, W. T. (1996). Ultrastructural evidence for increased contact between astrocytes and synapses in rats reared in a complex environment. *Neurobiology of Learning and Memory, 65,* 48–56.

Jose, P. E. (1990). Just-world reasoning in children's immanent justice judgments. *Child Development, 61,* 1024–1033.

Jusczyk, P. W., Friederiec, A. D., Wessels, J., Svenkerud, V. Y., and Jusczyk, A. M. (1993). Infants' sensitivity to the sound patterns of native language words. *Journal of Memory & Language, 32,* 402–420.

Jusczyk, P. W., Rosner, B. S., Cutting, J. E., Foard, F., & Smith, L. B. (1977). Categorical perception of non-speech sounds by two-month-old infants. *Perception and Psychophysics, 21,* 50–54.

Jussim, L., & Eccles, J. S. (1992). Teacher expectations: II. Construction and reflection of student achievement. *Journal of Personality & Social Psychology, 63,* 947–961.

Kagan, J. (1983). Stress and coping in early development. In N. Garmezy & M. Rutter (Eds.), *Stress, coping and development in children.* New York: McGraw-Hill.

Kagan, J. (1989). Temperamental contributions to social behavior. *American Psychologist, 44,* 668–674.

Kagan, J. (1994). *Galen's prophecy.* New York: Basic Books.

Kagan, J., Arcus, D., Snidman, N., Feng, W. Y., Hendler, J., & Greene, S. (1994). Reactivity in infants: A cross-national comparison. *Developmental Psychology, 30,* 342–345.

Kagan, J., & Moss, H. A. (1962). *Birth to maturity: A study in psychological development.* New York: Wiley.

Kagan, J., Reznick, S., & Snidman, N. (1987). The physiology and psychology of behavior inhibition in children. *Child Development, 58,* 1459–1473.

Kagan, J., Snidman, N., & Arcus, D. M. (1992). Initial reactions to unfamiliarity. *Current Directions in Psychological Sciences, 1,* 171–174.

Kagan, J., & Zentner, M. (1996). Early childhood predictors of adult psychopathology. *Harvard Review of Psychiatry, 3,* 341–350.

Kagan, J. J., Kearsley, R. B., & Zelazo, P. R. (1978). *Infancy: Its place in human development.* Cambridge, MA: Harvard University Press.

Kagan, J. S. (1969). Inadequate evidence and illogical conclusions. *Harvard Educational Review, 39,* 274–277.

Kahen, V., Katz, L. F., & Gottman, J. M. (1994). Linkages between parent-child interaction and conversations of friends. From family to peer group: Relations between relationships [Special issue]. *Social Development, 3,* 238–254.

Kail, R. (1991). Processing time declines exponentially during childhood and adolescence. *Developmental Psychology, 27,* 259–266.

Kail, R. (1995). Processing speed, memory, and cognition. In F. E. Weinert & W. Schneider (Eds.), *Memory performance and competencies: Issues in growth and development* (pp. 71–88). Mahwah, NJ: Erlbaum.

Kail, R., & Park, Y. (1994). Processing time, articulation time, and memory span. *Journal of Experimental Child Psychology, 57,* 281–291.

Kaitz, M., Meirov, H., Landman, I., Eidelman, A. I. (1993). Infant recognition by tactile cues. *Infant Behavior & Development, 16,* 333–341.

Kaitz, M., Shiri, S., Danziger, S., Hershko, Z., & Eidelman, A. I. (1994). Fathers can also recognize their newborns by touch. *Infant Behavior & Development, 17,* 205–207.

Kaler, S. R., & Kopp, C. B. (1990). Compliance and comprehension in very young toddlers. *Child Development, 61,* 1997–2003.

Kalichman, S. C. (1996). *Answering your questions about AIDS.* Washington, DC: American Psychological Associaton.

Kandel, D. (1973). Adolescent marijuana use: Role of parents and peers. *Science, 181,* 1067–1070.

Kanner, L. (1943). Autistic disturbances of affective contact. *Nervous Child, 2,* 217–250.

Kanner, L. (1973). How far can autistic children go in matters of social adaptation? In L. Kanner (Ed.), *Childhood psychosis: Initial studies and new insights.* Washington, DC: Winston.

Kanner, L. (1992). Follow-up study of 11 autistic children originally reported from 1943. *Focus on Autistic Behavior, 7*(5), 1–11.

Kaplan, C. A., & Hussain, S. (1995). Use of drugs in child and adolescent psychiatry. *British Journal of Psychiatry, 166,* 291–298.

Karnofsky, D. A. (1965). Drugs as teratogens in animals and man. *Annual Review of Pharmacology, 5,* 477–482.

Katchadourian, H. (1977). *The biology of adolescence.* San Francisco: Freeman.

Katz, L. F., & Gottman, J. M. (1993). Patterns of marital conflict predict children's internalizing and externalizing behaviors. *Developmental Psychology, 29,* 940–950.

Katz, L. F., & Gottman, J. M. (1996). Spillover effects of marital conflict: In search of parenting and co-parenting mechanisms. In J. P. McHale & P. A. Cowan (Eds.), *Understanding how family-level dynamics affect children's development: Studies of two-parent families* (pp. 57–76). San Francisco: Jossey-Bass.

Katz, L. F., & Gottman, J. M. (1997). Buffering children from marital conflict and dissolution. *Journal of Clincial Child Psychology, 26,* 157–171.

Katz, L. F., Kramer, L., & Gottman, J. M. (1992). Conflict and emotions in marital, sibling, and peer relationships. In C. U. Shantz & W. W. Hartup (Eds.), *Conflict in child and adolescent development* (pp. 122–149). Cambridge, England: Cambridge University Press.

Katz, V. L., Jenkins, T., Haley, L., & Bowes, W. A. (1991). Catecholamine levels in pregnant physicians and nurses: A pilot study of stress and pregnancy. *Obstetrics & Gynecology, 77,* 338–342.

Kaufman, A. S., & Kaufman, N. L. (1983). *Kaufman assessment battery for children: Interpretive manual.* Circle Pines, MN: American Guidance Service.

Kaufman, J., & Zigler, E. (1987). Do abused children become abusive parents? *American Journal of Orthopsychiatry, 57,* 186–192.

Kauffman, J. M. (1993). *Characteristics of emotional and behavioral disorders of children and youth* (5th ed.). New York: Macmillan/Merrill.

Kaye, K. L. & Bower, T. G. R. (1994). Learning and intermodal transfer of information in newborns. *Psychological Science, 5,* 286–288.

Kazdin, A. E. (1982). Applying behavioral principles in the schools. In C. R. Reynolds & T. B. Gutkin (Eds.), *The handbook of school psychology* (pp. 501–529). New York: Wiley.

Kazdin, A. E. (1989). Identifying depression in children: A comparison of alternative selection criteria. *Journal of Abnormal Child Psychology, 17,* 437–453.

Kazdin, A. E. (1993). Changes in behavioral problems and prosocial functioning in child treatment. *Journal of Child & Family Studies, 2,* 5–22.

Kazdin, A. E., French, N. H., & Unis, A. S. (1983). Child, mother and father evaluations of depression in psychiatric inpatient children. *Journal of Abnormal Child Psychology, 11,* 167–180.

Keating, D. P. (1990). Adolescent thinking. In J. Adelson (Ed.), *Handbook of adolescent psychology.* New York: Wiley.

Kee, D. W. (1994). Developmental differences in associative memory: Strategy use, mental effort, and knowledge-access interaction. In H. W. Reese (Ed.), *Advances in child development and behavior* (Vol. 25, pp. 7–32). New York: Academic Press.

Kee, D. W., & Howell, S. (1988, April). *Mental effort and memory development.* Paper presented at the meeting of the American Educational Research Association, New Orleans, LA.

Keefer, C. H., Dixon, S., Tronick, E. Z., & Brazelton, T. B. (1991). Cultural mediation between newborn behavior and later development: Implications for methodology in cross-cultural research. In J. K. Nugent, B. M. Lester, & T. B. Brazelton (Eds.), *The cultural context of infancy: Vol. 2. Multicultural and interdisciplinary approaches to parent-infant relations* (pp. 39–61). Norwood, NJ: Ablex.

Keegan, R. T. (1996, Summer). Creativity from childhood to adulthood: A difference of degree and not of kind. In M. A. Runco (Ed.), *Creativity from childhood through adulthood: The developmental issues* [Special issue]. *New Directions for Child Development,* No. 72, 57–66.

Keenan, K., Loeber, R., Zhang, Q., Stouthamer-Loeber, M., & Van Kammen, W. B. (1995). The influence of deviant peers on the development of boys' disruptive and delinquent behavior: A temporal analysis. *Development and Psychopathology, 7,* 715–726.

Keeney, T. J., Cannizzo, S. R., & Flavell, J. H. (1967). Spontaneous and induced rehearsal in a recall task. *Child Development, 38,* 953–966.

Keller, M., & Wood, P. (1989). Development of friendship reasoning: A study of interindividual differences in intraindividual change. *Developmental Psychology, 25,* 820–826.

Keller, M. B., Klein, D. N., Hirshfield, R. M., Kocsis, J. H., McCullough, M., et al. (1995). Results of the DSM-IV mood disorders field trial. *American Journal of Psychiatry, 152,* 843–849.

Kelley, M. L., Sanchez-Hucies, J., & Walter, R. (1993). Correlates of disciplinary practices in working- to middle-class African-American mothers. *Merrill-Palmer Quarterly, 39,* 252–264.

Kellman, P. J., & Banks, M. S. (1998). Infant visual perception. In W. Damon (Gen. Ed.), D. Kuhn, & R. S. Siegler (Vol. Eds.), *Handbook of child psychology. Vol. 2. Cognition, perception, and language.* New York: Wiley.

Kendall, P. C. (Ed.). (1991). *Child and adolescent therapy: Cognitive-behavioral procedures.* New York: Guilford Press.

Kendall, P. C., Chansky, T. E., Kane, M. T., Kim, R., Kortlander, E., Ronan, K., Sessa, F., & Siqueland, L. (1992). *Anxiety disorders in youth: Cognitive-behavioral interventions.* Needham Heights, MA: Allyn & Bacon.

Kendall, P. C., & Panichelli-Mindel, S. M. (1995). Cognitive-behavioral treatment. *Journal of Abnormal Child Psychology, 23,* 107–124.

Kendall, P. C., Vitousek, K. B., & Kane, M. (1991). Thought and action in psychotherapy: Cognitive-behavioral approaches. In M. Hersen, A. E. Kazdin, & A. S. Bellack (Eds.), *The clinical psychology handbook* (2nd ed., Vol. 120, pp. 596–626). New York: Pergamon Press.

Kennedy, W. A. (1969). A follow-up normative study of Negro intelligence and achievement. *Monographs of the Society for Research in Child Development, 34*(2, Serial No. 126).

Kennell, J., Klaus, M., McGrath, S., Robertson, S., & Hinckley, C. (1991). Continuous emotional support during labor in a U.S. hospital. *Journal of the American Medical Association, 265,* 2197–2201.

Kennell, J. H., & McGrath, S. K. (1993, September), *Labor support by a doula plus father vs father alone for middle class couples: The effect on perinatal outcomes.* Paper presented at the meeting of the Society for Behavioral Pediatrics, Providence, RI.

Kerns, K. A. (1994). A longitudinal examination of links between mother-child attachment and children's friendships in early childhood. *Journal of Social and Personal Relationships, 11,* 379–381.

Kessen, W., Leutzendoff, A. M., & Stoutsenberger, K. (1967). Age, food deprevation, non-nutritive sucking and movement in the human newborn. *Journal of Comparative and Physiological Psychology, 63,* 82–86.

Kestenbaum, J., Farber, E., & Sroufe, L. A. (1989). Individual differences in empathy among preschoolers: Relation to attachment history. In N. Eisenberg (Ed.), *Empathy and related emotional responses. New Directions for Child Development* (No. 44). San Francisco: Jossey-Bass.

Khatri, P., Kupersmidt, J., & Patterson, C. (1994, April). Aggression and peer victimization as predictors of self-report of behavioral and emotional adjustment. Poster presented at the biennial meeting of the Conference in Human Development, Pittsburgh, PA.

Kimball, M. M. (1986). Television and sex role attitudes. In T. M. Williams (Ed.), *The impact of television: A natural experiment in three communities* (pp. 265–301). Orlando, FL: Academic Press.

Kimball, M. M. (1989). A new perspective on women's math achievement. *Psychological Bulletin, 105,* 198–214.

Kindermann, T. A., McCollam, T. L., & Gibson, E., Jr. (1995). Peer networks and students' classroom engagement during childhood and adolescence. In K. Wentzel & J. Juvonen (Eds.), *Social motivation: Understanding children's school adjustment.* New York: Cambridge University Press.

Kirksey, A., & Wasynczuk, A. Z. (1993). Morphological, biochemical, and functional consequences of vitamin B6 deficits during central nervous system development. *Annals of the New York Academy of Sciences, 678,* 62–80.

Kisilevsky, B. S., & Muir, D. W. (1991). Human fetal and subsequent newborn responses to sound and vibration. *Infant Behavior and Development, 14,* 1–26.

Klahr, D. (1989). Information-processing approaches. In R. Vasta (Ed.), *Annals of child development: Vol. 6. Six theories of child development: Revised formulations and current issues* (pp. 133–185). Greenwich, CT: JAI Press.

Klahr, D., & MacWhinney, B. (1998). Information processing. In W. Damon (Ed.), D. Kuhn, & R. Siegler (Vol. Eds.), *Handbook of child psychology, Vol. 2. Cognition, perception and language.* (5th ed.). New York: Wiley.

Klahr, D., & Wallace, J. G. (1976). Cognitive development: An information processing view. Hillsdale, NJ: Erlbaum.

Klaus, M. H., & Kennell, J. H. (1982). *Parent-infant bonding.* St. Louis: Mosby.

Klaus, M. H., Kennell, J. H., & Klaus, P. H. (1995). *Bonding: Building the foundations of secure attachment and independence.* Reading, MA: Addison-Wesley.

Kleiman, G., & Humphrey, M. (1982). Word processing in the classroom. *Compute, 22,* 96–99.

Kleiman, G. M. (1984). *Brave new schools: How computers can change education.* Reston, VA: Reston Publishing.

Klesges, R., Malott, J., Boschee, P., & Weber, J. (1986). The effects of parental influences on children's food intake, physical activity and relative weight. *International Journal of Eating Disorders, 5,* 335–345.

Knight, G. P., Johnson, L. G., Carlo, G., & Eisenberg, N. (1994). A multiplicative model of the dispositional antecedents of a prosocial behavior. Predicting more of the people more of the time. *Journal of Personality and Social Psychology, 66,* 178–183.

Kobayashi, Y. (1994). Conceptual acquisition and change through social interaction. *Human Development, 37,* 233–241.

Koblinsky, S. A., & Sugawara, A. I. (1984). Nonsexist curricula, sex of teacher, and children's sex-role learning. *Sex Roles, 10,* 357–367.

Kochanska, G. (1991). *Affective factors in mothers' autonomy-granting to their five-year-olds: Comparisons of well and depressed mothers.* Paper presented at the meetings of the Society for Research in Child Development, Seattle, WA.

Kochanska, G. (1993a). Socialization and temperament in the development of guilt and conscience. *Child Development, 64,* 325–347.

Kochanska, G. (1993b). Toward a synthesis of parental socialization and child temperament in early development of conscience. *Child Development, 64,* 325–347.

Kochanska, G. (1995). Children's temperament, mother's discipline, and security of attachment: Multiple pathways to emerging internalization. *Child Development, 66,* 597–615.

Kochanska, G., Murray, K., & Coy, K. (1997). Inhibitory control as a contributor to conscience in childhood: From toddler to early school age. *Child Development, 68,* 263–277.

Kochanska, G., & Thompson, R. A. (1997). The emergence and development of conscience in toddlerhood and early childhood. In J. E. Grusec & L. Kuczynski (Eds.), *Parenting and children's internalization of values* (pp. 53–77). New York: Wiley.

Kochenderfer, B. J., & Ladd, G. W. (1996a). Peer victimization: Cause or consequences of school maladjustment. *Child Development, 67,* 1305–1317.

Kochenderfer, B. J., & Ladd, G. W. (1996b). Peer victimization: Manifestations and relations to school adjustment. *Journal of School Psychology, 34,* 267–283.

Kohlberg, L. (1963a). The development of children's orientations towards a moral order: 1. Sequence in the development of moral thought. *Vita Humana, 6,* 11–33.

Kohlberg, L. (1963b). Moral development and identification. In H. W. Stevenson (Ed.), *Child psychology. Sixty-second Yearbook of the National Society for the Study of Education.* Chicago: University of Chicago Press.

Kohlberg, L. (1969). *Stages in the development of moral thought and action.* New York: Holt.

Kohlberg, L. (1985). *The psychology of moral development.* San Francisco: Harper & Row.

Kohlberg, L., & Candee, D. (1984). The relationship of moral judgment to moral action. In W. M. Kurtines & J. L. Gewirtz (Eds.), *Morality, moral behavior and moral development.* New York: Wiley.

Kohlberg, L. A. (1966). A cognitive-developmental analysis of children's sex-role concepts and attitudes. In E. E. Maccoby (Ed.), *The development of sex differences* (pp. 82–173). Stanford, CA: Stanford University Press.

Kohn, M. L., & Schooler, C. (1983). *Work and personality: An inquiry into the impact of social stratification.* Norwood, NJ: Ablex.

Kohnstamm, G. A. (1989). Temperament in childhood: Cross-cultural and sex differences. In G. A. Kohnstamm, J. E. Bates, & M. K. Rothbart (Eds.), *Temperament in childhood* (pp. 483–508). West Sussex: Wiley.

Kolb, B. (1989). Brain development, plasticity & behavior. *American Psychologist, 44,* 1203–1212.

Koocher, G., & D'Angelo, E. J. (1992). Evolution of practice in child psychotherapy. In

I. Freedheim (Ed.), *History of psychotherapy* (pp. 457–492). Washington, DC: American Psychological Association.

Koolstra, C. M., van der Voort, T. H. A., & van der Kamp, L. J. (1997). Television's impact on children's reading comprehension and decoding skills: A 3-year panel study. *Reading Research Quarterly, 32,* 128–152.

Kopp, C. B. (1982). The antecedents of self-regulation. *Developmental Psychology, 18,* 199–214.

Kopp, C. B. (1983). Risk factors in development. In M. M. Haith & J. Campos (Eds.), *Infancy and developmental psychobiology: Vol. 2. Handbook of child psychology.* New York: Wiley.

Kopp, C. B. (1987). The growth of self-regulation: Caregivers and children. In N. Eisenberg (Ed.), *Contemporary topics in developmental psychology.* New York: Wiley.

Kopp, C. B. (1992). Emotional distress and control in young children. In N. Eisenberg & R. A. Fabes (Eds.), *Emotion and its regulation in early development.* San Francisco: Joseey-Bass.

Kopp, C. B. (1994). *Baby steps: The "whys" of your child's behavior in the first two years.* New York: W. H. Freeman.

Kopp, C. B., & Kaler, S. R. (1989). Risk in infancy: Origins and implications. *American Psychologist, 44,* 224–230.

Kopp, C. B., & Wyer, N. (1994). Self-regulation in normal and atypical development. In D. Cicchetti & S. L. Toth (Eds.), *Rochester symposium on developmental psychopathology: Vol. 5. Disorders and dysfunctions of the self* (pp. 31–56). Rochester, NY: University of Rochester Press.

Korner, A. (1974). The effect of the infant's state, level of arousal, sex and ontogenic stage on the caregiver. In M. Lewis & L. Rosenblum (Eds.), *The effect of the infant on its caregiver.* New York: Wiley.

Korner, A. F. (1989). Infant stimulation: The pros and cons in historical perspective. *Bulletin of National Center for Clinical Infant Programs, 10,* 11–17.

Korner, A. F., & Thoman, E. (1970). Visual alertness in neonates as evoked by maternal care. *Journal of Experimental Child Psychology, 10,* 67–78.

Kotelchuck, M. (1995). Reducing infant mortality and improving birth outcomes for families of poverty. In H. E. Fitzgerald, B. M. Lester & B. S. Zuckerman (Eds.), *Children of poverty: Research, health, and policy issues, Reference books on family issues* (Vol. 23, pp. 151–166). New York: Garland Publishing.

Kotovsky, L., & Baillargeon, R. (1994). Calibration-based reasoning about collision events in 11-month-old infants. *Cognition, 51,* 107–129.

Kraemer, H. C., Korner, A., Andes, T., Jacklin, C. N., & Dimiceli, S. (1985). Obstetric drugs and infant behavior: A re-evaluation. *Journal of Pediatric Psychology, 10,* 345–353.

Kramer, L., & Gottman, J. M. (1992). Becoming a sibling—with a little help from my friends. *Developmental Psychology, 28,* 685–699.

Krashen, S. (1975). The critical period for language acquisition and its possible bases. In D. Aaronson & R. W. Reiber (Eds.), *Annals of the New York Academy of Sciences: Vol. 263.*

Developmental psycholinguistics and communication disorders (pp. 211–224). New York: New York Academy of Sciences.

Kraus, N., McGee, T. J., Carrell, T. D., Zecler, S. G., Nicol, T. G., & Koch, D. B. (1996). Auditory neurophysiologic responses and discrimination deficits in children with learning problems. *Science, 273,* 971–973.

Kreutzer, M. A., Leonard, C., & Flavell, J. H. (1975). An interview study of children's knowledge about memory. *Monographs of the Society for Research in Child Development, 40,* 1–60.

Krogman, W. M. (1972). *Child growth.* Ann Arbor: University of Michigan Press.

Kruesi, M. J., Hibbs, E. D., Zahn, T. P., & Keysor, C. S. (1992). A 2-year prospective follow-up study of children and adolescents with disruptive behavior disorders: Prediction by cerebrospinal fluid 5-hydroxyindoleacetic acid, homovanillic acid and autonomic measures? *Archives of General Psychiatry, 49,* 429–435.

Kubey, R., & Csikszentmihalyi, M. (1990). *Television and the quality of life.* Hillsdale, NJ: Erlbaum.

Kuchner, J. F. R. (1980). *Chinese-American and European-American: A cross-cultural study of infant and mother.* Unpublished doctoral dissertation. University of Chicago.

Kuczaj, S. A. (1982). *Language development: Syntax and semantics* (Vol. 1). Hillsdale, NJ: Erlbaum.

Kuczynski, L. (1983). Reasoning, prohibitions, and motivations for compliance. *Developmental Psychology, 19,* 126–134.

Kuczynski, L., & Kochanska, G. (1990). Development of children's noncompliance strategies from toddlerhood to age 5. *Developmental Psychology, 26,* 398–408.

Kuczynski, L., Kochanska, G., Radke-Yarrow, M., & Girnius-Brown, O. (1987). A developmental interpretation of young children's noncompliance. *Developmental Psychology, 23,* 799–806.

Kuczynski, L., Marshall, S., & Schell, K. (1997). Value socialization in a bidirectional context. In J. E. Grusec & L. Kuczynski (Eds.), *Parenting and children's internalization of values: A handbook of contemporary theory* (pp. 23–50). New York: Wiley.

Kuhl, P. K., Andruski, J. E., Christovich, I. A., Christovich, L. A., et al. (1997). Cross-language analysis of phonetic units in language addressed to infants. *Science, 277,* 684–686.

Kuhl, P. K., & Miller, J. D. (1975). Speech perception by the chinchilla: voice-voiceless distinction in alveolar plosive consonants. *Science, 190,* 69–72.

Kuhl, P. K., Williams, K. A., Lacerda, F., Stevens, K. N., & Lindblom, B. (1992). Linguistic experience alters phonetic perception in infants by 6 months of age. *Science, 255,* 606–608.

Kuhn, D. (1991). Reasoning, higher order in adolescence. In R. M. Lerner, A. C. Petersen, & J. Brooks-Gunn (Eds.), *Encyclopedia of adolescence* (Vol. 2). New York: Garland.

Kuhn, D. (1998). Afterword to Volume 2: Cognition, perception, and language. In W. Damon (Gen. Ed.), D. Kuhn, & R. S. Siegler (Vol. Eds.), *Handbook of child psychology: Vol. 2. Cognition, perception, and language* (pp. 979–981). New York: Wiley.

Kumanyika, S. (1993). Ethnicity and obesity development in children. In C. L. Williams & S. Y. S. Kimm (Eds.), *Prevention and treatment of childhood obesity* (pp. 81–92). Annals of the New York Academy of Sciences, Vol. 699. New York: The New York Academy of Sciences.

Kunkel, D., & Canepa, J. (1994). Broadcasters license renewal claims regarding children's educational programming. *Journal of Broadcasting and Electronic Media, 38*, 397–416.

Kunkel, D., & Roberts, D. (1991). Young minds and marketplace values: Issues for children's television advertising. *Journal of Social Issues, 47*, 57–72.

Kunzinger, E. L., & Witryol, S. L. (1984). The effects of differential incentives on second-grade rehearsal and free recall. *The Journal of Genetic Psychology, 144*, 19–30.

Kurtz, B. E., & Borkowski, J. G. (1987). Development of strategic skills in impulsive and reflective children: A longitudinal study of metacognition. *Journal of Experimental Child Psychology, 43*, 129–148.

La Barbera, J. D., Izard, C. E., Vietze, P., & Parisi, S. A. (1976). Four- and six-month-old infants' visual responses to joy, anger, and neutral expressions. *Child Development, 47*, 535–538.

Labarthe, J. C. (1997). Are boys better than girls at building a tower or a bridge at 2 years of age? *Archives of Disease in Childhood, 77*, 140–144.

Lackovic-Grgin, K., Dekovic, M., & Opačic, G. (1994). Pubertal status, interaction with significant others, and self-esteem of adolescent girls. *Adolescence, 29*, 681–700.

Ladd, G. W. (1981). Effectiveness of a social learning method for enhancing children's social interaction and peer acceptance. *Child Development, 52*, 171–178.

Ladd, G. W., & Emerson, E. S. (1984). Shared knowledge in children's friendships. *Developmental Psychology, 20*, 932–940.

Ladd, G. W., & Golter, B. S. (1988). Parents' management of preschooler's peer relations: Is it related to children's social competence? *Developmental Psychology, 24*, 109–117.

Ladd, G. W., & LeSieur, K. D. (1995). Parents and children's peer relationships. In M. H. Bornstein (Ed.), *Handbook of parenting: Vol. 4. Applied and practical parenting* (pp. 377–410). Mahwah, NJ: Erlbaum.

Ladd, G. W., Muth, S., & Hart, C. H. (1992). Parent's management of children's peer relations: Facilitating and supervising children's activities in the peer cultures. In R. D. Parke & G. W. Ladd (Eds.), *Family-peer relationships: Modes of linkage.* Hillsdale, NJ: Erlbaum.

Lagerspetz, K. M. J., & Bjorkqvist, K. (1994). Indirect aggression in boys and girls. In L. R. Huesmann (Ed.), *Aggressive behavior: Current perspectives* (pp. 131–150). New York: Plenum Press.

Lamb, M. E. (1977). Father-infant and mother-infant interaction in the first year of life. *Child Development, 48*, 167–181.

Lamb, M. E. (Ed.). (1987). *The father's role: Cross-cultural perspectives.* New York: Wiley.

Lamb, M. E. (1996). *The role of the father in child development* (3rd ed.). New York: Wiley.

Lamb, M. E. (1998). Nonparental child care: Context, quality, correlates and consequences. In W. Damon (Ed.), *Handbook of child psychology* (4th ed.). New York: Wiley.

Lamb, M. E., & Campos, J. (1982). *Development in infancy.* New York: Random House.

Lamb, M. E., Easterbrooks, A., & Holden, G. W. (1980). Reinforcement and punishment among preschoolers: Characteristics, effects and correlates. *Child Development, 51*, 1230–1236.

Lamb, M. E., Frodi, A. M., Hwang, P., & Frodi, M. (1982). Varying degrees of paternal involvement in infant care: Attitudinal and behavioral correlates. In M. E. Lamb (Ed.), *Nontraditional families.* Hillsdale, NJ: Erlbaum.

Lamb, M. E., & Roopnarine, J. L. (1979). Peer influences on sex role development in preschoolers. *Child Development, 50*, 1219–1222.

Lamb, M. E., Suomi, S. J., & Stephenson, G. R. (1979). *Social interaction analysis: Methodological issues.* Madison, WI: University of Wisconsin Press.

Lambert, M. C., Weisz, J. R., & Knight, F. (1989). Over- and undercontrolled clinic referral problems of Jamaican and American children and adolescents: The culture general and the culture specific. *Journal of Consulting & Clinical Psychology, 57*, 467–472.

Lambert, S. R., & Drack, A. V. (1996). Infantile cataracts. *Survey of Ophthalmology, 40*, 427–458.

Lambert, W. E. (1987). The effects of bilingual and bicultural experiences on children's attitudes and social perspectives. In P. Homel, M. Palij, & D. Aranson (Eds.), *Childhood Bilingualism.* Hillsdale, NJ: Erlbaum.

Lambiotte, J. G., Dansereau, D. F., O'Donnell, A. M., Young, M. D., Skaggs, L. P., Hall, R. H., & Rocklin, T. R. (1987). Manipulating cooperative scripts for teaching and learning. *Journal of Educational Psychology, 79*, 424–430.

Lander, E. S. (1996). The new genomics: Global views of biology. *Science, 274*, 536–538.

Landers, C. (1989). A psychobiological study of infant development in South India. In J. K. Nugent, B. M. Lester, & T. B. Brazelton (Eds.), *The cultural context of infancy: Vol. 1. Biology, culture, and infant development* (pp. 169–207). Norwood, NJ: Ablex.

Landesman-Dwyer, S., & Sackett, G. P. (1983, April). *Prenatal nicotine exposure and sleep-wake patterns in infancy.* Paper presented at the biennial meeting of the Society for Research in Child Development, Detroit.

Landry, S. H. (1995). The development of joint attention in premature, low birth weight infants: Effects of early medical complications and maternal attention-directing behaviors. In C. Moore & P. J. Dunham (Eds.), *Joint attention and its role in development.* Hillsdale, NJ: Erlbaum.

Lane, H. (1976). *The wild boy of Aveyron.* Cambridge, MA: Harvard University Press.

Laney, M. D. (1990). Perspectives and interventions. In M. Lewis & S. Miller (Eds.), *Handbook of developmental psychopathology.* New York: Plenum.

Langlois, J. H. (1985). From the eye of the beholder to behavior reality: The development of social behaviors and social relations as a function of physical attractiveness. In C. P. Herman (Ed.), *Physical appearance, stigma, and social behavior.* Hillsdale, NJ: Erlbaum.

Langlois, J. H., & Downs, C. A. (1979). Peer relations as a function of physical attractiveness: The eye of the beholder or behavioral reality? *Child Development, 50*, 409–418.

Langlois, J. H., & Downs, C. A. (1980). Mothers, fathers and peers as socialization agents of sex-typed play behaviors in young children. *Child Development, 51*, 1237–1247.

Langlois, J. H., Roggman, L. A., Casey, R. J., Ritter, J. M., Rieser-Danner, L. A., & Jenkins, V. Y. (1987). Infant preferences for attractive faces: Rudiments of a stereotype? *Developmental Psychology, 23*, 363–369.

Langlois, J. H., Roggman, L. A., & Rieser-Danner, L. A. (1990). Infants' differential social responses to attractive and unattractive faces. *Developmental Psychology, 26*, 153–159.

Langlois, J. H., & Stephan, C. (1981). Beauty and the beast: The role of physical attractiveness in the development of peer relations and social behavior. In S. S. Brehm, S. H. Kassin, & F. X. Gibbons (Eds.), *Developmental social psychology.* New York: Oxford University Press.

Larrance, D. T., & Twentyman, C. T. (1983). Maternal attributions and child abuse. *Journal of Abnormal Psychology, 92*, 449–457.

Larson, R. (1997). The emergence of solitude as a constrictive domain of experience in early adolescence. *Child Development, 68*, 80–93.

Larson, R., & Lampman-Petraitis, C. (1989). Daily emotional states as reported by children and adolescents. *Child Development, 60*, 1250–1260.

Larson, R., & Richards, M. H. (1994). *Divergent realities: The emotional lives of mothers, fathers and adolescents.* New York: Basic Books.

Lasken, D. (1998, January 13). It's time to abandon bilingual education. *The New York Times,* p. A19.

Laursen, B., Hartup, W. W., & Koplas, A. L. (1996). Towards understanding peer conflict. *Merrill-Palmer Quarterly, 42*, 76–102.

Lave, J. (1977). Cognitive consequences of traditional apprenticeship training in West Africa. *Anthropology & Education Quarterly, 8*, 177–180.

Lazar, I., & Darlington, R. (1982). Lasting effects of early education: A report from the Consortium of Longitudinal Studies. *Monographs of the Society for Research in Child Development, 47*, 1–151.

Leahy, A. M. (1935). Nature-nurture and intelligence. *Genetic Psychology Monographs, 17*, 235–308.

Leaper, C. (1994). Exploring the consequences of gender segregation on social relationships. In C. Leaper (Ed.), *Childhood gender segregation: causes & consequences. New Directions for child development. No. 65* (pp. 67–86). San Francisco, CA: Jossey-Bass.

Leaper, C., Anderson, K. J., & Sanders, P. (1998). Moderators of gender effects on parents' talk to their children: A meta-analysis. *Developmental Psychology.*

Leaper, C., Leve, L., Strasser, T., & Schwartz, R. (1995). Mother-child communication sequences: Play activity, child gender, and marital status effects. *Merrill-Palmer Quarterly, 41*, 307–327.

Lee, V. E., Brooks-Gunn, J., & Schnur, E. (1988). Does Head Start work? A 1-year follow-up comparison of disadvantaged children attending Head Start, no preschool, and other preschool programs. *Developmental Psychology, 24*, 210–222.

Lee, V. E., Brooks-Gunn, J., Schnur, E., & Liaw, F. (1990). Are Head Start effects sustained? A longitudinal follow-up comparison of disadvantaged children attending Head Start, no preschool, and other preschool programs. *Child Development, 61*, 495–507.

Lefrancois, G. R. (1973). *Of children.* Belmont, CA: Wadsworth.

Lei, T., & Cheng, S. (1989). A little but special light on the university of moral judgment development. In L. Kohlberg, D. Candee, & A. Colby (Eds.), *Rethinking moral development.* Cambridge, MA: Harvard University Press.

Leibert, R. M., & Baron, R. A. (1972). Some immediate effects of televised violence on children's behavior. *Developmental Psychology, 6*, 469–475.

Leichtman, M. D., & Ceci, S. J. (1995). The effects of stereotypes and suggestions on preschoolers' reports. *Developmental Psychology, 31*, 758.

Leiderman, P. H. (1983). Social ecology and childbirth: The newborn nursery as environmental stressor. In N. Garmezy & M. Rutter (Eds.), *Stress, coping and development in children.* New York: McGraw-Hill.

Leinbach, M. D., & Fagot, B. I. (1992). *Gender-schematic processing in infancy: Categorical habituation to male and female faces.* Unpublished manuscript. University of Oregon, Eugene.

Leippe, M. R., & Romanczyk, A. (1989). Reactions to child (versus adult) eyewitnesses: The influence of jurors' preconceptions and witness behavior. *Law & Human Behavior, 13*, 103–132.

Leming, J. S. (1978). Cheating behavior, situational influence and moral development. *Journal of Educational Research, 71*, 214–217.

Lenneberg, E. H. (1967). *Biological foundations of language.* New York: Wiley.

Lenneberg, E. H., Rebelsky, F. G., & Nichols, I. A. (1965). The vocalizations of infants born to deaf and hearing parents. *Human Development, 8*, 23–37.

Lepper, M., & Hoddell, M. (1988). Intrinsic motivation in the classroom. In C. Ames & R. Ames (Eds.), *Research on motivation in education* (Vol. 3, pp. 73–107). New York: Academic.

Lepper, M. R. (1985). Microcomputers in education: Motivation and social issues. *American Psychologist, 40*, 1–18.

Lepper, M. R., Greene, D., & Nisbett, R. (1973). Test of the "overjustification hypothesis." *Journal of Personality and Social Psychology, 28*, 129–137.

Lepper, M. R., & Gurtner, J. (1989). Children and computers: Approaching the twenty-first century. *American Psychologist, 44*, 170–178.

Lepper, M. R., Woolverton, M., Mumme, D. L., & Gurtner, J. L. (1993). Motivational techniques of expert human tutors: Lessons for the design of computer-based tutors. In S. P. Lajoie & S. J. Derry (Eds.), *Computers as cognitive tools: Technology in education* (pp. 75–105). Hillsdale, NJ: Erlbaum.

Lerner, J. V. (1994). Maternal employment and children's socio-emotional development. In J. V. Lerner (Ed.), *Working women and their families* (pp. 54–86). Thousand Oaks, CA: Sage.

Lerner, R. M. (1984). *On the nature of human plasticity.* New York: Cambridge University Press.

Lerner, R. M., & Lerner, J. V. (1983). Temperament-intelligence reciprocities in early childhood: A contextual model. In M. Lewis (Ed.), *Origins of intelligence: Infancy and early childhood* (2nd ed., pp. 399–421). New York: Plenum.

Leslie, A. M. (1994). ToMM, ToBy, and Agency: Core architecture and domain specificity. In L. A. Hirschfeld & S. A. Gelman (Eds.), *Mapping the mind: Domain specificity in cognition and culture* (pp. 119–148). New York: Cambridge University Press.

Leslie, A. M., & Keeble, S. (1987). Do six-month-old infants perceive causality? *Cognition, 25*, 265–288.

Leslie, A. M., & Roth, D. (1993). What autism teaches us about metarepresentation. In S. Baron-Cohen, H. Tager-Flusberg, & D. J. Cohen (Eds.), *Understanding other minds: Perspectives on autism.* Oxford, England: Oxford University Press.

Lesser, G. S., Fifer, G., & Clark, D. H. (1965). Mental abilities of children from different social class and cultural groups. *Monographs of the Society for Research in Child Development, 30*(4, Serial No. 102), 1–115.

Lester, B., Hoffman, J., & Brazelton, T. B. (1985). The rhythmic structure of mother-infant interaction in term and preterm infants. *Child Development, 56*, 15–27.

Lester, B. M. (1988). Neurobehavioral assessment of the infant at risk. *Early identification of infants with developmental disabilities.* New York: Grune & Stratton.

Lester, B. M. (1991). *Neurobehavioral syndromes in cocaine exposed newborn infants.* Paper presented at the meeting of the Society for Research in Child Development, Seattle, WA.

Lester, B. M., Als, H., & Brazelton, T. B. (1982). Regional obstetric anesthesia and newborn behavior: A reanalysis toward synergistic effects. *Child Development, 53*, 687–692.

Lester, B. M., Boukydis, C. F. Z., Garcia Coll, C. T., Hole, W., & Peuker, M. (1992). Infantile colic: acoustic cry characteristics, maternal perception of cry, and temperament. *Infant Behavior and Development, 15*, 15–26.

Lester, B. M., Corwin, M., & Golub, H. (1988). Early detection of the infant at risk through cry analysis. In J. N. Newman (Ed.), *The psychological control of mammalian vocalization.* Hillsdale, NJ: Erlbaum.

Lester, B. M., & Dreher, M. (1989). Effects of marijuana use during pregnancy on newborn cry. *Child Development, 60*, 765–771.

Lester, B. M., McGrath, M. M., Garcia Coll, C., Brem, F. S., Sullivan, M. C., & Mattis, S. G. (1995). Relationship between risk and protective factors developmental outcomes and the home environment at four years of age in term and preterm infants. In H. E. Fitzgerald, B. M. Lester, & B. Zuckerman (Eds.), *Children of poverty, research, health and policy issues.* New York: Garland Press.

Levine, L., Tuber, S. B., Slade, A., & Ward, M. J. (1991). Mothers' mental representations and their relationship to mother-infant attachment. *Bulletin of the Menninger Clinic, 55*, 454–469.

Levine, L. J. (1995). Young children's understanding of the causes of anger and sadness. *Child Development, 66*, 697–709.

Levitt, M. J., Weber, R. A., & Clark, M. C. (1986). Social network relationships as sources of maternal support and well-being. *Developmental Psychology, 22*, 310–316.

Levy, G. D. (1989). Developmental and individual differences in preschoolers' recognition memories: The influences of gender schematization and verbal labeling of information. *Sex Roles, 21*, 305–324.

Levy, G. D. (1994). High and low gender schematic children's release from proactive interference. *Sex roles, 30*, 93–108.

Lewinsohn, P. M., & Rohde, P. (1993). The cognitive-behavioral treatment of depression in adolescents: Research and suggestions. *The Clinical Psychologist, 46*, 177–183.

Lewinsohn, P. M., Rohde, P., & Seeley, J. R. (1993). Psychosocial characteristics of adolescents with a history of suicide attempts. *Journal of the American Academy of Child and Adolescent Psychiatry, 32*, 600–668.

Lewis, M. (1983). On the nature of intelligence: Science or bias? In M. Lewis (Ed.), *Origins of intelligence: Infancy and early childhood* (2nd ed., pp. 1–24). New York: Plenum.

Lewis, M. (1989). Cultural differences in children's knowledge of emotional scripts. In C. Saarni & P. L. Harris (Eds.), *Children's understanding of emotion.* New York: Cambridge University Press.

Lewis, M. (1991). *Shame, the exposed self.* New York: Free Press.

Lewis, M. (1992). *Shame: The exposed self.* New York: The Free Press.

Lewis, M., Alessandri, S., Sullivan, M. W. (1992). Differences in shame and pride as a function of children's gender and task difficulty. *Child Development, 63*, 630–638.

Lewis, M., & Brooks, J. (1974). Self, other and fear: Infants' reactions to people. In M. Lewis & L. Rosenblum (Eds.), *The origins of fear.* New York: Wiley.

Lewis, M., & Freedle, R. (1973). The mother-infant dyad. In P. Pliner, L. Kranes, & T. Alloway (Eds.), *Communication and affect: Language and thought.* New York: Academic.

Lewis, M., & Michaelson, L. (1985). *Children's emotions and moods.* New York: Plenum.

Lewis, M., Ramsey, D. S., & Kawakami, K. (1993). Differences between Japanese infants and Caucasian American infants in behavioral and cortisol response to inoculation. *Child Development, 64*, 1722–1731.

Lewis, M. & Wilson, C. D. (1972). Infant development in lower-class American families. *Human Development, 15,* 112–127.

Liaw, F., & Brooks-Gunn, J. (1994). Cumulative familial risks and low birthweight children's cognitive and behavioral development. *Journal of Clinical Child Psychology, 23,* 360–372.

Liben, L., & Downs, R. (1993). Understanding person-space-map relations: Cartographic and developmental perspectives. *Developmental Psychology, 39,* 739–752.

Liben, L. S. (1991). Adults' performance on horizontality tasks: Conflicting frames of reference. *Developmental Psychology, 27,* 285–294.

Liben, L. S., & Bigler, R. S. (1987). Reformulating children's gender schemata. In L. S. Liben & M. L. Signorella (Eds.), *Children's gender schemata.* San Francisco: Jossey-Bass.

Liben, L. S., & Downs, R. M. (1989). Understanding maps as symbols: The development of map concepts in children. In H. W. Reese (Ed.), *Advances in child development and behavior* (Vol. 22, pp. 145–201). New York: Academic Press.

Liben, L. S., & Golbeck, S. L. (1980). Sex differences in performance on Piagetian spatial tasks: Differences in competence or performance. *Child Development, 51,* 594–597.

Liberman, I. Y., Shankweiler, D., Liberman, A. M., Fowler, C., & Fischer, F. W. (1976). Phonetic segmentation and recoding in the beginning reader. In A. S. Reber & D. Scarborough (Eds.), *Reading: Theory and practice.* Hillsdale, NJ: Erlbaum.

Lieberman, A. F., Weston, D. R., & Paul, J. H. (1991). Preventive intervention and outcome with anxiously attached dyads. *Child Development, 62,* 199–209.

Lieberman, E., Lang, J. M., Frigoletto, F., Jr., Richardson, D. K., Rengin, S. A., & Cohen, A. (1997). Epidural analgesic, intrapartum fever, and neonatal sepsis evaluation. *Pediatrics, 99,* 415–419.

Liebert, R. M., & Baron, R. A. (1972). Some immediate effects of televised violence on children's behavior. *Developmental Psychology, 6,* 469–475.

Liebert, R. M., & Sprafkin, J. (1988). *The early window: Effects of television on children and youth.* New York: Pergamon.

Liederman, P. H., Landsman, M., & Clark, C. (1990, March). *Making it or blowing it: Coping strategies and academic performance in a multiethnic high school population.* Paper presented at the biennial meeting of the Society for Research on Adolescence, Atlanta.

Liker, J. K., & Elder, G. (1983). Economic hardship and marital relations in the 1930s. *American Sociological Review, 48,* 343–359.

Lin, C., Verp, M. S., & Sabbagha, R. E. (1993). *The high risk fetus: Pathophysiology, diagnosis, management.* New York: Springer/Verlag.

Lindberg, M. (1980). Is knowledge base development a necessary and sufficient condition for memory development? *Journal of Experimental Child Psychology, 30,* 401–410.

Lindell, S. G. (1988). Education for childbirth: A time for change. *Journal of Obstetrics, Gynecology and Neonatal Nursing, 17,* 108–112.

Linn, M. C., & Hyde, J. S. (1989). Gender, mathematics, and science. *Educational Researcher, 18,* 17–27.

Linn, M. C., & Hyde, J. S. (1991). Trends in cognitive and psychosocial gender differences. In R. M. Lerner, A. C. Petersen, & J. Brooks-Gunn (Eds.), *The encyclopedia of adolescence.* New York: Garland.

Linn, S., Lieberman, E., Schoenbaum, S. C., Monson, R. R., Stubblefield, P. G., & Ryand, K. J. (1988). Adverse outcomes of pregnancy in women exposed to diethylstilbestrol in utero. *Journal of Reproductive Medicine, 33,* 3–7.

Linney, J. A., & Seidman, E. (1989). The future of schooling. *American Psychologist, 44,* 336–340.

Lipscomb, T. J., McAllister, H. A., & Bregman, N. J. (1985). A developmental inquiry into the effects of multiple models on children's generosity. *Merrill-Palmer Quarterly, 31,* 335–344.

Lipsett, S. P. (1990). Learning and memory in infants. *Merrill-Palmer Quarterly, 36,* 53–66.

Lipsitt, L. P., & Werner, J. S. (1981). The infancy of human learning processes. In E. Gollin (Ed.), *Developmental plasticity.* New York: Academic Press.

Little, G. A. (1992). The fetus at risk. In F. A. Hoekelman, S. B., Friedman, N. M., Nelson, & H. M., Seidel (Eds.), *Primary pediatric care* (2nd ed.). St. Louis: Mosby Yearbook.

Little, R. (1975). *Maternal alcohol use and resultant birth weight.* Unpublished doctoral dissertation. Johns Hopkins University, Baltimore, MD.

Liu, L. L., Clemens, C. J., Shay, D. K., Davis, R. L., & Novack, A. H. (1997). The safety of newborn early discharge. *The Journal of the American Medical Association, 278,* 293–298.

Livesley, W. J., & Bromley, D. B. (1973). *Person perception in childhood and adolescence.* London, England: Wiley.

Localio, A. R., Lawthers, A. G., Bengston, J. M., Herbert, L. E., Weaver, S. L., Brennan, T. A., & Landis, J. R. (1993). Relationship between malpractice claims and caesarean delivery. *Journal of the American Medical Association, 269,* 366–373.

Loeber, R., & Hay, D. F. (1993). Developmental approaches to aggression and conduct problems. In M. Rutter & D. F. Hay (Eds.), *Development through life: A handbook for clinicians* (pp. 488–516). Oxford: Blackwell Scientific Publications.

Loehlin, J. C., Willerman, L., & Horn, J. M. (1988). Human behavior genetics. *Annual Review of Psychology, 39,* 101–133.

Lollis, S. P., & Ross, H. S. (1992). Parents' regulation in children's peer interactions: Direct influences. In R. D. Parke & G. W. Ladd (Eds.), *Family-peer relationships: Modes of linkage.* Hillsdale, NJ: Erlbaum.

Loney, J., Kramer, J., & Milich, R. (1981). The hyperkinetic child grows up: Predictors of symptoms, delinquency, and achievement at follow-up. In K. D. Gadow & J. Loney (Eds.), *Psychosocial aspects of drug treatment for hyperactivity.* Boulder, CO: Westview.

Lorch, E. P., Bellack, D. R., & Augsbach, L. H. (1987). Young children's memory for televised stories: Effects of importance. *Child Development, 58,* 453–463.

Loudal, L. T. (1989). Sex role messages in television commercials: An update. *Sex Roles, 21,* 715–724.

Lovaas, O. I. (1987). Behavioral treatment and normal educational and intellectual functioning in young autistic children. *Journal of Consulting and Clinical Psychology, 55,* 3–9.

Lovaas, O. I., & Smith, P. (1988). Intensive behavioral treatment for young autistic children. In B. Lahey & A. Kazdin (Eds.), *Advances in clinical child psychology* (Vol. 2). New York: Plenum.

Lovaas, O. I., Smith, T., & McEachin, J. J. (1989). Clarifying comments on the young autism study: Reply to Schopler, Short, and Mesiboo. *Journal of Consulting and Clinical Psychology, 57,* 165–167.

Lovaas, O. I., Young, D. B., & Newsom, C. D. (1978). Childhood psychosis: Behavioral treatment. In B. B. Wolman (Ed.), *Handbook of treatment of mental disorders in childhood and adolescence.* Englewood Cliffs, NJ: Prentice-Hall.

Loveland, K. A. (1987). Behavior of young children with Down syndrome before the mirror: Exploration. *Child Development, 58,* 768–778.

Lovett, S. B., & Pillow, B. H. (1995). Development of the ability to distinguish between comprehension and memory: Evidence from strategy-selection tasks. *Journal of Educational Psychology, 87,* 523–536.

Lovett, S. B., & Pillow, B. H. (1996). Development of the ability to distinguish between comprehension and memory: Evidence from goal-state evaluation tasks. *Journal of Educational Psychology, 88,* 546–562.

Lozoff, B. (1989). Nutrition and behavior. *American Psychologist, 44,* 231–236.

Luecke-Aleksa, D., Anderson, D. R., Collins, P. A., & Schmitt, K. L. (1995). Gender constancy and television viewing. *Developmental Psychology, 31,* 773–780.

Lummis, M., & Stevenson, H. W. (1990). Gender differences in beliefs and achievement: A cross-cultural study. *Developmental Psychology, 26,* 254–263.

Luria, A. R. (1971). Towards the problem of the historical nature of psychological processes. *International Journal of Psychology, 6,* 259–272.

Luthar, S., Burack, J., Ciccetti, D., & Weisz, J. (1997). *Developmental psychopathology: Perspectives in adjustment risk and disorder.* New York: Cambridge University Press.

Luthar, S. S. (1991). Vulnerability and resilience: A study of high-risk adolescents. *Child Development, 62,* 600–616.

Luthar, S. S., & Zigler, E. (1991). Vulnerability and competence: A review of research on resilience in childhood. *American Journal of Orthopsychiatry, 61,* 6–22.

Lutiger, B., Graham, K., Einarson, T. R., & Koren, G. (1991). Relationship between gestational cocaine use and pregnancy outcome: A meta-analysis. *Teratology, 44,* 405–414.

Lykken, D. T., McGue, M., Tellegen, A., & Bouchard, T. J., Jr. (1992). Genetic traits that may not run in families. *American Psychologist, 47*(12), 1565–1577.

Lynch, M. P., Eilers, R. E., Oller, D. K., & Urbano, R. C. (1990). Innateness, experience, and music perception. *Psychological Science, 1,* 272–276.

Lyon, T. D., & Flavell, J. H. (1993). Young children's understanding of forgetting over time. *Child Development, 64,* 789–800.

Lyons-Ruth, K., Alpern, L., & Repacholi, B. (1993). Disorganized infant attachment classification and maternal psychosocial problems as predictors of hostile-aggressive behavior in the preschool classroom. *Child Development, 64,* 572–585.

Lyons-Ruth, K., Connell, D. B., Gruenbaum, H. U., & Botein, S. (1990). Infants at social risk: Maternal depression and family support services as mediators of infant development and security of attachment. *Child Development, 61,* 85–98.

Lyons-Ruth, K., Easterbrooks, M. A., & Cibelli, C. D. (1997). Infant attachment strategies, infant mental lag, and maternal depressive symptoms: Predictions of internalizing and externalizing problems at age 7. *Developmental Psychology, 33,* 681–692.

Lyons-Ruth, K., Easterbrooks, M. A., & Davidson, C. (1995, April). *Disorganized attachment strategies and mental lag in infancy: Prediction of externalizing problems at seven.* Paper presented at biennial meeting of the Society for Research in Child Development, Indianapolis.

Lyons-Ruth, K., Repacholi, B., McLeod, S., & Silva, E. (1991). Disorganized attachment behavior in infancy: Short-term stability, maternal and infant correlates, and risk-related subtypes. *Development and Psychopathology, 3,* 377–396.

Lytton, H. (1980). *Parent-child interaction: The socialization process observed in twin and singleton families.* New York: Plenum.

Lytton, H., & Romney, D. M. (1991). Parents' differential socialization of boys and girls: A meta-analysis. *Psychological Bulletin, 109,* 267–296.

Maccoby, E. E. (1988). Gender as a social category. *Developmental Psychology, 24,* 755–765.

Maccoby, E. E. (1990). Gender and relationships: A developmental account. *American Psychologist, 45,* 513–521.

Maccoby, E. E., & Jacklin, C. (1980). Sex differences in aggression: A rejoinder and reprise. *Child Development, 51,* 964–980.

Maccoby, E. E., & Jacklin, C. N. (1974). *The psychology of sex differences.* Stanford, CA: Stanford University Press.

Maccoby, E. E, & Jacklin, C. N. (1987). Gender segregation in childhood. In H. W. Reese (Ed.), *Advances in child development and behavior* (Vol. 20, pp. 239–288). New York: Academic.

Maccoby, E. E., & Martin, J. A. (1983). Socialization in the context of the family: Parent-child interaction. In E. M. Hetherington (Ed.), *Socialization, personality, and social development: Vol. 4. Handbook of child psychology.* New York: Wiley.

Maccoby, E. E., & Mnookin, R. (Eds.). (1992). *Dividing the child.* Cambridge, MA: Harvard University Press.

MacDonald, K. (1993). Parent-child play: An evolutionary perspective. In K. MacDonald (Ed.), *Parent-child play: Descriptions and implications* (pp. 113–143). Albany, NY: SUNY Press.

MacDonald, K., & Parke, R. D. (1984). Bridging the gap: The relationship between parent-child play and peer interactive competence. *Child Development, 55,* 1265–1277.

MacDonald, K., & Parke, R. D. (1986). Parent-child physical play: The effects of sex and age of children and parents. *Sex Roles, 15,* 367–378.

Macfarlane, J. A. (1975). Olfaction in the development of social preferences in the human neonate. In M. A. Hofer (Ed.), *Parent-infant interaction.* Amsterdam: Elsevier.

MacFarlane, J. W., Allen, L., & Honzik, M. P. (1954). *A developmental study of the behavior problems of normal children between 21 months and 14 years of age.* Berkeley and Los Angeles: University of California Press.

MacMillan, D. L., Keogh, B. K., & Jones, R. L. (1986). Special education research on mildly handicapped learners. In M. C. Wittrock (Ed.), *Handbook of research on teaching* (3rd ed.). New York: Macmillan.

Magai, C., & McFadden, S. H. (1995). *The role of emotions in social and personality development.* New York: Plenum.

Magnusson, D. (1988). Individual development from an interactional perspective: A longitudinal study. In D. Magnusson (Ed.), *Paths through life* (Vol. 1). Hillsdale, NJ: Erlbaum.

Magnusson, D. (1996). (Ed.). *The life-span development of individuals: Behavioral, neurobiological and psychosocial perspectives.* Cambridge, England: Cambridge University Press.

Magnusson, D. (1996). Towards a developmental science. In D. Magnusson (Ed.), *The lifespan development of individuals.* Cambridge, England: Cambridge University Press.

Magnusson, D., & Stattin, H. (1998). Person-context interaction theories. In W. Damon (Ed.), *Handbook of child psychology* (Vol. 1). New York: Wiley.

Main, M. (1973). *Exploration, play and level of cognitive functioning as related to child-mother attachment.* Unpublished doctoral dissertation. Johns Hopkins University, Baltimore, MD.

Main, M., & Cassidy, J. (1988). Categories of response to reunion with the parent at age 6: Predictable from infant attachment classification and stable over a 1-month period. *Developmental Psychology, 24,* 415–426.

Main, M., & Hesse, E. (1990). Parents' unresolved traumatic experiences are related to infant disorganized attachment status: Is frightened and/or frightening parental behavior the linking mechanism? In M. T. Greenberg, D. Cicchetti, & E. M. Cummings (Eds.), *Attachment in the preschool years: Theory, research, and intervention* (pp. 161–182). Chicago, IL: University of Chicago Press.

Main, M., Kaplan, N., & Cassidy, J. (1985). Security in infancy, childhood, and adulthood: A move to the level of representation. *Monographs of the Society for Research in Child Development, 50,* 66–104.

Main, M., & Solomon, J. (1989). Procedures for identifying infants as disorganized/disoriented during the Ainsworth strange situation. In M. Greenberg, D. Cichetti, & M. Cummings (Eds.), *Attachment in the preschool years.* Chicago: University of Chicago Press.

Main, M., & Solomon, J. (1990). Procedures for identifying infants as disorganized/disoriented during the Ainsworth strange situation. In M. Greenberg, D. Cicchetti, & E. M. Cummings (Eds.), *Attachment in the preschool years: Theory, research and intervention* (pp. 121–160). Chicago: University of Chicago Press.

Main, M., & Weston, D. (1981). The quality of the toddler's relationship to mother and father: Related to conflict behavior and readiness to established new relationships. *Child Development, 52,* 932–940.

Maisels, M. J., & Kring, E. (1997). Early discharge from the newborn nursery—Effect on scheduling of follow-up visits by pediatricians. *Pediatrics, 100,* 72–74.

Malatesta, C. Z. (1982). The expression and regulation of emotion: A lifespan perspective. In T. Field & A. Fogel (Eds.), *Emotion and early interaction* (pp. 1–24). Hillsdale, NJ: Erlbaum.

Malatesta, C. Z., Culver, C., Tesman, J., & Shepard, B. (1989). The development of emotional expression during the first two years of life: Normative trends and patterns of individual differences. *Monographs of the Society for Research in Child Development, 54,* 1–2.

Malatesta, C. Z., Grigoryev, P., Lamb, C., Albin, M., & Culver, C. (1986). Emotion socialization and expressive development in preterm and full-term infants. *Child Development, 57,* 316–330.

Malatesta, C. Z., & Haviland, J. (1982). Learning display rules: The socialization of emotional expression in infancy. *Child Development, 53,* 991–1003.

Malatesta, C. Z., & Haviland, J. (1985). Signals, symbols, and socialization. In M. Lewis & C. Saarni (Eds.), *The socialization of emotions.* New York: Plenum.

Malatesta, C. Z., & Izard, C. E. (1984). The facial expression of emotion: Young, middle-aged and older adult expressions. In C. Z. Malatesta & C. E. Izard (Eds.), *Emotion in adult development* (pp. 253–273). Beverly Hills: Sage.

Malcolm, L. A. (1970). Growth of the Asai child of the Madang district of New Guinea. *Journal of Biosocial Science, 2,* 213–226.

Malinosky-Rummell, R., & Hansen, D. J. (1993). Long-term consequences of childhood physical abuse. *Psychological Bulletin, 114,* 68–79.

Mallick, S. K., & McCandless, B. R. (1966). A study of catharsis on aggression. *Journal of Personality and Social Psychology, 4,* 591–596.

Mancus, D. S. (1992). Influence of male teachers on elementary school children's stereotyping of teacher competence. *Sex Roles, 26(3/4),* 109–128.

Mandler, J. M. (1998). Representation. In W. Damon (Gen. Ed.), D. Kuhn, & R. S. Siegler (Vol. Eds.), *Handbook of child psychology: Vol. 2. Cognition, perception, and language* (pp. 255–308). New York: Wiley.

Mandler, J. M., & Bauer, P. J. (1988). The cradle of categorization: Is the basic level basic? *Cognitive Development, 3,* 247–264.

Manez, J. (1987). *Perception of impending collision in 3- to 6-week-old infants.* Unpublished doctoral dissertation. University of Minnesota.

Mangelsdorf, S., Gunnar, M., Kestenbaum, R., Lang, S., & Andreas, D. (1990). Infant proneness-to-distress, temperament, maternal personality and mother-infant attachment: Associations and goodness of fit. *Child Development, 61,* 820–831.

Mangelsdorf, S., Watkins, S., & Lehn, L. (1991, April). *The role of control in the infant's appraisal of strangers.* Paper presented at the biennial meeting of the Society for Research in Child Development, Seattle, Washington.

Mangelsdorf, S. C., Shapiro, J. R., & Marzolf, D. (1995). Developmental and temperamental differences in emotion regulation in infancy. *Child Development, 66,* 1817–1828.

Mann, J., Ten Have, T., Plunkett, J. W., & Meisels, S. J. (1991). Time sampling: A methodological critique. *Child Development, 62,* 227–241.

Maratsos, M. (1983). Some current issues in the study of the acquisition of grammar. In P. H. Mussen (Ed.), *Handbook of child psychology* (Vol. 3). New York: Wiley.

Maratsos, M. (1989). Innateness and plasticity in language acquisition. In M. Rice & R. L. Shiefelbusch (Eds.), *The teachability of language.* Baltimore, MD: Brooks/Cole.

Maratsos, M. (1998). The acquisition of grammar. In W. Damon (Gen. Ed.), D. Kuhn, & R. S. Siegler (Vol. Eds.), *Handbook of child psychology: Vol. 2. Cognition, perception, and language* (5th ed., pp. 421–466). New York: Wiley.

Maratsos, M., & Chalkley, M. A. (1980). The internal language of children's syntax: The ontogenesis and representation of syntactic categories. In K. E. Nelson (Eds.), *Children's language* (Vol. 2). New York: Gardner Press.

Marcella, S., & McDonald, B. (1990). The infant walker: An unappreciated household hazard. *Connecticut Medicine, 54,* 127–129.

Marcus, D. E., & Overton, W. F. (1978). The development of cognitive gender constancy and sex-role preferences. *Child Development, 49,* 434–444.

Marcus, G. F. (1993). Negative evidence in language acquisition. *Cognition, 46,* 53–85.

Marean, G. C., Werner, L. A., & Kuhl, P. K. (1992). Vowel categorization by very young infants. *Developmental Psychology, 28,* 396–405.

Marini, Z., & Case, R. (1989). Parallels in the development of preschoolers' knowledge about their physical and social worlds. *Merrill-Palmer Quarterly, 35,* 63–87.

Marini, Z. A. (1992). Synchrony and asynchrony in the development of children's scientific reasoning. In R. Case (Ed.), *The mind's staircase: Exploring the conceptual underpinnings of children's thought and knowledge* (pp. 55–74). Hillsdale, NJ: Erlbaum.

Markman, E. M. (1973). Facilitation of part-whole comparisons by use of the collective noun "family." *Child Development, 44,* 837–840.

Markman, E. M. (1977). Realizing that you don't understand: A preliminary investigation. *Child Development, 48,* 986–992.

Markman, E. M. (1979). Realizing that you don't understand: Elementary school children's awareness of inconsistencies. *Child Development, 50,* 643–655.

Markman, E. M. (1989). *Categorization and naming in children.* Cambridge, MA: MIT Press.

Markman, E. M. (1991). The whole object, taxonomic and mutual exclusivity assumptions as initial constraints on word meanings. In J. P. Byrnes & S. A. Gelman (Eds.), *Perspectives on language and cognition: Interrelations in development* (pp. 72–106). Cambridge: Cambridge University Press.

Markman, E. M. (1994). Constraints on word meaning in early language acquisition. In L. Gleitman & B. Landau (Eds.), *The acquisition of the lexicon* (pp. 199–229). Cambridge, MA: MIT Press/Elsevier.

Markman, E. M., & Hutchinson, J. E. (1984). Children's sensitivity to constraints on word meaning: Taxonomic versus thematic relations. *Cognitive Psychology, 16,* 1–27.

Markman, E. M., & Siebert, G. (1976). Classes and collections: Internal organization resulting in holistic properties. *Cognitive Psychology, 8,* 561–577.

Martens, R. (1986). Youth sports in the USA. In M. Weiss & D. Gould (Eds.), *Competitive sport for children and youth.* Champaign, IL: Human Kinetics.

Martin, B., & Hoffman, J. A. (1990). Conduct disorders. In M. Lewis and S. Miller (Eds.), *Handbook of developmental psychopathology.* New York: Plenum.

Martin, C. L. (1992). New directions for assessing children's gender knowledge. *Developmental Review, 13,* 184–204.

Martin, C. L. (1993). New directions for investigating children's gender knowledge. *Developmental Review, 13,* 184–204.

Martin, C. L., Eisenbud, L., & Rose, H. (1995). Children's gender-based reasoning about toys. *Child Development, 52,* 1119–1134.

Martin, C. L., & Halverson, C. F. (1981). A schematic-processing model of sex typing and stereotyping in children. *Child Development, 52,* 1119–1134.

Martin, C. L., & Halverson, C. F. (1983). The effects of sex-typing schemas on young children's memory. *Child Development, 54,* 563–574.

Martin, C. L., & Little, J. K. (1990). The relation of gender understanding to children's sex-typed preferences and gender stereotypes. *Child Development, 61,* 1427–1439.

Martin, H. (1976). *The abused child.* Cambridge, MA: Ballinger.

Martin, J. A. (1981). A longitudinal study of the consequences of early mother-infant interaction: A microanalytic approach. *Monographs of the Society for Research in Child Development, 46* (3, Serial No. 190).

Martin, J. B. (1987). Molecular genetics: Applications to the clinical neurosciences. *Science, 238,* 765–772.

Martin, T. R., & Bracken, M. B. (1986). The association of low birthweight with passive smoke exposure in pregnancy. *American Journal of Epidemiology, 124,* 633–642.

Martinez, F. D., Wright, A. L., & Taussig, L. M. (1994). The effect of paternal smoking on the birthweight of newborns whose mothers do not smoke. *American Journal of Public Health, 84,* 1489–1491.

Martini, F. H. (1995). *Anatomy and physiology* (3rd ed.). Upper Saddle River, NJ: Prentice Hall.

Martini, M. (1994). Peer interactions in Polynesia: A view from the Marquesas. In J. Roopnarine, J. Johnson, & F. Hooper (Eds.), *Children's play in diverse cultures.* New York: SUNY Press.

Martorell, R. (1984). Genetics, environment and growth: Issues in the assessment of nutritional status. In A. Velasquez & H. Bourges (Eds.), *Genetic factors in nutrition.* Orlando, FL: Academic Press.

Martorell, R., Mendoza, F. S., Baisden, K., & Pawson, R. G. (1994). Physical growth, sexual maturation, and obesity in Puerto Rican children. In G. Lamberty & C. G. Coll (Eds.), *Puerto Rican women and children: Issues in health, growth, and development.* New York: Plenum.

Marzolf, D. P., & DeLoache, J. S. (1994). Transfer in young children's understanding of spatial representations. *Child Development, 65*(1), 1–15.

Mash, E. J., Johnston, C., & Kovitz, K. A. (1983). A comparison of the mother-child interactions of physically abused and nonabused children during play and task situations. *Journal of Clinical Child Psychology, 12,* 337–346.

Massey, C. M., & Gelman, R. (1988). Preschooler's ability to decide whether a photographed unfamiliar object can move itself. *Developmental Psychology, 24,* 307–317.

Masten, A. S., & Braswell, L. (1990). Developmental psychopathology: An integrative framework for understanding behavior problems in children and adolescents. In P. R. Martin (Ed.), *Handbook of behavior therapy and psychological science: An integrative approach.* New York: Pergamon.

Matas, L., Arend, R., & Sroufe, L. A. (1978). Continuity of adaptation in the second year. The relationship between quality of attachment and later competence. *Child Development, 49,* 547–556.

Matteson, D. R. (1991). Attempting to change sex role attitudes in adolescents: Explorations of reverse effects. *Adolescence, 26,* 885–898.

Maurer, D., & Maurer, C. (1988). *The world of the newborn.* New York: Basic Books.

Maurer, D., & Salapatek, P. (1976). Developmental changes in the scanning of faces by young infants. *Child Development, 47,* 523–527.

Mayes, L., & Zigler, E. (1992). An observational study of the affective concomitants of mastery in infancy. *Journal of Child Psychology & Psychiatry & Applied Disciplines, 33,* 659–667.

Mayes, L. C. (1995). Substance abuse and parenting. In M. Bornstein (Ed.). *Handbook of parenting* (Vol. 4). Mahwah: Erlbaum.

Mayes, L. C., & Bornstein, M. H. (1996). The context of development for young children from cocaine-abusing families. In P. M. Kato & T. Mann (Eds.), *Handbook of diversity issues in health psychology* (pp. 69–95). New York: Plenum Press.

McCall, R. B., Applebaum, M. I., & Hogarty, P. S. (1973). Developmental changes in mental performance. *Monographs of the Society for Research in Child Development, 38* (3, Serial No. 150), 1–84.

McCall, R. B., Hogarty, P. S., & Hurlburt, N. (1972). Transitions in infant sensorimotor development and the prediction of childhood IQ. *American Psychologist, 27,* 728–748.

McCall, R. B., & Mash, C. W. (1995). Infant cognition and its relation to mature intelligence. In R. Vasta (Ed.), *Annals of child development: A research annual* (Vol. 10, pp. 27–56). London, England: Jessica Kingsley Publishers.

McCartney, K., Harris, M. J., & Berniere, F. (1990). Growing up and growing apart: A developmental meta-analysis of twin studies. *Psychological Bulletin, 107,* 226–237.

McCauley, E., Ito, J., & Kay, T. (1986). Psychosocial funtioning in girls with Turner syndrome and short stature. *Journal of the American Academy of Child Psychiatry, 25,* 105–112.

McCauley, E., Kay, T., Ito, J., & Treeler, R. (1987). The Turner syndrome: Cognitive defects, affective discrimination and behavior problems. *Child Development, 58,* 464–473.

McClintock, M. K., & Herdt, G. (1996). Rethinking puberty: The development of sexual attraction. *Current Directions in Psychological Science, 5,* 178–183.

McCormick, C., & Mauer, D. M. (1988). Unimanual hand preferences in 6-month-olds: Consistency and relation to familial handedness. *Infant Behavior and Development, 11,* 21–29.

McCoy, J. K., Brody, G. H., & Stoneman, Z. (1994). A longitudinal analysis of sibling relationships as mediators of the link between family processes and youths' best friendships. *Family relations, 43,* 400–408.

McDavid, J. W., & Harari, H. (1966). Stereotyping of names and popularity in grade school children. *Child Development, 37,* 453–457.

McDonald, M. A., Sigman, M., Espinosa, M. P., & Neumann, C. G. (1994). Impact of a temporary food shortage on children and their mothers. *Child Development, 65,* 404–416.

McDowell, D., O'Neill, R., & Parke, R. D. (1998). *Display role use and social competence.* Unpublished manuscript. University of California: Riverside.

McGinty, M. J., & Zafran, E. I. (1988). *Surrogacy: Constitutional and legal issues.* Cleveland, OH: The Ohio Academy of Trial Lawyers.

McGraw, M. (1940). Neuromuscular development of the human infant as exemplified in the achievement of erect locomotion. *Journal of Pediatrics, 17,* 747–771.

McGreal, C. E. (1985, April). *The grandparent-grandchild relationship during the neonatal period.* Paper presented at the biennial meeting of the Society for Research in Child Development, Toronto, Canada.

McGue, M., & Bouchard, T. J. (1987). Genetic and environmental determinants of information processing and special mental abilities: A twin analysis. In R. J. Sternberg (Ed.), *Advances in the psychology of human intelligence* (Vol. 5). Hillsdale, NJ: Erlbaum.

McGuffey's Eclectic Primer. (1896). Rev. ed. Eclectic Educational Series. New York: American Book Company.

McHale, S. M., Bartko, W. T., Crouter, A. C., & Perry-Jenkins, M. (1990). Children's housework and psychosocial functioning: The mediating effects of parents' sex-role behaviors and attitudes. *Child Development, 61,* 1413–1426.

McKenna, J. J., & Mosko, S. (1990). Evolution and the sudden infant death syndrome (SIDS). *Human Nature, 1,* 291–330.

McKenna, J. J., & Mosko, S. (1993). Evolution and infant sleep: An experimental study of infant-parent co-sleeping and its implications for SIDS. *Acta Paediatrica, 389* (Suppl.), 31–36.

McKenzie, B. E., Tootell, H. E., & Day, R. H. (1980). Development of visual size constancy during the first year of human infancy. *Developmental Psychology, 16,* 163–174.

McKey, R. H., Condelli, L., Ganson, H., Barrett, B. J., McConkey, C., & Plantz, M. (1985). The impact of head start on children, families and communities. Washington, DC: US Government Printing Office.

McLanahan, S., & Sandefur, G. (1994). *Growing up with a single parent.* Cambridge, MA: Harvard University Press.

McLloyd, V., Jayaratne, T., Ceballo, R., & Borguez, J. (1994). Unemployment and work interruption among African-American single mothers: Effects on parenting and adolescent socio-emotional functioning. *Child Development, 65,* 562–589.

McLloyd, V. C. (1990). The impact of economic hardship on black families and children: Psychological distress, parenting and socioemotional development. *Child Development, 61,* 311–346.

McLloyd, V. C., Jayaratne, R. E., Ceballo, R., & Borquez, J. (1994). Unemployment and work interruption among African-American single mothers: Effects on parenting in adolescent socioemotional functioning. *Child Development, 65,* 562–589.

McManus, I. C., & Bryden, M. P. (1991). Geschwind's theory of cerebral lateralization: Developing a formal, causal modcl. *Psychological Bulletin, 110,* 237–253.

McNeill, D. (1970). *The acquisition of language: The study of developmental psycholinguistics.* New York: Harper & Row.

McPherson, D. (1993). *Gay parenting couples: Parenting arrangements, arrangement satisfaction, and relationship satisfaction.* Unpublished doctoral dissertation, Pacific Graduate School of Psychology, Palo Alto, CA.

Mead, M. (1935). *Sex and temperament in three primitive societies.* New York: Morrow.

Mednick, S. A., Schulsinger, H., & Schulsinger, F. (1975). Schizophrenia in children of schizophrenic mothers. In A. Davies (Ed.), *Child personality and psychopathology* (Vol. 2, pp. 221–252). New York: Wiley.

Medrich, E. A. (1981). *The serious business of growing up: A study of children's lives outside the school.* Berkeley: University of California Press.

Mehler, J., Dupoux, E., Nazzi, T., & Dehaene-Lambertz, G. (1996). Coping with linguistic diversity: The infant's viewpoint. In J. L. Morgan & K. Demuth (Eds.), *Signal to syntax: Bootstrapping from speech to grammar in early acquisition* (pp. 101–116). Mahwah, NJ: Erlbaum.

Mehler, J., Jusczyk, P., Lambertz, G., Halsted, N., Bertoncini, J., & Amieltison, C. (1988). A precursor of language acquisition in young infants. *Cognition, 29,* 143–178.

Meicler, M., & Gratch, G. (1980). Do 5-month-olds show object conception in Piaget's sense? *Infant Behavior and Development, 3,* 265–282.

Meier, R. P., & Newport, E. L. (1990). Out of the hands of babes: On a possible sign advantage in language acquisition. *Language, 66*(1), 1–23.

Meisel, J. M. (1995). Parameters in acquisition. In P. Fletcher & B. MacWhinney (Eds.), *The handbook of child language.* Oxford: Blackwell.

Meisels, S. (1996). Performance in context: Assessing children's achievement at the outset of school. In A. J. Sameroff & M. M. Haith (Eds.), *The five-to-seven shift* (pp. 407–434). Chicago: University of Chicago Press.

Meisels, S. J. (1992). Doing harm by doing good: Iatrogenic effects of early childhood enrollment and promotion policies. *Early Childhood Research Quarterly, 7,* 155–174.

Meltzoff, A. N. (1981). Imitation, intermodal coordination and representation in early infancy. In G. Butterworth (Ed.), *Infancy and epistemology.* Brighton: Harvester Press.

Meltzoff, A. N. (1988a). Infant imitation and memory: Nine-month-old infants in immediate and deferred tests. *Child Development, 59,* 217–225.

Meltzoff, A. N. (1988b). Infant imitation after a 1-week delay: Long-term memory for novel acts and multiple stimuli. *Developmental Psychology, 24,* 470–476.

Meltzoff, A. N. (1990). Towards a developmental cognitive science. *Annals of the New York Academy of Sciences, 608,* 1–37.

Meltzoff, A. N., & Borton, R. W. (1979). Intermodal matching by human neonates. *Nature, 282,* 403–404.

Meltzoff, A. N., & Moore, M. K. (1983). Newborn infants imitate adult facial gestures. *Child Development, 54,* 702–709.

Meltzoff, A. N., & Moore, M. K. (1994). Imitation, memory and the representation of persons. *Infant Behavior and Development, 17,* 83–99.

Mennella, J. A., & Beauchamp, G. K. (1993). The effects of repeated exposure to garlic-flavored milk on the nursling's behavior. *Pediatric Research, 34,* 805–808.

Mennella, J. A., & Beauchamp, G. K. (1996). The human infants' response to vanilla flavors in mother's milk and formula. *Infant Behavior & Development, 19,* 13–19.

Mercer, J. R. (1971). Sociocultural factors in labeling mental retardates. *Peabody Journal of Education, 48,* 188–203.

Mercer, J. R. (1972, September). IQ: The lethal label. *Psychology Today,* p. 44.

Meredith, H. V. (1975). Somatic changes during prenatal life. *Child Development, 46,* 603–610.

Mervis, C., & Mervis, J. (1982). Leopards are kitty cats: Object labeling by mothers for their thirteen-month-olds. *Child Development, 53,* 267–273.

Mervis, C. B., & Bertrand, J. (1994). Acquisition of the novel name-nameless category principle. *Child Development, 65,* 1646–1662.

Michel, G. F., & Moore, C. L. (1995). *Developmental psychobiology: An interdisciplinary science.* Cambridge, MA: MIT Press.

Mickelson, R. (1990). The attitude-achievement paradox among black adolescents. *Sociology of Education, 63,* 44–61.

Milham, J., Widmayer, S., Bauer, C. R., & Peterson, L. (1983, April). *Predicting cognitive deficits for preterm, low birthweight infants.* Paper presented at the biennial meeting of the Society for Research in Child Development, Detroit.

Miller, C. L., Heysek, P. J., & Whitman, T. L. (1995, March). *Cognitive readiness to parent and intellectual-emotional development in the children of adolescent mothers.* Poster session presented at 61st biennial meeting of the Society for Research in Child Development, Indianapolis.

Miller, G. A. (1956). The magical number seven, plus or minus two: Some limits on our capacity for processing information. *Psychological Review, 63,* 81–97.

Miller, J. G., & Bersoff, D. M. (1992). Culture and moral judgment: How are conflicts between justice and interpersonal responsibilities resolved? *Journal of Personality and Social Psychology, 62,* 541–554.

Miller, J. G., Bersoff, D. M., & Harwood, R. L. (1990). Perceptions of social responsibilities in India and in the United States: Moral imperatives or personal decisions? *Journal of Personality & Social Psychology, 58,* 33–47.

Miller, J. L., & Eimas, P. D. (1994). Observations on speech perception, its development, and the search for a mechanism. In J. C. Goodman & H. C. Nusbaum (Eds.), *The development of speech perception: The transition from speech sounds to spoken words* (pp. 37–56). Cambridge, MA: MIT Press.

Miller, K. F., & Baillargeon, R. (1990). Length and distance: Do preschoolers think that occlusion brings things together? *Developmental Psychology, 26,* 103–114.

Miller, K. F., Smith, C. M., Zhu, J., & Zhang, H. (1995). Preschool origins of cross-national differences in mathematical competence: The role of number-naming systems. *Psychological Science, 6,* 56–60.

Miller, L. T., & Vernon, P. A. (1997). Developmental changes in speed of information processing in young children. *Developmental Psychology, 33,* 549–554.

Miller, P., & Sperry, L. L. (1987). The socialization of anger and aggression. *Merrill-Palmer Quarterly, 33,* 1–31.

Miller, P. A., Eisenberg, N., Fabes, R. A., & Shell, R. (1996). Relations of moral reasoning and vicarious emotion to young children's prosocial behavior toward peers and adults. *Developmental Psychology, 32*(2), 210–219.

Miller, P. H. (1990). The development of strategies of selective attention. In D. F. Bjorklund (Ed.), *Children's strategies: Contemporary views of cognitive development* (pp. 157–184). Hillsdale, NJ: Erlbaum.

Miller, P. H. (1993). *Theories of developmental psychology* (3rd ed.). New York: Freeman.

Miller, P. H., & Aloise-Young, P. A. (1995). Preschoolers' strategic behavior and performance on a same-different task. *Journal of Experimental Child Psychology, 60,* 284–303.

Miller, P. H., & Seier, W. L. (1994). Strategy utilization deficiencies in children: When, where, and why. In H. W. Reese (Ed.), *Advances in child development and behavior* (Vol. 25, pp. 107–156). New York: Academic Press.

Miller, P. H., & Weiss, M. G. (1981). Children's attention allocation, understanding of attention, and performance on the incidental learning task. *Child Development, 52,* 1183–1190.

Miller, S. (1973). Ends, means and galumphing: Some leitmotifs at play. *American Anthropologist, 75,* 87–98.

Miller-Jones, D. (1989). Culture and testing. Children and their development: Knowledge base, research agenda, and social policy application. [Special Issue]. *American Psychologist, 44,* 360–366.

Mills, D. L., Coffey-Corina, S. A., & Neville, H. J. (1994). Variability in cerebral organization during primary language acquisition. In G. Dawson & K. W. Fischer (Eds.), *Human behavior and the developing brain.* New York: Guilford Press.

Milstein, R. M. (1980). Responsiveness in newborn infants of overweight and normal weight parents. *Appetite, 1,* 65–74.

Minami, M., & McCabe, A. (1995). Rice balls and bear hunts: Japanese and North American family narrative patterns. *Journal of Child Language, 22,* 423–446.

Minuchin, P. (1985). Families and individual development: Provocations from the field of family therapy. Family development [Special Issue]. *Child Development, 56,* 289–302.

Minuchin, P. P., & Shapiro, E. K. (1983). The school as a context for social development. In P. H. Mussen (Eds.), *Handbook of child psychology* (Vol. 4). New York: Wiley.

Mischel, W., & Patterson, C. J. (1978). Effective plans for self-control. In W. A. Collins (Ed.), *Minnesota symposia on child psychology* (Vol. 2). Hillsdale, NJ: Erlbaum.

Mischel, W., Shoda, Y., & Peake, P. K. (1988). The nature of adolescent competencies predicted by preschool delay of gratification. *Journal of Personality and Social Psychology, 54,* 687–696.

Mistretta, C. M., & Bradley, R. M. (1985). Development of the sense of taste. In E. M. Blass (Ed.), *Handbook of behavioral neurobiology* (pp. 205–236). New York: Plenum.

Mitchell, E. A., Ford, R. P. K., Stewart, A. W., Taylor, B. J., Bescroft, D. M., Thompson, J. M. P., Scragg, R., Hassall, I. B., Barry, D. M. J., Allen, E. M., & Roberts, A. P. (1993). Smoking and the sudden infant death syndrome. *Pediatrics, 91,* 893–896.

Mize, J., & Ladd, G. W. (1990). Toward the development of successful social skills for preschool children. In S. R. Asher & J. D. Coie (Eds.), *Peer rejection in childhood.* New York: Cambridge University Press.

Moely, B. E., Olson, F. A., Halwes, T. G., & Flavell, J. H. (1969). Production deficiency in young children's clustered recall. *Developmental Psychology, 1,* 26–34.

Moffitt, A. R. (1971). Consonant cue perception by twenty to twenty-four week old infants. *Child Development, 42,* 717–732.

Moffitt, T. E. (1993). Adolescence-limited and life-course-persistent antisocial behavior: A developmental taxonomy. *Psychological Review, 100,* 674–701.

Moffitt, T. E., Caspi, A., Belsky, J., & Silva, P. A. (1992). Childhood experience and the onset of menarche: A test of a sociobiological model. *Child Development, 63,* 47–58.

Moffitt, T. E., Caspi, A., Harkness, A. R., & Silva, P. A. (1993). The natural history of change in intellectual performance: Who changes? How much? Is it meaningful? *Journal of Child Psychology & Psychiatry & Allied Disciplines, 34,* 455–506.

Mohn, G., & van Hof-van Duin (1986). Development of binocular and monocular visual fields of human infants during the first year of life. *Clinical Visual Science, 1,* 51–64.

Mohr, P. J. (1979). Parental guidance of children's viewing of evening television programs. *Journal of Broadcasting, 23,* 213–228.

Molfese, D. L. (1973). Cerebral asymmetry in infants, children, and adults: Auditory evoked responses to speech and musical stimuli. *Journal of the Acoustical Society of America, 53,* 363.

Molfese, D. L., & Betz, J. C. (1988). Electrophysiological indices of the early development of lateralization for language and cognition, and their implications for predicting later development. In D. L. Molfese & S. J. Segalowitz (Eds.), *Brain lateralization in children: Developmental implications* (pp. 171–190). New York: Guilford Press.

Molfese, D. L., & Molfese, V. J. (1979). Hemisphere and stimulus differences as reflected in the cortical responses of newborn infants to speech stimuli. *Developmental Psychology, 15,* 505–511.

Molfese, D. L., & Molfese, V. J. (1980). Cortical response of preterm infants to phonetic and nonphonetic speech stimuli. *Developmental Psychology, 16,* 574–581.

Molfese, D. L., & Molfese, V. J. (1985). Electrophysiological indices of auditory discrimination in newborn infants: The bases for predicting later language development? *Infant Behavior and Development, 8,* 197–211.

Molfese, D. L., Morse, P. A., & Peters, C. J. (1990). Auditory evoked responses to names for different objects: Cross-modal processing as a basis for infant language acquisition. *Developmental Psychology, 26,* 780–795.

Molfese, D. L., & Segalowitz, S. J., (Eds.), (1988). *Brain lateralization in children.* New York: Guilford Press.

Money, J. (1987). Propaedeutics of dioecious G-I/R: Theoretical foundations for understanding dimorphic gender-identity/role. In J. M. Reinisch, L. A. Rosenblum, & S. A. Sanders (Eds.), *Masculinity/femininity: Basic perspectives.* New York: Oxford University Press.

Money, J. (1993). Specific neurocognitional impairments associated with Turner (45, X) and Klinefelter (47, XXY) syndromes: A review. *Social Biology, 40,* 147–151.

Money, J., & Annecillo, C. (1987). Crucial period effect in psychoendocrinology: Two syndromes abuse dwarfism and female (CVAH) hermaphroditism. In M. H. Bornstein (Ed.), *Sensitive periods in development: Interdisciplinary perspectives.* Hillsdale, NJ: Erlbaum.

Money, J., & Ehrhardt, A. A. (1972). *Man and woman, boy and girl.* Baltimore, MD: Johns Hopkins University Press.

Montie, J. E., & Fagan, J. F. (1988). Racial differences in IQ: Item analysis of the

Stanford-Binet at 3 years. *Intelligence, 12,* 315–332.

Moon, C., Cooper, R. P., & Fifer, W. P. (1993). Two-day-olds prefer their native language. *Infant Behavior & Development, 16,* 495–500.

Moore, D. R., & Arthur, J. L. (1989). Juvenile delinquency. In T. Oklendick & M. Hersen (Eds.), *Handbook of childhood psychopathology.* New York: Plenum.

Moore, K. L. (1989). *Before we are born.* Philadelphia: Saunders.

Moore, K. L., & Persaud, T. V. N. (1993). *Before we are born* (4th ed.). Philadelphia: Saunders.

Morelli, G. A., Rogoff, B., Oppenheim, D., & Goldsmith, D. (1992). Cultural variation in infants' sleeping arrangements: Questions of independence. *Developmental Psychology, 28,* 604–613.

Morelli, G. A., & Tronick, E. Z. (1992). Male care among Efe foragers and Lese farmers. In B. Hewlett (Ed.), *Father-child relations: Cultural and biosocial contexts* (pp. 231–262). New York: Aldine de Gruyther.

Morgan, G. A., & Ricciuti, H. (1969). Infants' responses to strangers during the first year. In B. M. Foss (Ed.), *Determinants of infant behavior* (Vol. 4, pp. 253–272). London: Methuen.

Morgan, J. L. (1990). Input, innateness, and induction in language acquisition. *Developmental Psychology, 23,* 661–678.

Morgan, J. L. (1994). Converging measures of speech segmentation in preverbal infants. *Infant Behavior and Development, 17,* 387–403.

Morgan, J. L., Bonamo, K. M., & Travis, L. L. (1995). Negative evidence on negative evidence. *Developmental Psychology, 31,* 180–197.

Morgan, J. L., & Demuth, K. (1996). *Signal to syntax: Bootstrapping from speech to grammar in early acquisition.* Mahwah, NJ: Erlbaum.

Morgan, J. L., & Saffran, J. R. (1995). Emerging integration of sequential and suprasegmental information in preverbal speech segmentation. *Child Development, 16,* 911–936.

Morrison, F. J., Holmes, D. L., & Haith, M. M. (1974). A developmental study of the effect of familiarity on short-term visual memory. *Journal of Experimental Child Psychology, 18,* 412–425.

Morrongiello, B. A., Hewitt, K. L., & Gotowiec, A. (1991). Infant discrimination of relative distance in the auditory modality: approaching versus receding sound sources. *Infant Behavior Development, 14,* 187–208.

Mosedale, L. (1991). Fathers in the delivery room. *Self,* April, 104–108.

Moshman, D. (1998). Cognitive development beyond childhood. In W. Damon (Gen. Ed.), D. Kuhn & R. S. Siegler (Vol. Eds.), *Handbook of child psychology: Vol. 2. Cognition, perception, and language* (pp. 947–978). New York: Wiley.

Moss, H. (1967). Sex, age and state as determinants of mother-infant interaction. *Merrill-Palmer Quarterly, 13,* 19–36.

Moss, M., Colombo, J., Mitchell, D. W., & Horowitz, F. D. (1988). Neonatal behavioral organization and visual discrimination at 3 months of age. *Child Development, 59,* 1211–1220.

Mounts, N. S., & Steinberg, L. (1995). An ecological analysis of peer influences on adolescent grade point average and drug use. *Developmental Psychology, 31,* 915–922.

Mueller, E. (1989). Toddlers' peer relations: Shared meaning and semantics. In W. Damon (Ed.), *Child development today and tomorrow.* San Francisco: Jossey-Bass.

Mueller, E., & Brenner, J. (1977). The origins of social skills and interaction among playgroup toddlers. *Child Development, 48,* 854–861.

Mueller, E., & Lucas, T. A. (1975). A developmental analysis of peer interaction among toddlers. In M. Lewis & L. A. Rosenblum (Eds.), *Friendship and peer relations.* New York: Wiley.

Muir, D., & Clifton, R. (1985). Infants' orientation to location of sound sources. In G. Gottlieb & N. Krasnegor (Eds.), *Measurement of audition and vision in the first year of postnatal life. A methodological overview.* Norwood, NJ: Ablex.

Muir, D., & Field, T. M. (1979). Newborn infants orient to sounds. *Child Development, 50,* 431–436.

Mumme, D. L., Fernald, A., & Herrera, C. (1996). Infant's responses to facial & emotional signals in a social referencing paradigm. *Child Development, 67,* 3219–3237.

Munroe, R. H., Shimmin, H. S., & Munroe, R. L. (1984). Gender understanding and sex role preference in four cultures. *Developmental Psychology, 20,* 673–682.

Munsinger, H. (1975). The adopted child's IQ: A critical review. *Psychological Bulletin, 82,* 623–659.

Murray, F. B. (1981). The new conservation paradigm. In I. Siegel, D. Brodzinsky, & R. Golinkoff (Eds.), *New directions in Piagetian research and theory.* Hillsdale, NJ: Erlbaum.

Murray, T. A. (1996). *The worth of a child.* Berkeley, CA: University of California Press.

Mutz, D. C., Roberts, D. F., & van Vuuren, D. P. (1993). Reconsidering the displacement hypothesis: Television's influence on children's time use. *Communication Research, 20,* 51–75.

Myers, A. W., & Cohen, R. (1990). Cognitive-behavioral approaches to child psychopathology. In M. Lewis & S. Miller (Eds.), *Handbook of developmental psychopathology.* New York: Plenum.

Myers, D. G. (1992). *Psychology* (3rd ed.). New York: Worth.

Myers, N. A., Clifton, R. K., & Clarkson, M. G. (1987). When they were young: Almost-threes remember two years ago. *Infant Behavior and Development, 10,* 123–132.

Myles-Worsley, M., Cromer, C. C., & Dodd, D. H. (1986). Children's preschool script reconstruction: Reliance on general knowledge as memory fades. *Developmental Psychology, 22,* 22–30.

Nachmias, M., Gunnar, M., Mangelsdorf, S., Parritz, R. H., & Buss, K. (1996). Behavioral inhibition and stress reactivity: The moderating role of attachment security. *Child Development, 67,* 508–522.

Nader, P. R. (1993). The role of the family in obesity: Prevention and treatment. In C. L. Williams & S. Y. S. Kimm (Eds.),

Prevention and treatment of childhood obesity (pp. 147–153). Annals of the New York Academy of Sciences, Vol. 699. New York: The New York Academy of Sciences.

Naigles, L. (1990). Children use syntax to learn verb meanings. *Journal of Child Languages, 17,* 357–374.

Naigles, L. (1995). The use of multiple frames in verb learning via syntactic bootstrapping. *Cognition, 58,* 221–251.

Naigles, L., & Gelman, S. (1995). Overextensions in comprehension and production revisited: Preferential-looking in a study of dog, cat, and cow. *Journal of Child Language, 22,* 19–46.

Nash, S. C., & Feldman, S. S. (1981). Sex role and sex-related attributions, constancy and change across the family life cycle. In M. E. Lamb & A. L. Brown (Eds.), *Advances in developmental psychology* (Vol. 1). Hillsdale, NJ: Erlbaum.

National Center for Health Statistics. (1976). *NCHS growth charts.* Washington, DC.

National Committee to Prevent Child Abuse. (1997). *Current trends in child abuse reporting and fatalities: Results of the 1996 annual 50-state survey.* Chicago: Author.

National Institute of Child Health and Human Development, Early Child Care Network. (1997). The effects of infant child care on infant-mother attachment security: Results of the NICHD study of early child care. *Child Development, 68,* 860–879.

National March of Dimes Foundation report on pregnancy-related diseases. (1996). White Plains, NY: March of Dimes Foundation.

Naus, M. J. (1982). Memory development in the young reader: The combined effects of knowledge base and memory processing. In W. Otto & S. White (Eds.), *Reading expository text.* New York: Academic.

Neal, M. V. (1968). Vestibular stimulation and developmental behavior of the small premature infant. *Nursing Research Report, 3,* 2–5.

Neapolitan, D. M., & Huston, A. C. (1994). *Educational content of children's programs on public and commercial television.* Lawrence: Center for Research on the Influences of Television on Children, University of Kansas.

Needham, A., & Baillargeon, R. (1993). *Reasoning about support in 3 month old infants.* Unpublished manuscript. University of Illinois at Champaign-Urbana.

Needleman, H. L., Leviton, A., & Bellinger, D. (1982). Lead-associated intellectual deficits. *New England Journal of Medicine, 306,* 367.

Neimark, E., Slotnick, N. S., & Ulrich, T. (1971). Development of memorization strategies. *Developmental Psychology, 5,* 427–432.

Neisser, U., Boodoo, G., Bouchard, T. J., Boykin, A. W., Brody, N., Ceci, S. J., Halpern, D. F., Loehlin, J. C., Perloff, R., Sternberg, R. J., & Urbina, S. (1995). *Intelligence: Knowns and unknowns.* Washington, DC: American Psychological Association.

Nelson, C. A. (1987). The recognition of facial expressions in the first two years of life. *Child Development, 58,* 889–909.

Nelson, K. (1973). Structure and strategy in learning to talk. *Monographs of the Society for Research in Child Development, 38* (1, 2).

Nelson, K. (1978). Aspects of language acquisition and form use from age 2 to age 20. *Annual Progress in Child Psychiatry and Child Development*, 165–188.

Nelson, K. (1988). Constraints on word learning? *Cognitive Development, 3*, 221–246.

Nelson, K. (1989). Strategies for first language teaching. In M. L. Rice & R. L. Schiefelbusch (Eds.), *The teachability of language.* Baltimore, MD: Brooks/Cole.

Nelson, K. (1993). Events, narratives, memory: What develops? In C. A. Nelson (Ed.), *Memory and affect in development. The Minnesota symposia on child psychology* (Vol. 26, pp. 1–24). Hillsdale, NJ: Erlbaum.

Nelson, K., Carskadden, G., & Bonvillian, J. D. (1973). Syntax acquisition: Impact of experimental variation in adult verbal interaction with the child. *Child Development, 44*, 497–504.

Nelson, K. E., Welsh, J., Camarata, S. M., Butkovsky, L., & Camarata, M. (1995). Available input for language-impaired children and younger children of matched language levels. *First Language, 15*, 1–17.

Netley, C. T. (1986). Summary overview of behavioral development in individuals with neonatally identified X and Y aneuploidy. *Birth Defects, 22*, 293–306.

Neuspiel, D. R., Hamel, S. C., Hochberg, E., Greene, J., & Campbell, D. (1991). Maternal cocaine use and infant behavior. *Neurotoxicology and Teratology, 13*, 229–233.

Neville, B., & Parke, R. D. (in press). Waiting for paternity. *Sex Roles.*

Neville, H. J. (1991). Neurobiology of cognitive and language processing: Effects of early experience. In K. R. Gibson & A. C. Petersen (Eds.), *Brain maturation and cognitive development: Comparative and cross-cultural perspectives* (pp. 355–380). New York: Aldine de Bruyter.

Neville, H. J., Mills, D. L., & Lawson, D. S. (1992). Fractioning language: Different neural subsystems with different sensitive periods. *Cerebral Cortex, 2*, 244–258.

Nevin, M. M. (1988). Dormant dangers of DES. *The Canadian Nurse, 84*, 17–19.

Newcomb, A. F., Bukowski, W. M., & Pattee, L. (1993). Children's peer relations: A meta-analytic review of popular, rejected, neglected, controversial, and average sociometric status. *Psychological Bulletin, 113*, 99–128.

Newcomb, M. D., & Bentler, P. M. (1988). The impact of family context, deviant attitudes, and emotional distress on adolescent drug use: Longitudinal latent-variable analyses of mothers and their children. *Journal of Research in Personality, 22*, 154–176.

Newcomb, M. D., & Bentler, P. M. (1989). Substance use and abuse among children and teenagers. *American Psychologist, 44*, 242–248.

Newcomb, M. D., Muddahian, E., & Bentler, P. M. (1986). Risk factors for drug use among adolescents: Concurrent and longitudinal analyses. *American Journal of Public Health, 76*, 525–531.

Newcombe, N., & Huttenlocher, J. (1992). Children's early ability to solve perspective-taking problems. *Developmental Psychology, 28*, 635–643.

Newcomer, S., & Udry, J. R. (1987). Parental marital status effects on adolescent sexual behavior. *Journal of Marriage and the Family, 48*, 235–240.

Newell, K., Scully, D. M., McDonald, P. V., & Baillargeon, R. (1989). Task constraints and infant grip configurations. *Developmental Psychobiology, 22*, 817–832.

Newman, D., Riel, M., & Martin, L. (1983). Cultural practices and Piagetian theory: The impact of a cross-cultural program. In D. Kuhn & J. Meacham (Eds.), *On the development of developmental psychology.* Basel, Switzerland: Karger.

Newport, E. L. (1990). Maturational constraints on language learning. *Cognitive Science, 14*, 11–28.

Newport, E. L. (1991). Constraining concepts of the critical period for language. In S. Carey & R. Gelman (Eds.), *The epigenesis of mind: Essays on biology and cognition* (pp. 111–130). Hillsdale, NJ: Erlbaum.

NHLBI Growth and Health Study Research Group. (1992). *American Journal of Public Health, 82*, 1613–1620.

Nicholls, J. G. (1984). Achievement motivation: Conceptions of ability, subjective experience, task choice, and performance. *Psychological Review, 91*, 328–346.

Nicholls, J. G., & Miller, A. T. (1983). *Children's achievement motivation.* Greenwich, CT: Guilford Press.

Nickolls, K. B., Cassel, J., & Kaplan, B. H. (1972). Psychosocial assets, life crisis and the prognosis of pregnancy. *American Journal of Epidemiology, 95*, 431–441.

Niemark, E. D. (1981). Confounding with cognitive style factors: An artifact explanation for the apparent nonuniversal incidence of formal operations. In I. Siegel, D. Brodzinsky, & R. Golinkoff (Eds.), *New directions in Piagetian research and theory.* Hillsdale, NJ: Erlbaum.

Niemiec, R., & Walberg, H. J. (1987). Comparative effects of computer assisted instruction: A synthesis of reviews. *Journal of Educational Commuting Research, 3*, 19–37.

Nigg, J. T., & Goldsmith, H. H. (1994). Genetics of personality disorders: Perspectives from personality and psychopathology research. *Psychological Bulletin, 115*, 346–380.

Nightingale, E. O., & Meister, S. B. (1987). *Prenatal screening, policies, and values: Three examples of neural tube defects.* Cambridge, MA: Harvard University Press.

Nikken, P., & Peeters, A. L. (1988). Children's perceptions of television reality. *Journal of Broadcasting and Electronic Media, 32*, 441–452.

Ninio, A., & Snow, C. (1996). *Pragmatic development.* Boulder, CO: Westview Press.

Nisan, M., & Kohlberg, L. (1982). Universality and variation in moral judgment: A longitudinal and cross-sectional study in Turkey. *Child Development, 53*, 865–876.

Nolen-Hoeksema, S., Wolfson, A., Mumme, D., & Guskin, K. (1995). Helplessness in children of depressed and nondepressed mothers. *Developmental Psychology, 31*, 377–387.

Nord, C. W., Moore, K. A., Morrison, D. R., Brown, B. V., & Myers, D. E. (1992). Consequences of teenage parenting. *Journal of School Health, 62*, 310–318.

Novak, G. (1996). *Developmental Psychology: Dynamic systems and behavioral analysis.* Reno, NV: Context Press.

Nsamenang, A. B., & Lamb, M. E. (1994). Socialization of Nso children in the Bamenda Grassfields of Northwest Cameroon. In P. M. Greenfield & R. R. Cocking (Eds.), *Cross cultural roots of minority child development.* Hillsdale, NJ: Erlbaum.

Nucci, L. P. (1996). Morality and the personal sphere of action. In E. Reed, E. Turiel, & T. Brown (Eds.), *Values and knowledge* (pp. 41–60). Hillsdale, NJ: Erlbaum.

Nucci, L. P., Camino, C., & Milnitsky-Sapiro, C. (1996). Social class effects on northeastern Brazilian children's conceptions of areas of personal choice and social regulation. *Child Development, 67*, 1223–1242.

Nucci, L. P., & Turiel, E. (1978). Social interactions and the development of social concepts in preschool children. *Child Development, 49*, 400–407.

Nucci, L. P., & Weber, E. (1995). Social interactions in the home and the development of young children's conceptions of the personal. *Child Development, 66*, 1438–1452.

Nugent, J. K., Lester, B. M., & Brazelton, T. B. (Eds.). (1989). *Biology, culture, and development.* Norwood, NJ: Ablex.

Nurcombe, B. (1992). The evolution and validity of the diagnosis of major depression in childhood and adolescence. In D. Cicchetti & S. Toth (Eds.), *Developmental perspectives on depression. Rochester symposium on developmental psychopathology* (Vol. 4, pp. 1–28). Rochester, NY: University of Rochester Press.

Nwokah, E. E., Hsu, H., Dobrowolska, O., & Fogel, A. (1994). The development of laughter in mother-infant communication: Timing parameters and temporal sequences. *Infant Behavior & Development, 17*, 23–35.

Oakes, L. M. (1994). The development of infants' use of continuity cues in their perception of causality. *Developmental Psychology, 30*, 869–879.

Oakes, L. M., & Cohen, L. B. (1994). Infant causal perception. In C. Rovee-Collier & L. Lipsitt (Eds.), *Advances in infancy research* (Vol. 9). Norwood, NJ: Ablex.

O'Brien, M., Huston, A. C., & Risley, T. (1983). Sex-typed play of toddlers in a day care center. *Journal of Applied Developmental Psychology, 4*, 1–9.

Ochs, E. (1988). *Culture and language development.* Cambridge: Cambridge University Press.

Oden, S., & Asher, S. R. (1977). Coaching children in social skills for friendship making. *Child Development, 48*, 495–506.

Oehler, J. M., Eckerman, C. D., & Wilson, W. H. (1988). Social stimulation and the regulation of premature infant's state prior to term age. *Infant Behavior and Development, 12*, 341–356.

Oetting, E. R., & Beauvais, F. (1990). Adolescent drug use: Findings of national and local surveys. *Journal of Consulting and Clinical Psychology, 58*, 385–394.

Ogbu, J. (1981). Origins of human competence: A cultural-ecological perspective. *Child Development, 52*, 413–429.

Ogbu, J. (1988). Black education: A cultural-ecological perspective. In H. P. McAdoo (Ed.),

Black families (pp. 169–186). Beverly Hills, CA: Sage.

Ogbu, J. (1994). From cultural differences to differences in cultural frame of reference. In P. Greenfield & R. R. Cocking (Eds.), *Cross-cultural roots of minority child development* (pp. 365–392). Hillsdale, NJ: Erlbaum.

Okamoto, Y., & Case, R. (1996). Exploring the microstructure of children's central conceptual structures in the domain of number. In R. Case & Y. Okamoto (Eds.), The role of central conceptual structures in the development of children's thought. *Monographs of the Society for Research in Child Development, 61,* Serial No. 246 Nos. 1 & 2.

O'Leary, K. D. (1980). Pills or skills for hyperactive children. *Journal of Applied Behavior Analysis, 13,* 191–204.

O'Leary, K. D., & O'Leary, S. G. (Eds.). (1977). *Classroom management.* New York: Pergamon.

Oller, D. K., & Eilers, R. E. (1988). The rate of audition in infant babbling. *Child Development, 59,* 441–449.

Oller, D. K., Wieman, L. A., Doyle, W. J., & Ross, C. (1976). Infant babbling and speech. *Journal of Child Language, 3,* 1–11.

Olson, G. M., & Sherman, T. (1983). Attention, learning and memory in infants. In P. H. Mussen (Ed.), *Handbook of child psychology* (4th ed., Vol. 2). New York: Wiley.

Olweus, D. (1979). Stability and aggressive reaction patterns in males: A review. *Psychological Bulletin, 86,* 852–875.

Olweus, D. (1982). Development of stable aggressive reaction patterns in males. In R. Blanchard & C. Blanchard (Eds.), *Advances in the study of aggression* (Vol. 1). New York: Academic.

Olweus, D. (1989). Bully/victim problems among school children: Basic facts and effects of a school-based intervention program. In K. Rubin & D. Pepler (Eds.), *The development and treatment of childhood aggression.* Hillsdale, NJ: Erlbaum.

Olweus, D. (1992). Bullying among schoolchildren: Intervention and prevention. In R. D. Peters, R. J. McMahon, & V. L. Quinsey (Eds.), *Aggression and violence throughout the life span* (pp. 100–125). Newbury Park, CA: Sage.

Olweus, D. (1993). *Bullying and school: What we know and what we can do.* Oxford: Blackwell.

Olweus, D., Mattson, A., Schalling, D., & Low, H. (1988). Circulating testosterone levels and aggression in adolescent males: A causal analysis. *Psychosomatic Medicine, 50,* 261–272.

Omark, D. R., Strayer, F. F., & Freedman, D. G. (1980). *Dominance relations.* New York: Garland.

Oppenheim, D., Sagi, A., & Lamb, M. (1988). Infant-adult attachments on the kibbutz and their relation to socioemotional development four years later. *Developmental Psychology, 24,* 427–433.

Orenstein, S. R. (1992). Throwing out the baby with the bedding. *Clinical Pediatrics, 31,* 546–548.

Orlick, T., Zhou, Q., & Partington, J. (1990), Co-operation and conflict within Chinese and Canadian kindergarten settings. *Canadian Journal and Behavioural Science, 22,* 20–25.

Ornstein, P. A., Larus, D. M., & Clubb, P. A. (1992). Understanding children's testimony: Implications of research on the development of memory. In R. Vasta (Ed.), *Annals of Child Development* (Vol. 8). London: Jessica Kingsley Publishers.

Ornstein, P. A., Medlin, R. G., Stone, B. P., & Naus, M. J. (1985). Retrieving for rehearsal: An analysis of active rehearsal in children's memory. *Developmental Psychology, 21,* 633–641.

O'Rourke, J. F. (1963). Field and laboratory: The decision making behavior of family groups in two experimental conditions. *Sociometry, 26,* 422–435.

Osterweil, D. A. (1991). *Correlates of relationship satisfaction in lesbian couples who are parenting their first child together.* Unpublished doctoral dissertation, California School of Professional Psychology, Berkeley/Alameda.

O'Sullivan, J. T. (1996). Children's metamemory about the influence of conceptual relations on recall. *Journal of Experimental Child Psychology, 62,* 1–29.

O'Sullivan, J. T., & Pressley, M. (1984). Completeness of instruction and strategy transfer. *Journal of Experimental Child Psychology, 38,* 275–288.

Overton, W. F., & Byrnes, J. P. (1991). Cognitive development. In R. M. Lerner, A. C. Petersen, & J. Brooks-Gunn (Eds.), *Encyclopedia of adolescence* (Vol. 1). New York: Garland.

Paik, H., & Comstock, G. (1994). The effects of television violence on antisocial behavior: A meta-analysis. *Communication Research, 21,* 516–546.

Palincsar, A. S., & Brown, A. L. (1984). Reciprocal teaching of comprehension fostering and comprehension monitoring activities. *Cognitive and Instruction, 1,* 117–175.

Palincsar, A. S., & Brown, A. L. (1987). Enhancing instructional time through attention to metacognition. *Journal of Learning Disabilities, 20,* 66–75.

Papalia, D. E., & Olds, S. W. (1996). *A child's world: Infancy through adolescence* (7th ed.). New York: McGraw-Hill.

Parke, R. D. (1977). Punishment in children: Effects, side effects and alternative strategies. In H. Hom & P. Robinson (Eds.), *Psychological processes in early education* (pp. 71–97). New York: Academic.

Parke, R. D. (1988). Families in life-span perspective: a multilevel developmental approach. In E. M. Hetherington, R. M. Lerner, & M. Perlmutter (Eds.), *Child development in life span perspective* (pp. 159–190). Hillsdale, NJ: Erlbaum.

Parke, R. D. (1990). In search of fathers: A narrative of an empirical journey. In I. Sigel & G. Brody (Eds.), *Methods of family research* (Vol. 1, pp. 153–188). Hillsdale, NJ: Erlbaum.

Parke, R. D. (1996). *Fatherhood.* Cambridge, MA: Harvard University Press.

Parke, R. D., & Buriel, R. (1998). Socialization in the family: Ethnic and ecological perspectives. In W. Damon (Gen. Ed.) & N. Eisenberg (Vol. Ed.), *Handbook of child psychology: Vol. 3. Social, emotional and personality development.* New York: Wiley.

Parke, R. D., Burks, V., Carson, J., Neville, B., & Boyum, L. (1994). Family-peer relationships:

A tripartite model. In R. D. Parke & S. Kellam (Eds.), *Advances in family research: Vol. 4. Family relationships with other social systems* (pp. 115–145). Hillsdale, NJ: Erlbaum.

Parke, R. D., MacDonald, K. B., Beitel, A., & Bhavnagri, N. (1988). The role of the family in the development of peer relationships. In R. D. Peters & R. J. McMahon (Eds.), *Social learning and systems approaches to marriage and the family* (pp. 17–44). New York: Brunner/Mazel.

Parke, R. D., & Neville, B. (1995). Late-timed fatherhood: Determinantes and consequences for children and families. In J. L. Shapiro, M. J. Diamond, & M. Greenberg (Eds.), *Becoming a father: Contemporary, social, developmental, and clinical perspectives,* (Vol. 8, pp. 104–116). New York: Springer.

Parke, R. D., & O'Leary, S. E. (1976). Father-mother-infant interaction in the newborn period: Some findings, some observations and some unresolved issues. In K. Riegel & J. Meacham (Eds.), *The developing individual in a changing world: Social and environmental issues* (Vol. 2). The Hague: Mouton.

Parke, R. D., & O'Neil, R. (1997). The influence of significant others on learning about relationships. In S. Duck (Ed.), *Handbook of personal relationships* (2nd ed., pp. 29–60). New York: Wiley.

Parke, R. D., & O'Neil, R. (1998). Social relationships across contexts: Family-peer linkages. In W. A. Collins & B. Laursen (Eds.), *Minnesota symposium on child psychology* (Vol. 30). Hillsdale, NJ: Erlbaum.

Parke, R. D., O'Neil, R., Spitzer, S., Isley, S., Welsh, M., Wang, S., Lee, J., Strand, C., & Cupp, R. (1997). A longitudinal assessment of sociometric stability and the behavioral correlates of children's social acceptance. *Merrill-Palmer Quarterly, 43,* 635–662.

Parke, R. D., & Slaby, R. G. (1983). The development of aggression. In E. M. Hetherington (Ed.), *Handbook of child psychology: Vol. 4. Socialization, personality and social development.* New York: Wiley.

Parker, J. G., & Asher, S. R. (1987). Peer acceptance and later personal adjustment: Are low accepted children at risk? *Psychological Bulletin, 102,* 357–389.

Parker, J. G., & Asher, S. R. (1993). Friendship and friendship quality in middle childhood. *Developmental Psychology, 29,* 611–621.

Parker, J. G., & Gottman, J. M. (1989). Social and emotional development in a relational context: Friendship interaction from early childhood to adolescence. In T. J. Berndt & G. W. Ladd (Eds.), *Peer relationships in child development.* New York: Wiley.

Parker, S. M., & Barrett, D. E. (1992). Maternal type A behavior during pregnancy, neonatal crying and infant temperament: Do type A women have type A babies? *Pediatrics, 89,* 474–479.

Parkhurst, J. T., & Asher, S. R. (1992). Peer rejection in middle school: Subgroup differences in behavior, loneliness and interpersonal concerns. *Developmental Psychology, 28,* 231–241.

Pasamanick, B., & Knoblock, H. (1966). Retrospective studies on the epidemiology of reproductive casualty: Old and new. *Merrill-Palmer Quarterly, 12,* 7–26.

Pascalis, O., De Schonen, S., Morton, J., Deruelle, C., & Fabre-Grenet, M. (1995). Mother's face recognition by neonates: A replication and extension. *Infant Behavior and Development, 18,* 79–85.

Pascual-Leone, J. (1980). Constructive problems for constructive theories. In R. H. Kluwe & H. Spada (Eds.), *Developmental models of thinking.* New York: Academic.

Pascual-Leone, J. A. (1989). Constructive problems for constructive theories: The current relevance of Piaget's work and a critique of information processing simulation psychology. In H. Spada & R. Kluwe (Eds.), *Developmental models of thinking.* New York: Academic.

Patterson, C. J. (1982). Self-control and self-regulation in childhood. In T. M. Field et al. (Eds.), *Review of human development.* New York: Wiley.

Patterson, C. J. (1992). Children of gay and lesbian parents. *Child Development, 63,* 1025–1042.

Patterson, C. J. (1995a). Families of the lesbian baby boom: Parents' division of labor and children's adjustment. *Developmental Psychology, 31,* 115–123.

Patterson, C. J. (1995b). Lesbian mothers, gay fathers, and their children. In A. R. D'Augelli & C. J. Patterson (Eds.), *Lesbian, gay and bisexual identities across the lifespan: Psychological perspectives* (pp. 262–290). New York: Oxford University Press.

Patterson, C. J., & Chan, R. W. (1997). Gay fathers. In M. E. Lamb (Ed.), *The role of the father in child development* (pp. 245–260). New York: Wiley.

Patterson, C. J., & Kister, M. C. (1981). Development of listener skills for referential communication. In W. P. Dickerson (Eds.), *Children's oral communication skills.* New York: Academic.

Patterson, D., & Barnard, K. (1990). Parenting of low birthweight infants. *Infant Medical Health Journal, 11,* 37–56.

Patterson, G. R. (1982). *Coercive family process.* Eugene, OR: Castalia Press.

Patterson, G. R. (1993). Orderly change in a stable world: The antisocial trait as chimera. *Journal of Consulting & Clinical Psychology, 61,* 911–919.

Patterson, G. R. (1995). Coercion—a basis for early age of onset for arrest. In J. McCord (Ed.), *Coercion and punishment in long-term perspective* (pp. 81–105). New York: Cambridge University Press.

Patterson, G. R. (1996). Some characteristics of a developmental theory for early-onset delinquency. In M. F. Lenzenweger & J. J. Haugaard (Eds.), *Frontiers of developmental psychopathology* (pp. 81–124). New York: Oxford University Press.

Patterson, G. R. (1997). Performance models for parenting: A social interactional perspective. In J. E. Grusec & L. Kuczynki (Eds.), *Parenting & children's internalization of values* (pp. 193–226). New York: Wiley.

Patterson, G. R., & Bank, L. (1989). Some amplifying mechanisms for pathologic processes in families. In M. Gunnar & E. Thelen (Eds.), *Systems and development:*

The Minnesota symposium on child psychology (Vol. 22, pp. 167–209). Hillsdale, NJ: Erlbaum.

Patterson, G. R., & Capaldi, D. M. (1991). Antisocial parents: Unskilled and vulnerable. In P. A. Cowan & E. M. Hetherington (Eds.), *Family transitions.* Hillsdale, NJ: Erlbaum.

Patterson, G. R., DeBarshyshe, B., & Ramsey, R. (1989). A developmental perspective on antisocial behavior. *American Psychologist, 44,* 329–335.

Patterson, G. R., Forgatch, M. S., Yoeger, K. L., & Stoolmiller, M. (in press). Variables that initiate and maintain an early-onset trajectory for juvenile offending. *Development and Psychopathology.*

Patterson, G. R., Reid, J. B., & Dishion, T. J. (1992). *A social learning approach: Vol. 4. Antisocial boys.* Eugene, OR: Castalia Press.

Patterson, G. R., & Stouthamer-Loeber, M. (1984). The correlation of family management practices and delinquency. *Child Development, 55,* 1299–1307.

Payne, J. S., Kauffman, J. M., Brown, G. B., & DeMott, R. M. (1974). *Exceptional children in focus.* Columbus, OH: Merrill.

Pearl, R. (1985). Children's understanding of others' need for help: Effects of problem explicitness and type. *Child Development, 56,* 735–745.

Pearson, B. Z., Fernández, S. C., Lewedeg, V., & Oller, D. K. (1997). The relation of input factors of lexical learning by bilingual infants (ages 8 to 30 months). *Applied Psycholinguistics, 18,* 41–58.

Pearson, B. Z., Fernández, S. C., & Oller, D. K. (1993). Lexical development in bilingual infants and toddlers: Comparison to monolingual norms. *Language Learning, 43,* 93–120.

Pearson, J. L., Hunter, A. G., Ensminger, M. E., & Kellam, S. G. (1990). Black grandmothers in multigenerational households. *Child Development, 61,* 434–442.

Peck, M. N., & Lundberg, O. (1995). Short stature as an effect of economic and social conditions in childhood. *Social Science and Medicine, 41,* 733–738.

Pedersen, F. A., Zaslow, M., Cain, R., & Anderson, B. (1980). *Cesarean birth: The importance of a family perspective.* Paper presented at the International Conference on Infant Studies, New Haven, CT.

Pedersen, F. A., Zaslow, M. J., Cain, R. L., & Anderson, B. J. (1981). Cesarean childbirth: Psychological implications for mothers and fathers. *Infant Mental Health Journal, 2,* 257–263.

Peevers, B. H., & Secord, P. F. (1973). Developmental changes in attribution of descriptive concepts to persons. *Journal of Personality & Social Psychology, 27,* 120–128.

Pegg, J. E., Werker, J. F., & McLeod, P. J. (1992). Preference for infant-directed over adult-directed speech: Evidence from 7-week-old infants. *Infant Behavior and Development, 15,* 325–345.

Pepler, D., Corter, C., & Abramovitch, R. (1982). Social relations among children. Comparisons of siblings and peer interaction. In K. Rubin & H. S. Ross (Eds.), *Peer relationships and social skills in childhood* (pp. 209–227). New York: Springer-Verlag.

Perry, B. D. (1997). Incubated in terror: Neurodevelopmental factors in the "cycle of violence." In J. D. Osofsky (Ed.), *Children in a violent society* (pp. 124–149). New York: The Guilford Press.

Perry, D. G., Perry, L. C., & Weiss, R. J. (1989). Sex differences in the consequences children anticipate for aggression. *Developmental Psychology, 25,* 312–320.

Perry, D. G., Williard, J. C., & Perry, L. C. (1990). Peers' perceptions of the consequences that victimized children provide aggressors. *Child Development, 61,* 1310–1325.

Peters, A. M. (1983). *The units of language.* New York: Cambridge University Press.

Peters, M. F. (1981). Parenting in black families with young children: A historical perspective. In H. McAdoo (Ed.), *Black families.* Newbury Park, CA: Sage.

Petersen, A. C. (Ed.). (1993). *Understanding child abuse and neglect.* Washington: National Academy Press.

Petersen, A. C., & Gitelson, I. B. (1984). *Toward understanding sex-related differences in cognitive performance.* New York: Academic.

Petersen, A. C., Sarigiani, P. A., & Kennedy, R. E. (1991). Adolescent depression: Why more girls? Special Issue: The emergence of depressive symptoms during adolescence. *Journal of Youth & Adolescence, 20,* 247–271.

Petersen, A. C., & Taylor, B. (1980). The biological approach to adolescence. In J. Adelson (Ed.), *Handbook of adolescent psychology.* New York: Wiley.

Petitto, L. (1993). On the ontogenetic requirements for early language acquisition. In B. de Boysson-Bardies, S. de Schonen, P. W. Jusczyk, P. McNeilage, & J. Morton (Eds.), *Developmental neurocognition: Speech and face processing in the first year of life* (pp. 365–383). Dordrecht, Netherlands: Kluwer Academic Press.

Petitto, L., & Marenette, P. (1991). Babbling in the manual mode: Evidence for the ontongeny of language. *Science, 251,* 1493–1496.

Petraitis, J., Flay, B. R., & Miller, T. Q. (1995). Reviewing theories of adolescent substance use: Organizing pieces in the puzzle. *Psychological Bulletin, 117,* 67–86.

Pettit, G. S., Bakshi, A., Dodge, K. A., & Coie, J. D. (1990). The emergence of social dominance in young boys' play groups: Developmental differences and behavioral correlates. *Developmental Psychology, 26,* 1017–1025.

Pettit, G. S., & Bates, J. E. (1989). Family interaction patterns and children's behavior problems from infancy to 4 years. *Developmental Psychology, 25,* 413–420.

Pettit, G. S., & Mize, J. (1993). Substance and style: Understanding the ways in which parents teach children about social relationships. In Steve Duck (Ed.), *Learning about relationships. Understanding relationship processes* (Vol. 2. pp. 118–151). Newbury Park, CA: Sage.

Pfiffner, L. J., & Barkley, R. A. (1990). Educational placement and classroom management. In R. A. Barkley (Ed.), *Attention-Deficit hyperactivity disorder: A handbook for diagnosis and treatment* (pp. 498–539). New York: Guilford.

Phillips, D. (1991). With a little help: Children in poverty and child care. In A. Huston (Ed.), *Children and poverty.* New York: Cambridge University Press.

Phillips, J. (1969). *The origin of intellect: Piaget's theory.* San Francisco: Freeman.

Phillips, R. B., Sharma, R., Premachandra, B. R., Vaughn, A. J., & Reyes-Lee, M. (1996). Intrauterine exposure to cocaine: Effect on neurobehavior of neonates. *Infant Behavior & Development, 19,* 71–81.

Piaget, J. (1932). *The moral judgment of the child.* New York: Harcourt, Brace.

Piaget, J. (1960). *The child's conception of the world.* London: Routledge.

Pianta, R., Egeland, B., & Erickson, M. F. (1989). The antecedents of maltreatment: Results of the mother-child interaction research project. In D. Cicchetti & V. Carlson (Eds.), *Child maltreatment: Theory and research on the causes and consequences of child abuse and neglect* (pp. 203–253). New York: Cambridge University Press.

Pick, H. (1992). E. J. Gibson's contributions to developmental psychology. *Developmental Psychology, 28,* 787–794.

Pickens, J. N. (1994). Perception of auditory-visual distance relations by 5-month-old infants. *Developmental Psychology, 30,* 537–544.

Pinker, S. (1989). *Learnability and cognition: The acquisition of argument structure.* Cambridge, MA: MIT Press.

Pinker, S. (1994). *The language instinct: How the mind creates language.* New York: Morrow.

Pipp, S. Easterbrooks, M. A., & Harmon, R. J. (1992). The relation between attachment and knowledge of self and mother in one-year-old infants. *Child Development, 63,* 738–750.

Pleck, J. H. (1984). Husbands' paid work and family roles: Current research issues. In H. Lapata & J. H. Pleck (Eds.), *Research in the inter-weave of social roles. Vol. 3. Families and jobs.* Greenwich, CT: JAI Press.

Pleck, J. H. (1993). Are "family-supportive" employer policies relevant to men? In J. C. Hood (Ed.), *Men, work, and family: Vol. 4. Research on men and masculinities* (pp. 217–237). Newbury Park, CA: Sage.

Plomin, R. (1986). *Development, genetics, and psychology.* Hillsdale, NJ: Erlbaum.

Plomin, R. (1989). Environment and genes: Determinants of behavior. *American Psychologist, 44,* 105–111.

Plomin, R. (1990a). *Nature & nurture: An introduction to human behavioral genetics.* Pacific Grove, CA: Brooks/Cole.

Plomin, R. (1990b). The role of inheritance in behavior. *Science, 248,* 183–188.

Plomin, R. (1995). Genetics and children's experiences in the family. *Journal of Child Psychology and Psychiatry, 36,* 33–68.

Plomin, R., & Bergeman, C. S. (1991). The nature of nurture: Genetic influence on "environmental" measures. *Behavioral and Brain Sciences, 14,* 373–385.

Plomin, R., & Daniels, D. (1987). Why are children in the same family so different from one another? *The Behavioral and Brain Sciences, 10,* 1–16.

Plomin, R., & DeFries, J. C. (1985). *Origins of individual differences in infancy.* New York: Academic.

Plomin, R., & McClearn, G. E. (Eds.). (1993). *Nature, nurture and psychology.* Washington, DC: American Psychological Association.

Plomin, R., McClearn, G. E., Pedersen, N. L., Nesselroade, J. R., & Bergeman, C. S. (1988). Genetic influence on childhood family environment perceived retrospectively from the last half of the life span. *Developmental Psychology, 24,* 738–745.

Plomin, R., & Petrill, S. A. (1997). Genetics and intelligence: What's new? *Intelligence, 24,* Special issue, 53–78.

Pollitt, E. (1994). Poverty and child development: Relevance of research in developing countries to the United States. *Child Development, 65,* 283–295.

Pollitt, E., Gorman, K., & Metallinos-Katsaras, E. (1992). Long-term developmental consequences of intrauterine and postnatal growth retardation in rural Guatemala. In G. J. Suci & S. R. Robertson (Eds.), *Future directions in infant development research* (pp. 43–70). New York: Springer-Verlag.

Pomerantz, E. M., & Ruble, D. N. (in press). A multidimensional perspective of control: Implications for the development of sex differences in self-evaluation and depression. In J. Heckhausen & C. Dweck (Eds.), *Motivation and self-regulation across the life span.*

Pomerleau, A., Bolduc, D., Malcuit, G., & Cossette, L. (1990). Pink or blue: Environmental gender stereotypes in the first two years of life. *Sex Roles, 22,* 359–367.

Porac, C., & Coren, S. (1981). *Lateral preferences and human behavior.* New York: Springer-Verlag.

Porges, S. W. (1995). Orienting in a defensive world: Mammalian modifications of our evolutionary heritage. A Polyvagal theory. *Psychophysiology, 32,* 301–318.

Porter, R. H., Makin, J. W., Davis, L. B., & Christensen, K. M. (1992). Breast-fed infants respond to olfactory cues from their own mother and unfamiliar lactating females. *Infant Behavior and Development, 15,* 85–93.

Posada, G., Gao, Y., Wu, F., Posada, R., Tascon, M., Schöelmerich, A., Sagi, A., Kondo-Ikemura, K., Haaland, W., & Synnevaag, B. (1995). The secure-base phenomenon across cultures: Children's behavior, mothers' preferences, and experts' concepts. In E. Waters, B. E. Vaughn, G. Posada, & K. Kondo-Ikemura (Eds.), *Caregiving, cultural, and cognitive perspectives on secure-base behavior and working models: New growing points of attachment theory and research. Monographs of the Society for Research in Child Development, 60*(2–3, Serial No. 244).

Postlethwait, J. H., & Hopson, J. L. (1995). *The nature of life* (3rd ed.). New York: McGraw-Hill.

Poulson, C. L. (1984). Operant theory and methodology in infant vocal conditioning. *Journal of Experimental Child Psychology, 38,* 103–113.

Power, T. G., & Parke, R. D. (1982). Play as a context for early learning: Lab and home analyses. In L. M. Laosa & I. E. Sigel (Eds.), *The family as a learning environment.* New York: Plenum.

Power, T. G., & Parke, R. D. (1986). Patterns of early socialization: Mother- and father-infant interaction in the home. *International Journal of Behavioral Development, 9,* 331–341.

Power, T. G., & Shanks, J. A. (1989). Parents as socializers: Maternal and paternal views. *Journal of Youth & Adolescence, 18,* 203–220.

Powlishta, K. K. (1989). *Salience of group membership: The case of gender.* Unpublished doctoral dissertation. Stanford University, Stanford, CA.

Pratt, M. W., Kerig, P., Cowan, P. A., & Cowan, C. P. (1988). Mothers and fathers teaching 3 year olds: Authoritative parenting and adult scaffolding of young children's learning. *Developmental Psychology, 24,* 832–839.

Pressley, M., Cariglia-Bull, T., Deane, S., & Schneider, W. (1987). Short-term memory, verbal competence, and age as predictors of imagery instructional effectiveness. *Journal of Experimental Child Psychology, 43,* 194–211.

Purcell, P., & Stewart, L. (1990). Dick and Jane in 1989. *Sex Roles, 22,* 177–185.

Putallaz, M. (1987). Maternal behavior and sociometric status. *Child Development, 58,* 324–340.

Putallaz, M., Costanzo, P. R., & Smith, R. B. (1991). Maternal recollections of childhood peer relationships: Implications for their children's social competence. *Journal of Social and Personal Relationships, 8,* 403–422.

Putallaz, M., & Gottman, J. M. (1981). Social skills and peer acceptance. In S. R. Asher & J. M. Gottman (Eds.), *The development of children's friendships.* New York: Cambridge University Press.

Putallaz, M., & Heflin, A. H. (1990). Parent-child interaction. In S. R. Asher & J. D. Coie (Eds.), *Peer rejection in childhood.* New York: Cambridge University Press.

Quay, L. C., & Jarrett, O. S. (1986). Teachers' interactions with middle- and lower SES preschool boys and girls. *Journal of Educational Psychology, 78,* 495–498.

Quinn, P. C., Cummins, M., Kase, J., Martin, E., & Weissman, T. K. (1996). Development of categorical representations for above and below spatial relations in 3- to 7-month-old infants. *Developmental Psychology, 32,* 942–950.

Rabinowitz, F. M., Grant, M. J., Howe, M. L., & Walsh, C. (1994). Reasoning in middle childhood: A dynamic model of performance on transitivity tasks. *Journal of Experimental Child Psychology, 58,* 252–288.

Radke-Yarrow, M., Cummings, E. M., Kuczynski, L., & Chapman, M. (1985). Patterns of attachment in two- and three-year-olds in normal families and families with parental depression. *Child Development, 56,* 884–893.

Radke-Yarrow, M., & Zahn-Waxler, C. (1983). Roots, motives and patterns in children's prosocial behavior. In J. Reykowski, T. Karylowski, D. Bar-Tal, & E. Staub (Eds.), *Origins and maintenance of prosocial behaviors.* New York: Plenum.

Radke-Yarrow, M., Zahn-Waxler, C., & Chapman, M. (1983). Children's prosocial dispositions and behavior. In E. M. Hetherington (Ed.), *Handbook of child psychology: Vol. 4. Socialization, personality and social development.* New York: Wiley.

Radziszewska, B., & Rogoff, B. (1988). Influence of adult and peer collaborators on the development of children's planning skills. *Developmental Psychology, 24,* 840–848.

Ragozin, A. S., Bashman, R. B., Crnic, K. A., Greenberg, M. T., & Robinson, N. M. (1982). Effects of maternal age on the parenting role. *Developmental Psychology, 18,* 627–634.

Raine, A., Brennan, P., & Mednick, S. A. (1994). Birth complications combined with early maternal rejection at age one year predispose to violent crime at age 18 years. *Archives of General Psychiatry, 51,* 984–988.

Rakic, P. (1991). Plasticity of cortical development. In S. E. Brauth, W. S. Hall, & R. J. Dooling (Eds.), *Plasticity of development.* Cambridge, MA: MIT Press.

Rakic, P. (1995). Corticogensis in human and nonhuman primates. In M. S. Gazzaniga (Ed.), *The cognitive neurosciences* (pp. 127–145). Cambridge, MA: MIT Press.

Ramey, C. T., Bryant, D. M., Campbell, F. A., Sparling, J. J., & Wasik, B. H. (1988). Early intervention for high-risk children: The Carolina early intervention program. In R. H. Price, E. Cowen, R. Lorien, & J. Ramos-McKay (Eds.), *Fourteen ounces of prevention: A casebook for practitioners.* Washington, DC: American Psychological Association.

Ramey, C. T., & Campbell, F. A. (1992). Poverty, early childhood education and academic competence: The Abecedarian experiment. In A. Huston (Ed.), *Children in poverty* (pp. 190–221). NY: Cambridge University Press.

Ramey, C. T., Campbell, F. A., & Blair, C. (in press). Enhancing the life course for high-risk children: Results from the Abecedarian project. In J. Crane (Ed.), *Social programs that really work.* New York: Sage.

Ramey, C. T., Lee, M. W., & Burchinal, M. R. (1989). Developmental plasticity and predictability: Consequences of ecological change. In M. Bornstein & N. A. Krasnegor (Eds.), *Stability and continuity in mental development* (pp. 217–234). Hillsdale, NJ: Erlbaum.

Ramey, C. T., & Ramey, S. L. (1992). Early educational intervention with disadvantaged children—to what effect? *Applied and Preventive Psychology, 1,* 130–140.

Ramey, C. T., & Ramey, S. L. (in press). Early intervention and early experience. *American Psychologist.*

Ramey, C. T., Ramey, S. L., Gaines, K. R., & Blair, C. (1995). Two-generation early intervention programs: A child development perspective. In S. Smith (Ed.), *Two-generation programs for families in poverty: A new intervention strategy* (pp. 202–215). Norwood, NJ: Ablex.

Ramirez, O. (1989). Mexican-American children and adolescents. In J. T. Gibbs & L. N. Huang (Eds.), *Children of color.* San Francisco: Jossey-Bass.

Rapoport, J. L. (1996). *DSM-IV training guide for diagnosis of childhood disorders.* New York: Brunner/Mazel.

Rapoport, J. L., Buchsbaum, M. S., Zahn, T. P., Weingartner, H., Ludlow, C., & Mikkelson, E. J. (1978). Dextroamphetamine: Cognitive

and behavioral effects in normal prepubertal boys. *Science, 199,* 560–563.

Raudenbusch, S. W. (1984). Magnitude of teacher expectancy effects on pupil IQ as a function of credibility of expectancy induction: A synthesis from 18 experiments. *Journal of Experimental Psychology, 76,* 85–97.

Ray, J. W., & Klesges, R. C. (1993). Influences on the eating behavior of children. In C. L. Williams & S. Y. S. Kimm (Eds.), *Prevention and treatment of childhood obesity* (pp. 57–69). Annals of the New York Academy of Sciences, Vol. 699. New York: The New York Academy of Sciences.

Reid, P. T., Tate, C. S., & Berman, P. W. (1989). Preschool children's self-presentations in situations with infants: Effects of sex and race. *Child Development, 60,* 710–714.

Reid, R., Maag, J. W., & Vasa, S. F. (1993). Attention deficit hyperactivity as a disability category: A critique. *Exceptional Children, 60,* 198–214.

Reilly, T. W., Entwisle, D. R., & Doering, S. G. (1987). Socialization into parenthood: A longitudinal study of the development of self evaluations. *Journal of Marriage and the Family, 49,* 295–308.

Reiss, A. L., & Freund, L. (1990). Fragile X syndrome, DSM-III-R, and autism. *Journal of American Academy of Child and Adolescent Psychiatry, 29,* 885–891.

Reiss, D. (1989). The represented and practicing family: Contrasting visions of family continuity. In A. J. Sameroff & R. N. Emde (Eds.), *Relationship disturbances in early childhood* (pp. 191–220). New York: Basic Books.

Reiss, D., Hetherington, E. M., & Plomin, R. (1994). The separate social worlds of teenage siblings. In E. M. Hetherington, D. Reiss, & R. Plomin (Eds.), *The separate world of siblings: Impact of non-shared environments on development.* Hillsdale, NJ: Erlbaum.

Reiss, D., & Klein, D. (1987). Paradigm and pathogenesis. In T. Jacob (Ed.), *Family interaction and psychopathology: Theories, methods, and findings* (pp. 203–205). New York: Plenum.

Reiss, D., Plomin, R., & Hetherington, E. M. (1991). Genetics and psychiatry: An unheralded window on the environment. *American Journal of Psychiatry, 148,* 283–291.

Reissland, N. (1988). Neonatal imitation in the first hour of life. Observations in rural Nepal. *Developmental Psychology, 24,* 464–469.

Reite, M., Cullum, C. M., Stocker, J., Teale, P., et al. (1993). Neuropsychological test performance and MEG-based brain lateralization: Sex differences. *Brain Research Bulletin, 32,* 325–328.

Remschmidt, H. E., Schulz, E., Martin, M., & Warnke, A. (1994). Childhood-onset schizophrenia: History of the concept and recent studies. *Schizophrenia Bulletin, 20,* 727–745.

Renninger, K. A. (1998). Developmental psychology and instruction: Issues from and for practice. In W. Damon (Gen. Ed.), I. E. Sigel, & K. A. Renninger (Vol. Eds.), *Handbook of child psychology: Child psychology in practice* (Vol. 4, pp. 211–274). New York: Wiley.

Renshaw, P. D., & Asher, S. R. (1983). Children's goals and strategies for social interaction. *Merrill-Palmer Quarterly, 29,* 353–374.

Renshaw, P. D., & Brown, P. J. (1993). Loneliness in middle childhood: Concurrent and longitudinal predictors. *Child Development, 64,* 1271–1284.

Resnick, M. B., Stralka, K., Carter, R. L., Ariet, M., Bucciarelli, R. L., Furlough, R. R., Evass, J. H., Curran, J. S., & Ausbon, W. W. (1990). Effects of birthweight and socio-demographic variables on mental development of neonatal intensive care unit survivors. *American Journal of Obstetrics and Gynecology, 162,* 374–378.

Resnick, S. M., Berenbaum, S. A., Gottesman, I. I., & Bouchard, T. J. (1986). Early hormonal influences on cognitive functioning in congenital adrenal hyperplasia. *Developmental Psychology, 22,* 191–198.

Rest, J. R. (1979). *Development in judging moral issues.* Minneapolis: University of Minnesota Press.

Rest, J. R. (1983). Morality. In J. Flavell & E. Markman (Eds.), *Handbook of child psychology: Vol. 3. Cognitive development.* New York: Wiley.

Rest, J. R. (1986). *Moral development: Advances in research and theory.* New York: Praeger.

Rest, J. R., Davison, M. L., & Robbins, S. (1978). Age trends in judging moral issues: A review of cross-sectional longitudinal and sequential studies of the Defining Issues Test. *Child Development, 49,* 263–279.

Restak, R. M. (1984). *The brain.* NewYork: Bantam.

Revelle, G. L., Wellman, H. M., & Karabenick, J. D. (1985). Comprehension monitoring in preschool children. *Child Development, 56,* 654–663.

Reynolds, W. M. (1994). Depression in adolescents. In T. Ollendick & R. Prinz (Eds.), *Advances in clinical child psychology* (Vol. 16, pp. 261–316).

Rheingold, H., & Eckerman, C. (1970). The infant separates himself from his mother. *Science, 168,* 78–83.

Rheingold, H. L. (1982). Little children's participation in the work of adults, a nascent prosocial behavior. *Child Development, 53,* 114–125.

Rheingold, H. L., & Cook, K. V. (1975). The content of boys' and girls' rooms as an index of parent behavior. *Child Development, 46,* 459–463.

Rheingold, H. L., & Eckerman, C. O. (1973). The fear of strangers hypothesis: A critical review. In H. Reese (Ed.), *Advances in child development and behavior* (Vol. 8, pp. 185–222). New York: Academic.

Rheingold, H. L., Hay, D. F., & West, M. J. (1976). Sharing in the second year of life. *Child Development, 47,* 1148–1158.

Rhode, G., Jenson, W. R., & Reavis, K. (1993). *Tough kid book.* Lonmont, CO: Sopris West.

Rice, M. L. (1989). Children's language acquisition. *American Psychologist, 44,* 149–156.

Rice, M. L. (1990). Preschoolers QUIL: Quick incidental learning of words. In G. Gontiramsdem & C. Snow (Eds.), *Children's language* (Vol. 7). Hillsdale, NJ: Erlbaum.

Rice, M. L., Huston, A. C., Truglio, R. T., & Wright, J. C. (1990). Words from Sesame Street: Learning vocabulary while viewing. *Developmental Psychology, 26,* 421–428.

Richardson, E., Kupertz, S. S., Winsberg, B. G., Maitinsky, S. & Wendell, N. (1988). Effects of methylphenidate dosage in hyperactive reading-disabled children: II. Reading achievement. *Journal of the American Academy of Child and Adolescent Psychiatry, 27,* 78–87.

Richardson, T. M., & Benbow, C. P. (1990). Long-term effects of acceleration on the social-emotional adjustment of mathematically precocious youths. *Journal of Educational Psychology, 82,* 464–470.

Richters, J., & Martinez, P. (1993). The NIMH community violence project: Children's distress symptoms associated with violence exposure. *Psychiatry, 56,* 22–35.

Riciutti, H. N. (1993). Nutrition and mental development. *Current Directions in Psychological Science, 2,* 43–46.

Riese, M. L. (1990). Neonatal temperament in monozygotic and dizygotic twin pairs. *Child Development, 61,* 1230–1237.

Riesen, A. H. (1947). The development of visual perception in man and chimpanzee. *Science, 106,* 107–108.

Ritter, P. L., Mont-Reynaud, R., & Dornbusch, S. M. (1990). *Minority parents and their youth: Concern, encouragement and support for school achievement.* Unpublished manuscript, Stanford University.

Robbins, L. C. (1963). The accuracy of parental recording of aspects of child development and of child rearing practices. *Journal of Abnormal and Social Psychology, 66,* 261–270.

Roberton, M. A., & Halverson, L. E. (1984). *Developing children: Their changing movement.* Philadelphia: Lea & Febiger.

Roberton, M. A., & Halverson, L. E. (1988). The development of locomotor coordination: Longitudinal change and invariance. *Journal of Motor Behavior, 20,* 197–241.

Roberts, R. J. (1981). Errors and the assessment of cognitive development. *New Directions for Child Development, 12,* 237–238.

Robins, L., & McEvoy, L. (1990). Conduct problems and substance abuse. In L. N. Robins & M. Rutter (Eds.), *Straight and devious pathways from childhood to adulthood.* Cambridge: Cambridge University Press.

Robinson, A., Bender, B. G., & Linden, M. G. (1992). Prenatal diagnosis of sex chromosome abnormalities. In A. Milunsky (Ed.), *Genetic disorders and the fetus: Diagnosis, prevention and treatment.* Baltimore: Johns Hopkins University Press.

Robinson, J. (1988). Who's doing the housework? *American Demographics, 10,* 24–28.

Robinson, J. L., Kagan, J., Reznick, J. S., & Corley, R. (1992). The heritability of inhibited and uninhibited behavior. A twin study. *Developmental Psychology, 28,* 1030–1037.

Robinson, L. A., & Klesges, R. C. (1997). Ethnic and gender differences in risk factors for smoking onset. *Health Psychology, 16,* 499–505.

Roche, A. F. (Ed.). (1979). Secular trends: Human growth, maturation, and development, *Monographs of the Society for Research in Child Development, 44* (Serial No. 179).

Rodin, J. (1981). Current status of the internal-external hypothesis for obesity: What went wrong? *American Psychologist, 36,* 361–372.

Roffwarg, H. P., Muzio, J. N., & Dement, W. C. (1966). Ontogenetic development of the human sleep-dream cycle. *Science, 152,* 604–619.

Rogoff, B. (1990). *Apprenticeship in thinking: Cognitive development in social context.* New York: Oxford University Press.

Rogoff, B. (1998). Cognition as a collaborative process. In W. Damon (Gen. Ed.), D. Kuhn, & R. S. Siegler (Vol. Eds.), *Handbook of child psychology, Vol. 5. Cognition, perception & language.* New York: Wiley.

Rogoff, B., & Mistry, J. (1990). The social and functional context of children's remembering. In R. Fivush & J. A. Hudson (Eds.), *Knowing and remembering in young children* (pp. 197–222). New York: Cambridge University Press.

Rogoff, B., & Waddell, K. J. (1982). Memory for information organized in a scene by children from two cultures. *Child Development, 53,* 1224–1228.

Rolland-Cachera, M. F., Deheeger, M., Bellisle, F., Sempe, M., Guilloud-Bataille, M., & Patoid, E. (1984). Adiposity rebound in children: A simple indicator for predicting obesity. *American Journal of Clinical Nutrition, 39,* 129–135.

Romski, M. A., & Sevcik, R. A. (1996). *Breaking the speech barrier: Language development through augmented means.* Baltimore: Brookes.

Roopnarine, J. (1992). Father-child play in India. In K. MacDonald (Ed.), *Parent-child play.* Albany: State University of New York Press.

Rosch, E., & Mervis, C. B. (1975). Family resemblances: Studies in the internal structure of categories. *Cognitive Psychology, 7,* 573–605.

Rosch, E., Mervis, C. B., Gray, W. D., Johnson, D. M., & Boyes-Braem, P. (1976). Basic objects in natural categories. *Cognitive Psychology, 8,* 382–439.

Rose, S. A. (1994). Relation between physical growth and information processing in infants born in India. *Child Development, 65,* 889–903.

Rose, S. A., & Feldman, J. F. (1995). Prediction of IQ and specific cognitive abilities at 11 years from infancy measures. *Developmental Psychology, 31,* 685–696.

Rose, S. A., Feldman, J. F., Wallace, I. F., & McCarton, C. (1989). Infant visual attention: Relation to birth status and developmental outcome during the first 5 years. *Developmental Psychology, 25,* 560–576.

Rosen, L. A., O'Leary, S. G., & Conway, G. (1985). The withdrawal of stimulant medication for hyperactivity: Overcoming detrimental attributions. *Behavior Therapy, 16,* 538–544.

Rosenblum, T., & Pinker, S. (1983). Word magic revisited: Monolingual and bilingual children's understanding of the word-object relationships. *Child Development, 54,* 773–780.

Rosenhan, D. (1972). Prosocial behavior of children. In W. W. Hartup (Ed.), *The young child* (Vol. 2, pp. 340–359). Washington, DC: National Association for the Education of Young Children.

Rosenstein, D., & Oster, H. (1988). Differential facial response to four basic tastes in newborns. *Child Development, 59,* 1555–1568.

Rosenthal, R. (1994). Interpersonal expectancy effects: A 30 year perspective. *Current Directions in Psychological Science, 3,* 176–179.

Rosenthal, R., & Jacobsen, L. (1968). *Pygmalion in the classroom.* New York: Holt.

Rosenzweig, M. R. (1966). Environmental complexity, cerebral change, and behavior. *American Psychologist, 21,* 321–332.

Rosenzweig, M. R., & Bennett, E. L. (1970). Effects of differential environments on brain weights and enzyme activities in gerbils, rats, and mice. *Developmental Psychobiology, 2,* 87–95.

Rosenzweig, M. R., Leiman, A. S., & Breedlove, S. M. (1996). *Biological psychology.* Sunderland, MA: Sinauer Associates.

Ross, D. M., & Ross, S. A. (1982). *Hyperactivity.* New York: Wiley.

Ross, H. S., & Conant, C. L. (1992). The social structure of early conflict: Interactions, relationships, and alliances. In C. U. Shantz & W. W. Hartup (Eds.), *Conflict in child and adolescent development.* Cambridge: Cambridge University Press.

Ross, H. S., Conant, C., Cheyne, J. A., & Alevizos, E. (1992). Relationships and alliances in the social interactions of kibbutz toddlers. *Social Development, 1,* 1–17.

Ross, H. S., & Goldman, B. D. (1977). Infants' sociability toward strangers. *Child Development, 48,* 638–642.

Rothbart, M. (1981). Measurement of temperament in infancy. *Child Development, 52,* 569–578.

Rothbart, M., & Bates, J. (1998). Temperament. In W. Damon (Gen. Ed.) & N. Eisenberg (Vol. Ed.), *Handbook of child psychology: Vol. 3. Social and emotional development* (5th ed.). New York: Wiley.

Rothbart, M. K. (1989) Behavioral approach and inhibition. In J. Steven Reznick (Ed.), Perspectives on behavioral inhibition. The John D. and Catherine T. MacArthur Foundation series on mental health and development, (pp. 139-157). Chicago, IL: University of Chicago Press.

Rothbart, M. K. (1989). Temperament in childhood: A framework. In G. A. Kohnstamm, J. E. Bates, & M. K. Rothbart (Eds.), *Temperament in childhood.* (pp. 59-73). Chichester, England: Wiley & Sons.

Rothbart, M. K., Ahadi, S. A., & Hershey, K. L. (1994). Temperament and social behavior in childhood. *Merrill-Palmer Quarterly, 40,* 21–39.

Rovee-Collier, C., & DuFault, D. (1991). Multiple contexts and memory retrieval at three months. *Developmental Psychobiology, 24,* 39–49.

Rovee-Collier, C. K. (1986). *Infants and elephants: Do they ever forget?* Paper presented at a Science and Public Policy Seminar, Washington, DC.

Rovee-Collier, C. K. (1987). Learning and memory in infants. In J. D. Osofsky (Ed.), *Handbook of infant development* (pp. 98–148). New York: Wiley.

Rovee-Collier, C. K., & Lipsitt, L. P. (1982). Learning, adaptation and memory in the newborn. In P. Stratton (Ed.), *Psychobiology of the human newborn.* New York: Wiley.

Rovee-Collier, C. K., & Shyi, G. (1992). A functional and cognitive analysis of infant long-term retention. In C. J. Brainard, M. L. Howe, & V. Reyna (Eds.), *Development of long-term retention* (pp. 3–55). New York: Springer-Verlag.

Rovet, J., & Netley, C. (1983). The triple X chromosome syndrome in childhood: Recent empirical findings. *Child Development, 54,* 831–845.

Rozin, P. (1996). Towards a psychology of food and eating: From motivation to module to model to marker, morality, meaning, and metaphor. *Current Directions in Psychological Science, 5,* 18–24.

Rubenstein, J. L., Huren, T., Horssman, D., Rubin, C., & Stockler, C. (1988, March). *Suicidal behavior in normal adolescents. Risk and protective factors.* Paper presented at the biennial meeting of the Society for Research in Adolescence, Alexandria, VA.

Rubin, J. Z., Provenzano, F. J., & Luria, A. (1974). The eye of the beholder: Parents' views on sex of newborns. *American Journal of Orthopsychiatry, 43,* 720–731.

Rubin, K. H. (1982). Non-social play in preschoolers: Necessarily evil? *Child Development, 53,* 651–657.

Rubin, K. H., Bukowski, W., & Parker, J. G. (1998). Peer interactions, relationships, and groups. In W. Damon (Gen. Ed.) & N. Eisenberg (Vol. Ed.), *Handbook of child psychology: Vol. 3. Social, emotional, and personality development* (5th ed., pp. 619–700). New York: Wiley.

Rubin, K. H., Fein, G. G., & Vandenberg, B. (1983). Play. In P. H. Mussen (Ed.), *Handbook of child psychology* (Vol. 4). New York: Wiley.

Rubin, K. H., & LeMare, L. (1990). Social withdrawal in childhood: Assessment issues and social commitments. In S. R. Asher & J. D. Coie (Eds.), *Children's status in the peer group.* New York: Cambridge University Press.

Rubin, Z. (1980). *Children's friendships.* Cambridge, MA: Harvard University Press.

Rubin, Z., & Sloman, J. (1984). How parents influence their children's friendship. In M. Lewis (Ed.), *Beyond the dyad.* New York: Plenum.

Ruble, D. N. (1987). The acquisition of self-knowledge: A self-socialization perspective. In N. Eisenberg (Ed.), *Contemporary topics in developmental psychology.* New York: Wiley.

Ruble, D. N. (1988). Sex role development. In M. H. Bornstein & M. E. Lamb (Eds.), *Developmental psychology: An advanced textbook* (2nd ed., pp. 411–460). Hillsdale, NJ: Erlbaum.

Ruble, D. N. (1994). A phase model of transitions: Cognitive and motivational consequences. In M. Zanna (Ed.), *Advances in experimental social psychology* (Vol. 26, pp. 163–214). New York: Academic Press.

Ruble, D. N., & Martin, C. L. (1998). Gender development. In W. Damon (Gen. Ed.) & N. Eisenberg (Vol. Ed.), *Handbook of child psychology* (Vol. 3, pp. 933–1016). New York: Wiley.

Rudy, G. S., & Goodman, G. S. (1991). The effects of participation on children's reports: Implications for children's testimony. *Developmental Psychology, 27,* 527–538.

Ruff, H. A., & Lawson, K. R. (1990). Development of sustained focused attention in young children during free play. *Developmental Psychology, 26,* 85–93.

Runco, M. A. (1996, Summer). Personal creativity: Definition and developmental issues. In M. A. Runco (Ed.), *Creativity from childhood through adulthood: The developmental issues* [Special issue]. *New Directions for Child Development,* No. 72, 3–30.

Rush, D., & Callahan, K. R. (1989). Exposure to passive cigarette smoking and child development: A critical review. In D. E. Hutchings (Ed.), *Prenatal abuse of licit and illicit drugs. Annals of the New York Academy of Sciences* (Vol. 562, pp. 74–100). New York: New York Academy of Sciences.

Rushton, J. P., Fulker, D. W., Neale, M. C., Nias, D. K. B., & Eysenck, H. J. (1986). Altruism and aggression: The heritability of individual differences. *Journal of Personality and Social Psychology, 50,* 1192–1198.

Russ, S. W. (1996, Summer). Development of creative processes in children. In M. A. Runco (Ed.). *Creativity from childhood through adulthood: The developmental issues* [Special issue]. *New Directions for Child Development,* No. 72, 31–42.

Russell, A., & Finnie, V. (1990). Preschool children's social status and maternal instructions to assist group entry. *Developmental Psychology, 26,* 603–611.

Russell, A., Russell, G., & Midwinter, D. (1992). Observer effects on mothers and fathers: Self-reported influence during a home observation. *Merrill-Palmer Quarterly, 38,* 263–283.

Rutter, M. (1983a). Cognitive deficits in the pathogenesis of autism. *Journal of Child Psychology and Psychiatry, 24,* 513–531.

Rutter, M. (1983b). School effects on pupil progress: Research findings and policy implications. *Child Development, 54,* 1–29.

Rutter, M. (1987). Psychosocial resilience and protective mechanisms. *American Journal of Orthopsychiatry, 51,* 316–331.

Rutter, M. (1989). Isle of Wight revisited: Twenty-five years of child psychiatric epidemiology. *Journal of the American Academy of Child and Adolescent Psychiatry, 28,* 633–653.

Rutter, M. (1990). Psychosocial resilience and protective mechanisms. In J. Rolf, A. S. Masten, D. Cicchetti, K. H. Nuechterlein, & S. Weintraub (Eds.), *Risk and protective factors in the development of psychopathology* (pp. 181–214). New York: Cambridge University Press.

Rutter, M. (1992). Nature, nurture and psychopathology. In B. Tizard & V. Varma (Eds.), *Vulnerability and resilience in human development.* London: Jessica Kingsley.

Rutter, M. (1995). Relationships between mental disorders in childhood and adulthood. *Acta Psychiatrica Scandinavica, 91,* 73–85.

Rutter, M. (1996). Transitions and turning points in developmental psychopathology: As applied to the age span between childhood and mid-adulthood. *International Journal of Behavioral Development, 19,* 603–626.

Rutter, M., Quinton, D., & Yule, B. (1977). Family pathology and disorder in children. London: Wiley.

Rutter, M., & Rutter, M. (1993). *Developing minds.* New York: Basic Books.

Rutter, M., & Schopler, E. (1987). Autism and pervasive developmental disorders: Concepts and diagnostic issues. *Journal of Autism and Developmental Disorders, 17,* 159–186.

Ryan, K. J. (1989). Ethical issues in reproductive endocrinology and infertility. *American Journal of Obstetrics and Gynecology, 160,* 1415–1417.

Rymer, R. (1993). *Genie: A scientific tragedy.* New York: HarperCollins.

Saarni, C. (1989). Children's understanding of strategic control of emotional expression in social transactions. In C. Saarni & P. Harris (Eds.), *Children's understanding of emotions.* New York: Cambridge University Press.

Saarni, C. (1990). Emotional competence: How emotions and relationships become integrated. In R. A. Thompson (Ed.), *Socioemotional development* (Nebraska Symposium on Motivation, Vol. 36). Lincoln: University of Nebraska Press.

Saarni, C., Mumme, D. L., & Campos, J. J. (1998). Emotional development: Action, communication, and understanding. In W. Damon (Gen. Ed.) & N. Eisenberg (Vol. Ed.), *Handbook of child psychology: Vol. 3. Social, emotional, and personality development* (pp. 237–310). New York: Wiley.

Sachs, J. (1985). Prelinguistic development. In J. Berko-Gleason (Ed.), *The development of language.* Columbus, OH: Merrill.

Sadeh, A. (1996). Stress, trauma, and sleep in children. *Child & Adolescent Psychiatric Clinics of North America, 5,* 685–700.

Saffran, J. R., Aslin, R. N., & Newport, E. L. (1996). Statistical learning by 8-month-old infants. *Science, 274,* 1926–1928.

Sagi, A. (1990). Attachment theory and research from a cross-cultural perspective. *Human Development, 33,* 10–22.

Sagi, A., van IJzendoorn, M. H., Aviezer, O., Donnell, I., Koren-Karie, N., Joels, T., & Harel, Y. (1995). Attachments in a multiple-caregiver and multiple infant environment: The case of the Israeli kibbutzim. In E. Waters, B. E. Vaughn, G. Posada, & K. Kondo-Ikemura (Eds.), *Caregiving, cultural, and cognitive perspectives on secure-base behavior and working models: New growing points of attachment theory and research. Monographs of the Society for Research in Child Development, 60*(2–3, Serial No. 244).

Sagi, A., van IJzendoorn, M. H., Aviezer, O., Donnell, F., & Mayseless, O. (1994). Sleeping out of home in a kibbutz community arrangement: It makes a difference for infant-mother attachment. *Child Development, 65,* 992–1004.

Sahin, N. (1990, September). *Preliminary report on the summative evaluation of the Turkish co-production of Sesame Street.* Paper presented at the International Conference on Adaptations of SESAME STREET. Amsterdam, The Netherlands.

Salapatek, P. (1969, December). *The visual investigation of geometric pattern by the one- and two-month-old infant.* Paper presented at the meeting of the American Association for the Advancement of Science, Boston.

Salapatek, P., & Kessen, W. (1966). Visual scanning of triangles by the human newborn.

Journal of Experimental Child Psychology, 3, 155–167.

Sallis, J. F., McKenzie, T. L., Alcaraz, J. E., Kolody, B., Hovell, M. F., & Nader, P. R. (1993). Project SPARK: Effects of physical education on adiposity in children. In C. L. Williams & S. Y. S. Kimm (Eds.), *Prevention and treatment of childhood obesity* (pp. 127–136). Annals of the New York Academy of Sciences, Vol. 699. New York: The New York Academy of Sciences.

Salomon, G., & Perkins, D. N. (1987). Transfer of cognitive skills from programming when and how? *Journal of Education Computing Research, 3,* 149–169.

Sameroff, A., Seifer, R., Baldwin, A., & Baldwin, C. (1993). *Continuity of risk from childhood to adolescence.* Unpublished paper. University of Rochester.

Sameroff, A. J. (1972). Learning and adaptation in infancy. A comparison of models. In H. Reese (Ed.), *Advances in child development and behavior* (Vol. 7). New York: Academic.

Sameroff, A. J. (1983). Developmental systems: Contexts and evolution. In P. H. Mussen (Ed.), *Handbook of child psychology.* New York: Wiley.

Sameroff, A. J. (1989). General systems and the regulation of development. In M. R. Gunnar & E. Thelen (Eds.), *Systems and development.* (Vol. 22, pp. 219–235). Hillsdale, NJ: Erlbaum.

Sameroff, A. J. (1994). Developmental systems and family functioning. In R. D. Parke & S. G. Kellam (Eds.), *Exploring family relationships with other social systems* (pp. 199–214). Hillsdale, NJ: Erlbaum.

Sameroff, A. J. (1994). Developmental systems and family functioning. In R. D. Parke & S. G. Kellam, *Exploring family relationships with other social contexts* (pp. 199–214). Hillsdale, NJ: Erlbaum.

Sameroff, A. J., & Chandler, M. J. (1975). Reproductive risk and the continuum of caretaking casualty. In F. Horowitz (Ed.), *Review of child development research* (Vol. 4). Chicago: University of Chicago Press.

Sameroff, A. J., & Seifer, R. (1983). Familial risk and child competence. *Child Development, 54,* 1254–1268.

Sameroff, A. J., Seifer, R., Barocas, R., Zax, M., & Greenspan, S. (1987). Intelligence quotient scores of 4-year-old children: Social-environmental risk factors. *Pediatrics, 79,* 343–350.

Sameroff, A. J., & Zax, M. (1973). Perinatal characteristics of the offspring of schizophrenic women. *Journal of Nervous and Mental Disease, 46,* 178–185.

Sanderson, J. A., & Siegal, M. (1991). *Loneliness in young children.* Unpublished manuscript. University of Queensland, Brisbane, Australia.

Santrock, J. W., & Sitterle, K. A. (1987). Parent-child relationships in step mother families. In K. Posley & M. Ihinger-Tallman (Eds.), *Remarriage and step parenting: Current research and theory* (pp. 135–154). New York: Guilford.

Sarnthein, J., vonStein, A., Rappelsberger, P., Petsche, H., Rauscher, F. H., & Shaw, G. (1997). Persistent patterns of brain activity: An EEG coherence study of the positive effect of music on spatial-temporal reasoning. *Neurological Research, 19,* 107–116.

Sassone, D., Lambert, N. M., & Sandoval, J. (1981). *The adolescent status of boys previously identified as hyperactive.* Unpublished manuscript. University of California.

Savin-Williams, R. (1987). *Adolescence: An ethological perspective.* New York: Springer-Verlag.

Saxby, L., & Bryden, M. P. (1984). Left-ear superiority in children for processing auditory emotional material. *Developmental Psychology, 20,* 72–80.

Saxby, L., & Bryden, M. P. (1985). Left visual field advantage in children for processing visual emotional stimuli. *Developmental Psychology, 20,* 253–261.

Saxe, G. B. (1982). Developing forms of arithmetic thought among the Oksapmin of Papua New Guinea. *Developmental Psychology, 18,* 583–594.

Saxe, G. B. (1988). The mathematics of child street vendors. *Child Development, 59,* 1415–1425.

Saxe, G. B., Guberman, S. R., & Gearhart, M. (1987). Social processes in early number development. *Monographs of the Society for Research in Child Development, 52,* 162.

Scarr, S. (1992). Developmental theories for the 1990s: Development and individual differences. *Child Development, 63,* 1–19.

Scarr, S. (1996). How people make their own environments: Implications for parents and policy makers. *Psychology, Public Policy & Law, 2,* 204–228.

Scarr, S., & McCartney, K. (1983). How people make their own environments: A theory of genotype environment effects. *Child Development, 54,* 424–435.

Scarr, S., Phillips, D., & McCartney, K. (1990). Facts, fantasies and the future of child care in the United States. *Psychological Science, 1,* 26–35.

Scarr, S., & Weinberg, R. A. (1976). IQ test performance of black children adopted by white families. *American Psychologist, 31,* 726–739.

Scarr, S., & Weinberg, R. A. (1977). Intellectual similarities within families of both adopted and biological children. *Intelligence, 1*(2), 170–191.

Scarr, S., & Weinberg, R. A. (1983). The Minnesota adoption studies: Genetic differences and malleability. *Child Development, 54,* 260–267.

Schaal, B., Tremblay, R. E., Soussignan, R., & Susman, E. J. (1996). Male testosterone linked to high social dominance but low physical aggression in early adolescence. *Journal of the American Academy of Child & Adolescent Psychiatry, 19,* 1322–1330.

Schaefer, C. (1997). Defining verbal abuse of children: A survey. *Psychological Reports, 80,* 626.

Schaffer, H. R. (1971). *The growth of sociability.* London: Penguin.

Schaffer, H. R. (1974). *The development of sociability.* New York: Penguin.

Schaffer, H. R. (1977). *Mothering.* Cambridge, MA: Harvard University Press.

Schaffer, H. R. (1996). *Social development.* Cambridge, MA: Blackwell.

Schaffer, H. R., & Emerson, P. E. (1964). The development of social attachments in infancy. *Monographs of the Society for Research in Child Development, 29*(3, Serial No. 94).

Schaivi, R. C., Thelgaard, A., Owen, D., & White, D. (1984). Sex chromosome anomalies, hormones and aggressivity. *Archives of General Psychiatry, 41,* 93–99.

Schank, R. C., & Abelson, R. P. (1977). *Scripts, plans, goals and understanding.* Hillsdale, NJ: Erlbaum.

Schardein, J. L. (1985). *Chemically induced birth defects.* New York: Dekker.

Schellenberg, E. G., & Trehub, S. E. (1996). Natural musical intervals: Evidence from infant listeners. *Psychological Science, 7,* 272–277.

Schieffelin, B. B., & Ochs, E. (1987). *Language socialization across cultures.* New York: Cambridge University Press.

Schiff, M. & Lewontin, R. (1986). *Education and class.* Oxford, England: Clarendon Press.

Schlossman, S., & Cairns, R. B. (1993). Problem girls: Observations on past and present. In G. Elder, Jr., J. Modell, & R. D. Parke (Eds.), *Children in time and place.* New York: Cambridge University Press.

Schneider, B. H., Smith, A., Poisson, S. E., & Kwan, A. B. (1997). Cultural dimensions of children's peer relations. In S. Duck (Ed.), *Handbook of personal relationships* (2nd ed., pp. 121–146). New York: Wiley.

Schneider, W., & Bjorklund, D. F. (1998). Memory. In W. Damon (Gen. Ed.), and D. Kuhn, & R. S. Siegler (Vol. Eds.), *Handbook of child psychology: Vol. 2. Cognition, perception, and language* (pp. 467–521). New York: Wiley.

Schnoll, S. H. (1986). Pharmacologic basis of perinatal addiction. In I. J. Chasnoff (Ed.), *Drug use in pregnancy: mother and child.* Lancaster, England: MTP Press.

Schofield, J. W. (1981). Complementary and conflicting identities: Images and interaction in an interracial school. In S. R. Asher & J. M. Gottman (Eds.), *The development of children's friendships.* New York: Cambridge University Press.

Schofield, J. W. (1995). *Computers and classroom culture.* New York: Cambridge University Press.

Schofield, J. W. (1997). Psychology: Computers and classroom social processes—a review of the literature. *Social Science Computer Review, 15,* 27–39.

Scholnick, E. K., Fein, G. G., & Campbell, P. F. (1990). Changing predictors of map use in way finding. *Developmental Psychology, 26,* 188–193.

Schultz, M. S. (1991). *Linkages among both parents, work roles, parenting style and children's adjustment to school.* Paper presented at the meeting of the Society for Research in Child Development. Seattle, WA.

Schwartz, D., Dodge, K. A., & Coie, J. D. (1993). The emergence of chronic peer victimization in boys' play groups. *Child Development, 64,* 1755–1772.

Schwartz, R. G., & Leonard, L. B. (1984). Words, objects and actions in early lexical acquisition. *Journal of Speech and Hearing Research, 27,* 119–127.

Schwartz-Bickenbach, D., Sculte-Hobein, B., Abt, S., Plum, C., & Nau, H. (1987). Smoking and passive smoking during infancy. *Toxicology Letters, 35,* 73–81.

Scribner, S. (1985). Vygotsky's use of history. In J. V. Wertsch (Ed.), *Culture, communication and cognition: Vygotskian perspectives.* New York: Cambridge University Press.

Sears, R. R. (1975). Your ancients revisited. In E. M. Hetherington (Ed.), *Review of child development research* (Vol. 5). Chicago: University of Chicago Press.

Seashore, M. J., Leifer, A. D., Barnett, C. R., & Leiderman, P. H. (1973). The effects of denial of early mother-infant interaction on maternal self-confidence. *Journal of Personality and Social Psychology, 26,* 369–378.

Secord, P. F., & Peevers, B. H. (1974). The development and attribution of person concepts. In T. Mischel (Ed.), *Understanding other persons.* Totowa, NJ: Rowman and Littlefield.

Sedlack, A. (1989). *National incidence of child abuse and neglect.* Paper presented at the meeting of the Society for Research in Child Development. Kansas City, KS.

Seier, W. L. (1994). The effects of a fantasy context, an obligation schema, and a rationale on children's conditional reasoning. *British Journal of Developmental Psychology, 12,* 507–522.

Seitz, V. (1988). Methodology. In M. Lamb & M. Bornstein (Eds.), *Developmental psychology: An advanced textbook.* Hillsdale, NJ: Erlbaum.

Seitz, V. (1990). Intervention programs for impoverished children: A comparison of educational and family support models. *Annals of Child Development, 7,* 73–103.

Seitz, V., Rosenbaum, L. K., & Apfel, N. H. (1985). Effects of family support intervention: A ten-year follow-up. *Child Development, 56,* 376–391.

Seligman, M. (1970). On the generality of the laws of learning. *Psychological Review, 77,* 406–418.

Seligman, M. E. P. (1973, June). Fall into helplessness. *Psychology Today,* pp. 43–48.

Seligman, M. E. P. (1974). Depression and learned helplessness. In R. J. Friedman & M. M. Katz (Eds.), *The psychology of depression: Contemporary theory and research.* Washington, DC: Winston-Wiley.

Selman, R. L. (1980). *The growth of interpersonal understanding.* New York: Academic.

Selman, R. L., & Byrne, D. F. (1974). A structural-developmental analysis of levels of role taking in middle childhood. *Child Development, 45,* 803–806.

Selman, R. L., & Jacquette, D. (1978). Stability and oscillation in interpersonal awareness: A clinical-developmental analysis. In C. B. Keasey (Ed.), *The XXV Nebraska symposium on motivation.* Lincoln: Univ. of Nebraska Press.

Senghas, A. (1995). The development of Nicaraguan Sign Language via the language acquisition process. In D. MacLaughlin & S. McEwen (Eds.), *Proceedings of BUCLD 19* (pp. 543–552). Somerville, MA: Cascadilla Press.

Serbin, L. A., Polwishta, K. K., & Gulko, J. (1993). The development of sex-typing in middle childhood. *Monographs of the Society for Research in Child Development, 58* (Serial No. 232).

Shaffer, R. (1996). *Social development.* New York: Blackwell.

Shakin, M., Shakin, D., & Sternglanz, S. H. (1985). Infant clothing: Sex labeling for strangers. *Sex Roles, 12,* 955–963.

Shantz, C. V. (1983). Social cognition. In J. H. Flavell & E. M. Markman (Eds.), *Handbook of child psychology: Cognitive development* (Vol. 3). New York: Wiley.

Shatz, M. (1983). Communication. In P. H. Mussen (Eds.), *Handbook of child psychology* (Vol. 3). New York: Wiley.

Shatz, M. (1994). Theory of mind and the development of socio-linguistic intelligence in early childhood. In C. Lewis & P. Mitchell (Eds.), *Children's early understanding of mind: Origins and development* (pp. 311–329). Hillsdale, NJ: Erlbaum.

Shatz, M., & Gelman, R. (1973). The development of communication skills: Modifications in the speech of young children as a function of listener. *Monographs of the Society for Research in Child Development, 38* (5, Serial No. 152), 1–37.

Shaywitz, B. A., Shaywitz, S. E., Pugh, K. R., & Constable, R. T. (1995). Sex differences in the functional organization of the brain for language. *Nature, 373,* 607–609.

Shelton, B. A. (1992). *Women, men, and time: Gender differences in paid work, house work, and leisure.* New York: Greenwood.

Shepardson, D. P., & Pizzini, E. L. (1992). Gender bias in female elementary teachers' perceptions of the scientific ability of students. *Science Education, 76*(2), 147–153.

Sherman, J. A. (1980). Mathematics, spatial visualization and related factors: Changes in girls and boys, grades 8–11. *Journal of Educational Psychology, 72,* 476–482.

Sherman, M. & Key, C. B. (1932). The intelligence of isolated mountain children. *Child Development, 3,* 279–290.

Shields, P. J., & Rovee-Collier, C. (1992). Long-term memory for context-specific category information at six months. *Child Development, 63,* 245–259.

Shiffman, S. (1993). Smoking cessation treatment: Any progress? *Journal of Consulting and Clinical Psychology, 61,* 718–722.

Shirley, M. M. (1931). *The first two years, a study of twenty-five babies: I Postural & locomotor development.* Minneapolis, MN: University of Minnesota Press.

Shoda, Y., Mischel, W., & Peake, P. K. (1990). Predicting adolescent cognitive and self-regulatory competencies from preschool delay of gratification: Identifying diagnostic conditions. *Developmental Psychology, 26,* 978–986.

Shrum, W., & Cheek, N. H. (1987). Social structure during the school years: Onset of the degrouping process. *American Sociological Review, 52,* 218–223.

Shweder, R. A., Goodnow, J., Hatano, G., LeVine, R. A., Markus, H., & Miller, P. (1998). The cultural psychology of development: One mind, many mentalities. In W. Damon (Gen. Ed.) & R. M. Lerner (Vol. Ed.), *Handbook of child psychology* (Vol. 1, pp. 865–938). New York: Wiley.

Shweder, R. A., & Haidt, J. (1993). The future of moral psychology: Truth, intuition, and the pluralist way. *Psychological Science, 4,* 360–356.

Shweder, R. A., & Much, M. C. (1987). Determinants of meaning: Discourse and moral socialization. In W. M. Kurtines & J. L. Gewiretz (Eds.), *Moral development*

through social interaction. New York: Wiley.

Siddiqui, A. (1995). Object size as a determinant of grasping in infancy. *Journal of Genetic Psychology, 156,* 345–358.

Siegel, A. W., & White, S. H. (1975). The development of spatial representatives of large scale environments. In H. W. Reese (Eds.), *Advances in child development and behavior* (Vol. 10). New York: Academic.

Siegel, M. (1987). Are sons and daughters treated more differently by fathers than mothers? *Developmental Review, 7,* 183–209.

Siegler, R. S. (1978). The origins of scientific reasoning. In R. S. Siegler (Ed.). *Children's thinking: What develops?* Hillsdale, NJ: Erlbaum.

Siegler, R. S. (1983). Information processing approaches to development. In P. Mussen (Ed.), *Manual of child psychology.* New York: Wiley.

Siegler, R. S. (1987). The perils of averaging data over strategies: An example from children's addition. *Journal of Experimental Psychology: General, 116,* 250–264.

Siegler, R. S. (1991). *Children's thinking* (2nd ed.). Englewood-Cliffs, NJ: Prentice-Hall.

Siegler, R. S. (1992). The other Alfred Binet. *Developmental Psychology, 28,* 179–190.

Siegler, R. S. (1994). Cognitive variability: A key to understanding cognitive development. *Current Directions in Psychological Science, 3,* 1–5.

Siegler, R. S. (1998). *Children's thinking* (3rd ed.). Upper Saddle River, NJ: Prentice-Hall.

Sigel, I. E. (1998). Practice and research: A problem in developing communication and cooperation: An outlook. In W. Damon (Gen. Ed.), I. E. Sigel, & K. A. Renninger (Vol. Eds.), *Handbook of child psychology: Vol. 4. Child psychology in practice.* New York: Wiley.

Sigman, M. (1995). Nutrition and child develop-ment: More food for thought. *Current Directions in Psychological Science, 4,* 52–55.

Sigman, M., & Mundy, P. (1989). Social attachments in autistic children. *Journal of the American Academy of Child and Adolescent Psychiatry, 28,* 74–81.

Signorella, M. L., Bigler, R. S., & Liben, L. S. (1993). Developmental differences in children's gender schemata about others: A meta-analytic review. *Developmental Review, 13,* 147–183.

Signorielli, N. (1993). Television, the portrayal of women, and children's attitudes. In G. L. Berry & J. K. Samen (Eds.), *Children and television: Images in a changing sociocultural world.* Newbury Park, CA: Sage.

Silverstein, B., Petersen, B., & Perdue, L. (1986). Some correlates of the thin standard of bodily attractiveness for women. *International Journal of Eating Disorders, 5,* 895–906.

Simmons, R. G., & Blyth, D. A. (1987). *Moving into adolescence: The impact of pubertal change and school context.* Hawthorne, NY: Aldine.

Simmons, R. G., Blyth, D. A., & McKinney, K. L. (1984). The social and psychological effects of puberty on white females. In J. Brookes-Gunn & A. C. Peterson (Eds.), *Girls at puberty: Biological, psychological and social perspectives.* New York: Plenum.

Simmons, R. G., Blyth, D. A., Van Cleave, E. F., & Bush, D. M. (1979). Entry into early adolescence: The impact of school structure, puberty, and early dating on self-esteem. *American Sociological Review, 44,* 948–967.

Simmons, R. G., Burgeson, R., Carlson-Ford, S., & Blyth, D. A. (1987). The impact of cumulative change in early adolescence, *Child Development, 58,* 1220–1234.

Simons, R. L., Conger, R. D., & Whitbeck, L. B. (1988). A multistage social learning model of the influences of family and peers upon adolescent substance use. *The Journal of Drug Issues, 18,* 293–315.

Singer, D. G., & Singer, J. L. (1994). *Barney and friends as education and entertainment: Phase 3: A national study: Can preschoolers learn through exposure to Barney and Friends?* New Haven, CT: Yale University Family Television Research and Consultation Center.

Singer, J. L. (1977, August). *Television, imaginative play and cognitive development: Some problems and possibilities.* Paper presented at the meeting of the American Psychological Association, San Francisco.

Singer, J. L., & Singer, D. G. (1980). *Imaginative play in preschoolers: Some research and theoretical implications.* Paper presented at the meeting of the American Psychological Association, Montreal.

Singer, J. L., & Singer, D. G. (1981). *Television, imagination and aggression: A study of preschoolers.* Hillsdale, NJ: Erlbaum.

Singer, J. L., Singer, D. G., Desmond, R., Hirsch, B., & Nicol, A. (1988). Family mediation and children's cognition, aggression and comprehension of television: A longitudinal study. *Journal of Applied Developmental Psychology, 9,* 329–347.

Sizer, T. (1984). *Horace's compromise: The dilemma of the American high school.* Boston: Houghton Mifflin.

Skinner, B. F. (1957). *Verbal behavior.* New York: Appleton-Century-Crofts.

Skodak, M., & Skeels, H. (1949). A final follow-up study of one hundred adopted children. *Journal of Genetic Psychology, 75,* 85–125.

Slaby, R. G., & Frey, K. S. (1975). Development of gender constancy and selective attention to same-sex models. *Child Development, 46,* 849–856.

Slaby, R. G., & Guerra, N. G. (1988). Cognitive mediators of aggression in adolescent offenders: I. Assessment. *Developmental Psychology, 24,* 580–588.

Slade, A. (1987). Quality of attachment & early symbolic play. *Developmental Psychology, 23,* 78–85.

Slater, A., Mattock, A., & Brown, E. (1990). Size constancy at birth: Newborn infants' responses to retinal and real size. *Journal of experimental child psychology, 49,* 314–322.

Slater, A. M., & Morison, V. (1985). Shape constancy and slant perception at birth. *Perception, 14,* 337–344.

Slaughter, D. T. (1988). Ethnicity, poverty, and children's educability: A developmental perspective. *Science and Public Policy Seminars.* Washington, DC.

Slaughter-Defoe, D. T., Nakagawa, K., Takanishi, R., & Johnson, D. J. (1990). Toward cultural/ecological perspectives on schooling and achievement in African- and Asian-American children. *Child Development, 61,* 363–383.

Slavin, R. E. (1995). Enhancing intergroup relations in schools: Cooperative learning and other strategies. In W. D. Hawley & A. W. Jackson (Eds.), *Toward a common destiny: improving race and ethnic relations in America* (pp. 291–314). San Francisco, CA: Jossey-Bass.

Slavin, R. E. (1996). Research on cooperative learning and achievement: What we know, what we need to know. *Contemporary Educational Psychology, 21,* 43–69.

Slavin, R. E., & Madden, N. A. (1979). School practices that improve race relations. *American Educational Research Journal, 16,* 169–180.

Slobin, D. I. (1968). Imitation and grammatical development in children. In N. S. Endler, L. R. Boulter, & H. Osser (Eds.), *Contemporary issues in development in psychology.* New York: Holt.

Slobin, D. I. (1979). *Psycholinguistics.* Glenview, IL: Scott, Foresman.

Slobin, D. I. (1982). Universal and particular in the acquisition of language. In L. R. Gleitman & H. E. Wanner (Eds.), *Language acquisition: The state of the art.* New York: Cambridge University Press.

Slobin, D. I. (1985). *The cross-linguistic study of language acquisition* (Vols. 1 & 2). Hillsdale, NJ: Erlbaum.

Slobin, D. I. (Ed.). (1992). *The cross-linguistic study of language acquisition: Vol. 3.* Hillsdale, NJ: Erlbaum.

Sluckin, A. M., & Smith, R. K. (1977). Two approaches to the concept of dominance in preschool children. *Child Development, 48,* 917–923.

Smetana, J. G. (1984). Toddler's social interaction regarding moral and conventional transgressions. *Child Development, 55,* 1767–1776.

Smetana, J. G. (1989). Toddlers' social interactions in the context of moral and conventional transgressions in the home. *Developmental Psychology, 25,* 499–508.

Smetana, J. G. (1995). Morality in context: Abstractions, ambiguities, and applications. In R. Vasta (Ed.), *Annals of child development* (Vol. 10, pp. 83–130). London: Jessica Kingsley.

Smetana, J. G. (1997). Parenting and the development of social knowledge reconceptualized: A social domain analysis. In J. E. Grusec & L. Kuczynski (Eds.), *Parenting and children's internalization of values* (pp. 162–192). New York: Wiley.

Smetana, J. G., & Asquith, P. (1994). Adolescents' and parents' conceptions of parental authority and adolescent autonomy. *Child Development, 65,* 1147–1162.

Smetana, J. G., & Braeges, J. L. (1990). The development of toddler's moral and conventional judgements. *Merrill-Palmer Quarterly, 36,* 329–346.

Smetana, J. G., & Letourneau, K. J. (1984). Development of gender constancy and children's sex-typed free play behavior. *Developmental Psychology, 20,* 691–696.

Smiley, P. A. (1989). *Individual differences in preschoolers' task persistence.* Poster presented at the biennial meeting of the Society for Research in Child Development, Kansas City, MO.

Smith, B. A., & Blass, E. M. (1996). Taste-mediated calming in premature, preterm and full term human infants. *Developmental Psychology, 32,* 1084–1089.

Smith, B. A., Fillion, T. J., & Blass, E. M. (1990). Orally mediated sources of calming in 1- to 3-day-old human infants. *Developmental Psychology, 26,* 731–737.

Smith, C. L. (1979). Children's understanding of natural language hierarchies. *Journal of Experimental Child Psychology, 27,* 437–458.

Smith, D. J., Stevens, M. E., Sudanagunta, S. P., Bronson, R. T., Makhinson, M., Watabe, A. M., O'Dell, T. J., Fung, J., Weier, H. U., Chang, J. F., & Rubin, E. M. (1997). Functional screening of 2Mb of human chromosome 21q22.2 in transgenic mice implicates minibrain in learning defects associated with Down syndrome. *Nature Genetics, 16,* 28–36.

Smith, F. (1992). Learning to read: The never-ending debate. *Phi Delta Kappan, 74,* 432–441.

Smith, H. (1992). The detrimental health effects of ionizing radiation. *Nuclear Medicine Communications, 13,* 4–10.

Smith, I. M., & Bryson, S. E. (1994). Imitation and action in autism: A critical review. *Psychological Bulletin, 116,* 259–273.

Smith, L. B., & Thelen, E. (1993). (Eds.). *A dynamic systems approach to development.* Cambridge, MS: MIT Press.

Smith, P. K., & Connolly, K. J. (1980). *The ecology of preschool behavior.* New York: Cambridge University Press.

Smith, P. K., & Sloboda, J. (1986). Individual consistency in infant-stranger encounters. *British Journal of Developmental Psychology, 4,* 83–92.

Smith, S. (Ed.) (1995). *Two-generation programs for families in poverty: A new intervention strategy.* Norwood, NJ: Ablex.

Smith, T. M. (1994). Adolescent pregnancy. In R. Simeonsson (Ed.). *Risk, resilience, and prevention: Promoting the well-being of all children.* Baltimore: Brooks Publishing.

Smollar, J., & Youniss, J. (1982). Social development through friendship. In K. H. Rubin & H. S. Ross (Eds.), *Peer relationships and social skills in childhood.* New York: Springer-Verlag.

Snarey, J. (1987, June). A question of morality. *Psychology Today,* pp. 6–8.

Snarey, J. (1993). *How fathers care for the next generation: A four decade study.* Cambridge, MA: Harvard University Press.

Snarey, J. R., Reimer, J., & Kohlberg, L. (1985). Development of social-moral reasoning among kibbutz adolescents: A longitudinal cross-cultural study. *Developmental Psychology, 21,* 3–17.

Snow, C. E. (1989). Understanding social interaction and language acquisition: Sentences are not enough. In M. H. Bornstein & J. S. Bruner (Eds.), *Interaction in human development* (pp. 83–104). Hillsdale, NJ: Erlbaum.

Snow, C. E., & Hoefnagel-Hohle, M. (1978). The critical period for language acquisition: Evidence from second language learning. *Child Development, 49,* 1114–1128.

Snyderman, M., & Rothman, S. (1988). *The IQ controversy, the media, and public policy.* New Brunswick, NJ: Transaction Books.

Soar, R. S., & Soar, R. M. (1979). Emotional climate and management. In P. L. Peterson & H. J. Walberg (Eds.), *Research on teaching concepts, findings and implications.* Berkeley, CA: McCutchan.

Society for Research in Child Development. (1993). Ethical standards of research with children. In *Directory of Members* (pp. 337–339). Ann Arbor, MI: SRCD.

Soken, H. H., & Pick, A. D. (1992). Intermodal perception of happy and angry expressive behaviors by seven-month-old infants. *Child Development, 63,* 787–795.

Sokolov, J. L. (1993). A local contingency analysis of the fine-tuning hypothesis. *Developmental Psychology, 29,* 1008–1023.

Sommer, K. S., Keogh, D., & Whitman, T. L. (1995, March). *Prenatal predictors of cognitive and emotional development in children of adolescent mothers.* Poster session presented at 61st biennial meeting of the Society for Research in Child Development, Indianapolis.

Sontag, L.W. (1944). Differences in modifiability of fetal behavior and physiology. *Psychosomatic Medicine, 6,* 151–154.

Sorahan, T., Lancashire, R. J., Hulten, M. A., Peck, I., & Stewart, A. M. (1997). Childhood cancer and parental use of tobacco: deaths from 1953 to 1955. *British Journal of Cancer, 75,* 134–138.

Sosa, R., Kennell, J., Klaus, M., Robertson, S., & Urrutia, J. (1980). The effect of a supportive companion on perinatal problems, length of labor and mother-infant interaction. *New England Journal of Medicine, 303,* 597–600.

Sostek, A. M., & Anders, T. F. (1981). The biosocial importance and environmental sensitivity of infant sleep-wake behaviors. In K. Bloom (Ed.), *Prospective issues in infancy research.* Hillsdale, NJ: Erlbaum.

Southern, W. T., Jones, E. D., & Stanley, J. C. (1994). Acceleration and enrichment: The context and development of program options. In K. A. Heller, F. J. Monks, & H. A. Passow (Eds.), *International handbook of research and development of giftedness and talent.* Oxford: Pergamon Press.

Spangler, G., & Grossman, K. E. (1993). Biobehavioral organization in securely & insecurely attached infants. *Child Development, 64,* 1439–1450.

Spearman, C. (1927). *The abilities of man.* New York: Macmillan.

Speer, J. R., & Flavell, J. H. (1979). Young children's knowledge of the relative difficulty of recognition and recall memory tasks. *Developmental Psychology, 15,* 214–217.

Spelke, E. S. (1987). The development of intermodal perception. In P. Salapatek & L. Cohen (Eds.), *Handbook of infant perception: Vol. 2. From perception to cognition* (pp. 233–274). New York: Academic.

Spelke, E. S. (1991). Physical knowledge in infancy: Reflections on Piaget's theory. In S. Carey & R. Gelman (Eds.), *The epigenesis of mind: Essays on biology and cognition.* Hillsdale, NJ: Erlbaum.

Spelke, E. S. (1994). Initial knowledge: Six suggestions. *Cognition, 50,* 431–445.

Spelke, E. S., & Cortelyou, A. (1981). Perceptual aspects of social knowing: Looking and listening in infancy. In M. E. Lamb & L. R. Sherrod (Eds.), *Infant social cognition* (pp. 6–84). Hillsdale, NJ: Erlbaum.

Spelke, E. S., Katz, G., Purcell, S. E., Ehrlich, S. M., et al. (1994). Early knowledge of object motion: Continuity and inertia. *Cognition, 51,* 131–176.

Spelke, E. S., & Newport, E. (1998). Nativism, empiricism, & the development of knowledge. In W. Damon (Gen. Ed.) & R. Lerner (Vol. Ed.), *Handbook of child psychology* (Vol. 1, pp. 275–340). New York: Wiley.

Spellacy, W. N., Miller, S. J., & Winegar, A. (1986). Pregnancy after 40 years of age. *Obstetrics and Gynecology, 68,* 452–454.

Spence, J. T. (1985). Gender identity and its implications for concepts of masculinity and femininity. In T. B. Sonderegger (Ed.), *Nebraska symposium on motivation: Psychology and gender* (Vol. 32). Lincoln: University of Nebraska Press.

Spergel, I. A., Ross, R. E., Curry, G. D., & Chance, R. (1989). *Youth gangs: Problem and response.* Washington, DC: Office of Juvenile Justice and Delinquency Prevention.

Sperling, G. (1960). The information available in brief visual presentations. *Psychological Monographs, 74.*

Spiker, D., & Ricks, M. (1984). Visual self-recognition in autistic children: Developmental variations. *Child Development, 55,* 214–225.

Springer, S. P., & Deutsch, G. (1989). *Left brain, right brain* (3rd ed.). New York: Freeman.

Springer, S. P., & Deutsch, G. (1993). *Left brain, right brain.* New York: W. H. Freeman.

Sroufe, L. A. (1979). Emotional development in infancy. In J. Osofsky (Ed.), *Handbook of infancy.* New York: Wiley.

Sroufe, L. A. (1983). Individual patterns of adaptation from infancy to preschool. In M. Perlmutter (Ed.), *Minnesota symposium on child psychology* (Vol. 16). Hillsdale, NJ: Erlbaum.

Sroufe, L. A. (1996). *Emotional development: The organization of emotional life in the early years.* New York: Cambridge University Press.

Sroufe, L. A., Carlson, E., & Shulman, S. (1993). The development of individuals in relationships: From infancy through adolescence. In D. C. Funder, R. D. Parke, C. Tomlinson-Keasey, & K. Widaman, (Eds.), *Studying lives through time: Approaches to personality and development.* Washington, DC: American Psychological Association.

Sroufe, L. A., & Fleeson, J. (1986). Attachment and the construction of relationships. In W. W. Hartup & Z. Rubin (Eds.), *Relationships & development* (pp. 51–71). Hillsdale, NJ: Erlbaum.

Sroufe, L. A., Waters, E., & Matas, L. (1974). Contextual determinants of infant affectional response. In M. Lewis & L. Rosenblum (Eds.), *Origins of fear.* New York: Wiley.

Sroufe, L. A., & Wunsch, J. P. (1972). The development of laughter in the first year of life. *Child Development, 43,* 1326–1344.

St. Clair, P. A., Smeriglio, V. L., Alexander, C. S., & Celentano, D. D. (1989). Social network structure and prenatal care utilization. *Medical Care, 27*(8), 823–831.

St. Peters, M. (1993). *The ecology of mother-child interaction.* Unpublished doctoral dissertation, University of Kansas, Lawrence.

St. Peters, M., Fitch, M., Huston, A. C., Wright, J. D., & Eakins, D. (1991). What do young children watch with their parents? *Child Development, 62,* 1409–1423.

Stangor, C., & Ruble, D. (1989). Differential influences of gender schemata and gender constancy on children's information processing and behavior. *Social Cognition, 7,* 353–372.

Stanley, J. C. (1976). Concern for intellectually talented youths: How it originated and fluctuated. *Journal of Clinical Child Psychology, 5,* 38–42.

Stanley, J. C., & Benbow, C. P. (1983). SMPY's first decade: Ten years of posing problems and solving them. *Journal of Special Education, 17,* 11–25.

Stanovich, K. E. (1994). Romance and reality. *The Reading Teacher, 47,* 280–291.

Stark, K. D., Napolitano, S., Swearer, S., & Schmidt, K. (1996). Issues in the treatment of depressed children. *Applied & Preventive Psychology, 5,* 59–83.

Starr, A. S. (1923). The diagnostic value of the audio-vocal digit memory span. *Psychological Clinic, 15,* 61–84.

Stattin, H., & Magnusson, D. (1990). *Pubertal maturation in female development* (Vol. 2). Hillsdale, NJ: Erlbaum.

Stechler, G., & Halton, A. (1982). Prenatal influences on human development. In B. Buolman (Ed.), *Handbook of developmental psychology* (pp. 175–189). Englewood Cliffs, NJ: Prentice-Hall.

Steckel, Richard. (1997). Ohio State University. As reproduced in "2000: The Millennium Notebook," *Newsweek,* June 2, p. 10.

Stein, N. L., & Trabasso, T. (1989). Children's understanding of changing emotional states. In C. Saarni & P. Harris (Eds.), *Children's understanding of emotion.* New York: Cambridge University Press.

Stein, Z. A., & Susser, M. W. (1976). Prenatal nutrition and mental competence. In J. D. Lloyd-Still (Ed.), *Malnutrition and intellectual development* (pp. 39–80). Littleton, MA: Publishing Sciences Group.

Steinberg, L. (1986). Latchkey children and susceptibility to peer pressure. An ecological analysis. *Developmental Psychology, 22,* 433–439.

Steinberg, L. (1987). Impact of puberty on family relations: Effects of pubertal status and pubertal timing. *Developmental Psychology, 23,* 451–460.

Steinberg, L. (1990). Interdependence in the family: Autonomy, conflict and harmony in the parent-adolescent relationship. In S. S. Feldman & G. L. Elliot (Eds.), *At the threshold: The developing adolescent* (pp. 255–276). Cambridge, MA: Harvard University Press.

Steinberg, L. (1996). *Beyond the classroom.* New York: Simon & Schuster.

Steinberg, L., Catalano, R., & Dooley, D. (1981). Economic antecedents of child abuse and neglect. *Child Development, 52,* 975–985.

Steinberg, L., Darling, N. E., & Fletcher, A. C. (1995). Authoritative parenting and adolescent adjustment: An ecological journey. In P. Moen, G. H. Elder, Jr., & K. Luscher (Eds.), *Examining lives in contest: Perspectives on the ecology of human development* (pp. 423–466).

Washington: American Psychological Association.

Steinberg, L., Dornbusch, S. M., & Brown, B. B. (1992). Ethnic differences in adolescent achievement: An ecological perspective. *American Psychologist, 47,* 723–729.

Steinberg, L., Mounts, N. S., Lamborn, S. D., & Dornbusch, S. M. (1991). Authoritative parenting and adolescent adjustment across varied ecological niches. *Journal of Research on Adolescence, 1,* 19–36.

Steiner, J. E. (1979). Human facial expression in response to taste and smell stimulation. In H. W. Reese & L. P. Lipsitt (Eds.), *Advances in child development and behavior* (Vol. 13). New York: Academic.

Steinglass, P. (1987). A systems view of family interaction and psychopathology. In T. Jacob (Ed.), *Family interaction and psychopathology: Theories, methods, and findings* (pp. 25–65). New York: Plenum.

Steinschneider, A. (1975). Implications of the sudden infant death syndrome for the study of sleep in infancy. In A. D. Pick (Ed.), *Minnesota symposia on child psychology,* (Vol. 9). Minneapolis, MN: University of Minnesota Press.

Stenberg, C., & Campos, J. (1989). *The development of anger expressions during infancy.* Unpublished manuscript. University of Denver, Denver, Colorado.

Stenberg, C., Campos, J., & Emde, R. N. (1983). The facial expression of anger in seven-month-old infants. *Child Development, 54,* 178–184.

Stephan, W. G., & Rosenfield, D. (1982). Racial and ethnic stereotypes. In A. Miller (Ed.), *In the eye of the beholder.* New York: Praeger.

Stern, D. (1977). *The first relationship.* Cambridge, MA: Harvard University Press.

Stern, D. N. (1974). Mother and infant at play: The dyadic interaction involving facial, vocal, and gaze behaviors. In M. Lewis & L. A. Rosenblum (Eds.), *The effect of the infant on its caregiver.* New York: Wiley.

Stern, M., & Karraker, K. H. (1989). Sex stereotyping of infants: A review of gender labeling studies. *Sex Roles, 20,* 501–522.

Sternberg, R. J. (1985). *Beyond IQ: A triarchic theory of human intelligence.* Cambridge, England: Cambridge University Press.

Sternberg, R. J. (1988). *The triarchic mind.* New York: Viking.

Sternberg, R. J. (1989). *Mechanisms of cognitive development* (2nd ed.). New York: Cambridge University Press.

Sternberg, R. J., Conway, B. E., Ketron, J. L., & Bernstein, M. (1981). People's conceptions of intelligence. *Journal of Personality and Social Psychology, 41,* 37–55.

Sternberg, R. J., & Lubart, T. I. (1992). Buy low and sell high: An investment approach to creativity. *Current Directions in Psychological Science, 1,* 1–5.

Sternberg, R. J., & Lubart, T. I. (1995). *Defying the crowd: Cultivating creativity in a culture of conformity.* New York: Free Press.

Sternberg, R. J., & Wagner, R. K. (1993). The g-ocentric view of intelligence and job performance is wrong. *Current Directions in Psychological Science, 2,* 1–6.

Sternberg, R. J., & Wagner, R. K. (1994). *Mind in context.* New York: Cambridge University Press.

Sternberg, R. J., Wagner, R. K., & Okagaki, L. (1993). Practical intelligence: The nature and role of tacit knowledge in work and at school. In H. W. Reese & W. Puckett (Eds.), *Advances in lifespan development* (pp. 205–227). Hillsdale, NJ: Erlbaum.

Sternberg, R. J., Wagner, R. K., Williams, M. W., & Horvath, J. A. (1995). Testing common sense. *American Psychologist, 50,* 912–927.

Stevenson, H. W., Chen, C., & Lee, S. Y. (1993). Mathematics achievement of Chinese, Japanese, and American children: Ten years later. *Science, 259,* 53–58.

Stevenson, H. W., Chen, C., & Uttal, D. H. (1990). Beliefs and achievement: A study of black, white, and hispanic children. *Child Development, 61,* 508–523.

Stevenson, H. W., & Stigler, J. W. (1992). *The learning gap.* New York: Summit Books.

Stevenson, J., & Fielding, J. (1985). Ratings of temperament in families of young twins. *British Journal of Developmental Psychology, 3,* 143–152.

Stewart, R. B., Mobley, L. A., Van Tuyl, S. S., & Salvador, W. A. (1987). The firstborns adjustment to the birth of a sibling: A longitudinal assessment. *Child Development, 58,* 341–355.

Stipek, D. (1993). *Motivation to learn.* Boston: Allyn & Bacon.

Stipek, D. (1996). Motivation and instruction. In R. C. Calfeo & D. C. Berliner (Eds.), *Handbook of educational psychology.* New York: Macmillan.

Stipek, D., & McCroskey, J. (1989). Investing in children: Government and workplace policies for parents. *American Psychologist, 44,* 416–423.

Stoch, M. B., Smyth, P. M., Moodie, A. D., & Bradshaw, D. (1982). Psychosocial outcome and findings after gross undernourishment during infancy: A 20-year developmental study. *Developmental Medicine & Child Neurology, 24,* 419–436.

Stocker, C., & Dunn, J. (1990). Sibling relationships in childhood: Links with friendships and peer relationships. *British Journal of Developmental Psychology, 8,* 227–244.

Stone, R. (1990, August 20). An artificial eye may be within sight. *The Washington Post,* p. A3.

Stone, R. (1992). Can a father's exposure to lead lead to illness in his children? *Science, 258,* 31.

Straker, G., Mendelsohn, M., Moosa, F., & Tudin, P. (1996). Violent political contexts and the emotional concerns of township youth. *Child Development, 67,* 46–54.

Straughan, R. (1986). Why act on Kohlberg's moral judgments? In S. Modgil & C. Modgil (Eds.), *Lawrence Kohlberg: Consensus and controversy.* Philadelphia: Falmer Press.

Straus, M., & Donnelly, D. (1994). *Beating the devil out of them: Corporal punishment in American families.* New York: Lexington Books.

Strayer, F. F. (1980). Current problems in the study of human dominance. In D. Omark, F. F. Strayer, & D. Freedman (Eds.), *Dominance relations.* New York: Garland.

Strayer, F. F. (1984). Biological approaches to the study of the family. In R. D. Parke, R. Emde, H. Macadoo, & G. P. Sackett (Eds.), *Review of child development research: Vol. 7. The family.* Chicago: University of Chicago Press.

Strayer, F. F., & Strayer, J. (1976). An ethological analysis of social agonism and dominance relations among preschool children. *Child Development, 47,* 980–989.

Strayer, J., & Roberts, W. (1988). Children's empathy and role-taking: Child and parental factors and relations to prosocial behavior. *Journal of Applied Developmental Psychology, 10,* 227–239.

Streissgath, A. P., Barr, H. M., Carmichael-Olson, H., Sampson, P. D., Bookstein, F. L., & Burgess, D. M. (1994). Drinking during pregnancy decreases word attach and arithmetic scores on standardized test: Adolescent data from a population based prospective study. *Alcohol: Clinical and Experimental Research, 18,* 248–254.

Streissgath, A. P., Bookstein, F. L., Sampson, P. D., & Barr, H. M. (1993). *The enduring effects of prenatal alcohol exposure on child development, birth through seven years: A partial least-squares solution.* Ann Arbor: University of Michigan Press.

Streissgath, A. P., Bookstein, F. L., Sampson, P. D., & Barr, H. M. (1995). Attention: Prenatal alcohol and continuities of vigilance and attentional problems from 4 through 14 years. *Development & Psychopathology, 1,* 419–446.

Streissguth, A. P., Sampson, P. D., & Barr, H. M. (1989). Neurobehavioral dose-response effects of prenatal alcohol exposure in humans from infancy to adulthood. *Annals of the New York Academy of Sciences, 562,* 145–158.

Streri, A., & Pecheux, M. (1986). Tactual habituation and discrimination of form in infancy: A comparison with vision. *Child Development, 57,* 100–104.

Strommen, E. F. (1994). Children's use of mouse-based interfaces to control virtual travel. *Proceedings of the National Educational Computing Conference,* 149–151.

Stunkard, A. J. (1958). The management of obesity. *New York Journal of Medicine, 58,* 79–87.

Stunkard, A. J., Foch, T. T., & Hrubeck, Z. (1986). A twin study of human obesity. *Journal of the American Medical Association, 256,* 51–54.

Stunkard, A. J., Sorenson, T. I., Hanis, C., Teasdale, T. W., Chakraborty, R., Schull, W. J., & Schulsinger, F. (1986). An adoption study of human obesity. *New England Journal of Medicine, 314,* 193–198.

Sue, S., & Okazaki, S. (1990). Asian-American educational achievements: A phenomenon in search of an explanation. *American Psychologist, 45,* 913–920.

Suess, G. L. (1987). *Consequences of early attachment experiences on competence in preschool.* Unpublished doctoral dissertation. Universitat Regensberg, West Germany.

Sugarman, S. (1987). *Piaget's construction of the child's reality.* Cambridge, England: Cambridge University Press.

Sullivan, H. S. (1953). *The interpersonal theory of psychiatry.* New York: Norton.

Sullivan, M. L. (1993). Culture and class as determinants of out-of-wedlock childbearing and poverty during late adolescence. *Journal of Research on Adolescence, 3,* 295–316.

Sulloway, F. J. (1995). Birth order and evolutionary psychology: A meta-analytic overview. *Psychological Inquiry, 6,* 75–80.

Suomi, S. J., & Harlow, H. F. (1972). Social rehabilitation of isolate-reared monkeys. *Developmental Psychology, 6,* 487–496.

Super, C. M., & Harkness, S. (1981). The infant's niche in rural Kenya and metropolitan America. In L. L. Adler (Ed.), *Cross-cultural research at issue* (pp. 47–55). New York: American Press.

Super, C. M., Herrera, M. G., & Mora, J. O. (1990). Long-term effects of food supplementation and psychosocial intervention on the physical growth of Columbian infants at risk of malnutrition. *Child Development, 61,* 29–49.

Swain, I. U., Zelazo, P. R., & Clifton, R. K. (1993). Newborn infants' memory for speech sounds retained over 24 hours. *Developmental Psychology, 29,* 312–323.

Swensen, A. (1983). Toward an ecological approach to theory and research in child language acquisition. In W. Fowler (Ed.), *Potentials of childhood* (Vol. 2). Lexington, MA: Heath.

Tagatz, G. E. (1976). *Child development and individually guided education.* Reading, MA: Addison-Wesley.

Tager-Flusberg, H. (1985). Putting words together: Morphology and syntax in the preschool years. In J. Berko-Gleason (Ed.), *The development of language.* Columbia: Bell D. Howell.

Tamis-LeMonda, C. S., & McLure, J. (1995). Infant visual expectation in relation to feature learning. *Infant Behavior and Development, 18,* 427–434.

Tanguey, J. P., & Fischer, K. W. (Eds.). (1995). *Self-conscious emotions.* New York: Guilford.

Tanner, J. (1990). *Fetus into man: Physical growth from conception to maturity.* Cambridge, MA: Harvard University Press.

Tanner, J. M. (1970). Physical growth. In P. H. Mussen (Ed.), *Carmichael's manuscript of child psychology* (Vol. 1, pp. 77–155). New York: Wiley.

Tanner, J. M. (1978). *Fetus into man: Physical growth from conception to maturity.* Cambridge, MA: Harvard University Press.

Tardiff, T. (1993). *Audit-to-child speech and language acquisition in Mandarin Chinese.* Unpublished doctoral dissertation. New Haven, CT.

Tardiff, T. (1996). Nouns are not always learned before verbs: Evidence from Mandarin speakers' early vocabularies. *Developmental Psychology, 32,* 492–504.

Tauber, K. (1990, September). Desegregation of public school districts: Persistence and change. *Phi Delta Kappan,* pp. 18–24.

Tavris, C. (1992). *The mismeasure of woman.* New York: Simon & Schuster.

Taylor, A. R., Asher, S. R., & Williams, G. A. (1987). The social adaptation of mainstreamed mildly retarded children. *Child Development, 58,* 1321–1334.

Taylor, M. (1988). Conceptual perspective taking: Children's ability to distinguish what they know from what they see. *Child Development, 59,* 703–718.

Tellegan, A., Lykken, D. T., Bouchard, T. J., Wilcox, K., Segal, N., & Rowe, S. (1988). Personality similarity in twins reared apart and together. *Journal of Social and Personality Psychology, 54,* 1031–1039.

Teller, D. Y. (1997). First glances. The vision of infants. The Friedenwald Lecture. *Investigative Ophthalmology & Visual Science, 38,* 2183–2203.

Teller, D. Y., & Bornstein, M. H. (1984). Infant color vision. In P. Salapatek & L. B. Cohen (Eds.), *Handbook of infant perception.* New York: Academic.

Terman, D. L., Larner, M. B., Stevenson, C. S., & Behrman, R. E. (1996). Special education for students with disabilities. *The Future of Children, 6,* 4–24.

Terman, L. M. (1954). The discovery and encouragement of exceptional talent. *American Psychologist, 9,* 221–230.

Terry, R., & Coie, J. D. (1991). A comparison of methods for defining sociometric status among children. *Developmental Psychology, 27,* 867–880.

Teti, D. M., Gelfand, D., Messinger, D. S., & Isabella, R. (1995). Maternal depression and the quality of early attachment: An examination of infants, preschoolers and their mothers. *Developmental Psychology, 31,* 364–376.

Thakwray, D. E., Smith, M. C., Bodfish, J. W., & Meyers, A. W. (1993). A comparison of behavioral and cognitive-behavioral interventions for bulimia nervosa. *Journal of Consulting and Clinical Psychology, 61,* 639–645.

Tharp, R. G. (1989). Psychocultural variables and constants: Effects on teaching and learning in schools. *American Psychologist, 44,* 349–359.

Tharp, R. G. (1994). Intergroup differences among Native Americans in socialization and child cognition: An ethnogenetic analysis. In P. M. Greenfield & R. R. Cocking (Eds.), *Cross-cultural roots of minority child development.* Hillsdale, NJ: Erlbaum.

Tharp, R. G., & Gallimore, R. (1988). *Rousing minds to life: Teaching, learning, and schooling in social context.* New York: Cambridge University Press.

Thelen, E. (1988). Self-organization in developmental processes: Can systems approaches work? In M. Gummar (Ed.), *Systems in development: Minnesota symposia in child psychology* (Vol. 22). Hillsdale, NJ: Erlbaum.

Thelen, E. (1992). Development as a dynamic system. *Current Directions in Psychological Science, 6,* 189–193.

Thelen, E., Corbetta, D., & Spencer, J. P. (1996). Development of reaching during the first year: Role of movement speed. *Journal of Experimental Psychology: Human Perception and Performance, 22,* 1059–1076.

Thelen, E., Corbetta, D., Kamm, K., Spencer, J. P., Schneider, K., & Zernicke, R. F. (1993). The transition to reaching: Mapping intention and intrinsic dynamics. *Child Development, 64,* 1058–1098.

Thelen, E., & Fisher, D. M. (1982). Newborn stepping: An explanation for a "disappearing reflex." *Developmental Psychology, 18,* 760–775.

Thelen, E., & Smith, L. B. (1994). *A dynamic systems approach to the development of cognition and action.* Cambridge, MA: MIT Press.

Thelen, E., & Ulrich, B. D. (1991). Hidden skills: A dynamic systems analysis of treadmill stepping during the first year. *Monographs of the Society for Research in Child Development, 58* (Serial No. 223), No. 1.

Thelen, E., Ulrich, B. D., & Niles, D. (1987). Bilateral coordination in human infants: Stepping on a split-belt treadmill. *Journal of Experimental Psychology, 13,* 1405–1410.

Thevenin, D. M., Eilers, R. E., Oller, D. K., & LaVoie, L. (1985). Where's the drift in babbling drift? A cross-linguistic study. *Applied Psycholinguistics, 6,* 3–15.

Thoman, E. (1987). Self-regulation of stimulation by prematures with a breathing blue bear. In J. Gallagher & C. Ramey (Eds.), *The malleability of children.* Baltimore/London: Paul H. Brookes.

Thoman, E. B., Hammond, K., Affleck, G., & Desilva, H. N. (1995). The breathing bear with preterm infants: Effects on sleep, respiration, and affect. *Infant Mental Health Journal, 16,* 160–168.

Thomas, A., & Chess, S. (1977). *Temperament and development.* New York: Bruner/Mazel.

Thomas, A., & Chess, S. (1986). The New York Longitudinal Study: From infancy to early adult life. In R. Plomin & J. Dunn (Eds.), *Changes, continuities and challenges.* Hillsdale, NJ: Erlbaum.

Thomas, A., Chess, S., & Korn, S. J. (1982). The reality of difficult temperament. *Merrill-Palmer Quarterly, 28,* 1–20.

Thomas, M. H., & Drabman, R. S. (1977, August). *Effects of television violence on expectations of others' aggression.* Paper presented at the annual meeting of the American Psychological Association, San Francisco.

Thompson, D. F., Molison, K. L., & Elliott, M. (1988, April). *Adult selection of children's toys.* Paper presented at the annual meeting of the Eastern Psychological Association, Buffalo, NY.

Thompson, L., & Walker, A. J. (1989). Gender in families. *Journal of Marriage and the Family, 51,* 845–871.

Thompson, R. (1990). Vulnerability in research: A developmental perspective on research risk. *Child Development, 61,* 1–16.

Thompson, R. A. (1987). Development of children's inferences of the emotions of others. *Developmental Psychology, 23,* 124–131.

Thompson, R. A. (1989). Causal attributions and children's emotional understanding. In C. Saarni & P. L. Harris (Eds.), *Children's understanding of emotions.* New York: Cambridge University Press.

Thompson, R. A. (1994). *Fatherhood and divorce: The future of children.* Los Altos, CA: Center for the Future of Children.

Thompson, R. A. (1995). *Preventing child maltreatment through social support: A critical analysis.* Thousand Oaks, CA: Sage.

Thompson, R. A. (1998). Early sociopersonality development. In W. Damon (Gen. Ed.) & N. Eisenberg (Vol. Ed.), *Handbook of child psychology: Vol. 3. Social, emotional, and personality development* (pp. 25–104). New York: Wiley.

Thompson, R. A., Lamb, M. E., & Estes, D. (1982). Stability of infant-mother attachment and its relationship to changing life circumstances in an unselected middle-class sample. *Child Development, 53,* 144–148.

Thornberry, T. P., Krohn, M. D., Lizotte, A. J., & Chard-Wierschem, D. (1993). The role of juvenile gangs in facilitating delinquent behavior. *Journal of Research in Crime and Delinquency, 30,* 55–87.

Thorne, B. (1986). Girls and boys together . . . but mostly apart: Gender arrangements in elementary schools. In W. W. Hartup & Z. Rubin (Eds.), *Relations and relationships.* Hillsdale, NJ: Erlbaum.

Thurber, C. A., & Weisz, J. R. (1997). "You can try or you can just give up": The impact of perceived control and coping style on childhood homesickness. *Developmental Psychology, 33,* 508–517.

Thurstone, L. (1952). Creative talent. In L. Thurstone (Ed.), *Applications of psychology.* New York: HarperCollins.

Thurstone, L. L. (1938). *Primary mental abilities.* Chicago: University of Chicago Press.

Tinsley, B. J. (1992). Multiple influences on the acquisition and socialization of children's health attitudes and behavior: An integrative review. *Child Development, 63,* 1043–1069.

Tinsley, B. J., Holtgrave, D. R., Erdley, C. A., & Reise, S. P. (1997). A multi-method analysis of risk perceptions and health behaviors in children. *Educational and Psychological Measurement, 57,* 197–209.

Tinsley, B. J., & Parke, R. D. (1988). The role of grandfathers in the context of the family. In P. Bronstein & C. P. Cowan (Eds.), *Fatherhood today: Men's changing roles in the family* (pp. 236–252). New York: Wiley.

Tirosh, E., & Canby, J. (1993). Autism with hyperplexia: A distinct syndrome? *American Journal on Mental Retardation, 98,* 84–92.

Tobin-Richards, M., Boxer, A. O., & Petersen, A. C. (1983). The psychological impact of pubertal change: Sex differences in perceptions of self during early adolescence. In J. Brooks-Gunn & A. C. Petersen (Eds.), *Girls at puberty: Biological, psychological, and social perspectives.* New York: Plenum.

Tomada, G., & Schneider, B. H. (1997). Relationship aggression, gender and peer acceptance: Invariance across culture, stability over time, and concordance among informants. *Developmental Psychology, 33,* 601–609.

Tomasello, M. (1995). Language is not an instinct. *Cognitive Development, 10,* 131–156.

Tomlinson-Keasey, C. (1990). Developing our intellectual resources of the 21st century: Educating the gifted. *Journal of Educational Psychology, 82,* 399–403.

Tomlinson-Keasey, C., & Keasey, C. B. (1974). The mediating role of cognitive development in moral judgment. *Child Development, 45,* 291–298.

Trabasso, T., Issen, A. M., Dolecki, P., McLanahan, A., Riley, C., & Tucker, T. (1978). How do children solve class-inclusion problems? In R. S. Siegler (Ed.), *Children's thinking: What develops?* Hillsdale, NJ: Erlbaum.

Trabasso, T., Stein, N., & Johnson, L. R. (1981). Children's knowledge of events: A causal analysis of story structure. In G. Bower (Ed.), *Learning and motivation* (Vol. 15). New York: Academic.

Trainor, L. J. (1996). Infant preferences for infant-directed versus non-infant directed playsongs and lullabies. *Infant Behavior and Development, 19,* 83–92.

Treffers, P. E., Eskes, M., Kleiverda, G., Van Alten, D. (1990). Home births and minimal medical interventions. *Journal of the American Medical Association, 264,* 2207–2208.

Trehub, S. E., & Trainor, L. J. (1993). Listening strategies in infancy: The roots of music and language development. In S. McAdams & E. Bigand (Eds.), *Thinking in sound: The cognitive psychology of human audition* (pp. 278–327). New York: Oxford University Press.

Trehub, S. E., Unyk, A. M., & Trainor, L. J. (1993). Maternal singing in cross-cultural perspective. *Infant Behavior and Development, 16,* 285–295.

Trevarthan, W. (1987). *Human birth: An evolutionary perspective.* New York: Aldine de Gruyter.

Triandis, H. C. (1990). Cross-cultural studies of individualism and collectivism. *Nebraska Symposium on Motivation, 39,* 41–133.

Trickett, P. K. (1997). Sexual and physical abuse and the development of social competence. In S. S. Luthar, J. A. Burack, D. Cicchetti, & J. Weiz (Eds.), *Developmental psychopathology perspectives on risk and disorder* (pp. 390–416). New York: Cambridge University Press.

Trickett, P. K., Aber, J. L., Carlson, V., & Cicchetti, D. (1991). The relationship of socioeconomic status to the etiology and developmental sequelae of physical child abuse. *Developmental Psychology, 27,* 148–158.

Trickett, P. K., & Kuczynski, L. (1986). Children's misbehavior and parental discipline in abusive and nonabusive families. *Developmental Psychology, 22,* 115–123.

Trickett, P. K., & Putnam, F. W. (1998). The developmental impact of sexual abuse. In P. Trickett & C. Schellenbach (Eds.), *Violence against children in the family and the community.* Washington: APA Books.

Trickett, P. K., & Susman, E. J. (1988). Parental perceptions of childrearing practices in physically abusive and non-abusive families. *Developmental Psychology, 24,* 270–277.

Tronick, E. Z. (1989). Emotions and emotional communication in infants. *American Psychologist, 44,* 112–119.

Tronick, E. Z., Thomas, R. B., & Daltabuit, M. (1994). The Quechua manta pouch: A caretaking practice for buffering the Peruvian infant against the multiple stressors of high altitude. *Child Development, 65,* 1005–1013.

Truglio, R. T. (1990). *The socializing effects of prime-time television on adolescents' learning about sexuality.* Report to Center for Population Options, University of Kansas, Lawrence.

Truss, T. J. (Ed.). (1981, October). *Child health and human development: An evaluation and assessment of the state of the science* (NIH Publication No. 82-2304). Washington, DC: U.S. Department of Health and Human Services.

Tuchmann-Deuplessis, H. (1965). Design and interpretation of teratogenic tests. In J. N. Robson, J. M. Sullivan, & R. L. Smith (Eds.), *Symposium of embryopathic activity of drugs* (pp. 56–87). Boston: Little, Brown.

Tulkin, S. R., & Kagan, J. (1972). Mother-child interaction in the first year of life. *Child Development, 43,* 31–41.

Turiel, E. (1966). An experimental test of the sequentiality of development stages in the child's moral judgments. *Journal of Personality and Social Psychology, 3,* 611–618.

Turiel, E. (1983). *The development of social knowledge: Morality and convention.* New York: Cambridge University Press.

Turiel, E. (1998). The development of morality. In W. Damon (Ed.) & N. Eisenberg (Vol. Ed.), *Handbook of child psychology: Social, emotional, and personality development.* (pp. 863–932). New York: Wiley.

Turiel, E., Killen, V., & Helwig, F. (1988). Morality: Its structure, functions and vagaries. In J. Kagan and S. Lamb (Eds.), *The emergence of morality in young children.* Chicago: University of Chicago Press.

Turkewitz, G. (1991). Perinatal influences on the development of hemispheric specialization and complex information processing. In M. J. S. Weiss, & P. R. Zelazo (Eds.), *Newborn attention: Biological constraints and the influence of experience.* Norwood, NJ: Ablex.

Turkheimer, E. (1991). Individual and group differences in adoption studies of IQ. *Psychological Bulletin, 110,* 392–405.

Turner, C. W., & Goldsmith, D. (1976). Effects of toy guns and airplanes on children's antisocial free play behavior. *Journal of Experimental Child Psychology, 21,* 303–315.

Turner, J. S., & Rubinson, L. (1993). *Contemporary human sexuality.* Englewood Cliffs, NJ: Prentice Hall.

Turner, P. J., & Gervai, J. (1995). A multidimensional study of gender typing in preschool children and their parents: Personality, attitudes, preferences, behavior & cultural differences. *Developmental Psychology, 31,* 759–772.

Turner-Bowker, D. M. (1996). Gender stereotyped description in children's picture books: Does "Curious Jane" exist in literature? *Sex Roles, 35,* 461–488.

Twain, M. (1976). The adventures of Tom Sawyer. In L. Teacher (Ed.), *The unabridged Mark Twain.* Philadelphia: Running Press.

Udvari, S., Schneider, B. H., Labovitz, G., & Tassi, F. (1995, August). *A multidimensional view of competition in relation to children's peer relations.* Paper presented at the American Psychological Association. New York, NY.

Ungerer, J. A., Brody, L. R., & Zelazo, P. R. (1978). Long-term memory for speech in 2- to 4-week-old infants. *Infant Behavior and Development, 7,* 177–186.

UNICEF. (1996). *Executive summary: Summary assessment of Plaza Sésamo IV-Mexico. [English translation of Spanish.]* Unpublished report. Mexico City.

United States Department of Commerce. (1996, October). *Statistical Abstract of the United States, 1996. The National Data Book* (116th ed.). Washington, DC: U.S. Department of Commerce.

U.S. Department of Education, National Center for Educational Statistics. (1997). *Children with special educational needs.* Washington, DC: US Government Printing Office.

United States Department of Health and Human Services. (1996). *Health in the United States, 1995*. Public Health Service, Centers for Disease Prevention and Control, National Center for HIV Statistics. (DHHS Publication No. (PHS) 85-2270). Hyattsville, MD: U.S. Department of Health and Human Services, p. 86.

U.S. Department of Justice. (1989). *Crime in the United States, 1988*. Washington, DC: Government Printing Office.

Uzgiris, I. C. (1989). Infants in relation: Performers, pupils and partners. In W. Damon (Ed.), *Child development: Today and tomorrow*. San Francisco: Jossey-Bass.

Valian, V. (1986). Syntactic categories in the speech of young children. *Developmental Psychology, 22*, 562–579.

Valsiner, J. (Ed.). (1989). *Child development in cultural context*. Toronto, Canada: Hogrefe and Huber.

Vandell, D., & Wilson, K. (1987). Infants' interactions with mother, siblings and peer contacts and relations between interaction systems. *Child Development, 58*, 176–186.

Vandell, D. L., Henderson, V. K., & Wilson, K. S. (1989). A longitudinal study of children with varying quality day care experiences. *Child Development, 59*, 1286–1292.

Van Den Bergh, B. R. H. (1992). Maternal emotions during pregnancy and fetal and neonatal behavior. In J. G. Nijhuis (Ed.), *Fetal behavior: Development and perinatal aspects*. New York: Oxford University Press.

Van den Boom, D. (1990). Preventive intervention and the quality of mother infant interaction and infant exploration in irritable infants. In W. Koops, H. J. G. Soppe, J. L. Van der Linden, P. C. M. Molenaar, & J. J. F. Schroots (Eds.), *Developmental psychology behind the dikes: An outline of developmental psychological research in the Netherlands*. Delft, Netherlands: Uitgeverij Eburon.

Van Den Oord, E. J. C. G., Verhhulst, F. C., & Boomsma, D. I. (1992). *A genetic study of maternal and paternal ratings of problem behaviors in three-year-old twins*. Unpublished manuscript.

Vander, A. J., Sherman, J. H., & Luciano D. S. (1994). *Human physiology*. 6th ed. New York: McGraw-Hill.

van IJzendoorn, M. H. (1995). Associations between adult attachment representations and parent-child attachment, parental responsiveness and clinical status: A meta-analysis on the productive validity of the Adult Attachment Interview. *Psychological Bulletin, 117*, 387–403.

van IJzendoorn, M. H., & Bakermans-Kranenburg, M. J. (1996). Adult attachment interview distinctions in mothers, fathers, adolescents and clinical groups: A meta-analytic search for normative data. *Journal of Consulting and Clinical Psychology, 64*, 8–21.

van IJzendoorn, M. H., Sage, A., & Lamberman, M. W. E. (1992). The multiple caretaker paradox: Data from Holland & Israel. In R. C. Planta (Ed.) *Beyond the parent: The role of other adults in children's lives* (pp. 5–24). San Francisco: Jossey-Bass.

Van Tiunen, I., & Wolfe, S. M. (1993). *Unnecessary caesarean sections: Halving a national epidemic*. Washington, DC: Public Citizens Health Research Group.

Vasey, M. W. (1993). Development and cognition in childhood anxiety: The example of worry. In T. Ollendick & R. Prinz (Eds.), *Advances in clinical child psychology* (Vol. 15, pp. 1–40). New York: Plenum Press.

Vaughn, B. E., Kopp, C. B., & Krakow, J. B. (1984). The emergence and consolidation of self-control from eighteen to thirty months of age: Normative trends and individual differences. *Child Development, 55*, 990–1004.

Vaughn, B. E., & Langlois, J. H. (1983). Physical attractiveness as a correlate of peer status and social competence in preschool children. *Developmental Psychology, 19*, 561–567.

Vaughn, B. E., Stevenson-Hinde, J., Waters, E., Kotsaftis, A., Lefever, G. B., Shouldice, A., Trudel, M., & Belsky, J. (1992). Attachment security and temperament in infancy and early childhood: Some conceptual clarifications. *Developmental Psychology, 28*, 463–473.

Vaughn, B. E., & Waters, E. (1981). Attention structure, sociometric status, behavioral correlates and relationships to social competence. *Developmental Psychology, 17*, 275–288.

Vaughn, B. E., & Waters, E. (1990). Attachment behavior at home and in the laboratory: Q-sort observations and Strange Situation classifications of one-year-olds. *Child Development, 61*, 1965–1973.

Verp, M. S. (1993). Environmental causes of pregnancy loss and malformation. In C. Lin, M. S. Verp, & R. E. Sabbagha (Eds.). *The high-risk fetus: Pathophysiology, diagnosis, and management*. New York: Springer-Verlag.

Voorhees, C. V., & Mallnow, E. (1987). Behavioral teratogenesis: Long-term influences on behavior from early exposure to environmental agents. In J. D. Osofsky (Ed.), *Handbook of infant development* (2nd ed., pp. 913–971). New York: Wiley.

Vosniadou, S. (1987). Children and metaphors. *Child Development, 58*, 870–885.

Vurpillot, E. (1968). The development of scanning strategies and their relation to visual differentiation. *Journal of Experimental Child Psychology, 6*, 632–650.

Vygotsky, L. S. (1934). *Thought and language*. Cambridge, MA: MIT Press.

Vygotksy, L. S. (1967). *Vaobraszeniye i tvorchestvo v deskom voraste* [Imagination and creativity in childhood]. Moscow: [Originally published 1930].

Vygotsky, L. S. (1978). *Thought and language*. Cambridge, MA: MIT Press.

Wachs, T. D. (1992). *The nature of nurture*. Newbury Park, CA: Sage.

Waddington, C. H. (1962). *New patterns in genetics and development*. New York: Columbia University Press.

Waddington, C. H. (1966). *Principles of development and differentiation*. New York: Macmillan.

Wadman, M. (1996, December 16), The DNA hard sell. *New York Times*.

Wahler, R. G. (1967). Infant social attachments: A reinforcement theory interpretation and investigation. *Child Development, 38*, 1079–1088.

Wahler, R. G., & Dumas, J. E. (1987). Family factors in childhood psychology: Toward a coercion-neglect model. In T. Jacob (Ed.), *Family interaction and psychopathology: Theories, methods, and findings* (pp. 581–625). New York: Plenum.

Walden, T. (1991). Infant social referencing. In J. Garber & K. Dodge (Eds.), *The development of emotional regulation and dysregulation*. New York: Cambridge University Press.

Walden, T. A., & Ogan, T. A. (1988). The development of social referencing. *Child Development, 59*, 1230–1240.

Walker, A. (1980). *Perception of expressive behavior by infants*. Unpublished doctoral dissertation. Cornell University, Ithaca, NY.

Walker, H. M. (1995). *The acting out child: Coping with classroom disruption*. Longmont, CO: Sopris West.

Walker, L. J. (1988). The development of moral reasoning. *Annals of Child Development, 5*, 33–78.

Walker, L. J. (1989). A longitudinal study of moral reasoning. *Child Development, 60*, 157–166.

Walker, L. J., deVries, B., & Trevethan, J. D. (1987). Moral stages and moral orientations in real-life and hypothetical dilemmas. *Child Development, 58*, 842–858.

Walker, L. J., Pitts, R., Hennig, K., & Matsuba, M. K. (1995). Reasoning about morality and real-life moral problems. In M. Killen & D. Hart (Eds.), *Morality in everyday life: Developmental perspectives* (pp. 371–407). New York: Cambridge University Press.

Wallach, M. A., & Kogan, N. (1965). *Modes of thinking in young children: A study of the creativity-intelligence distinction*. New York: Holt, Rinehart and Winston.

Walton, G. E., Bower, N. J. A., & Bower, T. G. R. (1992). Recognition of familiar faces by newborns. *Infant Behavior and Development, 15*, 265–269.

Wartella, E. (1995). The commercialization of youth: Channel One in context. *Phi Delta Kappan*, 448–451.

Wartner, A. G., Grossman, K., Fremmer-Bombik, E., & Suess, G. (1994). Attachment patterns at age six in South Germany: Predictability from infancy and implications for preschool behavior. *Child Development, 49*, 483–494.

Waterman, A. S. (Ed.). (1985). *Identity in adolescence: Progress and contents*. San Francisco: Jossey-Bass.

Waters, E., & Deane, K. E. (1985). Defining and assessing individual differences in attachment relationships: Q-methodology and the organization of behavior in infancy and early childhood. *Monographs of the Society for Research in Child Development, 50*, 41–65.

Waters, E., Vaughn, B. E., Posada, G., & Kondo-Ikemura, K. (1995). Caregiving, cultural, and cognitive perspectives on secure-base behavior and working models: New growing points of attachment theory and research. *Monographs of the Society for Research in Child Development, 60*, (2–3, Serial No. 244).

Waters, E., Vaughn, G., & Egeland, B. (1980). Individual differences in infant-mother attachment relationships at age one: Antecedents in neonatal behavior in an urban economically disadvantaged sample. *Child Development, 51*, 208–216.

Waters, H. F., & Malamud, P. (1975). "Drop that gun, Captain Video." *Newsweek, 85*(10), 81–82.

Watkins, B. A., Calvert, S. L., Huston-Stein, A., & Wright, J. C. (1980). Children's recall of television material: Effects of presentation mode and adult labeling. *Developmental Psychology, 16,* 672–674.

Watson, J. B. (1926). What the nursery has to say about instincts. In C. Murcheson (Ed.), *Psychologies of 1925* (pp. 1–35). Worcester, MA: Clark University Press.

Watson, J. B. (1928). *Psychological care of infant and child.* New York: Norton.

Waxman, S., & Gelman, R. (1986). Preschoolers' use of superordinate relations in classification and language. *Cognitive Development, 1,* 139–156.

Waxman, S. R., Shipley, E. F., & Shepperson, B. (1991). Establishing new subcategories: The role of category labels and existing knowledge. *Child Development, 62,* 127–138.

Wechsler, D. (1952). *Wechsler Intelligence Scale for Children.* New York: Psychological Corporation.

Wechsler, D. (1958). *The measurement and appraisal of adult intelligence* (4th ed.). Baltimore: Williams & Wilkins.

Wegman, M. E. (1993). Annual summary of vital statistics—1992. *Pediatrics, 92,* 743–754.

Wegman, M. E. (1994). Annual summary of vital statistics—1993. *Pediatrics, 93,* 771–782.

Wegman, M. E. (1995). Annual summary of vital statistics—1994. *Pediatrics, 94,* 792–803.

Wehren, A., & DeLisi, R. (1983). The development of gender understanding: Judgments and explanations. *Child Development, 54,* 1568–1578.

Weinberg, M. K. (1992). Boys and girls: Sex differences in emotional expressivity and self-regulation during early infancy. Paper presented in L. J. Bridges (Chair), *Early emotional self-regulation: New approaches to understanding developmental change and individual differences.* Symposium presented at the International Conference on Infant Studies (ICIS), Miami, FL.

Weinberg, R. A. (1989). Intelligence and IQ: Landmark issues and great debates. *American Psychologist, 44,* 98–104.

Weinberg, R. A., Scarr, S., & Waldman, I. D. (1992). The Minnesota Transracial Adoption Study: A followup of IQ test performance at adolescence. *Intelligence, 16,* 117–135.

Weiner, I. B. (1982). *Psychopathology from infancy through adolescence.* New York: Wiley.

Weinraub, M., & Lewis, M. (1977). The determinants of children's responses to separation. *Monographs of the Society for Research in Child Development, 42* (Serial No. 172).

Weisfeld, G. E., Muczenski, D. M., Weisfeld, C. C., & Omark, D. (1987). Stability of boys' social success among peer over an eleven-year period. *Contributions to Human Development, 18,* 58–80.

Weisner, T., & Gallimore, R. (1977). My brother's keeper: Child and sibling caretaking. *Current Anthropology, 18,* 169–190.

Weisner, T. S., & Wilson-Mitchell, J. E. (1990). Nonconventional family lifestyles and multischematic sex typing in six year olds. *Child Development, 61,* 1915–1933.

Weiss, G., Hechtman, L., Perman, T., Hopkins, J., & Weiner, A. (1979). Hyperactive children as young adults: A controlled prospective 10 year follow-up of the psychiatric status of 75 hyperactive children. *Archives of General Psychiatry, 36,* 675–681.

Weiss, G., & Hechtman, L. T. (1986). *Hyperactive children grown up.* New York: Guilford.

Weiss, G., & Hechtman, L. T. (1993). *Hyperactive children grown up* (2nd ed.). New York: Guilford.

Weissberg, R., & Greenberg, M. (1998). School and community competence-enhancement and prevention programs. In W. Damon (Gen. Ed.), I. Sigel, & K. A. Renninger (Vol. Eds.), *Handbook of child psychology: Vol. 4. Child psychology in practice.* New York: Wiley.

Weissberg, R. P., Caplan, M. Z., & Sivo, P. J. (1989). A new conceptual framework for establishing school-based competence promotion programs. In L. A. Bond & B. E. Compas (Eds.), *Primary prevention and promotion in the schools.* Newbury Park, CA: Sage.

Weisz, J. R. (1989). Culture and the developmental of children psychopathology. In D. Cicchetti (Ed.), *Rochester symposium on developmental psychopathology: Vol. 1. The emergence of discipline* (pp. 3–22). New York: Cambridge University Press.

Weisz, J. R., Suwanlert, S., Chaiyasit, W., Weiss, B., Walter, B. R., & Anderson, W. W. (1988). Thai and American perspectives on over- and under-controlled child behavior problems: Exploring the threshold model among parents, teachers, and psychologists. *Journal of Consulting and Clinical Psychology, 56,* 601–609.

Weitzman, N., Birns, B., & Friend, R. (1985). Traditional and nontraditional mothers' communication with their daughters and sons. *Child Development, 56,* 894–898.

Wellman, H. M. (1977). Preschoolers' understanding of memory relevant variables. *Child Development, 48,* 1720–1723.

Wellman, H. M. (1978). Knowledge of the interaction of memory variables: A developmental study of metamemory. *Developmental Psychology, 14,* 24–29.

Wellman, H. M. (1990). *The child's theory of mind.* Cambridge: MIT Press.

Wellman, H. M., & Bartsch, K. (1988). Young children's reasoning and beliefs. *Cognition, 30,* 239–277.

Wellman, H. M., Collins, J., & Glieberman, J. (1981). Understanding the combinations of memory variables: Developing conceptions of memory limitations. *Child Development, 52,* 1313–1317.

Wellman, H. M., & Gelman, S. A. (1992). Cognitive development: Foundational theories of core domains. *Annual Review of Psychology, 43,* 337–375.

Wellman, H. M., & Gelman, S. A. (1998). Knowledge acquisition in foundational domains. In W. Damon (Gen. Ed.), D. Kuhn, & R. S. Siegler (Vol. Eds.), *Handbook of child psychology: Vol. 2. Cognition, perception, and language* (pp. 523–573). New York: Wiley.

Wellman, H. M. , & Lempers, J. D. (1977). The naturalistic communicative abilities of two-year-olds. *Child Development, 48,* 1052–1057.

Wells, A. S. (1995). Reexamining social science research on school desegregation: Long-term versus short-term effects. *Teachers College Record, 96,* 691–706.

Wender, P. H., Rosenthal, D., Kety, S. S., Schulsinger, S., & Welner, J. (1974). Cross-fostering: A research strategy for clarifying the role of genetic and experimental factors in the etiology of schizophrenia. *Archives of General Psychiatry, 30,* 121–128.

Werker, J. F. (1989). Becoming a native listener. *American Scientist, 77,* 54–59.

Werker, J. F., & McLeod, P. J. (1989). Infant preference for both male and female infant-directed talk: A developmental study of attentional and affective responsiveness. *Canadian Journal of Psychology, 43,* 230–246.

Werker, J. F., Pegg, J. E., & McLeod, P. J. (1994). A cross-language investigation of infant preference for infant-directed communication. *Infant Behavior & Development, 17,* 323–333.

Werker, J. F., & Polka, L. (1993). Developmental changes in speech perception: New challenges and new directions. *Journal of Phonetics, 21,* 83–101.

Werner, E. (1995). Resilience in development. *Current Directions in Psychological Science, 4,* 81–85.

Werner, E. E. (1984). Resilient children. *Young Children, 40,* 68–72.

Werner, E. E. (1988). Individual differences, universal needs: A 30-year study of resilient high risk infants zero to three. *Bulletin of National Center for Clinical Infant Programs, 8,* 1–5.

Werner, E. E. (1989). High-risk children in young adulthood: A longitudinal study from birth to 32 years. *American Journal of Orthopsychiatry, 59,* 72–81.

Werner, E. E. (1991). The children of Kauai: Resiliency and recovery in adolescence and adulthood. *Journal of Adolescent Health, 13,* 262–268.

Werner, E. E. (1993). Risk, resilience, and recovery: Perspectives from the Kauai Longitudinal Study. *Development and Psychopathology, 5,* 503–515.

Werner, E. E., Bierman, J. M., & French, F. F. (1971). *The children of Kauai.* Honolulu: University of Hawaii.

Werner, E. E., & Smith, R. S. (1977). *Kauai's children come of age.* Honolulu: University of Hawaii.

Werner, E. E., & Smith, R. S. (1982). *Vulnerable but invincible: A longitudinal study of resilient children and youth.* New York: McGraw-Hill.

Werner, E. E., & Smith, R. W. (1992). *Overcoming the odds: High risk children from birth to adulthood.* Ithaca, NY: Cornell University Press.

Werner, J. S., & Siqueland, E. R. (1978). Visual recognition memory in the preterm infant. *Infant Behavior and Development, 1,* 79–84.

Wertsch, J., V. & Kanner, B. G. (1992). A sociocultural approach to intellectual development. In *Intellectual development.* R. J. Sternberg, C. A. Berg, (Eds.) Cambridge University Press, New York, NY. pp. 328–349.

Wertsch, J. S. V. (1985). *Vygotsky and the social formation of mind.* Cambridge: Harvard University Press.

Wertsch, J. V., & Tulviste, P. (1992). L. S. Vygotsky and contemporary developmental psychology. *Developmental Psychology, 28,* 543–553.

Wertsch, J. V. & Tulviste, P. (1994). Lee Semyonovich Vygotsky and contemporary psychology. In R. D. Parke, P. A. Ornstein, J. J. Rieser, & C. Zahn-Waxler (Eds.), *A century of developmental psychology.* Washington, D.C.: American Psychological Association.

Wetstone, H. (1977). *About word words and thing words: A study of metalinguistic awareness.* Paper presented at the second annual Boston University Conference on Language Development, Boston.

Whalen, C. K. (1989). Attention deficit and hyperactivity disorders. In T. Hollendick & M. Hersen (Eds.), *Handbook of child psychopathology* (pp. 131–169). New York: Plenum.

Whalen, C. K., & Henker, B. (1991). Therapies for hyperactive children: Comparisons, combinations and compromises. *Journal of Consulting and Clinical Psychology, 59,* 126–137.

Whalen, C. K., Henker, B., & Granger, D. A. (1990). Social judgment processes in hyperactive boys. *Journal of Abnormal Child Psychology, 18,* 297–316.

Whinney, D. (1993). AIDS & AIDS diagnosis for children with perinatally acquired HIV. *Journal of Acquired Immune Deficiency Syndromes, October,* 1139–1144.

Whitall, J., & Clark, J. E. (1994). The development of bipedal interlimb co-ordination. In S. P. Swinnen, J. Massion, & H. Heuer (Eds.), *Interlimb co-ordination: Neural, dynamical and cognitive constraints.* San Diego, CA: Academic Press.

White, B. L. (1967). An experimental approach to the effects of environment on early human behavior. In J. P. Hill (Ed.), *Minnesota symposia on child psychology* (Vol. 1). Minneapolis, MN: University of Minnesota Press.

White, C. B., Bushnell, N., & Regnemer, J. L. (1978). Moral development in Bahamian school children: A 3-year examination of Kohlberg's stages of moral development. *Developmental Psychology, 14,* 58–65.

Whitehurst, G. J., Fischel, J. E., Caulfield, M. B., DeBaryshe, B. D., & Valdex-Menchaca, M. C. (1989). Assessment and treatment of early experience language delay. In P. R. Zelazo & R. Barr (Eds.), *Challenges to developmental paradigms: Implication for assessment and treatment* (pp. 113–135). Hillsdale, NJ: Erlbaum.

Whitesell, N. R., & Harter, S. (1989). Children's reports of conflict between simultaneous opposite-valence emotions. *Child Development, 60,* 673–682.

Whiting, B. B., & Whiting, J. W. M. (1975). *Children of six cultures: A psychocultural analysis.* Cambridge, MA: Harvard University Press.

Whiting, B., & Edwards, C. (1988). *Children of different worlds. The formation of social behavior.* Cambridge, MA: Harvard University Press.

Whitney, M. P., & Thoman, E. B. (1994). Sleep in premature and fullterm infants from 24-hour home recordings. *Infant Behavior & Development, 17,* 223–234.

Wiegman, O., Kuttschreuter, M., & Baarda, B. (1992). A longitudinal study of the effects of television viewing on aggressive and prosocial behaviors. *British Journal of Social Psychology, 31,* 147–164.

Wierson, M., Long, P. J., & Forehand, R. L. (1993). Toward a new understanding of early menarche: The role of environmental stress in pubertal timing. *Adolescence, 28,* 913–924.

Wiesenfeld, A., Malatesta, C., & DeLoach, L. (1981). Differential parental response to familiar and unfamiliar infant distress signals. *Infant Behavior and Development, 4,* 281–295.

Wiesner, T. S. (1993). Overview: Sibling similarity and difference in different cultures. In C. W. Nuckolls (Ed.), *Siblings in South Asia: Brothers and sisters in cultural context.* (pp. 1–17). New York: Guilford Press.

Wilkie, C. F., & Ames, E. W. (1986). The relationship of infant crying to parental stress in the transition to parenthood. *Journal of Marriage and the Family, 48,* 545–550.

Wilkinson, A. C. (1984). Children's partial knowledge of the cognitive skill of counting. *Cognitive Psychology, 16,* 28–64.

Williams, E., Radin, N., & Allegro, T. (1992). Sex role attitudes of adolescents reared primarily by their fathers: An 11-year follow-up. *Merrill-Palmer Quarterly, 38,* 457–476.

Williams, J. E., & Best, D. L. (1990). *Measuring sex stereotypes: A multinational study* (rev. ed.). Newbury, CA: Sage.

Williams, R. L. (1970). Black pride, academic relevance and individual achievement. *Counseling Psychologist, 2,* 18–22.

Williams, T. H., & Handford, A. G. (1986). Television and other leisure activities. In T. H. Williams (Ed.), *The impact of television: A natural experiment in three communities.* Orlando, FL: Academic.

Williams, T. M. (Ed.). (1986). *The impact of television: A natural experiment in three communities.* Orlando, FL: Academic Press.

Williams, T. M., Baron, D., Phillips, S., Travis, L., & Jackson, D. (1986, August). *The portrayal of sex roles on Canadian and U.S. television.* Paper presented to the International Association for Mass Communication Research, New Delhi, India.

Williams, W. M., & Ceci, S. J. (1997). Are Americans becoming more or less alike? Trends in race, class, and ability differences in intelligence. *American Psychologist, 52,* 1226–1235.

Willinger, M., Hoffman, H. T., & Hartford, R. B. (1994). Infant sleep position and risk for sudden infant death syndrome. *Pediatrics, 93,* 814–819.

Wilson, B. J., Hoffner, C., & Cantor, J. (1987). Children's perceptions of effectiveness of techniques to reduce fear from mass media. *Journal of Applied Developmental Psychology, 8,* 39–52.

Wilson, B. J., & Weiss, A. J. (1993). The effects of sibling coviewing on preschooler's reactions to a suspenseful movie scene. *Communication Research, 20,* 214–248.

Wilson, E. O. (1975). *Sociobiology: The new synthesis.* Cambridge, MA: Belknap Press of Harvard University Press.

Wilson, G. L. (1991). Comment: Suicidal behavior—Clinical considerations and risk factors. *Journal of Consulting and Clinical Psychology, 36,* 869–873.

Wilson, M. N. (1989). Child development in the context of the black extended family. *American Psychologist, 44,* 380–385.

Wilson, R. S. (1983). The Louisville twin study: Developmental synchronies in behavior. *Child Development, 54,* 298–316.

Wilson, R. S., & Harpring, E. B. (1972). Mental and motor development in infant twins. *Developmental Psychology, 7,* 277–287.

Wilson, R. S., & Matheny, A. P., Jr. (1986). Behavior-genetics research in infant temperament: The Louisville Twin Study. In R. Plomin & J. Dunn (Eds.), *The study of temperament: Changes, continuities, and challenges* (pp. 81–97). Hillsdale, NJ: Erlbaum.

Wilson, W. J. (1995). Jobless ghettos and the social outcomes of youngsters. In P. Moen, G. H. Elder, & K. Luscher (Eds.), *Examining lives in context* (pp. 4257–4544). Washington, DC: American Psychological Association Press.

Wimmer, H. (1980). Children's understanding of stories: Assimilation by a general schema for actions or coordination of temporal relations. In F. Wilkening, J. Becker, & T. Trabasso (Eds.), *Information integration by children.* Hillsdale, NJ: Erlbaum.

Winn, M. (1990, April 29). New views of human intelligence. *The New York Times Magazine,* pp. 16–17, 28, 30.

Winner, E. (1988). *The point of words: Children's understanding of metaphor and irony.* Cambridge, MA: Harvard University Press.

Winner, E., McCarthy, M., Kleinman, S., & Gardner, H. (1979). First metaphors. In D. Wolf (Eds.), *Early symbolization: New directions for child development.* San Francisco CA: Jossey-Bass.

Wintre, M. G., & Vallance, D. D. (1994). A developmental sequence in the comprehension of emotions: Intensity, multiple emotions and valence. *Developmental Psychology, 30,* 509–514.

Witelson, S. F. (1977). Developmental dyslexia: Two right hemispheres and none left. *Science, 195,* 309–311.

Witelson, S. F. (1978). Sex differences in the neurology of cognition: Psychological, social, educational and clinical implications. In S. Sullerto (Ed.), *La fait feminin.* Paris: Fayard.

Witelson, S. F. (1983). Bumps on the brain: Neuroanatomical asymmetries as a basis for functional symmetries. In S. Segalowitz (Ed.), *Language functions and brain organization* (pp. 117–144). New York: Academic.

Witelson, S. F., & Swallow, J. A. (1987). Individual differences in human brain function. *National Forum, 67,* 17–24.

Wober, J. M. (1992). Text in a texture of television: Children's homework experience. *Journal of Educational Television, 18,* 23–34.

Wolf, A. M., Gortmaker, S. L., Cheung, L., Gray, H. M., Herzog, D. B., & Colditz, G. A. (1993). Activity, inactivity, and obesity: Racial, ethnic, and age differences among schoolgirls. *American Journal of Public Health, 83,* 1625–1627.

Wolfe, D. A., & Jaffe, P. (1991). Child abuse and family violence as determinants of child psychopathology. *Canadian Journal of Behavioral Science, 23,* 282–299.

Wolff, P. H. (1966). The causes, controls and organizations of behavior in the neonate. *Psychological Issues, 5* (1, Whole No. 17).

Wolff, P. H. (1987). *The development of behavioral states and the expression of emotions in early infancy: New proposals for investigation.* Chicago: University of Chicago Press.

Wolin, S. J., & Bennett, L. A. (1984). Family rituals. *Family Process, 23,* 401–420.

Wolin, S. J., Bennett, L. A., & Jacobs, J. S. (1988). Assessing family rituals. In E. Imber-Black, J. Roberts, & R. Whiting (Eds.), *Rituals in family therapy* (pp. 230–256). New York: Norton.

Wood, D., Bruner, J., & Ross, G. (1976). The role of tutoring in problem solving. *Journal of Child Psychology and Psychiatry, 17,* 89–100.

Woods, N. B. (1972). The unsupervised child of the working mother. *Developmental Psychology, 6,* 14–25.

Woodward, A. L., & Markman, E. M. (1998). Early word learning. In W. Damon (Gen. Ed.), R. S. Siegler, & D. Kuhn (Vol. Eds.), *Handbook of child psychology: Vol. 2.* Cognition perceptions of language (5th ed., pp. 371–420). New York: Wiley.

Woodward, J. Z., & Aslin, R. N. (1990, April). *Segmentation cues in maternal speech to infants.* Paper presented at the 7th biennial meeting of the International Conference on Infant Studies, Montreal, Quebec, Canada.

Woody-Ramsey, J., & Miller, P. H. (1988) The facilitation of selective attention in preschoolers. *Child Development, 59,* 1497–1503.

World Health Organization. *World Health Statistics Annual, 1992* (p. A-15). Geneva, Switzerland: World Health Organization, 1993.

Wright, J. C., & Huston, A. C. (1995). *Effects of educational TV viewing of lower income preschoolers on academic skills, school readiness, and school adjustment one to three years later.* Report to Children's Television Workshop, Center for Research on the Influences of Television on Children, University of Kansas, Lawrence.

Wright, J. C., Huston, A. C., Reitz, A. L., & Plemyat, S. (1994). Young children's perception of television reality: Determinants and developmental differences. *Developmental Psychology, 30,* 229–239.

Wright, J. C., St. Peters, M., & Huston, A. C. (1990). Family television use and its relation to children's cognitive skills & social behavior. In J. Bryant (Ed.), *Television and the American Family* (pp. 221–252). Hillsdale, NJ: Erlbaum.

Wymelenberg, S. (1990). *Science and babies: Private decisions, public dilemmas.* Washington, DC: National Academy Press.

Wynn, K. (1992). Addition and subtraction by human infants. *Nature, 358,* 749–750.

Wyshak, G., & Frisch, R. E. (1982). Evidence for a secular trend in age of menarche. *New England Journal of Medicine, 306,* 1033–1035.

Yarmey, A. D., & Jones, H. P. (1983). Accuracy of memory of male and female eyewitnesses to a criminal assault and rape. *Bulletin of the Psychonomic Society, 21,* 89–92.

Yau, J., & Smetana, J. G. (1996). Adolescent-parent conflict among Chinese adolescents in Hong Kong. *Child Development, 67,* 1262–1275.

Yonas, A., Arterberry, M. E., & Granrud, C. E. (1987). Space perception in infancy. *Annals of Child Development* (Vol. 4, pp. 1–34). Greenwich, CT: JAI Press.

Young, C., McMahon, J., Bowman, V., & Thompson, D. (1989). Maternal reasons for delayed prenatal care. *Nursing Research, 38*(4).

Young, W. C., Goy, R. W., & Phoenix, C. H. (1967). Hormones and sexual behavior. *Science, 143,* 212–218.

Youngblade, L. M., & Dunn, J. (1995). Individual differences in young children's pretend play with mother and sibling: Links to relationships and understanding other people's feelings and beliefs. *Child Development, 66,* 1472–1492.

Youniss, J. (1980). *Parents and peers in social development.* Chicago: University of Chicago Press.

Yuill, N., & Perner, J. (1988). Intentionality and knowledge in children's judgments of actors' responsibility and recipients' emotional judgment. *Developmental Psychology, 24,* 358–365.

Yussen, S. R., & Berman, L. (1981). Memory predictions for recall and recognition in first, third, and fifth grade children. *Developmental Psychology, 17,* 224–229.

Zahn-Waxler, C., Denham, S., Ianotti, R. J., & Cummings, E. M. (1992). Peer relations in children with a depressed caregiver. In R. D. Parke & G. W. Ladd (Eds.), *Family-peer relationships: Modes of linkage.* Hillsdale, NJ: Erlbaum.

Zahn-Waxler, C., Kochanska, G., Krupnick, J., & McKnew, D. (1990). Patterns of guilt in children of depressed and well mothers. *Developmental Psychology, 26,* 51–59.

Zahn-Waxler, C., Radke-Yarrow, M., & King, R. A. (1979). Child rearing and children's prosocial initiations toward victims of distress. *Child Development, 50,* 319–330.

Zahn-Waxler, C., Radke-Yarrow, M., Wagner, E., & Chapman, M. (1992). Development of concern for others. *Developmental Psychology, 28,* 126–136.

Zahn-Waxler, C., Robinson, J., & Emde, R. (1992). The development of empathy in twins. *Developmental Psychology, 28,* 1038–1047.

Zahn-Waxler, C., & Wagner, E. (1993). Caregivers' interpretations of infant emotions: A comparison of depressed and well mothers. In R. Emde, J. Osofsky, & P. Butterfield (Eds.), *Clinical infant reports: The I feel pictures* (pp. 175–184). Madison, CT: International Universities Press.

Zajonc, R. B., Marcus, H., & Marcus, G. B. (1979). The birth order puzzle. *Journal of Personality and Social Psychology, 37,* 1325–1341.

Zajonc, R. B., & Mullally, P. R. (1997). Birth order: Reconciling conflicting effects. *American Psychologist, 52,* 685–699.

Zarbatany, L., Hartmann, D. P., & Rankin, D. B. (1990). The psychological functions of preadolescent peer activities. *Child Development, 61,* 1067–1080.

Zegoib, L. E., Arnold, S., & Forehand, R. (1975). An examination of observer effects in parent-child interactions. *Child Development, 46,* 509–512.

Zeifman, D., Delaney, S., & Blass, E. M. (1996). Sweet taste, looking and calm in 2- and 4-week old infants: The eyes have it. *Developmental Psychology, 32,* 1090–1099.

Zelazo, N. A., Zelazo, P. R., Cohen, K. M., & Zelazo, P. D. (1988, April). *Specificity of practice effects on elementary neuromotor patterns.* Paper presented at the International Conference on Infant Studies, Washington, D.C.

Zelazo, P. (1972). Smiling and vocalizing: A cognitive emphasis. *Merrill-Palmer Quarterly, 18,* 349–365.

Zelazo, P. R. (1983). The development of walking: New findings and old assumptions. *Journal of Motor Behavior, 15,* 99–137.

Zelazo, P. R., Kearsley, R. B., & Ungerer, J. A. (1984). *Learning to speak: A manual for parents.* Hillsdale, NJ: Erlbaum.

Zelazo, P. R., Zelazo, N. A., & Kolb, S. (1972). "Walking" in the newborn. *Science, 176,* 314–315.

Zentner, M. R., & Kagan, J. (1996). Perception of music by infants. *Nature, 383,* 29.

Zerbe, K. J. (1993). *The body betrayed: Women, eating disorders, and treatment.* Washington, D.C.: American Psychiatric Press.

Zigler, E., Abelson, W. D., Trickett, P. K., & Seitz, V. (1982). Is an intervention program necessary in order to improve economically disadvantaged children's IQ scores? *Child Development, 53,* 340–348.

Zigler, E., & Seitz, V. (1982). Social policy and intelligence. In R. J. Sternberg (Ed.), *Handbook of human intelligence* (pp. 586–641). Cambridge, England: Cambridge University Press.

Zill, N. (1986). *Happy, healthy and insecure.* New York: Cambridge University Press.

Zill, N. (1988). Behavior, achievement and health problems among children in step families. In E. M. Hetherington & J. D. Arasten (Eds.), *Impact of divorce, single parenting and step parenting on children* (pp. 235–268). Hillsdale, NJ: Erlbaum.

Zill, N. (1991, Winter). U.S. children and their families: Current conditions and recent trends, 1989. *SRCD Newsletter,* pp. 1–3.

Zill, N. (1995). National surveys as data resources for public policy research on poor children. In P. Lindsay Chase-Lansdale & J. Brooks-Gunn (Eds.), *Escape from poverty: What makes a difference for children?* (pp. 272–290). New York: Cambridge University Press.

Zimmerman, M. A., & Arunkumar, R. (1994). Resiliency research: Implications for schools and policy. *Social Policy Report, 8*(4), 1–18.

Zisserman, L. (1992). The effects of deep pressure on self-stimulating behaviors in a child with autism and other disabilities. *American Journal of Occupational Therapy, 46,* 547–551.

Zuckerman, B., & Breshahan, K. (1991). Developmental and behavioral consequences of prenatal drug and alcohol exposure. *Pediatric Clinics of North America, 38,* 1387–1406.

Zuckerman, B., Frank, D., Hingson, R., Amaro, H., Devenson, S. M., Kayne, H., Parker, S., Vinci, R., Aboagye, K., Fried, L., Cabral, H., Timperi, R., & Bauchner, H. (1989). Effects of maternal marijuana and cocaine use on fetal growth. *New England Journal of Medicine, 12,* 762–768.

Zukow, P. (1989). Siblings as effective socializing agents: Evidence from central Mexico. In P. Zukow (Ed.), *Sibling interaction across cultures.* New York: Springer-Verlag.

Credits

Illustrations and Tables

Figure 1-4 from *Child Development in a Social Context* by Kopp, J. and Krakow, J., p. 648. Copyright © 1982 Addison Wesley Publishing Company, Inc. Reprinted with permission of Addison Wesley Longman.

Figure 3-3 from *Nature, 171,* by Watson, J.D. and Crick, F.H.C., "Molecular structure of nucleic acid: A structure for deoxyribose nucleic acid," pp. 737–738. Copyright © 1953 Macmillan Magazines Limited and Dr. James D. Watson. Reprinted with permission.

Table 3-5 from *Science, 212* by Bouchard, T.J. and McGue, M., "Familial Studies of Intelligence: A Review" pp. 1055–1059. Copyright © 1981 American Association for the Advancement of Science. Adapted with permission.

Figure 3-7 from *Handbook of Mental Deficiency: Psychological Theory and Research* (N. Ellis, Ed., McGraw-Hill, Inc.) by Gottesman, I. (1963), "Genetic aspects of intelligent behavior." Reprinted by permission of the author.

Figure 3-8 from *Individual Development and Evolution: The Genesis of Novel Behavior* by Gottleib, G., figure 14–3, p. 186 Copyright © 1992 Oxford University Press, Inc. Used by permission of Oxford University Press, Inc.

Figure 3-9 from *American Journal of Mental Deficiency,* Vol. 71 by Baumeister, A.A. (1967), "The effects of dietary control on intelligence in phenylketonuria," pp. 840–847. Reprinted by permission of the American Association on Mental Retardation.

Figure 3-10 from *Developmental Psychology, 7,* by Wilson, R.S. and Harpring, E.B. "Mental and motor development in infant twins," pp. 277–287. Copyright © 1972 American Psychological Association. Adapted with permission.

Figure 4-1 from *Nature of Life,* 3rd ed., 1995 by Postlethwait, J. and Hopson, J., "Concept Integrator: The Marvel of Human Development," pp. 348–349. Published by The McGraw-Hill Companies. Reprinted by permission of J. Postlethwait and J. Hopson.

Figure 4-5 from *Human Physiology,* 6th ed. by Vander, A.J., Sherman, J.H., and Luciano, D.S., p. 683. Copyright © 1994 The McGraw-Hill Companies. Adapted by permission.

Table 4-3 from *Current Research in Anesthesia and Analgesia, 32,* by Apgar, V.A., "A proposal for a new method of evaluation of the newborn infant," p. 267. Copyright © 1953. Published by John Wiley & Sons, Inc.

Figure 4-6 from *Infancy* by Field, T., p. 117. Copyright © 1990 by the President and Fellows of Harvard College. Reprinted by permission of the publisher, Harvard University Press, Cambridge, MA.

Figure 5-1 from *Prospective Issues in Infancy Research* K. Bloom (Ed.) by Sostek, A.M. and Anders, T.F., "The biosocial importance and environmental sensitivity of infant sleep-wake behaviors," p. 108. Copyright © 1981 Lawrence Erlbaum Associates, Inc. Reprinted with permission.

Figure 5-2 from *Science, 152* by Roffwarg, H.P., Muzio, J.N., & Dement, W.C. "Ontogenetic development of the human sleep-dream cycle," p. 604. Copyright © 1966 American Association for the Advancement of Science. Adapted with permission.

Figure 5-3 from *Journal of Experimental Child Psychology, 10,* by Korner, A.F. and Thoman, E., "Visual alertness in neonates as evoked by maternal care," pp. 67–78. Copyright © 1970 Academic Press, Inc. Reprinted with permission.

Figure 5-4 from *The World of the Newborn* by Maurer, D. and Maurer, C., "Visual discrimination in infants" (1988). Reprinted with permission.

Figure 5-6 from *Journal of Experimental Child Psychology, 37,* by Bertenthal, B.I., Proffitt, D.R. and Cutting, J.E., "Infant sensitivity to figural coherence in biochemical motions," pp. 213–230. Copyright © 1984 Academic Press, Inc. Reprinted with permission.

Figure 5-7 from *Child Development, 47* by Maurer, D. and Salapatek, P., "Developmental changes in the scanning of faces by young infants," pp. 523–527. Copyright © 1976 Society for Research in Child Development, Inc. Reprinted with permission.

Figure 5-8 from *Child Development, 59,* by Dannemiller, J.L. and Stephens, B.F., "A critical test of infant pattern perception models," pp. 210–216. Copyright © 1988 Society for Research in Child Development, Inc. Reprinted with permission.

Figure 5-11 from *Nature, 181,* by Meltzoff, A.N. and Borton, R.W., "Intermodal matching by human neonates," pp. 403–404. Copyright © 1979 Macmillan Magazines Limited. Reprinted with permission.

Figure 5-15 from *American Psychologist, 51,* by Bauer, P.J., "What do infants recall of their lives?", pp. 29–41. Copyright © 1996 American Psychological Association. Adapted with permission.

Figure 6-2 from *Biological Psychology* by Rosenzweig, M.R., Leiman, A.L. and Breedlove, S.M., p. 100. Copyright © 1996 Sinauer Associates, Inc. Reprinted with permission.

Figure 6-3 from *Nature of Life,* 3rd ed., 1995 by Postlethwait, J. and Hopson, J., Figure 32.8A, p. 718. Published by The McGraw-Hill Companies. Reprinted by permission of J. Postlethwait and J. Hopson.

Figure 6-6 from *American Psychologist, 46,* by Fox, N.A. "If it's not left, it's right: Electroencephalograph asymmetry and the development of emotion," pp. 863–872. Copyright © 1991 American Psychological Association. Adapted with permission.

Figure 6-7 from *Biological Psychology* by Rosenzweig, M.R., Leiman, A.L. and Breedlove, S.M., p. 652. Copyright © 1996 Sinauer Associates, Inc. Reprinted with permission.

Figure 6-8 from *Newsweek,* Special Issue (Your Child, Spring/Summer 1997), by Begley, S., pp. 28–29, "How to build a baby's brain." Copyright © Newsweek, Inc. All rights reserved. Reprinted with permission.

Figure 6-9 from *Science, 176* by Zelazo, P.R., Zelazo, N.A., and Kolb, S., "'Walking' in the newborn" pp. 314–315. Copyright © 1972 American Association for the Advancement of Science. Adapted with permission.

Figure 6-10 from *Child Development, 45* by Adelson, E. and Fraiberg, S., pp. 114–126. Copyright © 1974 Society for Research in Child Development, Inc. Reprinted with permission.

Figure 6-12 from *Newsweek,* June 2, 1997, "2000, The Millenium Notebook." Copyright © 1997 Newsweek, Inc. All rights reserved. Reprinted with permission.

Figure 6-13 from *Health Psychology, 14* by Epstein, L., Valoski, A., Wing, R. and McCurley, J., "Ten-year outcome of behavioral family-based treatment for childhood obesity," pp. 373–383. Copyright © 1994 American Psychological Association. Reprinted with permission.

Figure 6-14 from *Health Psychology, 14* by Epstein, L., Valoski, A., Wing, R. and McCurley, J., "Effects of decreasing sedentary behavior and increasing activity of weight change in obese children," pp. 109–115. Copyright © 1995 American Psychological Association. Reprinted with permission.

Figure 6-15 from *The Nature of Life,* 3rd ed. by Postlethwait, J.H. and Hopson, J.L. (1995), p. 716. Published by the McGraw-Hill Companies. Adapted by permission of J. Hopson.

Figure 6-16 from *Monographs of the Society for Research in Child Development, 44* (Serial No. 179) by Roche, A.F., "Secular trends: Human growth, maturation, and development." Copyright © 1979 Society for Research in Child Development, Inc. Reprinted with permission.

Figure 6-17 from *Girls at Puberty: Biological, Psychological, and Social Perspectives* by Tobin-Richards, M., Boxer, A.O. and Petersen, A.C., "The psychological impact of pubertal change: Sex differences in perceptions of self during early adolescence" (1984) Brooks-Gunn, J. and Petersen, A.C. (Eds.). Reprinted by permission of Plenum Publishing Corporation.

Figure 7-1 from *Determinants of Infant Behavior*, Vol. 3 (B.M. Foss, Ed.) by Gewirtz, J.L. (1967), "The course of infant smiling in four child-rearing environments in Israel," pp. 105–248.

Table 7-1 from *Emotional Development* by Sroufe, L.A. (1996), pp. 68–70. Adapted by permission from Cambridge University Press.

Figure 7-2 from *Child Development, 43* by Sroufe, L.A. and Wunsch, J.P., "The development of laughter in the first year of life," pp. 1326–1344. Copyright © 1972 Society for Research in Child Development, Inc. Reprinted with permission.

Figure 7-3 from *Psychological Issues*, Vol. 10, No. 37 by Emde, R.M., Gaensbauer, T.J. and Harmon, R.J., "Emotional expression in infancy: A biobehavioral study." Reprinted by permission of International Universities Press.

Table 7-3 from *Social Development* by Schaffer, R., Table 15, p. 129. Copyright © 1996 Blackwell Publishers, Oxford UK. Reprinted with permission.

Figure 7-4 from *The Origins of Fear* by Lewis, M. and Brooks, J., "Self, other and fear: Infants' reactions to people." Copyright © 1974. Published by John Wiley & Sons, Inc.

Table 7-4 from *Social Development* by Schaffer, R., Table 16, p. 136. Copyright © 1996 Blackwell Publishers, Oxford UK. Reprinted with permission.

Table 7-5 from *Review of Child Development Research*, Vol. 3, Table 1 by Ainsworth, M.D., "The development of infant-mother attachment," Caldwell, B. and Ricciuti, H. (Eds.). Copyright © 1973. Reprinted by permission of The University of Chicago Press.

Figure 7-6 from *Developmental Psychology, 33,* by Thurber, C. and Weisz, J. "You can try or just give up: The impact of perceived control and coping style on childhood homesickness," pp. 508–517. Copyright © 1997 American Psychological Association. Adapted with permission.

Figure 7-7 from *Child Development, 63,* by Lewis, M., Alessandri, S. and Sullivan, M.W., "Differences in shame and pride as a function of children's gender and task difficulty", p. 633. Copyright © 1992 Society for Research in Child Development, Inc. Reprinted with permission.

Figure 7-8 from *Social Cognition and the Acquisition of Self* by Lewis, M. and Brooks-Gunn, J. (1979). Reprinted by permission of Plenum Publishing Corporation.

Table 7-9 from *Social Development* by Schaffer, R., Table 22, p. 158. Copyright © 1996 Blackwell Publishers, Oxford UK. Reprinted with permission.

Figure 8-1 from *Cognitive Science, 14,* by Newport, E.L. (1990), "Maturational constraints on language learning," pp. 11–28. Published by Ablex Publishing Corporation.

Figure 8-2 from *Theories in Cognitive Psychology* (R.L. Solso, Ed.) by Huttenlocher, J., "The origins of language comprehension." Copyright © 1974 Lawrence Erlbaum Associates, Inc. Reprinted with permission.

Table 8-2 from *Contemporary Issues in Developmental Psychology* by Endler, N.S., Osser, H. and Boulter, L.R. "Some imitations produced by Adam & Eve," by Slobin, D.C., p. 414, Table 8–2. Copyright © 1968 Holt, Rinehart and Winston. Reprinted by permission of the publisher.

Figure 8-3 from *Breaking the Speech Barrier: Language Development through Augmented Means* by Romski, M. and Sevcik, R.A. (1996), pp. 28 & 56. Reprinted by permission of the publisher, Brookes Publishing Co., P.O. Box 10624, Baltimore, MD 21285–0624.

Figure 8-4 from *Meaningful Differences in the Everyday Experience of Young American Children* by Hart, B. and Risley, T. (1995), pp. 48 & 60. Reprinted by permission of the publisher, Brookes Publishing Co., P.O. Box 10624, Baltimore, MD 21285–0624.

Table 8-4 from *Language Development* by Hoff-Ginsberg, E., "Examples of children's overextended word uses," p. 101, table 3.2. Copyright © 1997 Brooks/Cole Publishing Company, Pacific Grove, CA 93950, a division of International Thomson Publishing Inc. By permission of the publisher. Based on Rescorla, L.A., *Journal of Child Language, 7,* pp. 321–335, and Bowerman, M., *The development of communication,* pp. 263–287, Waterson & Show (Eds.). Chichester: Wiley.

Table 8-5 from *The Acquisition of Language: The Study of Developmental Psycholinguistics* by McNeill, D. Copyright © 1970 Scott Foresman-Addison Wesley. Reprinted with permission.

Figure 8-6 from *Signing: How to Speak with Your Hands* by Costello, E. Copyright © 1983 by Elaine Costello. Reprinted by permission of Bantam Books, a division of Bantam Doubleday Dell Publishing Group, Inc.

Table 8-6 from *Psycholinguistics* by Slobin, D.I. Copyright © 1979 Scott Foresman-Addison Wesley. Adapted with permission.

Figure 8-7 from *Developmental Psychology, 10 ,* Entwisle, D.R. and Frasure, N.E. "A contradiction resolved: children's processing of syntactic cues," pp. 852–857. Copyright © 1974 American Psychological Association. Adapted with permission.

Figure 9-1 from *Cognition, 23,* by Baillargeon, R., "Representing the existence and the location of hidden objects: Object permanence in 6- and 8-month-old infants," pp. 21–41 (1986). Reprinted with kind permission from Elsevier Science - NL, Sara Burgerhartstraat 25, 1055 KV Amsterdam, The Netherlands.

Figure 9-2 from *Current Directions in Psychological Science*, Vol. 3 (1994) by Baillargeon, R., "How do infants learn about the physical world?," pp. 133–139. Reprinted by permission of Cambridge University Press.

Figure 9-3 from *Current Directions in Psychological Science*, Vol. 3 (1994) by Baillargeon, R., "How do infants learn about the physical world?," pp. 133–139. Reprinted by permission of Cambridge University Press.

Table 9-3 from *1977 Nebraska Symposium on Motivation in Child Psychology, 5th ed.* (Keasy, C.B. (Ed.)) by Selman, R. and Jaquette, D., "Stability and oscillation in interpersonal awareness: A clinical-developmental analysis," Table 1, p. 266. Adapted by permission of The University of Nebraska Press, Lincoln, NE.

Figure 9-4 from *The Origin of Intellect: Piaget's Theory* by Phillips, J. Copyright © 1969 by W.H. Freeman and Company. Reprinted with permission.

Figure 9-5 from *Of Children* by LeFrancois, G.R., p. 305. Copyright © 1973 Wadsworth Publishing Company. Reprinted with permission.

Figure 9-6 from *International Journal of Psychology, 19* by Dasen (1984), p. 410. Reprinted by permission of International Union of Psychological Science.

Figure 9-7 from *Child Development* by Selman, R.L. and Byrne, D.L., "A structural developmental analysis of levels of role-taking in middle childhood." Copyright © 1972 Society for Research in Child Development, Inc. Adapted with permission.

Figure 9-8 from *Developmental Psychology, 24,* by Radziszewska and Rogoff, "Influence of adult and peer collaborators on the development of children's planning skills," pp. 840–848. Copyright © 1988 American Psychological Association. Adapted with permission.

Figure 9-9 from *Cross Cultural Roots of Child Development* (Greenfield, P.M. & Cocking, R.R., Eds.) by Blake, I.K. Copyright © 1994 Lawrence Erlbaum Associates, Inc. Reprinted with permission.

Figure 9-10 from *Cross Cultural Roots of Child Development* (Greenfield, P.M. & Cocking, R.R., Eds.) by Blake, I.K. Copyright © 1994 Lawrence Erlbaum Associates, Inc. Reprinted with permission.

Figure 10-1 from *Advances in the Psychology of Learning and Motivation Research and Theory, 2* by Atkinson, R.C., and Shiffrin, R.M., "Human memory: A proposed system and its control processes." Reprinted by permission of Academic Press.

Figure 10-2 from *Children's Thinking*, 3rd ed. by Siegler, R. Copyright © 1998 Prentice-Hall, Inc., Upper Saddle River, NJ. Reprinted with permission.

Table 10-2 from *Acta Psychologica*, 92, by Davidson, D., "The effects of decision characteristics on children's selection search of predecisional information", p. 268. Copyright © 1996.

Figure 10-3 from *Children's Thinking: What Develops?* (Siegler, R.S., Ed.) "Knowledge structures and memory development," by Chi, M.T.H. Copyright © 1978 Lawrence Erlbaum Associates, Inc. Reprinted with permission.

Figure 10-5 from *Intellectual Development: Birth to Adulthood* by Case, R. (1985) Reprinted by permission of Academic Press.

Figure 10-8 from *Journal of Experimental Psychology, 6* by Vurpillot, E. (1968), "The development of scanning strategies and their relation to visual differentiation," pp. 632–650. Reprinted by permission of Academic Press.

Figure 10-9 from *Journal of Experimental Psychology* by Miller, P. and Aloise-Young (1995). Reprinted by permission of Academic Press.

Figure 10-10 from *Intellectual Development: Birth to Adulthood* by Case, R. (1985) Reprinted by permission of Academic Press.

Figure 10-12 from *Developmental Psychology, 33,* by Coyle, T.R. and Bjorklund, D.F. Copyright © 1997 American Psychological Association. Reprinted with permission.

Figure 10-13 from *American Psychologist* by Gentner, D. and Markman, A.B. Copyright © 1997 American Psychological Association. Adapted with permission.

Figure 10-15 from *Psychological Science* by Miller, K.F., Smith, C.M., Zhu, J., and Zhang, H. (1995). Reprinted by permission of Blackwell Publishers, Malden MA.

Figure 10-16 from *Child Development, 64* by Flavell, J.H., Green, F.L., and Flavell, E.R. "Children's understanding of the stream of consciousness." Copyright © 1993 Society for Research in Child Development, Inc. Adapted with permission.

Figure 11-1 from *Origins of Intelligence* (Lewis, M., Ed.) by Honzik, M. (1976), "Value and limitations of infant tests: An overview." Reprinted by permission of Plenum Publishing Corporation.

Figure 11-2 from *American Psychologist* (Nov.) by Williams, W.M. and Ceci, S.J. "Are Americans becoming more or less alike?" p. 129. Copyright © 1997 American Psychological Association. Adapted with permission.

Table 11-2 from *Current Directions in Psychological Sciences, 2,* by Sternberg, R.J. and Wagner, R.K., pp. 1–6. Copyright © 1983 Basic Books, a division of HarperCollins Publishers. Reprinted with permission.

Table 11-3 from *Frames of Mind: The Theory of Multiple Intelligences* by Gardner, H. Copyright © 1984, 1985 by Howard Gardner. Reprinted by permission of Basic Books, a division of HarperCollins Publishers.

Figure 11-4 from *American Psychologist, 31* by Scar, S. and Weinberg, R.A., "IQ test performance of black children adopted by white families," pp. 726–739. Copyright © 1976 American Psychological Association. Reprinted with permission.

Figure 11-5 from *Advances in Motivation and Achievement, 9* (Pintrich, P., & Maehr, M., Eds.) by Chen, C., Stevenson, H.W., Hayward, C., and Burgess, S. (1995) "Culture and academic achievement: Ethnic and cross-national differences," pp. 119–151. Reprinted by permission of JAI Press Inc.

Figure 11-6 from *Advances in Motivation and Achievement, 9* (Pintrich, P., & Maehr, M., Eds.) by Chen, C., Stevenson, H.W., Hayward, C., and Burgess, S. (1995) "Culture and academic achievement: Ethnic and cross-national differences," pp. 119–151. Reprinted by permission of JAI Press Inc.

Figure 11-7 from *Science, 259,* by Stevenson, H.W., Chen, C., and Lee, S.Y., p. 55. Copyright © 1993 American Association for the Advancement of Science. Reprinted with permission.

Figure 11-8 from *Social Programs That Work* (J. Crane, Ed.) by Ramey, C.T., Ramey, S.T., & Blair, C. "Enhancing the life course for high-risk children. Copyright © 1998 Russell Sage Foundation. Reprinted with permission.

Figure 11-9 from *Social Programs That Work* (J. Crane, Ed.) by Ramey, Campbell, & Blair. Copyright © 1998 Russell Sage Foundation. Reprinted with permission.

Table 12-1 from *Genetic Psychology Monographs, 75* by Baumrind, D., pp. 43–88. Reprinted with permission of the Helen Dwight Reid Educational Foundation. Published by Heldref Publications, 1319 Eighteenth St., N.W., Washington, D.C. 20036–1802. Copyright © 1967.

Table 12-2 from *The State of America's Children Yearbook, 1998.* Copyright © 1998 Children's Defense Fund. Reprinted with permission. All rights reserved.

Figure 12-3 from *Genetics Psychology Monographs, 75* by Baumrind, D.,"Child care practices anteceding three patterns of preschool behavior," pp. 43–88. Adapted with permission of the Helen Dwight Reid Educational Foundation. Published by Heldref Publications, 1319 Eighteenth St., N.W., Washington, D.C. 20036–1802. Copyright © 1967.

Figure 12-4 from *Disorders and Dysfunctions of the Self, 5* (Cichetti, D. & Toth, S.L., Eds.) by Kopp, C.B. and Wyer, N. p. 35, Rochester Symposium on Developmental Psychological Pathology. Copyright © 1994 Lawrence Erlbaum Associates, Inc. Reprinted with permission.

Figure 12-7 from *Child Development,* 47, by Conger, R.D., Conger, K.J., Elder, G.J., Jr., Lorenz, F.O., Simons, R.L., and Whitbeck, L.B., "A family process model of economic hardship and adjustment of early adolescent boys," pp. 526–541. Copyright © 1992 Society for Research in Child Development, Inc. Reprinted with permission.

Figure 12-10 from *Developmental Psychology* by Patterson, C.J. "Families of the lesbian baby boom." Copyright © 1995 American Psychological Association. Adapted with permission.

Figure 12-11 from *The State of America's Children Yearbook, 1998.* Copyright © 1998 Children's Defense Fund. Reprinted with permission. All rights reserved.

Figure 12-13 from *Child Development,* 67, by Garbarino, J. and Kostelny, K., "The effects of political violence on Palestinian children's behavior problems: A risk accumulation model," pp. 33–45. Copyright © 1996 Society for Research in Child Development, Inc. Reprinted with permission.

Figure 13-1 from *Developmental Psychology, 11* by Eckerman, C.O., Whatley, J.L. and Kutz, S.L. "Growth of social play with peers during the second year of life," pp. 42–49. Copyright © 1975 American Psychological Association. Reprinted with permission.

Table 13-1 from *Child Development, 68* by Farver, J. and Shin, Y.L. "Social pretend play in Korean and Anglo-American preschoolers," pp. 544–566. Copyright © 1997 Society for Research in Child Development, Inc. Reprinted with permission.

Figure 13-2 from *Developmental Psychology, 17* by Ellis, S., Rogoff, B. and Cromer, C., "Age segregation in children's social interactions," pp. 399–407. Copyright © 1981 American Psychological Association. Reprinted with permission.

Figure 13-3 from *Child Development, 68* by Farver, J. and Shin, Y.L. "Social pretend play in Korean and Anglo-American preschoolers." Copyright © 1997 Society for Research in Child Development, Inc. Adapted with permission.

Table 13-3 from *Child Development, 48* by Oden, S. and Asher, S.R., "Coaching children in social skills for friendship making," pp. 495–506. Copyright © 1977 Society for Research in Child Development, Inc. Reprinted with permission.

Figure 13-4 from *Psychological Bulletin, 115* by Crick, N.R. and Dodge, K.A. "A review and reformulation of social information processing mechanisms in children's social adjustment." pp. 74–101. Copyright © 1994 American Psychological Association. Reprinted with permission.

Table 13-4 from *Monographs of the Society for Research in Child Develoment, 48* (Serial No. 201) by Gottman, J.M. "How children become friends." Copyright © 1983 Society for Research in Child Development, Inc. Adapted with permission.

Figure 13-5 from *Monographs of the Society for Research in Child Develoment, 51* (2 Serial No. 213) by Dodge, K.A., Petit, G.S., McLaskey, C.L. and Brown, M.M. "Social competence in children," p. 40. Copyright © 1986 Society for Research in Child Development, Inc. Adapted with permission.

Table 13-5 from *Conversations of Friends* by Gottman, J.M. and Mettetal, G. (1986) "Speculations on social and affective development: Friendship and acquaintanceship through adolescence." Reprinted by permission of Cambridge University Press.

Figure 13-6 from *Child Development, 55* by Asher, S.R., Hymel, S. and Renshaw, P.D. "Loneliness in children," pp. 1456–1464. Copyright © 1984 Society for Research in Child Development, Inc. Reprinted with permission.

Figure 13-7 from *Developmental Psychology, 24* by Caspi, A., Elder, G. and Bem, D., "Moving against the world: Life course patterns of shy children," pp. 824–831. Copyright © 1988 American Psychological Association. Reprinted with permission.

Figure 13-9 from *Developmental Psychology, 22* by Steinberg, L.,"Latch-key children and susceptibility to peer pressure: An ecological analysis," pp. 433–439. Copyright © 1986 American Psychological Association. Reprinted with permission.

Figure 13-10 from *Pathways through Adolescence* (Crockett, L.J. & Crouter, A.C., Eds.) by Brown, B.B., and Huang, B. "Examining parenting practices in different peer practices." Copyright © 1995 Lawrence Erlbaum Associates, Inc. Reprinted with permission.

Figure 14-1 from *Big School, Small School* by Barker, R.G. and Gump, P.V. (1964). Reprinted by permission of Stanford University Press.

Figure 14-3 from *Child Development, 66* by Chen, C., and Stevenson, H.W., "Motivation and mathematics achievement: A comparative

Photographs

(Photo research by Inge King)

Chapter 11

Opener: PhotoDisc/Education, Volume 24 ; **p. 420 (left):** © Peter Buckley/Photo Researchers; **p. 420 (right):** © Harry Cutting/Monkmeyer; **p. 434:** © Sybil Shackman/Monkmeyer; **p. 438:** © L. Merrim/Monkmeyer; **p. 443:** © Paul Conklin/PhotoEdit; **p. 455:** © Christopher Hornsby, Courtesy of Milo Mottola, Totally Kid Carousel.

Chapter 12

Opener: PhotoDisc/Family and Lifestyles, Volume 15; **p. 463:** © Jack Spratt/The Image Works; **p. 469:** © George Goodwin/Monkmeyer; **p. 478:** PhotoDisc/Volume 10, Sports & Recreation; **p. 485:** © Tony Freeman/PhotoEdit; **p. 496:** © Deborah Davis/PhotoEdit; **p. 505:** © David Young-Wolff/PhotoEdit.

Chapter 13

Opener: PhotoDisc/Education, Volume 24 ; **p. 520:** PhotoDisc, Weekend Living, Volume 38; **p. 521:** PhotoDisc/People & Lifestyles, Volume 2; **p. 527:** © Bob Daemmrich/Stock, Boston; **p. 528:** © Jeff Greenberg/The Image Works; **p. 546:** © Jeff Greenberg/PhotoEdit; **p. 549 (top):** PhotoDisc/People and Lifestyles, Volume 2; **p. 549 (bottom):** PhotoDisc/Education, Volume 24.

Chapter 14

Opener: © Steve Skjold; **Fig. 14-2 a, b:** MCGUFFFEY'S ECLECTIC PRIMER, Revised Edition, American Book Company, 1896; **p. 561:** © Ed Bock/The Stock Market; **p. 566:** © Laura Dwight/PhotoEdit; **p. 567:** © Bob Daemmrich/The Image Works; **p. 569:** © Mug Shots/The Stock Market; **p. 575:** © Mary Kate Denny/PhotoEdit.

Chapter 15

Opener: David Frazier Photo Library; **p. 588 (left):** © Michal Heron/Woodfin Camp & Associates; **p. 588 (right)** © Martha Cooper/Peter Arnold, Inc.; **p. 596 (top):** PhotoDisc/Family and Lifestyles, Volume 15; **p. 596 (middle and bottom):** PhotoDisc/People and Lifestyles, Volume 2; **p. 600 (left):** © Miro Vintoniv/Stock, Boston; **p. 600 (right):** © Palmer Brilliant/The Picture Cube; **p. 605 (left):** © Charles Gupton/Stock, Boston; **p. 605 (right):** © Corroon/Monkmeyer; **p. 608:** © Hella Hammid/Photo Researchers; **p. 609:** © Bob Daemmrich/The Image Works.

Chapter 16

Opener: PhotoDisc/People and Lifestyles, Volume 2; **p. 624:** © Philip Jon Bailey/The Picture Cube; **p. 637:** © Tony Freeman/PhotoEdit; **p. 643:** © David Young-Wolff/PhotoEdit; **p. 656:** © David S. Strickler/Monkmeyer; **p. 658:** © Bruce Davidson/Magnum Photos.

Name Index

Index page numbers appearing in boldface correspond to the *Developmental Psychopathology Module* published in conjunction with this text.

Subject Index

Index page numbers appearing in boldface correspond to the *Developmental Psychopathology Module* published in conjunction with this text.